T0372997

SHEFFIELD WEDNESDAY

THE COMPLETE RECORD

1867-2011

SHEFFIELD WEDNESDAY

THE COMPLETE RECORD 1867-2011

JOHN BRODIE & JASON DICKINSON

DB PUBLISHING

First published in Great Britain in 2011 by The Derby Books Publishing Company Limited, 3 The Parker Centre, Derby, DE21 4SZ.

Paperback edition published in Great Britain in 2012 by The Derby Books Publishing Company Limited, 3 The Parker Centre, Derby, DE21 4SZ.

ISBN 978-1-78091-220-2

Printed and bound by Copytech (UK) Limited, Peterborough.

Contents

Foreword	7
Introduction	8
Sheffield Wednesday History	10
Wednesday Grounds	70
Matches to Remember	85
Wednesday's 125 Greatest Players	122
Managers	240
League Season	290
Wednesday's League Record Against Other Clubs	540
First Team 1889–2011	543
Non-Competitive & Minor Cup Ties 1867–2011	546
Player Of The Year	578
Club Sponsors	578
Season Ticket Prices – Post War	579
Average Attendance	580
Finance	582
Reserve Team Seasonal Records 1891–2011	584
Second/Third/A Team/Youth Friendlies & Minor Cups	588
Miscellaneous Games	609
Seasonal Third/A Team Results 1921–64	610
Seasonal Youth Team Records 1948–2011	611
Sheffield Wednesday In The Youth Cup	613
Youth Tournaments	617
Sheffield Wednesday Internationals	620
Player Database	636
Roll of Honour	668

Acknowledgements

Any publication that includes the words 'Complete Record' in its title requires the help, patience and expertise of countless individuals and organisations. We would therefore like to thank, in no particular order, the following and apologise in advance for anyone we have omitted. Such a volume would not be possible without the help and patience of our 'other halves', so thanks to Jill Brodie (especially for the proofreading) and Michelle Dickinson (particularly for her proofreading and putting up with Jason's untidy office). Also thanks to John's children, Andrew and Jessica, for their help, and to all at Derby Books, especially Alex Morton.

All at Sheffield Wednesday, especially Trevor Braithwait, Colin Wood and Elaine Murphy, plus all the staff at Sheffield Local Studies, where we have spent many, many hours over the last 20 years. Thanks to Keith Howard, Chris Edwards and Mick Fellows for programme covers, historians Tony Brown, Mick Grayson, Pete Law and Stuart Basson, plus Keith Farnsworth for his initial recommendation. A big thank you to cross-city historian Denis Clarebrough for his invaluable assistance with the grounds chapter and use of photos. Also thanks to John Quinn, Len Ashurst, Peter Eustace, John Pearson, Don Megson, Gerry Young, Ron Springett, John Hemmingham, Richard Letts plus Howard Wilkinson for writing the foreword. Thank you to Tommy Crawshaw (for photographs of his grandfather's medals) and Peter Holme (of the National Football Museum).

Our biggest thank you is to Lee Hicklin, who has diligently proofread and cross-checked the majority of this book from his extensive records.

Jason Dickinson and John Brodie
June 2011

FOREWORD

By Howard Wilkinson

If there is a more comprehensive history of Sheffield Wednesday Football Club than the one produced by John Brodie and Jason Dickinson, I would love to see it. I cannot begin to contemplate the hours of painstaking research it must have taken to produce such an array of interesting information and fascinating facts. Clearly, each of the near 700 pages must have been a labour of extreme love.

I joined 'The Owls' as a young player in 1962. Every Friday morning the manager would walk into the first-team dressing-room and pin five team sheets on the green baize notice board, on each of which were printed the First, Reserve, Yorkshire League, Northern Intermediate and County Senior League teams, including 12th man – a total of 60 players, all playing the next day! No one in that dressing room could possibly have conceived that 49 years later those players, those games and those competitions would be part of such a prestigious publication. Multiply that snapshot by several thousand times and you get some idea of the enormous amount of information gathered between the first and last page. The history of the club, its different grounds, every manager, every first-team player are in here somewhere. If a game was played, involving Sheffield Wednesday's first team, anywhere, any time, it is included – League, Cup competitions, Testimonials, Benefits and even abandoned games have their place. Extra bonuses include profiles of the '125 greatest players', details of every manager and complete records of reserve and youth-team football.

Of course, facts and statistics do not tell the whole story, but they do help us to remember parts of the overall story. For instance my first game at Hillsborough, in March 1950 for a Second Division game against Preston North End, saw Derek Dooley make his debut, and I was stood at the front of a packed Spion Kop in a 49,222 crowd, the majority of the fans sporting a flat cap! The legendary Tom Finney headed the only goal, and he also fractured his cheekbone in the first half but came back on after treatment to play the rest of the game. Almost three years later Derek was to lose a leg, the result of a tragic accident when playing away, by strange coincidence, against Preston North End again!

Similarly, details of our two League Cup quarter-final games against Liverpool in 1984, for instance, immediately took me back in time. The first game at Hillsborough was only played because fans, ground-staff, coaches, and I managed to clear terraces and the pitch of snow and ice. In front of almost 50,000 fans my side earned a deserved 2–2 draw, and we could not get enough tickets for the replay at Anfield, the first time the Owls had played at the famous venue since the late 1960s. Although beaten 3–0, Wednesday fans sang through the whole of the second half and long after the game was over – 'We'll be back, we'll be back, we'll be back!' Back we were the following season, after promotion, and an unbelievable performance and goals by Imre Varadi and Gary Shelton gave us an historic victory, prompting another never to be forgotten second-half chorus of 'We said we'd be back and we are, we said we'd be back and we are, we said we'd be back and we are!' That's the great thing about books like this, they stir the memory. These days superlatives are used far too cheaply, but as record books go, this book will surely take some beating. Enjoy the read.

Howard Wilkinson
Sheffield Wednesday Player, Manager & Chairman
April 2011

Introduction

It is now almost 25 years since Breedon Books published the first Complete Record on Sheffield Wednesday back in 1987. The Owls' place in English football and indeed the whole structure of the domestic game has changed dramatically in the intervening years, and it is perhaps timely for this revised and updated version to be published for a new generation of Wednesday fans to enjoy. For many amateur statisticians, their interest in the history of Sheffield Wednesday was triggered by the publication of the original volume, written by respected journalist Keith Farnsworth, with assistance from Wednesday fan Keith Littlewood.

In the intervening years, John and I have both spent countless hours researching the fascinating history of Sheffield Wednesday through a variety of sources, gleaning documented facts and sometimes even anecdotal trivia from regular trips to Sheffield Central Library. We have also trawled the club's minute books, consulted with fellow football historians and even visited the National Football Museum in Preston. The compilation and checking of facts and figures can be a laborious and often frustrating experience, especially when research in the pre-war *Sheffield Telegraph* and *Sheffield Independent* newspapers would often produce different scorers, or even different team line ups. The history of every club is littered with errors – up until 1999 it was still thought that Wednesday's first ever match was in December 1867, when they had in fact played several times before that date. Often when an error appears in print it is never corrected, but we hope, with this volume, that we have resolved any previous misnomers, anomalies and inaccuracies, and also added extra information, ensuring that this publication is as close as possible to an historically accurate reflection of the club's competitive playing record since first entering the FA Cup back in 1880.

We have checked (and double-checked) all the records included in this book, and apologise in advance for any errors or omissions that may still have slipped through the net – these are often spotted just after the work hits the bookshelves! We are sure that the biography of the top 125 players to appear for Wednesday will cause much debate among supporters, and it was not a simple task deciding who would make the list and which players fell by the wayside. Not unlike the 25 memorable games also described, the choice is, of course, subjective and may sometimes fail to include either the reader's favourite player or their favourite match, or even both! Still, we hope that there will be something for everyone and that the book will encourage conversation and debate.

We also hope that fans enjoy the rather unique, and exhaustive, appendix, which is included at the rear of this Complete Record. This extra information is effectively a summary of over 20 years of research into our club – including every pre-League game played by Wednesday, full seasonal records for reserve, third and youth teams, average crowds, financial records and even season ticket prices. We are unaware of any book on a football club published so far that can boast such a wealth of additional information within its pages.

Sheffield Wednesday FC is, of course, one of the oldest clubs in British soccer, and celebrated its 144th birthday in 2011. After being 'born' from The Wednesday Cricket Club in 1867, the club became a dominant force on the local amateur football scene in the 1880s, winning countless honours, before becoming an established side in the Football League, having won all of England's major domestic competitions. The Owls have now played over 4,400 games in English League football since making their debut in September 1892, with the League Championship having been secured on four occasions: in 1903, 1904, 1929 and 1930. A plethora of divisional honours have also been recorded, including five second-tier titles, while the team has twice earned promotion from step three in the pyramid system, the last promotion won through the Play-offs on a memorable day in Cardiff in 2005.

Wednesday first entered 'The English Cup' back in 1880, and the world-renowned trophy was jubilantly brought back to the City of Sheffield by Wednesday in 1896, 1907 and 1935. The Owls have also been finalists on three additional occasions, twice since World War Two.

The League Cup has also been won (in 1991), and Wednesday have played European football in several seasons, beginning with a run to the latter stages of the modern-day Europa League in the early 1960s, before being knocked out by the mighty Barcelona.

The club's unique name has also helped to make Sheffield Wednesday famous on the world football stage. Their fame was also aided by early forays into foreign lands – it is now 100 years since the club first toured abroad – while the countless famous players who have pulled on the blue-and-white-striped shirt have also helped to keep Wednesday in the public eye. The club was one of the first to employ a professional player, were founder members of the Premiership in 1992, and have led the way in ground development from the day they bought a swampy field that became their first real home, Olive Grove. Since then, the club has spent heavily on its home stadium of Hillsborough, which has been proud to host games in both the World Cup and European Championship Finals, in 1966 and 1996 respectively.

There is no doubt that Wednesday have experienced their fair share of highs and lows, with the last dozen years being particularly harsh on the loyal fans, who nevertheless continue to attend Hillsborough in impressive numbers. We sincerely hope that whoever updates this volume, maybe in another 25 years, will be able to reflect on several glorious seasons of subsequent success, which will see the Owls become a Premiership club again and put them back among the elite in the English game, where we, the fans, believe that they truly deserve to be.

Jason Dickinson/John Brodie
Summer 2011

Sheffield Wednesday History

It is unlikely that the club's founding fathers could have envisaged that The Wednesday Football Club would grow into one of England's most famous teams and evolve into the multi-million pound operation of today. The football club, of course, was born out of The Wednesday Cricket Club, formed back in 1820, and was officially founded on Wednesday 4 September 1867 at the Adelphi Hotel, whereupon the modern-day Crucible Theatre stands. During the meeting, brewery traveller John Pashley rose to his feet and proposed 'that a football club be formed in connection with the cricket club, and that no body of persons shall be empowered to sever the two clubs without the unanimous consent of the general meeting, six days notice to be given to every member of the club.' The motion was seconded by William Littehales, who would later become the club's honorary secretary, with financial agent Ben Chatterton elected president and John Marsh voted secretary and playing captain. Also elected onto the committee was one Charles Stokes, who, over 20 years later, would also be a major influence in the formation of Sheffield United. Around 60 members joined the fledgling club that night, the colours of blue and white were adopted and plans were made to start the club's first ever season. The club secured a playing field in the Highfields district of Sheffield and, after holding an inter-club practice game, The Wednesday played their first ever match, beating the Mechanics Club at Norfolk Park, in October 1867.

The popularity of association football had been growing steadily during the mid-1850s, and Wednesday arrived onto a thriving Sheffield football scene that included the likes of Sheffield FC (formed 1857), Hallam, Broomhall and Heeley. The city became the spiritual home of the sport and one of the first known Cup competitions further enhanced that opinion – the Cromwell Cup being offered as a prize in 1868. Conceived by Oliver Cromwell, a local theatre manager, the tournament was only open to clubs that had been formed for less than two years, and Wednesday beat MacKenzie Football Club 4–0 in the semi-final to set up a Bramall Lane meeting with Garrick. Around 600 supporters attended the subsequent Final and watched as the 90 minutes ended goalless before Wednesday scored a 'golden goal' to lift their first piece of silverware – Captain John Marsh being carried from the field by jubilant Wednesday fans. At the end of the season Wednesday held their first fundraising event – a sports day at Bramall Lane – and within a year of formation had quickly earned a loyal following on the burgeoning Sheffield football scene.

In those early days football was, of course, a purely amateur pastime, and Wednesday would not travel out of the city until winning at the St Andrews Football Club ground in November 1870. The year of 1870 also saw the famous Clegg brothers, William and Charles, join the club, while Henry Hawksley became club president. During those years the club

This undated image, *c.*1880, is possibly the earliest photograph of the Wednesday team.

would have relied solely on member donations to finance its operation, and it was perhaps indicative of those times when an October 1871 friendly – against Mackenzie Football Club at Wednesday's new Myrtle Road ground – was abandoned after the ball burst and no replacement could be found! As the 1870s progressed, The Wednesday started to emerge as one of the best clubs in Sheffield, and this allowed them to invite 'foreign' opposition to Sheffield for relatively high-profile friendly encounters – Nottingham Forest attracting a bumper 1,000 gate to Bramall Lane for one such game in March 1876. This period also saw the club lose the services of secretary-captain and founder member, John Marsh, who returned to his birthplace of Thurlstone. In his place Wednesday appointed William Littlehales as secretary, while William Stacey was handed the role of captain.

After the undoubted success of the FA Cup, introduced by the Football Association in 1871, the Sheffield FA decided that it was time for their own knockout cup, so in 1876 the Sheffield Challenge Cup was introduced. Goals from F. Butler (2) and Tomlinson secured a 3–1 win for Wednesday against Parkwood Springs in the first ever game in the new tournament, and their popularity in the city gathered pace as the club won through to the Bramall Lane Final. A tremendous crowd of 8,000 packed into the cricket ground for that inaugural Final, and they witnessed a thriller as Wednesday recovered from a three-goal deficit to force extra-time and scramble through a decisive goal from Skinner to win the new £50 trophy and delight their followers in the boisterous crowd. It was also of great significance that the winning side contained James Lang in its ranks, as the Scotsman is considered to be the first ever professional player in English football. At the time, professionalism was frowned upon and Lang was officially employed at a business owned by a Wednesday committee member. He later admitted, however, that he just read the paper all day while at 'work' and was, in fact, in the city purely to play for Wednesday.

The Cup win raised the club's profile immeasurably, and in the following season Wednesday arranged 'challenge matches' with Derby, Nottingham Forest, Spital Chesterfield and Glasgow Rangers – the latter winning 2–1 at Bramall Lane in February 1878. The Sheffield Challenge Cup was retained, and by the end of the 1870s the club had become firmly established as the most popular side in Sheffield – players such as Bob Gregory and Billy Mosforth (nicknamed the 'Little Wonder') becoming early heroes for that first generation of Wednesday fans. Victory in the inaugural Final of the Wharncliffe Charity Cup in 1879 strengthened their position and preceded an era that would totally transform the club and set in motion changes that would eventually result in FA Cup football; the adoption of professionalism; the purchase of their first 'proper' ground; and entry into their first League competition.

With Arthur Dickinson becoming a dominant force behind the scenes, the club took the momentous decision to enter the FA Cup in the summer of 1880 and was handed a long trip to Scottish club Queen's Park in the first round. Their scheduled opponents withdrew from the competition, however, and Wednesday started their FA Cup history with a 4–0 win at Blackburn Rovers – a victory that raised more than a few eyebrows in the football world. Their first run in the competition ended at the quarter-final stage, but a year later Wednesday reached the semi-finals for the first time, losing to Blackburn Rovers in a replay, and were now firmly established as Cup fighters of some renown. A third consecutive last eight place was secured in 1883 and, although they exited at that stage, a side now containing the likes of Tom Cawley, Jack Hunter and Harry Winterbottom won both the Sheffield Challenge Cup and the Wharncliffe Charity Cup to keep the club at the forefront of Sheffield football.

The football club officially split from the cricket section in 1883, and the football section would then experience some lean years that almost ended in their demise by the middle of the 1880s. Early exits in the FA Cup tarred their playing image, and on-field problems were highlighted by some terrible defeats – Wednesday losing 8–2 to Derby County at Bramall Lane and losing 9–0 and 16–0 to Lancashire side Halliwell. Off the field, the club was also struggling, having failed to replace William Littlehales as secretary. It was left to player Jack Hudson to temporarily fill the role, but the club was embarrassed in 1886 when their application for the FA Cup was submitted too late and they were refused entry. It was the dark cloud of professionalism, gaining ground across the Pennines, however, that would soon threaten the very existence of Wednesday.

The lack of FA Cup football severely damaged the club's standing, and perhaps of more importance was that several of their 'star' players decided to appear for local works team Lockwood Brothers, after they successfully applied to play in the Cup. The Lockwood Brothers side caused a mini sensation by the reaching the quarter-finals, while Wednesday officials were left struggling to even raise a team of 11 players for friendly games. The whole situation came to a dramatic climax in April 1887 when, with Wednesday still adamant that they would not adopt professionalism, several prominent players were instrumental in the formation of a new side, Sheffield Rovers. The newcomers immediately agreed to turn professional and quickly played the requisite number of games to be allowed to compete in the following season's FA Cup. The future of The Wednesday Football Club was now in the balance and would be resolved by two meetings held over the following few days. The first took place at Sheffield Rovers, where prominent Wednesday player, Tom Cawley, expressed the opinion that the players should give Wednesday one last chance to agree to switch from amateur to professional. His suggestion was agreed and, at a subsequent special meeting of the club, the players simply stated that either Wednesday gave in to their demands or they would defect en masse to Sheffield Rovers. The possible loss of their major players would, overnight, strip Wednesday of their hard-won status as the best club in the city, and in the end they had no choice but to accede, paying five shillings for home games and seven shillings for away games – a new era had begun.

The calendar year of 1887 was certainly pivotal in the history of Sheffield Wednesday as a few weeks later the club's officials agreed to take a lease on some swampy land just off Queens Road. This eventually became known as Olive Grove, the club's first real home, but perhaps more crucial was that Wednesday could now generate the income required, by being able to charge an admission fee to their games, to maintain their new-found professional status. The club hosted 25 games in their first season at Olive Grove, and set an early attendance record when the visit of Preston North End, in an FA Cup tie, saw around 9,000 crammed into the ground. Wednesday now regularly faced the top sides in the English game – the likes of West Bromwich Albion, Aston Villa and Blackburn Rovers – but the formation of the Football League in 1888 resulted in a huge change in the English game. Wednesday were one of several clubs to apply for membership of the new competition, but after failing to gain election they had to be content with their staple diet of high-profile challenge games and success in local Cup competitions. In comparison to the 'glamour' of the FA Cup and the competitive environment of League football, however, interest in these minor games was on the wane. Club president, John Holmes, therefore became a major figure in the formation of the Football Alliance League, the Wednesday official being elected as president of the new competition.

The arrival of competitive football proved hugely popular at Olive Grove and Wednesday enjoyed a fantastic first season, winning the inaugural Championship and also returning to form in the FA Cup. In the 'English Cup' the side reached their second semi-final, but this time progressed through to the showpiece Final, before being beaten by renowned Cup fighters Blackburn Rovers. Despite finishing bottom of the Alliance League in 1890–91, the crowds at Olive Grove actually increased, such was the public's appetite for football. The season was particularly memorable for the FA Cup meeting with Halliwell, which resulted in a club record 12–0 victory. The season was also of significance as in December 1890 Wednesday played the newly formed Sheffield United for the first time, beating their new rivals 2–1 at Olive Grove. In September 1891 the club faced non-British opposition for the first time when a Canadian touring side proved a novelty for an excellent crowd of around 6,000 inside Olive Grove. During the 1891–92 season Wednesday played a total of 60 games and, finishing fourth in the Alliance League, they re-applied to the Football League after plans were announced to extend the competition to two divisions. Wednesday's reputation ensured that they were subsequently voted into the Football

The Wednesday 1892–93.

League, going straight into the First Division, with neighbours United being elected into the new Second Division.

In preparation for the challenge that League football would provide, Wednesday upgraded both their facilities and playing staff, adding quality men like Harry Davis and Alec Brady to a side that already contained the 'Olive Grove Flyer' Fred Spiksley, Harry Brandon and Sheffield-born warhorse, Billy Betts. The next era in the history of the club started on the first Saturday in September 1892, when a goal from captain Tom Brandon was enough to give Wednesday a perfect start to their League career with a 1–0 win at Notts County. The club's first home game in League football ended with a resounding 5–2 win over Accrington, and the club enjoyed a great start to life in their new surroundings, sitting third in the table at the dawn of the new year. They did eventually fall away to finish their debut season in 12th position, winning on the final day to avoid inclusion in the 'test matches' – a forerunner of the modern-day Play-off system, where teams from the two divisions met to decide promotion and relegation. The 1892–93 season also saw Wednesday involved in a three-game 'protest' match in the FA Cup, a common occurrence at the time, where the defeated club would appeal the result, for a wide variety of reasons, and the Football Association would order the game to be replayed. It was Derby County who lodged an appeal after they lost 3–2 at Olive Grove, and it was then Wednesday's turn to follow suit after they lost in the re-staged game at Derby. A 4–2 win at Olive Grove eventually settled the tie, and not long after the governing body introduced the sensible rule of only allowing a protest before a tie, stamping out the practice instantly.

In the summer of 1893 the club became a limited company, issuing 50 £5 shares, and in the next two seasons Wednesday lost consecutive FA Cup semi-finals to Bolton Wanderers and West

Bromwich Albion, while finishing mid-table in the First Division. The following season proved the greatest so far in the club's history, as they not only equalled their best League finish – eighth in the First Division – but also reached the Final of the FA Cup. With the inspirational leadership of captain Jack Earp, Wednesday recorded wins over Southampton St Mary's, Sunderland, Everton and Bolton Wanderers to set up a meeting with Wolverhampton Wanderers at the Sydenham Grounds, Crystal Palace. Cup fever gripped the blue-and-white half of Sheffield and hundreds of fans packed the platform at Midland Station to give their heroes a rousing send-off. For the vast majority of Wednesday fans who followed their team to London the following morning, it was their first experience of the capital city and it was reported that many could be found in Hyde Park, standing open-mouthed as the gentry and pretty young ladies in their stylish dresses passed by! Of the 13 Wednesday players that travelled, Bob Ferrier and James Jamieson missed out on a dramatic Cup Final. Fred Spiksley scored within a minute of the 4 o'clock kick-off, but the game was quickly tied. After 18 minutes had elapsed, however, Wednesday were back in the lead, legendary winger Spiksley netting again, to the delight of the fans sporting the blue-and-white favours. There was no further scoring, and when the referee blew his whistle – at exactly 5.42pm – it was left to Earp to become the first Wednesday player to collect a major English trophy. On that afternoon around 4,000 fans were inside Olive Grove watching the reserves play, and they waited patiently until a telegram was read out, informing them of the glorious victory. When the team returned to Sheffield on the following Monday, the city streets were thronged with jubilant supporters, and such was the sheer numbers that a tour of the city was curtailed. Thousands of fans then packed into the Empire Palace to watch various speeches and presentations to end three days of celebration.

After the Cup victory win, Wednesday posted consecutive top-six finishes, but the summer of 1898 saw the club's very existence put in doubt once again. This time it was not professionalism that threatened their future, but the possibility of losing their Olive Grove ground, which in turn could cost the club their precious League status. Against this backdrop, the 1898–99 season proved a disaster, as the club failed to win a single game away from home and were eventually relegated, finishing bottom of the First Division. The season failed to provide any significant memories for the Wednesday fans, although the home meeting with Aston Villa in November

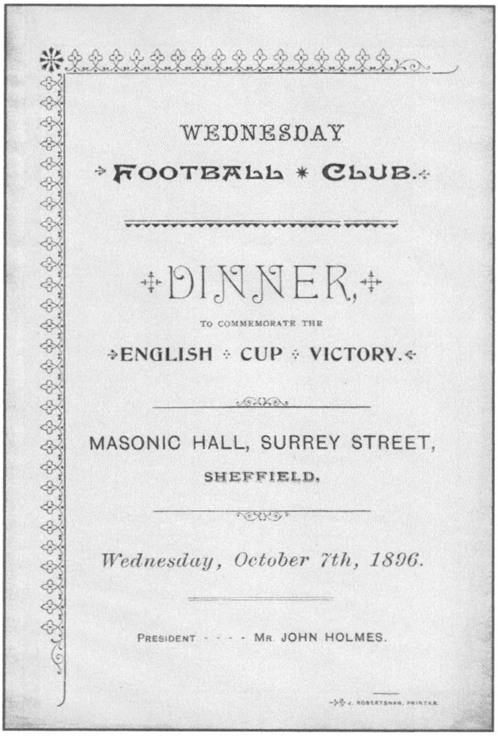

WEDNESDAY
FOOTBALL CLUB.

DINNER,
TO COMMEMORATE THE
ENGLISH CUP VICTORY.

MASONIC HALL, SURREY STREET,
SHEFFIELD.

Wednesday, October 7th, 1896.

PRESIDENT - - - - MR. JOHN HOLMES.

1896 FA Cup dinner menu.

IN LOVING MEMORY
OF
Sheffield W.
Once a Fighting Cup Team
But now dead and departed.
To Win the Cup was our ambition,
But owing to such opposition,
We have left it to a better Team
Now it is too late to Scream.
R.I.P.

A funeral card issued after a bad Cup run in 1900.

1898 did enter the record books after being abandoned with just over 10 minutes remaining to play. Incredibly, the Football League decided not to order the whole game to be replayed, instead asking the teams to reconvene on a later date to play out the remaining minutes! This duly occurred in March 1899, with the sides then playing an abridged benefit game for Wednesday player Harry Davis.

Relegation from the First Division and the loss of Olive Grove meant that the spring of 1899 was not a happy period for Wednesday supporters. Good news was soon forthcoming, however, as the club announced that they had purchased a piece of meadowland at Owlerton and that plans were in place to build a ground fit to host League soccer. To aid the move, Wednesday were turned into a limited liability company (LLC) – George Senior becoming Wednesday's first chairman – and a share issue was announced, which it was hoped would raise £5,000. A total of 22 directors were elected to the new board, including the Clegg brothers, Arthur Dickinson and John Holmes, while a vital appointment was that of trainer Paul Firth.

With changes on and off the field, supporters began to look forward to the new season, although the jury was undecided as to whether the move 'out of the city' would prove a disaster or a masterstroke. Fans could buy a season ticket for the new season from the club's offices in Barkers Pool, and Wednesday held their traditional pre-season public trial matches at the Niagara Grounds while the final touches were applied to Owlerton. Any fears about the location of the club's new home were quickly allayed, however, thanks to a bumper attendance on the opening day of the season. Wednesday enjoyed a tremendous debut campaign at Owlerton, winning all 17 home games to run away with the Second Division title – the Owls are one of only a handful of teams to have achieved this feat. Wednesday were unbeaten until the final day of the 19th century – a run of 14 games from the start of the season – and twice recorded 6–0 home wins (against Luton Town and Burton Swifts). Promotion was secured with three games still to play, while the Championship was clinched on the final day, after Middlesbrough were beaten. Wednesday's only defeat at their new home came against neighbours United in arguably the fiercest derby meeting of all time. The two city sides were drawn together in the second round of the FA Cup, but heavy snow caused the first tie, at Bramall Lane, to be abandoned, with the score 0–0 after 50 minutes of play. The restaged game ended 1–1, so the teams reconvened at Owlerton, where home player George Lee suffered a broken leg in the first half. United then nudged ahead from the penalty spot early in the second period. With tackles flying in from all directions, Wednesday man Pryce was sent off and, amazingly, with five minutes left the home side went down to eight men after Ambrose Langley was sent from the field! The visitors scored late on to confirm the victory, while the local press described the encounter as 'a game of wild excitement, which sadly tarnished the image of Sheffield Football.'

For their first season back in the First Division, Wednesday broke their transfer record to pay £200 for Scottish forward Andrew Wilson, while FA Cup-winning captain, Jack Earp, moved to Stockport County. The club also decided to publish a regular matchday programme for the first time and won their first two home games in the top division, before Preston ended their proud 100 per cent home record. The club would finish in a comfortable eighth position in their first season back, despite failing to win a single away fixture, with newcomer Wilson grabbing 13 goals for his new side. In the summer of 1901 Wednesday entered a side into the strong Midland League, with the reserves trouncing Derby County reserves 13–1 in their opening game! At first-team level, however, the consensus among Wednesday fans was that the side needed to be strengthened, despite the emergence of Harry Chapman and the purchase of Jack Lyall. This opinion was proven correct as another mid-table finish, combined with an early FA Cup exit, resulted in a few murmurs of discontent among the club's supporters. The shareholders even called a special meeting to register their disappointment that Wednesday had failed to build on their promotion to the top flight, even suggesting the revolutionary idea of appointing a full-time manager to ease the burden of secretary Arthur Dickinson. That 'respectful' rebellion would quickly fade away though, as in the next two seasons Wednesday won the League title not once, but twice! Despite the club signing several players in the summer, it was effectively the 'old guard' that would take Wednesday to their first ever top-flight title, winning 3–2 at Sheffield United on the opening day and winning seven times on the road. When Wednesday completed their League programme they sat atop the First Division, but could not celebrate as the only club who could overtake them, Sunderland, still had a game to play – at rivals Newcastle United. A week later a bumper 16,000 crowd watched Wednesday beat Notts County 2–0 to win the Plymouth Bowl, and after receiving their gold medals the players waited for news from the North East. Several thousand fans were also waiting at Owlerton – watching the reserve team play – and celebrations started in both Sheffield and Devon when the news was relayed that Sunderland had lost 1–0 and Wednesday were League champions of England. After a short tour of South Wales, the team returned home and was driven through the streets of Sheffield to the great acclaim of the fans.

Almost 12 months later Wednesday were again waiting for a result from elsewhere to know if they had retained the Championship. Two days previously the club had ended their Owlerton campaign unbeaten with 14 wins from 17 games, and sat one point clear of their nearest rivals, Manchester City. Wednesday still had one more game to play – at Derby County on the final Saturday of the season – but their rivals from across the Pennines would complete their fixtures early with a visit to Everton. Supporters and players once again waited for news, and it was time to celebrate when it was announced that Everton had

The Wednesday 1906–07.

won 1–0 and Wednesday were only the third club to retain the title. Their Championship rivals had beaten Wednesday in the semi-finals of the FA Cup, but the season had still been the greatest for the club by a considerable margin since election to the League in 1892.

A third consecutive title seemed a mere formality when Wednesday started the next season with seven wins on the bounce, scoring 20 times in the process. Unfortunately, the club's watertight defence – which had conceded only 28 times in the previous campaign – suddenly sprung a leak and Wednesday would win only seven more games to the end of the season, slipping down the table to finish in ninth place. Another FA Cup semi-final appearance ended in defeat to Newcastle United. Illness and injury were highlighted as a reason for their relatively poor season and the club enjoyed a much better 1905–06 campaign, finishing in third place, with a double over Sheffield United being relished by Wednesday fans. On Boxing Day 1905 Jimmy Stewart became the first Wednesday player to score four times in a League fixture, and he also ended the season with 20 League goals: the first player to achieve this feat for the club. The club was again challenging at the top of the First Division late in 1906, but they slipped down in dramatic style as their Cup exploits took centre stage. The run to an eventual Final meeting with Everton started at non-League Southampton, but it needed a goal from Andrew Wilson in the very last minute to force an Owlerton replay. The run then looked set to end after Sunderland forced a replay, but, in front of a record Roker Park crowd, Wednesday went through, despite

Tommy Crawshaw.

Fred Spiksley.

playing the final 20 minutes with 10 men after Harry Davis suffered a broken leg. Ten days later Owlerton's ground record was also smashed when over 37,000 watched Liverpool beaten to set up a semi-final meeting with Woolwich Arsenal. A brace from 'Andra' Wilson secured a 3–1 win and it was again time for the 'northern hordes' to plan a grand day out in London. Hundreds duly filled the open-topped buses to tour around the capital, but these outings were just to fill time before the main event: the FA Cup Final meeting with Everton. Over 84,000 packed into the Sydenham grounds at Crystal Palace, and it would be the Wednesday supporters who would return home joyful, as a first-half goal from Jimmy Stewart and a late winner from George Simpson secured a 2–1 win, with captain Tommy Crawshaw lifting the trophy aloft. An estimated crowd of 50,000 filled the streets of Sheffield to welcome home the victorious team and when the Cup was held aloft on the Town Hall balcony it received a tumultuous reception.

After two League titles and an FA Cup inside four years, Wednesday fans had to be content with several top-six finishes in the period up to the start of World War One, but no major honours. In fact, after lifting the Cup Wednesday fell to several humiliating defeats in the competition, starting with a first-round exit to non-League Norwich City; 500 Wednesday fans made the pilgrimage to Newmarket Road, only to see the home side win 2–0 on an icy pitch. A third-round exit to Second Division Glossop followed in February 1909 – the Derbyshire side winning 1–0 at Owlerton – before it was the turn of Southern League clubs Northampton Town and Coventry City to knock Wednesday out on Sheffield soil.

Off the field, the club mourned the passing of John Holmes, who had joined the committee back in 1868, while there was a mini sensation when outstanding inside-forward Jimmy Stewart refused to sign a new deal in the summer of 1908 and subsequently moved to home-town club Newcastle United. Many of the old guard also departed, with Tommy Crawshaw moving to Chesterfield, Harry Davis retiring, and long-term trainer Paul Firth not being retained. Wednesday broke their transfer record to pay £1,000 for centre-forward David McLean in February 1911, while at the end of the 1910–11 season the club embarked on their first ever overseas tour – a party of 14 players, four directors and two trainers visiting Denmark and Sweden. During the tour the club played their first ever Sunday game while Wednesday, as expected, won all five games on the trip, including a match against the Danish national side.

Although the club failed to secure any honours in the immediate pre-World War One era, the scoring exploits of David McLean and the near miss of 1912–13 cannot pass without further comment. The Scotsman is rightly regarded as the club's first truly prolific centre-forward, and in his first full season he scored 25 First Division goals (including four in an 8–0 win over Sunderland) in just 37 games, as the Owls finished fifth in the division.

A photograph from Wednesday's first overseas tour, to Denmark and Sweden in May 1911.

His importance to the team was undeniable and in the dramatic 1912–13 season he became the first Wednesday player to score 30 League goals in a season. He missed only two games during the season – one being the Owls' all-time record defeat in competitive football: 10–0 at Aston Villa – as a side containing Tom Brittleton, Teddy Davison, Andrew Wilson and Jimmy Spoors sat at the top of the First Division with just four games remaining after thrashing Bradford City 6–0 at Owlerton. A third title in 10 seasons looked set to be Wednesday's, but a draw at Manchester City saw the club slip to second, before a highly damaging home defeat to Newcastle United put the matter out of their hands. A home win over West Bromwich Albion proved academic as rivals Sunderland won, and defeat at Everton in the final game of the campaign meant that the Owls finished down in third – scant reward for a season where the team scored an average of almost two goals per game. The season was also highly significant with regard to the club's nickname, as up until that point they were simply known as the Blades. When player George Robertson presented the club with a mascot in the shape of an Owl, however, Wednesday officials reiterated that they hoped the gift would not lead to them being known as 'the Owls'. The figure was placed under the North Stand, and after Wednesday won their next four games without conceding a goal a new nickname was well and truly born!

The season that followed could not have been of greater contrast, with McLean again at the centre of the events. On this occasion though it was his lack of appearances in a Wednesday shirt that triggered a poor season, which ended with the club just outside of the relegation places. In the summer of 1913 McLean had demanded a three-year deal (unheard of in those times), and when the club refused he returned to Scotland to sign for non-League side Forfar. The loss of their star striker was a blow, and only the opening of the club's new South Stand and the official renaming of the ground to 'Hillsborough' moved the fans' topic of conversation off the McLean saga. One player who was still in the blue-and-white-shirt, record top scorer Andrew Wilson, enjoyed a benefit game in November 1913, with the home game against Bradford City being designated for the long-serving inside-forward. Wilson treated his playing comrades to cigars and champagne before receiving the gate receipts of £450 (around £40,000 in current prices).

By Christmas the Owls were struggling near the foot of the table, although the new year brought a run in the FA Cup and the eventual return to the fold of McLean. The second-round FA Cup tie at Hillsborough entered the club's history for all the wrong reasons as, despite the Owls winning 1–0, the match was marred by the collapse of a retaining wall at the Penistone Road end of the ground. Spectators and debris fell from the embankment onto the fans below and the game was stopped so that the injured could be treated. Thankfully, despite several broken bones, there were no fatalities, although 75 people were admitted into hospital, with the club eventually paying over £500 in compensation to the victims. After the game, Wolves appealed complaining that the referee had called time early and that the game should have been abandoned, but the FA dismissed their appeal and allowed Wednesday to progress to a last-16 meeting with Southern League Brighton. Unfortunately, the Owls exited in the next round – with almost 57,000, a record crowd for the City of Sheffied, watching Aston Villa score the only goal of the tie. A point in their penultimate home game of the season guaranteed First Division survival for Wednesday, and there was a marked improvement in fortunes during the 1914–15 season. The Owls were perched at the top of the table after seven different players scored in a 7–0 romp over Bolton Wanderers on 1 March 1915. Earlier in the season the football authorities, somewhat against public opinion, had decided to continue with the season after Britain entered World War One, but Wednesday would not be the last champions before the League closed for the duration of the conflict. They only won twice in their final 10 games of the campaign to slip down to a highly disappointing seventh place.

When national football ceased in 1915 many clubs closed down for the duration of the war and, in fact, Wednesday voted for football not to continue at all. They were outvoted, however, and immediately started to make plans for the first season of wartime soccer. The side that represented the club was almost unrecognisable from the pre-war team, as first-team regulars Jimmy Blair, George Robertson, David McLean, Teddy Davison and Sam Kirkman all became unavailable as Britain concentrated on the war effort. The Owls were placed in the Midland Section of the wartime League, but simply keeping the club afloat proved a challenge for the long-serving Arthur Dickinson, as he tried to recruit 11 players for each game and keep the club's finances on an even keel. Thankfully, although crowds had dwindled significantly, it was an FA announcement that would hand a financial lifeline to many clubs – the governing body informed

David McLean.

clubs that no player should receive payment for playing and that any player could play for any team at any time, at his own convenience. With this edict in place, Wednesday only posted relatively minor financial losses during the war years, which were absorbed by the retained profit brought forward from peacetime football. On the field, the club called upon the services of countless players who were attached to other clubs and fielded an astonishing 46 different players in the 1915–16 season. Almost 15,000 soldiers were admitted into Wednesday games for free in that season, and servicemen were a regular sight on the Hillsborough terraces throughout the duration of the conflict.

After that transitional season, Wednesday attempted to gather together a much stronger side – also re-engaging Ambrose Langley as trainer – but a failure to win any games on their travels meant that they had to settle for a lower mid-table finish. Two games did stand out from the norm. The home meeting with Bradford City in February 1917 was abandoned after 85 minutes when two players started a fight. The referee broke up the pair, but they started scrapping again, and within minutes part of the crowd was involved in the fisticuffs and the pitch was flooded with spectators. The players and officials fought their way back into the dressing rooms, with the Owls probably glad that the scenes had not taken place in peacetime football! The other match of note was the final game of the season, when a hat-trick from Jack Burkinshaw helped Wednesday to their biggest win during the war – 7–1 against Lincoln City. The saddest news of the wartime period for Wednesday came in April 1918, when it was reported that pre-war amateur attacker, Vivian Simpson, had been killed in France while fighting for his country.

As World War One started to turn in the direction of the Allied Forces, the final season of wartime football was greeted with much more optimism than before, and in November

A wartime team from 1918.

1918 some normality returned to the football field after the armistice was signed, signalling the end of the conflict. Fans instantly poured back into football stadiums, and 55,000 watched the two derby meetings with Sheffield United over the Christmas period. The season finished with Wednesday posting another lowly position, but national football was on the horizon and Owls fans were set to experience an unforgettable season, for all the wrong reasons.

After an enforced break of four seasons, English football returned to normality in 1919, but Wednesday had an early sign of the problems to come when crucial players Jimmy Blair and David McLean both refused to accept the terms offered. Not unlike the situation with McLean a few years earlier, Blair returned home to Scotland and signed for a non-League outfit, Alloa Athletic in this instance. His compatriot, McLean, did eventually re-sign, but it quickly became apparent that the Owls were going to struggle in the top flight, failing to taste victory until their seventh match of the season. Despite a derby win over Sheffield United, the club slumped to the bottom of the League and McLean was sold to Bradford Park Avenue after scoring over 100 goals for Wednesday. Lady Luck had also deserted the Owls, with Sam Kirkman contracting malaria and the Wednesday committee men coming under increasing pressure for constantly changing the team and failing to invest in quality players. Despite bringing several new faces into the side, none made a tangible difference, and the gloom around Hillsborough deepened further when non-League Darlington knocked Wednesday out of the FA Cup.

When the club finally acted – surprisingly paying a record fee for Blackpool defender George Wilson – it was unfortunately too late, and with five games still to play the Owls were relegated to the Second Division. The use of 41 players – a club record – and an excessive reliance on pre-war players seemed to be the major reasons for the failure and it was obvious that a major restructuring was required for the club to regain their former glories. The fall out from the relegation was significant: 21 players were either released or transferred, including Tom Brittleton, and at the club AGM Owls stalwart Arthur Dickinson announced that he was resigning from his role of secretary-manager after 29 years in the position. Dickinson's final act was to successfully organise the first ever England international staged at Hillsborough – a sensational 5–4 win over Scotland – in April 1920. To replace Dickinson, the club turned to his former assistant, Bob Brown, who moved from Portsmouth back to Sheffield. The new manager started his career at Hillsborough with three consecutive goalless matches, and one of his first acts was to sell Jimmy Blair to Cardiff City for a club record transfer fee. After a poor first half of the season, the signing of centre-forward Sam Taylor proved an inspired acquisition, as his partnership with Johnny McIntyre – who finished the season with 27 League goals – bore fruit, with the side winning five games in a row and thrashing FA Cup finalists Wolves 6–0 at Hillsborough to eventually finish 10th.

The early 1920s was a period in which Bob Brown slowly rebuilt the side, bringing in several players who would become legends at Wednesday and help the club to great success in the latter part of the decade. In Brown's first four seasons in charge the Owls registered top-10 finishes without ever really challenging for promotion, and Wednesday fans had to show a degree of patience as Brown searched for that elusive winning formula. The arrival

The Wednesday team from 1921–22.

of Jimmy Trotter, near the end of the 1921–22 season, proved a crucial capture, and the new-look Wednesday side really started to take shape when Rees Williams and Jack Brown were added to the playing staff.

The 1922–23 season was memorable for the FA Cup meeting with Barnsley at Hillsborough, when unprecedented interest in the tie resulted in a mammoth crowd of 66,103 packing into the ground – a record for both the Owls and the City of Sheffield. The summer of 1923 saw the club's reserve side accepted into the Central League, while players Billy Felton and Rees Williams were each fined £5 by the League management committee after they missed the train for a mid-week game at Port Vale in August 1923. The club's trainer, Jerry Jackson, was forced to play, but he retired just before the interval and the Owls lost 2–0.

The dawn of the 1924–25 campaign was greeted with great enthusiasm by Wednesday fans, as several summer signings – including Arthur Prince and Billy Marsden – plus the arrival of new trainer Chris Craig, raised hopes that the Owls would finally challenge for promotion. On the opening day of the season Wednesday became the first club to play at Crystal Palace's new Selhurst Park ground (a goal from new signing Marsden securing a 1–0 win), but results were inconsistent and the club eventually slipped down the rankings to finish in a disappointing 14th position. A link with the past was also broken during that campaign, as in September 1924 The Wednesday Cricket Club disbanded, citing the lack of a home ground as the major reason for their demise. The one real positive to emerge from the season was the increasingly prolific form of Jimmy Trotter, who became the first player to score five times in a League fixture – achieving the feat at home to Bob Brown's old club, Portsmouth, in December 1924. The arrival of Harold Hill also further strengthened the ranks, while another new face was Blackpool captain Matt Barrass, who had scored a hat-

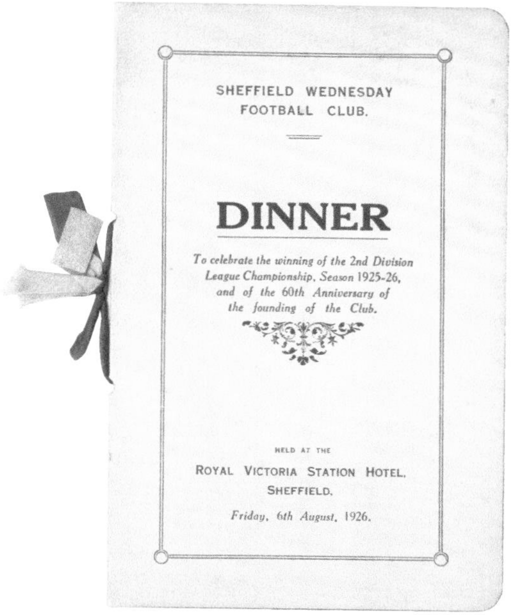

SHEFFIELD WEDNESDAY
FOOTBALL CLUB.
DINNER
To celebrate the winning of the 2nd Division League Championship, Season 1925-26, and of the 60th Anniversary of the founding of the Club.
HELD AT THE
ROYAL VICTORIA STATION HOTEL,
SHEFFIELD.
Friday, 6th August, 1926.

Menu from the dinner celebrating the 1925–26 Second Division title sucess.

trick at Hillsborough a few weeks earlier as Wednesday lost 6–2 – equalling their worst ever home loss at the time.

In the 1925–26 season the wait was finally over for Wednesday supporters as Brown's side made a great start, winning seven of their opening 10 League games to sit second in the table. This time the club did not fall away and, after beating Chelsea in November 1925, they went top of the Second Division table. A run of eight wins in nine games over the Christmas and New Year period ensured that the club remained in the top two promotion positions for the remainder of the season, returning to the summit in early March. A last-minute penalty save from Jack Brown – in a crucial promotion clash at Chelsea – secured a vital point, and it was left to top scorer Jimmy Trotter to score both goals in a 2–0 win at Southampton and clinch promotion back to the top flight. A week later the Championship was secured as Wednesday took their goal tally to a club record 88 – an astonishing 37 of those coming from the boots of Jimmy Trotter. The prolific attacker may have grabbed the headlines, but it was perhaps crucial that seven players – Matt Barrass, Ernie Blenkinsop, Jack Brown, captain Frank Froggatt, Billy Marsden, Jimmy Trotter and Rees Williams – all appeared in at least 40 League fixtures, building a team pattern that was an important part of their success.

For their first season back in the top flight the Owls decided against adding to their successful promotion side, although a handful of players did leave the club, including legendary goalkeeper Teddy Davison. The summer AGM involved a debate about the club's name (an issue that would be resolved three years later), while Richard Sparling's seminal work on the club, *The Romance of the Wednesday,* hit the bookstores of Sheffield. The fixture list handed the club a plum start to the season – a home tie with Sheffield United – but two late goals was enough to hand the Blades the opening day spoils. Wednesday's defence was generous to a fault in those early weeks, conceding seven at Spurs and five at Leicester, but thankfully a fine home record meant that the Owls remained in mid-table for most of the campaign. The club actually failed to record a single success on their travels, which included a defeat at Bramall Lane watched by the Blades' biggest crowd ever. It was deadly marksman Jimmy Trotter who again took all the plaudits with 37 League goals – a tally that has never been bettered by an Owls player in the top flight. He finished as top scorer in the First Division and netted almost half of the club's 75 goals in their 42-game League campaign. Although fans did not realise it at the time, the most important events of the season came in the transfer market, where Bob Brown's eye for talent hit the jackpot by capturing the signatures of Mark Hooper, Jack Allen and Alf Strange in the spring of 1927. Former England international Jimmy Seed joined from Tottenham in the close season, but Wednesday fans were shocked when the new campaign opened with a 4–0 drubbing at Everton. Unfortunately, the expected push for honours never materialised and it quickly became obvious that the Owls would be more occupied with events at the bottom end of the table than at the top end! In November 1927 the club took direct action again as they smashed their transfer record to capture the signature of Blackburn Rovers and England centre-forward Ted Harper. The newcomer made a truly sensational start to his Hillsborough career, becoming the only Owls player to score a League hat-trick on his debut – achieving this rare feat in a 6–4 win at Derby County. Unfortunately, his presence in the side failed to have a long-term effect, and by early March 1928 Wednesday looked certain to be relegated, sitting seven points adrift at the bottom with only 10 games remaining. It was at this point that the history of Sheffield Wednesday took a decidedly upward curve as, despite the situation looking hopeless, they suddenly started on a winning streak. Inspired and cajoled by captain Jimmy Seed, Wednesday netted nine goals in consecutive home fixtures, and four consecutive League wins in April pulled the club within touching distance of the teams immediately above them. It was then that their game in hand came into the frame, as a dramatic last-minute equaliser from Seed at Arsenal secured a valuable point and moved the Owls all the way up to 19th position in the table. The relegation dogfight thus went to the final day of the season and, in one of the most sensational finishes ever seen in English football, a total of only two points separated the bottom 10 teams. Wednesday duly recorded their eighth win from their final 10 League games and escaped relegation.

The incredible finish to the 1927–28 season not only saved the club's First Division place, but directly led to arguably the greatest period in Wednesday's long history. The side that finished the previous season simply continued where they had left off, with goals galore from Jack Allen taking the club to the summit of the division by late November. It was a position that Wednesday would not relinquish, and a side containing some of the greatest players to ever wear the blue-and-white shirt went into the final home match of the season, with their nearest rivals, Leicester City, one point behind. A goal from visitors Burnley stunned the expectant Hillsborough crowd, but Jack Allen, with his 35th and final goal of the season, levelled matters before half-time, leaving the 33,314 crowd awaiting news from elsewhere. The game at Hillsborough finished in a draw, but the celebrations began when news filtered through that the Foxes had also drawn, handing the League Championship to Bob Brown's troops. To complete an unforgettable season, the reserve team won the Central League title, while the senior side could bask in their success during a three-week post-season tour of Switzerland. From a position of power, Wednesday added exciting inside-forward Harry Burgess from Stockport County, while the summer of 1929 saw The Wednesday Football Club officially change its title to Sheffield Wednesday Football Club. A tremendous 4–0 win at Portsmouth started their defence of the League Championship crown, but Wednesday fans were shocked when Arsenal became the first team to win at Hillsborough since February 1928. In sharp contrast to the previous season when the club only won three times on the road, Wednesday had already won four away games by early

October and, with the legendary forward line of Hooper, Seed, Allen, Burgess and Rimmer in full flow, the Owls settled into second position. A point at home to Portsmouth in the final game of 1929 lifted Wednesday to the top of the table, and the quality of the side was no more apparent than in early April when, despite having Strange, Blenkinsop, Marsden and Hooper on England duty, they won 3–1 at Liverpool. In the end, Wednesday simply ran away with a second consecutive title, breaking the divisional points record (60) and scoring a club record 105 League goals. They also finished a huge 10 points clear of their nearest rival (a position comparable to Manchester United finishing 15 points clear of Chelsea in the modern-day Premiership). The only blot on an outstanding season was the club's failure to record the prestigious League and Cup double, controversially losing 2–1 to Huddersfield Town in the FA Cup semi-final with the referee denying the Owls a last-minute equaliser by blowing his whistle as Allen's shot headed for the net!

Not long after the title celebrations ended, the club were stunned when England international Billy Marsden was seriously hurt while playing for his country against Germany. His injuries were so severe that he was detained in a German hospital for several weeks and sadly never returned to the Wednesday team, being forced to retire a few months later. His loss was a blow to Bob Brown's plans of completing a hat-trick of titles, and a chance of early silverware disappeared when Arsenal won the Charity Shield at Stamford Bridge. The Gunners would prove to be the club's major rival for the League Championship and they quickly opened up a sizeable lead at the top of the division, winning a crunch game at Hillsborough in November 1929, a few days after club stalwart Arthur Dickinson passed away. The Owls' all-time record League win – 9–1 against Birmingham City – did, however, see Wednesday take back first place. The two clubs exchanged positions until the Owls' title hopes took a dive thanks to three straight defeats in February 1931. That sudden loss of form proved costly and, despite scoring 102 League and Cup goals, the club had to be content with third position as Arsenal set a new points record for the First Division, finishing 14 points ahead of Wednesday.

For the next two seasons Wednesday remained in the top echelons of the English game, finishing in third place on both occasions. It looked like a third title in four seasons was a mere formality at the beginning of the 1931–32 campaign, as Wednesday scored 20 goals in winning their first four fixtures, including an opening day 6–1 win at Blackburn Rovers. Without the leadership of Jimmy Seed (who had taken the manager's job at Clapton Orient), they slipped down to mid-table, before a late revival hoisted them into the top three, six points behind eventual champions, Everton. Eight away wins

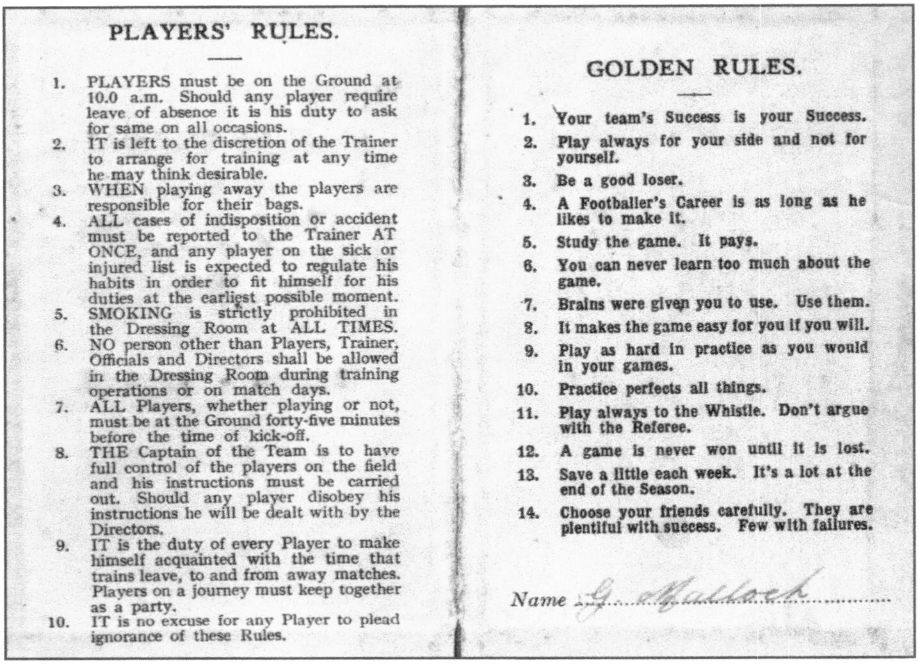

PLAYERS' RULES.

1. PLAYERS must be on the Ground at 10.0 a.m. Should any player require leave of absence it is his duty to ask for same on all occasions.
2. IT is left to the discretion of the Trainer to arrange for training at any time he may think desirable.
3. WHEN playing away the players are responsible for their bags.
4. ALL cases of indisposition or accident must be reported to the Trainer AT ONCE, and any player on the sick or injured list is expected to regulate his habits in order to fit himself for his duties at the earliest possible moment.
5. SMOKING is strictly prohibited in the Dressing Room at ALL TIMES.
6. NO person other than Players, Trainer, Officials and Directors shall be allowed in the Dressing Room during training operations or on match days.
7. ALL Players, whether playing or not, must be at the Ground forty-five minutes before the time of kick-off.
8. THE Captain of the Team is to have full control of the players on the field and his instructions must be carried out. Should any player disobey his instructions he will be dealt with by the Directors.
9. IT is the duty of every Player to make himself acquainted with the time that trains leave, to and from away matches. Players on a journey must keep together as a party.
10. IT is no excuse for any Player to plead ignorance of these Rules.

GOLDEN RULES.

1. Your team's Success is your Success.
2. Play always for your side and not for yourself.
3. Be a good loser.
4. A Footballer's Career is as long as he likes to make it.
5. Study the game. It pays.
6. You can never learn too much about the game.
7. Brains were given you to use. Use them.
8. It makes the game easy for you if you will.
9. Play as hard in practice as you would in your games.
10. Practice perfects all things.
11. Play always to the Whistle. Don't argue with the Referee.
12. A game is never won until it is lost.
13. Save a little each week. It's a lot at the end of the Season.
14. Choose your friends carefully. They are plentiful with success. Few with failures.

Name [illegible]

The players' rule book from the 1930s.

helped their cause, although their successes were marred by a 9–3 mauling at Everton, where Dixie Dean scored five for the Merseyside outfit. The club's form was far more consistent in the following season and Wednesday remained inside the top three positions from December until the end of the campaign. Unfortunately, a single win in their final nine games ruined any chance of regaining the title and they had to be content with only adding the Scunthorpe Hospital Cup to their trophy cabinet! Centre-forward Jack Ball also netted 10 times from the penalty spot during the campaign, setting a club record that would last for almost 50 years. The major news during the early stages of the 1933–34 season was the departure, after over 13 years in charge, of manager Bob Brown. He was replaced on a temporary basis by his assistant, Joe McClelland, but his departure would effectively end a golden period in the club's history; his eventual replacement, Billy Walker, would preside over a tremendous FA Cup win, but would also take the club into the Second Division.

One of Walker's first acts was, controversially, to sell top scorer Jack Ball to Manchester United, with Scottish forward Neil Dewar travelling in the opposite direction. An eventual mid-table finish in the First Division was accompanied by a run to the last 16 of

Shirt badge from the 1934–35 season.

the FA Cup, which resulted in the ground record at Hillsborough being smashed when 72,841 packed in for a fifth-round meeting with Manchester City. The season did, however, contain some sad news, as long-time trainer Chris Craig died after a brief illness, with the club holding a benefit match for his dependants. There were minor changes to the club's playing staff in the summer of 1934 and the season proved to be the last hurrah for several of the players who had brought the club major success. After a poor start, the Owls moved into the top six positions in time for Christmas, before the FA Cup grabbed all the headlines. Victories over Oldham Athletic, Wolves and Norwich City set up a quarter-final clash with old foes Arsenal at Hillsborough. The ground was again packed to the rafters, as goals from Rimmer and Hooper secured a semi-final meeting with Burnley. A superb display duly clinched the club's fourth FA Cup Final appearance and a first visit to the new Empire (Wembley) Stadium. By the time that Wednesday faced West Bromwich Albion in the Final, the Owls had moved up to fourth place in the table and would eventually finish one place higher. A crowd of 10,000 Wednesday fans made the journey to Wembley for the 1935 FA Cup Final and they saw a thrilling match, which was tied at two goals apiece with just three minutes left on the clock. Wednesday winger Ellis Rimmer then put his side ahead, however, and became the first player to score in every round of the Cup in the same season. He quickly added a fourth goal and celebrations began back home in Sheffield. A week later Wednesday paraded the Cup before their delighted fans at the last home game of the season, and hopes were high among those supporters that the season would just be the start of a second golden era, this time under Billy Walker.

Unfortunately, those fans were to be sadly disappointed as Wednesday experienced a torrid time over the next two seasons, which culminated in the almost unthinkable relegation from the First Division in 1937. The club made a reasonable start to the 1935–36 season, winning the Charity Shield against Arsenal at Highbury, but as autumn turned to winter wins become more and more infrequent. The side seemed to need an injection of new blood, but Owls fans were dismayed when centre-forward Jack Palethorpe was sold to Aston Villa. His departure left the club with only one striker – Neil Dewar – and by the end of the year Wednesday had slumped alarmingly to just two places off the bottom. A short Cup run helped lift the spirits around Hillsborough, but a team that had achieved so much just a few months earlier was suddenly looking vulnerable, with an obvious over-reliance on their ageing stars. A shocking 5–0 defeat at Middlesbrough on Easter Monday dropped the Owls into the relegation places for the first time, but a tremendous win at Stoke City soon saw them climb back out. A point in their final home game proved sufficient to secure safety, but did not prevent a post-mortem in the close season. In the summer of 1936 manager Billy Walker promised fans that his team would use an 'all up' attacking strategy, which would be reminiscent of the glory days only a few years earlier. In an attempt to stem the tide he made several forays into the transfer market, signing Roy Smith, Derwick Goodfellow, James McCambridge and Allenby Driver. The club's increasingly beleaguered manager had simply failed to bring in any players of First Division quality, however, and the club would suffer a terrible season, winning only nine games and being relegated after losing 5–1 against a Manchester City side that needed a victory to secure the League Championship. Both the manager and the club's board were harshly criticised during the season, with the latter being roundly condemned when they sold club captain Ronnie Starling to Aston Villa part way through the campaign. It was also seen by many fans as an admission of failure when manager Walker employed the services of a sports psychologist in an attempt to improve his players' mental toughness.

The close season saw Wednesday fail to strengthen sufficiently, and their published accounts proved what fans had suspected: the club had made a large profit, mainly by selling high and buying low. That tactic was clearly a recipe for disaster, and with a new trainer at the helm – Sam Powell replacing the departed George Irwin – Wednesday made an awful start to life back in the Second Division, slumping to the bottom of the League after a 4–1 derby defeat at Barnsley. Time had clearly run out for Billy Walker and he resigned 24 hours after the Oakwell debacle. The side was picked by the board of directors until new man Jimmy McMullan took over in January 1938. The new manager arrived at a club in turmoil, and he could not avoid criticism when the directors seemingly forced the sale of outstanding young prospect George Drury to Arsenal. Even the club's relatively mild-mannered shareholders threatened to organise a protest meeting, but Wednesday quickly tried to placate their disgruntled supporters by entering the transfer market to sign internationals Charlie Napier and Bill Fallon. Despite the arrival of the new recruits, the club went into their final game of the season, at Tottenham, just one point off the relegation places. Thankfully, the threat of regional football abated when Bill Fallon and George Hunt put the Owls 2–0 ahead at the interval, and they held on to stave off relegation and bring the curtain down on a season of drama, controversy and disappointment.

To the credit of Wednesday's manager, the side seemed transformed when the new season kicked off, seemingly improved by the capture of David Russell and winger Idris Lewis. A pre-season win over Sheffield United – one of a series of friendly games organised to celebrate the 50th birthday of the Football League – lifted the fans' spirits, and after five games Wednesday sat atop the Second Division table. After a small slump they revived, thanks to Doug Hunt's six-goal bonanza against Norwich City, and became serious contenders for the two promotion places. In the FA Cup Wednesday played eight times, but amazingly failed to reach the quarter-finals, losing to Chelsea in a fifth-round second replay at Highbury. It was therefore back to League matters and the race for promotion eventually went to the wire, with Blackburn Rovers and Sheffield's two professional clubs chasing the prize. When the regular season came to a close Rovers were champions and Wednesday sat in second place, but, crucially, the Blades still had a game left to play. The game was at home to Tottenham Hotspur and a week later a contingent of Wednesday fans were inside Bramall Lane to cheer on the North London side. Unfortunately, those supporters must have caught the early tram home as United trounced Spurs 6–1 to agonisingly deny the Owls a return to the big time.

The build-up to the 1939–40 season was dominated by world events, as the ever-menacing threat of Adolf Hitler's Germany loomed more and more into view. With the clouds of war forming, football tried to continue as normal. At Hillsborough the only transfer activity of note was the departure of club legend Mark Hooper, who signed for neighbours Rotherham United. In the summer months the club hosted a professional tennis competition – dubbed 'three hours of Wimbledon' – and the new season started with a disappointing 3–0 reverse at Luton Town. Football took a back seat on Sunday 3

September 1939, however, when British Prime Minster Neville Chamberlain announced that the country was now at war with Germany. All sporting activities were immediately banned while the authorities decided what course of action should be taken. The decision was made to continue with football, with new regional Leagues organised and crowd restrictions enforced – 8,000 fans or half of the ground's capacity, whichever was lower. The Owls found themselves in the hastily arranged East Midlands Regional League, although all player contracts had been cancelled and even manager Jimmy McMullan was now only part-time after gaining employment in a Sheffield factory. Those early war years were extremely difficult for all football clubs and Wednesday was no exception; a generally apathetic public were, understandably, more interested in the war effort than the game of football. Wednesday only just survived the 1939–40 season, and chairman William Turner expressed at the club's AGM that Wednesday would have to sign several amateur players in the summer if they were to fulfil their vow of fielding a team in the following season.

The Sheffield Blitz dominated the 1940–41 season, and after Bramall Lane was damaged Wednesday's neighbours made Hillsborough their home for several months. Without doubt, the highlight of the war years, from a football point of view, came in the 1942–43 season when a side containing Jackie Robinson and Frank Melling pushed for League and Cup honours. With secretary Eric Taylor now effectively in charge, the Owls would score over 100 goals in 39 games, and the highlights included: an 8–2 trouncing of Sheffield United; a 10–2 win at Mansfield Town; and a run to the Final of the League North War Cup. With early crowd restrictions lifted, a wartime record crowd of almost 48,000 was inside Hillsborough for the second leg of the Final against Blackpool, but it would be the Lancashire club that lifted the trophy. The club could not have hoped to repeat the feats of that season, especially as Melling was unavailable and Robinson made only the occasional appearance, and it was a mid-table finish as the war in Europe started to swing the way of the Allied forces. In the summer of 1944 William Fearnehough was elected as the club's new chairman, continuing a strong family link that dated back to his father, Walter, who was a founder member of Wednesday back in 1867. The close season also saw Wednesday win a five-a-side competition held in Millhouses Park, with youngster Redfern Froggatt earning rave reviews. One of the highlights of the 1944–45 season was the first win at Bramall Lane since 1933, while the continuing problems of wartime soccer were illustrated when the Owls could only raise nine senior players for a game at Notts County. They had no choice but to field two youngsters, with goalkeeper Harry Donaldson playing on the right wing! On 8 May 1945 victory in Europe was declared, and 24 hours later Wednesday met the Blades at the rebuilt Bramall Lane in a specially arranged VE game.

Wednesday in hoops during the 1945–46 season.

The world of football made its first step on the road to regaining its pre-war status quo in the summer of 1945 with the introduction of a Football League North and South, with the Owls facing 21 different clubs on a home and away basis. The Central League, which was a regional competition anyway, was reintroduced and Wednesday would be the first post-war winners, securing the Championship for the second time. The first team also enjoyed a very encouraging season and finished fifth in the League, while also reaching the last 16 of the FA Cup. For the only time in the competition's history, all the Cup ties from the first round up until the semi-finals were played on a two-leg basis, with the Owls netting 16 goals and beating York City and Mansfield Town. This set up a mouth-watering clash with Stanley Matthews' Stoke City, but there was no fairy-tale ending – the First Division side knocked out Wednesday.

The previous season had perhaps lulled the club into a false sense of security, as there was virtually no transfer activity in the summer that preceded the return of national soccer. Off the field, future club secretary Eric England joined the club as assistant to Eric Taylor, while pre-war players Sam Powell and Tommy Walker were appointed to the roles of trainer and assistant trainer respectively. The fixture list for the new season was an exact repeat of the abandoned 1939–40 season, and the seven-year gap was emphasised by a Wednesday line up for the opening game against Luton Town that contained only Jackie Robinson from the 1939 team. It quickly became obvious that the Owls would not be launching an immediate promotion push to the top division, as they had a bad start and struggled for the whole season, badly affected by a long, harsh winter. The sale of star Jackie Robinson, for a club record fee to Sunderland, certainly did not help the club's chance, although the crucial

Back playing in stripes in the 1946–47 season.

signings of Doug Hunt and Jimmy Dailey provided enough quality and experience to eventually lift the club away from immediate danger. Over 41,000 packed into Hillsborough for the Boxing Day meeting with Bury, but the natives were restless and Wednesday's response was to officially advertise the post of team manager. It was duly announced that Sheffield United's trainer, Doug Livingstone, had been appointed, but the Owls were left somewhat red-faced after he had a change of heart and declined the position. A new trainer, William Knox, was appointed, with Eric Taylor remaining in the role of secretary-manager. Two wins over top-flight opposition in the FA Cup lifted spirits, but the early weeks of 1947 were hard for both fans and players as match after match was postponed or played on a snowbound pitch. It was not until late May that Wednesday secured their Second Division status – a Tommy Ward goal being enough against Manchester City – but the season had still been a huge disappointment; chairman Fearnehough admitted that it had been the

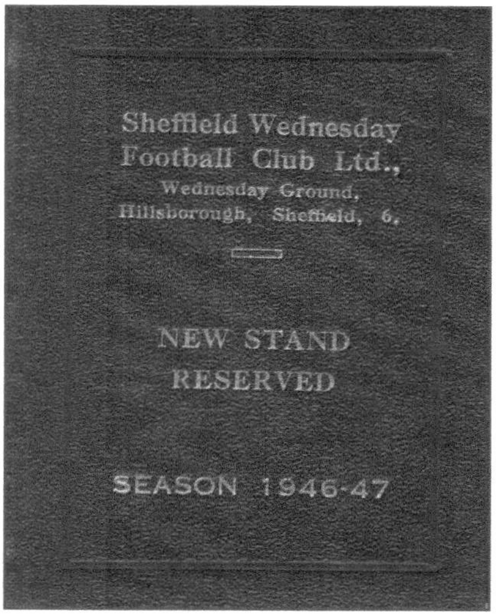

1946–47 season ticket.

worst in the club's history. The wretched season actually ended on 7 June 1947, with Chesterfield player George Milburn netting a hat-trick of penalties in a 4–2 defeat at Saltergate – the latest date on which the club has ever fulfilled a League fixture.

Over the remainder of the 1940s the club became determined to win promotion from the Second Division and the purse strings were loosened considerably in an attempt to achieve that ambition. The club transfer record was smashed with Eddie Quigley, the first big signing, joining from Bury for £12,000 in 1947. After going close to promotion in 1948 (a loss at Newcastle United in front of over 66,000 fans being a crucial turning point), Wednesday broke their transfer record again, paying £20,000 for Eddie Kilshaw early in the following season. Football in general was experiencing a post-war boom in attendances and this was shown in February 1949, when nearly 50,000 fans packed into Hillsborough for a Sheffield County Cup tie against Sheffield United. Unfortunately, despite Eddie Gannon arriving for another impressive fee, the Owls finished 13 points away from the two promotion places and also lost the services of talented winger, Kilshaw, who was forced to retire injured after just 19 games in the blue-and-white stripes.

The club's financial statements showed a big loss for the 1948–49 season, reflecting the fact that Wednesday had spent heavily in their attempt to achieve success, but the board vowed that promotion was a priority. Owls supporters therefore hoped that a return to the First Division, after a 13-year absence, could finally become reality, and thankfully they were not to be disappointed this time. Wednesday started the new campaign confidently, as a four-goal haul, including a hat-trick inside five minutes, by Eddie Quigley helped to beat local rivals Chesterfield. The 1–0 win at Preston North End was significant in that Wednesday winger Charlie Tomlinson scored the only goal of the match after just 12 seconds – believed to be the quickest ever goal for the club. The side was unbeaten from mid-October until mid-January – a run of 13 games – although the match at Coventry City was abandoned when fog descended on Highfield Road. Former Sheffield United winger Walter Rickett signed from Blackpool, and the Owls were then involved in a transfer that set a new British record: Eddie Quigley moved to Preston North End for £26,000, enabling Wednesday to double their money in the process. Also to sign was full-back Norman Curtis, while there was sadness when trainer William Knox died suddenly at his home. The club's attempts to replace Quigley ended with the capture of Hugh McJarrow, while on the field of play Wednesday climbed to second position after an Easter Monday win over Bury. An attack of promotion nerves followed – the club needed either a win or a 0–0 draw in their final game of the season, at home to champions Tottenham Hotspur, to clinch promotion. Both Sheffield United (who had finished their fixtures) and Southampton could still overhaul the Owls, but on a nervous afternoon at Hillsborough over 50,000 fans watched with bated breath as the 0–0 scoreline was achieved, securing promotion back to the First Division. In the end, the margin of success could not have been tighter, with Wednesday beating their city rivals to promotion by a difference in goal average (goals scored divided by goals conceded) of 0.008.

Promotion back to the top flight would set in motion a decade that would become known as the 'yo-yo years' due to the fact that Wednesday won the Second Division title on three separate occasions, but were also relegated three times. The run of mixed luck only

Derek Dooley.

ended when Harry Catterick was appointed manager in 1958. The 1950–51 campaign proved to be a long, hard season for the club, as an opening-day thrashing at Chelsea set the tone. A tremendous win over reigning champions Portsmouth in the first home game proved a false dawn and, with just one solitary game remaining of the season, the Owls were bottom of the division and needed a minor miracle to escape immediate relegation back from whence they had come. To help their relegation battle the club had surprised the football world by smashing the British transfer record to sign Jackie Sewell for £35,000, after sensational moves for Sheffield United star Jimmy Hagan and England International Nat Lofthouse had broken down. The new man netted six goals in the final 10 games of the season, including two in the final day 6–0 win over Everton. Before the game Wednesday knew that they had to win by at least six clear goals to have a chance, but sadly their rivals, Chelsea, won 4–0 to send Wednesday back down on goal average, this time by a difference in goal average of 0.044.

The 1951–52 season was dominated by one man, Derek Dooley, who rampaged through opposition defences to plunder a club record of 47 goals as his side won the Second Division title. The towering centre-forward was not actually introduced into the side until early October, as manager Eric Taylor searched for a winning formula after an unpredictable start had left Wednesday way down in 17th position and still licking their wounds after a 7–3 humiliation at Bramall Lane. The Sheffield-born attacker duly netted a brace as Barnsley were beaten and he never looked back, grabbing five second-half goals against Notts County and setting a club record by scoring in nine consecutive League matches. Crowds flocked to Hillsborough to watch him, and Wednesday set a new record crowd for a League fixture when over 65,000 watched the Blades record a season double. The derby setback proved an isolated disappointment, as promotion was clinched at Coventry City and the title secured on the final day of the season, with the Owls taking their goal tally to exactly 100. The club then took part in friendly matches in the Lake District and Switzerland, before bringing the curtain down on one of the greatest seasons in their history.

Fans were eager to see how Wednesday, and more particularly Dooley, would cope with life in the First Division, and the Owls sat in mid-table after a Dooley goal won the final game of 1952. A run of four straight defeats then pushed the club back down the table, but the losses paled into insignificance with the tragic events of 14 February 1953. The day could not have started worse as the news broke that morning that chairman William Fearnehough had passed away, aged 74. With the club in mourning, the Owls lost 1–0 at Deepdale, but it was the incident in the 59th minute that would change the life of one individual and have far-reaching implications for the short-term fortune of Sheffield Wednesday – the minute that Derek Dooley collided with the Preston goalkeeper and broke

Programme and ticket from Derek Dooley's testimonial game.

his right leg. Normally, this would mean a few months on the sidelines for the unfortunate player, but sadly this was not case; the key striker contracted gas gangrene and 48 hours later was forced to have his leg amputated in order to save his life. The world of football was stunned at the news, and Owls supporters could hardly believe what had happened to one of the most-loved players in the club's long history. One of the main reasons that fans had flocked to Hillsborough in the early 1950s (in the 1952–53 season Wednesday posted their highest ever average attendance) was the sight of Dooley, and it was certainly no coincidence that crowds dropped significantly after the dramatic end to his playing career. The season was played out in a somewhat sombre mood, although the players did just enough to keep Wednesday in the First Division.

The summer of 1953 saw the club play its final public trial match as the traditional pre-season fixture was consigned to the history books. The club tried, in vain, to find a suitable replacement for Dooley, with Jack Shaw and Clarrie Jordan manfully trying to fill his sizeable boots. The new season again brought a lower mid-table finish in the top flight, with the highlight being a run to the semi-finals of the FA Cup. In the third-round replay against neighbours United at Bramall Lane, Wednesday defender Vin Kenny became the first Owls player to be sent off in post-war football, but the derby spoils went to the blue-and-white side of the city. The Cup run eventually ended at Maine Road, Manchester, where finalists Preston won thanks to two goals in the second period. The 1954 close season saw floodlights installed at Hillsborough for the first time; Colonel Craig being appointed chairman in place of the deceased James Longden; and trainer-coach Alan Brown departing after accepting the managerial position at Burnley. Despite all these changes (crucially there were no incoming transfers and this inactivity proved to be the club's downfall), Wednesday quickly slipped down the League and won only eight games in the whole season to finish a massive 11 points from safety. Only Jackie Sewell, with 14 goals, reached double figures in a season where Derek Dooley's testimonial game produced the biggest match attendance (55,000) and over 40,000 people filled the ground when HM Queen Elizabeth II made a rare visit to a football stadium. A 7–0 County Cup disaster at Rotherham United signalled the end of a truly forgettable season, which resulted in Wednesday back in the worryingly familiar surrounds of the Second Division. The summer of 1955 saw the appointment of Doctor Andrew Stephen to the role of club chairman, and Stephen, knighted in 1972, would serve with distinction for the next 18 years.

The pattern of promotion, consolidation and relegation was repeated in the next three seasons, beginning with the Second Division title in 1956. In marked contrast to previous summers, Wednesday brought in several new players pre-season, signing Albert Broadbent, Walter Bingley, Gerry Young, Don Gibson, Ron Staniforth and Roy Shiner to totally revamp the first team. The new men quickly gelled with the likes of Albert Quixall, Alan Finney and Redfern Froggatt as the team slowly moved up the League table to reach the top two by December 1955. They continued to win as the New Year dawned, and a resounding 5–2 victory at Bury in the final away game not only secured promotion, but also the Championship, with 33 goals from new signing Shiner playing a major part in the success. The club made a good start to life back in the top flight, before five consecutive defeats pushed them down into the lower reaches of the League table, and five weeks without a home fixture due to adverse weather conditions did not help the club's fortunes. Thankfully, three wins in their final three fixtures of the season ensured a lower mid-table finishing position. Off the field, secretary-manager Eric Taylor was handed a new five-year contract, while the club's youth side won through to the FA Youth Cup semi-finals for the first time, losing heavily over two legs to West Ham United.

Any hopes of the club improving on that finish were quickly dashed as the 1957–58 season started in chaotic fashion, with a flu bug decimating the club's playing staff and forcing the two opening games of the season, at home to Manchester City and away to Newcastle United, to be postponed. The virulent nature of the infection forced the ground to shut down, and when the season did start Wednesday fielded a weakened side in terms of both personnel and fitness. The Owls never really recovered from that disrupted start and, after slipping to the bottom of the League, they were eventually relegated – a 5–0 win on the final day not being enough to save them. The season was plagued

Supporters' club year book from 1956–57.

The Wednesday squad from 1957–58.

with several other problems, as a goalkeeping crisis saw the club use four different men between the sticks before the arrival of future England international Ron Springett solved the problem. A run in the FA Cup did lift some of the gloom, and when the fifth-round draw took the Owls to Old Trafford hopes were high of springing an upset. Following the death of several Manchester United players and officials in the tragic Munich Air Disaster, however, the game became highly significant as the first post-Munich game for the Manchester club. The delayed tie was played in a highly emotional atmosphere, and Wednesday could not respond to a patched-up United side that rose to the occasion to record a 3–0 win.

The third relegation of the decade saw a real summer of change at Hillsborough as it was finally decided to split the secretary-manager role into two separate positions, with current incumbent Eric Taylor appointed in the single role of club secretary. After a failed attempt to prise Tottenham Hotspur assistant manager, Bill Nicholson, from the North London club, the Owls crossed the Pennines to hand a three-year contract to Rochdale manager, Harry Catterick. Behind the scenes, former players Tom Walker and Sam Powell were released from their backroom roles, while the Owls' youth team moved from local football into the regional Northern Intermediate League. New manager Catterick made an immediate impression at Wednesday, and a dozen games into the new season his charges were sitting at the top of the Second Division. It was a position they would not relinquish, despite star man Albert Quixall moving to Manchester United for a British record of £45,000 in the early weeks of the campaign. Promotion was clinched with four games still to play, and a 5–0 home win over Barnsley, strangely watched by the lowest crowd of the season, clinched the third title of the 1950s. Top scorer was again Roy Shiner, with 28, with four other players also recording double figures in the goal chart.

The appointment of Harry Catterick proved an inspired decision by the club's board of directors as the circle of promotion and relegation was firmly ended; Wednesday finished the following season in fifth place in the First Division – their best final position since the mid-1930s. A tremendous opening-day win at Arsenal quickly proved that the side could survive in the top flight, and Wednesday hit the headlines in the pre-Christmas period as a 7–0 win over League leaders West Ham United was followed by a four-goal success at Chelsea and then five goals in a Hillsborough win over Arsenal. Over 50,000 fans watched the FA Cup tie against Midland League Peterborough United, and after beating the non-League side the Owls went all the way to the semi-finals, where they narrowly lost to Blackburn Rovers at the final hurdle before Wembley. Back in the League, the club remained in the top six from mid-January until the end of the season, with 'the yo-yo years' now confined to the record books. With crowds averaging almost 33,000, expectations had been raised significantly and Owls fans were not to be disappointed, as Wednesday finished in their highest position in post-war soccer – runners-up in the First Division. After an exhausting post-season tour behind the old 'Iron Curtain', manager Catterick was involved in almost no transfer activity, with the only moves being out of the club (Norman Curtis was the biggest name to move to pastures new). A summer share issue raised capital to build the new North Stand, with the old stand demolished before the season was only a few weeks old. The timing of the stadium development was unfortunate, as the record attendance at Hillsborough for a League fixture would surely have been beaten in November 1960 when League leaders Spurs visited second-placed Wednesday. Still, over 56,000 fans packed into the three-sided ground to enjoy a classic game, with the Owls ending their visitors' unbeaten start to the campaign with a thrilling 2–1 win. With the likes of Don Megson, John Fantham, Tony Kay and Ron Springett at the height of their powers, the Owls were a real force in the top flight. Other than the win over Spurs, the season contained many

Wednesday in Tbilisi, USSR, during their post-season tour, 1960.

A Typhoo tea card of Sheffield Wednesday from 1960.

highlights, with a remarkable 7–2 FA Cup win at Manchester United perhaps being the pick of the crop. The reserve side also won the Central League for the third time, but the exciting season was tinged with tragedy, as on Boxing Day 1960 a coach transporting the Owls side from a game at Arsenal crashed on an icy road near Huntingdon. The majority of the passengers escaped unhurt, but young professional Dougie McMillan was not so fortunate and was trapped in the wreckage. In order to save his life, the attending medical team had no choice but to amputate his right leg at the crash scene. Similarities with Derek Dooley were obvious, as he became the second player in less than seven years to have his playing career ended in such tragic circumstances.

On the field of play the future was certainly looking bright for Wednesday supporters, but all was not well behind the scenes and those same fans were dismayed when Catterick resigned, joining Everton a few weeks before the end of the 1960–61 season. A new era began under new boss, Vic Buckingham, with a visit to Amsterdam to face his old side, Ajax,

Sheffield Wednesday in Nigeria, May 1961.

Action from the quarter-final tie against Barcelona.

and the friendly encounter entered the record books as the first ever pre-season game played by Wednesday. The Owls started the 1961–62 season well, topping the early League table, and when competitive European football arrived at Hillsborough, French side Lyon were beaten 7–6 on aggregate. That success in Europe coincided with a mini-slump in the League, but the Owls bounced back to hold a top-six position, as Italian side AS Roma were beaten to reach the quarter-finals and a glamour tie against Spanish giants Barcelona. In October 1961 the club held a benefit game for the unfortunate Doug McMillan, while the Owls' reserve team recorded their biggest ever Central League win – a 14–0 trouncing of neighbours Barnsley at Hillsborough. The greatly anticipated meeting with Barcelona was almost postponed due to the weather, but the game was eventually played on the arranged date, with the Owls registering a 3–2 success. A crowd of 75,000 Spaniards watched the second leg in the Camp Nou and, despite a brave display from the Owls, the English team eventually exited the tournament 4–3 on aggregate. Back in the bread and butter of the League, Wednesday ended the season with four consecutive wins to secure a finish of sixth place in what was a great first season at the helm for Buckingham.

One story dominated the summer of 1962 (apart from the capture of prolific centre-forward David Layne), as the Fairs Cup committee invited Wednesday, plus two other English sides, to compete in the tournament in the new season. The Football Association and the Football League did not agree with the decision, however, nominating their own choice and effectively banning the Owls from entering the tournament. The draw was even made for the first round – Wednesday coming out of the hat to face Victoria Cologne – and despite Wednesday appealing to the English authorities, they were met with a stubborn refusal to budge and European football eventually slipped through the club's fingers. The intransigence of the English authorities rebounded on the clubs they represented, as an understandably unimpressed Fairs Cup committee reduced their invite to just one club and the Owls had to wait another year before re-entering the competition.

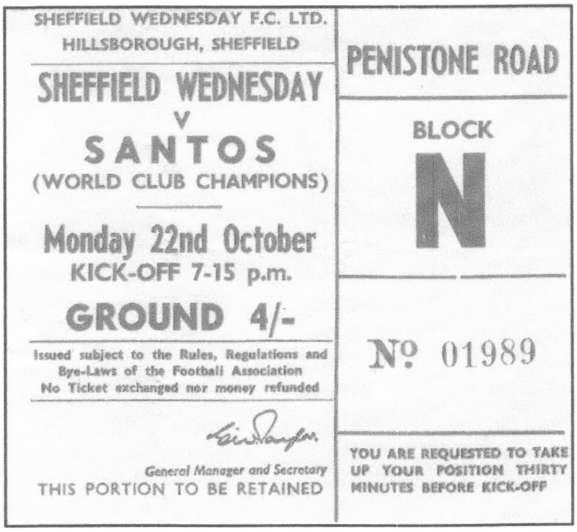

Ticket from the match against Santos.

Away from the summer controversy, the 1962–63 season saw Hillsborough confirmed as one of the venues for the 1966 World Cup Finals. In the same month the club were in hot water after fans ran onto the pitch and cushions were thrown from the stands when David Layne was sent off in a home game against Aston Villa. The visit of Brazilian superstar Pele and his Santos team also grabbed the headlines as over 45,000 watched the Owls lose 4–2 to the World Club champions. The League and Cup campaign was effectively ruined by one of the worst winters on record, the Owls not playing a single League game for almost two months! Almost half of the season's League fixtures were crammed into the final two months and several wins in that period ensured the club posted a second consecutive top-six finish. The Owls finished sixth again in 1964, for the third consecutive season, although they were humbled at Fourth Division Newport County in the third round of the FA Cup and exited the Fairs Cup after losing both legs against German side Cologne. The events of April 1964 proved a pivotal moment in the history of Sheffield Wednesday, however, as Vic Buckingham departed from Hillsborough and the club was brought into disrepute as the infamous bribes scandal story hit the newspaper stands. The departure of the Owls' manager was a shock to fans, with behind-the-scenes problems being cited as the main reason for his contract being terminated. Secretary Eric Taylor was

Sheffield Wednesday in 1962–63.

put in charge, and a few days later he was faced with the onerous task of speaking to the Wednesday fans the day after the *Sunday People* printed a story that implicated David Layne and Peter Swan, plus former player Tony Kay, in a match-fixing scandal. The allegations rocked the English game to the core, and for Wednesday the revelations were an unmitigated disaster as, after the players were found guilty and jailed, the FA imposed a life ban on the pair. The Owls therefore lost top scorer Layne and outstanding England international defender Swan, a blow from which, arguably, they never fully recovered.

The club's search for a new boss must have been subliminally affected by the great success of pre-war manager Bob Brown, as they shortlisted St Johnstone boss, Robert Brown, and Sunderland supremo Alan Brown! It was the latter that was appointed, surprisingly, after he had just led Sunderland to promotion from the Second Division, and he immediately recruited David Smith, who had been working in Libya, to the position of coach. The new man made a winning start to his Owls career and Wednesday sat in mid-table as the campaign reached the halfway point. The club's biggest win of the season – 5–1 at home to Burnley –was certainly remembered by forward Mark Pearson as it was later discovered that he had played most of the game with a broken leg. The injury effectively ended his Owls career, especially after he broke the same leg in his comeback game a few months later. The win over Burnley was a definite high point, but a few days later the club experienced a real low as they travelled to Denmark to play a game under the banner of the 'British week' trade celebrations. They faced part-time Aarhus and promptly lost 4–1 as a distinctly unhappy Alan Brown watched on. The side did, however, redeem themselves a few days later after holding an extremely strong German select side to a draw in Dusseldorf.

Sheffield Wednesday in 1965–66.

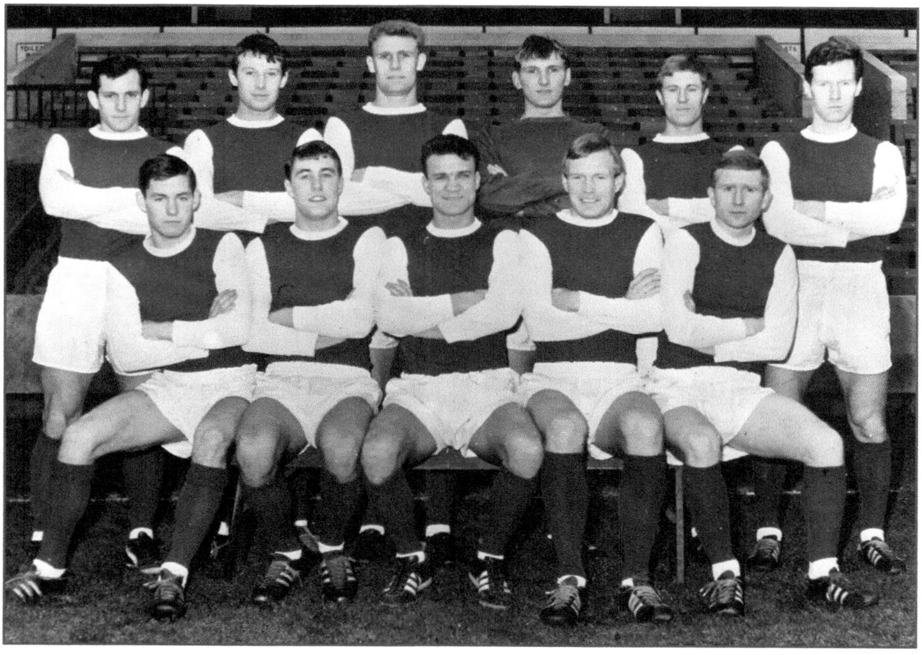

Defeat in the final three games of the 1964–65 season meant a final position of eighth – the first time since earning promotion back to the top division that Wednesday had finished outside of the top six.

It was obvious that the club was in transition and the 1965–66 season gave real hope that a new generation of young players would help the club to challenge for the major honours. The Owls kicked-off in their new non-striped home kit, which left the traditionalists choking on their half-time Bovril. Inconsistent League form would eventually leave the club down in the lower reaches of the division, with only three wins on their travels not helping their final position. Their patchy League form was, however, forgotten as the Owls went all the way to the 1966 FA Cup Final, playing every round of the tournament away from home. New signing Jim McCalliog and emerging youngster Graham Pugh scored in the shock semi-final win over Chelsea, and the Cup looked set to return to Sheffield as Wednesday raced into a 2–0 lead at Wembley. It was not to be, however, and manager, Alan Brown was bristling with pride at the full-time whistle, despite his young side having lost 3–2. It was at the end of this game that captain Don Megson started a tradition by taking his vanquished team on a lap of honour around the Wembley pitch. The run to Wembley was quickly followed by an exhaustive three-week tour of the Far East, and a season that had started with a pre-season trip to Bulgaria in July 1965 finally came to a close in mid-June 1966! It was the turn of the World Cup to take centre stage a few weeks later, with the Owls hosting games involving West Germany, Switzerland, Uruguay, Spain and Argentina. England's success in the Jules Rimet Trophy boosted the popularity of domestic football and crowds increased at all levels at the start of the 1966–67 season – the Owls' average for the season increasing by an astonishing 32 per cent on the 1965–66 campaign! A great start to the season saw the club top of the First Division table after an unbeaten seven game run, but once again they failed to maintain their good start and by the time the Christmas decorations were being unboxed, Wednesday had slipped down into mid-table. The season also saw Wednesday agree to enter the Football League Cup for the first time, although a last-minute home loss to Rotherham United was not exactly the perfect start to life in the competition. The penalty scored by Peter Eustace in a defeat at Southampton was noteworthy as it was the first spot-kick awarded to Wednesday since December 1964 – an incredible run of 82 games. The new year brought the FA Cup, and a third-round win over Queen's Park

The community song sheet from the 1966 FA Cup Final.

SHEFFIELD WEDNESDAY F. C. LTD.
HILLSBOROUGH, SHEFFIELD
FOOTBALL LEAGUE — DIVISION 1
SHEFFIELD WEDNESDAY
v
LEICESTER CITY
Saturday, 3rd Sept.
KICK-OFF 3-0 p.m.
General Manager and Secretary
RES. SEAT 7/6
Issued subject to the Rules, Regulations and Bye-Laws of the Football Association
No Ticket exchanged nor money refunded
THIS PORTION TO BE RETAINED
NORTH STAND
PENISTONE ROAD
ENTRANCE
O
GANGWAY
L
To the LEFT
ROW
SEAT
5
213
YOU ARE REQUESTED TO TAKE UP YOUR SEAT 15 MINUTES BEFORE KICK-OFF

Ticket from the 1966–67 season.

Rangers coincided with the official launch of a new club mascot – Ozzie the Owl. Sixteen-year-old goalkeeper Gary Scothorn became the club's youngest player when he appeared in the next Cup tie – a home win over Mansfield Town – before the run ended in agonising defeat as Chelsea scored an injury-time winner at Stamford Bridge. The Cup run provided a welcome distraction from an inconsistent League campaign, and the spring of 1967 saw Alan Brown clear out several of his coaching staff, with David Smith, John Logan, Hugh Swift and Keith Bannister all shown the door. Newcomers included Jack Marshall as assistant manager and Lawrie McMenemy as coach. The penultimate home game of the season saw a resounding 7–0 win over Burnley, with Jack Whitham becoming the first substitute to score for the club, netting a brace against the Lancashire team. At the end of the season the Owls embarked on another ambitious tour, this time playing five games in the sweltering heat of Mexico City; for the second season running there was hardly any time to catch a breath before the new season started.

The summer of 1967 saw the unique swap deal that resulted in the Springett brothers swapping clubs, with older sibling, Ron, moving back to Queen's Park Rangers and Peter moving north. The year also marked the centenary of the club, and the home game with Fulham on 6 September was officially designated as the celebration match. The club cut ticket prices in half for the game, although supporters did not know until they reached the turnstiles, and those that did attend were given a gift of a centenary badge. Unfortunately, partly due to an ongoing bus dispute, the attendance was one of the lowest of the whole season (26,511), as the 4–2 win kept Wednesday at the top of the fledgling First Division table, rather fittingly considering the occasion. Great starts to the season were a common theme for Wednesday in the 1960s, but, unfortunately, in the majority of cases such successful beginnings could not be maintained. The 1967–68 season proved no different, as only two League wins from mid-December until the end of the season resulted in the club plunging down the League table to finish just above the relegation zone. Manager Alan Brown had also walked out in February to rejoin Sunderland, and his assistant, Jack Marshall, would eventually be handed the role on a permanent basis after a brief spell as caretaker manager. He was faced with the task of restocking a first-team squad somewhat lacking in real quality, and despite a great start to the 1968–69 season, including a thrilling 5–4 win over Manchester United, the club's League form was again poor after Christmas – Wednesday recording only one win and Marshall departing before the campaign was at an end. Other than the aforementioned win over Matt Busby's Manchester United, the season was memorable for two FA Cup meetings with fierce rivals Leeds United. Over 52,000 watched the sides draw at Hillsborough, and Wednesday were the underdogs for the Elland Road replay. Young winger Brian Woodall grabbed all the headlines, however, as his brace helped the Owls to a 3–1 win in a tie, which was watched by over 100,000 fans. Unfortunately, Wednesday exited to Second Division Birmingham City in the next round and were left to concentrate on their woeful League record – the club's lack of a goalscorer was evident by an awful record of just nine goals in the final 19 games of the season. The only bright spot for the disgruntled fans was the late-season signing of Scottish teenager Tommy Craig, with Wednesday paying Aberdeen £100,000 and not only breaking their own transfer record, but also setting a record British fee for a teenager.

For the third time in eight years Wednesday went into the summer recess without a manager and the club's forward line was depleted even further as John Ritchie returned to Stoke City. The sale of Ritchie proved to be the last act for caretaker manager Eric Taylor, as a few days later the club appointed locally born Danny Williams to the vacant position. His arrival was generally perceived to be a positive appointment, as the former Swindon Town boss had led his Third Division club to a shock League Cup win just a few weeks before. One of his first acts was to sell unsettled attacker Jim McCalliog to Wolves for a club record £70,000, and unfortunately it was an acute lack of firepower that would leave the club at the wrong end of the First Division for the whole of the 1969–70 season. A pre-season home defeat to Scottish minnows Airdrie was certainly not the start that the new manager would have liked, and three consecutive League defeats at the start of the season reiterated what a hard task Williams, with no top-flight experience, was faced with. The Owls subsequently traded several players as the season progressed, signing Tony Coleman, Jackie Sinclair and Harold Wilcockson, but a shocking FA Cup home defeat to a Kevin Keegan-inspired Scunthorpe United side only served to deepen the crisis at Hillsborough. A brief rally in February and early March lifted the club out of the bottom two relegation

The 1969–70 team.

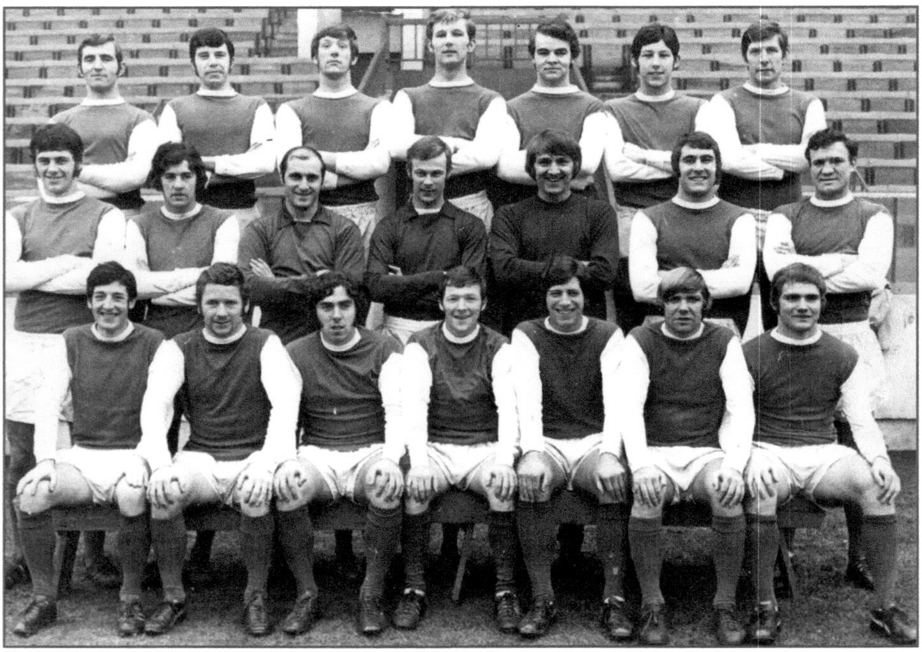

places, but their fate was decided in the final match of the season – against Manchester City at Hillsborough. The visitors had one eye on the Final of the European Cup Winners Cup, but even with over 45,000 packed inside the old ground, the team of 1970 could not raise their game, and the ensuing loss sent Wednesday spiralling back into the Second Division.

Hopes were high in the summer of 1970 that Wednesday could bounce straight back, and the capture of John Sissons and Sammy Todd, both from First Division clubs, backed up that view. The club's backroom was also much changed, with former players Tom McAnearney and Albert Broadbent departing, and ex-Manchester City trainer Dave Ewing being appointed as coach. Unfortunately, despite an opening-day win, it quickly became obvious that Wednesday simply did not possess the required quality in their ranks to mount a promotion push, and the departure of Wilf Smith early in the season further weakened the paper-thin squad. The club's fortunes waned further when an outbreak of influenza swept through Hillsborough and newcomer Ewing resigned to take a job in Scottish soccer. Record signing Tommy Craig then handed in a transfer request soon after the Owls had squandered a 4–1 lead at Hull City to draw, and in late January the axe fell on Williams after he had failed to halt the club's decline. Wednesday curried favour with their supporters by appointing club legend Derek Dooley as the new manager, but the 1950s goalscoring hero admitted that the road back to the First Division would be long and arduous. Once again, a chronic lack of goals meant that the Owls flirted with the wrong end of the Second Division table, but of greatest worry to the club must have been a drop of over 40 per cent in average home crowds as supporters deserted the club in droves. It was clear that the side needed to be overhauled but, off the field, finances had started to rear their ugly head as the club reported a sizeable loss. It would be the start of severe financial problems which would leave the club on the verge of bankruptcy by the middle of the 1970s. Despite this background, Dooley would vastly improve the team over the two years that followed, with the likes of John Holsgrove, Brian Joicey, David Sunley and Willie Henderson joining the ranks. The 1971–72 season proved a season of consolidation for Wednesday, as Dooley's side flirted with the top-10 positions before finishing in lower mid-table. The return of Pele and Santos produced the biggest home crowd of the campaign (almost 37,000), while John Sissons found himself on the losing side in a League fixture at Burnley, despite grabbing a hat-trick. The campaign was also memorable for Sunday League goalkeeper Trevor Pearson, as the amateur player appeared for the Owls in four games after the club suffered an injury crisis that deprived them of all their senior custodians.

The 1972–73 campaign was, without doubt, the club's best season of the decade, as Dooley's all-attacking side took the Owls to the top of both the League and entertainment tables. Former player Peter Eustace returned to the club for a second spell, while disgraced duo, Peter Swan and David Layne, returned on a trial basis. The club also appointed their first full-time physiotherapist, Geoff Eggerton, and a bumper opening-day crowd of over 23,000 delighted in a 3–0 win over Fulham. The Owls stayed atop the Second Division table until late September, before a loss of form resulted in a fall towards mid-table. A tremendous run in the FA Cup, however, subsequently boosted their League form, as First Division Crystal Palace were beaten in a second replay at Villa Park to set up a fifth-round clash with Chelsea. Almost 47,000 packed into Hillsborough for the game and the Owls took the lead, before eventually exiting 2–1. Wednesday had climbed steadily into the top six in the League, and were definitely on the fringes of the promotion race as the clocks went forward – in the process, 15-year-old goalkeeper Peter Fox became the club's youngest ever player after recording a clean sheet in a 2–0 home win over Orient. Three defeats in their last five games ruined any chance of regaining their First Division status and it was rather unfortunate that their finishing position – 10th– was the lowest that they had stood all season. It had certainly been a season of progress, although a final-day Hillsborough crowd of less than 9,000 suggested that perhaps the fans were still to be completely convinced.

The 1973–74 campaign proved a pivotal season for Sheffield Wednesday as, despite sanctioning more transfer activity against a backdrop of mounting losses, the club only just escaped relegation to the Third Division and were roundly condemned for the treatment of Derek Dooley. The arrival of experienced centre-half Ken Knighton seemed to have strengthened the first-team squad, but a poor start was exacerbated by a chronic injury crisis and a mystery stomach bug that decimated Dooley's squad. The club actually appealed, unsuccessfully, for a late October game at Notts County to be postponed due to the crisis. An 8–2 thrashing in the League Cup at Queen's Park Rangers certainly did not help the situation, but in hindsight it was the appointment of Matt Sheppard as chairman in early December that proved critical to the managerial career of Derek Dooley. As Christmas approached, the Owls sat just above the relegation zone, but after a creditable draw at Crystal Palace the board of directors held an emergency meeting to discuss several matters, including the results, coaching, tactics, fitness, the injury crisis and the flu outbreak. The outcome of that meeting stunned the football world, as on Christmas Eve 1973 Wednesday sacked one of the greatest players in their history. The sheer timing of his dismissal caused outcry and without doubt further damaged the club's reputation, which was still recovering from the bribes scandal of the mid-1960s. Not long after, the club sold both John Sissons and Peter Grummitt and then discovered that 'Mr Sheffield Wednesday' Eric Taylor intended to retire at the end of the season. His long-time assistant, Eric England, would succeed Taylor, but the

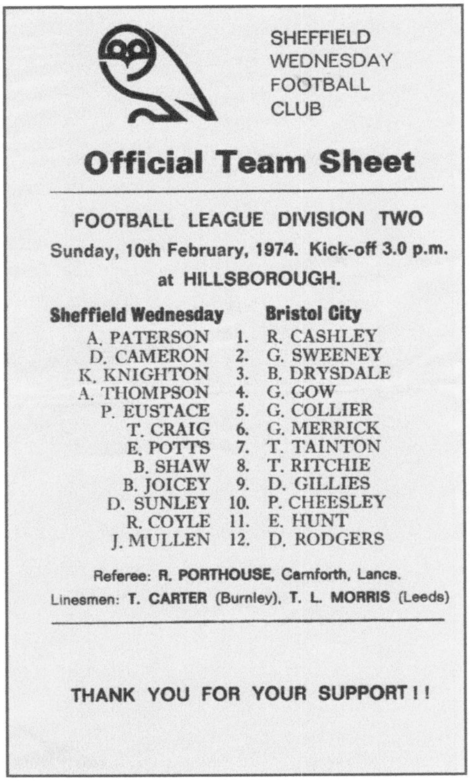
SHEFFIELD WEDNESDAY FOOTBALL CLUB

Official Team Sheet

FOOTBALL LEAGUE DIVISION TWO

Sunday, 10th February, 1974. Kick-off 3.0 p.m.

at HILLSBOROUGH.

Sheffield Wednesday		Bristol City
A. PATERSON	1.	R. CASHLEY
D. CAMERON	2.	G. SWEENEY
K. KNIGHTON	3.	B. DRYSDALE
A. THOMPSON	4.	G. GOW
P. EUSTACE	5.	G. COLLIER
T. CRAIG	6.	G. MERRICK
E. POTTS	7.	T. TAINTON
B. SHAW	8.	T. RITCHIE
B. JOICEY	9.	D. GILLIES
D. SUNLEY	10.	P. CHEESLEY
R. COYLE	11.	E. HUNT
J. MULLEN	12.	D. RODGERS

Referee: R. PORTHOUSE, Carnforth, Lancs.

Linesmen: T. CARTER (Burnley), T. L. MORRIS (Leeds)

THANK YOU FOR YOUR SUPPORT ! !

The team sheet from Wednesday's first Sunday fixture.

club's choice of their next manager proved a surprise to many. Incredibly to modern eyes, both Brian Clough and Ron Atkinson applied for the vacant post, but the Owls board instead handed the job to 38-year-old coach Steve Burtenshaw, who had no managerial experience whatsoever! The appointment proved disastrous as, despite a Ken Knighton goal saving the club from relegation in 1974, there was no escape a year later as Wednesday suffered arguably the worst season in their history.

The new manager released nine players in the summer of 1974, but the club were forced to announce large rises in season tickets prices due to spiralling costs, and would start the new season with just 3,000 fans having purchased season passes. Those fans that stayed away were proven correct, as the club experienced an awful season, quickly falling to the bottom of the table, with a League Cup loss at Fourth Division Scunthorpe United adding to the air of despondency around Hillsborough. With the club's finances reaching breaking point, the board sanctioned one last throw of the dice and Middlesbrough attacker Eric McMordie was captured on loan. His arrival helped Wednesday to climb out of the relegation places, but his eventual return to his parent club effectively ended the Owls' chances of remaining in the division, and the departure of crowd favourite Tommy Craig in the same month was the final nail in the club's relegation coffin. McMordie's six goals in nine games ensured that he finished the season as top scorer, as incredibly Wednesday failed to win any of their final 17 games of the campaign and scored only twice! The club was relegated at Nottingham Forest with five games still to play, and when Brian Joicey netted a last-minute equaliser against Oxford United, it was the Owls' first goal for 14 hours and 10 minutes. When the wretched season finally ended, Wednesday had recorded their lowest ever points tally – two fewer than the equally disastrous 1919–20 season – and there was genuine doubt about the club's very existence. The local newspaper even launched a 'Save our Owls' campaign, and the club officials must have wondered how they could ever hope to stop the rot as Wednesday slid into England's third tier for the first time in the club's history.

Unfortunately for Owls fans, the slump would continue, as life in the Third Division was little better than in the higher grade. Both on and off the field, the club was in deep crisis and finances were now almost at breaking point, with the club's overdraft increasing daily. Stringent cost-cutting measures were therefore implemented, with several backroom staff made redundant, including chief scout Fred Scott and physiotherapist Geoff Eggerton. The Owls also announced that what little money they had would be ploughed into producing home-grown talent, while several senior players left for pastures new. It was perhaps typical of the club's luck that the chance of earning some much-needed extra revenue fell through when legendary American stuntman motorcyclist, Evil Knievel, was forced to cancel his scheduled show at Hillsborough after being injured at Wembley! The club's AGM was a very sombre affair and shareholders must have been in despair when chairman Matt Sheppard commented that 'Wednesday are in serious trouble, both from a financial and footballing point of view'. Only 2,050 season tickets were sold for the 1975–76 season, and poor form in pre-season continued when the League restarted, with Wednesday losing their first ever game in the Third Division away to Southend United, despite leading at the break. The Owls quickly slid towards the wrong end of the League before two events would, in

Advert for the 1976 shareholder scheme.

hindsight, start the club's long-term recovery from those dark days. The first event was the resignation of Matt Sheppard, citing pressure of his work, and the appointment of tough, no-nonsense Sheffield businessman Bert McGee to the position. Within a few days ailing manager Burtenshaw was sacked, and Gillingham boss, Len Ashurst, and his ex-Marine assistant, Tony Toms, arrived at Hillsborough. The dire financial straits the club were experiencing – they only had £5 left on their overdraft at one point – meant that the new manager had little or nothing to work with, and his back room staff became almost non-existent when Youth Development Officer George McCabe was made redundant. The horrendous year of 1975 ended with the Owls having only recorded four wins, but thankfully 1976 would be kinder to Owls fans, as their club scrambled from the lower

The 1976 share prospectus.

reaches of the Third Division to give themselves a chance of avoiding the unthinkable drop into the basement division. A run of four consecutive 1–0 home wins in the spring of 1976 dragged Wednesday to within one place of safety, and their fate eventually rested upon the final match played in the division – a rearranged home game against Southend United at Hillsborough. A point was all that was needed by the Owls, while their visitors from Essex knew that nothing but a win would save them from the drop. A crowd of over 25,000 (more than double the season average) showed their support and thankfully, despite a second-half fightback from Southend, Wednesday secured the desired result and staved off a second consecutive relegation, from which they may never have recovered.

Another big loss was posted for the 1975–76 season and, much to the dismay of Wednesday fans, the club increased season tickets prices again. The only positive to arise was that, for the first time, those aforementioned financial statements did show a sharp rise in commercial activity, helping to cut the loss from a year earlier. The wage bill had also been cut by 50 per cent, but against this backdrop Len Ashurst's team enjoyed a great pre-season, winning the newly introduced Shipp Cup and making a respectable start to the new season. A League Cup win at Second Division Wolverhampton Wanderers brought the club's name back into the public domain for the right reasons, and the club would enjoy a hugely improved campaign. The Owls spent virtually all of the season in the top 10, rising as high as fourth place on two occasions, and a true goalscorer finally emerged – youngster Rodger Wylde netting 25 times in League and Cup football and forming a great partnership with Tommy Tynan. Off the field, a share issue raised vital revenue, although the head of the shareholders commented that 'The directors have proved they don't know how to spend money. Why should we give them some more to throw away?' New signings included Bob

The 1977–78 squad.

Bolder, Dave Rushbury, Denis Leman and Jeff Johnson, although the unfortunate Neil O'Donnell was forced to retire, with Wednesday hosting a benefit game against former club Norwich City on his behalf. Crucially, for the first time in three years, the word of relegation was not on the lips of Wednesday fans and there was genuine optimism that Ashurst could lead the club back into the Second Division.

It was therefore a shock to all parties concerned, especially after Ian Porterfield had been added to the squad, that Wednesday could only boast five points from their first 10 League games and sat rock bottom of the division! It was unfortunate that fortunes on the pitch had suddenly waned, as off the field the news was much brighter, with a new club lottery, introduced by commercial manager and former player Dennis Woodhead, providing the Owls with their first profit for many years – an astonishing figure of over £130,000! A good run in the League Cup was not enough to save Len Ashurst and, despite all his good work behind the scenes, he was fired just before a home game against Chesterfield. The caretaker job was handed to Ken Knighton, but the news quickly emerged that former England World Cup winner Jack Charlton was in the frame for the vacant position. He duly took charge, becoming Wednesday's fifth manager in just seven years. The new man was in charge on arguably the blackest day in the club's history – a Saturday in December 1977 when Wednesday, bottom of the Third Division, were knocked out of the FA Cup at non-League Wigan Athletic. The club eventually moved out of the bottom four positions in mid-January 1978 and became increasingly difficult to beat.

For the first time for many seasons, Wednesday were in a position to pay a sizeable fee for a player and £45,000 was duly spent to secure the services of midfielder Brian Hornsby from Shrewsbury Town. The newcomer was instrumental in a run of four consecutive wins that lifted the Owls towards mid-table, and 35 goals from the Tynan-Wylde partnership ensured a comfortable finish. The next campaign did not produce the hoped-for tilt at promotion, but would be remembered fondly by Owls fans due to an amazing FA Cup tie against eventual winners, Arsenal. The pre-season period saw Wednesday lose the services of Richard Walden, but Ray Blackhall was recruited to take his place and the club's youth policy started to reap rich dividends – Mark Smith having already made his senior bow and Mel Sterland signing as a new apprentice. With the club's finances much improved, Jack Charlton was constantly looking to improve his squad and a club record £165,000 bid for Welsh International Leighton James only floundered when he signed for a higher-ranked club. One player to leave was Tommy Tynan, although Mike Pickering and John Lowey replenished the increasingly strong squad. Wednesday spent the majority of their Third Division campaign around lower mid-table and it would be their Cup exploits that significantly increased their national profile and also provided a springboard for a promotion push a few months later. Replay wins over Scunthorpe United and Tranmere Rovers earned Wednesday a third-round tie with Arsenal and, after fans had cleared the Hillsborough pitch of snow, the tie ended 1–1, with Owls supporters constantly pelting visiting 'keeper Pat Jennings with snowballs for the whole 90 minutes! A last-minute Liam Brady equaliser denied the Owls a win at Highbury in the replay and the teams subsequently re-convened at Filbert Street, Leicester for a second replay. At the time the country was in the midst of a big freeze and Leicester's investment in large tarpaulin sheets ensured that the national press could feature the subsequent three replays in their sports pages. The first tie ended 2–2 after extra-time and this classic Cup meeting produced a thrilling 3–3 draw in the fourth instalment. A fifth game ensured that the tie became the third longest in FA Cup history, but it was a game too far for the plucky Owls side as over 30,000 fans – including several thousand from Sheffield – watched the Gunners secure a 2–0 victory. The income generated from the Cup run helped to finance the signing of maverick winger Terry Curran from First Division Southampton, and the side that Jack built was finally ready to take off.

Thousands of Owls fans travelled to Oakwell for the opening game of the 1979–80 season and they were rewarded with a 3–0 win – new signings Andy McCulloch and Ian Mellor among the scorers. An unlucky defeat to top-flight Manchester City in the League Cup followed – City scoring twice in the final two minutes at Maine Road to knock Wednesday out. The Owls' performances over the two-legged tie suggested that a promotion challenge was a real possibility and, after a slow start, they moved into the top six before the eagerly awaited Boxing Day clash with Sheffield United. The subsequent 4–0 win over the Blades has become legendary among Owls fans and, more importantly, the result provided a huge boost to a Wednesday side that went on an unbeaten run of 16 games soon after. A victory at home to Wimbledon in early March 1980 took the Owls to the top of the table, and full-back Mark Smith broke Jack Ball's long-standing record when he netted his 11th penalty of the season in early April. A defeat at Bury put promotion back in the melting pot, but a tremendous win at promotion rivals Blackburn Rovers delighted a travelling army of around 10,000 Owls fans. The late Ian Mellor header at Ewood Park proved vital, as four days later, despite a 1–0 defeat at Exeter City, Wednesday were promoted from the Third Division when rivals Chesterfield lost at Millwall. Almost 33,000 attended the final game of the season, and most of them invaded the pitch at the final whistle to celebrate and strip the players of virtually every item of clothing!

Not since the afterglow of the 1966 FA Cup Final had Wednesday fans enjoyed their summer recess so thoroughly. The club made little alteration to the first-team squad in the summer of 1980 – Charlton keeping his faith with the players that had earned the club promotion. The club accounts showed that Wednesday had recorded their biggest ever profit and that, somehow, Charlton had got the Owls promoted with a surplus on transfer dealing of almost £150,000! Over 26,000 attended the opening-day League win over Newcastle United, and the Owls would be strong at Hillsborough all season, not tasting defeat until the final day of January 1981. That strong form ensured the club remained in the higher reaches of the Second Division table, and in early March they were serious contenders to record back-to-back promotions. Six defeats in the final seven games of the season ruined that dream, unfortunately, as the side slipped to 10th position – still a terrific finish considering that Wednesday had only just been promoted. The season also saw Wednesday break their transfer record to pay £250,000 for Yugoslav Ante Mirocevic, while there were distasteful scenes in an away game at Oldham when so-called supporters rioted after fans' favourite Terry Curran had been sent off. The club was hit with various sanctions by the Football Association, which included the closure of Hillsborough's terraces for four games, an away fans ban for four matches (which was beaten by hundreds of inventive

Wednesdayites) and an order to pay £12,000 in compensation to their next four away opponents. The campaign also saw the latest ever postponement of a Hillsborough League fixture when a 25 April 1981 game with West Ham United was snowed off. Despite the poor end to the previous campaign, the capture of Gary Bannister and Gary Megson resulted in Wednesday being installed as one of the favourites for promotion, and four consecutive wins at the start of the 1981–82 campaign proved the bookmakers correct. A harsh winter meant that Wednesday did not play a League game for six weeks between early December and mid January, but when League football restarted the Owls hit the ground running, moving into the third promotion place in late March. A tremendous run of form saw Charlton's side consolidate that precious third spot, and with just three games remaining Wednesday only had promotion to lose. Unfortunately, that proved to be the case, as a draw at Rotherham United and defeat at Bolton Wanderers meant that a last-day win over promotion rivals Norwich City proved merely academic. Ironically, if the new system of three points for a win had not been introduced then the Owls, not the Canaries, would have been promoted to the top division.

After the promotion dream died Jack Charlton decided to overhaul his senior squad and released several players who had helped win promotion in 1980, including Ian Mellor, Ray Blackhall and Dave Grant. Crowd favourite Terry Curran also departed, with the controversial attacker moving across the city to Bramall Lane – Charlton seething after Sheffield United were ordered to pay £100,000 by a transfer tribunal when the Owls had asked for £250,000. New men included the vastly experienced Mike Lyons and Wednesday were again fast out of the blocks when the new season started, winning five of their opening six League games to immediately settle into a top-three position. Unfortunately, the club

The Wednesday team in 1982–83.

would fall away to eventually finish seven points off the top three in a season when Cup football dominated the headlines. A run to the quarter-finals of the League Cup – for the first time – ended with a narrow defeat at top-flight Arsenal, while wins over lower League opposition took the club into the last 16 of the FA Cup for the first time in a decade. A win over fellow Second Division clubs Cambridge United and Burnley (5–0 in a memorable quarter-final replay) set up a Highbury meeting with First Division strugglers Brighton & Hove Albion. On a red-hot day in North London the mass of Wednesday fans would be disappointed as, despite an equaliser from Mirocevic (his last goal for the club), a late winner from Michael Robinson ended the Wembley dream.

The summer of 1983 saw the end of an era, as after six successful seasons at the helm manager Jack Charlton decided to take a break from the world of football, tendering his resignation. The Owls' first choice was locally born Graham Taylor, but it was eventually Notts County manager Howard Wilkinson who was installed as boss, quickly appointing Peter Eustace and physiotherapist Alan Smith to his backroom team. The new manager was then involved in a whirlwind of transfer activity, with the likes of Andy McCulloch and Bob Bolder departing and Martin Hodge, Iain Hesford, Imre Varadi and Lawrie Madden arriving. The new-look Wednesday side would make an incredible start to the new season, setting a new club record by remaining unbeaten for the first 18 competitive games. The new all-action, hard-running Owls side did not particularly find favour with the football purists, but Wednesday fans were delighted as Wilkinson's side remained in first place until New Year's Eve. In that period over 41,000 packed into Hillsborough to watch promotion rivals Newcastle United beaten 4–2, while progress was made in the League Cup with Wednesday earning a January quarter-final home date with Liverpool. Secretary Eric England also retired, with former Sheffield United Chief Executive Dick Chester taking his place. The new year brought an FA Cup win over First Division Coventry City, while the aristocrats from Liverpool were given a huge fright in front of almost 50,000, with the Owls at one point leading 2–1 after being denied a blatant penalty for a handball by Alan Hansen. The game eventually finished 2–2 and 12,000 fans travelled over the snowy Pennines to back their side in a subsequent 3–0 defeat at Anfield. The run in the FA Cup ended in the quarter-finals when Southampton won 5–1 in a replayed tie – the first game at Hillsborough being the first match to be televised live from the old ground. All eyes then returned to the fight for promotion, and a crucial win at Newcastle United, thanks to Gary Shelton's overhead kick, brought the First Division within touching distance. A defeat at Middlesbrough meant that the champagne stayed on ice, but the bubbly was flowing three days later when a penalty from life-long Owls fan Mel Sterland was enough to beat Crystal Palace and put Wednesday back into the top flight after a 14 year absence. A win at Huddersfield Town then pulled the Owls five points clear in the race for the Championship, but they would ultimately come up short on goal difference, as Chelsea won their final two games.

With the ghost of 1970 banished forever, Wilkinson made plans for First Division football, although the departure of 22-goal top scorer Gary Bannister was a surprise and a disappointment to most Owls fans. Another departure was that of Gary Megson, with reinforcements including Lee Chapman, Brian Marwood and Andy Blair. Watched by over

31,000, Wednesday started the season with a great win over Brian Clough's Nottingham Forest, and the side's reputation grew when the Owls returned to Anfield and registered a stunning 2–0 win at the home of the European Champions. The tremendous start lifted Wednesday to their highest position for almost 25 years, second in the top flight, while the League Cup produced further drama as Wednesday lost a three-goal Hillsborough lead in a replayed home fifth-round tie against Chelsea, before grabbing a last-minute equaliser to force a 4–4 draw. The club exited at Stamford Bridge in the third tie and then controversially went out of the FA Cup at the last-16 stage, before a good run of form in April ensured a highly creditable eighth-place finish, just three points shy of fifth place. For the second summer running the Owls had to replace their top scorer, as Imre Varadi moved to West Bromwich Albion for a club record £285,000 fee. This mattered little though, as Wilkinson's team ended the campaign in fifth position, which in pre-Heysel days would have secured a UEFA Cup place. Arguably, the game of the season came in November when runaway League leaders Manchester United, led by Ron Atkinson, suffered their first defeat, watched by over 48,000 fans, as a Chapman goal won the game for Wednesday. The management team all signed new five-year contracts at the dawn of 1986 and then oversaw an FA Cup run, which took the club all the way to a semi-final meeting with Everton. Virtual unknown Carl Shutt netted three times in the latter stages of the competition and then scored the equaliser in the Villa Park semi-final, forcing extra-time, before Graeme Sharp fired the Merseyside club to Wembley. The best finish by an Owls side since 1951–52 ensured a top-six position and firmly re-established the club in the top echelons of the English game.

After several seasons of success, the 1986–87 campaign seemed almost tame by comparison as the Owls finished mid-table in the First Division and exited the FA Cup at the quarter-final stage. It was, however, noticeable that the Hillsborough purse strings seemed to have been tightened by the club's board, as Wilkinson only brought in untried youngsters and lower League players, but the side still occupied a top-six position by Christmas. The club's run in the League Cup had ended with a heavy defeat at Everton, but not before former dustman Colin Walker had entered the record books as the first Wednesday player to score a treble after being introduced from the substitutes bench. He achieved the feat in a 7–0 win at Stockport, just two days after Oxford United had been hit for six in a League encounter at Hillsborough. The Owls had also entered the newly introduced Full Members Cup for the first time, while the FA Cup run – somewhat marred by a horrendous injury suffered by central-defender Ian Knight against Chester – would mask a poor second half to the League campaign. Eventual winners Coventry City ended Wednesday's run in the competition, before a late rally ensured a lower mid-table finish in the League, prior to a four-game post-season tour of Canada. The club would experience a summer of sheer frustration in the transfer market, as several big-money moves broke down for a wide variety of reasons. Incredibly, one player who did sign, former England international David Armstrong, changed his mind after 72 hours, with the Owls agreeing to tear up his freshly penned contract! It was generally believed that the club's wage structure was the root of the problem and the 1987–88 season perhaps reflected this opinion, as quality football was at a premium as the club ended in mid-table. A 5–1 home defeat to Champions Liverpool on the final day of the season certainly highlighted the need for new recruits, but the increasingly frustrated Wilkinson was running out of patience, and just a few weeks into the 1988–89 season he tendered his resignation. Top scorer Lee Chapman had been sold in the summer, further weakening the squad, and the only newcomer had been David Hodgson, a free-transfer capture from an obscure Spanish club. Defender Mel Sterland even started the season in the forward line, such was the club's paucity of talent – although Wilkinson did manage to re-recruit both Imre Varadi and Chris Turner before he departed. The side was therefore left to Peter Eustace on a temporary basis as the club searched for a new boss. Unfortunately, their search resulted in several very public rejections and Eustace was eventually handed the reigns on a permanent basis. His appointment would rank alongside that of Steve Burtenshaw, as the former Owls midfielder lasted only 109 days in a disastrous tenure. Problems quickly mounted both on and off the pitch, with the almost panic buy of Wilf Rostron and Darren Wood failing to placate a disgruntled fan base. By this time, Mel Sterland had been stripped of his beloved captaincy, several players had submitted transfer requests and Imre Varadi had been suspended after his wife called a local radio station to complain about his manager! The inevitable parting of ways occurred in early February 1989, with Wednesday in the relegation places and Eustace fighting somewhat of a lone battle. With virtually no money available for transfers and the playing squad threadbare, the club's next move stunned and delighted Wednesday fans, as high-profile, big-spending Ron Atkinson breezed into Hillsborough. It would be the beginning of another renaissance.

His first three months at Hillsborough were tinged with the tragedy of the Hillsborough disaster, which resulted in 96 Liverpool fans being killed at the semi-final against Nottingham Forest. Before the tragic events of 15 April 1989 'Big Ron' had smashed the Owls' transfer record when paying his old club, West Bromwich Albion, £750,000 for midfielder Carlton Palmer. He had also sanctioned the move of Mel Sterland to Glasgow Rangers, and various moves in the transfer market ensured a win at home to Middlesborough on the final Saturday of the season, which cemented the club's First Division status. He duly signed a one-year contract at Wednesday and set about revamping the side and totally changing the style of play. The pairing of David Hirst and new signing Dalian Atkinson proved crucial and, despite a poor start, the addition of Roland Nilsson, John Sheridan and Phil King soon resulted in a revival – lifting Wednesday towards mid-table safety. Wednesday fans were now warming to Atkinson's attractive style of football, and even during their early-season struggles the team still managed to record their highest ever away win (8–0 at Aldershot in the League Cup) and beat Sheffield United 3–2 in a thrilling Full Members Cup game at Hillsborough. As spring dawned, Owls fans were already looking forward to the next season, but what happened next surprised everyone concerned, as four defeats in five games suddenly left this new-look side requiring a point on the season's final day to guarantee First Division football. On an emotional Hillsborough afternoon the team slumped to a 3–0 defeat, and a win for relegation rivals Luton Town meant that Wednesday fans, manager Ron Atkinson and new chairman Dave Richards watched on in utter disbelief as the side were relegated to the Second Division. To compound matters, city rivals United took their place in the top flight, and in the

The Wednesday team photograph from the start of the 1990–91 season.

immediate aftermath of the relegation 'Big Ron' vowed to stay on as Wednesday boss and get the club promoted straight back to the First Division. The season that followed was one of the most exciting in modern times, as after Dalian Atkinson left for a club record £1.7 million fee and was replaced by Paul Williams, the Owls made a terrific start, remaining unbeaten for the opening 12 League fixtures. The side was evolving into arguably the club's best team since the war and, with Danny Wilson and John Harkes now first-team regulars and captain Nigel Pearson leading by example, the Owls spent virtually the complete season in the three promotion positions. While their tilt at promotion continued, Wednesday also enjoyed runs in both of the major domestic Cup competitions, reaching the last 16 of the FA Cup before crashing out at Third Division Cambridge United. But it was the League Cup that grabbed all the headlines, as five goals from Pearson, including one in the memorable home semi-final win over Chelsea, helped underdogs Wednesday to beat three top-flight sides to reach the Wembley Final. The events of 21 April 1991 need no real explanation, other than that John Sheridan's goal brought the club their first major honour since the FA Cup win on the same ground back in 1935. After the win over Manchester United the Owls turned their attention back to securing promotion, and with Notts County gaining ground fast, this was not a foregone conclusion. Luckily for Wednesday, the 1990–91 season saw three sides promoted automatically from the second tier, as the size of the First Division was increased, and that third promotion slot was eventually secured on an emotional night at Hillsborough, when a brace from 32-goal top scorer David Hirst helped his side to a 3–1 win over Bristol City. For the first time in the club's long history, Wednesday secured two senior trophies in the same season, while to complete a memorable campaign the club's reserve side lifted the Central League title and the youth team reached the FA Youth Cup Final for the first and only time.

Wednesday fans' unbridled optimism for the new season was somewhat deflated in the summer of 1991, when manager Atkinson was courted by Doug Ellis at Aston Villa. Fans celebrated when 'Big Ron' decided to stay, but a few weeks later their delight turned to anger as he finally did resign. It was Trevor Francis who would become the club's first player-manager, and he quickly recruited Paul Warhurst from Oldham and then broke

The team at the start of the 1991–92 season, with the League Cup and the Central League Championship Cup.

Wednesday's transfer record, paying £1.2 million for England goalkeeper Chris Woods. Wednesday started the 1991–92 season with a home defeat to Atkinson's Villa, played in a highly emotional atmosphere, but their entertaining brand of football soon moved the club into the top six positions, in what was the final season before the introduction of the Premiership. Owls fans were stunned when midfielder Carlton Palmer scored a first-half hat-trick in the home game with Queen's Park Rangers, although their grip on the League Cup ended with a replay loss at Southampton. A spell of snowy weather coincided with the arrival, on trial, of former French international Eric Cantona, and despite impressing he eventually moved to Leeds United – a managerial *faux pas* that Francis would live to regret. An early FA Cup exit followed, before an astonishing game at Highbury where Wednesday, level at 1–1 with 18 minutes remaining, managed to lose 7–1! Despite that defeat and a record 6–1 home loss to Leeds United, the Owls continued to challenge at the top end of the First Division. Only one loss in their final 10 games meant that an unlikely Championship win was even a possibility, but that was ended when a certain Mark Bright equalised for Crystal Palace in the club's final away match. Although the title had gone, the point at Selhurst Park secured UEFA Cup football for Wednesday – quite a remarkable achievement for a newly promoted team and a sign of how Atkinson, and then Francis, had completely transformed the side in just three years. Honours eluded the club in their first season back in the big time and this also proved to be the case in 1992–93, but only after quite an astonishing season. The arrival of Chris Waddle proved to be the club's high-profile signing of the close season, while Wednesday were one of the 22 founder members of the Premiership after BSkyB paid £304 million for the broadcasting rights. Despite making progress in the League Cup and UEFA Cup, the club's early-season form was patchy and it would not be until the new year that they became re-established in the top 10 places. A controversial exit to German side Kaiserslautern ended their enjoyable run in Europe and, with new signing Mark Bright quickly finding his goal touch, the Owls showed signs of recovery prior to the busy Christmas period. A tremendous run of seven consecutive League victories followed – the best sequence since the Dooley-inspired side of 1951–52 – and this form was also repeated in the FA and League Cup. They would, of course, reach both domestic Finals, with central-defender Paul Warhurst being called up to the England

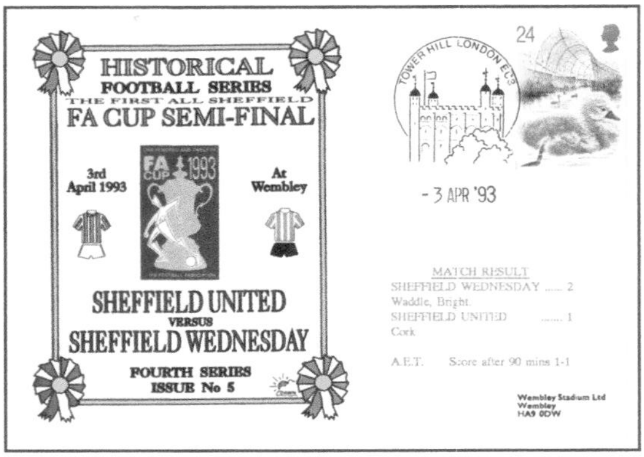

First day cover, celebrating the first all Sheffield FA Cup semi-final, 1993.

squad as a forward after he was successfully switched to the attack. Semi-final wins over Sheffield United and Blackburn Rovers secured two Wembley Finals, but the season would end in disappointment as old foes Arsenal denied the Owls on both occasions. Despite the ultimate disappointment, after a 63-game campaign it was still a season to treasure, with Chris Waddle being voted Player of the Season by the Football Writers Association – the first time that an Owls player had been awarded the honour in its 45-year existence.

The following summer saw the club break their transfer record to purchase both Andy Sinton and Des Walker, although they also received their highest ever fee – £3 million – when Warhurst moved to Blackburn Rovers. The new season started with record season ticket sales, but after a poor start Wednesday would need another mid-season surge to move to a final finishing position of seventh. The Owls also reached the semi-final of the League Cup, losing 5–1 on aggregate to Manchester United, but it had been a season of problems, both on and off the pitch. On the season's final day Wednesday fans waved goodbye to Roland Nilsson and they must have wondered what was in store for the future, as many of the players recruited by Atkinson started to depart for pastures new. In hindsight, the 1993–94 campaign proved a pivotal moment in the club's early Premiership years, as the following season was a struggle that would cost Trevor Francis his job. The departure of Carlton Palmer and Nigel Worthington was seen by Owls fans as a retrograde step, and their replacements, Ian Taylor and Ian Nolan, struggled to fill the void. The likes of Dan Petrescu and Klas Ingesson later increased the size of the squad, but Wednesday spent all of the season outside of the top six positions and even flirted with relegation, especially after Nottingham Forest won 7–1 at Hillsborough in Wednesday's record all-time home defeat. Only three wins in the final 15 League games (with their form reminiscent of those late-season slumps of the 1960s) heaped pressure on Francis, but it was a surprise to many when he departed, by mutual consent, on FA Cup Final day. The club's 15th manager since the war proved to be Luton Town boss David Pleat, although he was not in charge when the Owls made a late entry into the Intertoto Cup – a scratch side losing to FC Basel in Switzerland in late June 1995. Moving out of Hillsborough was Chris Bart-Williams, while Pleat's first captures were Anderlecht captain Marc Degryse and Welsh midfielder Mark Pembridge. Unfortunately, Pleat's first season proved a major disappointment, as the club spent a large majority in the bottom half of the division before eventually earning a last-day point to secure their status. One highlight was a 6–2 home win over Yorkshire rivals Leeds United, while the club broke the bank again by paying a combined £4.5m fee for Yugoslav duo, Darko Kovacevic and Dejan Stefanovic. Another link with the successful side of the early 1990s was broken when John Sheridan left on loan, and incredibly only David Hirst remained from the side that won the League Cup just five years before.

It was clearly obvious to David Pleat that action was needed and the summer of 1996 saw several backroom changes, which included the departure of Danny Bergara (head coach), Frank Barlow (reserve team manager) and Mick Mills (chief scout). Former player Martin Hodge became the club's first ever full-time goalkeeping coach, while Peter Shreeves arrived to fill the shoes of Bergara. Record signing Darko Kovacevic also left, joining Spanish football in a £2.3 million deal. Despite failing to secure any big-name signings in the close season, Wednesday made a terrific start in the League, winning their first four games to top the Premiership. New attacker Andy Booth and youth product Richie Humphreys were among the early goalscorers, but the club then failed to win for 10 competitive games, slipping down to mid-table and being knocked out of the League Cup by minnows Oxford United. Crowd favourite Chris Waddle moved to Scottish football, while at the club's AGM the board was fiercely criticised for apparent deterioration in quality of the first-team squad. Within a few days, however, Italian Benito Carbone arrived for a club record £3 million fee, and the Owls then embarked on remarkable run that saw them lose only once in 17 Premiership matches. During that sequence of results, the Owls came back from a two-goal deficit to win 3–2 at Southampton, the first time that this had been achieved by a Wednesday side since 1963! A late charge for UEFA Cup qualification was dashed by three defeats in their final four games, while an FA Cup run to the quarter-finals ended in disappointment when Wimbledon won at Hillsborough in front of the television cameras. The season also saw the arrival of London investment company Charterhouse Development Capital Funds onto the Hillsborough scene, as they bought a 20 per cent stake in Wednesday in return for £17 million. The club was valued at £42.5 million and the deal was duly sanctioned by the shareholders at an Extraordinary General Meeting. The major transfer news of the 1997 pre-season was the club record capture of fiery Italian winger Paulo Di Canio, with Wednesday paying £3 million for his signature, and also the transfer of £1.5 million-rated Regi Blinker to Glasgow Celtic. It would be a desperately poor start to the new season, with a 7–2 hammering at Blackburn Rovers starting to ring alarm bells around Hillsborough. An embarrassing League Cup exit to Grimsby Town followed and Wednesday sat bottom of the Premiership after conceding six goals at Old Trafford. Just before that game David Hirst had left for Southampton, and just after the game David Pleat's reign came to an end. The club appointed Peter Shreeves as caretaker manager, and amazingly he won his only game in charge – 5–0 against Bolton Wanderers. The surprise return of Ron Atkinson galvanised the side and three consecutive wins effectively retained the club's top-flight status – Wednesday just finishing above the relegation zone after a season of struggle. The club, surprisingly, did not offer Atkinson a new contract at the end of the season and instead recruited the services of former player Danny Wilson.

Known as 'Didwell' as a player at Wednesday, Wilson recruited Dutch midfield star Wim Jonk during his early weeks at the helm, but then had to discipline Carbone after he arrived late for pre-season training. Carbone's misdemeanour paled into insignificance, however, after his compatriot, Di Canio, pushed over referee Paul Alcock after he had been sent off

Wednesday at the start of the 1999–2000 season, their last year in the Premiership.

in the home game against Arsenal. He was subsequently banned for 11 matches by the Football Association, fined £10,000 and never played another game for the Owls – moving to West Ham for a cut price fee a few months later. The loss of the talented Roman was a blow to the club, but the form of Carbone ensured that Wednesday remained comfortable and eventually finished in mid-table in a satisfactory first season for Wilson. Some late-season transfer activity resulted in Richard Cresswell arriving for almost £1 million, while virtual unknown Phil Scott arrived from Scottish football on a lucrative contract. The signing of two more players from Scottish soccer, Phil O'Donnell and Simon Donnelly, plus the arrivals of Gilles De Bilde and Gerald Sibon, were hailed as crucial signings by the club and manager. Unfortunately, none of Wilson's captures made the desired impression on the top flight, resulting in a calamitous season for Wednesday. The club made an appalling start – winning only one of their first 17 League fixtures – and the Owls quickly slipped into the relegation zone, with only the poor form of Watford denying them bottom position. Injuries to all three Scots left the playing squad somewhat threadbare, as did the sale of Emerson Thome, and despite the ever-consistent form of Des Walker and midfield talents of Niclas Alexandersson, the Owls never climbed out of the bottom three places. Off the field of play, chairman Dave Richards resigned to take over as boss of the Premiership, with Howard Culley elected in

ONE HUNDRED YEARS AT HILLSBOROUGH
2nd September 1899-1999
100
With compliments from Sheffield Wednesday F.C.
to commemorate this special occasion

Badge given to the fans to celebrate 100 years at Hillsborough.

his place. Back on the field of play, a defeat at Watford spelled the end of Wilson's tenure in the hot seat, and with caretaker manager Peter Shreeves *in situ*, a late rally raised hopes of avoiding the drop. A draw at Arsenal – where the Owls had led 3–1 – confirmed relegation, however, and a 4–0 win on the final day of the season was merely academic. The balmy days of the early 1990s now seemed light years away, with the club now without a manager and back in the second tier after 10 years of top-flight soccer.

Attempts to recruit Joe Kinnear as the club's next manager proved unsuccessful, and local businessman Dave Allen was co-opted onto the board of directors. The board subsequently survived an EGM vote of no confidence, and a week later former Bradford City manager Paul Jewell was appointed to the vacant managerial position. Caretaker manager Shreeves was retained as assistant manager, while Chris Waddle resigned from the coaching staff after failing to gain the top job. Meanwhile, there was some good news as the club announced a £1 million shirt sponsorship with Spanish lollipop maker Chupa Chups. With the majority of their first-team squad still on lucrative contracts, it was seen as vital that Wednesday regained their top-flight place as soon as possible, and for most of the season the Owls looked destined to exit the division. Unfortunately, their efforts put them at the wrong end of the division, as a club record run of eight consecutive defeats from early September to late October 2000 dumped Wednesday into early relegation trouble. The season had started in dramatic style when Kevin Pressman was sent off after just 13 seconds in the opening fixture, but with many of the club's high earners on the treatment table Wednesday struggled from the start, and a second consecutive relegation looked likely. It was notable that Charterhouse also exited the Hillsborough scene – director Geoff Arbuthnott resigning in January 2001 after their investment seemed to fail (director Dave Allen would buy their 36 per cent stake a few weeks later). On the field of play, pressure was mounting on Paul Jewell as he tried, unsuccessfully, to find a winning formula. That pressure, at both boardroom and pitch level, finally told in February 2001, when on the morning of a game at Wimbledon it was announced that chairman Howard Cully had resigned with immediate effect (Geoff Hulley eventually taking his place). Paul Jewell was subsequently fired after a 4–1 defeat dumped the club to the bottom of the First Division. Former assistant Peter Shreeves was handed control and he performed a minor miracle, taking the Owls to six wins in their next eight games, helped by the signings of the experienced Trond Soltvedt and the returned Carlton Palmer. Shreeves was even named Manager of the Month for March and in May 2001 and was rewarded with a two-year contract. Unfortunately, the club's fortunes did not significantly improve in the following season, as manager Shreeves resigned after 13 League games and his replacement, Terry Yorath, presided over the remainder of a season that ended with Wednesday just outside of the relegation zone. A run to the League Cup semi-finals was a definite highlight for the despairing Owls supporters, with top-flight Sunderland and Aston Villa knocked out, before a fifth-round drubbing of fellow First Division side Watford set up a two-legged meeting with Premiership Blackburn Rovers. The tie proved a bridge too far for the brave Wednesday side, losing 6–3 on aggregate, but it was hoped that the confidence gained would finally trigger a promotion challenge in 2002–03.

In an attempt to improve the club's fortunes, Yorath spent the summer of 2002 trawling the transfer market, although deepening financial problems already meant that he was trading at a reduced level in comparison to many clubs in the division. A total of 10 players were released, including Phil Scott, while Brentford top scorer Lloyd Owusu and Chelsea's Leon Knight, on a season-long loan, came into the club. Unfortunately, the new season began like the previous three, with Wednesday quickly dropping to the wrong end of the League table. Only two wins before Christmas meant that relegation to the third tier seemed inevitable, with manager Yorath having resigned on Halloween and the Owls third bottom of the First Division. Chief scout Bill Green and player David Burrows were in charge for the subsequent home game against Derby County, before Chris Turner arrived to fill the managerial role on a permanent basis. A week later he recruited another former Owls player, Colin West, as his assistant, but the new management team faced a huge task in turning around the club's fortunes. Wednesday's chances of avoiding relegation were not helped in January 2003 when, due to financial reasons, six-goal top scorer Gerald Sibon returned to Dutch football on a free transfer. A late-season rally, including a dramatic injury-time winner at Champions-elect Portsmouth, raised hopes, but a damaging draw at home to Grimsby Town meant that the Owls needed a win at Brighton to keep their hopes alive. Sadly, a first-half goal from Grant Holt proved insufficient as the home side drew level, and the full-time whistle sent Wednesday into the lower tier. Ironically, a few days later the team won 7–2 at Burnley to record the club's biggest ever away goals tally win in League football, but it was scant consolation as Wednesday suffered a second relegation in three years. At the season's end the Owls again cleared the decks with eight senior players shown the door, including high-earners Donnelly and O'Donnell, while Wednesday had a new chairman – Dave Allen stepping up to replace Geoff Hulley. Owls fans hoped that the club's rapid decline would finally be ended in the Second Division, and Turner's new-look side made a great start, losing only one of the first seven games, to sit second in the division. New recruits included Guylain Ndumbu-Nsungu, Adam Proudlock and Graeme Lee, but by late October the season had started to fall apart, and defeat in the final four games of the season resulted in a final finishing position of 16th – the Owls' second-lowest League ranking of all time. A run to the Northern Final of the Football League Trophy had briefly taken attention away from poor League form, but fans and management knew that the summer of 2004 would be vital, as the club's fall from grace needed to be arrested sooner rather than later.

It was left to manager Chris Turner to perform major surgery on the side, as an end-of-season cull resulted in a total of 13 players being released – the highest number since the end of the disastrous 1919–20 campaign. Players released included Alan Quinn, Steve Haslam, Kevin Pressman and Leigh Bromby, while the summer was dominated by the failed takeover of the club by former Chelsea owner Ken Bates. In hindsight, Turner's signings in that summer were rather inspired, as he captured the signatures of future crowd favourites Steve MacLean, JP McGovern, Glenn Whelan, Lee Bullen and Lee Peacock. Unfortunately for the former Owls custodian, his new side failed to gel quickly enough, and after slipping into the bottom half of the table, despite having made an excellent start, he was 'relieved of his duties' soon after the final whistle of a 1–0 home loss to Bournemouth. New manager, on a three-year contract, was Paul Sturrock, and he immediately signed Hasney Aljofree on loan from his former club Plymouth Argyle. The new manager's Wednesday career started

Wednesday win the Cardiff Play-off in 2005.

with an encouraging 3–0 win at Wrexham, and the huge impact made by loan signing Kenwyne Jones inspired a move up to fourth place by the end of the calendar year. Forward MacLean became the first Owls player to hit three goals in an away League game since John Sissons achieved the feat in the early 1970s – in a 4–0 victory at Belle Vue – and fans were in a positive frame of mind for the first time for several years. The club would remain in the top six positions for the remainder of the 2004–05 season, clinching a place in the end-of-season Play-offs after a dramatic late win at promotion rivals Hull City in the final away match of the campaign. The club's first experience of the Play-offs resulted in a semi-final meeting with Brentford, and a narrow home win provided the springboard for a truly memorable night at Griffin Park – goals from Peacock and Brunt securing a 3–1 aggregate win. With Wembley still being redeveloped, all the major matches in the English domestic calendar were being staged at Cardiff's Millennium Stadium, and it was to the Welsh capital that a record-breaking 40,000 Wednesday fans flocked. It would be an unforgettable afternoon for those massed ranks of Owls fans, as their club recovered from a 2–1 deficit with just a few minutes remaining to force extra-time, and eventually gained promotion to the Championship thanks to a 4–2 win.

For the first time in several years, Wednesday fans enjoyed the summer break and watched on as Sturrock recruited the likes of Burton O'Brien, Frankie Simek and Plymouth captain Graham Coughlan. Unfortunately, his plans for the new season received an early blow when main scorer MacLean suffered a broken leg in a pre-season friendly match, and life in the higher tier proved much harder than many supporters had imagined. A lack of goals, unsurprising considering MacLean's absence, proved their major problem, and Wednesday would fail to score in seven consecutive League games in the run-up to the

Wednesday in 2006.

Christmas fixtures. This left the Owls in the relegation zone for the majority of the season, although the January arrival of Marcus Tudgay and Deon Burton did provide some goalscoring pedigree. The club also suffered in the goalkeeping department, as David Lucas, loan signing Nicky Weaver and Chris Adamson were between the sticks before the crucial loan capture of Scott Carson from Liverpool. It was a world-class display from Carson that took the Owls to a terrific win at Wolves, and the club stayed just above the bottom three places to set up a relegation six-pointer at Brighton. At the scene of the club's relegation three years before, Wednesday saved themselves, as the resultant three-point haul not only relegated their hosts but also the two sides below them in the Championship table. The Owls ended the season with the highest average crowd outside of the Premiership (24,853), and with the club's status secured, Sturrock entered the transfer market again, with Kenny Lunt, Madjid Bougherra and Wade Small among the new arrivals. Despite a poor start to the season, leaving Wednesday in the lower reaches of the table, Sturrock signed a new contract until 2010 and it was therefore a shock to the large majority of Wednesday supporters when he was sacked after a 4–0 defeat at Colchester just a few weeks later. The loss left Wednesday just outside of the relegation zone, but those worries were quickly forgotten as caretaker, academy director Sean McAuley, presided over a 10-point haul from just four games. It was a strange situation for new boss Brian Laws, as he took control of a team full of confidence and winning games – the exact opposite of what a new manager usually encounters! The new man at the helm knew not to tinker with the side and Wednesday continued to win, while loan goalkeeper Mark Crossley became the first ever custodian to score for the club in a competitive match. A poor start to 2007, which included five straight defeats, looked to have finished hopes of a late charge for the Play-off positions. A tremendous run of form lifted the club to within touching distance of the top six positions, however, and it was only defeat at Birmingham City in the final away game that finally ended hopes of Premiership football.

The 2007–08 shop catalogue.

The summer of 2007 saw the departure of Chris Brunt to West Bromwich Albion for an initial £2.5 million fee, while the somewhat injury-prone Frances Jeffers arrived. The pre-season preparations were disrupted by the £1 million damage caused to the ground by the huge floods that hit the city of Sheffield on 25 June, and Wednesday fans suffered a further blow when their side experienced the worst start to a season in their long history. After a highly encouraging 2006–07 season fans were in high spirits and fully expected a tilt at promotion, so it was therefore a major shock when Laws' side promptly lost their first six games of the new season! That terrible start would dog the club for the remainder of the season and, despite a rally in the autumn, inspired by the goals of Akpo Sodje, Wednesday slipped back down the table and into the final relegation place with just two games to play. A relegation six-pointer at Leicester City was won, and then in front of over 36,000 the Owls beat Norwich City to preserve that hard-won Championship status. The following summer was very low-key with only James O'Connor signed on a permanent basis, and with finances still an issue the club went into the new season hoping that the squad would be strong enough. Considering the struggles of the previous campaign, the new season was a pleasant surprise to Owls fans as the club held a comfortable midtable position throughout, with the first derby double over neighbours Sheffield United in 95

The team photograph from the start of the 2009–10 season.

years being a definite highlight. The early weeks of 2009 also saw several off-field appointments, including Nick Parker in the role of chief executive and Lee Strafford in the position of chairman, filling the void that had been created back in November 2007 when Dave Allen resigned from the board. Former player and manager Howard Wilkinson was then appointed to the unpaid role of 'technical advisor', with a remit of helping to bring much-needed investment into Hillsborough, while a few weeks later former club physiotherapist Alan Smith also returned to Wednesday in a consultant role. Off the field, news was completed with the announcement that for the first time the Owls would gift their shirt sponsorship, with the Sheffield Children's Hospital the recipients.

All the changes both on and off the pitch meant that Wednesday fans welcomed the new season with optimism, despite the Owls not having spent any money in the transfer market, and a reasonable start left the club in midtable after the opening six games. Sadly, that proved only a temporary position as the team suddenly started to lose both form and confidence, slipping quickly down the Championship table as Laws tried, in vain, to stop the rot. A winless run of eight games heaped severe pressure on Laws and the situation came to a head when the team lost meekly at Leicester City, with Wednesday and their manager parting company. The defeat at the Walkers Stadium pushed the Owls into the bottom three, and caretaker manager Sean McAuley was then in charge for two games, earning a highly creditable draw against eventual champions Newcastle United in one of those fixtures. The onset of snow caused the next fixture to be postponed, and when the Owls played again, at Barnsley, they had new manager Alan Irvine at the helm. He had joined along with assistant Rob Kelly and coach Billy Barr, and made an instant impression as the Owls won four of his first six games in charge to climb to the dizzy heights of 18th position by early February. Unfortunately, his early influence quickly wore off and Wednesday then won only two of their next 15 games to slide back into deep trouble at the foot of the Championship table. The club's status eventually rode on the final game of the season against Crystal Palace in front of the BBC cameras at Hillsborough. Two years earlier the Owls won their final game to save themselves, but it was not to be in 2010 as the 2–2 draw sent Wednesday back into League One, just five years after that glorious day in Cardiff.

The club's relegation would have a massive effect on Wednesday from both playing and financial perspectives. On the playing side, Irvine released six players before practically recruiting a brand-new side – the likes of Neil Mellor, Paul Heffernan, Giles Coke and Clinton Morrison adding to a squad, which on paper looked more than capable of getting the club straight back into the Championship. A terrific start, including a 5–0 win at Hartlepool United, backed that theory, but pre-Christmas form would be inconsistent, with the club's financial crisis growing ever deeper. After averting a winding-up order, issued by HMRC, the club's search for investment became increasingly urgent, with the very real threat of administration hanging over the Owls. A fraught court appearance in mid-November saw the club earn themselves another 14 days to find an investor, although Wednesday's future now seemed in acute peril. Thankfully, on 27 November 2010, after many false dawns, the news that Wednesday fans had been waiting to hear was finally announced – the Milan Mandaric group had agreed to save the club. The deal meant that the Serbian-born US citizen became sole owner of Sheffield Wednesday and the club could move forward debt free, ending almost

Milan Mandaric.

a decade of financial constraints that had dogged every manager since relegation from the Premiership. In Mandaric's first public appearance at Hillsborough his new team read the script by winning 6–2, although a 5–1 defeat at Exeter a week later showed the other side of Irvine's team. A severe cold snap then forced several games to be cancelled, and with the River Don frozen for the first time in living memory, Wednesday had to postpone both of their Christmas home fixtures as they were hit with a raft of burst pipes in every part of Hillsborough.

The month of January saw the club busy in the transfer market with manager Irvine given the funds by Milan Mandaric to bring several players into Hillsborough, beginning with the capture of French born Reda Johnson from Plymouth Argyle. The new man made his debut, alongside fellow new boy Michael Morrison, in a surprise FA Cup win at Championship Bristol City – a significant result as amazingly this was the first ever time that the Owls had ever won on an opponents home ground in the competition against a higher rank club! Further transfers resulted in Darren Purse and Luke Boden leaving the club with Gary Madine and Mark Reynolds arriving. There was also movement behind the scenes as Chief Executive, Nick Parker, left with Paul Aldridge taking his place, in addition to the role of vice-Chairman. Also departing the board of Directors was Howard Wilkinson, who had fulfilled his wish of facilitating the club's takeover.

Unfortunately despite the influx of new players the Owls' League form remained poor and a run of five consecutive away defeats heaped pressure on Alan Irvine. He had guided Wednesday to the last 16 of the FA Cup for the first time in 11 years but with the club slipping out of play off contention the axe was wielded for the first time by the new Chairman, Irvine departing the day after a damaging 5-3 defeat at Peterborough United. Within 48 hours former player, Gary Megson, was handed the task of reviving the club's promotion push but fortunes would only get worse before they got better – Megson not tasting his first win until late February and only witnessing a maiden home win on the opening Saturday of April. This terrible run ruined any chances of promotion and at one point Wednesday slipped worryingly towards the relegation zone in League One, before the loan arrivals of centre halves, Danny Batth and Rob Jones, steadied the ship somewhat. After finally finding some form at Hillsborough, Wednesday moved up the table as the season came to a close although a final day loss pushed them back into a lower mid-table finish – the third worst in their entire history. However Owls fans are never lacking in optimism and hopes are high Wednesday will be amongst the front runners for promotion when the 2011-12 season reaches its climax.

Wednesday Grounds

Hillsborough has now been the home of Wednesday for over 110 years, but prior to 1899 the club led a somewhat nomadic existence, using several grounds before moving into Olive Grove in 1887:

Highfields	1867–70
Myrtle Road	1870–77
Bramall Lane	1873–87
Sheaf House	1877–81/1885–87
Hunter's Bar/Robert's Farm/Rustling's Farm	1882–85
Olive Grove	1887–99
Owlerton/Hillsborough	1899–present

Highfields 1867–70

It has generally been accepted that the site of the club's first playing pitch was where the current Highfields Library is situated, near to the junction of London Road and Abbeydale Road as you travel south out of the city. Recent research suggests, however, that the actual ground was more likely to have been to the south of the library. Back in the 1860s the Highfield area was predominantly open green space with the occasional buildings, such as Highfield House, Mount Pleasant and Highfield Terrace. Below Mount Pleasant, which still stands today, were the Cremorne Gardens, although it is probable that Wednesday played east of the gardens, across London Road, which did not follow the route of the modern-day thoroughfare. The gardens disappeared many generations ago, with modern-day Mount Pleasant Road running north to south, where the gardens used to be.

It would perhaps be correct to suggest, however, that it is more likely that the fledgling Wednesday club began on a pitch that was directly to the east of the Cremorne Gardens, with the Highfield Library to the north and Asline Road to the south – roughly where Highfield Place, Holland Road and Colver Road were subsequently built. The field in question would have been just below St Barnabas Church and in all likelihood would have boasted a slight slope, near to where the Medical Centre now stands. This assumption is further supported by the fact that back in the 1850s a private residence called Parkfield House was prominent on the map. This is significant as it was at this address, the home of local solicitor Harry Chambers, that the historic meeting to form Sheffield Football Club was held in October 1857. The owner of the house was a player and secretary for Sheffield FC and later became a senior member of the Football Association. The area where Wednesday first played may have belonged to Mr Chambers, and it is reasonable to assume that a man so enthusiastic a player and follower of the comparatively new game of association football would have been sympathetic to a newly founded Wednesday FC.

An 1850s map of Highfields.

Unfortunately, no contemporary evidence has ever been found regarding the club's first ground, and it would have been a rather crude roped-off pitch at best, with no facilities whatsoever. One of the club's first ever players – future club and FA chairman Charles Clegg – was quoted years later saying that in those early years he had to get changed behind a hedge and pay a young lad a few pennies to mind his clothes!

The actual location of that first pitch will probably forever remain a mystery, with the only certainty being that it was in the Highfields district of Sheffield and provided the springboard for the club to flourish and expand in those difficult and challenging early years. The club's first ever game – an inter-club practice match on 12 October 1867 – was played at Highfields, and it remained the club's base until March 1870 when Dronfield held Wednesday to a 1–1 draw, Ward scoring the final goal for Wednesday at their first home.

The approximate site of the Highfields ground today.

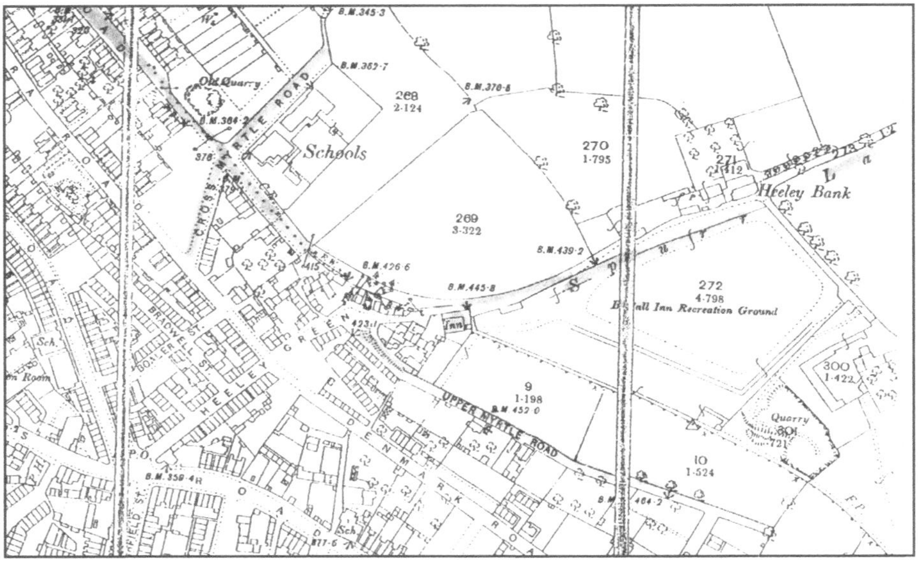

A map from 1884, showing Myrtle Road.

Myrtle Road 1870–77

The club's second home was situated on open land adjacent to Myrtle Road, to the south of the newly built Queens Road and Midland Railway line. The teams kicked away from Myrtle Road, down a sloping pitch below an old quarry. The exact spot is likely to have been between Myrtle Road and Midhill Road, near to the Heeley City Farm. This belief is reinforced by a contemporary match report in 1873, for a game against Broomhall, where the reporter stated that Wednesday 'won the toss and kicked from the road'. The seminal work by Richard Sparling, *The Romance of the Wednesday,* also mentions that the club 'moved and played on a hilly pitch overlooking Olive Grove'. More contemporary evidence mentioned Wednesday kicking 'from the road end, on a sloping pitch' and it now seems certain that this was the site of the club's second home – it is also believed that Wednesday shared the pitch with the MacKenzie Club. A receipt from the era has luckily survived and this showed that Wednesday paid just over £8 in rent for the 1875–76 season, which included the posts, nails and labour!

Like their first 'ground', Myrtle Road would simply have been a rather unkempt pitch with minimal facilities, but the seven years that the club spent at the Heeley venue ensured that Wednesday could increase their

The approximate site of the Myrtle Road ground today.

membership and maintain a presence in an area where a fan base was slowly growing. A second team game in October 1870 kicked-off the Myrtle Road era, and in their final season (1876–77) the club secured the newly introduced Sheffield Challenge Cup, although all the games were played away from home. Despite having left Myrtle Road, the club actually returned in January 1882, playing two friendly games against Exchange and Spital Chesterfield.

Bramall Lane 1872–87

The Wednesday Cricket Club was one of several local sides involved in the grand plan to build a large permanent cricket ground on Bramall Lane, on land leased from the Duke of Norfolk for a rent of £70 per annum. A committee was formed in January 1854 to officially launch the project, and thanks to the large number of subscribers work quickly began on the new ground. It was officially opened in April 1855 when two representative sides, drawn from the six cricket clubs that would use the ground, played a challenge match. A 10ft-high wall was erected around the new enclosure and the eight-and-a-half-acre site boasted refreshment facilities and covered enclosures for spectators. The new ground quickly became home to the newly formed Yorkshire County Cricket Club and was rightly lauded as one of the finest sporting grounds in England. Football was first played there in 1862, and by the end of the decade the increasing popularity of the winter game meant that association football began to feature regularly.

In 1872 turnstiles were installed at the ground and it was perhaps no coincidence that The Wednesday FC almost immediately hired the ground for a friendly game against Derbyshire in November of the same year. In the mid-1870s the ground was extended and dressing rooms added, and by the early 1880s Wednesday were playing the majority of their home fixtures at Bramall Lane. These included their first ever home FA Cup tie – versus Staveley in December 1881 – and countless high-profile 'challenge' matches against the likes of Queens Park, Blackburn Rovers and Notts County. Wednesday continued to regularly use Bramall Lane until they finally moved to Olive Grove in 1887. When Wednesday secured their own ground the Bramall Lane committee faced a considerable loss of revenue

Bramall Lane.

The Sheaf House.

and made the decision to form a new football club to be based at Bramall Lane. It was not until 1889 that the plan came to fruition with the formation of Sheffield United.

Sheaf House 1877–81/1885–87

Success in local football meant another move, at the start of the 1877–78 season, with the Sheaf House grounds being Wednesday's fourth home. The name derived from the grand house built by Daniel Brammall in 1816 – the modern-day Sheaf House Hotel – and it was behind the house that a sports ground was subsequently developed. The ground, effectively between Bramall Lane and Shoreham Street, was occasionally used by Yorkshire County Cricket Club, and Wednesday spent five years at the venue, playing Exchange Brewery in their first game at their new home in a October 1877 Sheffield Challenge Cup

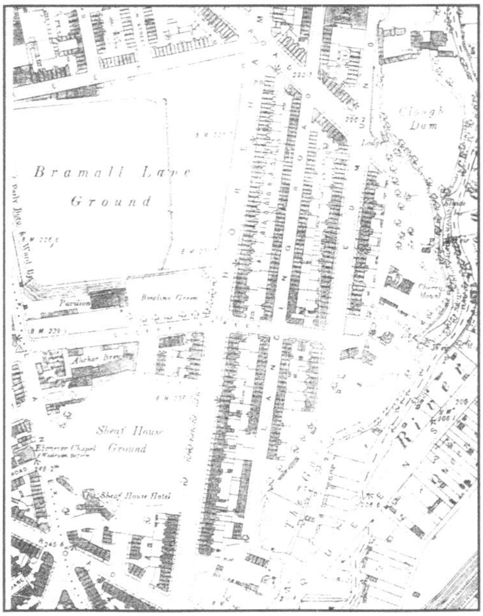

A 1890s map showing Bramall Lane and the Sheaf House grounds.

tie. Wednesday settled into their new home in the latter part of the 1870s and in March 1880 held a successful four-a-side medal competition on the ground, losing 1–0 to Heeley in the Final.

Rather curiously, however, Wednesday then virtually deserted the venue and only a single match was played there in the 1880–81 season, with Bramall Lane becoming the club's preferred option as they started to dominate the Sheffield football scene and outgrow the basic surroundings of Sheaf House. This was not, however, the end of Wednesday's connection with Sheaf House, as in the two years immediately preceding their move to Olive Grove the club returned to the ground and played several friendly games, including matches against Derby County and Notts County.

Hunter's Bar/Robert's Farm/Rustling's Farm 1882–85

After leaving Sheaf House early in the 1880s, Wednesday began to play minor home matches just off modern-day Ecclesall Road, near to the Hunter's Bar roundabout. In contemporary match reports the ground was generally described as Hunter's Bar or Robert's Farm, the latter relating to the farmland close to the main road. It was also occasionally given the name of Rustling's Farm, which was situated next to the present-day junction of Ecclesall Road and Rustlings Road, which runs around the southern side of the park. Described as 'near to the bathing dam in Endcliffe Park', the pitch was highly likely to have been close to where the Hallamshire Tennis Club is now situated. Fans' memories of the location point directly to Endcliffe Park, which was first opened in 1884 when the weir was damned to create bathing pools for the public.

The new pitch was first used in November 1882, but in three years the club's first team played only a handful of games, with the venue mainly utilised for reserve team football. Over 25 second-team games are known to have been played on the ground during that period, but all the major games were still played at Bramall Lane. The venue was last used in December 1885 for a Sheffield Challenge Cup tie against Hallam, with Wednesday now just 18 months away from securing a 'proper' ground that they could call their own.

Olive Grove 1887–99

After playing at various venues in the first 20 years of their existence, the decision to become a professional football team in April 1887 also created the necessity of a ground that could generate sufficient income to pay their newly acquired wage bill. Moving into Bramall Lane did not seem an option, as on many occasions Wednesday were sometimes left with less than one sixth of the gate receipts after the opposing club and the ground had taken their slice of the financial cake – for big games such as FA Cup ties, it is believed that the receipts were equally shared between the two

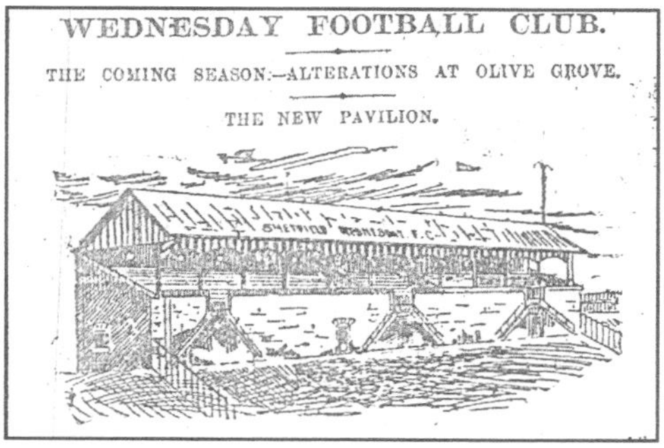

The Olive Grove stand.

Action from Wednesday v Aston Villa 1897–98 at Olive Grove.

clubs and the venue. Therefore, in the summer of 1887 the Wednesday officials took the brave move of agreeing a seven-year lease with the Duke of Norfolk for a swampy piece of land through which a footpath and brook ran, just off Queens Road on the southern side of the Midland Railway line, which had been opened in 1870. The Wednesday officials split into a ground committee and management committee and ignored people who said that the move was too far away from the town centre and that they would not even get 200 fans to make the trip! The club's new ground, 'Olive Grove', took its name from a house of the same name that lay a little way to the north-east of the ground, and as soon as the ink was dry on the contract the club started work on bringing their new home up to scratch.

Wednesday were not actually the first tenants of Olive Grove, as a junior club called Nether FC had previously utilised the land – future Wednesday goalkeeper Jim Smith being among their playing ranks. During the junior club's tenure at Olive Grove, several springs bubbled just under the playing surface, while a footpath ran straight across the pitch from the north end and continued by a footbridge over the railway and through the gardens on Queens Road. Wednesday were faced with the same problems when they took possession of the land and during the summer months they spent around £5,000 to bring the ground up to a minimum standard. The footpath was diverted, the brook covered, the field drained and the whole pitch enclosed. The club also erected a large shed on the north-west side of the ground, which could accommodate around 1,000 spectators. The new ground could be entered over the railway bridges at either Charlotte Road or Myrtle Road, although the latter involved a walk along a somewhat rough footpath to reach the ground – the current Olive Grove Road was constructed a few years later. The venue boasted a rather uneven playing surface that measured 110 x 70 yards, surrounded by a 6ft cinder track. All the club's hard work came to fruition in September 1887 when, for a guarantee of £10, Lancashire giants Blackburn Rovers visited to officially open Wednesday's first real home. A healthy crowd of around 2,000 paid threepence each to witness the dawning of a new era and they were rewarded with a sparkling match, as Wednesday recovered from a three goal deficit to draw 4–4.

An impending FA Cup tie against Preston North End in January 1888 resulted in further improvements to the ground, as a brook that bordered the elevated side of the ground was covered, thus creating a slope which provided an excellent vantage point for 1,500 fans. A new stand was also hastily erected to boost capacity, while several drays were strategically placed to provide even more viewing opportunities. A smallpox scare caused the tie to be postponed, but a record crowd of around 9,000 attended the rearranged game, firmly disproving those sceptics who had derided the club's move to Olive Grove.

Election into the Football League in 1892 resulted in Wednesday undertaking major improvements to Olive Grove, the majority of the works completed by Sheffield contractors Mastin & Sons. The largest expense was the building of an impressive new 1,000-seated stand, which was said to be one of the best in the whole Football League. The brick structure measured 179ft long by 18ft wide and it could boast dressing, bath, committee and refreshment rooms. Prior to this stand being erected, the players had changed at the nearby Queens Road public house, *The Earl of Arundel and Surrey*, and walked to the ground in their full playing kit, while the officials met at their committee rooms at the Cambridge Hotel in the city centre. At the front of the new stand railings were erected to create a standing enclosure, for which an extra sixpence would be charged, although this also gave the supporter the option of using the seating facilities. At the Sheffield end of Olive Grove, the standing area was raised and extended, while similar improvements were made at the Heeley end. In addition to the construction work, the notoriously uneven playing surface was levelled, re-laid and extended to measure a full 125 by 76 yards, of which the playing surface was much smaller at 115 by 76 yards. The complete overhaul for the impending season was believed to have cost around £2,000, but Wednesday believed that the expense would be justified by an anticipated increase in attendances. The club now boasted one of the finest enclosures in the country, and an admission fee of sixpence (2½p) was set for the dawn of a new era.

As Wednesday became an established side in the Football League they continued to improve Olive Grove, but just after the club had lifted the FA Cup in 1896 rumours started to circulate that the club might be forced to move from their new and improved ground. Those fears were allayed, however, when it was confirmed that only a 10-yard strip of land next to the railway line was owned by the Midland Railway Company, and the remainder had been purchased by the Sheffield Corporation. Sadly though, in the summer of 1898 it was announced that the club's lease on Olive Grove, which was due to expire on 29 September 1898, would not be renewed, as the Railway Company needed to extend the railway line. The club was granted permission by both parties to use the ground for the 1898–99 season, but then they would need to find a new ground if League soccer was to continue.

In August 1898 the local press reported that Wednesday were set to sign a 20-year lease on their former Sheaf House ground, having agreed a nominal rent with prospective landlords Mappin's Brewery. All the club needed was the consent of the magistrates at the forthcoming 'Brewster Sessions', but when the final day passed and the club had not submitted an application, it emerged that the brewery company had suddenly demanded a much larger rent. Wednesday felt their desperation at securing a new home was being taken advantage of, and it was back to square one as the whole deal collapsed. A home defeat to Newcastle brought the curtain down on the Olive Grove years, but a new ground was on the horizon – far away from their traditional heartland.

Owlerton/Hillsborough 1899–present

With Olive Grove set to be lost and Sheaf House no longer an option, Wednesday officials were faced with the real possibility of the club being homeless at the end of the 1898–99 season. The club's first act was to canvass their supporters, and for the home game against Aston Villa in November 1898 over 10,000 cards were distributed to canvass opinion as to which area Wednesday should move to. It was not a surprise that Carbrook, relatively close to the city centre, should top the poll with 4,767 votes, with Owlerton trailing in second place with 4,115. As the final season at Olive Grove drew ever nearer, Wednesday fans waited for news and finally, in April 1899, the club announced that they had secured a 10-acre freehold plot of meadowland on the north side of the River Don at High Bridge, Owlerton for £4,500. Considering the result of the supporters poll, it was a surprise to many that the club had decided to move 'out of the city' and the decision was considered an almighty risk – at the time Owlerton was a sparsely populated district, poorly served by public transport and with very few amenities. The move effectively meant that many fans would have to walk from the existing horse tram terminus at Hillsborough Bridge to watch their favourites. But early crowds at Owlerton compared favourably to Olive Grove, vindicating the club's decision, and this was helped by the extension of the tram to the area in 1901.

The land purchase price eventually rose to £4,783 with a £3,300 mortgage, secured in the name of director Charles Clegg, who provided the majority of the monies required. Bought from famous Sheffield silversmiths James Dixon, the land was bordered to the south by the River Don and to the west by Leppings Lane, with the soon-to-be-named Penistone Road on the easterly border. Work began apace as soon as the ink was dry on the contract, with regular contractor Mastin & Sons employing some 70 or 80 men on-site in order to

Owlerton, 1902.

complete the required works in time for the opening League game of the impending new season. The first expense was £730 for the 'laying out' of the ground, and then the former stand at Olive Grove, which had been dismantled a few weeks earlier, was promptly re-erected brick by brick on the River Don side of the new enclosure. The new pitch was raised by as much as 2ft to bring the 115 by 75-yard playing surface level, although it did slightly slope to the Leppings Lane end. Railings were installed around the pitch and a fence was erected from High Bridge to Leppings Lane, with the majority of the ground becoming enclosed and entrances constructed at both ends – at the time the club had no plans to build any accommodation behind either of the goals, they would simply be banked up. The new ground was officially christened 'Wednesday Football Ground, Owlerton', and the stage was set for another new era to commence.

An excellent crowd attended the opening League game at Owlerton, and within a few weeks the ground was improved further as a new stand was built on the Wadsley Bridge side, designed by Sheffield architects W.H. Lancashire & Sons and again built by Mastin & Sons. The new structure was a part-steel, part-brick building, with the former material sourced from Glasgow company A.J. Main. The new stand was 290ft in length and seated a total of 3,000 fans, with the construction purposely designed 'with a tendency to the crescent formation in order to afford a free and uninterrupted view from all vantage points.' The sub-structure was brick and timber, with a galvanised iron roof being supported by several steel pillars 28ft apart, although the latter feature did somewhat spoil the aforementioned view! Directly in front of the seated area the land was banked up to create a standing enclosure for 2,500 spectators, and the new stand was the first of its kind in the country as all the entrances to the seats and facilities were at the rear. Entrances were also built to each section to ensure equal distribution of fans. Nothing had been overlooked and the new stand even included a press section, accommodating around 50 reporters, while underneath were roomy dressing rooms (26ft 6in by 24ft) and bathrooms, containing not only baths, but also luxury showers with hot and cold water. At the time the Wednesday directors noted that the visiting team received the same-sized dressing rooms as the home club, and they hoped that this would be adopted at other clubs. Other facilities included a tea and coffee room, toilets for both sexes, a cycle room, referee's room and a refreshment room, franchised to a Mr and Mrs Donohue for £70. A large entrance door and turnstiles were erected on Penistone Road, and the total cost to Wednesday was £2,674, although this bought them arguably the most modern stand built at that point in English football. The new stand was partially opened for the home game against Luton Town in January 1900 and the club's operations moved across from the 'Olive Grove' stand a few weeks later. In 1902 the club extended the roof to cover the standing area, adding 10 pillars as support, while the whole structure was effectively completed a year later when the grassy bank was replaced by terracing. The Leppings Lane end of the ground also saw a more modest covered stand erected, which provided standing room for 3,000 fans. Measuring 240ft wide by 33ft deep, the structure was built at the top of a small grassy bank, 50ft from the pitch railings, with a corrugated iron roof keeping the elements off the fans. This stand was eventually extended and joined up to the North Stand.

Hillsborough, 1913.

The early construction of the North Stand showed that Wednesday were determined to make Owlerton one of the best grounds in the country, and in 1913 they announced ambitious plans to erect a new South Stand. Designed by famous architect and engineer Archibald Leitch – who designed stands at many clubs, including Glasgow Rangers, Arsenal, Manchester United, Chelsea and Everton – the new stand was described as 'the greatest structure on any football ground' and ran the whole length of the riverside at Owlerton. Wednesday stretched their finances, spending the equivalent of around £1.5 million at today's prices, but when completed there was additional seating for some 5,600 fans and around 11,000 places in the enclosure to the front of the stand. The old Olive Grove stand had been downgraded to a 'threepenny' stand when the North Stand was built, and was duly sold to the builders of the new South Stand, Freckingham & Sons, for the princely sum of £65. They demolished the building and erected a stand that included luxury dressing rooms, offices and even a billiards room. When the stand was partially opened – for the game against Derby County in September 1913 – it did not actually have a roof, but hundreds of fans still sat in the rain to try out the new structure. Two months later the stand was in full use, and just prior to Christmas the words 'The Wednesday Football Club Ltd' appeared on the roof and sometime later a decorative ball bearing the club's 1866 date of formation was added above the name – it was not until many years later that it was discovered that Wednesday were actually formed in 1867. The teams and officials all moved from the North Stand to the new South Stand in January 1914 and have, of course, remained next to the River Don ever since.

In the summer of 1914 the club spent £800 to extend and install concrete terracing at the Kop end of what was commonly known as Hillsborough, but it would not be until 1927 that further significant changes occurred. The alterations were all at the Leppings Lane end of the ground, with a small stand being erected in the north-west corner at a cost of £2,373. A year later the old stand was demolished to make way for a terrific new stand, boasting a standing capacity of 12,000 (5,000 uncovered), which boosted the ground capacity to over 80,000. The new edifice cost £7,233, with Wednesday again employing Freckingham & Co to construct the stand, which contained 90 tonnes of steelwork, 20,000 roof slates, toilets, refreshment rooms and store rooms. The building was completed when a large scoreboard was erected on the roof, updating fans of the latest scores around the country. The construction meant that Hillsborough boasted covered accommodation for 20,000, the largest of any UK ground at the time. It was not until 1954 that further improvements were made to Hillsborough, when the Kop was extended and upgraded and Husband & Co were paid £150,000 to install floodlights for the first time.

The club were again at the forefront of stand construction in 1960 when they announced plans to built a ground-breaking cantilever North Stand with seating for 10,008 supporters. In order to finance the projected cost, the club issued £150,000 worth of debenture stock with an attractive interest rate of six per cent, which the public bought in £100 blocks. The greatest stand since Arsenal's East Stand was built in the 1930s therefore grew from the ashes of the demolished old stand, with Hillsborough a three-sided ground for the majority of the 1960–61 season. The inconvenience was worthwhile, however, as when FA chairman Sir Stanley Rous officially opened the structure before the August 1961 game against Bolton Wanderers, Wednesday boasted one of the finest stands in world football. Built the full length of the pitch, the stand measured 362ft wide by 124ft deep, and the huge cantilever roof projected a full 16ft beyond the first row of seats, ensuring protection from driving rain. Materials used included 508 tonnes of steel, 115,000 bricks and 30 miles of beechwood seating.

An artists impression of the new cantilever stand in 1960.

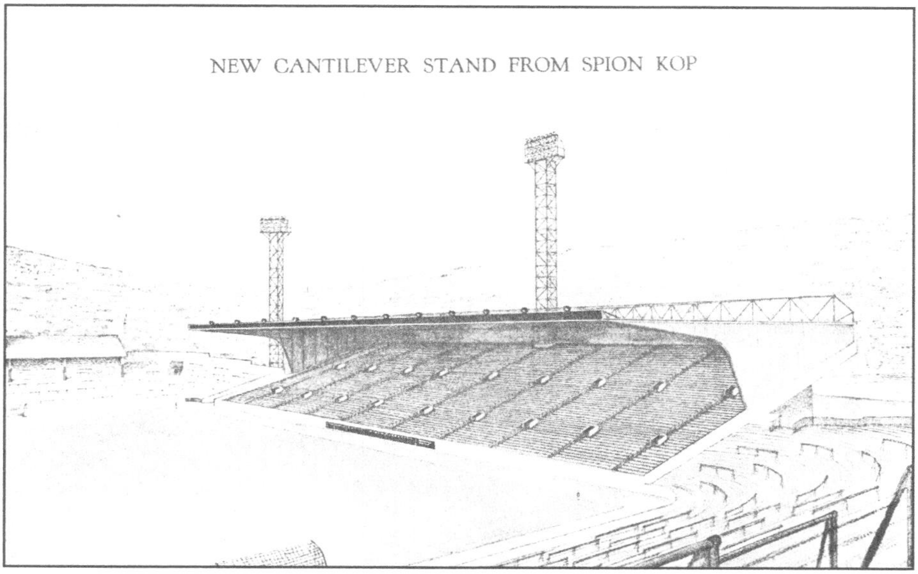

When the club was allocated games in the 1966 World Cup Finals it resulted in changes to two sides of the increasingly modern ground. The biggest change came at the Leppings Lane end, as Wednesday replaced the 1920s structure with a 4,471-seater construction with a large standing area at the front. Built by Rotherham-based Tarmac Civil Engineering and designed by Husband & Co, the total project cost £109,036, with the new stand opened for the World Cup match between Switzerland and West Germany in July 1966. Incidentally, seven months later the old north-west stand was demolished to make way for new terracing, at a cost of £29,000. The other building work undertaken pre 1966 was the transformation of the South Stand enclosure from terracing to 3,356 seats, at a cost of £27,600. The new seated South Stand was used for the first time for the home game against Liverpool in November 1965.

The club's fall from grace in the 1970s meant that ground development took a back seat, but soon after Wednesday regained their top-flight place they announced the plans that diehard Wednesday fans had waited to hear for many years – the Kop was to be covered! Architects Eastwood & Partners were engaged and Ackroyd & Abbott contracted to put a roof over the traditional home end of Hillsborough. A £500,000 grant from the Football Trust contributed greatly to the estimated total £850,000 cost, and a 'Raise The Roof Fun Run' was attended by thousands of fans in April 1986, while the team's run to the FA Cup semi-finals also put some welcome cash into the coffers. The works commenced after the final game of the 1985–86 season and the Kop was greatly extended, giving the area a more symmetrical look, as opposed to the rather humpback shape of the uncovered Kop. A huge crane was brought on-site (part of the old Kop, near to the North Stand, was demolished so the machine could get into the ground) and this lifted the huge steel bars that supported the metal roof. When the works were completed the club had the largest covered standing area in Europe (22,000), and the visit of Everton for the opening home game of the 1986–87 season saw around 15,000 curious fans pack into the newly roofed area of Hillsborough. The new addition was officially opened by HM the Queen in December 1986, with over 40,000 inside the ground to witness the royal seal of approval.

The disaster at the stadium in 1989 led to huge changes in English grounds, and Wednesday closed the Leppings Lane terrace for two years while the capacity of the Kop was slashed to below the pre-roof era. In the summer of 1990 over £400,000 was spent on ground improvements, which included £70,000 on new crush barriers for the Kop, £30,000 on fire alarms and £10,000 on emergency lighting. The Leppings Lane terrace was redeveloped and opened in August 1991 with 2,494 tip-up blue seats, an extended roof, new turnstiles and a police room – total cost being around £850,000, with a £480,000 grant received towards the project. The summer of 1992 saw a £200,000 undersoil heating system installed, while 12 months later there were yet more changes as both the Kop and north-west corner were converted to all-seaters. A grand total of 11,210 seats were installed on the Kop, complete with an Owl design and the words 'The Owls', with usual contractors Ackroyd & Abbott being handed the task, and 8,500 fans bought season tickets for the area for the following season. The final alteration to the west end of the ground resulted in 1,382 seats being installed in the north-west area, taking the ground capacity to an all-seated 35,726.

Hillsborough in 1999.

The club's honour of being chosen as a host ground for the 1996 European Championships resulted in a massive project being launched to extend and renovate the South Stand. The first phase of the redevelopment started straight after the final home match of the 1992–93 season, against Liverpool, when workmen from contractors Ackroyd & Abbott came on-site to remove the old South Stand roof. In its place was erected a huge 500-tonne single-span girder that literally towered over the old South Stand, with the new roof stretching all the way back to the edge of the River Don. All the wooden seating was subsequently replaced with the modern plastic variety, with the bill for the first part of the works totalling £1.8 million – a grant of over half of the sum (£960,000) being received from the Football Trust. Phase two of the development was completed during the 1995–96 season when, at a cost of £5 million, Wednesday fitted just over 3,000 seats in what is now called the Grandstand and created 30 executive boxes. The club also refurbished the interior to create several hospitality suites, and when the work was the finished the old South Stand was virtually obliterated, buried under the mass of steel, concrete and plastic. One homage to the past did survive though, as the decorative ball that was erected back in 1913 was restored to its rightful place on what was now one of the most modern stands in the English game.

Hillsborough in 2011.

The North Stand at Hillsborough.

The upgrade of Hillsborough continued in the summer of 1997, when the rather uncomfortable wooden seating in the North Stand was ripped out and just under 10,000 plastic seats installed, with 'SWFC' strategically spelt out in white among the blue seats. Sadly, a decade later the devastating floods of June 2007 caused untold damage to the interior of both the South and North Stand. At one point the pitch was under several feet of water, with the dressing rooms and boardroom all being invaded by a tide of water and mud. The club shop, ticket office and lower levels of the North Stand were also badly affected, with over £1 million claimed on the club's insurance to rectify all the damage caused by the sudden downpour. There is no doubt that Hillsborough is now totally unrecognisable from that September afternoon in 1899 when Owlerton was opened, but for every subsequent generation of fans it has been considered the club's spiritual home and it is highly unlikely that this opinion will ever change.

Current capacities:

North Stand	9,255
West Stand	6,658
North West Corner	1,337
Kop	11,210
South Stand (lower)	8,275
Grandstand	3,077
TOTAL	39,812

Matches to Remember

MATCH TO REMEMBER 1 — 10 MARCH 1877

THE WEDNESDAY 4 HEELEY 3

Sheffield Challenge Cup Final. Played at Bramall Lane (12-a-side game)

One of the oldest Cup competitions in the world, the Sheffield Challenge Cup, was introduced by the Sheffield FA in 1876, The Wednesday FC appearing in the first ever game played in the new tournament. The new trophy was designed by a local art student, F. Fidler, after the FA offered a £5 prize for the best idea.

Wednesday had beaten Parkwood Springs 3–1 at home, Kimberworth 1–0 away, Attercliffe 1–0 away and, in the semi-final, Exchange 3–1 at Bramall Lane to set up a Final tie with Heeley, also at Bramall Lane.

Before an estimated crowd of 8,000 Wednesday lost the toss of the coin and Wednesday's Bill Stacey kicked off, playing into a fierce wind. After some end to end play, a scrimmage occurred near the Wednesday goal and Martin was able to deflect the ball in past Stacey to put Heeley ahead. From the restart the ball was again put into the Wednesday goalmouth, where it hit a Wednesday defender on his back and went in for an own-goal, putting Heeley two goals ahead. Before half-time, in trying to clear his lines, Stacey headed into his own goal to put Heeley 3–0 ahead at the break.

Wednesday started the second half with the wind in their favour and Bishop put over a cross, from which Frank Butler was able to pull a goal back. Soon after, William Clegg shot just over, before another Bishop cross reached Tom Butler, who reduced the arrears to just a single goal. Then William Clegg netted from Frank Butler's pass to bring the scores level and send Wednesday's fans wild. Near the end, a Heeley player handled the ball to prevent a certain goal, but Wednesday were unable to turn the ball in from the resultant free-kick.

At the end of the match, and with the score tied at 3–3, the players met in the centre of the field to decide whether to play on or to replay. As a grand dinner was arranged that night for the presentation of the Cup and medals, plus the fact that the crowd were wanting a result, an extra half hour was the outcome.

Wednesday started the first half with the wind in their favour again, but were unable to take advantage. In the second half of extra-time, with the advantage of the wind now in Heeley's favour, Wednesday put up a great show to keep them out and, with a few minutes left, Bill Skinner was able to turn another Bishop cross past the Heeley 'keeper to make Wednesday the first winner of this new Cup.

During the evening event at the Imperial Hotel on Castle Street, the President of the Sheffield Association, Mr Shaw, who was also the match referee, presented the Cup to Wednesday's President and the medals to Wednesday's players.

It is perhaps fitting that the Final of the competition, now known as the Senior Cup, is currently held at Hillsborough, the home of the inaugural winners.

The Wednesday: F. Stacey, W.H. Stacey (captain), E. Buttery, W.E. Cregg, T. Butler, H. Muscroft, J. Bingley, F.M. Butler, T. Bishop, W.E. Skinner, J.J. Lang, J.C. Cregg.

Heeley: W. Beard, T.A. Tomlinson, P. Andrews, J. Deans (captain), R. Martin, J. Tomlinson. F. Brownhill, T. Leslie, J. Hunter, J. Thorpe, H.M. Barrington, J. Lindley.

Referee: Mr J.C. Shaw. Umpires: Mr W.R. Wake and Mr J.W. Barber.

MATCH TO REMEMBER 2 — 3 SEPTEMBER 1892

NOTTS COUNTY 0 THE WEDNESDAY 1

First Division

For Wednesday's first ever game in the Football League they travelled to the Castle Grounds, the temporary home of Notts County due to the unavailability of their Trent Bridge ground. The Midland Railway Company laid on special trains for Wednesday's fans to travel, but sadly, as a result of the crowded trains a young man slipped between the train and the platform and was seriously injured.

Just before kick-off, with many fans not yet in the ground the large crowds outside knocked down part of a barrier and many gained free admission. Just before the game was due to start the fans encroached onto the field, forcing the players to leave the pitch and delaying the kick-off by 25 minutes. In front of around 13,000 fans Notts started well, but Wednesday's defence held firm and soon a great pass led to Spiksley having a shot that Toone in the Notts goal saved well. Wednesday soon got the upper hand in the opening stages and Davis and Brown both went close to scoring. A Spiksley shot from out wide landed on top of the crossbar before, at the end of 11 minutes of play, a Wednesday corner led to the ball reaching Tom Brandon, Wednesday's captain, and he duly had the honour of scoring Wednesday's first ever League goal. Play then fluctuated from end to end, with both 'keepers having to make saves before half-time arrived, but Wednesday managed to stay 1–0 ahead. During the break two mounted policemen were brought to the ground to ensure that the crowd were kept off the field of play.

The second half was delayed due to heavy rain, but eventually restarted at 11 minutes to five. Within minutes Brady's shot almost extended Wednesday's lead and then Spiksley saw his effort ruled out for offside. Wednesday had the better of the play during the rest of the game, but the County defence held firm to leave the final score 1–0 in the visitors' favour – Wednesday's first ever League victory.

Notts County: G. Toone, A. Whitelaw, J. Hendry, J. Parke, D. Calderhead, A. Shelton, A.C. McGregor, E. Docherty, James Osward, H. Walkerdine, H.B. Daft.

The Wednesday: J. Allan, T. Brandon, A.C. Mumford, A. Hall, W. Betts, H. Brandon, F. Spiksley, A. Brady, H. Davis, R.N. Brown, W. Dunlop

Referee: Mr W.H. Jope (Wednesbury)

MATCH TO REMEMBER 3 — 18 APRIL 1896

THE WEDNESDAY 2 WOLVERHAMPTON WANDERERS 1

FA Cup Final

Wednesday went into their second FA Cup Final as favourites, as opponents Wolves were struggling near the foot of the First Division table and, due to injury, were also without the services of their first-choice goalkeeper. A crowd of 48,836 gathered at the Crystal Palace grounds – including a large following from Sheffield – and the crowd were stunned when Wednesday scored within 30 seconds of the start. Fred Spiksley shot low past the Wolves goalkeeper from a Brash cross, scoring what was the fastest ever FA Cup Final goal and perhaps still holds that record, as no truly accurate records were kept from those times.

After 8 minutes, however, Wolves were back in the game when Black equalised with an overhead kick, following a free-kick, with Henderson following up on the line to make sure that it went in. Soon after this Black netted again, but was given offside. Then, after 20 minutes, Crawshaw saw his shot blocked, only for Brady to pick up the rebound and pass to Spiksley, whose shot struck a post and rolled into the net. At half-time Wednesday led by the odd goal of three.

After 12 minutes of the second half Dunn of Wolves scored from an indirect free-kick, but this was disallowed as no one else had touched the ball, and both sides went close to adding more goals as both 'keepers made some fine saves. Near the end of the match Wednesday's Tommy Crawshaw brought inside-forward Davis back into

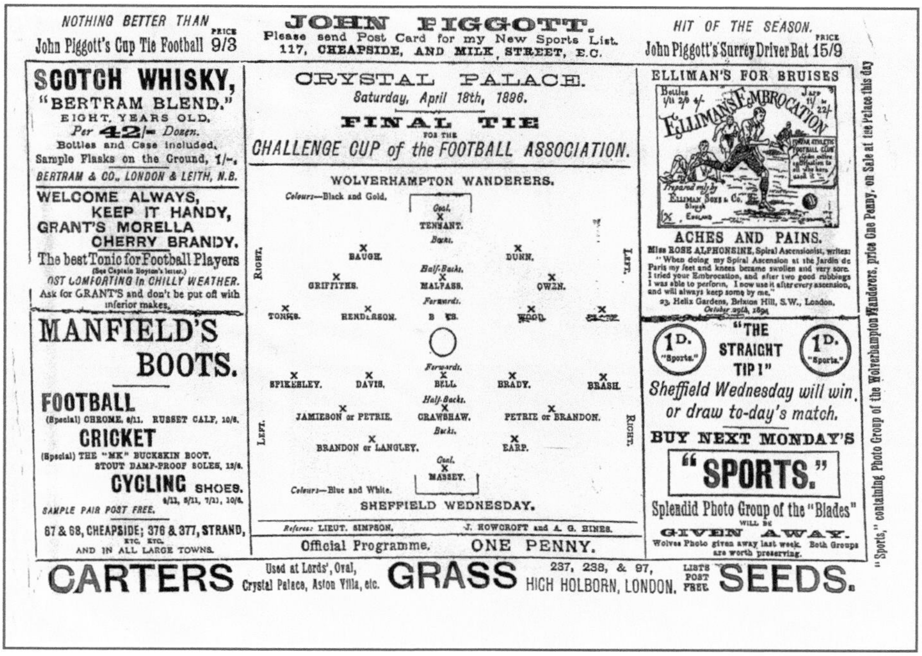

NOTHING BETTER THAN
John Piggott's Cup Tie Football PRICE 9/3

JOHN PIGGOTT.
Please send Post Card for my New Sports List.
117, CHEAPSIDE, AND MILK STREET, E.C.

HIT OF THE SEASON.
John Piggott's Surrey Driver Bat PRICE 15/9

SCOTCH WHISKY,
"BERTRAM BLEND."
EIGHT YEARS OLD.
Per 42/- Dozen.
Bottles and Case included.
Sample Flasks on the Ground, 1/-.
BERTRAM & CO., LONDON & LEITH, N.B.

WELCOME ALWAYS,
KEEP IT HANDY,
GRANT'S MORELLA
CHERRY BRANDY.
The best Tonic for Football Players
(See Captain Boyton's letter.)
MOST COMFORTING in CHILLY WEATHER.
Ask for GRANT'S and don't be put off with inferior makes.

MANFIELD'S
BOOTS.
FOOTBALL
(Special) CHROME, 8/11. RUSSET CALF, 10/6.
CRICKET
(Special) THE "MK" BUCKSKIN BOOT.
STOUT DAMP-PROOF SOLES, 13/6.
CYCLING SHOES.
6/11, 8/11, 7/11, 10/6.
SAMPLE PAIR POST FREE.
67 & 68, CHEAPSIDE; 376 & 377, STRAND,
ETC. ETC.
AND IN ALL LARGE TOWNS.

CRYSTAL PALACE.
Saturday, April 18th, 1896.
FINAL TIE
FOR THE
CHALLENGE CUP of the FOOTBALL ASSOCIATION.

WOLVERHAMPTON WANDERERS.
Colours—Black and Gold.
Goal. TENNANT.
Backs. BAUGH. DUNN.
Half-Backs. GRIFFITHS. MALPASS. OWEN.
Forwards. TONKS. HENDERSON. WOOD.
RIGHT. LEFT.

Forwards. SPIKESLEY. DAVIS. BELL. BRADY. BRASH.
Half-Backs. JAMIESON or PETRIE. CRAWSHAW. PETRIE or BRANDON.
Backs. BRANDON or LANGLEY. EARP.
Goal. MASSEY.
Colours—Blue and White.
LEFT. RIGHT.
SHEFFIELD WEDNESDAY.

Referee: LIEUT. SIMPSON. J. HOWCROFT and A. G. HINES.
Official Programme. ONE PENNY.

ELLIMAN'S FOR BRUISES
Bottles 1/1½ 2/9 4/- Jars 11/- 22/-
ELLIMAN'S EMBROCATION
Prepared only by ELLIMAN SONS & Co. Slough ENGLAND
ACHES AND PAINS.
Miss ROSE ALPHONSINE, Spiral Ascensionist, writes:
"When doing my Spiral Ascension at the Jardin de Paris my feet and knees became swollen and very sore. I tried your Embrocation, and after two good rubbings I was able to perform. I now use it after every ascension, and will always keep some by me."
23, Helix Gardens, Brixton Hill, S.W., London.
October 29th, 1894.

1D. "Sports." "THE STRAIGHT TIP!" 1D. "Sports."
Sheffield Wednesday will win, or draw to-day's match.
BUY NEXT MONDAY'S
"SPORTS."
Splendid Photo Group of the "Blades"
WILL BE
GIVEN AWAY.
Wolves Photo given away last week. Both Groups are worth preserving.

"Sports," containing Photo Group of the Wolverhampton Wanderers, price One Penny, on Sale at the Palace this day

CARTERS Used at Lords', Oval, Crystal Palace, Aston Villa, etc. GRASS 237, 238, & 97, HIGH HOLBORN, LONDON. LISTS POST FREE. SEEDS.

Tommy Crawshaw's 1896 FA Cup Medal.

defence so that the Wednesday captain could be utilised in a stopper centre-half role. This may have been the first time this system had been used, but the tactic successfully kept the Wolves at bay and the final whistle blew with Wednesday winning the competition at their 15th attempt.

As the teams were leaving the field Wolves 'keeper, Tennant, asked, 'When do we replay?' When Spiksley's winning goal had entered the net, the ball had rebounded back out and Tennant had then booted it away. Somehow, he had failed to notice that the match had restarted from the centre circle!

Wednesday were duly awarded the new FA Cup from Lord Kinnaird, the President of the Football Association. The original Cup had been stolen in 1895 from a Birmingham store after Aston Villa had won it. Wednesday returned to Sheffield on the Monday and huge crowds gathered around the city centre, cheering the team all the way to the Royal Hotel, where a celebratory dinner was held in their honour.

The Wednesday: J. Massey, M.J. Earp, A. Langley, H. Brandon, T.H. Crawshaw, R. Petrie, A. Brash, A. Brady, L. Bell, H. Davis, F. Spiksley.

Wolves: W. Tennant, R. Baugh, T. Dunn, H. Griffiths, A.W. Malpass, W. Owen, J. Tonks, C.J. Henderson, W.E. Beats, H. Wood, D.G. Black.

Referee: Lieut. W. Simpson (Finsbury Barracks, London).

MATCH TO REMEMBER 4 — 2 SEPTEMBER 1899

THE WEDNESDAY 5 CHESTERFIELD TOWN 1

Second Division

This was the first game to be played at the new Owlerton home of The Wednesday, with near neighbours from the Derbyshire town of Chesterfield providing the opposition for the historic occasion. Wednesday had just been relegated from the top flight, while Chesterfield Town had just been voted into the Football League from the Midland League. After losing the much-loved Olive Grove to the development of the Railway system, the club took a chance in moving out of central Sheffield into the sparsely populated area of Owlerton. Thankfully, a bumper 12,000 crowd allayed any fears that the hard core of the club's support would not travel a few miles to watch their favourites.

The Lord Mayor of Sheffield, William Clegg (who was also Wednesday's chairman and a former player), officially kicked off at 3 o'clock before running off the field. The first goal at the new enclosure, from Chesterfield's Herbert Munday, arrived after 10 minutes – hence coining the phrase 'Munday scored versus Wednesday on a Saturday'. The visiting inside-forward almost scored again soon after – his goal being disallowed – but Wednesday hit back to level matters after

The team for the first game at Hillsborough.

33 minutes through 'Olive Grove Flyer' Fred Spiksley. Five minutes later Wednesday had turned the game around, with Bob Ferrier's goal putting his side ahead at the interval.

In the second half, after having an effort from Spiksley ruled out for offside, Wednesday added a third goal by Harry Millar on 64 minutes from an effort that hit the underside of the bar and rebounded back into play – the goal being awarded after the referee had consulted both of his linesmen. Just after this, Chesterfield were frustrated when Munday netted, but play was pulled back for an earlier foul committed by Wednesday man Jack Earp. After 78 minutes the win was confirmed when Millar ran onto an Archie Brash pass to make the score 4–1, and the great start to life at Owlerton was rounded off three minutes later when, from Spiksley's pass, Brash fired home goal number five. Wednesday would win all their League games at their new ground on the way to the Second Division title, while Chesterfield finished in a creditable seventh place.

The Wednesday: J. Massey, M.J. Earp (captain), A. Langley, R. Ferrier, T.H. Crawshaw, H. Ruddlesdin, A. Brash, J. Pryce, H. Millar, J. Wright, F. Spiksley.

Chesterfield: J. Hancock, J.E. Pilgrim, D.J. Fletcher, W. Ballantyne, J. Bell, E. Downie, W. Morley, F.W. Thacker, W.H. Gooing, H. Munday, G. Geary.

Referee: J.W. Horrocks (Bury).

MATCH TO REMEMBER 5 — 12 NOVEMBER 1904

THE WEDNESDAY 5 EVERTON 5

First Division

Visitors to Owlerton, Everton, were fresh from a five-goal bombardment the previous week, while although Wednesday were one place higher than the Liverpool club – third in the top division – they went into this game on the back of three consecutive defeats. It was therefore no surprise that within two minutes Everton's Alex Young had put the visitors a goal up, beating Richard Jarvis who was playing only his second first-team game. After 10 minutes,

The WEST END CLOTHIERS' COMPANY, LTD.,
For HIGH-CLASS TAILORING 41, HIGH STREET.
at POPULAR PRICES. SHEFFIELD.

Sheffield Wednesday v. Everton.

Vol. 5 Played at Owlerton, Sheffield, November 12th, 1904. No. 11

Wednesday.

Right Wing. Left Wing.

1
Jarvis
BACKS:
2 Layton 3 Burton
HALF-BACKS:
4 Ferriar 5 Crawshaw 6 Ruddlesdin
FORWARDS:
7 Davis 8 Stewart (J.) 9 V. S. Simpson or Malloch 10 Wilson (Centre). 11 Simpson

Referee: Mr. F. Heath, Birmingham.

Should any Alteration be made, a notice will be sent round giving the name of the substituted player, and the number of the position in which he will play.

Published by J. WALTHAM, 11 Vincent Road, Sheffield.

Linesmen: Messrs. Wooley and North.
FORWARDS:
12 H. P. Hardman 13 Settle 14 Young 15 McDermott 16 Sharp
HALF-BACKS:
17 Abbott 18 Taylor 19 J. B. Ashworth
BACKS:
20 Crelley 21 Balmer
22
Scott

Left Wing. Right Wing.

Everton.

The WEST END CLOTHIERS' COMPANY, Ltd.,
TROUSERS from 10/6 Per Pair, TO MEASURE.

The WEST END CLOTHIERS' COMPANY, Ltd.,
REAL INDIGO DYED SERGE SUITS, from 37/6 TO MEASURE.

however, Harry Davis finished off a cross from Georgie Simpson to quickly pull his side level. After an injury to Ashworth had left Everton with 10 men for eight minutes, they almost fell behind when Everton 'keeper, Billy Scott, saved from Georgie Simpson's shot at the second attempt, with Wednesday claiming that the ball had crossed the line. Just before half-time Settle scored in a scrimmage, and two minutes later he netted again after Jarvis had caught the ball but was barged into the net. A fourth goal arrived soon after, Hardman scoring with a low shot, and there was still time for the Toffeemen to score a fifth, through Abbott, to leave Wednesday fans in a despondent mood at the half-time break.

With Wednesday four goals in arrears at the interval, few would have anticipated what drama the second half would bring. Wednesday started the half well, but were still 5–1 behind after 63 minutes. The Owls were given a lifeline, however, when Balmer tripped Georgie Simpson in the area and Wednesday were awarded a penalty-kick. Unfortunately, Scott pushed Stewart's penalty out, but thankfully he followed in to score the rebound, with Scott being hurt in the ensuing melee. He was beaten again five minutes later when Georgie Simpson waltzed around him and rolled the ball into the empty net. Scott now left the field – Abbott taking his place in the goal – and with 10 men Everton were faced with hanging on to their two-goal lead as Wednesday attacked furiously. Inside-forward Jimmy Stewart then fired against a post, but with 10 minutes remaining Viv Simpson netted, following a corner-kick, to make the score 4–5. Both sides then went down to 10 men when Harry Davis was sent off for punching Hardman, but there was still time for a dramatic last-minute twist when Bob Ferrier fired home a thunderous free-kick that finished up in the back of the net to seal an amazing comeback, much to the joy of the home fans.

The Wednesday: T.R. Jarvis, W. Layton, H.A. Burton, R. Ferrier, T.H. Crawshaw (captain), H. Ruddlesdin, H. Davis, J. Stewart, A. Wilson, V.S. Simpson, G. Simpson.

Everton: W. Scott, W. Balmer, J. Crelley, S.B. Ashworth, J.D. Taylor, W. Abbott, J.S. Sharp, T. McDermott, A.S. Young, J. Settle, H.P. Hardman.

Referee: F. Heath (Small Heath, Birmingham).

MATCH TO REMEMBER 6 — 20 APRIL 1907

THE WEDNESDAY 2 EVERTON 1

FA Cup Final

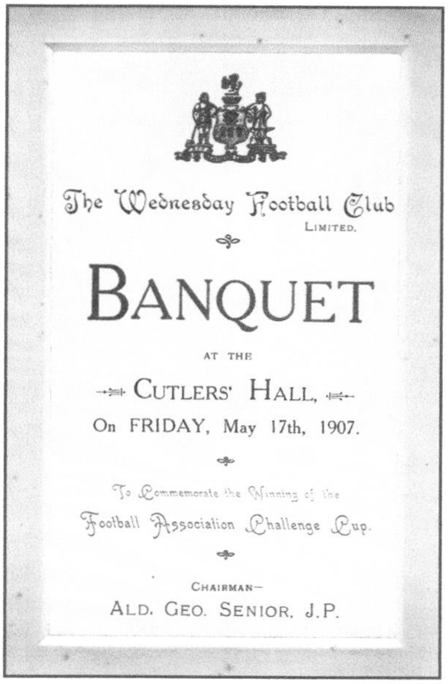

The Wednesday faced Cup-holders Everton in the 1907 FA Cup Final before a huge crowd of 84,594. Wednesday were missing Harry Davis, who had broken his leg in an earlier round, while Everton had 10 of the same side that had lifted the trophy the year before.

Taylor won the toss for Everton and they kicked-off with the wind at their backs and, in the opening minutes, Abbott headed against Wednesday's bar. After 10 minutes play Georgie Simpson put Wednesday ahead, but this was ruled out by the officials for an infringement. After 21 minutes of play, however, Harry Chapman's shot was fumbled by the Everton 'keeper and appeared to go in, but Jimmy Stewart made sure by banging it into the net in a goalmouth scramble. The goal was credited to Stewart – after the match, referee Nat Whittaker stated that he had awarded the goal after Chapman's shot, but history has always credited Stewart with the opening goal in the showpiece match. Both teams had further chances in the first period before Jack Lyall, running out of goal, lost the ball and William Bartlett had to get back to clear from the goalline. A few minutes later both Harry Burton and Willie Layton failed to cut out Hardman's centre, which eventually landed at the feet of Jack Sharp, who gave Lyall no chance with his shot to pull Everton level after 38 minutes.

In the second half both teams had chances. The best fell to Bolton, whose shot was brilliantly saved by

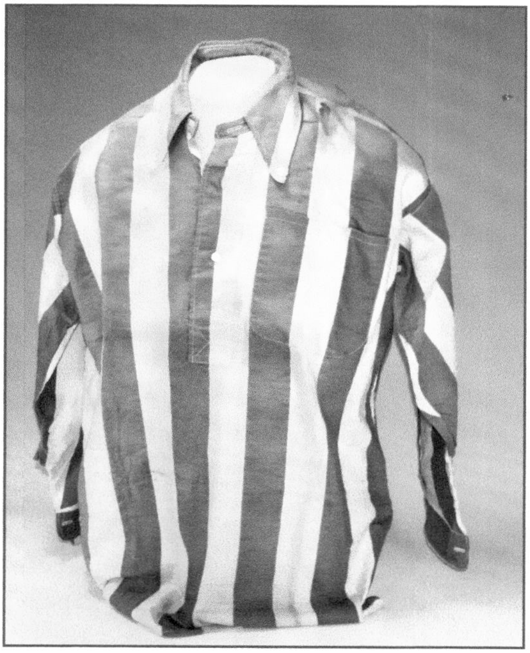

1907 FA Cup Final shirt.

Tommy Crawshaw's 1907 FA Cup medal.

Lyall to keep Wednesday level. As time was running out, Andrew Wilson chased a long ball to the byline, near the corner flag, where he beat Jock Taylor and crossed to Simpson, stood at the far post, who headed in what proved to be the winning goal on 86 minutes. With so little time for Everton to launch a comeback, the Cup was Wednesday's for a second time, with captain Tommy Crawshaw entering club history as the only man to win the famous trophy on two occasions.

The Wednesday: J. Lyall, W. Layton, H.A. Burton, J.T. Brittleton, T.H. Crawshaw (captain), W. Bartlett, H. Chapman, F. Bradshaw, A. Wilson, J. Stewart, G. Simpson.

Everton: W. Scott, W. Balmer, R. Balmer, H. Makepeace, J. Taylor (captain), W. Abbott, J. Sharp, H. Bolton, A. Young, J. Settle, H. Hardman.

Referee: Mr N. Whittaker (Brockley, London).

MATCH TO REMEMBER 7 — 13 DECEMBER 1930

SHEFFIELD WEDNESDAY 9 BIRMINGHAM FC 1

First Division

A crowd of only 21,226 attended this game, despite Wednesday having scored 30 goals in their last seven games. The missing fans would have cause to regret their absence, however, as Sheffield Wednesday recorded the highest ever League victory in their long history, the comprehensive win also taking the club top of the First Division table.

Wednesday nearly went a goal down in the first minute when Ernie Blenkinsop slipped, allowing Horsman to get away and cross to Briggs, but luckily Tommy Walker was able to clear the danger. By half-time Wednesday had netted five times, with Harry Burgess opening the scoring after 16 minutes when he netted with a diving header from Mark Hooper's cross. After 29 minutes it was 2–0 when Jack Ball fired home a spectacular 30-yard shot into the roof of the net, and two minutes later the home side netted again, Ellis Rimmer heading in from Hooper's corner-kick. Hooper then turned from creator to goalscorer after 38 minutes when he ran onto Rimmer's pass and scored from the rebound after Hibbs had pushed his first shot out. The first-half goal-fest ended with four minutes remaining on the clock when Ball lobbed over Hibbs, although there was still time for Jimmy Seed to hit a terrific shot that flew just over the bar.

The shell-shocked visitors started the second half with their forward line reshuffled, but within five minutes Wednesday had added to the score when Jimmy Seed played a one-two with Hooper and swooped to head in the latter's low cross on 49 minutes. Birmingham then had a shot punched away by Brown, before a totally dominant Wednesday side had yet

Vol. 31. —PRICE 2d.— No. 9.

THE HIPPODROME

THE MOST POPULAR SHEFFIELD HALL.

TWICE NIGHTLY :-: 6.30 and 8.40.

THE LATEST, BRIGHTEST and BEST.

Manager: W. B. GIBSON.

Sheffield Wednesday v. Birmingham

Played at Hillsborough, Sheffield, SATURDAY, December 13th, 1930.

Sheffield Wednesday.

Right Wing. Left Wing.

Goal. 1 Brown

Backs. 2 Walker 3 Blenkinsop

Half-Backs. 4 Strange 5 Leach 6 Wilson

Forwards. 7 Hooper 8 Seed 9 Ball 10 Burgess 11 Rimmer

Referee: Mr. J. Roscoe (Bolton).

Should any alteration be made, a notice will be sent round giving the name of the substituted player, with the number of the position in which he will play.

Linesmen: Messrs. J. Williams (Barnsley) & L. Heath (Sutton-in-Ashfield). (Blue & White Flag) (Red & White Flag)

Forwards. 16 Curtis 15 Briggs 14 Fillingham 13 Crosbie 12 Horsman

Half-Backs. 19 Cringan 18 Morrall 17 Stoker

Backs. 21 Booton 20 Liddell

Goal. 22 Hibbs

Left Wing. Right Wing.

Birmingham.

THE HIPPODROME 6.30 THE HIPPODROME 8.40

more chances to add to the scoreline. The Blues grabbed a consolation goal after 61 minutes, however, when Briggs saw his mishit shot in a breakaway roll over the line. This stirred Wednesday back into action and they netted three goals in 10 minutes through a Hooper shot (63 mins), a Seed effort (70 mins) and a header from Hooper that hit a post and went in (73 mins). The ninth goal meant that Wednesday had surpassed their previous record mark – 8–0 against Sunderland on Boxing Day 1911. Birmingham's Crosland did hit the bar late on, but Wednesday then had two chances to record double figures with Tommy Walker's spot-kick hit straight at the 'keeper, who saved easily, before Ball went clear just before the end but shot wide.

Sheffield Wednesday: J.H. Brown, T. Walker, E. Blenkinsop, A.H. Strange, T. Leach, C. Wilson, M. Hooper, J. Seed (captain), J. Ball, H. Burgess, E.J. Rimmer.

Birmingham: H. Hibbs, G. Liddell, H. Booton, L. Stoker, G. Morrall, J. Cringan, W. Horsman, J. Crosbie, T. Fillingham, G.R. Briggs, E. Curtis.

Referee: J. Roscoe (Bolton).

MATCH TO REMEMBER 8 27 APRIL 1935

SHEFFIELD WEDNESDAY 4 WEST BROMWICH ALBION 2

FA Cup Final

Wednesday reached their fourth FA Cup Final by beating Oldham at home 3–1, Wolves away 2–1, Norwich away 1–0, Arsenal at home by 2–1 and then Burnley, in the Villa Park semi-final, 3–0.

The referee started the game at two minutes to three, and at the time of the scheduled kick-off Wednesday were already one goal to the good, as Jack Palethorpe met Mark Hooper's cross before firing in a low shot for a sensational start to the game in front of a crowd of 93,204. After 20 minutes West Brom hit back when Wally Boyes met Joe Carter's cross and hit a stunning shot into the roof of the goal. The man who provided the assist for the goal was the only Sheffield-born player on the pitch. The half-time interval arrived with the score still a tie at 1–1.

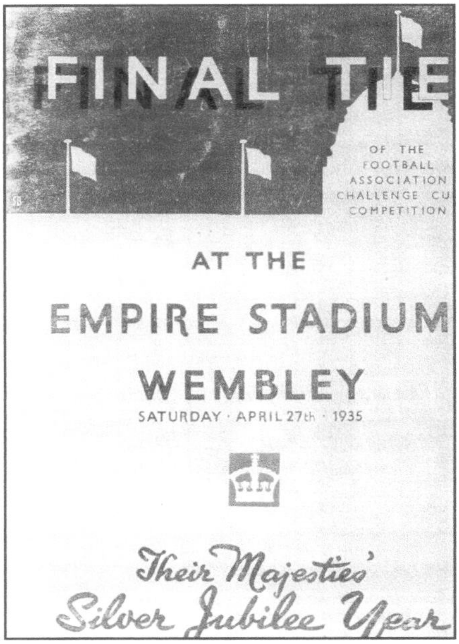

FINAL TIE
OF THE FOOTBALL ASSOCIATION CHALLENGE CUP COMPETITION
AT THE
EMPIRE STADIUM
WEMBLEY
SATURDAY · APRIL 27th · 1935
Their Majesties'
Silver Jubilee Year

After 69 minutes of the second half, Ronnie Starling, the Wednesday captain, beat Bill Richardson to the ball, and his pass found Hooper, who beat three defenders and hit a low shot, which hit a post and went in, putting the Owls back into the lead. Then, with 15 minutes to go, Sandford's shot from 20 yards was deflected off Walt Millership and beat Jack Brown to bring the tie level again. With time running out, Joe Carter hit a post and then Billy G. Richardson, put clear by Boyes, shot wide. Up until the Final Wednesday winger Ellis Rimmer had scored in every round in the Cup run, and he maintained his unique record when heading home from Sharp's cross, after 85 minutes, to put his side back ahead. Two minutes later the Cup was on its way to Sheffield for the third time when Harold Pearson pushed out Hooper's shot and Rimmer fired home the rebound to rubber-stamp the victory. Incidentally, Rimmer had a lucky mascot, which he put on his dressing-room peg before each round of the Cup, but this had been left in Sheffield

Captain Ron Starling receiving the FA Cup from the The Prince of Wales.

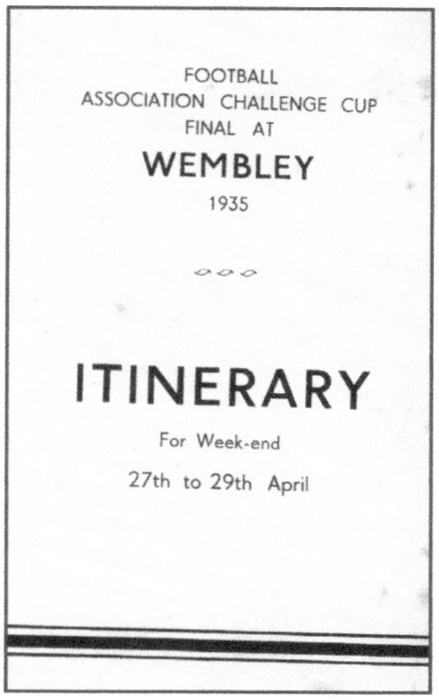
FOOTBALL
ASSOCIATION CHALLENGE CUP
FINAL AT
WEMBLEY
1935

ITINERARY
For Week-end
27th to 29th April

when Wednesday travelled down to London on the Thursday. Trainer Sam Powell found it as he was leaving Hillsborough on the Saturday morning, and it eventually arrived at Wembley at half-time, allowing the superstitious winger to reunite with his lucky charm.

Captain Ronnie Starling was presented with the Cup by the Prince of Wales, who later became King Edward VIII before abdicating the throne a few months later. Wednesday arrived back in Sheffield to a great welcome from their fans and were honoured with an official reception at the Town Hall, where the team showed off the Cup from the balcony, to huge cheers from the assembled masses.

Sheffield Wednesday: J.H. Brown, J. Nibloe, A.E. Catlin, W. Sharp, W. Millership, H. Burrows, M. Hooper, J. Surtees, J. Palethorpe, R.W. Starling (captain), E.J. Rimmer.

West Bromwich Albion: H. Pearson, G. Shaw, H. Trentham, J. Murphy, W. Richardson, J. Edwards, T. Glidden, J. Carter, W.G. Richardson, E. Standford, W. Boyes.

Referee: A.E. Fogg (Bolton).

MATCH TO REMEMBER 9 — 19 NOVEMBER 1938

SHEFFIELD WEDNESDAY 7 NORWICH CITY 0

Second Division

Neither side went into this game in particularly good form, with Norwich without an away point all season and Wednesday faring little better, boasting only 14 points from as many games. It was therefore a shock to the 16,963 fans inside Hillsborough when the Owls went goal crazy, with centre-forward Doug Hunt becoming the only man in club history to score a double hat-trick in a competitive fixture.

Jackie Robinson and Doug Hunt.

The first chance fell to Hunt inside the opening minute, before the visitors effectively went down to 10 men after 13 minutes when City player Len Fleck tried to clear a ball but only succeeded in kicking his own player, Peter Burke, with his victim limping around the pitch for the remainder of the match. Wednesday quickly took advantage of this and four minutes later they opened the scoring, Hunt netting from Bill Fallon's cross. After 25 minutes it was 2–0 as Hunt, looking offside, ran onto a through ball before slotting home. City did have the ball in the net a few minutes later, only for O'Reilly's effort to be ruled out by the linesman. By half-time, however, Hunt had netted twice more, his hat-trick goal arriving after 39 minutes when he fired home a left-foot shot from Jackie Robinson's pass. His fourth goal, to make it 4–0 to Wednesday, came a minute prior to the break, when Hunt beat Smalley before netting.

The visitors kept Hunt at bay for the opening 20 minutes of the second period, but he was then in the right place at the right time when his header from Fallon's corner struck a post but rebounded straight back at his feet. Goal number five for Hunt equalled the previous club record – 1920s forward Jimmy Trotter having twice achieved the feat. After 80 minutes the Owls reached 6–0, but this time is was Fallon's turn to score as he was on hand to net when Len Massarella's shot struck an upright. The seventh goal proved to be the record-breaker, as with just three minutes remaining on the clock Hunt emerged to

grab his sixth goal and complete the rout. Unsurprisingly, the game became known as Hunt's match, but Jackie Robinson was also in imperious form, giving a near-perfect display of the art of the inside-forward. Hunt also grabbed a hat-trick at Luton Town a week later, but only scored another nine until the end of the season, as Wednesday just missed on promotion to the top flight.

Sheffield Wednesday: D. Goodfellow, J. Ashley, F. Lester, D. Russell, H. Hanford, H. Burrows, L. Massarella, J. Robinson, D. Hunt, C. Napier, W. Fallon.

Norwich City: H. Dukes, L. Flack, J. Taylor, B. Robinson, P. Burke, T. Smalley, J. Church, H. Ware, J. O'Reilly, W. Furness, F. Manders.

Referee: W. Daly (Kent).

MATCH TO REMEMBER 10 — 8 MAY 1943

SHEFFIELD WEDNESDAY 1 BLACKPOOL 2

Wartime League North Cup Final Second Leg

A last-minute equaliser from Blackpool's Eddie Burbanks in the first leg of the War Cup Final at Bloomfield Road ensured that the teams went into the Hillsborough second leg all square, after having shared four goals. This set the scene for an eagerly awaited second leg, with demand for tickets greater than any other Owls game during the war years – fans started to queue at every turnstile at the ground from 11 o'clock in the morning and the attendance reached 47,657, generating receipts of £5,965 (some reserve tickets were even traded on the black market).

Before the game, the teams were introduced to Mr Will Cuff, the League President, and the First Lord of the Admiralty Mr Albert Alexander, who was also the MP for

Wednesday team before the War Cup Final v Blackpool in 1943.

Hillsborough at the time. The game started with both teams having chances, but the sides were evenly matched. The turning point of the match came after 24 minutes, when Walt Millership brought down Jock Dodds to concede a free-kick just outside the penalty area. The Blackpool captain duly picked himself up and watched as his low shot went through the Owls' wall, deflected off Millership and skidded along the greasy pitch to slip under Wednesday 'keeper, Albert Morton. This goal appeared to visibly affect Wednesday's confidence and they never appeared to totally recover from the blow. Before half-time Morton had to tip George Farrow's shot onto the bar, and Frank Melling had Wednesday's best chance of the half with an angled shot that Reg Savage was able to save.

Wednesday started brightly in the second half, with the large crowd behind them, and Jackie Robinson just failed in an attempt to reach Melling's pass. During the second half, Albert Morton had to make good saves from both Ronnie Dix and Tom Gardner before, in the 76th minute, Gardner effectively sealed the Cup for Blackpool when he took advantage of a defensive mix-up to score a second. In a last throw of the dice, Wednesday pushed defender Millership into the attack and he set up a chance for Jackie Robinson to head a brilliant goal after 86 minutes. Unfortunately, it proved a mere consolation as Blackpool held on to lift the trophy.

In addition to medals, the Blackpool players were given War Savings Certificates each, while Wednesday gave each of them a safety razor and a set of blades. Grimsby Town also sent a consignment of fish for their tea after the game!

Sheffield Wednesday: A. Morton, A.J. Ashley, K.J. Gadsby (Leeds), D.W. Russell, W. Millership, J. Cockroft (West Ham), W. Reynolds, J. Robinson, F. Melling, J. Thompson, H.M. Swift.

Blackpool: R. Savage (Queen of the South), A.L. Pope (Hearts), H. Hubbick (Bolton), G.H. Farrow, L.E. Hayward, H. Johnston, T. Gardner (Burnley), R.W. Dix (Tottenham), J. Dodds (captain), R.J. Finan, W.E. Burbanks (Sunderland).

Referee: Mr F.W. Wort (Liverpool).

MATCH TO REMEMBER 11 — 3 NOVEMBER 1951

SHEFFIELD WEDNESDAY 6 NOTTS COUNTY 0

Second Division

The phenomenon that was Derek Dooley really came into the limelight on this winter afternoon in 1951. The bustling centre-forward had been recalled by Wednesday boss Eric Taylor for the home game with Barnsley in early October, with the Owls struggling in the Second Division, lying down in 17th place. He duly scored a brace as Wednesday registered a 2–1 win, but only netted once more in the three games prior to Notts County visiting Hillsborough. On a rainy afternoon in front of a bumper 46,570 crowd, Wednesday and Derek really got into gear.

Both sides had chances in a fairly even first half before, on 44 minutes, Jackie Sewell, the former Notts County player, headed Walter Rickett's corner past Roy Smith, who had played for Wednesday for 12 years, to give the Owls a half-time lead. Wednesday kicked towards the Kop end at Hillsborough in the second period and it proved to be the making of Derek Dooley, as he netted all five goals scored by the Owls in the second half.

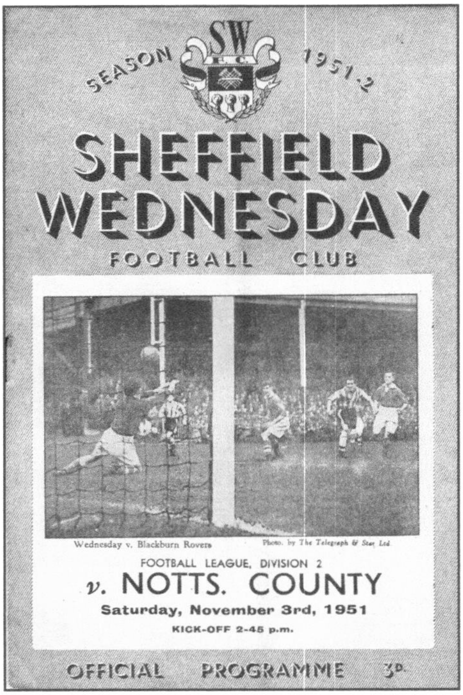

Derek Dooley.

Goal number one saw Dooley go past Leuty and Deans to fire in an unstoppable shot on 53 minutes, before 12 minutes later he ran onto Eddie Gannon's pass to fire home a low shot. Despite Jackie Sewell being a virtual passenger on the wing after picking up an injury, the Owls continued to dominate, although County did have a goal chalked off for an infringement. Three minutes later, Derek completed his hat-trick after his shot was knocked away by Smith but Derek coolly followed in to score from the rebound. He followed this up with his fourth goal, his third in five minutes, by heading in from Walter Rickett's centre. With five minutes left, Dooley netted from Alan's Finney's pass for his fifth, Wednesday's sixth, to become the second player since World War Two to net five in a game for Wednesday – Jimmy Dailey having achieved the feat against Barnsley in September 1947.

The legendary attacker finished the season with an astonishing 46 League goals, setting a remarkable record that will probably never be beaten, as Wednesday stormed to the Second Division title. He also set the record of scoring in nine consecutive League games, another Wednesday club record.

Sheffield Wednesday: D. McIntosh, K. Bannister, M. Kenny, E. Gannon, E. Packard, G. Davies, A. Finney, J. Sewell, D. Dooley, A. Quixall, W. Rickett.

Notts County: R. Smith, T. Deans, A. Southwell, G. Brunt, L. Leuty, P. Robinson, K. McPherson, J. Jackson. T. Lawson, R. Wylie, R. Crookes.

Referee: F.H. Garrard (Preston).

MATCH TO REMEMBER 12 — 28 NOVEMBER 1959

SHEFFIELD WEDNESDAY 7 WEST HAM UNITED 0

First Division

West Ham United arrived at Hillsborough as First Division leaders, but mid-table Wednesday turned the table on its head by recording a stunning 7–0 success.

The crowd of 38,307 witnessed a sensational start as Wednesday raced into a three-goal lead in the first 10 minutes of the game. The opening goal came with just three minutes on the clock when Keith Ellis knocked on a Don Megson free-kick for Johnny Fantham to head past visiting 'keeper Noel Dwyer. Six minutes later the Owls doubled

Alan Finney and John Fantham who scored four of the seven goals.

their lead with Fantham netting, deflecting Derek Wilkinson's free-kick home, from inside a crowded penalty area. It was Wilkinson's turn to get on the score sheet next, as he turned in Alan Finney's low cross to leave the London side reeling. Hammers defender John Bond then had to clear off the line from a Keith Ellis header, before a fourth goal arrived after just 25 minutes when Ellis outjumped the West Ham defence to head Bobby Craig's cross down for Finney to net. The Owls continued to totally dominate play and almost netted a fifth before the break as an Ellis header drifted just inches wide

During the second half Wednesday continued to be a potent attacking force, but it was not until the 65th minute that they added to their half-time advantage, Bobby Craig, on his home debut, shooting home after good work by Ellis and Fantham. It was then time for Ron Springett to make a rare save from Mike Grice's low shot, following Malcolm Musgrove's corner. It was soon 6–0, however, as Alan Finney made a fine run down the wing before crossing brilliantly for Ellis to head past Dwyer after 72 minutes. Eight minutes later, Finney, from Tony Kay's pass, scored his second goal, Wednesday's seventh, while the only blot on a memorable day came near the end when key man Tony Kay was hurt and had to be carried from the field

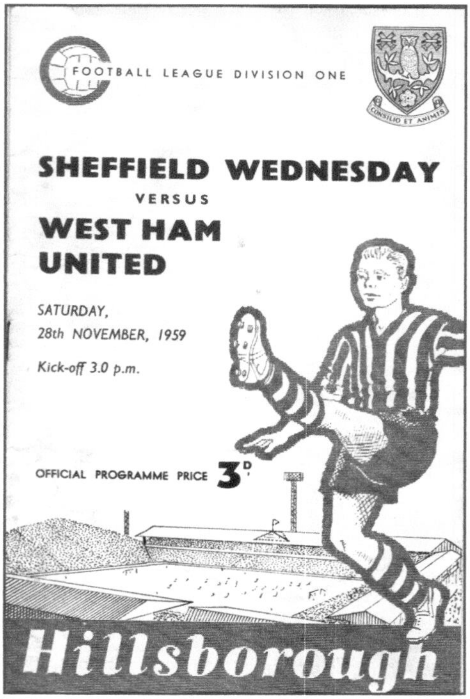

Wednesday remained unbeaten until the end of 1959, moving up to eighth in the table, and eventually finished in their highest final position since the mid-1930s, fifth in the top division. The defeat sent West Ham on a downward spiral and they ended the season in 14th place.

Sheffield Wednesday: R.D. Springett, P. Johnson, D.H. Megson, T. McAnearney, P. Swan, A.H. Kay, D. Wilkinson, R. Craig, K.D. Ellis, J. Fantham, A. Finney (captain).

West Ham United: N.M. Dwyer, J.F. Bond, N.E. Cantwell, A. Malcolm, K. Brown, J. Smith, M.J. Grice, P.A. Woosnam, H.R. Obeney, J.H. Dick, M. Musgrove.

Referee: T.H. Cooper (Bolton).

MATCH TO REMEMBER 13 — 1 FEBRUARY 1961

MANCHESTER UNITED 2 SHEFFIELD WEDNESDAY 7

FA Cup Fourth-Round Replay

UNITED REVIEW
MANCHESTER UNITED FOOTBALL CLUB
MANCHESTER UNITED v. SHEFFIELD WEDNESDAY
Kick-off 7-30 pm
FA Cup – Replay
WEDNESDAY 1st FEBRUARY
4d.
NUMBER 21
(SPECIAL ISSUE)
SEASON
OFFICIAL
1960-61
PROGRAMME
UNITED v. SPURS — 16th JANUARY, 1961
One of the two goals that spiked Spurs. Pearson takes a back-heel from centre-forward Gregg and slams it past Brown whilst right back Barton watches in dismay. Where's Dawson? In goal! Final score? United 2 Spurs 0.
Photo by courtesy of the Daily Mail

After the teams had drawn 1–1 at Hillsborough on the previous Saturday, they reconvened at Old Trafford, with the home fans fully expecting their side to press home their ground advantage. They could only watch in disbelief, however, as Wednesday inflicted upon United their biggest defeat at Old Trafford since World War Two. The Owls took just two minutes to take the lead when Johnny Fantham ran through a crowd of players to blast the ball home from five yards. United were quickly on level terms though, as within two minutes Nobby Stiles' pass found future Owl, Mark Pearson, whose low shot flew in past Ron Springett. After conceding that quick equaliser, Wednesday subsequently took control of the game, and on the half hour Alan Finney hit a 20-yard shot that United 'keeper, Ronnie Briggs, caught but then let slip from his grasp, only able to watch as the ball rolled into the net. Three minutes later Maurice Setters conceded a free-kick near his penalty area, and he was made to pay for his indiscretion as Derek Wilkinson's free-kick was headed in by Keith Ellis. It took Wednesday only four more minutes to add to their lead as brilliant play from Bobby Craig set up Ellis to shoot home, with Briggs getting his hand to it but unable to keep the shot out. It was the Owls' third goal in just seven minutes and took them to a commanding 4–1 lead at the interval.

John Fantham netting Wednesday's fifth.

In the second half Ralph O'Donnell, in trying to head clear, hit his own bar, before Fantham ran onto a free-kick and went on to shoot home after 52 minutes. An Alex Dawson long-range shot through a crowd of players then pulled a goal back for United on 63 minutes and the home side visibly rallied after this, with only two great saves from Springett keeping out shots from John Giles and ex-Wednesday player Albert Quixall. After 74 minutes, however, Wednesday effectively ended the tie when Keith Ellis headed in from Alan Finney's cross, the sixth goal prompting a mass exodus by disgruntled United fans. They missed Alan Finney completing the rout with 10 minutes remaining when he drifted into the penalty area to head in Craig's cross off a post.

Note: The last time Wednesday had scored seven in a match was against West Ham the previous season, the opposition's team included Noel Cantwell, who had signed from West Ham earlier in the season

Manchester United: W.R. Briggs, S.A. Brennan, N. Cantwell, M.E. Setters, W.A. Foulkes, J.J. Nicholson, A. Quixall, N.P. Stiles, A.D. Dawson, M. Pearson, R. Charlton.

Sheffield Wednesday: R.D. Springett, P. Johnson, D.H. Megson, T. McAnearney, R. O'Donnell, A.H. Kay, D. Wilkinson, R. Craig, K.D. Ellis, J. Fantham, A. Finney.

Referee: Mr P.G. Brandwood (Kidderminster).

MATCH TO REMEMBER 14 — 22 OCTOBER 1962

SHEFFIELD WEDNESDAY 2 SANTOS 4

Friendly

During the 1950s the installation of floodlights all around England prompted clubs to invite exotic foreign opposition and Wednesday hosted several such games, the likes of Vasas, Budapest, Juventus and Napoli all visiting during that decade. These games were still popular in the early 1960s and Wednesday were rewarded for their initiative in inviting Brazilian side Santos – including star man Pele – as the game attracted a bumper 49,058 fans to Hillsborough. The Owls just about broke even, however, due to the financial demands of the superstars from South America, but this was forgotten as fans were treated to a game that was talked about for many years by the supporters lucky enough to get tickets to this legendary match.

Santos arrived as reigning World Club champions, but only goalkeeper Gilmar was part of the side that had won the World Cup just a few months earlier, Pele having missed out on the showpiece due to an

Pele.

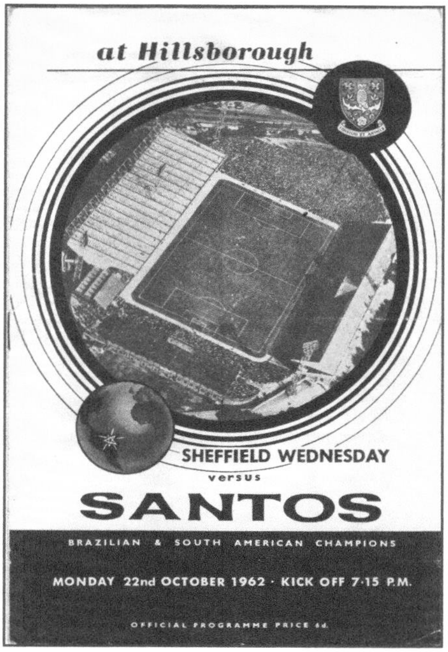

injury. The brilliant Brazilian was regarded as the world's greatest player and there is no doubt that it was his talents that fans had flocked to see. The first 45 minutes provided some breathless action for supporters, with Santos going ahead after just two minutes when Pele sent Pagao down the wing with a superb 40-yard pass, and Pagao's centre flew over Peter Swan's head for Coutinho to sweep a low shot past Ron Springett. In the fifth minute David Layne saw his header tipped over the bar by Gilmar, and Wednesday were holding their own until Pele beat Don Megson to the ball and showed some fancy footwork before slipping a short pass to Coutinho, who fired home after 28 minutes. The Owls got themselves back into the game just two minutes later through Billy Griffin who, at full speed, ran onto Eddie Holliday's cross to fire in. Within another three minutes Wednesday levelled when David Layne got up highest to head in another Holliday cross off a post. Layne then went close with a shot just wide before he was hurt two minutes after netting and had to be replaced by Gerry Young.

The visitors then stepped up a gear and by half-time had re-established their two-goal advantage, Coutinho completing his hat-trick after 40 minutes when he wriggled through a crowded penalty area and dummied Springett to score. On the stroke of half-time, Pele himself netted as he ghosted past players before Tony Kay brought him down in the area. It would be arguably the most talked about penalty-kick ever scored at Hillsborough as Pele took the spot-kick and, as Eric Taylor, the Wednesday General Manager, stated afterwards, 'Pele did the foxtrot, a two-step and a tango as he took the penalty, and then stopped before sending Springett the wrong way.' The first-half entertainment was impossible to repeat and there were no more goals in the second period, despite the Owls creating several chances. Visiting 'keeper, Gilmar, brilliantly saved Holliday's shot and then saved Colin Dobson's penalty. Also, Billy Griffin and Alan Finney had shots that both rebounded from the goal frame, but Santos rode their luck to secure the victory.

Sheffield Wednesday: R.D. Springett, P. Johnson, D.H. Megson, T. McAnearney, P. Swan, A.H. Kay (captain), A. Finney, C. Dobson, D.R. Layne (G.M. Young 35 mins), W. Griffin, E. Holliday.

Santos: Gilmar, Mauro, Dalmo, Olavo, Lima, Formiga (Carlos), Pagao, Mengalvio, Coutinho, Pele, Dorval.

Referee: M. Kitabdjian (France).

The 1966 Cup Final team.

MATCH TO REMEMBER 15 — 14 MAY 1966

SHEFFIELD WEDNESDAY 2 EVERTON 3

FA Cup Final

Wednesday had reached the FA Cup Final by uniquely playing all their games away from home, beating Reading 3–2, Newcastle United 2–1, Huddersfield Town 2–1, Blackburn Rovers 2–1 and Chelsea, in the semi-final at Villa Park, 2–0. During their run to Wembley, Wednesday had worn their all-white change strip in every tie and this continued in the Final as they lost the toss for choice of shirts, opponents Everton picking their all-blue jerseys. The Owls had to start with Sam Ellis at centre-half (making his Cup debut aged just 18), as Vic Mobley was still out injured, while Everton's Manager, ex-Wednesday boss Harry Catterick, also had selection problems, although the omission of England international Pickering was a shock. It provided an opportunity for a virtual unknown called Mike Trebilcock – an opportunity that he grasped in spectacular style.

SHEFFIELD WEDNESDAY
FOOTBALL CLUB
BANQUET
to celebrate the occasion of the Fifth appearance of the Club in the Final of the Football Association Challenge Cup
SATURDAY, 14th MAY, 1966
HOTEL RUSSELL, LONDON

The 100,000 crowd saw Wednesday take an early lead when David Ford flicked a throw-in onto Jim McCalliog, whose low shot was slightly deflected off Ray Wilson, past Gordon West in the Everton goal – this was the first goal that the Merseyside club had conceded in their Cup run. Later, Everton's Alex Young was offside as he put the ball into the net, and on 18 minutes Everton appealed in vain for a penalty when Ron Springett dived on the ball as Alex Young tried to go round him in the box. Wednesday had the upper hand for most of the first half, and half-time arrived with Wednesday still one goal in the lead.

After 11 minutes of the second half, the famous old trophy looked set to be the Owls' when Johnny Fantham made a run past two defenders and watched as his shot was pushed away by West, only for David Ford to run in and put Wednesday into a two-goal lead. Wednesday seemed to lose their concentration temporarily and allowed Everton back into the game, as Mike Trebilcock scored two minutes later, hitting in a shot after the ball had been headed down to him. The hopes of Cup glory started to fade five minutes later when a free-kick was knocked out to Trebilcock on the edge of the area, who drilled a shot past Springett. In the 73rd minute Everton's sensational comeback was complete, as a long clearance down the middle of the field somehow rolled under Gerry Young's boot, allowing Derek Temple to run on and fire a low shot past Springett to give Everton the lead.

Wednesday came close to scoring on two occasions, but Everton held firm and the Cup was lost. After the game captain Don Megson took the Wednesday team on a lap of honour – the first losing team to do this. Wednesday returned to Sheffield to a packed crowd of over 100,000 fans, who gave them a tremendous welcome as if they had won the Cup.

Sheffield Wednesday: R.D. Springett, W.S. Smith, D.H. Megson (captain), P. Eustace, S. Ellis, G.M. Young, J.D. Quinn, J. Fantham, J. McCalliog, D. Ford, J.G. Pugh.

Everton: G. West, T. Wright, R. Wilson, J. Gabriel, B. Labone, B. Harris, A. Scott, M. Trebilcock, A. Young, C. Harvey, D. Temple.

Referee: J.K. Taylor (Wolverhampton).

MATCH TO REMEMBER 16 — 31 AUGUST 1968

SHEFFIELD WEDNESDAY 5 MANCHESTER UNITED 4

First Division

The visit to Hillsborough of reigning European champions Manchester United fired the imagination of Wednesday fans, with a bumper crowd of 51,931 welcoming a star-studded United team that included eight of the side that beat Benfica at Wembley to become the first English team to win the European Cup. Such household names as Bobby Charlton, Denis Law and George Best were on show for the Red Devils, but after just two minutes they were behind when Tony Dunne failed to cut out David Ford's forward pass and Jack Whitham hit a great shot from outside the area that flashed past Alex Stepney. Soon after, Dunne was forced to leave the field injured, substitute Francis Burns taking his place, and after 11 minutes of play the scores were level – Best, European Player of the Year, firing home after a great individual run. Three minutes later the visitors went ahead as Wednesday 'keeper Peter Springett could only push out a Best shot for Law to crash the loose ball into the net.

The play continued to switch from end to end and it was 2–2 when John Ritchie headed home from David Ford's centre. The fans must have been breathless by now and the scoring did not abate, a United free-kick being headed on by Brian Kidd for Law to hit in a first-time shot off the cross bar. Next, Alex Stepney saved brilliantly from Ford to keep United in front, and the Owls then struck the woodwork again, Ford being the unlucky man. With eight minutes left of the first half, the match seemed to have swung convincingly in the visitors direction, as Law knocked on a low centre from Kidd to allow Bobby Charlton to fire home one of his trademark shots from outside of the penalty area. Wednesday were not finished though, and an incredible 45 minutes ended 4–3 to United as Whitham netted again for the Owls, driving home from John Fantham's centre.

It took Wednesday just two minutes of the second half to draw level, but they needed help from visiting player Stiles as he headed into his own net when trying to clear the ball from Ford's free-kick. The

SHEFFIELD WEDNESDAY
FOOTBALL CLUB
FOOTBALL LEAGUE—DIVISION 1
MANCHESTER UNITED
On Saturday, 31st August, 1968, kick-off 3.0 p.m.
OFFICIAL PROGRAMME - PRICE ONE SHILLING
at Hillsborough

Jack Whitham who scored a hat-trick.

club's electronic scoreboard credited Whitham, who was close to Stiles, as the scorer, but it was clearly all the work of England World Cup winner Stiles! After 56 minutes Wednesday fans went wild as Don Megson's 30-yard shot crashed into the net to put the Owls ahead. The celebrations were cut short by an offside flag, however. Both sides were pushing for a winner and Springett had to dive full length to save Charlton's shot. With 15 minutes remaining, this amazing game was decided when Stepney could not hold onto Ford's low centre and Whitham was on hand to complete his hat-trick and give the Owls a 5–4 win. Wednesday had to hang on as United pressed for an equaliser – at times, everyone apart from Stepney was in the Wednesday half – but the Owls almost grabbed a sixth with five minutes remaining when Ritchie spurned a simple chance, firing high into the Kop. With three minutes left Nobby Stiles' shot beat Springett, but Vic Mobley got back to turn the goal-bound shot from off the line for a corner. It was the last action in arguably the greatest game ever played at Hillsborough.

Sheffield Wednesday: R.D. Springett, G. Young, D.H. Megson (captain), S. Ellis, V.J. Mobley, P. Eustace, J. Whitham, J. McCalliog, J.H. Ritchie, D. Ford, J. Fantham. Unused Sub: A. Warboys.

Manchester United: A.C. Stepney, S.A. Brennan, A.P. Dunne (F. Burns 3 mins), J. Fitzpatrick, D. Sadler, N.P. Stiles, W. Morgan, B. Kidd, R. Charlton, D. Law, G. Best.

Referee: W.S. Castle (Sedgley, Worcs).

MATCH TO REMEMBER 17 29 APRIL 1976

SHEFFIELD WEDNESDAY 2 SOUTHEND UNITED 1

Third Division

After suffering relegation to the third tier in 1975, the Owls were then faced with the unthinkable 12 months later – a drop into the Fourth Division for the first time. Their fate, both on and off the field, therefore rested on their final game of the 1975–76 season, at home to relegation rivals Southend United. As long as Wednesday avoided defeat they would be safe, and Owls fans returned to Hillsborough in the club's hour of need – a crowd of 25,802 giving the club their biggest home crowd of the season by a considerable margin. The match was equally important for Southend as they needed a win to avoid relegation, so the scene was set for a nail-biting finale to the season. The game had originally been scheduled for FA Cup semi-final day, but, with one of those games being played at Hillsborough, the match was rearranged for after

Mick Prendergast who scored the first goal.

the final day of the season – poor old Aldershot were just outside the drop zone, but knew that whatever the result in Sheffield they would still be relegated.

With nerves on edge in the crowd, Wednesday challenged Southend from the off, and after 16 minutes Mike Prendergast (who was struggling with an ankle injury) saw Sean Rafter tip his header onto a post. Then, on 29 minutes, Hillsborough went into rapturous celebrations as Prendergast drove home Eric Potts' flick from Neil O'Donnell's low-drilled cross from the right wing. Six minutes later Ian Nimmo headed down Phil Henson's free-kick to little Eric Potts, who hammered in a half-volley to seemingly put the Owls in command. Just before the break Stuart Parker hit Wednesday's bar, and there was still time for Prendergast to fire O'Donnell's cross onto the bar. There were no further chances before the break, however, with Wednesday just 45 minutes from safety.

The second half became increasingly tense after United pulled a goal back through Alan Moody after 61 minutes, but with time running out boss Len Ashurst was seen still urging his side on and waving to the players to go forward as they dropped deeper in an attempt to protect their precious lead. Thankfully, the Owls did hold on and celebrations started at the final whistle, with the fans rushing onto the pitch to congratulate their side. After the players reached the safety of the dressing room, the fans were calling for them to come back out and give a salute, which they did from the directors' box, waving to the supporters, who were singing *We are the Champions* and *You'll Never Walk Alone.*

Sheffield Wednesday: P.D. Fox, R.F. Walden, B. Shaw, J. Mullen, D.S. Cusack, N. O'Donnell, R.J. Wylde, P.M. Henson, I.W. Nimmo, M.J. Prendergast, E.T. Potts. Unused Sub: G. Hull.

Southend United: S. Rafter, D. Worthington, A.C. Ford, A. Little, A.P.F. Hadley, A. Moody, K. Foggo (R.A. Pountney H/T), T.J. Nicholl, S.J. Parker, P.D. Sylvester, A. Taylor.

Referee: E.R. Garner (Maghull, Liverpool).

MATCH TO REMEMBER 18 — 26 DECEMBER 1979

SHEFFIELD WEDNESDAY 4 SHEFFIELD UNITED 0

Third Division

Sheffield United's relegation, at the end of the previous season, meant that the teams would meet for the first time in a Third Division game and the first League meeting since a 0–0 draw at Hillsborough in April 1971. The Blades went into the game as League leaders and were certainly favourites against an Owls side that were sat in sixth place. A record crowd for the division (49,309) packed into Hillsborough for the 11 o'clock Boxing Day encounter, with the match also generating record receipts of over £70,000. What followed has entered Wednesday history as 'the Boxing Day massacre' as United were totally overwhelmed, with the home side showcasing their true ability and registering a stunning 4–0 success.

The early play gave little indication of the final score as play fluctuated from end to end, with the best chance being created after 29 minutes when Andy McCulloch watched his header cleared off the line by visiting defender Tony Kenworthy. Then, with five minutes to the break, Ian Mellor, who just minutes before had been inches wide with a diving header, picked up a pass, ran forward and, with his weaker leg, hit a stunning 25-yard drive that flew past United's 'keeper, Derek Richardson. The tremendous strike sparked wild scenes of celebration among the Owls fans, although those same supporters held their collective breathes a few minutes later when Bob Bolder pushed a Jeff Bourne shot onto the crossbar and John MacPhail could only fire the loose ball straight at Bolder from close range.

Mark Smith scoring a penalty in the Boxing day game v Sheffield United.

The Owls led 1–0 at the break and almost doubled their lead after 57 minutes when a Mellor shot hit the post and Jeff King's effort from the rebound crashed against the crossbar. In trying to stop King's shot, United captain Mick Speight was injured and had to be replaced by substitute John Cutbush. The loss of their captain was a blow to the Blades and six minutes later it was 2–0, McCulloch beating Kenworthy and, as Richardson ran out, crossing for Terry Curran to dive forward and head into the empty net. Two minutes later Curran ran onto Brian Hornsby's pass and sprinted away to find Jeff King, who fired past the United 'keeper from 15 yards, sending the Wednesday fans into ecstasy. Wednesday completed the rout in the 87th minute when Richardson pulled Curran down in the area, and Mark Smith (a lifelong Wednesday fan) slotted home the penalty to give the Wednesday fans a late Christmas present they would always remember.

During the game, the Wednesday Kop started singing 'massacre, massacre', and this was eventually extended into the song that is still heard today on a matchday at Hillsborough. The loss proved a crushing blow for the Blades as they fell away to finish down in 12th place, while Wednesday surged to promotion

Sheffield Wednesday: R.J. Bolder, R. Blackhall, C. Williamson, M.C. Smith, M. Pickering (captain), B. Hornsby, J.D. King, J.D. Johnson, A. McCulloch, I. Mellor, E. Curran. Unused Sub: D. Leman.

Sheffield United: D.W. Richardson, M. Speight (captain) (W.J. Cutbush 57 mins), L. Tibbott, A.D. Kenworthy, J. MacPhail, J.M. Matthews, L. de Goey, J.A. Bourne, B.D. Butlin, P. Garner, A. Sabella.

Referee: P. Partridge (Bishop Auckland).

MATCH TO REMEMBER 19 — 29 SEPTEMBER 1984

LIVERPOOL 0 SHEFFIELD WEDNESDAY 2

First Division

After gallantly losing 3–0 at Anfield in a League Cup tie in January 1984, the travelling Wednesday fans sang 'We'll be back, we'll be back', and after winning promotion the Owls did return, for a top-flight engagement eight months later. Before a crowd of 40,196, those visiting fans, numbering 5,000, were in fine voice again, as following a stunning 2–0 win they gleefully sang 'We told you we'd be back and we are!'

Liverpool had just completed a hat-trick of First Division titles and had lifted the Championship seven times in the previous nine years (in addition to being European Cup and League Cup holders), so the visit of newly promoted Wednesday seemed just a routine three-point haul for the all-conquering Reds side. Football does

Imre Varadi who scored the first goal against Liverpool.

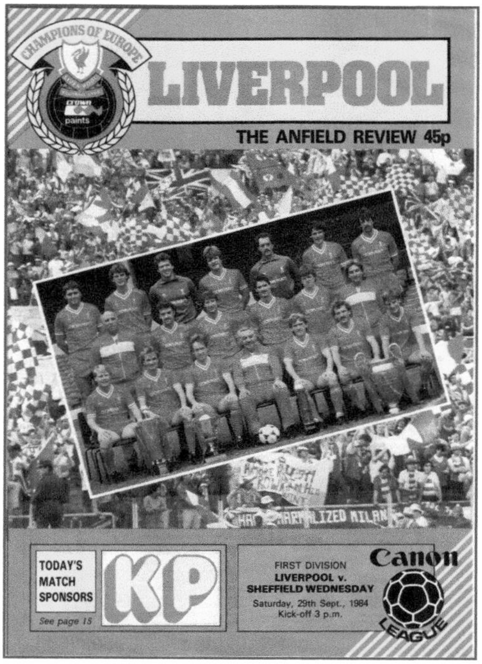

have a habit of springing the odd surprise, however, and the Owls, with just a single point on the road up until that game, shocked the Anfield regulars by taking a surprise lead after eight minutes, thanks to a characteristic moment of madness from 'keeper Bruce Grobbelaar. He raced out of his goal in an attempt to kick clear from the onrushing Imre Varadi, but proceeded only to strike the ball against the Wednesday man and then, from out near the touchline, Varadi managed to reach the loose ball first and steer it into the unguarded net from an acute angle. With former Everton captain Mick Lyons at the heart of Wednesday's defence, they held firm against a Liverpool side that was missing top scorer Ian Rush, with Paul Walsh going close when his header struck a post. Alan Kennedy then saw his goal disallowed for offside, and several other efforts before the break were either blocked, just wide or stoutly defended to ensure that the Owls remained ahead at the half-time interval.

Liverpool came at Wednesday again in the second half and were denied a penalty when Lyons appeared to foul Walsh. Then, John Wark hit a post from 8 yards, before Wednesday went further in front when Mel Sterland drove a low shot that Grobbelaar dived to save, only for the ball to rebound out to Gary Shelton, who fired home the rebound under the body of Grobbelaar. Liverpool still came forward, but Lee Chapman nearly scored a third when he headed Marwood's cross just wide. The Wednesday fans then started to sing 'What's it like to be outclassed?' as they held out for a famous win.

Liverpool: B. Grobbelaar, P. Neal, A. Kennedy, M. Lawrenson, R. Whelan, A. Hansen, K. Dalglish, S. Lee, P. Walsh, J. Wark (J. Molby 60 mins), S. Nicol.

Sheffield Wednesday: S. Hodge, M. Sterland, P. Shirtliff, M. Smith, M. Lyons (captain), J. Ryan (L. Madden 66 mins), B. Marwood, A. Blair, I. Varadi, L. Chapman, G. Shelton.

Referee: T.J. Holbrook (Wolverhampton).

MATCH TO REMEMBER 20 — 3 OCTOBER 1989

ALDERSHOT 0 SHEFFIELD WEDNESDAY 8

Football League Cup Second Round, Second Leg

After Aldershot held Wednesday to a 0–0 draw at Hillsborough two weeks previously, an upset seemed to be on the cards as Wednesday were bottom of the First Division, with

Steve Whitton scoring one of his four goals in the League Cup win at Aldershot.

only two goals from Dalian Atkinson to show from seven League and Cup games. Wednesday went on to record their biggest ever away win, however, and their biggest victory since beating Birmingham 9–1 back in December 1930.

It was the home side who almost scored first when Glen Burvill's cross was headed just wide by Gerry Williams. In the 24th minute the Owls sneaked in front on aggregate, however, as Steve Whitton tapped in after David Coles had failed to hold onto Dalian Atkinson's cross. Wednesday were suddenly in the mood for goals, and seven minutes later Atkinson ran onto a poor back pass from Ian Stewart to fire in the second before the floodgates opened and Wednesday netted twice more before the break – Whitton grabbing his second after 40 minutes with a header from Craig Shakespeare's corner and Dalian Atkinson smashing in a 20-yard effort from Dave Bennett's cross to give Wednesday a 4–0 lead on the stroke of half-time.

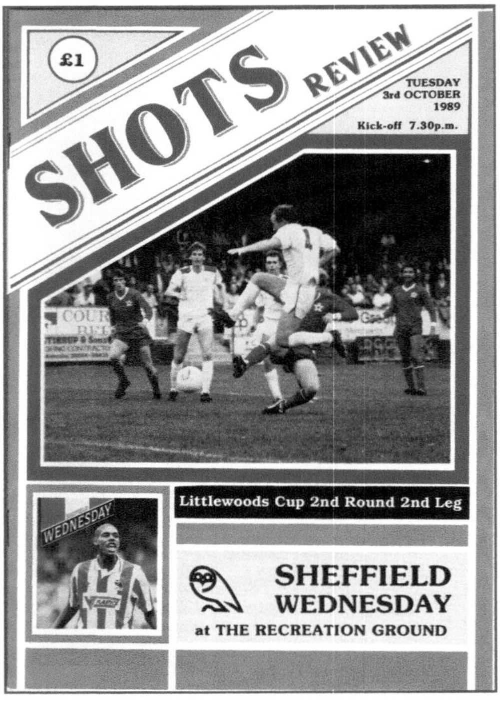

Owls forward Atkinson completed his hat-trick on 48 minutes, hitting in a cross volley from 12 yards, and four minutes later Steve Whitton also scored his third, playing a one-two with David Hirst before firing in the return ball. Whitton then went one better, running on to tap home after a defensive mistake. By now, the Owls fans were reaching for the record books and the score became eight with 10 minutes left to play as Craig Shakespeare fired home from Imre Varadi's cross to end a night to forget for the Hampshire club – unsurprisingly, the defeat was Aldershot's worst home reverse in their history. It was unfortunate that only 4,011 fans were inside the Recreation Ground on that historic night, although the 200 loyal fans from Sheffield were amply rewarded for their long trip south.

Aldershot: D. Coles, K. Brown, I. Phillips, G. Burvill, C. Smith, S. Wignall, S. Claridge, D. Puckett, I. Stewart (P. Coombes 62 mins), G. Williams (D. Anderson 62 mins), A. Randall.
Sheffield Wednesday: K. Pressman, J. Newsome, N. Worthington, C. Palmer (D. Hirst 41 mins), P. Shirtliff, L. Madden, D. Bennett, A. Harper, S. Whitton (I. Varadi 72 mins), D. Atkinson, C. Shakespeare.
Referee: P.A. Durkin (Portland, Dorset).

MATCH TO REMEMBER 21 — 21 APRIL 1991

SHEFFIELD WEDNESDAY 1 MANCHESTER UNITED 0

League Cup Final

Second Division Wednesday went into the 1991 League Cup Final, sponsored by Rumbelows, rated as underdogs against top-flight Manchester United. The Owls had reached the showpiece Final by beating First Division sides Derby County, Coventry City and Chelsea, but Alex Ferguson's United looked set to win the League Cup for the first time in their history. For the Sunday Final, Wednesday boss Ron Atkinson was at his inventive best, inviting comedian Stan Boardman onto the team bus for the journey from the team hotel to Wembley Stadium. His pre-match routine put the players at ease, and when the bus turned into Wembley Way all that could be seen was a sea of blue and white, with Boardman famously

John Sheridan scoring v Manchester United 1991 League Cup Final.

commenting, 'You're not gonna let them down today. You can't let this lot down. They want to see you with the Cup!'

The game quickly evolved into a contest between United danger man Lee Sharpe and Wednesday's right-sided partnership of Roland Nilsson and John Harkes – the latter becoming the first US player to appear in a major domestic Cup Final in England. United failed to make any inroads in a quiet opening 20 minutes, and when they tried to attack down the middle of the field they found John Sheridan and Danny Wilson in fine form. Then, with 37 minutes on the clock, Wednesday fans celebrated wildly as Nigel Worthington's free-kick was headed out by an under-pressure Gary Pallister to John Sheridan, who hit a terrific shot from 22 yards that 'keeper Les Sealey could only touch onto the far post and watch as the ball deflected into the net to put the Owls ahead.

The Owls led by Sheridan's terrific strike at the break, and they almost doubled that advantage six minutes into the half, but Steve Bruce was able to block Worthington's drive. United then had the ball in the net when Mark Hughes bundled Chris Turner into the goal from Mike Phelan's cross, but referee Ray Lewis was on hand to award Wednesday a free-kick. With Wednesday fans counting down every second, they held their collective breathes with just nine minutes remaining when Chris Turner saved brilliantly to tip Brian McClair's header, from Denis Irwin's cross, over the crossbar. With time ticking away, each second seemed an eternity for the Wednesday fans, but they could soon celebrate as the final whistle was blown, confirming that Wednesday had won their first major Cup for 56 years and were the first Second Division side to win the League Cup since Aston Villa back in 1975.

Wednesday's inspirational captain, Nigel Pearson, received the Cup from Rumbelows Employee Of The Year, Tracey Bateman, and then led the team on a lap of honour in front of their ecstatic fans – United supporters having long since departed Wembley to leave the Owls' fans to enjoy their very special moment. A few weeks later promotion was achieved to complete a remarkable season in the club's history.

Sheffield Wednesday: C. Turner, R. Nilsson, P. King, J. Harkes (L. Madden 88 mins), P. Shirtliff, N. Pearson (captain), D. Wilson, J. Sheridan, D. Hirst, P. Williams, N. Worthington. Unused Sub: T. Francis.

Manchester United: L. Sealey, D. Irwin, C. Blackmore, S. Bruce, N. Webb (M. Phelan 56 mins), G. Pallister, B. Robson, P. Ince, B. McClair, M. Hughes, L. Sharpe. Unused Sub: J. Donaghy.

Referee: R.S. Lewis (Great Bookham).

MATCH TO REMEMBER 22 — 3 APRIL 1993

SHEFFIELD WEDNESDAY 2 SHEFFIELD UNITED 1

FA Cup Semi-final

With both Wednesday and United having drawn their FA Cup sixth-round games, they knew in advance that a win in their respective replays would set up a Steel City derby in the semi-final. The Blades duly beat Blackburn Rovers, and 24 hours later the Owls overcame Derby County to make the mouth-watering prospect of a clash between the two Sheffield teams become a reality. When the FA announced that only the London derby between Spurs and Arsenal would be switched to Wembley and the Sheffield clubs would play their tie at Elland Road, however, there was uproar in the city. Eventually, the FA was forced to change their decision, and Sheffield was like a ghost town as many fans shared coaches to the National Stadium, resulting in an attendance of 75,365

The two teams walked out onto the Wembley pitch to a cascade of noise and thousands of balloons as both sets of fans produced a memorable welcome. The teams kicked-off and there was a truly sensational start as Wednesday were awarded a free-kick when John Pemberton fouled Mark Bright 30 yards from goal, and Chris Waddle fired home a spectacular long-range goal that left United 'keeper, Alan Kelly, grasping thin air as the ball flew into the net, sending Wednesday fans into

Match action from the F.A.Cup Semi-Final 1993 at Wembley.

raptures. The Owls dominated the first half with Paul Warhurst twice hitting the woodwork, but just before the whistle for half-time Alan Cork ran onto Franz Carr's through pass and his mishit shot went in, with Chris Waddle running back in vain to try and clear the ball off the line.

The second half saw United's 'keeper produce an outstanding save to prevent David Hirst's shot, from just 8 yards, going in, and then somehow kept out Mark Bright's close-range effort as the match went into extra-time. The tension mounted for the Wednesday fans who, after dominating the match, now feared that United could steal it. Kelly again made another great save, blocking Hirst's shot from 5 yards with his legs, and Wednesday twice had the ball in the net, the offside flag denying them on both occasions. Then, in the 107th minute of the game, John Harkes hit a corner to Mark Bright who, unmarked six yards out, headed in at the near post.

This produced an almighty roar from the blue half of the stadium, which was a mixture of both joy and relief, and Wednesday held on to secure arguably the most famous Sheffield derby win of all-time.

Sheffield Wednesday: C. Woods, R. Nilsson, N. Worthington, C. Palmer, J. Harkes, V. Anderson, D. Wilson, C. Waddle, P. Warhurst (D. Hirst 61 mins), M. Bright, J. Sheridan (G. Hyde 110 mins).

Sheffield United: A. Kelly, K. Gage, D. Whitehouse, J. Gannon, B. Gayle, J. Pemberton, F. Carr, M. Ward (A. Littlejohn 96 mins), A. Cork, B. Deane, G. Hodges (J. Hoyland 90 mins).

Referee: K. Morton (Bury St Edmunds).

MATCH TO REMEMBER 23 15 MAY 1993

SHEFFIELD WEDNESDAY 1 ARSENAL 1

FA Cup Final

Having already lost 2–1 to Arsenal in the League Cup Final, there was revenge in the air for the Owls when the two sides were paired together in the FA Cup Final. In front of a 79,347 Wembley crowd, Wednesday were appearing in their first Final in the competition since the 1966 loss to Everton, but were without their inspirational captain, Nigel Pearson, who had broken his leg a few weeks earlier, and defensive stalwart Peter Shirtliff. The absences meant that Paul Warhurst was forced to drop back into his old position of centre-half, after he had scored 18 goals from his new position at the heart of the club's attack. In the opening 12 minutes David Seaman had to twice make saves, first tipping Carlton Palmer's header over, and then saving from a Chris Waddle 25-yard curling free-kick. After 21 minutes Arsenal, who were at this time second best, managed to get ahead when Andy Linighan headed Paul Davis' free-kick to Ian Wright at the back post to head in the opening goal. The Gunners retained their lead until the whistle sounded for half-time.

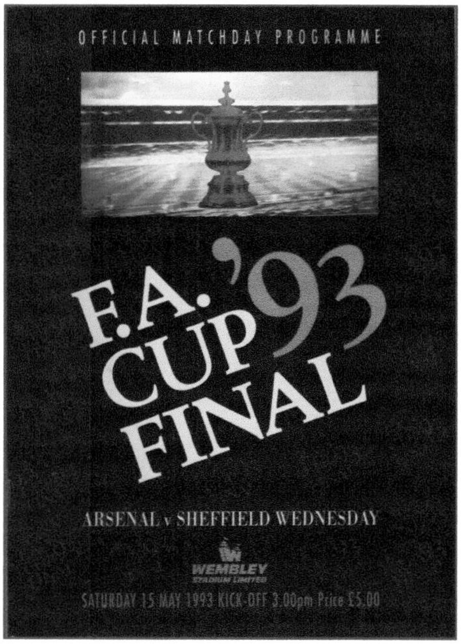

The second half started with Wednesday looking for an equaliser, and in the first two minutes of the half David Hirst came close with a header that was knocked out for a corner, which Seaman beat away to safety. Waddle then went close with a driven cross shot, but two minutes later, on 62 minutes, Wednesday were level. A John Sheridan cross was headed on by Mark Bright for John Harkes, who stooped to head the ball back across the area for David Hirst. The Owls forward just beat David Seaman to the ball and poked it past him to equalise the scores. The remainder of normal time was relatively uneventful, with Arsenal dropping back to defend as the game drifted toward full-time. In the final minute Chris Woods was forced to tip over Ian Wright's volley, while during extra-time the only action of note was a Roland Nilsson 30-yard shot that Seaman fumbled out for a corner just before the end of the game.

The teams therefore reconvened at Wembley on the following Thursday, and it proved a heartbreaking evening for Owls fans as substandard Wednesday lost in the last minute of extra-time, when Chris Woods failed to keep out Andy Linighan's header to seal a 2–1 win after Waddle had equalised Wright's opening goal.

Sheffield Wednesday: C. Woods, R. Nilsson, N. Worthington, C. Palmer, D. Hirst, V. Anderson (G. Hyde 85 mins), C. Waddle (C. Bart-Williams 111 mins), P. Warhurst, M. Bright, J. Sheridan, J. Harkes.

Arsenal: D. Seaman, L. Dixon, N. Winterburn, A. Linighan, T. Adams, R. Parlour (A. Smith 64 mins), P. Davis, P. Merson, J. Jensen, I. Wright (D. O'Leary 90 mins), K. Campbell.

Referee: K.P. Barratt (Coventry).

MATCH TO REMEMBER 24 29 MAY 2005

SHEFFIELD WEDNESDAY 4 HARTLEPOOL UNITED 2

Play-off Final

After beating Brentford 3–1 on aggregate in the semi-finals, Wednesday faced Hartlepool United in the League One Play-Off Final at Cardiff's Millennium Stadium. Backed by a record following of over 40,000 Wednesday fans in a 59,808 crowd, the Owls emerged from the tunnel to a rapturous welcome, with blue and white balloons almost obscuring the playing surface. Wednesday had finished fifth in League One, while United had ended the season just one point, and one place, behind.

Wednesday quickly got into their stride and had the better of the opening chances, but on the stroke of half-time Craig Rocastle exchanged passes with Lee Peacock and after reaching the byline crossed to the far post, where Jon-Paul McGovern gleefully hammered the ball home to trigger wild scenes of celebrations among the blue-and-white hordes.

It was the turn of the Hartlepool fans to celebrate just two minutes into the second period, however, as a throw in from former Owl Ritchie Humphreys skimmed off the head of Owls captain Lee Bullen and fell nicely for Eifion Williams to head in an equaliser at the far post. The quick leveller spurred on the north-east side and Owls fans could only watch on as both Anthony Sweeney and Joel Porter went close to putting United ahead. The Owls did hit back, with McGovern firing against the side netting and Chris Brunt sending a 30-yard free-kick just wide, but Wednesday fans' grand day out in Wales looked to be turning sour as in the 72nd minute Jon Daly, who had only been on the pitch a minute, was on hand to head in from a Gavin Strachan free-kick.

Paul Sturrock and Lee Bullen lead Wednesday out at Cardiff.

Wednesday boss Paul Sturrock then had no choice but to go for broke and introduced three substitutes into the fray. Seven minutes later his changes paid off as Drew Talbot ran through into the area, before being pulled back by Hartlepool defender Chris Westwood. The result was a penalty for Wednesday and a red card for Westwood, with top scorer Steve MacLean given the onerous task of pulling his side level from 12 yards. The Scot had been absent from the first team due to injury for 12 weeks prior to the Final, but his shock selection in the matchday 16 proved inspirational as he scored from the spot to level the game at 2–2.

Suddenly, the match had swung dramatically in the Owls' favour, and in the dying minutes of the game both Richard Wood and Chris Brunt had efforts blocked by frantic defending. There was no further scoring in normal time, however, and the tie went into the extra 30 minutes to decide which side would secure Championship football for the 2005–6 season. Within three minutes of the extra period the Owls nudged in front, as Glenn Whelan blocked Michael Nelson's clearance and went on to fire in a tremendous low shot to put Wednesday back in front. The Owls then kept possession as Hartlepool, with 10 men, started to visibly run out of steam, but Wednesday fans held their collective breaths when, with just four minutes remaining, Sweeney ran clean through, only to be denied a shot by a great late tackle by skipper Lee Bullen. The stage was then set for youngster Drew Talbot, who, after heading the ball forward, ran half the length of

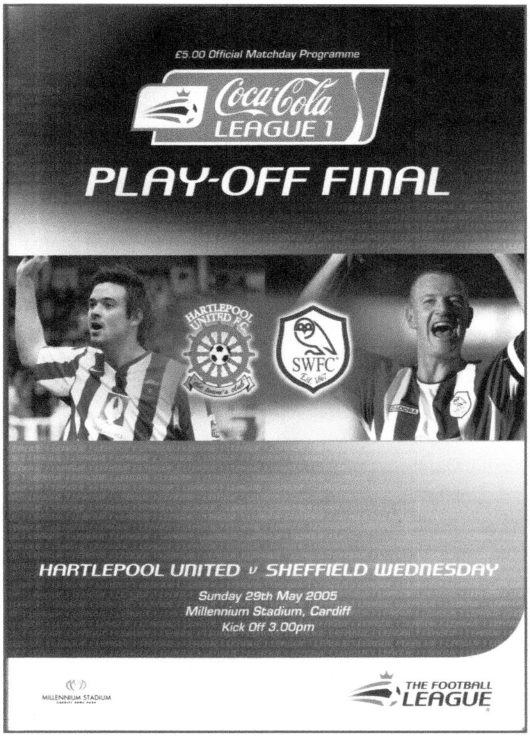

the pitch before rounding the advancing goalkeeper and slotting the ball into the net to clinch promotion. The already celebrating fans went into overdrive with their cheering, dancing, hugging and flag-waving, and were in full voice as the trophy was handed over – 40,000 fans singing the Wednesday anthem, *Hi Ho Sheffield Wednesday,* on one of the most memorable days in the club's long history.

Sheffield Wednesday: D. Lucas, A. Bruce (P. Collins 75 mins), L. Bullen (captain), R. Wood, P. Heckingbottom, J-P. McGovern, G. Whelan, C. Rocastle, C. Brunt, L. Peacock (A. Talbot 75 mins), J. Quinn (S. MacLean 75 mins). Unused Subs: C. Adamson, S. Adams.

Hartlepool United: D. Konstantopoulos, M. Barron (D. Craddock 62 mins), M. Nelson, C. Westwood, M. Robson, R. Humphreys (captain), G. Strachan, A. Sweeney, T. Butler (E. Williams 31 mins), A. Boyd, J. Porter (J. Daly 70 mins). Unused Subs: J. Provett, M. Tinkler.

Referee: P.T. Crossley (Kent).

MATCH TO REMEMBER 25 — 7 FEBRUARY 2009

SHEFFIELD UNITED 1 SHEFFIELD WEDNESDAY 2

Championship

A late comeback from Sheffield United had denied the Owls a long-awaited double in the 2007–08 season, but Wednesday ended a 95-year wait by achieving the desired feat in the season that followed. A strike from Steve Watson had given the Owls a 1–0 win over the Blades in October 2008, and a crowd of 30,786 were then inside Bramall Lane, plus 9,000 Wednesday fans watching the action on a big screen back at Hillsborough, to witness Brian Laws' side make modern-day history.

The lunchtime game started in a sensational fashion as Wednesday fan Tommy Spurr hammered his side into the lead after just 46 seconds, converting Michael Gray's cutback from near the byline. Owls fans had little time to enjoy their team's advantage, however, as just four minutes later United's Italian loan player, Arturo Lupoli, headed a long throw from Halford onto the bar and watched the ball bounce down and go over the line, despite the best attempts of Richard Wood to keep the ball out. Then, on 19 minutes, Leigh Bromby, following

Tudgay netting the winner v Sheffield United at Bramall Lane.

another long throw, hit a post, before Wednesday's top scorer, Marcus Tudgay, produced a real moment of magic. He intercepted Kilgallon's poorly headed clearance, 40 yards from goal, and ran forward a further 15 yards before unleashing a simply stunning shot that flew into the top far corner of the net, giving Paddy Kenny no chance, before turning to run the length of the pitch to celebrate with the Wednesday fans.

In the second half, with United desperate to get an equaliser, they were lucky not to go further behind, as on 49 minutes, Tudgay flicked a header from a throw-in to Leon Clarke, whose volleyed shot beat the 'keeper, only to hit the far post. Both teams had half chances, but none were taken, and as the clock ticked down the Wednesday fans started to realise that it would take a late, late goal for the Blades to salvage a draw. In the final minute of normal time the hosts appealed in vain for a penalty-kick, but it needed a brilliant save from Lee Grant, from Billy Sharp's rising shot, to earn the Owls a deserved win and place their names in the history books.

Sheffield United: P. Kenny, K. Naughton, L. Bromby, M. Kilgallon, G. Naysmith, G. Halford, B. Howard (L. Hendrie 78 mins), N. Montgomery (captain), S. Quinn, A. Lupoli (J. Ward 52 mins), D. Webber (B. Sharp 73 mins). Unused subs. D. Cotterill, S. Jihai.

Sheffield Wednesday: L. Grant, L. Buxton, M. Beevers, R. Wood (captain), T. Spurr, J. Johnson (S. Watson 90 mins), J. O'Connor, D. Potter, M. Gray, L. Clarke, M. Tudgay. Unused Subs: R. Hinds, S. McAllister, L. Boden, W. Small.

Referee: M.R. Halsey (Lancashire).

Wednesday's 125 Greatest Players

ALLEN, John William Alcroft 'Jack'

(1927–31)

Centre-forward, 5ft 9½in, 12st (1927)
Born: 31 January 1903 Newburn, Newcastle
Died: 19 November 1957 Burnopfield, County Durham
Signed from: Brentford, 8 March 1927, £750
Transferred: Newcastle United, 8 June 1931, £3,500
Career: Prudhoe Castle, Leeds United, Brentford, Wednesday, Newcastle United, Bristol Rovers, Gateshead, Ashington
Debut: 9 April 1927 v Aston Villa (h) First Division
Last appearance: 24 January 1931 v Barnsley (a) FA Cup
Appearances/Goals: League 104/76, FAC 10/9

Prolific centre-forward Jack Allen was without doubt one of the finest attackers in Sheffield Wednesday's long history. After a mixed time at Brentford, the Geordie was glad of a fresh start when Bob Brown acquired his services for Wednesday, and he was a vital member of the side that pulled off the 'great escape' in 1928, Allen scoring nine times from the inside-left position. When Brown switched Allen to centre-forward, early in the 1928–29 season, it proved an inspired positional change as in the number-nine shirt he terrorised the top-flight defences, smashing home 35 goals in 37 League games as the Owls won the First Division title. The deadly attacker continued in the same vein in the 1929–30 campaign, scoring an incredible 39 goals in League and Cup football as Wednesday retained the title in fine style and also came close to the double – losing a controversial FA Cup semi-final to Huddersfield Town. Despite his incredible scoring record, the Owls still purchased Jack Ball in the summer of 1930 and, somewhat incredibly, Allen soon lost his place to the newcomer and spent the majority of the 1930–31 season in the reserve team! The rigid formation prevalent in the era – a strict 2–3–5 formation with just one centre-forward – seemed to be the main reason for Allen's fall from favour. The pacy attacker, noted for his deadly left foot, was understandably unhappy at his lack of first-team football, and after being placed on the transfer list he moved to his hometown club, Newcastle United, in the summer of 1931. He scored twice as United won the FA Cup in 1932, with his first goal causing a furore in what became known as 'the over-the-line incident' – many believed the ball had crossed the touchline before reaching Allen. After a spell at Bristol Rovers, he ended his playing days at League side Ashington, prior to becoming a pub licensee back in County Durham.

ATHERTON, Peter

(1994–2000)
Defender/midfielder, 5ft 11in, 13st 12lb (1997)
Born: 6 April 1970 Orrell
Signed from: Coventry City, 3 June 1994, £800,000 (T.)
Transferred: Bradford City, 4 July 2000, Free
Career: Wigan Athletic, Coventry City, Wednesday, Bradford City, Birmingham City (loan), Halifax Town
Debut: 20 August 1994 v Tottenham Hotspur (h) FA Premiership
Last appearance: 14 May 2000 v Leicester City (h) FA Premiership
Appearances/Goals: League 214/9, FAC 18/0, FLC 16/0, Euro 3/0

Utility player Peter Atherton was a mainstay of the Wednesday side of the mid-to-late 1990s, appearing in a variety of positions which included right-back, centre-half and midfield. He had made his name, winning an England Under-21 cap in the process, as a right-back under Terry Butcher at Coventry City, and was an established top-flight player when he arrived at Hillsborough in the summer of 1994. He was signed as a direct replacement for departed full-back Roland Nilsson but started the season at the heart of the Owls' defence after Wednesday captured the signature of Romanian Dan Petrescu. It would be David Pleat who switched the consistent Atherton back to his more accustomed right-back role before he eventually developed into a deep-lying defensive midfield player, sitting just in front of the traditional back four. It was in this role that Atherton captained the Owls in the late 1990s, and by the end of the decade he held, somewhat unexpectedly, the record as the player with the most appearances in the Premiership, since its inception in 1992. He remained an automatic choice as the decade drew to a close, but relegation in 2000 spelt the end of his Owls career, Atherton moving to Premiership Bradford City on a 'Bosman' free transfer. He reverted to defensive duties in West Yorkshire but after losing his first-team place re-joined his old boss, Trevor Francis, when Birmingham City secured his capture on a three-month loan in February 2001. A change of management at Valley Parade resulted in Atherton regaining his first-team place, prior to joining Halifax Town in 2005. He officially retired after 14 games but made an emergency appearance in October 2007, a few months after being appointed assistant manager at the non-League club.

BALL, John Thomas 'Jack'

(1930–33)

Centre-forward, 5ft 10in, 11st 10lb (1930)
Born: 13 September 1907 Banks, Nr. Southport
Died: 2 February 1976 Luton
Signed from: Manchester United, 29 July 1930, £1,300
Transferred: Manchester United 29 December 1933, exchange for N. Dewar
Career: Banks Juniors, Croston FC, Southport, Darwen, Chorley, Manchester United, Wednesday, Manchester United, Huddersfield Town, Luton Town, Excelsior Roubaix, Vauxhall Motors, St Albans City
Debut: 8 September 1930 v Chelsea (h) First Division
Last appearance: 23 December 1933 v Stoke City (a) First Division
Appearances/Goals: League 132/90, FAC 3/4

Forward Jack Ball followed in the footsteps of his immediate predecessor, Jack Allen, and 1920s hotshot Jimmy Trotter as deadly goalscorers for the club in the inter-war period. After replacing Allen as the club's first-choice centre-forward – early in the 1930–31 season – he was an outstanding success, finishing top goalscorer in every season that he wore the blue-and-white shirt. He had originally started his career in minor football in Lancashire, but such was his scoring record with Chorley – netting 58 goals in 42 games in his debut campaign – that several League sides chased his signature. He eventually signed for Manchester United, but after a reasonable first season his new employers hit financial problems and Jack crossed the Pennines to sign for Bob Brown's Wednesday. His prowess in front of goal ensured the Owls challenged for all the major honours during his time at Hillsborough, but he only had a Charity Shield runners'-up medal to show for his time in Sheffield. During the 1932–33 season he scored 10 times from 15 penalties – setting a record that was not bettered for almost 50 years – but it would be the arrival of new manager Billy Walker that would spell the end for Ball. The new boss was determined to sign Manchester United centre-forward Neil Dewar, and it was Ball who was used to prise the Scotsman from Old Trafford: Ball returning to Manchester in a swap deal. His second spell at Old Trafford was unproductive for Ball, and it was not until he joined Luton in October 1934 that he rediscovered his goalscoring boots. A controversial move to French soccer followed next for Jack before he returned home to work for Vauxhall Motors, captaining the Works team. He was later employed by a wholesale manufacturing chemist and after retiring helped out at his son's public house.

BANNISTER, Gary

(1981–84)

Forward, 5ft 8½in, 11st 3lb (1981)

Born: 22 July 1960 Collins Green, Warrington

Signed from: Coventry City, 27 July 1981, £80,000

Transferred: Queen's Park Rangers, 26 July 1984, £200,000 (T.)

Career: Coventry City, Detroit Express (loan), Wednesday, Queen's Park Rangers, Coventry City, West Bromwich Albion, Oxford United (loan), Nottingham Forest, Stoke City, Hong Kong Rangers, Lincoln City, Darlington, Porthleven

Debut: 29 August 1981 v Blackburn Rovers (a) Second Division

Last appearance: 12 May 1984 v Cardiff City (a) Second Division

Caps: England Under-21 (1)

Appearances/Goals: League 117+1/55, FAC 12/4, FLC 13/7

Pacy and clinical attacker Gary Bannister was a darling of Owls fans in the early 1980s. Arguably Jack Charlton's best buy, Bannister holds the unique record of having scored 22 goals in each of his three seasons at Hillsborough (a 20 goals per season feat last achieved by Jack Ball in the 1930s) and that consistent scoring led Wednesday to an FA Cup semi-final in 1983 before promotion back to the top flight a year later. During the course of his time at Hillsborough he formed attacking partnerships with the likes of Terry Curran, Andy McCulloch and Imre Varadi but outscored all his rivals to enter the club's annals as one of the greatest goalscorers in recent history. It was ironic that after helping Wednesday back into the First Division, after an absence of 14 years, he turned down a new contract in the summer of 1984, and Owls fans were disappointed when he joined fellow top-flight side Queen's Park Rangers – a transfer tribunal deciding that Wednesday should receive a club-record sum of £200,000 for his services. It would be several more years before the Owls could boast a prolific scorer such as 'Banno', and his former fans could only watch with envy as Bannister continued to score freely for the West London club, grabbing 72 goals in just 172 games for Rangers. Sadly for Bannister his move, to former club Coventry City, proved a disappointment, and he would make several moves over the ensuing years, failing to replicate his success at Hillsborough and Loftus Road. He enjoyed an Indian Summer while player-coach at Darlington in the mid-

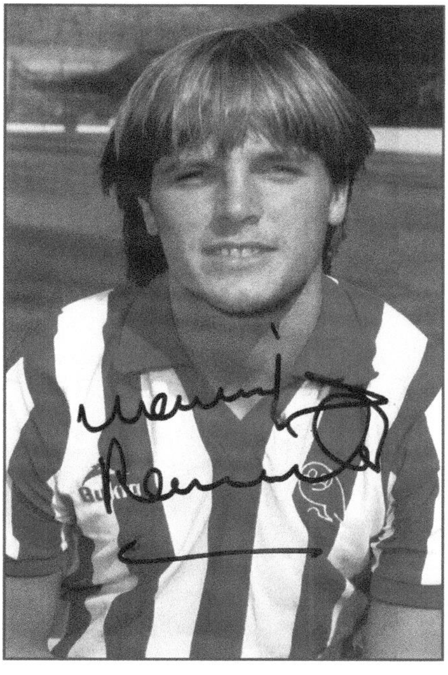

1990s as his goals from a new midfield position helped the Quakers to Wembley for the Third Division Play-off Final. Unfortunately his side lost 1–0 to Plymouth Argyle, and a neck injury forced his retirement from professional soccer a few months later. He later moved to Cornwall – working in the hotel trade – and continued to play for a local amateur side as he passed his 40th birthday.

BANNISTER, Keith

(1945–53)
Half-back, 5ft 10in, 11st 4lb (1946)
Born: 27 January 1923, Sheffield
Signed from: Sheffield YMCA, 17 February 1945
Transferred: Chesterfield, 19 June 1953, £750
Career: Sheffield YMCA, York City (guest), Wednesday, Chesterfield, King's Lynn, Macclesfield Town
Debut: 25 December 1946 v Bury (a) Second Division
Last appearance: 6 September 1952 v Charlton Athletic (h) Second Division
Appearances/Goals: League 75/0, FAC 3/0

After serving his country for five years in the RAF, during World War Two, Keith Bannister returned home to sign professional forms with Wednesday – putting his signature to a contract when the Owls stopped for a meal on the way home from a wartime fixture. His early appearances in a Wednesday shirt came on the left side of defence – at half-back and full-back – before he eventually settled into the right-back role, in the winter of 1950. A bad injury then curtailed his progress before in October 1951 manager Eric Taylor called up both Bannister and his great friend, Derek Dooley, for their first starts of the campaign. It proved an inspired move and the duo were ever present as the two-footed Bannister captained Wednesday to the Second Division Championship. Unfortunately, he was denied the honour of leading the Owls out in the opening game of the following season as the no-nonsense defender tore ligaments in the pre-season public practice game. This setback proved a precursor to a nightmare season for Bannister, as his place was initially taken by Norman Jackson prior to Vin Kenny becoming first-choice right-back. In fact, the former captain made only a solitary appearance in the 1952–53 season, and just over a year after leading his side to a divisional title he was sold to neighbours Chesterfield. He played in Cheshire non-League soccer until retiring in 1960 and worked as a salesman and for an insurance company for the remainder of his working life. His link with Wednesday was not severed entirely, however, as in 1961 he was appointed part-time coach to the club's youth side and from 1967 scouted for the club. For six years in the 1980s he was the club's sports and recreation manager before moving to the United States, to be near his daughter. While over the Pond he played over-40s soccer for a San Diego side before returning home to Sheffield.

BART-WILLIAMS, Christopher Gerald 'Chris'

(1991–95)
Midfielder, 5ft 11in, 11st 10lb (1992)
Born: 16 June 1974, Freetown, Sierra Leone
Signed from: Leyton Orient, 15 November 1991, £575,000
Transferred: Nottingham Forest, 1 July 1995, £2.5 million (T.)
Career: Leyton Orient, Wednesday, Nottingham Forest, Charlton Athletic, Ipswich Town, Leeds United (trial), Apoel Nicosia, Marsaxlokk
Debut: 23 November 1991 v Arsenal (h) First Division
Last appearance: 7 May 1995 v Manchester United (a) Premiership
Caps: England B (1), Under-21 (14)
Appearances/Goals: League 95+29/16, FAC 9+3/2, FLC 10+6/4, Euro 1+2/2, Other 0+1/0

Although born in Africa, Chris Bart-Williams was brought up in London and became hot property after making his League debut for Leyton Orient at the tender age of just 16. The England Youth international had scouts flocking to Brisbane Road, and just four months after signing his first professional contract he was snapped up by top-flight Wednesday. His new boss, Trevor Francis, had also made his senior debut at the age of just 16 – for Birmingham City in 1970 – and it was thought that he could aid the youngster in his sudden elevation into the top echelon of the English game. The Owls boss certainly had great confidence in the teenager as just a few days after moving north he made his debut. That display astonished Wednesday fans as the youngster showed a maturity and calmness that belied his age, and he became an integral part of the Wednesday squad for the next four years. Although not blessed with pace, his intelligence on the ball and ability to 'pick a pass' ensured he won several Under-21 caps for his adopted country, while at Hillsborough, and was part of the squad that qualified for Europe in 1992 and reached both domestic Cup Finals a year later. While mainly utilised in a midfield role, Bart-Williams (unsurprisingly nicknamed 'Bartman') appeared on several occasions in attack – netting a hat-trick in a 5–2 home win over Southampton in April 1993 – and was seen by many Wednesday fans as the long-term replacement for John Sheridan. However, he did not remain to fulfil that prophecy as after a mixed 1994–95 season he opted to leave for pastures new, joining Nottingham Forest, with Wednesday receiving one of the highest transfer fees ever decided at a tribunal, after the two clubs could not agree upon a fee. From a financial perspective the deal proved lucrative for the Owls, but it could also be said that the club never replaced Bart-Williams' creativity. He was a regular for Forest throughout the remainder of the 1990s but then experienced disappointing spells at both Charlton and Ipswich Town before dropping out of the English game altogether in 2005. He subsequently moved to the US, where he now coaches male and female soccer teams.

BETTS, William 'Billy'

(1883–95)

Centre/half-back, 5ft 7in, 11st 2lb (1890)
Born: 26 March 1864, Sheffield
Died: 8 August 1941, Sheffield
Signed from: Heeley 1883
Transferred: Retired 1895
Career: Pitsmoor (Christchurch), Parkwood Rovers, Clarence, Pyebank Rovers, Heeley, Wednesday, Lockwood Brothers, Wednesday
Debut: 6 January 1883 v Nottingham Forest (a) FA Cup
Last appearance: 13 April 1895 v Preston North End (a) First Division
Caps: England Full (1)
Appearances/Goals: League 50/3, FAC 33/1

Defender Billy Betts was one of the club's outstanding players from the Victorian age. He appeared in several of the games that marked the club's progress in the 19th century, from being one of the first players to sign professional forms in 1887 to appearing in both the first Football Alliance and Football League matches played by Wednesday, in 1889 and 1892 respectively. In total he appeared in over 300 games and was an ever present as Wednesday won the FAL title in 1890, as well as being in the side that reached the FA Cup Final for the first time, losing 6–1 to Blackburn Rovers. The fearless Betts once broke his nose during a game but continued after treatment, and it was this attitude that ensured he was a firm favourite of the Olive Grove regulars of the period. A superb header of the ball and accomplished cricketer, Billy also worked

ful-time during the week – as a stoker in Neepsend Gas Works – and remained a first choice until he was replaced by another Wednesday great, Tommy Crawshaw, in the mid-1890s. After retiring from the field of play, he was appointed part-time groundsman and in the early 1920s coached the A team and was briefly assistant trainer to the first team. His grandson, Dennis Woodhead, was a regular for the club in the late 1940s and early 1950s.

BLAIR, James 'Jimmy'

(1914–19 & 1919–20)

Left-back, 5ft 9in, 11st 7lb (1920)
Born: 11 May 1888, Glenboig, Scotland
Died: 28 February 1964, Sheffield
Signed from: Clyde, 14 May 1914, £1,975
Transferred: Alloa United, August 1919
Signed from: Alloa United, 24 October 1919, £250
Transferred: Cardiff City, 19 November 1920, £3,500
Career: Bonnyrigg Thistle, Glasgow Ashfield, Clyde, Wednesday, Clydebank

(guest), Glasgow Rangers (guest), Alloa United, Wednesday, Cardiff City, Bournemouth & Boscombe United, Sheppey United
Debut: 26 September 1914 v Bradford Park Avenue (h) First Division
Last appearance: 13 November 1920 v West Ham United (a) Second Division
Caps: Scotland Full (2)
Appearances/Goals: League 57/0, FAC 4/0

The Owls paid a club record fee for Scotsman Jimmy Blair, and there is no doubt that he was one of the finest left-backs to ever represent the club. Unfortunately for Wednesday fans, a combination of events meant that they saw relatively little of the cool, clever and reliable defender. After impressing greatly in his debut season, as Wednesday finished seventh in the old First Division, the onset of World War One meant that Blair returned home and played as a guest for several teams – winning the 1918 Scottish Championship with Glasgow Rangers. When national football returned in 1919 it was fully expected that Blair would return to Sheffield to continue his English career, but Wednesday fans were shocked when he declined to return and instead signed for junior side Alloa United. The reason behind the decision was a disagreement over his benefit – he wanted the wartime period to count but Wednesday refused – and incredibly when the dispute was resolved the Owls had to pay a fee to get Jimmy back! During the disastrous relegation season of 1919–20, he was one of the few shining lights, but Blair was still unsettled in Sheffield and was transfer listed in November 1920. Within a few days Cardiff City secured his services – the Owls receiving a club record fee – and he enjoyed great success in South Wales, leading City to promotion from the Second Division in 1921 and the FA Cup Final in 1925, losing to Sheffield United. After over 200 games for City, Blair ended his playing days as a player-manager in Kent non-League football while he was a pub licensee for 20 years, from 1928 to 1948. He later moved back to Sheffield, to be near his daughter, and was a season ticket holder at Hillsborough in the 1950s.

BLENKINSOP, Ernest 'Ernie'

(1923–34)
Left-back, 5ft 8½in, 11st 8lb (1923)
Born: 20 April 1902, Cudworth, Barnsley
Died: 24 April 1969, Sheffield
Signed from: Hull City, 20 January 1923, £1,150
Transferred: Liverpool, 15 March 1934, £6,500
Career: Cudworth United Methodist Club, Cudworth Village, Hull City, Wednesday, Liverpool, Cardiff City, Buxton, Halifax Town (guest), Bradford Park Avenue (guest), Bradford City (guest), Hurst (guest)
Debut: 27 January 1923 v Bury (a) Second Division

Last appearance: 10 March 1934 v Wolverhampton Wanderers (h) First Division
Caps: England Full (26), Football League (8)
Appearances/Goals: League 393/5, FAC 31/0

Arguably the greatest left-back in the Owls' history, Ernie Blenkinsop was a first-team regular at Wednesday for over a decade, helping the club to two League titles in 1929 and 1930, as well as a Second Division Championship in 1926. The stylish and polished full-back rose from the relative obscurity of the second tier to win 26 caps for his country, standing only second to Ron Springett as the most-capped England international for the club. He was actually in Hull City's reserve team when Bob Brown's legendary eye for talent brought him to Hillsborough, and his debut actually came at right-back. A week later his home debut – in front of a then record crowd of over 66,000 versus Barnsley in the FA Cup – resulted in a switch to left-back, and he never looked back. After losing his place, his outstanding form in reserve-team football prompted a recall, and he forged a successful full-back partnership with Billy Felton and, later, with Tommy Walker. When 'Blenki' was sold to First Division rivals Liverpool there was an outcry from Owls fans as 'The Prince of Full-backs' was not only the club captain but also a current England international. It was thought by many that new manager Billy Walker judged Blenkinsop as a long-term threat to his own position and that the club record fee received could in no way compensate for his loss. When he returned in Liverpool colours he was not only given a standing ovation from the fans but was cheered onto the pitch by the players! After a spell as player-coach at Cardiff City, Ernie retired from League soccer while at the start of World War Two he returned to Sheffield, scouting for Wednesday as well as coaching Sheffield FC. After ill health meant he could no longer work in the steel industry, Ernie spent the remainder of his life serving behind the bar, running the Sportsman's Inn at Crosspool until his passing in 1969.

BOLDER, Robert John 'Bob'

(1977–83)
Goalkeeper, 6ft 3in, 11st 13lb (1978)
Born: 2 October 1958, Dover
Signed from: Dover Athletic, 9 March 1977, £1,000
Transferred: Liverpool, 4 August 1983, £125,000
Career: Dover Athletic, Wednesday, Liverpool, Sunderland, Luton Town (loan), Charlton Athletic, Margate, Dagenham & Redbridge
Debut: 27 December 1977 v Rotherham United (h) Third Division

Last appearance: 14 May 1983 v Crystal Palace (h) Second Division
Appearances/Goals: League 196/0, FAC 12/0, FLC 16/0

Goalkeeper Bob Bolder was initially rejected by Charlton Athletic when a teenager, mainly because he was considered too small and scrawny, but in his late teenage years he grew to over six foot in height, and summer months spent as a farm labourer ensured his physique increased proportionally. His playing career started with Kent club Dover Athletic, and he was brought to Hillsborough by Len Ashurst, the Owls manager's previous spell as Gillingham boss suggesting that Bolder had already been scouted by the Gills. Within a few months Bolder was established as number-two to Chris Turner in the Hillsborough pecking order. When Jack Charlton decided to replace fans's favourite Chris Turner with Bolder – ironically because he thought Turner was too small – the new first-choice custodian received a hostile reception. However he soon won over his critics and was between the sticks as the Owls won promotion from the Third Division in 1980, his rival having been sold to Sunderland in 1979. From October 1980 until the end of the 1982–83 season, Bolder appeared in 133 consecutive games for Wednesday – including the 1983 FA Cup semi-final loss to Brighton – and his consistency meant that several clubs were interested in his services, when he was one of four players to reject new contracts. When Liverpool made a move for his signature it was no surprise that he jumped at the chance of joining the Anfield club. The move proved to be somewhat frustrating for Bolder as he failed to dislodge Bruce Grobbelaar from the first team and did not make a senior appearance for the Reds. He did earn a

European Cup-winners' medal in 1985 – he was reserve 'keeper – before a loan spell to Sunderland was converted to a full transfer. His career turned full circle when he signed for Charlton Athletic in 1986, and he appeared in almost 300 games for the Valiants, the most successful spell of his career. Highlights included an appearance at Wembley in the Full Members' Cup Final, while the Owls provided the opposition for his benefit match in 1995. He is now the community officer at the Valley.

BOOTH, Andrew David 'Andy'

(1996–2001)
Forward, 6ft, 12st 6lb (1996)
Born: 6 December 1973, Huddersfield
Signed from: Huddersfield Town, 4 July 1996, £2.7 million
Transferred: Huddersfield Town, 22 March 2001, £175,000
Career: Huddersfield Town, Wednesday, Tottenham Hotspur (loan), Huddersfield Town

Debut: 17 August 1996 v Aston Villa (h) Premiership
Last appearance: 17 March 2001 v Burnley (h) First Division
Appearances/Goals: League 124+9/28, FAC 9+1/5, FLC 10+1/1

The name of Andy Booth will be inexorably linked with his home-town club Huddersfield Town for whom he recorded 452 appearances, scoring exactly 150 goals. It was his form during his first spell at the Terriers that alerted several top-flight clubs, including Liverpool, to his attributes, but it was Wednesday boss David Pleat who took the plunge to sign him, the Owls paying a whopping fee for his services. The new boy enjoyed an encouraging debut season at Wednesday, scoring 13 times as the club finished an unexpected seventh in the Premiership, having led the table after gaining maximum points from their opening four games. Unfortunately, the remainder of his career at Wednesday was dogged with injury and loss of form – a first-half hat-trick against Bolton Wanderers in November 1997 being a definite highlight – and it would be fair to say he never really proved himself at a higher level. Although not blessed with pace, his terrific ability in the air and wholehearted attitude ensured he did not fall out of favour with Wednesday fans, despite his goals record being relatively poor. When he did move from Hillsborough his destination was a surprise as he joined fellow Premiership club Tottenham Hotspur on loan – the fact that David Pleat was director of football at White Hart Lane being a major factor. Soon after returning to Wednesday he was sold back to Huddersfield Town and suffered an agonising last-day relegation from the second tier two months later. After reaching the Play-offs in 2002 the Terriers went into administration and were

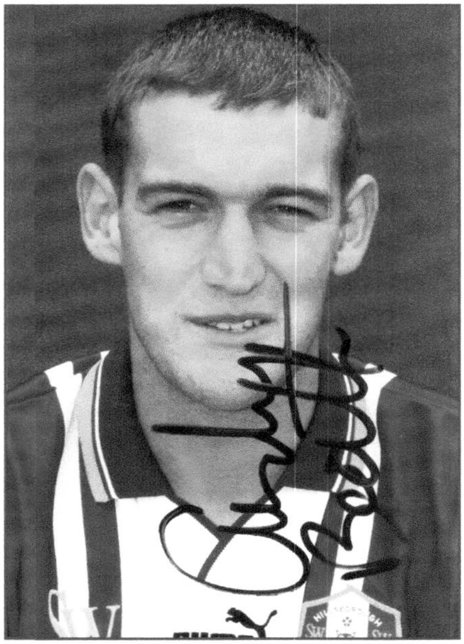

relegated to the basement division, with Booth a frustrated spectator as injury ravaged his season. He was awarded a testimonial in 2006 – Town playing Real Sociedad – and netted on his final appearance in professional football, prior to moving into his new role as club ambassador.

BRADSHAW, Francis 'Frank'

(1905–10)
Inside-forward, 5ft 9½in, 11st 10lb (1907)
Born: 31 May 1885, Sheffield
Signed from: Oxford Street Sunday School, January 1905
Transferred: Northampton, May 1910, £700
Career: Oxford Street Sunday School, Wednesday, Northampton, Everton, Arsenal
Debut: 23 April 1906 v Everton (h) First Division
Last appearance: 19 February 1910 v Notts County (h) First Division
Caps: England Full (1), Football League (2)
Appearances/Goals: League 87/38, FAC 8/2

Brilliant inside-forward Frank Bradshaw was without doubt one of the finest footballers that Sheffield has produced. Unfortunately, his career at Hillsborough was dogged with injury and he failed to achieve the success his talent surely merited. As a teenager he played in Sheffield junior football, while training to be a silversmith, before signing amateur forms for The Wednesday in 1904. His form in reserve-team soccer eventually led to a senior debut, although despite netting twice he was unceremoniously dropped for the following game. He then experienced his first spell on the sidelines – being injured in a pre-season practice match – but the 'big, dashing and clever' attacker recovered to reclaim a first-team place in the latter part of the 1906–07 season. This coincided with Wednesday's run to the FA Cup Final, and Bradshaw was the youngest member, aged 23, of the side that beat Everton to lift the famous trophy. For the next two seasons Frank was at the peak of his game – being an automatic choice for the number-eight shirt – and his form also brought international honours, although despite scoring a hat-trick as England won 11–1 in Austria he was only picked on one further occasion, injury meaning he could not take up the opportunity. Another long spell on the sidelines in the 1909–10 season, due to a persistent knee cartilage injury, resulted in the Owls hierarchy deciding – in hindsight incorrectly – that his career in the top flight was effectively over and sold Frank to non-League Northampton Town. He was perhaps lucky that the Cobblers manager at the time was a young Herbert Chapman, who of course became one of the greatest managers of all time in the English game, and he immediately sent the inside-forward to a London specialist. He quickly repaired the damage, and incredibly Bradshaw continued to play senior football until 1923, 13 years after Wednesday had decided he did not have a future! He spent only one season at Northampton before finishing First Division runner-up with Everton and playing over 200 times for Arsenal. He ended his playing days at full-back and was later, briefly, manager at Football League side Aberdare Athletic before moving to Somerset. He was a FA coach for many years before being employed by British Aerospace until his retirement.

BRANDON, Harold 'Harry'

(1890–98)

Half-back, 5ft 5in, 12st 2lb (1896)
Born: 26 March 1873, Kilbirnie, Ayrshire
Signed from: Glasgow Clyde, 12 December 1890
Transferred: Chesterfield Town, 18 October 1898
Career: Haywood Wanderers, Paisley St Mirren, Glasgow Clyde, Wednesday, Chesterfield Town
Debut: 17 January 1891 v Halliwell (h) FA Cup

Last appearance: 16 April 1898 v Wolverhampton Wanderers (a) First Division
Caps: Alliance League (1)
Appearances/Goals: League 147/15, FAC 25/1

One of four members of the Brandon family to play for Wednesday, Harry easily made the greatest impact. The wholehearted defender made his name in Scottish football before travelling to Sheffield for a trial in 1890, playing against Sheffield United in the first-ever meeting between the two city clubs. He appeared under the assumed name of Todd, so as not to alert any rivals, and was quickly signed to a professional contract after fans had chaired him off the pitch. His competitive debut for Wednesday came in the club's biggest ever win – 12–0 versus Halliwell – and Harry became an automatic choice for several seasons, appearing in Wednesday's first-ever League fixture as well as winning the FA Cup in 1896. His versatility also made him a valuable member of the team as he actually played in every position possible – including as goalkeeper in a reserve game – and his obvious commitment to the cause made him a popular figure among the Olive Grove regulars. A healthy crowd of 3,000 watched his benefit game against Notts County in 1897 before he completed his playing career with a short spell at neighbours Chesterfield Town. After retiring he worked at Barnsley colliery and coached in local football.

BRAYSHAW, Edward 'Teddy'

(1884–91)

Left-back, 5ft 6½in, 11st 8lb (1890)
Born: 1863, Kirkstall
Died: 20 November 1908, Wortley
Signed from: Walkley, 1884
Transferred: Retired, 1891
Career: All Saints, Pyebank, Walkley, Wednesday, Lockwood Brothers, Sheffield Rovers, Grimsby Town
Debut: 8 November 1884 v Long Eaton Rangers (a) FA Cup
Last appearance: 14 February 1891 v West Bromwich Albion (h) FA Cup
Caps: England Full (1)
Appearances/Goals: FA Cup 21/0

Full-back Teddy Brayshaw was both influential and instrumental in the club's switch from amateur status to professional in 1887. Brayshaw, whose father was an eminent detective, was a stalwart of Sheffield football in the 1880s, regularly appearing for the local FA in representative football. A carpenter by trade, Brayshaw remained amateur throughout his time with The Wednesday but was a major player when the notion of turning professional came to a head. Several players of the time realised that the club would die if the change was not made and

Teddy was one of several men who formed Sheffield Rovers to effectively force the issue. He duly played in the opening game at Olive Grove in 1887 and was a vital member of the side that won the inaugural Championship of the new Football Alliance League in 1890, as well as playing in the FA Cup Final loss to Blackburn Rovers. Various injuries started to disrupt his career in his later years with Wednesday, and he slowly drifted from the first-team scene as the new era of League football came onto the horizon. The fracture of several small bones in his left foot eventually forced his early retirement, although he did briefly attempt a comeback with Grimsby Town, prior to entering the pub trade. Sadly, ill health forced his retirement in 1907 and within 12 months he had passed away, just 45 years of age.

BRIGHT, Mark Abraham

(1992–97)
Forward, 6ft, 12st 12lb (1996)
Born: 6 June 1962, Stoke
Signed from: Crystal Palace, 11 September 1992, £875,000
Transferred: Sion, 17 January 1997, £70,000
Career: Leek Town, Port Vale, Leicester City, Crystal Palace, Wednesday, Millwall (loan), Sion, Charlton Athletic
Debut: 12 September 1992 v Nottingham Forest (a) Premiership
Last appearance: 2 September 1996 v Leicester City (h) Premiership
Appearances/Goals: League 112+21/48, FAC 13/7, FLC 20+1/11, EURO 3/4

Attacker Mark Bright was a member of the highly entertaining Owls side of the early 1990s, leading the club's scoring charts in four consecutive seasons. After starting his career in Staffordshire non-League football, Bright entered the professional ranks at Port Vale and came to the fore at Crystal Palace, where he formed a deadly partnership with Ian Wright – Bright actually scoring more goals than his co-striker during their the time together. In total he amassed 114 goals, in 286 games, for the Eagles, but when Wright was sold he was soon to follow, joining the Owls in a deal that saw the £500,000-rated Paul Williams move in the opposite direction. With the likes of John

Sheridan and Chris Waddle pulling the strings in midfield, there was certainly no lack of goalscoring opportunities for Bright at Wednesday, and he proved a consistent scorer as the club challenged for the game's top honours. Although not blessed with searing pace, Bright's ability in the air and all-round contribution to the side ensured he remained an automatic choice under Trevor Francis, his most famous goal being the extra-time winner in the 1993 FA Cup semi-final at Wembley. Despite his goals record, he was used sparingly by new manager David Pleat with newcomers Marc Degryse and Darko Kovacevic preferred in attack. This eventually led to his departure, early in 1997, with his final appearance being the home victory over Leicester City that left the Owls top of the Premiership, with 12 points from 12 games. His destination, Swiss club Sion, was certainly a surprise and unfortunately the move proved disastrous as his new club failed to pay Wednesday the initial instalment of the agreed transfer fee and FIFA decreed that Bright could not play until the issue was resolved. By the time Wednesday had started legal proceedings against Sion, Bright had already returned home to sign for Charlton – the Addicks paying the Owls £30,000 to solve the issue. Around the same time he married Pop Star Michelle Gayle and enjoyed a swansong at the Valley, helping his new side clinch a place in the Premiership in 1998. He retired a year later and is now heard regularly as a match summariser for BBC Radio Five Live.

BRITTLETON, James Thomas 'Tommy'

(1905–20)

Half-back, 5ft 9½in, 12st 4lb (1913)
Born: 23 April 1882, Winsford, Cheshire
Died: 22 February 1955, Winsford, Cheshire
Signed from: Stockport County, 6 January 1905, £300
Transferred: Stoke FC, 21 May 1920, Free
Career: Winsford Juniors, Winsford Celtic, Winsford United, Stockport County, Wednesday, Stoke FC, Winsford Celtic, Winsford United
Debut: 14 January 1905 v Bury (h) First Division
Last appearance: 1 May 1920 v Oldham Athletic (h) First Division
Caps: England Full (5), Football League (2)
Appearances/Goals: League 342/30, FAC 30/3

Once described as 'the perfect footballer', Tommy Brittleton was one of the finest players of his generation, spending over 15 years at Wednesday after coming to the fore while at Stockport County, during the early part of the 20th century. He had actually built his early reputation as an intelligent inside-forward, but it would be in the

modern-day defensive midfield role that he would star for the Owls and win caps for his country. His path to Hillsborough was certainly unique as he was recommended to Wednesday by a referee who had taken charge of a game in which Brittleton had excelled! In fact, that was his second transfer on recommendation as his initial move from Winsford to Stockport took place when a County fan noticed his obvious talents and urged his club to sign him! Wednesday broke their transfer record to sign Brittleton, and he initially replaced the injured Harry Chapman in the number-eight shirt. However in the ensuing months Brittleton – an early exponent of the long throw in – settled into a half-back role, replacing Herrod Ruddlesdin in the Wednesday line-up. Noted for his tireless running, superb tackling ability and unselfish play, Tommy remained in the Owls side until the commencement of World War One, being a member of the side that lifted the FA Cup in 1907, and just missed out on the League title in 1913. During that period he won various representative honours, although he turned down the FA's offer to tour South Africa in 1911 so he could spend the summer fishing – he was once described as the 'biggest home bird you could ever meet'. During the hostilities he appeared in 129 games for Wednesday and at the time became the oldest player to represent the club in a competitive fixture when he made an emergency appearance against Oldham in 1920, aged 38 years and 8 days. When he was awarded a free transfer by Wednesday – in recognition of his services – it was thought that would end his days in League soccer, but incredibly he would play for a further five years for Stoke FC and was player-coach from 1921. He was later player-manager back at Winsford and worked in the chemical industry prior to becoming a landlord in his home town.

BROWN, John Henry 'Jack'

(1923–37)

Goalkeeper, 5ft 10in, 12st 6lb (1935)
Born: 19 March 1899, Worksop
Died: 9 April 1962, Sheffield
Signed from: Worksop Town, 23 February 1923, £360
Transferred: Hartlepool United, 17 September 1937, Free
Career: Netherton United, Worksop Wesley, Worksop Town, Wednesday, Hartlepool United
Debut: 21 April 1923 v Coventry City (a) Second Division
Last appearance: 20 March 1937 v Liverpool (h) First Division
Caps: England Full (6), Football League (2)
Appearances/Goals: League 465/0, FAC 42

For the large majority of the period between the two World Wars, the commanding figure of Jack Brown guarded the Wednesday net from opposition raids. The goalie, who only switched from centre-forward to 'keeper in his late teenage years, had first risen to prominence with Midland League Worksop Town in the early 1920s where his heroic

display, in January 1923, earned his side a 0–0 FA Cup draw at Tottenham Hotspur. Despite losing 9–0 in the replay, also held at White Hart Lane, Town knew they would not be able to hold onto their prize asset and Brown duly moved to Hillsborough a few weeks later. He was signed as back up to Teddy Davison but after featuring occasionally in the next two seasons he looked set to be released in May 1925 as the Owls tried to sign a replacement from Newport County. However, that deal was delayed and the club effectively had no choice but to re-sign Brown, as he was required for a County Cup game. This proved a slice of luck for Wednesday as in the season that followed the broad shouldered stopper was ever present as the Second Division title was secured in fine style. Over the years that followed Brown proved an outstanding 'keeper – he was one of only three players to appear in more than 500 games for the club – and earned two League Championship medals plus an FA Cup-winners' medal in 1935. He was virtually ever present for 12 seasons before being replaced by Roy Smith in March 1937. He was at the veteran stage at this point – he was one day past his 38th birthday when he made his farewell appearance – and would play just one more competitive game, for Hartlepool, before retiring. After leaving the game he held a variety of jobs, including publican and newsagent, and is without doubt an all-time Wednesday great.

BRUNT, Christopher 'Chris'

(2004–07)

Winger, 6ft 1in, 11st 8lb (2004)

Born: 14 December 1984, Belfast

Signed from: Middlesbrough, 2 March 2004, Free

Transferred: West Bromwich Albion, 15 August 2007, £2.75 million

Career: St Andrews, Middlesbrough, Wednesday, West Bromwich Albion

Debut: 17 March 2004 v AFC Bournemouth (h) Second Division

Last appearance: 11 August 2007 v Ipswich Town (a) Championship

Caps: Northern Ireland Full (10), Under-23 (1), Under-21 (1)

Appearances/Goals: League 113+27/23, FAC 4/0, FLC 4+1/0, Other 2+2/1

Mercurial winger Chris Brunt was a product of the Middlesbrough Academy but moved to Hillsborough after failing to break into the first team at the Riverside. Comparisons with another winger from the North East, Chris Waddle, were obvious as Brunt possessed the same languid, rather ungainly playing style and was also tall and pencil slim. He made an instant impression when crashing home a terrific free-kick on his full debut and was voted Player of the Month by Owls fans in April with Wednesday awarding the youngster a new contract, as reward for his encouraging start to life in League soccer. He was in and out of the side in his first

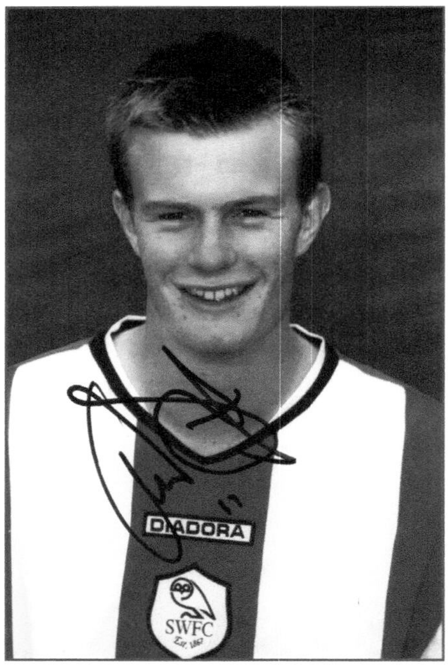

full season but played in the team that clinched promotion back to the Championship, at Cardiff, in May 2005. As Brunt's form became more consistent he became a regular at Wednesday and started to attract top-flight scouts to Hillsborough to view the left-footed, left-sided wingman in action. During his time at Wednesday he netted some outstanding goals, including a near 40-yard effort at Hillsborough against Coventry City and memorable long-range goal in a 3–2 win at rivals Leeds United. The unassuming Brunt became the subject of transfer speculation in the summer of 2007, and after refusing several bids for his services the Owls could not resist the offer from West Bromwich Albion of an initial £2.5 million, rising to £3 million depending on appearances. He duly helped Albion win promotion to the Premiership in 2008 and was top scorer as they were relegated back down to the Championship a year later. Twelve months later he was again instrumental in Albion winning promotion for the second time in three years, to earn Brunt another season at the top level of the English game.

BULLEN, Lee (2004–08)

Defender, 6ft 2in, 12st 7lb (2004)
Born: 29 March 1971, Edinburgh
Signed from: Dunfermline Athletic, 24 May 2004, Free
Transferred: Released, 30 June 2008
Career: Dunfermline Athletic, Penicuik Athletic, Meadowbank Thistle, Stenhousemuir, Whitburn, Stanmore CYC, Kui-Tan, Golden AA, South China AA, PAE Kalamata, Dunfermline Athletic, Wednesday, Falkirk
Debut: 7 August 2004 v Colchester United (h) League One
Last appearance: 26 April 2008 v Leicester City (a) Championship

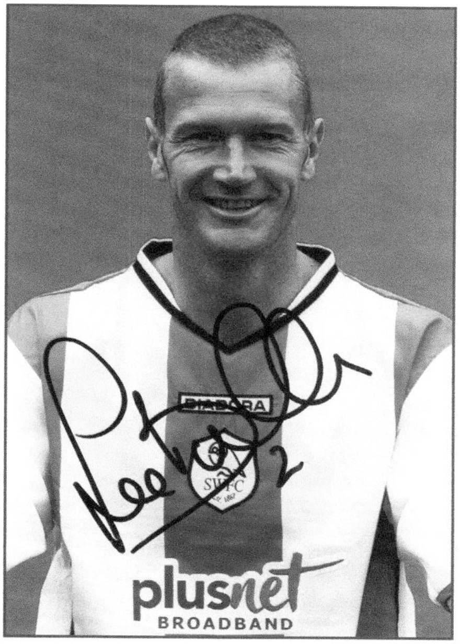

Appearances/Goals: League 108+26/8, FAC 4+1/1, FLC 4+1/0, Others 4/0

The playing career of Lee Bullen took the Scot all over the world, but it would be on a sunny day in South Wales when he would experience the highlight of his playing career. That day, of course, was the 2005 Championship Play-off Final when the popular defender captained Wednesday to a 4–2 win over Hartlepool United, witnessed by a 40,000-strong travelling army of delirious Owls fans. In that debut season with Wednesday, Bullen had showed his versatility by playing in several different positions – scoring in consecutive games when utilised as a forward – and his career with the Owls was perhaps unique as he played in all 10 outfield positions and even experienced a spell in goal, replacing the injured David Lucas at Millwall in 2006; keeping a clean sheet as his side secured a vital 1–0 win in a relegation 'six-pointer'. His wholehearted attitude ensured 'Bully' stayed four seasons at Wednesday and proved an invaluable squad member to both Paul Sturrock and Brian Laws. Injury meant he missed a farewell appearance at Hillsborough but he was given a rousing send off by the Wednesday fans, prior to accepting a playing contract with Scottish side Falkirk in the summer of 2008. He was later appointed to the coaching staff and, when time permits, makes the long trip to see Wednesday in action. His experience with Wednesday was actually his only one in English football as after initially failing to make the grade at Dunfermline he reverted to part-time status while working for a Building Society in Edinburgh. A move to Australian club Stanmore in 1991 started his globe trekking exploits as he then played football in Hong Kong and Greece before returning home to Scotland – while playing in the Far East he actually played against an England touring side in 1996 when he was selected for a Golden XI side. His career came full circle when he signed for Dunfermline in January 2000 with the highlight being a sub appearance in the 2004 Scottish Cup Final loss to Glasgow Celtic at Hampden Park.

BURGESS, Harry

(1929–35)
Inside left, 5ft 8in, 11st 7lb (1929)
Born: 20 August 1904, Alderley Edge, Cheshire
Died: 6 October 1957, Wilmslow, Cheshire
Signed from: Stockport County, 21 June 1929, £3,500
Transferred: Chelsea, 15 March 1935, £4,000
Career: Wilmslow Albion, Alderley Edge, Stockport County, Sandbach Ramblers (loan), Wednesday, Chelsea, Brentford (guest), Reading (guest), Fulham (guest), Southampton (guest), Stockport County (guest)
Debut: 14 September 1929 v Aston Villa (h) First Division
Last appearance: 20 February 1935 v Liverpool (a) First Division
Caps: England Full (4)
Appearances/Goals: League 215/70, FAC 18/7

Twenty four years after Wednesday raided Stockport County for the services of Tom Brittleton, the Owls captured another outstanding talent when they secured the signature of inside-forward Harry Burgess. The new boy provided yet more inspiration to an Owls side that were already reigning League champions and, with Burgess scoring and creating dozens of chances, Wednesday romped away with the League title again, setting a new record winning margin. He finished second only to the great Jack Allen in that 1929–30 season, and in his first three seasons at Hillsborough the side scored over 100 League and Cup goals in every campaign. Unsurprisingly, he became a huge crowd favourite, although it would be fair to say that Owls fans of the era must have been spoilt for choice as to their favourite player, due to the abundance of talent in the blue-and-white shirt! His signing was yet another masterstroke from

legendary Wednesday boss Bob Brown but after being a regular for five years a fall out with new boss Billy Walker, in December 1934, effectively ended his Wednesday career with Harry sold to Chelsea soon after. It was perhaps more than coincidence that a certain Bob Brown was scouting for the Londoners at the time! The left-sided attacker had started his playing career in non-League soccer, while working as a carpenter, before being recruited by Stockport from his village side. He crashed home 28 goals in his first full season for County – as a centre-forward – and increased that tally to 31 two years later, remarkable considering he had moved to the left wing! This form, of course, had scouts flocking to Edgley Park and the move into the top division was almost inevitable. During the war years, Harry served in the police and after retiring from football in 1945 he worked for the MoD prior to becoming a publican in Wilmslow. A keen cricketer and golfer, he passed away at the relatively young age of 53 and was unable to enjoy his retirement.

BURTON, Henry Arthur 'Harry'

(1902–09)

Left-back, 5ft 10½in, 12st (1907)
Born: 1881, West Bromwich
Died: 28 August 1923, Sheffield
Signed from: Attercliffe FC, August 1902, £10
Transferred: West Bromwich Albion, 28 March 1909, £850*
* Joint fee with G. Simpson
Career: Huntsman's Garden Schoolboys, Attercliffe FC, Wednesday, West Bromwich Albion, Scunthorpe and Lindsay United
Debut: 10 October 1903 v Wolverhampton Wanderers (a) First Division
Last appearance: 27 March 1909 v Manchester City (a) First Division
Appearances/Goals: League 171/0, FAC 27/0

Although born in the West Midlands, Harry Burton grew up in Sheffield and joined the Owls as understudy to the great Ambrose Langley. However, injury soon ended the career of Langley, and Burton stepped seamlessly into his boots, the two-footed full-back quickly forging a reputation as the fastest full-back in the English game. In his first season in the first team he helped Wednesday to their second consecutive League title and went on to appear in the 1907 FA Cup Final as Everton were beaten to lift the trophy. He formed a terrific full-back partnership with Willie Layton and was unlucky not to win representative honours during a six-year run in the senior side. His time at Wednesday came to a rather abrupt halt in the spring of 1909 as just a few weeks after a disastrous home defeat to minnows Glossop North End in the FA Cup – in which Harry had the proverbial nightmare in scoring an own-goal and missing a penalty – he was sold to his home-town club, West Bromwich, along with winger George Simpson. The transfer caused quite a stir among Owls fans as the players dropped a division to join the promotion-chasing Baggies, with many fans also questioning the sale of two assets to the side. Unfortunately, only a few months after moving to Albion he suffered a serious injury that effectively ended his days as a professional player, although he did manage to play another season in non-League soccer before his injured knee forced a permanent retirement. He duly returned to Sheffield to gain employment but just 10 years later passed away, at only 42 years of age.

CARBONE, Benito 'Benny'

(1996–99)
Forward, 5ft 6in, 10st 8lb (1998)
Born: 14 August 1971, Bagnara Calabra, Italy
Signed from: Inter Milan, 14 October 1996, £3 million
Transferred: Aston Villa, 21 October 1999, £250,000
Career: Torino, Reggina (loan), Casertana (loan), Ascoli (loan), Napoli, Inter Milan, Wednesday, Aston Villa, Bradford City, Derby County (loan), Middlesbrough (loan), Como, AC Parma, Catanzaro, Vicenza, Sydney FC (guest), Pavia
Debut: 19 October 1996 v Blackburn Rovers (h) Premiership
Last appearance: 19 September 1999 v Newcastle United (a) Premiership
Appearances/Goals: League 86+10/25, FAC 7/1, FLC 3+1/0

Bought by David Pleat from Italian giants Inter Milan, Benito Carbone was the club's record signing when he joined early in the 1996–97 season. The highly talented and diminutive forward – known for his superb close control and pace – started his Owls career in the forward line before moving to what in football parlance is called 'the hole', sitting just behind the front two strikers.

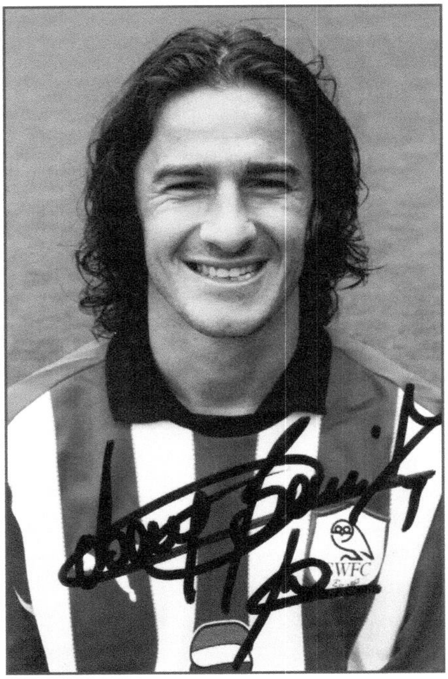

Despite his 'record signing' tag, Wednesday fans were still surprised at Carbone's sheer work rate and wholehearted displays, and he became an instant hit as the Owls finished the season in seventh place. The arrival of his compatriot, Paulo Di Canio, meant that Benny was often a substitute during the early part of the following season, but when Ron Atkinson returned as manager the flamboyant duo were automatic choices. The next season, under new boss Danny Wilson, he was a regular and scored some tremendous long-range goals. His career at Hillsborough hit the rocks in spectacular style at the start of the 1999–2000 season as he refused to be named as a substitute in a game at Southampton, promptly leaving the Dell and flying home to Italy! His relationship with Wednesday fans had already been tested in the previous pre-season when he reported several weeks late for pre-season training and the 'taxi for Mr Carbone' incident meant an acrimonious departure to Aston Villa occurred soon after, Wednesday losing almost £2.5 million on the temperamental Italian. His early career had seen Carbone play for several different Italian League sides, replacing Diego Maradona at Napoli, and win 20 Under-21 caps for his country prior to arriving at the San Siro. After leaving Hillsborough, he helped Villa to the 2000 FA Cup Final, losing to Chelsea, and was then one of several high-profile signings made by Bradford City in the summer of 2000. Relegation from the Premiership, a year later, sent City into financial meltdown, and despite Carbone being named Player of the Year he was eventually sent on loan to Derby County, playing alongside Fabrizio Ravanelli. After three months he returned to City and was fined two weeks wages after, again, refusing to be a substitute. He returned home in 2002 and is now the 'star name' player at minnows Pavia FC.

CATLIN, Arthur Edward 'Ted'

(1930–46)
Left-back, 5ft 10in, 10st 10lb (1935)
Born: 11 January 1911, South Bank, nr. Middlesbrough
Died: 28 November 1990, Sheffield
Signed from: South Bank, 13 November 1930
Transferred: Released, 1946
Career: Middlesbrough (amateur), South Bank, Wednesday, Charlton Athletic (guest), Stockport County (guest)
Debut: 28 March 1931 v Leicester City (h) First Division
Last appearance: 29 April 1939 v Tottenham Hotspur (h) Second Division
Caps: England Full (5), Football League (1)
Appearances/Goals: League 206/0, FAC 21/0

The momentous task of replacing Ernie Blenkinsop in the Wednesday side fell to Ted Catlin, who had served a four-year

apprenticeship in Wednesday's reserve side prior to becoming an automatic choice. Before Blenkinsop's departure, Catlin had only tended to play when his rival was away on international duty, but his form was such that in the mid-1930s Ted was also capped by his country. The full-back retained his first-team spot until the onset of World War Two in 1939, at which point Catlin joined the Army, being stationed in Scotland and then Southern England. Illness meant he was invalided out of the forces in 1943, and Catlin would return to Sheffield, playing almost 100 wartime matches for Wednesday (including the first leg of the 1943 War Cup Final) while working in local industry. After his playing days came to an end – Hugh Swift taking over at left-back – Catlin became a Sheffield licensee while also working as a part-time scout for the Owls. He was promoted to chief scout in 1957 but within a few months was demoted back to his previous role after 'failing to fulfil his duties'. He remained a publican for the remainder of his life; passing away while serving behind the bar.

CAWLEY, Thomas Edward

(1880–92)

Forward, 5ft 9in, 10st (1890)
Born: 2 January 1860, Sheffield
Died: 28 January 1933, Sheffield
Signed from: Parkwood/Burton Star, 1880
Transferred: Retired 1892
Career: St Michael's Juniors, Parkwood/Burton Star, Wednesday, Sheffield Rovers, Lockwood Brothers
Debut: 5 November 1881 v Providence (a) FA Cup
Last appearance: 23 January 1892 v Bolton Wanderers (h) FA Cup
Appearances/Goals: FAC 37/22

Although an outstanding player on the Sheffield football scene in the 1880s, Tom Cawley will perhaps be more remembered for his off-the-field actions than any of his deeds on the playing field. As The Wednesday officials refused to usher in a new era, by turning professional in 1887, several players, including Cawley, formed a rival side named Sheffield Rovers. This new club was intended to turn professional and enter the following season's FA Cup competition. However, at one meeting of the Wednesday members it was Tom Cawley who made an impassioned speech, in favour of professionalism, in one final effort to make the club's hierarchy re-think their decision. Thankfully, for modern-day supporters the committee did change their minds, as if they had not it would be highly likely that Wednesday would have fallen by the wayside as professional clubs started to dominate the game. As a player, Cawley was conspicuous in an era of 'kick and rush' football as he was blessed with great skill and ball control. In addition he was known to be an inordinately fair player and was a much-respected figure among his 19th-century peers. He first appeared for Wednesday in a challenge match against Scottish club Queens Park, in 1880, and remained with the club as they purchased Olive Grove, won the inaugural Football Alliance League title in 1890 and also reached FA Cup Final in the same year. An all-round sportsman who excelled at cricket, Cawley appeared in a staggering 28 representative games for the Sheffield FA but just missed out on a full cap for England, despite once scoring four times in a selection trial match! He eventually became assistant trainer for the Owls while his son, also called Tom, appeared for Wednesday during World War One.

CHAPMAN, Henry 'Harry'

(1899–1911)

Inside-forward, 5ft 6in, 11st 7lb (1907)
Born: 19 January 1878, Kiveton Park, Sheffield
Died: 29 September 1916
Signed from: Attercliffe, 1899
Transferred: Hull City, 27 April 1911, £200
Career: Kiveton Park, Worksop Town, Grimsby Town (trial), Attercliffe, Wednesday, Hull City

Debut: 16 February 1901 v Blackburn Rovers (h) First Division
Last appearance: 28 January 1911 v Notts County (a) First Division
Appearances/Goals: League 270/93, FAC 29/7

Attacker Harry Chapman was held in such high esteem during for the opening decade of the 20th century that he was given the title of 'the finest inside-forward of his day not to be capped'. It was a mystery to Wednesday fans why he never represented England (although the legendary Steve Bloomer was in situ in the national side), as he was without doubt the finest inside-forward of the pre-World War One era. After arriving from local football, the diminutive Chapman quickly formed a terrific partnership with winger Harry Davis – the duo were nicknamed 'the marionettes' – and over the years proved to be a highly versatile player, a rare facet for a player from that era. His incredible work rate and enthusiasm, allied with pace and a great tactical brain, made him almost the perfect player, and he was pivotal as

Wednesday won back-to-back League titles in 1903 and 1904 and the FA Cup in 1907. Unsurprisingly, he was greatly respected by his peers and idolised by the Owlerton faithful during his 10 years in top-flight football. He remained an automatic choice for over a decade and played for a further two seasons, after being appointed player-coach at Hull City, before a knee injury forced his retirement. In March 1913 he was appointed manager, but his story had a sad ending as, aged just 38, Chapman died of the dreaded tuberculosis, followed soon after by his wife, leaving two orphaned children.

CHAPMAN, Lee Roy

(1984–88)

Forward, 6ft 2in, 13st 3lb (1984)
Born: 5 December 1959, Lincoln
Signed from: Sunderland, 12 July 1984, £100,000
Transferred: Niort, 30 June 1988, £290,000 (T.)
Career: Stoke City, Stafford Rangers (loan), Plymouth Argyle (loan), Arsenal, Sunderland, Wednesday, Niort, Nottingham Forest, Leeds United, Portsmouth, West Ham United, Southend United (loan), Ipswich Town, Leeds United (loan), Swansea City
Debut: 25 August 1984 v Nottingham Forest (h) First Division
Last appearance: 7 May 1988 v Liverpool (h) First Division
Appearances/Goals: League 147+2/62, FAC 17+1/10, FLC 17/6, Other 2+1/0

If a player was ever more suited to a team's style of play then it was Lee Chapman and Wednesday in the mid-1980s. The old-fashioned style centre-forward had arrived at Hillsborough as a replacement for fans' favourite Gary Bannister and initially seemed quite an awkward and ungainly player to Owls fans, as he was not particularly adept with the ball at his feet; however, he was bought by Howard Wilkinson for a reason, and over the next four seasons Chapman would lead the Owls attack superbly, being an ideal focal point for Wednesday's direct style of play. His wholehearted displays ensured he also became popular with Owls fans who watched Chapman mature as a player during four seasons at the club – he was voted Player of the Year in 1987 and for a so called 'target man' his goal tally was remarkable. Before arriving at Wednesday his career had been on somewhat of a downward curve as a big money (£500,000) move to Arsenal in 1983 had proven disastrous and he fared little better during a six month stay at Sunderland. His career was certainly resurrected at Hillsborough and it was therefore a surprise to Wednesday fans when he rejected a new contract in the summer of 1988 and looked set to move to Greek football. However, his destination proved a surprise as he signed for obscure French side Niort, with the fee to be decided by a UEFA transfer tribunal. The move then

became somewhat farcical as the French club admitted they could not the pay the £290,000 fee set by the independent panel. The whole sorry episode ended with Chapman back in England as a Nottingham Forest player and Niort making a £60,000 profit on the whole episode!
Honours started to flow for Chapman on his return to England as he won the League Cup and Full Members' Cup at Forest before winning a League Championship medal, under old boss Wilkinson, at Leeds United – coming back to haunt Wednesday with a hat-trick in a televised 6–1 win at Hillsborough. He duly married TV star Leslie Ash and ended his playing days in May 1996, with an admirable 253 goals to his name, from 679 games. He now owns several bars and restaurants, all over the UK.

CRAIG, Thomas Brooks 'Tommy'

(1969–74)

Midfielder, 5ft 7in, 11st 7lb (1970)
Born: 21 November 1950, Glasgow
Signed from: Aberdeen, 7 May 1969, £100,000
Transferred: Newcastle United, 20 December 1974, £120,000
Career: Avon Villa, Drumchapel Amateurs, Aberdeen, Wednesday, Newcastle United, Aston Villa, Swansea City, Carlisle United, Hibernian
Debut: 12 May 1969 v Tottenham Hotspur (h) First Division
Last appearance: 14 December 1974 v Oldham Athletic (h) Second Division
Caps: Scotland Under-23 (1)
Appearances/Goals: League 210+4/38, FAC 9+1/1, FLC 9/1

The 1970s were generally regarded as the worst decade in Wednesday's history, both on and off the field. For the long-suffering fans there was only a handful of players

that helped relieve the gloom, with Tommy Craig being arguably top of that short list. His signing in May 1969 – by caretaker manager Eric Taylor – grabbed the headlines as the fee (£100,000) broke the British record for a teenager, and it did not take long for Wednesday fans to realise that the money was well spent on the 18-year-old. The Glaswegian possessed an outstanding left foot, tremendous shooting ability and did not look out of place in the top-flight during his first full season at Hillsborough. Unfortunately for Craig he moved to Wednesday just when the club was starting its descent down the divisions, and within a year of joining the Owls were relegated to the Second Division. Over the following seasons, Craig was a jewel in the club's midfield, but Wednesday's struggles continued and he slowly started to stagnate as the club's squad became weaker and weaker, Wednesday only avoiding the drop into the third tier in 1974 by winning their final game. The club, of course, were relegated a year later, but halfway through the season Wednesday decided it was time to let their only real asset move on, and Tommy signed for top-flight Newcastle United. His old sparkle returned at St James' Park and he would captain United in the 1976 League Cup Final loss to Manchester City. A spell at Aston Villa was subsequently ruined by injury, and Tommy returned to Scotland to end his playing days in Edinburgh. Since hanging up his boots, Craig has held a wide variety of coaching positions, working for Hibs, Celtic, Aberdeen and Newcastle, and spent just under six months as head coach at Belgium club Charleroi before being dismissed in April 2010.

CRAWSHAW, Thomas Henry 'Tommy'

(1894–1908)

Half-back, 5ft 11in, 12st (1896)
Born: 27 December 1872, Sheffield
Died: 25 November 1960, Sheffield
Signed from: Heywood Central, 24 April 1894
Transferred: Chesterfield Town, June 1908
Career: Park Grange, Attercliffe, Heywood Central, Wednesday, Chesterfield Town, Castleford
Debut: 1 September 1894 v Everton (a) First Division
Last appearance: 7 March 1908 v Sheffield United (h) First Division
Caps: England Full (10), Football League (8)
Appearances/Goals: League 418/24, FAC 47/2

Sheffield-born defender Tommy Crawshaw is without doubt a legend in the club's long history, being the only man to twice win the FA Cup while wearing the blue-and-white stripes. Crawshaw was one of the outstanding players of his generation and is arguably the Owls' greatest-ever captain. Once described as a 'glorious spoiler of the game', Tommy had countless qualities, including superb heading ability, deceptive pace and a commitment to the cause that was unswerving. He led his side by example and in 14 years at The Wednesday not only lifted the aforementioned FA Cups but also led his side to the Second Division title in 1900 and then to consecutive First Division crowns in the early part of the 20th century. Understandably, he was a huge crowd favourite and proved a greater leader than his predecessor, Billy Betts, whom he had been brought in to effectively replace in 1894. He made his debut on the opening day of the 1894–95 campaign and within a year was not only a First Division regular but had already won the first of 10 caps for England, making his debut against Ireland in March 1895. The centre half-back teamed up with Bob Ferrier and Herrod Ruddlesdin to form a famous back line, and even though Tommy had passed his 36th birthday he called upon on all his experience and resolve to captain Wednesday to the Cup Final win over Everton in 1907. Age did eventually start to catch up with the inspirational Crawshaw in the following season, but when he was granted a free transfer there was no shortage of clubs queuing up to secure his signature. He eventually moved to neighbours Chesterfield Town – it was thought his signing was the sole reason the Derbyshire club was re-elected into the Football League a few weeks later – and after ending his playing days was employed as secretary at Glossop, until the start of World War One in 1914. He later ran a newsagents and was a publican in the city before hitting hard times in the early 1950s, Wednesday coming to his financial aid by depositing the equivalent of 10

weeks wages in a bank account so their old player could get back on his feet. Thankfully, he recovered and lived to the grand old age of 88 before passing away in Wharncliffe Hospital.

CURRAN, Edward Terrance 'Terry'

(1979–82)

Winger/forward, 5ft 10in, 11st 3lb (1980)

Born: 20 March 1955, Kinsley, Nr. Pontefract

Signed from: Southampton, 29 March 1979, £85,000

Transferred: Sheffield United, 28 July 1982, £100,000 (T.)

Career: Doncaster Rovers, Nottingham Forest, Bury (loan), Derby County, Southampton, Wednesday, Sheffield United, Everton, Orebro, Huddersfield Town, Panionios, Hull City (trial), Sunderland, Matlock Town (trial), Grantham Town, Grimsby Town, Chesterfield, Goole Town

Debut: 31 March 1979 v Watford (a) Third Division

Last appearance: 15 May 1982 v Norwich City (h) Second Division
Appearances/Goals: League 122+3/35, FAC 3/0, FLC 10/4

With the notable exception of Tommy Craig and Roger Wylde, the 1970s were barren years for charismatic and exciting forwards in a blue-and-white shirt. However, the arrival of Yorkshire-born forward Terry Curran saw his popularity rise to such heights that it exceeded the praise lavished on both of his immediate predecessors. The maverick attacker had just appeared for Southampton in the 1979 League Cup Final prior to joining the Owls, and the club paid a relatively hefty fee to obtain his services. However, the money was well spent as Curran quickly became established in a Jack Charlton-built side that would eventually take the Owls out of the Third Division in 1980. There is no doubt that Curran was one of the most flamboyant players to ever represent the club, and he became a huge cult hero among Owls supporters – you could redeem tokens in the local newspaper for a poster of 'TC' and join his fan club or even purchase his single *Singing the Blues.* His 24 goals in the promotion season – including a spectacular strike in the derby game at Sheffield United – did little to dampen his popularity, and he was duly named in the PFA divisional team for the campaign. His sending off at Oldham, in September 1980, was the trigger for the infamous riot that resulted in Wednesday suffering FA sanctions, and as the months passed his relationship with manager 'Big Jack' started to become strained, with Curran almost asking for a move in December 1981. The two settled their differences, but Curran was never a player to let the grass grow under his feet – his spell at Hillsborough was his longest at any club –

and after his contract expired in the summer of 1982 he ended his days at Hillsborough. With Curran, controversy was never far away, and he certainly grabbed the headlines again as, much to the consternation of Owls fans, he signed for none other than Sheffield United! The clubs wrangled over the transfer fee, Wednesday wanting £250,000 and the Blades offering a derisory £50,000, and the tribunal-decided fee of £100,000 left Jack Charlton fuming. His spell across the city proved unproductive, and he then enjoyed a period at Everton, winning the title in 1985, although he did not appear in enough games to earn a medal. Spells in Swedish and Greek soccer followed, but Curran could never really recapture his form at Wednesday and played for a variety of League, and non-League, sides before retiring in December 1988 after a short spell at Goole Town. He lasted just five weeks as boss at Manchester-based side Mossley before quitting football altogether to buy a transport café on the A1. This eventually developed into several businesses and Curran effectively retired on the proceeds when the site was sold to a developer. He still harbours a return to management though, his usually being the first letter to land at Hillsborough whenever the club begins a search for a new manager! He has been youth coach at several South Yorkshire sides and is currently employed at Rotherham United's Centre of Excellence.

CURTIS, Norman William

(1950–60)
Left-back, 5ft 8½in, 11st (1950)
Born: 10 September 1924, Dinnington
Died: 7 September 2009, York
Signed from: Gainsborough Trinity, 23 January 1950, £1,250
Transferred: Doncaster Rovers, 25 August 1960, £1,000
Career: Gainsborough Trinity, Wednesday, Doncaster Rovers, Buxton
Debut: 25 November 1950 v Bolton Wanderers (h) First Division
Last appearance: 6 February 1960 v Everton (h) First Division
Appearances/Goals: League 310/21, FAC 14/0

Full-back Norman Curtis revelled in the nickname of 'Cannonball' during a decade at Hillsborough when he continued the club's fine tradition of left-backs – following Ernie Blenkinsop and Ted Catlin and preceding Don Megson and Nigel Worthington. After starting his working life as a butcher's boy in Dinnington, Curtis joined the Royal Navy in 1942 and served with distinction as a gunner/wireless operator – spending 324 hours airborne and thankfully emerging from the conflict unscathed. After being de-mobbed he was signed by former Football League side Gainsborough Trinity and worked as an engineer while playing part-time for the Lincolnshire club. He replaced Hugh Swift in the Owls side and, although a quiet man off the field, he took no prisoners on the pitch, proving a fearsome opponent for opposition players unlucky enough to face the two-footed Curtis, during almost a decade in the first team at Hillsborough. Possessing natural pace and the ability to tackle decisively, Curtis won three Second Division Championship medals at Wednesday and was also the club's emergency goalkeeper – he once saved two penalties in a game at Preston North End although the side still lost 6–0, after losing goalie Dave McIntosh to injury. His nickname derived from his unique penalty-taking technique that saw 'Cannonball' usually run from his own half, after a forward had placed the ball on the penalty spot, to smash home past the, frankly scared, goalkeeper! The full-back, who was a wicket-keeper batsman for Lincolnshire CCC during the summer months, eventually lost his place to the emerging Don Megson in 1960 and subsequently moved to take over as player-manager at neighbours Doncaster Rovers. After the Rovers chairman started to exert an influence on player selection, he resigned in July 1961, being appointed to the same role at non-League Buxton. He later ran a sporting goods store in Gainsborough and worked for a Harrogate-based brewery until retiring to York.

DAVIS, Henry 'Harry'

(1900–08)

Winger, 5ft 4in, 11st 10lb (1900)
Born: November 1879, Wombwell, Barnsley
Died: October 1945, Sheffield
Signed from: Barnsley, 22 January 1900, £200
Transferred: Released, April 1908
Career: Wombwell, Ardsley Parish Church, Barnsley, Wednesday
Debut: 3 February 1900 v Newton Heath (a) Second Division
Last appearance: 27 February 1907 v Sunderland (a) FA Cup
Caps: England Full (3), Football League (1)
Appearances/Goals: League 213/59, FAC 22/8

Fortunately for historians, the careers of the two Harry Davis's that played for Sheffield Wednesday did not run concurrent, the two men appearing between 1892 and 1907 but never sharing a dressing room. The Barnsley-born Harry Davis was somewhat of a teenage prodigy and his second club, Ardsley, became so concerned that they would lose their prize

asset that they persuaded the 15-year-old Harry to sign a professional contract. Those concerns were well founded, and two years later Davis moved to Oakwell for the princely sum of £5. The diminutive player with the big heart quickly repaid the Barnsley committee by scoring 25 times in just 56 games and duly joined the Owls part-way through the 1899–1900 season, with the Reds receiving 40 times the amount they had paid for the attacker. He was tried in several attacking positions in his early years at Hillsborough but eventually settled into a role on the right wing, forming a terrific right-sided partnership with Harry Chapman. He quickly became a firm favourite with Owlerton fans – who nicknamed Harry 'Joe Pluck' due to his whole-hearted commitment on the field – and helped Wednesday to consecutive League titles in 1903 and 1904. He was also a great entertainer and would often have the Wednesday fans roaring with laughter due to his propensity, when tackled, to slide for 10 yards or more with his arms and legs in the air! Of course, behind the frivolity was a composed attacker, who possessed a deadly shot, and Davis was capped three times by England, in 1903, while also representing the Football League. His whole-hearted attitude did result in Harry receiving more than his fair share of injuries, and he was forced to miss two FA Cup semi-finals and the 1907 Final before an accidental collision with future Owl, English McConnell, in a Cup tie at Sunderland brought his career to a premature end. He was then briefly assistant trainer at Wednesday before entering the licensing trade and then serving his country in World War One. For the remainder of his working life Harry ran a newsagents shop in Sheffield.

DAVISON, John Edward 'Teddy'

(1908–26)

Goalkeeper, 5ft 7in, 11st 10lb (1913)
Born: 2 September 1887, Gateshead
Died: February 1971, Wortley
Signed from: Gateshead Town, 14 April 1908, £300
Transferred: Mansfield Town, 1 June 1926
Career: Gateshead St Chad's, Gateshead Town, Wednesday, Mansfield Town
Debut: 10 October 1908 v Bristol City (h) First Division
Last appearance: 20 December 1924 v Hull City (a) Second Division
Caps: England Full (1)
Appearances/Goals: League 397/0, FAC 27/0

It is relatively rare that a great player becomes a great manager, but this was true in the case of Wednesday goalkeeper Teddy Davison. The diminutive custodian was arguably more revered for his spells in management than his playing career, but he was truly outstanding in both vocations, spending over 20 years on the field of play and 30 years in the manager's chair. He was scouted by future Wednesday boss Bob Brown – the club's North East scout at the time – from non-League football and after saving a penalty in a trial match he was handed a professional contract by the Owls' hierarchy. Within 18 months Davison had replaced Jack Lyall as first-choice goalkeeper at Owlerton, and he reigned as undisputed number one for almost 15 years. Unfortunately for Davison, he joined the Owls just after they had won the FA Cup and left just before they won their next major honour – the 1926 Second Division title – so he failed to earn any medals. One of nine children, Davison began his working life in the typesetting department of a Newcastle newspaper, but after choosing football as his career he never looked back – his terrific reflexes, superb anticipation and raw courage marking 'Teddy' as one of the greatest custodians of his generation. He became the smallest goalkeeper to play for England when winning his solitary cap in 1922, and he became so respected among his peers that he became known as 'Honest Ted'. It was,

therefore, no surprise when he volunteered for active service during World War One, with Teddy joining the Field Royal Artillery. He spent two years in the French trenches – only playing twice for the Owls while home on leave – but thankfully survived the carnage to reclaim his first-team place when the hostilities ceased. His Wednesday career eventually came to an end when another Owls legend, Jack Brown, took his place, and Davison immediately moved into management, taking over as player-manager at Midland League Mansfield Town in 1926. After success with the Stags and then Chesterfield he accepted a lucrative offer to return to Sheffield to take up the position of Sheffield United boss. More success followed at Bramall Lane – including an appearance in the 1936 FA Cup Final – and he remained in management until finally retiring, aged 71, after a second spell at Saltergate. Known as 'the George Washington of Sheffield football', he still worked as a scout before finally retiring after leaving an indelible mark on the English game.

DI CANIO, Paolo

(1997–99)

Winger, 5ft 9in, 11st 9lb (1998)
Born: 9 July 1968, Rome, Italy
Signed from: Glasgow Celtic, 8 August 1997, £4.5 million
Transferred: West Ham United, 28 January 1999, £2 million
Career: Rinascita 79, Pro Tevere Roma, Lazio, Ternana (loan), Juventus, Napoli (loan), AC Milan, Glasgow Celtic, Wednesday, West Ham United, Charlton Athletic, Lazio, Cisco Roma
Debut: 9 August 1997 v Newcastle United (a) Premiership
Last appearance: 26 September 1998 v Arsenal (h) Premiership
Appearances/Goals: League 39+2/15, FAC 3/0, FLC 4/2

The man with the 'fluttering feet', Roman Paolo Di Canio is without doubt one of the most colourful and controversial characters in the club's long history. He combined his outrageous talent with a streak of unpredictability, a dash of charisma and a drop of Latin temperament which made Di Canio a player that was never out of the limelight, for both positive and negative reasons. His career had started at his home-town club Lazio, where he became established and subsequently moved to Juventus for a whopping £3 million fee in 1990. His terrific ability on the ball made sure he was always a fans' favourite at every club he served and on his day Di Canio was virtually unstoppable – a much faster version of Chris Waddle would perhaps be an ideal description of the fiery right-winger! He won the UEFA Cup with Juve' in 1993 and then moved to another giant of the Italian game, AC Milan, for another large fee. Frustrated at not being able to secure a starting berth at

the San Siro, he moved to Celtic where he was named PFA Player of the Year and became an instant cult hero among the Parkhead fans. A fall out with the Celtic management resulted in Di Canio failing to report for pre-season training in July 1997, and within a few weeks David Pleat had paid £4.5 million for his services – a Wednesday club record that still stands today. Dutch winger Regi Blinker, valued at £1.5 million, switched clubs as part of the transfer, and the famous sideburns joined his compatriot Benny Carbone in a blue-and-white shirt. When Ron Atkinson took over as Owls boss in November 1997 he immediately put both men into the starting line up, and Di Canio flourished, scoring an unbelievable goal at Southampton when he seemed to dribble past the entire Saints defence before firing home an outrageous winner. Sadly, Wednesday's love affair with the Italian would only end in bitter acrimony, following the events of a September 1998 home game with Arsenal. His well-documented push on referee Paul Alcock, which resulted in the official's comical tumble to the turf, landed Di Canio in seriously hot water with the FA – he had previously been fined £1,000 for baring his buttocks after scoring in a game at Wimbledon in August 1997! His misdemeanour resulted in a 10-match ban and £10,000 fine and spelt the end of his career at Wednesday, with Di Canio refusing to return from Italy when his ban came to an end. The two parties then became deadlocked, with the inevitable conclusion being his sale to a Premiership rival for a knockdown fee. He enjoyed a great spell at the Hammers, scoring one of the greatest Premiership goals of all time and, somewhat ironically, winning the FIFA Fair Play award in 2001. He returned home in 2004 and announced his retirement in March 2008.

DOOLEY, Derek MBE

(1947–53)

Centre-forward, 6ft 3in, 12st 8lb (1948)
Born: 13 December 1929, Sheffield
Died: 5 March 2008, Sheffield
Signed from: Denaby United, 16 June 1947
Transferred: Retired injured, February 1953
Career: Sheffield YMCA, Firth Park YM, Lincoln City (amateur), Denaby United, Wednesday, Dundee United (guest)
Debut: 11 March 1950 v Preston North End (h) Second Division
Last appearance: 14 February 1953 v Preston North End (a) First Division
Appearances/Goals: League 61/62, FAC 2/1

Many players may have scored or appeared in more games for Wednesday, but for sheer impact Derek Dooley would surely top the list. After beginning his playing career in local Sheffield football, Dooley signed amateur forms for Lincoln City – appearing in two League games – but it was a reserve-team appearance for the Imps that led the ginger-haired attacker to Hillsborough. He was recommended by opponent, and former Owl, Walt Millership and in the season that followed started to score freely in the club's Yorkshire League side. When he started to impress in reserve-team football he was given a League debut but that proved a disappointing experience for the tall, bustling and powerful attacker. However 49 goals in the 1950–51 season, for the second and third teams, eventually earned Dooley a run in the side in October 1951, and within months he was the talk of not just Sheffield football fans but countrywide. In the remainder of the 1951–52 season Dooley scored an incredible 47 goals in just 31 games, setting a club season scoring record that surely will never be bettered. The down-to-earth and likeable Dooley became a scoring phenomena, and crowds flocked in their thousands to see him play. With a

powerful shot in both feet, pace and an eye for an opening, he terrorised virtually every defender he faced in the second tier, and despite a sticky start to his career in the top-flight he had scored 16 goals in 25 games prior to that fateful day on 14 February 1953, when his young life was shattered. The dramatic events that ended his roller-coaster career started when he collided with Preston goalkeeper George Thompson and suffered a broken right leg, which left Dooley in Preston Royal Infirmary. However, his condition then suddenly started to deteriorate, as a gash on his leg became infected from gas gangrene, and despite various treatments the doctors had no choice but to amputate his leg to save Dooley's life. The tragic news stunned the nation's football fans, with Wednesday supporters reacting in almost disbelief that their star forward would never play again. For Dooley it was a heartbreaking moment, but he showed true Yorkshire grit by looking to the future and, with the aid of a false leg, started working at a local bakery – his testimonial match at Hillsborough raised £15,000 (around £300,000 today) and was the first game played under floodlights at the ground. He eventually became Wednesday's first Development Fund manager, and after being the subject of ITV's *This is Your Life* he was a popular appointment as team manager in January 1971. He preached attacking football, and his side enjoyed a top-half finish in 1972–73 before a combination of injury and illness saw the Owls struggle in the following campaign. The events of Christmas Eve 1973 then stunned the football world again as he was controversially dismissed, with the shameful timing being the main reason for the criticism. Unsurprisingly, he was bitter at his departure, and it would be almost 20 years before he returned to Hillsborough, in the official capacity of managing director of Sheffield United. He had crossed the city in 1974 as commercial manager and was co-opted onto the board in 1983 and twice served as chairman. He was made a 'freeman of the city' in 1993, awarded the MBE in 2003, and after he passed away in 2008 the city of Sheffield named a new section of road 'The Derek Dooley Way' in recognition of a man who was loved and respected by both sets of Sheffield football fans.

EARP, Martin John 'Jack'

(1893–1900)

Right-back, 5ft 9in, 11st 12lb (1894)
Born: 6 September 1872, Nottingham
Signed from: Nottingham Forest, 29 September 1893
Transferred: Stockport County, 26 July 1900
Career: Nottingham Forest (amateur), Everton (amateur), The Corinthians (amateur), Wednesday, Stockport County
Debut: 7 October 1893 v Stoke FC (a) First Division
Last appearance: 31 March 1900 v Leicester Fosse (h) Second Division
Caps: Football League (1)
Appearances/Goals: League 155/7, FAC 19/1

Right-back from the Victorian age who holds a unique place in the club's history, being the first man to lift the FA Cup for Wednesday. He achieved the feat in 1896 when he captained The Wednesday to a 2–1 win over Wolves at the Sydenham Grounds, Crystal Palace. During the early part of his career Earp was strictly amateur, playing for several sides during that period, and had in fact signed amateur forms at Wednesday before deciding to turn professional, after being released by Nottingham Forest. He quickly became a regular at Olive Grove, earning the respect of both players and fans as well as being handed the club captaincy. Although totally right-footed, Earp matured into one of the finest full-backs in England with his 'let's get stuck in' mentality ensuring he was always in the thick of the action. He replaced Tom Brandon in the first team and formed a terrific partnership with fellow full-back Ambrose Langley as Wednesday found their feet in the Football League. He remained as captain until the club was forced to move from Olive Grove in 1899, with Willie Layton taking his place in the senior side. He played only five times as Wednesday won the Second Division title a year later and subsequently led Stockport County in the first League game in their history. He would play only 17 times for County before emigrating to South Africa in 1901, joining the police force.

ELLIS, Keith Duncan

(1953–63)

Forward, 6ft ¾in, 11st 12lb (1955)
Born: 6 November 1935, Sheffield
Signed from: Edgar Allen's, 9 April 1955
Transferred: Scunthorpe United, 4 March 1964, £7,300
Career: Edgar Allen's, Wednesday, Scunthorpe United, Cardiff City, Lincoln City
Debut: 19 March 1955 v Preston North End (h) First Division
Last appearance: 26 October 1963 v Aston Villa (h) First Division
Appearances/Goals: League 102/52, FAC 14/7, Euro 2/1

Although never mentioned in the same breath as Bronco Layne or John Fantham, the scoring record of attacker Keith Ellis was quite remarkable. The tall, bulky forward – who possessed tremendous heading ability – maintained an average of just over a goal every two games during a decade at Wednesday. The Owls had quickly snapped him up after playing just a handful of games for his works side, initially signing amateur forms, and it would be two years before he turned professional, after training to be a draughtsman. When he did break into the senior side his career was interrupted by National Service and then by centre-forward Roy Shiner. However, when Harry Catterick gave Ellis a chance he rewarded his boss in fine style by scoring 33 times as

Wednesday finished fifth, and then second, in the old First Division – the highlight of that scoring sequence being a treble in the famous 7–2 FA Cup win at Manchester United in February 1961. Unfortunately, he did not have the chance to add to his tally as a clash of personalities with new manager Vic Buckingham meant Ellis was banished to the reserve team, playing only a handful of games prior to joining Scunthorpe United. Surprisingly, he failed to recapture his goal touch after leaving Hillsborough and within two years had retired from football altogether. He returned home to South Yorkshire and was a publican before being employed as a sales manager for a major brewery, up to his retirement.

ELLIS, Samuel 'Sam'

(1964–72)
Half-back, 6ft, 11st 7lb (1966)
Born: 12 September 1946, Ashton-under-Lyne
Signed from: WH Smith (Manchester), 12 September 1964
Transferred: Mansfield Town, January 1972, £5,000
Career: Snipe Wanderers, WH Smith (Manchester), Wednesday, Mansfield Town, Lincoln City, Watford
Debut: 4 April 1966 v Blackpool (h) First Division
Last appearance: 7 September 1971 v Carlisle United (a) League Cup
Caps: England Under-23 (3)
Appearances/Goals: League 155+3/1, FAC 13/0, FLC 11/0

Defender Sam Ellis will always be associated with the 1966 FA Cup Final as aged just 19, and with only 10 first-team games for the club, he secured a place in the dramatic 3–2 defeat to Everton at Wembley. It was an injury to first-choice half-back Vic Mobley that opened the door for the flame-haired Ellis, and he grabbed the opportunity with both hands. It would be the start of a successful career for the youngster that would end with over 400 League games to his name at four different League sides. The tall and powerful stopper

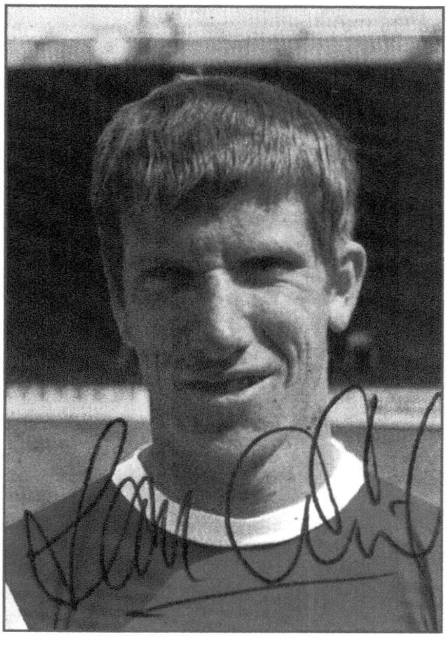

was a regular for Wednesday during the remainder of the decade but lost his place following relegation in 1970. His last appearance came in a disastrous 5–0 Cup defeat at Carlisle United, but he enjoyed better times at Lincoln City, helping Graham Taylor's side to the Fourth Division title in 1976 and even finishing top scorer one season with 13 goals (taking the penalty kicks admittedly helping his total). He earned the nickname 'Super Sam' at Sincil Bank and after 33 goals in 176 games won the basement division Championship again, with Watford in 1979, before retiring. Since then Ellis has remained in the game in a variety of different management and coaching roles, including Blackpool and Bury manager, and in recent years has been assistant manager to Kevin Blackwell, initially at Leeds United and then at Bramall Lane.

FANTHAM, John (1956–69)

Inside-forward, 5ft 8in, 11st 7lb (1964)
Born: 6 February 1939, Sheffield
Signed from: Amateur, 1 October 1956
Transferred: Rotherham United, 9 October 1969, £4,000
Career: Wednesday, Rotherham United, Macclesfield Town
Debut: 1 February 1958 v Tottenham Hotspur (h) First Division
Last appearance: 20 September 1969 v West Ham United (a) First Division
Caps: England Full (1), Under-23 (1), Football League (3)
Appearances/Goals: League 381+7/146, FAC 33+1/11, FLC 6/4, Euro 6/5

Post-war record goalscorer John Fantham initially joined the Owls at the age of 15 before being signed as a professional a year later. Brought up in the Sheffield district of Pitsmoor, Fantham excelled at many sports

and was close to becoming a professional cricketer – he represented Yorkshire boys – before beginning a career in football. After gaining experience in the club's youth and reserve sides, he made his senior debut at inside-right, as a replacement for the injured Albert Quixall. Boasting a powerful shot, true goalscorer's instinct and great vision, Fantham became a first-team regular following the departure of Quixall to Manchester United, in September 1958, although it would be in the role of inside-left where he would play the majority of his Owls career. He was a vital member of the Wednesday side that won the Second Division title in 1959 and then challenged Spurs for the 1961 League title, the Owls eventually finishing as runners-up. Dangerous both inside and outside of the penalty area, he helped Wednesday reach the last eight of the Fairs Cup in 1962 and appeared at Wembley in the 1966 FA Cup Final as Wednesday bravely lost 3–2 to Everton. If a certain Jimmy Greaves had not been blocking his path to the England side, he would almost certainly have won more than a solitary cap for his country, and throughout the 1960s he remained a potent force in the top division – without doubt one of the finest players the city of Sheffield has produced. When Fantham netted his 149th goal for the club he surpassed the post-war record held by his predecessor at inside-left, Redfern Froggatt, and while still a player at Wednesday he started his own hairdressing business. After ending his playing days at non-League Macclesfield Town he settled back in Sheffield, starting his own machine tool business.

FERRIER, Robert 'Bob'

(1894–1906)

Half-back/Inside-forward, 5ft 5in, 10st 7lb (1896)

Born: 13 August 1872, Dumbarton

Died: 11 December 1947

Signed from: Dumbarton, 1894

Transferred: Released, 1906

Career: L'Homme qui rit, Dumbarton, Wednesday

Debut: 1 September 1894 v Everton (a) First Division

Last appearance: 26 April 1905 v Newcastle United (h) First Division

Appearances/Goals: League 308/18, FAC 21/2

The club's side during their first 20 years of League football was characterised by a succession of highly talented Scottish imports. The well worn path started way back in the 1870s with James Lang, and one of the most successful was undoubtedly Bob Ferrier, who remained at The Wednesday for a total of 12 years, after arriving from Dumbarton in the summer of 1894. Nicknamed 'Rabbie' in his homeland, Ferrier was spotted by Wednesday scouts north of the border and duly moved to Sheffield for the start of the club's third season of League football. Although mainly recognised as an outstanding defender, it was as an inside-right that Ferrier made his name at Wednesday, forming a great partnership with Archie Brash as Wednesday reached the 1896 FA Cup Final. Possessing a 'capital long shot', great close control and stamina, Ferrier was unfortunate to miss out on a winners' medal at the Crystal Palace Final, being named only as reserve. He remained a first choice for the club, as part of the forward line, until January 1898 when his career took an unlikely turn. For a FA Cup tie at Sunderland, Wednesday lost regular half-back Harry Brandon to injury and it was decided to use Ferrier as a temporary replacement. However, he made such an impact in his new role that he would never revert back to the attack, adapting to his new defensive role with gusto and handing Wednesday a ready-made replacement for the ageing Brandon. He proved a key player as Wednesday won the Second Division in 1900 and then secured consecutive League titles during the early part of the 20th century. He eventually lost his place during the 1904–05 season, to Herrod Ruddlesdin, and overcame the death of his young wife to help the reserve side to the runners'-up spot in the Midland League in 1906 before returning home to Scotland. He gained employment in shipbuilding on his return home and scouted for the Owls between the two World Wars.

FINNEY, Alan

(1950–66)

Winger, 5ft 8in, 10st 7lb (1950)
Born: 31 October 1933, Langwith, Notts
Signed from: Armthorpe Youth Club, 31 October 1950, £50
Transferred: Doncaster Rovers, 13 January 1966, £3,500
Career: Armthorpe Youth Club, Wednesday, Doncaster Rovers, Alfreton Town, Doncaster Dentists
Debut: 24 February 1951 v Chelsea (h) First Division
Last appearance: 1 January 1966 v Leeds United (a) First Division
Caps: England B (1), Under-23 (3)
Appearances/Goals: League 455/81, FAC 39/6, Euro 10/1

One of only three players in the club's history to have appeared in over 500 first-team games, right-winger Alan Finney was an automatic choice for virtually 15 seasons, after being de-mobbed from National Service in 1951. The pencil-thin, quick and tricky attacker also possessed a quality rare for a winger, consistency, and after making his debut in the same game as Albert Quixall the pair were key players during the 'yo-yo years' of the 1950s, as Wednesday were promoted four times and relegated on three occasions. The former Doncaster and Yorkshire boys player – who was born in Nottinghamshire but brought up in Doncaster – became a huge crowd favourite at Hillsborough and was ever present as the outstanding Owls side of the early 1960s finished runners-up to double winners Tottenham Hotspur in 1961. He played in the first-ever England Under-23 international – against Italy in Bologna in January 1954 – and was also prominent as the club took their first forays into European club football in the early 1960s. Father time finally started to catch up with Finney during the mid-1960s, and he was unlucky that Wednesday's run to the 1966 FA Cup Final, and ground developments linked to the World Cup, meant that he could not host his promised testimonial match at Hillsborough against Sheffield United. The Owls eventually faced his new club, Doncaster Rovers, in his benefit game at Belle Vue, just a few days after the FA Cup Final, with Rovers winning 6–5 in a 'no tackle' match. He won a Fourth Division title with Rovers before retiring from the professional game in 1967 and played in non-League football while being employed at Armthorpe Colliery. He later ran his own bookmakers business in Doncaster, and his post-war appearance record will in all probability never be bettered.

FORD, David

(1963–69)

Forward, 5ft 7in, 10st 7½lb (1966)
Born: 2 March 1945, Sheffield
Signed from: Trainee, 15 January 1963
Transferred: Newcastle United, 16 December 1969, £30,000 (swap for Jackie Sinclair)
Career: Wednesday, Newcastle United, Sheffield United, Halifax Town
Debut: 23 October 1965 v Sunderland (h) First Division
Last appearance: 13 December 1969 v Leeds United (a) First Division
Caps: England Under-23 (2)
Appearances/Goals: League 117+5/31, FAC 10/5, FLC 3/1

Attacker David Ford holds the distinction of being Sheffield Wednesday's first-ever used substitute, although his career at Hillsborough in the 1960s was blighted by injury. An outstanding athlete at grammar school, Ford had looked set to become a civil servant before his mother wrote to Wednesday to request a trial for her offspring. This proved successful, and after signing apprentice forms in January 1962

he became a regular in Derek Dooley's Northern Intermediate League side. After helping the club to the FA Youth Cup semi-finals in 1963, he started to make waves in the reserve side, and such was his form that Wednesday included the teenager on their pre-season tour of Germany in the following year. His sheer speed and shooting ability marked him out as rare talent, but a knee injury suffered on tour effectively wiped out his whole season. He recovered from that setback to make his senior debut and would become an exciting regular, scoring for Wednesday in the 1966 FA Cup Final loss to Everton. He also scored a hat-trick in a 7–0 romp over Burnley in May 1967 but suffered ill fortune again a few months later when he was injured in a road traffic accident that tragically killed his fiancée. In addition to the emotional impact, Ford spent 10 weeks on the treatment table, and he struggled to regain his earlier form as the 1960s drew to a close. It was still a disappointment to Owls fans when he left for Newcastle United, but he was back in Sheffield within 14 months, signing for Sheffield United. After helping the Blades to promotion in 1971, he ended his playing days at Halifax Town and still runs his Sheffield-based plumbing and heating business, maintaining strong links with Wednesday.

FROGGATT, Redfern

(1943–62)

Inside-forward, 5ft 11in, 11st 1lb (1948)
Born: 23 August 1924, Sheffield
Died: 26 December 2003, Sheffield
Signed from: Sheffield YMCA, 11 November 1943
Transferred: Stalybridge Celtic, August 1962
Career: Sheffield YMCA, Wednesday, Stalybridge Celtic
Debut: 5 January 1946 v Mansfield Town (a) FA Cup

Last appearance: 30 April 1960 v West Ham United (a) First Division
Caps: England Full (4), B (1), Football League (1)
Appearances/Goals: League 434/139, FAC 24/9

When Redfern Froggatt captained Wednesday to the Second Division Championship in 1959 he followed in the footsteps of his father, Frank, who achieved the feat back in 1926 during a relatively brief spell at Hillsborough. His father played fewer than 100 games for the Owls, but Redfern was one of the best inside-forwards of his generation, winning four caps for his country during the early 1950s – playing alongside his cousin, Jack, in every game. His qualities were numerous, with 'Red' earning the reputation as an all-round player who was equally adept at scoring himself or creating chances for his colleagues. His intelligence on the field marked him out as one of the Owls' best players of the immediate post-war period, as Wednesday struggled to get out of the Second Division and then bounced between the top divisions during the 1950s. Although his first 'official' game for the Owls came in a 1946 FA Cup tie, he had made his first-team bow over three years earlier – in February 1943 – after being spotted playing for Sheffield YMCA in a Millhouses Park five-a-side tournament. He held a reserve occupation during the war so was able to represent Wednesday on 80 occasions prior to the national Football League restarting in September 1946. From that point on, Froggatt was a first-team regular, and even when he looked set to lose his place in the side he would use his versatility by simply changing positions – a third of his goals came while he was playing as a right-winger, although he is commonly recognised as an inside-left. After setting a

new post-war mark for appearances and goals, he would play mainly reserve-team soccer in his final two seasons at Hillsborough before becoming a 'big-name' signing for non-League Stalybridge Celtic. After retiring from the game, he worked as a sales rep for an oil company, before living in Sheffield for the remainder of his life.

GANNON, Edward 'Eddie'

(1949–55)
Half-back, 5ft 9½in, 11st 9lb (1949)
Born: 3 January 1921, Dublin, Eire
Died: 31 July 1989, Dublin, Eire
Signed from: Notts County, 10 March 1949, £15,000
Transferred: Shelbourne, 21 April 1955, Free
Career: Star 'O'Connell' Celtic, Creighton Rovers, Dublin Pearse Street, Distillery, Shelbourne, Notts County, Wednesday, Shelbourne
Debut: 12 March 1949 v Grimsby Town (a) Second Division

Last appearance: 2 April 1955 v Cardiff City (h) First Division
Caps: Eire Full (11)
Appearances/Goals: League 204/4, FAC 15/0

Wednesday had to fight off competition from several clubs to capture the signature of Irish international wing-half Eddie Gannon, but he gave the club great service over a period of five years. The studious and unassuming Dubliner had actually not played any competitive football until the age of 18, but after being handed a trial in Irish soccer he graduated quickly through the ranks in his homeland to win a Championship medal with Shelbourne in 1944. His form was such that it was inevitable that he would move to English football, and he would win the first of his 14 caps for Eire during his spell at the Meadow Lane club. He would enjoy the best years of his career at Wednesday, with his attacking forays from defence creating countless chances for the likes of Jackie Sewell and Derek Dooley. Like the majority of the men who played for the Owls in the 1950s, he experienced a few promotion and relegation seasons, while in the latter part of his career in England he actually lived in Dublin and flew over for games! Well known for his generous nature – he once gifted 11 of his international jerseys to an Irish youth side that could not afford to buy a kit – Gannon eventually returned home to become player-manager at Dublin side Shelbourne. Despite being in his mid-30s he was capped a final time by his country, and after managing Irish side Bolton Athletic he was employed in the power industry for the remainder of his working life.

GRANT, Lee Anderson

(2007–10)

Goalkeeper, 6ft 4in, 13st 11lb (2007)
Born: 27 January 1983, Hemel Hempstead
Signed from: Derby County, 1st July 2007, Free
Transferred: Burnley, 27 July 2010, u/d
Career: Derby County, Burnley (loan), Oldham Athletic (loan), Wednesday, Burnley
Debut: 11 August 2007 v Ipswich Town (a) Championship
Last appearance: 2 May 2010 v Crystal Palace (h) Championship
Appearances/Goals: League 136/0, FAC 4/0, FLC 5/0

Following the departure of Kevin Pressman in 2004 the Owls struggled to find a suitable replacement, using several loan players including Brad Jones, Scott Carson, Paul Gallagher and Mark Crossley. It was not until Brian Laws captured the signature of Derby County reserve-team player Lee Grant, in the summer of 2007, that the problem position was finally solved. Despite a somewhat shaky start to his Wednesday career, being challenged by fellow newcomer Rob Burch, the stopper eventually became established as the club's first-choice 'keeper and slowly improved season upon season. A brilliant shot stopper, Grant matured into one of the

best goalkeepers in the Championship and was named fans' and players' Player of the Year as the Owls suffered relegation in 2010. He had started as a trainee at Derby County and, in almost six years as a professional, totalled 79 appearances for the Derbyshire-based club. In addition, he was sent on loan spells to both Burnley (one game) and Oldham (16 games) prior to becoming the undisputed number one at Hillsborough. After 136 consecutive appearances for the club he was bought by former manager, Brian Laws, for Burnley in the summer of 2010.

GREGORY, Robert 'Bob'

(1873–84)
Centre-forward
Born: third quarter, 1853, Sheffield
Died: October 1910, Sheffield
Signed from: Hallam FC, 1873
Transferred: Hallam FC, 1884
Career: Oxford Street (Sheffield), Hallam, Wednesday, Hallam
Debut: 18 December 1880 v Blackburn Rovers (a) FA Cup
Last appearance: 1 December 1883 v Staveley (a) FA Cup
Appearances/Goals: FAC 17/14

It would be fair to say that Bob Gregory was the club's first prolific centre-forward and a hero to the Wednesday fans of the era. The native Sheffielder, like his contemporaries, was amateur throughout his playing career and, after becoming a regular at Wednesday during the late 1870s, scored a hat-trick in the club's FA Cup debut – a resounding 4–0 win at Blackburn Rovers in 1880. He was also the first Wednesday player to score five times in a senior fixture – achieving the feat against Spilsby in 1882 – and led the club's attack in the first 17 games played in the new national Cup competition. Described as being 'difficult to knock off the ball' and a 'great dribbler', Gregory won several local honours while in Wednesday colours, including three Wharncliffe Charity Cups and two Sheffield Challenge Cups, and was a major factor in the club growing to

become the dominant force in Sheffield football. He was also picked for a North v South trial game in 1881 – a game that was used by the FA to help pick players for the national side – and was captain for The Wednesday on numerous occasions. Wednesday staged a benefit match for Gregory, at Bramall Lane in 1883, and he eventually returned to Sheffield-based side Hallam, a team he also played cricket for during the summer months.

HARKES, John Andrew

(1990–93)
Defender/midfielder, 5ft 10in, 11st 10lb (1993)
Born: 8 March 1967, Kearny, New Jersey, US
Signed from: US Soccer Federation, 3 December 1990, $185,000
Transferred: Derby County, 17 August 1993, £800,000
Career: Missouri Athletic Club, US Soccer Federation, Wednesday (trial), Blackburn Rovers (trial), Glasgow Celtic (trial), Wednesday (loan), Wednesday (perm.), Derby County, US Soccer Federation, West Ham United (loan), Washington D.C. United, Nottingham Forest (loan), New England Revolution, Columbus Crew
Debut: 31 October 1990 v Swindon Town (h) League Cup
Last appearance: 20 May 1993 v Arsenal (N) FA Cup Final Replay
Caps: US Full (12)
Appearances/Goals: League 59+22/7, FAC 12+1/1, FLC 17/3, Euro 4/0, Other 3/0

Although he spent fewer than three years at Wednesday, US international John Harkes was one of the most popular players of recent times. He was a relative unknown when he first arrived at Hillsborough, for a trial in January 1990, and was soon forgotten when he returned to the US team camp in preparation for Italia '90. Manager, Ron Atkinson remained undecided, however, and the likeable Harkes returned on loan in September 1990, after having appeared in all three games played by his country in Italy. Although primarily a midfielder, it was a long-term injury to regular right-back, Roland Nilsson, that launched Harkes's English League career as 'Big Ron' utilised the newcomer at full-back. He duly impressed greatly – grabbing the headlines with an amazing long-range strike in a League Cup tie at Derby County – and the Owls made the transfer permanent, paying his national association a fee as they held his registration. The hard work and 100 per cent commitment shown by Harkes quickly endeared him to Wednesday fans, and he proved a capable replacement for Nilsson. When the Swede regained fitness, Harkes moved back into midfield and played a pivotal role, along with Nilsson, as Wednesday snuffed out the threat of Manchester United winger Lee Sharpe to lift the League Cup in 1991. During his time in the blue-and-white shirt, Harkes became the first US National to appear in a

domestic Cup Final and then the first to score – netting in the 1993 League Cup Final defeat to Arsenal. He was a first-team regular throughout the memorable early 1990s, helping the club to third spot in the top division and into UEFA Cup football, but contracted 'itchy feet' in the summer of 1993, refusing two contract offers from Wednesday. He eventually left, for Derby County, but experienced a mixed time at the Baseball Ground, later admitting that he should never have left Hillsborough. He later returned to his homeland to help launch the new MLS competition and captained DC United to the inaugural Championship. The title was retained a year later, and Harkes was now captain of his country – eventually winning 90 caps for the Stars and Stripes. He was later re-signed by his old boss, Ron Atkinson, for a brief spell at Nottingham Forest but would end his career back in the US, winning the domestic Cup with Columbus Crew in 2002. He now works as a commentator for ESPN on their coverage of the MLS.

HENDERSON, William 'Willie'

(1972–74)

Winger, 5ft 4in, 11st 2lb (1972)

Born: 24 January 1944, Baillieston, Scotland

Signed from: Durban City, 10 July 1972, £750

Transferred: Contract cancelled, 29 April 1974

Career: Edinburgh Athletic, Glasgow Rangers, Durban City, Wednesday, Miami Toros (loan), Hong Kong Rangers, Carolina Hill, Sliema Wanderers (trial), Airdrie

Debut: 12 August 1972 v Fulham (h) Second Division

Last appearance: 27 April 1974 v Bolton Wanderers (h) Second Division

Appearances/Goals: League 42+6/5, FAC 5/0, FLC 3/0

Diminutive winger Willie Henderson was a shining light during the dark days of the 1970s, entertaining fans with his swashbuckling wing play and notoriously bad eyesight! The right-sided attacker had made his name during over a decade at Scottish giants Glasgow Rangers, 'the wee blue train' appearing in over 300 games and winning a plethora of trophies, including League titles, both domestic Cups and an appearance in the 1967 Cup-Winners' Cup Final loss to Bayern Munich. He remained first choice at Ibrox until the early 1970s and then left for a spell in South African football, after Tommy McLean took his place in the Rangers side. It was from the Southern Hemisphere club that Henderson arrived at Wednesday, manager Derek Dooley capturing his signature, and it became part of club folklore that Willie's vision was so poor that after receiving the ball he would dribble towards the touchline, with his head down, and only cross when he could actually see the white line! His exciting forays made the Owls an attractive side during the 1972–73 season as they

challenged for promotion before falling away to finish in 10th place. His second season at Wednesday was badly affected by injury although he played his part in the final game of the season where a win secured the Owls' Second Division status. At the end of the season he left to become a player-manager in the Far East and remained in South East Asia for almost four years, prior to returning home to end his playing days in Scottish soccer. After spending several years in Spain he returned to Glasgow where he now runs a bar, as well as helping Rangers on a matchday, entertaining corporate clients.

HIRST, David Eric

(1986–97)
Forward, 5ft 11in, 13st 10lb (1997)
Born: 7 December 1967, Cudworth, Barnsley
Signed from: Barnsley, 11 August 1986, £300,000
Transferred: Southampton, 17 October 1997, £2 million
Career: Barnsley, Wednesday, Southampton, Brunsmeer Athletic (sun.)
Debut: 23 August 1986 v Charlton Athletic (a) First Division
Last appearance: 4 October 1997 v Everton (h) Premiership
Caps: England Full (3), B (3), Under-21 (7)
Appearances/Goals: League 261+33/106, FAC 12+7/6, FLC 26+9/11, Euro 3/1, Other 7/4

Among the top 10 greatest scorers in the Owls' history, David Hirst spent 11 years at Wednesday, after joining as a raw 18-year-old from neighbours Barnsley, for what proved a bargain fee. His tremendous pace, lethal left foot and eye for a chance marked him as the best striker to represent the club since the days of Bronco Layne, in the early 1960s, and arguably proved to be Howard Wilkinson's best buy during his five years

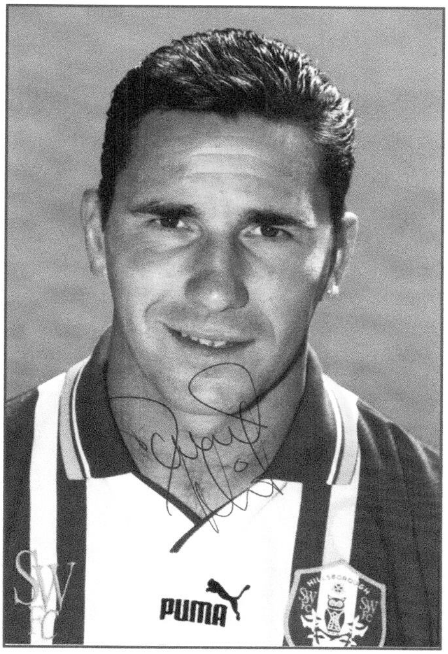

at the helm in the mid-1980s. The lethal attacker made a dream home debut when scoring with his first touch, after being introduced as a substitute, in the 2–2 draw with Everton in August 1986. During his first season provided several glimpses of the talent that would develop during his time with Wednesday. He was never really a regular under Wilkinson, and it needed the arrival of Ron Atkinson for Hirst to became an established first-team player – forming a great partnership with Dalian Atkinson in the 1989–90 season that ended with Hirst named as fans' Player of the Year, but the Owls were relegated from the top flight. That surprise relegation hastened his strike partner's move to Spanish football, but 'Big Ron' struck gold when he teamed new signing Paul Williams with Hirst. The duo clicked immediately, and Hirst would score a total of 32 goals in the 1990–91 season as Wednesday bounced straight back to the First Division and won their first major trophy since 1935 – the Barnsley-born forward playing in the League Cup Final win over Manchester United. His form was such that Hirst received his first call-up for the national side – scoring against New Zealand while on tour – and was being mentioned in the same breath as Alan Shearer, with Wednesday reputed to have refused a club record bid from Manchester United for his services. He continued to score freely in an injury hit season back in the top flight, and unfortunately that would be the story of his remaining years with the Owls, spells in the first team punctuated by various injury problems. When fit and on form, Hirst was comparable with any forward of his generation and played a part in the memorable 1992–93 season when the Owls reached both domestic Cup Finals, the hugely popular number nine netting in the 1–1 FA Cup Final draw against Arsenal. It was a persistent Achilles problem that held Hirst back, and in fact in the last five years of his time at Wednesday he recorded only 28 of the total 128 goals he scored while at Hillsborough. Wednesdayites were sad to see him leave, for a sizeable fee, to Southampton but within three years he had announced his retirement from the game, after failing to start a first-team game for 18 months. He later played in Sheffield Sunday football, alongside Chris Waddle, and is now a regular face behind the scenes at Hillsborough, running various social events and helping with corporate hospitality.

HODGE, Martin John

(1983–88)

Goalkeeper, 6ft 2in, 13st 7lb (1983)
Born: 4 February 1959, Southport
Signed from: Everton, 22 August 1983, £50,000
Transferred: Leicester City, 26 August 1988, £250,000
Career: Southport Trinity, Plymouth Argyle, Everton, Preston North End (loan), Oldham Athletic (loan), Gillingham (loan), Preston North End (loan), Wednesday, Leicester City, Hartlepool United, Rochdale, Plymouth Argyle
Debut: 27 August 1983 v Swansea City (a) Second Division
Last appearance: 12 March 1988 v Manchester United (a) First Division
Appearances/Goals: League 197/0, FAC 25/0, FLC 24/0, Other 3/0

When Martin Hodge arrived from Everton, initially on loan, it was expected he would act solely as understudy to new signing, England Under-21 goalkeeper Iain Hesford. However, the careers of both players took completely different paths as after Hodge was picked for the opening game of the 1983–84 season he would appear in a club-record 214 consecutive games, while Hesford never played a competitive match for the Owls! He became a vital cog in Howard Wilkinson's style of play – Hodge taking the majority of the free-kicks awarded in his half of the field – and his terrific shot-stopping ability and

consistency meant he came agonisingly close to a call-up for the 1986 England World Cup squad. He remained a first choice for several seasons at Hillsborough, being one of only a handful of goalkeepers to be beaten by a fellow custodian when Coventry's Steve Ogrizovic scored a freak goal past him in October 1986. The 1987–88 season proved to be an unhappy one for Hodge as poor form and injury meant he lost his first-team place to the emerging Kevin Pressman, and his Owls career came to a close when he joined Leicester City on loan. His ill luck continued in the East Midlands as he was injured in his first game for the Foxes, after signing permanently, and spent several weeks on the treatment table. He would end his playing days back at his first club, Plymouth Argyle, and in 1996 returned to Wednesday, after being appointed as the Owls' first-ever full-time goalkeeping coach. He later spent two torrid seasons in charge of the reserve team before being appointed first-team coach in June 2001. He was dismissed, along with manager Terry Yorath, in October 2002 and was then goalie coach at both Rochdale and Leeds United before being appointed scout for Watford.

HOOPER, Mark

(1927–39)
Winger, 5ft 5in, 10st 7lb (1927)
Born: 14 July 1901, Darlington
Died: 9 March 1974, Sheffield
Signed from: Darlington, 21 January 1927, £1,950
Transferred: Rotherham United, 1939
Career: Cockfield Colliery, Darlington, Wednesday, Rotherham United
Debut: 22 January 1927 v Leicester City (h) First Division
Last appearance: 7 May 1938 v Tottenham Hotspur (a) Second Division
Appearances/Goals: League 384/124, FAC 39/11

If the title of the 'greatest winger in Wednesday's history' was decided then there is no doubt that inter-war player Mark Hooper would finish high, if not take the accolade outright. One factor that could tip the award in his favour – which was also shared by his contemporary Ellis Rimmer – was an incredible goals record as the diminutive winger netted an astonishing 135 times, averaging almost a goal every three games! The slightly built attacker – he wore only size 4 boots – had first come to the fore with village side Cockfield who earned national headlines in the early 1920s when they progressed all the way to the last four of the highly prestigious FA Amateur Cup. He eventually turned professional with Darlington in 1924, but not before Wednesday boss Bob Brown had made a rare error of judgement, the club's legendary manager deciding that the wingman was simply too small. It was an opinion that was soon to change though as Hooper would grab a hat-trick against the

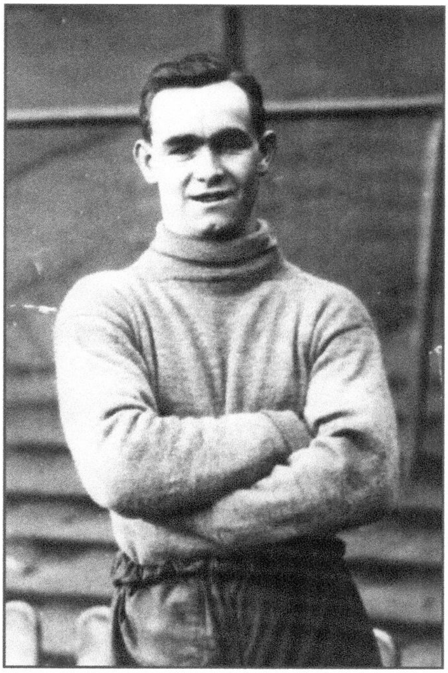

Owls in a March 1926 win at the Feethams and within a year was signing for First Division Wednesday. He replaced Welshman Rees Williams on the right wing and would effectively remain there for over a decade, helping Wednesday through the greatest period in their history. He possessed the heart of a lion, being fearless against players much taller and heavier, and was a real 'bag of tricks', possessing tremendous ball control, deceptive speed, terrific crossing ability and a fierce shot. League titles and an FA Cup win followed – Hooper netting in the 1935 Cup Final win over West Bromwich Albion – while he also set a new club record of 189 consecutive appearances, which was only bettered by Martin Hodge in the early 1980s. An operation to remove his cartilage, in May 1937, severely curtailed his senior appearances and he acted as player-coach in the club's A team for two seasons before leaving the Owls just before World War Two. A year after joining Rotherham United, he officially retired from the field of play but remained at Millmoor for a further 18 years, initially as second-team trainer and then first-team trainer until retiring in 1958, following a major operation. For the remainder of his life he ran his sweet and tobacconists shop near to the Wednesday ground, which had first been opened back in the 1930s when he will still a regular for the Owls.

HUNT, Douglas Arthur

(1938–46)

Centre-forward, 5ft 10in, 11st 8lb (1935)
Born: 19 May 1914, Shipton Bellinger, Hampshire
Died: 30 May 1989, Yeovil
Signed from: Barnsley, 1 March 1938, £3,875
Transferred: Clapton Orient, April 1946, £620
Career: Winchester City, Southampton (amat.), Northfleet United, Tottenham Hotspur, Barnsley, Wednesday, Brentford (guest), Tottenham Hotspur (guest), Aldershot (guest), Fulham (guest), West Ham United (guest), Clapton Orient, Gloucester City
Debut: 5 March 1938 v Manchester United (h) Second Division
Last appearance: 29 April 1939 v Tottenham Hotspur (h) Second Division
Appearances/Goals: League 42/30, FAC 6/1

Although forward Doug Hunt played in only one full peacetime season for Wednesday, he wrote himself into the club's history books as the only player to have scored six times in a single game for the club. He achieved the feat in the November 1938 Second Division home game against Norwich City, scoring after 17, 25, 39, 44, 65 and 87 minutes to set a unique mark. The month proved a remarkable period for the attacker as Hunt had scored four times a few days prior to the game – in a County Cup game against Rotherham United – and seven days later had to be content with just three goals as Wednesday won 5–1 at Luton Town! In total he would score 25 times in that 1938–39 campaign as Wednesday were just beaten to a promotion place by neighbours United. Unfortunately, Owls fans never had the opportunity to see if the tall and well-built attacker could continue his rich vein of scoring as after war was declared, in September 1939, he would only appear in the occasional wartime fixture, prior to joining the Armed forces. Although still signed to Wednesday, he played as a guest for a variety of southern-based teams during the hostilities – winning the London Cup with Brentford in 1942 – before briefly returning to Hillsborough after being de-mobbed in 1945. He appeared in a handful of League North games during the transitional 1945–46 season but left to become player-coach at Leyton Orient. After his playing days ended, he spent a remarkable 28 years as trainer coach to non-League Yeovil Town, prior to retiring in 1986.

HYDE, Graham

(1988–99)

Midfielder, 5ft 7in, 11st 11lb (1996)
Born: 19 November 1970, Doncaster
Signed from: Trainee, 17 May 1988
Transferred: Birmingham City, 5 February 1999, Free
Career: Wednesday, Birmingham City, Chesterfield (loan), Peterborough United (loan), Bristol Rovers, Hereford United, Worcester City, Hednesford Town, Halesowen Town, Fleet Town
Debut: 14 September 1991 v Manchester City (a) First Division
Last appearance: 22 August 1998 v Tottenham Hotspur (a) Premiership
Appearances/Goals: League 126+46/11, FAC 13+5/2, FLC 17+3/2, Euro 7/0, Other 1/1

Tigerish midfield player who progressed through the ranks to become a first team regular during the mid-1990s. While a first

year professional, Hyde was in the club's youth side that won the NIL Cup in 1989, and two years later he won a Championship medal as the reserve side lifted the Central League title, appearing alongside the likes of Jon Newsome and David Wetherall. The success of the second team proved a springboard to senior football for the small but competitive player, and he duly became a regular under the reign of Trevor Francis, appearing in both of the Wembley Cup Final losses in 1993. In Francis's last two seasons at the helm, Hyde was an automatic choice, but the arrival of David Pleat changed his status with injuries, poor form and the form of Mark Pembridge all contributing to several spells on the sidelines for the popular Yorkshire-born player. Disciplinary problems during the 1997–98 season also meant he spent several weeks suspended and when old teammate, Danny Wilson, was put in charge his first-team opportunities seemingly disappeared altogether. Therefore, after 10 years as a professional at Hillsborough, he left for Birmingham City where another former colleague, Trevor Francis, was manager. He enjoyed a season in the Blues first team but would eventually drift into the lower reaches of the Football League before dropping into Conference football. He ended his playing days under the management of another former Wednesday player, Andy Sinton, at Hampshire side Fleet Town.

JOHNSON, Jeffrey David 'Jeff'

(1976–81)

Midfielder, 5ft 8in, 11st 7lb (1978)
Born: 26 November 1953, Cardiff
Signed from: Crystal Palace, 1 July 1976, Free
Transferred: Newport County, 30 July 1981, £60,000
Career: Clifton Athletic, Manchester City, Swansea City (loan), Crystal Palace, Wednesday, Newport County, Gillingham, Port Vale, Barrow
Debut: 14 August 1976 v Grimsby Town (a) League Cup
Last appearance: 8 May 1981 v West Ham United (h) Second Division
Appearances/Goals: League 175+5/6, FAC 14/1, FLC 17/2

Welsh Under-23 international Jeff Johnson was one the finest free transfer signings in Wednesday's history, being an automatic choice for five seasons as the club dragged themselves back out of the Third Division in the late 1970s. Crystal Palace manager Malcolm Allison had, somewhat hastily, released the stylish midfielder, and Owls boss Len Ashurst quickly secured his signature. He had appeared in 87 games for the Eagles and under Ashurst, and his successor Jack Charlton, Johnson was one of the first names on the team sheet and was named fans' Player of the Year in the 1979–80 promotion season. He remained a regular during the club's first season back in the second tier of English football but duly signed for Len Ashurst again, his old boss being in charge of then League side Newport County. Incidentally, he was the final player to be sold from the side that Jack Charlton had inherited in October 1977. After dropping into non-League football at Barrow, a broken leg ended his playing days, and he is now a taxi driver in Manchester after having obtained his PSV licence soon after hanging up his boots.

JOHNSON, Peter 'Charlie'

(1957–65)

Full-back, 5ft 9in, 10st 8lb (1961)
Born: 31 July 1931, Rotherham
Signed from: Rotherham United, 24 December 1957, £6,000
Transferred: Peterborough United, 1 July 1965, Free
Career: Rawmarsh Welfare, Rotherham United, Wednesday, Peterborough United

Debut: 25 December 1957 v Preston North End (h) First Division
Last appearance: 2 January 1965 v Sheffield United (a) First Division
Appearances/Goals: League 181/6, FAC 19/0, Euro 7/0

Full-back Peter Johnson made his name with home-town club Rotherham United, although he was utilised in a variety of positions by the Millers, including a spell at centre-forward that brought 'Charlie' a League hat-trick in November 1956. The Owls were mainly impressed by his defensive qualities, however, and after failing to secure his signature in 1954 – Johnson did not want to play for any other club but Rotherham – they finally got their man on Christmas Eve 1957, winger Albert Broadbent travelling in the opposite direction as part of the deal. The new signing did not immediately become a regular at Wednesday, but the departure of veteran Ron Staniforth opened the door to the first team, and Johnson was an ever present in four consecutive seasons in the early 1960s as the Owls reached the FA Cup semi-finals in 1960, finished runners-up to Spurs a year later and reached the last eight of the Fairs Cup in 1962. It would actually be an off-the-field event that effectively ended his time as a first-team regular as during the club's 1964 pre-season tour of West Germany he fell out with manager Alan Brown, on a non-footballing matter. The incident cast a shadow over the remainder of his Wednesday career and after just two more senior games for the club he was replaced by Brian Hill and left for Peterborough less than 12 months later. After his career came to a close he owned a Tailors shop back in Rotherham and worked at the Templeborough Steel Works until his retirement.

JOICEY, Brian

(1971–76)

Forward, 5ft 11in, 12st 2lb (1974)
Born: 19 December 1945, Winlanton, County Durham
Signed from: Coventry City, 27 August 1971, £55,000
Transferred: Barnsley, July 1976, Free
Career: Clara Vale, Ashington, Blyth Spartans, Tow Law Town, North Shields, Coventry City, Wednesday, Barnsley, Frickley Athletic, Matlock Town, Royal Oak Coal Aston (Sun.)
Debut: 31 August 1971 v Middlesbrough (a) Second Division
Last appearance: 20 March 1976 v Rotherham United (a) Third Division
Appearances/Goals: League 144+1/48, FAC 7+3/4, FLC 9+2/1

After having played all of his early career in north-east amateur football, Brian Joicey was elevated into the professional ranks at the relatively late age of 23, after scoring the only goal of the game as North Shields

won the prestigious FA Amateur Cup at Wembley. He made a bright start in the full-time game at Coventry City but was subsequently rescued from the Sky Blues' reserves by Owls boss Derek Dooley. The move proved a fillip for both parties, as the swashbuckling forward became an instant favourite with Wednesday fans, scoring 16 times in his debut season. He bettered that tally in the 1972–73 season, netting 20 goals, and will forever be remembered for his FA Cup treble against top-flight Crystal Palace, at Villa Park, that sent the London side tumbling out of the competition. As the Owls' fortunes started to slump further, Joicey's form also suffered although he did net another famous goal in the club's history – his 90th-minute equaliser against Oxford United in April 1975 triggered wild scenes of celebration as Wednesday had not scored for eight games! After dropping into the reserve side, he moved to neighbours Barnsley where, after rediscovering his scoring form, his professional career came to a dramatic close in November 1978. After being kicked in the kidneys during a game at York City he later collapsed, after suffering a stroke, and was forced to hang up his boots. In the same season the determined Joicey was back playing, in non-League soccer, while he worked in the car sales trade for the rest of his working life.

KAY, Anthony Herbert 'Tony'

(1954–62)

Halfback, 5ft 8in, 10st 7lb (1954)
Born: 13 May 1937, Sheffield
Signed from: Trainee, 22 May 1954
Transferred: Everton, 27 December 1962, £60,000
Career: Wednesday, Everton
Debut: 8 April 1955 v Bolton Wanderers (a) First Division
Last appearance: 22 December 1962 v Everton (h) First Division
Caps: England Under-23 (7), Football League (3)
Appearances/Goals: League 179/10, FAC 18/0, Euro 6/0

Unfortunately for outstanding wing-half Tony Kay, his career will always be blighted by the bribes scandal that rocked British soccer in 1964. Along with former Owls teammates, Bronco Layne and Peter Swan, the FA banned him for life, after being

found guilty of betting on his own side to lose a top-flight fixture. Before his career came to a shuddering halt, Kay had become established at the top of the English game, winning the First Division title with Everton and earning his solitary cap for England in 1963. The former Sheffield boys player had originally been seconded to the Owls in 1952, and after a two-year 'apprenticeship' he turned professional, making his senior debut within 12 months. His highly competitive nature, superb passing ability and strong tackling ensured he quickly became a first-team regular at Hillsborough, and he became a member of the famous back line, along with Swan and Tom McAnearney, that took the club to the Second Division title in 1959. The trio also powered Wednesday to First Division runners'-up spot behind the great Spurs side two years later before his shock departure to Everton, his old boss Harry Catterick breaking the bank to obtain his services. He spent four months in jail because of the bribes scandal and worked as a bookmaker after his release, prior to moving to Spain. He returned to England in 1986 and ran a Sports Centre in London, while also playing for an Arsenal old boys team until his 62nd year, before retiring to Merseyside.

KEAN, Frederick William 'Fred'

(1920–28)

Halfback, 5ft 8in, 12st (1935)
Born: 1898–99, Sheffield
Died: 28 October 1973, Sheffield
Signed from: Portsmouth, June 1920
Transferred: Bolton Wanderers, 13 September 1928, £5,600
Career: Soldiers and Sailors Federated Team, Crookes United, Sheffield FC, Hallam, Portsmouth, Wednesday, Bolton Wanderers, Luton Town, Sutton Town
Debut: 28 August 1920 v Barnsley (a) Second Division
Last appearance: 8 September 1928 v Sunderland (h) First Division
Caps: England Full (7), Football League (4)
Appearances/Goals: League 230/8, FAC 17/0

Local product Fred Kean's route to Wednesday started in Sheffield junior football, just after World War One, but it was a move to Southern League Portsmouth that resulted in a somewhat bizarre move to Hillsborough – Portsmouth manager Bob Brown selling Kean to the Owls and promptly following him to Wednesday a few days later! The club's legendary boss clearly had plans for inside-forward Kean, and he was quickly switched to a defensive position. The move proved the making of Kean, as he was outstanding in his new role, being capped for England within three years of moving back to his home town. The no-nonsense defender, who had a distinctive upright running stance, helped Wednesday to the 1926 Second Division title and was duly

handed the captaincy as the Owls retained their newly won top-flight place a year later; however near the end of the 1927–28 season he lost his first-team place to Tony Leach and lost the captain's armband to veteran Jimmy Seed. This surprising turn of events led to Kean handing in a transfer request, and Wednesday fans were dismayed when he left for a club record fee soon after. He would win the FA Cup with Wanderers in 1929 and end his playing days as player-coach in non-League soccer, prior to becoming a publican back in Sheffield. Throughout his life he lived with the false accusation that he was drunk during a 6–2 home loss, on Boxing Day 1924, and was still asked about that day years after he had hung up his boots!

KING, Phillip Geoffrey 'Phil' (1989–94)

Full-back, 5ft 10in, 12st (1989)
Born: 28 December 1967, Bristol
Signed from: Swindon Town, 3 November 1989, £400,000
Transferred: Aston Villa, 1 August 1994, £250,000
Career: Exeter City, Torquay United, Swindon Town, Wednesday, Notts County (loan), Aston Villa, West Bromwich Albion (loan), Swindon Town, Blackpool (loan), Brighton & Hove Albion, Kidderminster Harriers, Bath City, Cinderford Town, Clifton FC (Sun.), Dolphin FC (Sun.)
Debut: 4 November 1989 v Nottingham Forest (a) First Division
Last appearance: 2 April 1994 v Everton (h) Premiership
Caps: England B (1)
Appearances/Goals: League 124+5/2, FAC 9/0, FLC 17/0, Euro 4/0

Popular full-back Phil King will always be remembered for his outstanding left-wing partnership with Nigel Worthington, which was a vital part of the Owls' success of the early 1990s. The duo became one of the most-feared pairings in English football, with King occupying the left-back role so 'Irish' could provide the attacking impetus. He was one of several signings made by Ron Atkinson late in 1989 – Roland Nilsson and John Sheridan being two others – and the consistent and steady defender duly helped the Owls to promotion and League Cup glory in 1991 before helping Wednesday become an established force in the First Division. Despite being fined two weeks wages in February 1992 – after refusing to play in a home game after a row with assistant boss Ritchie Barker – he still remained first choice at Hillsborough, and he was named Player of the Year by fans for the 1991–92 season. The following season was ruined by a cruciate knee ligament injury, and when he regained fitness King found his way back to the first team blocked by Nigel Worthington – his former partner having dropped back into his old full-back role after the big money arrival of left-winger Andy Sinton. This spelt the beginning of the end for King, and after going onto a week-to-week contract he left for a loan spell at Notts County. He eventually rejoined his old boss, Ron Atkinson, at Aston Villa and famously scored the winning penalty kick in a UEFA Cup triumph over Inter Milan at Villa Park. After dropping into Sunday League football at the end of his career, he now runs a Swindon-based pub and retains strong links with Wednesday, helping the club with fund-raising activities and always proving a popular host whenever the Owls visit the Wiltshire town.

KOVACEVIC, Darko

(1995–96)
Forward, 6ft, 1in, 12st (1995)
Born: 18 November 1973, Kovin, Yugoslavia
Signed from: Red Star Belgrade, 11 December 1995, £2.5 million
Transferred: Real Sociedad, 18 June 1996, £4.6 million
Career: Radnicki Kovin, Proleter Zrenjanin, Red Star Belgrade, Wednesday, Real Sociedad, Juventus, Lazio, Real Sociedad, Olympiacos
Debut: 23 December 1995 v Southampton (h) Premiership
Last appearance: 8 April 1996 v Arsenal (h) Premiership
Caps: Yugoslavia Full (4)
Appearances/Goals: League 8+8/4, FAC 1/0

When you consider that Yugoslavian international Darko Kovacevic is the club's all-time record sale, at £4.6 million, it is perhaps surprising that he made little impact during a brief spell at Hillsborough. After scoring freely with Red Star Belgrade he was targeted, along with teammate Dejan Stefanovic, by Owls manager David Pleat, and the club duly agreed a £4.5 million double transfer in

October 1995. However red tape then almost saw the deal collapse altogether, and it was almost eight weeks before the duo arrived in Sheffield to officially put pen to paper on lucrative contracts. The tall, imposing attacker made a promising start to his Owls career – scoring twice on his home debut – but he was used sparingly by Wednesday as Kovacevic became used to life both on and off the pitch in England. He did, however, show signs that Wednesday had purchased a supreme finisher and outstanding target man, so it was therefore a shock to most Owls fans when the club accepted a 'get your money back' offer from Spanish club Real Sociedad in the summer of 1996. His move to sunnier climes proved highly successful for Darko, and after scoring 41 League goals in 95 League games he was bought by Italian giants Juventus in 1999 for a staggering £12 million – the move to the Turin club triggering an extra £2.1 million into Hillsborough's coffers due to a sell-on clause. He netted 20 times in his first season at Juventus and continued to represent his country – now known as Serbia – before his career came to a premature end after he was diagnosed with a heart problem in 2009. He underwent a successful operation but was forced to end his career, returning to Spain with his family.

LANGLEY, Ambrose

(1893–1905)
Left-back, 5ft 11½in, 14st (1896)
Born: 10 March 1870, Horncastle, Lincolnshire
Died: 29 January 1937, Sheffield
Signed from: Everton, summer 1893
Transferred: Hull City, 26 April 1905
Career: Horncastle Town, Blue Star/Horncastle Gridirons, Boston Town, Grimsby Town, Middlesbrough Ironopolis, Everton, Wednesday, Hull City
Debut: 2 September 1893 v Sunderland (h) First Division
Last appearance: 19 December 1903 v Newcastle United (h) First Division
Caps: Football League (1)
Appearances/Goals: League 295/14, FAC 23/0

Ambrose Langley was a full-back who was a star of the club's early years in the Football League. Part of the famous 'three Ls' back line – along with Jack Lyall and Willie Layton – Langley had made his name in local Lincolnshire football before winning back-to-back Northern League Championship medals with Middlesbrough Ironopolis. An unsuccessful spell at League side Everton followed, and doubts about his fitness then brought his career to a crossroads. However, Wednesday took a chance on his 'dodgy knee', and they were rewarded with 12 years' service to the blue-and-white shirt. The totally committed and uncompromising left-back eventually replaced Jack Earp in the Owls' first team and won both the First and Second Division title at Wednesday, in addition to the FA Cup in 1896. He possessed a somewhat short fuse and was sent off in the infamous FA Cup tie against Sheffield United in 1900 and even had to settle out of court on one occasion when he 'accidentally' elbowed a Preston fan in the face – giving him two black eyes – after Ambrose was barracked in a game at the Lancashire side! He was eventually appointed player-manager at Hull City and almost led The Tigers into the top flight in 1910 before returning to Hillsborough in 1913 to become assistant to secretary Arthur Dickinson. After World War One he took the reins at Huddersfield Town – losing the 1920 FA Cup Final to Aston Villa – before leaving football altogether to become a publican back in Sheffield.

LAYNE, David Richard 'Bronco'

(1962–64 & 1972–73)
Centre-forward, 5ft 10in, 11st 11lb (1963)
Born: 29 July 1939, Sheffield

Signed from: Bradford City, 30 May 1962, £22,500
Transferred: Contract cancelled, January 1965
Signed from: 28 July 1972
Transferred: Retired, March 1973
Career: Sheffield United (Yth), English Steel, Rotherham United, Swindon Town, Bradford City, Wednesday, Thorpe Arch Open Prison, Wednesday, Hereford United (loan), Matlock Town
Debut: 18 August 1962 v Bolton Wanderers (h) First Division
Last appearance: 8 April 1964 v Stoke City (a) First Division
Appearances/Goals: League 74/52, FAC 4/1, EURO 3/5

The infamous bribes scandal of 1964 not only tarnished the club's good name but also damaged the Owls' fortunes on the field as they lost the outstanding talents of both Bronco Layne and Peter Swan. The former had terrorised the top-flight defences for two seasons, after arriving from an equally prolific spell at Bradford City, and many Wednesday fans still rate Layne as the best centre-forward to appear

for the club in post war soccer. His bustling style and rocket-like shot took Wednesday fans back to the days of Derek Dooley, and his 52 First Division goals set him alongside the likes of David McLean and Jack Allen as the one of most prolific strikers in top-flight football for the Owls. The former Sheffield boys player had started his career as a youngster at Sheffield United but left Bramall Lane to work in the steel industry. He returned to football as a part-time player at Rotherham United, and 28 goals in only 41 League games for Swindon Town earned him the nickname of 'Bronco' after a popular TV cowboy of the time – this was after he fired home a free-kick and was said to have 'the hardest shot in the west'.
His form at the Wiltshire club persuaded Bradford City to break their transfer record to obtain his signature, and they duly trebled their money when he moved to Hillsborough 18 months later. His tremendous form at Wednesday suggested that an England call-up would not be very far away but the scandal effectively ended his career, Layne serving a four-month prison sentence. His contract at Wednesday was cancelled but when the FA lifted his ban, in 1972, he returned to Hillsborough in an attempt to re-launch his career after eight years in the shadows. After a successful trial period he was awarded a one-year deal but would play only a handful of games for the reserves before an ankle injury meant he was forced to concentrate on his role of publican, a profession he continues to this day.

LAYTON, William 'Willie'

(1896–1910)
Full-back, 5ft 7½in, 12st 4lb (1907)
Born: 1875, Gornall, Staffs.
Died: April 1944, Australia
Signed from: Blackwell Colliery, September 1895

Transferred: Retired, 1910
Career: Blackwell Colliery, Chesterfield, Wednesday, St Lawrence
Debut: 8 January 1898 v Everton (a) First Division
Last appearance: 25 September 1909 v Tottenham Hotspur (a) First Division
Caps: Football League (1)
Appearances/Goals: League 331/2, FAC 30/0

The unswerving loyalty of Willie Layton to The Wednesday stemmed from a fateful day in November 1895 when the promising young full-back was due to work his usual shift down the mineshaft of Blackwell Colliery, in Derbyshire. However Layton, who was on amateur forms at Wednesday, decided not to work, as he wanted to be fresh for the following day's game. On the same night an underground explosion killed seven miners, and Willie vowed never to play for another club. He was handed a professional contract a few months later and after serving a long apprenticeship in the second team replaced Jack Earp at right-back after the first game of the 1899–1900 season. He remained an ever present as Wednesday coasted to the Second Division Championship and the sturdy, pacy and whole-hearted Layton would remain a rock at the heart of the club's defence for the next decade – joining with Lyall and Langley to form the famous 'three Ls' backline. The model professional won back-to-back League titles at the start of the 20th century and added the FA Cup to his medal haul in 1907 before finally retiring from the game in 1910. Layton – famous for his scissor kick that he used regularly to clear his lines – then became a publican while also signing up for a local village team. However, he stunned his regulars when he suddenly emigrated to Australia in 1912, leaving his wife and children behind! He never returned, marrying a girl he met on the ship, and worked as a miner in Sydney before illness meant he was unable to work for the final 10 years of his life.

LYALL, John 'Jack'

(1901–09)
Goalkeeper, 6ft 1½in, 12st 7lb (1908)
Born: 16 April 1881, Dundee
Died: 17 February 1944, Detroit, USA
Signed from: Jarrow, 27 February 1901, £100 *(Joint fee with Gosling)*
Transferred: Manchester City, 15 September 1909, £650
Career: Jarrow, Wednesday, Manchester City, Dundee, Ayr United, Jarrow, Palmer's (Jarrow)
Debut: 21 September 1901 v Bolton Wanderers (h) First Division
Last appearance: 29 March 1909 v Sunderland (h) First Division
Caps: Scotland Full (1)
Appearances/Goals: League 263/0, FAC 32/0

The final member of the 'three Ls' defensive line was Scottish goalkeeper Jack Lyall, the tall and commanding custodian

arriving from North East junior football just past the turn of the 20th century. His form 'between the sticks' meant he quickly became a big favourite with Owlerton fans, and he won both the League Championship and FA Cup while in Wednesday colours – such was his form that he received a call-up to the England squad only for the FA to realise that he was in fact Scottish! The confusion had arisen because his parents had brought Jack to England when he was just a few months old. He remained a first-team regular until the arrival of another club legend, Teddy Davison, and eventually left for Second Division Manchester City after almost 300 appearances for Wednesday. While at City he famously turned down an FA offer to tour South Africa, with a representative side, as he commented that he would rather go fishing! He returned to his birthplace in 1911, signing for Dundee, and ended his playing days back in North East non-League football before joining the forces in 1916. Prior to being posted to the Far East, he would guest for the Owls, while in 1927 he moved to the US – working as a plasterer for the remainder of his life.

LYONS, Michael Joseph 'Mike'

(1982–85)

Defender, 6ft, 12st 2lb (1982)
Born: 8 December 1951, Liverpool
Signed from: Everton, 24 June 1982, £80,000
Transferred: Grimsby Town, 11 November 1985, £25,000
Career: Everton, Wednesday, Grimsby Town
Debut: 28 August 1982 v Middlesbrough (h) Second Division
Last appearance: 29 October 1985 v Swindon Town (a) League Cup
Appearances/Goals: League 129/12, FAC 15/2, FLC 20/2

The signing of veteran Mike Lyons by Jack Charlton proved an inspirational capture as the central-defender not only led the club out of the Second Division in 1984 but also helped them consolidate in the top-flight. He had previously spent almost 13 years at Everton, amassing a colossal 460 games, and looked set to remain at Goodison Park for the remainder of his career before 'Big Jack'

brought Lyons to Hillsborough. This highly competitive and combative central-defender became an instant hit with Wednesday fans and inspired the side to great success under Howard Wilkinson – when he left for a role as player-manager at Grimsby Town the Owls sat third in the top-flight. He failed to bring any success to the Mariners and after being sacked in June 1987 he spent four years back at Everton as reserve team manager. After short coaching spells at Wigan Athletic and Huddersfield Town, he effectively left these shores for good, securing the position of Brunei national team manager. He eventually arrived in Australia, via a spell coaching in Singapore, where he was boss at Canberra Cosmos before taking charge of Southampton's Perth-based Academy in 2000. When this was closed in 2002 he returned to Brunei for a third spell in charge before being appointed manager at Perth-based club Stirling Lions in 2004. The Lions are part of West Ham's Academy structure, but Lyons was sacked from his role in April 2010.

McANEARNEY, Thomas 'Tom'

(1951–65)

Wingback, 5ft 9½in, 10st 2lb (1955)
Born: 6 January 1933, Lochee, Dundee
Signed from: Dundee North End, 20 October 1951, £490
Transferred: Peterborough United, 1 November 1965, £5,000
Career: Dunkeld Amateurs, St Stevens Amateurs, Dundee North End, Wednesday, Peterborough United, Aldershot
Debut: 3 September 1952 v Liverpool (h) First Division
Last appearance: 20 February 1965 v Everton (h) First Division
Appearances/Goals: League 352/19, FAC 23/2, Euro 7/1

One of two McAnearney brothers to play for Wednesday, Tom enjoyed the far greater success. After arriving from Scottish junior football in 1950, initially signing amateur forms, he progressed through the ranks to become a first-team regular in the late 1950s – he also served a two-year apprenticeship as a bricklayer and fulfilled his mandatory two years National Service during the decade. The Scot possessed terrific tackling ability, pace and intelligence, which meant Tom was regarded as one of the best defenders in the English game. He was part of the Swan-Kay-McAnearney back line that led the club to the Second Division title in 1959, First Division runners-up in 1961 and into the last eight of European competition a year later. He eventually lost his first-team place to the rapidly emerging Peter Eustace, and after a spell at Peterborough he ended his playing days at Aldershot – the Hampshire club breaking their transfer record to obtain his services. His final 18 months at

Aldershot was as player-manager, and Tom returned to Hillsborough in October 1968 after being appointed assistant-manager to Jack Marshall. A few months later he served as caretaker boss before reverting to his previous role under new manager, Danny Williams. A brief spell as Bury manager followed before almost a decade back at Aldershot, leading the Shots to promotion from the Third Division in 1973 and a memorable run to the last 16 of the FA Cup in 1979. His career in the game ended with a coaching spell at Chelsea before Tom became a postman back in Aldershot, prior to retiring back to Sheffield.

MACLEAN, Steven George 'Steve'

(**2004–07**)

Forward, 5ft 10in, 11st 1lb (2004)

Born: 23 August 1982, Edinburgh, Scotland

Signed from: Glasgow Rangers, 8 July 2004, £125,000

Transferred: Cardiff City, 1 July 2007, Free

Career: Glasgow Rangers, Scunthorpe United (loan), Sheffield Wednesday, Cardiff City, Plymouth Argyle, Aberdeen (loan), Oxford United

Debut: 7 August 2004 v Colchester United (h) League One

Last appearance: 6 May 2007 v Norwich City (h) Championship

Appearances/Goals: League 60+23/32, FAC 3/1, FLC 2/0, Other 1+1/2

Popular forward Steve MacLean made a huge impression in his debut season at Wednesday, as he not only became the first man to score 20 goals in a season for over a decade but also became the first player to score an away League hat-trick for over 30 years, when grabbing three in a 4–0 derby win at Doncaster Rovers in December 2004. He had started his career at Glasgow Rangers but came to the fore during a remarkable one-season loan at Scunthorpe United where he plundered 28 goals in all competitions, including three trebles, and finished divisional top scorer. It was obvious that his services would be much in demand and it was Chris Turner who paid his parent club a bargain fee in the summer of 2004 for the supreme penalty box predator. He scored regularly during the early part of the season and had 19 goals to his name before a broken foot, suffered in Match 2005, looked to have ended his season prematurely. However, he proved to be a shock inclusion in the matchday squad for the Play-off Final in Cardiff and duly came off the bench to convert the crucial penalty that tied the score at 2–2 against Hartlepool United – maintaining a 100 per cent record of seven penalties scored during the season. This goal took him to the notable 20-goal mark and of course the Owls went on to secure elevation to the Championship. A broken leg, suffered in pre season, ruined the 2005–06 season for MacLean but he netted regularly in the campaign that followed as Brian Laws' side just missed out on the Play-offs. Fans were dismayed when he was allowed to leave for Cardiff City in 2007, but MacLean has struggled to reproduce his Hillsborough form since leaving Wednesday, failing to secure a regular first-team berth and finding goals in short supply.

McCULLOCH, Andrew 'Andy'

(1979–83)

Forward, 6ft 2in, 13st 6lb (1979)
Born: 3 January 1950, Northampton
Signed from: Brentford, 22 June 1979, £60,000
Transferred: Crystal Palace, 1 August 1983, £20,000
Career: Fleet Town, Tottenham Hotspur (trial), Walton & Hersham, Queen's Park Rangers, Cardiff City, Oxford United, Brentford, Oakland Stompers (loan), Wednesday, Crystal Palace, Aldershot
Debut: 11 August 1979 v Hull City (h) League Cup
Last appearance: 14 May 1983 v Crystal Palace (h) Second Division
Appearances/Goals: League 122+3/44, FAC 10/4, FLC 14/1

Tall and commanding attacker Andy McCulloch was a popular player among Owls fans during the Jack Charlton era. He arrived from Brentford in the summer of 1979, and the brave and bustling forward led the club's attack for four seasons, as 'Big Jack' led the club out of the Third Division and to the fringes of the top flight. He had started his career in non-League soccer and eventually broke into League football at QPR, scoring 10 times in 30 appearances. It was his record of almost 50 goals for Brentford that attracted the Owls to his abilities and he scored 18 times as Wednesday were promoted from the third tier in 1980. After partnering Gary Bannister for two seasons he refused a new contract and returned to London, ironically signing for his final opponents in an Owls

shirt, Crystal Palace. He received a standing ovation from Wednesday supporters on his return to Hillsborough in a Palace shirt but a serious knee injury, suffered in 1985, brought his career to a premature end. In the following year he started his own commercial cleaning business in Surrey, which still flourishes today, and is manager of Kingston District League minnows Esher United.

McINTOSH, David 'Dave/Mac'

(1947–58)

Goalkeeper, 5ft 10½in, 11st 2lb (1947)
Born: 4 May 1925, Girvan, Ayrshire
Died: 24 July 1995, Glenrothes
Signed from: Girvan Ayrshire, 2 October 1947, Free
Transferred: Doncaster Rovers, 16 January 1958, Free
Career: Girvan Ayrshire, Wednesday, Doncaster Rovers
Debut: 3 April 1948 v Fulham (a) Second Division
Last appearance: 7 December 1957 v Aston Villa (h) First Division
Appearances/Goals: League 293/0, FAC 15/0

Just a short while after leaving the Navy, goalie Dave McIntosh was recommended to Wednesday by a Rotherham United director and after impressing greatly during a trial period was handed a professional contract by Eric Taylor. By the end of the season the fearless and outstanding custodian had made his senior debut and would remain the club's first-choice goalkeeper for almost a decade as Wednesday climbed out of the Second Division in 1950 and then experienced the 'yo-yo years' of the 1950s. Affectionately known as 'Mac', the Scot replaced Roy Smith at Hillsborough, and only injury kept McIntosh out of the first team – he had the misfortune to break his arm twice inside a 12-month period. He won Second Division title medals in both 1952 and 1956, and he was one of four 'keepers the club used during the 1957–58 season before Ron Springett arrived from QPR. The manager who signed McIntosh for Doncaster Rovers, Peter Docherty, actually resigned before he could see his new capture make his debut while 'Mac' stayed for two seasons at Rovers, appearing in 15 games before retiring in 1959. His final appearance was actually a game back at Hillsborough – in an April 1959 County Cup tie against the Owls – and he subsequently moved back to Scotland, working as a delivery driver for a distillery until his retirement.

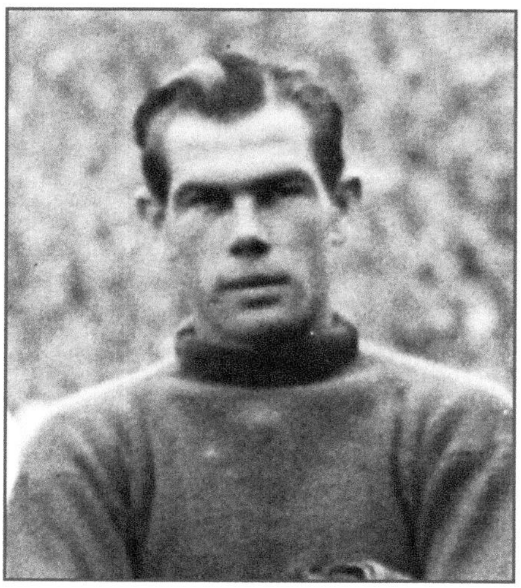

McLEAN, David Prophet 'Davie' (1911–19)

Centre-forward, 5ft 7½in, 11st 10lb (1911)
Born: 13 December 1887, Forfar
Died: 21 December 1967, Forfar
Signed from: Preston North End, 16 February 1911, £1,000
Transferred: Bradford Park Avenue, 23 October 1919, £2,000
Career: Forfar Half Holiday, Forfar West End, Glasgow Celtic (trial), Forfar Celtic, Forfar Athletic, Glasgow Celtic, Forfar Athletic (loan), Ayr (loan), Preston North End, Wednesday, Forfar Athletic (loan), Dykehead (guest), Third Lanark (guest), Glasgow Rangers (guest), Bradford Park Avenue, Dundee, Forfar Athletic, Dundee, Forfar Athletic, Dykehead
Debut: 18 February 1911 v Bury (h) First Division
Last appearance: 6 September 1919 v Middlesbrough (a) First Division
Caps: Scotland Full (1)
Appearances/Goals: League 135/88, FAC 12/12

Without doubt one of the greatest forwards in the club's long history, Davie McLean was an outstanding penalty box predator who became the first man to score 30 League goals in a season for Wednesday, achieving the feat in 1912–13. He had scored a mere 25 goals in the previous season and therefore fans were stunned when he returned home to Forfar after the Owls had refused his request for a guaranteed benefit of £450! The two sides became so entrenched that McLean started to play back at old club Forfar Athletic and when he finally returned to Sheffield, in December 1913, Wednesday had to pay a

transfer sum (£250) to re-sign their legendary attacker on professional forms. On his return he was instantly back into the scoring groove and by the end of the season had scored in excess of 20 League goals for the third consecutive campaign. If the onset of war in 1914 had not placed football on the sidelines it is quite possible that McLean could have even challenged Andrew Wilson in the all-time scoring stakes, due to his astonishing goals-per-game ratio, but it was not to be and after spending the majority of the hostilities back in Scotland (scoring 29 goals as Rangers finished runners-up in 1919) he returned to Sheffield after a gap of over four years. He only appeared in three more games for Wednesday before being sold for a club-record fee. He duly played alongside his brother, George, at Bradford Park Avenue before returning home to Scotland. He spent the remainder of his life back in Forfar, assuming the role of local celebrity, and was a publican for the majority of those years.

MADDEN, Lawrence David 'Lawrie'

(1983–91)

Defender, 5ft 11in, 13st 11lb (1984)
Born: 28 September 1955, Hackney
Signed from: Millwall, 24 August 1983, Free
Transferred: Wolverhampton Wanderers, 15 August 1991, Free
Career: Arsenal (Am.), Manchester University, Mansfield Town (N/C), Boston United, Tottenham Hotspur (trial), Charlton Athletic, Millwall, Wednesday, Leicester City (loan), Derby County (trial), Wolverhampton Wanderers, Darlington (N/C), Chesterfield, Emley
Debut: 27 August 1983 v Swansea City (a) Second Division
Last appearance: 8 May 1991 v Bristol City (h) Second Division
Appearances/Goals: League 200+12/2, FAC 20+1/0, FLC 26+2/3, Other 5/0

The arrival of central-defender Lawrie Madden, in the summer of 1983, received little coverage in the local press as the journeyman Londoner seemed simply to be a back-up player brought into the squad

by new manager Howard Wilkinson. However, this could not have been further from the truth as the incredibly consistent Madden started the opening game of the new season and would play over 250 first-team games in an eight-year stay at Hillsborough. His no-nonsense defending and dogged personality ensured he earned the respect of the Wednesday fans, and there was no doubt that when Madden was absent from the side he was badly missed – a 5–0 home FA Cup collapse to Everton in 1988 proving the point emphatically as Madden had played in the previous three draws, but injury meant he missed the fourth tie. He was perhaps most fondly remembered by Owls fans for his late cameo appearance as a right-winger in the 1991 League Cup Final win over Manchester United! The scholarly Madden had devoted the early years of his career to a combination of football (turning down a professional contract with Arsenal) and study – gaining a degree in Economics and Social Studies at Manchester University – and enjoyed the best years of a mixed career in the blue-and-white of Wednesday. He recorded his 500th League game at Chesterfield and now works in the Sheffield area as a freelance journalist.

MARSDEN, William 'Billy'

(1924–31)

Half-back, 5ft 9in, 11st 3lb (1924)

Born: 10 November 1901, Silksworth, Co. Durham

Died: 20 September 1983, Sheffield

Signed from: Sunderland, 17 May 1924, £450

Transferred: Retired, 1931

Career: Ryhope FC, Silksworth Colliery, Sunderland, Wednesday

Debut: 30 August 1924 v Crystal Palace (a) Second Division

Last appearance: 3 May 1930 v Manchester City (h) First Division

Caps: England Full (3), Football League (1)

Appearances/Goals: League 205/9, FAC 16/0

Brilliant half-back Billy Marsden saw his career cruelly cut short by a serious injury suffered while representing his country. The fateful game was a meeting with Germany in Berlin, in May 1930, and after challenging for a high ball with a teammate he suffered truly horrific injuries – a broken neck and spinal damage that put his life in danger. It was only the skill of a German surgeon that saved Billy and after six weeks in hospital he returned to Sheffield in an attempt to salvage his career. Unfortunately despite playing a handful of reserve team games he could not return to senior football and at the age of 30 was forced to quit the game. He received £750 compensation from the FA (the Owls were paid £2,000!) and a few weeks after Wednesday played a benefit match on his behalf, in September 1931, he left for a coaching appointment in Holland. He remained abroad, apart from a brief spell as Gateshead trainer, until forced to escape the invading German

forces in 1940 and worked as a publican back in Sheffield after the hostilities ended – he was the last surviving member of the Owls side that won consecutive titles between the war to pass away. Before his forced retirement Marsden had been a peerless member of the all-conquering Wednesday side of the late 1920s, after having served his apprenticeship under the great Charles Buchan at Sunderland. He was yet another outstanding signing by Wednesday boss Bob Brown, and described as 'tall, speedy and strong' he was ever present as the club won the Second Division title in 1926 – he had been converted by Brown from an inside-forward to left half-back, even though he was right-footed. The Strange-Leach-Marsden backline became one of England's best defensive trios, and they helped the club to those aforementioned top-flight Championships before fate dealt Billy a cruel hand during his third cap for England.

MARWOOD, Brian

(1984–88)

Winger, 5ft 7in, 11st (1984)

Born: 5 February 1960, Seaham Harbour, Sunderland

Signed from: Hull City, 9 August 1984, £115,000 (T.)

Transferred: Arsenal, 23 March 1988, £600,000

Career: Hull City, Wednesday, Arsenal, Sheffield United, Middlesbrough, Swindon Town, Barnet

Debut: 25 August 1984 v Nottingham Forest (h) First Division

Last appearance: 19 March 1988 v Portsmouth (h) First Division

Appearances/Goals: League 125+3/27, FAC 19/3, FLC 13/5, Other 0+1/0

Right-winger Brian Marwood was a mainstay of the Owls side in the mid-1980s, after signing from his first club, Hull City. His capture by Howard Wilkinson proved an inspired signing as Marwood fitted perfectly into the club's style of play, providing a constant stream of quality crosses for the likes of Lee Chapman and Garry Thompson to feed off. He was also a consistent scorer, and his accuracy from set plays meant he was a major factor as the Owls finished in the top half of the First Division in his first two seasons and also reached the FA Cup semi-final; his absence from that game being thought by many as the reason for the Owls' loss to Everton. He was certainly missed when he was not in from the side, and his form meant that Marwood reached the fringes of the England squad – it was not until he moved to Arsenal for an Owls club-record fee that he won his one and only full England cap (in the same game as fellow one cap wonder Mel Sterland). He won the First Division title with the Gunners in 1989, but injury then curtailed appearances, and after a short spell at Bramall Lane he retired in 1994 to take the role of PFA Chairman. He now holds the position of football administrator at Premiership Manchester City.

MASSEY, James 'Jimmy'

(1893–1901)

Goalkeeper, 5ft 10in, 10st 9lb (1896)
Born: 1869, Wolverhampton
Died: December 1960, Mexborough
Signed from: Doncaster Rovers, 1893
Transferred: Denaby United, 1901
Career: Denaby United, Doncaster Rovers, Wednesday, Denaby United, South Kirkby Colliery
Debut: 3 November 1894 v Aston Villa (h) First Division
Last appearance: 9 February 1901 v Bury (h) FA Cup
Appearances/Goals: League 159/0, FAC 14/0

West Midlands-born custodian Jimmy Massey was the club's second 'regular' goalkeeper after joining the Football League in 1892. After serving an apprenticeship in the reserve team, he took over from Bill Allan in 1896 (he was suffering from a broken finger when he made his debut!) and remained undisputed first choice until the dawn of the new century. He quickly became a big favourite with Olive Grove regulars with his bravery in the area and tremendous form, subsequently helping the club to FA Cup glory in 1896. He appeared in the opening game at Hillsborough, in September 1899, and won a Second Division Championship medal at the end of the season, although he had lost his place to Frank Stubbs after playing in the first 29 matches of the campaign. As injuries took their toll on his fitness, he missed the whole of the 1901–02 season, after being released, before re-launching his career back at his old side, Denaby United. He worked in the coal mines until retirement – losing an eye in an accident at Barnburgh Colliery – and was the final member of the aforementioned FA Cup-winning side to pass away, when he died at the grand old age of 91.

MEGSON, Donald Harry 'Don'

(1953–70)

Left-back, 5ft 10in, 11st 4lb (1956)
Born: 12 June 1936, Sale, Cheshire
Signed from: Mossley, 19 June 1953, £50
Transferred: Bristol Rovers, 14 March 1970, Free
Career: Mossley, Wednesday, Bristol Rovers
Debut: 14 November 1959 v Burnley (h) First Division
Last appearance: 24 January 1970 v Scunthorpe United (h) FA Cup
Caps: Football League (1)
Appearances/Goals: League 386/6, FAC 41/1, FLC 5/0, Euro 10/0

After signing as an amateur in 1952, Don Megson waited over seven years before finally making his senior bow for the Owls. However, after manager Harry Catterick had switched Megson to left-back – after

he had completed his National Service in 1959 – the former Lancashire boys player never looked back, becoming one of the greatest full-backs in Wednesday's history. He quickly became an automatic choice for the club and subsequently helped the Owls to finish runners-up to the great Spurs side in 1961. Qualities such as terrific distribution, no-nonsense tackling ability and great strength made him almost unchallenged for the whole of the 1960s in the Wednesday side while 'Meg' also played the game with great passion and pure enjoyment. He was, of course, a huge favourite with Wednesday fans – older supporters suggesting that only Ernie Blenkinsop was a superior left-back – and he made history in the 1966 FA Cup Final when he became the first captain to take his side on a lap of honour around the Wembley pitch, despite the Owls losing to Everton. His last appearance was an unhappy finale, the shocking FA Cup loss to minnows Scunthorpe United, but over 11,000 fans attended his testimonial game a few months later to say goodbye – he had been granted a free transfer in March 1970 in recognition of his service to Wednesday. He retired from playing after two years at Bristol Rovers and was then manager for five years before a short spell in charge of US side Portland Timbers. He was also briefly in charge at Bournemouth before retiring back to Sheffield, scouting occasionally for his son, Gary.

MEGSON, Gary John

(1981–84 & 1985–89)

Midfielder, 5ft 10in, 11st 6lb (1983)
Born: 2 May 1959, Manchester
Signed from: Everton, 7 August 1981, £108,500
Transferred: Nottingham Forest, 2 August 1984, £170,000
Signed from: Newcastle United, 20 December 1985, £60,000
Transferred: Manchester City, 5 January 1989, £250,000
Career: Frampton Rangers, Parkway Juniors, Mangotsfield, Plymouth Argyle, Everton, Wednesday, Nottingham Forest, Newcastle United, Wednesday, Manchester City, Norwich City, Lincoln City, Shrewsbury Town
Debut: 29 August 1981 v Blackburn Rovers (a) Second Division
Last appearance: 2 January 1989 v Coventry City (a) First Division
Appearances/Goals: League 230+3/25, FAC 27/6, FLC 23/2, Other 3/0

Following in the footsteps of his father was flame-haired midfielder Gary Megson who initially joined the Owls under the reign of Jack Charlton in the early 1980s. In his first spell at Hillsborough Megson Junior missed only three games and his energetic displays at the heart of the club's engine room drove Wednesday to the brink of promotion twice, plus an FA Cup semi-final, before 1984 brought the long-awaited elevation back to the 'big time'.

Surprisingly, he would not follow the club into the First Division as the lure of working under Brian Clough proved too strong – Megson signing for Nottingham Forest. Unfortunately, the move was disastrous, and he failed to play a game and was even publicly criticised by the somewhat unpredictable Clough. His career was resurrected under Jack Charlton at Newcastle United, and he duly returned to Wednesday, being re-signed by Howard Wilkinson. He was quickly back into the groove at Hillsborough – Wednesday finishing fifth and reaching the last four of the FA Cup again – but a very public falling out with new manager Peter Eustace resulted in a swift departure to Manchester City! Since ending his playing days as a non-contract player at Shrewsbury Town, Gary has held several managerial roles, including being in charge at Norwich City, Blackpool, Stockport County, Stoke City and West Bromwich Albion. He left his last position – as manager at Premiership Bolton Wanderers – in December 2009.

MILLERSHIP, Walter 'Harry or Walt'

(1930–46)

Forward/half-back, 5ft 10in, 11st 9lb (1930)
Born: 8 June 1910, Warsop Vale, Nottinghamshire
Died: 1978, Brimington, nr Chesterfield
Signed from: Bradford Park Avenue, 10 March 1930, £2,600
Transferred: Denaby United, 24 May 1946, Free
Career: Warsop Main, Welbeck Athletic, Shirebrook, Bradford Park Avenue, Wednesday, Doncaster Rovers (guest), Sheffield United (guest), Denaby United
Debut: 5 April 1930 v Liverpool (a) First Division
Last appearance: 15 April 1939 v Nottingham Forest (h) Second Division
Appearances/Goals: League 210/25, FAC 26/9

Due to his no-nonsense tackling and robust play, half-back Harry Millership was handed the nickname of 'Battleship' by Owls fans. He had originally been signed by manager Bob Brown as an inside-

forward and was mainly confined to second -team football during his first three seasons at Wednesday. However, when regular half-back Tony Leach was injured near the end of the 1932–33 season, boss Brown took the inspired decision to try Millership as a temporary replacement. He appeared in three games, before returning to the reserves, but before 1933 had elapsed he had taken Leach's place and remained first choice for the remainder of the decade. Dubbed 'the best centre-half never to have played for England', Harry appeared for Wednesday in their 1935 FA Cup win over West Bromwich Albion and also played over 150 games for the club during the war years (including the 1943 War Cup Final), while employed in a local munitions factory. The rugged defender is also credited with spotting a young Derek Dooley –playing against the centre-forward for Denaby United – while after hanging up his boots he became a publican in the Chesterfield area. He later returned to his original job as a miner, remaining in that profession until retiring in 1969.

MOBLEY, Victor John 'Vic'

(1961–69)
Defender, 6ft ½in, 13st 12lb (1964)
Born: 11 October 1943, Oxford
Signed from: Oxford City, 1 September 1961, £50
Transferred: Queen's Park Rangers, 30 September 1969, £55,000
Career: Oxford City, Wednesday, Queen's Park Rangers
Debut: 4 April 1964 v Wolverhampton Wanderers (a) First Division
Last appearance: 16 August 1969 v Wolverhampton Wanderers (h) First Division
Caps: England Under-23 (13), Football League (1)
Appearances/Goals: League 187/8, FAC 19/0, FLC 4/0

Vic Mobley was a commanding central-defender who started his career in amateur football before turning professional at the age of 17. His terrific passing ability and command in the air saw Mobley act as understudy to Peter Swan during his early years at Hillsborough, but the infamous bribes scandal of 1964 dramatically ended the career of Swan, allowing Mobley to take the place of the disgraced England star. It was a first-team place that he would hold onto for the following five seasons, although lady luck was not always on his side – an injury denied him a full cap for England while he was forced to miss the 1966 FA Cup Final after damaging ankle ligaments in the semi-final at Villa Park. Known as a 'gentle giant' he appeared in 111 consecutive games before a somewhat abrupt departure in 1969 – Mobley returning from a day trip to Queen's Park Rangers with his transfer forms ready to be counter-signed! His playing career lasted only another two years before arthritis forced his early retirement, in April 1971, and he spent two years on the QPR coaching staff before working as a carpenter. He emigrated to New Zealand in 1975 and is now a retired former insurance consultant, living in Auckland.

MOSFORTH, William H. 'Billy'

(1875–88)

Winger, 5ft 3in, 11st (1888)
Born: 2 January 1858, Sheffield
Died: 11 July 1929, Sheffield
Signed from: Amateur, 1875
Transferred: Amateur, 1888
Career: Sheffield Albion, Ecclesfield, Wednesday, Norfolk Park, Crookes, Exchange, Providence, Hallam, Walkley, Heeley, Lockwood Brothers, Sheffield United, Owlerton
Debut: 18 December 1880 v Blackburn Rovers (a) FA Cup
Last appearance: 30 January 1888 v Preston North End (h) FA Cup
Caps: England Full (9)
Appearances/Goals: FAC 25/6

Mosforth was an outstanding winger of the Victorian age, who is arguably the greatest player to play for The Wednesday in their pre-League era. In an age when individualism was king, diminutive and lightening quick Mosforth was a superstar in the English game – he was nicknamed 'The Little Wonder' by adoring Wednesday fans, dazzled by his speed, tremendous dribbling ability and amazing capacity to score from virtually any angle on the pitch. In those pre professional days Mosforth played for a variety of sides during his career, first playing for Wednesday at the age of 17 in 1875, and would win nine full caps for England. He started his playing career alongside the famous Clegg brothers at the Albion Club but, with Mosforth at the fore, Wednesday rose to become the dominant force in Sheffield, winning a multitude of local honours, including the Sheffield Challenge Cup and Wharncliffe Charity Cup. An engraver by trade, Billy appeared in the club's first-ever FA Cup tie, in 1880, and also in the opening game at Olive Grove in 1887 – he was instrumental in the club adopting professionalism in the same year. The 'pocket dynamo' was truly a real crowd entertainer and perhaps one of the main reasons why association football rose in popularity to such an extent in the 1880s. He later appeared in the first-ever game of the newly formed Sheffield United FC and became a publican in the city.

NILSSON, Roland Nils Lennart

(1989–94)

Right-back, 5ft 11in, 11st 10lb (1989)
Born: 27 November 1963, Helsingborg, Sweden
Signed from: IFK Gothenburg, 5 December 1989, £375,000
Transferred: Helsingborg IF, 9 May 1994, Free
Career: Helsingborg IF, IFK Gothenburg,

Wednesday, Helsingborg IF, Coventry City, Helsingborg IF
Debut: 9 December 1989 v Luton Town (h) First Division
Last appearance: 7 May 1994 v Manchester City (h) Premiership
Caps: Sweden Full (31)
Appearances/Goals: League 151/2, FAC 15/0, FLC 16/1, Euro 1+1/0, Other 2/0

Swedish right-back Roland Nilsson was a virtual unknown to Wednesday fans when Ron Atkinson swooped for his signature in December 1989. However, over the five years that followed he became one of the most popular players in modern times. The totally unflappable Scandinavian boasted an incredible level of fitness, impeccable timing and tremendous tackling ability, while his capacity to read the game ensured 'Rolo' was without doubt one of the finest defensive players in the English game during his time at Hillsborough. He was described by 'Big Ron' as the 'best professional I have ever worked with' and his commitment to the cause was no better typified than the 1993 FA Cup Final replay when Nilsson played for Sweden and flew back to appear for the Owls just 24 hours later! His display in the 1991 League Cup Final win over Manchester United is credited by many as the main reason Wednesday lifted the trophy – alongside John Harkes, he marked danger man Lee Sharpe out of the game – and 12 months later helped the Owls to qualify for Europe, after finishing third in the final season of the old First Division. It was, therefore, a sad day for Wednesdayites when Nilsson announced he wanted to return home in November 1993, a request that the club initially rejected; however, a compromise was reached, and it was an emotional day on the final afternoon of the 1993–94 season when Nilsson said his farewells before re-

joining home-town club Helsingborg. A few weeks later he was in the Sweden side that finished third in the World Cup Finals and three years later he made a surprise return to English soccer, being signed by his old boss Atkinson for Coventry City. Whenever he returned to Hillsborough in Sky Blue colours he was given a standing ovation by Wednesday fans while his career came to a close in 1999 when he suffered a punctured lung and broken ribs during a match at Arsenal. He later spent a short spell as manager back at Coventry but since 2002 has coached back in his home country, initially with GAIS Gothenburg and then Malmo FF.

PALMER, Carlton Lloyd

(1989–94 & 2001)
Midfielder, 6ft 2in, 12st 4lb (1989)
Born: 5 December 1965, Regis, nr. Oldbury
Signed from: West Bromwich Albion, 22 February 1989, £750,000
Transferred: Leeds United, 1 July 1994, £2.75 million

Signed from: Coventry City, 13 February 2001, Loan
Transferred: Coventry City, May 2001, loan return
Signed from: Coventry City, 3 September 2001, Free
Transferred: Released, 24 October 2001
Career: Whiteheath, St Michael's, Oldbury, Newton Albion, Netherton, Dudley Town, West Bromwich Albion, Wednesday, Leeds United, Southampton, Nottingham Forest, Coventry City, Watford (loan), Wednesday (loan), Wednesday, Stockport County, Darlington, Dublin City, Mansfield Town
Debut: 25 February 1989 v Wimbledon (a) First Division
Last appearance: 20 October 2001 v Walsall (h) First Division
Caps: England Full (18), B (5), Under-21 (4)
Appearances/Goals: League 226+1/14, FAC 18+1/0, FLC 31/3, Euro 3+1/0, Other 5/1

A vital member of the successful Owls side of the early 1990s, Carlton Palmer formed a terrific midfield partnership with John Sheridan. While his colleague received the

plaudits for his quality distribution, Palmer played the equally important role of winning the ball and breaking down opposition attacks through his tireless box-to-box displays. The duo powered the club to promotion and League Cup success in 1991, although Palmer missed Wembley after being sent off two weeks earlier at Portsmouth. He remained a first choice at Hillsborough for Wednesday's first three seasons back in the top flight and was unfortunately on the losing side in both domestic Cup Finals in 1993. It would be fair to say that goalscoring was not Carlton's strong point, so it was therefore a shock when he grabbed a first-half Hillsborough hat-trick, against Queen's Park Rangers in September 1991, to leave Wednesday fans speechless! While at Wednesday the industrious ball winner won his first cap for England – his inclusion in the International set up being harshly criticised by the tabloids – and appeared in the 1992 European Championships. A fall out with boss Trevor Francis triggered a move up the M1 to Leeds United where he was a regular, under the tutelage of Howard Wilkinson, as the West Yorkshire club qualified for Europe. After 129 games he joined old teammate David Hirst at Southampton and even at the age of 33 commanded a fee of £1.1 million when he later moved to Nottingham Forest. A surprise return to Hillsborough followed, Palmer helping the Owls to stave off relegation from the First Division (Championship) in 2001 while on loan. He returned in September of the same year, for a third spell, but an apparent fall out with caretaker boss Terry Yorath resulted in his contract being paid up and Palmer signing as player-manager for Stockport County. He resigned as player-manager of Mansfield Town in September 2005, marking the end of his career in football management, and Palmer has since run his own estate agents business and now works as a pundit for various TV channels while also teaching football at a Dubai-based boarding school. In June 2010 he appeared on a celebrity edition of *Come Dine With Me*, winning the £1,000 prize for charity.

PEARSON, Nigel Graham

(1987–94)
Defender, 6ft 1in, 13st 3lb (1988)
Born: 21 August 1963, Nottingham
Signed from: Shrewsbury Town, 16 October 1987, £250,000
Transferred: Middlesbrough, 19 July 1994, £500,000
Career: Heanor Town, Shrewsbury Town, Wednesday, Middlesbrough
Debut: 17 October 1987 v Nottingham Forest (a) First Division
Last appearance: 18 September 1993 v Southampton (h) Premiership
Appearances/Goals: League 176+4/14, FAC 15/1, FLC 17+2/5, Euro 3/0, Other 7/0

The glorious 1990–91 campaign was inspired by the leadership of captain Nigel Pearson, who lifted the League Cup trophy above his head on that memorable afternoon in the spring of 1991. He arrived from the relative obscurity of lower-League Shrewsbury Town – it was his impressive and commanding display against the Owls in a League Cup tie that led directly to his arrival at Hillsborough a few weeks later. He became an automatic choice at the heart of the club's defence and when 'Big Ron' arrived at the helm Pearson improved further, helping Wednesday to reach great heights during the early 1990s. He was deservedly named Man of the Match in that Cup win over Manchester United at Wembley and contributed a terrific 12 goals from defence during the entire 1990–91 campaign, the majority being scored in the run to the Final. He remained a vital player under Trevor Francis but missed out on both Wembley Finals in 1993 after fracturing his leg in the League Cup semi-final at Blackburn Rovers. Another leg break – in September 1993 – proved a further setback, and it was permanent, as far his Owls career was concerned, as he duly moved to Middlesbrough in the following summer. He regained his fitness on Teesside and immediately captained Boro to the First Division (Championship) title before suffering the agony of the 1996–97 season when his side lost in both domestic Cup Finals and were also relegated from the Premiership. He also wore the captain's armband in their 1998 League Cup Final loss before starting a coaching career at Carlisle United. As his reputation as a coach started to grow, Pearson moved up the ladder and impressed greatly when he helped Southampton escape the Championship trap door. This did not go unnoticed, and he then enjoyed two outstanding seasons at Leicester City, leading them to the League One title in 2009 and an appearance in the Championship Play-off semi-final before surprisingly leaving to take over at Hull City.

PRENDERGAST, Michael John 'Mick'

(1967–78)
Forward, 5ft 8in, 12st (1973)
Born: 24 November 1950, Denaby Main
Died: 30 April 2010, Mexborough
Signed from: Trainee, 24 November 1967
Transferred: Barnsley, 9 March 1978, £14,000
Career: Wednesday, Barnsley, Halifax Town (loan), Mexborough Town, Denaby United, The Gate (Sun.)
Debut: 9 April 1969 v Newcastle United (a) First Division
Last appearance: 7 March 1978 v Chester (h) Third Division
Appearances/Goals: League 170+14/53, FAC 7+1/2, FLC 15/4

A product of the youth system at Wednesday, striker Mick Prendergast spent over a decade at Hillsborough, but a catalogue of injuries restricted his first-team appearances to less than 200. He was a tireless and popular front runner who initially signed professional forms on his 17th birthday before finishing the 1968–69 season as reserve-team top scorer, in addition to making his senior bow. Following relegation in 1970, he enjoyed his most prolific campaign, netting 16 times, and was named supporters' Player of the Year in 1973 before suffering a broken leg that kept him out for the whole of the disastrous 1974–75 season. After recovering from the fracture, 'Prendo' entered the club's record books as the first man to score a goal for Wednesday in the third tier of the English game. In 1977 his loyalty was rewarded with a testimonial match against top-flight Leicester City, but soon after he signed for neighbours Barnsley. The former Yorkshire boys player ended his playing days in non-League soccer, but his story had an unhappy ending as at the age of just 36 he became registered disabled after having a hip replacement and passed away, in Mexborough Montagu Hospital, in 2010.

PRESSMAN, Kevin Paul

(1985–2004)
Goalkeeper, 6ft 1in, 14st 2lb (1988)
Born: 6 November 1967, Fareham
Signed from: Trainee, 6 November 1985
Transferred: Released, 30 June 2004
Career: Brunsmeer (Sun.), Middlewood Rovers, Wednesday, Stoke City (Loan), West Bromwich Albion (Loan), Leicester City, Leeds United (N/C), Coventry City (N/C), Mansfield Town, Portadown, Scunthorpe United
Debut: 5 September 1987 v Southampton (a) First Division
Last appearance: 8 May 2004 v Queen's Park Rangers (h) Second Division
Caps: England B (3), Under-21 (1), Youth (8)

Appearances/Goals: League 400+4/0, FAC 21/0, FLC 46/0, Euro 1/0, Other 6/0

Over the years, the Owls boasted several outstanding and long-serving goalkeepers, such as Teddy Davison and Ron Springett, and Kevin Pressman was another custodian who fitted that description. Although born in Hampshire, his family moved to the Sheffield area when he was only eight years old and he was subsequently spotted by an Owls scout and started to play for the club's nursery side, Middlewood Rovers. After fighting off competition from several major clubs, Wednesday signed him to schoolboy forms in 1981, and he went on to win caps at schools level for England. Within a year of signing apprentice forms, he was upgraded to full professional and made a winning senior debut at The Dell, Southampton. Competition from the likes of Martin Hodge and Chris Turner meant he acted the role of understudy during the late 1980s. The brilliant shot stopper, who commanded his penalty area, became first choice under Ron Atkinson, at the start of the 1989–90 season, but a cruciate knee ligament injury checked his progress. He was virtually out in the cold for two seasons after the club spent over £1 million to bring England 'keeper Chris Woods to Sheffield. However, the resilient Pressman eventually wrestled the number-one jersey off his rival and was even called-up for the full England squad in March 1998, such was his outstanding form. A challenge from Pavel Srnicek followed, but after re-claiming the jersey he would be unchallenged as first choice as Wednesday moved down into League One in 2003. A new deal in 2001 saw the burly custodian handed a new contract, which included a role as goalkeeping coach, and he remained player-coach until relinquishing the latter role to concentrate

on his football in January 2003. He was one of 13 players released by Chris Turner at the end of the 2003–04 season and played for a variety of clubs, some on a non-contract basis, which included Irish club Portadown and his final club, Scunthorpe United. He was assistant manager/goalkeeping coach for the Iron before being dismissed in March 2011.

QUIGLEY, Edward 'Eddie'

(1947–49)

Inside-forward, 5ft 9in, 11st 4lb (1947)
Born: 13 July 1921, Bury
Died: 16 April 1997, Blackpool
Signed from: Bury, 9 October 1947, £12,000
Transferred: Preston North End, December 1949, £26,000
Career: Bury, Wednesday, Preston North End, Blackburn Rovers, Bury, Mossley
Debut: 11 October 1947 v Plymouth Argyle (a) Second Division
Last appearance: 26 November 1949 v Luton Town (h) Second Division
Appearances/Goals: League 74/49, FAC 4/3

As a youngster Eddie Quigley had high hopes of becoming a professional cricketer, but it would be as a footballer

that he excelled. He signed for home-town club Bury during World War Two – Quigley served in the armed forces for the majority of the war years – and it was Wednesday manager Eric Taylor who brought the outstanding inside-forward to Hillsborough, setting a new club-record fee for both buying and selling club. His attributes included superb passing capability and the ability to think quickly when the ball was at his feet. He played in a deeper position than the traditional inside-forward and specialised in long cross-field passing and accurate and powerful long-range shooting. He proved an inspired signing by the Owls and on two occasions netted four goals in a single game while averaging over a goal every game during his time at Hillsborough. His career at Wednesday was not without problems, though, as he was stripped of the captaincy in March 1949, as a disciplinary measure, although fans were still stunned when later in the year he left for Preston – the *Lilywhites* paying a British record transfer fee for his services. Despite winning England B honours and a Second Division Championship medal, his time at Deepdale was not a roaring success, but he rediscovered his scoring touch at Blackburn Rovers – netting 95 times in 166 games for the Ewood Park club. He later spent five years as player-manager at Manchester-based non-League side Mossley and was on the coaching staff back at Bury. He was also in charge of Blackburn Rovers for just over three years and finally retired after a spell as chief scout at Blackpool in the early 1980s.

QUINN, John David

(1959–67)

Forward, 5ft 6½in, 10st 7½lb (1966)
Born: 30 May 1938, St Helens
Signed from: Prescot Cables, 29 April 1959, £1,250
Transferred: Rotherham United, 24 November 1967, £25,000
Career: St Helens Town, Prescot Cables, Burnley (trial), Everton (trial), Wednesday, Rotherham United, Worksop Town, Goole Town
Debut: 26 September 1959 v Luton Town (h) First Division
Last appearance: 11 November 1967 v Chelsea (a) First Division
Appearances/Goals: 165+8/20, FAC 14+1/3, FLC 3+1/0, Euro 2/1

John Quinn was a forward who was working as a welder and playing in amateur football before being spotted by Wednesday scouts in the late 1950s. He was quickly signed to a professional contract at Hillsborough, and within a few months was making his senior debut in the English top-flight. His two-year National Service interrupted his early progress, but the consistent and dependable utility-forward

saw his patience rewarded when new boss Alan Brown was appointed, Quinn becoming an automatic choice. His greatest asset was his sheer versatility – he appeared in every position except for centre-half and goalkeeper – and earned the respect of his peers due to his cheerful and outgoing demeanour. He was later dubbed the 'Mighty Quinn' (after a 1968 Manfred Mann song) by Rotherham fans and played his part in the young team reaching the 1966 FA Cup Final. As that young side started to break up, Quinn moved onto neighbours Rotherham United – the Millers' boss Tommy Docherty breaking their transfer record to buy him – but his time at Millmoor was virtually ruined by a serious Achilles tendon injury that kept him on the sidelines for almost two years. He appeared in just over 100 games for Rotherham before retiring from League soccer at Halifax Town in 1975. He was later controversially sacked as Halifax boss and returned to Sheffield to play in local football before hanging up his boots, aged 38, in October 1978. He then ran a Sports shop, with old teammate Gerry Young, near to Hillsborough before selling the business to work from home. A keen golfer, his 'Johnny Quinn's All Stars' charity side raised thousands of pounds for worthy causes.

QUIXALL, Albert

(1948–58)

Inside-forward, 5ft 7¾in, 11st (1954)
Born: 9 August 1933, Sheffield
Signed from: Meynell Youth Club, 24 August 1950
Transferred: Manchester United, 18 September 1958, £45,000
Career: Meynell Youth Club, Wednesday, Manchester United, Oldham Athletic, Stockport County, Altrincham
Debut: 24 February 1951 v Chelsea (h) First Division
Last appearance: 17 September 1958 v Sunderland (h) Second Division
Caps: England Full (5), B (3), Under-23 (1), Football League (3)
Appearances/Goals: League 241/63, FAC 19/2

Outstanding attacker Albert Quixall was a star of the 1950s Wednesday side, eventually being sold for a British record fee when he moved to Manchester United in 1958. His early promise was shown by two schoolboy caps for England and he initially worked as an apprentice joiner – at the firm of a Wednesday director – while a part-time professional at Hillsborough. He turned full-time in August 1950 and went on to make his senior debut in the season that followed, quickly becoming the 'golden boy' of Sheffield soccer due to his superb football brain, perfect ball control, outstanding skill, blond hair and boyish looks. At the tender age of 20 he won the first of five full caps for England and won a multitude of representative honours while being a regular in the Owls side that bounced between the two top divisions in the 1950s – Quixall winning two Second Division title medals while at Hillsborough. Every season outside of the top flight meant it became more and more difficult for the Owls to hold onto their prize asset, but when he did finally leave he became one of Manchester United's first post-Munich signings as Matt Busby tried to re-build his decimated squad. His final appearance came in a 6–0 home win against Sunderland, and understandably Owls fans were extremely disappointed to see Quixall leave, after his submission of a transfer request has caused a rush of top-flight clubs to the negotiating table. He netted 51 goals in 165 games for United – winning the FA Cup in 1963 – and after his playing career came to a close in non-League soccer, he settled in the area, starting his own successful scrap metal business.

RIMMER, Ellis James

(1928–38)

Winger, 5ft 10in, 11st 7lb (1928)
Born: 2 January 1907, Birkenhead
Died: 16 March 1965, Formby
Signed from: Tranmere Rovers, 16 February 1928, £1,850
Transferred: Ipswich Town, 16 August 1938, £450
Career: Parkside, Northern Nomads, Everton (Am.), Whitchurch, Tranmere Rovers, Wednesday, Ipswich Town
Debut: 25 February 1928 v Newcastle United (h) First Division
Last appearance: 12 March 1938 v Stockport County (a) Second Division
Caps: England Full (4)
Appearances/Goals: League 381/122, FAC 36/18

Winger Ellis Rimmer joins the names of Fred Spiksley, Mark Hooper and Chris Waddle as arguably the greatest wingmen in the Owls' long history. He could even make a claim as the best of all time due to his quite phenomenal goalscoring record which saw Rimmer net an astonishing 140 goals in a decade at Wednesday – placing the Lancastrian fifth in the club's all-time top scorers list. He formed an irresistible partnership with fellow wing wizard Mark

Hooper, and they powered the club to the success of the late 1920s and early 1930s. Rimmer won the League title twice while in Wednesday colours and joined a select band of players to have scored in every round of the FA Cup, when he helped the club to secure the trophy in 1935. He not only scored a plethora of goals himself but also was a major supplier to the three 'Jacks' – Allen, Ball and Palethorpe – who led the Owls attack during Rimmer's career at Hillsborough. His success at Wednesday was a far cry from his early days as an amateur at Everton – he only progressed as far as the third team – and it was with another local club, Tranmere Rovers, that he was given his debut in senior football. His 21 goals in 61 games alerted Wednesday manager Bob Brown to his talents and just over two years after moving across the Pennines he was being capped at full international level by England. His time at Wednesday ended when he signed for newly elected League side Ipswich Town, although he appeared in only four matches for the Suffolk club before retiring from the game. He was later a publican in Sheffield before returning to Merseyside, where he ran a hostelry in Formby.

RITCHIE, John Henry

(1966–69)

Centre-forward, 6ft 1½in, 13st 7lb (1966)
Born: 12 July 1941, Kettering
Died: 23 February 2007, Stoke
Signed from: Stoke City, 11 November 1966, £80,000
Transferred: Stoke City, 7 July 1969, £27,500
Career: Monn & Felton Boot & Shoe Works, Ennannett United, Kettering Town, Stoke City, Wednesday, Stoke City, Stafford Rangers
Debut: 12 November 1966 v Manchester United (a) First Division

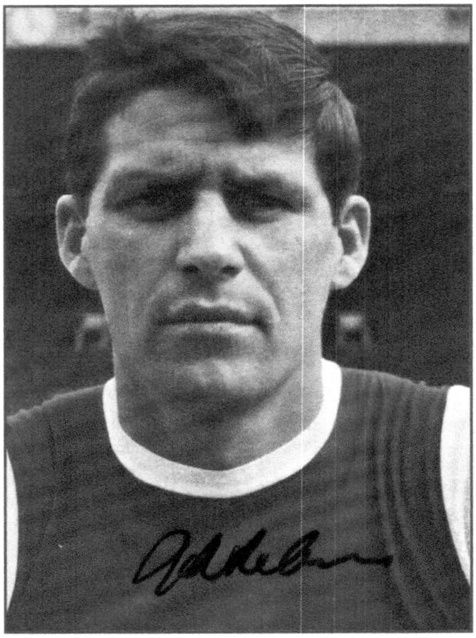

Last appearance: 12 May 1969 v Tottenham Hotspur (h) First Division
Caps: Football League (1)
Appearances/Goals: League 88+1/34, FAC 12/10, FLC 5/1

The Owls broke their club transfer record to obtain the services of stylish and prolific scorer John Ritchie. For Wednesday fans the capture must certainly have been a relief, as in previous games against Stoke City Ritchie had plundered seven goals from just 10 appearances! His playing career had started at a Kettering shoe factory, where he was employed, and it was his form for the town's senior non-League club that led directly to a transfer to Stoke City. He made a huge impact for the Staffordshire club in his first full season, setting a club record of netting in nine consecutive games, as well as helping City to the 1964 League Cup Final. His subsequent move to Hillsborough was a huge shock to Stoke fans, while Wednesday supporters were delighted to finally have an orthodox centre-forward in their team. Despite only joining in November, he finished joint top scorer in his first season – with 15 goals – and was outright top scorer in 1967–68 before the departure of manager Alan Brown proved somewhat unsettling for the tall, bustling attacker. He duly returned to Stoke, for a cut-price fee, and was quickly back among the goals – his overall tally for City totalled a club record 176 goals in 343 competitive games. He was in the side that won Stoke's only major honour – the 1972 League Cup – and also appeared in two FA Cup semi-finals. A double fracture of his leg, suffered in September 1974, proved the death knell for his career as he managed only a handful of games in non-League soccer before being forced to retire. He then concentrated on his pottery business, running the enterprise until his retirement due to ill health in 2003. He passed away, due to complications from Alzheimers disease, four years later.

ROBINSON, John 'Jackie'

(1934–46)

Inside-forward, 5ft 8in, 10st 1lb (1935)
Born: 10 August 1917, Shiremoor, Northumberland
Died: 31 July 1972, Shiremoor
Signed from: Shiremoor, October 1934, £20 10s
Transferred: Sunderland, 11 October 1946, £6,800
Career: New Biggin Juniors, West Wylam Colliery, Shiremoor, Wednesday, Newcastle United (guest), Darlington (guest), Hartlepool United (guest), Middlesbrough (guest), Sunderland, Lincoln City
Debut: 22 April 1935 v West Bromwich Albion (a) First Division
Last appearance: 21 September 1946 v Chesterfield (h) Second Division
Caps: England Full (4), Football League (1)
Appearances/Goals: League 108/34, FAC 11/5

It was unfortunate for brilliant inside-forward Jackie Robinson that he reached his playing peak during the years that spanned World War Two. Despite having appeared in just over 100 peacetime games for Wednesday, he is still, rightly, regarded as one of the finest players to ever pull on the blue-and-white shirt. His record of 90 goals in just 110 wartime games gives an insight into his talents and for decades after he left the club, fans still lavished praise on Jackie – he possessed superb passing ability, tremendous pace, a deceptive body swerve and, of course, a remarkable eye for goal. He had initially been spotted accidentally by Wednesday boss Billy Walker – he had attended a match to watch another player – but was quickly tied to Hillsborough, borrowing Ronnie Starling's boots and scoring the winner at West Bromwich Albion on his debut, in the week leading up the FA Cup Final meeting with the same side. He became a first-team regular during the 1936–37 season and was the only real positive to take from a campaign that ended in relegation from the top flight. His form was such that Robinson won his first full cap for England soon after – netting in an 8–0 win over Finland – and then appeared in the infamous match in Germany where the English players were controversially forced to give the Nazi salute, prior to kick-off. When war was declared in September 1939, Jackie returned home to his native North East and served in the Home Guard, while playing as a guest for several local sides; however, he returned to Sheffield and enjoyed a remarkable 1942–43 season, netting an astonishing six hat-tricks, as Wednesday reached the Final of the North War Cup. His haul included a treble in a record 8–2 romp over Sheffield United in February 1943 and it was hoped that this form could be replicated when the war years finally ended. However, after just a handful of post war games he was surprisingly sold to First Division Sunderland – his fee was later reduced after it was found that he had lied about his age to prolong his playing career! He enjoyed three successful seasons on Wearside before a broken leg ended his playing days at Lincoln City in 1949. He worked as a builder and then a publican before passing away, aged just 55, in the early 1970s.

RUDDLESDIN, Herrod 'Ruddy'

(1898–1908)

Half-back, 5ft 7in, 11st 2lb (1901)
Born: 1875–76 Birdwell, Barnsley
Died: 26 March 1910, Birdwell
Signed from: Birdwell, April 1898
Transferred: Northampton Town, May 1908
Career: Birdwell, Wednesday, Northampton Town
Debut: 10 September 1898 v Nottingham Forest (h) First Division
Last appearance: 19 October 1907 v Aston Villa (h) First Division
Caps: England Full (3)
Appearances/Goals: League 259/7, FAC 26/0

Locally born Herrod Ruddlesdin was actually considered to be a promising left-winger when he signed from non-League football. However it was quickly decided that he was far more suited to the role of left half-back, a position he would occupy with great distinction for the decade he was on the Owls' books. Despite being small in stature, his intelligent and consistent play endeared him to Wednesday fans of the era, 'good old Ruddy' being a familiar phrase uttered about his qualities. Alongside Bob Ferrier and Tommy Crawshaw, Ruddlesdin formed a solid back line that took the club out of the Second Division in 1900 and then on to consecutive League titles during the early part of the 20th century. His form also earned the defender full caps for his country and if he was not struck down with the terrible illness of consumption then his career at Wednesday could have been prolonged further. Unfortunately he started to struggle from the effects of the disease during the 1906–07 season and could only play a single game in the following season before the ex-miner was forced to end his League career, signing for Herbert Chapman at Southern League Northampton Town. Sadly, he was too ill to ever appear for the Cobblers and was only 34 years of age when he was taken by consumption.

SEED, James Marshall 'Jimmy'

(1927–31)
Inside-forward, 5ft 10in, 11st 9lb (1930)
Born: 25 March 1895, Blackhill, Durham
Died: 16 July 1966, Farnborough
Signed from: Tottenham Hotspur, 2 August 1927, Part-Ex for A. Lowdell
Transferred: Retired, April 1931
Career: Whitburn, Sunderland, Mid Rhondda, Tottenham Hotspur, Wednesday
Debut: 27 August 1927 v Everton (h) First Division
Last appearance: 4 April 1931 v Blackpool (a) First Division
Appearances/Goals: League 134/33, FAC 12/5

Every great Wednesday side has had within their ranks a player who has inspired his colleagues, the likes of Nigel Pearson and Lee Bullen being two modern-day examples. This was also true back in the late 1920s when the Owls won back-to-back League titles, with veteran forward Jimmy Seed providing that all-important spark of inspiration. Wednesday's legendary manager, Bob Brown, bought some truly outstanding players while he was in charge at Hillsborough, but it could be argued that none were greater than the capture of Seed, virtually on a free transfer. In his first season at Hillsborough, his influence – on a relatively young Wednesday side – slowly grew as the season progressed and he helped the club to pull off the remarkable 'great escape' in the spring of 1928. The momentum from that escape was continued into the following season and the 34-year-old Hampshire-born attacker led Wednesday to their third League title in 1929. His remarkable fitness ensured he was again a regular as the club walked away with the title again in 1930 – finishing the equivalent of 15 points clear in modern terms – and Brown said that if his captain was unable to play he should 'just throw your shirt onto the pitch' as if to symbolise his importance. His advancing years eventually caught up with Seed and he duly left in 1931, to take up the position of Clapton Orient manager, firmly established in the annuals of club history as one of the greatest ever captains. His career had started in his native North East, signing for Sunderland after scoring regularly in amateur football. He was a regular for the *Black Cats* before World War One but was unfortunately gassed while fighting for his country and rather harshly released on his return. He re-launched his career in Welsh soccer and was soon back in League football, winning

the Second Division title and then the FA Cup with Spurs in the early 1920s. He later fell out of favour at White Hart Lane, after his request to be released was rebuffed, and he was effectively the make-weight in the deal that took Arthur Lowdell to Tottenham from Hillsborough. When his playing days came to a close he became a success off the field, being in charge of Charlton Athletic for 24 years – from May 1933 until January 1957 – and in 1947 bringing the FA Cup to the Valley for the only time in the club's history.

SEWELL, John 'Jackie'

(1951–55)

Inside-forward, 5ft 9in, 10st 11lb (1951)
Born: 24 January 1927, Kell, near Whitehaven
Signed from: Notts County, 15 March 1951, £35,000
Transferred: Aston Villa, 2 December 1955, £23,000
Career: Kells Centre, Workington (guest), Notts County, Wednesday, Aston Villa, Hull City, City of Lusaka, Zambia
Debut: 17 March 1951 v Liverpool (a) First Division
Last appearance: 26 November 1955 v West Ham United (h) Second Division
Caps: England Full (6), Football League (4)
Appearances/Goals: League 164/87, FAC 11/5

It seems unbelievable to modern eyes that Wednesday, in the decade immediately after the end of World War Two, were involved in several transfer deals that broke the English record. The last time the Owls were involved, as a buying club, came in 1951 when, in an attempt to extricate themselves from the foot of the top-flight table, they splashed out £35,000 for the services of exciting attacker Jackie Sewell. It was a calculated gamble by the Owls board, but unfortunately it did not have the desired effect as despite Sewell scoring six times in 10 games they were still relegated to the second tier. However Wednesday, and Sewell, quickly bounced back and the attacker with a powerful shot, and tremendous work rate, was even capped at full international level, despite playing in the Second Division. The title was duly captured, and Sewell continued to score on a regular basis although the Owls were relegated again in 1955. He eventually moved back into the top flight and was in the Aston Villa side that beat Manchester United to win the 1957 FA Cup. He ended his English League career with highly impressive figures of 227 goals in 510 games before moving to modern-day Zimbabwe in 1961. He remained in Africa for 12 years, playing for a side he was asked to form and later being player-coach for the national team. He returned to the UK in 1973 and worked for a Nottingham-based car dealer until his retirement in 1987. At the age of 83 he launched his biography, signing copies when Notts County faced the Owls at Meadow Lane in October 2010.

SHELTON, Gary

(1982–87)
Midfielder, 5ft 7in, 10st (1982)
Born: 21 March 1958, Nottingham
Signed from: Aston Villa, 25 March 1982, £50,000
Transferred: Oxford United, 23 July 1987, £135,000
Career: Parkhead United, Walsall, Aston Villa, Notts County (loan), Wednesday, Oxford United, Bristol City, Rochdale (loan), Chester City
Debut: 27 March 1982 v Orient (h) Second Division
Last appearance: 9 May 1987 v Wimbledon (h) First Division
Caps: England Under-21 (1)
Appearances/Goals: League 195+3/18, FAC 23+1/3, FLC 18/3, Other 1/0

Midfielder Gary Shelton was a vital member of the Owls side of the mid-1980s and was an extremely popular figure among Owls fans, due to his whole-hearted displays and no-nonsense tackling. He was initially signed on loan by Jack Charlton – after he failed to nail down a regular berth at Aston Villa – and was an instant hit to ensure the move was made permanent a few weeks later. He was Player of the Year in the 1983–84 promotion season, and his attitude to the game was no better typified than his nickname of 'Stretch' which referred to the countless occasions he had been carried off the field, only to return to the action a few minutes later! After the Owls promotion he helped them to two top 10 finishes in the First Division – netting in a memorable 2–0 win at Anfield in September 1984 – before leaving for Oxford United (then a top-flight side themselves). During two years at United he suffered the pain of relegation but was then an inspirational figure for Bristol City, during almost five years at the West Country club. At his final club, Chester City, he became their oldest-ever player when made his final appearance, in February 1998, just short of his 40th birthday. A move into coaching followed for Shelton and he teamed up with old teammate, Gary Megson, as assistant manager as West Bromwich Albion won promotion to the Premiership in both 2002 and 2004.

SHERIDAN, John Joseph

(1989–96)
Midfielder, 5ft 10in, 10st 8lb (1993)
Born: 1 October 1964, Stretford, Manchester
Signed from: Nottingham Forest, 2 November 1989, £500,000
Transferred: Bolton Wanderers, 12 November 1996, £225,000
Career: Manchester City (Trainee), Leeds United, Nottingham Forest, Wednesday, Birmingham City (loan), Bolton Wanderers, Huddersfield Town (trial), Doncaster Rovers, Oldham Athletic

Debut: 4 November 1989 v Nottingham Forest (a) First Division
Last appearance: 7 September 1996 v Chelsea (h) Premiership
Caps: Eire Full (29), Under-23 (1)
Appearances/Goals: League 187+10/25, FAC 17+1/3, FLC 24/3, Euro 2/1, Other 3/1

The outstanding team of the early 1990s contained a plethora of players that could claim to be some of the greatest to ever represent the Owls. Men such as Nilsson, Waddle and Hirst helped to make that relatively short era a time of flowing, attacking football and goals galore. At the heart of that team, and probably the most popular player in the club's recent history, was playmaker John Sheridan. The stylish central midfielder had arrived at Wednesday after Ron Atkinson had ended his nightmare spell at Nottingham Forest where unpredictable Reds boss Brian Clough had effectively left 'Shezza' out in the cold. He had arrived at the City Ground for a hefty fee, after forging a reputation as the best midfield player outside the top flight, after 267 games for Leeds United. He was only given a solitary game by Clough and was delighted when 'Big Ron' ended his brief and unhappy time at Forest. His move to Wednesday proved perfect for both player and club with Sheridan becoming a darling of the fans as the Owls won promotion, and the League Cup in 1991 with his 37th minute strike at Wembley securing the club's first major honour since 1935. He was then the creative force as Wednesday finished third in 1992 and reached both domestic Cup Finals a year later. At his peak Sheridan's superb passing skills and incredible vision made him one of the most outstanding midfield players of his generation and his Wednesday partnership with Carlton Palmer proved a match made in heaven. While at Wednesday, Sheridan also played in both the 1990 and 1994 World Cup Finals for Eire – his Dublin-born parents being the link – while he was known for some spectacular goals, a stunning free kick at Luton Town probably being his best. He remained a first choice at Wednesday until the arrival of David Pleat in 1995 and then spent a spell on loan at Birmingham City before eventually moving to Bolton Wanderers. His popularity at Hillsborough continues to be high to this day, and while still a player he received a standing ovation from Owls fans whenever he appeared in opposition. His playing career eventually came to a close at Oldham Athletic, and he was then manager of the Boundary Park club from 2006 until 2009, reaching the League One Play-offs in 2007 and being in contention for promotion before leaving in March 2009. He was appointed Chesterfield boss in June 2009 and was in charge as the Spireites started life in their new B2Net Stadium in 2010.

SHINER, Roy Albert James

(1955–59)

Centre-forward, 5ft 8½in, 12st 3lb (1955)
Born: 15 November 1924, Seaview, Isle of Wight
Died: 28 October 1988, Isle of Wight
Signed from: Huddersfield Town, 18 July 1955*
Transferred: Hull City, 2 November 1959, £6,500
Career: Ryde ATC Corps, East Cowes Victoria, Ryde Sports, Portsmouth (trial), Wolverhampton Wanderers (trial), Cheltenham Town, Huddersfield Town, Wednesday, Hull City, Cheltenham Town
Debut: 20 August 1955 v Plymouth Argyle (h) Second Division
Last appearance: 26 September 1959 v Luton Town (h) First Division
Appearances/Goals: League 153/93, FAC 7/3
* *Shiner/Staniforth exchange for Conwell/Marriott*

Although he started his career as a full-back, Roy Shiner made his name as a free-scoring centre-forward during the 1950s.

His career had started in amateur football on the Isle of Wight and he did not turn fully professional until signing for Huddersfield Town in 1951 – the Terriers almost calling off the deal when they discovered he was three years older than they had originally believed! He failed to really become established at the West Yorkshire club but a display against the Owls' reserve side convinced Eric Taylor to take a chance on the imposing attacker and he was rewarded as Shiner was ever present and netted 33 times as the Second Division title was secured in 1956. He continued to score regularly in the higher grade and his never say die attitude ensured he was a great favourite with Wednesday supporters of the era. He plundered another 28 goals as the Owls won the second tier again in 1959 and it was only after Keith Ellis took his place, early in the following season, that Shiner eventually moved on – despite his advancing years several clubs chased his signature with Hull City winning the race. He netted a brace on his debut for City and appeared in 22 games before returning to Cheltenham Town where he was briefly player-manager in October 1961. One of only a handful of Isle of Wight players to play League soccer for the Owls – his father, Albert, played a single game for Derby County – Shiner returned to his birthplace and became a partner in a building contractor. He quickly returned to football as a manager and was subsequently in charge of various clubs on the island, winning a multitude of honours, and also raised thousands of pounds for charity in his role as secretary of two fund raising teams.

SHIRTLIFF, Peter Andrew

(1978–86 & 1989–93)

Defender, 6ft 1in, 12st 2lb (1982)
Born: 6 April 1961, Sheffield
Signed from: Trainee, 30 October 1978

Transferred: Charlton Athletic, 6 August 1986, £125,000
Signed from: Charlton Athletic, 26 July 1989, £500,000
Transferred: Wolverhampton Wanderers, 18 August 1993, £250,000
Career: Wednesday, Charlton Athletic, Wednesday, Wolverhampton Wanderers, Barnsley, Carlisle United (loan)
Debut: 12 August 1978 v Doncaster Rovers (a) League Cup
Last appearance: 8 May 1993 v Blackburn Rovers (a) Premiership
Appearances/Goals: League 292/8, FAC 25+1/4, FLC 35+2/1, Euro 1/0, Other 3/0

Born in the Sheffield district of Chapeltown, Peter Shirtliff supported Wednesday as a youngster and would graduate from the youth ranks to become one of the club's most popular and consistent defenders of the post war period – over 350 senior games placing him comfortably in the club's all-time top 20 appearance makers. He was one of many players to progress from the successful youth team of the late 1970s and first broke into the senior side during Jack Charlton's reign as manager. He was a vital member of the 1983–84 team that won promotion to the First Division, under Howard Wilkinson, and remained a first choice before his first spell at Hillsborough ended after a disagreement over a testimonial game, with a move to Charlton Athletic. He scored the winning goal that kept the Addicks in the top division in 1987 – in the promotion/relegation Play-off match against Leeds United – but after just over 100 games he returned to Hillsborough, being re-signed by Ron Atkinson for a sizeable fee. His second spell in Wednesday colours started with a shock relegation from the First Division, but Shirtliff was then a prominent member – alongside captain Nigel Pearson – of the Owls defence that helped the club to promotion and Wembley success; Peter playing in the League Cup Final win over Manchester United. He was then a regular as the Owls qualified for Europe 12 months later, after finishing third in the First Division, but injury then denied him the chance of an appearance in the 1993 FA Cup Final. He had also suffered a broken arm a few weeks earlier, and the double setback signalled the end of his Wednesday career, Shirtliff moving to Wolves a few weeks later. The strong, committed centre-half was a key member of the Wolves side for two seasons before a short playing spell at Barnsley preceded a move into coaching at Oakwell, Shirtliff eventually becoming assistant manager. He later held a variety of coaching roles at the likes of Mansfield Town and Tranmere Rovers before being appointed assistant manager – to old teammate Danny Wilson – at Swindon Town in 2009. He helped Town to the 2010 League One Play-off Final but was sacked, along with Wilson, in March 2011.

SIMPSON, George 'Georgie'

(1902–09)

Left-winger, 5ft 6in, 10st 5lb (1907)
Born: 1883, Jarrow
Signed from: Jarrow FC, 2 May 1902, £10
Transferred: West Bromwich Albion, 29 March 1909, £850 (joint fee with H. Burton)
Career: Jarrow, Wednesday, West Bromwich Albion, North Shields
Debut: 14 March 1903 v Blackburn Rovers (h) First Division
Last appearance: 29 March 1909 v Sunderland (h) First Division
Appearances/Goals: League 142/30, FAC 22/9

It was never going to be easy for the left-winger that replaced Wednesday legend Fred Spiksley, but George Simpson proved himself a more than capable successor, helping the club to the First Division Championship in 1904 before heading home the goal, against Everton, that brought the FA Cup back to Sheffield three years later. After being plucked from North East non-League football, the fearless and speedy attacker appeared in just a solitary game in his first season but became an established first-team player during the 1903–04 campaign and remained so until losing his place to Frank Foxall six seasons later. He was still out of the side when, along with Harry Burton, he was sold to Second Division promotion-chasing West Bromwich Albion – the double transfer causing somewhat of a sensation in Sheffield football as the joint fee was considered quite exorbitant by 1909 standards. The sale by Wednesday proved quite prudent, in hindsight, as Simpson failed to become established and within a year had dropped out of League soccer altogether, joining amateur club North Shields.

SMITH, Mark Craig

(1978–87)

Centre-half, 6ft, 12st 6lb (1978)
Born: 21 March 1960, Sheffield
Signed from: Trainee, 21 March 1978
Transferred: Plymouth Argyle, 22 July 1987, £170,000
Career: Middlewood Rovers, Wednesday, Plymouth Argyle, Barnsley, Notts County, Port Vale (loan), Huddersfield Town (loan), Chesterfield (loan), Lincoln City (loan)
Debut: 29 April 1978 v Colchester United (a) Third Division
Last appearance: 9 May 1987 v Wimbledon (h) First Division
Caps: England Under-21 (5)
Appearances/Goals: 281+1/16, FAC 39/3, FLC 29/1

Mark Smith was a stylish central-defender who was among the crop of first-team players to emerge from the successful late 1970s youth team. The local-born talent had joined the Owls straight from school and was initially utilised in midfield before a switch into defence, by youth coach Ken Knighton, effectively launched his career.

He graduated to the first team, under Jack Charlton, and was a fixture in the side as Wednesday won promotion from the Third Division in 1980 and reached the top flight in 1984 – his form in the higher grade in the early 1980s also resulted in several Under-21 caps for his country. He will perhaps mainly be remembered by Wednesday fans for the aforementioned 1980 promotion campaign when he converted 11 penalty kicks – breaking a club record that had been held by centre-forward Jack Ball for almost 50 years. After the Owls reached the First Division, Smith had to fight for his first-team place with the likes of Lawrie Madden, Peter Shirtliff and Mick Lyons and he eventually left for Plymouth Argyle, after enjoying a testimonial season at Hillsborough. The Devon club broke their transfer record to obtain his services, and Smith was a regular for two seasons before returning to South Yorkshire to sign for Barnsley. He was given a warm reception when he returned to Hillsborough with the Reds, despite scoring at the Kop end, in April 1991 and his first taste of coaching came as youth-team boss at Lincoln City in 1994. He returned to Oakwell as reserve-team boss in August 1998 and later received great acclaim in 2003 when he led the Academy side to the last four of the FA Youth Cup and runners-up position in the League. He duly came back to Wednesday in the same role a few weeks later and was caretaker boss at Hillsborough for one game in 2004 – between Chris Turner and Paul Sturrock. He continued his success at Youth level by taking the Owls' youngsters to runners-up spot in 2005 but was controversially dismissed a year later after the club overhauled its coaching structure. He returned to professional football in 2007, joining Sheffield United, and is now their development coach, while also taking an active part in looking after the Blades' reserve side, alongside another former Owl, Sam Ellis.

SMITH, Wilfred Samuel 'Wilf'

(1963–70)

Right-back, 5ft 10in, 11st 3lb (1966)

Born: 3 September 1946, Neumunster, Germany

Signed from: Trainee, 4 September 1963

Transferred: Coventry City, 31 August 1970, £100,000

Career: Wednesday, Coventry City, Brighton & Hove Albion (loan), Millwall (loan), Bristol Rovers, Chesterfield, Atherstone United

Debut: 19 December 1964 v Blackpool (h) First Division

Last appearance: 15 August 1970 v Charlton Athletic (h) Second Division

Caps: England Under-23 (6), Youth (6), Football League (3)

Appearances/Goals: League 207/4, FAC 21/1, FLC 6/0

Although Wilf Smith spent the vast majority of his childhood growing up in

Sheffield, he was actually christened Wolfgang Smith, in Germany in September 1964. His British father, serving in the Army, was based in Germany where he met and married a local girl. It was only after the family moved to England that they changed their son's forename, by deed poll, to make it easier for him to settle into school. After leaving school at the age of 14, he turned down an approach from Sheffield United, signing amateur forms at Wednesday instead. He was elevated to professional status on his 15th birthday and started to work as an apprentice electrician while he graduated through the ranks at Wednesday. After making his debut at the age of 18, replacing Gerry Young at left half-back, the strong and quick defender excelled at right-back, appearing in the dramatic 1966 FA Cup Final defeat to Everton and eventually amassing 234 competitive games for the Owls. He was a full-back that also loved to

get forward, although he only netted five goals for Wednesday, and when the club was relegated in 1970 he was a prime asset that it was difficult for Wednesday to keep. This proved the case and he duly became the costliest full-back in the British game when transferring to top-flight Coventry City for £100,000 in August 1970. He remained a consistent performer for City, totalling 151 games in five years, before his League career came to close at Chesterfield in 1977, following a major operation on his ankle. After leaving the game of football he started his own retail business, selling household items and garden tools, in the Leicestershire area, and retired in 2007 after selling his business.

SPIKSLEY, Frederick 'Fred'

(1891–1904)

Winger, 5ft 6in, 10st 4lb (1896)
Born: 25 January 1870, Gainsborough
Died: 28 July 1948, Goodwood, Sussex
Signed from: Gainsborough Trinity, February 1891
Transferred: Glossop, October 1904, Free
Career: Gainsborough Jubilee Swifts, Gainsborough Trinity, Wednesday, Glossop, Leeds City, Watford
Debut: 23 January 1892 v Bolton Wanderers (h) FA Cup
Last appearance: 18 April 1903 v West Bromwich Albion (h) First Division
Caps: England Full (7), Football League (2)
Appearances/Goals: League 292/100, FAC 29/15

Christened the 'Olive Grove Flyer' by adoring Wednesday fans, winger Fred Spiksley was an outstanding talent of the club's early years in the Football League. He arrived at Wednesday just before they gained League status after impressing for Midland League team Gainsborough Trinity – during the 1887–88 season he scored in every single home match played by the Lincolnshire side. His capture by

Wednesday was a story of chance as he was due to sign for Accrington but found himself stranded in Sheffield, on his way back from Lancashire, after missing his last train home. He duly bumped into Wednesday player Fred Thompson in a Sheffield hotel and Spiklsey promised he would not sign for Accrington until the Owls had spoken to him – soon after he joined Wednesday at a wage of £3 per week, plus a job at the *Sheffield Telegraph.* It was the start of a remarkable career that saw Fred remain a first choice for Wednesday for almost a dozen seasons and win seven caps for England, scoring a hat-trick for his country against Scotland. In an era when individualism was still more prevalent than teamwork, the nimble-footed, sharp-shooting and lightening-quick Spiksley was a jewel in the Wednesday side. He was one of the 11 players who appeared for the Owls in their first-ever League fixture, in September 1892, and scored twice – one after just 30 seconds – in the 1896 FA Cup Final as The Wednesday won the Cup for the first time. He combined with Alec Brady to form a superb left-wing partnership and after helping the club bounce straight back into the First Division in 1900, after being relegated and losing their Olive Grove home, he played his part during the 1902–03 campaign as the First Division title was secured for the first time. A leg injury finally ended his playing days at Wednesday and he played a further two years before being appointed secretary at London-based non-League side Southern United. His post-playing career was so colourful that a whole book could easily be produced as Fred travelled all over the world to coach and manage a wide variety of sides. Just a few years after leaving Wednesday he was declared bankrupt but later coached in Sweden, Germany, Mexico, England, Spain (at Barcelona) and Switzerland. He remained fit and active in his later years – competing in sprinting competitions well into his 70s – and it was while indulging in his favourite pastime – horse racing – that he passed away at Ladies Day at Goodwood Races, allegedly after backing the winner!

SPOORS, James 'Jimmy'

(1908–20)

Right-back, 5ft 9½in, 11st 4lb (1913)
Born: 1887–88 Jarrow
Died: 7 February 1960, Sheffield
Signed from: Jarrow, April 1908, £10
Transferred: Barnsley, 11 June 1920, £350
Career: Jarrow, Wednesday, Barnsley
Debut: 7 November 1908 v Middlesbrough (h) First Division
Last appearance: 5 April 1920 v Bolton Wanderers (h) First Division
Appearances/Goals: League 255/5, FAC 17/0

Defender Jimmy Spoors was yet another talent that was spotted by the Owls' legendary manager Bob Brown, when he was acting purely as North East scout in the early part of the 20th century. During the period Wednesday raided the Jarrow club for several players that would become regulars in the top flight and strong, no-nonsense centre full-back Jimmy Spoors was no exception. After a season in reserve-team football, he graduated to the first team when Willie Layton decided to retire, and he was virtually unopposed as first choice until League football was mothballed in 1915 as the 'Great War' raged in Europe. Spoors, who boasted terrific pace and a polished playing manner, served in the Army during the conflict, being posted in Italy, and appeared in a handful of games for the Owls during rare visits back to Sheffield. When the hostilities came to a close, Spoors returned to the first team at Hillsborough, but an ageing team suffered a disastrous 1919–20 campaign, which ended in relegation from the First Division. The full-back escaped the huge cull at the end of the season – Wednesday releasing 21 players – but his days were numbered and after just 18 more games he signed for neighbours Barnsley. He was utilised as an emergency centre-forward at Oakwell and holds the distinction of being the first Tykes player to net a League hat-trick away from home, achieving the feat at Birmingham in March 1921. He netted nine times in the last 11 games of that season but appeared only once more, in an FA Cup tie, prior to spending a season as player-manager to the reserve side and being released in 1922. Later in life he became a publican in the area.

SPRINGETT, Ronald Derrick 'Ron'

(1958–67)

Goalkeeper, 5ft 10in, 12st 11lb (1961)
Born: 22 July 1935, Fulham
Signed from: Queen's Park Rangers, 13 March 1958, £10,000
Transferred: Queen's Park Rangers, 22 May 1967, £16,000
Career: Victoria United, Queen's Park Rangers, Wednesday, Queen's Park Rangers, Southampton (loan), Valley United (Sun.)
Debut: 15 March 1958 v Bolton Wanderers (h) First Division
Last appearance: 15 May 1967 v Leeds United (a) First Division
Caps: England Full (33), Football League (9)
Appearances/Goals: League 345/0, FAC 28/0, FLC 1/0, Euro 10/0

A handful of players can lay claim to the title of Wednesday's greatest-ever goalkeeper and Ron Springett would certainly be in that elite group. It would not be unfair to say the brilliantly agile and brave goalie, with lightening-quick reflexes, is the club's best custodian since the war as he was first choice at Hillsborough from the day he arrived until he uniquely swapped clubs with brother Peter in 1967. In the intervening years Springett actually lived in London, training in the capital alongside his brother at QPR, and commuted to Sheffield

for games – this perhaps showed how highly he was rated by Wednesday. He joined as a hugely promising 20-year-old with Wednesday having suffered a 'keeper crisis during the 1957–58 season as four different men had worn the green jersey, with varying degrees of success. The arrival of Ron resolved the situation, and within 18 months he was capped at full international level as Wednesday won the Second Division Championship. He subsequently became undisputed number one for both club and country, helping the Owls to First Division runners'-up spot in 1961 and playing for England in the 1962 World Cup Finals in Chile. He also appeared for England in the famous 9–3 rout of the Scots in April 1961, and his 33 caps for England is a record haul for any player while on the Owls' books. While in Wednesday colours he appeared in every European game played by the club in the early 1960s and was also in the side that bravely lost 3–2 to Everton in the 1966 FA Cup Final. After losing his international shirt to Gordon Banks he had to watch from the sidelines as England lifted the Jules Rimet Trophy in 1966, and it was not until June 2009 that he was presented with a winners' medal, after Fifa had decided to award medals retrospectively. He eventually moved from Hillsborough in 1967 with the Springett name remaining in the Owls goal as younger sibling Peter took over from Ron. The popular goalie returned later in the year for a well-attended testimonial game and as a show of gratitude he presented Wednesday with his first-ever England cap. He played only 45 games after leaving Wednesday, retiring in 1969, although he did appear in a handful of Sunday League games, as a centre-forward, before retiring from football altogether. He later ran a sports shop, in the shadow of Loftus Road, and then ran his own decorating and gardening business until his retirement.

SPURR, Thomas 'Tommy'

(2006–present)

Left-back, 6ft 1in, 11st 5lb (2007)
Born: 30 September 1987, Leeds
Signed from: Trainee, 1 July 2006
Career: Wednesday
Debut: 22 April 2006 v Reading (h) Championship
Appearances/Goals: League 186+6/5, FAC 10/2, FLC 7/0, OTHER 2/0

Popular full-back Tommy Spurr joined the Owls at the tender age of just seven and eventually progressed through the youth ranks to become an Academy Scholar at Hillsborough. It was primarily as a centre-half that Spurr impressed in youth and reserve-team football, but when he made his senior bow it was as an emergency left-back, in the 1–1 home draw with Reading – he had been voted Academy Player of the Year in 2004–05. His whole-hearted attitude and terrific tackling ability immediately ensured his popularity among Wednesday fans, and he became a regular at left-back throughout the 2006–07 season, as various injuries decimated the first-team squad. Although his positional move to left-back was supposed to be only a temporary change, the tall and athletic Spurr has subsequently made the full-back role his own and is now rightly considered to be first choice for the club. His progress was rewarded in December 2006 with a new three-year deal, and he was handed a new lucrative four-year contract in September 2009 – the Owls having rejected two offers for his services from big spending Queen's Park Rangers in December 2007. Although not a prolific goalscorer, Tommy has made a habit of netting some spectacular goals, and his first-minute goal against Sheffield United, in the February 2009 win at Bramall Lane, helped the Owls to an historic first double over United for 95 years. The goal was extra special for the impressive defender as he supported Wednesday as a youngster, while his parents are away match regulars, watching their son and supporting the Owls. He remained a regular for the majority of the 2010/11 season before falling out of favour under new manager, Gary Megson, after a bad home defeat to Brentford

STARLING, Ronald William 'Ronnie'

(1932–37)

Inside-right, 5ft 9½in, 11st 5lb (1935)
Born: 11 October 1909, Pelaw-on-Tyne
Died: 17 December 1991, Sheffield
Signed from: Newcastle United, 25 June 1932, £3,250
Transferred: Aston Villa, 6 January 1937, £6,900
Career: Usworth Colliery, Washington Colliery, Hull City, Newcastle United, Wednesday, Aston Villa, Northampton Town (guest), Walsall (guest), Wednesday (guest), Nottingham Forest (guest), Beighton Miners Welfare
Debut: 27 August 1932 v Blackpool (h) First Division
Last appearance: 2 January 1937 v Wolverhampton Wanderers (h) First Division
Caps: England Full (1)
Appearances/Goals: League 176/30, FAC 17/0

Although rightly remembered as the last player to lift aloft the FA Cup for Wednesday, talented inside-forward Ronnie Starling was an outstanding player in his own right, being described as 'the man with fluttering feet'. He was a somewhat unorthodox inside-right and soon after joining the Owls many fans called for him to be dropped from the side. However, manager Billy Walker resisted those calls and after moving Ronnie to inside-left, and handing him the captain's armband, Starling formed an outstanding wing partnership with Ellis Rimmer, becoming one of the most talked about attackers in the English game. Many supporters were surprised that Ronnie was only capped once for his country while at Hillsborough. During his five years with Wednesday, the former Durham boys

player enjoyed the best period of his playing career, winning the aforementioned England cap and of course leading his side to Wembley success in the 1935 FA Cup Final against West Bromwich Albion. He added a Charity Shield winners' medal to his collection later in the year but when the Owls were struggling near the foot of the First Division, in January 1937, he was effectively sacrificed after the club had fought off interest from several clubs for the rapidly emerging Jackie Robinson. His departure – the fee was a new record for the Owls – was roundly criticised and within a few months the Owls were relegated and almost dropped into regional soccer 12 months later. He subsequently led Aston Villa to the Second Division title in 1938 and continued to play throughout the war years for a variety of clubs, including two appearances back in Wednesday colours. After the war he spent two years as Nottingham Forest trainer before launching a comeback, aged 41, at Sheffield-based Yorkshire League side Beighton. After finally hanging up his boots he ran a newsagents shop, near to Wednesday's home ground, while also playing in charity matches until his 60th year. After retiring, he became a regular on the golf course before passing away in a Sheffield nursing home, a few months after watching his old side return to Wembley and win their first major honour since Ronnie's side 56 years earlier.

STERLAND, Melvyn 'Mel'

(1979–89)

Full-back, 5ft 11in, 12st 7lb (1981)
Born: 1 October 1961, Sheffield
Signed from: Trainee, 5 October 1979
Transferred: Glasgow Rangers, 3 March 1989, £800,000
Career: Middlewood Rovers, Wednesday, Glasgow Rangers, Leeds United, Boston United, Denaby United, Universal Drilling (Sun.), Hollinsend Amateurs, Hallam
Debut: 17 May 1979 v Blackpool (h) Third Division
Last appearance: 25 February 1989 v Wimbledon (a) First Division
Caps: England Full (1), B (1), Under-21 (7), Football League (1)
Appearances/Goals: League 271+8/37, FAC 34+1/5, FLC 30/7, Other 3/0

Home-grown attacking full-back Mel Sterland was arguably the most popular Wednesday player of the 1980s. After progressing through the youth ranks at Hillsborough – mainly being utilised in a forward role – he made a goalscoring debut as a raw 17-year-old in 1979, but it was in a right-back role that he would be best remembered by Owls fans. It was Wednesday coach John Harris who converted Sterland to full-back and from that point he never looked back, earning Under-21 honours for England and becoming an automatic choice for the club. It was his penalty-kick, in the home game against Crystal Palace in April 1984,

that secured promotion to the First Division and his rampaging runs from right-back earned Mel the nickname of 'Zico' from Owls fans – manager Jack Charlton also coined the, rather less flattering, nickname of the 'flying pig'! Soon after helping the club to promotion, he was part of the successful England Under-21 side that won the 1984 European Championships. He remained a vital member of the Wednesday side as they impressed in the higher grade and showed his versatility by spending the first few weeks of the 1988–89 season in a forward role – as a youngster he had netted 144 goals in a single season for his two junior sides! He duly became the first Wednesday player to win a full cap for England since Ron Springett, but when manager Peter Eustace controversially stripped him of his beloved captain's armband he asked to be placed on the transfer list. It was new manager Ron Atkinson who actually sold Mel to Glasgow Rangers, for a club-record fee, with the money effectively paying for the purchase of Carlton Palmer. A brief spell in Glasgow earned Sterland a League Championship medal, and he repeated the feat under old boss, Howard Wilkinson, as new club Leeds United won the Second and First Division titles in consecutive seasons in the early 1990s. Persistent injury problems eventually forced the whole-hearted player to quit the professional game in 1994, although he continued to play in non-League soccer, being employed as player-manager at Boston United, Denaby United and Stalybridge Celtic. He survived life-saving surgery in 2003 – after a blood clot travelled from his leg to his lungs – and in 2008 put his life story into print with the publication of his autobiography *Boozing, Betting & Brawling*. He is now a regular around Hillsborough on a matchday, contributing a column to the matchday programme and remains a firm favourite with Owls fans.

STEWART, James 'Jimmy'

(1902–08)

Inside-forward, 5ft 8in, 10st 8lb (1902)
Born: 1883, Gateshead
Died: 23 May 1957, Durham
Signed from: Gateshead NER, 29 April 1902, £32
Transferred: Newcastle United, 1 August 1908, £1,000
Career: Todds Nook (Newcastle), Gateshead NER, Wednesday, Newcastle United, Glasgow Rangers, North Shields
Debut: 14 February 1903 v Grimsby Town (h) First Division
Last appearance: 25 April 1908 v Everton (a) First Division
Caps: England Full (2)
Appearances/Goals: League 123/52, FAC 18/8

Attacker Jimmy Stewart was another outstanding player to arrive at Owlerton from the hotbed of North East football in the early part of the 20th century. He was

invited for trials, along with teammate George Simpson, and after just a single game for the reserves he was handed a professional contract, such was his obvious ability. After a season of reserve-team football he broke into Wednesday's first team during the Championship-winning season of 1903–04, and Stewart – nicknamed 'Tadger' – became an instant hit. He quickly developed into one of the finest inside-forwards in the English game, and he duly helped the club to the FA Cup semi-finals in 1905 before scoring in both the semi-final and Final in 1907 as Wednesday won the trophy for the second time. He also scored on his debut for England – against Wales in 1907 – but Owls fans were shocked in the summer of 1908 when he refused to sign a new contract, despite being offered the maximum wage allowed at the time by the FA. He subsequently returned to the North East, and his delicate skills powered Newcastle United to the League title in his debut season. He missed out on an appearance in the 1910 FA Cup Final for the Geordies but did appear in the Final replay defeat to Bradford City a year later. He subsequently spent a season with Glasgow giants Rangers, scoring 10 goals in 19 games, before his career came to a close with a spell as player-manager at non-League North Shields. Away from football he worked as a commercial traveller and publican before being employed as an accountant, while also scouting for Derby County.

STRANGE, Alfred Henry 'Alf' (1927–35)

Half-back, 5ft 8ins, 11st 6lbs (1927)
Born: 2 April 1900, Marehay, Nr Ripley
Died: October 1978 Ripley
Signed from: Port Vale, 17 February 1927, £1,230 plus Harry Anstiss
Transferred: Bradford Park Avenue, 10 May 1935, £200
Career: Marehay Colliery, Ripley Town, Wednesday (trial), Portsmouth, Port Vale, Wednesday, Bradford Park Avenue, Ripley Town, Raleigh, Corsham United
Debut: 19 February 1927 v Sunderland (H) First Division
Last Appearance: 22 April 1935 v West Bromwich Albion (A) First Division
Caps: England Full (20), Football League (2)
Appearances/Goals: League 253/22, FAC 20/0

Alf Strange was yet another outstanding player to appear for the club in the period between the two World Wars. Despite initially having joined Wednesday as a highly rated inside-forward, it would be a change to right half-back, near the end of his second season at Hillsborough, that would totally transform the career of the Derbyshire-born player. Over the five seasons that followed, Strange missed only six games and his tremendous form in the Owls rearguard subsequently led to a multitude of caps for his country. An

integral member of the famous Wednesday back line, along with Tony Leach and Billy Marsden, he was imperious for the Owls as the club won back-to-back League titles and constantly challenged for England's top honours. His many qualities made Strange one of the finest half-backs of his generation with superb passing skills and long-range shooting ability just an example of his attributes.

Like many of his contemporaries, he started his working life at his local pit and actually almost joined the Owls in 1918 after attending a Hillsborough trial. He subsequently secured a deal at Portsmouth and arrived back at Wednesday, via Port Vale, with the Owls paying a hefty fee for his services. He was an automatic choice at Wednesday for almost five seasons until experiencing an injury ravaged 1933–34 campaign, which saw Alf suffer a broken foot before fracturing his leg in a top-flight match at Liverpool. On his comeback he broke his other leg and then the form of Horace Burrows and Wilf Sharp kept him in the reserves as the Owls reached Wembley in 1935. He moved to Bradford at the end of the season but his fitness was poor and it was no real surprise when he retired from the professional game a few months later. He continued to play at an amateur level into his mid-40s and later returned to the mines before retiring back to Ripley, where he tended to his chickens with memories of glory times in an Owls shirt.

SWAN, Peter

(1953–65 & 1972–73)

Centre-half, 6ft, 11st 2lb (1954)

Born: 8 October 1936, South Elmsall

Signed from: Ground staff, 19 November 1953

Transferred: Contract cancelled, April 1965

Signed from: Free agent, 28 July 1972

Transferred: Bury, 26 July 1973, Free

Career: Wednesday, Bury, Matlock Town, Worksop Town

Debut: 5 November 1955 v Barnsley (a) Second Division

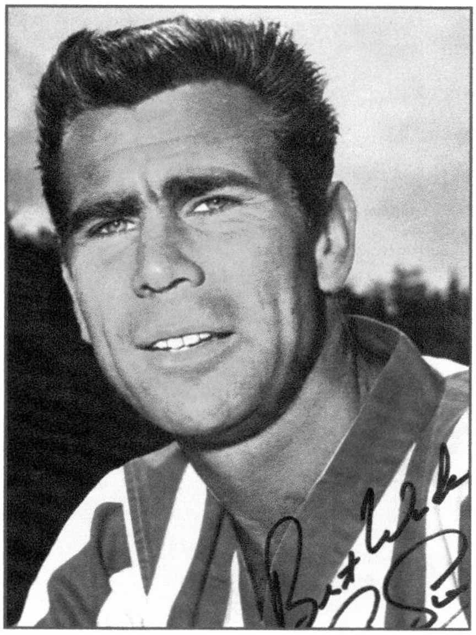

Last appearance: 11 November 1972 v Oxford United (h) Second Division
Caps: England Full (19), Under-23 (3), Youth (1), Football League (6)
Appearances/Goals: League 273+2/0, FAC 14/0, FLC 2/0, Euro 10/0

Unfortunately for outstanding defender Peter Swan, his playing career will always be associated with the betting scandal in 1964 that not only left his career in tatters but also that of his teammate Bronco Layne. Before that moment Swan had been capped on numerous occasions for his country and was a crucial member of the Wednesday side that was promoted out of the Second Division in 1959 before pushing for the major honours in the early 1960s. The Swan-Kay-McAnearney back line was almost unrivalled in the English game, and the long-legged, dominant wing-half was an automatic choice for six seasons, also playing for England on a regular basis. It was, therefore, a massive blow to both club and player when the news story broke that he was involved in a match fixing scandal – Swan had bet for the Owls to lose at Ipswich Town in 1962. After being found guilty, he was banned 'sine die' by the Football Association and worked at a local bakery and as a publican before his ban was surprisingly lifted in 1972. He was given a second chance by the Owls, and after signing a one-year deal he appeared briefly back in the senior side – taking his tally of games to over the 300 mark – but time was not on his side and the 36-year-old ended his League career at Bury, scoring on his debut for the Shakers after failing to score a single goal for Wednesday! After being appointed player-manager at Matlock Town, he appeared at Wembley in their FA Trophy Final victory over Scarborough and ended his playing days at Worksop Town before concentrating on the licensing trade. He worked as a publican until his retirement and in September 2006 published his biography entitled *Putting the Record Straight.*

SWIFT, Humphrey Mills 'Hugh'

(1944–51)
Left-back, 5ft 11in, 11st 8lb (1948)
Born: 22 January 1921, Sheffield
Died: 24 January 1970, Sheffield
Signed from: Lopham Street WMC, 1944
Transferred: Retired, 11 August 1951
Career: Burngreave O. B., Lopham Street WMC, Wednesday, Sheffield United (guest)
Debut: 5 January 1946 v Mansfield Town (a) FA Cup
Last appearance: 26 February 1951 v Manchester United (h) First Division
Caps: England B (1)
Appearances/Goals: League 181/0, FAC 14/0

It was on the left wing that Hugh Swift was a star in Sheffield youth football, being crowned the city's best schoolboy player

when being awarded the prestigious Clegg Shield during the war years. At the time he was appearing for Sheffield-based Burngreave Old Boys but eventually began to train regularly with Wednesday, attending newly introduced evening training sessions. However, his career failed to progress as it was expected to, and he eventually stopped attending the sessions after being told he was too frail to make the grade. He duly returned to local amateur soccer, but his second chance came in February 1942 when he was asked to guest for the Owls in a wartime League fixture. It was a chance that Swift needed, and he impressed sufficiently to be tied to amateur forms in September 1942. He quickly became an almost ever present during the 1942–43 season, but just before the War North Cup Final his career changed direction as he was utilised as an emergency left-back, in place of the injured Ted Catlin, and subsequently shackled the great Stanley Matthews in the first leg of the Final. It would be at left-back that Swift remained for the rest of his career, with his ability with both feet, pace and trademark sliding tackling ensuring he was undisputed as Wednesday's left-back in the immediate post war years. Between December 1946 and April 1949 he was part of a 109 consecutive game partnership with right-back Frank Westlake, and he captained Wednesday to promotion from the Second Division in 1950. Sadly, with Hugh tipped to win full international honours, his career hit the buffers as a double fracture of his jaw in a game at Coventry City proved an initial setback before knee problems left him on the sidelines. Unfortunately, due to Swift having suffered Rheumatic fever as a teenager, leaving him with a heart murmur, his knees started to swell constantly and he had no choice but to retire altogether from the sport in 1951, aged just 30 years old. Thankfully, Swift had never become a full-time professional at Hillsborough, so he was able to fall back on his career with a Sheffield Silversmiths, owned by Wednesday president William Turner. He was also retained by the club, on full wages, as a scout and also coached at Hillsborough until February 1967 when he was a victim of a clear out by manager Alan Brown. Within a year he was back at Wednesday, as youth coach, and remained on the staff until his untimely death, just two days past his 59th birthday, in 1970.

TROTTER, James William 'Jimmy'

(1922–30)

Centre-forward, 5ft 8in, 11st 6lb (1922)
Born: 25 November 1899, Easington
Died: 17 April 1984, St Albans
Signed from: Bury, 17 February 1922, £1,907
Transferred: Torquay United, 5 June 1930, £500
Career: Parsons Turbine Works, Bury, Wednesday, Torquay United, Watford
Debut: 13 February 1922 v Wolverhampton Wanderers (h) Second Division
Last appearance: 2 February 1929 v Sheffield United (a) First Division
Appearances/Goals: League 153/109, FAC 6/5

Prolific centre-forward Jimmy Trotter was plucked from amateur football by Bury and subsequently sold to Wednesday when the Lancashire club hit financial problems and had no choice but to part with their prized asset. He scored 20 goals in his first full season at Wednesday, but these were all for the reserve side that won the Championship of the Midland League in 1923. He acted as understudy to Sid Binks at first-team level, and it would not be until his rival left for

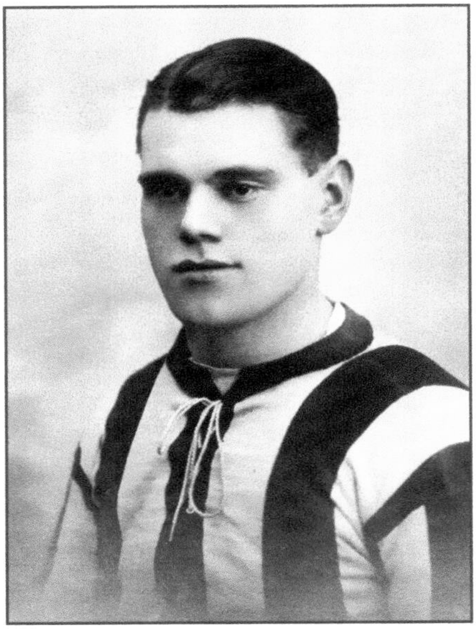

Huddersfield Town, in September 1924, that Trotter was finally given a prolonged run in the first team. He quickly started to find the net on a regular basis, and he entered the record books in December 1924 by becoming the first Owls player to score five times in a League game, achieving the feat at home to Portsmouth. He was then virtually unstoppable as Wednesday won the Second Division title in 1926, and his top-flight tally of 37 goals in the 1926–27 season still stands today as the highest seasonal haul in the top division by an Owls player. He was taken to their hearts by Wednesday fans with the song 'Trot, Trot, Trotter, score a little goal for me' often heard reverberating around Hillsborough when Jimmy was in full flow. As the 1920s came to a close, Trotter lost his first-team place to Jack Allen, although his 21 goals for the reserves in the 1928–29 season ensured that the second team repeated the feat of the senior side by winning the League Championship. The North East-born forward spent another season in the reserves before moving to the 'English Riveria' when signing for Torquay United. He would spend only a season in Devon, though, and ended his playing days at Watford before moving into coaching when old teammate Jimmy Seed recruited him for the role of trainer to Charlton's A team in 1934. He would remain at The Valley for over 20 years – he was promoted to first-team trainer a year after joining – and also served as England trainer during the reign of Walter Winterbottom. He graduated to manager in September 1956, but relegation in his second season at the helm and when the Valiants failed to re-gain their First Division status he was dismissed in October 1961, retiring from football altogether.

TUDGAY, Marcus

(2006–2010)

Forward, 5ft 9in, 11st 7lb (2007)

Born: 3 February 1983, Shoreham, Sussex

Signed from: Derby County, 1 January 2006, u/d

Sold: Nottingham Forest, 25 November 2010, u/d

Career: Derby County, Wednesday, Nottingham Forest

Debut: 2 January 2006 v Crewe Alexandra (h) Championship

Last Appearance: 20 November 2010 v MK Dons (A) League One

Appearances/Goals: League 178+17/49, FAC 6+1/1, FLC 5+1/1, Other 1+2/1

Utility-forward Marcus Tudgay was signed by Owls boss Paul Sturrock on the first day of the 2006 transfer window. His move from County was initially a loan deal, but the move was subsequently made permanent just five days later with the Owls paying an undisclosed fee for his services. He had joined the Rams straight from school and made his senior debut in August 2002 before becoming a first-team regular, being utilised as an out-and-out striker or wide midfielder. He netted on his Wednesday debut in a 3–0 win over Crewe Alexandra

and scored some vital goals as the Owls avoided relegation from the Championship – netting in the final-day win at old club Derby County (his final goal for the Rams had coincidentally been against Wednesday in November 2004). He missed the start of the 2006–07 season after, somewhat bizarrely, severing tendons in his foot after stepping on glass at a family barbecue and spent several weeks on the sidelines after the injury required surgery. He did, however, bounce back and finished joint top scorer as Wednesday surged up the League table, under new manager Brian Laws, and just fell short of securing a Play-off position. An excellent 'link' player, Tudgay has continued to score regularly, and his terrific long-range strike at Bramall Lane in February 2009 ensured he entered the club annuals as Wednesday ended that 95-year wait for a double over United – he was also voted PFA fans' Player of the Season. He struggled to re-capture his old form during the relegation season of 2009–10, and despite passing the 50-goal mark for the Owls he subsequently left, in a loan deal, to Championship side Nottingham Forest in November 2010. This was made permanent on 5 January 2011, ending a five-year association with the Owls.

VARADI, Imre 'Ray'

(1983–85 & 1988–90)

Forward, 5ft 8½in, 11st 11lb (1983)
Born: 8 July 1959, Paddington, London
Signed from: Newcastle United, 26 August 1983, £170,000
Transferred: West Bromwich Albion, 19 July 1985, £285,000 (T)
Signed from: Manchester City, 30 September 1988, £100,000
Transferred: Leeds United, 2 February 1990, £45,000 (exchange for C. Bradshaw)
Career: Letchworth Garden City, Tottenham Hotspur (trial), Cambridge United (trial), Sheffield United, Everton, Benfica (trial), Newcastle United, Wednesday, West Bromwich Albion, Manchester City, Wednesday, Leeds United, Luton Town (loan), Oxford United (loan), Rotherham United, Mansfield Town (N/C), Boston United, Scunthorpe United (N/C), Boston United, Matlock Town, Guiseley, Denaby United, Stalybridge Celtic, Universal Drilling (Sun.), Sheffield FC.
Debut: 27 August 1983 v Swansea City (a) Second Division
Last appearance: 21 October 1989 v Tottenham Hotspur (a) First Division
Appearances/Goals: League 86+12/36, FAC 9/7, FLC 12+1/3, Other 1/0

Livewire forward Imre Varadi started his playing career in non-League soccer, and it was not until the age of 17 that he joined a League club for the first time, signing a professional contract for Sheffield United. Varadi, whose surname was a product of a Hungarian father and Italian mother, made an immediate impact at Bramall Lane, and after just 10 games, and four goals, he was

sold to Everton for a quick profit. He failed to become established at the Merseyside club but became a huge favourite at his next side, Newcastle United, where he grabbed 42 goals in just 90 games. When he was sold, somewhat against his will, to Wednesday in the summer of 1983, the Geordie supporters were not amused and when Varadi netted twice against Newcastle, at Hillsborough in November 1983, he made his feelings known by failing to celebrate. By this time he was a vital member of Howard Wilkinson's side that would earn promotion back to the top-flight, along with Newcastle, in 1984 and he grabbed 21 League and Cup goals in the following season, with the quick and prolific forward becoming a firm favourite with Wednesday fans. Owls fans were therefore disappointed when in the summer of 1985 he rejected the Owls' offer of a new contract and instead signed for West Bromwich Albion – a transfer tribunal setting the fee. He finished the season as top marksman for Albion and then Manchester City but suffered relegation with both clubs before being re-signed by Wednesday. However, his second stint at Hillsborough was by no means a happy one as he quickly fell out with new manager Peter Eustace and was actually suspended by Eustace after asking for a transfer! The arrival of a new manager, Ron Atkinson, did little to improve his position at Wednesday, and he departed after failing to start a first-team game for 10 months. It was his old boss Howard Wilkinson who took him to Elland Road, and Varadi helped United to the Second Division title before appearing for a plethora of lower-League sides during the remainder of his career. He was assistant manager to Mel Sterland at both Boston United and Stalybridge Celtic and is now a FIFA registered agent, while also appearing regularly as a match summariser for BBC Radio Sheffield.

WADDLE, Christopher Roland 'Chris'

(1992–96)

Winger, 6ft, 11st 5lb (1995)

Born: 14 December 1960, Felling

Signed from: Olympic Marseille, 17 July 1992, £1 million

Transferred: Falkirk, 13 September 1996, Free

Career: Sheffield United (trial), Coventry City (Yth), Pelaw Juniors, Whitehouse Social Club (Sun.), Sunderland (trial), Pelaw Social Club, Clarke Chapman, Leam Lane Social Club (Sun.), Tow Law Town, Sunderland (trial), Newcastle United, Tottenham Hotspur, Olympic Marseille, Wednesday, Falkirk, Bradford City, Sunderland, Burnley, Hollinsend Amateurs, Brunsmeer, Torquay United, Hilltop, Davy Sports, Brunsmeer, Worksop Town, Parkgate (loan), Staveley, Glapwell, South Normanton Athletic, Stocksbridge Park Steels, Staveley, South Normanton Athletic, Staveley, MBNA, Greenhill White Hart

Debut: 15 August 1992 v Everton (a) Premiership

Last appearance: 5 May 1996 v West Ham United (a) Premiership
Appearances/Goals: League 94+15/10, FAC 12+1/3, FLC 19/0, Euro 5+1/2

Despite joining the Owls near the end of his glittering career, mercurial winger Chris Waddle subsequently became one of the most popular players of recent times with Wednesday fans. His outstanding form in his debut campaign for Wednesday left Owls fans, and many in the national media, calling for his recall to the England side and he was duly voted as the 'Football Writers Player of the Year' – the only time a Wednesday player has been awarded the prestigious honour. The 1992–93 season, of course, ended in ultimate disappointment, but Waddle's spectacular goal in the FA Cup semi-final against Sheffield United and goal in the Final replay against Arsenal ensured his name is firmly etched in the club's history. A few months later his devastating masterclass of wing play – against West Ham United at Hillsborough – saw the match in question dubbed as 'Waddle's game', and he

continued to be a first-team regular at Wednesday until the arrival of David Pleat in the summer of 1995. He subsequently rejected the club's offer of a player-coach role, and after a mixed 1995–96 season he eventually made the surprise free transfer move to Scottish First Division side Falkirk. After just five games north of the border he signed for Bradford City – playing against the Owls in a February 1997 FA Cup tie – and later joined boyhood heroes Sunderland. After a relatively unsuccessful spell as player-manager at Burnley, Waddle ended his senior career at Torquay United before returning to Hillsborough to join the coaching staff in December 1998. He was promoted to reserve-team manager in July 1999 but left in the following summer after failing to win the race for the vacant managerial position. After leaving Wednesday, the affable Geordie continued to appear in local football – turning out for HSBC in the Wragg Over-35 League in 2010 – and is now a regular voice on BBC Radio, working as a match summariser. As a youngster, the lanky teenager had famously worked in a factory that produced spices for pies and sausages, while playing non-League football. His first break came when he joined Northern League Tow Law Town and his form was such that Newcastle United signed Waddle to a professional deal in July 1980. The raw 19-year-old took time to adapt to his new surroundings, but he was soon a vital member of the United side that won promotion from the old Second Division in 1984, alongside the likes of Kevin Keegan, Peter Beardsley and Terry McDermott. Waddle's career then started to gather pace and a first full cap for England preceded a £650,000 move to Tottenham Hotspur. He became an established international at White Hart Lane, although he failed to secure any major honours, losing in the 1987 FA Cup Final to Coventry City. He then famously scored a top 10 hit, in collaboration with Glenn Hoddle, with *Diamond Lights* before becoming the most expensive British footballer when moving to French club Olympic Marseille for £4.25 million in July 1989. A year later he experienced the agony of missing a penalty in the World Cup semi-final against West Germany, but in Southern France he was a superstar, helping OM to three League titles and the 1991 European Cup Final. He came out of retirement again, in December 2010, to join Sheffield Sunday League club Greenhill White Hart, just short of his 50th birthday.

WALKER, Desmond Sinclair 'Des'

(1993–2001)
Centre-half, 5ft 11in, 11st 13lb (1997)
Born: 26 November 1965, Hackney
Signed from: Sampdoria, 14 July 1993, £2.75 million
Transferred: Released, 30 June 2001
Career: Nottingham Forest, Sampdoria, Wednesday, Burton Albion, Nottingham Forest, Mansfield Town
Debut: 14 August 1993 v Liverpool (a) Premiership
Last appearance: 21 April 2001 v Barnsley (h) First Division
Caps: England Full (1)
Appearances/Goals: League 307/0, FAC 24/0, FLC 28/0, Euro 3/0

Although Des Walker cost a large fee, by 1993 standards, there is no doubt that Wednesday received full value for their monies. The former England star returned from an unhappy spell in Italian football, where he was inexplicably often played at full-back, to sign for Trevor Francis's Wednesday side, who at the time were being tipped as title contenders after a memorable 1992–93 season. For the next eight years the lightening quick central-defender was a veritable rock at the heart of the club's defence, almost solely keeping the opposition out at times as the Owls started to slide down the Premiership table and eventually into the First Division. His coolness under pressure, terrific tackling ability and sheer speed marked Walker down as one of the finest defenders of his generation, and he was a firm favourite among Wednesday with the cry 'you'll never beat Des Walker' heard on virtually every matchday. Despite his tremendous form during eight years at Hillsborough, he added only a solitary cap to bring his final England tally to 58, with seemingly far inferior players being called up by the national manager. It is likely that Walker would have remained at Wednesday for the rest of his career if financial problems had not besieged the club after relegation in 2000 – the club could not afford to renew his contract in the summer of 2001, and he sadly departed as a free agent. He made a surprise comeback at non-League Burton Albion – managed by former teammate Nigel Clough – and actually rejoined his first club, Nottingham Forest, where he enjoyed an 'Indian summer', captaining the Reds to the First Division Play-offs in

2003. It was, of course, at Forest that he is arguably best known as under Brian Clough he became a Forest legend, amassing 346 competitive games and his solitary goal in over 20 years as a professional – versus Luton Town on New Year's Day 1992. He twice won the League Cup while in Forest colours, although he unfortunately scored an own-goal in the 1991 FA Cup Final as Spurs lifted the old trophy. His outstanding displays for England at Italia '90 prompted several top European clubs to chase his signature, but it was another two years before Genoa based Sampdoria eventually paid £1.5 million for his services. Luckily for the Owls, ex-Sampdoria player Trevor Francis was able to pull a few Italian strings when the race to bring Walker back to England started, and his arrival was seen as a huge coup for the club. Unfortunately, his qualities could not lead the Owls to honours, and after his playing days finally ended Walker joined the coaching staff at the City Ground – remaining there until Gary Megson took charge in January 2005.

WALKER, Thomas 'Tommy'

(1926–37)

Full-back, 5ft 9½in, 11st 8lb (1926)

Born: 4 March 1902, Cross Crols, Stirlingshire

Died: 7 March 1973, Sheffield

Signed from: Bradford City, 24 February 1926, £1,900

Transferred: To Staff, April 1936

Career: Cross Crols, Haverbridge Rechabities, Sternburn Thistle Juveniles, California Celtic Juniors, Bowness, Vale of Grange, Bradford City, Wednesday

Debut: 3 April 1926 v Hull City (h) Second Division

Last appearance: 22 April 1935 v West Bromwich Albion (a) First Division

Appearances/Goals: League 258/3, FAC 29/0

As a player and then coach, Scot Tommy Walker spent a remarkable 41 years at Hillsborough, after initially signing as a player near the end of the club's Second Division title-winning season of 1925–26. The right-back had originally been spotted in Scottish junior soccer back in his homeland by Bradford City and was no doubt glad to escape the hard life of a miner to turn professional – he was almost killed while working underground when a roof caved in and he had to crawl on his stomach to reach safety. He went straight into the first team at Wednesday and formed a formidable full-back partnership with the great Ernie Blenkinsop as the Owls won back-to-back League titles, with the athletic Walker showing many attributes, including the ability to read the game well and outpace many an attacking forward. He linked well with winger Mark Hooper and produced countless quality crosses for the likes of Jack Allen and Jack Ball to power the Owls to success. In September 1929 he became the first Scot to represent the Sheffield FA, but his career at Hillsborough came to a shuddering halt in 1935 after a major fall out with manager Billy Walker, prior to an FA Cup third-

round tie at Wolves. He was instantly dropped and played only twice more before moving onto the coaching staff in April 1936. He was initially handed the role of third-team trainer but within a year was promoted to look after the club's reserve side. He remained on the payroll until March 1967 when manager Alan Brown re-vamped his backroom staff, with Tommy an unfortunate casualty. After leaving Hillsborough he was allowed to live in a property owned by the Owls until his death six years later.

WARHURST, Paul

(1991–93)

Defender/Forward, 6ft 1in, 12st 8lb (1992)
Born: 26 September 1969, Stockport
Signed from: Oldham Athletic, 10 July 1991, £750,000
Transferred: Blackburn Rovers, 3 September 1993, £2.75 million
Career: Manchester City, Oldham Athletic, Wednesday, Blackburn Rovers, Crystal Palace, Bolton Wanderers, Stoke City, Bolton Wanderers, Chesterfield, Barnsley, Queen's Park Rangers, Carlisle United (N/C), Notts County (trial), Grimsby Town, Chester City (trial), Blackpool, Forest Green Rovers, Wrexham, Barnet, Northwich Victoria
Debut: 17 August 1991 v Aston Villa (h) First Division
Last appearance: 25 August 1993 v West Ham United (a) Premiership
Caps: England Under-21 (1)
Appearances/Goals: League 60+6/6, FAC 7+1/5, FLC 9/4, Euro 4/3, Other 1/0

It will never be known what course the Wednesday career of Paul Warhurst would have taken if he had not been picked as an emergency striker for the September 1992 top-flight game at Nottingham Forest. Up until that moment, the stylish and lightening-quick player had forged a reputation as a right-back, becoming much sought after a string of impressive displays for Oldham Athletic as they accompanied the Owls out of the Second Division in 1991. He also appeared in the 1990 League Cup Final for the Latics but was one of Trevor Francis' first signings after he took over the managerial duties from Ron Atkinson. The Owls equalled their transfer record to obtain his services, and after being switched to centre-half he quickly became a firm favourite among Wednesday fans. Any player who could run 100m in under 11 seconds would be dangerous for any side, and his surges from defence were a common feature of the exciting 1991–92 season as the Owls finished third in the top-flight. His early form for Wednesday earned Warhurst an England Under-21 cap, but it would be a goalscoring debut in the forward line that led to his career being turned upside down and Warhurst receiving a call-up to the full England side as a forward! A few days after his surprise goal at the City Ground, he netted twice in a UEFA Cup romp over Spora Luxembourg although he needed the life-saving treatment of physiotherapist Alan Smith after he

collapsed and swallowed his tongue. He recovered sufficiently to score in the second leg, but it was then the 'calm before the storm' as he reverted to his former position at the heart of the club's defence. However, in the new year he was pushed up front once again and subsequently proved a modern-day sensation as his goals helped the Owls to both domestic Cup Finals and then saw Warhurst become the first player since Redfern Froggatt to net in seven consecutive games. A groin injury denied him the chance of a full cap for England, and his Owls career seemingly hit the buffers when he refused to play in the FA Cup Final unless it was in a forward role. He did eventually appear in the showpiece occasion but his days at Wednesday looked numbered despite a £3 million switch to Blackburn Rovers failing to materialise. A few weeks later, though, the deal was resurrected, and he departed Hillsborough after a more than eventful two years at the club. Soon after moving to Ewood Park he suffered a broken leg, and a succession of persistent injuries meant he never really made an impact, scoring only four times in 74 games for Rovers. By the late 1990s he had metamorphosed into a central midfield player, but his brief glory days were behind Warhurst as he appeared for a variety of clubs – including just 72 hours at Carlisle United – before dropping into Conference football in 2005.

WHELAN, Glenn David

(2004–08)
Midfielder, 6ft, 12st 5lb (2005)
Born: 13 January 1984, Dublin
Signed from: Manchester City, 1 July 2004, Free
Transferred: Stoke City, 31 January 2008, £500,000
Career: Manchester City, Bury (loan), Wycombe Wanderers (trial), Wednesday, Stoke City

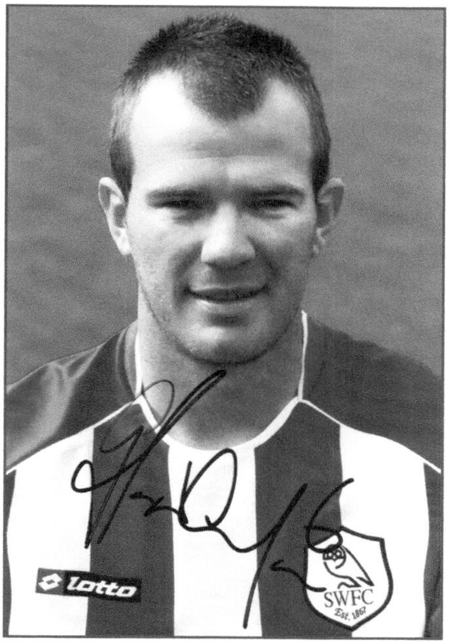

Debut: 21 August 2004 v Huddersfield Town (h) League One
Last appearance: 29 January 2008 v Wolverhampton Wanderers (a) Championship
Caps: Eire B (1), Under-21 (13),
Appearances/Goals: League 136+6/12, FAC 6/1, FLC 8/2, Other 3/1

When Manchester City released central midfield player Glenn Whelan, after just a solitary first-team appearance, his career seemed at a crossroads. However, he was duly signed by Wednesday boss Chris Turner, and within four years the talented Whelan was winning a full International cap for the Republic of Ireland. A sending off in a Manchester City reserve game meant Whelan missed the first three games of the 2004–05 season and a red card, in only his seventh appearance for Wednesday, also hampered his early weeks at Hillsborough. Despite these early setbacks it was obvious to Owls fans that Turner had pulled off somewhat of a coup by securing the Dubliner's signature and he quickly became an integral part of the Owls side that pushed for promotion in League One. Turner had dubbed him 'the next John Sheridan' but it would be his successor, Paul Sturrock, who would reap the benefits of his talents as Whelan showed an increasing range of passing abilities and a real eye for goal. It proved a memorable first season at Wednesday, and Whelan was voted Eire Under-21 Player of the Year while he scored a terrific goal at the Millennium Stadium, Cardiff as the Owls beat Hartlepool United to win the divisional Play-off Final. He continued to be a vital member of the Wednesday side as the club consolidated in the Championship and just missed out on a Play-off place in 2007. He was named the club's Player of the Year for the 2006–07 season, but as Wednesday struggled at the wrong end of the table in 2008 he became a highly saleable asset with his contract due to expire in the summer. It was, therefore, no real surprise that Wednesday accepted an offer from Premiership Stoke City, and he departed with the good wishes of Wednesday fans. It was becoming obvious that Whelan was a Premiership player, and after moving to Staffordshire he has became a regular for City while also becoming a first choice for his country.

WILKINSON, Derek

(1953–65)

Winger, 5ft 9in, 10st 7lb (1953)
Born: 4 June 1935, Stalybridge
Signed from: Dukinfield Town, 14 November 1953, £100
Transferred: Retired, May 1965
Career: Stalybridge Celtic, Dukinfield Town, Wednesday
Debut: 13 November 1954 v Cardiff City (a) First Division
Last appearance: 7 November 1964 v Manchester United (a) First Division
Caps: Football League (2)
Appearances/Goals: League 212/53, FAC 15/4, Euro 4/0

After being signed from Lancashire minor football, winger Derek Wilkinson became an almost ever present in Wednesday's reserve side as he slowly built a reputation as a fast, direct and 100 per cent committed winger, who could also adapt to any role in the forward line. He had initially joined Wednesday on a part-time basis, while continuing to work as a French polisher and training with Stalybridge Celtic, but he turned full-time and duly secured a regular first-team spot in the late 1950s, netting 11 times as Wednesday lifted the Second Division title in 1959. He was a popular player with both his peers and Owls fans and helped the club to the semi-finals of the FA Cup (1960), runners'-up spot behind Spurs (1961) and the last eight of the Fairs Cup (1962). Unfortunately, the wholehearted attacker then started to be dogged by a succession of injuries and his appearances started to diminish as the 1960s progressed. Sadly he was forced to

retire, aged just 29, in 1965 when he failed to recover from a serious groin injury. A crowd of just over 10,000 attended his testimonial match against an All Star XI in 1966, and by this time he had returned home to Manchester to re-start his career as a French polisher. From 1978, until his retirement in 2000, he drove a forklift truck at a Stockport-based company and now lives out his retirement in the area.

WILSON, Andrew 'Andra'

(1900–20)
Forward, 5ft 10in, 13st 6lb (1913)
Born: 10 December 1880, Lendalfoot, Ayrshire
Died: 13 March 1945, Patterton Farm, nr. Irvine
Signed from: Glasgow Clyde, 1 May 1900, £200
Transferred: Retired, 1920
Career: Irvine Meadow, Glasgow Clyde, Wednesday
Debut: 1 September 1900 v Manchester City (a) First Division
Last appearance: 10 March 1920 v Liverpool (a) First Division
Caps: Scotland Full (6)
Appearances/Goals: League 502/198, FAC 44/17

Purely from a statistical point of view, there is little doubt that Andrew Wilson was the club's greatest-ever player, topping both the all-time appearances and goals list. The Owls broke their transfer record to obtain his services in the opening year of the 20th century, and he would stay a total of 21 years at Wednesday, appearing in first-team football in all but his final season in an Owls shirt. His attributes were many, including a powerful shot and dedication to the cause, and despite not playing organised football as a youngster he was soon snapped up by Clyde, after winning several Cups with junior side Irvine Meadow. He spent only a single season in Glasgow before taking the well-trodden path south of Hadrian's Wall after his team were relegated from the Scottish First Division in 1900. Although his early career had seen Wilson utilised at left-back and on the right wing – he personally believed the former position to be his best – he went straight into the Wednesday side at centre-forward (replacing Harry Millar) and was an instant hit, netting 13 times to finish his debut season as top scorer. Incredibly, he would go on to register double-figures goals in every season until World War One brought an end to National football in 1915! For the first 10 years of his Wednesday career he wore the number-nine centre-forward shirt, winning two League titles and the FA Cup, but when James Murray arrived in 1910 he was switched to inside-forward. He duly excelled in his new position – forming a deadly partnership with David McLean – and continued to score freely as the club just missed out on a third League title in 1913. His burly frame made 'Andra' difficult to knock off the ball, and his all-round talents made him one of the greatest players of the pre-World War One period. He effectively retired at the end of the war years, after netting another 25 goals in 75 games for the Owls during the conflict, and was handed a new role in the summer of 1919 as coach to the reserve side and scout. He did make one further senior appearance – as an emergency forward in a defeat at Liverpool – and then spent a further season at Hillsborough before being appointed Bristol Rovers manager in June 1921. He spent five years in the West Country and was later manager at both Oldham Athletic and Stockport County before returning home to Scotland to live out his remaining years.

WILSON, George

(1920–25)
Half-back, 5ft 8½in, 11st 7lb (1920)
Born: 14 January 1892, Kirkham, Preston
Died: 25 November 1961, Blackpool
Signed from: Blackpool, 11 March 1920, £2,500
Transferred: Nelson, 13 July 1925, £2,350
Career: Sacred Heart School, Catholic College, Kirkham Sunday School League, Willow's Rovers, Fleetwood, Morecambe, Blackpool, Wednesday, Nelson
Debut: 13 March 1920 v Liverpool (h) First Division
Last appearance: 21 March 1925 v Middlesbrough (a) Second Division
Caps: England Full (12), Football League (4)
Appearances/Goals: League 184/4, FAC 12/0

In modern-day football the thought of a Championship player being an England regular, as well as captain, seems almost ridiculous. However, back in the early 1920s Wednesday centre-back George Wilson achieved such a feat, winning a dozen caps for his country between 1921 and 1924. The son of a Blackpool police detective, Wilson broke into senior football at his home-town club and became a first-team regular just before the start of World War One. He subsequently fought for Britain on the killing fields of Europe, winning a Belgian Medal of Honour for his gallantry. When the hostilities ended he went straight back into the Tangerine's first team and was also handed the captaincy. He was quickly emerging as one of the finest defenders of his generation and there was a scramble of clubs when the intelligent, energetic and expansive pivot was surprisingly placed on the transfer list in the spring of 1920. It was relegation-threatened Wednesday who broke their transfer record to obtain his services, but his arrival failed to save the club from the drop, and George would spend his entire Wednesday career in the second tier of the English game. New manager Bob Brown instantly recognised his qualities, and he was made captain before winning his first England cap. He matured into the Owls' greatest centre-back since Tommy Crawshaw and was an automatic choice at the heart of the defence as Wednesday,

unsuccessfully, tried to win promotion back to the First Division. After enjoying a record benefit year in 1925, Wilson and the club's hierarchy fell out over terms for the new season, and it quickly became apparent that he had played his last game in the blue-and-white shirt. It was his destination that shocked the football world as he duly signed for Division Three (North) minnows Nelson, the Lancashire side paying what was a record fee for both sides. It was thought that the offer of the licence of the Prince of Wales Public House was the major reason for the surprise switch, but Wilson stayed only two seasons before hanging up his boots and returning home to Blackpool.

WOOD, Richard Mark

(2003–09)

Central-defender, 6ft 3in, 11st 11lb (2003)
Born: 5 July 1985, Ossett, West Yorkshire
Signed from: Trainee, 21 March 2003
Transferred: Coventry City, 18 November 2009, £500,000
Career: Ossett Trinitarians, Wednesday, Coventry City
Debut: 21 April 2003 v Brighton & Hove Albion (a) First Division
Last appearance: 7 November 2009 v Queen's Park Rangers (h) Championship
Appearances/Goals: League 162+9/7, FAC 3+2/0, FLC 6+1/1, Other 5+1/0

Commanding central-defender Richard Wood was no doubt left with contrasting emotions after his first senior appearance for the Owls, as the club suffered relegation from the Championship after failing to win at Brighton. The Yorkshire-born defender subsequently netted his first goal for Wednesday in the amazing 7–2 win at Burnley and became established in the first team in the lower grade. He had originally been spotted playing in the Wakefield and District League, at the tender age of 10, and progressed through Wednesday's youth ranks to sign a three-year scholarship contract in July 2001. Within two years, he was tied to a professional deal and would make his aforementioned first-team bow, aged 17, in April 2003. His first full season at senior level was interrupted by a stress fracture of his foot, but Wood was then paired with Graeme Lee at the heart of the Owls defence as they fought to earn promotion from League One. He later formed an even better partnership with Lee Bullen, and the teenager was outstanding as Hartlepool United were beaten 4–2 in Cardiff to win promotion in 2005. His prowess in the air and great powers of recovery meant he remained a regular under both Paul Sturrock and Brian Laws, having signed a new two-year deal in June 2005. After almost 200 games for Wednesday he eventually joined fellow Championship club Coventry City, initially on loan, in November 2009. The move was made permanent on 4 January 2010, and boss Chris Coleman soon handed Wood the captain's armband.

WOODHEAD, Dennis

(1945–55)

Winger, 5ft 9in, 12st 9½lb (1946)

Born: 12 June 1925, Sheffield

Died: 26 July 1995, Sheffield

Signed from: Amateur, 19 April 1945, Free

Transferred: Chesterfield, 9 September 1955, £2,000

Career: Edgar Allen's, Hillsborough Boys Club, Wednesday, Chesterfield, Derby County, Southport, Derby County, Frickley Colliery, Worksop Town, Retford Town

Debut: 24 May 1947 v Newcastle United (h) Second Division

Last appearance: 5 March 1955 v Everton (h) First Division

Appearances/Goals: 213/72, FAC 13/3

A few months after signing amateur forms for Wednesday, winger Dennis Woodhead volunteered for the RAF and would serve his country with distinction through the remainder of World War Two, flying 31 operational bombing flights over Germany in his role as a flight engineer. The Owls were so keen to tie Woodhead to a professional form that he actually put pen to paper in India, where he was stationed with the RAF. After finally being demobbed in April 1947 he quickly made his first senior start for the club and the left-winger with a powerful shot was soon an automatic choice on the left flank. A grandson of 19th century Owls player Billy Betts, Woodhead also earned a reputation for his scoring from out wide although his career was interrupted in August 1949 when he suffered a broken leg against Leicester City at Hillsborough. He returned to fitness to aid the club's promotion from the Second Division in 1950 and went on to claim a Second Division title medal two years later and an FA Cup semi-final appearance in 1954. He formed an exciting wing partnership with Red Froggatt at Wednesday, but after relegation in 1955 he moved to neighbours Chesterfield, netting a hat-trick on his debut in a 7–2 win over Rochdale. His stay at Saltergate was brief, and he later helped Derby County to promotion from regional Third Division soccer prior to dropping into non-League football. He ran a sweet shop and sold insurance after becoming a part-time player, and after a short spell working back at Chesterfield he returned to Wednesday as commercial manager in 1971, replacing former teammate Derek Dooley. He remained in the role until taking early retirement in 1987.

WORTHINGTON, Nigel

(1984–94)

Left-back/midfield, 5ft 11in, 12st 6lb (1985)

Born: 4 November 1961, Ballymena, Northern Ireland

Signed from: Notts County, 7 February 1984, £100,000

Transferred: Leeds United, 4 July 1994, £325,000 (T)

Career: Ballymena United, Linfield (guest), Notts County, Wednesday, Leeds United, Stoke City, Blackpool

Debut: 25 February 1984 v Brighton & Hove Albion (h) Second Division
Last appearance: 7 May 1994 v Manchester City (h) Premiership
Caps: Northern Ireland Full (50)
Appearances/Goals: League 334+4/12, FAC 29/1, FLC 41/1, Euro 3/1, Other 6/0

If the word 'consistency' were searched for in a dictionary then the name of Nigel Worthington would no doubt be used as an example of the adjective. From re-joining his former Notts County boss, Howard Wilkinson, at Hillsborough in 1984, he was virtually an ever present in the Wednesday side until he was signed yet again by Wilkinson, for Leeds, 10 years later. The unflappable and composed Irishman arrived at the club as a left-back and remained in this position for the remainder of the 1980s until the arrival of Ron Atkinson triggered a move to the left side of midfield. He duly formed an outstanding partnership with Phil King, which was a key feature of the club's successful side of the early 1990s, and was in the Owls side that lifted the League Cup in 1991 and then lost both domestic Cup Finals in 1993. He had

helped the Owls to promotion from the old Second Division in 1984 – appearing in the final 14 games of the season – and looked set to leave for champions Arsenal in 1989 before deciding to stay at Hillsborough. The popular Worthington, nicknamed 'Irish' by Wednesday supporters, enjoyed a testimonial match in 1993 before rejecting a new contract and departing up the M1 in the summer that followed. Before arriving at Wednesday he had built his reputation in Irish football, playing for Ballymena while working in a tyre factory, and won the Irish Cup with Linfield before moving to English soccer in 1981 for a hefty £100,000 fee. He was voted Northern Ireland Young Player of the Year, and after joining Wednesday he would also be the first winner of the senior award, when this was introduced in 1992. Throughout his years in Wednesday colours, Worthington was a regular for his country, playing in the 1986 World Cup Finals, and his cap total of 50 stands as the highest number won by an Owls player. Despite later moving into a midfield role at Wednesday, he remained at left-back for Northern Ireland, taking his cap tally to 66 before retiring from the international scene. He appeared in the 1995 League Cup Final for Leeds but was only really a squad player, moving to Stoke before taking over as player-manager of Blackpool in 1997. He spent two years at the helm and was then in charge for six more seasons at Norwich City before a brief spell as caretaker boss at Leicester City. He was appointed manager of his country in June 2007 and remains in that role today.

WYLDE, Rodger James

(1971–80)

Forward, 6ft 1in, 12st (1978)
Born: 8 March 1954, Sheffield
Signed from: Trainee, 1 July 1971
Transferred: Oldham Athletic, 29 February 1980, £75,000

Career: Wednesday, Burnley (loan), Oldham Athletic, Sporting Lisbon, Sunderland, Barnsley, Rotherham United (loan), Stockport County
Debut: 18 November 1972 v Middlesbrough (h) Second Division
Last appearance: 16 February 1980 v Chesterfield (h) Third Division
Appearances/Goals: League 157+12/54, FAC 15/4, FLC 10/8

Popular 1970s attacker who graduated through the youth ranks during the reign of Derek Dooley, Wylde originally signed schoolboy forms in 1968 after his schoolteacher, an Owls fan, had sent the United supporting teenager for a trial at Hillsborough! After impressing in youth and reserve-team football – scoring a double hat-trick for the second team in an August 1972 Central League game – he duly made his senior bow, but the polished striker, with excellent close control, did not really become established until the arrival of Len Ashurst as manager in 1975. He went on to form a deadly partnership with Tommy Tynan and was nicknamed 'Oscar' by Wednesday fans as he plundered 56 goals during a three-season spell as first-choice striker – finishing top scorer with 25 goals in all competitions during the 1976–77 campaign. The purchase of Terry Curran and Andy McCulloch by new boss Jack Charlton meant Wylde's opportunities became limited, and just a few weeks before the Owls clinched promotion back to the Second Division he was sold, somewhat reluctantly, to Oldham Athletic. He scored freely for the Greater Manchester club – 51 goals in 113 matches – and then spent a year in the Portuguese sun at Sporting Lisbon. His old manager Len Ashurst then gave Wylde his only experience of top-flight football, the former Sheffield boys player appearing in 11 games for Sunderland with one of his three goals being scored in a 1–1

draw at Anfield. He ended his playing days at Stockport County, but while on their books he gained a BSc (Hons) Degree in physiotherapy at Salford University and was appointed to the role at County in June 1989. He remains in that job over 20 years later and was inducted into the club's Hall of Fame in 2006.

YOUNG, Gerald Morton 'Gerry'

(1955–71)

Centre-half/forward, 5ft 10½in, 11st 9lb (1964)
Born: 1 October 1936, Harton, South Shields
Signed from: Hawthorn Leslie, 14 May 1955
Transferred: Retired, July 1971
Career: Newcastle United (Amat.),

Hawthorn Leslie, Wednesday
Debut: 2 March 1957 v Blackpool (a) First Division
Last appearance: 2 January 1971 v Tottenham Hotspur (a) FA Cup
Caps: England Full (1)
Appearances/Goals: League 307+2/13, FAC 17/2, FLC 10/1, Euro 8/4

It was while playing for his works side, Hawthorn Leslie, that Gerry Young was spotted by a Wolves scout who was unsuccessful in persuading the teenager to attend a trial at the Black Country club. However, their loss was the Owls gain as the scout phoned Eric Taylor at Wednesday to recommend his find. The trainee electrician duly signed part-time professional forms – turning full-time after finishing his trade apprenticeship – and started to feature regularly in reserve-team soccer before making a senior debut, at inside-forward, in a defeat at Blackpool. Despite Young scoring trebles against Manchester United and AS Roma (in the Fairs Cup), he failed to really secure a permanent place in the club's first team, and it was the sale of star wing-half, Tony Kay, that provided a change of fortunes. In a reverse of Paul Warhurst's switch in the early 1990s, Young would move from the forward line into a defensive position. He made such an impact that within 18 months he was capped at full international level by England, although a ruptured thigh denied him a second cap and also allowed Bobby Moore to take his place. He remained a constant in the club's first team for the remainder of the 1960s, and during the middle of the decade he appeared in 80 consecutive games. His sheer professionalism endeared him to his peers (he was married on a matchday morning before catching the train for a game at Birmingham in the afternoon), while his great positional sense and no-nonsense defending made him popular with supporters. Unfortunately for Young, he will probably be best remembered for his mis-control in the 1966 FA Cup Final that led to Everton's winning goal, but he provided great service to the Owls over a 20-year period. Soon after being appointed reserve-team manager at Hillsborough, in April 1971, he retired from the field of play and was briefly caretaker manager in 1973, between the reigns of Derek Dooley and Steve Burtenshaw. He remained on the club's coaching staff until October 1975 when he was dismissed, along with Burtenshaw, as the club struggled at the foot of the old Third Division. He later joined forces with old teammate, John Quinn, to open a sporting goods store just a stone's throw from Hillsborough with Young specialising in sporting trophies. The premises closed in 2001, with Young continuing to trade from home.

MANAGERS

Arthur Joshua Dickinson: 1871–1920

Died 5 November 1930

Although Arthur Dickinson was never actually Wednesday's official manager, it would be unfair not to include him in this section due to his tireless work behind the scenes and sheer unswerving dedication to the club's well-being and progression, both on and off the field of play. He had initially joined The Wednesday committee in 1876, and when the club turned professional in 1887 he was handed the role of honorary financial secretary, before becoming full honorary secretary in 1891. In those pre-league days his duties were far-reaching and he would often travel over Hadrian's Wall to scout for Scottish players. One such trip, to Dunbarton in September 1891, was taken with agent John Wilson and ended with Arthur running from a baying mob of Dumbarton fans and having to stay in a Glasgow hotel for two days while he made himself presentable, after suffering two black eyes and a bloody nose and mouth!

When the club was elected into the Football League in 1892 Dickinson became the only honorary secretary in the competition and he remained so for the remainder of his time at Wednesday. He was actually only a part-time employee at Wednesday as Arthur's paid employment was as a salesman for a leading Sheffield cutlery firm, which took him overseas on many occasions in order to expand and develop the famous Sheffield cutlery brand. His great love was Wednesday, however, and he was highly influential in the club rising from local football to the top of the English game, effectively picking the side that reached three FA Cup Finals (the first in 1890 as a non-league side), won the Football Alliance League, the Second Division Championship and then back-to-back Football League titles in the early part of the 20th century.

In 1899 he oversaw the club's conversion to a limited liability company – receiving the very first share – and in the Olive Grove days Arthur was often known to stash all the match receipts from a home game under his sofa until the banks reopened on the Monday morning! He was, of course, also the organisational flair behind the club's purchase of meadowland at Owlerton in 1899, and then helped to construct from scratch a ground that became the envy of almost

every club in the Football League. It would not be an understatement to say that without Dickinson, The Wednesday may not have progressed from their amateur status to the club we know today. In addition to his many duties at Wednesday, Arthur also served on a plethora of football committees, including the highly influential FA Council, and held an almost encyclopaedic knowledge of the rules and regulations of the English game.

His tireless work kept the Owls in business during the difficult years of World War One, but after 44 years service to Wednesday he finally tendered his resignation on 18 May 1920, after the Owls had suffered a disastrous season that culminated in relegation from the First Division. In the previous month Arthur, a master administrator, had been proud to successfully stage England's famous 5–4 win over Scotland at Hillsborough and, despite having officially resigned from his position at Wednesday, he remained a familiar face around the ground. He often acted as a courier for the match receipts to the bank after games – he had managed to arrange for the banks to stay open after games so that he would no longer have to hide the takings in his house until the following Monday morning!

The day after the Owls had faced the Blades in a Sheffield County Cup game at Hillsborough, Arthur travelled to London to attend a Football League management committee meeting. After booking into his hotel he was walking with an Everton official when he suddenly collapsed and died instantly, without uttering a single word. His colleague thought that he had simply fainted, but sadly, on 5 November 1930, aged 79, one of the most influential figures in the 144-year history of Sheffield Wednesday passed away, leaving a remarkable legacy.

Robert (Bob) Brown: 1920–1933

Died 7 March 1935

It was while working in a north-east shipyard that legendary Owls manager Bob Brown first became associated with The Wednesday, being appointed the club's scout for the region in August 1905. He had previously appeared for a variety of amateur sides in the area, including Hebburn Argyle, and his expert knowledge ensured that over the next three years he recommended a stream of top-quality players to Wednesday's hierarchy. In 1908 he moved to Sheffield after being appointed general assistant to Arthur Dickinson, but in June 1911 he left Owlerton to take over as secretary-manager of Portsmouth, the south-coast side having just been relegated from the top division of the Southern League.

His impact at Portsmouth was immediate as he brought several players into the club, including former Wednesday men Frank Stringfellow and Michael

Dowling, and immediately won promotion at the first time of asking, finishing second behind Merthyr Town. Success continued when, in the first season after World War One, he guided Portsmouth to the First Division title and election into the Football League – Pompey becoming founder members of the new Third Division. After a disagreement over future policy, however, he subsequently resigned his position and moved to fellow League new boys Gillingham.

Within weeks though, he was enticed to rejoin Wednesday as their first official secretary-manager, and he faced a major job in rebuilding a team that had just been relegated from the First Division. In fact, it took him six seasons to earn promotion back to the top division, but the team that Brown built then took Wednesday to the greatest period in their history. A dramatic escape from relegation in 1928 proved the catalyst as the Owls won six and drew two of their final eight games of the season to record an astonishing revival. The form showed in the latter end of that season simply continued when the 1928–29 campaign began and, with new signing Jimmy Seed an inspiration, Wednesday won the Championship for only the third time in their history. In the following season Brown's side was virtually invincible and won the title again, setting a new record margin when finishing the season a huge 10 points clear of their nearest challengers. The Owls also came agonisingly close to becoming the first side to complete the 'double' in the 20th century, but as a highly controversial refereeing display in the semi-final against Huddersfield Town not only allowed the Terriers a goal after a blatant handball, but then saw the official blow the final whistle as the ball was in flight, from the boot of Jack Allen, to tie the game at 2–2!

Brown – ably assisted by trainer Chris Craig – then led Wednesday to third place in the table in the next three seasons, signing players who would be instrumental in helping Wednesday to win the FA Cup in 1935. Brown, however, who was a tough disciplinarian but had the respect of his players, was struck down with a personal tragedy in the summer of 1933 when his wife, who some years earlier had a major operation and was still not back to full health, had a seizure on a holiday and sadly passed away, leaving Brown a broken man and a shadow of his former self.

He returned to Hillsborough, but fell ill during a Central League game versus Everton on September 9th 1933, and after being diagnosed with high blood pressure he was ordered to take bed rest for a fortnight. Just twelve days later, on September 21 1933, the reign of Bob Brown at Wednesday came to a somewhat premature end as he tendered his resignation due to ill health. He did eventually regain some semblance of health, and later scouted for several teams. It was while on a scouting mission for Chelsea, as he was about to board a train at Leeds, however, that he collapsed and was rushed to hospital on 7 March 1935, after having suffered a cerebral haemorrhage. Sadly, he died a day later, ironically just a week before Wednesday beat Burnley in the FA Cup semi-final on their way to winning the trophy. Like his immediate predecessor, Arthur Dickinson, Brown's spell in charge at Hillsborough ranked him firmly as one of the greatest Wednesday managers of all-time.

Joseph (Joe) Bentley McClelland: 1933 (Caretaker)

Died 2 July 1964

Born in 1884, Joe McClelland was secretary of the Halifax and District

Association in 1911 when Halifax Town was formed, and later that year became the club's first ever secretary-manager. He guided them to seventh position in the Yorkshire Combination League in their first season and in the next campaign Town moved into the strong Midland League. The West Yorkshire side was duly elected into the Football League in 1921 and Joe remained at the Shay for a further decade, prior to accepting an offer from Wednesday to become assistant to Bob Brown, joining on 31 July 1931.

In September 1933, following the resignation of Bob Brown, Wednesday set their sights on securing the services of Charlton Athletic manager and former inspirational Owls player Jimmy Seed as his replacement. When Seed decided to remain at the Valley, however, Wednesday handed McClelland the role of secretary-manager at Hillsborough on a temporary basis, while the committee reconsidered their options. McClelland was in charge of the Wednesday side for a total of 11 games, but won only twice before Billy Walker was handed the position on a permanent basis in December 1933.

He returned to his former role of assistant after Walker was installed, but resigned on 30 October 1934 due to ill health. After recovering from his ailments he joined Lincoln City in June 1936 as their secretary-manager, and remained in the Lincolnshire City for the remainder of his life, helping the Imps to stay together during the difficult years of the World War Two. At the age of 63, in July 1946, he gave the reins to a younger man and moved upstairs to become club secretary. He eventually retired from football altogether in 1949 and his service was rewarded when City played a benefit match on his behalf. For the remainder of his working life he was employed by Lincoln-based engineering firm, Ruston Hornsby, and later in life was awarded a long-service medal by the Football Association.

He passed away on 2 July 1964 in Lincoln St George hospital, after having lived in an old people's home for two years due to his failing health.

William (Billy) Henry Walker: December 1933–November 1937

Died 28 November 1964

Born at Wednesbury, Staffordshire on 29 October 1897, Billy Walker was the son of former Wolves player, George Walker, but a career in the game looked unlikely as he almost died from the dreaded consumption as a teenager. He recovered from the illness to play for his school football side, King's Hill, however, and his early promise was rewarded with a cap at schoolboy level for England. On leaving school, Billy gained employment at an engineering firm and started playing for several local teams, including Fallings

Heath, Hednesford Town, Darlaston, Wednesbury Old Park and Wednesbury Old Athletic. In March 1915 he signed amateur forms for Aston Villa, but, mainly due to the onset of war, Walker did not progress to professional status until May 1919. He was a regular for neighbours Birmingham FC during the final season of the war years, but it would be as a Villa player that he made his name and enjoyed a highly successful career.

The outstanding inside-forward netted twice on his debut for Villa and ended his first senior campaign with an FA Cup winners medal after Huddersfield Town were beaten 1–0 in the Final. He also appeared in the 1924 FA Cup Final – only the second Final staged at Wembley – but was this time on the losing side as Newcastle United won the trophy. Ironically, just five days before the Final, Villa had thrashed the Geordies 6–1, with Billy grabbing a treble! It was a busy period for Walker as a fortnight before the Final he became the first player to net for England in an international at Wembley Stadium. Over the next decade Walker became established as one of the finest players in the English game and won 18 full caps for his country, as well as amassing a highly impressive 244 goals in 531 games for Aston Villa – he still remains atop the all-time goalscoring charts for Villa.

When he was appointed secretary-manager at Wednesday on 8 December 1933 there was general surprise among supporters, as Walker had no experience of management whatsoever, and he immediately retired from the field of play to concentrate on his new challenge. Wednesday had been somewhat of a rudderless ship between the departure of Bob Brown and the arrival of Walker, slipping all the way down the First Division table to 19th position. The new man made an immediate impact, winning his first three games in charge, and taking the Owls on a tremendous 12-game unbeaten run to pull the club away from the danger zone, ending the season in mid-table.

His second season brought great success as Wednesday not only finished third in the top flight, but also beat West Bromwich Albion 4–2 to lift the FA Cup for the third and, to date, final time. In that first full season he parted with several players who were real favourites with fans, such as Jack Ball, Harry Burgess and Ernie Blenkinsop, and, in hindsight, despite the Cup win, their replacements were inadequate, as the Owls only just avoided relegation in 1936. His inability to replace the stars of old was harshly shown 12 months later as Wednesday were relegated from the top division, and by November 1937 the Owls had slumped alarmingly to second bottom in the old Second Division. A disastrous defeat at Barnsley subsequently resulted in Walker being confronted by a group of angry

shareholders and a day later he tendered his resignation.

In January 1938 he was appointed manager of Chelmsford City, who were turning from amateur status to semi-professional and wanted Walker to help them to achieve this aim. He remained at the Essex club for only a year, however, resigning in October 1938, before taking over as secretary-manager at Third Division South club Nottingham Forest. He joined the City Ground side in March 1939 and stayed for 21 years, even playing for Forest on several occasions during World War Two, including some games as a goalkeeper. While in charge he took Forest into the Second Division – winning the regional south title in 1951 – and then won promotion to the top flight in 1957. He also guided his side to the 1959 FA Cup, where Roy Dwight (the uncle of Elton John) was among the scorers as Luton Town were beaten at Wembley. He resigned from his role at Forest in June 1960, but remained on the club's committee until suffering a stroke in October 1963. Sadly, he never really recovered and his health deteriorated further before he died in a Nottingham hospital on 28 November 1964.

James (Jimmy) McMullan: January 1938–April 1942

Died 28 November 1964

Born in Denny, a small village in Stirlingshire, Scotland on 26 March 1895, Jimmy McMullan started his working life as a miner, playing football for his village team, Denny Hibernian. He moved on to play for Third Lanark for a short time, but in November 1913, aged 18, he signed for Partick Thistle and went straight into the first team, making his debut against Kilmarnock in a 4–2 home win. McMullan stayed with Partick, playing during the war

years, but was unlucky in 1921, thanks to an injury suffered while playing for Scotland, when he missed the 1921 Scottish Cup Final as Partick beat Rangers – this match became known as the 'Boycott Final' due to the Scottish Football Association doubling the admission price from one to two shillings (5 pence to 10 pence). There was also a miners strike at the time, all of which resulted in less than 30,000 fans watching the game, which was a very poor attendance in those times.

A dispute with Partick then preceded a sensational move to Kent League side Maidstone United – the club's chairman, Herbert Sharp, travelled to Scotland to secure McMullan as player-manager despite the fact that the Scotsman did not even know where Maidstone was! In McMullan's first season in charge Maidstone won an amazing five trophies – the Kent League, Kent Senior Cup, Chatham Cup, Gilbert Parker Shield and the Thames & Medway Combination. He helped the side to the Senior Cup and the League again a year later, and it was obvious he would soon be back in senior football – re-signing for Partick Thistle in the summer of 1923.

In February 1926 he moved to First Division Manchester City for a reputed fee of £4,700 and blossomed into a brilliant inside-left at Maine Road. He lost the 1926 FA Cup Final in City colours and a week later the club suffered relegation to the Second Division, although they returned to the big time in 1928 after securing the Second Division Championship. In the same year he captained the Scotland side that stunned England 5–1 at Wembley – earning the team the nickname of 'Wembley Wizards'– and in 1933 was again on the losing side in a FA Cup Final, Everton beating City 3–0.

At the end of the season McMullan applied for the manager's job at Second Division Oldham and was appointed, but only stayed for a year. He did take them to the Lancashire Senior Cup Final, losing to Bolton at his old ground Maine Road, and during his year in charge Oldham faced Wednesday in a FA Cup fourth-round tie, holding them to a 1–1 draw at Boundary Park, before being beaten in the replay.

Known as a man of considerable charm and modesty, McMullan's next role was as the first ever manager of Aston Villa, appointed in May 1934. Unfortunately, despite being given a considerable 'war chest' by Villa, the club suffered relegation for the first time in their history and Jimmy duly tendered his resignation in October 1936. The diminutive McMullan – he stood only 5ft 5ins tall – was always in demand though, and after less than a month out of work he joined Notts County as manager on 10 November 1936.

Having just missed out on promotion from Third Division South, he was still in charge of the League's oldest club when he was interviewed for the vacant job at Hillsborough in December 1937. A few days later his club agreed to release McMullan, and he officially joined Wednesday three days into 1938. He took over with the Owls struggling in 17th position in the old Second Division, and he ensured that Wednesday avoided the ignominy of suffering relegation into regional soccer by averaging a point a game until the end of the season. The signings of Charlie Napier and Doug Hunt contributed greatly to a successful 1938–39 campaign as Wednesday chased promotion all season, before being agonisingly beaten to the second promotion spot by fierce rivals Sheffield United after they won their final game of the season.

Unfortunately, his good start to life in the Hillsborough hot seat then came to an abrupt end as Germany invaded Poland and World War Two engulfed Europe. All contracts were declared null and void and Jimmy started to work in a local factory, while continuing to manage the Owls on a part-time basis. With players called-up and the public lukewarm to football, it was a challenge for McMullan to keep Wednesday competitive in the early years of the conflict and his temporary contract was not renewed in the summer of 1942. Surprisingly, McMullan never returned to football in any capacity and continued to work in Sheffield industry until his retirement, passing away in a Wadsley Bridge residential home on 28 November 1964 – the same day that his immediate predecessor at Hillsborough, Billy Walker, died.

Eric Woodhouse Taylor: April 1942–July 1958

Died 23 September 1974

Eric Taylor was born on a Wednesday, on 22 May 1912, and would go on to become a great ambassador for the club, being the driving force behind the almost total redevelopment of Hillsborough, which resulted in the ground being widely recognised as one of the best in the country. Eric was also a member of the Sheffield and Hallamshire Association's civic council for 30 years.

Born in the Birley Carr district of Sheffield in May 1912, Taylor started his working life in a law firm, before seeing an advertisement in the local paper for an office boy at a city football team. When he applied he did not know if the job was with Wednesday or United, but was overjoyed to discover that it was at 'his' team, Sheffield Wednesday. His passion for the club had started at an early age, and Eric and his school friends would often slip into the ground to watch the final few minutes of matches once the gates were opened to allow fans to leave.

Once he had secured the position – in September 1929 – he learned that his role had been created as a reward for legendary secretary-manager Bob Brown, after he had secured the First Division title a few months earlier. He learned quickly from Brown, and when Joe McClelland left in October 1934 Taylor was soon promoted to assistant secretary to newcomer Billy Walker. He then served under Jimmy McMullan, but such was Taylor's progress, despite his relatively tender years, that he was asked to take over as part-time team manager in April 1942 – at the time Eric was working at Howell's Tube Works and had no option but to fit both roles into a busy working week!

Just over a year into his new post, Taylor guided Wednesday to the 1943 North War Cup Final, losing to Blackpool over two legs, and his growing stature was rewarded when he was officially named as full-time secretary-manager on 14 June 1945. Taylor was certainly not a 'tracksuit' manager and left the day-to-day coaching of the team to

his various trainers, Sam Powell, Laurie McMenemy, Alan Brown, Bill Knox and Jack Marshall among others. After a brush with relegation in the first post-war season, Taylor slowly rebuilt the Wednesday side, culminating in 1950 when the Owls finished runners-up behind Tottenham Hotspur to reclaim the First Division place they had lost 13 years earlier. In the immediate post-war years Taylor showed his eye for talent by bringing some great players to Hillsborough, such as Jackie Sewell, Ron Springett, Roy Shiner and the imperious Derek Dooley, with the Owls being involved in several deals that set a new British transfer fee mark.

Of course, the 1950s have become known as the 'yo-yo years' and three promotions from the Second Division (two as champions) were counterbalanced with relegation from the top flight in 1951, 1955 and 1958. As the game of football started to become somewhat of a global brand, the pressures on Taylor's time increased, and after the third relegation of the decade the Owls board decided that it was time to relieve that pressure and advertise for a separate team manager. After Harry Catterick was appointed, Eric became secretary/general manager and over the years that followed he showed his remarkable flair for administration and organisation by developing Hillsborough. In his new role Taylor set about remodelling and improving the ground, and before the final plans came together and were submitted he visited many other grounds around the world in a knowledge-gaining mission to be sure that the improvements would provide the club with the most up-to-date and very best facilities that were available at that time.

In April 1964 Taylor had the unenviable task of addressing the crowd during half-time at the Wednesday and Spurs game, after it had emerged that two of Wednesday's players – Peter Swan and Bronco Layne – were alleged to have been involved in a bribes scandal. A dyed-in-the-wool Owls fan with a strict moral code, his impassioned speech that night came from the heart and is still remembered by supporters who were inside Hillsborough.

During the 1960s Hillsborough not only hosted several FA Cup semi-finals and a full England international, but Taylor was one of the proudest men in Sheffield when the ground was chosen to host games in the 1966 World Cup Finals. The likes of Switzerland, West Germany and Uruguay appeared on the Hillsborough turf and his organisation was voted the best of all the provincial grounds during that memorable summer. Such was his reputation that the North American National Professional Soccer League offered Taylor a lucrative salary in September 1966 to become their executive secretary. Eric refused the offer to stay with Wednesday, however, but, tragically, within a year he was involved in a car accident that left him seriously injured and fighting for his life.

He thankfully recovered to return to his job at Hillsborough, but sadly for Taylor his work off the pitch had not been replicated on the field of play, as Wednesday tumbled out of the First Division in 1970 and to the brink of the Third Division in 1974. Before the end of the 1973–74 campaign Taylor had announced his intention to retire when his contract expired on 30 June 1974, and he was appointed vice-president on his departure after a remarkable 45 years on the staff at Wednesday. He intended to act on a consultancy basis for the Owls, but started to suffer increasingly poor health and just a few months after retiring, at the relatively young age of just 62, died on 23 September 1974. His passing was mourned across the football community and the esteem in which he was held was demonstrated a few weeks later when England manager Don Revie brought a strong national side to Hillsborough to play in a testimonial match in honour of 'Mr Sheffield Wednesday', Eric Taylor.

Henry (Harry) Catterick: August 1958–April 1961

Died 9 March 1985

When Eric Taylor relinquished the suffix of his secretary-manager title in the summer of 1958, Wednesday appointed the little-known Rochdale boss Harry Catterick as the club's first ever full-time team manager. In fact, his appointment proved a real master stroke and Catterick is now rightly regarded as one of the club's greatest managers.

Born in Darlington on 26 November 1919, the teenage Harry started his playing career as an amateur for Stockport County, while also appearing for Cheadle Heath Nomads, before he penned a professional contract with Everton at the age of 18. His move to Goodison Park was the start of a love affair with the Merseyside club that would stay with Catterick for the rest of his life, and would eventually result in Wednesday losing his valuable services in 1961.

As a player Catterick did not break into Everton's first team until the years of World War Two, after the Toffeemen lost the services of Tommy Lawton and Bob 'Bunny' Bell. When peacetime football returned Harry found that his way to the first team was blocked by Jock Dodds. Catterick spent the majority of his 14 years at Goodison Park in the shadows, amassing just 71 appearances and scoring 24 goals without ever being an established first-team player. He suffered two broken arms in the immediate post-war years, which certainly did not help his hopes of breaking into the senior side, and he rejected several offers to move elsewhere, deciding instead to stay and fight for his place.

In December 1951 he moved to become player-manager of Crewe Alexandra, although the player part of his title disappeared at the end of the 1952–53 season, after 11 goals in 24 appearances. This coincided with his move to Rochdale in June 1953, where in five seasons he kept the Lancashire club above the re-election zone without ever climbing above 10th position. He must therefore have applied for the Wednesday post more in hope than expectation, but despite there being better-known candidates for the position, he greatly impressed Owls chairman, Dr Andrew Stephen, and the rest of the Wednesday board and was offered the role.

He officially took over on 1 September 1958, after gaining his release from Rochdale, although he had actually started

in the middle of August, at the commencement of the new season. Incidentally, he was replaced at Spotland by Wednesday's trainer Jack Marshall, who would return to Hillsborough as manager in the late 1960s. The new man made an immediate impression on the Wednesday fans and in his first season led the club to the Championship of the old Second Division, despite selling 'golden boy' Albert Quixall to Manchester United for a British record fee in September 1958. Promotion was secured with still four games to be played, and Wednesday ended a terrific season on a high after neighbours Barnsley were beaten 5–0 at Hillsborough on the last day of the season.

Catterick was a single-minded, tough and uncompromising character, but he was highly respected by his players and was not afraid to introduce several individuals from the club's youth team – the likes of John Fantham, Peter Swan and Tony Kay. His second season in charge saw the Owls finish fifth in the First Division, as well as losing to Blackburn Rovers in the FA Cup semi-final, and the 1960–61 season proved to be Harry's nadir at Wednesday, as his team chased the great Tottenham side all season in a race for the Championship. Unfortunately, the season also saw Catterick and the Wednesday hierarchy start to disagree on certain matters, and as the campaign progressed the situation deteriorated, culminating in Catterick's shock resignation in April 1961 with four games of the seasons still to play, citing interference from the board. In later life Catterick said that if he had been able to sign centre-forward Joe Baker (the Owls board had failed to sanction his purchase) then Wednesday would have won the First Division title, as his success at Wednesday had not involved any major transfer buys. The parallels with future boss Howard Wilkinson are striking, as both men effectively resigned due to a lack of investment in the team and would then win the top-flight titles soon after leaving Hillsborough.

It was his old club, Everton, that Catterick joined 10 days later, and the irony was not lost on Wednesday fans when his first game in charge was against the manager-less Owls at Hillsborough. Wednesday fans booed him when he took his seat in the directors' box and watched on as his new side sent Wednesday to only their second home loss of the whole season. He was handed a free rein at Goodison Park and, after securing former Owls coach Tommy Eggleston as his right-hand man, he subsequently returned to Wednesday in December 1962 to buy captain Tony Kay for £60,000. At the end of that 1962–63 season Everton raced away to win the First Division title, and Catterick watched in 1966 as his side came from two goals behind to beat Wednesday in the FA Cup Final. His stylish and entertaining brand of football delighted the Goodison Park regulars and he signed some true club legends – men such as Colin Harvey, Howard Kendall and Alan Ball. Wednesday fans could only watch on enviously as Everton reached the 1968 FA Cup Final, losing to West Bromwich Albion, finished third in the top flight in 1969 and then won the title again 12 months later. Catterick – dubbed the 'silent man of football' – was still in charge at the Blues in January 1972 when he suffered a heart attack while driving home from Sheffield. He was eventually moved 'upstairs' to become general manager in April 1973.

He remained in that position until the start of the 1975–76 campaign, when the departure from Preston of Bobby Charlton resulted in Catterick being handed the Deepdale hot seat. After two seasons, where Preston finished in the top half of the table, he decided to call it a day, retiring from football in the summer of 1977. It was perhaps fitting that Catterick died on 9 March 1985 at his beloved Goodison Park after watching Everton and Ipswich draw 2–2 in the FA Cup. His legacy was truly great, with the fans of two different clubs considering Harry Catterick to be one of their greatest managers – an accolade enjoyed only by a select few.

Victor (Vic) Frederick Buckingham: May 1961–April 1964

Died 26 January 1995

To fill the managerial vacancy created by the departure of Harry Catterick, the Wednesday board looked abroad to Holland and appointed Ajax manager, Englishman Vic Buckingham. In his younger days Buckingham had played for Greenwich schools, before signing for Tottenham Hotspur, appearing for their junior team and also their nursery side, Northfleet. He made his senior debut for Spurs, at centre-half, during the 1935–36 season and amassed 128 appearances in the five seasons immediately preceding World War Two.

Buckingham – born on 23 October 1915 in Greenwich – served in the Royal Air Force during the conflict and played as a guest for a wide variety of clubs, including Crewe, Fulham and Portsmouth, while also playing occasionally for his parent club, Tottenham. He also twice appeared for the England national side – against Wales on both occasions in the 1940–41 campaign – although caps were not officially awarded during the hostilities.

At the end of the war Buckingham enjoyed his first experience of life off the field when he spent the summer of 1946 in Norway, coaching Moss FC. He subsequently coached both Spurs' junior side (Stanmore FC) and the club's youth side, before officially retiring from the field of play in 1949. It was already obvious that the flamboyant Londoner would enjoy a successful career in management and this began with a short period as coach to famous amateur side Pegasus (a team drawn from the universities of Oxford and Cambridge). This included a victory in the 1951 Amateur Cup Final, an amazing crowd of 100,000 watching the students beat Bishop Auckland at Wembley. This success increased Buckingham's profile considerably, and he was quickly handed his first managerial role in League soccer after being appointed Bradford Park Avenue manager in June 1951.

He lifted Avenue to eighth place in the old Third Division North, but resigned in January 1953, joining First Division West Bromwich Albion the following month. Less than four weeks after hanging up his boots Buckingham was now managing in the top flight, and he continued to impress, leading Albion to runners-up spot in his first full season (1953–54) and also FA Cup glory at Wembley – beating Preston 3–2 to secure the famous old 'tin pot'. The debonair boss had quickly earned a reputation for playing open and attacking football, and he led the Baggies to a FA Cup semi-final and two top-six finishes before his shock resignation in June 1959.

His next destination was a surprise as he moved to Dutch club Ajax Amsterdam, clearly deciding that he wanted to test his managerial qualities by experiencing time on foreign shores. The Dutch title was secured in his maiden season and the national Cup followed a year later as Buckingham continued a coaching career that had seen almost total success – he is also widely regarded as the man who 'discovered' Johann Cryuff. With his two-year contract with Ajax set to end in the summer of 1961, he agreed to take over at Plymouth Argyle, although was unable to take up the post immediately due to his commitments with the Amsterdam side. In the interim, however, he heard from a friend that the Hillsborough post had suddenly become vacant and managed to persuade Argyle to release him from their verbal agreement and was officially appointed Owls manager on 8 May 1961.

The club's sixth manager officially started in his new role on 1 June and took over an Owls side that had just finished First Division runners-up, with expectations high for another tilt at the title. Buckingham's management methods and skills were thought to be ahead of his time, having been influenced by the England manager Walter Winterbottom, with whom he had come into contact during his Middlesex FC days. During his time at Hillsborough he was inclined to let his players have a free rein and play to the situation, but underneath his laid-back persona was a steely determination to win. This was proven in March 1962 when he sensationally slated his own players in the local media, the front-page story quoting Buckingham as saying, 'It's just not good enough, as a team they have got no skill and in the long run hard work will never make up for that deficit.'

What the players thought of the outburst was never reported, but he enjoyed a relatively successful first campaign in the Wednesday hot seat, finishing sixth and taking the club to the last eight of the Fairs Cup, losing to Barcelona over two legs. He also finished sixth in his two other seasons in charge, but towards the end of his spell, in the spring of 1964, 'keeper Ron Springett submitted a transfer requesting, citing personal grievances with his manager. This was rejected by the board after Springett had met with them, and when Buckingham was asked after the meeting if he would be resigning, or if the club would ask him to go, he stated, 'Both are possible.' Various players experiencing off-field problems did not help his cause and it was also reported that he enjoyed an uneasy relationship with his chief scout, Jack Mansell.

Within days, Wednesday's assistant manager, Gordon Clark, left Hillsborough to take up the managerial position at Peterborough United and it seemed that the writing was on the wall for Buckingham. On 9 April 1964 he was informed that his contract would not be renewed when it expired on 31st May, and three days later the club was rocked when on 12 April 1964 the infamous bribery affair was exposed by a national Sunday newspaper, citing two current Wednesday players and one former player as being involved.

It was no surprise that Vic did not stay until the end of the season, former manager Eric Taylor stepping in as caretaker manager, and within days he was reappointed at former club Ajax on a lucrative three-year deal. He only stayed until January 1965 though, when he returned to take over at Fulham, also signing a three-year deal. That period proved a test of his managerial qualities as the London club struggled at the wrong end of the table and were eventually relegated. A man widely regarded as one of the finest coaches of his generation would spend the rest of his career in foreign lands, in charge at Greek club Ethnikos for two years before taking over at Barcelona in January 1970. He helped 'Barca' to recover from a slump in form and led them to Spanish Cup success, before having to resign due to a recurring back problem. In March 1972 he did return to football, being appointed manager at Seville, but only stayed for a brief spell before moving back to Greece to coach his former club. Buckingham returned to England to retire and, until his death in Chichester, Sussex on 26 January 1995, he still kept an interest in football and was a shareholder at West Bromwich Albion.

Alan Winstone Brown: August 1964–February 1968

Died 9 March 1996

Alan Brown was born in Consett on 26th August 1914, and grew up in the village of Corbridge in Northumberland. At school he played rugby in the morning and appeared for a local junior team, Spen

Black and White Football Club, in the afternoon. The club produced several players who went on to play for League teams, such as Jackie Milburn (Newcastle United), Bob Cowen (Leeds United) and Arthur Egglestone (Sheffield United). After being recommended to Huddersfield Town by his cousin, England international Austen Campbell, he signed professional forms for the Terriers in March 1933, appearing in 57 League games before leaving to take up a position in the police force.

When World War Two began he joined the Royal Air Force, where he played several sports, in addition to football. He appeared in inter-services representative soccer games, while still playing for Huddersfield, and also made guest appearances for Liverpool, Manchester United and Notts County. In 1945 he was the 12th man for England against Scotland at Villa Park, while in February 1946 Burnley broke their transfer record by paying £25,000 to take Brown to Turf Moor.

He was immediately made captain and the half-back led the Clarets in a memorable 1946–47 season, which ended with an extra-time defeat to Charlton Athletic in the FA Cup Final. The Lancashire side also finished Second Division runners-up, conceding a paltry 29 goals on their way to promotion, and in October 1947 Brown was captain of the Football League side that beat their Irish League counterparts 4–3 in Dublin. A year later, in October 1948, he was transferred to Notts County for £12,500, but after only six months he asked to be released from his contract, having made just 13 League appearances for them.

He subsequently returned to the police force, while also running his own restaurant in Burnley. On 23 January 1951, however, he started a long and relatively successful career as a coach after being appointed by Eric Taylor at Hillsborough – Sheffield was not unknown to Brown, as during the war years he had spent some time there as a physical training instructor and also coached for the Sheffield and Hallamshire FA. He replaced the deceased Bill Knox, who had died at the age of just 44 in February 1950, and was given a valuable apprenticeship at Wednesday, remaining for four years before taking over as manager at his old club, Burnley, in August 1954.

During three seasons at Burnley, Brown earned a reputation as a very astute manager and a tough disciplinarian, and he secured three top-10 finishes for the Clarets, despite having to work with one of the smallest budgets in the First Division. He duly returned to his native North East in July 1957 when he was appointed manager at Sunderland – a club who were recovering from an enquiry into alleged illegal payments to their playing staff. Unfortunately, in his first season Sunderland accompanied Wednesday in

being relegated from the top flight – the first ever relegation the Wearside club had suffered in their history. Over the next six seasons Brown battled to haul Sunderland back into the top flight, introducing such players as Brian Clough and future Owls boss Len Ashurst, and he finally succeeded in 1964.

The Sunderland boss then caused a minor sensation by resigning from his position in July 1964, and signing a five-year contract at Sheffield Wednesday! He officially started at Hillsborough on 1 August 1964 and led the Owls to a creditable 8th-place finish in his debut campaign. Although he boasted somewhat of a steely exterior, there was genuine warmth behind his persona and he acted as a father figure to the extremely young side that won through to the 1966 FA Cup Final. His feeling for his young charges was shown in his passionate and proud speech in praise of the youngsters after Everton had stormed back to win 3–2 at Wembley. He was also a highly principled man, and during the period leading up to the Final the no-nonsense Brown threatened to resign when some of his players requested more Cup tickets than was the official allocation. He decided that he would stick by the FA rules and resign on principle if the players were not prepared to accept the ruling – the players in question later apologised to Brown.

The season that followed saw a swell of support for Wednesday after the Cup heroics, but after a good start they fell away to record a final finishing position of 11th. By early September of the 1967–68 season the Owls were flying high at the top of the table – fittingly, as the club was celebrating its centenary year – but that early-season form did not continue, with the loss of key man David Ford – he was injured in a car crash that killed his fiancée – a key factor in the slump. With the Owls in the bottom half of the table and Sunderland now without a manager after they sacked Ian McColl, Brown tendered his resignation to the Wednesday board on 8 February 1968. He denied that he would be taking over at Sunderland, but a few days after his resignation was accepted he was, unsurprisingly, appointed as Sunderland manager. In 1970 a Sunderland side managed by Brown again accompanied Wednesday out of the First Division, and he remained in charge until being fired in November 1972 after a poor start to the season. Nine of his players at Sunderland would go on to win the 1973 FA Cup as a Second Division team, beating First Division Leeds United.

Brown returned to football in 1973 to coach Norwegian team Ham-Kam Hamar, taking them to runners-up spot in their top division, before retiring at the end of the season and moving to Bodmin, Cornwall. He was enticed out of retirement to become chief coach at Plymouth, however, and helped Argyle to the runners-up spot in the Third Division, and promotion in 1975. Brown stayed with Plymouth until 1977 when he retired once again, moving to North Devon, where he wrote a coaching book called *Team Coach*, which was published with financial assistance from Wednesday, Sunderland, Burnley and other individuals from his past, including Derek Dooley, Jack Whitham, Peter Eustace and Brian Clough. He later moved to the Devonshire town of Barnstaple, where he passed away on 9 March 1996.

John (Jack) Gilmour Marshall: February 1968–March 1969

Died 6 January 1998

Jack Marshall, known by some as 'Jolly Jack', was born of Scottish parents in Bolton, Lancashire on 29 May 1917. His early football career started with Bacup Borough, where he was spotted by Burnley scouts and duly signed professional forms for the Clarets in November 1936. His other career option, as a poultry farmer, fell by the wayside and he made his debut for Burnley during the 1938–39 season, before, like so many other players, he lost the best years of his career to World War Two. During the conflict he joined the Royal Air Force and was posted to Cairo, Egypt, severely curtailing any chances of regular wartime soccer. After the war he struggled to get back into the Burnley side and after only 27 senior appearances was forced to retire in 1949 after failing to recover from a serious leg injury.

He then worked as a scout for Bolton Wanderers, while also studying massage and physiotherapy, in addition to working for an engineering company, and later filled the same role at Bury and Stoke City. In January 1955 he was appointed by Wednesday to the role of chief scout and physiotherapist. He worked under Eric Taylor at Hillsborough, replacing the

departed Alan Brown, and also assisted England manager Walter Winterbottom with the national B side.

Like his predecessor, Marshall moved directly from Wednesday into his first managerial role, taking over as boss at Rochdale in October 1958. He did, of course, replace Harry Catterick at Spotland, but could not stop his new side slipping into the bottom division (it would be 2010 before they were promoted back!). After another season he was allowed to accept the post of manager at First Division Blackburn Rovers, but not until Rochdale had a new man in charge. He was therefore at the helm until the seventh game of the 1960–61 season, before taking over the hot seat at Ewood Park in September 1960. He had to rebuild a team that had reached the FA Cup Final in the previous season – beating Wednesday in the semi-final – and was not afraid to experiment with various positional changes, with both Fred Pickering and Keith Newton benefiting greatly by going on to win caps for England. A quarter-final FA Cup defeat to Wednesday in March 1966 was followed a few weeks later by relegation from the First Division, and Marshall started the 1966–67 campaign without a contract, despite bringing in some new personnel. Ex-Owl Eddie Quigley was brought into the club to take over as coach and in February 1968, amidst some internal turmoil, Marshall resigned as manager and accepted the post of assistant to Alan Brown at Wednesday.

Within days of Marshall joining the Owls staff. Brown rendered his shock resignation and Marshall was appointed as caretaker manager. Within 72 hours though, he somewhat reluctantly agreed to accept the position on a permanent basis, being officially appointed on 11 February 1968. After being unsuccessful in obtaining new players for the side, he tinkered with both team formation and tactics, and this was just enough to ensure that the Owls avoided dropping into the Second Division. At the start of the following season Marshall suffered a bout of illness, and was in hospital having his appendix removed when Hillsborough was witness to arguably the greatest game ever seen at the old ground – Wednesday's 5–4 win over European Champions Manchester United. A few days later they came back down to earth with a bump, however, as Fourth Division Exeter City dumped the Owls out of the League Cup. Over the ensuing weeks, several players submitted transfer requests and Marshall struggled manfully to lift the gloom that seemed to hang around the club. A 5–0 home defeat to Arsenal in March 1969 proved the final straw and, although Wednesday were actually 10th in the First Division following the loss, the pressure began to build on Marshall. He subsequently discovered that Wednesday did not intend to renew his contract when it was due to expire in the summer of 1969, and tendered his resignation from the post on 18 March 1969.

On 1 July 1969 he returned to Bury, this time as manager, but experienced a short and traumatic period in charge. A plethora of new directors came into the club soon after he was appointed and the writing was quickly on the wall. Marshall and his assistant, Jimmy Meadows, were fired after just 11 weeks in charge, with financial reasons being given as an excuse. In July of 1970 he took up the role of physiotherapist at his old team, Blackburn Rovers, where he would remain before retiring in 1979 and returning to his old Bolton roots. He later moved back to South Yorkshire and passed away in Rotherham on 6 January 1998.

Daniel (Danny) Thomas Williams: July 1969–January 1971

Like many of his contemporaries, Danny Williams left school at the age of 14 to work at a local coal mine. He worked at the pit head at Silverwood Colliery, while also playing football for the colliery side and Wath Wanderers, the latter acting as a nursery side for Wolverhampton Wanderers at the time. Born in Rotherham (20 November 1924 in Thrybergh), Williams began to train with Sheffield United part way through World War Two, and in the spring of 1943 he was offered an official trial with his home-town team, Rotherham United. He duly signed as a part-time professional with the Millers and started a career in the game that would stretch until his retirement over 40 years later.

He would remain at Rotherham United for an astonishing 23 years – as player, coach, trainer and eventually manager. He was a hard-working wing-half and he turned down several offers from the likes of Arsenal to remain at Millmoor, amassing 461 League appearances – a club record that still stands today. It was not until 1951, when the working regulations implemented during the war ended, that he could turn full-time with United. In the same year he was part of the outstanding Rotherham side that won the Championship of the old Third Division North, while four years later he was a crucial member of the side that agonisingly missed out on a place in the top flight on goal average. His playing career came to a close at the end of the 1959–60 season and he was immediately appointed player-coach of the club's reserve side.

In 1962, he informed Rotherham that he was leaving to concentrate on the sports shop that he had opened while still a player, but in the meantime manager Tom Johnson moved to Grimsby Town and Danny was asked to take over his role. He accepted the

offer and remained manager until January 1965, when he resigned as a matter of principle after several of his talented young players were sold against his will. He actually decided to retire from the game after leaving Millmoor, but after moving to Bournemouth he soon found he was missing the day-to-day involvement and accepted the position of Swindon Town manager in August 1965. His impact at the Wiltshire club was astonishing as in the 1968–69 season he took the club to promotion from the old Third Division (League One), while also stunning the world of football by winning the League Cup at Wembley, beating hot favourites Arsenal 1–0.

He was now on the radar of many bigger clubs and was offered and accepted the position of manager at Wednesday, joining on 17 July 1969. His move to Hillsborough was universally welcomed by Wednesday supporters, but in hindsight the happy-go-lucky Williams joined the Owls at exactly the wrong time, with the club already on a slide that would end in Third Division football six years later. His lack of knowledge regarding top-flight football almost certainly counted against Williams, but internal strife, an unhappy dressing room and several big-name players coming to the end of their illustrious careers were problems that he simply inherited. He sold several players that were anxious to leave Hillsborough, but many of their replacements – the majority from the lower leagues – failed to be of the desired quality, and Wednesday not only suffered relegation from the First Division in 1970, but also experienced Cup humiliations against Scunthorpe United and Bournemouth. With the club out of the FA Cup and lying 13th in the Second Division, Williams' relatively short spell in charge came to an end on 15 January 1971, as the board acted swiftly in an attempt to stop the club's slide down the Leagues. It would be a further two years before the two parties finally agreed a compensation deal, the former boss accepting a golden handshake of £10,000 (almost £100,000 in today's prices).

After leaving Hillsborough he was appointed manager at struggling Mansfield Town in November 1971, but was unable to stop them from dropping out of the Third Division at the end of the season. He was eventually lured back to Swindon Town in March 1974, and was in charge until being moved 'upstairs' in May 1978. He returned briefly as caretaker manager at the start of the 1980–81 season when Wilf Trantor resigned, but was soon back in his previous role, remaining until retiring to Bournemouth in May 1985.

Derek Dooley: January 1971–December 1973

(Also see Players section)

The coaching career of Derek Dooley started at Wednesday in the 1960s, when he coached the club's young players in the

evenings – at the time he worked full-time as an assistant sales manager at Gunstones Bakery. He eventually joined the club on a full-time basis as their inaugural development fund manager, and when Danny Williams was sacked in January 1971 he was asked to take over. His decision to accept the role was, like his predecessor, highly popular with Owls fans, and over the next 18 months he totally re-vamped the Wednesday side.

The likes of Brian Joicey, Willie Henderson, John Holsgrove and Dave Clements were all brought to Hillsborough by the pipe-smoking and reflective Dooley, and his new side gelled immediately at the start of the 1972–73 season, going on to the top of the Second Division table and winning many plaudits for their stylish brand of football. His swashbuckling side lifted some of the gloom that had surrounded Hillsborough since relegation in 1970 and, although the Owls did eventually fall away to finish in 10th place, the season gave renewed hope to Wednesday fans.

Unfortunately, the 1973–74 campaign was beset with problems, as a mystery virus and apparent loss of form meant that the team was at the wrong end of the table from their opening-day loss at Swindon Town. The odd win kept Wednesday out of the relegation places, but with the Christmas programme on the horizon, there was genuine hope that fortunes would change in the new year. Dooley, however, would not be in charge for the Boxing Day fixture at home to Hull City, as on Christmas Eve he was sensationally relieved of his post. Wednesday chairman Matt Sheppard, who had only been elected chairman 18 days earlier, will always be associated with Dooley's sacking, which was roundly condemned by both local and national media. Unsurprisingly, it would be almost two decades before Dooley could return to the ground, such was his obvious feelings after the manner of his dismissal.

Stephen (Steve) Burtenshaw: January 1974–October 1975

After neither Danny Williams nor Derek Dooley had succeeded in reviving the club's fortunes in the early 1970s, Wednesday turned to the relatively unknown Steve Burtenshaw. Born in Portslade-by-Sea, Sussex on 23 November 1935, Burtenshaw had captained both Brighton and Sussex boys as a teenager, as well as attending a trial for the England schools side. He won the FA County Youth Cup in 1952 and duly joined the ground staff at Brighton, turning professional in November 1952. He followed in the footsteps of his two elder brothers, Charlie and Bill, who were both professional footballers, although he initially served his compulsory national service and was stationed in Germany, where he appeared for the army's soccer team.

A solid half-back, Burtenshaw recorded a total of 252 appearances for Albion over a period of 15 years at the club, winning a Third Division Championship medal in the 1957–58 season. In 1964 he was handed the title of player/assistant coach, and continued to appear at first-team level until December 1966. After finally hanging up his boots he duly moved to Arsenal in December 1967 after accepting the position of reserve-team coach, and was promoted to first-team coach when Don Howe moved to become West Bromwich Albion manager in July 1971. He was on the move again in September 1973 as he resigned from his role at Highbury to swap places with Bobby Campbell at Queen's Park Rangers.

During his relatively short spell as a coach he had built a big reputation and, despite only working at Queen's Park Rangers for a matter of months, he was appointed Wednesday manager on 28 January 1974. His appointment was a real shock to Wednesday fans, who were hoping for a high-profile manager to lift the club from its mini slump, and at the time the 38-year-old became the youngest ever manager at Hillsborough. Unfortunately, his radical coaching methods did not impress the club's players and his management skills were called into question as he tried to keep Wednesday in the Second Division. He initially pulled the Owls away from the drop zone, but a shocking 8–0 defeat in their final away game of the season, at Jack Charlton's champions Middlesborough, put the club back in danger. Their survival therefore went to the final game, where a Ken Knighton goal was enough to preserve their status. The 1974–75 season proved an unmitigated disaster for Burtenshaw and Wednesday, however, as the club won only five games, failed to taste success from December 1974 until the end of the season, and were relegated at Nottingham Forest on 1 April 1975 with five games still to play. It was surprising to many Owls supporters that their now-beleaguered manager was still in charge when the club's first ever season in the Third Division commenced in August 1975. He did only last eight games of the new season though – Chairman Bert McGee wielding the axe to end his disastrous reign on 1 October – as Wednesday quickly slipped to the wrong end of the division after recording just two victories.

In the summer of 1976 he joined Everton as a coach, and in January 1977 he became caretaker manager when Billy Bingham was sacked. His four games in charge saw Everton lose both League matches, draw in the FA Cup and hold Bolton to a draw in the first leg of the League Cup semi-final before a new manager, Gordon Lee, was appointed. Burtenshaw was promoted to the role of assistant manager, but his managerial career looked in tatters when he lasted only 10 months of a three-year contract back at former club Queen's Park Rangers before being sacked in May 1979. He subsequently returned to another former

club, Arsenal, to become youth coach, and later served as caretaker manager in March 1986 when Don Howe resigned. When George Graham took over, Burtenshaw became the club's chief scout, while in 1995 he was implicated, along with Graham, in an illegal payments enquiry concerning the move of Danish international John Jensen to Highbury in 1992. The pair were found guilty by the Football Association, with Burtenshaw, by then chief scout back at Queen's Park Rangers, fined a total of £10,000 for his involvement with infamous football agent Rune Hauge.

In January 2001 he suffered a stroke, but recovered sufficiently to become a scout for Kevin Keegan at Manchester City in August 2001. He later retired from football, but returned to help out with some scouting for Arsenal, a role he continues to fulfil to this day.

Leonard (Len) Ashurst: October 1975–October 1977

Born in Liverpool on 10 March 1939, Len Ashurst was the manager that finally started the long-awaited revival that eventually took the club out of the Third Division in 1980. As a youngster, Ashurst had appeared for Liverpool boys and in the 1953–54 season was left-back in the side that won the English Schools Trophy, beating their Southampton counterparts 8–1 on aggregate. In the summer of 1954 he joined Liverpool's ground staff and kept busy throughout the calendar year, representing Lancashire at cricket as well as starting to work as an apprentice compositor in the printing trade at a firm in the centre of Liverpool.

Ashurst played for his country at youth level in the 1956–57 season, winning seven caps, but soon after was unfortunately released by Liverpool. Shortly afterwards, however, he signed amateur forms for Wolverhampton Wanderers, but his stay in the Black Country was brief as George Curtis, who had been in charge of the England youth side, tried to capture his signature for Sunderland, where Curtis was employed as coach. The matter became somewhat complicated, as to gain his release from Molineux he had to play a single game for Liverpool side Prescot Cables, before officially moving to Wearside. His first manager at Sunderland was none other than Alan Brown, who had cut his coaching teeth at Wednesday. Ashurst stayed a Sunderland player until March 1971, amassing over 400 appearances and winning an England Under-23 cap against West Germany in 1961 in the process. He was a permanent fixture in the Sunderland side that gained promotion from the Second Division in 1964, finishing runners-up behind Leeds United, and was twice managed by Brown, who returned to Roker Park in 1968 after four years at Wednesday. He was awarded a deserved benefit – facing neighbours Newcastle United in his fundraising game – and by the time he departed for Hartlepool United in 1971, had become a naturalised 'Mackem'.

His first job in management could not have been tougher for Ashurst as when he joined Hartlepool they were bottom of the League. He initially joined as player-manager and faced the challenge with gusto, adopting the role of player, manager and trainer. He did manage to haul United off the bottom spot, but they still had to apply for re-election at the end of the season, gaining enough votes to retain their League membership. During his time in charge Ashurst improved Hartlepool's League position each season, and in June 1974 his hard work was rewarded when he took over at newly promoted Gillingham.

It was from the Kent club that he

arrived at Hillsborough on 16 October 1975, but the move was not without problems after Ashurst had walked out on Gillingham to take the vacant position at Hillsborough – in February 1976 the Owls were issued with a writ, citing an illegal approach for Ashurst, and the whole matter was only settled in July 1977 when Wednesday paid £5,000 in compensation. On the field of play, the new manager steadied the ship and hit the headlines in January 1976 when his coach, former marine Tony Toms, took the players up onto the Yorkshire Moors for a night of survival training! That early example of a team-building exercise resulted in Wednesday winning their next match 2–0 against Chester, and a late season run of consecutive home wins was enough to avoid the unthinkable relegation into the basement division.

In the months that followed Ashurst cleared out several players and laid the foundations for a youth policy that would produce a fruitful bounty under the reign of Jack Charlton. The 1976–77 season proved a much better campaign for the long-suffering Wednesday fans as the team rallied to finish in eighth position, winning over 20 League games in a season for the first time since 1961–62. Unfortunately, the next season started badly, and after 10 games – five draws and five defeats – Wednesday were rooted to the bottom of the Third Division. Despite his hard work behind the scenes, a manager is usually judged on first-team results and it was therefore left to Bert McGee, Wednesday's chairman, to dismiss a club manager for the second time in two years, Ashurst cleared out his desk on 5 October 1977.

He was unemployed for a few months before accepting the position of Newport County manager in June 1978, and in his first season he took Newport to 8th in the table. He followed that by steering County to promotion from the Fourth Division and also winning the Welsh Cup, beating Shrewsbury Town 5–1 over the two legs, discovering a young John Aldridge in the process. The victory ensured qualification for the old European Cup Winners Cup, and they grabbed national headlines in the 1980–81 season by winning through to the last eight of the prestigious competition, only losing to East German side Carl Zeiss Jena 3–2 on aggregate. Despite his success at County, he was sacked in February 1982, mainly due to financial pressures, but was quickly employed by neighbours Cardiff City. He could not save the Bluebirds from relegation, but took them straight back up a year later, before taking the opportunity to manage his former club, Sunderland – joining in March 1984. He successfully saved his new club from relegation from the top flight and then led them to the 1985 League Cup Final at Wembley, losing 1–0 to Norwich City. Unfortunately, his side was also relegated and he paid the price, being sacked at the season's end.

A spell of coaching abroad followed, at Kuwait Sporting Club and Qatar-based Wakrah Sport Club, while he enjoyed a brief six-week spell as assistant to ex-Owl Jimmy Mullen at Blackpool. In August

1989 he moved back home for a second spell as Cardiff City manager, but after relegation and severe cost-cutting he departed again in the summer of 1991. A spell at non-League Weymouth and some time spent coaching in Malaysia followed, before Len returned to his former club in Qatar. During a pre-season tour, travelling to the Gaza Strip from Iraq, the team bus was attacked with a large boulder thrown through the coach window, killing the co-driver. Ashurst was also injured, but after hospital treatment was released. His final management post was at Southern League Weston-super-Mare – Wednesday signing the club's goalkeeper, Stuart Jones, on Ashurst's recommendation – before he resigned in August 1998 to become a FA Academy assessor for the southern region. He was later a match delegate for the Premiership and, after retiring back to the North East, published his 2009 autobiography, *Left Back in Time*.

John (Jack) Charlton OBE: October 1977–May 1983

Former World Cup winner Jack Charlton continued the good work of Len Ashurst when he was appointed Wednesday boss on 8 October 1977. Affectionately known as 'Big Jack', Charlton had been invited by the club's directors to attend a home game against Chesterfield, with a view to taking over as manager. The word that Charlton was in the stands spread like wildfire around the ground and against this background the Owls recorded their first win of the season. Charlton had decided not to accept the role, however, but because of the fans reaction to him, he had a sudden change of heart and instead accepted.

Born on 8 May 1935 in Ashington, Northumberland, Jack was from a real 'footballing' family, with four uncles playing professional football and his mum's cousin, Jackie Milburn, a legend at Newcastle United. Of course, his brother, Bobby, became arguably the most famous Charlton of them all. As a youngster, Jack played for the Ashington YMCA side, but after attending trials at Leeds United he turned them down, instead starting work at the nearby Linton pit. He quickly realised that colliery life was not for him, however, and decided instead to join the police force, at which point fate took a hand. His interview with the police was scheduled for the Friday, but he was subsequently offered another trial by Leeds United, who wanted Jack to play for their youth side on the Saturday. He chose to go to Leeds and never looked back, joining the club's ground staff and staying with United for the entire length of his playing career.

After completing his compulsory national service in Germany, the no-nonsense, rugged centre-half helped Leeds United to promotion from the Second Division in 1956, behind champions Wednesday, and although they were relegated in 1960 he was a key figure when they bounced back four years later. The next season saw the West Yorkshire club finish second in the First Division, as well as losing the 1965 FA Cup Final, and by the time Charlton retired in the 1972–73 campaign, Leeds had become established as a major force in the game. During that spell they won a plethora of honours, including the League title, FA Cup, League Cup and Fairs Cup, plus finishing League runners-up on four occasions and reaching the finals in both domestic Cup competitions. He was nicknamed 'Giraffe' (thanks to his 6ft 2in frame) during his playing days and accrued a massive 629 first-team appearances for Leeds – an incredible total for any player of any era. During the height of his powers he was also capped on 35 occasions by England – making his debut in 1965 against Scotland – and, of course, along with his brother, was part of the national side that lifted the Jules Rimet Trophy on that memorable afternoon in the summer of 1966.

He retired from international football after the 1970 World Cup Finals, and after retiring from the domestic game he was approached to take over as manager of Second Division Middlesbrough. He was duly appointed in May 1973 and enjoyed a tremendous first season as Boro romped to the Championship, finishing a huge 15 points clear of runners-up Luton Town. Success continued for Charlton as he led his charges to seventh place in the top flight – just five points behind the champions – and a year later took them to the semi-finals of the League Cup. In 1975 he won the Anglo-Scottish Cup, but resigned in April 1977, stating that he wanted more time with his family and felt that four years was more than long enough to spend at any one club. He therefore took a break from the game, indulging in his favourite pastimes of hunting and fishing, but after returning from a family holiday in the Caribbean he publicly stated that he wanted to get back into football.

It was because of that statement that Owls director Roy Whitehead invited Charlton to Hillsborough and Jack became the club's 10th post-war manager. His first task was to steer the club from the foot of the Third Division table, and based on defensive solidity he achieved that feat, Wednesday climbing to a relatively comfortable final position of 14th. As his side evolved, a combination of exciting youth products and terrific signings, the Owls finished in the same position in 1979, although on this occasion relegation was never a worry. The titanic FA Cup marathon with eventual winners, Arsenal, can be seen, in hindsight, as a real turning

point as, despite the Gunners eventually winning through, the experience gained by the players and the overall raising of the club's profile gave Wednesday a huge fillip, both on and off the field. Another turning point came on Boxing Day 1979, when Wednesday, sixth in the table, thrashed League leaders Sheffield United and went on to mount a promotion challenge that ended successfully a few months later. Charlton would break his 'four year rule' by remaining at Hillsborough until the summer of 1983 and twice came close to taking the club back into the First Division, agonisingly missing out in 1982 as the new three-points-for-a-win rule saw Norwich City take the third promotion slot – Wednesday would have gone up under the old two-point rule. He also led the club to the 1983 FA Cup semi-final and left with the good wishes of Wednesday fans.

After taking a break from the game he returned to Middlesbrough as caretaker manager in March 1984, but after successfully avoiding relegation he resigned the position. That same summer, relative Jackie Milburn helped him to secure the manager's position at Newcastle United, but Jack was somewhat reluctant to accept and he was never really popular with the 'Toon Army', eventually resigning during the following pre-season after receiving abuse from Newcastle supporters. He vowed never to return to club management, but then came the opportunity to take charge, on a part-time basis, of the Republic of Ireland national side. A change in eligibility rules by FIFA proved a massive boost to Ireland and Jack pieced together a disparate bunch of players that duly qualified for the 1988 European Championships. A win over England in those Finals raised Jack's popularity and he was an honorary Irishman by the time he resigned in December 1995, after almost 10 years in charge and appearances in the 1990 and 1994 World Cup Finals.

He then returned to his native Northumberland and now enjoys his retirement, while also attending the occasional after-dinner speaking engagement. He was awarded the OBE in 1974, made a Freeman of Dublin in 1994 and inducted into the English Football Hall of Fame in 2005.

Howard Wilkinson: June 1983–October 1988

Sheffield-born Howard Wilkinson holds a unique place in the history of Sheffield Wednesday as he is the only man to serve as a player, manager and chairman. Born in the Netherthorpe district of the city on 13 November 1943, he started his football career playing for his school team, Abbeydale Boys Grammar, and duly appeared for England schools against Scotland schools. Other early representative honours included games for the Sheffield and Hallamshire County team and five caps at youth level for his country. He made appearances for Sheffield United as an amateur, but after joining Sheffield-based non-league side Hallam he eventually signed for his boyhood heroes, Sheffield Wednesday, on 25 June 1962.

The young winger then served a two-year apprenticeship with the club's reserve side before breaking into the first team, making his debut at home to Chelsea in September 1964. He enjoyed a successful first season at senior level, appearing in exactly one third of the club's First Division games, but struggled to maintain his early promise and added only eight more games to his tally before moving to Brighton & Hove Albion for a £6,000 fee on 9 July 1966. His relatively modest playing career in League soccer came to a close on the south coast, where he scored 19 goals in 129 appearances prior to being appointed player-coach at Boston United in May 1971.

His move to Lincolnshire was the start of a highly successful career as coach and manager, which would see Howard not only manage Wednesday, but also take charge of the England side. While at Boston he gained a degree in Physical Education from the University of Sheffield, and returned to his old Sheffield school to gain some experience. In 1972 his manager at Boston, Jim Smith, left to join Colchester United and Wilkinson took over as player-manager, taking the club to two Northern Premier League titles in 1973 and 1974, plus a Northern Premier League Cup win in 1975. A spell at Manchester club Mossley followed for Wilkinson and he continued to collect trophies, lifting the Manchester Senior Cup before he was appointed FA Regional Director of Coaching for the North East. As part of his new title he also managed England's semi-professional side, winning the Four Nations title in 1979.

The inevitable move into League football came in December 1979, when Wilkinson was appointed to the coaching staff at Notts County. He duly moved up to assistant manager at Meadow Lane – being promoted to England Under-21 manager at the same time – and was handed the managerial hot seat in July 1982, when boss Jimmy Sirrel was appointed manager at Sheffield United. His early promise led to his appointment at Second Division Wednesday on 24 June 1983, and he duly added ex-Owl Peter Eustace and highly rated physio Alan Smith to his backroom staff. He joined a club that had been outside of the top flight for 13 years, but his all-action, all-running side quickly went to the top of the early League tables and did not taste defeat until the 16th match of the 1983–84 season, setting a new club record. Wednesday remained in the promotion places throughout the season, and a Mel Sterland penalty in the home game with Crystal Palace in April 1984 took the club back into the First Division.

His direct style of football upset some critics, but for Wednesday fans he could do no wrong, as Wilkinson took the Owls to final finishing positions of eighth and fifth in the higher division, as well as to the FA Cup semi-finals in 1986. The UEFA ban on English clubs, after the Hysel disaster, denied the club European football in the 1986–87 season, and his achievements led to offers for his services: Saudi Arabian side Al-Ittihad Club willing to pay Wilkinson a reputed £500,000 fee just to join and an astonishing £1 million annual salary. After his early successes with Wednesday, Wilkinson realised that investment in the side was needed to keep the club at the 'business end' of the top division, but he became frustrated when backing was not forthcoming from the boardroom – Chairman Bert McGee, who turned around the club's finances during his time at the helm, being perhaps understandably reticent about loosening the Hillsborough purse strings. The side then started to show signs of that lack of investment, and a 5–1 home loss on the final day of the 1987–88 season – admittedly against champions Liverpool – left Wednesday fans somewhat disgruntled as they went into the summer recess.

After rejecting approaches from Greek side PAOK Salonika, Wilkinson did eventually leave Wednesday when ambitious Leeds United were given permission by the Owls board to speak to Howard regarding their vacant managerial position. He duly resigned on 10 October 1988, and in his first full season took the West Yorkshire club to the Second Division title in 1990. Wednesday fans could then only watch and wonder as his newly promoted side won the final First Division title, before the formation of the Premiership a year later, pipping Wednesday to the Championship. He also took Leeds to the 1996 League Cup Final, but he was severely criticised by United fans after losing to Aston Villa, and was sacked in September after a poor start to the season.

He was quickly appointed as the Football Association's inaugural technical director in January 1997, with a remit to oversee the coaching and training methods at all levels of the English game. During this time he was briefly caretaker manager of the national side on two separate occasions – losing 2–0 against France in February 1999 and drawing 0–0 in Finland in 2000 – and was also handed the job of Under-21 manager. After six matches in charge, however, he resigned in June 2001.

In October 2002 Wilkinson resigned from his FA post to take over at Sunderland, three days after they had sacked Peter Reid. His stay on Wearside was brief though, as he was sacked after only six months in charge, leaving in March 2003 with Sunderland at the bottom of the table. He then moved abroad, taking charge of Chinese club Shanghai Shenhua in March 2004, but left after only two months, citing personal reasons for his resignation. In October that year he became first-team coach at Leicester City on a temporary basis, and in December moved back to his old club, Notts County, as a non-executive director. He was duly appointed chairman of the League Managers Association in September 2007, and returned to Hillsborough as technical advisor in January 2009. When chairman Lee Strafford resigned in May 2010, Howard was appointed interim chairman until the end of the season, but agreed to remain in the role in the summer that followed. He was subsequently a key figure as the club was finally taken over and saved from administration in November 2010. He remained on a three man board of directors before leaving the club in January 2011, just 48 hours before Alan Irvine departed Hillsborough.

Peter Eustace: October 1988–February 1989

Born in the Sheffield district of Stocksbridge on 31 July 1944, Peter Eustace started his working life as an apprentice mechanical engineer at the local steelworks plant. He was soon drafted into the works team, which was a real force in the old Yorkshire League at the time. When former Owls player Frank Slynn gained employment at the company, he spotted Eustace and arranged for the teenager to attend a trial at Wednesday. He became the youngest player to win a Championship medal when Stocksbridge Works were successful in 1959, and he subsequently signed apprentice forms at Hillsborough in March 1961, turning professional in June 1962.

Within three years he was a regular in the side, showing great maturity at the heart of the Owls side and was a major player as Wednesday reached the Final of the FA Cup in 1966 – the young side losing 3–2 to Everton after having been two goals

ahead. His form resulted in a call-up to the full England squad in 1968, but Lady Luck deserted Eustace as he suffered a knee injury after colliding with a friend while skiing on the hills around Stocksbridge, and missed out on a probable appearance for his country – he was called-up twice more, but never earned that elusive full cap. When new manager Danny Williams was appointed in 1969 he stated that Eustace was the team's best player, but then promptly sold him in January 1970, Wednesday receiving a club record fee of £95,000, with Peter actually being voted Player of the Year by Owls fans, despite him leaving midway through the campaign.

He was seen by the Hammers as a replacement for World Cup winner Martin Peters, but Eustace failed to fully reproduce his Hillsborough form and, in March 1972, returned to South Yorkshire after joining Rotherham United on loan. He duly returned to Wednesday for a second spell at the start of the 1972–73 season, and after completing a three-month loan period he rejoined on a permanent basis, the Owls paying a £13,900 fee for his services. Unfortunately, Wednesday struggled in his first two full seasons back in the blue-and-white stripes, and after suffering a disastrous relegation to the Third Division in 1975 Eustace moved to Peterborough United. His League career effectively ended after a full season at The Posh, although he did later return to Wednesday for a brief trial period in May 1976, before retiring after appearing for Worksop Town.

After his playing days ended Eustace started to work for his father-in-law's building firm back in Stocksbridge, before returning to the game in 1979 when he was appointed trainer at Sunderland, managed by former teammate Ken Knighton. The duo took the Wearside club to promotion to the First Division in 1980, and in July 1983 he returned to his boyhood team, Sheffield Wednesday, as assistant manager to the new Owls boss, Howard Wilkinson. Like at Sunderland, he achieved immediate success, and he and his old teammate led Wednesday back into the top flight after an absence of 14 years.

When Wilkinson resigned in October 1988, Eustace was appointed caretaker manager and won his two games in charge as Wednesday searched, unsuccessfully, for a replacement. The club were rebuffed on several occasions by managerial targets and eventually decided to offer Eustace the vacant position on a full-time basis. Unfortunately, his spell in charge was one of the most turbulent of any Owls manager in the club's history. He lasted just 109 days and won just one home game – an FA Cup tie against minnows Torquay United – and faced criticism from both inside and outside of the club. He was put out of his misery on 15 February 1989 after the Owls had slipped from mid-table into the relegation zone, with his time at the helm the shortest of any Wednesday boss.

He bounced back from his Hillsborough tribulations to be appointed coach at Leyton Orient and, after a spell in the same capacity at Charlton Athletic, he was named as assistant to Frank Clark, back at Orient. When the club's manager became managing director of the club in the summer of 1991, Eustace was named as his replacement and remained in the role until being shown the door in April 1994. He then experienced a spell out of the game – running a public house in the picturesque Derbyshire village of Hope – before returning in 1999 as an international scout for Premiership West Ham United. His area included Scotland and Scandinavia, and he worked under Harry Redknapp for two years before working as an independent scout. He returned to Hillsborough as chief scout in

July 2003, but was made redundant three years later as the club cut costs. His appeal to take Wednesday to an industrial tribunal for unfair dismissal was rejected and he duly teamed up again with Redknapp, who was now in charge at Portsmouth, as a scout. Just after Pompey won the 2008 FA Cup Final he returned north and is now employed as chief scout at Hartlepool United.

Ronald (Ron) Frederick Atkinson: February 1989–June 1991 and November 1997–May 1998

In hindsight, the arrival of Ron Atkinson was a real turning point in the club's recent history, as Wednesday were transformed from a drab, defensive side into an attacking team, full of top-quality players, that challenged for the game's top honours in the early 1990s. The flamboyant Atkinson was born in Liverpool on 18 March 1939, but spent the majority of his childhood in the city of Birmingham after his family relocated there when he was a toddler. As a boy he appeared for his school football team, Lea Village, and after gaining employment at a tool company he also started to play for their works side. It was while representing his employers that he was spotted by his boyhood idols, Aston Villa, and was subsequently signed as a part-time professional

Unfortunately, he was released in 1959, along with his brother, Graham, and seemed destined for a playing career outside of the Football League after signing for non-League Headington United. A central-defender, Ron was appointed captain, and in his first season led his new club to runners-up position in the old Southern League, behind champions Bath City. His side was unsuccessful in obtaining enough votes to gain membership of the Football League, but they would become an irresistible force as they won back-to-back titles under their new name of Oxford United. The League still evaded them though, and it required the sad demise of Accrington – who resigned from the League in February 1962 – for Oxford to be elected by a large majority. Atkinson – known as 'The Tank' during his playing days – duly led United into the Football League, and by 1968, thanks to two promotions, they had reached the Second Division. He totalled almost 400 games for Oxford, although he was part-time for several years during that period, working as a sales representative for a large building firm.

A short spell at Witney Town preceded his first managerial appointment as player-manager of Kettering Town in December 1971. He quickly took The Poppies into the Southern League and then walked away with the title in 1973, a year before he broke into League management at Cambridge United. He was unable to play for United as Kettering had retained his registration, so Atkinson concentrated solely on his managerial role, leading Cambridge to the Championship of the Fourth Division in 1977. While in charge at United he famously sold a player to Barry Fry for a case of champagne, and his larger-than-life personality added to his obvious managerial ability made sure that Atkinson would not remain in the lower leagues for much longer. He was duly enticed away by First Division West Bromwich Albion in January 1978. At the Hawthorns he built one of the finest teams in the club's history, led by the 'three degrees': Cyrille Regis, Brendan Batson and Laurie Cunningham. They reached the last four of the FA Cup and 'Big Ron' then took Albion to third place in the top flight, just behind Liverpool and Nottingham Forest. They also reached the quarter-finals of the UEFA Cup, narrowly losing to

Red Star Belgrade, and remained a consistent top-six side before Atkinson was appointed Manchester United manager in June 1981.

It was at Old Trafford that Ron increased his reputation of being a big-spending, bejewelled manager and he twice won the FA Cup with United, beating Brighton in 1983 and Everton two years later. The Red Devils had not won a League title since the 1960s, however, and it was his failure to deliver that crown that ultimately led to his dismissal in November 1986. It was the first sacking of Atkinson's career and it was almost a year before he was back in the game, returning to West Bromwich Albion for a second spell. After just six weeks, however, he was offered the chance to work abroad and resigned, moving to Jesus Gil's Atletico Madrid. It is doubtful that Ron was unaware of Señor Gil's propensity for sacking managers, but the lure of the sun was too much! He actually lasted just 96 days, despite taking the Spanish club from near the foot of the table to third place, with the name of Ron being added to Gil's many victims.

It was therefore from sunny Spain that Atkinson breezed into Hillsborough, joining Wednesday as the successor to Peter Eustace on 15 February 1989. He signed a contract until the end of the season, but after securing the club's First Division survival he penned a new deal in the summer of 1989 as he set about totally revamping the Wednesday team. Early signings included Carlton Palmer, John Sheridan and Roland Nilsson and Wednesday started to play an entertaining brand of football not seen at the club since the early 1960s. Sadly, a late slump resulted in a shock last-day relegation in 1990, but Ron vowed to get Wednesday back, and the 1990–91 season provided Owls fans with memories galore. With David Hirst now paired with Paul Williams – Dalian Atkinson having been sold for a club record £1.75 million to Spanish soccer – and the likes of John Harkes, Danny Wilson and Phil King in the ranks, Wednesday stormed to promotion from the old Second Division and enjoyed a memorable day at Wembley, beating Manchester United to lift the League Cup in April 1991.

With fans debating what impact Big Ron's side could make on the top division, they were stunned when Atkinson sensationally quit Wednesday after being offered the manager's job at boyhood heroes, Aston Villa. Then, on a highly emotional day at Hillsborough, he was persuaded by Wednesday officials to reverse his decision and attended the parade through Sheffield to celebrate the previous season's success. Six days later, however, he changed his mind again (a decision he would regret in later life) and this time there was no turning back, with Atkinson joining Villa and leaving Owls fans deeply disappointed and angry. He led

Villa to Premiership runners-up spot in 1993 and won the League Cup in 1994 – beating Manchester United in a domestic Final for the second time – but was shown the door after failing to bring sustained success to Villa Park. In January 1995 he was appointed manager of struggling Coventry City, and with some of his renowned 'wheeler-dealing' he led them to safety with games to spare. He subsequently brought in several high-profile players, but results were not forthcoming and his reign came to an end in November 1996 as he made way for Gordon Strachan and was handed the title of Director of Football.

On 14 November 1997 he made a surprise return to the Hillsborough hot seat following the departure of David Pleat, and although his reaction from fans was initially mixed, he soon convinced the doubters, helped by four straight wins on arrival! He steered Wednesday to Premiership survival and had made arrangements for former captain Nigel Pearson to be groomed as his eventual successor, but those plans never came to fruition as Big Ron discovered that the club did not intend to renew his contract at the end of the 1997–98 season. His final game in charge therefore came at Crystal Palace, where a young Clinton Morrison scored the injury-time winner for Crystal Palace.

Atkinson then spent time working in the media before coming back into football management, taking over at struggling Nottingham Forest in January 1999. He failed to keep them in the Premiership, however, and left in June that year. He continued to work in the media as a match summariser, until in April 2004 he was forced to resign after making an off-air comment which was accidentally broadcast. He appeared later for Sky TV and commentated for a UK digital channel during the 2006 World Cup. In January 2007 he returned to Kettering Town as Director of Football, but left in April 2007 after the departure of the club manager. He was briefly a consultant at Halesowen Town and now lives out his retirement, while also working as a pundit for a betting company.

Trevor John Francis: June 1991–May 1995

The only player–manager in Wednesday's history, Trevor Francis was appointed in the summer of 1991, following the sensational departure of Ron Atkinson. It was Big Ron who had originally brought Francis to Hillsborough, solely as a player, in January 1990 and the Owls board decided to hand the former England international the hot seat. The Owls were newly promoted to the top flight and Francis added the likes of Paul Warhurst, Chris Bart-Williams and Chris Woods to the exciting side that Atkinson had built. The team he inherited

from his predecessor hit the ground running in the First Division and enjoyed a tremendous season, finishing third and just missing out on winning the title. The side did qualify for Europe and Francis subsequently secured the headline signing of Chris Waddle as the Owls challenged for the major honours.

The side played some of the best football seen by Wednesday fans for many years in the 1992–93 season, but was desperately unfortunate to lose in both domestic Cup Finals, memorably beating Sheffield United in the Steel City FA Cup semi-final at Wembley. Francis was, unsurprisingly, accused of bringing success with a side that Atkinson had built, but his transfer record at Wednesday was good – he also signed Des Walker, although the likes of Nigel Jemson were perhaps not so successful. The big-money purchase of the aforementioned Walker and Andy Sinton in the summer of 1993 saw the club ready to storm the Championship, but a terrible start resulted in the club eventually finishing seventh for the second consecutive season. The 1994–95 season proved a highly challenging one for Francis, as several of the old guard moved onto pastures new and their replacements did not immediately gel, leading to a season of struggle and some high-profile personality clashes between Francis and some of his senior players. Despite only just avoiding relegation, however, it was still a surprise when he was sacked at the end of the season – a record 7–1 home defeat to Nottingham Forest in April 1995 certainly not helping his cause.

His route to Hillsborough had started in his hometown of Plymouth on 19 April 1954, and saw the young forward impress in youth football before joining Birmingham City as an apprentice in July 1969. He turned professional two years later, but had already made a huge impact on the English game, becoming the youngest ever player to score four goals in one League game. The deadly and pacey attacker became a legend at City, totalling 133 goals in 329 games, and helped City to promotion from the Second Division in 1972, as well as reaching the last four of the FA Cup. The Blues reached the top 10 in the First Division during Francis's spell and they again lost in the FA Cup semi-finals in 1975, while he was also called-up for the full England side in 1977 after having won several caps at Under-23 level. In the summer of 1978 he joined US club Detroit Express on loan, and hit 19 goals in just 22 NASL matches before returning to Birmingham.

In February 1979 he became the most expensive footballer in the British game – Brian Clough's Nottingham Forest paying £1 million for his services in February 1979. The actual fee was set at £999,999, so he was not tagged as the first £1 million player, but various taxes took his fee beyond the magic mark. Within a few weeks Francis was the toast of Nottingham, as his first game in the European Cup happened to be in the Final and he famously scored the winning goal. At the end of the season Francis, to the dismay of Clough, returned to Detroit, scoring an average of a goal every game in 14 appearances, before returning home after the new season had already commenced. He was absent through injury for the 1980 European Cup Final and experienced an injury-hit 1980–81 season before moving to Manchester City for £1.2 million in September 1981. After netting twice on his debut, he was out injured for several matches and netted 12 times in his debut season, before moving to Italian football, signing for Genoa-based club Sampdoria in July 1982. He moved to Italy after appearing for England in the 1982

World Cup Finals in Spain, and would win a total of 52 full caps for his country.

During four years in Serie A, Francis helped his new side to the Italian Cup in 1985, before moving to fellow Italian side Atalanta in July 1986. He duly joined Glasgow Rangers in September 1987, remaining just six months before moving to Queen's Park Rangers as a non-contract player in February 1988. He was appointed player-manager at Loftus Road in December 1988 after Jim Smith left to take over at Newcastle United. His short spell at Rangers proved a turbulent time for Francis as, despite scoring on a regular basis, he encountered several disciplinary problems with his playing staff – famously fining a player for being at the birth of his child – and was dismissed in 1990. Sheffield Wednesday boss Ron Atkinson then threw him a lifeline, signing Francis as a non-contract player, and his cameo appearances, mainly from the bench, helped the Owls to clinch promotion to the top flight and win the League Cup – Francis being an unused substitute at Wembley.

After leaving Wednesday he worked as a TV pundit, before in May 1996 he made an emotional return to old club Birmingham City after being appointed manager at St Andrews. He led them to three First Division play-offs, but failed on each occasion, and in the 2001 League Cup Final was unlucky as Liverpool scored a last-minute equaliser to force the tie into extra-time, and then broke Birmingham's hearts by winning the trophy in a penalty shoot-out.

He left by mutual consent in October 2001, and in the following month took charge at Crystal Palace, but this proved to be his final managerial position to date, as he left on Good Friday 2003. Since then he has been a regular face on TV, working as a match pundit for the likes of Sky Sports and Al Jazeera Sports.

David John Pleat: June 1995–November 1997

Nottingham-born David Pleat, born 15 January 1945, was brought up on the Clifton estate, which at the time was the largest council estate in Europe. He was schooled at the Mundella Grammar School and at the age of 15, having just played and scored for the England Schoolboys at Wembley, he was signed as an apprentice by his boyhood heroes, Nottingham Forest, who had former Owls boss Billy Walker at the helm. While in Forest colours he was capped at England youth level and in 1962 turned professional with Forest. He would only appear in six senior games for the Nottingham club, before the winger was sold to Luton Town in 1964 for a fee of £8,000.

He was virtually constant in the side in his first season at Kenilworth Road, but Town were relegated to the old Fourth Division and Pleat suffered a broken leg just three days before the start of the following season. He subsequently returned from injury too early and made only three appearances, triggering a back problem that would dog the attacker for the rest of his playing career. He was eventually handed a free transfer to Shrewsbury Town in May 1967, and worked at a bookmakers in the summer of 1968, prior to joining Exeter City. He was in the side that sensationally knocked Wednesday out of the League Cup four days after the Owls had beaten European Champions Manchester United 5–4 at Hillsborough, but continued to suffer several niggling injuries and, after a spell with Peterborough United, he dropped out of senior football in 1971 to become player-manager at Nuneaton Town.

His stay at Nuneaton was only brief and, after working as a freelance journalist, he returned to old club, Luton Town, as coach. He remained at The Hatters until December 1977, when he was promoted to chief coach, and within two months he had taken over from Harry Haslam as first-team manager. He enjoyed great success with Luton Town, his attack-minded side running away with the Second Division title in 1982, and famously ran onto the Manchester City pitch a year later when his side won 1–0 at Maine Road to retain their newly won status. Two years later his side lost to Everton in the FA Cup semi-finals, and after taking Town to ninth place in 1986 on limited resources, he was offered and accepted the manager's position at Tottenham Hotspur. He totally changed Spurs' playing style – moving to a five-man midfield with Clive Allen playing up front on his own – and Spurs finished third in the First Division, with Allen scoring 33 times. The club also lost in the semi-finals of the League Cup – to rivals Arsenal – and a memorable season ended in ultimate disappointment when Coventry City defeated Spurs in the FA Cup Final.

It was off-field problems that ended his tenure at White Hart Lane in October 1987, with Pleat resigning after lurid newspaper allegations about his private life. He came back into the game at Leicester City in December 1987, but failed to mount a promotion challenge from the Second Division and was dismissed in January 1991, with City on the brink of relegation to the Third Division for the first time in their history. A second spell at Luton Town followed, but his new side were immediately relegated from the top flight and only just avoided the drop in the two seasons that followed. It was against this background that Pleat was, rather surprisingly, offered the job at Hillsborough, and a legal battle ensued, with Luton Town chairman, David Kohler, immediately obtaining a court injunction

to stop Pleat from joining Wednesday. It needed the intervention of a FA arbitration panel to decide a compensation package and Pleat then finally took charge at Hillsborough.

His first season at Wednesday almost ended in relegation from the Premiership, but the Owls started the following campaign with enthusiasm, and after victories in the first four games they sat atop the division. They did eventually fall away to finish in a creditable seventh place, with £3 million record signing Benito Carbone in the side. In August 1997 he smashed the Owls' transfer record to pay Glasgow Rangers £4.5 million for the outstanding talents of Paulo Di Canio, but the club started badly and fortunes did not improve. By now his general people-management skills were being called into question, and with problems starting to mount off the field, Wednesday slumped to the bottom of the Premiership. A 6–1 defeat at Manchester United in November 1997, proved his final game in charge and

Pleat returned to Spurs as Director of Football. He remained at While Hart Lane until July 2004 – acting as caretaker manager in September 2003 – before being appointed as advisor to Portsmouth manager Alain Perrin in April 2005. A few months later he became a Football Consultant to his former club, Nottingham Forest, and was then employed in the same role at Spanish club UD Marbella, while also working as a co-commentator on Radio 5 Live. He is still a regular voice on radio, as well as writing a regular column in *The Guardian* newspaper.

Daniel (Danny) Joseph Wilson: July 1998–March 2000

Born on New Year's Day 1960 in Wigan, Danny Wilson was on the books of Sunderland as an associate schoolboy, but it would be with his hometown club that Danny broke into senior football. At the time, Wigan were still a Northern Premier League side and the tigerish midfielder appeared for the Latics in their final season as a non-League side, before signing for Bury in September 1977. The Greater Manchester club donated the princely sum of £1,000 into the Wigan coffers for the services of the teenage Wilson and he rewarded their faith by remaining a virtual constant in the side for three seasons, only missing a game due to suspension after being red-carded in a 5–1 defeat at Wednesday in February 1980.

In the following summer he was transferred to Chesterfield for a £150,000 fee and helped them to win the Anglo-Scottish Cup, beating Notts County over two legs, in his maiden season at Saltergate. He remained at Chesterfield until January 1983 when, due to financial problems, his club was forced to accept a cash-plus-player offer from Nottingham Forest for his signature. Under Brian Clough at Forest he scored on his debut and remained in the side for the next nine games, but after that run ended he never made another appearance! He subsequently spent time on loan at Scunthorpe United in October 1983 and appeared in six games, before a further loan spell at Brighton ended with a permanent transfer. He enjoyed a great spell at Brighton and was soon made captain, before winning the first of his 24 full caps for Northern Ireland. He duly moved into the top flight with Luton Town in 1987, and a few months later he was part of the entertaining Town side that shocked Arsenal 3–2 – Wilson equalising the scores at 2–2 – at Wembley to win the 1988 League Cup. In the same season they reached the semi-finals of the FA Cup and were back at Wembley in the spring of 1989, this time losing 3–1 to Forest in the League Cup Final.

The calendar year of 1990 proved a bittersweet time for Wilson, as on the final day of the 1989–90 season he helped the Hatters escape the relegation trapdoor, sending Wednesday down in the process, before joining Ron Atkinson's Owls side in August 1990. He quickly became a favourite with Wednesday fans, and his 100 per cent commitment to the cause (he famously played in a game at Manchester City despite suffering from two broken ribs) was a vital factor in the glorious season of promotion and League Cup glory that followed. He would also help the Owls into Europe, scoring at Hillsborough in a UEFA Cup tie against Kaiserslautern, and to both domestic Cup finals in 1993, prior to moving to Barnsley as player-coach in June 1993, after 14 goals in 137 appearances for Wednesday.

He was effectively assistant to Viv Anderson at Oakwell, but within a year he was elevated to manager after Anderson

left to join old teammate Bryan Robson at Middlesbrough. After just missing out on the First Division play-offs in 1996, Danny retired from playing, and within the year he had taken Barnsley, on very limited resources, into the Premiership for the first time in their history. He had quickly earned a reputation as one of the best young managers in the game and this opinion was only slightly damaged when he failed to keep the Tykes in the higher grade. He was subsequently headhunted by Owls chairman, Dave Richards, and Wilson was asked to step into the shoes vacated by Ron Atkinson, officially being appointed on 6 July 1998. He enjoyed a reasonable debut season at Wednesday, leading the club to 12th position in the Premiership, and suffered the blow of losing star man Paulo Di Canio – the fiery Italian failed to report back to Hillsborough after his ban for pushing over a referee had been discharged. Unfortunately, it was then that Wilson's career at Wednesday took a decidedly disastrous turn, as he signed several players that were not only injury prone, but would drain the club of wages for many years to come (a financial problem that was only solved 11 years later when the club were taken over by Milan Mandaric). The likes of Phil O'Donnell, Simon Donnelly and Phil Scott were hardly seen on the field of play in that 1999–00 season and, with Wednesday sliding towards the First Division, Wilson was sacked in March 2000, a month after Dave Richards had himself resigned.

In the summer of 2000 he signed a four-year contact with Bristol City, but after twice guiding his side to the play-offs he was released in the summer of 2004, joining MK Dons in December of the same year. After a close shave with relegation he was sacked when they were eventually relegated a year later, and then spent just over two years as manager at Hartlepool United (June 2006–December 2008). He moved to take over at Swindon Town and led them to the 2010 League One play-off Final, losing 1–0 to Millwall in the showpiece occasion at Wembley. With Swindon at the wrong end of the League One table, after having reached the Play-off Final in 2010, he resigned in March 2011.

Paul Steven Jewell: June 2000–Feb 2001

Born in Liverpool on 28 September 1964, Paul Jewell attended De La Salle School before commencing an apprenticeship with First Division Liverpool. Due to fierce competition at Anfield, the striker failed to make a first-team appearance for the Reds and was eventually forced to move elsewhere to secure first-team football, transferring to Wigan Athletic for a £15,000 fee in December 1984. He would total 137 League games for the Lancashire side, scoring 35 goals, before Bradford City manager Terry Dolan took Jewell to Valley Parade in June 1988. He became a real crowd favourite for the Bantams and would play the remainder of his career for City, except for a loan spell at Grimsby Town in 1995, amassing over 250 games and scoring 50 plus goals. He helped them to promotion from the Second Division in 1996, appearing in his final game as a player during the season.

Jewell had been co-opted onto the coaching staff before officially hanging up his boots, and was then promoted to assistant to Chris Kamara. When the City boss was dismissed in January 1998, the club turned to Jewell on a temporary basis, and he took his charges away from danger and into a final finishing position of 13th in the old Second Division. It was expected by many supporters that City would appoint a big name, but they duly handed a permanent deal to Jewell and also handed the rookie boss a war chest in an attempt to gain promotion to the Premiership for the first time. The new boss twice smashed the club's transfer record – spending £1 million on Lee Mills and £1.3 million on Isaiah Rankin – and despite a poor start they mounted a serious challenge for promotion. After adding Dean Windass and Stuart McCall to the side, they duly clinched the runners-up spot, behind Sunderland, for a return to the top flight for the first time in 77 years.

Against all the odds, Jewell managed to keep City in the higher grade, with a dramatic last-day win over Liverpool securing that treasured Premiership status. A disagreement with chairman Geoffrey Richmond, however, dramatically ended his tenure at Valley Parade, Jewell resigning and subsequently being appointed manager at Hillsborough on 21 June 2000 – City and Wednesday eventually agreeing a compensation package after Jewell had been placed on gardening leave by Bradford. Wednesday fans warmly welcomed his arrival at Hillsborough, but

it was unlikely that Jewell realised the paucity of the side he was inheriting and the financial problems that the club would suffer following relegation from the top flight a few weeks earlier. A poor start was followed by a shocking run of eight consecutive defeats in the League – an unwanted club record – and, despite memorable League Cup wins over Sheffield United and West Ham United, Jewell found the job a constant struggle. With Wednesday bottom of the First Division, he was mercilessly sacked on 12 February 2001 following a shocking 4–1 defeat at Wimbledon. His managerial qualities, before and after Wednesday, suggested that Jewell was not totally to blame for his disastrous spell in charge and after moving to ambitious Wigan Athletic he emphasised that point.

He joined Second Division Wigan in June 2001 and, backed by multimillionaire Dave Whelan, he took his new side to the Championship in 2003, and just missed out on the First Division play-off lottery a year later. On the final day of the 2004–05 season Wigan duly won promotion to the Premiership for the first time, and they have retained that status ever since, losing to Manchester United in the 2006 League Cup Final. On the final day of the 2006–07 season he steered his side to a win at Bramall Lane, which saved their status and sent the Blades down, but 24 hours later Jewell tendered his resignation. He was appointed manager at struggling Derby County in November 2007, but could not effect their form, the Derbyshire club falling out of the Premiership with a record low of 11 points – his only win during the season being against Wednesday in an FA Cup penalty shoot-out at Hillsborough. After failing to mount a promotion push from the Championship, he resigned on New Year's Eve 2008 and spent time working as a TV pundit, before being appointed manager of Ipswich Town on 10 January 2011.

Terence (Terry) Charles Yorath: October 2001–October 2002

Born in Cardiff on 27 March 1950, Terry Yorath played soccer for Cardiff boys, but when he was picked to play for Wales at both soccer and rugby union he actually wanted to follow rugby, only being persuaded to change his mind by his father and elder brother. When he informed his school that he had chosen to follow the football code, he was immediately banned from playing rugby and cricket at school – a somewhat draconian decision that made a teenage Yorath determined to become a professional football player. He subsequently started to train twice a week with his local side, Cardiff City, but he eventually signed apprentice forms with Leeds United at Easter 1965. Aged 17, he signed professional forms at the West Yorkshire club, but despite being capped at Under-23 level for Wales, he was only a fringe player for the first few years of his professional career. He had only appeared in a handful of senior games for Leeds when he won the first of 59 full caps for Wales – in November 1969 – although he did appear in the 1973 FA Cup Final when Second Division Sunderland recorded a shock 1–0 win over hot favourites United. He became more of a regular as United won the Championship in 1974, and by the mid-1970s he was captain for both Leeds and his country, playing for the former in the 1975 European Cup Final defeat to Bayern Munich.

He eventually amassed just under 200 appearances for Leeds, before a transfer fee of £125,000 took Yorath to his second club, Coventry City, in August 1976. The fiery midfielder later played alongside Ricky Villa and Ossie Ardiles during an 18-month stay at Tottenham Hotspur, before his former teammate Johnny Giles – manager at Vancouver Whitecaps – tempted Yorath to the North American Soccer League in February 1981. He remained in western Canada for two seasons and gained his first experience of coaching with the club's indoor five a-side team. He returned to England in December 1982 after being appointed player-coach at Bradford City, and in his second full season he helped City to the Championship of the Third Division. Sadly, the final match of the season, which was seen as a chance to celebrate the capture of the title, turned into one of the darkest days in British football when a fire gutted the main stand, taking 56 lives and injuring countless others.

In July 1986 he returned to his homeland after being appointed manager of Swansea City, and in 1988 they gained promotion through the play-off system. At the same time he was handed the reins of the Welsh national side on a part-time basis, but he caused uproar in his day job when he walked out on Swansea to become manager back at Bradford City in February 1989. An injunction issued by Swansea after his resignation was eventually quashed when Bradford City paid the Football League-imposed fine, but, unfortunately for Yorath, he was only in the role for a short time – a consortium taking over the club and dismissing Yorath in 1990. Previous wounds had healed sufficiently for Yorath to return to Swansea as manager, and he steered the South Wales club to safety after relegation looked inevitable. At the time he was still juggling his club role with his international position and this eventually led to his dismissal in December 1991; his chairman was concerned that he could not fulfil both roles, although nine consecutive defeats was also a factor!

He was immediately appointed full-time manager of the national side, and he enjoyed arguably the best years of his backroom career. Working alongside Peter Shreeves, he took Wales to within a whisker of both Euro '92 and the 1994 World Cup Finals, but his national association was impatient and he was sacked in 1993. His spell as full-time boss of Wales was also tinged with tragedy, as in 1992 his 15-year-old son, Daniel, was kicking a ball around at home with his father when he collapsed and died in Yorath's arms due to a rare heart condition. It was a tragedy from which Yorath never fully recovered.

He was subsequently general and football manager at Cardiff City, and in 1995 was handed the role of national team manager of Lebanon. Incredibly, within two years they overtook Wales in the FIFA ranking list and he returned to British soccer in October 1997, becoming assistant manager to Peter Jackson at Huddersfield Town. He was later coach back at Bradford

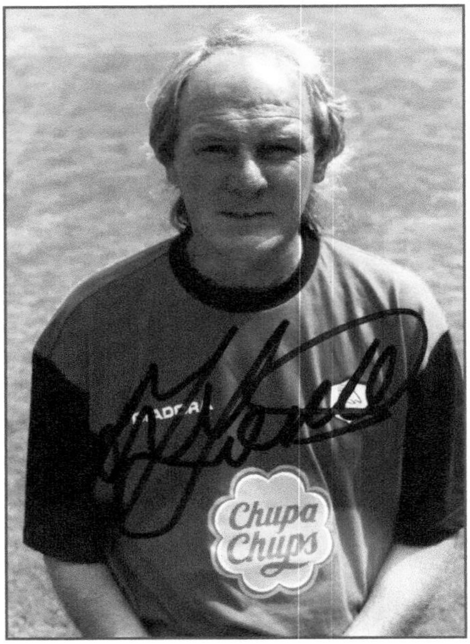

City – working alongside Paul Jewell – before resigning in the summer of 2000 to join his former boss at Wednesday. After Jewell's departure he remained assistant-manager to Peter Shreeves, but was then appointed caretaker manager in October 2001. After a month in the role he was officially handed the job until the end of the 2001–02 season and would lead Wednesday to First Division safety in a final position of 17th. Sadly, the following season started badly for Wednesday and Yorath, and the home game with Millwall on 30 October 2002 proved his final game in charge. With the Owls losing and with five minutes remaining, a female fan tapped Yorath on the shoulder and said, 'Terry, you're a lovely man, but please do the best thing for Wednesday and resign.' The following day he tendered his resignation.

After a time away from football he returned in June 2003 to Huddersfield Town as assistant to Peter Jackson again, and ended the season by beating Mansfield Town on penalties to win promotion by the play-off system. The next season saw Huddersfield miss out on the Play-offs by a single point, and they lost to Barnsley at the semi-final stage a year later. In December 2006 Yorath left Town by mutual consent and in June 2008 was appointed Director of Football at Margate, where his older bother had once played. He eventually took over as manager, but resigned in September 2009 due to the financial problems the club was suffering, and officially retired from the game.

Peter Shreeves: February–June 2000 (caretaker) and February–October 2001

Welshman Peter Shreeves first arrived at Wednesday in June 1996 after being appointed by David Pleat as first-team coach. He moved from a similar role at Chelsea, and played his part as the Owls just missed out on a place in Europe, finishing seventh in the Premiership in 1997. Between the reigns of Pleat and Ron Atkinson, in November 1997 he was caretaker manager for a solitary game – a stunning 5–0 Premiership home win over Bolton Wanderers – but left by mutual consent in September 1998, rejoining Atkinson at Nottingham Forest. He returned in February 2000 as a temporary replacement for sacked manager Danny Wilson, and following the arrival of Paul Jewell he was appointed as assistant manager to the Liverpudlian. When Jewell was shown the door, it was left to Shreeves to save Wednesday from relegation to the Second Division, a task that he achieved thanks to the inspirational form of new signings Trond Soltvedt and Carlton Palmer. In May 2001 he was rewarded with a new two-year contract, but with resources increasingly limited it proved an uphill struggle for the experienced Shreeves and, after a 2–1 home defeat to Preston left the club in the relegation places, he resigned on 17 October 2001.

His journey to Hillsborough had started in the South Wales village of Neath, where he was born on 30 November 1940. He was brought up in the London borough of Islington – he was born in Wales as his mother had been evacuated there during the early stages of World War Two – and starting playing football with amateur side Finchley. He subsequently appeared in 113 games for Reading as an inside-forward, but was forced to retire from the professional game after suffering a broken leg. He then appeared for non-League Chelmsford City and also played for Wimbledon, while also working as a taxi driver, before commencing his coaching career in 1974 at Charlton Athletic. He was appointed youth team manager at London rivals Tottenham Hotspur three years later, and was promoted to reserve team manager, and then to assistant manager to Keith Burkinshaw. He helped Spurs to UEFA Cup glory in 1984 and a few weeks later he was appointed manager. He led

Spurs to third place in his first season, but was sacked in favour of David Pleat in March 1986, with Spurs sat in 10th position in the top flight. During the years that followed, Shreeves was coach at Queen's Park Rangers, briefly manager back at Spurs, assistant manager at Watford, assistant to the Welsh national side, and then assistant to Glenn Hoddle at Chelsea.

After leaving Wednesday for the second time, he took charge at Conference side Barnet in February 2002, but after failing to lead the North London side to the play-offs, he resigned after just a year in charge. He then started to work outside of the club game for the first time in his career after being appointed to a Premiership delegate team that reported on all aspects of the competition. He returned to club football in June 2009 after being appointed Director of Football at Conference side Grays Athletic, and duly returned to Barnet as coach in January 2010. He left when manager and ex-Owl Ian Hendon was sacked at the end of the 2009–10 season.

Christopher (Chris) Robert Turner: November 2002–September 2004

Former player Chris Turner became the club's fifth manager in less than three years when Owls chairman Dave Allen appointed him on 7 November 2002. He inherited an Owls side that was already struggling at the wrong end of the First Division table, and he watched his new charges lose meekly, 3–0 at Norwich City, in his first game in charge. He duly managed to take the Owls to eight victories to the end of the season, but that reasonable record was not enough to save Wednesday from the drop, the club being relegated at Brighton on Easter Monday 2003 with two games still to play. A few

days later his side recorded a somewhat bizarre 7–2 win at Burnley, which stands as the club's all-time record away success in League football.

Hopes were high among Owls fans that Turner could lead the club straight back into the second tier, and four wins in the opening six League matches duly saw Wednesday in second spot in the early tables. Unfortunately, this proved a false dawn, and from early October until the dawn of the new year Wednesday failed to win a League fixture and dropped alarmingly down the table. It was generally accepted that many of the players that Turner had inherited were simply not good enough and, after finishing the season in 16th position (the second-worst League placing in Wednesday's history), Turner mercilessly culled the playing staff, releasing 13 players and virtually signing a completely new team. In hindsight, many of his summer signings, the likes of Steve McLean, JP McGovern, Lee Bullen and

Glenn Whelan, proved to be a great success, but unfortunately for Turner they did not gel immediately and, with patience in short supply at Hillsborough, he was sacked on 18 September 2004, after a 1–0 home defeat to Bournemouth had left Wednesday in the lower half of the League One table.

His departure ended an association with Wednesday that had started back in March 1975, when a teenage Turner signed apprentice forms at Hillsborough. The Sheffield-born goalkeeper quickly progressed through the ranks and duly made a senior debut at the age of just 17 in an August 1976 League Cup fixture at Grimsby Town. He would appear in an astonishing 52 League and Cup games in that first season and his form was rewarded with several caps at England youth level. When new manager Jack Charlton brought Bob Bolder to the club, the pair became fierce rivals, with local lad Turner having the backing of a vocal majority among Owls fans. It was the taller and heavier Bolder, however, that eventually won the race to become the undisputed winner, and Turner was eventually sold to Sunderland, after a loan spell at Lincoln City, for £75,000 in July 1979.

Turner's qualities quickly came to the fore for the Wearside club and he was a first-team regular for several seasons, amassing 223 games in six years at Sunderland. A move to Manchester United followed in August 1985, where he competed with Gary Bailey and Jim Leighton for the position of 'keeper. After 79 games for the Manchester giants, his career turned full circle as Howard Wilkinson re-signed Turner for Wednesday. He arrived as cover for Kevin Pressman and the pair would constantly swap the goalkeeper shirt over the next three years, with Turner taking over from his rival halfway through the memorable 1990–91 season and appearing for the Owls in the League Cup Final triumph over Manchester United. The arrival of £1 million goalkeeper Chris Woods in the summer of 1991 effectively brought the curtain down on Turner's playing career at Wednesday after 205 games, and a few weeks later, in October, he was a makeweight in the deal that brought starlet Chris Bart-Williams from Leyton Orient. While still on the playing staff at the London club, he was handed the role of assistant manager and eventually became co-manager, sharing the duties with John Sitton between 1994 and 1995. After leaving Leyton Orient he was briefly a player with Leicester City, before being appointed youth team manager at Wolverhampton Wanderers.

His first sole managerial post came in 1999, when he was appointed manager at Hartlepool United. At the time his new club were bottom of the entire Football League, but he duly saved them from a drop into the conference and they became serious contenders for promotion to League One, eventually gaining promotion in 2003. Of course, Turner had left by then, after being handed the reins at Wednesday, and it was Mike Newell who picked up the baton from Turner to lead United into the higher grade. After leaving Hillsborough Turner took over at Stockport County, but his new side were bottom of League One, and on this occasion he could not stop their slide into the basement division. The following season proved an unmitigated disaster for Turner as County plunged down the division, and he was sacked the day after a 6–0 Boxing Day defeat to local rivals Macclesfield Town left Stockport five points adrift at the foot of the table.

He returned to Hartlepool United in February 2006, in a newly created position of Director of Sport, but returned to the manager's chair on a caretaker basis in December 2008, following the departure of Danny Wilson. He suddenly resigned from

Hartlepool in August 2010 and a few weeks later became the public face behind an ultimately unsuccessful bid to buy Sheffield Wednesday.

Paul Whitehead Sturrock: September 2004–October 2006

Born in the small Aberdeenshire village of Allon on October 10 1956, Paul Sturrock's career in football started purely by accident, as one day the 14-year-old travelled to watch minnows Grandtully Vale and ended the afternoon on the field of play! The team was short of two players, and manager Jimmy Crerar asked Sturrock if he could play and if his bespectacled friend could warm the substitute bench. He duly netted twice in the game and was immediately signed, scoring a further 20 times in that season. In 1972 he started to appear regularly for Perthshire Amateur League club Vale of Atholl, and he started to make his name after moving to Perth-based club Bankfoot Juniors. He duly attended trials at Morton and St Johnstone, although it was surprising that he did not give up the game after being told at the latter that he would never be anything other than a farmer, in reference to his background!

Thankfully, his manager at Bankfoot was also a scout for Dundee United and the obviously talented youngster was signed as an apprentice in July 1974, on wages of £3 per week. It would be a match made in heaven for player and club as Sturrock would play for no other team in his professional career, appearing in 571 competitive games and scoring 170 times, before injury forced his retirement in May 1989. During that period, Sturrock – affectionately nicknamed 'Luggy' by United fans – matured into one of the greatest Scottish attackers of his generation, winning 20 full caps for Scotland and appearing in the 1986 World Cup Finals in Mexico. He helped his club to the Scottish League title in 1983 and was part of an outstanding Dundee United team that reached the 1984 European Cup semi-finals and lost in the 1987 UEFA Cup Final to an IFK Gothenburg side containing a certain Roland Nilsson in their ranks. The decade was, without doubt, the greatest in the club's history as they also twice lifted the League Cup, in 1980 and 1981, were finalists twice more and also lost on four separate occasions in the Final of the Scottish Cup.

After his playing days ended, the Tannadice legend was co-opted onto the club's coaching staff in June 1989, and after gaining some off-field experience he was handed the manager's job at St Johnstone in November 1993. He immediately revamped their training routine and invested in home-grown talent, an ethos that saw the Saints promoted to the Scottish Premier League in 1997, finishing a mammoth 20 points clear of second-placed Airdrie. His success continued as he secured fifth place in the top division for St Johnstone, before the emotional pull of Dundee United proved too strong, with Sturrock taking the manager's job in September 1998. He continued his previous success by guiding United to third place in the League by Christmas 1999, only for the United board to sell his top scorer, Billy Dodds, and then watch the side slide down the League to finish third from bottom. Just two games into the new season he tendered his resignation and began a career in the English game that continues to this day.

He was appointed boss at Plymouth Argyle in October 2000, taking over from caretaker manager Kevin Summerfield, and took the club to unparalleled success, amassing a record points haul of 102 in the 2001–02 season as Argyle lifted the Third

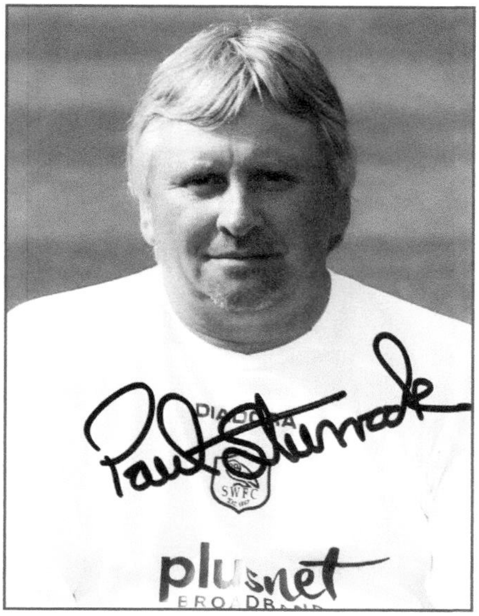

Division title – Sturrock being named Manager of the Season by the Football League. After a season of consolidation Argyle challenged for promotion in 2003–04 and a double over Wednesday helped them to top the division. The Devon club would eventually earn promotion to the Championship, but Sturrock was not there to see the celebrations, leaving for Southampton after watching Argyle beat the Owls in his final match in charge. His move to St Mary's gave Sturrock his first opportunity in the top echelons of the English game, but after replacing fellow Scot Gordon Strachan in the hot seat, he would experience a decidedly unhappy time on the south coast. He was in charge for only 13 games at Southampton and left by mutual consent in August 2004.

It was at this point that Sturrock arrived at Hillsborough, being appointed Sheffield Wednesday manager on 23 September 2004. He brought his old backroom team at Plymouth to Sheffield, and there was an immediate improvement in results as the Owls started to show the form that previous boss, Chris Turner, had expected. The inspirational loan signings of Kenwyne Jones and Joey O'Brien provided a huge boost to the team and, with young players Glenn Whelan and Chris Brunt starting to gain a foothold in League soccer, Wednesday moved up the League One table, onto the coat-tails of the top two clubs. The likeable Scot motivated and inspired his previously under-performing squad, and they challenged for the promotion places before eventually falling away to finish in the play-offs for the first time in Wednesday's history. A two-legged win over Brentford set up a truly memorable day in Cardiff, where over 40,000 Owls fans cheered their side to ultimate victory over Hartlepool United and promotion to the Championship.

Despite Sturrock's side suffering a multitude of injury problems, Wednesday retained that newly won Championship status – a win at Brighton sending their hosts and two other sides down – and looked to rebuild for a more successful 2006–07 season. He signed a new four-year contract in September 2006, but bizarrely he lasted only a few weeks into that new agreement, being shown the door on 19 October 2006 after a 4–0 loss at Colchester United had left the Owls bottom of the Championship. His departure was widely condemned by Wednesday supporters, who jammed the phone lines of a local radio station in protest, but Sturrock was only out of work for a short time, joining Swindon Town as manager in November 2006. He led the Wiltshire club to promotion from League Two in 2007, but just a year after joining he resigned to rejoin former club Plymouth Argyle – in the summer of 2008 he had revealed that he suffers from a mild form of Parkinson's disease.

After failing to lift Argyle from the lower reaches of the Championship table, he was relieved of his managerial duties in

December 2009, moving into a newly created role of Business Development Manager. He subsequently resigned in April 2010, but eventually came back into the game as Southend United manager three months later. With manager Steve Tilson on gardening leave, Sturrock appointed former Owls man Graham Coughlan as player-coach, and soon recruited the services of his son, Blair, who had played for his father at both Plymouth and Swindon.

Brian Laws: November 2006–December 2009

Born in Wallsend, Tyne and Wear on 14 October 1961, Brian Laws began his playing career by appearing at schoolboy level for both Wallsend and Northumberland, while being a regular for Wallsend Boys Club. As a youngster he attended trails at Newcastle United, West Bromwich Albion, Leicester City and Coventry City, but it was with Burnley that he signed apprentice forms in 1978. He was elevated to the professional ranks a year later and broke into the first team, at right-back, during the 1980–81 season, making his debut on 30 August 1980 in Burnley's Third Division fixture at Charlton Athletic. He missed only one game until the end of the season and won a Championship medal in 1982, before new manager John Bond sold Laws to Huddersfield Town for £50,000 in August 1983.

He was on the move again in March 1985 when Middlesbrough paid £30,000 for his services. He duly scored the vital goal that saved the Teeside club from relegation a few weeks later, but the club could not avoid the drop a year later, slipping into the Third Division. The summer of 1986 proved to be a time of real crisis for Middlesbrough, as they were on the verge of being liquidated and losing their membership of the Football League. They eventually reformed, although in July 1986 Laws had famously applied to the Football League to have his contract cancelled – due to his club's perilous financial state – so that he could leave on a free transfer. When the club was saved, Laws remained on the playing staff and was part of the Boro side that earned promotion to the Second Division in 1987 and then returned to the top flight a year later, with Laws not featuring in the two-legged play-off Final when Boro overcame Chelsea.

Despite the club being saved, finances were still not particularly healthy at Middlesbrough, and a row with manager Bruce Rioch over the length of a new contract ended in a transfer to Brian Clough's Nottingham Forest for £120,000 in 1988. During his time at Forest, Laws would learn greatly from the enigma that was Clough, who on arrival famously said to the new recruit, 'I've never seen you play, son. I'm going on the recommendation of Ronnie Fenton. So if you're crap, Ronnie signed you. If you're good, I signed you.'

He would enjoy the best years of his playing career at the City Ground, appearing in 140 League games for Forest, winning the League Cup and Full Members Cup in his debut season, in addition to finishing third in the top flight and reaching the last four of the FA Cup – Laws playing for the Reds at Hillsborough in that fateful abandoned semi-final against Liverpool. He helped his side to retain the League Cup in 1990 and featured twice more in major Cup finals – Forest losing in the 1991 FA Cup Final and the 1992 League Cup Final. He subsequently appeared in Forest's first ever game in the newly formed Premiership, but the season proved a disaster for the Nottingham side as they suffered relegation to the Football League and Brian Clough tendered his resignation. His first-team opportunities were limited as Forest bounced back into the top flight and, after appearing in just six games, he moved to take over as player-manager of Grimsby Town.

His spell in charge at Town was initially successful, but deteriorated after Laws allegedly broke the jaw of Italian striker Ivano Bonetti after throwing a plate of chicken wings at him after a defeat at Luton Town in February 1996! A poor start to the 1996–97 season resulted in Laws being fired by the Mariners, after a 3–0 home defeat to bottom side Oldham Athletic left Town in the relegation zone. After leaving Grimsby he briefly resurrected his playing career, appearing 11 times for Darlington and twice for Scunthorpe United, before being appointed manager of Scunthorpe United in February 1997. He continued to appear for United during the early days of his managerial career, primarily as a substitute, and enjoyed a terrific 1998–99 season as his side won promotion to the old Second Division (League One) via a 1–0 Wembley Pay-off Final victory over Leyton Orient. With limited resources, he could not stop Scunthorpe from being relegated a year later, and his time at Glanford Park seemed to have ended when he was sacked in March 2004, after a poor run of results had ended with a damaging home loss to bottom club Carlisle United. There was a power struggle behind the scenes at United, however, and when new owners took over, Laws was reinstated, 20 days after being shown the door. He duly led them to promotion for a second time in May 2005, before his almost 10-year stay at United finally did come to an end, joining the Owls on 6 November 2006.

Most new managers inherit a side low on confidence and struggling to secure a win, but when Laws took over the Owls were flying under caretaker manager Sean McAuley, and had secured 10 points from a possible 12 during his temporary tenure. The side continued that form for the remainder of the season and climbed from the lower reaches of the Championship to just miss out on a play-off spot – defeat at Birmingham City in the penultimate game of the season ending their hopes. Unfortunately, the start of the following season proved an unmitigated disaster as the Owls set an unwanted club record by losing their first six games of the new campaign. That terrible start handicapped the side for the rest of the season and a relegation battle ensued, safety only being achieved on the final day of the season thanks to a 4–1 Hillsborough win over Norwich City. A mid-table finish in 2008–09 was perhaps overshadowed by arguably the greatest achievement by Laws in over three years at Wednesday – a double over Sheffield United for the first time in 95 years. It certainly earned Laws kudos among the Wednesday fans, and

hopes were high in the summer of 2009 that Wednesday could genuinely become play-off contenders. Unfortunately, a reasonable start was not continued, and as the side started to slide down the table, pressure started to mount on Laws, despite fans backing their increasingly beleaguered boss. When that fan support started to crack thanks to a 3–0 defeat at Leicester City in December 2009, Laws knew it was time to go, and he left the club by mutual consent on the following day.

He was quickly back in the game after rather surprisingly being handed the reins at Premiership Burnley in January 2010. He stepped into the shoes vacated by Owen Coyle, but could not keep the Lancashire club in the top flight, losing 15 of the club's remaining 18 League games, and suffered relegation back into the Championship after a brief taste of life in England's top division. In the summer of 2010 the Burnley board agreed that Laws would be in charge for the following season, as the Clarets attempted to regain their Premiership place. After less than a year in the job, he was fired over the 2010 Christmas period, with Burnley sat just outside the Play-off positions.

James Alan Irvine: January 2010–February 2011

Born on 12 July 1958, in Glasgow, Alan Irvine seemed set for a career outside of football when he studied for the qualifications required to become an insurance broker. However, while pursuing that career option he also started to play on a regular basis for Glasgow-based amateur side Queens Park, Irvine being the archetypal tricky winger. A move to Everton, after 88 appearances between 1977 and 1981 for Queens Park, meant Irvine would remain in football for the remainder of his career. He played under Howard Kendall at Goodison Park and appeared 60 times before being transferred to Crystal Palace in the summer of 1984. He enjoyed the best playing spell of his career at the south-east London club, amassing 109 appearances and scoring 12 goals, before returning to Scotland to sign for Dundee United. His playing career came to a close at Blackburn Rovers where after helping his side gain promotion to the Premiership in 1992, under Kenny Dalglish, he officially retired before Rovers took their place in the newly formed top division of the English game.

After hanging up his boots for the Ewood Park club, he was handed the role of youth-team coach and duly followed Dalglish to Newcastle United, where Irvine became Academy Director, after a time as first-team coach. In 2002, 18 years after he had departed Everton, he returned to Merseyside after being appointed assistant manager to David Moyes. During Irvine's spell at Everton, the club twice finished in the top six of the Premiership, and he was quickly earning a reputation as one of the finest young coaches in the English game.

His first sole managerial role eventually occurred in November 2007 when he took the difficult decision to leave Everton and became boss at struggling Championship side, Preston North End. When he joined, the club was just one place off the relegation zone, but he guided North End to a respectable final position of 15th, before revamping the playing squad in the summer that followed. It was a different Preston side that took the field in the next campaign, and a dramatic last-day victory, over Queen's Park Rangers, saw his side snatch the final Play-off position, squeezing into sixth place. Unfortunately, Preston were beaten over two legs by Sheffield United and suffered somewhat of a 'hangover' at the start of the 2009–10 season, struggling to recapture the form of the previous campaign. A run of only one win in 10 games saw the pressure mount on Irvine, but it was a major shock to both Preston fans and football supporters in general when he was dismissed in December 2009, despite having won over 40 per cent of the 110 matches while he was at the helm.

On 8 January 2010, Irvine was handed the difficult job of lifting Wednesday from the foot of the Championship table, signing a three-and-a-half-year contract at Hillsborough. He made an instant impact, winning at Barnsley in his first game in charge and was named Manager of the Month for January after recording four wins out of his opening five games. A home win over Blackpool, in early February 2010, moved the Owls clear of the bottom three places, but unfortunately Wednesday would win only two more games until the final day of the season, setting up a 'winner takes all' home meeting with Crystal Palace. Despite a crowd of almost 38,000 packing Hillsborough on that fateful day, the Owls could not gain the required win and dropped back into League One, after an absence of five years.

The summer of 2010 saw Irvine totally restructure his side, signing several experienced players, such as Clinton Morrison, Paul Heffernan, Gary Teale and Nicky Weaver. His new look side started the season well, a 5–0 away win at Hartlepool in August securing Irvine another Manager of the Month accolade, before dropping into mid-table as off-the-field problems seemingly started to affect the side. His team reached the Northern semi-final of the Football League Trophy and sat in a Play-off position as Christmas approached, but despite bringing several players into the club in the January transfer window League form was poor. A run to the last 16 of the FA Cup did somewhat mask the problems, but a fifth consecutive away League defeat – 5–3 at Peterborough United – signalled the end of Irvine's reign as he departed 24 hours later.

Gary John Megson (February 2011 - present)

(Also see players section)

Former player and boyhood Wednesday fan, Gary Megson, became the first managerial appointment of Chairman Milan Mandaric when he was offered, and accepted, the position of Owls boss, on 4th February 2011. It was the third time that Megson had been offered such a role by Mandaric as he had previously worked under him at Leicester City while back in 2000 he landed the position of Portsmouth boss only to pull out, in the interests of his young family. Megson described his return to Hillsborough as his 'dream job' while he had previously failed to land the role after being interviewed following the departure of Paul Sturrock.

It was while still a player that Megson secured his first coaching role, being appointed player-coach at Norwich City in January 1994. He stepped up to the role of

assistant-manager, to John Deehan, six months later and was then caretaker boss for a three-month period after Deehan resigned in April 1995. After leaving Carrow Road he returned to simply playing – for Lincoln City and Shrewsbury Town – before a brief spell as assistant manager at Bradford City ended when he was recruited by Norwich City as a replacement for the departed Martin O'Neill. Unfortunately his first experience of management was not a happy one for Megson as he won only five of 27 games and was fired in June 1996. A few weeks later he took the role of Blackpool manager and in what proved his only season he led the Tangerines to seventh place, four points from a play off position, in the Second Division (League One). Another move occurred in the summer of 1997 as the departure of Dave Jones, to Southampton, created a vacancy at Stockport County, which was subsequently filled by Megson. He finished eighth and then sixteenth in his two seasons at Edgeley Park and was sacked in June 1999 with County Chairman Brendan Elwood accusing Megson of applying for other managerial posts while he was still in charge of County. He then enjoyed a reasonable start as manager of Second Division (League One) Stoke City but was unfortunate when the club was taken over by an Icelandic consortium and they quickly brought in the manager of the Iceland National side, Gudjon Thordarson, to replace Megson.

During a short period out of the game has was linked with several jobs, including Sheffield United manager, before being appointed as successor to Brian Little at

West Bromwich Albion in March 2000. A successful first season at the Hawthorns ended with qualification for the First Division (Championship) play offs although Bolton Wanderers won 5-2 on aggregate in the semi-final. His stock had certainly risen while in charge of the Baggies and his name was linked with several high profile jobs before he was named First Division Manager of the Year in 2002 after leading Albion to runners up position, behind Manchester City, and a place in the Premiership. Albion came straight back down but twelve months later they finished second again, this time behind Megson's former club Norwich City. Unfortunately Megson's relationship with the Albion Chairman. Jeremy Peace, had by this time started to deteriorate and after a public fall out he departed in October 2004 with the Baggies just outside the relegation places in the top-flight. He subsequently took over as Nottingham Forest boss in January 2005 but after failing to save them from relegation he left by mutual consent just over a year later.

Stoke City manager Tony Pulis brought him back into the game, in July 2007, when he appointed Megson to his coaching staff. A few weeks later, in September 2007, he was appointed Leicester City boss by Mandaric and ironically his first win as City boss came at Hillsborough a few days later. However his tenure at the Walkers Stadium was extremely brief as after Mandaric twice refused permission for Megson to talk to Premiership Bolton Wanderers, about their vacant managerial position, he promptly resigned and took over at the Lancashire side. When Megson took charge Bolton was bottom of the Premiership, with only five points from ten games, but he dragged them to safety, as well as reaching the last 16 of the UEFA Cup. He duly made several big money signings in the summer that followed and despite a poor start he led them to a creditable finishing position of 13th. He was again highly active in the transfer market in the summer of 2009 but when Bolton started poorly again the Reebok fans started to jeer during games, leading to a very public fall-out between Megson and his club's fans. The honorary Yorkshireman and the Bolton fans had never particularly seen eye to eye and Megson was relieved of his duties in December 2009. The two parties could not agree a compensation package so he was placed on 'gardening leave' in December 2009, effectively meaning Megson spent an additional year, on full pay, on Bolton's payroll before becoming a free agent again in 2011. He was subsequently offered the manager's job at Ipswich Town but refused the role after Town would not sanction the appointment of his backroom staff.

Within a few weeks he returned to Wednesday for a third spell and was handed the task of reviving the club's promotion challenge. Unfortunately he inherited a team on the slide and the Owls slipped perilously close to the relegation zone as Megson tried to find a winning formula. Thankfully a late flurry of victories banished the spectre of League Two football and Megson, backed by the financial means of Mandaric, vowed to bring the good times back to the long suffering Wednesday fans.

1880-87

Pre-League FA Cup

Manager: Arthur Dickinson

Did you know that?

1867–68. Wednesday's first game was an inter-club practice match played on 12 October 1867. The club won their first Cup in February 1868 when the Garrick club was defeated in the Final of the Cromwell Cup. The match was an early example of the use of the 'golden goal' as, after the tie was 0–0 at the end of 90 minutes, the game continued until Wednesday scored to secure the Cup.

1872. Up until 1872, Wednesday used to present a gallon of beer to the winning team and a half gallon to the losers.

1875–76. When James Lang moved from Scotland to Sheffield he became Wednesday's first unofficial professional. He was given employment by a Wednesday official, Walter Fearnhough, in his knife-making company, but actually had no duties apart from playing football.

1876–77. On 10 March 1877, Wednesday won the Sheffield Challenge Cup, beating Heeley 4–3 after being three goals in arrears at one point – the winner being scored in extra-time.

1877–78. On 18 February 1878 Glasgow Rangers played only their second game outside of Scotland when they defeated Wednesday 2–1 at Bramall Lane, Sheffield. Two days before, they had beaten Nottingham Forest 4–2.

Match No.	Date	Venue	Opponents	Round	Result	HT Score	Position	Scorers	Attendance
1880-81									
1		A	Queen's Park, Glasgow	1R				Walk over as Queen's Park withdrew	
2	Dec 18	A	Blackburn Rovers	2R	4-0	0-0		Gregory (3), Winterbottom	2,000
3	Jan 8	A	Turton (near Bolton)	3R	2-0	1-0		Gregory, Rhodes	2,000
4	Feb 5	A	Darwen (Lancs)	4R	2-5	0-0		Gregory (2)	4,500
									App
									Goals
1881-82									
5	Nov 5	A	Providence***	1R	2-0	0-0		Cawley, Anthony	
6	Dec 28	H	Staveley*	3R	2-2	1-1		Rhodes, Cawley	2,000
7	Jan 7	A	Staveley +	3R Re	0-0	0-0			1,000
8	9	A	Staveley**	3R 2Re	5-1	2-1		Rhodes (4), Cawley	2,000
9	21	H	Heeley*	4R	3-1	1-0		Rhodes, Cawley, Mosforth	4,000
10	Feb 7	H	Upton Park, London*	5R	6-0	2-0		Rhodes, Cawley (3), Mosforth (2)	3,000
11	Mar 6	A	Blackburn Rovers#	S/F	0-0	0-0			6,000
12	15	A	Blackburn Rovers##	S/F Re	1-5	1-1		Suter (og)	10,000
* Played at Bramall Lane ** Played at Lockwood's Ground. *** Played at Quibell's Field.									App
# Played at Huddersfield. ## Played at Manchester + After extra-time (Bye in round 2)									Goals
1882-83									
13	Nov 4	H	Spilsby (Lincolnshire)*	1R	12-2	5-2		Gregory (5), Cawley (3), Newbould (3), Anthony	800
14	Dec 2	A	Lockwood Brothers	2R	6-0	4-0		Anthony, Newbould, Gregory (2), Cawley, Mosforth	1,300
15	Jan 6	A	Nottingham Forest	3R	2-2	0-0		Gregory, Harrison	3,000
16	13	H	Nottingham Forest*	3R Re	3-2	3-0		Harrison (2), Mosforth	2,000
17	Feb 12	H	Notts County*	4R	1-4	1-3		Bentley	2,000
* Played at Bramall Lane									App
									Goals
1883-84									
18	Dec 1	A	Staveley	2R	1-3	0-3		Winterbottom	2,000
									App
									Goals
1884-85									
19	Nov 8	A	Long Eaton Rangers	1R	1-0	1-0		Cawley	Large
20	Jan 3	H	Nottingham Forest*	3R	1-2	0-2		Sayer	3,000
* Played at Bramall Lane, (Bye in round 2)									App
									Goals
1885-86									
21	Oct 31	A	Long Eaton Rangers	1R	0-2	0-1			700
									App
									Goals

Anthony G "Nudger"	Bentley Willis	Betts Billy	Bingley Jack	Brayshaw Teddy	Bowns George	Buttery Edward	Buttery Thomas	Cawley Tom	Dungworth Jack	Gregory Bob	Fletcher Henry	Harrison W	Hesson J	Hiller Carl	Hiller Walpole	Hudson Jack	Hunter Jack	Jeeves Jack	Lang James	Ledger H	Malpass Arthur	Morley Lance	Mosforth William	Moss William	Newbould Herbert	Nicholson George	Rhodes E	Sayer Jim	Shaw Bernard	Smith Jim	Stacey William	Stevens J	Stratford Chas	Ulyett George	Watson J	West Fred	Wilkinson Henry	Wilson S	Winterbottom Harry	Wortley George
						3	2			9						5	4		8		6		10		11						1								7	
			8			3				9	6					5	4		10	1	2		11				7													
						6	2			9							5		8		3		10		11						1		4						7	
			1			3	2			3	1					2	3		3	1	3		3		2		1				2		1						2	
										6																	1												1	

11			10			3		9		7						6				1	5		8								2		4							
7						5		11		6										1	2		8				9						4			10	3			
7						3		9		6						4				1	2		10				11									8	5			
						3		10		6						4				1	2		8				11					7				9	5			
						3		9		7						5				1	2		8				11					4				10	6			
						6		8		7						5				1	2		10				9					4				11	3			
						7		9		3						6			5	1	8		2									4				11	10			
						7		9		3						6			5	1	8		2									4				11	10			
3			1			8		8		8						7			2	8	8		8				5				1	5	2			7	7			
1								7															3				7													

7								8		9						4				1	5		11		10						3		6				2			
7								9		8						5				1	4		11		10						3		6				2			
	5	3						8		9		7				4				1			11		10								6				2			
	5	3						8		9		7				4				1			11		10								6				2			
	5	3			7			8		9						4							11		10								6	1			2			
2	3	3			1			5		5		2				5				4	2		5		5						3		5	1			5			
2	1							4		8		3											2		4															

								8		5				7		6		2			3	1	11		10								4						9	
								1		1				1		1		1			1	1	1		1								1						1	
																																							1	

	6			4				9					10								3		11					7		1			5					2	8	
	6			4				8							10								7					9		1			5					2	11	3
	2			2				2					1		1						1		2					2		2			2					2	2	1
								1																				1												

				6	5			9	4							2							11	3		10			7	1					8					
				1	1			1	1							1							1	1		1			1	1					1					

1887-89

Pre-League FA Cup

Manager: Arthur Dickinson

Did you know that?

1886–87. Wednesday submitted their FA Cup entry too late and therefore were not able to take part in the competition. However, several of their players went to play for a local works team, Lockwood Brothers, and reached the quarter-final, losing after a replay to West Bromwich Albion. This indirectly led to Wednesday adopting professionalism on 22 April 1887.

1887–88. On 24 March 1888, in a friendly at Lincoln, Tom Cawley was sent-off for fouling Jimmy Slater; however, it was pointed out that in fact it was Slater who had hurt himself fouling Cawley. The referee called him back, but as a matter of principle the Wednesday player refused.

1888–89. On 26 January 1889, in a Gainsborough Charity Cup game, future Wednesday player Fred Spiksley, playing for Gainsborough against Wednesday, was hurt and had to leave the field with a broken bone in his leg.

OPENING MATCH at Olive Grove,

THE WEDNESDAY v. BLACKBURN ROVERS

BLACKBURN TEAM.

Left Wing.

H. Arthur.

A. Chadwick.

WEDNESDAY TEAM.

1886-87

Did not enter competition.

1887-88

Match No.	Date	Venue	Opponents		Round	Result	HT Score	Position	Scorers	Attendance
22	Oct 15	A	Belper	W	1R	3-2	3-0		Waller, Kinman, Cawley	1,500
23	Nov 5	A	Long Eaton Rangers	W	2R	2-1 #	0-1		Waller, Mosforth	1,500
24	Dec 17	A	Crusaders (Essex)	W	4R	1-0	1-0		Hiller	1,000
25	Jan 7	A	Nottingham Forest	W	5R	4-2	1-2		Ingram (3), Winterbottom	8,000
26	30	H	Preston North End	L	6R	1-3	0-1		Ingram	9,000

After extra-time. Score at full-time 1-1. (Bye in round 3)

App

Goals

1888-89

Match No.	Date	Venue	Opponents		Round	Result	HT Score	Position	Scorers	Attendance
27	Feb 2	A	Notts Rangers		1R	1-1	0-1		F Thompson	3,000
28	9	H	Notts Rangers		1R Re	3-0	0-0		Cawley, Dungworth (2)	6,000
29	16	H	Notts County		2R	3-2	1-0		Ingram, Cawley, Winterbottom	7,000
30	Mar 2	A	Wolverhampton W		3R	0-3	0-0			6,000

App

Goals

Beckett Albert	Betts Billy	Brayshaw Teddy	Cawley Tom	Cooper William	Dungworth Jack	Hiller Carl	Ingram Billy	Kinman	Mosforth William	Mumford Albert	Smith Jim	Thompson Fred	Waller George	Webster Fred	Winterbottom Harry	Wise F	Woolhouse Harry
	4		10	6	5			7	11		1	3	9	8		2	
6	5	3	9		4	10			11		1	2	8		7		
	5	2	8		4	11	10		7		1	3	6		9		
	5	2	10		4	9	7		11		1	3	6		8		
	5	2	10		4	9	8		11		1	3	6		7		
1	5	4	5	1	5	4	3	1	5		5	5	5	1	4	1	
			1			1	4	1	1				2		1		

Beckett Albert	Betts Billy	Brayshaw Teddy	Cawley Tom	Cooper William	Dungworth Jack	Hiller Carl	Ingram Billy	Kinman	Mosforth William	Mumford Albert	Smith Jim	Thompson Fred	Waller George	Webster Fred	Winterbottom Harry	Wise F	Woolhouse Harry
	5	3	10		4		8			11	1	2	6		7		9
	5	3	10		4		8			11	1	2	6		7		9
	5	3	10		4		8			11	1	2	6		7		9
	5	3	10		4		8			11	1	2	6		7		9
	4	4	4		4		4			4	4	4	4		4		4
			2		2		1					1			1		

1889-90

Football Alliance

Manager: Arthur Dickinson

Did you know that?

Final League Position: 1st

Wednesday won the new Football Alliance League and reached the FA Cup Final as a non-League team.

Match No.	Date	Venue	Opponents		Round	Result	HT Score	Position	Scorers	Attendance
1	Sep 7	H	Bootle	W		2-1	2-1	-	Ingram (2)	2,000
2	14	A	B'Ham St George	W		2-0	2-0	2nd	Woolhouse (2)	700
3	28	A	Long Eaton Rangers	L		0-2	0-1	2nd		
4	Oct 12	H	Crewe	W		6-4	4-2	2nd	Winterbottom (4) Cawley, Ingram	3,000
5	19	A	Small Heath	D		2-2	1-2	2nd	Cawley, Mumford	3,000
6	26	A	Bootle	L		1-4	1-4	4th	Ingram	3,000
7	Nov 16	H	Long Eaton Rangers	W		9-1	4-0	6th	Cawley, (2 own-goals), Bennett, Ingram (4), Betts	2,000
8	30	H	Newton Heath	W		3-1	0-1	2nd	Ingram, Cawley, (Hay og)	5,000
9	Dec 7	A	Grimsby	W		4-0	1-0	1st	Bennett (2), Ingram, White	2,000
10	21	H	Small Heath	W		9-1	5-1	1st	Bennett (4), Cawley (5)	1,500
11	26	A	Sunderland Albion	W		3-2	1-1	1st	Cawley (2), Scrimmage	6,000
12	28	H	Nottingham Forest	W		3-1	0-0	1st	Mumford (2), Woolhouse	5,500
13	30	H	Darwen	W		4-1	2-1	1st	Woolhouse, Ingram (2), Bennett	4,500
14	Jan 4	A	Nottingham Forest	W		3-1	1-1	1st	Bennett, Ingram, Betts	2,000
15	11	A	Darwen	L		3-4	0-3	1st	Woolhouse, Scrimmage, Mumford	4,000
16	Feb 8	A	Crewe	L		0-2	0-0	1st		4,000
17	Mar 15	A	Walsall Town Swifts	D		2-2	0-0	1st	Ingram (2)	3,500
18	22	H	Grimsby	W		4-3	4-0	1st	Ingram (2), Winterbottom, Mumford	6,000
19	Apr 5	H	B'Ham St George	L		0-5	0-2	1st		5,000
20	8	H	Walsall Town Swifts	W		4-0	1-0	1st	Mumford, Bennett (2), Hiller	3,000
21	12	H	Sunderland Albion	W		4-1	4-1	1st	Ingram (2), Hiller, Mumford	4,000
22	26	A	Newton Heath	W		2-1	2-1	1st	Ingram, Bennett	4,500

2 x Scrimmage — App

Three own-goals — Goals

FA Cup

Match No.	Date	Venue	Opponents		Round	Result	HT Score	Position	Scorers	Attendance
23	Jan 18	H	London Swifts	W	Rd 1	6-1	2-1		Bennett (2), Cawley, Winterbottom, Mumford (2)	6,000
24	Feb 1	H	Accrington	W	Rd 2	2-1	1-1		Cawley, Winterbottom	10,000
25	15	H	Notts County	W	Rd 3	5-0	3-0		McMillian (og), Cawley (2), Bennett, Mumford	5,000
26	22	H	Notts County	L	Replay	2-3	1-2		Ingram (2)	12,000
27	Mar 3	N	Notts County	W	2 Re'py	2-1	2-0		Cawley, Winterbottom	10,000
28	8	N	Bolton Wanderers	W	S/Final	2-1	0-0		Winterbottom, Mumford	15,000
29	29	N	Blackburn Rovers	L	Final	1-6	0-4		Bennett	20,000

Match 25 Protest by County upheld — App

Match 26 Protest by Wednesday upheld — One own-goal — Goals

Match 27 Played at Derby — Included two protest games

Match 28 Played at Perry Barr, Birmingham

Match 29 Played at Kennington Oval, London

Bennett Mickey	Betts Billy	Brayshaw Teddy	Cawley Tom	Cutts C	Drabble S	Dungworth Jack	Gill T	Hazelwood Fred	Hiller Walpole	Ingram William	Morley Hayden	Mumford Albert	Parkin J	Smith Jim	Thompson Fred	Waller George	White A	Winterbottom Harry	Woolhouse Harry
	5	6	10			4		3		8		9		1	2			7	11
	5	3	10			4				8		9		1	2	6		7	11
	5	6	10			4		3				9		1	2		8	7	11
	5	3	10			4				8		9		1	2	6		7	11
	5	3	10			4				8		9		1	2	6		7	11
	5	3	10		7	4				8		9		1	2	6			11
9	5	3	10			4				8		11		1	2	6		7	
9	5	3	10			4				8		11		1	2	6		7	
9	5	3	10			4				8				1	2	6	11	7	
9	5	3	10			4				8		11		1	2	6		7	
9	5		10			4				8		11	3	1	2	6		7	
9	5	3	10			4				8		2		1		6		7	11
9	5	3				4				8	2	10		1		6		7	11
9	5	3	6			4				8	2	10		1				7	11
9	5		3			4				8	2	10		1		6		7	11
9	5	3	11			4				8	2	10		1		6		7	
9	5	3	10			4	6			8	2			1				7	11
	5	3	10			4				8	2	9		1		6		7	11
9	5	3	10			4				8		11		1	2	6		7	
9	5		6			4			7	8		11		1	2	3			10
9	5		10			4	6		7	8		3		1	2				11
9	5	3	6	10		4			7	8				1	2				11
15	22	18	21	1	1	22	2	2	3	21	6	19	1	22	15	16	2	18	15
12	2		11						2	20		7					1	5	5

Bennett Mickey	Betts Billy	Brayshaw Teddy	Cawley Tom	Cutts C	Drabble S	Dungworth Jack	Gill T	Hazelwood Fred	Hiller Walpole	Ingram William	Morley Hayden	Mumford Albert	Parkin J	Smith Jim	Thompson Fred	Waller George	White A	Winterbottom Harry	Woolhouse Harry
9	5	3	10			4				8	2	11		1		6		7	
9	5	3	10			4				8	2	11		1		6		7	
9	5	3	10			4				8	2	11		1		6		7	
9	5	3	10			4				8	2	11		1		6		7	
	5	3	10			4				8	2	9		1		6		7	11
	5	3	10			4				8	2	9		1		6		7	11
9	5	3	10			4				8	2	11		1		6			7
5	7	7	7			7				7	7	7		7		7		6	3
4			5							2		4						4	

League Table

	P	W	D	L	F	A	Pts
SHEFFIELD WEDNESDAY	22	15	2	5	70	39	32
Bootle	22	13	2	7	66	39	28
Sunderland Albion*	22	12	2	8	67	44	28
Grimsby Town	22	12	2	8	58	47	26
Crewe Alexandra	22	11	2	9	68	59	24
Darwen	22	10	2	10	70	75	22
Birmingham St George	22	10	3	9	67	52	21
Newton Heath	22	9	2	11	40	44	20
Walsall Town Swifts	22	8	3	11	44	59	19
Small Heath	22	6	5	11	44	67	17
Nottingham Forest	22	6	5	11	31	62	17
Long Eaton Rangers	22	4	2	16	35	73	10

*** Sunderland Albion were awarded the two points for a match they lost at Birmingham St George. Consequently, some versions of the table show the two clubs having played 21 games, with the goals (5-3 to St George) removed.**

Long Eaton Rangers resigned and joined the Midland League

Stoke were not re-elected by the Football League and took Long Eaton's place for 1890/91

1890-91

Football Alliance

Manager: Arthur Dickinson

Did you know that?

Final League Position: 12th

On 15 December 1890 Wednesday met Sheffield United for the first time. Wednesday beat their local rivals 2–1, at Olive Grove, thanks to goals from the two Harrys (Woolhouse and Winterbottom). A crowd of 10,000 also saw Harry Brandon play under the assumed name of Todd.

Wednesday beat Halliwell, a team from the Bolton area, 12–0 to record their highest FA Cup win on 17 January 1891 at Olive Grove. Originally, Halliwell were drawn at home, but the game was switched to Sheffield. After the game, Halliwell lodged a protest on the state of the ground.

Match No.	Date	Venue	Opponents		Round	Result	HT Score	Position	Scorers	Attendance
1	Sep 20	A	Sunderland Albion	L		1-3	1-0	8th	Mumford	6,000
2	27	A	Walsall Town Swifts	L		1-2	1-0	10th	Bennett	2,000
3	Oct 11	H	Small Heath	D		3-3	2-2	10th	Ingram, Winterbottom, Woolhouse	6,500
4	18	H	Crewe Alexandra	L		4-6	2-3	11th	Mumford (2), Woolhouse (2)	3,000
5	25	A	B'ham St Georges	L		3-5	1-4	12th	Siddons (og), B. Brandon, Mumford	1,000
6	Nov 1	H	Nottingham Forest	L		0-2	0-0	12th		8,000
7	8	A	Darwen	L		1-7	0-2	12th	Mumford	1,500
8	15	H	Grimsby Town	W		2-1	0-0	12th	Mumford, B. Brandon	8,000
9	22	H	Walsall Town Swifts	D		2-2	2-1	12th	Woolhouse (2)	6,000
10	Dec 13	H	Stoke	L		2-4	0-2	12th	Woolhouse, B. Brandon	6,000
11	29	H	Darwen	W		7-3	4-3	12th	Woolhouse (3), Mumford (3), Betts	6,000
12	Jan 10	A	Small Heath	L		1-7	0-3	12th	B. Brandon	1,500
13	24	H	Newton Heath	L		1-2	1-1	12th	B. Brandon	3,000
14	Feb 21	A	Newton Heath	D		1-1	1-0	12th	Woolhouse	4,000
15	Mar 7	A	Grimsby Town	L		0-3	0-0	12th		2,000
16	9	H	Bootle	D		1-1	1-1	12th	Scrimmage	1,500
17	14	A	Crewe Alexandra	L		0-2	0-1	12th		600
18	21	A	Nottingham Forest	D		0-0	0-0	12th		2,000
19	23	A	Bootle	L		0-5	0-1	12th		2,000
20	28	H	B'ham St Georges	W		4-0	3-0	12th	Gibson (3), Gemmell	4,000
21	Apr 4	A	Stoke	L		1-5	1-2	12th	Gemmell	2,000
22	6	H	Sunderland Albion	W		4-2	3-0	12th	Betts, Woolhouse (2), H. Brandon	1,000

1 x Scrimmage | Apps

One own-goal | Goals

FA Cup

Match No.	Date	Venue	Opponents		Round	Result	HT Score	Position	Scorers	Attendance
23	Jan 17	H	Halliwell	W	1R	12-0	5-0		Cawley (2), B. Brandon, Woolhouse (5), H. Brandon, Mumford (2), Ingram	1,000
24	31	H	Derby County	W	2R	3-2	0-1		Hodder, Winterbottom (2)	8,000
25	Feb 14	H	West Bromwich A.	L	3R	0-2	0-1			16,871

Apps

Goals

Bennett Harry	Bennett Mickey	Betts Billy	Brandon Harry	Brandon James	Brandon Bob	Brayshaw Teddy	Cawley Tom	Dungworth Jack	Fenwick A	Ferguson J	Gemmell Duncan	Gibson J	Hodder William	Ingram William	Kennedy J	McConnachie J	McWatt H	Morley Hayden	Mumford Albert	Richardson R	Robertson R	Scott P	Smith Jim	Thompson Fred	Webster A	Winterbottom Harry	Woolhouse Harry
	9	5				3	6	4						8					10				1	2	7		11
	8	5				3	6	4					9					2	10				1			7	11
		5				3	6	4					9	8				2	10				1			7	11
		5				6		4					9	8				2	10		7		1	3			11
		5			9	3	6	4					10		7				8				1	2			11
					9	3	6	4					7		11				5				1	2		10	8
		5			9		6	4					11	8				3	7				1	2			10
	8	5			9		6	4					11					3	7				1	2			10
	8	5			9		6	4					11					3	7				1	2			10
4		5			9		6						11				1	3	8					2		7	10
		5	4		9		6	3					11						8				1	2		7	10
	10	5	4		9	3	6		1				11	8										2		7	
	8	5	4		9		6							7				3	11				1	2			10
		5	4		9	3	6							8								11	1	2		7	10
		5	4	7	9	3	6							8					11				1	2			10
		5	4	7	9	3	6							8					11				1	2			10
		5	4	7	9		6						11						3				1	2		8	10
			4	7	9	2	6			5	8								3	11			1				10
			4		9	2	6			5	8		7						3	11			1				10
		5	4	8						6	7	9				2			3	10			1				11
5			4		8					6	7	9				2			3	10			1				11
		5	4	8						6	7	9				2			3	10			1				11
2	6	18	12	6	16	12	18	10	1	5	5	3	13	9	2	3	1	8	20	5	1	1	20	15	1	8	21
	1	2	1		5						2	3		1					9							1	12

Bennett Harry	Bennett Mickey	Betts Billy	Brandon Harry	Brandon James	Brandon Bob	Brayshaw Teddy	Cawley Tom	Dungworth Jack	Fenwick A	Ferguson J	Gemmell Duncan	Gibson J	Hodder William	Ingram William	Kennedy J	McConnachie J	McWatt H	Morley Hayden	Mumford Albert	Richardson R	Robertson R	Scott P	Smith Jim	Thompson Fred	Webster A	Winterbottom Harry	Woolhouse Harry
		5	4		9	3	6							11					8				1	2		7	10
		5	4			3	6						9	11					8				1	2		7	10
		5	4		9	3	6						11						8				1	2		7	10
		3	3		2	3	3						2	2					3				3	3		3	3
			1		1		2						1	1					2							2	5

League Table

	P	W	D	L	F	A	Pts
Stoke	22	13	7	2	57	39	33
Sunderland Albion	22	12	6	4	69	28	30
Grimsby Town	22	11	5	6	43	27	27
Birmingham St George	22	12	2	8	64	62	26
Nottingham Forest*	22	9	7	6	66	39	23
Darwen	22	10	3	9	64	59	23
Walsall Town Swifts	22	9	3	10	34	61	21
Crewe Alexandra	22	8	4	10	59	67	20
Newton Heath	22	7	3	12	37	55	17
Small Heath	22	7	2	13	58	66	16
Bootle	22	3	7	12	40	61	13
SHEFFIELD WEDNESDAY	22	4	5	13	39	66	13

Nottingham Forest had two points deducted 23/10/90 for playing an unregistered player (TH Widdowson v Bootle, 6/9/90)

Stoke and Darwen were elected to the Football League

Sunderland Albion resigned to play only in the Northern League

Ardwick, Burton Swifts and Lincoln City were elected for 1891/92

1891-92

FOOTBALL ALLIANCE

Manager: Arthur Dickinson

Did you know that?

Final League Position: 4th

In 27 December 1891, when 'keeper Bill Allan joined Wednesday, it was found that the club had no boots big enough to fit him, so a local cobbler had to work all night to make him a pair. Wednesday duly beat Lincoln City 7–2 in a Football Alliance League game.

On 13 May 1892, Wednesday were voted into the Football League when the League was increased from 12 to 14 teams.

Match No.	Date	Venue	Opponents		Round	Result	HT Score	Position	Scorers	Attendance
1	Sep 19	H	Grimsby Town	W		4-2	1-1	6th	Woolhouse (3), J. Brandon	10,000
2	26	A	Walsall Town Swifts	L		1-2	0-2	8th	Thompson	3,500
3	Oct 10	A	Small Heath	D		1-1	0-0	6th	Gemmell	1,000
4	17	H	Burton Swifts	W		5-2	3-1	6th	Spiksley, Gemmell (2), Thompson, Mumford	9,000
5	24	A	Bootle	L		2-3	0-1	5th	Richardson, T. Brandon (pen)	2,000
6	31	H	Crewe Alexandra	W		4-1	1-0	5th	Thompson, Spiksley (2), Ingram	6,000
7	Nov 7	A	Nottingham Forest	D		1-1	0-0	5th	H. Brandon	3,000
8	14	A	B'Ham St Georges	W		4-2	1-1	3rd	McConachie, Stainsbie (og), Betts, Woolhouse	500
9	21	H	Walsall Town Swifts	W		4-0	3-0	3rd	Brown, Cawley, Gemmell, Thompson	3,000
10	28	H	Nottingham Forest	W		3-1	1-0	3rd	Gemmell, Brown, Richardson	12,000
11	Dec 5	A	Ardwick	W		4-0	3-0	2nd	Woolhouse (2), Gemmell (2)	6,000
12	12	H	Newton Heath	L		2-4	1-3	3rd	Brown, Woolhouse	4,000
13	19	A	Crewe Alexandra	L		1-2	0-0	3rd	Woolhouse	2,000
14	26	H	Ardwick	W		2-0	1-0	3rd	Thompson, Hall	12,000
15	28	H	Lincoln City	W		7-2	5-2	2nd	Thompson (2), Richardson, Woolhouse (2) McConachie, Brown	10,000
16	Jan 9	H	Small Heath	W		6-3	2-2	3rd	Brown (3), Richardson, Spiksley (2)	6,000
17	Feb 20	A	Newton Heath	D		1-1	1-0	3rd	Thompson	7,000
18	27	A	Burton Swifts	L		3-4	1-4	3rd	Richardson (2), Spiksley	Large
19	Mar 5	H	Bootle	W		4-1	2-0	3rd	Spiksley (2), Thompson, H. Brandon	5,000
20	12	A	Lincoln City	D		2-2	1-2	3rd	Gemmell, Brown	2,000
21	19	A	Grimsby Town	L		0-1	0-0	3rd		2,000
22	26	H	B'Ham St Georges	W		4-0	4-0	4th	Spiksley, H. Brandon, McConachie, T. Brandon	4,000
										Apps
									One own-goal	Goals
FA Cup										
23	Jan 23	H	Bolton Wanderers	W	1R	4-1	1-0		Spiksley (2), Richardson, Brown	16,500
24	30	H	Small Heath	W	2R	2-0	1-0		Richardson, Thompson	12,000
25	Feb 13	A	West Bromwich Alb	L	3R	1-2	0-2		Richardson	8,000
										Apps
										Goals

Allan Bill	Betts Billy	Brandon Harry	Brandon James	Brandon Tom	Brown Bob	Cawley Tom	Darroch Jack	Gemmell Duncan	Hall Alex	Ingram William	McConachie Robert	McReady	Mumford Albert	Richardson R	Smith Jim	Spiksley Fred	Thompson Gavin	Webster F	Winterbottom Harry	Woolhouse Harry
	5	4	8			6		7			2		3		1	11	9			10
	5	4		3		6	2	7					8	10	1	11	9			
	5	4	8	3		6	2	7					9	10	1	11				
	5	4		3		6	2	7					8	10	1	11	9			
	5	4		3		6	2						8	10	1	11	9		7	
	5					6	2			8	3		4	10	1	11	9		7	
	5	4				10	2	7	6		8		3		1	11	9			
	5	4						7	6		3	8	2		1	11	9			10
	5				8	11	2	7	6		4		3		1		9			10
	5				8		2	7	6		4		3	11	1		9			10
	5	3			8		2	7	6		4			11	1		9			10
	5	3			8		2	7	6		4				1	11	9			10
	5				8		2	7	6		4		3	11	1		9			10
	5	3			8			7	6		4		2	11	1		9			10
1	5				8		2	7	6		4		3	11			9			10
		6		3	8	4		7	2		5			10	1	11	9			
1	5	6		3	8			7	4		10		2			11	9			
1		6		3		5		7	4				2	10		11	9	8		
1	5	6		3	8			7	4				2	10		11	9			
1	5	6		3	8			7	4				2	10		11	9			
1	5	6		3	8			7	4				2	10		11	9			
1	5	6		3				7	4	8	9		2	10		11				
7	20	17	2	11	12	10	12	20	16	2	14	1	19	16	15	16	20	1	2	9
	1	3	1	2	8	1		8	1	1	3		1	6		9	9			10

Allan Bill	Betts Billy	Brandon Harry	Brandon James	Brandon Tom	Brown Bob	Cawley Tom	Darroch Jack	Gemmell Duncan	Hall Alex	Ingram William	McConachie Robert	McReady	Mumford Albert	Richardson R	Smith Jim	Spiksley Fred	Thompson Gavin	Webster F	Winterbottom Harry	Woolhouse Harry
1		4		2	8	5		7	6				3	10		11	9			
1	5	4		2	8			7	6				3	10		11	9			
1	5	4		2	7			8	6				3	10		11	9			
3	2	3		3	3	1		3	3				3	3		3	3			
					1									3		2	1			

League Table

	P	W	D	L	F	A	Pts
Nottingham Forest	22	14	5	3	59	22	33
Newton Heath	22	12	7	3	69	33	31
Small Heath	22	12	5	5	53	36	29
SHEFFIELD WEDNESDAY	22	12	4	6	65	35	28
Burton Swifts	22	12	2	8	54	52	26
Crewe Alexandra	22	7	4	11	44	49	18
Ardwick	22	6	6	10	39	51	18
Bootle	22	8	2	12	42	64	18
Lincoln City	22	6	5	11	37	65	17
Grimsby Town*	22	6	6	10	40	39	16
Walsall Town Swifts	22	6	3	13	33	59	15
Birmingham St George*	22	5	3	14	34	64	11

Grimsby Town had two points deducted on 10/01/92 for playing an ineligible player

***Birmingham St George had two points deducted on 17/9/91 for playing unregistered players Matthews and McGuffie in game 1**

All clubs except Birmingham St George joined the Football League.

Newton Heath, Nottingham Forest and Sheffield Wednesday were voted into the top division; the other 8 formed the new Division Two, with Burslem Port Vale, Darwen, Northwich Victoria and Sheffield United.

1892-93

Division One

Manager: Arthur Dickinson

Did you know that?

Final League Position: 12th

On 3 April 1893, Wednesday won their last game of the season 3–2 at home to Notts County and avoided the Test Match. This involved the bottom three clubs in Division One playing the top three clubs in the Second Division, and the three winners either remained in the top division or were promoted from the second tier.

Match No.	Date	Venue	Opponents		Round	Result	HT Score	Position	Scorers	Attendance
1	Sep 3	A	Notts County	W		1-0	1-0		T. Brandon	13,000
2	10	H	Accrington	W		5-2	3-0	2nd	R. Brown (2) Spiksley, Davis, Rowan	9,000
3	12	A	Preston North End	L		1-4	0-3	6th	R. Brown	1,200
4	17	A	Bolton Wanderers	L		0-1	0-1	6th		7,000
5	24	A	Accrington	L		2-4	2-1	10th	Davis, Rowan	4,000
6	Oct 1	H	Burnley	W		2-0	1-0	6th	R. Brown, Spiksley	12,000
7	3	H	Nottingham Forest	D		2-2	1-1	5th	Davis (2)	8,000
8	15	A	Blackburn Rovers	W		2-0	2-0	6th	Rowan (2)	3,500
9	22	H	Newton Heath	W		1-0	0-0	4th	Spiksley	6,000
10	29	H	Sunderland	W		3-2	2-2	4th	Hall (2), Brady	20,000
11	Nov 5	H	Bolton Wanderers	W		4-2	2-0	3rd	Rowan, Spiksley (2), Somerville (og)	18,000
12	19	H	Blackburn Rovers	L		0-3	0-1	5th		7,000
13	26	A	Everton	W		5-3	5-1	4th	Brady (2), Spiksley, R. Brown, Davis	15,000
14	Dec 1	A	Nottingham Forest	L		0-2	0-2	4th		3,000
15	3	H	Aston Villa	W		5-3	3-1	3rd	Spiksley, Rowan, Davis, Woolhouse, Mumford	6,000
16	10	H	Derby County	D		3-3	3-0	3rd	Rowan, H. Brandon, Spiksley	5,000
17	17	A	Stoke	L		0-2	0-0	3rd		6,000
18	24	A	Newton Heath	W		5-1	3-0	3rd	Rowan (2), Davis, Spiksley (2)	4,000
19	Jan 2	H	West Bromwich Alb	W		6-0	3-0	3rd	H. Brandon, Rowan, Brady, Brown, Spiksley (2)	15,500
20	7	A	Aston Villa	L		1-5	0-3	4th	McIntosh	4,000
21	14	H	Preston North End	L		0-5	0-2	4th		17,500
22	28	A	Sunderland	L		2-4	0-2	4th	Rowan, Spiksley	7,500
23	Feb 11	A	Wolverhampton W	L		0-2	0-1	5th		4,000
24	13	H	Everton	L		0-2	0-1	8th		5,000
25	Mar 11	H	Wolverhampton W	L		0-1	0-1	9th		8,000
26	18	A	West Bromwich Alb	L		0-3	0-1	11th		3,500
27	25	A	Derby County	D		2-2	1-2	10th	Rowan (2)	6,000
28	31	A	Burnley	L		0-4	0-3			8,500
29	Apr 1	H	Stoke	L		0-1	0-1	12th		4,500
30	3	H	Notts County	W		3-2	1-1	12th	T. Brandon, H. Brandon (2)	7,500
										Apps
									One own-goal	Goals

FA Cup

Match No.	Date	Venue	Opponents		Round	Result	HT Score	Position	Scorers	Attendance
31	Jan 21	H	Derby County * #	W	1st	3-2	0-1		Davis, Rowan, Spiksley	19,000
32	30	A	Derby County * +	L	Repy	0-1	0-0			14,000
33	Feb 2	H	Derby County	W	2nd R	4-2	3-1		Betts, Spiksley, Woolhouse (2)	10,000
34	4	H	Burnley	W	2nd	1-0	0-0		Spiksley	9,500
35	18	A	Everton	L	3rd	0-3	0-2			24,451
										Apps
										Goals

* Match replayed after protest
\# After extra-time. Score at full-time 2-2
\+ After extra-time. Score at full-time 0-0

Allan Bill	Betts Billy	Brady Alec	Brandon Harry	Brandon Tom	Brown James	Brown Robert	Chalmers Bruce	Darroch John	Davis Harry	Dunlop Walter	Hall Alex	McConachie R	McIntosh Thomas	Mumford Albert	Rowan Sandy	Spiksley Fred	Woolhouse Harry
1	5	10	4	2		8			9	7	6			3		11	
1	5	10	4	2		8			7		6			3	9	11	
1	5	10	4	2		8			7		6			3	9	11	
1	5	10	4	2		8			7		6			3	9	11	
1	5	10	4	2		8			7		6			3	9	11	
1	5	10	4	2		8			7		6			3	9	11	
1	5	10	4	2		8			7		6			3	9	11	
1	5	10	4	2		8		3	7		6				9	11	
1	5	10	4	2		8		3	7		6				9	11	
1	5	10	4	2		8		3	7		6				9	11	
1	5	10	4	2		8		3	7		6				9	11	
1	5	10	4	2		8			7		6			3	9	11	
1	5	10	4	2		8		3	7					6	9	11	
1	5	10	4	2		8		3	7					6	9	11	
1	5	8	4	2				3	7					6	9	11	10
1	5	10	4	2		8		3	7					6	9	11	
1	5	8	4	2				3	7					6	9	11	10
1	5	10	4	2		8	6	3	7						9	11	
1	5	10	4	2	3	8	6		7						9	11	
1	5			2	3	7	6				4		8		9	11	10
1	5	10	4	2		8	6		7					3	9	11	
1	5		4	2		8	6		10				7	3	9	11	
1			4	2		8	6	3	7		5			11	9		10
1	5		4	2		8	6	3	7				10		9		11
1	5	10	4	2		8	6	3	7						9	11	
1	5	10	4	2			6		7				8	3	9	11	
1		10	4	2			6		8		5		7	3	9	11	
1		11	4	2		10	6		8		5		7	3	9		
1	5	10	4	2			6		8			11	7	3	9		
1		10	4	2		9	6		8		5		7	3		11	
30	26	26	29	30	2	25	13	13	29	1	17	1	8	21	28	26	5
		4	4	2		6			7		2		1	1	13	13	1

Allan Bill	Betts Billy	Brady Alec	Brandon Harry	Brandon Tom	Brown James	Brown Robert	Chalmers Bruce	Darroch John	Davis Harry	Dunlop Walter	Hall Alex	McConachie R	McIntosh Thomas	Mumford Albert	Rowan Sandy	Spiksley Fred	Woolhouse Harry
1	5	10	4	2		8	6		7					3	9	11	
1	5		4	2		8	6	3	7						9	11	10
1	5		4	2		8	6	3	7						9	11	10
1	5		4	2		8	6	3	7						9	11	10
1	5		4	2		8	6		7					3	9	11	10
5	5	1	5	5		5	5	3	5					2	5	5	4
	1								1						1	3	2

League Table

	P	W	D	L	F	A	Pts
Sunderland	30	22	4	4	100	36	48
Preston North End	30	17	3	10	57	39	37
Everton	30	16	4	10	74	51	36
Aston Villa	30	16	3	11	73	62	35
Bolton Wanderers	30	13	6	11	56	55	32
Burnley	30	13	4	13	51	44	30
Stoke	30	12	5	13	58	48	29
West Bromwich Albion	30	12	5	13	58	69	29
Blackburn Rovers	30	8	13	9	47	56	29
Nottingham Forest	30	10	8	12	48	52	28
Wolverhampton W.	30	12	4	14	47	68	28
SHEFFIELD WEDNESDAY	30	12	3	15	55	65	27
Derby County	30	9	9	12	52	64	27
Notts County	30	10	4	16	53	61	24
Accrington	30	6	11	13	57	81	23
Newton Heath	30	6	6	18	50	85	18

1893-94

Division One

Manager: Arthur Dickinson

Did you know that?

Final League Position: 12th

During the season, Wednesday were involved in three abandoned League games, all within a period of six weeks. A snowstorm caused the home game against Stoke to be abandoned, after 70 minutes, and a week later the game at Darwen fell victim to the British weather, heavy rain and wind the reason on this occasion. It was Darwen again on 30 December, with fog the culprit this time.

With Wednesday near the bottom of the League, John Holmes, the club's President, offered Wednesday's players £50 to share if they could win five out of their last six games. They subsequently did just that to finish safe in 12th position.

Match No.	Date	Venue	Opponents		Round	Result	HT Score	Position	Scorers	Attendance
1	Sep 2	H	Sunderland	D		2-2	1-2		Miller (2)	14,500
2	4	A	Wolverhampton W	L		1-3	0-2		Brady	5,000
3	9	A	Blackburn Rovers	L		1-5	1-4		Chalmers	8,000
4	16	H	Newton Heath	L		0-1	0-1	16th		7,000
5	23	A	Sunderland	D		1-1	0-1	16th	Betts	3,000
6	25	H	West Bromwich Alb	L		2-4	0-0	16th	Spiksley, Betts	6,000
7	30	H	Blackburn Rovers	W		4-2	3-1	13th	Davis, Webster, Spiksley, Miller	10,000
8	Oct 7	A	Stoke	L		1-4	1-2	16th	Miller	7,000
9	14	H	Derby County	W		4-0	0-0	15th	Brady (3), Davis	8,000
10	16	A	Sheffield United	D		1-1	1-1	11th	Spiksley	27,000
11	21	A	Derby County	D		3-3	2-2	11th	Spiksley, R. Brown, Miller	6,000
12	28	A	Nottingham Forest	L		0-1	0-1	14th		7,000
13	Nov 4	H	Everton	D		1-1	0-1	14th	Miller	9,000
14	13	H	Sheffield United	L		1-2	0-1	15th	Miller	13,000
15	27	A	West Bromwich Alb	D		2-2	2-1	14th	Davis, H. Brandon	3,500
16	Dec 2	H	Wolverhampton W	L		1-4	0-3	14th	Davis	6,000
17	7	H	Stoke	W		4-1	1-1	13th	Spiksley (2), H. Brandon, Smith	2,000
18	9	A	Aston Villa	L		0-3	0-0	14th		10,000
19	11	A	Darwen	L		1-2	1-2		Webster	2,000
20	16	H	Bolton Wanderers	W		2-1	2-1	13th	Webster, Spiksley	5,000
21	23	A	Everton	L		1-8	1-4	14th	Spiksley	15,000
22	25	A	Bolton Wanderers	D		1-1	1-0		Somerville (og)	6,000
23	26	H	Burnley	L		0-1	0-1	14th		14,000
24	Jan 6	H	Aston Villa	D		2-2	2-1	13th	Spiksley (2)	8,500
25	13	A	Newton Heath	W		2-1	1-0	13th	Woolhouse (2)	7,000
26	15	H	Darwen	W		5-0	1-0	12th	Webster (2), Woolhouse, Spiksley, Miller	4,000
27	Feb 6	H	Preston North End	W		3-0	1-0	12th	Earp, H. Brandon, Spiksley	10,000
28	Mar 5	H	Nottingham Forest	W		1-0	1-0	12th	Davis	3,500
29	23	A	Burnley	W		1-0	1-0	12th	Spiksley	8,500
30	26	A	Preston North End	L		0-1	0-0	12th		5,000
										Apps
									One own-goal	Goals

FA Cup

31	Jan 27	A	Woolwich Arsenal	W	1st	2-1	1-1		Spiksley (2)	10,000
32	Feb 10	H	Stoke	W	2nd	1-0	0-0		Woolhouse	16,000
33	24	H	Aston Villa #	W	3rd	3-2	1-1		Woolhouse (2), Spiksley	22,100
34	Mar 10	N	Bolton Wanderers *	L	S/F	1-2	0-1		Woolhouse	30,000
										Apps
										Goals

* Played at Fallowfield, Manchester

After extra-time

Division One Abandoned Matches

35	Nov 18	H	Stoke (70 mins Snow)			3-1	2-0		Brady, Spiksley, Davis	1,500
36	Nov 25	A	Darwen (15 mins Rain/Mud)				0-1			1,500
37	Dec 30	H	Darwen (58 mins Fog)			2-2	2-1		Spiksley, Brady	3,000

Allan Bill	Betts Billy	Brady Alec	Brandon Harry	Brown James	Brown Robert	Chalmers Bruce	Darroch John	Davis Harry	Earp Jack	Glen Bob	Jamieson Jim	Langley Ambrose	McIntosh Thomas	Mellars Billy	Miller John	Mumford Albert	Rowan Sandy	Shepherd James	Smith Jock	Spiksley Fred	Webster John	Woolhouse Harry
1		10	4		7	5	2				6	3			9				8	11		
1		10	4		8	5	2	7			6	3					9			11		
1		10	4		9	5				6		2	7			3			8	11		
1		10	4		6	5	2	8				3			9					11	7	
1	5	10		2		6		8				3						4	9	11	7	
1	5	10		2		6		8				3						4	9	11	7	
1	5		4	2		6		8				3			9				10	11	7	
1	5		4	3		6		8	2						9				10	11	7	
1	5	10	4					8	2		6	3			9					11	7	
1	5	10	4					8	2		6	3			9					11	7	
1		10	4		8	5			2		6	3			9				7	11		
1	5	10	4						2		6	3			9				8	11	7	
1	5	10	4					8	2		6	3			9					11	7	
1	5	10	4		6			8	2			3			9				7	11		
1	5	10	7		4			8	2		6	3							9	11		
1	5		7	3	4			8	2		6				9				10	11		
1	5	10	7	3	4			8	2		6								9	11		
1	5	10	7		4		3	8	2		6								9	11		
1	5	10	3		4			8	2		6								9	11	7	
1	5	10	3		4			8	2		6								9	11	7	
1		10			4	5		8	2		6	3							9	11	7	
1	5	10	2	3	4			8			6								9	11	7	
1	5	10	4	3	11			8	2		6								9		7	
1	5	10			6			8	2		4	3								11	7	9
1	5				4			8	2		6	3			9					11	7	10
1	5				4			8	2		6	3			9					11	7	10
1	5	10	4					8	2		6	3								11	7	9
1		10	4		5			8	2		6	3								11	7	9
1	5	10			8			9	2		6	3		4						11	7	
1	5	10	2		8			9			6	3				4				11	7	
30	23	25	23	8	21	10	4	26	21	1	23	22	1	1	13	2	1	2	18	29	21	5
	2	4	3		1	1		5	1						8				1	13	5	3

Allan Bill	Betts Billy	Brady Alec	Brandon Harry	Brown James	Brown Robert	Chalmers Bruce	Darroch John	Davis Harry	Earp Jack	Glen Bob	Jamieson Jim	Langley Ambrose	McIntosh Thomas	Mellars Billy	Miller John	Mumford Albert	Rowan Sandy	Shepherd James	Smith Jock	Spiksley Fred	Webster John	Woolhouse Harry
1	5	10			4			8	2		6	3								11	7	9
1	5	10	4					8	2		6	3								11	7	9
1	5	10	4					8	2		6	3								11	7	9
1	5	10	4					8	2		6	3								11	7	9
4	4	4	3		1			4	4		4	4								4	4	4
																				3		4

Allan Bill	Betts Billy	Brady Alec	Brandon Harry	Brown James	Brown Robert	Chalmers Bruce	Darroch John	Davis Harry	Earp Jack	Glen Bob	Jamieson Jim	Langley Ambrose	McIntosh Thomas	Mellars Billy	Miller John	Mumford Albert	Rowan Sandy	Shepherd James	Smith Jock	Spiksley Fred	Webster John	Woolhouse Harry
1	5	10	7		4			8	2		6	3							9	11		
1	5	10	7		4			8	2		6	3							9	11		
1	5	10	4	3				8	2		6								9	11	7	

League Table

	P	W	D	L	F	A	Pts
Aston Villa	30	19	6	5	84	42	44
Sunderland	30	17	4	9	72	44	38
Derby County	30	16	4	10	73	62	36
Blackburn Rovers	30	16	2	12	69	53	34
Burnley	30	15	4	11	61	51	34
Everton	30	15	3	12	90	57	33
Nottingham Forest	30	14	4	12	57	48	32
West Bromwich Albion	30	14	4	12	66	59	32
Wolverhampton W	30	14	3	13	52	63	31
Sheffield United	30	13	5	12	47	61	31
Stoke	30	13	3	14	65	79	29
SHEFFIELD WEDNESDAY	30	9	8	13	48	57	26
Bolton Wanderers	30	10	4	16	38	52	24
Preston North End	30	10	3	17	44	56	23
Darwen	30	7	5	18	37	83	19
Newton Heath	30	6	2	22	36	72	14

1894-95

Division One

Manager: Arthur Dickinson

Did you know that?

Final League Position: 8th

On 16 March 1895 Wednesday played West Bromwich Albion in the FA Cup semi-final at Derby and lost 2–0. The second goal was a penalty given away by Ambrose Langley on Billy Bassett by the corner flag (in those days the penalty area was the full width of the pitch).

Match No.	Date	Venue	Opponents		Round	Result	HT Score	Position	Scorers	Attendance
1	Sep 1	A	Everton	L		1-3	1-1		Petrie	25,000
2	3	H	Preston North End	W		3-1	2-0		Brandon, Davis, Earp	7,000
3	8	H	Blackburn Rovers	W		4-1	2-0	5th	Davis, Ferrier, Earp (pen), Brady	12,000
4	15	A	Derby County	W		2-1	2-0	3rd	Davis, Brash	6,000
5	22	H	Bolton Wanderers	W		2-1	1-1	3rd	Spiksley, Ferrier	10,000
6	29	A	Blackburn Rovers	L		1-3	0-2	4th	Woolhouse	7,000
7	Oct 6	H	Burnley	W		4-3	3-3	4th	Brash, Ferrier, Crawshaw, Brady	4,500
8	13	A	Wolverhampton W	L		0-2	0-2	8th		8,000
9	27	H	Sheffield United	L		2-3	2-2	7th	Spiksley, Davis	14,500
10	Nov 3	H	Aston Villa	W		1-0	0-0	6th	Brady	8,500
11	10	A	Burnley	L		0-3	0-3	8th		6,000
12	17	H	Wolverhampton W	W		3-1	3-1	7th	Davis, Brandon (pen), Brady	8,500
13	Dec 3	A	Aston Villa	L		1-3	0-1	9th	Woolhouse	5,000
14	8	A	Stoke	W		2-0	1-0	8th	Davis, Spiksley	3,000
15	15	H	Nottingham Forest	D		0-0	0-0	6th		6,000
16	26	H	Small Heath	W		2-0	2-0	6th	Crawshaw, Ferrier	14,000
17	29	H	Derby County	D		1-1	0-0	7th	Crawshaw	3,000
18	Jan 1	H	Everton	W		3-0	3-0	5th	Brandon, Davis (2)	18,000
19	5	H	Liverpool	W		5-0	3-0	5th	Spiksley (2), Woolhouse (2), Brandon	10,000
20	7	A	Bolton Wanderers	D		2-2	1-1	5th	Woolhouse, Spiksley	2,000
21	12	A	Sheffield United	L		0-1	0-1	5th		12,000
22	19	A	Nottingham Forest	L		1-2	1-1	6th	Ferrier	5,000
23	Feb 26	A	Sunderland	L		1-3	0-1	9th	Woolhouse	7,500
24	Mar 23	H	Sunderland	L		1-2	0-1	9th	Brady	6,000
25	25	A	Small Heath	D		0-0	0-0			3,000
26	30	A	Liverpool	L		2-4	1-2	8th	Priestley, Brash	6,000
27	Apr 1	H	West Bromwich Alb	W		3-2	0-1	8th	Jamieson, Brady, Brash	2,000
28	13	A	Preston North End	L		1-3	1-1	8th	Betts	4,000
29	17	H	Stoke	L		2-4	1-2	8th	Petrie, Spiksley	3,000
30	22	A	West Bromwich Alb	L		0-6	0-4	8th		8,217
										Apps
										Goals

FA Cup

Match No.	Date	Venue	Opponents		Round	Result	HT Score	Position	Scorers	Attendance
31	Feb 2	H	Notts County	W	1st	5-1	3-0		Brady, Brash (2), Spiksley, Ferrier	12,000
32	16	H	Middlesbrough	W	2nd	6-1	5-0		Davis (3), Brady, Spiksley (2)	4,000
33	Mar 2	H	Everton	W	3rd	2-0	2-0		Brady, Ferrier	28,000
34	16	N	West Bromwich Alb #	L	S/F	0-2	0-2			17,000
										Apps
										Goals

Played at County Ground, Derby

Abandoned Game after 75 minutes due to crowd interference

Match No.	Date	Venue	Opponents		Round	Result	HT Score	Position	Scorers	Attendance
35	Apr 6	H	Stoke			0-0	0-0			5,000

Allan Bill	Betts Billy	Brady Alex	Brandon Harry	Brash Archie	Crawshaw Tommy	Davis Harry	Earp Jack	Ferrier Bob	Fox William	Jamieson Jim	Langley Ambrose	Lowe H.G.	Massey Jack	Petrie Bob	Priestley R	Spiksley Fred	Sutherland George	Webster John	Woolhouse Harry
1		10		7	5	9	2	8		6	3			4		11			
1		10	4	7	5	9	2	8		6	3					11			
1		10	4	7	5	9	2	8		6	3					11			
1		10		7	5	9	2	8		6	3			4		11			
1		10		7	5	9	2	8		6	3			4		11			
1		10	4	7	5		2	8		6	3					11			9
1		10	4	7	5	9	2	8		6	3					11			
1		10	4	7	5	9	2	8		6	3					11			
1		10	4	7	5	9	2	8		6	3					11			
		10	4	7	5	9	2	8		6	3		1			11			
		10	9	7	5		2	8		6	3		1	4		11			
		10	4	7	5	9		8		6	3		1			11	2		
1			4	7	5	9	2	8		6	3					11			10
1			4	7	5	9	2	8		6	3	10				11			
1			9	7	5		2	8		6	3	10		4		11			
1		10	3	7	5	9	2	8		6				4		11			
1		10	3	7	5	9	2	8		6				4		11			
1		10	4	7	5	9	2	8		6	3					11			
1		10	7		5		2	8		6	3			4		11			9
1		10	7		5		2	8		6	3			4		11			9
1		10	7		5	9	2	8		6	3			4		11			
1			4	7	5	9	2	8			3			6		11			10
1		10	4	7	5	9	2	8		6	3								11
1		10	8	7	5	9	2			6	3			4		11			
1		10	7	8	5				9	6	3			4		11	2		
1		10	2	8	5				9	6	3			4	7	11			
1		10	2	8	5	9				6	3			4	7	11			
1	5	10	2	8		9			7	6	3			4		11			
1		10	2	8	5	9				6	3			4		11		7	
1		10	4			9			8	6	3			5		11	2	7	
27	1	26	27	26	28	23	23	23	4	29	28	2	3	18	2	29	3	2	6
	1	6	4	4	3	8	2	5		1				2	1	7			6

Allan Bill	Betts Billy	Brady Alex	Brandon Harry	Brash Archie	Crawshaw Tommy	Davis Harry	Earp Jack	Ferrier Bob	Fox William	Jamieson Jim	Langley Ambrose	Lowe H.G.	Massey Jack	Petrie Bob	Priestley R	Spiksley Fred	Sutherland George	Webster John	Woolhouse Harry
1		10	4	7	5	9	2	8			3			6		11			
1		10	4	7	5	9	2	8			3			6		11			
1		10	4	7	5	9	2	8			3			6		11			
1		10	4	7	5	9	2				3			6		11			8
4		4	4	4	4	4	4	3			4			4		4			1
		3		2		3		2								3			

Allan Bill	Betts Billy	Brady Alex	Brandon Harry	Brash Archie	Crawshaw Tommy	Davis Harry	Earp Jack	Ferrier Bob	Fox William	Jamieson Jim	Langley Ambrose	Lowe H.G.	Massey Jack	Petrie Bob	Priestley R	Spiksley Fred	Sutherland George	Webster John	Woolhouse Harry
1		10	2	7	5	9		8		6	3			4		11			

League Table

	P	W	D	L	F	A	Pts
Sunderland	30	21	5	4	80	37	47
Everton	30	18	6	6	82	50	42
Aston Villa	30	17	5	8	82	43	39
Preston North End	30	15	5	10	62	46	35
Blackburn Rovers	30	11	10	9	59	49	32
Sheffield United	30	14	4	12	57	55	32
Nottingham Forest	30	13	5	12	50	56	31
SHEFFIELD WEDNESDAY	30	12	4	14	50	55	28
Burnley	30	11	4	15	44	56	26
Bolton Wanderers	30	9	7	14	61	62	25
Wolverhampton W	30	9	7	14	43	63	25
Small Heath	30	9	7	14	50	74	25
West Bromwich Albion	30	10	4	16	51	66	24
Stoke	30	9	6	15	50	67	24
Derby County	30	7	9	14	45	68	23
Liverpool	30	7	8	15	51	70	22

1895-96

Division One

Manager: Arthur Dickinson

Did you know that?

Final League Position: 8th

On 18 April 1896, in the FA Cup Final against Wolves, Fred Spiksley scored the fastest goal in a Final and, as no accurate records of the times exist, it may still be the fastest goal to the present day.

Match No.	Date	Venue	Opponents		Round	Result	HT Score	Position	Scorers	Attendance
1	Sep 2	A	Everton	D		2-2	2-0		Bell, Crawshaw	14,000
2	7	H	Sheffield United	W		1-0	1-0	4th	Bell	15,000
3	14	A	Wolverhampton W	L		0-4	0-1	10th		6,000
4	28	A	Derby County	L		1-3	0-1	13th	Brash	10,000
5	Oct 5	H	West Bromwich Alb	W		5-3	2-1	12th	Spiksley (2), Brady, Earp (pen), Davis	8,000
6	12	H	Wolverhampton W	W		3-1	1-1	10th	Petrie, Brady, Brandon	10,000
7	19	H	Sunderland	W		3-0	2-0	8th	Davis (2), Bell	10,000
8	26	A	West Bromwich Alb	W		3-2	1-0	4th	Brash, Davis, Bell	5,500
9	Nov 2	H	Bolton Wanderers	D		1-1	0-0	6th	Sutcliffe (og)	7,000
10	9	A	Bury	L		1-6	1-4	8th	Brandon	4,000
11	16	H	Stoke	W		2-1	1-0	7th	Spiksley, Crawshaw	4,000
12	23	A	Blackburn Rovers	L		1-2	1-0	8th	Spiksley	5,000
13	30	H	Nottingham Forest	W		3-0	1-0	6th	Crawshaw, Brady, Brash	5,000
14	Dec 14	H	Burnley	W		1-0	1-0	6th	Brady	5,000
15	21	A	Stoke	L		0-5	0-3	7th		3,000
16	26	A	Sheffield United	D		1-1	1-0	8th	Ferrier	17,515
17	28	H	Derby County	L		0-4	0-1	8th		11,787
18	Jan 1	H	Preston North End	D		1-1	1-1	8th	Davis	9,000
19	4	A	Burnley	L		0-2	0-0	8th		3,500
20	11	H	Blackburn Rovers	W		3-0	1-0	7th	Spiksley, Richards, Bell	8,000
21	18	H	Aston Villa	L		1-3	1-1	7th	Spiksley	12,000
22	Feb 8	A	Small Heath	D		1-1	0-1	7th	Gooing	5,000
23	18	H	Everton	W		3-1	2-0	6th	Bell, Davis, Spiksley	10,000
24	22	H	Bury	L		1-3	1-1	6th	Spiksley	5,000
25	Mar 7	A	Sunderland	L		1-2	0-1	6th	Langley	6,000
26	14	A	Aston Villa	L		1-2	1-1	7th	Spiksley	10,000
27	Apr 4	H	Small Heath	W		3-0	3-0	9th	Davis, Bell, Spiksley	4,000
28	6	A	Preston North End	W		1-0	0-0	8th	Davis	3,000
29	7	A	Nottingham Forest	L		0-1	0-0	8th		6,500
30	25	A	Bolton Wanderers	L		0-2	0-2	8th		8,000
										Apps
									One own-goal	Goals

FA Cup

Match No.	Date	Venue	Opponents		Round	Result	HT Score	Position	Scorers	Attendance
31	Feb 1	A	Southampton St Mary	W	1st	3-2	2-1		Brady (2), Davis	8,000
32	15	H	Sunderland	W	2nd	2-1	2-0		Bell, Spiksley	22,000
33	29	H	Everton	W	3rd	4-0	2-0		Brash (2), Bell (2)	12,475
34	Mar 21	N	Bolton Wanderers *	D	S/F	1-1	0-1		Brash	37,000
35	28	N	Bolton Wanderers **	W	S/F Re	3-1	1-1		Crawshaw, Davis, Spiksley	15,000
36	Apr 18	N	Wolverhampton W #	W	Final	2-1	2-1		Spiksley (2)	48,836
										Apps
										Goals

* At Goodison Park, Liverpool
** At Trent Bridge, Nottingham
# Crystal Palace, London

Allan Bill	Bell Lawrie	Brady Alec	Brandon Harry	Brash Archie	Callaghan John	Crawshaw Tommy	Davis Harry	Earp Jack	Ferrier Bob	Gooing William	Jamieson Jim	Langley Ambrose	Massey Jack	Petrie Bob	Richards Anthony	Spiksley Fred
1	9	10		7		5		2	8		6	3		4		11
1	9	10		7		5		2	8		6	3		4		11
1	9	10		7		5		2	8		6	3		4		11
1		10	4	7		5	9	2	8		6	3				11
1	9	10	4	7		5	8	2				3		6		11
	9	10	4	7		5	8	2				3	1	6		11
	9		3	7		5	10	2	8		6		1	4		11
	9		4	7		5	10	2	8			3	1	6		11
	9	10	4	7		5	8	2			6	3	1			11
	9	10	4			5	7	2	8		6	3	1			11
1	9		4	7		5	10	2	8		6	3				11
1	9		4	7		5	10	2	8		6	3				11
1	9	10	4	7		5		2	8			3		6		11
1	9	10	4	7		5		2	8			3		6		11
1	9	10	4			5		2	8			3		6	7	11
1	9	10	4	7		5		2	8			3		6		11
1	9	10	4	7		5		2	8			3		6		11
1		10	4	7		5	9	2	8		6	3				11
1		10			4	5	9	2	8		6	3			7	11
1	9	8	4			5	10	2			6	3			7	11
	9	8	4			5	10	2			6	3	1		7	11
		8	3			5	10	2		9	6		1	4	7	11
	9			8		5	10	2	4		6	3	1		7	11
		10	4			5		2	8	9	6	3	1		7	11
	10	11		7	4			2	8	9	6	3	1	5		
	9	10		7		5		2	8		6	3	1	4		11
	9	8	4	7			10	2			6	3	1	5		11
	9		2	7	4		10		8		6	3	1	5		11
		10		7		5	9	2	8		6	3	1	4		11
	9	8	4			5	10	2	7			3	1	6		11
15	24	24	22	22	3	27	19	29	23	3	21	28	15	19	7	29
	7	4	2	3		3	8	1	1	1		1		1	1	10

Allan Bill	Bell Lawrie	Brady Alec	Brandon Harry	Brash Archie	Callaghan John	Crawshaw Tommy	Davis Harry	Earp Jack	Ferrier Bob	Gooing William	Jamieson Jim	Langley Ambrose	Massey Jack	Petrie Bob	Richards Anthony	Spiksley Fred
	9	8	3			5	10	2			6		1	4	7	11
	9	8	4			5	10	2	7		6	3	1			11
	9	8	3	7		5	10	2			6		1	4		11
	9	8	3	7		5	10	2			6		1	4		11
	9	8	4	7		5	10	2				3	1	6		11
	9	8	4	7		5	10	2				3	1	6		11
	6	6	6	4		6	6	6	1		4	3	6	5	1	6
	3	2		3		1	2									4

League Table

	P	W	D	L	F	A	Pts
Aston Villa	30	20	5	5	78	45	45
Derby County	30	17	7	6	68	35	41
Everton	30	16	7	7	66	43	39
Bolton Wanderers	30	16	5	9	49	37	37
Sunderland	30	15	7	8	52	41	37
Stoke	30	15	0	15	56	47	30
SHEFFIELD WEDNESDAY	30	12	5	13	44	53	29
Blackburn Rovers	30	12	5	13	40	50	29
Preston North End	30	11	6	13	44	48	28
Burnley	30	10	7	13	48	44	27
Bury	30	12	3	15	50	54	27
Sheffield United	30	10	6	14	40	50	26
Nottingham Forest	30	11	3	16	42	57	25
Wolverhampton W	30	10	1	19	61	65	21
Small Heath	30	8	4	18	39	79	20
West Bromwich Albion	30	6	7	17	30	59	19

1896-97

Division One

Manager: Arthur Dickinson

Did you know that?

Final League Position: 6th

On Boxing Day 1896 Wednesday met Sheffield United at Bramall Lane with a then record gate for a game in Sheffield of 30,000. The record receipts figure still remained, however, set at Olive Grove on 2 March 1895 in an FA Cup tie versus Everton.

Match No.	Date	Venue	Opponents		Round	Result	HT Score	Position	Scorers	Attendance
1	Sep 1	H	Liverpool	L		1-2	1-2	6th	Davis	10,000
2	5	A	Everton	L		1-2	1-0	16th	Davis	18,000
3	12	H	West Bromwich Alb	W		3-1	2-0	12th	Brash, Callaghan (2)	7,000
4	19	A	Blackburn Rovers	L		0-4	0-1	14th		6,000
5	26	H	Stoke	W		4-3	1-3	11th	Spiksley, Brady, Bell, Earp	5,000
6	Oct 3	A	West Bromwich Alb	W		2-0	1-0	9th	Spiksley, Brady	10,291
7	10	H	Sunderland	D		0-0	0-0	8th		10,000
8	17	A	Bury	D		1-1	0-1	8th	Davis	2,000
9	24	H	Everton	W		4-1	2-0	6th	Ferrier, Spiksley, Brady, Bell	4,000
10	31	A	Nottingham Forest	D		2-2	1-2	6th	Spiksley (2)	6,000
11	Nov 14	H	Aston Villa	L		1-3	0-1	7th	Brady	8,000
12	21	A	Aston Villa	L		0-4	0-0	10th		14,000
13	28	H	Derby County	W		2-0	1-0	9th	Spiksley (2)	10,000
14	Dec 5	A	Sunderland	D		0-0	0-0	8th		1,000
15	12	H	Wolverhampton W	D		0-0	0-0	9th		1,000
16	19	A	Burnley	D		1-1	1-1	8th	Brady	4,500
17	26	A	Sheffield United	L		0-2	0-1	9th		30,000
18	28	H	Blackburn Rovers	W		6-0	3-0	8th	Brash, Brady, Ferrier (3), Porter (og)	5,000
19	Jan 2	H	Preston North End	W		1-0	0-0	9th	Spiksley	12,000
20	9	A	Derby County	L		1-2	1-1	9th	Ferrier	5,000
21	23	A	Stoke	D		0-0	0-0	9th		4,000
22	Feb 20	A	Preston North End	D		2-2	0-1		Spiksley, Brash	5,000
23	27	H	Bolton Wanderers	D		0-0	0-0	8th		7,000
24	Mar 2	H	Sheffield United	D		1-1	1-0	8th	Brandon	11,500
25	6	H	Burnley	W		1-0	1-0	6th	Brash	5,000
26	13	A	Wolverhampton W	L		0-2	0-1	7th		5,000
27	Apr 3	A	Liverpool	D		2-2	1-0	7th	Davis, Brady	6,000
28	5	H	Nottingham Forest	W		3-0	2-0		Davis (2), Beech	1,900
29	10	A	Bolton Wanderers	L		1-2	1-1	7th	Spiksley	2,000
30	17	H	Bury	W		2-0	1-0	6th	Ferrier, Bell	1,000
										Apps
									One own-goal	Goals

FA Cup

Match No.	Date	Venue	Opponents		Round	Result	HT Score	Position	Scorers	Attendance
31	Jan 30	H	Nottingham Forest	L	1R	0-1	0-1			16,639
										Apps

Beech George	Bell Lawrie	Brady Alex	Brandon Harry	Brash Archie	Callaghan John	Crawshaw Tommy	Davis Harry	Earp Jack	Ferrier Bob	Gillies Alex	Jamieson Jim	Langley Ambrose	Massey Jack	Melia Jimmy	Petrie Bob	Regan Bill	Spiksley Fred
	9	8		7		5	10	2				3	1		6	4	11
	9	8		7		5	10				6	3	1	2	4		11
	9		2	7	10	5			8		6	3	1			4	11
	9	10	4	7		5		2	8			3	1		6		11
	9	10	4	7		5		2	8			3	1		6		11
	9	10	4	7		5		2	8		6	3	1				11
	9	8	4	7		5	10	2			6	3	1				11
	9	10		7		5	11	2	8		6	3	1			4	
	9	10	4			5	7	2	8		6	3	1				11
	9	10	4	7		5	8	2			6	3	1				11
	9	10	4	7		5	8	2			6	3	1				11
	9		4	7		5	10	2	8		6	3	1				11
	9	8	4	7		5	10	2			6	3	1				11
	9	8	4	7		5	10					3	1	2	6		11
	9	8		7		5	10				6	3	1	2	4		11
	9	8		7		5	10				6	3	1	2	4		11
	9	8		7		5	10	2			6	3	1		4		11
		10		7		5	9	2	8		6	3	1		4		11
		10		7		5	9	2	8		6	3	1		4		11
	11	10		7		5	9	2	8		6	3	1		4		
		10	4	7		5	9	2	8			3	1		6		11
		10	4	7			9	2	8		6	3	1		5		11
	9		4	7		5	10	2	8			3	1		6		11
		10	4	7		5	9	2	8			3	1		6		11
		10	4	7		5		2	8	9	6	3	1				11
		10	4	7		5		2	8	9	6	3	1				11
	7	10	4				9	2	8		6	3	1			5	11
10	7		4				9		8		6	3	1	2		5	11
		10	3	7		5	9		8		6	2	1			4	11
	9		2	7		5	10		8		6	3	1			4	11
1	22	25	21	27	1	27	24	22	20	2	23	30	30	5	15	7	28
1	3	7	1	4	2		6	1	6								10
	9	11	4	7		5	10	2	8			3	1		6		
	1	1	1	1		1	1	1	1			1	1		1		

League Table

	P	W	D	L	F	A	Pts
Aston Villa	30	21	5	4	73	38	47
Sheffield United	30	13	10	7	42	29	36
Derby County	30	16	4	10	70	50	36
Preston North End	30	11	12	7	55	40	34
Liverpool	30	12	9	9	46	38	33
SHEFFIELD WEDNESDAY	30	10	11	9	42	37	31
Everton	30	14	3	13	62	57	31
Bolton Wanderers	30	12	6	12	40	43	30
Bury	30	10	10	10	39	44	30
Wolverhampton W	30	11	6	13	45	41	28
Nottingham Forest	30	9	8	13	44	49	26
West Bromwich Albion	30	10	6	14	33	56	26
Stoke	30	11	3	16	48	59	25
Blackburn Rovers	30	11	3	16	35	62	25
Sunderland	30	7	9	14	34	47	23
Burnley	30	6	7	17	43	61	19

1897-98

Division One

Manager: Arthur Dickinson

Did you know that?

Final League Position: 5th

On 12 February 1898, in an FA Cup tie at Stoney Lane, West Bromwich, Wednesday's Ambrose Langley knocked the ball out for a throw-in and picked up the ball as it bounced back into play. The linesman gave a free-kick for handball, from which Albion netted for the only goal of the game.

Match No.	Date	Venue	Opponents		Round	Result	HT Score	Position	Scorers	Attendance
1	Sep 1	A	Aston Villa	L		2-5	1-2		Dryburgh, Davis	10,000
2	4	H	Sunderland	L		0-1	0-0	16th		6,000
3	11	A	Bury	L		0-3	0-2	16th		8,000
4	18	H	Liverpool	W		4-2	0-1	14th	Earp (pen), Kaye (2), Ferrier	8,000
5	25	A	Sunderland	L		0-1	0-1	16th		13,500
6	27	H	Aston Villa	W		3-0	1-0	11th	Spiksley (2), Ferrier	12,000
7	Oct 2	H	Notts County	W		3-1	2-1	8th	Kaye, Spiksley (2)	12,000
8	9	A	Bolton Wanderers	W		3-0	2-0	4th	Crawshaw, Brady, Spiksley	6,000
9	16	H	Sheffield United	L		0-1	0-1	8th		24,000
10	23	A	Blackburn Rovers	D		1-1	0-1	10th	Spiksley	5,000
11	Nov 13	H	Blackburn Rovers	W		4-1	1-1	9th	Kaye (2), Spiksley (2)	6,000
12	20	H	Bury	W		3-0	1-0	5th	Potts, Spiksley (2)	7,000
13	27	H	Bolton Wanderers	W		3-0	1-0	5th	Brady, Spiksley, Crawshaw	6,000
14	Dec 4	A	Notts County	D		0-0	0-0	5th		3,000
15	11	H	Preston North End	W		2-1	0-1	4th	Kaye, Brady	5,000
16	18	A	Preston North End	L		0-2	0-1	6th		4,000
17	25	H	Stoke	W		4-0	4-0	3rd	Kaye, Spiksley, Brandon, Crawshaw	12,500
18	27	A	Sheffield United	D		1-1	0-1	5th	Spiksley	37,389
19	Jan 1	H	Nottingham Forest	L		3-6	3-4	5th	Jamieson, Dryburgh, Brady	8,500
20	8	A	Everton	L		0-1	0-1	7th		14,000
21	15	H	Derby County	W		3-1	0-0	5th	Dryburgh, Spiksley (pen), Fryer (og)	8,000
22	22	A	Nottingham Forest	L		0-1	0-0	6th		8,000
23	Feb 5	H	Everton	W		2-1	0-0	5th	Jamieson, Langley	12,000
24	19	A	Derby County	W		2-1	0-0		Methven (og), Spiksley	8,000
25	Mar 5	H	Wolves	W		2-0	2-0	3rd	Brady (2)	8,000
26	12	A	West Bromwich Alb	W		2-0	1-0	3rd	Brady, Kaye	3,500
27	26	A	Stoke	L		1-2	1-0	3rd	Spiksley	1,000
28	Apr 9	H	West Bromwich Alb	W		3-0	0-0		Kaye, Brady, Spiksley	7,000
29	11	A	Liverpool	L		0-4	0-2			7,000
30	16	A	Wolves	L		0-5	0-1	5th		8,000
										Apps
									Two own-goals	Goals

FA Cup

Match No.	Date	Venue	Opponents		Round	Result	HT Score	Position	Scorers	Attendance
31	Jan 29	A	Sunderland	W	1R	1-0	0-0		Kaye	18,000
32	Feb 12	A	West Bromwich Alb	L	2R	0-1	0-0			16,000
										Apps
										Goals

Brady Alec	Brandon Harry	Brash Archie	Crawshaw Tommy	Davis Harry	Dryburgh William	Earp Jack	Ferrier Bob	Jamieson Jim	Kaye Albert	Langley Ambrose	Layton Willie	Mallinson W.H	Massey Jack	Melia Jimmy	Potts Harry	Regan Bill	Spiksley Fred	Stevenson Thomas
10	4		5	9	7	2	8			3			1			6	11	
10	4		5	9	7	2	8			3			1				11	6
	4		5	10	7	2	8		9	3			1			6	11	
	4	7	5	10		2	8	6	9	3			1				11	
	4	7	5	10		2	8	6	9	3			1				11	
10	4	7	5			2	8	6	9	3			1				11	
10	4	7	5			2	8	6	9	3			1				11	
10	4	7	5				8	6	9	3			1	2			11	
10	4	7	5			2	8	6	9	3			1				11	
10	4	7	5			2	8	6	9	3			1				11	
10	4	7	5			2	8	6	9	3			1				11	
8	4	7	5			2		6	9	3			1		10		11	
10	4	7	5			2	8	6	9	3			1				11	
10	4	7	5	8		2		6	9	3			1				11	
10	4	7	5			2	8	6	9	3			1				11	
10	4	7	5			2	8	6	9	3			1				11	
10	4	7	5			2	8	6	9	3			1				11	
10	4	7	5			2	8	6	9	3			1				11	
10	4	7	5		9	2	8	6					1	3			11	
10	4	7	5		9	2	8	6			3		1				11	
10	4	7	5		9	2	8	6			3		1				11	
10			5		8	2	7	6	9	3			1				11	4
10			5	8	7	2	4	6	9	3		1					11	
10			5	8	7	2	4	6	9	3			1				11	
10			5	8	7	2	4	6	9	3			1				11	
10			5	8	7	2	4	6	9	3			1				11	
10	2		5	8	7		4	6	9	3			1				11	
10	3		5	8	7	2	4	6	9				1				11	
10	6		5	8	7	2	4		9	3			1				11	
10	6		5	8	7	2	4		9	3			1				11	
27	25	18	30	14	15	28	28	25	25	26	2	1	29	2	1	2	30	2
8	1		3	1	3	1	2	2	9	1					1		17	

Brady Alec	Brandon Harry	Brash Archie	Crawshaw Tommy	Davis Harry	Dryburgh William	Earp Jack	Ferrier Bob	Jamieson Jim	Kaye Albert	Langley Ambrose	Layton Willie	Mallinson W.H	Massey Jack	Melia Jimmy	Potts Harry	Regan Bill	Spiksley Fred	Stevenson Thomas
10			5	8	7	2	4	6	9	3			1				11	
10			5	8	7	2	4	6	9	3			1				11	
2			2	2	2	2	2	2	2	2			2				2	
									1									

League Table

	P	W	D	L	F	A	Pts
Sheffield United	30	17	8	5	56	31	42
Sunderland	30	16	5	9	43	30	37
Wolverhampton W	30	14	7	9	57	41	35
Everton	30	13	9	8	48	39	35
SHEFFIELD WEDNESDAY	30	15	3	12	51	42	33
Aston Villa	30	14	5	11	61	51	33
West Bromwich Albion	30	11	10	9	44	45	32
Nottingham Forest	30	11	9	10	47	49	31
Liverpool	30	11	6	13	48	45	28
Derby County	30	11	6	13	57	61	28
Bolton Wanderers	30	11	4	15	28	41	26
Preston North End	30	8	8	14	35	43	24
Notts County	30	8	8	14	36	46	24
Bury	30	8	8	14	39	51	24
Blackburn Rovers	30	7	10	13	39	54	24
Stoke	30	8	8	14	35	55	24

1898-99

Division One

Manager: Arthur Dickinson

Did you know that?

Final League Position: 18th

With Wednesday beating Aston Villa 3–1 on 26 November 1898, and with 10 and a half minutes still to play, the match was abandoned due to poor light. The remaining 10 and a half minutes were played on 13 March 1899, with Wednesday netting again to finish 4–1 winners.

Match No.	Date	Venue	Opponents		Round	Result	HT Score	Position	Scorers	Attendance
1	Sep 3	A	Liverpool	L		0-4	0-1	18th		18,000
2	10	H	Nottingham Forest	W		2-1	1-1	14th	Hemmingfield, Dryburgh	11,000
3	17	A	Bolton Wanderers	D		0-0	0-0	13th		3,000
4	19	H	Preston North End	W		2-1	1-0	5th	Dryburgh, Hemmingfield	4,000
5	24	H	Derby County	W		3-1	0-0	2nd	Spiksley, Brady, Hemmingfield	11,000
6	Oct 1	A	West Bromwich Alb	L		0-2	0-1	6th		6,767
7	3	H	Sheffield United	D		1-1	1-1	3rd	Hemmingfield	16,000
8	8	H	Blackburn Rovers	L		1-2	1-1	7th	Dryburgh	14,000
9	15	H	Bury	W		3-2	3-1	6th	Hemmingfield (2), Dryburgh	6,000
10	22	A	Sunderland	L		0-2	0-1	8th		7,000
11	29	H	Wolverhampton W	W		3-0	3-0	7th	Kaye (3)	8,500
12	Nov 5	A	Everton	L		0-2	0-0	8th		15,000
13	12	H	Notts County	D		1-1	1-0	8th	Crawshaw	12,000
14	19	A	Stoke	L		0-1	0-1	10th		7,000
15	26	H	Aston Villa *	W		4-1	2-1	8th	Crawshaw, Dryburgh, Hemmingfield	16,500
16	Dec 3	A	Burnley	L		0-5	0-5	15th		6,000
17	17	A	Newcastle United	D		2-2	2-1	11th	Wright, Spiksley	15,500
18	26	A	Sheffield United	L		1-2	0-1	18th	Hemmingfield	32,500
19	31	H	Liverpool	L		0-3	0-1	18th		4,000
20	Jan 2	A	Bury	D		0-0	0-0	16th		6,000
21	7	A	Nottingham Forest	D		1-1	0-1	16th	Cole	9,000
22	14	H	Bolton Wanderers	W		1-0	0-0	16th	Davis	8,000
23	21	A	Derby County	L		0-9	0-4	16th		4,700
24	Feb 4	A	Blackburn Rovers	L		0-2	0-2	17th		4,000
25	14	H	West Bromwich Alb	L		1-2	0-0	17th	Beech	7,500
26	18	H	Sunderland	L		0-1	0-1	17th		12,000
27	25	A	Wolverhampton W	D		0-0	0-0	17th		4,000
28	Mar 4	H	Everton	L		1-2	0-0	17th	Crawshaw (pen)	7,000
29	11	A	Notts County	L		0-1	0-0	17h		5,000
30	25	A	Aston Villa	L		1-3	0-1	17th	Spiksley	15,000
31	27	H	Stoke	L		1-3	0-2	17th	Crawshaw (pen)	12,000
32	Apr 1	H	Burnley	W		1-0	0-0	17th	Wright (pen)	5,500
33	15	H	Newcastle United	L		1-3	1-1	18th	Hutton	4,000
34	22	A	Preston North End	D		1-1	0-1	18th	Wright	4,000
15A	Mar 13	H	Aston Villa *	W					Richards	3,000

* Match abandoned with the score at 3-1 to Wednesday after 79.5 minutes. Apps

The outstanding 10.5 minutes were played on March 13 when Wednesday added another goal Goals

to make the final score 4-1 (Players who played in both parts of the Aston Villa game are counted as one appearance. Those who played in one part of the game are also counted as one appearance)

FA Cup

Match No.	Date	Venue	Opponents		Round	Result	HT Score	Position	Scorers	Attendance
35	Jan 28	H	Stoke	D	1R	2-2	1-1		Crawshaw, Earp	20,000
36	Feb 2	A	Stoke	L	1R Re	0-2	0-1			11,000

Apps

Goals

Beech George	Bosworth Sam	Brady Alec	Cole William	Crawshaw Tommy	Davis Harry	Dryburgh William	Earp Jack	Ferrier Bob	Hemmingfield Bill	Hutton Robert	Jamieson Jim	Kaye Albert	Langley Ambrose	Layton Willie	Mallinson W.H	Massey Jack	McCafferty Michael	Potts Harry	Pryce Jack	Richards Fred	Ruddlesdin Harry	Spiksley Fred	Topham Jack	Wright Jocky
		10		5	8	7	2	4			6	9	3			1						11		
				5	10	7	2	4	9			8	3			1					6	11		
			8	5	10	7	2	4	9				3			1					6	11		
				5	10	7		4	9			8	3	2		1					6	11		
		8		5	10	7	2	4	9					3		1					6	11		
8				5	10	7	2	4	9					3		1					6	11		
		8		5	10	7	2	4	9					3		1					6	11		
				5		7	8	4	9			10	3	2		1					6	11		
		10		5	8	7		4	9				3	2		1					6	11		
		10		5	8	7	2	4	9					3		1					6		11	
				5	8	7	2	4	10			9	3			1					6	11		
					8	7	2	4	10			9	3	6		1					5	11		
				5	8	7	2	4	10			9	3			1					6	11		
		10		5	8	7	2	4	9					3		1					6	11		
				5	8	7	2		9		4			3		1					6	11		10
				5	8	7	2		9		4			3		1					6	11		10
			2	5	8			4	9			7	3			1					6	11		10
				5	8	7	2	4	9				3			1					6	11		10
				5	7			4	9			8	3	2		1					6	11		10
				5	8			4	9			7	3	2	1						6	11		10
			7	5	8			4				9	3	2		1					6	11		10
			7	5	8		2	4				9	3			1					6	11		10
				5		7	2	4	8			9	3			1					6	11		10
			7	5	8	10		4				9	3	2		1					6		11	
8				5		7	2	4				9	3			1					6		11	10
				5			2	4	9		6		3			1		8			11	7		10
				5	9	7	2	4				8		3		1					6		11	10
	7			5			2	4						3		1			9	8	6	11		10
	7			5	9		2	4						3		1			8		6	11		10
	7			5			2	4					3			1			9	8	6	11		10
				5	7		2	4		8			3			1			9		6	11		10
	7						2	4	9				3			1	5		8		6	11		10
	7			5			2	4		9			3			1			8		6	11		10
	7			5			2	4		9				3		1			8		6	11		10
	7			5			2	4					3			1			9	8	6	11		10
2	7	6	5	32	25	21	27	33	22	3	4	16	24	19	1	33	1	1	8	3	33	30	4	19
1		1	1	4	1	5			8	1		3								1		3		3

Beech George	Bosworth Sam	Brady Alec	Cole William	Crawshaw Tommy	Davis Harry	Dryburgh William	Earp Jack	Ferrier Bob	Hemmingfield Bill	Hutton Robert	Jamieson Jim	Kaye Albert	Langley Ambrose	Layton Willie	Mallinson W.H	Massey Jack	McCafferty Michael	Potts Harry	Pryce Jack	Richards Fred	Ruddlesdin Harry	Spiksley Fred	Topham Jack	Wright Jocky
		10	7	5	8		2	4					3			1					6		11	9
			7	5	8		2	4				9	3			1					6		11	10
		1	2	2	2		2	2				1	2			2					2		2	2
				1			1																	

League Table

	P	W	D	L	F	A	Pts
Aston Villa	34	19	7	8	76	40	45
Liverpool	34	19	5	10	49	33	43
Burnley	34	15	9	10	45	47	39
Everton	34	15	8	11	48	41	38
Notts County	34	12	13	9	47	51	37
Blackburn Rovers	34	14	8	12	60	52	36
Sunderland	34	15	6	13	41	41	36
Wolverhampton W	34	14	7	13	54	48	35
Derby County	34	12	11	11	62	57	35
Bury	34	14	7	13	48	49	35
Nottingham Forest	34	11	11	12	42	42	33
Stoke	34	13	7	14	47	52	33
Newcastle United	34	11	8	15	49	48	30
West Bromwich Albion	34	12	6	16	42	57	30
Preston North End	34	10	9	15	44	47	29
Sheffield United	34	9	11	14	45	51	29
Bolton Wanderers	34	9	7	18	37	51	25
SHEFFIELD WEDNESDAY	34	8	8	18	32	61	24

1899-1900

Division Two

Manager: Arthur Dickinson

Did you know that?

Final League Position: 1st

Wednesday were unbeaten for the whole League season at home (17 games), winning all their Owlerton games to win the title. They did lose in an FA Cup replay against local city rivals, Sheffield United.

Match No.	Date	Venue	Opponents		Round	Result	HT Score	Position	Scorers	Attendance
1	Sep 2	H	Chesterfield	W		5-1	2-1	4th	Spiksley, Ferrier, Millar (2), Brash	12,000
2	9	A	Gainsborough Trinity	W		2-0	1-0	1st	Millar, Wright	4,000
3	16	H	Bolton Wanderers	W		2-1	2-0	2nd	Spiksley, Millar	10,000
4	23	A	Loughborough Town	D		0-0	0-0	3rd		7,500
5	30	H	Newton Heath	W		2-1	1-1	3rd	Wright, Langley	8,000
6	Oct 7	A	Burton Swifts	W		5-0	1-0	3rd	Millar, Wright, Crawshaw, Spiksley, Lee	2,000
7	14	A	Lincoln City	W		2-1	1-0	3rd	Wright, Spiksley	5,000
8	21	H	Small Heath	W		4-0	4-0	1st	Wright (2), Millar, Spiksley	9,000
9	Nov 11	A	Woolwich Arsenal	W		2-1	2-0	2nd	Wright (2)	8,000
10	25	A	Leicester Fosse	D		0-0	0-0	1st		12,000
11	Dec 2	H	Luton Town	W		6-0	4-0	1st	Pryce (2), Spiksley (3), Wright	12,000
12	16	H	Walsall	W		2-0	1-0	1st	Spiksley, Millar	4,000
13	23	A	Middlesbrough	W		2-1	2-1	1st	Brash, Spiksley	6,000
14	25	A	New Brighton Tower	D		2-2	1-1	1st	Brash, Wright	5,500
15	30	A	Chesterfield	L		0-1	0-1	2nd		4,000
16	Jan 1	H	Grimsby Town	W		2-1	0-1	1st	Langley, Wright	15,000
17	6	H	Gainsborough Trinity	W		5-1	1-1	2nd	Millar (4), Brash	3,000
18	13	A	Bolton Wanderers	L		0-1	0-0	2nd		15,000
19	20	H	Loughborough Town	W		5-0	3-0	2nd	Millar, Wright (2), Topham, Langley (pen)	4,000
20	Feb 3	A	Newton Heath	L		0-1	0-0	2nd		11,000
21	12	A	Burslem Port Vale	W		3-0	1-0	4th	Millar (2), Wright	2,000
22	24	A	Small Heath	L		1-4	1-2	4th	Davis	9,000
23	27	H	Barnsley	W		5-1	2-0	1st	Brash, Davis, Wright (3).	3,000
24	Mar 3	H	New Brighton Tower	W		4-0	2-0	1st	Wright (2), Pryce, Brash	5,000
25	12	H	Burton Swifts	W		6-0	2-0	1st	Topham, Wright, Ferrier, Ruddlesdin, Crawshaw, Earp	3,000
26	17	H	Woolwich Arsenal	W		3-1	2-0	1st	Davis (2), Ruddlesdin	4,500
27	24	A	Barnsley	L		0-1	0-0	1st		5,000
28	31	H	Leicester Fosse	W		2-0	0-0	1st	Beech, Wright	13,500
29	Apr 7	A	Luton Town	W		1-0	0-0	1st	Langley	1,000
30	13	A	Grimsby Town	W		2-1	0-1	1st	Crawshaw, Wright	8,000
31	14	H	Burslem Port Vale	W		4-0	2-0	1st	Davis, Wright (3)	5,000
32	17	H	Lincoln City	W		1-0	1-0	1st	Ruddlesdin	6,000
33	21	A	Walsall	D		1-1	0-1	1st	Langley	3,000
34	28	H	Middlesbrough	W		3-0	1-0	1st	Davis (2), Pryce	4,000
										Apps
										Goals

FA Cup

35	Jan 27	H	Bolton Wanderers	W	1R	1-0	0-0		Wright	12,390
36	Feb 17	A	Sheffield United	D	2R	1-1	1-0		Brash	28,374
37	19	H	Sheffield United	L	2R Re	0-2	0-0			23,000
										Apps
										Goals

FA Cup match abandoned after 50 minutes (Snow)

38	Feb 10	A	Sheffield United	D	2R	0-0	0-0			32,381

Beech George	Bolsover Henry	Brash Archie	Crawshaw Percy	Crawshaw Tommy	Davis Harry "Pluck"	Earp Jack	Ferrier Bob	Hutton Robert	Langley Ambrose	Layton Willie	Lee George	Mallinson W.H	Massey Jack	Millar Harry	Pryce Jack	Ruddlesdin Harry	Simmons William	Spiksley Fred	Topham Jack	Wright Jocky
		7		5		2	4		3				1	9	8	6		11		10
		7		5			4		3	2			1	9	8	6		11		10
				5			4		3	2	7		1	9	8	6		11		10
		7		5			4		3	2			1	9	8	6		11		10
				5			4		3	2	7		1	9	8	6		11		10
				5			4		3	2	7		1	9	8	6		11		10
				5			4		3	2	7		1	9	8	6		11		10
				5			4		3	2	7		1	9	8	6		11		10
		7		5			4		3	2			1	9	8	6		11		10
		7		5			4		3	2			1	9	8	6		11		10
		7		5			4		3	2			1	9	8	6		11		10
		7		5			4		3	2			1	9	8	6		11		10
		7		5			4		3	2			1	9	8	6		11		10
		7		5			4		3	2			1	9	8	6		11		10
		7	4	5				8	3	2			1	9		6		11		10
		7	4	5					3	2			1	9	8	6		11		10
		7		5			4		3	2			1	9	8	6		11		10
		7		5			4		3	2			1	9	8	6		11		10
				5			4		3	2			1	9	8	6	7		11	10
		7		5	8		4		3	2			1		9	6			11	10
		7		5			4		3	2			1	9	8	6		11		10
10		7		5	9		4		3	2		1			8	6			11	
		7		5	9		4		3	2		1			8	6			11	10
		7		5	9		4		3	2		1			8	6			11	10
	1	7		5	8	2	4			3				9		6			11	10
	1	7		5	8	2	4			3				9		6		11		10
		7		5	9	2	4			3			1		8	6			11	10
9				5	7	2	4			3			1		8	6			11	10
		7		5	8		4		3	2			1	9	10	6				11
				5	7		4		3	2			1	9	8	6		11		10
		7		5	11		4		3	2			1	9	8	6				10
		7		5	11		4		3	2			1	9	8	6				10
		7		5	11		4		3	2			1	9	8	6				10
		7		5	11		4		3	2			1	9	8	6				10
2	2	26	2	34	14	5	32	1	30	33	5	3	29	28	31	34	1	21	8	33
1		6		3	7	1	2		5		1			14	4	3		10	2	25
		7		5			4		3	2			1	9	8	6			11	10
		7		5			4		3	2			1	9	8	6		11		10
		7		5			4		3	2	9	1			8	6			11	10
		3		3			3		3	3	1	1	2	2	3	3		1	2	3
		1																		1
		7		5			4		3	2			1	9	8	6		11		10

League Table

	P	W	D	L	F	A	Pts
SHEFFIELD WEDNESDAY	34	25	4	5	84	22	54
Bolton Wanderers	34	22	8	4	79	25	52
Small Heath	34	20	6	8	78	38	46
Newton Heath	34	20	4	10	63	27	44
Leicester Fosse	34	17	9	8	53	36	43
Grimsby Town	34	17	6	11	67	46	40
Chesterfield	34	16	6	12	65	60	38
Woolwich Arsenal	34	16	4	14	61	43	36
Lincoln City	34	14	8	12	47	43	36
New Brighton Tower	34	13	9	12	66	58	35
Burslem Port Vale	34	14	6	14	39	50	34
Walsall	34	12	8	14	50	55	32
Gainsborough Trinity	34	9	7	18	47	75	25
Middlesbrough	34	8	8	18	39	69	24
Burton Swifts	34	9	6	19	43	84	24
Barnsley	34	8	7	19	46	79	23
Luton Town	34	5	8	21	40	75	18
Loughborough	34	1	6	27	18	100	8

1900-01

Division One

Manager: Arthur Dickinson

Did you know that?

Final League Position: 8th

On 26 January 1901 Wednesday's home game against Bury in the first round of the FA Cup was postponed due to the death of Queen Victoria, on 22 January 1901. The next home game against Nottingham Forest, the following week, was also postponed.

Match No.	Date	Venue	Opponents		Round	Result	HT Score	Position	Scorers	Attendance
1	Sep 1	A	Manchester City	D		2-2	2-1		Wright (2)	20,000
2	8	H	Bolton Wanderers	W		1-0	0-0	7th	Wright	20,000
3	15	A	Bury	L		0-2	0-0	11th		11,000
4	22	H	Notts County	W		4-1	1-0	7th	Wright, Wilson (2), Crawshaw	17,500
5	29	A	Nottingham Forest	L		0-1	0-0	10th		12,000
6	Oct 6	H	Preston North End	L		0-1	0-1	10th		10,000
7	13	A	Blackburn Rovers	D		2-2	1-0	12th	Malloch, Wilson	3,000
8	27	A	Stoke	L		1-2	1-1	15th	Millar	6,000
9	Nov 3	H	Aston Villa	W		3-2	1-2	15th	Wilson, Wright, Davis	22,000
10	10	A	West Bromwich Alb	D		1-1	1-1	14th	Wright	10,338
11	17	H	Liverpool	W		3-2	3-2	12th	Crawshaw, Wilson (2)	10,000
12	24	A	Everton	D		1-1	1-1	12th	Davis	12,000
13	Dec 1	H	Newcastle United	D		2-2	1-1	13th	Malloch, Ferrier	12,000
14	8	A	Sunderland	L		0-1	0-1	14th		8,000
15	15	A	Sheffield United	L		0-1	0-0	14th		25,000
16	22	H	Derby County	W		2-1	1-0	12th	Malloch, Wright	6,000
17	26	A	Wolverhampton W	D		1-1	1-1	12th	Wilson	13,000
18	29	H	Manchester City	W		4-1	0-0	12th	Wilson, Pryce, Malloch, Davis	15,000
19	Jan 1	H	Wolverhampton W	W		2-0	1-0	10th	Wright, Pryce	20,000
20	5	A	Bolton Wanderers	D		1-1	0-0	11th	Wright	10,000
21	12	H	Bury	L		1-2	1-1	11th	Wilson	10,000
22	19	A	Notts County	L		0-2	0-1	12th		6,000
23	Feb 16	H	Blackburn Rovers	D		1-1	1-0	10th	Chapman	7,000
24	Mar 2	H	Stoke	W		4-0	2-0	11th	Wright, Davis, Wilson, Chapman	4,000
25	9	A	Aston Villa	L		1-2	0-1	13th	Spiksley	16,000
26	16	H	West Bromwich Alb	W		2-1	1-1	11th	Millar, Davis	9,000
27	23	A	Liverpool	D		1-1	0-1	10th	Spiksley	12,000
28	30	H	Everton	W		3-1	1-0	8th	Chapman (2), Spiksley	4,500
29	Apr 5	A	Preston North End	L		2-3	0-0	8th	Chapman, Spiksley	8,000
30	6	A	Newcastle United	D		0-0	0-0	8th		15,000
31	9	H	Nottingham Forest	W		4-1	1-1	8th	Wilson, Langley (pen), Layton, Crawshaw	18,000
32	13	H	Sunderland	W		1-0	0-0	8th	Wilson	14,000
33	27	A	Derby County	L		1-3	0-2	8th	Chapman	4,000
34	29	H	Sheffield United	W		1-0	0-0	8th	Wilson	11,000
										Apps
										Goals

FA Cup

Match No.	Date	Venue	Opponents		Round	Result	HT Score	Position	Scorers	Attendance
35	Feb 9	H	Bury	L	1R	0-1	0-0			27,000
										Apps

Chapman Harry	Cole William	Crawshaw Tommy	Davis Harry "Pluck"	Ferrier Bob	Fish Tom	Gosling William	Langley Ambrose	Layton Willie	McWhinnie William	Malloch Jock	Massey Jack	Millar Harry	Pryce Jack	Ruddlesdin Harry	Spiksley Fred	Stubbs Frank	Thackeray Fred	Wilson Andrew	Wright Jocky
		5		4			3	2	7	11	1		8	6				9	10
		5	7	4			3	2		11	1		8	6				9	10
		5	11	4			3	2	7		1		8	6				9	10
		5	7	4			3	2		11	1		8	6				9	10
		5		4			3	2	7	11	1		8	6				9	10
		5	7	4			3	2		11	1		8	6				9	10
	2	5	7	4			3			11			8	6		1		9	10
		5	7	4			3	2		11	1	9	8	6					10
		5	8	4			3	2		11	1			6	7			9	10
	2	5	7	4			3			11	1	8		6				9	10
		5	8	4			3	2	7	11	1			6				9	10
		5	8	4			3	2	7	11	1			6				9	10
		5	8	4			3	2	7	11	1			6				9	10
		5	8	4			3	2	7	11	1			6				9	10
		5	8	4			3	2	7	11	1			6				9	10
		5	7	4			3	2		11	1		8	6				9	10
		5	7	4			3	2		11	1		8	6				9	10
		5	7	4			3	2		11	1		8	6				9	10
		5	7	4			3	2		11	1		8	6				9	10
		5	7	4			3	2		11	1		8	6				9	10
		5	7	4			3	2		11	1		8	6				9	10
	2	5	7	4			3			10			8	6	11	1		9	
10		5		4			3	2	7				8	6	11	1		9	
8		5	7	4			3	2						6	11	1		9	10
8			7	4			3	2						6	11	1	5	9	10
8		5	7	4			3	2		11		9		6		1			10
8		5	7	4		3		2				9		6	11	1			10
8			7	4	6	3		2							11	1	5	9	10
8		5	7	4		3		2						6	11	1		9	10
8		5	7	4		2	3							6	11	1		9	10
8		5	7	4			3	2						6	11	1		9	10
8		5	7	4			3	2						6	11	1		9	10
8		5	7	4			3	2						6	11	1		9	10
8		5	7	4			3	2						6	11	1		9	10
12	3	32	31	34	1	4	31	30	9	22	20	4	16	33	13	14	2	31	32
6		3	5	1			1	1		4		2	2		4			13	10

Chapman Harry	Cole William	Crawshaw Tommy	Davis Harry "Pluck"	Ferrier Bob	Fish Tom	Gosling William	Langley Ambrose	Layton Willie	McWhinnie William	Malloch Jock	Massey Jack	Millar Harry	Pryce Jack	Ruddlesdin Harry	Spiksley Fred	Stubbs Frank	Thackeray Fred	Wilson Andrew	Wright Jocky
		5		4			3	2		11	1		8	6	7			9	10
		1		1			1	1		1	1		1	1	1			1	1

League Table

	P	W	D	L	F	A	Pts
Liverpool	34	19	7	8	59	35	45
Sunderland	34	15	13	6	57	26	43
Notts County	34	18	4	12	54	46	40
Nottingham Forest	34	16	7	11	53	36	39
Bury	34	16	7	11	53	37	39
Newcastle United	34	14	10	10	42	37	38
Everton	34	16	5	13	55	42	37
SHEFFIELD WEDNESDAY	34	13	10	11	52	42	36
Blackburn Rovers	34	12	9	13	39	47	33
Bolton Wanderers	34	13	7	14	39	55	33
Manchester City	34	13	6	15	48	58	32
Derby County	34	12	7	15	55	42	31
Wolverhampton W	34	9	13	12	39	55	31
Sheffield United	34	12	7	15	35	52	31
Aston Villa	34	10	10	14	45	51	30
Stoke	34	11	5	18	46	57	27
Preston North End	34	9	7	18	49	75	25
West Bromwich Albion	34	7	8	19	35	62	22

1901-02

Division One

Manager: Arthur Dickinson

Did you know that?

Final League Position: 9th

On 14 September 1901, in an away game at Notts County, Wednesday's 'keeper, Frank Stubbs, took a heavy knock to his head. It was stated later that he then punched a ball into his own net. Following that, he allegedly caught the ball before turning around and placing it in the back of his own net. Wednesday lost 6–1 (contemporary match reports from both Sheffield and Nottingham do not back this up, but Stubbs was clearly concussed). One report stated that he caught the ball and then was barged into the net.

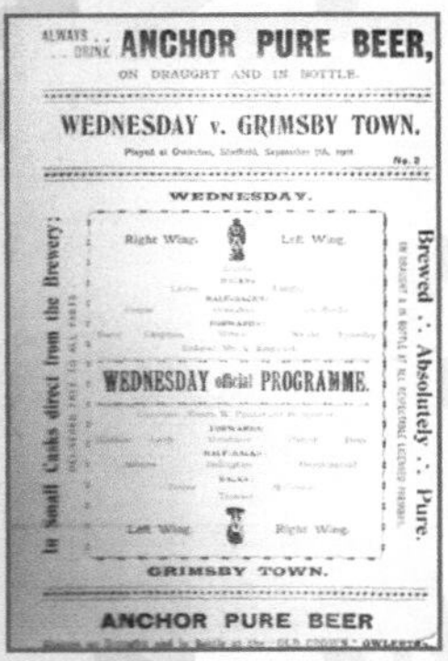

Match No.	Date	Venue	Opponents		Round	Result	HT Score	Position	Scorers	Attendance
1	Sep 7	H	Grimsby Town	W		3-1	0-1	6th	Wilson (2), Crawshaw	17,500
2	14	A	Notts County	L		1-6	1-0		Wright	12,000
3	21	H	Bolton Wanderers	W		5-1	2-0	8th	Wilson, Chapman (2), Brown (og), Davis	7,000
4	Oct 5	H	Wolverhampton W	D		1-1	1-0	12th	Wilson	7,500
5	12	A	Liverpool	W		2-1	0-1	7th	Chapman, Wilson	15,000
6	19	H	Newcastle United	D		0-0	0-0	7th		16,000
7	26	A	Aston Villa	L		1-4	0-1	12th	Wilson	30,000
8	Nov 2	H	Sheffield United	W		1-0	1-0	10th	Wilson	26,000
9	9	A	Nottingham Forest	D		1-1	1-1	11th	Chapman	9,000
10	16	H	Bury	W		4-1	3-0	5th	Dryburgh, Malloch (2), Spiksley	10,000
11	23	A	Blackburn Rovers	L		0-2	0-0	9th		7,000
12	30	H	Stoke	W		3-1	2-1	7th	Malloch, Chapman, Spiksley	8,500
13	Dec 7	A	Everton	L		0-5	0-2	9th		15,000
14	14	H	Sunderland	D		1-1	0-0	9th	Chapman	5,500
15	21	A	Small Heath	D		1-1	0-0	11th	Davis	8,000
16	26	H	Manchester City	W		2-1	0-0	9th	Wright, Spiksley	10,000
17	Jan 4	A	Grimsby Town	L		1-3	1-2	10th	Davis	6,000
18	11	H	Notts County	W		4-0	2-0	6th	Spiksley, Chapman, Wright, Moralee	9,500
19	18	A	Bolton Wanderers	L		1-3	0-1	11th	Davis	10,506
20	Feb 1	A	Wolverhampton W	L		0-1	0-0	11th		3,000
21	15	A	Newcastle United	L		1-2	0-2	14th	Chapman	15,000
22	22	H	Aston Villa	W		1-0	1-0	11th	Davis	14,000
23	Mar 1	A	Sheffield United	L		0-3	0-0	12th		28,426
24	8	H	Nottingham Forest	L		0-2	0-1	13th		9,000
25	15	A	Bury	L		0-2	0-2	14th		4,000
26	17	H	Derby County	W		2-0	0-0	13th	Dryburgh (2)	4,500
27	22	H	Blackburn Rovers	L		0-1	0-0	13th		8,000
28	28	A	Manchester City	W		3-0	1-0	12th	Beech, Chapman, Davis	25,000
29	29	A	Stoke	W		2-1	2-0	11th	Davis, Simpson	7,000
30	Apr 1	H	Liverpool	D		1-1	1-1		Wilson	15,000
31	5	H	Everton	D		1-1	0-0	9th	Beech	2,500
32	12	A	Sunderland	W		2-1	1-0	8th	Chapman, Simpson	10,000
33	19	H	Small Heath	L		1-2	1-1	8th	Spiksley	13,500
34	26	A	Derby County	D		2-2	1-0	9th	Wilson (2)	5,000
										Apps
									One own-goal	Goals

FA Cup

Match No.	Date	Venue	Opponents		Round	Result	HT Score	Position	Scorers	Attendance
35	Jan 25	A	Sunderland	L	1R	0-1	0-1			30,096
										Apps

Beech George	Chapman Harry	Crawshaw Percy	Crawshaw Tommy	Davis Harry 'Pluck'	Dryburgh William	Ferrier Bob	Fish Tom	Gosling William	Hutton Robert	Langley Ambrose	Layton Willie	Lyall Jack	Malloch Jock	Moralee Matt	Ruddlesdin Harry	Simpson Viv	Spiksley Fred	Stubbs Frank	Thackeray Fred	Wilson Andrew	Wright Jocky
	8		5	7		4				3	2				6		11	1		9	10
	8		5			4	6			3	2		7				11	1		9	10
	8		5	7		4				3	2	1			6		11			9	10
	8		5	7		4				3	2	1			6		11			9	10
	8		5	7		4				3	2	1	10		6		11			9	
	8		5	7		4				3	2	1			6		11			9	10
	8		5	7		4				3	2	1	10		6		11			9	
	8		5		7	4				3	2	1	11		6					9	10
9	8				7	4				3	2	1	11		6				5		10
	8		5		7	4				3	2	1	10		6		11			9	
	8		5		7	4				3	2	1	10		6		11			9	
	8		5		7	4				3	2	1	10		6		11			9	
	8		5		7	4				3	2	1	10		6		11			9	
	8		5	7		4	6			3	2	1	10				11			9	
			5	7		4	6	2		3		1	10				11			9	8
			5	7			6			3	2	1	10		4		11			9	8
		4		7			6			3	2	1	10				11		5	9	8
	10	4		7			6		9	3	2	1		5			11				8
		4	5	7						3	2	1	10		6		11			9	8
	8			7	9	4				3	2	1	11	5	6						10
	8		5	7	9	4				3	2	1	11		6						10
			5	7	8	4				3	2	1	11		6					9	10
	8		5	7		4				3	2	1			6		11			9	10
	8		5	7		4				3	2	1	11		6					9	10
	8		5	7		4				3	2	1	11		6					9	10
	8		5		7	4				3	2	1	11		6					9	10
	8		5	7	10	4				3	2	1	11		6					9	
10	8		5	7		4				3	2	1			6	9	11				
10	8		5	7		4				3	2	1			6	9	11				
10	8		5	7		4				3	2	1			6		11			9	
10	8		5	7		4				3	2	1			6	9	11				
10	8		5	7		4				3	2	1			6	9	11				
10	8		5	7		4				3	2	1			6	9	11				
10	8		5	7		4				3	2				6		11	1		9	
8	29	3	30	26	11	30	6	1	1	34	33	31	21	2	29	5	25	3	2	25	19
2	10		1	7	3								3	1		2	5			10	3

Beech George	Chapman Harry	Crawshaw Percy	Crawshaw Tommy	Davis Harry 'Pluck'	Dryburgh William	Ferrier Bob	Fish Tom	Gosling William	Hutton Robert	Langley Ambrose	Layton Willie	Lyall Jack	Malloch Jock	Moralee Matt	Ruddlesdin Harry	Simpson Viv	Spiksley Fred	Stubbs Frank	Thackeray Fred	Wilson Andrew	Wright Jocky
			5		7		4			3	2	1	10		6		11			9	8
			1		1		1			1	1	1	1		1		1			1	1

League Table

	P	W	D	L	F	A	Pts
Sunderland	34	19	6	9	50	35	44
Everton	34	17	7	10	53	35	41
Newcastle United	34	14	9	11	48	34	37
Blackburn Rovers	34	15	6	13	52	48	36
Nottingham Forest	34	13	9	12	43	43	35
Derby County	34	13	9	12	39	41	35
Bury	34	13	8	13	44	38	34
Aston Villa	34	13	8	13	42	40	34
SHEFFIELD WEDNESDAY	34	13	8	13	48	52	34
Sheffield United	34	13	7	14	53	48	33
Liverpool	34	10	12	12	42	38	32
Bolton Wanderers	34	12	8	14	51	56	32
Notts County	34	14	4	16	51	57	32
Wolverhampton W	34	13	6	15	46	57	32
Grimsby Town	34	13	6	15	44	60	32
Stoke	34	11	9	14	45	55	31
Small Heath	34	11	8	15	47	45	30
Manchester City	34	11	6	17	42	58	28

1902-03

Division One

Manager: Arthur Dickinson

Did you know that?

Final League Position: 1st

Wednesday were on a tour of South Wales, Bristol and Plymouth, having finished their League matches with a 3–1 win over WBA, and were one point ahead of Sunderland, who still had an away game at local rivals, Newcastle. With Newcastle winning 1–0, Wednesday finished as champions for the first time.

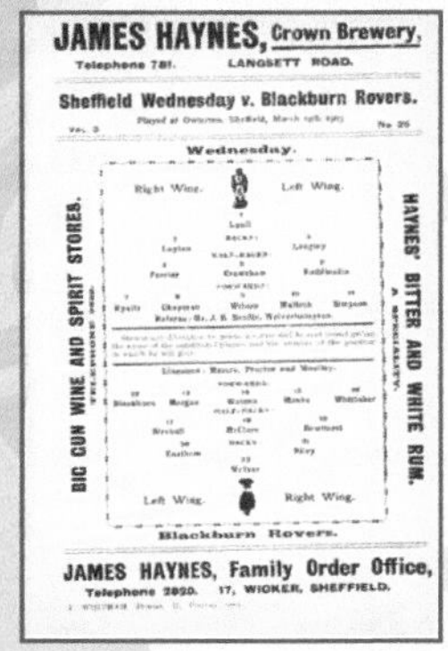

Match No.	Date	Venue	Opponents		Round	Result	HT Score	Position	Scorers	Attendance
1	Sep 1	A	Sheffield United	W		3-2	2-1		Spiksley, Wilson, Davis	20,113
2	6	A	Bolton Wanderers	W		2-0	0-0	2nd	Davis, Wilson	12,000
3	13	H	Middlesbrough	W		2-0	0-0	2nd	Wilson, Davis	20,000
4	20	A	Newcastle United	L		0-3	0-1	3rd		23,000
5	27	H	Wolverhampton W	D		1-1	1-1	3rd	Chapman (pen)	15,000
6	Oct 3	A	Notts County	W		3-0	2-0	1st	Spiksley (3)	5,000
7	4	A	Liverpool	L		2-4	1-2	3rd	Chapman, Spiksley	17,000
8	11	H	Sheffield United	L		0-1	0-0	8th		21,500
9	18	A	Grimsby Town	W		1-0	1-0	4th	Chapman	6,000
10	Nov 1	A	Nottingham Forest	W		4-1	2-1	5th	Wilson (2), Davis, Chapman (pen)	10,000
11	8	H	Bury	W		2-0	1-0	3rd	Wilson, Chapman	8,000
12	15	A	Blackburn Rovers	L		1-2	1-0	4th	Langley (pen)	7,000
13	22	H	Sunderland	W		1-0	1-0	4th	Chapman	12,000
14	29	A	Stoke	L		0-4	0-2	6th		10,000
15	Dec 6	H	Everton	W		4-1	2-1	4th	Wilson (3), Spiksley	10,000
16	13	H	Derby County	L		0-1	0-0	5th		14,000
17	20	A	West Bromwich Alb	W		3-2	1-0	4th	Chapman, Davis (2)	14,500
18	26	A	Aston Villa	L		0-1	0-1	5th		40,000
19	27	H	Notts County	W		2-0	1-0	5th	Davis, Chapman	25,000
20	Jan 1	H	Aston Villa	W		4-0	2-0	2nd	Wilson, Malloch, Ruddlesdin (2)	40,000
21	3	H	Bolton Wanderers	W		3-0	2-0	2nd	Davis (3)	10,000
22	10	A	Middlesbrough	L		1-2	1-0	2nd	Davis	8,000
23	17	H	Newcastle United	W		3-0	1-0	2nd	Chapman (2), Spiksley	10,000
24	24	A	Wolverhampton W	L		1-2	0-0	2nd	Davis	7,000
25	31	H	Liverpool	W		3-1	1-0	2nd	Chapman (1 + pen), Davis	15,000
26	Feb 14	H	Grimsby Town	D		1-1	1-0	2nd	Langley (pen)	8,000
27	28	H	Nottingham Forest	W		1-0	1-0	2nd	Langley (pen)	12,000
28	Mar 14	H	Blackburn Rovers	D		0-0	0-0	1st		9,000
29	21	A	Sunderland	W		1-0	0-0	1st	Wilson	28,000
30	28	H	Stoke	W		1-0	0-0	1st	Marrison	8,000
31	Apr 4	A	Everton	D		1-1	0-1	1st	Langley (pen)	12,000
32	6	A	Bury	L		0-4	0-2	1st		2,000
33	11	A	Derby County	L		0-1	0-1	1st		10,000
34	18	H	West Bromwich Alb	W		3-1	2-1	1st	Wilson, Langley (pen), Spiksley	15,500
										Apps
										Goals

FA Cup

Match No.	Date	Venue	Opponents		Round	Result	HT Score	Position	Scorers	Attendance
35	Feb 7	A	Blackburn Rovers	D	1R	0-0	0-0			12,000
36	12	H	Blackburn Rovers	L	1R Re	0-1	0-1			25,410
										Apps

Barron George	Beech George	Chapman Harry	Crawshaw Percy	Crawshaw Tommy	Davis Harry 'Pluck'	Ferrier Bob	Hounsfield Reg	Langley Ambrose	Layton Willie	Lyall Jack	Malloch Jack	Marrison Tom	Moralee Matt	Ruddlesdin Harry	Ryalls Joe	Simpson George	Simpson Viv	Spiksley Fred	Stewart Jimmy	Stubbs Frank	Thackeray Fred	Wilson Andrew
		8		5	7	4		3	2	1	10			6				11				9
		8		5	7	4		3	2	1	10			6				11				9
		8		5	7	4		3	2	1	10			6				11				9
		8		5	7	4		3	2	1	10			6				11				9
		8		5	7	4		3	2	1	10			6				11				9
		8		5		4	7	3	2	1	10			6				11				9
		8		5		4	7	3	2	1	10			6				11				9
		8			7	4		3	2	1	10		5	6				11				9
	8	7	4	5				3	2	1	10			6				11				9
		8		5	7	4		3	2	1	10			6				11				9
		8		5	7	4		3	2	1	10			6				11				9
				5	7	4		3	2	1	10			6			8	11				9
		8		5	7	4		3	2	1	10			6				11				9
		8		5	7	4		3	2	1	10			6				11				9
		8		5	7	4		3		1	10			6				11			2	9
	10	8		5	7	4		3	2	1	11			6								9
		8		5	7	4		3	2		10			6				11		1		9
		8		5	7	4		3	2	1	10			6				11				9
		8		5	7	4		3	2	1	10			6				11				9
		8		5	7	4		3	2	1	10			6				11				9
		8		5	7	4		3	2	1	10			6				11				9
		8		5	7	4		3	2	1	10			6				11				9
		8		5	7	4		3	2	1	10			6				11				9
		8		5	7	4		3	2	1	10			6				11				9
		8		5	7	4		3	2	1	10			6				11				9
	8	7		5		4		3		1				6				11	10		2	9
		8		5	7	4		3	2	1	10			6				11				9
		8		5		4		3	2	1	10			6	7	11						9
		8		5	7	4		3		1	10			6				11			2	9
				5	7	4		3		1	10	8		6				11			2	9
		8		5		4		3		1	10			6			7	11			2	9
7		8		5		4		3	2	1	10			6				11				9
		8		5	7	4		3	2	1	10			6				11				9
		8		5		4		3	2	1	10			6			7	11				9
1	3	32	1	33	26	33	2	34	29	33	33	1	1	34	1	1	3	32	1	1	5	34
		12			13			5			1	1		2				8				12

Barron George	Beech George	Chapman Harry	Crawshaw Percy	Crawshaw Tommy	Davis Harry 'Pluck'	Ferrier Bob	Hounsfield Reg	Langley Ambrose	Layton Willie	Lyall Jack	Malloch Jack	Marrison Tom	Moralee Matt	Ruddlesdin Harry	Ryalls Joe	Simpson George	Simpson Viv	Spiksley Fred	Stewart Jimmy	Stubbs Frank	Thackeray Fred	Wilson Andrew
		8		5	7	4		3	2	1	10			6				11				9
		8		5	7	4		3		1	10			6				11			2	9
		2		2	2	2		2	1	2	2			2				2			1	2

League Table

	P	W	D	L	F	A	Pts
SHEFFIELD WEDNESDAY	34	19	4	11	54	36	42
Aston Villa	34	19	3	12	61	40	41
Sunderland	34	16	9	9	51	36	41
Sheffield United	34	17	5	12	58	44	39
Liverpool	34	17	4	13	68	49	38
Stoke	34	15	7	12	46	38	37
West Bromwich Albion	34	16	4	14	54	53	36
Bury	34	16	3	15	54	43	35
Derby County	34	16	3	15	50	47	35
Nottingham Forest	34	14	7	13	49	47	35
Wolverhampton W	34	14	5	15	48	57	33
Everton	34	13	6	15	45	47	32
Middlesbrough	34	14	4	16	41	50	32
Newcastle United	34	14	4	16	41	51	32
Notts County	34	12	7	15	41	49	31
Blackburn Rovers	34	12	5	17	44	63	29
Grimsby Town	34	8	9	17	43	62	25
Bolton Wanderers	34	8	3	23	37	73	19

1903-04

Division One

Manager: Arthur Dickinson

Did you know that?

Final League Position: 1st

Wednesday were unbeaten at home in all League and Cup games and won the First Division Championship.

Match No.	Date	Venue	Opponents		Round	Result	HT Score	Position	Scorers	Attendance
1	Sep 2	A	West Bromwich Alb	W		1-0	0-0	1st	Chapman	9,000
2	5	H	Middlesbrough	W		4-1	2-1	1st	Malloch, Wilson, Chapman, G. Simpson	20,000
3	12	A	Liverpool	W		3-1	2-1	1st	Wilson (2), Davis	18,000
4	19	H	Bury	D		1-1	1-1	2nd	Wilson	18,000
5	26	A	Blackburn Rovers	D		0-0	0-0	2nd		10,000
6	Oct 3	H	Nottingham Forest	W		2-1	2-1	3rd	Wilson, Henderson (og)	15,000
7	10	A	Wolverhampton W	L		1-2	1-1	3rd	Davis	12,000
8	17	A	Sunderland	W		1-0	0-0	2nd	Wilson	15,000
9	24	H	West Bromwich Alb	W		1-0	1-0	2nd	Chapman	12,000
10	31	A	Small Heath	D		0-0	0-0	2nd		13,000
11	Nov 7	H	Everton	W		1-0	1-0	1st	Chapman	15,000
12	14	A	Stoke	L		1-3	1-1	2nd	Wilson	10,000
13	21	H	Derby County	W		1-0	1-0	2nd	G. Simpson	5,000
14	28	A	Manchester City	D		1-1	1-1	2nd	Chapman	8,000
15	Dec 12	A	Sheffield United	D		1-1	1-1	3rd	Wilson	32,014
16	19	H	Newcastle United	D		1-1	0-1	3rd	Langley (pen)	8,000
17	26	A	Aston Villa	L		1-2	1-1	4th	Wilson	49,500
18	Jan 1	H	Wolverhampton W	W		4-0	1-0	4th	Chapman (pen), V. Simpson (2), Malloch	18,000
19	2	A	Middlesbrough	W		1-0	0-0	2nd	Chapman (pen)	15,000
20	9	H	Liverpool	W		2-1	0-0	2nd	Crawshaw, Stewart	13,000
21	16	A	Bury	L		0-1	0-0	3rd		6,000
22	23	H	Blackburn Rovers	W		3-1	1-0	3rd	Chapman (2), Crawshaw	14,000
23	30	A	Nottingham Forest	W		1-0	1-0	1st	Wilson	15,000
24	Feb 13	H	Sunderland	D		0-0	0-0	1st		8,000
25	22	H	Notts County	W		2-0	1-0	1st	G. Simpson (2)	7,000
26	27	H	Small Heath	W		3-2	3-1	1st	Chapman, Davis, Hemmingfield	6,000
27	Mar 12	H	Stoke	W		1-0	0-0	1st	Chapman	12,000
28	26	H	Manchester City	W		1-0	1-0	1st	Chapman	25,000
29	Apr 2	A	Notts County	L		0-1	0-1	1st		12,000
30	4	A	Everton	L		0-2	0-1	1st		30,000
31	9	H	Sheffield United	W		3-0	2-0	1st	Chapman (2), G. Simpson	17,000
32	16	A	Newcastle United	L		0-4	0-3	2nd		20,000
33	23	H	Aston Villa	W		4-2	3-0	1st	Wilson, Chapman, Davis, G. Simpson	15,000
34	30	A	Derby County	W		2-0	1-0	1st	Chapman, Davis	5,000
										Apps
									One own-goal	Goals

FA Cup

Match No.	Date	Venue	Opponents		Round	Result	HT Score	Position	Scorers	Attendance
35	Feb 6	A	Plymouth Argyle	D	1R	2-2	1-1		Wilson (2)	18,371
36	10	H	Plymouth Argyle	W	1R Re	2-0	1-0		Davis, Chapman (pen)	18,845
37	20	H	Manchester United	W	2R	6-0	2-0		V Simpson (3), Davis (2), G Simpson	22,051
38	Mar 5	A	Tottenham Hotspur	D	3R	1-1	0-1		Davis	18,000
39	9	H	Tottenham Hotspur	W	3R Re	2-0	0-0		Davis, Chapman	30,011
40	19	N	Manchester City *	L	S/Final	0-3	0-2			53,000
										Apps
										Goals

* Played at Goodison Park, Liverpool

Bartlett Bill	Beech George	Burton Harry	Chapman Harry	Crawshaw Tommy	Davis Harry 'Pluck'	Eyre Isaac	Ferrier Bob	Hemmingfield Bill	Hoyland George	Jarvis Richard	Langley Ambrose	Layton Willie	Lyall Jack	Malloch Jock	Moralee Matt	Ruddlesdin Harry	Ryalls Joe	Simpson George	Simpson Viv	Stewart Jimmy	Wilson Andrew
			8	5	7		4				3	2	1	10		6		11			9
			8	5	7		4				3	2	1	10		6		11			9
			8	5	7		4				3	2	1	10		6		11			9
			8	5	7		4				3	2	1	10		6		11			9
			8	5	7		4				3	2	1	10		6		11			9
			8	5	7		4				3	2	1			6		11		10	9
		3	8		7		4					2	1		5	6		11		10	9
			8	5	7		4				3	2	1			6		11		10	9
		3	8	5	7		4					2	1	10		6		11			9
		3	8	5	7		4					2	1	10		6		11			9
		3	8	5	7		4					2	1	10		6		11			9
		3	8	5	7		4					2	1	10		6		11			9
		3	8	5	7		4					2	1	10		6		11			9
		3	8	5	7		4					2	1	10		6		11			9
		3	8	5	7		4					2	1	10		6		11			9
			8	5	7		4				3	2	1	11		6			10		9
		3	8	5	7		4					2	1	11		6			10		9
		3	8	5	7		4					2	1	11		6			10		9
		3	8	5	7		4					2	1	11		6				10	9
		3	8	5	7		4					2	1	11		6				10	9
		3	8	5	7			4				2	1	11		6			10		9
		3	8	5	7			4				2	1	11		6			10		9
		3	8	5	7		4					2	1	11		6			10		9
	9	3	8	5	7		4					2	1	11		6				10	
6		3	8	5	7		4					2	1					11	9	10	
		3	8	5	7		4	9				2	1			6		11		10	
6		3	8		7	9	4	5				2	1	10				11			
	10	3	8	5	7		4		9			2	1			6		11			
	10	3	8	5	7		4			1		2				6		11			9
	10	3	8	5			4	7				2	1			6		11			9
		3	8	5			4					2	1			6	7	11		10	9
		3	8	5	7		4					2	1			6		11		10	9
6		3	8	5	7		4					2	1	10				11			9
6		3	8	5	7			4				2	1	10				11			9
4	4	26	34	32	32	1	31	6	1	1	8	34	33	24	1	30	1	25	7	10	29
			16	2	5			1			1			2				6	2	1	11

Bartlett Bill	Beech George	Burton Harry	Chapman Harry	Crawshaw Tommy	Davis Harry 'Pluck'	Eyre Isaac	Ferrier Bob	Hemmingfield Bill	Hoyland George	Jarvis Richard	Langley Ambrose	Layton Willie	Lyall Jack	Malloch Jock	Moralee Matt	Ruddlesdin Harry	Ryalls Joe	Simpson George	Simpson Viv	Stewart Jimmy	Wilson Andrew
		3	8	5	7		4					2	1	11		6			10		9
		3	8	5	7		4					2	1	11		6			10		9
	9	3	8	5	7		4					2	1			6		11	10		
	9	3	8	5	7		4					2	1			6		11	10		
		3	8	5	7		4	9				2	1			6		11	10		
		3	8	5	7		4					2	1	10		6		11			9
	2	6	6	6	6		6	1				6	6	3		6		4	5		3
			2		5													1	3		2

League Table

	P	W	D	L	F	A	Pts
SHEFFIELD WEDNESDAY	34	20	7	7	48	28	47
Manchester City	34	19	6	9	71	45	44
Everton	34	19	5	10	59	32	43
Newcastle United	34	18	6	10	58	45	42
Aston Villa	34	17	7	10	70	48	41
Sunderland	34	17	5	12	63	49	39
Sheffield United	34	15	8	11	62	57	38
Wolverhampton W	34	14	8	12	44	66	36
Nottingham Forest	34	11	9	14	57	57	31
Middlesbrough	34	9	12	13	46	47	30
Small Heath	34	11	8	15	39	52	30
Bury	34	7	15	12	40	53	29
Notts County	34	12	5	17	37	61	29
Derby County	34	9	10	15	58	60	28
Blackburn Rovers	34	11	6	17	48	60	28
Stoke	34	10	7	17	54	57	27
Liverpool	34	9	8	17	49	62	26
West Bromwich Albion	34	7	10	17	36	60	24

1904-05

Division One

Manager: Arthur Dickinson

Did you know that?

Final League Position: 9th

At the start of the season Wednesday were seven games unbeaten and, combined with the last two games of the previous season, set a club record of nine games without defeat.

Match No.	Date	Venue	Opponents		Round	Result	HT Score	Position	Scorers	Attendance
1	Sep 3	A	Middlesbrough	W		3-1	1-1	4th	Wilson, Davis (2)	18,000
2	10	H	Wolverhampton W	W		4-0	0-0	3rd	Davis, Wilson (2), Chapman	13,000
3	17	A	Bury	W		4-1	2-0	3rd	Davis, Chapman (2), Wilson	8,000
4	24	H	Aston Villa	W		3-2	0-2	1st	Davis, Chapman, G. Simpson	20,000
5	Oct 1	A	Blackburn Rovers	W		1-0	0-0	1st	Davis	15,000
6	8	H	Nottingham Forest	W		2-0	1-0	1st	G. Simpson, Davis	15,000
7	15	H	Stoke	W		3-0	3-0	1st	Wilson, Chapman, G. Simpson	15,000
8	22	A	Sunderland	L		0-3	0-2	1st		25,000
9	29	H	Woolwich Arsenal	L		0-3	0-1	1st		15,000
10	Nov 5	A	Derby County	L		0-1	0-0	3rd		14,000
11	12	H	Everton	D		5-5	1-5	3rd	Davis, Stewart, G. Simpson, V. Simpson, Ferrier	12,000
12	19	A	Small Heath	L		1-2	0-1	7th	Wilson	15,000
13	26	H	Manchester City	W		2-1	2-0	4th	Wilson (2)	15,000
14	Dec 3	A	Notts County	D		2-2	0-0	5th	G. Simpson, Hoyland	8,000
15	10	H	Sheffield United	L		1-3	1-0	7th	Wilson	16,000
16	17	A	Newcastle United	L		2-6	0-2	9th	Wilson, G. Simpson	18,000
17	26	A	Nottingham Forest	L		1-2	1-1	11th	G. Simpson	15,000
18	27	H	Sunderland	D		1-1	0-1	11th	V. Simpson	18,000
19	31	H	Middlesbrough	W		5-0	3-0	8th	Chapman, Wilson (2), Stewart (2)	12,000
20	Jan 2	H	Preston North End	W		2-0	2-0	7th	Wilson, Chapman	18,000
21	7	A	Wolverhampton W	L		0-1	0-1	8th		8,000
22	14	H	Bury	W		4-0	2-0	8th	Stewart (2 + pen), Hemmingfield	16,000
23	21	A	Aston Villa	W		2-0	0-0	7th	Davis, Stewart	14,000
24	28	H	Blackburn Rovers	L		1-2	1-2	8th	Davis	16,000
25	Feb 11	A	Stoke	L		1-2	1-2	8th	Brittleton	8,000
26	25	A	Woolwich Arsenal	L		0-3	0-2	10th		20,000
27	Mar 11	A	Everton	L		2-5	1-1	10th	Brittleton, Davis	15,000
28	18	H	Small Heath	W		3-1	1-0	10th	Hemmingfield, Stewart, Wilson	12,000
29	Apr 1	H	Notts County	W		1-0	1-0	8th	Davis	8,000
30	3	H	Derby County	D		1-1	0-0	8th	Stewart	2,000
31	8	A	Sheffield United	L		2-4	0-1	8th	Stewart (2)	22,000
32	15	A	Manchester City	D		1-1	1-0	8th	Brittleton	20,000
33	22	A	Preston North End	L		0-1	0-1	9th		7,000
34	26	H	Newcastle United	L		1-3	1-0	9th	G. Simpson	12,000
										Apps
										Goals

FA Cup

Match No.	Date	Venue	Opponents		Round	Result	HT Score	Position	Scorers	Attendance
35	Feb 4	A	Blackburn Rovers	W	1R	2-1	1-1		Chapman, Hemmingfield	20,723
36	18	H	Portsmouth	W	2R	2-1	1-1		Stewart, Davis	36,413
37	Mar 4	A	Preston North End	D	3R	1-1	1-1		Wilson	11,067
38	9	H	Preston North End	W	3R Re	3-0	2-0		Stewart, Wilson, G. Simpson	24,848
39	25	N	Newcastle United *	L	S/Final	0-1	0-1			40,000
										Apps
										Goals

* At Hyde Road, Manchester

Bartlett Bill	Brittleton Tom	Burton Harry	Chapman Harry	Crawshaw Percy	Crawshaw Tommy	Davis Harry "Pluck"	Eaton Walter	Ferrier Bob	Hemmingfield Bill	Hoyland George	Jarvis Richard	Layton Willie	Lyall Jack	Malloch Jock	Marrison Tom	Ruddlesdin Harry	Simpson George	Simpson Viv	Slavin Hugh	Stewart Jimmy	Wilson Andrew
		3	8		5	7		4				2	1	10		6	11				9
6		3	8		5	7		4				2	1	10			11				9
6		3	8		5	7		4				2	1	10			11				9
6		3	8		5	7		4				2	1	10			11				9
6		3	8		5	7		4				2	1	10			11				9
6		3	8		5	7		4				2	1	10			11				9
6		3	8			7		4	5			2	1	10			11				9
6		3	8		5	7		4				2	1	10			11				9
6		3	8		5	7		4				2	1	10			11				9
		3			5	7		4				2	1	10		6	11			8	9
		3			5	7		4			1	2				6	11	10		8	9
		3			5	7		4				2	1			6	11	8		10	9
		3			5	7		4					1	10		6	11	8	2		9
		3			5			4		7		2	1	10	8	6	11				9
		3			5			4				2	1	10		6	11	7		8	9
		3			5	7		4		8		2	1			6	11	10			9
		3		4	5	7							1	10	8	6	11		2		9
		3		4	5	7					1				8	6	11	10	2		9
		3	8	4	5	7					1					6	11		2	10	9
6		3	8			7			5		1					4	11		2	10	9
		3	8		5	7		4					1		9	6	11		2	10	
6	8	3			5	7			9				1			4	11		2	10	
6	8	3			5	7			9				1			4	11		2	10	
6	8	3			5	7							1	11		4			2	10	9
6	8	3			5	7							1	11		4			2	10	9
6	8	3	7					4	5				1	11					2	10	9
6	8	3			5	7		4					1				11		2	10	9
6		3			5	7			8			2	1			4	11			10	9
6	8	3			5	7		4			1	2		11						10	9
6	8	3			5	7	2						1	11		4				10	9
6	8	3			5	7			9			2	1	11		4				10	
6	8	3			5	7						2	1			4	11			10	9
6	8	3			5	7						2	1	11		4				10	9
6	8				5	7		4				2	1				11		3	10	9
22	12	33	13	3	31	31	1	21	7	2	5	21	29	21	4	22	27	6	13	20	30
	3		7			12		1	2	1							8	2		11	14

Bartlett Bill	Brittleton Tom	Burton Harry	Chapman Harry	Crawshaw Percy	Crawshaw Tommy	Davis Harry "Pluck"	Eaton Walter	Ferrier Bob	Hemmingfield Bill	Hoyland George	Jarvis Richard	Layton Willie	Lyall Jack	Malloch Jock	Marrison Tom	Ruddlesdin Harry	Simpson George	Simpson Viv	Slavin Hugh	Stewart Jimmy	Wilson Andrew
6		3	8		5	7			9				1	11		4			2	10	
6		3	8		5	7			9				1			4	11		2	10	
6		3	8		5	7							1			4	11		2	10	9
6		3	8		5	7							1			4	11		2	10	9
6		3			5	7			8				1			4	11		2	10	9
5		5	4		5	5			3				5	1		5	4		5	5	3
			1			1			1								1			2	2

League Table

	P	W	D	L	F	A	Pts
Newcastle United	34	23	2	9	72	33	48
Everton	34	21	5	8	63	36	47
Manchester City	34	20	6	8	66	37	46
Aston Villa	34	19	4	11	63	43	42
Sunderland	34	16	8	10	60	44	40
Sheffield United	34	19	2	13	64	56	40
Small Heath	34	17	5	12	54	38	39
Preston North End	34	13	10	11	42	37	36
SHEFFIELD WEDNESDAY	34	14	5	15	61	57	33
Woolwich Arsenal	34	12	9	13	36	40	33
Derby County	34	12	8	14	37	48	32
Stoke	34	13	4	17	40	58	30
Blackburn Rovers	34	11	5	18	40	51	27
Wolverhampton W	34	11	4	19	47	73	26
Middlesbrough	34	9	8	17	36	56	26
Nottingham Forest	34	9	7	18	40	61	25
Bury	34	10	4	20	47	67	24
Notts County	34	5	8	21	36	69	18

1905-06

Division One

Manager: Arthur Dickinson

Did you know that?

Final League Position: 3rd

Wednesday's ground was closed by the FA on 16 February 1906 for six days because of crowd trouble during the Preston North End game on 27 January 1906.

Match No.	Date	Venue	Opponents		Round	Result	HT Score	Position	Scorers	Attendance
1	Sep 2	H	Manchester City	W		1-0	0-0	2nd	Stewart	25,000
2	4	A	Wolverhampton W	D		0-0	0-0	2nd		7,000
3	9	A	Bury	D		2-2	1-1	5th	Davis, Wilson	4,000
4	13	A	Newcastle United	W		3-0	1-0	2nd	Stewart (2), Wilson	20,000
5	16	H	Middlesbrough	W		3-0	2-0	2nd	Wilson, Stewart, Brittleton	20,000
6	23	A	Preston North End	W		1-0	1-0	2nd	Wilson	13,000
7	30	H	Newcastle United	D		1-1	0-1	1st	Crawshaw	20,000
8	Oct 7	A	Aston Villa	L		0-3	0-1	2nd		24,000
9	14	H	Liverpool	W		3-2	3-1	1st	Ruddlesdin, Stewart, Chapman	15,000
10	21	A	Sheffield United	W		2-0	1-0	1st	Chapman, Stewart	29,089
11	28	H	Notts County	W		3-1	2-0	1st	Wilson, G. Simpson, Stewart	12,000
12	Nov 4	A	Stoke	L		0-4	0-2	1st		15,000
13	11	H	Bolton Wanderers	L		1-2	0-0	1st	Brittleton	6,000
14	18	A	Woolwich Arsenal	W		2-0	1-0	1st	Chapman, Malloch	20,000
15	25	H	Blackburn Rovers	L		0-1	0-1	2nd		8,000
16	Dec 2	A	Sunderland	L		0-2	0-2	4th		10,000
17	9	H	Birmingham	W		4-2	3-0	3rd	Wilson (2), Chapman, G. Simpson	12,000
18	16	A	Everton	L		0-2	0-1	6th		15,000
19	23	H	Derby County	W		1-0	0-0	3rd	Ruddlesdin	12,000
20	26	H	Wolverhampton W	W		5-1	3-1	3rd	Stewart (4), Wilson	18,000
21	27	H	Nottingham Forest	W		1-0	1-0	2nd	Stewart	16,000
22	30	A	Manchester City	L		1-2	0-1	3rd	Wilson	25,000
23	Jan 6	H	Bury	D		1-1	1-1	2nd	Davis	4,000
24	20	A	Middlesbrough	D		2-2	1-2	3rd	Chapman (2)	10,000
25	27	H	Preston North End	D		1-1	0-0	3rd	Chapman	9,000
26	Feb 10	H	Aston Villa	D		2-2	0-1	4th	Davis (pen), Stewart	25,000
27	17	A	Liverpool	L		1-2	0-1	5th	Stewart	20,000
28	Mar 3	A	Notts County	W		3-1	2-1	4th	Wilson (2), Davis	10,000
29	17	A	Bolton Wanderers	L		0-1	0-1	6th		20,000
30	24	H	Woolwich Arsenal	W		4-2	3-1	5th	Stewart (3), Chapman	15,000
31	31	A	Blackburn Rovers	L		0-1	0-1	5th		10,000
32	Apr 7	H	Sunderland	D		3-3	1-2	6th	Wilson (2), G. Simpson	10,000
33	9	H	Stoke	W		2-0	0-0	6th	Wilson, G. Simpson	4,000
34	14	A	Birmingham	L		1-5	0-3	6th	Wilson	7,000
35	16	A	Nottingham Forest	W		4-3	3-0	4th	Stewart (3), Wilson	16,000
36	18	H	Sheffield United	W		1-0	0-0	3rd	Davis (pen)	12,500
37	23	H	Everton	W		3-1	1-1	3rd	Bradshaw (2), Tummon	6,000
38	28	A	Derby County	L		1-2	1-2	3rd	Brittleton	4,000
										Apps
										Goals

FA Cup

Match No.	Date	Venue	Opponents		Round	Result	HT Score	Position	Scorers	Attendance
39	Jan 13	H	Bristol Rovers	W	1R	1-0	1-0		G. Simpson	15,661
40	Feb 3	H	Millwall	D	2R	1-1	0-1		Stewart	21,511
41	8	A	Millwall	W	2R Re	3-0	2-0		G. Simpson, Davis (pen), Chapman	18,000
42	24	H	Nottingham Forest	W	3R	4-1	2-0		Wilson, Stewart, Chapman, G. Simpson	36,363
43	Mar 10	A	Everton	L	4R	3-4	1-4		G. Simpson, Bartlett, Davis (pen)	30,000
										Apps
										Goals

Bartlett Bill	Bradshaw Frank	Brittleton Tom	Burton Harry	Chapman Harry	Crapper Chris	Crawshaw Tommy	Davis Harry 'Pluck'	Hemmingfield Bill	Layton Willie	Lyall Jack	Malloch Jack	Reynolds Jack	Ruddlesdin Harry	Simpson George	Simpson Viv	Slavin Hugh	Stewart Jimmy	Tummon Oliver	Wilson Andrew
6			3	8		5	7		2	1			4	11			10		9
6			3	8		5	7		2	1			4	11			10		9
6			3	8		5	7		2	1			4	11			10		9
6			3	8		5	7		2	1			4	11			10		9
6		8	3			5	7		2	1			4	11			10		9
6		8	3			5	7		2	1			4	11			10		9
6		8	3			5	7		2	1			4	11			10		9
6		8	3			5	7		2	1			4	11			10		9
6			3	8		5	7		2	1			4	11			10		9
6				8		5	7		2	1			4	11		3	10		9
6				8		5	7		2	1			4	11		3	10		9
6				8		5	7		2	1			4	11		3	10		9
6		8	3			5	7		2	1			4	11			10		9
6		9	3	8		5	7		2	1	11		4				10		
6		9	3	8		5	7		2	1	11		4				10		
6		10	3	8		5	7		2	1			4	11					9
6			3	8		5	7			1			4	11		2	10		9
6			3	8		5	7			1			4	11		2	10		9
6			3	8		5	7		2	1			4	11			10		9
6			3	8		5	7		2	1	11		4				10		9
		4	3	8		5	7		2	1	11		6				10		9
6			3	8		5	7		2	1	11		4				10		9
		4	3	8		5	7		2	1	11		6				10		9
		4		8		5	7		2	1	11		6			3	10		9
6			3	8		5	7		2	1	11		4				10		9
6			3	8		5	7		2	1			4	11			10		9
6			3	8		5	7		2	1			4	11			10		9
6			3	8		5	7		2	1			4	11			10		9
6		8	3			5	7		2	1			4	11			10		9
6			3	8		5	7		2	1			4	11	9		10		
6			3	8		5	7		2	1			4	11			10		9
6		8	3			5			2	1		7	4	11			10		9
6		4	3	8		5	7		2	1				11			10		9
6		4	3	8		5	7			1	11					2	10		9
6		4	3	8		5	7			1	11					2	10		9
6		4	3			5	7	8	2	1	11						10		9
6	8	4			3	5	7		2	1							10	11	9
6		4	3	8		5	7		2	1							10	11	9
35	1	19	33	29	1	38	37	1	34	38	11	1	32	25	1	8	37	2	35
	2	3		8		1	5				1		2	4			20	1	16

6			3	8		5	7		2	1			4	11			10		9
6		8	3			5	7		2	1	11		4				10		9
6			3	8		5	7		2	1			4	11			10		9
6			3	8		5	7		2	1			4	11			10		9
6			3	8		5	7		2	1			4	11			10		9
5		1	5	4		5	5		5	5	1		5	4			5		5
1				2			2							4			2		1

League Table

	P	W	D	L	F	A	Pts
Liverpool	38	23	5	10	79	46	51
Preston North End	38	17	13	8	54	39	47
SHEFFIELD WEDNESDAY	38	18	8	12	63	52	44
Newcastle United	38	18	7	13	74	48	43
Manchester City	38	19	5	14	73	54	43
Bolton Wanderers	38	17	7	14	81	67	41
Birmingham	38	17	7	14	65	59	41
Aston Villa	38	17	6	15	72	56	40
Blackburn Rovers	38	16	8	14	54	52	40
Stoke	38	16	7	15	54	55	39
Everton	38	15	7	16	70	66	37
Woolwich Arsenal	38	15	7	16	62	64	37
Sheffield United	38	15	6	17	57	62	36
Sunderland	38	15	5	18	61	70	35
Derby County	38	14	7	17	39	58	35
Notts County	38	11	12	15	55	71	34
Bury	38	11	10	17	57	74	32
Middlesbrough	38	10	11	17	56	71	31
Nottingham Forest	38	13	5	20	58	79	31
Wolverhampton W.	38	8	7	23	58	99	23

1906-07

Division One

Manager: Arthur Dickinson

Did you know that?

Final League Position: 13th

Harry Chapman's cartilage was prone to coming out during matches, and he used to simply put it back into place without leaving the field and carry on playing!

Match No.	Date	Venue	Opponents		Round	Result	HT Score	Position	Scorers	Attendance
1	Sep 1	A	Bury	D		0-0	0-0			10,000
2	3	H	Newcastle United	D		2-2	1-2		Brittleton, Tummon	6,000
3	8	H	Manchester City	W		3-1	1-0	4th	Wilson, Stewart (2)	12,000
4	15	A	Middlesbrough	W		3-1	1-1	4th	Wilson, Chapman, G. Simpson	17,000
5	22	H	Preston North End	W		2-1	1-0	2nd	Stewart (2)	10,000
6	29	A	Newcastle United	L		1-5	0-1	6th	Wilson	30,000
7	Oct 6	H	Aston Villa	W		2-1	2-0	5th	Wilson, Chapman	22,000
8	13	A	Liverpool	W		2-1	0-0	5th	Wilson, Tummon	13,000
9	20	H	Bristol City	W		3-0	1-0	3rd	Davis (2), Wilson	20,000
10	27	A	Notts County	D		2-2	1-1	4th	V. Simpson, Stewart	14,000
11	Nov 3	H	Sheffield United	D		2-2	1-1	4th	Wilson (2)	12,000
12	10	A	Bolton Wanderers	D		0-0	0-0	2nd		15,000
13	17	H	Manchester United	W		5-2	2-0	3rd	G. Simpson, Crawshaw, Wilson (2), Stewart	7,000
14	24	A	Stoke	D		1-1	1-0	3rd	Wilson	5,000
15	Dec 1	H	Blackburn Rovers	W		3-1	1-1	2nd	Stewart, Wilson, G. Simpson	8,000
16	8	A	Sunderland	D		1-1	1-1	2nd	Davis (pen)	20,000
17	15	H	Birmingham	L		0-1	0-0	3rd		10,000
18	22	A	Everton	L		0-2	0-2	4th		20,000
19	25	H	Derby County	D		1-1	1-1	5th	Tummon	22,000
20	29	H	Bury	L		1-2	1-1	5th	Wilson	8,000
21	Jan 1	H	Woolwich Arsenal	D		1-1	0-1	5th	Wilson	16,000
22	5	A	Manchester City	W		1-0	0-0	5th	G. Simpson	25,000
23	19	H	Middlesbrough	L		0-2	0-1	6th		10,000
24	26	A	Preston North End	L		0-1	0-0	7th		8,000
25	Feb 9	A	Aston Villa	L		1-8	1-3	8th	Davis (pen)	25,000
26	16	H	Liverpool	L		2-3	1-0	10th	Davis (pen), V. Simpson	12,000
27	Mar 2	H	Notts County	L		1-3	1-3	10th	Wilson	10,000
28	16	H	Bolton Wanderers	W		2-0	0-0	11th	Wilson (2)	10,000
29	29	A	Woolwich Arsenal	L		0-1	0-0	11th		25,000
30	30	H	Stoke	L		0-1	0-0	14th		10,000
31	Apr 1	A	Derby County	L		0-1	0-1	14th		10,000
32	4	A	Sheffield United	L		1-2	0-1	14th	Maxwell	17,000
33	6	A	Blackburn Rovers	W		2-0	0-0	13th	Foxall, Bradshaw	6,000
34	10	A	Manchester United	L		0-5	0-4	14th		10,000
35	13	H	Sunderland	W		2-1	2-1	12th	Foxall, Maxwell	3,000
36	24	A	Bristol City	L		0-2	0-0	14th		16,000
37	25	A	Birmingham	D		1-1	0-0	12th	Hemmingfield	10,000
38	27	H	Everton	D		1-1	0-0	13th	Bradshaw	10,000
										Apps
										Goals

FA Cup

Match No.	Date	Venue	Opponents		Round	Result	HT Score	Position	Scorers	Attendance
39	Jan 12	H	Wolves	W	1R	3-2	0-1		Tummon, Stewart, G. Simpson	21,938
40	Feb 2	A	Southampton	D	2R	1-1	0-0		Wilson	15,000
41	7	H	Southampton	W	2R Re	3-1	2-0		Wilson (2), Stewart	27,367
42	23	H	Sunderland	D	3R	0-0	0-0			36,324
43	27	A	Sunderland	W	3R Re	1-0	0-0		G. Simpson	35,856
44	Mar 9	H	Liverpool	W	4R	1-0	0-0		Chapman	37,830
45	23	N	Woolwich Arsenal *	W	S/Final	3-1	1-1		Wilson (2), Stewart	36,000
46	Apr 20	N	Everton **	W	Final	2-1	1-1		Stewart, G. Simpson	84,584
										Apps
										Goals

* Played at St Andrews (Birmingham)

** Played at Crystal Palace, London

Bartlett Bill	Bradshaw Frank	Brittleton Tom	Burton Harry	Chapman Harry	Crawshaw Tommy	Crinson Bill	Davis Harry 'Pluck'	Foxall Frank	Hemmingfield Bill	Holbem Walter	Jameson Joe	Layton Willie	Lloyd Billy	Lyall Jack	Malloch Jock	Maxwell James	Proud Pattison	Reynolds Jack	Rollinson Frank	Ruddlesdin Harry	Simpson George	Simpson Viv	Slavin Hugh	Stewart Jimmy	Tummon Oliver	Wilson Andrew
6		8	3		5		7		4			2		1							11			10		9
6		8	3		5		7		4			2		1										10	11	9
6		8	3		5		7					2		1	11					4				10		9
6			3	8	5		7					2		1						4	11			10		9
6	8		3		5		7					2		1						4	11			10		9
6		8	3		5		7					2		1						4	11			10		9
6		4	3	8	5		7					2		1	11										10	9
6		4	3		5		7					2		1	11							8			10	9
6		4	3		5		7					2		1	10							8			11	9
6		4	3		5		7					2		1								8		10	11	9
6		4	3		5		7					2		1								8		10	11	9
6		4	3	8	5							2		1	11									10	7	9
6		4	3		5							2		1							11	8		10	7	9
6		4	3	8	5							2		1							11			10	7	9
6		4	3		5							2		1							11	8		10	7	9
6		4	3	8	5		10					2		1							11				7	9
6		4	3	8	5							2		1							11			10	7	9
6		5	3	8								2		1						4	11			10	7	9
6		5	3	8								2		1					10	4	11				7	9
6		4			5		7					2	8	1							11		3	10		9
6	8	4			5							2		1	10						11		3		7	9
		4			5	1						2	8		10					6	11		3		7	9
		4			5							2		1			6				11	8	3	10	7	9
		4		8			7			5		2		1	10					6	11		3			9
6		4		8	5		7					2		1	10						11		3			9
6		4	3	8			7			5		2		1							11	10				9
6	8	4	3							5		2		1						7	11			10		9
6	10	4	3	8						5				1							11		2		7	9
6	8	4	3		5							2		1		7					11			10		9
6	8	4	3							5		2		1				7			11			10		9
	8	4	3		5							2		1	10					6	11				7	9
	9		3		5			10			4	2	8	1		7				6	11					
	9		3					10	6	5	4		8	1	11	7							2			
	8		3		5				6		2		4	1	11	7								10		9
			3	8	5			10	6				4	1		7					11		2			9
6	8	3		7	5				4			2		1							11			10		9
6	9	4	3		5			11	8			2		1		7								10		
6	8	4			5			11				2		1		7							3	10		9
30	13	32	30	14	30	1	16	5	7	6	3	34	6	37	12	7	1	1	1	11	26	8	10	23	19	35
	2	1		2	1		5	2	1							2					4	2		7	3	17

Bartlett Bill	Bradshaw Frank	Brittleton Tom	Burton Harry	Chapman Harry	Crawshaw Tommy	Crinson Bill	Davis Harry 'Pluck'	Foxall Frank	Hemmingfield Bill	Holbem Walter	Jameson Joe	Layton Willie	Lloyd Billy	Lyall Jack	Malloch Jock	Maxwell James	Proud Pattison	Reynolds Jack	Rollinson Frank	Ruddlesdin Harry	Simpson George	Simpson Viv	Slavin Hugh	Stewart Jimmy	Tummon Oliver	Wilson Andrew
		4	3		5							2		1						6	11	8		10	7	9
6		4	3		5		7					2		1							11	8		10		9
6		4		8	5		7					2		1							11		3	10		9
6	9	4		8	5		7					2		1							11		3	10		
6	10	4	3	8	5		7					2		1							11					9
6		4	3	8	5							2		1							11	7		10		9
6	8	4	3	7	5							2		1							11			10		9
6	8	4	3	7	5							2		1							11			10		9
7	4	8	6	6	8		4					8		8						1	8	3	2	7	1	7
				1																	3			4	1	5

League Table

	P	W	D	L	F	A	Pts
Newcastle United	38	22	7	9	74	46	51
Bristol City	38	20	8	10	66	47	48
Everton	38	20	5	13	70	46	45
Sheffield United	38	17	11	10	57	55	45
Aston Villa	38	19	6	13	78	52	44
Bolton Wanderers	38	18	8	12	59	47	44
Woolwich Arsenal	38	20	4	14	66	59	44
Manchester United	38	17	8	13	53	56	42
Birmingham	38	15	8	15	52	52	38
Sunderland	38	14	9	15	65	66	37
Middlesbrough	38	15	6	17	56	63	36
Blackburn Rovers	38	14	7	17	56	59	35
SHEFFIELD WEDNESDAY	38	12	11	15	49	60	35
Preston North End	38	14	7	17	44	57	35
Liverpool	38	13	7	18	64	65	33
Bury	38	13	6	19	58	68	32
Manchester City	38	10	12	16	53	77	32
Notts County	38	8	15	15	46	50	31
Derby County	38	9	9	20	41	59	27
Stoke	38	8	10	20	41	64	26

1907-08

Division One

Manager: Arthur Dickinson

Did you know that?

Final League Position: 5th

After drawing with Nottingham Forest on 23 November 1907, Wednesday did not draw again until 20 April 1908 against Woolwich Arsenal – a total of 23 League and Cup games.

Match No.	Date	Venue	Opponents		Round	Result	HT Score	Position	Scorers	Attendance
1	Sep 2	A	Preston North End	D		1-1	1-0		Wilson	8,000
2	7	H	Newcastle United	W		3-1	1-0	5th	Stewart, Bradshaw, Wilson	18,000
3	14	A	Bristol City	W		2-0	0-0	4th	Chapman, Wilson	18,000
4	21	H	Notts County	W		2-0	1-0	3rd	Wilson, Brittleton	16,000
5	23	H	Bristol City	W		5-3	1-0	1st	Chapman, Wilson (2), Stewart (2)	8,500
6	28	A	Manchester City	L		2-3	1-1	3rd	Brittleton, Stewart	30,000
7	Oct 5	H	Preston North End	W		1-0	0-0	2nd	Brittleton	14,000
8	12	A	Bury	W		2-0	2-0	1st	Bradshaw, Stewart	10,000
9	19	H	Aston Villa	L		2-3	1-0	2nd	Chapman, Wilson	18,000
10	26	A	Liverpool	L		0-3	0-1	2nd		20,000
11	Nov 2	H	Middlesbrough	W		3-2	3-1	2nd	Chapman, Simpson, Stewart	18,000
12	9	A	Sheffield United	W		3-1	1-0	2nd	Brittleton, Simpson, Stewart	30,694
13	16	H	Chelsea	W		3-1	1-1	2nd	Simpson, Wilson, Chapman	10,000
14	23	A	Nottingham Forest	D		2-2	1-1	2nd	Tummon, Maxwell	12,000
15	30	H	Manchester United	W		2-0	0-0	2nd	Bartlett, Stewart	43,143
16	Dec 7	A	Blackburn Rovers	L		0-2	0-1	2nd		12,000
17	14	H	Bolton Wanderers	W		5-2	0-2	2nd	Stewart (2), Bradshaw, Brittleton, Wilson	5,000
18	21	A	Birmingham	L		1-2	1-2	2nd	Wilson	12,000
19	26	H	Sunderland	L		2-3	1-2	2nd	Napier, Stewart	20,000
20	28	H	Everton	L		1-2	0-1	3rd	Napier	20,000
21	31	H	Woolwich Arsenal	W		6-0	4-0	2nd	Bradshaw (3), Wilson, Brittleton (pen), Chapman	9,000
22	Jan 4	A	Newcastle United	L		1-2	1-0	3rd	Bradshaw	30,000
23	18	A	Notts County	W		2-1	0-1	3rd	Bradshaw, Bartlett	14,000
24	25	H	Manchester City	W		5-1	3-1	3rd	Bradshaw (2), Stewart (2), Chapman	11,000
25	Feb 8	H	Bury	W		2-0	1-0	2nd	Maxwell, Bolland	17,000
26	15	A	Aston Villa	L		0-5	0-3	3rd		12,000
27	Mar 7	H	Sheffield United	W		2-0	0-0	2nd	Wilson, Maxwell	20,000
28	9	H	Liverpool	L		1-2	1-1	2nd	Simpson	5,000
29	14	A	Chelsea	L		1-3	0-3	3rd	Wilson	35,000
30	21	H	Nottingham Forest	W		2-1	1-1	3rd	Wilson, Simpson	8,000
31	28	A	Manchester United	L		1-4	0-1	3rd	Wilson	30,000
32	Apr 4	H	Blackburn Rovers	W		2-0	1-0	2nd	Simpson, Maxwell	8,000
33	8	A	Middlesbrough	L		1-6	0-4	2nd	Wilson	15,000
34	11	A	Bolton Wanderers	L		1-2	1-2	3rd	Bradshaw	15,000
35	17	A	Sunderland	W		2-1	1-0	3rd	Wilson (2)	20,000
36	18	H	Birmingham	L		1-4	1-4	4th	Wilson	10,000
37	20	A	Woolwich Arsenal	D		1-1	0-0	5th	Bradshaw	16,000
38	25	A	Everton	D		0-0	0-0	5th		12,000
										Apps
										Goals
FA Cup										
39	Jan 11	A	Norwich City	L	1R	0-2	0-1			10,326
										Apps

Armstrong Harold	Bartlett Bill	Bolland Tommy	Bradshaw Frank	Brittleton Tom	Burton Harry	Chapman Harry	Crawshaw Tommy	Crinson Bill	Foxall Frank	Hibbert Henry	Holbem Walter	Jameson Joe	Layton Willie	Lloyd Billy	Lyall Jack	Maxwell James	Miller Walter	Napier Dan	Rollinson Frank	Ruddlesdin Harry	Simpson George	Slavin Hugh	Stewart Jimmy	Taylor Jock	Tummon Oliver	Wilson Andrew
	6			4	3	8	5						2		1	7					11		10			9
	6		8	4	3		5						2		1	7					11		10			9
	6		10	4	3	8	5						2		1	7					11					9
	6			4		8	5						2		1	7					11	3	10			9
	6			4	3	8	5						2		1	7					11		10			9
	6			4	3	8	5	1					2			7					11		10			9
	6		8	4	3	7					5				1						11	2	10			9
	6		8	4	3	7			11		5				1							2	10			9
			8	4	3	7	5								1					6	11	2	10			9
7	6		10	4	3	8					5		2		1						11					9
	6		8	4	3	7	5						2		1						11		10			9
	6		8	4	3	7	5						2		1						11		10			9
	6		8	4	3	7	5						2		1						11		10			9
	6		8	4	3	7					5		2		1	11							10		9	
	6		8	4	3	7	5						2		1						11		10			9
	6		8	4	3	7					5				1						11	2	10			9
	6		8	4	3	5									1	7					11	2	10			9
	6		8	4	3	7					5		2		1						11		10			9
	6		8	4	3	7							2		1			5			11		10			9
	6		8	4	3				11				2		1	7		5					10			9
			8	5	3	7							2		1			4			11		10	6		9
			8	4	3	7	5						2		1			6			11		10			9
	6	11	8	5	3								2		1	7		4					10			9
	6	11	9	5	3	8							2		1	7		4					10			
	6	11	9			8	5						2		1	7		4				3	10			
	6		8	5	3	7							2		1			4			11		10			9
	6		8	4	3		5						2		1	7					11		10			9
	6		8	5							3		2		1	7		4			11		10			9
	6			5	2	8						4	3		1	7					11		10			9
	6		5	4	3	8						2			1	7					11		10			9
	6		8	4									2		1	7	5				11	3	10			9
	6			4		8		1		5			2			7	9		10		11	3				
	6		8	4	3			1					2			7	5		10		11					9
	6	11	8	5	3	7							2	4	1				10							9
	6	7		5	3	8			11				2	4	1								10			9
	6	7				8			11	5			2	4	1							3	10			9
	6	11	8	5		10							2	4	1	7						3				9
	6	11	8	5		7					2			4	1							3	10			9
1	35	8	30	36	30	31	14	3	4	2	8	2	31	5	35	20	3	9	3	1	27	12	32	1	1	34
	2	1	12	6		7										4		2			6		13		1	19

Armstrong Harold	Bartlett Bill	Bolland Tommy	Bradshaw Frank	Brittleton Tom	Burton Harry	Chapman Harry	Crawshaw Tommy	Crinson Bill	Foxall Frank	Hibbert Henry	Holbem Walter	Jameson Joe	Layton Willie	Lloyd Billy	Lyall Jack	Maxwell James	Miller Walter	Napier Dan	Rollinson Frank	Ruddlesdin Harry	Simpson George	Slavin Hugh	Stewart Jimmy	Taylor Jock	Tummon Oliver	Wilson Andrew
	6		8	4	3	7	5						2		1						11		10			9
	1		1	1	1	1	1						1		1						1		1			1

League Table

	P	W	D	L	F	A	Pts
Manchester United	38	23	6	9	81	48	52
Aston Villa	38	17	9	12	77	59	43
Manchester City	38	16	11	11	62	54	43
Newcastle United	38	15	12	11	65	54	42
SHEFFIELD WEDNESDAY	38	19	4	15	73	64	42
Middlesbrough	38	17	7	14	54	45	41
Bury	38	14	11	13	58	61	39
Liverpool	38	16	6	16	68	61	38
Nottingham Forest	38	13	11	14	59	62	37
Bristol City	38	12	12	14	58	61	36
Everton	38	15	6	17	58	64	36
Preston North End	38	12	12	14	47	53	36
Chelsea	38	14	8	16	53	62	36
Blackburn Rovers	38	12	12	14	51	63	36
Woolwich Arsenal	38	12	12	14	51	63	36
Sunderland	38	16	3	19	78	75	35
Sheffield United	38	12	11	15	52	58	35
Notts County	38	13	8	17	39	51	34
Bolton Wanderers	38	14	5	19	52	58	33
Birmingham	38	9	12	17	40	60	30

1908-09

Division One

Manager: Arthur Dickinson

Did you know that?

Final League Position: 5th

Wednesday player, English McConnell, was given a monkey from a fan of the team in Southampton to be the club mascot. He was called 'Jacko', but the club lost his first match.

Match No.	Date	Venue	Opponents		Round	Result	HT Score	Position	Scorers	Attendance
1	Sep 1	A	Leicester Fosse	D		1-1	0-0		Wilson	15,000
2	5	A	Aston Villa	D		1-1	1-0	12th	Wilson	20,000
3	12	H	Notts County	W		2-0	0-0	4th	Chapman, Brittleton	20,000
4	19	A	Nottingham Forest	W		2-1	1-1	4th	Chapman, Wilson	16,000
5	26	H	Newcastle United	W		2-0	0-0	3rd	Bradshaw (2)	25,000
6	Oct 3	A	Sunderland	L		2-4	1-3	5th	Bradshaw (2)	30,000
7	10	H	Bristol City	W		2-0	2-0	4th	Rollinson, Lloyd	15,000
8	17	A	Chelsea	D		2-2	2-1	5th	Wilson (2)	35,000
9	24	H	Preston North End	W		1-0	1-0	4th	Chapman	12,000
10	31	A	Blackburn Rovers	D		2-2	1-0	3rd	Bradshaw (2)	22,000
11	Nov 7	H	Middlesbrough	W		3-2	3-2	3rd	Brittleton, Bradshaw, Wilson	15,000
12	14	A	Bradford City	D		0-0	0-0	2nd		20,000
13	21	H	Manchester City	W		3-1	2-0	2nd	Chapman (3)	11,000
14	28	A	Manchester United	L		1-3	1-1	4th	Bradshaw	20,000
15	Dec 5	H	Liverpool	L		2-3	1-1	4th	Wilson, Lloyd	10,000
16	12	A	Everton	L		0-1	0-0	4th		20,000
17	19	H	Bury	W		4-3	2-1	4th	Bradshaw (2), Lloyd, Wilson	6,000
18	25	H	Sheffield United	W		1-0	1-0	4th	Simpson	28,000
19	26	A	Sheffield United	L		1-2	1-0	4th	Bradshaw	38,408
20	28	H	Woolwich Arsenal	W		6-2	5-0	4th	Tummon (2), Wilson (3), Lloyd	12,000
21	Jan 1	H	Leicester Fosse	W		3-1	3-0	4th	Bradshaw, Wilson (2)	13,000
22	2	H	Aston Villa	W		4-2	1-0	3rd	Brittleton, Wilson, Tummon, Chapman	18,000
23	9	A	Notts County	L		0-1	0-0	3rd		12,000
24	23	H	Nottingham Forest	W		3-0	1-0	3rd	Wilson (2), Bradshaw	10,000
25	30	A	Newcastle United	L		0-1	0-0	3rd		35,000
26	Feb 13	A	Bristol City	D		1-1	0-0	3rd	Rollinson	10,000
27	27	A	Preston North End	L		1-4	0-3	3rd	Wilson	8,000
28	Mar 13	A	Middlesbrough	L		1-2	0-1	4th	Chapman	10,000
29	20	H	Bradford City	L		0-2	0-1	4th		16,000
30	22	H	Chelsea	W		5-1	2-1	3rd	Rollinson (2), Lloyd, Wilson, Brittleton	7,000
31	27	A	Manchester City	L		0-4	0-1	3rd		12,000
32	29	H	Sunderland	L		2-5	1-2	4th	Bradshaw, Simpson	4,000
33	Apr 3	H	Manchester United	W		2-0	1-0	4th	Bradshaw (2)	15,000
34	10	A	Liverpool	W		2-1	1-1	4th	Hunter, Foxall	20,000
35	12	A	Woolwich Arsenal	L		0-2	0-1	4th		12,000
36	17	H	Everton	W		2-0	1-0	4th	Bradshaw, Foxall	8,000
37	19	H	Blackburn Rovers	L		1-2	1-0	5th	Bradshaw	3,000
38	24	A	Bury	L		2-4	0-3	5th	Bradshaw, Layton	15,000
										Apps
										Goals

FA Cup

Match No.	Date	Venue	Opponents		Round	Result	HT Score	Position	Scorers	Attendance
39	Jan 16	H	Stoke	W	1R	5-0	4-0		Chapman, Wilson (2), Bradshaw (2)	7,893
40	Feb 6	A	Portsmouth	D	2R	2-2	0-1		Tummon (2)	27,853
41	11	H	Portsmouth	W	2R Re	3-0	2-0		Brittleton, Lloyd, Wilson	26,066
42	20	H	Glossop North End	L	3R	0-1	0-1			35,019
										Apps
										Goals

Armstrong Harold	Bartlett Bill	Bolland Tommy	Bradshaw Frank	Brittleton Tom	Burton Harry	Chapman Harry	Davison Teddy	Foxall Frank	Holbem Walter	Hunter Andrew	Jameson Joe	Kinghorn Henry	Layton Willie	Lloyd Billy	Lyall Jack	McConnell English	Napier Dan	O'Connell Patrick	Rollinson Frank	Simpson George	Slavin Hugh	Spoors Jimmy	Stringfellow Frank	Taylor Jock	Tummon Oliver	Wilson Andrew
7	6		10	4		8			3				2		1	5				11						9
7	6		10	4		8			3				2		1	5				11						9
7	6		10	4		8		11	3				2		1	5										9
7	6		10	4	3	8		11	2						1	5										9
7	6		10	4		8			3				2		1	5				11						9
	6		10	4		8		11	3				2	7	1	5										9
	6			4		8	1	11	3				2	7		5			10							9
	6		10	4		8		11	3				2	7	1	5										9
	6		10	4		8			3				2	7	1	5				11						9
	6		10	4		8		11	3				2	7	1	5										9
	6		10	4	3	8							2	7	1					11		5				9
	6		10	4	3	8							2	7	1	5				11						9
	6		10	4	3	8		11					2	7	1	5										9
	6		10	4	3	8		11	2					7	1							5				9
	6	11	10	4	3	8							2	7	1							5				9
	6	7	10	4	3	8		11					2		1	5										9
	6	11	10	4	3	8	1						2	7		5										9
	6		10	4	3	8							2	7	1	5				11						9
	6		10	4	3	8							2	7	1	5				11						9
			10	8	3				2					7	1	5	4							6	11	9
			10	4		8			3		2			7	1							5		6	11	9
			10	4	3	8			2					7	1							5		6	11	9
			10	4	3				2					7	1				8			5		6	11	9
	6		10	4	3	8		11					2		1	5									7	9
	6				3	8		11	2					4	1				10			5			7	9
	6			4		8			3				2	7	1				10	11		5				9
	6							10			3	1	2	7			4			11		5	8			9
	6	11	10	4	3	8			2						1							5	7			9
	6	11		4	3	8							2		1				10			5	7			9
	6			4	3		1	11	2					7					10			5	8			9
	6			4	3		1	11	2	7									10			5	8			9
			9	4		8			3	7			2		1				10	11		5		6		
	6		10			8	1	11	3	7			2	4		5										9
	6		10	4		8	1	11	3	7			2			5										9
	6		10			8	1	11	3	7				4		5					2					9
			10					11	3	7		1		4		5					2		8	6		9
	6		10	2					3	7		1		4					11			5	8			9
	6		10	4			1	11		7			2			5		8			3					9
5	32	5	31	33	19	30	8	19	26	8	2	3	25	25	27	23	2	1	9	11	3	15	7	6	6	37
			19	4		8		2		1			1	5					4	2					3	18

Armstrong Harold	Bartlett Bill	Bolland Tommy	Bradshaw Frank	Brittleton Tom	Burton Harry	Chapman Harry	Davison Teddy	Foxall Frank	Holbem Walter	Hunter Andrew	Jameson Joe	Kinghorn Henry	Layton Willie	Lloyd Billy	Lyall Jack	McConnell English	Napier Dan	O'Connell Patrick	Rollinson Frank	Simpson George	Slavin Hugh	Spoors Jimmy	Stringfellow Frank	Taylor Jock	Tummon Oliver	Wilson Andrew
	6		10	4	3	8							2	7	1	5									11	9
	6		10	4	3	8							2	7	1	5									11	9
	6			4	3	8							2	7	1	5			10						11	9
	6		10	4	3	8							2	7	1	5				11						9
	4		3	4	4	4							4	4	4	4			1	1					3	4
			2	1		1								1											2	3

League Table

	P	W	D	L	F	A	Pts
Newcastle United	38	24	5	9	65	41	53
Everton	38	18	10	10	82	57	46
Sunderland	38	21	2	15	78	63	44
Blackburn Rovers	38	14	13	11	61	50	41
SHEFFIELD WEDNESDAY	38	17	6	15	67	61	40
Woolwich Arsenal	38	14	10	14	52	49	38
Aston Villa	38	14	10	14	58	56	38
Bristol City	38	13	12	13	45	58	38
Middlesbrough	38	14	9	15	59	53	37
Preston North End	38	13	11	14	48	44	37
Chelsea	38	14	9	15	56	61	37
Sheffield United	38	14	9	15	51	59	37
Manchester United	38	15	7	16	58	68	37
Nottingham Forest	38	14	8	16	66	57	36
Notts County	38	14	8	16	51	48	36
Liverpool	38	15	6	17	57	65	36
Bury	38	14	8	16	63	77	36
Bradford City	38	12	10	16	47	47	34
Manchester City	38	15	4	19	67	69	34
Leicester Fosse	38	8	9	21	54	102	25

1909-10

Division One

Manager: Arthur Dickinson

Did you know that?

Final League Position: 11th

On 28 March 1910, in the home game against Bradford City, out of the 22 players, 14 were Scotsmen, two were Irish and the referee was also Scottish. Wednesday won 2–1.

Match No.	Date	Venue	Opponents		Round	Result	HT Score	Position	Scorers	Attendance
1	Sep 1	A	Everton	D		1-1	0-1		Brittleton	15,000
2	4	H	Middlebrough	L		1-5	1-1	14th	Chapman	10,000
3	11	A	Bristol City	D		1-1	1-1	14th	Bradshaw	10,000
4	18	H	Bury	L		1-4	0-1	16th	Kirkman	8,000
5	20	H	Everton	L		1-3	1-2	16th	Rollinson	7,000
6	25	A	Tottenham Hotspur	L		0-3	0-1	20th		25,000
7	Oct 2	H	Preston North End	W		4-1	2-0	18th	Rollinson (2), Kirkman, Foxall	10,000
8	9	A	Notts County	D		0-0	0-0	16th		16,000
9	16	H	Newcastle United	W		3-1	2-0	14th	Rollinson (3)	14,000
10	23	A	Liverpool	L		1-3	0-3	15th	Kirkman	30,000
11	30	H	Aston Villa	W		3-2	1-1	14th	Rollinson (2), Wilson	12,000
12	Nov 6	A	Sheffield United	D		3-3	2-2	12th	Kirkman (2), Chapman	28,830
13	13	H	Woolwich Arsenal	D		1-1	0-1	12th	Wilson	10,000
14	27	H	Chelsea	W		4-1	2-0	12th	Brittleton (pen), Wilson, Foxall, Kirkman	12,000
15	Dec 4	A	Blackburn Rovers	D		0-0	0-0	12th		12,000
16	11	H	Nottingham Forest	W		4-3	4-2	12th	Wilson (2), Foxall, Rollinson	14,000
17	18	A	Sunderland	L		0-2	0-1	12th		8,000
18	25	A	Manchester United	W		3-0	0-0	12th	Bradshaw (2), Foxall	25,000
19	27	H	Manchester United	W		4-1	2-1	12th	Tummon, Wilson (2) Kirkman	37,000
20	Jan 3	A	Bolton Wanderers	W		2-0	1-0	10th	Wilson, Rollinson	10,000
21	8	A	Middlebrough	L		0-4	0-1	10th		10,000
22	22	H	Bristol City	W		2-0	2-0	10th	Rollinson, Chapman	6,000
23	Feb 12	A	Preston North End	L		0-1	0-1	11th		7,000
24	19	H	Notts County	D		0-0	0-0	11th		12,000
25	26	A	Newcastle United	L		1-3	1-1	11th	Stringfellow	5,000
26	Mar 5	H	Liverpool	W		3-0	2-0	10th	Brittleton (2), Lloyd	12,000
27	9	A	Bury	L		2-3	0-1	11th	Stringfellow, Brittleton	5,000
28	12	A	Aston Villa	L		0-5	0-0	11th		12,000
29	14	H	Tottenham Hotspur	D		1-1	0-0	11th	Foxall	4,000
30	19	H	Sheffield United	L		1-3	1-0	11th	Brittleton	16,000
31	25	A	Bradford City	L		0-2	0-0	11th		12,000
32	26	A	Woolwich Arsenal	W		1-0	1-0	11th	Chapman	8,000
33	28	H	Bradford City	W		2-1	1-1	11th	Murray, Robertson	15,000
34	Apr 2	H	Bolton Wanderers	D		0-0	0-0	11th		8,000
35	9	A	Chelsea	L		1-4	1-1	11th	Wilson	25,000
36	16	H	Blackburn Rovers	W		2-1	1-0	11th	Hunter (2)	5,000
37	23	A	Nottingham Forest	W		6-0	4-0	11th	Murray, Wilson (2), Robertson (2), Chapman	5,000
38	30	H	Sunderland	W		1-0	0-0	11th	Chapman	9,000
										Apps
										Goals

FA Cup

Match No.	Date	Venue	Opponents		Round	Result	HT Score	Position	Scorers	Attendance
39	Jan 15	A	Northampton Town	D	1R	0-0	0-0			12,000
40	20	H	Northampton Town	L	1R Re	0-1	0-0			18,533
										Apps

Bartlett Bill	Bradshaw Frank	Brittleton Tom	Chapman Harry	Davison Teddy	Foxall Frank	Hamilton Henry	Holbem Walter	Hunter Andrew	Kinghorn Henry	Kirkman Sam	Layton Willie	Lloyd Billy	McConnell English	McSkimming Bob	Murray James	O'Connell Patrick	Robertson George	Rollinson Frank	Slavin Hugh	Spoors Jimmy	Stringfellow Frank	Taylor Jock	Tummon Oliver	Warren Peter	Weir Findley	Wilson Andrew
6	10	4	8	1	11		3	7			2									5						9
	10	4	8	1	11		3	7			2									5		6				9
6	10	4	8	1	11		3	7			2									5						9
6	9	4	8	1			3			7	2							10		5			11			
		4	8	1						7	2							10	3	5		6	11			9
		4	8	1						7	2							10	3	5		6	11			9
		4	8	1	11		3			7			5					10		2		6				9
	8	4		1	11		3			7			5					10		2		6				9
	8	4		1	11		3			7			5					10		2		6				9
		4	8	1	11		3			7						5		10		2		6				9
	8	4		1	11		3			7			5					10		2		6				9
		4	8	1	11		3			7			5					10		2		6				9
		4	8	1						7			5					10		2		6	11	3		9
6		4	8	1	11		3			7			5					10		2						9
6		4	8	1	11		3			7			5					10		2						9
6	8	4		1	11		3			7			5					10		2						9
6	10	5	8	1			3			7		4								2		11				9
6	10	5	8	1	11		3			7		4								2						9
6	10	5	8	1			3			7		4								2			11			9
6		4	8	1			3			7			5					10		2			11			9
		4	8	1			3			7			5					10		2		6	11			9
6			8	1		9	3			7		4	5					10		2			11			
6		5	8	1			3			7		4						10		2			11			9
	10	8				9	3		1	7		4	5							2			11		6	
6			7	1		10	3					4								2	8		11		5	9
		9				10	3		1	7		4	5							2	8		11		6	
11		9				10	3		1	7		4	5							2	8				6	
6					11	10	3		1	7		4	5							2	8					9
6					11	10			1	7		4		3		5				2	8					9
6		9	7		11		3		1			4				5		10		2	8					
		8							1	7		4	5	3	9		11	10		2					6	
			8						1	7		4	5	2	9		11	10		3					6	
			8						1	7		4	5	3	9		11			2					6	10
			8					7	1			4	5	3	9		11			2					6	10
		4	8						1			7	5	3	9		11			2		6				10
		5	8					7	1			4		3	9		11			2					6	10
		5	8					7	1			4		3	9		11			2					6	10
		5	8					7	1			4		3	9		11			2					6	10
17	12	31	28	24	16	7	26	7	14	28	6	20	21	9	8	3	8	20	2	38	6	13	12	1	11	30
	3	6	6		5			2		7		1			2		3	11			2		1			11

Bartlett Bill	Bradshaw Frank	Brittleton Tom	Chapman Harry	Davison Teddy	Foxall Frank	Hamilton Henry	Holbem Walter	Hunter Andrew	Kinghorn Henry	Kirkman Sam	Layton Willie	Lloyd Billy	McConnell English	McSkimming Bob	Murray James	O'Connell Patrick	Robertson George	Rollinson Frank	Slavin Hugh	Spoors Jimmy	Stringfellow Frank	Taylor Jock	Tummon Oliver	Warren Peter	Weir Findley	Wilson Andrew
6		4	8	1			3			7			5					10		2			11			9
6		4	8	1			3			7			5					10		2			11			9
2		2	2	2			2			2			2					2		2			2			2

League Table

	P	W	D	L	F	A	Pts
Aston Villa	38	23	7	8	84	42	53
Liverpool	38	21	6	11	78	57	48
Blackburn Rovers	38	18	9	11	73	55	45
Newcastle United	38	19	7	12	70	56	45
Manchester United	38	19	7	12	69	61	45
Sheffield United	38	16	10	12	62	41	42
Bradford City	38	17	8	13	64	47	42
Sunderland	38	18	5	15	66	51	41
Notts County	38	15	10	13	67	59	40
Everton	38	16	8	14	51	56	40
SHEFFIELD WEDNESDAY	38	15	9	14	60	63	39
Preston North End	38	15	5	18	52	58	35
Bury	38	12	9	17	62	66	33
Nottingham Forest	38	11	11	16	54	72	33
Tottenham Hotspur	38	11	10	17	53	69	32
Bristol City	38	12	8	18	45	60	32
Middlesbrough	38	11	9	18	56	73	31
Woolwich Arsenal	38	11	9	18	37	67	31
Chelsea	38	11	7	20	47	70	29
Bolton Wanderers	38	9	6	23	44	71	24

1910-11

Division One

Manager: Arthur Dickinson

Did you know that?

Final League Position: 6th

In May 1911 Wednesday travelled on their first overseas tour, visiting Gothenburg in Sweden to play two games and then three games in Copenhagen, Denmark. In the second game in Sweden, ex-Wednesday player Fred Spiksley ran the line on Wednesday's behalf. The referee in the Swedish games was Charles Bunyan, who had been the 'keeper for Hyde when Preston North End had recorded an English record score of 26–0 in an FA Cup tie.

Match No.	Date	Venue	Opponents		Round	Result	HT Score	Position	Scorers	Attendance
1	Sep 3	A	Tottenham Hotspur	L		1-3	1-1		Chapman	35,000
2	10	H	Middlesbrough	D		1-1	0-1		Chapman	12,000
3	17	A	Preston North End	W		3-1	3-0	11th	Chapman (2), Murray	10,000
4	24	H	Notts County	L		1-3	0-1	15th	Murray	12,000
5	Oct 1	A	Manchester United	L		2-3	1-1	17th	Robertson (2)	20,000
6	8	H	Liverpool	W		1-0	1-0	14th	Robertson	14,000
7	15	A	Bury	D		1-1	1-0	14th	Wilson	10,000
8	22	H	Sheffield United	W		2-0	2-0	11th	Chapman (2)	25,000
9	29	A	Aston Villa	L		1-2	1-1	13th	Chapman	20,000
10	Nov 5	H	Sunderland	D		1-1	0-1	12th	Brittleton	20,000
11	12	A	Woolwich Arsenal	L		0-1	0-0	13th		10,000
12	19	H	Bradford City	L		0-1	0-1	16th		10,000
13	26	A	Blackburn Rovers	L		1-6	1-2	19th	Wilson	10,000
14	Dec 3	H	Nottingham Forest	W		5-2	2-0	15th	Chapman (1 + pen), Rollinson, Wilson, Kirkman	3,000
15	10	A	Manchester City	W		2-1	1-1	13th	Wilson, Chapman	20,000
16	17	H	Everton	L		0-2	0-0	15th		7,000
17	24	A	Oldham Athletic	L		0-1	0-0			8,000
18	26	A	Bristol City	D		2-2	1-2	16th	Chapman, Weir	20,000
19	27	H	Newcastle United	L		0-2	0-1	18th		25,000
20	31	H	Tottenham Hotspur	W		2-1	1-0	17th	Stringfellow, Glennon	10,000
21	Jan 2	H	Bristol City	W		2-1	2-0	14th	Glennon (2)	5,000
22	7	A	Middlesbrough	W		1-0	1-0	17th	Stringfellow	12,000
23	21	H	Preston North End	D		0-0	0-0	12th		3,000
24	28	A	Notts County	L		0-2	0-2	14th		12,000
25	Feb 11	A	Liverpool	L		0-3	0-1	15th		12,000
26	18	H	Bury	W		1-0	1-0	14th	Spoors	16,000
27	25	A	Sheffield United	W		1-0	1-0	12th	McLean	23,000
28	Mar 4	H	Aston Villa	W		1-0	1-0	11th	Paterson	12,000
29	11	A	Sunderland	W		2-1	2-1	10th	Robertson, McLean	10,000
30	18	H	Woolwich Arsenal	D		0-0	0-0	10th		7,000
31	Apr 1	H	Blackburn Rovers	W		1-0	1-0	9th	Kirkman	6,000
32	4	A	Bradford City	L		2-5	1-1		Wilson (2)	7,000
33	8	A	Nottingham Forest	W		1-0	1-0	9th	Wilson	5,000
34	14	A	Newcastle United	W		2-0	0-0	9th	Wilson, Robertson	20,000
35	15	H	Manchester City	W		4-1	2-0	8th	Campbell, Stringfellow, Paterson, Robertson	9,000
36	17	H	Manchester United	D		0-0	0-0	7th		25,000
37	22	A	Everton	D		1-1	0-1	7th	Wright	12,000
38	29	H	Oldham Athletic	W		2-0	1-0	6th	Robertson, Wilson	4,000
										Apps
										Goals

FA Cup

Match No.	Date	Venue	Opponents		Round	Result	HT Score	Position	Scorers	Attendance
39	Jan 14	H	Coventry City	L	1R	1-2	1-1		Wilson	19,603
										Apps
										Goals

Bradley Martin	Brittleton Tom	Campbell Jimmy	Chapman Harry	Davison Teddy	Dowling Michael	Glennon Teddy	Holbem Walter	Kinghorn Henry	Kirkman Sam	Lloyd Billy	McSkimming Bob	McLean Davie	Murray James	O'Connell Patrick	Paterson Marr	Robertson George	Rollinson Frank	Spoors Jimmy	Stringfellow Frank	Warren Peter	Weir Findley	Wilson Andrew	Worrall Teddy	Wright Percy
	4		8				3	1	7		5		9			11		2			6	10		
	4		8				3	1	7		5		9			11		2			6	10		
	4		8		7		3	1			5		9			11		2			6	10		
	4		8		7		3	1			5		9			11		2			6	10		
	4		8		9			1	7	5	3					11		2			6	10		
	5		8	1	9				7	4	3					11		2			6	10		
8	9			1			3		7	4	5					11		2			6	10		
	9		8	1			3		7	4	5					11		2			6	10		
	9		8	1			3		7	4	5					11		2			6	10		
	9		8	1			3		7	4	5					11	6	2				10		
	9		8	1			3		7	4	5						11	2			6	10		
	8		7	1			3			4	5			9			11	2			6	10		
	4			1			3		7		5		9			11		2	8		6	10		
			8	1					7	4				5		11	10	2		3	6	9		
			8	1					7	4				5		11	10	2		3	6	9		
			8	1					7	4				5		11	10	2		3	6	9		
	5		8	1		10	3		7	4						11		2			6	9		
			8				3	1	7	4				5		11	10	2			6	9		
			8				3	1	7	4				5		11	10	2			6	9		
	4					9	3	1	7					5		11		2	8		6	10		
	4			1		9	3		7					5		11		2	8		6	10		
	4			1		9	3		7					5		11		2	8		6	10		
	4			1		9	3		7		5					11			8		6	10	2	
8			9	1			3		7		5			4		11					6	10	2	
	4			1	7		3			8	5				9	11		2			6	10		
	4	6		1	7						3	9			8	11		2			5	10		
	4	6		1					7		3	9			8	11		2			5	10		
	4	6		1					7		3	9			8	11		2			5	10		
	4	6		1					7		3	9			8	11		2			5	10		
	4	6		1					7		3	9			8	11		2			5	10		
	4	6		1					7		3	9			8	11		2			5	10		
	4	6		1					7		3	9			8	11		2			5	10		
	4	6		1	7						3	9			8	11		2			5	10		
	4	6		1					7		3	9			8	11		2			5	10		
	4	6		1					7		3				9	11		2	8		5	10		
	4	6		1					7		3				9	11		2	8		5	10		
	5	6		1					7	4	3	9			8			2				10		11
	4	6		1					7			9			8	11		2		3	5	10		
2	32	13	18	30	7	5	20	8	32	16	28	11	5	10	14	35	8	36	7	4	36	38	2	1
	1	1	11			3			2			2	2		2	7	1	1	3		1	9		1

Bradley Martin	Brittleton Tom	Campbell Jimmy	Chapman Harry	Davison Teddy	Dowling Michael	Glennon Teddy	Holbem Walter	Kinghorn Henry	Kirkman Sam	Lloyd Billy	McSkimming Bob	McLean Davie	Murray James	O'Connell Patrick	Paterson Marr	Robertson George	Rollinson Frank	Spoors Jimmy	Stringfellow Frank	Warren Peter	Weir Findley	Wilson Andrew	Worrall Teddy	Wright Percy
				1		9	3		7	4				5		11		2	8		6	10		
				1		1	1		1	1				1		1		1	1		1	1		
																						1		

League Table

	P	W	D	L	F	A	Pts
Manchester United	38	22	8	8	72	40	52
Aston Villa	38	22	7	9	69	41	51
Sunderland	38	15	15	8	67	48	45
Everton	38	19	7	12	50	36	45
Bradford City	38	20	5	13	51	42	45
SHEFFIELD WEDNESDAY	38	17	8	13	47	48	42
Oldham Athletic	38	16	9	13	44	41	41
Newcastle United	38	15	10	13	61	43	40
Sheffield United	38	15	8	15	49	43	38
Woolwich Arsenal	38	13	12	13	41	49	38
Notts County	38	14	10	14	37	45	38
Blackburn Rovers	38	13	11	14	62	54	37
Liverpool	38	15	7	16	53	53	37
Preston North End	38	12	11	15	40	49	35
Tottenham Hotspur	38	13	6	19	52	63	32
Middlesbrough	38	11	10	17	49	63	32
Manchester City	38	9	13	16	43	58	31
Bury	38	9	11	18	43	71	29
Bristol City	38	11	5	22	43	66	27
Nottingham Forest	38	9	7	22	55	75	25

1911-12

Division One

Manager: Arthur Dickinson

Did you know that?

Final League Position: 5th

On 3 April 1912, Hillsborough held their first semi-final at the ground, a replayed game between West Bromwich Albion and Blackburn Rovers, with Albion winning 1–0 in front of a 20,050 crowd.

Match No.	Date	Venue	Opponents		Round	Result	HT Score	Position	Scorers	Attendance
1	Sep 2	H	Preston North End	L		0-1	0-0			10,000
2	4	A	Tottenham Hotspur	L		1-3	1-2	17th	Wilson	20,000
3	9	A	Bury	D		2-2	2-2		Kirkman, McLean	10,000
4	16	H	Middlesbrough	L		0-2	0-1	20th		16,000
5	23	A	Notts County	L		0-1	0-0	20th		12,000
6	30	H	Tottenham Hotspur	W		4-0	2-0	20th	McLean, Burkinshaw, Wilson, Glennon	8,000
7	Oct 7	A	Manchester United	L		1-3	0-1	19th	McLean	30,000
8	14	H	Liverpool	D		2-2	0-0	19th	Glennon, Wilson	12,000
9	21	A	Aston Villa	W		3-2	0-1	17th	Brittleton, Kirkman, Glennon	13,570
10	28	H	Newcastle United	L		1-2	0-1	18th	McLean (pen)	17,000
11	Nov 4	A	Sheffield United	D		1-1	1-0	18th	Wilson	28,000
12	11	H	Oldham Athletic	W		1-0	0-0	16th	Robertson	12,000
13	18	A	Bolton Wanderers	L		2-4	2-2	18th	Kirkman, Wilson	18,000
14	25	H	Bradford City	W		4-2	2-0	17th	McLean (2), Kirkman, Robertson	18,000
15	Dec 2	A	Woolwich Arsenal	W		2-0	2-0	18th	McLean, Kirkman	8,000
16	9	H	Manchester City	W		3-0	2-0	17th	McLean (2), Glennon	12,000
17	16	A	Everton	L		0-1	0-1	14th		12,000
18	23	H	West Bromwich Alb	W		4-1	3-1	13th	Robertson, McLean (2), Glennon	13,000
19	25	A	Blackburn Rovers	D		0-0	0-0	13th		17,069
20	26	H	Sunderland	W		8-0	7-0	11th	Kirkman (2), McLean (4), Glennon (2)	29,925
21	30	A	Preston North End	W		3-2	2-1	8th	McLean (2), Wilson	10,000
22	Jan 1	A	Sunderland	D		0-0	0-0	9th		27,000
23	20	A	Middlesbrough	D		1-1	0-1	6th	Wilson	10,887
24	27	H	Notts County	W		3-0	1-0	6th	McLean (2), Robertson	8,000
25	Feb 10	H	Manchester United	W		3-0	0-0	4th	McLean, Wilson, Glennon	25,000
26	17	A	Liverpool	D		1-1	1-1	4th	Kirkman	15,000
27	24	H	Aston Villa	W		3-0	2-0	4th	Kirkman, Wilson, McLean	20,000
28	Mar 2	A	Newcastle United	W		2-0	1-0	3rd	Glennon, Wright	15,000
29	9	H	Sheffield United	D		1-1	0-0	2nd	Glennon	29,500
30	16	A	Oldham Athletic	L		0-1	0-0	2nd		10,000
31	18	H	Bury	W		2-1	2-0	5th	Glennon (2)	6,000
32	23	H	Bolton Wanderers	L		0-1	0-0	5th		6,000
33	30	A	Bradford City	L		1-5	1-3	5th	McDonald (og)	9,000
34	Apr 6	H	Woolwich Arsenal	W		3-0	2-0	5th	Wilson, Brittleton, Glennon	6,000
35	8	H	Blackburn Rovers	D		1-1	1-1	5th	McLean	15,000
36	13	A	Manchester City	L		0-4	0-2	5th		30,000
37	20	H	Everton	L		1-3	0-2	6th	Wilson	5,000
38	27	A	West Bromwich Alb	W		5-1	3-1	5th	McLean (3), Kirkman (2)	8,000
										Apps
									One own-goal	Goals

FA Cup

Match No.	Date	Venue	Opponents		Round	Result	HT Score	Position	Scorers	Attendance
39	Jan 13	A	Middlesbrough	D	1R	0-0	0-0			25,013
40	25	H	Middlesbrough	L	1R Re	1-2	1-1		McLean	30,468
										Apps
										Goals

Brittleton Tom	Burkinshaw Lol	Campbell Jimmy	Davison Teddy	Glennon Teddy	Kirkman Sam	Lloyd Billy	McLean Davie	McSkimming Bob	O'Connell Patrick	Paterson Marr	Robertson George	Spoors Jimmy	Warren Peter	Weir Findley	Wilson Andrew	Worrall Teddy	Wright Percy
4		6	1		7		9	3		8	11	2		5	10		
		6	1		7	4	9	3		8	11	2		5	10		
		6	1		7	4	9			8	11	2	3	5	10		
		6	1		7	4	9			8	11	2	3	5	10		
4	7	6	1	8			9	3			11	2		5	10		
4	7	6	1	8			9	3			11	2		5	10		
4	7	6	1	8			9	3			11	2		5	10		
4	7	6	1	8			9	3			11	2		5	10		
4		6	1	8	7		9	3			11	2		5	10		
4		6	1		7		9	3		8	11	2		5	10		
4		6	1	8	7		9	3			11	2		5	10		
4		6	1	8	7		9	3			11			5	10	2	
		6	1		7	4	9	3		8	11	2		5	10		
4		6	1	8	7		9				11	3		5	10	2	
4		6	1	8	7		9				11	3		5	10	2	
4		6	1	8	7		9				11	3		5	10	2	
4		6	1	8	7		9		5		11	3			10	2	
4		6	1	8	7		9				11	3		5	10	2	
4		6	1	8	7		9				11	3		5	10	2	
4		6	1	8	7		9				11	3		5	10	2	
4		6	1	8	7		9		5		11	3			10	2	
4		6	1	8	7		9		5			3		11	10	2	
		6	1	8	7		9		5		11	3		4	10	2	
		6	1	8	7	4	9	5			11	3			10	2	
		6	1	8	7		9	5			11	3		4	10	2	
		6	1	8	7		9	5			11	3		4	10	2	
4		6	1	8	7		9	5			11	3			10	2	
4		6	1	8	7		9	5				3			10	2	11
4		6	1	8	7		9	5			11	3			10	2	
4		6	1	8	7		9	5			11	3			10	2	
4		6	1	8	7		9				11	3		5	10	2	
		6	1	9	7	4		5		8	11	3				2	10
4		6	1	8	7		9	5			11	3			10	2	
4		6	1	8	7		9	5			11	3			10	2	
4		6	1	8	7		9	5			11	3			10	2	
4		6	1	8	7		9	5			11	3			10	2	
4		6	1	8	7		9	5			11	3			10	2	
4		6	1	8	7		9	5			11	3			10	2	
29	4	38	38	32	34	6	37	25	4	7	36	37	2	24	37	26	2
2	1			13	11		25				4				11		1

Brittleton Tom	Burkinshaw Lol	Campbell Jimmy	Davison Teddy	Glennon Teddy	Kirkman Sam	Lloyd Billy	McLean Davie	McSkimming Bob	O'Connell Patrick	Paterson Marr	Robertson George	Spoors Jimmy	Warren Peter	Weir Findley	Wilson Andrew	Worrall Teddy	Wright Percy
4		6	1	8	7		9		5		11	3			10	2	
4		6	1	8	7		9		5		11	3			10	2	
2		2	2	2	2		2		2		2	2			2	2	
							1										

League Table

	P	W	D	L	F	A	Pts
Blackburn Rovers	38	20	9	9	60	43	49
Everton	38	20	6	12	46	42	46
Newcastle United	38	18	8	12	64	50	44
Bolton Wanderers	38	20	3	15	54	43	43
SHEFFIELD WEDNESDAY	38	16	9	13	69	49	41
Aston Villa	38	17	7	14	76	63	41
Middlesbrough	38	16	8	14	56	45	40
Sunderland	38	14	11	13	58	51	39
West Bromwich Albion	38	15	9	14	43	47	39
Woolwich Arsenal	38	15	8	15	55	59	38
Bradford City	38	15	8	15	46	50	38
Tottenham Hotspur	38	14	9	15	53	53	37
Manchester United	38	13	11	14	45	60	37
Sheffield United	38	13	10	15	63	56	36
Manchester City	38	13	9	16	56	58	35
Notts County	38	14	7	17	46	63	35
Liverpool	38	12	10	16	49	55	34
Oldham Athletic	38	12	10	16	46	54	34
Preston North End	38	13	7	18	40	57	33
Bury	38	6	9	23	32	59	21

1912-13

Division One

Manager: Arthur Dickinson

Did you know that?

Final League Position: 3rd

Wednesday's nickname up to this season had been the Blades, but when Wednesday's player, George Robertson, was given a wooden owl as a gift, this was placed under the North Stand for their game against Liverpool on October 12 1912. The game was won, as was the next few home games. A local journalist wrote that he hoped that Wednesday would not get the nickname 'The Owls', but it stuck despite the club stating that their nickname was still the Blades.

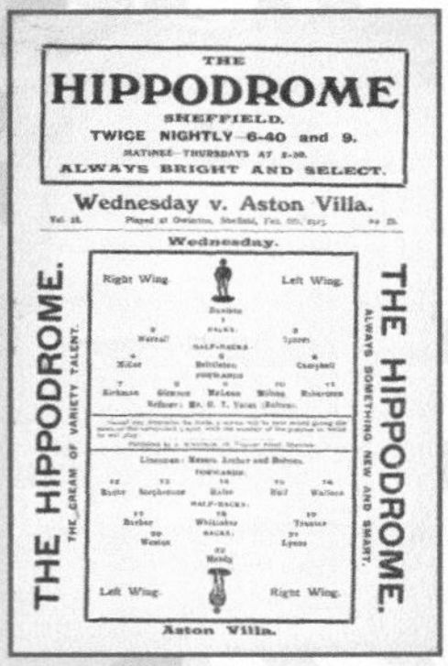

Match No.	Date	Venue	Opponents		Round	Result	HT Score	Position	Scorers	Attendance
1	Sep 2	H	Blackburn Rovers	W		2-1	2-1		McLean (2)	15,000
2	7	A	Tottenham Hotspur	W		4-2	0-0		Glennon (2), Robertson, Kirkman	28,000
3	14	H	Middlesbrough	W		3-1	2-0	3rd	Kirkman, McLean (2)	25,000
4	21	A	Notts County	W		2-1	2-1	3rd	McLean (2)	13,000
5	28	H	Manchester United	D		3-3	0-1	3rd	McLean (pen), Kirkman, Wilson	30,000
6	Oct 5	A	Aston Villa	L		0-10	0-6	4th		30,000
7	12	H	Liverpool	W		1-0	1-0	4th	Wright	20,000
8	19	A	Bolton Wanderers	L		0-3	0-1	7th		20,000
9	26	H	Sheffield United	W		1-0	1-0	5th	Glennon	15,500
10	Nov 2	A	Newcastle United	L		0-1	0-0	6th		25,000
11	9	H	Oldham Athletic	W		5-0	2-0	5th	Glennon, Kirkman (2), McLean (1 + pen)	15,000
12	16	A	Chelsea	W		4-0	2-0	4th	Wilson, Glennon (2), McLean	30,000
13	23	H	Woolwich Arsenal	W		2-0	1-0	3rd	McLean, Wilson	14,000
14	30	A	Bradford City	D		0-0	0-0	2nd		16,000
15	Dec 7	H	Manchester City	W		1-0	0-0	2nd	Wilson	20,000
16	14	A	West Bromwich Alb	D		1-1	0-0	2nd	McLean (pen)	15,000
17	21	H	Everton	L		1-2	1-1	3rd	McLean	14,500
18	25	H	Sunderland	L		1-2	1-1	5th	Robertson	37,000
19	26	A	Sunderland	W		2-0	2-0	3rd	McLean, Kirkman	10,000
20	28	H	Tottenham Hotspur	W		2-1	0-1	2nd	Robertson, Burkinshaw	30,000
21	Jan 1	H	Derby County	D		3-3	0-2	1st	McLean (2), Kirkman	40,000
22	4	A	Middlesbrough	W		2-0	1-0	1st	McLean, Robertson	13,575
23	18	H	Notts County	W		3-1	2-0	1st	McLean, Wilson, Glennon	15,000
24	25	A	Manchester United	L		0-2	0-2	1st		45,000
25	Feb 8	H	Aston Villa	D		1-1	1-1	1st	Wilson	41,000
26	15	A	Liverpool	L		1-2	1-2	3rd	McLean	25,000
27	24	H	Bolton Wanderers	D		2-2	1-0	1st	McLean (pen), Glennon	10,000
28	Mar 1	A	Sheffield United	W		2-0	1-0	1st	Robertson, McLean	35,419
29	15	A	Oldham Athletic	L		0-2	0-0			6,000
30	21	A	Blackburn Rovers	W		1-0	1-0	4th	Wilson	20,000
31	22	H	Chelsea	W		3-2	2-1	3rd	Wilson, Robertson, Kirkman	8,000
32	24	H	Derby County	W		4-1	1-0	3rd	Robertson (2), McLean (2)	12,000
33	29	A	Woolwich Arsenal	W		5-2	2-0	1st	Wilson, McLean (2), Kirkman, Glennon	5,000
34	Apr 5	H	Bradford City	W		6-0	3-0	1st	Glennon, Kirkman, McLean (2), Burkinshaw, Wright	16,000
35	12	A	Manchester City	D		2-2	0-1	2nd	Robertson, Glennon	30,000
36	14	H	Newcastle United	L		1-2	0-2	2nd	McLean (pen)	10,000
37	19	H	West Bromwich Alb	W		3-2	3-1	2nd	Glennon, McLean (2)	10,000
38	26	A	Everton	L		1-3	1-2	3rd	Robertson	15,000
										Apps
										Goals

FA Cup

Match No.	Date	Venue	Opponents		Round	Result	HT Score	Position	Scorers	Attendance
39	Jan 16	H	Grimsby Town	W	1R	5-1	2-1		McLean (4), Brittleton	26,442
40	Feb 1	A	Chelsea	D	2R	1-1	1-1		McLean	33,606
41	5	H	Chelsea	W	2R Re	6-0	3-0		McLean (2 + pen), Kirkman, Wilson (2)	35,860
42	22	A	Bradford Park Avenue	L	3R	1-2	1-1		Kirkman	24,000
										Apps
										Goals

Bralsford Chas	Brittleton Tom	Burkinshaw Lol	Campbell Jimmy	Davison Teddy	Glennon Teddy	Kirkman Sam	Lloyd Billy	McLean Davie	McSkimming Bob	Miller Jimmy	Robertson George	Spoors Jimmy	Wilson Andrew	Worrall Teddy	Wright Percy
	4		6	1	8	7		9	5		11	3	10	2	
	4		6	1	8	7		9	5		11	3	10	2	
	4		6	1	8	7		9	5		11	3	10	2	
	4		6	1	8	7		9	5		11	3	10	2	
	4		6	1	8	7		9	5		11	3	10	2	
	4		6	1		7	8		5		11	3	9	2	10
	4		6	1		7		9	5		11	3	10	2	8
	4		6	1		7		9	5		11	3	10	2	8
	4		6	1	8	7		9	5			3	10	2	11
	4		6	1	8	7		9	5			3	10	2	11
3	4		6	1	8	7		9	5		11		10	2	
	4		6	1	8	7		9	5		11	3	10	2	
	4		6	1	8	7		9	5		11	3	10	2	
	4		6	1	8	7		9	5		11	3	10	2	
	4		6	1	8	7		9	5		11	3	10	2	
	4		6	1	8	7		9	5		11	3	10	2	
3	4		6	1	8	7		9	5		11		10	2	
	4		6	1	8	7		9	5		11	3	10	2	
	4		6	1	8	7		9	5		11	3	10	2	
	4	7	6	1	8			9	5		11	3	10	2	
	4		6	1	8	7		9	5		11	3	10	2	
			6	1	8	7		9	5	4	11	3	10	2	
	4	7	6	1	8			9	5			3	10	2	11
	4	8	6	1	9	7			5		11	3	10	2	
	5		6	1	8	7		9		4	11	3	10	2	
	5		6	1	8	7		9		4	11	3	10	2	
	4		6	1	8	7		9	5		11	3	10	2	
	4		6	1	8	7		9	5		11	3	10	2	
	4		6	1	8	7		9	5			3	10	2	11
	4		6	1	8	7		9	5		11	3	10	2	
			6	1	8	7		9	5	4	11	3	10	2	
			6	1	8	7		9	5	4	11	3	10	2	
	4		6	1	8	7		9	5		11	3	10	2	
		10	6	1	8	7		9	5	4		3		2	11
	4		6	1	8	7		9	5		11	3	10	2	
	2	8	6	1		7		9	5	4	11	3	10		
	2		6	1	8	7		9	5	4	11	3	10		
	4		6	1	8	7		9	5		11	3	10	2	
2	34	5	38	38	34	36	1	36	36	8	33	36	37	36	8
		2			12	10		30			10		9		2

	4		6	1	8	7		9	5		11	3	10	2	
	4		6	1	8	7		9	5		11	3	10	2	
	4		6	1	8	7		9	5		11	3	10	2	
	4		6	1	8	7		9	5		11	3	10	2	
	4		4	4	4	4		4	4		4	4	4	4	
	1					2		8					2		

League Table

	P	W	D	L	F	A	Pts
Sunderland	38	25	4	9	86	43	54
Aston Villa	38	19	12	7	86	52	50
SHEFFIELD WEDNESDAY	38	21	7	10	75	55	49
Manchester United	38	19	8	11	69	43	46
Blackburn Rovers	38	16	13	9	79	43	45
Manchester City	38	18	8	12	53	37	44
Derby County	38	17	8	13	69	66	42
Bolton Wanderers	38	16	10	12	62	63	42
Oldham Athletic	38	14	14	10	50	55	42
West Bromwich Albion	38	13	12	13	57	50	38
Everton	38	15	7	16	48	54	37
Liverpool	38	16	5	17	61	71	37
Bradford City	38	12	11	15	50	60	35
Newcastle United	38	13	8	17	47	47	34
Sheffield United	38	14	6	18	56	70	34
Middlesbrough	38	11	10	17	55	69	32
Tottenham Hotspur	38	12	6	20	45	72	30
Chelsea	38	11	6	21	51	73	28
Notts County	38	7	9	22	28	56	23
Woolwich Arsenal	38	3	12	23	26	74	18

1913-14

Division One

Manager: Arthur Dickinson

Did you know that?

Final League Position: 18th

On 4 February 1914, in a second-round Cup replay with Wolverhampton Wanderers which Wednesday won 1–0, a newly built outer wall on the Penistone Road side of the ground collapsed without warning. Over 70 people needed medical treatment, many of whom had to be taken to the Royal Infirmary. The match was held up for a time, and the Wolves goalkeeper fainted and had to leave the field, taking no further part in the game.

Match No.	Date	Venue	Opponents		Round	Result	HT Score	Position	Scorers	Attendance
1	Sep 1	A	Bolton Wanderers	W		1-0	1-0		Glennon	26,321
2	6	H	Manchester United	L		1-3	1-1		J. Burkinshaw	32,000
3	13	A	Burnley	L		0-3	0-0	16th		20,000
4	20	H	Preston North End	W		2-1	1-1	12th	Wilson, Spoors (pen)	15,000
5	22	H	Oldham Athletic	L		1-2	1-0	13th	Glennon	15,000
6	27	A	Newcastle United	L		1-3	0-1	16th	Wilson	30,000
7	Oct 4	H	Liverpool	W		4-1	1-0	12th	Wilson, Kirkman, L. Burkinshaw, Robertson	25,000
8	11	A	Aston Villa	L		0-2	0-2	15th		22,000
9	18	H	Middlesbrough	W		2-0	2-0	11th	Robertson, J. Burkinshaw	15,000
10	25	A	Sheffield United	W		1-0	0-0	9th	Glennon	42,912
11	Nov 1	H	Derby County	L		1-3	0-1	10th	Spoors	20,000
12	8	A	Manchester City	W		2-1	1-0	10th	Kirkman, Wilson	25,000
13	15	H	Bradford City	L		1-3	0-1	10th	Wilson	20,000
14	22	A	Blackburn Rovers	L		2-3	0-2	13th	Wilson, Kirkman	25,000
15	29	H	Sunderland	W		2-1	1-1	10th	Robertson, Wilson	22,000
16	Dec 6	A	Everton	D		1-1	1-1	12th	Wilson	25,000
17	13	H	West Bromwich Alb	L		1-4	1-1	13th	Robertson	17,000
18	20	A	Tottenham Hotspur	D		1-1	1-1	13th	Wright	20,000
19	25	A	Chelsea	L		1-2	0-1	16th	Wright	40,000
20	26	H	Chelsea	W		3-0	1-0	13th	J. Burkinshaw, L. Burkinshaw, Campbell	38,000
21	27	A	Manchester United	L		1-2	0-1	17th	Spoors (pen)	10,000
22	29	H	Bolton Wanderers	D		1-1	1-0		McGregor	7,000
23	Jan 3	H	Burnley	L		2-6	0-2	17th	Brittleton, McGregor	25,000
24	17	A	Preston North End	L		0-5	0-3	18th		10,000
25	24	H	Newcastle United	D		0-0	0-0	18th		30,000
26	Feb 7	A	Liverpool	W		2-1	0-1	17th	McLean, J. Burkinshaw	20,000
27	14	H	Aston Villa	L		2-3	1-1	18th	Wilson (2)	30,000
28	28	H	Sheffield United	W		2-1	1-0	18th	Glennon, McLean	39,000
29	Mar 11	A	Derby County	D		1-1	1-0	15th	Wilson	10,000
30	14	H	Manchester City	D		2-2	1-0	15th	J. Burkinshaw, McLean (pen)	17,000
31	18	A	Middlesbrough	L		2-5	0-2	17th	McLean, Wilson	8,000
32	21	A	Bradford City	L		1-3	1-1	18th	Wilson	15,000
33	28	H	Blackburn Rovers	W		3-1	2-1	16th	L. Burkinshaw, McLean, Wilson	14,000
34	Apr 4	A	Sunderland	W		1-0	1-0	16th	McLean	12,000
35	11	H	Everton	D		2-2	0-1	17th	McLean (2)	14,000
36	14	A	Oldham Athletic	L		0-2	0-0	17th		10,000
37	18	A	West Bromwich Alb	D		1-1	1-1	18th	J. Burkinshaw	15,000
38	25	H	Tottenham Hotspur	W		2-0	0-0	18th	Wilson, McLean	10,000
										Apps
										Goals

FA Cup

Match No.	Date	Venue	Opponents		Round	Result	HT Score	Position	Scorers	Attendance
39	Jan 10	H	Notts County	W	1R	3-2	2-2		J. Burkinshaw, L. Burkinshaw, Brittleton	27,579
40	31	A	Wolverhampton W	D	2R	1-1	1-0		McLean	32,942
41	Feb 4	H	Wolverhampton W	W	2R Re	1-0	1-0		Kirkman	43,050
42	21	H	Brighton & Hove Alb	W	3R	3-0	0-0		McLean, Gill, J. Burkinshaw	38,997
43	Mar 7	H	Aston Villa	L	4R	0-1	0-1			56,991
										Apps
										Goals

Bentley Harry	Brelsford Chas	Brittleton Tom	Burkinshaw Jack	Burkinshaw Lol	Campbell Jimmy	Davison Teddy	Gill Jimmy	Glennon Teddy	Kirkman Sam	Lamb John	McGregor James	McLean Davie	McSkimming Bob	Miller Jimmy	Monaghan James	Nicholson Horace	Parkes David	Pickering John	Robertson George	Spoors Jimmy	Streets George	Wilson Andrew	Worrall Teddy	Wright Percy
		4	9		6			8	7				5						11	3	1	10	2	
		4	9		6	1		8	7				5						11	3		10	2	
		4	9		6	1		8	7				5						11	3		10	2	
			9		6	1		8	7				5	4					11	3		10	2	
			9		6	1		8	7	5				4					11	3		10	2	
			9		6	1		8	7	5				4					11	3		10	2	
				9	6	1		8	7				5	4					11	3		10	2	
	2			9	6	1		8	7				5	4						3		10		11
		2	8		6	1		9	7				5	4					11	3		10		
		2	8		6	1		9	7				5	4					11	3		10		
		2	8		6	1		9	7				5	4				11		3		10		
		2	8		6	1		9	7				5	4				11		3		10		
		2	8		6	1		9	7				5	4				11		3		10		
		2	8		6	1		9	7				5	4				11		3		10		
		4			6	1		8	7				5	9					11	3		10	2	
		4	8		6	1			7				5	9						3		10	2	11
		4	8		6	1							5	9	7				11	3		10	2	
		4	8		6	1					9		5	10	7					3			2	11
		4	8		6	1	7				9		5	10						3			2	11
		4	8	7	6	1					9		5	10						3			2	11
		4	8	7	6	1					9		5	10						3			2	11
	3	4	8	10		1			7		9		5	6									2	11
		4	8	7							9		5	10		6				3	1		2	11
	2	4	8	7		1						9	5	6						3		10		11
		4	8		6	1			7			9	5						11	3		10	2	
	2	4	8		6	1	11		7			9	5							3		10		
			8		6	1	11		7			9	5	4						3		10	2	
		4			6	1	11	8	7			9	5							3		10	2	
		4			6	1	11	8	7			9					5			3		10	2	
		4	10		6	1		8	7			9					5		11	3			2	
		4	8		6	1			7			9					5		11	3		10	2	
		4	8	7	6	1						9					5		11	3		10	2	
		4		7	6	1		8				9	2				5		11	3		10		
		4		7	6	1		8				9	2				5		11	3		10		
			8	7	6	1						9	2			4	5		11	3		10		
4			8	7		1						9	2			6	5		11	3		10		
		4	8	7		1						9	6				5		11	3		10	2	
		4	8	7		1						9	6				5		11	3		10	2	
1	4	30	31	14	32	36	5	20	24	2	6	15	32	22	2	3	10	4	21	37	2	31	25	9
		1	6	3	1			4	3		2	9							4	3		15		2

Bentley Harry	Brelsford Chas	Brittleton Tom	Burkinshaw Jack	Burkinshaw Lol	Campbell Jimmy	Davison Teddy	Gill Jimmy	Glennon Teddy	Kirkman Sam	Lamb John	McGregor James	McLean Davie	McSkimming Bob	Miller Jimmy	Monaghan James	Nicholson Horace	Parkes David	Pickering John	Robertson George	Spoors Jimmy	Streets George	Wilson Andrew	Worrall Teddy	Wright Percy
		4	8	7	6	1							5	10						3		9	2	11
		4	8	7	6	1						9	5							3		10	2	11
	2	4			6	1	11	8	7			9	5							3		10		
		4	8		6	1	11		7			9	5							3		10	2	
		4			6	1	11	8	7			9	5							3		10	2	
	1	5	3	2	5	5	3	2	3			4	5	1						5		5	4	2
		1	2	1			1		1			2												

League Table

	P	W	D	L	F	A	Pts
Blackburn Rovers	38	20	11	7	78	42	51
Aston Villa	38	19	6	13	65	50	44
Middlesbrough	38	19	5	14	77	60	43
Oldham Athletic	38	17	9	12	55	45	43
West Bromwich Albion	38	15	13	10	46	42	43
Bolton Wanderers	38	16	10	12	65	52	42
Sunderland	38	17	6	15	63	52	40
Chelsea	38	16	7	15	46	55	39
Bradford City	38	12	14	12	40	40	38
Sheffield United	38	16	5	17	63	60	37
Newcastle United	38	13	11	14	39	48	37
Burnley	38	12	12	14	61	53	36
Manchester City	38	14	8	16	51	53	36
Manchester United	38	15	6	17	52	62	36
Everton	38	12	11	15	46	55	35
Liverpool	38	14	7	17	46	62	35
Tottenham Hotspur	38	12	10	16	50	62	34
SHEFFIELD WEDNESDAY	38	13	8	17	53	70	34
Preston North End	38	12	6	20	52	69	30
Derby County	38	8	11	19	55	71	27

1914-15

Division One

Manager: Arthur Dickinson

Did you know that?

Final League Position: 7th

On 13 February 1915, in an away game against Manchester United, Wednesday's Jimmy Blair was kicked in the face, knocking him out completely, and had to be carried off with a broken jaw. Later in the same game, Paddy O'Connell missed the ball and kicked the referee, Mr W.J. Heath, instead, leaving him limping for the rest of the game.

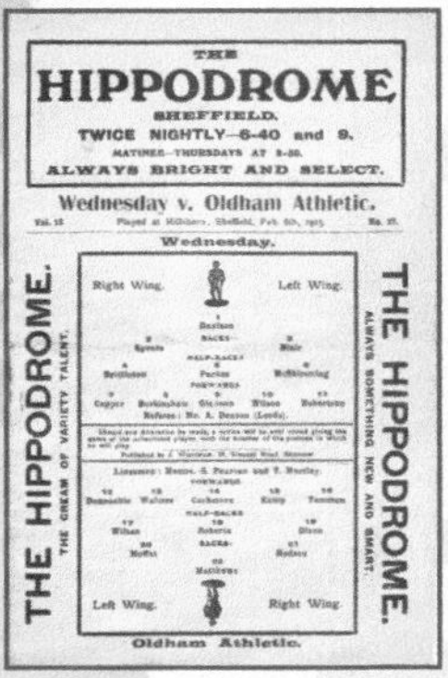

Match No.	Date	Venue	Opponents		Round	Result	HT Score	Position	Scorers	Attendance
1	Sep 1	H	Middlesbrough	W		3-1	1-0		Kirkman, Wilson (2)	12,000
2	5	A	Sheffield United	W		1-0	1-0	2nd	Wilson	25,000
3	9	A	Newcastle United	D		0-0	0-0			8,000
4	12	H	Aston Villa	W		5-2	4-0	1st	McLean (3), Glennon, Wilson	10,000
5	19	A	Liverpool	L		1-2	0-2	2nd	McLean	25,000
6	26	H	Bradford Park Avenue	W		6-0	2-0	1st	Kirkman, Glennon, McLean (2 + pen), Capper	15,000
7	Oct 3	A	Oldham Athletic	L		2-5	1-4	3rd	Wilson, McLean	12,300
8	10	H	Manchester United	W		1-0	0-0	2nd	Glennon	19,000
9	17	A	Bolton Wanderers	W		3-0	1-0	2nd	McLean (2), Glennon	20,000
10	24	H	Blackburn Rovers	D		1-1	1-1	2nd	McLean	24,000
11	31	A	Notts County	W		2-1	1-1	2nd	McLean (pen), Wilson	10,000
12	Nov 7	H	Sunderland	L		1-2	1-2	3rd	Capper	20,000
13	14	H	Manchester City	W		2-1	1-1	3rd	Glennon (2)	24,000
14	21	A	West Bromwich Alb	D		0-0	0-0	2nd		11,000
15	28	H	Everton	L		1-4	0-2	4th	McLean	14,000
16	Dec 5	A	Chelsea	D		0-0	0-0	5th		15,000
17	12	H	Bradford City	D		3-3	1-1	4th	Wilson, Brittleton, McLean	8,000
18	19	A	Burnley	W		3-2	3-1	3rd	McLean (2), Burkinshaw	6,000
19	25	H	Tottenham Hotspur	W		3-2	2-0	2nd	Burkinshaw, McLean, Wilson	25,000
20	26	A	Tottenham Hotspur	L		1-6	0-4	5th	McLean	8,000
21	Jan 1	H	Newcastle United	W		2-1	0-1	3rd	McLean, Bentley	10,000
22	2	H	Sheffield United	D		1-1	1-0	4th	Wilson	28,000
23	16	A	Aston Villa	D		0-0	0-0	2nd		7,500
24	23	H	Liverpool	W		2-1	1-1	3rd	McLean, Kirkman	12,000
25	Feb 6	H	Oldham Athletic	D		2-2	2-1	3rd	Wilson, Capper	20,000
26	13	A	Manchester United	L		0-2	0-0	3rd		7,000
27	27	A	Blackburn Rovers	D		1-1	1-1	4th	Glennon	7,000
28	Mar 1	H	Bolton Wanderers	W		7-0	3-0	1st	Parkes, Glennon, Gill, Robertson, Wilson, Capper, Bentley	7,000
29	6	H	Notts County	D		0-0	0-0	1st		11,000
30	13	A	Sunderland	L		1-3	0-1	1st	Robertson	12,000
31	17	A	Bradford Park Avenue	D		1-1	0-1	2nd	Glennon	7,000
32	20	A	Manchester City	L		0-4	0-1	4th		20,000
33	27	H	West Bromwich Alb	D		0-0	0-0	3rd		9,000
34	Apr 3	A	Everton	W		1-0	1-0	2nd	Kirkman	12,000
35	5	A	Middlesbrough	L		1-3	0-1	3rd	Wilson	11,000
36	10	H	Chelsea	W		3-2	1-1	3rd	McLean (2), Wilson	10,000
37	17	A	Bradford City	L		0-1	0-0	4th		10,000
38	24	H	Burnley	D		0-0	0-0	7th		10,000
										Apps
										Goals

FA Cup

Match No.	Date	Venue	Opponents		Round	Result	HT Score	Position	Scorers	Attendance
39	Jan 9	H	Manchester United	W	1R	1-0	0-0		Wilson	23,248
40	30	H	Wolverhampton W	W	2R	2-0	2-0		Robertson, Glennon	22,919
41	Feb 20	H	Newcastle United	L	3R	1-2	0-1		McLean	25,971
										Apps
										Goals

Bentley Harry	Blair Jimmy	Brittleton Tom	Burkinshaw Jack	Capper Freddy	Davison Teddy	Gill Jimmy	Glennon Teddy	Kirkman Sam	McLean Davie	McSkimming Bob	Parkes David	Robertson George	Spoors Jimmy	Wilson Andrew	Worrall Teddy
		4			1		8	7	9	6	5	11	3	10	2
4					1		8	7	9	6	5	11	3	10	2
4					1		8	7	9	6	5	11	3	10	2
4					1	11	8	7	9	6	5		3	10	2
4					1	11	8	7	9	6	5		3	10	2
4	3			11	1		8	7	9	6	5		2	10	
4	3			11	1		8	7	9	6	5		2	10	
4	3			11	1		8	7	9	6	5		2	10	
4	3			11	1		8	7	9	6	5		2	10	
4	3			11	1		8	7	9	6	5		2	10	
4	3			11	1		8	7	9	6	5		2	10	
4	3			11	1		8	7	9	6	5		2	10	
4	3			11	1		8	7	9	6	5		2	10	
4	3			11	1		8	7	9	6	5		2	10	
4				11	1		8	7	9	6	5		3	10	2
6		4			1		8	7	9		5	11	3	10	2
6		4			1		8	7	9		5	11	3	10	2
6		4	8		1			7	9	5		11	3	10	2
6		4	8		1			7	9	5		11	3	10	2
6		4	8		1			7	9	5		11	3	10	2
6		4			1		8	7	9	5		11	3	10	2
6		4			1		8	7	9	5		11	3	10	2
	3	4			1		8	7	9	6	5	11	2	10	
6	3	4			1		8	7	9		5	11	2	10	
	3	4	8	7	1		9			6	5	11	2	10	
	3	4	8	7	1				9	6	5	11	2	10	
6		4		7	1	8	9			3	5	11	2	10	
6		4		7	1	8	9			3	5	11	2	10	
6		4		7	1	8	9			3	5	11	2	10	
6		4	8	7	1		9			3	5	11	2	10	
6		4		7	1		8		9	3	5	11	2	10	
6		4		7	1		8		9	5		11	3	10	2
6		4		8	1	11		7	9	3	5		2	10	
6	3	4		8	1			7	9	5		11	2	10	
6	3	4		8	1			7	9	5		11	2	10	
6	3	4		7	1		8		9	5		11	2	10	
	3	4		7	1		8		9	6	5	11	2	10	
	3	4	8	7	1				9	6	5	11	2	10	
32	18	24	7	24	38	6	30	27	33	35	29	25	38	38	14
2		1	2	4		1	9	4	22		1	2		13	

6	2	4			1		8	7	9		5	11	3	10	
	2	4	8		1		9	7		6	5	11	3	10	
4				7	1		8		9	6	5	11	3	10	2
2	2	2	1	1	3		3	2	2	2	3	3	3	3	1
							1		1			1		1	

League Table

	P	W	D	L	F	A	Pts
Everton	38	19	8	11	76	47	46
Oldham Athletic	38	17	11	10	70	56	45
Blackburn Rovers	38	18	7	13	83	61	43
Burnley	38	18	7	13	61	47	43
Manchester City	38	15	13	10	49	39	43
Sheffield United	38	15	13	10	49	41	43
SHEFFIELD WEDNESDAY	38	15	13	10	61	54	43
Sunderland	38	18	5	15	81	72	41
Bradford Park Avenue	38	17	7	14	69	65	41
West Bromwich Albion	38	15	10	13	49	43	40
Bradford City	38	13	14	11	55	49	40
Middlesbrough	38	13	12	13	62	74	38
Liverpool	38	14	9	15	65	75	37
Aston Villa	38	13	11	14	62	72	37
Newcastle United	38	11	10	17	46	48	32
Notts County	38	9	13	16	41	57	31
Bolton Wanderers	38	11	8	19	68	84	30
Manchester United	38	9	12	17	46	62	30
Chelsea	38	8	13	17	51	65	29
Tottenham Hotspur	38	8	12	18	57	90	28

1915-16

Midland Section (Principal Tournament)

Manager: Arthur Dickinson

Did you know that?

Final League Position: 7th

On 1 January 1916 Wednesday's away game was abandoned as it was played in poor weather with a high wind. At half time, with Wednesday losing 1–0, the Wednesday players got into a hot bath and would not come out for the second half!

Match No.	Date	Venue	Opponents	Round	Result	HT Score	Position	Scorers	Attendance
1	Sep 4	H	Bradford Park Avenue		L 2-4	1-2		Wilson, Goodwin	5,000
2	11	A	Leeds City		L 1-2	1-1	12th	Harrop	8,000
3	18	H	Hull City		L 2-4	0-4	14th	Goodwin, Wilson	3,000
4	Oct 2	H	Barnsley		L 1-4	1-3	14th	Brittleton	5,000
5	9	A	Leicester Fosse		L 1-3	0-1	14th	Burkinshaw	5,000
6	16	H	Sheffield United		D 0-0	0-0	14th		11,000
7	23	A	Bradford City		W 1-0	0-0	14th	Harrop	8,000
8	30	H	Huddersfield Town		W 2-1	0-0	14th	Harrop (pen), Hatton	5,000
9	Nov 6	A	Grimsby Town		L 1-2	1-1	14th	Wilson	4,000
10	13	H	Notts County		W 4-1	2-0	12th	Glennon, Cawley (2), Wilson	4,000
11	20	A	Derby County		W 5-1	2-1	11th	Bentley, Capper (3), Cawley	1,000
12	27	H	Lincoln City		W 4-1	2-0	10th	Wilson (2), Glennon, Hatton	3,000
13	Dec 4	A	Bradford Park Avenue		W 2-1	0-0	7th	Wilson, Burkinshaw	2,500
14	11	H	Leeds City		D 0-0	0-0	8th		3,000
15	18	A	Hull City		W 3-1	2-0	8th	Hatton, Glennon, Cawley	2,000
16	25	H	Nottingham Forest		L 0-1	0-0	7th		18,000
17	27	A	Nottingham Forest		L 0-1	0-0	7th		10,000
18	Jan 8	H	Leicester Fosse		W 3-1	1-0	9th	Wilson, Burkinshaw, Cawley	3,500
19	15	A	Sheffield United		D 1-1	0-1	8th	Capper	14,000
20	22	H	Bradford City		W 1-0	1-0	8th	Burkinshaw (pen)	5,000
21	29	A	Huddersfield Town		D 2-2	1-0	7th	Wilson, Glennon	3,000
22	Feb 5	H	Grimsby Town		W 2-1	0-1	6th	Hatton, Wilson	5,000
23	12	A	Notts County		D 1-1	0-1	6th	Burkinshaw (pen)	2,500
24	19	H	Derby County		W 5-0	2-0	3rd	Hatton, Wilson (2), Islip, Harrop	2,500
25	Apr 21	A	Lincoln City		L 2-6	1-3	6th	Atkins, Hood	7,000
26	25	A	Barnsley		L 0-4	0-2	7th		4,432
									Apps
									Goals

MIDLAND SECTION (Subsidiary Tournament) POSITION 4th

Match No.	Date	Venue	Opponents	Round	Result	HT Score	Position	Scorers	Attendance
27	Mar 4	H	Lincoln City		D 2-2	0-1		Glennon (2)	2,500
28	11	A	Grimsby Town		D 0-0	0-0	3rd		300
29	18	A	Rotherham County		W 2-0	0-0	1st	Wilson (2)	8,000
30	25	H	Hull City		L 0-2	0-0	2nd		3,000
31	Apr 1	A	Sheffield United		D 1-1	1-0	4th	Wilson	15,000
32	8	A	Lincoln City		L 0-3	0-0	5th		2,000
33	15	H	Grimsby Town		W 2-1	1-0	4th	Burkinshaw (pen), Wilson	3,000
34	22	H	Rotherham County		W 3-2	3-1	2nd	Burkinshaw, Islip (2)	10,000
35	24	H	Sheffield United		L 0-1	0-1	3rd		14,000
36	29	A	Hull City		L 0-1	0-0	4th		3,000
									Apps
									Goals

Guest Players: Ball (Birmingham), McManus and Simmons (Hull), Sgt Major Brown (Crystal Palace), Goodwin (Exeter), Causer (Glossop), W. Jones, Atkins, Sheppard & Rodgers (Whitwell St Lawrence), Thompson (Preston), Cadman (Firth Park), Hood (Silverwood), Johnson (Bohemians), Stapleton (Mexborough Town), Hanwell (Grimesthorpe).

Match abandoned at half time poor weather

37	Jan 1	A	Barnsley		0-1

Atkins Jack	Ball Billy	Bentley Harry	Brandon Tom Jnr	Brelsford Charlie	Brelsford Tom	Brittleton Tom	Brown W	Burkinshaw Jack	Cadman A.P.	Capper Alf	Causer Arthur	Cawley Tom Jnr	Clarke Horace	Davison Teddy	Dickinson J	Downing Michael	Glennon Teddy	Goodwin Billy	Hanwell P.H.	Harrop Joe	Hatton G S	Hood H	Islip Ernie	Johnson G	Jones W	Lloyd Billy	McGregor A W	McManus Thomas	Mills K	Reed Percy	Rodgers A	Sheppard J	Simmons Harry	Smith J	Spoors Jimmy	Stapleton William	Streets George	Tasker Hiram	Thompson Bob	Watson W	Wilkinson H	Wilson Andrew	Womack Frank	Worrall Teddy				
		6				4				7							8	9		5																	1	11				10	3	2				
		6		2		4		11		7							8	9		5																	1					10	3					
		6		2	11	4				7							8	9		5																	1					10	3					
		6				4		8		7	1						9			5																3				11		10		2				
					4	2		8					6					9		5							7									3	1			11		10						
	2	6				4		9		7				1			8			5																				11		10	3					
					6	4				7							9			5	11									8						2	1					10	3					
					4	2							6				9			5	11						7			8						3	1					10						
		4		2	7							10	6							5	11															8	1					9	3					
		6				4				7		10					8			5	11															2	1					9	3					
		6		2	7	4				8		10								5	11																1					9	3					
		6				4				7		10					8			5	11															2	1					9	3					
		4				6		11				8	7				10			5																2	1					9	3					
				3	6	4				7		10		1			8			5	11															2						9						
				3		4		7				10		1			8			5	11							6								2						9						
				3	6	4		7				10					8			5	11															2	1					9						
				3	6			7				10	4				8			5	11														2		1					9						
					6	4		8		7		10		1						5	11															2						9	3					
					6	4		8		7		10		1			5				11															2						9	3					
				3	6	4		8				10					5				11					7										2	1					9						
				3	6	4		7				10					8			5	11															2	1					9						
				3	6	2		4		7		10		1						5	11		8																			9						
				3	6	2		4				10			7					5	11		8														1					9						
				3	6	2		4		7		10		1						5	11		8																			9						
10			5						7				9			3			4			8			11						6	2									1							
					6	3	9	4	7				11				5					10	8													2	1											
1	1	10	1	13	17	23	1	16	2	14	1	16	7	7	1	1	18	4	1	22	17	2	4		1	1	2	1		2	1	1			1	16	17	1		3	1	24	12	2				
1		1				1		5		4		5					4	2		4	5	1	1																			12						

				3	6	2		4		7		10		1			8			5			11																			9						
				3	7	2		4				10	6				8			5			11														1					9						
				3	6	2		4		8		10					5						11				7										1					9						
		4			6	2		8				10					5						11	7												3	1					9						
				3	6	2		4				10		1			5						11	7															8			9						
				3	6	4		8					11				5						10											7		2	1					9						
				3	6	4		8		9							5						11	7												2	1					10						
				3	6	4		8									5						10	7	11											2	1					9						
					7	3	9	4					6				5						8		11											2	1					10						
10					4	2							6				5						9		11				8				7				1					3						
1		1		7	10	10	1	9		3		5	4	2			10			2			10	4	3		1		1				1	1		5	8		1			10						
								2									2						2																			4						

		6		3		4		8		7							9			5	11															2	1					10						

1916-17

Midland Section (Principal Tournament)

Manager: Arthur Dickinson

Did you know that?

Final League Position: 13th

On 9 September 1916, Bradford Park Avenue travelled to Hillsborough with only four men. The others arrived at the ground later, but they were still a man short, so they borrowed Tom Cawley, who was a Leeds player but played as a guest for Wednesday. Wednesday lost 3–1, with Cawley netting twice.

In March 1917 Arnold Birch, who was interned in Holland during the war, was allowed to return back to Sheffield for a month due to a family death and turned out for Wednesday in seven matches before having to return to Holland.

Match No.	Date	Venue	Opponents	Round	Result	HT Score	Position	Scorers	Attendance
1	Sep 2	A	Chesterfield	D	1-1	1-1		Burkinshaw (pen)	5,500
2	9	H	Bradford Park Avenue	L	1-3	1-1	13th	Jones	5,000
3	16	A	Birmingham	L	1-4	1-2	16th	T. Brelsford	16,000
4	23	H	Hull City	W	2-1	0-0	14th	Islip, Glennon	4,000
5	30	A	Nottingham Forest	L	1-5	1-0	14th	Cawley	8,000
6	Oct 7	H	Barnsley	W	3-0	0-0	11th	Cawley, Glennon (2)	5,000
7	14	A	Leeds City	L	0-1	0-1	12th		5,000
8	21	H	Sheffield United	D	2-2	1-1	13th	Islip, Kirkman	15,000
9	28	A	Bradford City	D	1-1	0-0	13th	Jones	
10	Nov 4	H	Leicester Fosse	W	3-0	2-0	12th	T. Brelsford, Glennon, Cawley	3,000
11	11	A	Grimsby Town	L	0-1	0-1	11th		
12	18	H	Notts County	W	2-0	1-0	9th	Kirkman, Wilson	2,000
13	25	A	Rotherham County	D	0-0	0-0	9th		4,500
14	Dec 2	H	Huddersfield Town	D	0-0	0-0	9th		3,500
15	9	H	Chesterfield	W	3-1	2-0	7th	Oldacre (2), Glennon	4,000
16	16	A	Bradford Park Avenue*	L	1-3	1-2	8th	Glennon	2,000
17	23	H	Birmingham	L	0-2	0-1	10th		10,000
18	26	A	Lincoln City	L	0-4	0-2	13th		4,000
19	30	A	Hull City	L	0-1	0-0	13th		2,000
20	Jan 6	H	Nottingham Forest	L	1-4	1-2	14th	Wilson	3,000
21	13	A	Barnsley	L	0-2	0-2	14th		2,000
22	20	H	Leeds City	D	2-2	1-1	14th	Kirkman, Glennon	5,000
23	27	A	Sheffield United	L	0-1	0-0	14th		12,000
24	Feb 3	H	Bradford City#	W	1-0	1-0	14th	Glennon	5,000
25	10	A	Leicester Fosse	L	0-3	0-1	14th		1,000
26	17	H	Grimsby Town	W	3-1	1-0	14th	Edwards (pen), Butler (og), Capper	2,000
27	24	A	Notts County	L	0-1	0-1	14th		1,000
28	Mar 3	H	Rotherham County	W	1-0	0-0	14th	Wilson	10,000
29	10	A	Huddersfield Town	L	0-3	0-1	13th		1,000
30	Apr 28	H	Lincoln City	W	7-1	2-0	13th	Burkinshaw (3), Bell (2), Glennon, Kirkman	5,000
									Apps
								One own-goal	Goals

MIDLAND SECTION (Subsidiary Tournament) POSITION 10th

Match No.	Date	Venue	Opponents	Round	Result	HT Score	Position	Scorers	Attendance
31	Jan 1	H	Rotherham County	L	2-3	1-3		Spoors (pen), Wilson	12,000
32	Mar 24	A	Sheffield United	W	4-3	4-1	3rd	Burkinshaw, Glennon (2), Buddery	12,000
33	31	H	Barnsley	D	2-2	1-2	3rd	Brittleton, Wilson	3,000
34	Apr 9	A	Rotherham County	L	1-2	1-0		Wilson	7,000
35	14	H	Sheffield United	W	2-1	2-0	2nd	Brittleton, Glennon	10,000
36	21	A	Barnsley	D	1-1	0-0	10th	Bell	2,000
									Apps
									Goals

* Abandoned after 70 minutes (Score stands) Wednesday, late due to fog, and three men short borrow three from Bradford.

\# Abandoned after 85 minutes (Score stands) Torrance & Tom Brelsford were sent off for fighting which led to other players fighting and hundreds of spectators running onto the pitch.

Guest Players: Atkins (Whitwell), Bell (Cravens Club), Buddery (Portsmouth), Tom Cawley (Leeds City), A. Cooper (Beighton), Cowham (Patrick Thistle), Firby (Silverwood), W. Jones (Whitwell St Lawrence), Islip (Huddersfield), Robinson, W. Brown & Howie (Bradford PA), Newsome (Interned from Holland).

Atkins Jack	Ballance W	Batiste Walter	Bell Harold	Bingham W	Birch Arnold	Blackwell Ernest	Booth J W	Brelsford Ben	Brelsford Charlie	Brelsford Tom	Brittleton Tom	Brown W	Buddery Harold	Burkinshaw Jack	Capper Alf	Cawley Tom Jnr	Clarke Horace	Cooper Arthur	Cowham J	Dunn S	Edwards	Firby G	Gill Jimmy	Glennon Teddy	Grayson H	Harrop Joe	Helliwell J C	Howard F	Islip Ernie	Jones W	Kirkman Sam	Lamb Jack	Longbottom C	Lowe Edward	Lyall Jack	McGregor A W	Newsome P (Chubby)	Oldacre Percy	Peach S	Quayle W	Robertson George	Robinson J	Roulson Joe	Sanderson C L	Smith J	Spoors Jimmy	Stokes A J	Tasker Hiram	Thorpe Ted	Watson W	Wilson Andrew
									3	6	4			7		10										5			8	11					1											2					9
									3	6	4			7										9		5			8	11					1														2		10
									3	6				7		10								4		5			8	11					1														2		9
									3	6	2			4		10								8		5			9		7				1						11										
									3	6	2			4		10								8		5			7						1						11										9
									3	6	2			4	7	10								8		5									1						11										9
									3	6	2			4	7	10		1						8																						5				11	9
									3	6	2			4	8									9					10		7				1											5				11	
									3	6	4				7	10								8		5				11					1											2					9
									3	6	4				7	10								8		5			9	11					1											2					
10								2	3	6				4		8										5				11					1	7															9
									3	6	2			4	8	10								5					11		7				1																9
									3	6	2			4	7	10		1					8	5					11																						9
									3	6	2			4	7	10								8		5			11						1																9
									3	6	2				7	10								8		5			11						1			9													4
									3		2	10			7	9	4							5				6		11					1							8									
				4					3	10	7						6						8	5											1										11				2		9
8							11		3	4							6	1												10														5			7		2		9
								6	3								4	1		10										11	7									8						5			2		9
		8							3	6								1	7					4		5			11									9											2		10
	9								3							10	11							4		5								6	1	7													2		8
									3	6	2					10								9		5					7	4			1															11	8
									3		4		9											8		5			11					6	1	7													2		10
									3	6	4				8	10			7					5						11					1														2		9
									3		7		9			10		1				4				6																				5		11	2		8
									3	6	4		9		8	10		1	11		5										7																		2		
						1			3		4		9		7	10								6		5				11																			2		8
					1				3	6	5				7	11								9					10														4						2		8
					1				3		4		9			10								6		5				11			7																2		8
			10		1				3		4		9	8										5		11	6				7																		2		
2	1	1	1	1	3	1	1	2	30	22	24	1	6	13	14	22	5	7	3	1	1	1	2	24		19	1	1	14	12	7	1	1	2	19	3		2		1	3	1	1	1	1	7	1	1	15	3	24
			2							2					4	1	3				1			9					2	2	4							2													3

Atkins Jack	Ballance W	Batiste Walter	Bell Harold	Bingham W	Birch Arnold	Blackwell Ernest	Booth J W	Brelsford Ben	Brelsford Charlie	Brelsford Tom	Brittleton Tom	Brown W	Buddery Harold	Burkinshaw Jack	Capper Alf	Cawley Tom Jnr	Clarke Horace	Cooper Arthur	Cowham J	Dunn S	Edwards	Firby G	Gill Jimmy	Glennon Teddy	Grayson H	Harrop Joe	Helliwell J C	Howard F	Islip Ernie	Jones W	Kirkman Sam	Lamb Jack	Longbottom C	Lowe Edward	Lyall Jack	McGregor A W	Newsome P (Chubby)	Oldacre Percy	Peach S	Quayle W	Robertson George	Robinson J	Roulson Joe	Sanderson C L	Smith J	Spoors Jimmy	Stokes A J	Tasker Hiram	Thorpe Ted	Watson W	Wilson Andrew
									3	10							6	1				4			8				11		7															5			2		9
					1				3		4		9	8	7									10		5				11													6						2		
					1				3	6	4		9	7										8		5				11																			2		10
					1			6	3		4			8	9									5						11						7													2		10
					1				3		4			6	7									8		5			10												11								2		9
			10						3					4	7							6		8		5											11		1										2		9
			1		4			1	6	2	4		2	5	4		1	1				2		5	1	4			2	3	1					1	1		1		1		1			1			6		5
			1								2		1	1										3																						1					3

1917-18

Midland Section (Principal Tournament)

Manager: Arthur Dickinson

Did you know that?

Final League Position: 11th

On 27 April 1918 S. Peach, a goalkeeper of Wycliffe BC, appeared for Wednesday as a half-back in a game against Grimsby Town, and the next season he would also play as a winger.

Match No.	Date	Venue	Opponents	Round	Result	HT Score	Position	Scorers	Attendance
1	Sep 1	H	Leeds City	L	0-1	0-0	13th		8,000
2	8	A	Leeds City	L	0-5	0-3	14th		6,000
3	15	H	Nottingham Forest	L	0-3	0-0	15th		5,000
4	22	A	Nottingham Forest	L	1-3	0-0	15th	Glennon	3,000
5	29	H	Leicester Fosse	L	1-3	0-2	15th	Glennon	4,000
6	Oct 6	A	Leicester Fosse	W	2-1	2-0	12th	Wilson, Burkinshaw (pen)	3,000
7	13	A	Hull City	D	3-3	0-1	11th	Wilson, Glennon, Burkinshaw (pen)	1,000
8	20	H	Hull City	W	4-3	0-1	9th	Burkinshaw, Glennon (2), Bell	5,000
9	Nov 10	A	Barnsley	L	2-3	0-1	12th	Bell, Glennon	1,500
10	17	H	Barnsley	W	4-2	1-2	12th	Burkinshaw (1 + pen), Wilson, Kay (og)	6,000
11	24	A	Bradford Park Avenue	L	1-2	1-0	12th	Glennon	1,000
12	Dec 1	H	Bradford Park Avenue	W	3-1	0-1	10th	Brittleton, Armitage, Burkinshaw (pen)	4,000
13	8	H	Bradford City	W	3-0	1-0	10th	Armitage, Hinchcliffe (2)	6,000
14	15	A	Bradford City	L	1-3	0-1	10th	Armitage	1,500
15	22	H	Rotherham County	D	3-3	0-2	10th	Spratt, Armitage, Capper	3,000
16	25	A	Sheffield United	L	0-1	0-1	10th		32,000
17	26	H	Sheffield United	W	3-1	2-1	10th	McLean, Armitage, Glennon	20,000
18	29	A	Rotherham County	D	0-0	0-0	8th		3,000
19	Jan 5	H	Lincoln City	W	7-2	5-1	8th	Capper, Glennon, Armitage, Buddery, Spratt (2), Brittleton	3,500
20	12	A	Lincoln City	L	0-3	0-1	8th		1,500
21	26	A	Grimsby Town	D	0-0	0-0	9th		2,000
22	Feb 2	A	Birmingham	L	1-4	0-2	10th	Burkinshaw	10,000
23	9	H	Birmingham	L	0-2	0-0	10th		3,000
24	16	A	Notts County	L	0-3	0-1	11th		4,000
25	23	H	Notts County	W	2-1	1-0	11th	Glennon, Spratt	3,000
26	Mar 2	A	Huddersfield Town	L	0-4	0-1	11th		1,000
27	9	H	Huddersfield Town	W	3-1	1-1	11th	Glennon (3)	5,000
28	Apr 27	H	Grimsby Town	D	1-1	1-1	11th	Brittleton	3,000
									Apps
								One own-goal	Goals

MIDLAND SECTION (Subsidiary Tournament) POSITION 1st

Match No.	Date	Venue	Opponents	Round	Result	HT Score	Position	Scorers	Attendance
29	Jan 1	A	Barnsley	L	1-4	0-3		Glennon	2,500
30	Mar 16	A	Sheffield United	W	5-0	3-0	6th	Glennon (4), Burkinshaw	12,000
31	23	H	Sheffield United	W	2-1	2-1	4th	Glennon (2)	15,000
32	30	A	Rotherham County	D	0-0	0-0	2nd		
33	Apr 1	H	Barnsley	W	6-2	3-0	1st	Salt (3), Glennon, Burkinshaw (pen), Pearson	10,000
34	6	H	Rotherham County	D	1-1	0-1	1st	Burkinshaw	2,000
									Apps
									Goals

Guest Players: Buddery (Bradford), Hibbert (Birley Carr), McGregor (Queens Park), Maw (Firth Park), Peach (Wycliffe BC), Roulson (Birmingham), Doughty (Lincoln), Brown (Whitwell), Robinson (Clarion).

S. Peach (goalkeeper) played at no 6 v Grimsby on April 27

Armitage Len	Barratt P	Bell Harold	Bentley Harry	Blair Jimmy	Brelsford Charlie	Brelsford Tom	Brittleton Tom	Brown W	Buddery Harold	Bullock	Burkinshaw Jack	Capper Alf	Clarke Horace	Cooper Arthur	Cowham J	Davison Teddy	Donaldson A J	Doughty H	Ford S	Glennon Teddy	Godfrey Joby	Harrop Joe	Hibbert Billy	Hinchcliffe Alfred	Jones W	Lemons Charlie	McGregor A W	McLean David	McSkimming Bob	Maw J W	Parkes David	Peach S	Pearson Stanley	Price Arthur	Quayle W	Robinson G H	Rodgers A	Roulson Joe	Salt Harold	Smith J	Spoors Jimmy	Spratt Bert	Stapleton William	Streets George	Summers George	Thompson Bob	Thorpe Ted	Toulson A	Whitchurch Ernest	Wilson Andrew
		10			3		4						8	1	7					9		5			11													6									2			
	7	10			3	6	4							1						9		5					11								8												2			
		10			3		4				7			1						8		5					11											6									2			9
		10			3		2				4		11							8		5					7					1						6												9
		10			3		4				9	7		1						8		5					11											6									2			
		10			3		4	7			6			1						8		5								11													2							9
		10			3		4				6			1						8		5				7				11													2							9
		10			3		4				8	7				1				9		5								11								6					2							
		10			3		4				6	7		1						8		5								11													2							9
9			6		3		4				8	7		1						5																							2					11		10
9					3		4				8	7		1						6		5																				11	2							10
9					3		4				8	7		1						5				10																		11	6				2			
9					3		4				8	7		1						6		5		10																		11	2							
9					3		4				8	7		1						5		6		10																		11	2							
9					3		4				8	7		1						5		6		10														2				11								
				3			4				8	7		1						6		5						9	2													11								10
8				3			4					7		1						5								9	2									6				11								10
9					3		4							1								5		8														6				11	2				7			10
9					3		4		8			7								6		5		10																		11	2		1					
9					3		4											7		5				8																		11	6		1		2			10
9							4		7		8									6		5		10																		11	2		1		3			
9										10	4	7								6											5					1	3					11	2				8			
9					3		4		8			7					10			6		5																				11	2	1						
9							4				8								11	6		5																3					2		1		7			10
					3		4				8									9		5		10									7									11	2		1				6	
					3		4													9		5	11										7	8				6					2		1	10				
					3		4				8									10	9	5	11	6									7										2		1					
							4												9			5	8									6	7							10	3	11	2		1					
14	1	9	1	2	22	1	27	1	3	1	19	14	2	16	1	1	1	1	2	26	1	23	3	10	1	1	4	2	2	4	1	2	4	1	1	1	1	10		1	1	15	20	1	8	1	10	1	1	12
6		2					3		1		7	2								13				2				1														4								3

9					3		4					7								10		5																6				11	2		1	8				
					3		4		8		9									10		5											7					6				11	2		1					
					3		4				9	7								10		5		6																		11	2		1	8				
					3		4		8											9				6							5		7						10			11	2		1					
					3		4		9		6									10											5		7						8			11	2		1					
							4		8		7								11			5		6														3	10				2		1	9				
1					5		6		4		4	2							1	5		4		3							2		3					3	3			5	6		6	3				
											3									8													1						3											

1918-19

Midland Section (Principal Tournament)

Manager: Arthur Dickinson

Did you know that?

Final League Position: 11th

On 27 December 1918 Sheffield Wednesday played Sheffield United in a friendly game at Tankersley Cricket Ground in aid of the 'Welcome Home Fund' for servicemen. The game ended 2–2, with £23 being taken at the gate.

Match No.	Date	Venue	Opponents	Round	Result	HT Score	Position	Scorers	Attendance
1	Sep 7	A	Bradford Park Avenue	L	3-4	2-1		J. Burkinshaw, Ford, Glennon	4,000
2	14	H	Bradford Park Avenue	L	2-3	1-3		Glennon (2)	5,000
3	21	A	Hull City	D	0-0	0-0	13th		4,000
4	28	H	Hull City	W	3-1	1-0	12th	Glennon, Ford, J. Burkinshaw	4,000
5	Oct 5	A	Coventry City	L	0-2	0-1	14th		7,500
6	12	H	Coventry City	W	3-0	2-0	12th	J. Burkinshaw, Glennon, Ford	7,000
7	19	H	Barnsley	W	2-0	1-0	9th	J. Burkinshaw, Glennon	8,000
8	26	A	Barnsley	W	1-0	0-0	8th	Glennon	2,500
9	Nov 2	H	Leicester Fosse	L	0-2	0-2	9th		7,000
10	9	A	Leicester Fosse	L	3-7	1-5	12th	J. Burkinshaw (2), Glennon	3,000
11	16	H	Nottingham Forest	L	1-2	1-0	12th	Ford	8,000
12	23	A	Nottingham Forest	L	1-3	0-1	12th	Brelsford	6,000
13	30	H	Leeds City	L	0-2	0-0	13th		10,000
14	Dec 7	A	Leeds City	D	1-1	0-0	13th	Brittleton	9,000
15	14	A	Bradford City	W	2-1	1-1	13th	Cartledge, Roe	6,000
16	21	H	Bradford City	W	1-0	0-0	12th	Roe	10,000
17	25	H	Sheffield United	W	4-0	3-0		J. Burkinshaw, Brittleton, Pearson, McLean	20,000
18	26	A	Sheffield United	L	0-3	0-1	12th		35,000
19	28	A	Grimsby Town	W	2-0	1-0	11th	Roe, Stapleton (pen)	4,000
20	Jan 11	A	Lincoln City	W	4-1	2-1	11th	Glennon (2), J. Burkinshaw, Pearson	4,000
21	18	H	Lincoln City	W	4-2	2-2	10th	J. Burkinshaw (2 + pen), Roe	6,000
22	25	A	Rotherham County	D	1-1	1-0	10th	Brittleton	6,000
23	Feb 1	H	Rotherham County	D	0-0	0-0	9th		5,000
24	8	H	Birmingham	L	0-1	0-1	10th		13,000
25	15	A	Birmingham	L	2-4	1-2	11th	Capper, S. Lamb	10,000
26	22	H	Notts County	D	2-2	1-1	10th	Capper, J. Burkinshaw	8,000
27	Mar 1	A	Notts County	D	0-0	0-0	11th		12,000
28	8	H	Huddersfield Town	L	1-3	1-1	11th	S. Lamb	15,000
29	15	A	Huddersfield Town	L	1-2	1-2	11th	Glennon	5,000
30	Apr 22	H	Grimsby Town	W	5-2	4-2	11th	J. Burkinshaw (2), Glennon (2), Gill	9,500
									Apps
									Goals

MIDLAND SECTION (Subsidiary Tournament) POSITION 2nd

Match No.	Date	Venue	Opponents	Round	Result	HT Score	Position	Scorers	Attendance
31	Jan 1	H	Rotherham County	W	4-2	4-1	1st	Brittleton, Glennon (2), Godfrey	3,000
32	Mar 22	H	Sheffield United	L	0-2	0-1	3rd		18,000
33	29	A	Sheffield United	L	0-1	0-0	4th		23,000
34	Apr 19	A	Barnsley	W	2-1	0-1	2nd	Glennon, J. Burkinshaw	6,000
35	21	A	Rotherham County	D	1-1	0-1	2nd	J. Burkinshaw (pen)	
36	26	H	Barnsley	W	4-3	1-0	2nd	Gill (2), Bentley (2)	6,000
									Apps
									Goals

Guest Players: Godfrey (Forest), Hibbert (Birley Carr), Buddery (Bradford), Maw (Firth Park).

Andrews H	Baker Alf	Bentley Harry	Birch Arnold	Blair Jimmy	Brelsford Charlie	Brittleton Tom	Buddery Harold	Burkinshaw Jack	Burkinshaw Roy	Buxton W	Campbell Jimmy	Capper Alf	Cartledge A	Davison Teddy	Deans J	Elshaw A	Ford S	Frith W A	Gill Jimmy	Glennon Teddy	Godfrey Joby	Harrop Joe	Hibbert Billy	Hill G	Hinchcliffe Alfred	Kirkman Sam	Lamb Jack	Lamb Samual	McLean David	Maw J W	Nicholson Harry	Parkes David	Peach S	Pearson Stanley	Reed Percy	Roe Archie	Rutledge W	Salt Harold	Saunders H P	Spoors Jimmy	Spratt Bert	Stapleton William	Summers Percy	Thorpe Ted	Watson W	Wood J		
						4		9									7			10		5			6									8							11	2	1	3				
						4		9				8								10		5			6									7							11	2	1	3				
						4		8									9			10		5	11		6									7								2	1	3				
					3	4		8									9			10		5			6					11				7								2	1					
						4		8	9			11								10		5			6									7								2	1	3				
						3		8	9		4						11			10		5			6									7								2	1					
						4		8	9					1						10		5		3	6			11													7	2						
						4		8	9											10		5		3	6			11													7	2	1					
						3		4	9											10		5		6				11						7							8	2		1				
			1			4		8	9											5				6				11						7							10	2		3				
			1			4		8	9			7					11			5				6										10			2							3				
					3	4		8	9								10			6		5												7									1	2	11			
			1			4		8	10								9			5				3	6			11						7										2				
			1			4									3					10		5			6			11						7		9		8						2				
			1			3							9					4		10		5			6			11						7		8								2				
9			1	3		4		10														5			6			11						7		8								2				
			1	3		4		10												5					6			11	9					7		8								2				
			1	3		4		10									11			5					6				9					7		8								2				
			1			4									3					9		5			6								11	7		8						10		2				
						4		10												9		5			6			11						7		8						2	1	3				
								10										4				5			6			11						7		9		8				2	1	3				
			1			4		10														5			6			11						7		8		9				2		3				
			1			4		10				8										5						11			6			7		9						2		3				
			1		3	4	9					7										5			6			11						8		10						2						
			1		3	4		10				8								9		6						11				5		7								2						
						4		10				8								9		5			6			11						7					3				1	2				
						3		4		9										10		5			6									7		8						2	1			11		
			1		3	4				9										8		6						11				5		7								2				10		
			1			3		10				8								9		5			6		4	11						7								2						
	11		1			4		8			6								10	9		5				7														3		2						
1	1		16	3	5	29	1	25	9	2	2	8	1	1	2		8	2	1	25		25	1	6	22	1	1	18	2	1	1	2	1	27		12	1	3	1	1	6	21	12	20	1	2		
					1	3		14				2	1				4		1	13								2	1					2		4						1						

			1			4									3					10	9	5			6			11						7		8								2				
			1			3		10			6	8								9							4	11				5		7								2						
	11		1			4		8			6	7								10												5						9		3		2						
			1			4		10			6	8							11	9						7	5													3		2						
			1			4		10			6	8							11	9						7	5													3		2						
		8	1			4					6					11			10							7	5								9					3		2						
	1	1	6			6		4			5	4			1	1			3	5	1	1			1	3	4	2				2		2	1	1		1		4		5		1				
		2				1		2											2	3	1																											

1919-20

Division One

Manager: Arthur Dickinson

Did you know that?

Final League Position: 22nd

On 4 October 1919, Wednesday met Sheffield United at Bramall Lane in the 100th club match between the two sides.

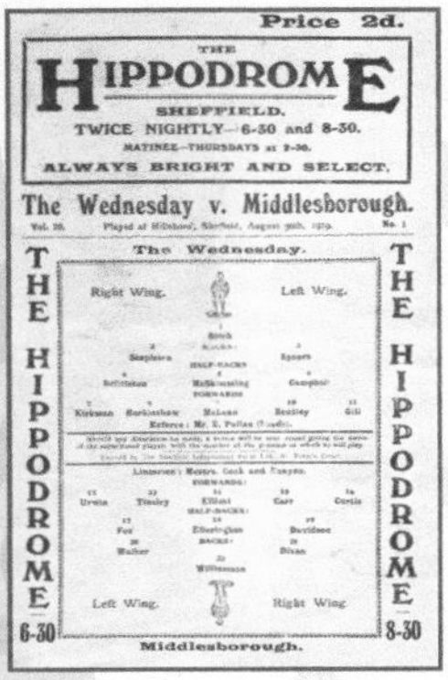
Price 2d.

THE HIPPODROME SHEFFIELD.

TWICE NIGHTLY—6-30 and 8-30.

ALWAYS BRIGHT AND SELECT.

The Wednesday v. Middlesborough.

The Wednesday.

Right Wing. Left Wing.

Left Wing. Right Wing.

THE HIPPODROME 6-30

THE HIPPODROME 8-30

Middlesborough.

Match No.	Date	Venue	Opponents	Round	Result	HT Score	Position	Scorers	Attendance
1	Aug 30	H	Middlesbrough	L	0-1	0-0			25,000
2	Sep 1	A	Manchester United	D	0-0	0-0			13,000
3	6	A	Middlesbrough	L	0-3	0-2	22nd		21,000
4	8	H	Manchester United	L	1-3	0-2	21st	Bentley	9,500
5	13	H	Notts County	D	0-0	0-0	21st		14,000
6	20	A	Notts County	L	1-3	0-1	21st	Gill	12,000
7	27	H	Sheffield United	W	2-1	1-1	20th	Campbell, Gill	30,000
8	Oct 4	A	Sheffield United	L	0-3	0-1	20th		40,000
9	11	H	Blackburn Rovers	D	0-0	0-0	22nd		15,000
10	18	A	Blackburn Rovers	L	0-1	0-0	20th		10,000
11	25	A	Manchester City	L	2-4	1-3	21st	Brittleton (2)	25,000
12	Nov 1	H	Manchester City	D	0-0	0-0	22nd		12,000
13	8	A	Derby County	L	1-2	0-2	22nd	Edmondson	9,000
14	15	H	Derby County	W	2-0	1-0	22nd	Gill, Spoors (pen)	9,000
15	22	A	West Bromwich Alb.	W	3-1	2-0	22nd	Price, Gill, Edmondson	31,000
16	29	H	West Bromwich Alb.	L	0-3	0-1	22nd		30,000
17	Dec 6	A	Sunderland	L	1-2	1-1	22nd	Edmondson	20,000
18	13	H	Sunderland	L	0-2	0-2	22nd		30,000
19	20	A	Arsenal	L	1-3	1-1	22nd	Binney	32,000
20	25	A	Bradford City	D	1-1	0-1	22nd	Gill	25,000
21	26	H	Bradford City	W	1-0	0-0	21st	McKay	35,000
22	27	H	Arsenal	L	1-2	1-1	21st	W. Harvey	30,000
23	Jan 1	A	Bolton Wanderers	L	0-2	0-1	22nd		35,500
24	3	A	Everton	D	1-1	1-1	22nd	McKay	30,000
25	17	H	Everton	W	1-0	0-0	22nd	Welsh	30,000
26	24	H	Burnley	W	3-1	1-0	22nd	Gill, Welsh (2)	20,000
27	Feb 7	H	Preston North End	L	0-1	0-0	22nd		14,000
28	14	A	Preston North End	L	0-3	0-2	22nd		20,000
29	17	A	Burnley	L	0-2	0-1	22nd		18,000
30	28	A	Bradford Park Avenue	L	0-3	0-2	22nd		15,000
31	Mar 10	A	Liverpool	L	0-1	0-1	22nd		15,000
32	13	H	Liverpool	D	2-2	2-0	22nd	McKay, Welsh	12,000
33	20	A	Chelsea	D	1-1	1-1	22nd	Gill	38,000
34	22	H	Newcastle United	L	0-1	0-0	22nd		10,000
35	Apr 3	A	Newcastle United	D	1-1	1-1	22nd	McIntyre	20,000
36	5	H	Bolton Wanderers	L	0-2	0-2	22nd		16,000
37	6	H	Chelsea	L	0-2	0-1	22nd		12,000
38	17	A	Aston Villa	L	1-3	1-1	22nd	Gill	25,000
39	19	H	Bradford Park Avenue	L	0-1	0-0	22nd		5,000
40	26	A	Oldham Athletic	L	0-1	0-1	22nd		11,750
41	29	H	Aston Villa	L	0-1	0-0	22nd		14,000
42	May 1	H	Oldham Athletic	W	1-0	0-0	22nd	W. Taylor	14,000
									Apps
									Goals

FA Cup

Match No.	Date	Venue	Opponents	Round	Result	HT Score	Position	Scorers	Attendance
43	Jan 14	A	Darlington	D	1R	0-0	0-0		12,016
44	19	H	Darlington	L	1R Re	0-2	0-1		52,388
									Apps

Armitage Len	Bentley Harry	Binney Chas	Birch Arnold	Blair Jimmy	Brelsford Tom	Bremall Charles	Brittleton Tom	Burkinshaw Jack	Campbell Jimmy	Capper Alf	Cooper Alf	Cooper Anthony	Davison Teddy	Edmondson Joe	Eggo Bert	Gill Jimmy	Harvey Edward	Harvey Billy	Hinchliffe Alf	Kirkman Sam	Kite Percy	Lamb Jack	McIntyre Johnnie	McKay Colin	McLean David	McSkimming Bob	O'Neill Harry	Parkes David	Pearson Stanley	Price Arthur	Reed Percy	Robertson George	Shelton George	Spoors Jimmy	Stapleton William	Sykes Joe	Taylor Sam	Taylor Billy	Welsh Fletcher	Whalley Johnny	Wilson Andrew	Wilson George
	10		1				4	8	6							11				7					9	5								3	2							
	6		1				4	8								10	11								9	5			7					3	2							
	6		1				4	8								10									9	5			7			11		3	2							
	4		1				2	9	6	7						10										5						11		3	8							
	8		1				4	10		7						9	11									5					6			3	2							
9			1							7	11	8				10						4				5					6			3	2							
			1				8	4	10	7	11					9										5					6			3	2							
			1				8	4	10	7	11					9										5					6			3	2							
9	4		1				8	10	6	7												5				2					11			3								
9	4		1				8	10	6													5				2					7	11		3								
	4						8		6				1	9				7								2	5			10		11		3								
	6			3			4	8		11			1	9				7								5				10					2							
	4			3			8		6				1	9			11	7								5				10					2							
		8	1	3			4		6					9		11				7						2				10				5								
			1	3			4	8	6					9		11		7												10	5			2								
			1	3			4	8	6					9		11		7												10	5			2								
	4		1	3			8		6					9		11		7									5			10				2								
	4			3					6	8			1	9		10		7									5					11		2								
	4	8	1	3			2	6	11					9				7						10				5														
	4	8	1	3				6						9		11		7						10				5							2							
		8	1	3				4	6							11		7						9				5		10					2							
		8	1	3				4	6							11		7						9				5		10					2							
		8	1	3				4	6					9			11	7										5		10					2							
		8	1	3				4	6							11		7						9						10	5				2							
		8	1	3			4			7						11			6					10		2		5											9			
		8		3			4		6	7			1			11								10				5							2				9			
				3			4		6				1			11				7				10				5							2		8		9			
	4			3			2		6				1	8						7						5				10			11						9			
				3			2						1		4	10				7										6	5		11				8		9			
		8		3			2			7			1		4									10						6	5		11						9			
	3	8			4				6	7			1	9																			11		2	5					10	
					4		2			7			1											10			3						11			6	8		9			5
				3	4		2			8			1			9		7					10							6			11									5
				3	4		2			8			1			9		7					10							6			11									5
				3	4					11			1			9		7					10							6				2						8		5
				3	5		4			10			1			9		7					6										11	2						8		
	2				5					4			1			10		7					6	9			3						11							8		
	2			3	4								1			9	11	7					6														10			8		5
				3	4					7			1	9			11						6												2		10			8		5
		8			4		2			7			1				11						6	9			3			10												5
							2			7			1		4		11						6				3										8	10	9			5
							3								4		11			7	1									6					2		8	10	9			5
3	18	12	21	25	10		30	18	22	21	3	1	20	14	4	27	9	19	1	6	1	3	9	12	3	16	7	8	2	19	11	5	9	18	20	2	7	2	9	5	1	9
	1	1					2		1					3		8		1					1	3						1				1				1	4			

Armitage Len	Bentley Harry	Binney Chas	Birch Arnold	Blair Jimmy	Brelsford Tom	Bremall Charles	Brittleton Tom	Burkinshaw Jack	Campbell Jimmy	Capper Alf	Cooper Alf	Cooper Anthony	Davison Teddy	Edmondson Joe	Eggo Bert	Gill Jimmy	Harvey Edward	Harvey Billy	Hinchliffe Alf	Kirkman Sam	Kite Percy	Lamb Jack	McIntyre Johnnie	McKay Colin	McLean David	McSkimming Bob	O'Neill Harry	Parkes David	Pearson Stanley	Price Arthur	Reed Percy	Robertson George	Shelton George	Spoors Jimmy	Stapleton William	Sykes Joe	Taylor Sam	Taylor Billy	Welsh Fletcher	Whalley Johnny	Wilson Andrew	Wilson George
		8	1	3				4	6							11		7						9		2				10	5											
		8	1	3		9	4		6	7						11								10		2					5											
		2	2	2		1	1	1	2	1						2		1						2		2				1	2											

League Table

	P	W	D	L	F	A	Pts
West Bromwich Albion	42	28	4	10	104	47	60
Burnley	42	21	9	12	65	59	51
Chelsea	42	22	5	15	56	51	49
Liverpool	42	19	10	13	59	44	48
Sunderland	42	22	4	16	72	59	48
Bolton Wanderers	42	19	9	14	72	65	47
Manchester City	42	18	9	15	71	62	45
Newcastle United	42	17	9	16	44	39	43
Aston Villa	42	18	6	18	75	73	42
Arsenal	42	15	12	15	56	58	42
Bradford Park Avenue	42	15	12	15	60	63	42
Manchester United	42	13	14	15	54	50	40
Middlesbrough	42	15	10	17	61	65	40
Sheffield United	42	16	8	18	59	69	40
Bradford City	42	14	11	17	54	63	39
Everton	42	12	14	16	69	68	38
Oldham Athletic	42	15	8	19	49	52	38
Derby County	42	13	12	17	47	57	38
Preston North End	42	14	10	18	57	73	38
Blackburn Rovers	42	13	11	18	64	77	37
Notts County	42	12	12	18	56	74	36
SHEFFIELD WEDNESDAY	42	7	9	26	28	64	23

1920-21

Division Two

Manager: Bob Brown

Did you know that?

Final League Position: 10th

On 15 January 1921, in an away game at Port Vale, the referee blew for half-time but, with the band coming on to play during half-time, he discovered that he had only played 42 minutes. He had to remove the band from the pitch so that the remaining three minutes could be played.

On 23 April 1921 the kick-off against Bury was delayed at Hillsborough due to the non-arrival of a linesman. Arnold Birch, the Wednesday reserve goalkeeper, took over as a linesman.

Match No.	Date	Venue	Opponents		Round	Result	HT Score	Position	Scorers	Attendance
1	Aug 28	A	Barnsley	D		0-0	0-0			15,000
2	30	H	Nottingham Forest	D		0-0	0-0			18,000
3	Sep 4	H	Barnsley	D		0-0	0-0	9th		25,000
4	11	H	Stoke	L		1-3	0-1	21st	McIntyre	25,000
5	18	A	Stoke	W		1-0	0-0	16th	McIntyre	20,000
6	25	H	Coventry City	W		3-0	1-0	13th	McIntyre (3)	25,000
7	Oct 2	A	Coventry City	W		3-2	1-2	10th	McIntyre (2), Binney	18,000
8	7	A	Nottingham Forest	L		2-4	2-1	10th	Wilson, McIntyre	10,000
9	9	H	Leeds United	W		2-0	1-0	8th	McIntyre (2)	25,000
10	16	A	Leeds United	L		0-2	0-1	10th		15,000
11	23	H	Birmingham	L		1-2	1-2	13th	McIntyre (pen)	25,000
12	30	A	Birmingham	L		0-4	0-2	17th		40,000
13	Nov 1	A	Rotherham County	L		0-2	0-1	17th		20,000
14	6	H	West Ham United	L		0-1	0-0	17th		20,000
15	13	A	West Ham United	L		0-4	0-3	18th		22,000
16	20	H	Fulham	W		3-0	1-0	18th	McIntyre, Dent, Binney	18,000
17	27	A	Fulham	L		0-2	0-1	18th		8,000
18	Dec 4	H	Cardiff City	L		0-1	0-0	19th		12,000
19	11	A	Cardiff City	L		0-1	0-0	20th		30,000
20	18	H	Leicester City	D		0-0	0-0	20th		15,000
21	25	H	Notts County	D		1-1	1-0	20th	Kean	27,000
22	27	A	Notts County	L		0-3	0-2	20th		26,000
23	Jan 1	A	Leicester City	L		1-2	1-2	20th	McIntyre (pen)	15,000
24	15	A	Port Vale	L		0-1	0-1	20th		10,000
25	22	H	Port Vale	W		1-0	1-0	20th	McIntyre	20,000
26	Feb 5	A	Blackpool	D		1-1	0-0	20th	Hall	10,000
27	7	H	Blackpool	L		0-1	0-0	20th		10,000
28	12	A	South Shields	W		3-2	0-1	20th	S. Taylor, Lofthouse (2)	15,000
29	19	H	South Shields	D		1-1	1-0	20th	S. Taylor	20,000
30	26	A	Hull City	D		1-1	1-1	20th	McIntyre	8,000
31	Mar 12	A	Wolverhampton W	W		2-1	0-0	20th	S. Taylor, McIntyre	22,160
32	21	H	Hull City	W		3-0	0-0	20th	McIntyre (2), Wilson	12,000
33	26	H	Stockport County	W		2-1	1-1	20th	McIntyre (2 pens)	25,000
34	28	H	Rotherham County	W		2-0	1-0	18th	McIntyre, S. Taylor	25,000
35	Apr 2	A	Stockport County	W		1-0	0-0	17th	McIntyre	10,000
36	9	H	Clapton Orient	D		1-1	0-1	14th	S. Taylor	15,000
37	11	H	Wolverhampton W	W		6-0	3-0	12th	McIntyre, Price, S. Taylor (2), Lofthouse, Smelt	14,000
38	16	A	Clapton Orient	L		0-1	0-1	13th		20,000
39	23	H	Bury	W		2-0	1-0	11th	S. Taylor, McIntyre	15,000
40	30	A	Bury	D		1-1	1-0	12th	McIntyre (pen)	8,000
41	May 2	H	Bristol City	D		2-2	2-0	11th	Smelt, McIntyre	15,000
42	7	A	Bristol City	W		1-0	0-0	10th	McIntyre	8,000
										Apps
										Goals

FA Cup

Match No.	Date	Venue	Opponents		Round	Result	HT Score	Position	Scorers	Attendance
43	Jan 8	H	West Ham United	W	1R	1-0	1-0		Price	49,125
44	29	A	Everton	D	2R	1-1	0-1		S. Taylor	44,000
45	Feb 3	H	Everton	L	2R Re	0-1	0-1			62,407
										Apps
										Goals

Armitage Harold	Bellas Jack	Binney Chas	Birch Arnold	Blair Jimmy	Brelsford Tom	Capper Alf	Cooper Joe	Davison Teddy	Dent Fred	Dunn John	Eggo Bert	Hall Harry	Harvey Edward	Kean Fred	Kell George	Levick Oliver	Lofthouse Jimmy	McIntyre Johnnie	O'Neill Harry	Price Arthur	Prior George	Reed Percy	Reeves Fred	Reilly John	Shelton George	Smelt John	Sykes Joe	Taylor Sam	Taylor Billy	Welsh Fletcher	Wilson George
				3				1		2	4			8			11	6						7					10	9	5
				3		7		1		2	4			8			11	6											10	9	5
				3				1		2	4			8			11	6				7							10	9	5
				3				1		2	4			8			11	9							7		6		10		5
		8		3		7		1		2	4						11	9		10							6				5
		8		3		7		1		2	4						11	9		10							6				5
		8		3		7		1		2	4						11	9		10							6				5
		8		3	4	7		1		2							11	9		10							6				5
	2	8		3				1			4						11	9		10					7		6				5
	2	8	1	3							4						11	9		10					7		6				5
	2	8		3				1			4						11	9	5	10					7		6				
	2	8		3				1			4		11					10			9				7		6				5
	2	8						1			4						11	9	3	10	7	5					6				
		8		3	10			1			4						11	9	2	6		5		7							
		8		3		7		1			4						11	9	2	10							6				5
	2	8				7		1	10		4						11	9	3								6				5
	2	8				7		1	10		4						11	9	3								6				5
	2	7				8		1	10		4						11	9	3	6											5
	2	7				8		1			4	9					11	10	3	6											5
	2	7						1	8		4	9	11					10	3	6											5
	2				4	7		1				9		8				10	3	6									11		5
	2				4	7		1				9		8				10	3	6									11		5
	2	8			4			1					11	10				9	3	6	7										5
	2				4			1				10		8			11		3	6					7			9			5
	2				4	7		1				8				6		10	3						11			9			5
	2				4			1				8			3		11	10		6						7		9			5
	3				4			1				8		7	2		11	10		6								9			5
	3				4			1				8			2		11	10		6						7		9			5
	3				4			1				8			2		11	10		6						7		9			5
	3				4	7		1				8			2		11	10		6								9			5
	2				4			1				8					11	10	3	6						7	5	9			
	2				4			1				8					11	10	3	6						7		9			5
	2				4			1				8					11	10	3	6						7		9			5
	2				4			1				8					11	10	3	6						7		9			5
	2				4			1				8					11	10	3	6						7		9			5
	2				4			1				8		5			11	10	3	6						7		9			
	2				4			1				8					11	10	3	6						7		9			5
	2				4			1				8					11	10	3	6						7		9			5
	2				4			1				8					11	10	3	6						7		9			5
	2				4			1				8		5			11	10	3	6			7					9			
2					4			1				8					11	10	3	6						7		9			5
2					4		9	1									11	10	3	6						7		8			5
2	30	17	1	14	24	14	1	41	4	8	19	22	3	11	5	1	36	41	26	34	3	3	1	2	7	14	14	19	6	3	36
		2							1			1		1			3	27		1						2		8			2

Armitage Harold	Bellas Jack	Binney Chas	Birch Arnold	Blair Jimmy	Brelsford Tom	Capper Alf	Cooper Joe	Davison Teddy	Dent Fred	Dunn John	Eggo Bert	Hall Harry	Harvey Edward	Kean Fred	Kell George	Levick Oliver	Lofthouse Jimmy	McIntyre Johnnie	O'Neill Harry	Price Arthur	Prior George	Reed Percy	Reeves Fred	Reilly John	Shelton George	Smelt John	Sykes Joe	Taylor Sam	Taylor Billy	Welsh Fletcher	Wilson George
	2				4	7		1						8				9	3	6					11				10		5
	2				4			1						8			11	10	3	6		7						9			5
	2				4			1						8	3		11	10		6		7						9			5
	3				3	1		3						3	1		2	3	2	3		2			1			2	1		3
																				1								1			

League Table

	P	W	D	L	F	A	Pts
Birmingham	42	24	10	8	79	38	58
Cardiff City	42	24	10	8	59	32	58
Bristol City	42	19	13	10	49	29	51
Blackpool	42	20	10	12	54	42	50
West Ham United	42	19	10	13	51	30	48
Notts County	42	18	11	13	55	40	47
Clapton Orient	42	16	13	13	43	42	45
South Shields	42	17	10	15	61	46	44
Fulham	42	16	10	16	43	47	42
SHEFFIELD WEDNESDAY	42	15	11	16	48	48	41
Bury	42	15	10	17	45	49	40
Leicester City	42	12	16	14	39	46	40
Hull City	42	10	20	12	43	53	40
Leeds United	42	14	10	18	40	45	38
Wolverhampton W	42	16	6	20	49	66	38
Barnsley	42	10	16	16	48	50	36
Port Vale	42	11	14	17	43	49	36
Nottingham Forest	42	12	12	18	48	55	36
Rotherham County	42	12	12	18	37	53	36
Stoke	42	12	11	19	46	56	35
Coventry City	42	12	11	19	39	70	35
Stockport County	42	9	12	21	42	75	30

1921-22

Division Two

Manager: Bob Brown

Did you know that?

Final League Position: 10th

During the season most of Wednesday's team were struck down with the flu epidemic that had hit Sheffield. Also nine of the squad had minor operations during the season.

Match No.	Date	Venue	Opponents		Round	Result	HT Score	Position	Scorers	Attendance
1	Aug 27	H	Barnsley	L		2-3	1-2	15th	McIntyre (pen), Ratcliffe	20,000
2	29	A	Derby County	W		1-0	1-0	18th	S. Taylor	12,000
3	Sep 3	A	Barnsley	L		0-2	0-1	19th		17,000
4	5	H	Derby County	D		1-1	0-1	18th	Lofthouse	18,000
5	10	A	Notts County	L		0-2	0-1	17th		15,000
6	17	H	Notts County	D		0-0	0-0	14th		15,000
7	24	A	Crystal Palace	D		2-2	2-2	17th	McIntyre, S. Taylor	15,000
8	Oct 1	H	Crystal Palace	W		1-0	0-0	14th	W. Taylor	22,000
9	8	H	Rotherham County	W		1-0	0-0	13th	Lofthouse	20,000
10	15	A	Rotherham County	D		0-0	0-0	13th		17,000
11	22	H	Bradford Park Avenue	W		2-1	2-0	10th	Ratcliffe, McIntyre	12,000
12	29	A	Bradford Park Avenue	L		1-2	0-1	13th	Brelsford	10,000
13	Nov 5	H	Fulham	L		1-4	0-1	14th	McIntyre	20,000
14	12	A	Fulham	L		1-3	0-1	16th	W. Taylor	25,000
15	19	A	Blackpool	W		2-0	0-0	15th	McIntyre (1 + pen)	5,000
16	26	H	Blackpool	W		5-1	3-0	14th	Brelsford, Lofthouse (2), Ratcliffe, McIntyre (pen)	12,000
17	Dec 3	H	Clapton Orient	D		0-0	0-0	14th		18,000
18	10	A	Clapton Orient	D		1-1	1-0	13th	McIntyre	17,000
19	24	A	Coventry City	D		2-2	0-0	14th	Ratcliffe (pen), Lofthouse	16,000
20	26	A	Leeds United	D		1-1	1-0	14th	S. Taylor	20,540
21	27	H	Leeds United	W		2-1	1-1	12th	Lofthouse, Wilson	25,000
22	31	A	Stoke	D		1-1	1-0	12th	W. Taylor	12,000
23	Jan 14	H	Stoke	L		0-1	0-0	15th		8,000
24	28	A	Wolverhampton W	D		0-0	0-0	14th		18,000
25	Feb 4	H	Nottingham Forest	L		0-4	0-2	15th		14,000
26	11	A	Nottingham Forest	L		0-2	0-2	17th		20,000
27	13	H	Wolverhampton W	W		3-1	0-0	14th	Trotter, Brelsford (pen), Petrie	16,000
28	18	H	Bristol City	W		1-0	0-0	13th	Petrie	20,000
29	25	A	Bristol City	L		1-3	0-2	15th	Wilson	14,000
30	Mar 4	H	South Shields	L		0-3	0-1	15th		15,000
31	11	A	South Shields	D		0-0	0-0	16th		12,000
32	13	H	Coventry City	W		3-2	2-1	12th	Binney (3)	10,000
33	18	A	Port Vale	L		0-1	0-0	15th		8,000
34	Apr 1	A	West Ham United	L		0-2	0-1	17th		20,000
35	3	H	Port Vale	W		2-0	0-0	14th	Brelsford (pen), Lowdell	10,000
36	8	H	West Ham United	W		2-1	1-0	13th	Lunn, Lofthouse	6,000
37	14	A	Hull City	D		0-0	0-0	12th		12,000
38	15	A	Bury	W		2-1	1-0	11th	Lunn, Lowdell	8,000
39	17	H	Hull City	D		0-0	0-0	10th		15,000
40	22	H	Bury	W		4-1	1-1	10th	Lunn (2), Kean, Lowdell	7,000
41	29	A	Leicester City	D		1-1	0-1	10th	Lofthouse	10,000
42	May 6	H	Leicester City	W		1-0	0-0	10th	Petrie	12,000
										Apps
										Goals
FA Cup										
43	Jan 7	A	Bradford Park Avenue	L	1R	0-1	0-0			21,880
										Apps

Armitage Harold	Armstrong Joe	Bellas Jack	Binney Chas	Birch Arnold	Bralsford Tom	Davison Teddy	Froggatt Frank	Gray George	Hall Harry	Holmes George	Kean Fred	Lamb Walter	Levick Oliver	Lofthouse Jimmy	Lowdell Arthur	Lunn Fred	Matthewson Tommy	McIntyre Johnnie	O'Neill Harry	Petrie Charlie	Price Arthur	Prior George	Ramsbottom Thomas	Ratcliffe Archie	Shelton George	Smelt John	Sykes Joe	Taylor Sam	Taylor Billy	Thompson Emil	Trotter Jimmy	Wilson George
					4	1								11				10	3		6	2		9		7		8				5
					4	1			8			2		11				10	3		6					7		9				5
	7				4	1			8			3		11				10	2		6							9				5
	8				4	1			7					11					3		6	2						9	10			5
					4	1			8					11				10	3		6	2						9		7		5
					4	1				2				11				8	3		6							9	10	7		5
					4	1				2				11				8	3		6							9	10	7		5
					4	1				2				11				8	3		6							9	10	7		5
	10				4	1				2				11				8	3		6							9		7		5
	10				4	1				2				11				8	3		6							9		7		5
	10				4	1	5			2				11				8	3		6			9						7		
	10				4	1				2				11				8	3		6			9						7		5
	10				4	1				2				11				8	3		6			9						7		5
					4	1				2				11				9	3		6							8	10	7		5
					8	1				2	4			11				10	3		6			9						7		5
					8	1			7	2	4			11				10	3		6			9								5
					8	1		2		3	4			11				10			6			9						7		5
					8	1		2			4			11				10			6		3	9						7		5
					6	1		2			4			11			7						3	10				8	9			5
					6	1		2			4			11							10		3	9	7			8				5
					6	1		2	7		4			11							10		3	9				8				5
			7			1		2			4		6	11									3	9				8	10			5
					6	1				2	4			11		9							3					8	10	7		5
		10			6	1		2			4			11	8	9							3							7		5
		10			6	1		2			4			11	8								3					9		7		5
					6	1				2	4			11	8	9				10			3							7		5
					6	1				2	4			11	8					10			3							7	9	5
					6	1				2	4			11	8					10		3								7	9	5
					6	1				2	4			11	8					10			3							7	9	5
					6	1				2				11	8					10			3				4			7	9	5
			7		6	1			9	2	4			11						10		3						8				5
			7	1	6				9	3	4			11						10		2						8				5
3			7		6	1	5		9		4			11						10		2						8				
			7		6	1		2			4			11	8					10		3								9		5
			7		6	1		2			4			11	8	9					10	3										5
			7		6	1	5	2			4			11	8	9					10	3										
			7			1	6	2			4			11	8	9					10	3										5
					6	1		2			4			11	8	9					10	3								7		5
					6	1		2			4			11	8	9					10	3						7				5
						1		2			4		6	11	8	9				10		3						7				5
						1	5	2			4		6	11	8	9				10		3						7				
					6	1		2			4			11	8	9				10		3						7				5
1	7	2	8	1	38	41	5	17	9	20	27	2	3	42	16	11	1	17	16	12	25	16	12	12	1	2	1	24	8	23	4	38
			3		4						1			8	3	4		8		3				4				3	3		1	2

Armitage Harold	Armstrong Joe	Bellas Jack	Binney Chas	Birch Arnold	Bralsford Tom	Davison Teddy	Froggatt Frank	Gray George	Hall Harry	Holmes George	Kean Fred	Lamb Walter	Levick Oliver	Lofthouse Jimmy	Lowdell Arthur	Lunn Fred	Matthewson Tommy	McIntyre Johnnie	O'Neill Harry	Petrie Charlie	Price Arthur	Prior George	Ramsbottom Thomas	Ratcliffe Archie	Shelton George	Smelt John	Sykes Joe	Taylor Sam	Taylor Billy	Thompson Emil	Trotter Jimmy	Wilson George
			8		6	1		2		3	4			11		9												10		7		5
			1		1	1		1		1	1			1		1												1		1		1

League Table

	P	W	D	L	F	A	Pts
Nottingham Forest	42	22	12	8	51	30	56
Stoke	42	18	16	8	60	44	52
Barnsley	42	22	8	12	67	52	52
West Ham United	42	20	8	14	52	39	48
Hull City	42	19	10	13	51	41	48
South Shields	42	17	12	13	43	38	46
Fulham	42	18	9	15	57	38	45
Leeds United	42	16	13	13	48	38	45
Leicester City	42	14	17	11	39	34	45
SHEFFIELD WEDNESDAY	42	15	14	13	47	50	44
Bury	42	15	10	17	54	55	40
Derby County	42	15	9	18	60	64	39
Notts County	42	12	15	15	47	51	39
Crystal Palace	42	13	13	16	45	51	39
Clapton Orient	42	15	9	18	43	50	39
Rotherham County	42	14	11	17	32	43	39
Wolverhampton W	42	13	11	18	44	49	37
Port Vale	42	14	8	20	43	57	36
Blackpool	42	15	5	22	44	57	35
Coventry City	42	12	10	20	51	60	34
Bradford Park Avenue	42	12	9	21	46	62	33
Bristol City	42	12	9	21	37	58	33

1922-23

Division Two

Manager: Bob Brown

Did you know that?

Final League Position: 8th

On 3 February 1923, in an FA Cup tie against Barnsley at home, a Barnsley corner flew straight into the net with no one else touching it. It was disallowed, as in those days the rules stated that you could not score directly from a corner. Wednesday went on to win 2–1.

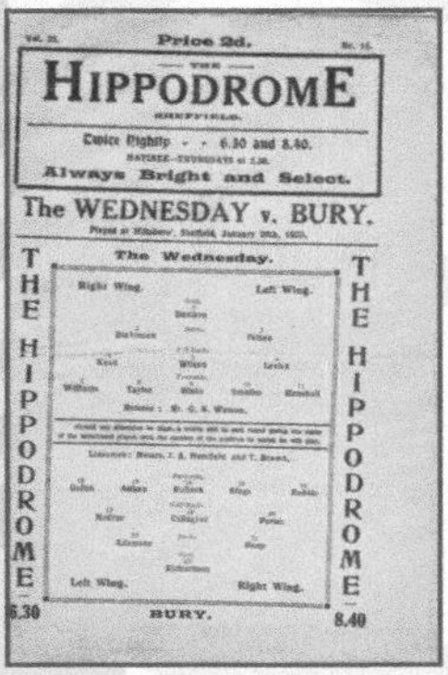

Match No.	Date	Venue	Opponents		Round	Result	HT Score	Position	Scorers	Attendance
1	Aug 26	A	Rotherham County	W		2-1	2-1		Lofthouse, Binks	20,000
2	28	H	Manchester United	W		1-0	1-0		Binks	20,000
3	Sep 2	H	Rotherham County	W		1-0	0-0	2nd	Evans (og)	30,000
4	4	A	Manchester United	L		0-1	0-0	6th		35,000
5	9	H	Derby County	D		0-0	0-0	7th		20,000
6	16	A	Derby County	D		1-1	0-0	9th	Lowdell	14,000
7	23	H	Notts County	L		0-1	0-0	9th		20,000
8	30	A	Notts County	L		0-1	0-0	10th		15,000
9	Oct 7	H	Fulham	W		1-0	1-0	9th	Binks (pen)	15,000
10	14	A	Fulham	L		0-1	0-0	13th		25,000
11	21	A	Clapton Orient	D		2-2	2-2	13th	Binks, Smailes	15,000
12	28	H	Clapton Orient	W		4-1	1-0	8th	Taylor (3), Lofthouse	15,000
13	Nov 4	H	Crystal Palace	W		3-1	0-0	5th	Taylor, Smailes, Binks	15,000
14	11	A	Crystal Palace	L		0-2	0-1	9th		10,000
15	18	A	Hull City	D		0-0	0-0	8th		8,000
16	25	H	Hull City	W		1-0	0-0	7th	Taylor	15,000
17	Dec 2	A	Leicester City	L		1-3	0-1	8th	Taylor	19,000
18	9	H	Leicester City	W		2-1	0-1	8th	Williams, Smailes	20,000
19	16	A	Barnsley	W		4-2	0-2	6th	Smailes (2), Taylor (2)	8,000
20	23	H	Barnsley	L		2-3	1-2	7th	Smailes, Taylor	30,000
21	25	H	Bradford City	D		2-2	1-1	8th	Smailes (2)	25,000
22	26	A	Bradford City	D		1-1	1-1	8th	Smailes	25,000
23	30	A	Blackpool	L		0-3	0-3	10th		8,000
24	Jan 1	H	Southampton	D		0-0	0-0	9th		30,000
25	6	H	Blackpool	L		2-3	1-0	11th	Binks, Smailes	20,000
26	20	H	Bury	W		2-0	1-0	9th	Smailes, Binks	20,000
27	27	A	Bury	L		0-4	0-2	10th		12,000
28	Feb 10	H	Stockport County	W		4-1	1-0	10th	Binks (3), Henshall	15,000
29	17	A	Leeds United	D		0-0	0-0	11th		14,000
30	Mar 3	A	West Ham United	L		1-2	0-2	12th	Taylor	16,000
31	15	A	Stockport County	W		1-0	0-0		Taylor	4,000
32	17	H	South Shields	W		2-0	2-0	11th	Harron, Binks	15,000
33	19	H	Leeds United	W		3-1	1-1	9th	Binks (pen), Brelsford, Smailes	11,000
34	24	A	South Shields	D		1-1	0-1	10th	Taylor	7,000
35	31	H	Wolverhampton W	W		1-0	1-0	10th	Brelsford	10,000
36	Apr 2	A	Southampton	D		1-1	0-1	9th	Taylor	16,000
37	7	A	Wolverhampton W	L		0-2	0-1	10th		10,000
38	14	H	Coventry City	W		3-0	0-0	8th	Sykes, Binks, Petrie	10,000
39	21	A	Coventry City	D		1-1	1-1	9th	Kean	12,000
40	28	H	Port Vale	W		2-0	0-0	7th	Smailes, Harron	12,000
41	30	H	West Ham United	L		0-2	0-2	7th		10,000
42	May 5	A	Port Vale	D		2-2	1-2	8th	Petrie (2)	5,000
										Apps
									One own-goal	Goals

FA Cup

Match No.	Date	Venue	Opponents		Round	Result	HT Score	Position	Scorers	Attendance
43	Jan 13	H	New Brighton	W	1R	3-0	1-0		Smailes, Binks (2)	36,082
44	Feb 3	H	Barnsley	W	2R	2-1	0-1		Smailes, Binks	66,103
45	24	A	Derby County	L	3R	0-1	0-0			16,400
										Apps
										Goals

Bellas Jack	Binks Sid	Binney Chas	Birch Arnold	Blenkinsop Ernest	Brelsford Tom	Brown Jack	Davison Teddy	Dickinson Walter	Felton Billy	Froggatt Frank	Gray George	Harron Joe	Henshall Harry	Kean Fred	Levick Oliver	Lofthouse Jimmy	Lowdell Arthur	Petrie Charlie	Prior George	Smailes Andrew	Sykes Joe	Taylor Sam	Trotter Jimmy	Williams Rees	Wilson George
	9				6		1				2			4		11	8	10	3					7	5
	9				6		1				2			4		11	8	10	3					7	5
	9				6		1				2			4		11	8	10	3					7	5
	9				6		1				2			4		11	8	10	3					7	5
	9				6		1				2			4		11	8		3			10		7	5
	9				6		1				2			4		11	8		3			10		7	5
	9				6		1				2			4		11	8		3				10	7	5
	9	10			6		1				2			4		11	8		3					7	5
	9	10			6		1				2			4		11	8		3			7			5
	9				6		1				2			4		11	8		3	10				7	5
3	9				6		1			5	2			4		11				10		8		7	
3	9				6		1				2			4		11				10		8		7	5
	9				6		1				2			4		11			3	10		8		7	5
	9				6		1				2			4		11			3	10		8		7	5
	9				6		1	3		5	2			4		11				10		8		7	
	9				6		1	3						4		11			2	10		8		7	5
	9				6		1	3						4		11			2	10		8		7	5
2	9				6		1	3					11	4						10		8		7	5
2	9				6		1	3					11	4						10		8		7	5
2	9				6		1	3					11	4						10		8		7	5
2					6		1						11	4					3	10		8	9	7	5
2	9	7	1		6								11	4					3	10		8			5
2	9		1		6								11	4					3	10		8		7	5
2	9		1		6				3				11	4						10		8		7	5
2	9		1		6				3				11	4						10		8		7	5
	9						1	2	3				11	4	6					10		8		7	5
	9			2			1		3				11	4	6					10		8		7	5
2	9			3			1						11	4			8			10	6			7	5
2	9			3			1			5			11	4			8			10	6			7	
	9			3			1		2				11	4						10	6	8		7	5
	9			3			1		2			11		4						10	6	8		7	5
	9			3			1		2			11	7	4						10	6	8			5
	9			3	4		1		2	5		11								10	6	8		7	
	9			3			1		2			11		4						10	6	8		7	5
	9			3	6		1		2			11		4						10		8		7	5
	9			3			1		2			11		4			7			10	6	8			5
	9			3			1		2			11		4			7			10	6	8			5
	9			3			1		2	5		11			6		7	10			4	8			
	9			3		1			2			11		4	6		7	10				8			5
				3			1		2	6		11		4			7	10		9		8			5
				3			1		2	6		11		4			7	10		9		8			5
2	9			3			1					11		4				10		6		8		7	5
13	39	3	4	16	27	1	37	7	16	7	15	12	14	40	4	17	18	9	17	31	10	33	2	33	37
	13				2							2	1	1		2	1	3		13	1	13		1	

Bellas Jack	Binks Sid	Binney Chas	Birch Arnold	Blenkinsop Ernest	Brelsford Tom	Brown Jack	Davison Teddy	Dickinson Walter	Felton Billy	Froggatt Frank	Gray George	Harron Joe	Henshall Harry	Kean Fred	Levick Oliver	Lofthouse Jimmy	Lowdell Arthur	Petrie Charlie	Prior George	Smailes Andrew	Sykes Joe	Taylor Sam	Trotter Jimmy	Williams Rees	Wilson George
2	9				6		1	3					11	4						10		8		7	5
2	9			3			1						11	4			8			10	6			7	5
2	9			3			1						11	4						10	6	8		7	5
3	3			2	1		3	1					3	3			1			3	2	2		3	3
	3																			2					

League Table

	P	W	D	L	F	A	Pts
Notts County	42	23	7	12	46	34	53
West Ham United	42	20	11	11	63	38	51
Leicester City	42	21	9	12	65	44	51
Manchester United	42	17	14	11	51	36	48
Blackpool	42	18	11	13	60	43	47
Bury	42	18	11	13	55	46	47
Leeds United	42	18	11	13	43	36	47
SHEFFIELD WEDNESDAY	42	17	12	13	54	47	46
Barnsley	42	17	11	14	62	51	45
Fulham	42	16	12	14	43	32	44
Southampton	42	14	14	14	40	40	42
Hull City	42	14	14	14	43	45	42
South Shields	42	15	10	17	35	44	40
Derby County	42	14	11	17	46	50	39
Bradford City	42	12	13	17	41	45	37
Crystal Palace	42	13	11	18	54	62	37
Port Vale	42	14	9	19	39	51	37
Coventry City	42	15	7	20	46	63	37
Clapton Orient	42	12	12	18	40	50	36
Stockport County	42	14	8	20	43	58	36
Rotherham County	42	13	9	20	44	63	35
Wolverhampton W	42	9	9	24	42	77	27

1923-24

Division Two

Manager: Bob Brown

Did you know that?

Final League Position: 8th

On 27 August 1923 two Wednesday players, Billy Felton and Rees Williams, missed the train to Stoke for the game against Port Vale. Trainer, Jerry Jackson, had to play on the wing, with the other place taken by travelling reserve, Charlie Petrie, as Wednesday lost 2–0. Jackson had to leave the field at half-time – he may be Wednesday's oldest player, as his date of birth has not been confirmed, and it is possible that he could have been 46 or even older.

On Christmas Day 1923 Wednesday player Tom Armitage was badly hurt in a reserve-team game. He tragically died, five days later, in a Sheffield hospital.

On Boxing Day 1923, with Hillsborough's pitch covered in snow, the goalposts were painted blue. Wednesday beat Coventry City 2–0.

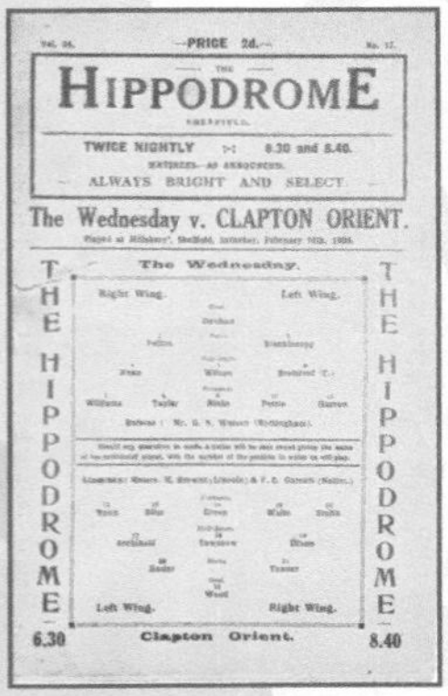

Match No.	Date	Venue	Opponents		Round	Result	HT Score	Position	Scorers	Attendance
1	Aug 25	H	Bradford City	D		0-0	0-0			25,000
2	27	A	Port Vale	L		0-2	0-2			14,000
3	Sep 1	A	Bradford City	L		1-4	1-3	20th	R. Williams	16,000
4	3	H	Port Vale	W		2-1	1-0	18th	Taylor (pen), Trotter	12,000
5	8	H	Southampton	D		1-1	1-1	19th	Petrie	20,000
6	15	A	Southampton	L		0-3	0-1	20th		9,000
7	22	H	Fulham	W		2-1	0-0	17th	Binks, Harron	15,000
8	29	A	Fulham	L		1-4	0-1	20th	Petrie	20,000
9	Oct 6	H	Blackpool	D		2-2	0-0	19th	Harron, Petrie	15,000
10	13	A	Blackpool	L		0-1	0-1	20th		12,000
11	20	A	Nelson	D		1-1	1-1	20th	Petrie	9,000
12	27	H	Nelson	W		5-0	4-0	17th	Petrie, Walker (2), Taylor (1 + pen)	18,000
13	Nov 3	A	Barnsley	D		0-0	0-0	18th		15,200
14	10	H	Barnsley	W		1-0	1-0	16th	Petrie	20,000
15	17	H	Hull City	W		1-0	1-0	12th	Petrie	15,000
16	24	A	Hull City	D		1-1	1-0	13th	Petrie	8,000
17	Dec 1	A	Stoke	D		1-1	0-1	10th	Binks	8,000
18	8	H	Stoke	W		3-0	1-0	9th	Kean, Petrie (2)	18,000
19	15	A	Crystal Palace	L		0-3	0-2	11th		10,000
20	22	H	Crystal Palace	W		6-0	3-0	10th	Binks (4), Petrie (2)	12,000
21	25	A	Coventry City	L		1-5	0-3		Binks	20,000
22	26	H	Coventry City	W		2-0	0-0	6th	Kean, Binks	30,000
23	29	A	Derby County	D		1-1	1-1	7th	Crilly (og)	16,626
24	Jan 5	H	Derby County	W		1-0	0-0	7th	Binks	28,000
25	19	H	Leeds United	D		0-0	0-0	7th		20,000
26	26	A	Leeds United	L		0-1	0-1	11th		14,000
27	Feb 9	A	Leicester City	L		1-2	1-2	13th	Binks	15,000
28	11	H	Leicester City	W		2-1	1-0	9th	Binks (2)	5,000
29	16	H	Clapton Orient	W		1-0	1-0	8th	Petrie	14,000
30	23	A	Clapton Orient	D		0-0	0-0	7th		20,000
31	Mar 1	H	Stockport County	W		3-0	1-0	6th	Walker, Binks, Petrie	10,000
32	8	A	Stockport County	L		0-1	0-0	9th		12,000
33	15	A	Oldham Athletic	L		0-2	0-1	9th		11,055
34	22	H	Oldham Athletic	L		1-2	0-0	12th	Taylor	15,000
35	29	A	South Shields	D		1-1	0-1	12th	Taylor	8,000
36	Apr 5	H	South Shields	W		5-0	3-0	11th	Taylor (3), Walker, Harron	15,000
37	12	A	Bury	L		0-5	0-1	12th		12,000
38	18	A	Bristol City	W		3-2	1-0	10th	Binks (3)	14,000
39	19	H	Bury	D		1-1	1-1	10th	Petrie	15,000
40	21	H	Bristol City	W		1-0	0-0	9th	Taylor	7,000
41	26	A	Manchester United	L		0-2	0-1	12th		20,000
42	May 3	H	Manchester United	W		2-0	0-0	8th	Walker, Ayres	10,000
										Apps
									One own-goal	Goals

FA Cup

Match No.	Date	Venue	Opponents		Round	Result	HT Score	Position	Scorers	Attendance
43	Jan 12	H	Leicester City	W	1R	4-1	4-0		Petrie, Binks, Taylor (2)	39,127
44	Feb 2	H	Bristol City	D	2R	1-1	1-0		Harron	38,238
45	6	A	Bristol City	L	2R Re	0-2	0-2			22,754
										Apps
										Goals

Ayres George	Binks Sid	Blenkinsop Ernest	Brelsford Tom	Brown Jack	Chapman Billy	Davison Teddy	Eyre Ron	Felton Billy	Froggatt Frank	Harron Joe	Jackson Jerry	Kean Fred	Levick Oliver	Lowdell Arthur	Petrie Charlie	Prior George	Smailes Andrew	Sykes Joe	Taylor Sam	Trotter Jimmy	Walker Billy	Williams Len	Williams Rees	Wilson George	Wilson Joe
	9	3		1				2				4	6				10		8				7	5	11
	9	3		1							7	2	6		4		10		8					5	11
		3		1				2				4	6	7			10		8	9			11	5	
		3		1				2		11		4	6		10				8	9			7	5	
		3		1				2		11		4	6		10				8	9			7	5	
	9	3		1				2		11		4		7	10		6		8					5	
	9	3		1				2		11		4			10		6		8				7	5	
	9	3		1				2	5	11		4			10		6		8				7		
	9	3		1				2	6	11		4			10				8				7	5	
	9	3				1		2	6	11		4			10				8				7	5	
		3	6			1		2	5	11		4			10				8		9		7		
		3	6			1		2		11		4			10				8		9		7	5	
		3	6			1		2		11		4			10				8		9		7	5	
	9	3	6			1		2		11		4			10				8				7	5	
	9	3	6			1		2		11		4			10				8				7	5	
		3	6			1		2		11		4			10				8		9		7	5	
	9	3	6			1		2		11		4			10				8				7	5	
	9	3	6			1		2		11		4			10				8				7	5	
	9	3	6			1		2		11		4			10				8				7	5	
	9	3	6			1		2		11		4			10						8		7	5	
	9	3	6			1		2		11		4			10						8		7	5	
	9	3				1		2	6	11		4			10				8				7	5	
	9	3				1		2	6	11		4			10				8				7	5	
	9	3				1		2	6	11		4			10				8				7	5	
	9	3				1		2	6	11		4			10				8				7	5	
	9	3				1			6	11		4			10				8			2	7	5	
	9	3	6			1				11		4			10						8	2	7	5	
	9	3	6			1		2										5		10	8	4	7		11
	9	3	6			1		2		11		4			10				8				7	5	
	9	3	6			1		2		11		4							8		10		7	5	
	9	3	6			1		2		11		4			10						8		7	5	
	9	3	6			1		2		11		4			10			5			8		7		
	9	3	6		7	1			5	11		4			10	2					8				
		3				1	9	2	5	11		4	6	7					10		8				
	9	3				1				11		4	6						10		8	2	7	5	
	9	3		1						11		4	6						10		8	2	7	5	
	9	3		1						11		4	6						10		8	2	7	5	
	9	3		1						11		4	6		10				8			2	7	5	
		3		1				2	6	11		4			10				8		9		7	5	
		3		1				2		11		4	6		10				8	9			7	5	
	9	3		1				2		11		4	6		10				8				7	5	
9		3		1	7			2		11		4	6						8		10			5	
1	31	42	18	16	2	26	1	34	12	38	1	41	13	3	33	1	6	2	35	5	18	7	37	36	3
1	16									3		2			15				9	1	5		1		

Ayres George	Binks Sid	Blenkinsop Ernest	Brelsford Tom	Brown Jack	Chapman Billy	Davison Teddy	Eyre Ron	Felton Billy	Froggatt Frank	Harron Joe	Jackson Jerry	Kean Fred	Levick Oliver	Lowdell Arthur	Petrie Charlie	Prior George	Smailes Andrew	Sykes Joe	Taylor Sam	Trotter Jimmy	Walker Billy	Williams Len	Williams Rees	Wilson George	Wilson Joe
	9	3				1		2	6	11		4			10				8				7	5	
	9	3				1		2	6	11		4			10				8				7	5	
	9	3				1		2	6	11		4		8							10		7	5	
	3	3				3		3	3	3		3		1	2				2		1		3	3	
	1									1					1				2						

League Table

	P	W	D	L	F	A	Pts
Leeds United	42	21	12	9	61	35	54
Bury	42	21	9	12	63	35	51
Derby County	42	21	9	12	75	42	51
Blackpool	42	18	13	11	72	47	49
Southampton	42	17	14	11	52	31	48
Stoke	42	14	18	10	44	42	46
Oldham Athletic	42	14	17	11	45	52	45
SHEFFIELD WEDNESDAY	42	16	12	14	54	51	44
South Shields	42	17	10	15	49	50	44
Clapton Orient	42	14	15	13	40	36	43
Barnsley	42	16	11	15	57	61	43
Leicester City	42	17	8	17	64	54	42
Stockport County	42	13	16	13	44	52	42
Manchester United	42	13	14	15	52	44	40
Crystal Palace	42	13	13	16	53	65	39
Port Vale	42	13	12	17	50	66	38
Hull City	42	10	17	15	46	51	37
Bradford City	42	11	15	16	35	48	37
Coventry City	42	11	13	18	52	68	35
Fulham	42	10	14	18	45	56	34
Nelson	42	10	13	19	40	74	33
Bristol City	42	7	15	20	32	65	29

1924-25

Division One

Manager: Bob Brown

Did you know that?

Final League Position: 14th

In September 1924 the Wednesday Cricket Club, from which the football section had formed in 1867, disbanded due to lack of funds and having no home pitch.

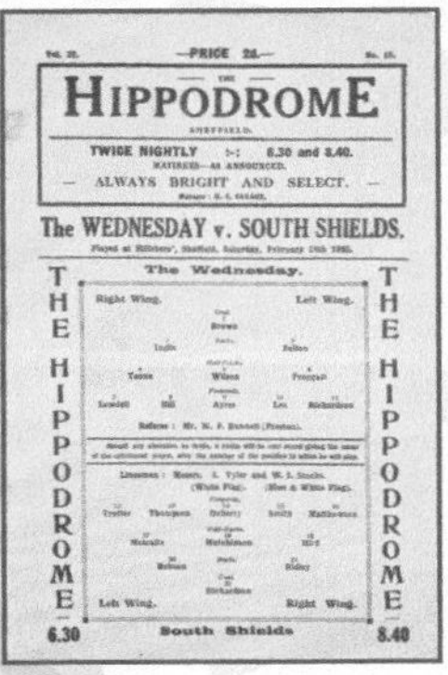

Match No.	Date	Venue	Opponents		Round	Result	HT Score	Position	Scorers	Attendance
1	Aug 30	A	Crystal Palace	W		1-0	1-0		Marsden	20,000
2	Sep 1	H	Derby County	L		0-1	0-0			30,000
3	6	H	Southampton	W		1-0	0-0	4th	R. Williams (pen)	30,000
4	8	A	Derby County	L		1-2	1-1	10th	Petrie	20,538
5	13	A	Chelsea	D		0-0	0-0	10th		40,000
6	20	H	Stockport County	W		3-0	1-0	7th	Ayres (3)	22,000
7	27	A	Manchester United	L		0-2	0-1	11th		30,000
8	Oct 2	A	Clapton Orient	L		0-1	0-1			8,000
9	4	H	Leicester City	L		1-4	0-2	16th	Trotter	18,000
10	11	A	Stoke	W		2-0	0-0	11th	Taylor, R. Williams	10,000
11	18	H	Coventry City	W		2-0	2-0	9th	Hill, Trotter	25,000
12	25	A	South Shields	W		1-0	1-0	9th	Trotter	7,000
13	Nov 1	H	Bradford City	D		3-3	1-2	8th	Trotter, R. Williams (pen), Ayres	15,000
14	8	A	Port Vale	L		0-1	0-0	10th		8,000
15	15	H	Middlesbrough	W		2-0	2-0	8th	Trotter (2)	13,983
16	22	A	Barnsley	L		0-3	0-1	9th		12,000
17	29	H	Wolverhampton W	W		2-0	0-0	9th	Marsden, Hill	16,668
18	Dec 6	A	Fulham	L		1-2	1-1	9th	Taylor	18,000
19	13	H	Portsmouth	W		5-2	2-1	7th	Trotter (5)	17,255
20	20	A	Hull City	L		2-4	1-2	8th	Taylor, Hill	10,000
21	25	H	Blackpool	L		2-6	0-4		Hill (2)	35,000
22	26	A	Blackpool	D		2-2	2-1	11th	Hill, Ayres	14,000
23	27	H	Crystal Palace	L		0-1	0-1	12th		15,500
24	Jan 1	H	Oldham Athletic	W		1-0	0-0	9th	Hill	15,300
25	3	A	Southampton	L		0-1	0-0	10th		7,000
26	17	H	Chelsea	W		2-1	1-1	8th	Trotter (2)	18,000
27	24	A	Stockport County	L		0-1	0-0	12th		15,000
28	Feb 7	A	Leicester City	L		1-6	0-2	13th	Trotter	25,000
29	14	H	Stoke	W		2-1	0-1	12th	Ayres, Hill	12,000
30	21	A	Coventry City	D		1-1	1-1	11th	Hill	14,242
31	23	H	Manchester United	D		1-1	1-1		Weaver	8,000
32	28	H	South Shields	L		0-1	0-1	11th		15,000
33	Mar 7	A	Bradford City	L		0-2	0-0	13th		12,000
34	14	H	Port Vale	L		0-1	0-0	14th		12,000
35	21	A	Middlesbrough	L		0-2	0-1	18th		8,000
36	28	H	Barnsley	W		1-0	0-0	17th	S. Powell	28,000
37	Apr 4	A	Wolverhampton W	L		0-1	0-1	19th		12,000
38	10	A	Oldham Athletic	D		1-1	1-1	19th	Trotter	11,667
39	11	H	Fulham	W		3-1	2-0	16th	S. Powell (3)	20,000
40	18	A	Portsmouth	D		1-1	1-1	16th	S. Powell	15,000
41	25	H	Hull City	W		5-0	2-0	15th	Trotter (2), Barrass, Marsden, Hill	16,500
42	May 2	H	Clapton Orient	D		0-0	0-0	14th		14,000
										Apps
										Goals

FA Cup

Match No.	Date	Venue	Opponents		Round	Result	HT Score	Position	Scorers	Attendance
43	Jan 10	H	Manchester United	W	1R	2-0	1-0		Hill (2)	35,079
44	31	A	Sheffield United	L	2R	2-3	2-2		Trotter (2)	40,256
										Apps
										Goals

Ayres George	Barrass Matt	Binks Sid	Blenkinsop Ernest	Brown Jack	Chapman Billy	Collier Bill	Davison Teddy	Felton Billy	Froggatt Frank	Harron Joe	Hill Harold	Inglis Bill	Kean Fred	Lowdell Arthur	Marsden Billy	Petrie Charlie	Powell Sam	Powell Billy	Prince Arthur	Richardson Eddie	Taylor Sam	Toone George	Trotter Jimmy	Weaver Alex	Williams Len	Williams Rees	Wilson George
10		9	3			6	1	2		11			4		8											7	5
10		9	3			6	1	2					4		8				11							7	5
		9	3			6	1	2		11			4		8	10										7	5
		9				6	1	3		11		2	4		8	10										7	5
		9				6	1	3		11		2	4		8	10										7	5
10		9				6	1	3		11		2	4								8					7	5
10		9				6	1	3		11		2	4								8					7	5
9						6	1	3		11		2	4	8		10			7								5
10			3				1	2		11			4	8					7			6	9				5
10						6	1	3		11		2									8	4	9			7	5
10					7	6	1	3		11	8	2	4										9				5
10					7		1	3		11	8	2	4					6					9				5
10							1	3			8	2	4					6	11				9			7	5
10							1	3			8	2	4					6	11				9			7	5
							1	3			8	2	4					6	11		10		9			7	5
							1	3			8	2	4		10			6	11				9			7	5
							1	3	5		8	2	4		10			6	7	11			9				
							1	3	5			2	4		10			6	7	11	8		9				
							1	3	5		8	2	4					6	7	11	10		9				
							1	3	5		8	2	4					6	7	11	10		9				
			3	1				2			8		4					6		11	10		9			7	5
10				1				3	6		8	2							7	11		4	9				5
10				1				3	6		8	2							11			4	9			7	5
10				1				3	5		8	2		7				6	11			4		9			
10				1				3	5		8	2		7				6	11			4		9			
			3	1					6		8	2		7				10		11		4	9				5
				1				3	6		8	2		7				10	11			4	9				5
				1				3	5			2		7	10			6		11	8	4	9				
10				1				3			8	2		7	9			6		11		4					5
10				1		6		3			8	2		7					11			4		9			5
9				1		6		3			8	2							11			4		10		7	5
9				1				3	6		8	2		7					11			4		10			5
10				1		6		3			9	2		7					11			4		8			5
				1		6		3			10	2		7					11			4	9			8	5
	10		3	1				2			8						9	6	11			4				7	5
	10		3	1				2	5		8						9	6	11			4				7	
	10		3	1				2	5		8						9	6	11			4				7	
	8		3	1				2	5						6		10		11			4	9			7	
	8		3	1				2	5				4				10	6	11				9			7	
	8		3	1				2	5		7			4	6		10		11				9				
	8		3	1					5		7			4	6		10		11				9		2		
	8		3	1				2	5		7			4	6		10		11				9				
20	8	7	14	22	2	14	20	40	19	11	28	29	21	15	14	4	8	20	29	9	9	19	24	6	1	21	28
6	1										10				3	1	5				3		17	1		3	

Ayres George	Barrass Matt	Binks Sid	Blenkinsop Ernest	Brown Jack	Chapman Billy	Collier Bill	Davison Teddy	Felton Billy	Froggatt Frank	Harron Joe	Hill Harold	Inglis Bill	Kean Fred	Lowdell Arthur	Marsden Billy	Petrie Charlie	Powell Sam	Powell Billy	Prince Arthur	Richardson Eddie	Taylor Sam	Toone George	Trotter Jimmy	Weaver Alex	Williams Len	Williams Rees	Wilson George
				1				3	6		8	2		7				10		11		4	9				5
				1				3			8	2		7				6		11	10	4	9				5
				2				2	1		2	2		2				2		2	1	2	2				2
											2												2				

League Table

	P	W	D	L	F	A	Pts
Leicester City	42	24	11	7	90	32	59
Manchester United	42	23	11	8	57	23	57
Derby County	42	22	11	9	71	36	55
Portsmouth	42	15	18	9	58	50	48
Chelsea	42	16	15	11	51	37	47
Wolverhampton W	42	20	6	16	55	51	46
Southampton	42	13	18	11	40	36	44
Port Vale	42	17	8	17	48	56	42
South Shields	42	12	17	13	42	38	41
Hull City	42	15	11	16	50	49	41
Clapton Orient	42	14	12	16	42	42	40
Fulham	42	15	10	17	41	56	40
Middlesbrough	42	10	19	13	36	44	39
SHEFFIELD WEDNESDAY	42	15	8	19	50	56	38
Barnsley	42	13	12	17	46	59	38
Bradford City	42	13	12	17	37	50	38
Blackpool	42	14	9	19	65	61	37
Oldham Athletic	42	13	11	18	35	51	37
Stockport County	42	13	11	18	37	57	37
Stoke	42	12	11	19	34	46	35
Crystal Palace	42	12	10	20	38	54	34
Coventry City	42	11	9	22	45	84	31

1925-26

Division Two

Manager: Bob Brown

Did you know that?

Final League Position: 1st

When Frank Froggatt was made captain for the new season, he was the first Sheffield born player to be given this job on a permanent basis since Tommy Crawshaw had held this post in 1907.

Match No.	Date	Venue	Opponents		Round	Result	HT Score	Position	Scorers	Attendance
1	Aug 29	H	Fulham	W		3-0	1-0		Lowdell (pen), Bedford, Powell	21,173
2	31	A	Stockport County	W		2-0	0-0	1st	Trotter, Blenkinsop (pen)	10,848
3	Sep 5	A	South Shields	D		1-1	0-1	4th	Barrass	10,312
4	7	A	Oldham Athletic	D		1-1	0-0	4th	Barrass	10,726
5	12	H	Preston North End	W		5-1	3-0	3rd	Trotter (4), Blenkinsop (pen)	25,159
6	19	A	Middlesbrough	L		0-3	0-1	7th		13,983
7	21	H	Stockport County	W		6-2	5-1	2nd	Ayres, Trotter (5)	12,761
8	26	H	Portsmouth	W		4-2	2-1	2nd	Barrass, Ayres (2), Trotter	22,966
9	Oct 3	A	Wolverhampton W	W		2-1	1-0	2nd	Blenkinsop (pen), Ayres	25,823
10	10	H	Swansea Town	W		3-1	1-1	2nd	Barrass, Bedford, Kean	27,992
11	17	H	Derby County	L		1-4	1-0	3rd	Trotter	31,445
12	24	A	Nottingham Forest	L		0-2	0-2	4th		12,244
13	31	H	Barnsley	W		3-0	2-0	4th	Trotter, Hill (2)	23,920
14	Nov 7	A	Port Vale	L		3-4	0-2	4th	Barrass, Prince, Hill	6,826
15	14	H	Darlington	W		4-0	2-0	4th	Trotter (3), Blenkinsop (pen)	19,726
16	21	A	Hull City	W		1-0	1-0	4th	Barrass	8,623
17	28	H	Chelsea	W		4-1	2-0	1st	Trotter, Hill (3)	23,827
18	Dec 5	A	Clapton Orient	D		0-0	0-0	2nd		11,279
19	12	H	Southampton	W		2-1	2-0	1st	Trotter, Hill	20,628
20	19	A	Blackpool	L		0-1	0-0	3rd		8,931
21	25	A	Bradford City	W		4-1	2-1		Barrass, Prince, Trotter (2)	18,267
22	26	H	Bradford City	W		5-1	2-0	2nd	Hill (2), Trotter (2), Barrass	37,409
23	28	H	Oldham Athletic	W		5-1	3-1	2nd	Barrass, Hill (2), Trotter (2)	25,933
24	Jan 2	A	Fulham	L		0-3	0-2	2nd		17,621
25	16	H	South Shields	W		1-0	0-0	2nd	Barrass	19,555
26	23	A	Preston North End	W		3-0	0-0	2nd	Barrass, Trotter, Prince	12,047
27	Feb 6	A	Portsmouth	W		2-1	1-0	2nd	Prince, Trotter	14,565
28	13	H	Wolverhampton W	W		2-1	2-0	1st	Barrass, Hill	29,398
29	22	H	Middlesbrough	W		2-0	2-0	1st	Trotter (2)	20,684
30	27	A	Derby County	L		1-4	1-2	1st	Prince	26,724
31	Mar 11	A	Swansea Town	D		2-2	2-1	2nd	Milne (og), Barrass	17,084
32	13	A	Barnsley	D		1-1	1-0	1st	Trotter	28,124
33	20	H	Port Vale	L		0-2	0-2	1st		24,965
34	22	H	Nottingham Forest	W		2-0	1-0	1st	Trotter, Prince	29,975
35	27	A	Darlington	L		1-5	1-2	1st	Trotter (pen)	9,406
36	Apr 3	H	Hull City	W		2-0	1-0	1st	Trotter, Wilkinson	29,075
37	5	A	Stoke City	W		1-0	1-0	1st	Trotter (pen)	18,387
38	6	H	Stoke City	W		2-0	1-0	1st	Powell, Wilkinson	28,679
39	10	A	Chelsea	D		0-0	0-0	1st		41,817
40	17	H	Clapton Orient	W		3-0	1-0	1st	Wilkinson, R. Williams, Trotter	21,227
41	24	A	Southampton	W		2-1	0-1	1st	Trotter (2)	8,619
42	May 1	H	Blackpool	W		2-0	2-0	1st	Trotter, Lowdell	20,575
										Apps
									One own-goal	Goals
FA Cup										
43	Jan 9	A	New Brighton	L	1R	1-2	1-1		Trotter	10,326
										Apps
										Goals

Ayres George	Barrass Matt	Bedford Lewis	Blenkinsop Ernest	Brown Jack	Felton Billy	Fletcher Brough	Froggatt Frank	Hill Harold	Kean Fred	Lowdell Arthur	Marsden Billy	McIlvenny Patrick	Powell Sam	Prince Arthur	Trotter Jimmy	Walker Tommy	Wilkinson Jack	Williams Len	Williams Rees
	8	11	3	1	2		5			4	6		10		9				7
	8	11	3	1	2		5		4		6		10		9				7
	8	11	3	1	2		5		4		6		10		9				7
	8	11	3	1	2		5		4		6		10		9				7
	8	11	3	1	2		5		4		6		10		9				7
	8	11	3	1	2		5		4		6		10		9				7
10	8	11	3	1	2		5		4		6				9				7
10	8	11	3	1	2		5		4		6				9				7
10	8	11	3	1	2		5		4		6				9				7
10	8	11	3	1	2		5		4		6				9				7
10	8	11	3	1	2		5		4		6				9				7
	8			1	2		5			4	6		10	11	9			3	7
	8		3	1	2		5	10	4	7	6			11	9				
	8		3	1	2		5	10	4		6			11	9				7
	8		3	1	2		5	10		4	6			11	9				7
	8		3	1	2		5	10		4	6			11	9				7
	8		3	1	2		5	10		4	6			11	9				7
	8		3	1	2		5	10		4	6			11	9				7
	8		3	1	2		5	10		4	6			11	9				7
	8		3	1	2		5	10		4	6	9		11					7
	8		3	1	2		5	10		4	6			11	9				7
	8		3	1	2		5	10		4	6			11	9				7
	8		3	1	2		5	10		4	6			11	9				7
	8		3	1	2		5	10		4	6			11	9				7
	8		3	1	2		5	10		4	6			11	9				7
	8		3	1	2		5	10		4	6			11	9				7
	8		3	1	2		5	10		4	6			11	9				7
	8		3	1	2		5	10		4	6			11	9				7
	8		3	1	2		5	10		4	6			11	9				7
	8		3	1	2		5	10		4	6			11	9				7
	8		3	1	2		5			4	6		10	11	9				7
	8		3	1	2		5			4	6		10	11	9				7
	8		3	1	2		5	10		4	6			11	9				7
	8		3	1	2		5	10		4	6			11	9				7
	8		3	1	2		5	10		4	6			11	9				7
	10		3	1		8	5		4		6				9	2	11		7
	10		3	1		8	5		4		6				9	2	11		7
	8		3	1			5		4		6		10		9	2	11		7
	10		3	1			5		4	8	6				9	2	11		7
	10		3	1			5		4	8	6				9	2	11		7
			3	1			5		4	8	6		10		9	2	11		7
			3	1			5		4	8	6		10		9	2	11		7
5	40	11	41	42	35	2	42	21	19	28	42	1	12	24	41	7	7	1	41
4	13	2	4					12	1	2			2	6	37		3		1

Ayres George	Barrass Matt	Bedford Lewis	Blenkinsop Ernest	Brown Jack	Felton Billy	Fletcher Brough	Froggatt Frank	Hill Harold	Kean Fred	Lowdell Arthur	Marsden Billy	McIlvenny Patrick	Powell Sam	Prince Arthur	Trotter Jimmy	Walker Tommy	Wilkinson Jack	Williams Len	Williams Rees
	8		3	1	2		5	10		4	6			11	9				7
	1		1	1	1		1	1		1	1			1	1				1
															1				

League Table

	P	W	D	L	F	A	Pts
SHEFFIELD WEDNESDAY	42	27	6	9	88	48	60
Derby County	42	25	7	10	77	42	57
Chelsea	42	19	14	9	76	49	52
Wolverhampton W	42	21	7	14	84	60	49
Swansea Town	42	19	11	12	77	57	49
Blackpool	42	17	11	14	76	69	45
Oldham Athletic	42	18	8	16	74	62	44
Port Vale	42	19	6	17	79	69	44
South Shields	42	18	8	16	74	65	44
Middlesbrough	42	21	2	19	77	68	44
Portsmouth	42	17	10	15	79	74	44
Preston North End	42	18	7	17	71	84	43
Hull City	42	16	9	17	63	61	41
Southampton	42	15	8	19	63	63	38
Darlington	42	14	10	18	72	77	38
Bradford City	42	13	10	19	47	66	36
Nottingham Forest	42	14	8	20	51	73	36
Barnsley	42	12	12	18	58	84	36
Fulham	42	11	12	19	46	77	34
Clapton Orient	42	12	9	21	50	65	33
Stoke City	42	12	8	22	54	77	32
Stockport County	42	8	9	25	51	97	25

1926-27

Division One

Manager: Bob Brown

Did you know that?

Final League Position: 16th

On 26 March in a home game against Manchester United one of the linemen failed to turn up, and Wednesday player, Billy Felton, ran the line!

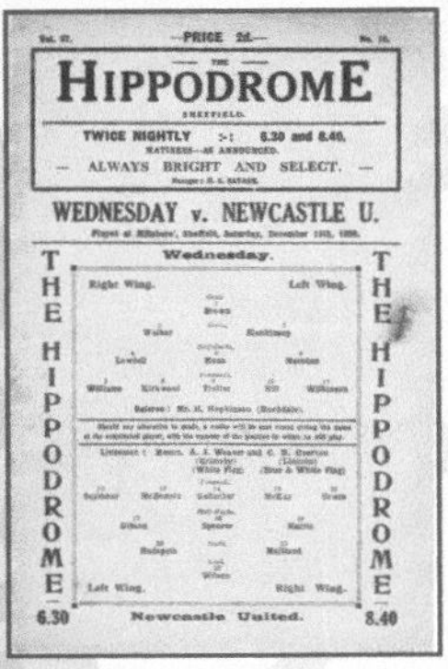

Match No.	Date	Venue	Opponents		Round	Result	HT Score	Position	Scorers	Attendance
1	Aug 28	H	Sheffield United	L		2-3	1-1		Trotter (2)	43,282
2	30	A	Tottenham Hotspur	L		3-7	1-2	20th	Anstiss, Trotter, Wilkinson	19,726
3	Sep 4	A	Leicester City	L		3-5	2-4	21st	Trotter, Hill, Froggatt	24,275
4	6	H	West Ham United	W		1-0	1-0	21st	Trotter (pen)	18,602
5	11	H	Everton	W		4-0	2-0	14th	Anstiss, Trotter (3)	22,889
6	13	A	Birmingham	D		0-0	0-0	13th		13,676
7	18	A	Blackburn Rovers	D		2-2	1-0	12th	Trotter (2)	21,401
8	25	H	Huddersfield Town	D		1-1	0-0	15th	Trotter	32,493
9	Oct 2	A	Sunderland	L		1-4	0-2	17th	Wilkinson	16,211
10	4	A	West Ham United	D		1-1	1-1	15th	Hill	9,770
11	9	H	West Bromwich Alb	W		2-1	1-0	13th	Trotter, Hill	15,508
12	16	H	Liverpool	W		3-2	1-1	11th	Anstiss, Wilkinson, Hill	24,535
13	23	A	Arsenal	L		2-6	0-2	12th	Anstiss, Hill	27,846
14	30	H	Derby County	W		2-1	0-1	10th	Wilkinson, Trotter	29,805
15	Nov 6	A	Manchester United	D		0-0	0-0	10th		16,166
16	13	H	Bolton Wanderers	W		2-1	1-1	10th	Trotter, Wilkinson	21,033
17	20	A	Aston Villa	D		2-2	1-2	8th	Trotter, Williams	14,889
18	29	H	Cardiff City	W		3-0	1-0	8th	Kirkwood, Hill (2)	16,986
19	Dec 4	A	Burnley	L		0-1	0-1	9th		18,349
20	11	H	Newcastle United	W		3-2	2-1	6th	Trotter (2), Hill	38,422
21	18	A	Leeds United	L		1-4	0-3	8th	Trotter	20,722
22	25	A	Bury	L		0-2	0-1	9th		19,836
23	28	H	Tottenham Hotspur	W		3-1	2-1	9th	Hill, Trotter (2)	35,529
24	Jan 1	H	Bury	L		1-3	1-2	11th	Hill	35,367
25	15	A	Sheffield United	L		0-2	0-1	11th		60,084
26	22	H	Leicester City	D		2-2	0-1	12th	Hill, Powell	19,796
27	Feb 5	H	Blackburn Rovers	L		0-3	0-2	16th		16,708
28	12	A	Huddersfield Town	L		3-4	1-1	15th	Anstiss (pen), Wilkinson (2)	22,329
29	19	H	Sunderland	W		4-1	3-1	15th	Trotter (3), Hooper	24,581
30	26	A	West Bromwich Alb	D		2-2	1-0	15th	Trotter (2)	17,091
31	Mar 2	A	Everton	L		1-2	0-2		Strange	19,455
32	5	A	Liverpool	L		0-3	0-2	15th		21,363
33	12	H	Arsenal	W		4-2	2-0	15th	Trotter (3), Leach	21,252
34	19	A	Derby County	L		0-8	0-2	16th		19,321
35	26	H	Manchester United	W		2-0	1-0	13th	Trotter (2)	11,997
36	Apr 2	A	Bolton Wanderers	L		2-3	1-2	15th	Trotter (2)	16,195
37	9	H	Aston Villa	W		3-1	1-1	14th	Trotter, Hooper, Strange	9,020
38	16	A	Cardiff City	L		2-3	1-1	18th	Trotter, Wilkinson	13,426
39	19	H	Birmingham	D		4-4	4-2	18th	Strange, Trotter (2), Hill	17,720
40	23	H	Burnley	W		2-1	0-1	16th	Kean, Strange	16,721
41	30	A	Newcastle United	L		1-2	1-1	17th	Strange	28,421
42	May 7	H	Leeds United	W		1-0	0-0	16th	Trotter	12,027
										Apps
										Goals

FA Cup

Match No.	Date	Venue	Opponents		Round	Result	HT Score	Position	Scorers	Attendance
43	Jan 8	H	Brighton & Hove Alb	W	1R	2-0	1-0		Hill, Trotter	24,945
44	29	H	South Shields	D	2R	1-1	0-1		Trotter	33,471
45	Feb 2	A	South Shields	L	2R Re	0-1	0-1			23,470
										Apps
										Goals

Allen Jack	Anstiss Harry	Blenkinsop Ernest	Brown Jack	Burridge Ben	Cruickshank Alex	Felton Billy	Froggatt Frank	Hill Harold	Hooper Mark	Kean Fred	Kirkwood Dan	Leach Tony	Lowdell Arthur	Marsden Billy	Marson Fred	Mellors Dick	Powell Sam	Strange Alf	Trotter Jimmy	Walker Tommy	Wilkinson Jack	Williams Rees
	8	3	1	6			5			4				10					9	2	11	7
	8	3	1	6			5			4				10					9	2	11	7
		3	1				5	10		4			8	6					9	2	11	7
		3	1			2		8		5			4	6			10		9		11	7
	10	3	1			2		8		5			4	6					9		11	7
	10	3	1		7	2		8		5			4	6					9		11	
	10	3	1		7	2		8		5			4	6					9		11	
	10	3	1			2		8		5			4	6					9		11	7
	10	3	1			2		8		5			4	6					9		11	7
	10	3	1					8		5			4	6					9	2	11	7
	10	3	1				5	8					4	6					9	2	11	7
	10	3	1					8		5			4	6					9	2	11	7
	10	3	1			2		8		5			4	6	11				9			7
		3	1					8		5			4	6			10		9	2	11	7
		3	1					8		5			4	6			10		9	2	11	7
		3	1	10				8		5			4	6					9	2	11	7
		3	1					8		5	10		4	6					9	2	11	7
		3	1					10		5	8		4	6					9	2	11	7
		3	1					10		5	8		4	6					9	2	11	7
		3	1					10		5	8		4	6					9	2	11	7
		3	1					10		5	8		4	6					9	2	11	7
		3	1					10		5	8		4	6					9	2	11	7
		3	1					10		5	8		4	6					9	2	11	7
		3	1					10		5	8		4	6					9	2	11	7
		3	1					10		5	8		4	6					9	2	11	7
		3	1					8	7	5			4	6			10		9	2	11	
		3	1						11	5		8	4	6	10				9	2		7
	9	3		5					7		8		4	6	10	1				2	11	
		3	1						7	5	8	4		6				10	9	2	11	
			1			3			7	5	8	4		6				10	9	2	11	
			1			3			7	5	8	4		6				10	9	2		11
			1			3			7	5	8	4		6				10	9	2		11
			1			3			7	5	8	4		6				10	9	2	11	
						3			7	5	8	4		6		1		10	9	2	11	
		3	1					10	7	5	8		4	6					9	2	11	
		3						10				5	4	6		1		8	9	2	11	7
10		3	1			2			7	5		4		6				8	9		11	
10		3	1			2			7	5		4		6				8	9		11	
		3	1					10		5		4		6				8	9	2	11	7
10		3	1			2			7	5		4		6				8	9		11	
10		3	1			2			7	5		4		6				8	9		11	
10		3	1			2			7	5		4		6				8	9		11	
5	12	37	39	4	2	17	4	27	15	39	17	14	28	42	3	3	4	13	41	30	38	28
	5						1	12	2	1	1	1					1	5	37		8	1

Allen Jack	Anstiss Harry	Blenkinsop Ernest	Brown Jack	Burridge Ben	Cruickshank Alex	Felton Billy	Froggatt Frank	Hill Harold	Hooper Mark	Kean Fred	Kirkwood Dan	Leach Tony	Lowdell Arthur	Marsden Billy	Marson Fred	Mellors Dick	Powell Sam	Strange Alf	Trotter Jimmy	Walker Tommy	Wilkinson Jack	Williams Rees
		3	1					10		5	8		4	6					9	2	11	7
		3	1					8		5			4	6			10		9	2	11	7
		3	1					10		5		8	4	6					9	2	11	7
		3	3					3		3	1	1	3	3			1		3	3	3	3
								1											2			

League Table

	P	W	D	L	F	A	Pts
Newcastle United	42	25	6	11	96	58	56
Huddersfield Town	42	17	17	8	76	60	51
Sunderland	42	21	7	14	98	70	49
Bolton Wanderers	42	19	10	13	84	62	48
Burnley	42	19	9	14	91	80	47
West Ham United	42	19	8	15	86	70	46
Leicester City	42	17	12	13	85	70	46
Sheffield United	42	17	10	15	74	86	44
Liverpool	42	18	7	17	69	61	43
Aston Villa	42	18	7	17	81	83	43
Arsenal	42	17	9	16	77	86	43
Derby County	42	17	7	18	86	73	41
Tottenham Hotspur	42	16	9	17	76	78	41
Cardiff City	42	16	9	17	55	65	41
Manchester United	42	13	14	15	52	64	40
SHEFFIELD WEDNESDAY	42	15	9	18	75	92	39
Birmingham	42	17	4	21	64	73	38
Blackburn Rovers	42	15	8	19	77	96	38
Bury	42	12	12	18	68	77	36
Everton	42	12	10	20	64	90	34
Leeds United	42	11	8	23	69	88	30
West Bromwich Albion	42	11	8	23	65	86	30

1927-28

Division One

Manager: Bob Brown

Did you know that?

Final League Position: 14th

This season became known as 'The Great Escape'. Seven points adrift and bottom with 10 games to go, Wednesday pulled themselves up, and with a win and a draw in the last two games they climbed to 14th place.

Match No.	Date	Venue	Opponents		Round	Result	HT Score	Position	Scorers	Attendance
1	Aug 27	A	Everton	L		0-4	0-2			39,485
2	29	H	Manchester United	L		0-2	0-2			17,944
3	Sep 3	H	Cardiff City	D		3-3	2-2	13th	Hooper, Trotter (pen), Allen	19,218
4	7	A	Manchester United	D		1-1	1-0		Trotter	18,759
5	10	A	Blackburn Rovers	L		1-3	0-1	20th	Allen	17,877
6	17	H	Bolton Wanderers	W		3-0	1-0	19th	Marsden, Trotter (2)	19,111
7	24	A	Sheffield United	D		1-1	1-1	19th	Trotter	43,144
8	Oct 1	A	Middlesbrough	D		3-3	2-2	20th	Allen, Hooper (2)	22,230
9	8	H	Birmingham	L		2-3	2-3	21st	Allen, Trotter	19,974
10	15	A	Newcastle United	L		3-4	3-2	21st	Allen, Hooper (pen), Harris (og)	29,886
11	22	H	Arsenal	D		1-1	0-1	22nd	Hooper	12,698
12	29	A	Burnley	L		1-3	0-1	22nd	Hooper (pen)	16,366
13	Nov 5	H	Bury	W		4-0	1-0	21st	Hill, Trotter, Seed, Wilkinson	16,808
14	12	A	Liverpool	L		2-5	2-2	21st	Kean, Wilkinson	24,253
15	19	H	Leicester City	L		1-2	0-2	21st	Trotter	15,969
16	26	A	Derby County	W		6-4	1-3	20th	Collins (og), Harper (3) Wilkinson, Hill	16,067
17	Dec 3	H	West Ham United	W		2-0	1-0	18th	Hooper, Harper	22,796
18	10	A	Portsmouth	D		0-0	0-0	20th		19,258
19	17	H	Sunderland	D		0-0	0-0	18th		19,755
20	24	A	Aston Villa	L		4-5	3-4	20th	Hooper (2), Harper, Seed	12,345
21	26	A	Huddersfield Town	L		0-1	0-0	21st		21,336
22	27	H	Huddersfield Town	L		0-5	0-2	22nd		41,824
23	31	H	Everton	L		1-2	1-1	22nd	Marsden	18,354
24	Jan 7	A	Cardiff City	D		1-1	0-0	22nd	Seed	9,208
25	21	H	Blackburn Rovers	W		4-1	3-0	22nd	Hill, Harper (2), Hooper	36,094
26	Feb 4	H	Sheffield United	D		3-3	1-0	22nd	Wilkinson (2), Harper	41,646
27	11	H	Middlesbrough	L		2-3	1-2	22nd	Hooper (pen + 1)	15,631
28	25	H	Newcastle United	D		0-0	0-0	22nd		25,462
29	29	A	Bolton Wanderers	L		0-2	0-1	22nd		9,786
30	Mar 7	A	Birmingham	L		0-1	0-0	22nd		12,076
31	10	H	Burnley	W		5-0	2-0	22nd	Wilson (2), Trotter, Rimmer (2)	12,401
32	17	A	Bury	L		2-4	1-2	22nd	Seed, Hooper (pen)	14,185
33	24	H	Liverpool	W		4-0	4-0	22nd	Seed, Hooper, Trotter, Rimmer	12,255
34	31	A	Leicester City	D		2-2	2-1	22nd	Prince, Trotter	18,634
35	Apr 6	A	Tottenham Hotspur	W		3-1	2-0	22nd	Seed, Hooper (2)	26,432
36	7	H	Derby County	D		2-2	0-0	22nd	Trotter, Seed	28,566
37	10	H	Tottenham Hotspur	W		4-2	3-1	22nd	Hooper (pen + 2), Seed	15,900
38	14	A	West Ham United	W		2-1	0-1	21st	Allen (2)	14,580
39	21	H	Portsmouth	W		2-0	1-0	21st	Trotter, Allen	14,536
40	28	A	Sunderland	W		3-2	2-2	22nd	Hooper (2), Trotter	19,339
41	May 2	A	Arsenal	D		1-1	0-0	19th	Seed	15,818
42	5	H	Aston Villa	W		2-0	0-0	14th	Allen, Trotter	36,636
										Apps
									Two own-goals	Goals
FA Cup										
43	Jan 14	H	Bournemouth	W	1R	3-0	1-0		Seed, Harper (2)	26,797
44	28	A	Swindon Town	W	2R	2-1	0-1		Seed, Harper	17,474
45	Feb 18	H	Sheffield United	D	3R	1-1	0-0		Wilkinson	57,076
46	22	A	Sheffield United	L	3R Re	1-4	0-1		Hooper (pen)	59,447
										Apps
										Goals

Allen Jack	Blenkinsop Ernest	Brown Jack	Burridge Ben	Felton Billy	Froggatt Frank	Harper Ted	Hill Harold	Hodgkiss Thomas	Hooper Mark	Kean Fred	Kirkwood Dan	Leach Tony	Marsden Billy	Marson Fred	Mellors Dick	Powell Sam	Prince Arthur	Rimmer Ellis	Seed Jimmy	Smith Norman	Strange Alf	Trotter Jimmy	Walker Tommy	Wilkinson Jack	Williams Rees	Wilson Charles
	3	1		2						5		4	6						8		10	9		11	7	
	3	1	6	2						5		4							8		10	9		11	7	
10	3		4	2	5				7				6	11	1				8			9				
	3		4	2	5		10		7				6	11	1				8			9				
10	3		4	2			8		7			5	6	11	1							9				
10	3		4	2					7	5			6	11	1						8	9				
10	3		4	2					7	5			6	11	1						8	9				
10	3		4	2					7	5			6	11	1						8	9				
10	3		4	2					7	5			6	11	1				8			9				
10	3		6	2					7	5		4			1				8			9		11		
10	3		6	2					7	5		4			1				8			9		11		
	3	1	4	2					7	5			6						10		8	9		11		
	3	1	4				8		7	5			6						10			9	2	11		
	3	1	4				8		7	5			6						10			9	2	11		
	3	1	4				8		7	5			6						10			9	2	11		
	3	1				9	8		7	5		4	6						10				2	11		
	3	1				9	8		7	5		4	6						10				2	11		
	3	1				9	8		7	5		4	6						10				2	11		
	3	1				9	8		7	5			6						10	4			2	11		
	3	1				9	8		7	5		4							10	6			2	11		
	3	1				9	8		7	5		4							10	6			2	11		
		1		3		9	8		7			5							6	4	10		2	11		
	3	1							7	5		4	8							6	10	9	2	11		
	3	1					8		7	5			6						10	4		9	2	11		
	3	1				9	8		7	5			6						10	4			2	11		
	3	1				9			7	5			6						10	4		8	2	11		
	3	1				9			7	5	8		6						10	4			2	11		
	3	1	6			9			7	5								11	10	4			2			8
	3	1	6			9			7	5								11	8	4			2			10
	3	1	6						7			5				9		11	8	4			2			10
		1	6					2	7			5						11	8	4		9	3			10
		1						2	7	4		5						11	8	6		9	3			10
10	3	1							7	4		5	6					11	8			9	2			
10	3	1										5	6				7	11	8	4		9	2			
10	3	1							7			5	6					11	8	4		9	2			
	3	1							7			5	6					11	8	4	10	9	2			
10	3	1							7	4		5						11	8		6	9	2			
10	3	1							7			5						11	8	4	6	9	2			
10	3	1							7			5						11	8	4	6	9	2			
10	3	1							7			5	6					11	8		4	9	2			
10	3	1							7			5	6					11	8		4	9	2			
10	3	1							7			5	6					11	8		4	9	2			
17	39	33	18	13	2	12	14	2	39	28	1	25	28	7	9	1	1	15	37	19	15	30	30	20	2	5
9						8	3		21	1			2				1	3	9			15		5		2
	3	1				9	8		7	5			6						10	4			2	11		
	3	1				9	8		7	5			6						10	4			2	11		
	3	1				9			7	5			6						10	4	8		2	11		
	3	1				9			7	5			6						10	4	8		2	11		
	4	4				4	2		4	4			4						4	4	2		4	4		
						3			1										2					1		

League Table

	P	W	D	L	F	A	Pts
Everton	42	20	13	9	102	66	53
Huddersfield Town	42	22	7	13	91	68	51
Leicester City	42	18	12	12	96	72	48
Derby County	42	17	10	15	96	83	44
Bury	42	20	4	18	80	80	44
Cardiff City	42	17	10	15	70	80	44
Bolton Wanderers	42	16	11	15	81	66	43
Aston Villa	42	17	9	16	78	73	43
Newcastle United	42	15	13	14	79	81	43
Arsenal	42	13	15	14	82	86	41
Birmingham	42	13	15	14	70	75	41
Blackburn Rovers	42	16	9	17	66	78	41
Sheffield United	42	15	10	17	79	86	40
SHEFFIELD WEDNESDAY	42	13	13	16	81	78	39
Sunderland	42	15	9	18	74	76	39
Liverpool	42	13	13	16	84	87	39
West Ham United	42	14	11	17	81	88	39
Manchester United	42	16	7	19	72	80	39
Burnley	42	16	7	19	82	98	39
Portsmouth	42	16	7	19	66	90	39
Tottenham Hotspur	42	15	8	19	74	86	38
Middlesbrough	42	11	15	16	81	88	37

1928-29

Division One

Manager: Bob Brown

Did you know that?

Final League Position: 1st

Wednesday won the League Championship, setting a new record of 52 points.

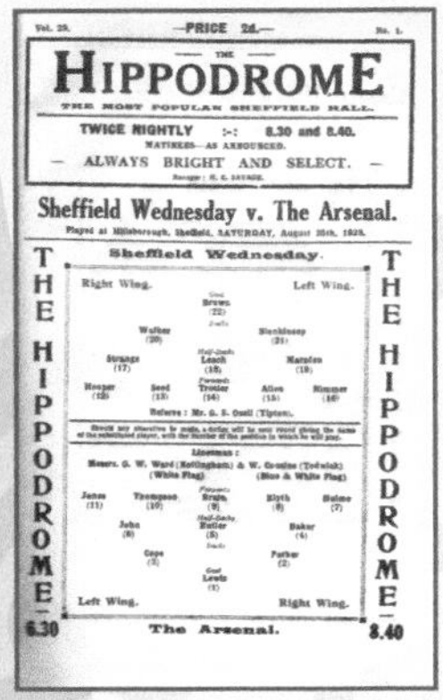

Match No.	Date	Venue	Opponents		Round	Result	HT Score	Position	Scorers	Attendance
1	Aug 25	H	Arsenal	W		3-2	1-1		Hooper (2), Marsden	23,684
2	29	A	Everton	D		0-0	0-0			39,011
3	Sep 1	A	Blackburn Rovers	L		1-4	0-3	13th	Seed	18,647
4	3	H	Everton	W		1-0	1-0	8th	Seed	24,322
5	8	H	Sunderland	W		2-1	1-0	5th	Trotter, Strange	25,716
6	15	A	Derby County	L		0-6	0-4	7th		22,762
7	22	H	Sheffield United	W		5-2	2-0	3rd	Allen (2), Hooper (2), Rimmer	44,699
8	29	H	Bolton Wanderers	D		0-0	0-0	7th		25,098
9	Oct 6	A	Portsmouth	L		2-3	0-1	10th	Allen, Hooper (pen)	22,732
10	13	H	Birmingham	W		3-0	1-0	7th	Allen (3)	21,677
11	20	A	Bury	W		4-0	2-0	4th	Allen (4)	12,273
12	27	H	Cardiff City	W		1-0	1-0	4th	Hooper	20,116
13	Nov 3	A	Leicester City	D		1-1	0-0	4th	Allen	29,522
14	10	H	Manchester United	W		2-1	1-0	3rd	Hooper, Gregg	18,113
15	17	A	Leeds United	W		2-0	0-0	2nd	Seed, Gregg	25,519
16	24	H	Liverpool	W		3-2	1-2	1st	Rimmer, Allen (2)	14,624
17	Dec 1	A	West Ham United	L		2-3	1-1	1st	Allen (2)	18,536
18	8	H	Newcastle United	W		3-1	1-0	1st	Allen (2), Hooper	23,835
19	15	A	Burnley	W		2-0	1-0	1st	Allen (2)	16,173
20	22	H	Aston Villa	W		4-1	3-0	1st	Hooper, Seed (2), Allen	24,822
21	25	H	Manchester City	W		4-0	3-0	1st	Allen (2), Hooper, Gregg,	45,093
22	26	A	Manchester City	D		2-2	0-0	1st	Allen (2)	42,826
23	29	A	Arsenal	D		2-2	0-2	1st	Gregg, Hooper	39,255
24	Jan 1	H	Huddersfield Town	D		1-1	0-0	1st	Gregg	57,143
25	5	H	Blackburn Rovers	W		1-0	0-0	1st	Allen	28,136
26	19	A	Sunderland	L		3-4	2-3	1st	Allen, Gregg, Seed	36,475
27	Feb 2	A	Sheffield United	D		1-1	1-1	1st	Hooper	44,576
28	9	A	Bolton Wanderers	D		2-2	0-2	1st	Blenkinsop, Allen	22,387
29	18	H	Derby County	W		5-0	3-0	1st	Gregg, Harper (3), Strange	16,026
30	23	A	Birmingham	L		1-4	1-1	1st	Harper	28,599
31	Mar 2	H	Bury	W		3-1	0-1	1st	Whitehouse, Harper, Seed	23,826
32	4	H	Portsmouth	W		2-1	2-0	1st	Hooper, Wilson	13,705
33	9	A	Cardiff City	L		1-3	1-2	1st	Allen	18,636
34	16	H	Leicester City	W		1-0	1-0	1st	Allen	30,176
35	23	A	Manchester United	L		1-2	0-1	1st	Hargreaves	27,095
36	30	H	Leeds United	W		4-2	2-0	1st	Rimmer (3), Seed	30,655
37	Apr 2	A	Huddersfield Town	D		0-0	0-0	1st		32,555
38	6	A	Liverpool	L		2-3	1-1	1st	Rimmer, Allen	28,878
39	13	H	West Ham United	W		6-0	4-0	1st	Strange (pen + 1), Hooper (2),Rimmer, Allen	22,596
40	20	A	Newcastle United	L		1-2	0-2	1st	Allen	26,401
41	27	H	Burnley	D		1-1	0-0	1st	Allen	33,314
42	May 4	A	Aston Villa	L		1-4	1-2	1st	Strange	12,510
										Apps
										Goals

FA Cup

Match No.	Date	Venue	Opponents		Round	Result	HT Score	Position	Scorers	Attendance
43	Jan 12	A	Wigan Borough	W	3R	3-1	1-0		Hooper, Allen (2)	30,651
44	26	A	Reading	L	4R	0-1	0-0			29,248
										Apps
										Goals

Allen Jack	Blenkinsop Ernest	Brown Jack	Burridge Ben	Felton Billy	Gregg Bob	Hargreaves Len	Harper Ted	Hatfield Ernie	Hill Harold	Hooper Mark	Kean Fred	Leach Tony	Marsden Billy	Rimmer Ellis	Seed Jimmy	Strange Alf	Trotter Jimmy	Walker Tommy	Whitehouse Jack	Wilkinson Jack	Wilson Charles
10	3	1								7		5	6	11	8	4	9	2			
10	3	1								7	5		6	11	8	4	9	2			
	3	1							10	7	5		6	11	8	4	9	2			
10	3	1								7	5		6		8	4	9	2		11	
	3	1			10					7	5		6		8	4	9	2		11	
10	3	1					9			7		5	6		8	4		2		11	
10		1		3			9			7		5	6	11	8	4		2			
10	3	1					9			7		5	6	11	8	4		2			
9	3	1			10					7		5	6	11	8	4		2			
9	3	1			10					7		5	6	11	8	4		2			
9	3	1	5		10					7			6	11	8	4		2			
9	3	1	5		10					7			6	11	8	4		2			
9	3	1			10					7		5	6		8	4		2		11	
9	3	1			10					7		5	6		8	4		2		11	
9		1		3	10					7		5	6	11	8	4		2			
9	3	1			10					7		5	6	11	8	4		2			
9	3	1			8					7		5	6	11		4		2			10
9	3	1			8					7		5	6	11		4		2			10
9	3	1			10					7		5	6	11	8	4		2			
9	3	1			10					7		5	6	11	8	4		2			
9	3	1			10					7		5	6	11	8	4		2			
9	3	1			10					7		5	6	11	8	4		2			
9	3	1			10					7		5	6	11	8	4		2			
9	3	1			10					7		5	6	11	8	4		2			
9	3	1			10					7		5	6	11	8	4		2			
9	3	1			10					7		5	6	11	8	4		2			
	3	1			10					7		5	6	11	8	4	9	2			
9	3	1			10					7		5	6	11	8	4		2			
	3	1			10		9			7		5	6	11	8	4		2			
	3	1		2	10		9			7		5	6	11	8	4					
	3	1					9			7		5	6	11	8	4		2	10		
	3	1								7		5	6	11	8	4		2	10		9
9	3	1								7		5	6		8	4		2	10	11	
9	3	1				11				7		5	6		8	4		2	10		
9	3	1				11				7		5	6		10	4		2	8		
9	3	1			10					7		5	6	11	8	4		2			
9	3	1			10					7		5	6	11	8	4		2			
9	3	1			10					7		5	6	11	8	4		2			
9		1			10			3		7		5	6	11	8	4		2			
9	3	1			10					7		5	6	11	8	4		2			
9	3	1			10					7		5	6	11	8	4		2			
9	3	1			10					7		5	6	11		4		2	8		
35	39	42	2	3	30	2	6	1	1	42	4	36	42	34	39	42	6	41	6	6	3
33	1				7	1	5			15			1	7	8	5	1		1		1

Allen Jack	Blenkinsop Ernest	Brown Jack	Burridge Ben	Felton Billy	Gregg Bob	Hargreaves Len	Harper Ted	Hatfield Ernie	Hill Harold	Hooper Mark	Kean Fred	Leach Tony	Marsden Billy	Rimmer Ellis	Seed Jimmy	Strange Alf	Trotter Jimmy	Walker Tommy	Whitehouse Jack	Wilkinson Jack	Wilson Charles
9	3	1			10					7		5	6	11	8	4		2			
9	3	1			10					7		5	6	11	8	4		2			
2	2	2			2					2		2	2	2	2	2		2			
2										1											

League Table

	P	W	D	L	F	A	Pts
SHEFFIELD WEDNESDAY	42	21	10	11	86	62	52
Leicester City	42	21	9	12	96	67	51
Aston Villa	42	23	4	15	98	81	50
Sunderland	42	20	7	15	93	75	47
Liverpool	42	17	12	13	90	64	46
Derby County	42	18	10	14	86	71	46
Blackburn Rovers	42	17	11	14	72	63	45
Manchester City	42	18	9	15	95	86	45
Arsenal	42	16	13	13	77	72	45
Newcastle United	42	19	6	17	70	72	44
Sheffield United	42	15	11	16	86	85	41
Manchester United	42	14	13	15	66	76	41
Leeds United	42	16	9	17	71	84	41
Bolton Wanderers	42	14	12	16	73	80	40
Birmingham	42	15	10	17	68	77	40
Huddersfield Town	42	14	11	17	70	61	39
West Ham United	42	15	9	18	86	96	39
Everton	42	17	4	21	63	75	38
Burnley	42	15	8	19	81	103	38
Portsmouth	42	15	6	21	56	80	36
Bury	42	12	7	23	62	99	31
Cardiff City	42	8	13	21	43	59	29

1929-30

Division One

Manager: Bob Brown

Did you know that?

Final League Position: 1st

On 3 August 1929 the Wednesday Football Club Limited changed its name to Sheffield Wednesday Football Club Limited by approval of the Board of Trade.

In the FA Cup semi-final on 22 March 1930 at Old Trafford, with Wednesday winning 1–0, Alec Jackson equalised after Lewis had handled the ball. Jackson then netted again to put Huddersfield in the Final, but not before Jack Allen had scored, with the whistle going as the ball went into the net. Some claimed that the half had only lasted 43 minutes!

Wednesday scored over a century of goals for the first time in a season, netting 105 League goals in retaining the First Division Championship and remaining unbeaten at home.

Match No.	Date	Venue	Opponents		Round	Result	HT Score	Position	Scorers	Attendance
1	Aug 31	A	Portsmouth	W		4-0	2-0		Rimmer (2), Allen (2)	27,537
2	Sep 2	H	Bolton Wanderers	W		1-0	1-0	1st	Allen	26,480
3	7	H	Arsenal	L		0-2	0-1	3rd		38,735
4	14	A	Aston Villa	W		3-1	1-0	3rd	Burgess, Allen (2)	36,209
5	21	H	Leeds United	L		1-2	0-2	9th	Seed	21,353
6	25	A	Bolton Wanderers	W		3-1	2-1	5th	Seed, Hooper, Allen	11,136
7	28	A	Sheffield United	D		2-2	2-1	3rd	Seed, Allen	47,039
8	Oct 5	A	Burnley	W		4-2	1-0	2nd	Marsden, Burgess (2), Hooper	17,294
9	12	H	Sunderland	D		1-1	1-0	2nd	Burgess	23,158
10	19	H	Huddesfield Town	W		3-1	2-0	2nd	Burgess, Allen, Rimmer	25,998
11	26	A	Birmingham	L		0-1	0-1	4th		27,221
12	Nov 2	H	Leicester City	W		4-0	1-0	4th	Burgess, Allen (3)	19,159
13	9	A	Newcastle United	W		3-1	2-0	3rd	Rimmer, Allen (2)	27,505
14	16	H	Manchester United	W		7-2	4-1	2nd	Rimmer (2), Allen (4), Hooper	14,264
15	23	A	West Ham United	D		1-1	1-0	2nd	Burgess	18,753
16	30	H	Liverpool	W		2-1	2-1	2nd	Strange, Hooper	19,701
17	Dec 7	A	Middlesbrough	L		1-4	1-3	2nd	Allen	21,265
18	14	H	Blackburn Rovers	W		4-0	2-0	2nd	Seed, Allen (2), Burgess	19,278
19	25	A	Everton	W		4-1	2-0	2nd	Allen, Hooper (3)	30,835
20	26	H	Everton	W		4-0	1-0	2nd	Burgess, Leach (2), Allen	45,559
21	28	H	Portsmouth	D		1-1	0-1	1st	Strange	23,548
22	Jan 1	A	Manchester City	D		3-3	2-0	1st	Rimmer, Allen, Seed	55,930
23	4	A	Arsenal	W		3-2	1-1	1st	Burgess (2), Seed	40,766
24	18	H	Aston Villa	W		3-0	1-0	1st	Rimmer, Marsden, Hooper	34,911
25	Feb 1	H	Sheffield United	D		1-1	1-1	1st	Burgess	54,459
26	4	A	Grimsby Town	W		5-0	2-0	1st	Allen, Burgess (2), Rimmer, Seed	12,514
27	8	H	Burnley	W		4-1	2-0	1st	McCluggage (og), Seed, Rimmer (2)	23,864
28	22	A	Huddesfield Town	L		1-4	1-2	1st	Burgess	27,001
29	Mar 8	A	Leicester City	L		1-2	0-1	2nd	Marsden	29,664
30	15	H	Newcastle United	W		4-2	3-0	1st	Rimmer (2), Allen, Burgess	9,350
31	29	H	West Ham United	W		2-1	1-1	1st	Hooper, Burgess	25,092
32	Apr 5	A	Liverpool	W		3-1	1-1	1st	Allen, Hooper, Burgess	35,563
33	9	A	Leeds United	L		0-3	0-2	1st		3,950
34	12	H	Middlesbrough	W		1-0	1-0	1st	Rimmer	23,087
35	14	A	Manchester United	D		2-2	0-2	1st	Allen (2)	12,806
36	19	A	Blackburn Rovers	W		1-0	0-0	1st	Hooper	17,768
37	21	A	Derby County	L		1-4	0-3	1st	Hooper	25,624
38	22	H	Derby County	W		6-3	2-0	1st	Allen (3), Rimmer, Millership, Hooper	41,218
39	26	H	Grimsby Town	W		1-0	0-0	1st	Jacobson (og)	22,524
40	28	H	Birmingham	D		1-1	1-0	1st	Strange	9,310
41	30	A	Sunderland	W		4-2	1-1	1st	Hooper (2), Burgess, Allen	26,351
42	May 3	H	Manchester City	W		5-1	3-1	1st	Allen, Hooper (3), Seed	22,293
										Apps
									Two own-goals	Goals

FA Cup

Match No.	Date	Venue	Opponents		Round	Result	HT Score	Position	Scorers	Attendance
43	Jan 11	H	Burnley	W	3R	1-0	0-0		Allen	31,794
44	25	A	Oldham Athletic	W	4R	4-3	2-2		Hooper, Allen (2), Seed	46,471
45	Feb 15	H	Bradford Park Avenue	W	5R	5-1	2-1		Seed, Rimmer, Allen, Bentley (og), Hooper	53,268
46	Mar 1	A	Nottingham Forest	D	6R	2-2	2-1		Rimmer, Allen	44,166
47	5	H	Nottingham Forest	W	6R Re	3-1	1-1		Seed, Allen (pen), Burgess	59,205
48	22	N	Huddersfield Town *	L	S/Final	1-2	1-1		Hooper	69,292
										Apps
									One own-goal	Goals

* At Old Trafford, Manchester

Allen Jack	Beeson George	Blenkinsop Ernest	Brown Jack	Burgess Harry	Burridge Ben	Gregg Bob	Hooper Mark	Jones Tommy	Leach Tony	Mackey Thomas	Marsden Billy	Mellors Dick	Millership Walt	Rimmer Ellis	Seed Jimmy	Smith Billy	Strange Alf	Walker Tommy	Whitehouse Jack	Wilkinson Jack	Wilson Charles
9		3	1			10	7		5		6			11			4	2	8		
9		3	1			10	7		5		6			11			4	2	8		
9		3	1			10	7		5		6			11			4	2	8		
9		3	1	10			7		5		6			11	8		4	2			
9		3	1	10			7		5		6			11	8		4	2			
9		3	1	10			7		5		6			11	8		4	2			
9		3	1	10			7		5		6			11	8		4	2			
9		3	1	10			7		5		6			11	8		4	2			
9		3	1	10			7		5		6			11	8		4	2			
9				10			7		5		6	1		11	8		4	2			3
9		3	1	10			7		5		6			11	8		4				2
9	2		1	10	6		7		5					11	8		4				3
9		3	1	10			7		5		6			11	8		4				2
9		3	1	10			7		5		6			11	8		4				2
9		3	1	10			7		5		6			11	8		4				2
9		3	1	10			7		5		6			11	8		4				2
9		3	1	10			7		5		6			11			4		8		2
9		3	1	10			7		5		6			11	8		4	2			
9		3	1	10			7		5		6			11	8		4	2			
9		3	1	10			7		5		6			11	8		4	2			
		3	1	9	5	10	7				6			11	8		4	2			
9		3	1	10			7		5		6			11	8		4	2			
9		3	1	10			7		5		6			11	8		4	2			
9		3	1	10			7		5		6			11	8		4	2			
9		3	1	10			7		5					11	8	6	4	2			
9		3	1	10			7		5		6			11	8		4	2			
9		3	1	10			7		5		6			11	8		4	2			
9		3	1	10			7		5		6			11	8		4	2			
9		3	1	10			7		5		6				8		4	2		11	
9		3	1	10			7		5		6			11	8		4	2			
9		3	1	10			7		5		6			11	8		4	2			
9			1	10			7	11	5				8		4	6		2			3
9		3	1	10			7		5		6		8	11			4	2			
9		3	1	10			7		5		6		8	11			4	2			
9		3	1	10			7		5		6		8	11			4	2			
9		3	1	10		8	7		5		6			11			4	2			
9		3	1	10			7		5		6		8	11			4	2			
9		3	1	10			7		5				8	11		6	4	2			
9		3	1	10			7		5					11	8	6	4	2			
9		3	1	10			7			5	6			11	8		4	2			
9		3	1	10			7		5		6			11	8		4	2			
9	2	3	1	10			7		5		6			11	8		4				
41	2	39	41	39	2	5	42	1	40	1	37	1	6	40	32	4	41	34	4	1	9
33				19			18		2		3		1	15	9		3				

Allen Jack	Beeson George	Blenkinsop Ernest	Brown Jack	Burgess Harry	Burridge Ben	Gregg Bob	Hooper Mark	Jones Tommy	Leach Tony	Mackey Thomas	Marsden Billy	Mellors Dick	Millership Walt	Rimmer Ellis	Seed Jimmy	Smith Billy	Strange Alf	Walker Tommy	Whitehouse Jack	Wilkinson Jack	Wilson Charles
9		3	1	10			7		5		6			11	8		4	2			
9		3	1	10			7		5		6			11	8		4	2			
9		3	1	10			7		5		6			11	8		4	2			
9		3	1	10			7		5		6			11	8		4	2			
9		3	1	10			7		5		6			11	8		4	2			
9		3	1	10			7		5		6			11	8		4	2			
6		6	6	6			6		6		6			6	6		6	6			
6				1			3		1					2	3						

League Table

	P	W	D	L	F	A	Pts
SHEFFIELD WEDNESDAY	42	26	8	8	105	57	60
Derby County	42	21	8	13	90	82	50
Manchester City	42	19	9	14	91	81	47
Aston Villa	42	21	5	16	92	83	47
Leeds United	42	20	6	16	79	63	46
Blackburn Rovers	42	19	7	16	99	93	45
West Ham United	42	19	5	18	86	79	43
Leicester City	42	17	9	16	86	90	43
Sunderland	42	18	7	17	76	80	43
Huddersfield Town	42	17	9	16	63	69	43
Birmingham	42	16	9	17	67	62	41
Liverpool	42	16	9	17	63	79	41
Portsmouth	42	15	10	17	66	62	40
Arsenal	42	14	11	17	78	66	39
Bolton Wanderers	42	15	9	18	74	74	39
Middlesbrough	42	16	6	20	82	84	38
Manchester United	42	15	8	19	67	88	38
Grimsby Town	42	15	7	20	73	89	37
Newcastle United	42	15	7	20	71	92	37
Sheffield United	42	15	6	21	91	96	36
Burnley	42	14	8	20	79	97	36
Everton	42	12	11	19	80	92	35

1930-31

Division One

Manager: Bob Brown

Did you know that?

Final League Position: 3rd

George Nevin was signed from Newcastle United on a free transfer after he had appealed to the Football League to have his valuation of £1,000 removed.

PRICE 2d.

HIPPODROME

TWICE NIGHTLY 6.30 and 8.40.

THE LATEST, BRIGHTEST and BEST

Sheffield Wednesday v. Sheffield United

Sheffield Wednesday.

Sheffield United.

Match No.	Date	Venue	Opponents		Round	Result	HT Score	Position	Scorers	Attendance
1	Aug 30	H	Newcastle United	W		2-1	0-1		Burgess, Weaver (og)	23,673
2	Sep 1	A	Aston Villa	L		0-2	0-0			27,622
3	6	A	Sheffield United	D		1-1	1-0	12th	Burgess	36,738
4	8	H	Chelsea	D		1-1	1-1	9th	Rimmer	21,282
5	13	A	Grimsby Town	W		3-2	1-1	8th	Rimmer (2), Ball	17,101
6	15	A	Chelsea	D		0-0	0-0	6th		51,690
7	20	H	Manchester United	W		3-0	1-0	5th	Ball (2), Rimmer	18,705
8	27	A	West Ham United	D		3-3	2-3	7th	Seed, Hooper (2)	26,487
9	Oct 4	H	Bolton Wanderers	W		1-0	0-0	6th	Burgess (pen)	21,310
10	11	A	Liverpool	W		2-1	0-0	5th	Ball, Hooper	39,278
11	18	H	Manchester City	D		1-1	1-0	5th	Ball	20,750
12	25	A	Derby County	W		3-2	2-0	3rd	Ball, Collins (og), Rimmer	23,511
13	Nov 1	H	Sunderland	W		7-2	3-2	3rd	Rimmer, Burgess, Ball (3), Hooper, Wilson	19,299
14	8	A	Leeds United	W		3-2	2-1	2nd	Rimmer, Walker (pen), Ball	22,040
15	15	H	Arsenal	L		1-2	1-1	3rd	Ball	43,671
16	22	A	Leicester City	W		5-2	3-1	3rd	Ball (3), Burgess (2)	18,794
17	29	H	Blackpool	W		7-1	4-0	2nd	Hooper (3), Seed, Ball, Rimmer, Burgess	17,393
18	Dec 6	A	Portsmouth	W		4-2	2-0	2nd	Rimmer, Wilson, Burgess, Walker (pen)	27,920
19	13	H	Birmingham	W		9-1	5-0	1st	Burgess, Ball (2), Rimmer, Hooper (3), Seed (2)	21,226
20	20	A	Blackburn Rovers	L		2-5	0-2	1st	Seed, Jones (og)	17,778
21	26	A	Middlesbrough	L		0-2	0-1	2nd		23,212
22	27	A	Newcastle United	W		2-1	1-1	2nd	Seed (2)	37,194
23	29	H	Middlesbrough	W		3-2	3-1	2nd	Ball (2), Rimmer	18,530
24	Jan 1	H	Huddersfield Town	W		2-1	2-1	2nd	Burgess, Rimmer	39,631
25	3	H	Sheffield United	L		1-3	1-1	2nd	Ball	33,322
26	17	H	Grimsby Town	W		4-1	3-0	1st	Rimmer, Allen, Burgess, Ball (pen)	19,729
27	28	A	Manchester United	L		1-4	0-2	2nd	Jones	6,077
28	31	H	West Ham United	W		5-3	2-1	1st	Wade (og), Burgess, Hooper, Rimmer (2)	16,796
29	Feb 7	A	Bolton Wanderers	D		2-2	1-1	2nd	Ball, Burgess	19,594
30	14	H	Liverpool	L		3-5	1-2	2nd	Ball (2), Stephenson	21,675
31	21	A	Manchester City	L		0-2	0-2	3rd		29,822
32	Mar 7	A	Sunderland	L		1-5	1-3	3rd	Hooper	14,987
33	14	H	Leeds United	W		2-1	1-0	3rd	Menzies (og), Rimmer	14,562
34	21	A	Arsenal	L		0-2	0-0	3rd		47,872
35	28	H	Leicester City	W		4-0	2-0	3rd	Ball (2), Rimmer (2)	10,525
36	Apr 4	A	Blackpool	W		4-0	1-0	3rd	Johnson, Burgess (3)	23,931
37	7	A	Huddersfield Town	D		1-1	0-1	3rd	Rimmer	22,601
38	11	H	Portsmouth	D		2-2	1-1	3rd	Stephenson, Hooper	13,400
39	18	A	Birmingham	L		0-2	0-0	3rd		16,441
40	20	H	Derby County	W		3-2	2-2	3rd	Hooper, Ball, Rimmer	5,141
41	25	H	Blackburn Rovers	L		1-3	1-2	3rd	Rimmer	5,101
42	May 2	H	Aston Villa	W		3-0	2-0	3rd	Stephenson (2), Rimmer	12,419
										App
									Five own-goals	Goals
FA Cup										
43	Jan 10	A	Gateshead	W	3R	6-2	4-2		Hooper, Allen, Ball (pen), Rimmer (2), Burgess	12,490
44	24	A	Barnsley	L	4R	1-2	0-1		Ball	24,032
										App
										Goals
FA Charity Shield played at Stamford Bridge, London										
45	Oct 8	N	Arsenal	L		1-2	0-2		Burgess pen)	20,000

Allen Jack	Ball Jack	Beeson George	Blenkinsop Ernest	Breedon Jack	Brown Jack	Burgess Harry	Catlin Ted	Davison Tommy	Dodds Sam	Gregg Bob	Hooper Mark	Johnson George	Jones Tommy	Leach Tony	Mackey Thomas	Mellors Dick	Millership Walt	Peacock Joe	Rimmer Ellis	Robson Thomas	Seed Jimmy	Smith Billy	Stephenson George	Strange Alf	Walker Tommy	Wilson Charles
9			3		1	10					7			5					11		8	6		4	2	
9			3		1	10					7			5					11		8	6		4	2	
9			3		1	10					7			5					11		8	6		4	2	
	9		3			10				8	7			5		1		6	11					4	2	
	9		3		1	10					7			5					11		8			4	2	6
	9		3		1					10	7			5					11		8			4	2	6
	9		3		1	10					7			5					11		8			4	2	6
9			3		1	10					7			5					11		8			4	2	6
9			3		1	10					7			5					11		8			4	2	6
	9		3		1	10					7			5					11		8			4	2	6
	9		3		1	10					7			5					11		8			4	2	6
	9		3		1	10					7			5					11		8			4	2	6
	9		3		1	10					7			5					11		8			4	2	6
	9		3		1	10					7			5					11		8			4	2	6
	9		3		1	10					7			5					11		8			4	2	6
	9				1	10			5		7						4		11		8	6			2	3
	9		3		1	10					7			5					11		8			4	2	6
	9		3		1	10					7			5					11		8			4	2	6
	9		3		1	10					7			5					11		8			4	2	6
	9		3		1	10					7			5					11		8			4	2	6
	9		3		1	10					7			5			8		11					4	2	6
	9		3	1		10					7			5					11		8			4	2	6
	9		3	1		10					7			5			8		11					4	2	6
	9		3	1		10					7			5			8		11					4	2	6
	9		3	1		10					7				5		8		11					4	2	6
10	9		3	1		8					7								11			6		4	2	5
	9		3	1		8					7		11	5								6		4	2	10
	9		3	1		10					7				5				11		8			4	2	6
	9		3	1		10		5			7								11				8	4	2	6
	9		3	1		10		5			7								11				8	4	2	6
	9		3		1	10		5			7								11				8	4	2	6
	9		3		1	10		5			7								11		8			4	2	6
	9	2	3		1	10		5			7								11		8			4		6
	9	2	3		1	10		5			7								11		8			4		6
	9				1		3				7			5					11	4	8		10		2	6
			3		1	10					7	9		5					11		8			4	2	6
	9		3		1	10					7			5					11				8	4	2	6
	9		3		1	10					7			5					11				8	4	2	6
	9		3		1	10					7			5					11				8	4	2	6
	9	2	3		1	8					7			5					11				10	4		6
	9	2	3		1	8					7			5					11				10	4		6
	9		3	1		8					7			5					11			6	10	4	2	
6	36	4	40	10	31	40	1	6	1	2	42	1	1	32	2	1	5	1	41	1	26	7	10	40	38	37
1	27					16					14	1	1						22		7		4		2	2

10	9		3	1		8					7			5					11					4	2	6
10	9		3	1		8					7			5					11					4	2	6
2	2		2	2		2					2			2					2					2	2	2
1	2					1					1								2							

	9		3		1	10					7			5					11		8			4	2	6

League Table

	P	W	D	L	F	A	Pts
Arsenal	42	28	10	4	127	59	66
Aston Villa	42	25	9	8	128	78	59
SHEFFIELD WEDNESDAY	42	22	8	12	102	75	52
Portsmouth	42	18	13	11	84	67	49
Huddersfield Town	42	18	12	12	81	65	48
Derby County	42	18	10	14	94	79	46
Middlesbrough	42	19	8	15	98	90	46
Manchester City	42	18	10	14	75	70	46
Liverpool	42	15	12	15	86	85	42
Blackburn Rovers	42	17	8	17	83	84	42
Sunderland	42	16	9	17	89	85	41
Chelsea	42	15	10	17	64	67	40
Grimsby Town	42	17	5	20	82	87	39
Bolton Wanderers	42	15	9	18	68	81	39
Sheffield United	42	14	10	18	78	84	38
Leicester City	42	16	6	20	80	95	38
Newcastle United	42	15	6	21	78	87	36
West Ham United	42	14	8	20	79	94	36
Birmingham	42	13	10	19	55	70	36
Blackpool	42	11	10	21	71	125	32
Leeds United	42	12	7	23	68	81	31
Manchester United	42	7	8	27	53	115	22

1931-32

Division One

Manager: Bob Brown

Did you know that?

Final League Position: 3rd

On 23 January 1932, in an FA Cup tie against Bournemouth, two Wednesday players netted hat-tricks. This was the first time this had been achieved in a competitive game for Wednesday. Harry Burgess got three and Harry Millership netted four in a 7–0 home win.

Match No.	Date	Venue	Opponents		Round	Result	HT Score	Position	Scorers	Attendance
1	Aug 29	A	Blackburn Rovers	W		6-1	2-1		Ball, Hooper, Stephenson (4)	15,819
2	31	H	Grimsby Town	W		4-1	1-1		Ball, Rimmer (2), Stephenson	16,734
3	Sep 5	H	Bolton Wanderers	W		7-1	3-1	1st	Burgess (2), Rimmer (1 + pen), Ball, Leach, Stephenson	14,544
4	9	A	Chelsea	W		3-2	1-2	1st	Ball, Smith, Rimmer	31,426
5	12	A	Middlesbrough	L		0-4	0-1	1st		24,050
6	19	H	Huddersfield Town	W		4-1	2-0	1st	Millership (2), Rimmer (pen +1)	24,326
7	21	H	Chelsea	D		2-2	2-0	1st	Ball, Burgess	11,809
8	26	A	Newcastle United	L		1-4	1-1	4th	Hooper	31,892
9	Oct 3	H	Aston Villa	W		1-0	1-0	2nd	Burgess	28,798
10	10	A	Leicester City	L		2-3	1-1	4th	Ball, Strange	30,100
11	17	A	Everton	L		3-9	1-2	6th	Rimmer, Hooper, Ball	38,186
12	24	H	Derby County	W		3-1	2-0	5th	Stephenson, Hooper, Ball	12,901
13	31	A	West Bromwich Alb	D		1-1	1-1	6th	Rimmer	31,414
14	Nov 7	H	Birmingham	W		5-1	2-0	3rd	Rimmer (2), Hooper, Ball (2)	17,438
15	14	A	Blackpool	W		2-1	1-0	3rd	Hooper, Rimmer	12,160
16	21	H	Sheffield United	W		2-1	2-1	2nd	Ball, Stephenson	25,823
17	28	A	Portsmouth	L		0-2	0-1	3rd		19,320
18	Dec 5	H	Arsenal	L		1-3	1-1	4th	Ball	23,265
19	12	A	Sunderland	L		1-3	1-1	6th	Ball	21,818
20	19	H	Manchester City	D		1-1	1-1	5th	Ball	7,431
21	25	A	Liverpool	L		1-3	0-3		Stephenson	27,096
22	26	H	Liverpool	D		1-1	0-1	10th	Stephenson	34,705
23	Jan 2	H	Blackburn Rovers	W		5-1	2-0	10th	Millership (3), Stephenson, Leach	12,792
24	16	A	Bolton Wanderers	W		4-2	1-1	8th	Millership (2), Strange, Rimmer	8,851
25	25	H	Middlesbrough	D		1-1	0-1	6th	Hooper	9,525
26	30	A	Huddersfield Town	L		1-6	1-3	8th	Rimmer	19,061
27	Feb 6	H	Newcastle United	W		2-0	1-0	8th	Millership (pen + 1)	16,270
28	20	H	Leicester City	W		3-1	2-1	6th	Rimmer, Ball (2)	11,391
29	24	A	Aston Villa	L		1-3	1-2	8th	Ball	12,045
30	27	H	Everton	L		1-3	0-2	8th	Stephenson	24,279
31	Mar 5	A	Derby County	W		1-0	1-0	6th	Rimmer	15,174
32	12	H	West Bromwich Alb	L		2-5	1-1	7th	W. Richardson (og), Rimmer	15,110
33	19	A	Birmingham	W		2-1	1-1	6th	Stephenson, Rimmer	17,271
34	25	A	West Ham United	W		2-1	0-0	5th	Rimmer, Ball	25,759
35	26	H	Blackpool	W		3-0	2-0	4th	Ball, Jones, Rimmer (pen)	13,101
36	28	H	West Ham United	W		6-1	1-1	3rd	Hooper (2), Jones (2), Strange, Leach	14,848
37	Apr 2	A	Sheffield United	D		1-1	0-1	4th	Ball	37,872
38	9	H	Portsmouth	W		3-1	1-1	3rd	Rimmer, Hooper, Burgess	8,037
39	16	A	Arsenal	L		1-3	1-2	4th	Hooper	25,220
40	23	H	Sunderland	W		3-2	2-1	2nd	Ball, Hooper, Jones	7,908
41	30	A	Manchester City	W		2-1	2-0	3rd	Burgess, Ball	16,322
42	May 7	A	Grimsby Town	L		1-3	0-2	3rd	Ball	16,049
										Apps
									One own-goal	Goals

FA Cup

Match No.	Date	Venue	Opponents		Round	Result	HT Score	Position	Scorers	Attendance
43	Jan 9	A	Tottenham Hotspur	D	3R	2-2	1-2		Burgess, Rimmer	41,511
44	13	H	Tottenham Hotspur	W	3R Re	3-1	1-0		Millership, Rimmer, Stephenson	30,000
45	23	H	Bournemouth	W	4R	7-0	2-0		Burgess (3), Millership (pen + 3)	32,600
46	Feb 13	H	Chelsea	D	5R	1-1	1-1		Stephenson	39,000
47	17	A	Chelsea	L	5R Re	0-2	0-1			60,004
										Apps
										Goals

Ball Jack	Beeson George	Blenkinsop Ernest	Breedon Jack	Brown Jack	Burgess Harry	Catlin Ted	Davison Tommy	Gowdy Billy	Hooper Mark	Jones Tommy	Leach Tony	Mackey Thomas	Malloch Gavin	Millership Walt	Rimmer Ellis	Robson Thomas	Short Jimmy	Smith Billy	Stephenson George	Strange Alf	Walker Tommy	Wilson Charles	Wright Vic
9		3		1	8				7		5				11			6	10	4	2		
9		3		1	8				7		5				11			6	10	4	2		
9		3		1	8				7		5				11			6	10	4	2		
9		3		1	8				7		5				11			6	10	4	2		
9		3		1	8				7		5				11			6	10	4	2		
9		3		1	8				7		5			10	11			6		4	2		
9		3		1	8				7		5			10	11			6		4	2		
9	2	3		1	8				7		5				11			6	10	4			
9	2	3		1	10		5		7						11			6		4			8
9	2	3		1	10				7		5				11			6		4			8
9	2			1	8	3	5		7						11	4		6	10				
9	2	3		1	8		5		7						11			6	10	4			
9	2	3		1	8		5		7						11			6	10	4			
9	2			1	8		5		7						11			6	10	4		3	
9	2	3		1	8		5		7						11				10	4		6	
9	2	3		1	8		5		7						11				10	4		6	
9	2	3		1	8		5		7						11			6	10	4			
9		3		1					7			5		8	11			6	10	4	2		
9		3		1	10		5		7					8	11			6		4	2		
9		3		1	10		5		7					8	11	4				6	2		
9		3		1	10				7		5		6		11				8	4	2		
9		3		1	10				7		5		6		11				8	4	2		
		3		1	10				7		5		6	9	11				8	4	2		
		3		1	10				7		5		6	9	11				8	4	2		
8		3		1	10				7		5		6	9	11					4	2		
		3		1	10				7		5		6	9	11				8	4	2		
		3		1	10		5		7				6	9	11				8	4	2		
9		3		1					7	10	5		6		11				8	4	2		
9		3		1					7	10	5		6		11				8	4	2		
9		3		1	10				7		5		6		11				8	4	2		
9		3		1					7		5		6	10	11				8	4	2		
9		3		1					7		5		6	10	11				8	4	2		
9		3	1		10				7		5		6		11				8	4	2		
9		3	1		10				8	7	5		6		11					4	2		
9		3	1		10				8	7	5		6		11					4	2		
9		3	1		10				8	7	5		6		11					4	2		
9		3	1		10				8	7	5		6		11					4	2		
9			1		10	3		4	7	8	5		6		11						2		
9		3	1		10				7	8	5		6		11					4	2		
9		3	1		10				7	8	5		6		11					4	2		
9			1		10	3				7	5		6		11		8			4	2		
9	3		1		10					7	5		6		11		8			4	2		
38	11	37	10	32	37	3	11	1	40	11	30	1	22	12	42	2	2	17	26	40	32	3	2
23					6				12	4	3			9	21			1	13	3			

Ball Jack	Beeson George	Blenkinsop Ernest	Breedon Jack	Brown Jack	Burgess Harry	Catlin Ted	Davison Tommy	Gowdy Billy	Hooper Mark	Jones Tommy	Leach Tony	Mackey Thomas	Malloch Gavin	Millership Walt	Rimmer Ellis	Robson Thomas	Short Jimmy	Smith Billy	Stephenson George	Strange Alf	Walker Tommy	Wilson Charles	Wright Vic
		3		1	10			6	7		5			9	11				8	4	2		
		3		1	10				7		5			9	11				8	4	2	6	
		3		1	10				7		5		6	9	11				8	4	2		
		3		1	10		5		7				6	9	11				8	4	2		
		3		1	10				7		5		6	9	11				8	4	2		
		5		5	5		1	1	5		4		3	5	5				5	5	5	1	
					4									5	2				2				

League Table

	P	W	D	L	F	A	Pts
Everton	42	26	4	12	116	64	56
Arsenal	42	22	10	10	90	48	54
SHEFFIELD WEDNESDAY	42	22	6	14	96	82	50
Huddersfield Town	42	19	10	13	80	63	48
Aston Villa	42	19	8	15	104	72	46
West Bromwich Albion	42	20	6	16	77	55	46
Sheffield United	42	20	6	16	80	75	46
Portsmouth	42	19	7	16	62	62	45
Birmingham	42	18	8	16	78	67	44
Liverpool	42	19	6	17	81	93	44
Newcastle United	42	18	6	18	80	87	42
Chelsea	42	16	8	18	69	73	40
Sunderland	42	15	10	17	67	73	40
Manchester City	42	13	12	17	83	73	38
Derby County	42	14	10	18	71	75	38
Blackburn Rovers	42	16	6	20	89	95	38
Bolton Wanderers	42	17	4	21	72	80	38
Middlesbrough	42	15	8	19	64	89	38
Leicester City	42	15	7	20	74	94	37
Blackpool	42	12	9	21	65	102	33
Grimsby Town	42	13	6	23	67	98	32
West Ham United	42	12	7	23	62	107	31

1932-33

Division One

Manager: Bob Brown

Did you know that?

Final League Position: 3rd

On 10 December 1932 Middlesbrough did not arrive until five minutes before kick-off but were ready in their kit, so the game started on time with Wednesday winning 2–1.

During this season, Jack Ball scored 10 penalties but also missed five. The only one that would have altered the result was against Chesterfield in the FA Cup, which ended 2–2 with Wednesday losing the replay.

—PRICE 2d.—
Sheffield Wednesday Football Club Limited.
SHEFFIELD WEDNESDAY
VERSUS
LIVERPOOL.
Played at Hillsborough, Sheffield, Saturday, December 24th, 1932.

Match No.	Date	Venue	Opponents		Round	Result	HT Score	Position	Scorers	Attendance
1	Aug 27	H	Blackpool	W		4-1	1-1		Hooper, Burgess (2), Ball (pen)	15,152
2	31	A	Everton	L		1-2	1-1	8th	Starling	28,007
3	Sep 3	A	Derby County	L		0-2	0-2	11th		18,163
4	5	H	Everton	W		3-1	1-0	8th	Leach, Ball, Rimmer	14,890
5	10	H	Blackburn Rovers	D		1-1	1-1	8th	Ball (pen)	14,454
6	17	A	Leeds United	L		2-3	1-2	12th	Ball, Starling	17,977
7	24	H	Sheffield United	D		3-3	2-2	11th	Ball, Rimmer, Hooper	24,804
8	Oct 1	H	West Bromwich Alb	W		3-1	3-1	10th	Ball, Leach, Hooper	10,775
9	8	A	Birmingham	L		1-2	1-2	12th	Hooper	14,999
10	15	H	Sunderland	W		3-1	2-0	9th	Ball, Murray (og), McDougall (og)	11,799
11	22	A	Wolverhampton W	W		5-3	3-1	9th	Rimmer, Ball (3 + pen)	24,361
12	29	H	Newcastle United	W		2-0	1-0	8th	Rimmer, Ball	9,496
13	Nov 5	A	Leicester City	D		0-0	0-0	8th		16,044
14	12	H	Portsmouth	W		2-1	1-0	7th	Strange, Leach	10,319
15	19	A	Chelsea	W		2-0	0-0	5th	Ball (2)	20,677
16	26	H	Huddersfield Town	W		2-1	2-0	4th	Hooper, Ball (pen)	17,890
17	Dec 3	A	Aston Villa	W		6-3	3-2	3rd	Ball (pen + 1), Leach, Strange, Starling, Burgess	31,518
18	10	H	Middlesbrough	W		2-1	1-1	2nd	Ball (pen), Strange	11,651
19	17	A	Bolton Wanderers	L		0-3	0-2	3rd		11,409
20	24	H	Liverpool	W		3-0	1-0	3rd	Burgess, Ball, Starling	14,948
21	26	A	Manchester City	D		2-2	1-2	3rd	Ball (pen + 1)	45,916
22	27	H	Manchester City	W		2-1	0-0	3rd	Rimmer, Hooper	37,589
23	31	A	Blackpool	W		4-3	0-1	3rd	Strange, Rimmer, Starling, Burgess	13,689
24	Jan 2	H	Arsenal	W		3-2	1-1	2nd	Leach, Ball (pen + 1)	65,345
25	7	H	Derby County	D		0-0	0-0	2nd		20,565
26	21	A	Blackburn Rovers	D		1-1	0-1	3rd	Millership	10,417
27	Feb 4	A	Sheffield United	W		3-2	1-1	3rd	Starling, Stephenson, Ball	32,608
28	8	H	Leeds United	W		2-0	2-0	2nd	Ball (2 pens)	9,585
29	11	A	West Bromwich Alb	L		0-2	0-0	3rd		20,863
30	25	A	Sunderland	W		2-1	2-1	2nd	Ball, Hooper	10,074
31	Mar 4	H	Wolverhampton W	W		2-0	1-0	2nd	Starling, Ball	12,982
32	11	A	Newcastle United	L		1-3	0-0	2nd	Ball	32,351
33	18	H	Leicester City	W		4-1	2-1	2nd	Ball (3), Burgess	13,964
34	25	A	Portsmouth	L		0-3	0-3	2nd		17,374
35	Apr 1	H	Chelsea	D		2-2	2-1	2nd	Jones, Rimmer	10,121
36	5	H	Birmingham	D		1-1	1-0	2nd	Ball	6,088
37	8	A	Huddersfield Town	L		0-4	0-3	2nd		11,972
38	14	A	Arsenal	L		2-4	1-2	2nd	Rimmer, Hooper	61,945
39	15	H	Aston Villa	L		0-2	0-1	2nd		16,700
40	22	A	Middlesbrough	D		1-1	1-0	3rd	Strange	10,640
41	29	H	Bolton Wanderers	W		2-0	1-0	3rd	Burgess (2)	4,810
42	May 6	A	Liverpool	L		1-4	1-1	3rd	Bradshaw (og)	11,355
										Apps
									Three own-goals	Goals

FA Cup

Match No.	Date	Venue	Opponents		Round	Result	HT Score	Position	Scorers	Attendance
43	Jan 14	H	Chesterfield	D	3R	2-2	2-1		Ball (2)	30,178
44	18	A	Chesterfield	L	3R Re	2-4	0-4		Millership (2)	19,652
										Apps
										Goals

Ball Jack	Beeson George	Blenkinsop Ernest	Bratley George	Breedon Jack	Brown Jack	Burgess Harry	Burrows Horace	Catlin Ted	Hooper Mark	Jones Tommy	Leach Tony	Malloch Gavin	Millership Walt	Nevin George	Rimmer Ellis	Smith Billy	Starling Ronnie	Stephenson George	Strange Alf	Walker Tommy
9		3		1		10			7		5	6			11		8		4	2
9		3		1		10			7		5	6			11		8		4	2
9		3		1		10			7		5	6			11		8		4	2
9		3		1		10			7		5	6			11		8		4	2
9		3		1		10			7		5	6			11		8		4	2
9	2	3		1		10			7		5	6			11		8		4	
9	2	3		1		10			7		5	6			11		8		4	
9	2			1		10		3	7		5	6			11		8		4	
9	2	3		1		10			7		5	6			11		8		4	
9	2	3			1	10				7	5	6			11		8		4	
9	2	3			1	10			7		5	6			11		8		4	
9	2	3			1	10			7		5	6			11		8		4	
9	2	3			1	10			7		5	6			11		8		4	
9		3			1	10			7		5	6			11		8		4	2
9	2	3			1	10			7		5	6			11		8		4	
9	2	3			1	10			7		5	6			11		8		4	
9	2	3			1	10			7		5	6			11		8		4	
9	2	3			1	10			7		5	6			11		8		4	
9	2	3			1	10			7		5	6			11		8		4	
9	2				1	10		3	7		5	6			11		8		4	
9	2				1	10		3	7		5	6			11		8		4	
9	2				1	10	6	3	7		5				11		8		4	
9	2				1	10		3		7	5	6			11		8		4	
9	2				1	10		3		7	5	6			11		8		4	
9	2				1	10		3		7	5	6			11		8		4	
					1		10			7	5	6	9	3	11		8		4	2
9	2				1			3		7	5	6			11		8	10	4	
9	2				1			3		7	5	6			11		8	10	4	
9	2		5		1			3		7		6			11		8	10	4	
9	2				1	10		3	7		5	6			11		8		4	
9	2				1	10		3	7		5	6			11		8		4	
9	2				1	10		3	7		5	6			11		8		4	
9	2	3	5		1	10			7			6			11		8		4	
9	2	3	5		1	10			7			6			11		8		4	
9	2				1	10		3	7	8		6	5		11	4				
9	2	3			1	10			7			6	5		11		8		4	
9	2				1	10	6	3		7			5		11		8		4	
9	2				1	10	6	3	7		5				11		8		4	
9	2				1	10	6	3	7		5				11		8		4	
9	2			1		10	6		7		5			3	11		8		4	
9	2	3		1		10	6		7		5				11		8		4	
9	2	3		1		10	6		7		5				11		8		4	
41	35	23	3	12	30	38	8	17	33	10	36	35	4	2	42	1	41	3	41	7
33						8			8	1	5		1		8		7	1	5	

Ball Jack	Beeson George	Blenkinsop Ernest	Bratley George	Breedon Jack	Brown Jack	Burgess Harry	Burrows Horace	Catlin Ted	Hooper Mark	Jones Tommy	Leach Tony	Malloch Gavin	Millership Walt	Nevin George	Rimmer Ellis	Smith Billy	Starling Ronnie	Stephenson George	Strange Alf	Walker Tommy
9	2				1	10		3	7		5	6			11		8		4	
					1			3	7		5	6	9		11		8	10	4	2
1	1				2	1		2	2		2	2	1		2		2	1	2	1
2													2							

League Table

	P	W	D	L	F	A	Pts
Arsenal	42	25	8	9	118	61	58
Aston Villa	42	23	8	11	92	67	54
SHEFFIELD WEDNESDAY	42	21	9	12	80	68	51
West Bromwich Albion	42	20	9	13	83	70	49
Newcastle United	42	22	5	15	71	63	49
Huddersfield Town	42	18	11	13	66	53	47
Derby County	42	15	14	13	76	69	44
Leeds United	42	15	14	13	59	62	44
Portsmouth	42	18	7	17	74	76	43
Sheffield United	42	17	9	16	74	80	43
Everton	42	16	9	17	81	74	41
Sunderland	42	15	10	17	63	80	40
Birmingham	42	14	11	17	57	57	39
Liverpool	42	14	11	17	79	84	39
Blackburn Rovers	42	14	10	18	76	102	38
Manchester City	42	16	5	21	68	71	37
Middlesbrough	42	14	9	19	63	73	37
Chelsea	42	14	7	21	63	73	35
Leicester City	42	11	13	18	75	89	35
Wolverhampton W	42	13	9	20	80	96	35
Bolton Wanderers	42	12	9	21	78	92	33
Blackpool	42	14	5	23	69	85	33

1933-34

Division One

Manager: Bob Brown/Billy Walker

Did you know that?

Final League Position: 11th

On 6 January 1934 Wednesday met an Arsenal side, at Highbury, who were mourning the loss of their legendary manager, Herbert Chapman, who had passed away a few hours earlier.

The FA Cup game against Manchester City on 17 February 1934 at Hillsborough set the record attendance for the ground – 72,841. One fan was killed in the crush and thousands were locked out.

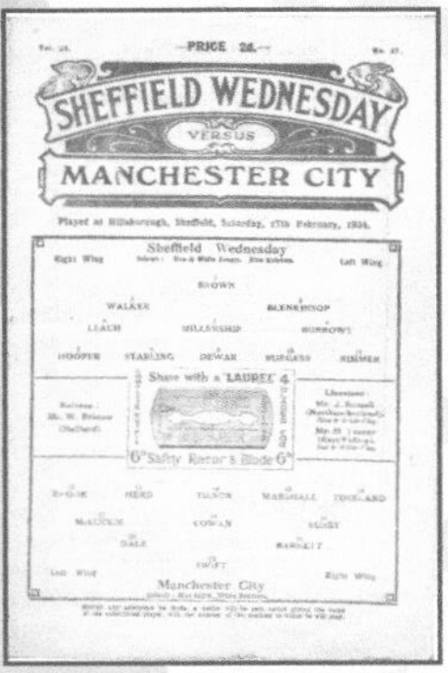

Match No.	Date	Venue	Opponents		Round	Result	HT Score	Position	Scorers	Attendance
1	Aug 26	A	Manchester City	W		3-2	2-1		Ball, Leach, Burgess	29,151
2	28	H	Aston Villa	L		1-2	1-1		Burgess	19,362
3	Sep 2	H	Arsenal	L		1-2	1-1	13th	Burgess	22,377
4	4	A	Aston Villa	L		0-1	0-1	18th		22,581
5	9	A	Everton	W		3-2	2-0	15th	Ball, Burgess (2)	33,340
6	16	H	Middlesbrough	W		3-0	2-0	10th	Hooper, Rimmer, Ball	12,670
7	23	A	Blackburn Rovers	L		1-3	0-1	16th	Ball	15,622
8	30	H	Newcastle United	W		3-1	1-0	11th	Ball (pen + 1), Rimmer	14,278
9	Oct 7	A	Leeds United	L		1-2	1-2	16th	Hooper	16,300
10	14	H	Derby County	D		1-1	0-1	18th	Millership	14,780
11	21	H	Sheffield United	L		0-1	0-1	19th		27,951
12	28	A	Wolverhampton W	L		2-6	1-3	19th	Ball, Starling	21,717
13	Nov 4	H	Chelsea	W		2-1	0-0	18th	Burrows, Burgess	10,830
14	11	A	Huddersfield Town	L		2-3	1-1	19th	Cooper, Starling	19,814
15	18	H	Portsmouth	L		1-2	0-1	20th	Starling	8,810
16	25	A	Sunderland	L		0-4	0-2	20th		14,638
17	Dec 2	H	Leicester City	D		1-1	1-1	19th	Strange	10,313
18	9	A	Liverpool	W		3-1	2-0	19th	Hooper (2), Rimmer	22,298
19	16	H	Tottenham Hotspur	W		2-1	1-0	17th	Hooper, Law	17,232
20	23	A	Stoke City	W		1-0	1-0	15th	Burgess	16,758
21	26	H	West Bromwich Alb	W		3-1	2-1	14th	Hooper, Law, Rimmer	33,675
22	27	A	West Bromwich Alb	D		1-1	0-0	12th	Hooper	32,795
23	30	H	Manchester City	D		1-1	1-0	11th	Starling	27,074
24	Jan 2	H	Birmingham	W		2-1	1-1	10th	Burgess (2)	12,754
25	6	A	Arsenal	D		1-1	1-1	10th	Dewar	45,156
26	20	H	Everton	D		0-0	0-0	10th		23,393
27	Feb 3	H	Blackburn Rovers	W		4-0	2-0	10th	Burgess, Dewar (2), Hooper	19,303
28	7	A	Middlesbrough	W		3-2	2-2	6th	Hooper, Dewar, Starling	9,069
29	10	A	Newcastle United	D		0-0	0-0	7th		23,023
30	24	A	Derby County	D		1-1	0-0	7th	Burgess	18,984
31	26	H	Leeds United	L		0-2	0-1			6,771
32	Mar 3	A	Sheffield United	L		1-5	1-0	8th	Burrows	32,318
33	10	H	Wolverhampton W	W		2-1	2-0	8th	Hooper, Walker (pen)	5,182
34	17	A	Chelsea	W		1-0	1-0	5th	Rimmer	31,606
35	24	H	Huddersfield Town	L		1-2	1-1	7th	Cooper	17,278
36	31	A	Portsmouth	W		2-0	1-0	6th	Dewar, Starling	20,373
37	Apr 3	A	Birmingham	L		0-3	0-1	7th		24,021
38	7	H	Sunderland	W		2-0	2-0	6th	Cooper, Dewar	11,799
39	14	A	Leicester City	L		0-2	0-0	8th		11,731
40	21	H	Liverpool	L		1-2	1-1	10th	Starling	13,633
41	28	A	Tottenham Hotspur	L		3-4	1-2	10th	Starling, Burgess, Dewar	20,322
42	May 5	H	Stoke City	D		2-2	1-0	11th	Oxley, Dewar	9,235
										Apps
										Goals
FA Cup										
43	Jan 13	A	Rotherham United	W	3R	3-0	2-0		Hooper, Dewar, Leach	21,198
44	27	A	Oldham Athletic	D	4R	1-1	0-1		Hooper	45,990
45	31	H	Oldham Athletic	W	4R Re	6-1	3-1		Dewar (3), Hooper, Rimmer, Burgess	41,311
46	Feb 17	H	Manchester City	D	5R	2-2	1-1		Rimmer, Dewar	72,841
47	21	A	Manchester City	L	5R Re	0-2	0-1			68,514
										Apps
										Goals

Ball Jack	Beeson George	Blenkinsop Ernest	Breedon Jack	Brolly Tom	Brown Jack	Burgess Harry	Burrows Horace	Catlin Ted	Cooper Sedley	Dewar Neil	Hooper Mark	Jones Tommy	Law Alex	Leach Tony	Malloch Gavin	Millership Walt	Oxley Bernard	Rimmer Ellis	Starling Ronnie	Strange Alf	Thompson Jackie	Walker Tommy
9	2	3	1			10	6				7			5				11	8	4		
9	2	3	1			10	6				7			5				11	8	4		
9	2	3	1			10	6				7			5				11	8	4		
9	2	3	1			10	6				7			5				11	8	4		
9	2	3			1	10	6				7					5		11	8	4		
9	2	3			1	10	6				7					5		11	8	4		
9	2	3			1	10	6				7					5		11	8	4		
9	2	3			1	10	6				7					5		11	8	4		
9	2	3			1		6				7			5		10		11	8	4		
		3		4	1		6				7	10		5		9		11	8			2
9	2	3			1	10	6				7			5				11	8	4		
9	2	3			1	10	6		11		7			5					8	4		
9	2				1	10	6	3	11		7			5					8	4		
9	2				1	10	6	3	11		7			5					8	4		
9	2	3			1	10	6		11		7			5					8	4		
9	2	3			1	8	6		11		7			5						4	10	
9	2	3			1		6		11		7			4		5				8	10	
	2	3			1	10	6				7		9	4		5		11		8		
	2	3			1	10	6				8	7	9	4		5		11				
9	2	3			1	10	6				7			4		5		11	8			
		3			1	10	6				7		9	4		5		11	8			2
		3			1	10	6				7		9	4		5		11	8			2
		3			1	10	6			9	7			4		5		11	8			2
		3			1	10	6				7		9	4		5		11	8			2
	2	3			1	10	6			9	7			4		5		11	8			
		3			1	10	6			9		7		4		5		11	8			2
		3			1	10	6			9	7			4		5		11	8			2
	2				1	10	6	3		9	7					5		11	8	4		
					1	10	6	3		9	7			4		5		11	8			2
					1	10	6	3		9	7					5		11	8	4		2
					1	10	6	3		9	7					5		11	8	4		2
					1	10	6	3		9	7			4		5		11	8			2
		3		4	1	10	6				7		9			5		11	8			2
			1			10	4	3			7		9		6	5		11	8			2
	2		1			10	4	3	11		7		9		6	5			8			
			1			10	4	3	11	9	7				6	5			8			2
			1			10	4	3	11	9		7			6	5			8			2
			1			10	4	3	11	9		7			6	5			8			2
			1			10	4	3	11	9		7			6	5			8			2
			1			10	4	3		9	7				6	5		11	8			2
			1			10	4	3		9	7				6	5		11	8			2
			1				4	3		9	7				6	5	10	11	8			2
17	22	26	13	2	29	38	42	16	11	16	38	6	8	25	9	32	1	31	38	20	2	20
7						12	2		3	8	10		2	1		1	1	5	8	1		1

Ball Jack	Beeson George	Blenkinsop Ernest	Breedon Jack	Brolly Tom	Brown Jack	Burgess Harry	Burrows Horace	Catlin Ted	Cooper Sedley	Dewar Neil	Hooper Mark	Jones Tommy	Law Alex	Leach Tony	Malloch Gavin	Millership Walt	Oxley Bernard	Rimmer Ellis	Starling Ronnie	Strange Alf	Thompson Jackie	Walker Tommy
		3			1	10	6			9	7			4		5		11	8			2
		3			1	10	6			9	7			4		5		11	8			2
		3			1	10	6			9	7			4		5		11	8			2
					1	10	6	3		9	7			4		5		11	8			2
					1		6	3		9	7			4		5		11	10	8		2
		3			5	4	5	2		5	5			5		5		5	5	1		5
						1				5	3			1				2				

League Table

	P	W	D	L	F	A	Pts
Arsenal	42	25	9	8	75	47	59
Huddersfield Town	42	23	10	9	90	61	56
Tottenham Hotspur	42	21	7	14	79	56	49
Derby County	42	17	11	14	68	54	45
Manchester City	42	17	11	14	65	72	45
Sunderland	42	16	12	14	81	56	44
West Bromwich Albion	42	17	10	15	78	70	44
Blackburn Rovers	42	18	7	17	74	81	43
Leeds United	42	17	8	17	75	66	42
Portsmouth	42	15	12	15	52	55	42
SHEFFIELD WEDNESDAY	42	16	9	17	62	67	41
Stoke City	42	15	11	16	58	71	41
Aston Villa	42	14	12	16	78	75	40
Everton	42	12	16	14	62	63	40
Wolverhampton W	42	14	12	16	74	86	40
Middlesbrough	42	16	7	19	68	80	39
Leicester City	42	14	11	17	59	74	39
Liverpool	42	14	10	18	79	87	38
Chelsea	42	14	8	20	67	69	36
Birmingham	42	12	12	18	54	56	36
Newcastle United	42	10	14	18	68	77	34
Sheffield United	42	12	7	23	58	101	31

1934-35

Division One

Manager: Billy Walker

Did you know that?

Final League Position: 3rd

Wednesday's winger, Ellis Rimmer, scored in every round of the Cup, including two goals in the Final, as they won the FA Cup. This match famously kicked-off two minutes early.

1934–35. On 12 February 1935 Wednesday's manager arranged a special practice match at Hillsborough, with the crowd standing around the touchline to get the players used to a small pitch and cramped conditions, in preparation for their FA Cup game at Norwich's ground, the Nest (the reserves ran out 4–1 winners before 8,000 fans).

Match No.	Date	Venue	Opponents		Round	Result	HT Score	Position	Scorers	Attendance
1	Aug 25	H	Stoke City	W		4-1	1-1		Dewar, Hooper, Turner (og), Rimmer	17,657
2	29	A	Chelsea	W		2-1	1-1	1st	Rimmer (2)	19,756
3	Sep 1	A	Manchester City	L		1-4	1-3	5th	Rimmer	44,704
4	3	H	Chelsea	W		3-1	1-1	1st	Burrows, Dewar, Rimmer	13,696
5	8	H	Middlesbrough	D		3-3	1-2	4th	Dewar, Burgess, Rimmer	16,103
6	15	A	Blackburn Rovers	L		1-2	0-1	6th	Burgess	14,334
7	22	H	Arsenal	D		0-0	0-0	8th		25,334
8	29	A	Portsmouth	L		1-2	1-1	11th	Dewar	17,358
9	Oct 6	H	Liverpool	W		4-1	1-0	9th	Burgess, Rimmer, Hooper (2)	17,935
10	13	A	Leeds United	D		0-0	0-0	9th		16,860
11	20	H	Wolverhampton W	W		3-1	2-1	6th	Hooper, Rimmer (2)	14,646
12	27	A	Huddersfield Town	L		0-4	0-3	8th		14,913
13	Nov 3	H	Derby County	W		1-0	1-0	7th	Burgess	19,401
14	10	A	Aston Villa	L		0-4	0-2	9th		20,300
15	17	H	Preston North End	W		2-1	1-0	7th	Rimmer, Burgess	16,000
16	24	A	Tottenham Hotspur	L		2-3	1-2	9th	Starling, Millership	25,103
17	Dec 1	H	Sunderland	D		2-2	1-0	9th	Dewar, Starling	22,880
18	8	A	Leicester City	W		1-0	1-0	7th	Burgess	13,288
19	15	H	Everton	D		0-0	0-0	7th		19,266
20	22	A	Grimsby Town	L		1-3	0-2	10th	Oxley	10,438
21	25	H	Birmingham	W		2-1	1-0	6th	Burgess, Oxley	24,090
22	26	A	Birmingham	W		4-0	1-0	6th	Palethorpe (2 + pen), Rimmer	24,499
23	29	A	Stoke City	D		1-1	0-0	9th	Burrows	19,386
24	Jan 1	H	West Bromwich Alb	W		2-1	0-0	5th	Surtees, Millership	30,055
25	5	H	Manchester City	W		1-0	0-0	4th	Oxley	31,356
26	19	A	Middlesbrough	L		3-5	2-1	6th	Hooper, Burgess, Rimmer	9,378
27	28	H	Blackburn Rovers	D		2-2	1-1		Crook (og), Rimmer	8,043
28	Feb 2	A	Arsenal	L		1-4	0-0	7th	Palethorpe	57,922
29	9	H	Portsmouth	W		3-0	2-0	7th	Palethorpe, Surtees, Cooper	17,396
30	20	A	Liverpool	W		2-1	1-1	4th	Burgess, Starling	14,500
31	23	H	Leeds United	W		1-0	0-0	4th	Rimmer	19,591
32	Mar 4	A	Wolverhampton W	D		2-2	0-1	4th	Starling (pen), Palethorpe	12,966
33	9	H	Huddersfield Town	D		1-1	0-0	4th	Rimmer	19,819
34	20	A	Derby County	L		0-4	0-2	4th		15,120
35	23	H	Aston Villa	W		2-1	2-1	4th	Starling (pen), Dewar	12,495
36	30	A	Preston North End	L		1-2	1-1	4th	Hooper	17,656
37	Apr 6	H	Tottenham Hotspur	W		4-0	2-0	4th	Law (2), Palethorpe, Rimmer	12,158
38	13	A	Sunderland	D		2-2	2-1	4th	Palethorpe, Rimmer	22,900
39	20	H	Leicester City	D		1-1	0-1	4th	Sharp	15,654
40	22	A	West Bromwich Alb	D		1-1	1-1	4th	Robinson	34,060
41	May 1	A	Everton	D		2-2	1-1	3rd	Hooper, Burrows (pen)	7,802
42	4	H	Grimsby Town	W		1-0	0-0	3rd	Rimmer	21,046
										Apps
									Two own-goals	Goals

FA Cup

Match No.	Date	Venue	Opponents		Round	Result	HT Score	Position	Scorers	Attendance
43	Jan 12	H	Oldham Athletic	W	3R	3-1	1-0		Palethorpe, Rimmer, Surtees	26,662
44	26	A	Wolverhampton W	W	4R	2-1	1-0		Palethorpe, Rimmer	50,362
45	Feb 16	A	Norwich City	W	5R	1-0	0-0		Rimmer	25,007
46	Mar 2	H	Arsenal	W	6R	2-1	1-1		Hooper, Rimmer	66,945
47	16	N	Burnley*	W	S/Final	3-0	1-0		Rimmer (2), Palethorpe	56,625
48	Apr 27	N	West Bromwich Alb #	W	Final	4-2	1-1		Palethorpe, Hooper, Rimmer (2)	93,204
										Apps
										Goals

* At Villa Park, Birmingham
# At Wembley

Baird Walter	Brown Jack	Burgess Harry	Burrows Horace	Catlin Ted	Cooper Sedley	Dewar Neil	Hill Haydn	Hooper Mark	Law Alex	Malloch Gavin	Millership Walt	Nibloe Joe	Nicholls Harry	Oxley Bernard	Palethorpe Jackie	Rimmer Ellis	Robinson Jackie	Sharp Wilf	Smith Tom	Starling Ronnie	Strange Alf	Surtees Jack	Walker Tommy	Wright Jim
	1	10	4	3		9		7		6	5	2				11				8				
	1	10	4	3		9		7		6	5	2				11				8				
	1	10	4			9		7		6	5	3				11				8			2	
	1	10	4			9		7		6	5	3				11				8			2	
	1	10	4			9		7		6	5	3				11				8			2	
	1	10	4	3		9				6	5	2		7		11				8				
	1	10	4	3		9					5	2	6	7		11				8				
	1		4	3		9		7		6	5	2		10		11				8				
	1	10	4	3		9		7		6	5	2				11				8				
	1	10	4	3		9		7		6	5	2				11				8				
	1	10	4	3		9		7		6	5	2				11				8				
	1	10	4	3		9		7		6	5	2				11				8				
	1	10	6					7			5	3	4	9		11				8			2	
	1	10	6		7						5	3	4	9		11				8			2	
3	1	10	4			9		7		6	5	2				11				8				
	1	10	4			9		7		6	5	3				11				8			2	
	1	10	4			9				6	5	3		7		11				8			2	
	1	10	6			9					5	3		7		11		4		8			2	
	1	10	6								5	3		7	9	11		4		8			2	
	1	10	6		11						5	3		7	9			4		8			2	
	1	10	6		11						5	3		7	9			4				8	2	
	1		6	3				7			5				9	11		4		8		10	2	
	1		6	3				7			5				9	11		4		10		8	2	
	1		6	3							5			7	9	11		4		10		8	2	
	1		6	3							5			7	9	11		4		10		8	2	
	1	9	6	3				7			5					11		4		10		8	2	
	1		6	3				7			5					11		4	9	10		8	2	
	1	10	6	3				7			5	2			9	11		4				8		
	1		6	3	7						5	2			9	11		4		10		8		
	1	8	6	3				7			5	2			9	11		4		10				
	1		6	3				7			5	2			9	11		4		10		8		
	1		6	3							5	2		7	9	11		4		10		8		
	1		6	3				7			5	2			9	11		4		10		8		
	1		6		7			10			5				9	11		4				8	2	3
	1		6	3		9		7			5	2				11		4		10		8		
	1		6	3	11	9		7			5	2						4		10		8		
			6	3			1		7		5	2			9	11		4		10		8		
			6	3			1	7			5	2			9	11		4		10		8		
	1		6	3				7			5	2			9	11		4		10		8		
	1		6	3				7			5				9	11	10				4	8	2	
	1		6	3	11			7			5	2			9			4		10		8		
	1		6	3				7			5	2			9	11		4		10		8		
1	40	23	42	29	7	18	2	29	1	14	42	34	3	13	20	38	1	24	1	38	1	21	19	1
		9	3		1	6		7	2		2			3	8	18	1	1		5		2		

Baird Walter	Brown Jack	Burgess Harry	Burrows Horace	Catlin Ted	Cooper Sedley	Dewar Neil	Hill Haydn	Hooper Mark	Law Alex	Malloch Gavin	Millership Walt	Nibloe Joe	Nicholls Harry	Oxley Bernard	Palethorpe Jackie	Rimmer Ellis	Robinson Jackie	Sharp Wilf	Smith Tom	Starling Ronnie	Strange Alf	Surtees Jack	Walker Tommy	Wright Jim
	1		6	3				7			5				9	11		4		10		8	2	
	1		6	3				7			5	2			9	11		4		10		8		
	1		6	3				7			5	2			9	11		4		10		8		
	1		6	3				7			5	2			9	11		4		10		8		
	1		6	3				7			5	2			9	11		4		10		8		
	1		6	3				7			5	2			9	11		4		10		8		
	6		6	6				6			6	5			6	6		6		6		6	1	
								2							4	8						1		

League Table

	P	W	D	L	F	A	Pts
Arsenal	42	23	12	7	115	46	58
Sunderland	42	19	16	7	90	51	54
SHEFFIELD WEDNESDAY	42	18	13	11	70	64	49
Manchester City	42	20	8	14	82	67	48
Grimsby Town	42	17	11	14	78	60	45
Derby County	42	18	9	15	81	66	45
Liverpool	42	19	7	16	85	88	45
Everton	42	16	12	14	89	88	44
West Bromwich Albion	42	17	10	15	83	83	44
Stoke City	42	18	6	18	71	70	42
Preston North End	42	15	12	15	62	67	42
Chelsea	42	16	9	17	73	82	41
Aston Villa	42	14	13	15	74	88	41
Portsmouth	42	15	10	17	71	72	40
Blackburn Rovers	42	14	11	17	66	78	39
Huddersfield Town	42	14	10	18	76	71	38
Wolverhampton W	42	15	8	19	88	94	38
Leeds United	42	13	12	17	75	92	38
Birmingham	42	13	10	19	63	81	36
Middlesbrough	42	10	14	18	70	90	34
Leicester City	42	12	9	21	61	86	33
Tottenham Hotspur	42	10	10	22	54	93	30

1935-36

Division One

Manager: Billy Walker

Did you know that?

Final League Position: 20th

In a friendly game played against a French Northern League team in Lille, France, on 1 December 1935, the two match balls, laced together, were dropped from a plane as it flew overhead. Wednesday lost 3–2. The balls were the smaller sized four ones that were used on the Continent at this time. (The French team comprised Polish, French, English and Spanish players).

Match No.	Date	Venue	Opponents		Round	Result	HT Score	Position	Scorers	Attendance
1	Aug 31	A	Aston Villa	W		2-1	0-0		Palethorpe, Hooper	48,637
2	Sep 2	A	Bolton Wanderers	D		1-1	0-0		Palethorpe	21,655
3	7	H	Wolverhampton W	D		0-0	0-0	9th		21,381
4	9	H	Bolton Wanderers	D		2-2	2-0	4th	Hooper, Palethorpe	13,349
5	14	A	Arsenal	D		2-2	1-1	8th	Rimmer, Palethorpe	59,492
6	16	H	Huddersfield Town	L		1-2	1-1	9th	Rimmer	14,164
7	21	A	Portsmouth	L		2-3	2-2	13th	Palethorpe, Rimmer	23,613
8	28	H	Preston North End	W		1-0	1-0	10th	Hooper	17,106
9	Oct 5	A	Brentford	D		2-2	0-1	9th	Sharp, Dewar	25,338
10	12	H	Derby County	W		1-0	1-0	8th	Hooper	34,646
11	19	H	Birmingham	W		3-1	1-1	6th	Millership, Dewar, Rimmer	13,840
12	26	A	Sunderland	L		1-5	0-2	8th	Dewar	32,890
13	Nov 2	H	West Bromwich Alb	L		2-5	1-1	9th	Dewar, Hooper	22,597
14	9	A	Leeds United	L		2-7	1-6	15th	Dewar (2)	19,897
15	16	H	Grimsby Town	W		3-0	1-0	11th	Dewar, Surtees, Starling	20,241
16	23	A	Manchester City	L		0-3	0-2	13th		36,781
17	30	H	Chelsea	W		4-1	1-1	10th	Dewar (2), Hooper, Burrows (pen)	16,014
18	Dec 7	A	Blackburn Rovers	L		2-3	1-3	12th	Dewar (2)	9,815
19	14	H	Stoke City	L		0-1	0-1	14th		14,070
20	21	A	Liverpool	L		0-1	0-1	14th		11,969
21	26	A	Everton	L		3-4	2-2	18th	Hooper, Surtees, Burrows	32,768
22	28	H	Aston Villa	W		5-2	2-2	17th	Starling, Hooper, Dewar, Rimmer, Surtees	25,371
23	Jan 4	A	Wolverhampton W	L		1-2	0-1	20th	Rimmer	25,450
24	18	H	Arsenal	W		3-2	2-1	19th	Dewar, Rimmer, Hooper	35,576
25	Feb 1	A	Preston North End	W		1-0	0-0	19th	Dewar	15,828
26	3	H	Everton	D		3-3	1-0	17th	Rimmer (3)	5,938
27	8	H	Brentford	D		3-3	0-3	17th	Starling (2), Dewar	21,470
28	12	H	Portsmouth	L		0-1	0-0	17th		6,135
29	19	A	Derby County	L		1-3	1-0	18th	Grosvenor	14,491
30	29	H	Leeds United	W		3-0	0-0	16th	Rimmer, Dewar, Luke	6,589
31	Mar 7	A	Chelsea	W		2-1	1-1	13th	Starling, Rimmer	27,221
32	14	H	Sunderland	D		0-0	0-0	13th		32,450
33	24	A	Grimsby Town	L		0-4	0-3	18th		7,887
34	28	H	Manchester City	W		1-0	0-0	15th	Luke	21,540
35	Apr 4	A	West Bromwich Alb	D		2-2	2-0	17th	Rimmer, Dewar	17,719
36	11	H	Blackburn Rovers	D		0-0	0-0	18th		15,569
37	13	A	Middlesbrough	L		0-5	0-1	21st		18,621
38	14	H	Middlesbrough	D		0-0	0-0	19th		21,157
39	18	A	Stoke City	W		3-0	2-0	18th	Dewar (2), Starling	16,453
40	22	A	Birmingham	L		1-4	1-2	18th	Luke	9,089
41	25	H	Liverpool	D		0-0	0-0	17th		7,630
42	May 2	A	Huddersfield Town	L		0-1	0-0	20th		8,101
										Apps
										Goals

FA Cup

43	Jan 11	A	Crewe Alexandra	D	3R	1-1	1-1		Surtees	9,755
44	15	H	Crewe Alexandra	W	3R Re	3-1*	0-0		Dewar, Rimmer, Surtees	15,995
45	27	H	Newcastle United	D	4R	1-1	1-1		Dewar	25,355
46	29	A	Newcastle United	L	4R Re	1-3	0-1		Rimmer	27,653
										Apps
										Goals

* After extra-time.

FA Charity Shield

47	Oct 23	A	Arsenal	W		1-0	0-0		Dewar	13,400

Match abandoned due to snow after 34 minutes

48	Feb 22	A	Birmingham City				0-1			5,000

Ashley Jack	Bargh George	Brown Jack	Bruce Bob	Burrows Horace	Catlin Ted	Cooper Sedley	Dewar Neil	Grosvenor Tommy	Hanford Harry	Hill Haydn	Hooper Mark	Hull John	Luke Charlie	Malloch Gavin	Millership Walt	Nibloe Joe	Palethorpe Jackie	Rhodes Dick	Rimmer Ellis	Robinson Jackie	Sharp Wilf	Starling Ronnie	Surtees Jack	Wright Jim
		1		6	3						7				5	2	9		11		4	10	8	
		1		6	3						7				5	2	9		11		4	10	8	
		1		6	3						7				5	2	9		11		4	10	8	
	8	1		6	3						7				5	2	9		11		4	10		
		1		6	3						7				5	2	9		11		4	10	8	
		1		6	3						7				5	2	9		11		4	10	8	
		1		6	3						7				5	2	9		11		4	10	8	
	10	1		6	3						7				5	2	9		11		4	8		
		1		6	3		9				7				5	2			11	8	4	10		
		1	10	6	3		9				7				5	2			11		4	8		
		1	10	6	3		9				7				5	2		4	11			8		
		1	10	6	3		9				7				5	2		4	11			8		
		1	10	6	3		9				7				5	2		4	11			8		
		1	10	6	3	11	9				7				5	2		4				8		
		1		6	3		9				7				5	2			11		4	10	8	
		1		6	3		9				7				5	2			11		4	10	8	
		1		6	3		9				7				5	2			11	8	4	10		
		1		6	3		9				7				5	2			11	8	4	10		
		1		5	3		9				7			6		2			11	8	4	10		
				6	3		9			1	7				5	2			11		4	10	8	
				6	3		9			1	7				5	2			11		4	10	8	
		1		6	3		9				7				5	2			11		4	10	8	
		1		6	3		9				7				5	2			11		4	10	8	
		1		6	3		9				7				5	2			11		4	10	8	
		1		10	3		9								5	2		6	11		4	7	8	
	4	1		6	3		9				7				5	2			11			10	8	
		1		6			9				7				5	2			11		4	8	10	3
	7	1		6			9					4			5	2			11			10	8	3
	10	1		4	3		9	8					7	6	5	2			11					
		1		6	3		9	8	5				7		4	2			11			10		
		1		6	3		9	8	5				7		4	2			11			10		
		1			3		9	8	5				7	6	4	2			11			10		
		1			3		9	8	5				7	6	4	2			11			10		
		1		6	3		9	8	5				7		4	2			11			10		
		1		6	3		9	8	5				7			2			11		4	10		
		1		6	3		9	8	5				7		4	2			11			10		
		1		6	3		9		5		7		10			2			11		4	8		
		1		6	3		9	8			7				5	2		4	11			10		
3		1		6			9	8					7		5	2		4	11			10		
3		1		6			9	8					7		5	2		4	11			10		
		1		6	3			9	5				7			2		4	11	8		10		
9		1		6	3			8	5				7			2		4	11			10		
3	5	40	5	40	38	1	32	13	10	2	28	1	13	4	37	42	8	10	41	5	24	41	17	2
				2			19	1			9		3		1		5		13		1	6	3	

Ashley Jack	Bargh George	Brown Jack	Bruce Bob	Burrows Horace	Catlin Ted	Cooper Sedley	Dewar Neil	Grosvenor Tommy	Hanford Harry	Hill Haydn	Hooper Mark	Hull John	Luke Charlie	Malloch Gavin	Millership Walt	Nibloe Joe	Palethorpe Jackie	Rhodes Dick	Rimmer Ellis	Robinson Jackie	Sharp Wilf	Starling Ronnie	Surtees Jack	Wright Jim
		1		6	3		9				7				5	2			11		4	10	8	
		1		6	3		9				7				5	2			11		4	10	8	
		1		6	3		9				7				5	2			11		4	10	8	
		1		6			9				7				5	2			11		4	10	8	3
		4		4	3		4				4				4	4			4		4	4	4	1
							2												2				2	

Ashley Jack	Bargh George	Brown Jack	Bruce Bob	Burrows Horace	Catlin Ted	Cooper Sedley	Dewar Neil	Grosvenor Tommy	Hanford Harry	Hill Haydn	Hooper Mark	Hull John	Luke Charlie	Malloch Gavin	Millership Walt	Nibloe Joe	Palethorpe Jackie	Rhodes Dick	Rimmer Ellis	Robinson Jackie	Sharp Wilf	Starling Ronnie	Surtees Jack	Wright Jim
		1	10	6	3		9				7				5	2		4	11			8		

Ashley Jack	Bargh George	Brown Jack	Bruce Bob	Burrows Horace	Catlin Ted	Cooper Sedley	Dewar Neil	Grosvenor Tommy	Hanford Harry	Hill Haydn	Hooper Mark	Hull John	Luke Charlie	Malloch Gavin	Millership Walt	Nibloe Joe	Palethorpe Jackie	Rhodes Dick	Rimmer Ellis	Robinson Jackie	Sharp Wilf	Starling Ronnie	Surtees Jack	Wright Jim
		1		4	3		9	8					7	6	5	2			11			10		

League Table

	P	W	D	L	F	A	Pts
Sunderland	42	25	6	11	109	74	56
Derby County	42	18	12	12	61	52	48
Huddersfield Town	42	18	12	12	59	56	48
Stoke City	42	20	7	15	57	57	47
Brentford	42	17	12	13	81	60	46
Arsenal	42	15	15	12	78	48	45
Preston North End	42	18	8	16	67	64	44
Chelsea	42	15	13	14	65	72	43
Manchester City	42	17	8	17	68	60	42
Portsmouth	42	17	8	17	54	67	42
Leeds United	42	15	11	16	66	64	41
Birmingham	42	15	11	16	61	63	41
Bolton Wanderers	42	14	13	15	67	76	41
Middlesbrough	42	15	10	17	84	70	40
Wolverhampton W	42	15	10	17	77	76	40
Everton	42	13	13	16	89	89	39
Grimsby Town	42	17	5	20	65	73	39
West Bromwich Albion	42	16	6	20	89	88	38
Liverpool	42	13	12	17	60	64	38
SHEFFIELD WEDNESDAY	42	13	12	17	63	77	38
Aston Villa	42	13	9	20	81	110	35
Blackburn Rovers	42	12	9	21	55	96	33

1936-37

Division One

Manager: Billy Walker

Did you know that?

Final League Position: 22nd

On Christmas Day 1936 Wednesday lost to Brentford 2–1 in London in a game that started at 11.15am. The next day, they had to play Sunderland at Roker Park, about 280 miles away, in a 2 o'clock kick-off, losing 2–1 again.

Match No.	Date	Venue	Opponents		Round	Result	HT Score	Position	Scorers	Attendance
1	Aug 29	H	Sunderland	W		2-0	0-0		Hooper, Starling	27,016
2	Sep 2	A	Everton	L		1-3	1-2		Luke	31,586
3	5	A	Wolverhampton W	L		3-4	2-2	17th	Dewar (2), Starling (pen)	29,335
4	10	H	Everton	W		6-4	3-1	9th	Dewar (3), Rimmer (2), Luke	16,677
5	12	H	Derby County	L		2-3	2-0	16th	Dewar, Hooper	25,921
6	17	H	Huddersfield Town	D		2-2	0-2	14th	Starling, Luke	18,452
7	19	A	Manchester United	D		1-1	1-0	14th	Starling	40,933
8	26	H	Portsmouth	D		0-0	0-0	13th		20,312
9	Oct 3	H	Preston North End	L		0-1	0-0	16th		18,090
10	10	A	Arsenal	D		1-1	0-1	16th	Hooper	46,421
11	17	A	Chelsea	D		1-1	1-1	18th	Hooper	34,488
12	24	H	Stoke City	D		0-0	0-0	16th		22,169
13	31	A	Charlton Athletic	L		0-1	0-1	19th		12,930
14	Nov 7	H	Grimsby Town	W		2-1	1-0	16th	Robinson, Dewar	19,636
15	14	A	Liverpool	D		2-2	2-0	15th	Dewar, Drury	22,221
16	21	H	Leeds United	L		1-2	1-1	17th	Drury	18,411
17	28	A	Birmingham	D		1-1	0-0	18th	Green	17,993
18	Dec 5	H	Middlesbrough	W		1-0	0-0	17th	Hooper	18,826
19	19	H	Manchester City	W		5-1	2-1	16th	Robinson (2), Drury (2), Hooper	19,821
20	25	A	Brentford	L		1-2	0-1	18th	Robinson	26,560
21	26	A	Sunderland	L		1-2	0-0	18th	Hooper	48,786
22	28	H	Brentford	L		0-2	0-0	19th		20,374
23	Jan 2	H	Wolverhampton W	L		1-3	1-1	20th	Shelley	17,819
24	9	A	Derby County	L		2-3	2-0	20th	Dewar, Thompson	16,132
25	23	H	Manchester United	W		1-0	1-0	19th	Millership	9,021
26	Feb 3	A	Portsmouth	L		0-1	0-1	20th		6,454
27	6	A	Preston North End	D		1-1	1-1	19th	Thompson	17,316
28	13	H	Arsenal	D		0-0	0-0	19th		35,813
29	20	H	Chelsea	D		1-1	0-1	17th	Ashley	16,459
30	Mar 6	H	Charlton Athletic	W		3-1	3-1	18th	Ashley, Luke, Robinson	17,586
31	13	A	Grimsby Town	L		1-5	1-3	19th	Ashley	9,978
32	20	H	Liverpool	L		1-2	1-1	19th	Thompson	19,918
33	26	A	Bolton Wanderers	L		0-1	0-1	20th		26,780
34	27	A	Leeds United	D		1-1	1-0	20th	Thompson	20,776
35	29	H	Bolton Wanderers	W		2-0	0-0	19th	Thompson (2)	30,859
36	Apr 3	H	Birmingham	L		0-3	0-1	20th		21,555
37	5	A	Stoke City	L		0-1	0-1	20th		11,676
38	10	A	Middlesbrough	L		0-2	0-2	22nd		16,477
39	17	H	West Bromwich Alb	L		2-3	0-0	22nd	Millership, Dewar	12,002
40	21	A	West Bromwich Alb	W		3-2	1-1	21st	Rimmer, Drury, Shelley	10,806
41	24	A	Manchester City	L		1-4	0-3	22nd	Rimmer	50,985
42	May 1	A	Huddersfield Town	L		0-1	0-0	22nd		5,809
										Apps
										Goals

FA Cup

Match No.	Date	Venue	Opponents		Round	Result	HT Score	Position	Scorers	Attendance
43	Jan 16	H	Port Vale	W	3R	2-0	2-0		Robinson, Drury	27,450
44	30	A	Everton	L	4R	0-3	0-2			35,807
										Apps
										Goals

Ashley Jack	Brown Jack	Burrows Horace	Catlin Ted	Dewar Neil	Drury George	Goodfellow Derwick	Green Albert	Grosvenor Tommy	Hanford Harry	Hooper Mark	Luke Charlie	McCambridge Jimmy	Millership Walt	Moss Frank	Nibloe Joe	Rhodes Dick	Rimmer Ellis	Robinson Jackie	Roy Jack	Shelley Albert	Smith Roy	Starling Ronnie	Surtees Jack	Thompson Jackie	Webster Walter
	1	6	3	9					5	10	7				2	4	11					8			
	1	6	3	9					5	10	7				2	4	11					8			
	1	6	3	9					5	10	7				2	4	11					8			
2	1	6	3	9					5	10	7					4	11					8			
2	1	6	3	9					5	10	7					4	11					8			
		6	3	9		1			5	10	7		4		2		11					8			
		6	3			1			5	10	7		9		2	4	11					8			
		6	3	9		1				10	7		5		2	4	11					8			
		6	3			1			5		7				2	4	11	10				8	9		
	1	6	3							7		9	5		2	4	11					8		10	
3	1	6							5	7					2	4	11					9	8	10	
	1	6	3							8	7		5		2	4	11					9		10	
	1	6	3					8		7		9	5		2	4	11							10	
	1	6	3	9	7					10			5		2	4	11	8							
	1	6	3	9	7					10			5	4	2		11	8							
3		6		9	7	1	11			10			5	4	2			8							
	1	6	3	9	7		11			10			5	4	2			8							
	1	6	3		7		11			10			5	4	2			8				9			
2	1	6	3		7					10			5	4			11	8				9			
2	1	6	3		7					10			5	4			11	8				9			
2	1	6	3		7					10			5	4			11	8				9			
2	1	6	3		7					10			5	4			11	8				9			
2	1	6	3		7								5	4			11	8		9		10			
	1		3	9	7				5	10				4	2	6		8						11	
2	1	6	3	9					5	10	7		4				11							8	
2	1	6	3				11		5		7					4		8		9				10	
9	1	6	3						5		7		4		2			8	11					10	
9	1	6	3						5	10	7		4		2			8	11						
9	1	6	3		7								5	4	2			8	11					10	
9	1		3						5		7		6	4	2			8	11					10	
9	1		3						5		7		6	4	2			8	11					10	
9	1		3						5		7		6	4	2			8	11					10	
2			3	9	7			4	5	10						6	11	8			1				
2			3		8			6	5		7			4			11	10			1			9	
2			3		8			6	5	7				4			11	10			1			9	
2			3		8			6	5	7			9	4			11	10			1				
2			3				11	6	5	7	10					4		8			1				9
2			3		10				5				8	4		6	11	7			1			9	
2			3	10	7				5				8	4		6	11	9			1				
2			3	10	7			4	5							6	11	8		9	1				
2		6	3	9	10			4	5		7						11	8			1				
2			3	9	10			4	5		7					6	11	8			1				
27	27	29	40	18	21	5	5	9	27	28	21	2	26	19	23	21	30	29	6	3	10	18	2	15	1
3				10	5		1			7	4		2				4	5		2		4		6	

Appearances / Goals																									
	1	6	3	9	7					10			5	4	2		11	8							
2	1	6	3	9				8	5	10	7					4	11								
1	2	2	2	2	1			1	1	2	1		1	1	1	1	2	1							
					1													1							

League Table

	P	W	D	L	F	A	Pts
Manchester City	42	22	13	7	107	61	57
Charlton Athletic	42	21	12	9	58	49	54
Arsenal	42	18	16	8	80	49	52
Derby County	42	21	7	14	96	90	49
Wolverhampton W	42	21	5	16	84	67	47
Brentford	42	18	10	14	82	78	46
Middlesbrough	42	19	8	15	74	71	46
Sunderland	42	19	6	17	89	87	44
Portsmouth	42	17	10	15	62	66	44
Stoke City	42	15	12	15	72	57	42
Birmingham	42	13	15	14	64	60	41
Grimsby Town	42	17	7	18	86	81	41
Chelsea	42	14	13	15	52	55	41
Preston North End	42	14	13	15	56	67	41
Huddersfield Town	42	12	15	15	62	64	39
West Bromwich Albion	42	16	6	20	77	98	38
Everton	42	14	9	19	81	78	37
Liverpool	42	12	11	19	62	84	35
Leeds United	42	15	4	23	60	80	34
Bolton Wanderers	42	10	14	18	43	66	34
Manchester United	42	10	12	20	55	78	32
SHEFFIELD WEDNESDAY	42	9	12	21	53	69	30

1937-38

Division Two

Manager: Billy Walker/Jimmy McMullan

Did you know that?

Final League Position: 17th

When Wednesday played Aston Villa on 18 September 1937 it was found that Bob Curry was not registered at the time. Wednesday escaped a point deduction but were still fined for their misdemeanour.

Match No.	Date	Venue	Opponents		Round	Result	HT Score	Position	Scorers	Attendance
1	Aug 28	A	Chesterfield	L		0-1	0-0			25,086
2	Sep 2	H	Fulham	W		2-1	2-0		Drury, Robinson	16,511
3	4	H	Swansea Town	D		1-1	1-0	11th	Ware	18,739
4	6	A	Fulham	D		0-0	0-0	9th		11,352
5	11	A	Norwich City	L		1-3	1-2	15th	Hooper	19,548
6	16	H	Tottenham Hotspur	L		0-3	0-1	19th		13,263
7	18	H	Aston Villa	L		1-2	1-1	20th	Matthews	20,565
8	25	A	Bradford Park Avenue	D		1-1	1-0	20th	Rimmer	17,674
9	Oct 2	H	West Ham United	W		1-0	0-0	17th	Rimmer	19,987
10	9	A	Southampton	L		2-5	2-2	18th	Matthews (2)	19,542
11	16	H	Sheffield United	L		0-1	0-0	20th		52,523
12	23	A	Manchester United	L		0-1	0-1	21st		16,379
13	30	H	Stockport County	D		3-3	3-0	21st	Robinson, Rimmer (2)	14,272
14	Nov 6	A	Barnsley	L		1-4	1-3	22nd	Thompson	11,309
15	13	H	Luton Town	W		4-0	1-0	20th	Robinson, Luke, Rimmer, Thompson	16,815
16	20	A	Coventry City	W		1-0	1-0	20th	Driscoll	28,254
17	27	H	Nottingham Forest	L		0-2	0-1	20th		17,133
18	Dec 4	A	Newcastle United	L		0-1	0-0	20th		9,502
19	11	H	Bury	W		2-0	1-0	20th	Roy, Driscoll	10,492
20	18	A	Burnley	D		1-1	0-1	19th	Robinson	13,722
21	25	A	Plymouth Argyle	W		4-2	3-2	19th	Drury, Thompson, Rimmer, Matthews	17,389
22	27	H	Plymouth Argyle	D		1-1	1-0	19th	Matthews	20,560
23	Jan 1	H	Chesterfield	W		1-0	1-0	17th	Driver	43,199
24	15	A	Swansea Town	D		1-1	1-1	17th	Massarella	6,052
25	22	H	Norwich City	W		1-0	1-0	12th	Burrows (pen)	12,690
26	29	A	Aston Villa	L		3-4	1-2	13th	Massarella, Matthews, Drury	35,603
27	Feb 5	H	Bradford Park Avenue	W		1-0	0-0	13th	Matthews	24,838
28	12	A	West Ham United	L		0-1	0-1	14th		19,320
29	19	H	Southampton	D		0-0	0-0	14th		17,781
30	26	A	Sheffield United	L		1-2	1-1	16th	Drury	50,011
31	Mar 5	H	Manchester United	L		1-3	0-2	15th	Massarella	37,156
32	12	A	Stockport County	L		1-2	1-0	19th	Hunt	15,282
33	19	H	Barnsley	L		0-1	0-0	20th		34,629
34	26	A	Luton Town	D		2-2	1-1	21st	Robinson, Fallon	13,216
35	Apr 2	H	Coventry City	W		2-1	0-1	21st	Robinson, Hunt	25,956
36	9	A	Nottingham Forest	W		1-0	1-0	17th	Hunt	15,526
37	16	H	Newcastle United	W		3-0	1-0	18th	Robinson, Massarella (2)	30,137
38	18	A	Blackburn Rovers	L		0-1	0-1	20th		14,978
39	19	H	Blackburn Rovers	D		1-1	1-0	18th	F. Walker	28,207
40	23	A	Bury	L		0-2	0-2	20th		7,258
41	30	H	Burnley	W		2-1	2-1	19th	Hunt (1 + pen)	19,553
42	May 7	A	Tottenham Hotspur	W		2-1	2-0	17th	Fallon, Hunt	13,367
										Apps
										Goals

FA Cup

Match No.	Date	Venue	Opponents		Round	Result	HT Score	Position	Scorers	Attendance
43	Jan 8	H	Burnley	D	3R	1-1	0-1		Millership	33,006
44	11	A	Burnley	L	3R Re	1-3	1-2		Drury	25,933
										Apps
										Goals

Ashley Jack	Burrows Horace	Catlin Ted	Chedgzoy Syd	Curry Bob	Driscoll Jack	Driver Allenby	Drury George	Fallon Bill	Goodfellow Derwick	Green Albert	Hanford Harry	Hooper Mark	Hunt Doug	Lester Fred	Luke Charlie	Massarella Len	Matthews Ernie	Millership Walt	Moss Frank	Napier Charlie	Nibloe Joe	Rhodes Dick	Rimmer Ellis	Robinson Jackie	Roy Jack	Smith Roy	Thompson Jackie	Walker Cyril	Walker Fred	Ware Harry	Westlake Frank
	6	3	7				8		1		5										2	4	11	10						9	
2		3	7				10		1		5								6			4	11	8						9	
2		3	7				10		1		5								6			4	11	8						9	
2	6	3							1		5	10			7							4	11	8						9	
2	6	3							1		5	10			7							4	11	8						9	
2		3	7				8		1	11	5	10					9					4							6		
2		3		10					1		5	8			7		9		4			6	11								
2		3							1			7					9	5				6	11	8			10			4	
2									1			7					9	5			3	6	11	8	10					4	
2									1			7					9	5			3	6	11	8	10					4	
2							10		1								9	5			3	6	11	8			7			4	
4					10		6		1					3				5			2			7			11	8		9	
4							6		1					3				5			2		11	8	7		9			10	
4		3					6		1						7			5			2		11	8			9			10	
2	6	3					4		1						7			5					11	10			9	8			
2	6	3			10		4		1						7			5					11				9	8			
2	6	3			10		4		1						7			5					11				9	8			
9	6	3					10		1						7			5			2	4	11	8							
9	6	3			10				1									5			2	4	11	8	7						
9	6	3			10				1									5			2	4	11	8	7						
	6	3					10		1								9	5			2	4	11		7		8				
	6	3					10		1								9	5			2	4	11		7		8				
	6	3				8	10		1								9	5			2	4	11		7						
2	6	3				8	10		1		9					7		5				4			11						
2	6	3				8	10		1							7	9	5				4	11								
2	6	3					10		1							7	9	5				4	11				8				
4	6	3					10		1							7	9	5			2		11				8				
2	6	3					10		1							7	9	5				4	11				8				
2	6	3				8	10		1							7	9	5				4	11								
2	6	3					10		1							7	11	5				4		8			9				
2	6	3					10		1				9			7	11	5				4		8							
2	6	3							1				9			7		5				4	11	8			10				
2	6	3						11	1				9			7		5		10		4		8							
4		3						11					9			7		5		10				8		1			6		2
2	6	3						11					9			7		5		10				8		1			4		
2	6	3						11					9			7		5		10				8		1			4		
2	6	3						11					9			7		5		10				8		1			4		
2	6	3						11					9			7		5		10				8		1			4		
2	6	3						11					9			7		5						8		1	10		4		
	6	3						11					9			7		5			2			8		1	10		4		
	6	3						11	1				9			7		5		10	2			8					4		
	6	3						11	1		5	7	9								2			8			10		4		
35	30	37	4	1	5	4	23	10	35	1	9	8	12	2	8	18	16	34	3	7	17	26	27	29	9	7	18	4	10	12	1
	1				2	1	4	2				1	6		1	5	7						6	7	1		3		1	1	
9	6	3				8	10		1									5			2	4	11		7						
4	6	3			8	9	10		1			7						5			2		11								
2	2	2			1	2	2		2			1						2			2	1	2		1						
							1											1													

League Table

	P	W	D	L	F	A	Pts
Aston Villa	42	25	7	10	73	35	57
Manchester United	42	22	9	11	82	50	53
Sheffield United	42	22	9	11	73	56	53
Coventry City	42	20	12	10	66	45	52
Tottenham Hotspur	42	19	6	17	76	54	44
Burnley	42	17	10	15	54	54	44
Bradford Park Avenue	42	17	9	16	69	56	43
Fulham	42	16	11	15	61	57	43
West Ham United	42	14	14	14	53	52	42
Bury	42	18	5	19	63	60	41
Chesterfield	42	16	9	17	63	63	41
Luton Town	42	15	10	17	89	86	40
Plymouth Argyle	42	14	12	16	57	65	40
Norwich City	42	14	11	17	56	75	39
Southampton	42	15	9	18	55	77	39
Blackburn Rovers	42	14	10	18	71	80	38
SHEFFIELD WEDNESDAY	42	14	10	18	49	56	38
Swansea Town	42	13	12	17	45	73	38
Newcastle United	42	14	8	20	51	58	36
Nottingham Forest	42	14	8	20	47	60	36
Barnsley	42	11	14	17	50	64	36
Stockport County	42	11	9	22	43	70	31

1938-39

Division Two

Manager: Jimmy McMullan

Did you know that?

Final League Position: 3rd

Wednesday finished the season by beating Spurs 1–0 at home, which put them in second place, but city rivals Sheffield United, in third place, still had a game to play the following week at home against Spurs, which they won 6–1. This dropped Wednesday to third spot, and they missed out on promotion by one point.

Match No.	Date	Venue	Opponents		Round	Result	HT Score	Position	Scorers	Attendance
1	Aug 27	H	Bury	W		2-0	1-0		Hunt, Robinson	24,568
2	29	A	Tottenham Hotspur	D		3-3	1-1	6th	Hunt, Whatley (og), Robinson	28,586
3	Sep 3	A	West Ham United	W		3-2	1-1	5th	Hunt (2), Napier	23,400
4	8	H	Blackburn Rovers	W		3-0	2-0	2nd	Fallon, Robinson, Napier	23,036
5	10	H	Tranmere Rovers	W		2-0	0-0	1st	Lowes, Lewis	32,600
6	17	A	Chesterfield	L		1-3	0-1	4th	Fallon	21,879
7	24	H	Swansea Town	D		1-1	1-0	3rd	Robinson	23,632
8	Oct 1	A	Bradford Park Avenue	L		1-3	1-0	4th	Massarella	13,002
9	8	H	Manchester City	W		3-1	1-1	4th	Robinson, Fallon, Hunt (pen)	25,372
10	15	A	Southampton	L		3-4	3-3	8th	Napier (3)	17,231
11	22	H	Coventry City	D		2-2	1-1	7th	Driver, Lewis	24,007
12	29	A	Sheffield United	D		0-0	0-0	8th		44,909
13	Nov 5	H	Newcastle United	L		0-2	0-0	9th		25,358
14	12	A	West Bromwich Alb	L		1-5	0-4	14th	Hunt	18,298
15	19	H	Norwich City	W		7-0	4-0	11th	Hunt (6), Fallon	16,963
16	26	A	Luton Town	W		5-1	2-1	7th	Hunt (3), Massarella, Fallon	15,936
17	Dec 3	H	Plymouth Argyle	L		1-2	0-1	10th	Hanford	22,144
18	10	A	Nottingham Forest	D		3-3	2-3	8th	Robinson, Massarella (2)	15,540
19	17	H	Burnley	W		4-1	1-0	8th	Robinson, Massarella, Fallon, Hunt (pen)	12,259
20	24	A	Bury	W		3-2	2-1	7th	Hunt, Lewis, Robinson	8,459
21	27	H	Fulham	W		5-1	2-0	6th	Millership, Lewis (2), Keeping (og), Robinson	46,743
22	31	H	West Ham United	L		1-4	1-3	8th	Millership	29,070
23	Jan 2	A	Blackburn Rovers	W		4-2	2-0	7th	Millership (3), Robinson	33,100
24	14	A	Tranmere Rovers	W		4-1	1-1	5th	Millership, Driver, Lewis (2)	8,762
25	28	A	Swansea Town	W		1-0	0-0	5th	Hunt	10,317
26	Feb 4	H	Bradford Park Avenue	W		2-0	0-0	4th	Hunt, Robinson	25,261
27	18	H	Southampton	W		2-0	2-0	3rd	Hunt (2)	26,329
28	25	A	Coventry City	L		0-1	0-1	4th		22,786
29	Mar 4	H	Sheffield United	W		1-0	0-0	3rd	Fallon	48,983
30	11	A	Newcastle United	L		1-2	1-0	5th	Millership	28,578
31	18	H	West Bromwich Alb	W		2-1	2-0	3rd	Robinson, Fallon	31,061
32	20	H	Chesterfield	D		0-0	0-0	3rd		18,823
33	25	A	Norwich City	D		2-2	1-1	3rd	Toseland, Robinson	14,336
34	Apr 1	H	Luton Town	W		4-1	2-1	2nd	Hunt (pen), Fallon, Robinson, Toseland	27,646
35	7	A	Millwall	L		0-2	0-1	4th		37,585
36	8	A	Plymouth Argyle	D		1-1	0-1	4th	Robinson	17,649
37	10	H	Millwall	W		3-1	1-0	2nd	Napier (2), Millership	34,804
38	15	H	Nottingham Forest	D		1-1	1-0	3rd	Davies (og)	24,747
39	17	A	Fulham	D		2-2	2-0	2nd	Lowes, Fallon	10,784
40	22	A	Burnley	W		2-1	2-1	2nd	Hunt (2)	9,953
41	26	A	Manchester City	D		1-1	1-0	2nd	Napier	25,955
42	29	H	Tottenham Hotspur	W		1-0	0-0	3rd	Napier	27,639
										Apps
									Three own-goals	Goals

FA Cup

Match No.	Date	Venue	Opponents		Round	Result	HT Score	Position	Scorers	Attendance
43	Jan 7	H	Yeovil & Petters Utd	D	3R	1-1	1-0		Robinson	24,466
44	12	A	Yeovil & Petters Utd	W	3R Re	2-1	1-1		Lewis, Napier	14,359
45	21	H	Chester	D	4R	1-1	1-0		Millership	29,237
46	25	A	Chester	D	4R Re	1-1	0-0		Robinson	18,996
47	30	N	Chester *	W	4R 2Re	2-0	0-0		Robinson, Hunt	15,321
48	Feb 11	A	Chelsea	D	5R	1-1	1-0		Robinson	60,920
49	13	H	Chelsea **	D	5R Re	0-0	0-0			47,549
50	20	N	Chelsea #	L	5R 2Re	1-3	0-2		Fallon	51,879
										Apps
										Goals

* At Maine Road, Manchester. ** After extra-time.
# At Highbury, London

Ashley Jack	Burrows Horace	Catlin Ted	Dillon Francis	Driver Allenby	Fallon Bill	Goodfellow Derwick	Hanford Harry	Hunt Doug	Lester Fred	Lewis Dai	Lowes Arnold	Massarella Len	Millership Walt	Napier Charlie	Pickering Bill	Robinson Jackie	Russell Dave	Smith Roy	Thompson Jackie	Toseland Ernie
2	6	3			11	1	5	9		7				10		8	4			
2	6	3			11	1	5	9		7				10		8	4			
2	6	3			11	1	5	9		7				10		8	4			
2	6	3			11	1	5	9		7				10		8	4			
2	6	3			11	1	5			7	9			10		8	4			
2	6	3			11	1	5	9		7				10		8	4			
2	6	3			11	1	5			7	9			10		8	4			
2	6				11	1	5		3			7		10		8	4		9	
2	6				11	1	5	9	3			7		10		8	4			
	6	3			11	1	5	9	2			7		10		8	4			
2	6			8		1	5	9	3	11		7		10			4			
2	6		7			1		9		11			5	10	3	8	4			
2	6		7		11	1		9					5	10	3	8	4			
2	6				11	1		9		7			5	10	3	8	4			
2	6				11	1	5	9	3			7		10		8	4			
2	6				11	1	5	9	3			7		10		8	4			
2	6				11	1	5	9	3			7		10		8	4			
2	6				11	1	5	9	3			7		10		8	4			
2	6				11	1	5	9	3			7		10		8	4			
2	6					1	5	9	3	11		7		10		8	4			
2	6					1	5		3	11		7	9	10		8	4			
2	6					1	5		3	11		7	9	10		8	4			
2	6						5		3	11		7	9	10		8	4	1		
2	6			10	11		5		3	7			9			8	4	1		
2	6		7		11		5	9	3					10		8	4	1		
2	6	3	7		11		5	9						10		8	4	1		
2	6	3	7				5	9		11				10		8	4	1		
2	6	3	7				5	9		11				10		8	4	1		
2	6	3	7		11		5	9						10		8	4	1		
2	6	3			11		5			7			9	10		8	4	1		
2	6	3			11		5						9	10		8	4	1		7
2	6	3			11		5	9						10		8	4	1		7
2	6	3			11		5	9						10		8	4	1		7
2	6	3			11		5	9						10		8	4	1		7
2	6	3			11		5	9						10		8	4	1		7
2	6	3			11		5						9	10		8	4	1		7
2	6	3			11		5						9	10		8	4	1		7
2	6	3			11		5						9	10		8	4	1		7
2	6	3			11		5	9			8			10			4	1		7
2	6	3			11		5	9			8			10			4	1		7
2	6	3			11		5	9			8			10			4	1		7
2	6	3			11		5	9			8			10			4	1		7
41	42	25	7	2	34	22	39	30	15	18	6	13	12	41	3	37	42	20	1	12
				2	10		1	24		7	2	5	8	9		15				2

Ashley Jack	Burrows Horace	Catlin Ted	Dillon Francis	Driver Allenby	Fallon Bill	Goodfellow Derwick	Hanford Harry	Hunt Doug	Lester Fred	Lewis Dai	Lowes Arnold	Massarella Len	Millership Walt	Napier Charlie	Pickering Bill	Robinson Jackie	Russell Dave	Smith Roy	Thompson Jackie	Toseland Ernie
2	6						5		3	11		7	9	10		8	4	1		
2	6				11		5	9	3	7				10		8	4	1		
2	6				11		5		3			7	9	10		8	4	1		
2	6		7		11		5	9	3					10		8	4	1		
2	6	3	7		11		5	9						10		8	4	1		
2	6	3			11		5	9		7				10		8	4	1		
2	6	3			11		5	9		7				10		8	4	1		
2	6	3			11		5	9		7				10		8	4	1		
8	8	4	2		7		8	6	4	5		2	2	8		8	8	8		
					1			1		1			1	1		4				

League Table

	P	W	D	L	F	A	Pts
Blackburn Rovers	42	25	5	12	94	60	55
Sheffield United	42	20	14	8	69	41	54
SHEFFIELD WEDNESDAY	42	21	11	10	88	59	53
Coventry City	42	21	8	13	62	45	50
Manchester City	42	21	7	14	96	72	49
Chesterfield	42	20	9	13	69	52	49
Luton Town	42	22	5	15	82	66	49
Tottenham Hotspur	42	19	9	14	67	62	47
Newcastle United	42	18	10	14	61	48	46
West Bromwich Albion	42	18	9	15	89	72	45
West Ham United	42	17	10	15	70	52	44
Fulham	42	17	10	15	61	55	44
Millwall	42	14	14	14	64	53	42
Burnley	42	15	9	18	50	56	39
Plymouth Argyle	42	15	8	19	49	55	38
Bury	42	12	13	17	65	74	37
Bradford Park Avenue	42	12	11	19	61	82	35
Southampton	42	13	9	20	56	82	35
Swansea Town	42	11	12	19	50	83	34
Nottingham Forest	42	10	11	21	49	82	31
Norwich City	42	13	5	24	50	91	31
Tranmere Rovers	42	6	5	31	39	99	17

1939-40

Division Two

Manager: Jimmy McMullan

Did you know that?

On 30 March 1940 Walter Rickett, playing for Sheffield United against Wednesday in his first derby game, and his home debut, scored with his first touch in the first minute. After the war, Rickett, who had been transferred to Blackpool, would return to Sheffield and play for Wednesday 97 times.

Match No.	Date	Venue	Opponents	Round	Result	HT Score	Position	Scorers	Attendance
1	Aug 26	A	Luton Town	L	0-3	0-3			11,900
2	28	H	Barnsley	W	3-1	1-0		Napier (2), Hunt	23,810
3	Sep 2	H	Plymouth Argyle	L	0-1	0-0	16th		12,079

Apps
Goals

War was declared on Sunday 3rd September 1939 and all sport was suspended

EAST MIDLANDS REGIONAL DIVISION POSITION 9th

4	Oct 21	A	Doncaster Rovers	D	2-2	1-1		Millership, Ward	6,006
5	28	H	Notts County	D	1-1	0-1		Driver	4,000
6	Nov 4	A	Grimsby Town	L	2-3	0-2		Massarella, Hunt (pen)	2,000
7	11	A	Chesterfield	L	0-4	0-2	9th		5,028
8	18	H	Barnsley	D	1-1	1-1	10th	Ward	4,005
9	25	A	Mansfield Town	L	3-5	2-3	10th	Millership, Dillon, Hunt (pen)	1,600
10	Dec 2	H	Sheffield United	L	2-3	1-1	11th	Driver, Millership	5,500
11	9	A	Nottingham Forest	D	1-1	0-0	9th	Driver	3,116
12	23	H	Mansfield Town	W	2-0	1-0	8th	Ward, Millership	2,000
13	26	H	Chesterfield	W	2-1	1-1	5th	Massarella,Driver	5,200
14	Jan 13	H	Rotherham United	L	0-1	0-1	7th		1,700
15	Mar 2	A	Rotherham United	D	1-1	0-0	8th	Lowes	2,500
16	16	A	Barnsley	L	0-2	0-1	8th		2,800
17	22	A	Lincoln City	L	2-4	2-1	9th	Thompson, Millership	5,372
18	23	H	Grimsby Town	W	2-1	2-1	9th	Thompson (2)	3,975
19	30	A	Sheffield United	L	3-4	0-3	9th	Hoyle (2), Burrows	10,013
20	Apr 6	H	Nottingham Forest	W	2-1	0-0	9th	Ward, Thompson (pen)	4,641
21	May 4	H	Doncaster Rovers	L	1-3	0-1	9th	Ward	2,000
22	9	H	Lincoln City	L	2-3	1-2	9th	Scholfield, Hoyle	752
23	18	A	Notts County	W	4-1	2-1	9th	Millership (3), Ward	4,000

Apps
Goals

LEAGUE NORTH CUP

24	Apr 20	A	Leeds United	L	3-6	1-3		Massarella, Hunt (1 + pen)	8,065
25	27	H	Leeds United	W	3-2	2-0		Napier (2 + pen)	9,506

Apps
Goals

* Guest player from Arsenal
** Guest player from Grenoside FC

Ashley Jack	Burrows Horace	Catlin Ted	Collett Ernie *	Dillon Francis	Driver Allenby	Ellison Irving	Fallon Bill	Hanford Harry	Hoyle Ernest **	Hunt Doug	Lester Fred	Lewis Dai	Lowes Arnold	Massarella Len	Millership Walt	Morton Albert	Mulrenan Bernard	Napier Charlie	Packard Edgar	Pickering Bill	Robinson Jackie	Rogers Alf	Russell Dave	Scholfield Ernest	Smith Roy	Thompson Jackie	Toseland Ernie	Walker Fred	Ward Tommy
2	6	3						5		9		11						10			8		4		1		7		
2	6	3						5		9		11						10			8				1		7	4	
2	6	3			8		11	5		9								10							1		7	4	
3	3	3			1		1	3		3		2						3			2		1		3		3	2	
										1								2											

Ashley Jack	Burrows Horace	Catlin Ted	Collett Ernie *	Dillon Francis	Driver Allenby	Ellison Irving	Fallon Bill	Hanford Harry	Hoyle Ernest **	Hunt Doug	Lester Fred	Lewis Dai	Lowes Arnold	Massarella Len	Millership Walt	Morton Albert	Mulrenan Bernard	Napier Charlie	Packard Edgar	Pickering Bill	Robinson Jackie	Rogers Alf	Russell Dave	Scholfield Ernest	Smith Roy	Thompson Jackie	Toseland Ernie	Walker Fred	Ward Tommy
2								5		9	3			11	10								4		1		7	6	8
2	6	3			8					9			10	11					5				4		1		7		
2				7				5		9	3			11	10						8		4		1			6	
2								5		9	3			11	10						8		4		1	7			6
2	6	3			8					9				11					5				4		1		7		10
2	6			7			11	5		9	3				10								4		1				8
2	6				8					9	3				10				5				4		1		7		11
2	6	3			8					9			7		10				5				4		1				11
2		3			8								10	7	9				5				4		1			6	11
2	6	3			8					9				7	10				5				4		1				11
2	6			7					9		3		8		5								4		1	10			11
2			6										8	11	9				5	3			4		1	10			7
2	6	3	5										8	11	10	1							4			9			7
2	6		5											11	9	1	7			3			4			10			8
2	6		5						9					11		1	7			3			4			10			8
2	6		5						9					11	10	1	7			3			4						8
2	6		5						9						10	1	7			3			4			8			11
2	6	3	5			11			9					7	10	1							4						8
2		3	6		8				9				10			1			5			7		11					4
2	6		5												9	1				3		7	4	11		10			8
20	14	8	9	3	7	1	1	4	6	9	6		7	13	16	8	4		8	6	2	2	19	2	12	8	4	3	18
	1			1	4				3	2			1	2	8									1		4			6

Ashley Jack	Burrows Horace	Catlin Ted	Collett Ernie *	Dillon Francis	Driver Allenby	Ellison Irving	Fallon Bill	Hanford Harry	Hoyle Ernest **	Hunt Doug	Lester Fred	Lewis Dai	Lowes Arnold	Massarella Len	Millership Walt	Morton Albert	Mulrenan Bernard	Napier Charlie	Packard Edgar	Pickering Bill	Robinson Jackie	Rogers Alf	Russell Dave	Scholfield Ernest	Smith Roy	Thompson Jackie	Toseland Ernie	Walker Fred	Ward Tommy
2	6		5							9				11	3	1					8		4			10	7		
2	6	3	5											11		1		10			8		4			9	7		
2	2	1	2							1				2	1	2		1			2		2			2	2		
										2				1				3											

1940-41

North Regional League

Manager: Jimmy McMullan

Did you know that?

Final League Position: 34th

On 14 September 1940, when Wednesday played Notts County at Hillsborough, all of the visiting players were guest players as Wednesday won 3–1.

On Christmas Day 1940 Sheffield United played Wednesday in a wartime home game. It was, in fact, played at Hillsborough, as Bramall Lane had been severely damage by a bombing raid a few weeks earlier. The game ended goalless.

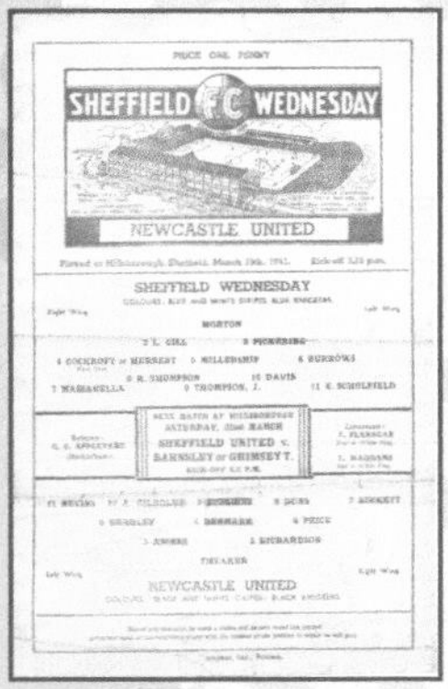

Match No.	Date	Venue	Opponents		Round	Result	HT Score	Position	Scorers	Attendance
1	Aug 31	H	Huddersfield Town	W		1-0	1-0		Wynn	3,197
2	Sep 7	A	Halifax Town	D		1-1	1-0		Ward	2,000
3	21	A	Huddersfield Town	L		0-5	0-3	32nd		2,214
4	28	H	Chesterfield	L		0-5	0-3	34th		3,898
5	Oct 5	A	Middlesbrough	L		4-5	2-2		Robinson (2), J. Thompson (2)	2,200
6	12	H	Barnsley	D		2-2	2-1		J. Thompson (pen + 1)	3,525
7	19	H	Halifax Town	W		4-2	1-1		J. Thompson (2), Scholfield, Millership	2,075
8	26	A	Barnsley	L		0-5	0-4	33rd		2,588
9	Nov 2	H	Middlesbrough	W		6-3	4-1		Robinson (2), J. Thompson (2), Ward, R. Thompson	1,163
10	9	A	Doncaster Rovers	D		4-4	3-1	32nd	J. Thompson (2), Ward, R. Thompson	1,370
11	16	H	Rotherham United	D		1-1	0-0	28th	Ward	3,440
12	23	A	Chesterfield	L		0-2	0-0	31st		3,002
13	30	H	Bradford Park Avenue	W		4-3	3-1		J. Thompson, Robinson (2), Scholfield	2,234
14	Dec 7	A	Rotherham United	L		0-1	0-1			2,974
15	25	A	Sheffield United *	D		0-0	0-0			6,757
16	28	A	Bradford City	W		4-2	4-1		Ward, Massarella, Beardshaw (og), Rogers	1,408
17	Jan 4	H	Rotherham United	W		4-2	1-1		Curry, Ward (3)	1,000
18	11	A	Doncaster Rovers **	L		0-4	0-2			2,604
19	18	A	Grimsby Town	L		1-2	1-2		Burgin	1,500
20	25	A	Newcastle United	L		1-7	0-6		Robinson	2,500
21	Mar 1	A	Barnsley	L		1-7	0-3		J. Thompson	2,197
22	8	A	Lincoln City	L		1-4	0-3		Ward	1,500
23	15	H	Newcastle United	W		2-0	0-0		Massarella, Scholfield	1,371
24	22	A	Leeds United	L		2-3	2-1		Scholfield, J. Thompson	1,500
25	29	H	Burnley	L		0-2	0-0	33rd		1,257
26	Apr 5	A	Burnley	L		0-2	0-0	33rd		1,880
27	12	H	Chesterfield	W		3-1	3-0		Drury, Lowes, J. Thompson	4,071
28	14	H	Sheffield United	W		3-1	2-0		Starling (2), Drury	7,606
29	19	H	Nottingham Forest	D		1-1	1-0		J. Thompson	2,378
30	26	A	Chesterfield	L		0-1	0-1	34th		2,000

* Away game played at Hillsborough — Apps

** Also County Cup Preliminary round — One own-goal — Goals

LEAGUE WAR CUP (PRELIMINARY ROUND)

Match No.	Date	Venue	Opponents		Round	Result	HT Score	Position	Scorers	Attendance
31	Feb 1	A	York City	L	Pri R	0-7	0-5			2,500
32	8	H	York City #	W	Pri R	2-1	2-0		Robinson, J. Thompson	2,000

\# Played at Scunthorpe — Apps

Goals

Guest players: M.Burgin (WBA), J. Cockroft (West Ham), G. Drury (Arsenal), T. Johnson (Sheffield United) R. Starling (Aston Villa) & J. Wynn (Rochdale)

Ashley Jack	Burgin Maynell	Burrows Horace	Catlin Ted	Cockroft Joe	Curry Bob	Davis Alec	Driver Allenby	Drury George	Gill Len	Herbert Frank	Johnson Ted	Lowes Arnold	Massarella Len	Millership Walt	Morton Albert	Packard Edgar	Pickering Bill	Robinson Jackie	Roebuck Norman	Rogers Alf	Russell Dave	Scholfield Ernest	Smith Alan	Smith Roy	Starling Ronnie	Thompson Jackie	Thompson Ron	Turner Bradley	Ward Tommy	Westlake Frank	Wynn Jim
		6												5	1		3		7	8	2	11				10			4		9
		6	2											5	1		3		7	8		11				10			4		9
		6							2	4				5	1		3		7			11				10	8		9		
	8	6							2			4		9	1	5	3					11				10			7		
2		6								4				5	1		3	8		7		11				10			9		
2		6								4				5			3	8	7			11				10		1	9		
2	9	6												5			3		7		4	11				10		1	8		
2		6					8			4				5	1		3		7			11				10			9		
2		6							4					5			3	8				11				10	7	1	9		
2		6	3						4					5				8				11				10	7	1	9		
2		6							4					5	1		3			8		11				10	7		9		
2		6							4					5	1		3		7	10		11					8		9		
2		6							4					5	1		3	8	7			11				10			9		
2		6			10					4				5	1		3			8		11					7		9		
2		6		4	10								7	5	1		3			8		11							9		
2		6		4	10								7	5	1		3			8		11							9		
2		6		4	8								7	5	1		3					11				10			9		
2		6		4	8								7			5	3					11		1		10			9		
2	9	5		4				10	6			8	11		1				7											3	
	9				4				2	6				5	1		3	8	7			11				10					
2		5		4				10	6				11				3			8						9	7	1			
2		5		4				8	6				7		1							11					9		10	3	
		6		4		10			2				7	5	1		3					11				9	8				
		6		4					2				7	5	1		3			10		11				9	8				
2		6		4				9					7	5	1		3	8				11				10					
		5				6	9	8	2	4					1		3		7			11				10					
				4		6		7	2			9	11		1	5	3								8	10					
				4				9		6			7		1	5	3					11			8	10				2	
				4		6		9			5		7				3			8		11		1		10				2	
		6		4		8		10	2					5	1		3			9		11	7								
18	4	26	2	14	6	5	2	9	16	8	1	3	13	22	23	4	27	7	11	12	2	27	1	2	2	23	10	5	19	4	2
	1				1			2				1	2	1				7		1		4			2	15	2		9		1
2	9	6		4	11			8					7	5	1		3									10					
2		6		4				9					7	5	1		3	8				11				10					
2	1	2		2	1			2					2	2	2		2	1				1				2					
																		1								1					

1941-42

Football League North (1st Competition)

Manager: Jimmy McMullan

Did you know that?

Final League Position: 16th

On 4 April 1942, in an away game at Leeds, Wednesday fielded a forward line of amateur players, with two scoring in a 2–1 win.

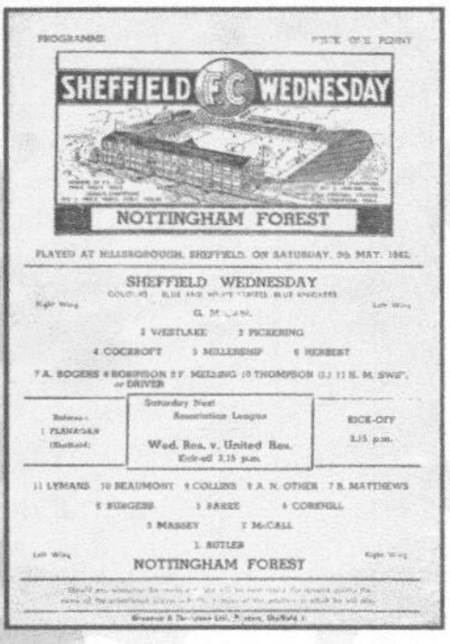

Match No.	Date	Venue	Opponents		Round	Result	HT Score	Position	Scorers	Attendance
1	Aug 30	H	Rotherham United	W		1-0	0-0		Thompson (pen)	3,679
2	Sep 6	A	Rotherham United	L		1-4	1-1		Drury	2,300
3	13	A	Grimsby Town	D		1-1	0-0		Thompson	2,000
4	20	H	Grimsby Town	L		0-2	0-1			3,534
5	27	H	Lincoln City	D		1-1	1-0		Melling	3,959
6	Oct 4	A	Lincoln City	L		0-6	0-6			4,116
7	11	A	Doncaster Rovers	D		2-2	1-0		Thompson (2)	2,554
8	18	H	Doncaster Rovers	W		5-2	1-0		Roebuck, Lowes, Drury (2), Melling	940
9	25	H	Sheffield United	L		1-3	0-0		Millership	8,907
10	Nov 1	A	Sheffield United	D		3-3	1-1		Robinson (3)	9,149
11	8	A	Mansfield Town	L		0-4	0-2			1,236
12	15	H	Mansfield Town	W		2-0	2-0		Melling (2)	2,305
13	22	H	Chesterfield	D		1-1	0-1		Robinson	3,591
14	29	A	Chesterfield	W		1-0	0-0		Burgin	1,717
15	Dec 6	A	Barnsley	L		3-4	1-0		Burgin, Melling, Robinson	1,300
16	13	H	Barnsley	W		3-0	1-0		Melling (2), Burgin	2,806
17	20	H	Newcastle United	W		4-2	3-1		Herbert (pen), Rogers, Melling, Drury	3,375
18	25	A	Newcastle United	W		4-2	2-1	16th	Burgin, Robinson (2), Rogers	10,000

Apps
Goals

FOOTBALL LEAGUE NORTH (2nd Competition) #

Match No.	Date	Venue	Opponents		Round	Result	HT Score	Position	Scorers	Attendance
19	Dec 27	H	Everton	L	*	0-3	0-2			11,721
20	Jan 3	A	Everton	L	*	0-2	0-1			5,000
21	10	H	Bradford City	L	*	0-1	0-0			3,884
22	Feb 21	H	Burnley	W	*	3-1	1-1		Thompson, Rogers, Melling	1,472
23	28	A	Burnley	L	*	0-3	0-2			2,043
24	Mar 14	A	Leicester City	L	*	1-5	1-2		Rogers	6,500
25	21	H	Bury	D	*	2-2	0-2		Burgin, Thompson	2,850
26	28	A	Bury	L	*	2-8	0-2		Rogers, Melling	1,746
27	Apr 4	A	Leeds United	W		2-1	1-1		Howsam, Nelson	3,000
28	6	A	Bolton Wanderers	D		3-3	0-1		Cockroft (pen), Howsam, Burgin	2,000
29	11	H	Leicester City	W		4-1	3-0		Nelson (2), Melling, Howsam	3,416
30	18	A	Leicester City	W		1-0	1-0		Cockroft (pen)	3,000
31	25	A	Sheffield United	L		0-3	0-3			8,102
32	May 2	A	Nottingham Forest	L		1-2	0-1		Thompson (pen)	1,888
33	9	H	Nottingham Forest	W		3-1	2-0		Burgin, Driver, Thompson	2,402

Did not play enough games to be placed in the table.
* Also League War Cup qualifying competition

Apps
Goals

Guest players: C. Hanks (Bolton W), B. Jones (Tranmere R), G. Laking (Middlesbrough), J. Wynn (Rochdale)

Armeson Laurence	Ashley Jack	Burrows Horace	Burgin Maynell	Catlin Ted	Cockroft Joe	Driver Allenby	Drury George	Gill Len	Hanks Charlie	Herbert Frank	Howsam Alfred	Jones Benny	Laking George	Lane Robert E	Lowes Arnold	McCabe George	Melling Frank	Millership Walt	Morton Albert	Nelson Bernard	Packard Edgar	Padgett Herbert	Pickering Bill	Robinson Jackie	Roebuck Norman	Rogers Alf	Scholfield Ernest	Smith Alan	Smith Roy	Swift Hugh	Thompson Jackie	Walker Cyril	Ward Tommy	Westlake Frank	Wynn Jim
	2			3	4		8			6					9			5	1						11	7					10				
6	2			3	4		8		9							1		5							11	7							10		
					4		8		9	6		11	2			1		5													10			3	7
	2				4		8	6	9				3					5	1						11						10				7
	2				4		8			6							9	5					3		11	7			1		10				
	2			6	4		8						3				9	5	1						11						10	7			
	2	6			4		7						3		9			5	1								11				10		8		
	2				4		7			6			3		8		9				5				11				1		10				
	2				4		7			6			3				9	5						8	11				1		10				
					4					6			2				9	5	1					8	11			7			10			3	
	2				4		7			6			3				9	5	1					8	11						10				
					4		8			6			2				9	5	1				3		11	7					10				
					4	7		2		6							9	5	1				3	8			11				10				
			10		4					6			2	7			9	5					3		11	8			1						
			10		4					6			2				9	5	1				3	8	11	7									
			10		4					6			2			1	9	5					3		11	7						8			
			10		4	8	11	2		6							9	5	1				3			7									
			9		4					6			2					5	1				3	8		7	11				10				
1	9	1	5	3	18	2	12	3	3	14		1	13	1	3	3	12	17	11		1		8	6	13	9	3	1	4		13	2	2	2	2
			4				4			1					1		8	1						7	1	2					4				
					4		7			6			2				9	10	1		5		3	8			11								
					4					6	7		2		8		9	5					3				11		1		10				
	2				4		11			6	7				10		9	5	1				3	8											
					4		10			6			2				9	5	1			8	3			7					11				
			10		4		8			6			2				9	5	1				3			7				11					
					4		11			6			2		10		9	5				8	3			7			1						
	2		9		4					6								5	1			8	3			7		11			10				
	3		8		5		10	4		6			2				9		1							7	11								
					4					6	11		2			1	9	5		10		8	3			7									
	2		9		4					6	11							5	1	10			3			7					8				
			8		4					6	11		2				9	5	1	10			3			7									
					4					6	11		2				9	5	1	10			3			7					8				
					4	8				6			2				9	10	1		5		3			7	11								
					4	8				6			2			1	9	5		11			3			7					10				
			9		4	8				6						1		5					3			7				11	10			2	
	4		6		15	3	6	1		15	6		11		3	3	12	14	10	5	2	4	14	2		12	4	1	2	2	7			1	
			3		2	1					3						3			3						3					4				

1942-43

Football League North (1st Competition)

Manager: Eric Taylor

Did you know that?

Final League Position: 3rd
Final League Position: 5th

On 13 February 1943 Frank Melling scored twice as Wednesday beat Sheffield United 8–2 in a wartime game at Hillsborough. After the war, Melling became a director at Bramall Lane.

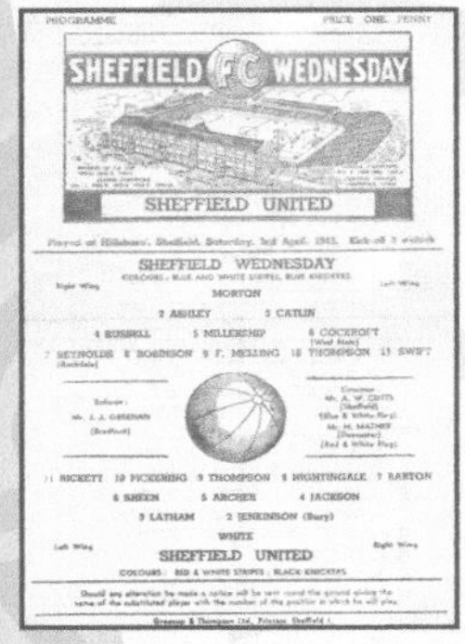

Match No.	Date	Venue	Opponents		Round	Result	HT Score	Position	Scorers	Attendance
1	Aug 29	A	Doncaster Rovers	W		3-1	1-0		Melling (2), Robinson	2,689
2	Sep 5	H	Doncaster Rovers	W		3-2	3-1		J.Thompson (2), Melling	3,817
3	12	H	Rotherham United	W		4-1	2-0		Melling (3), Cockroft (pen)	5,070
4	19	A	Rotherham United	D		2-2	1-2		Melling, Robinson	4,400
5	26	H	Bradford Park Avenue	W		1-0	0-0	4th	Cockroft (pen)	5,870
6	Oct 3	A	Bradford Park Avenue	D		3-3	0-2		J. Thompson, Cockroft (pen), R. Thompson	3,500
7	10	A	Grimsby Town	L		0-2	0-0			2,370
8	17	H	Grimsby Town	W		2-0	1-0		Vincent (og), Melling	7,703
9	24	H	Barnsley	W		5-1	2-0		Robinson (2), J. Thompson (2), Melling	7,550
10	31	A	Barnsley	W		3-0	2-0		Robinson, Melling, J. Thompson	4,774
11	Nov 7	H	Mansfield Town	W		9-1	2-1		Robinson (3), Burgin (4), J. Thompson, Swift	9,569
12	14	A	Mansfield Town	W		10-2	2-1	3rd	Burgin (3), Robinson (3), Reynolds, Swift, J.Thompson, Webber (og)	2,600
13	21	A	Notts County	D		2-2	2-2		Cockroft (pen), Burgin	3,000
14	28	H	Notts County	W		3-1	3-1	3rd	Robinson (3)	9,776
15	Dec 5	A	Chesterfield	L		1-5	1-2		Driver	2,500
16	12	H	Chesterfield	W		6-0	3-0		Reynolds, Melling (3), Swift (2)	10,876
17	19	H	Sheffield United	W		4-0	1-0		Reynolds, Robinson (2), Melling	18,942
18	25	A	Sheffield United	L		0-3	0-2	3rd		34,455
										Apps
									Two own-goals	Goals

FOOTBALL LEAGUE NORTH (2nd Competition)

Match No.	Date	Venue	Opponents		Round	Result	HT Score	Position	Scorers	Attendance
19	Dec 26	H	Lincoln City	W	*	4-3	3-3		Robinson (3), Reynolds	19,787
20	Jan 2	A	Lincoln City	W	*	3-0	3-0		Robinson, J. Thompson, Swift	3,640
21	9	A	Nottingham Forest	D	*	1-1	0-1		Millership	4,365
22	16	H	Nottingham Forest	D	*	1-1	1-1		J. Thompson	9,983
23	23	H	Rotherham United	W	*	3-2	2-1		Robinson (3)	10,068
24	30	A	Rotherham United	D	*	1-1	0-0		Melling	7,000
25	Feb 6	A	Sheffield United	L	*	1-3	1-1		Robinson	18,677
26	13	H	Sheffield United	W	*	8-2	6-1		Robinson (3), J. Thompson (2), Melling (2), Reynolds	18,232
27	20	H	Grimsby Town	D	*	2-2	1-1		Melling, Cockroft (pen)	12,852
28	27	A	Grimsby Town	W	*	2-1	2-0		Everitt, J. Thompson	4,000
29	Mar 6	H	Bradford City	W	**	1-0	0-0		Reynolds	17,588
30	13	A	Bradford City	D	**	1-1	0-1		Robinson	9,009
31	20	A	Nottingham Forest	L	**	0-1	0-1			13,404
32	27	H	Nottingham Forest	W	**	5-1	2-0		Melling (4), Robinson	23,518
33	Apr 3	H	Sheffield United	W	**	3-2	1-1		Robinson (2), Melling	37,550
34	10	A	Sheffield United	D	**	0-0	0-0			43,718
35	17	H	York City	W	S/F	3-0	2-0		Robinson (2), Hodgson (og)	35,253
36	24	A	York City	D	S/F	1-1	0-1		J. Thompson	16,350
37	26	A	Rotherham United	L		1-2	1-2		Herbert	2,500
38	May 1	A	Blackpool	D	F	2-2	1-1		Cockroft (pen), Robinson	28,000
39	8	H	Blackpool	L	F	1-2	0-1		Robinson	47,657
										Apps
									One own-goal	Goals

* Knock out Cup Qualifying
** LEAGUE NORTH Knock out rounds.

Guest players: W. Reynolds (Rochdale), J. Smith (Sheffield United), G. Laking (Middlesbrough), K. Rossington (Sheffield United)

Ardron Wally	Ashley Jack	Burgin Maynell	Catlin Ted	Cockroft Joe	Driver Allenby	Everitt Richard	Fox Oscar	Froggatt Redfern	Gabby Ken	Gill Len	Hainsworth Len	Herbert Frank	Laking George	Lowes Arnold	Melling Frank	Millership Walt	Morton Albert	Reynolds Walter	Robinson Jackie	Rogers Alf	Rossington Ken	Russell Dave	Schofield Ernest	Searson Harry	Smith Jack	Swift Hugh	Thompson Jackie	Thompson Ron	Westlake Frank	Ward Tommy
	2		3	6											9	5	1	7	8			4				11	10			
		8	3	6								4	2		9	5	1	7								11	10			
		10	3	6								4			9	5	1	7								11		8	2	
	2		3	6								4		10	9	5	1	7	8							11				
	2		3	6											9	5	1	7	8			4				11	10			
	2		3	6											9	5	1	7				4				11	10	8		
	2		3	6								4			9	5	1	7	8							11	10			
	2		3							4		6			9	5	1	7	8							11	10			
	2		3	6								4			9	5	1	7	8							11	10			
	2		3	6								4			9	5	1	7	8							11	10			
	2	9	3	6								4				5	1	7	8							11	10			
	2	9	3	6								4				5	1	7	8							11	10			
	2	9	3	6								4				5	1	7	8							11	10			
	2		3	6								4			9	5	1	7	8							11	10			
	2		3	6	8							4			9	5	1	7								11	10			
	2		3	10								6			9	5	1	7	8			4				11				
	2		3	6								4			9	5	1	7	8	10						11				
	2		3	6								10			9	5	1	7	8			4				11				
	16	5	18	17	1					1		15	1	1	15	18	18	18	14	1		5				18	13	2	1	
		8		4	1										14			3	16							4	8	1		

Ardron Wally	Ashley Jack	Burgin Maynell	Catlin Ted	Cockroft Joe	Driver Allenby	Everitt Richard	Fox Oscar	Froggatt Redfern	Gabby Ken	Gill Len	Hainsworth Len	Herbert Frank	Laking George	Lowes Arnold	Melling Frank	Millership Walt	Morton Albert	Reynolds Walter	Robinson Jackie	Rogers Alf	Rossington Ken	Russell Dave	Schofield Ernest	Searson Harry	Smith Jack	Swift Hugh	Thompson Jackie	Thompson Ron	Westlake Frank	Ward Tommy
	2		3	6						4					9	5	1	7	8							11	10			
	2		3	6						4					9	5	1	7	8							11	10			
	2		3	6						4					9	5	1	7	8							11	10			
	2		3	6								4			9	5	1	7	8							11	10			
	2		3	6						4					9	5	1	7	8							11	10			
	2		3	6						4					9	5	1	7	8							11	10			
	2		3	6						4					9	5	1	7	8							11	10			
	2		3	6											9	5	1	7	8			4				11	10			
	2		3	6				8							9	5	1	7				4				11	10			
	2		3	6		9				4						5	1	7	8							11	10			
	2		3	6		9				4					8	5	1	7								11	10			
	2		3	6												5	1	7	8			4				11	10			9
	2		3	6							10				9	5	1	7	8			4				11				
	2		3	6											9	5	1	7	8			4				11	10			
	2		3	6											9	5	1	7	8			4				11	10			
	2		3	6											9	5	1	7	8			4				11	10			
9			3	6												5		7	8			4			1	11	10		2	
9	2		3	6												5		7	8			4			1	11	10			
	2		3			9	8			6		10				5		7			4		11	1						
	2		3	6											9	5	1	7	8			4				11	10			
	2			6					3						9	5	1	7	8			4				11	10			
2	20		20	20		3	1	1	1	9	1	2			16	21	18	21	18		1	11	1	1	2	20	19		1	1
				2		1						1			9	1		3	19							1	6			

1943-44

Football League North (1st Competition)

Manager: Eric Taylor

Did you know that?

Final League Position: 40th
Final League Position: 30th

During this season, Wednesday had 40 players in the armed services.

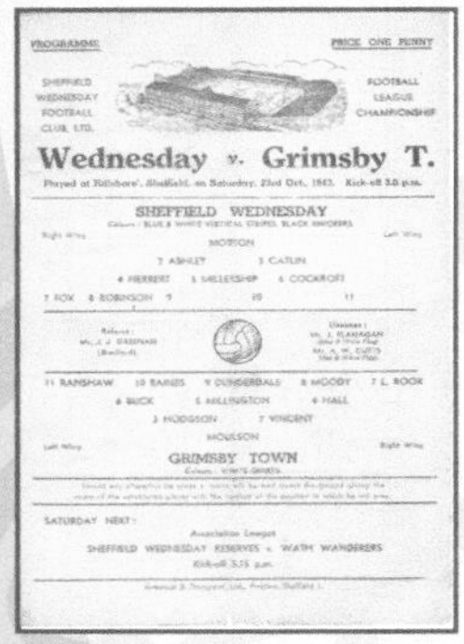

Match No.	Date	Venue	Opponents		Round	Result	HT Score	Position	Scorers	Attendance
1	Aug 28	A	Barnsley	L		1-3	1-1		Robinson	4,057
2	Sep 4	H	Barnsley	W		3-1	1-0		Ward, Robinson, J. Thompson	10,252
3	11	H	Doncaster Rovers	D		2-2	1-2		Ward, Millership	8,365
4	18	A	Doncaster Rovers	L		1-3	0-0		Robinson	6,840
5	25	A	Bradford Park Avenue	L		1-3	1-1		Robinson	4,305
6	Oct 2	H	Bradford Park Avenue	L		2-3	2-0		Ward, Swift	10,120
7	9	A	Rotherham United	L		1-5	1-2		Beddows	7,000
8	16	H	Rotherham United	D		1-1	1-1		Beddows	9,846
9	23	H	Grimsby Town	L		2-3	2-0		Ward, Robinson (pen)	11,806
10	30	A	Grimsby Town	W		3-1	2-0		Robinson, Wright, Ward	2,500
11	Nov 6	A	Mansfield Town	W		2-0	0-0		Rogers, Robinson (pen)	4,424
12	13	H	Mansfield Town	L		2-3	1-2		Wright, Rogers	9,721
13	20	H	Notts County	W		1-0	0-0		Wright	8,251
14	27	A	Notts County	D		0-0	0-0			2,500
15	Dec 4	H	Chesterfield	W		5-0	1-0		Ashley, Barton, Robinson (2), Rogers	8,872
16	11	A	Chesterfield	L		1-3	0-2		Reynolds	2,395
17	18	H	Sheffield United	L		0-2	0-1			12,855
18	25	A	Sheffield United	D		1-1	0-0	40th	Robinson	23,863
										Apps
										Goals

FOOTBALL LEAGUE NORTH (2nd Competition)

Match No.	Date	Venue	Opponents		Round	Result	HT Score	Position	Scorers	Attendance
19	Dec 27	A	Chesterfield	W	*	2-0	0-0		Robinson (pen), Reynolds	9,500
20	Jan 1	H	Chesterfield	W	*	3-1	3-0		Russell, Ashley, Rogers	12,195
21	8	H	Nottingham Forest	D	*	0-0	0-0			11,137
22	22	H	Derby County	W	*	3-1	3-1		Reynolds, Wright, Froggatt	8,482
23	29	A	Derby County	L	*	1-4	1-2		Cockroft (pen)	10,000
24	Feb 5	A	Leicester City	D	*	1-1	0-1		Froggatt	8,200
25	12	H	Leicester City	L	*	0-3	0-2			19,320
26	19	H	Notts County	W	*	2-0	1-0		Cockroft (pen), Wright	10,070
27	26	A	Notts County	W	*	5-1	2-0	19th	Wright (3), Driver, Rogers	3,000
28	Mar 4	A	Bradford Park Avenue	L	**	0-5	0-3			11,209
29	11	H	Bradford Park Avenue	L	**	1-2	1-1		Rogers	12,830
30	18	A	Rotherham United	L	^	1-3	1-1	37th	Froggatt	5,000
31	25	H	Rotherham United	D	^	0-0	0-0			10,213
32	Apr 1	A	Lincoln City	L	#	1-2	1-1		Driver	3,803
33	8	H	Lincoln City	W	#	2-0	0-0		Driver, Massarella pen)	8,000
34	10	H	Huddersfield Town	D		2-2	1-1		Massarella (1 + pen)	10,555
35	15	H	Huddersfield Town	W	##	2-1	1-1		Rogers, Massarella (pen)	9,230
36	22	A	Huddersfield Town	L	##	1-5	1-3		Fox	3,448
37	29	H	York City	W		2-1	1-0		Froggatt, Rogers	5,180
38	May 6	A	York City	L		3-4	2-2	30th	J. Thompson, Rogers (2)	3,919
										Apps
										Goals

* Also League Cup Qualifying compeitions ** League Cup Knock out rounds
^ Also County Cup.
# Also combined counties cup 1st round ## semi/final

Guest players: H. Barton (Sheffield United), S. Burton (West Ham), J. Cockroft (West Ham), J. Curnow (Hull City) H.Donaldson (Notts County) G Hinsley (Bradford City) W.Reynolds (Rochdale) N.Wilkinson (Stoke) H.Wright (Wolves) G Laking (Middlesbrough) F.Wright (C.Palace)

Ashley Jack	Barton Harry	Beddows John	Briscoe Jim	Brown Wilf	Burton Stan	Catlin Ted	Cockroft Joe	Curnow Jack	Donaldson Harry	Driver Allenby	Drury Bill	Everitt Richard	Fox Oscar	Froggatt Redfern	Gabsby Ken	Goodson Harry	Hall Arthur	Herbert Frank	Hinsley George	Hunt Doug	Ibbotson Wilf	Laking George	Lowes Arnold	McCarter Jimmy	Massarella Len	Millership Walt	Morton Albert	Napier Charlie	Poulston Len	Pickering Bill	Reynolds Walter	Robinson Jackie	Rogers Alf	Russell Dave	Scholfield Ernest	Swift Hugh	Thompson Jackie	Thompson Ron	Wakley Ivor	Ward Tommy	Westlake Frank	Wilkinson Norman	Wiseman Ken	Woodhead Dennis	Wright Frank	Wright Horace		
2							6															7			5	1			3		8		4		11	10			9								
2						3	6											5											1					7	8		4		11	10			9								
2																				6								5						3	7	8		4		11	10			9			1					
2						3	6					9				5														1					7	8		4		11	10											
2						3	6					9																	5							7	8		4		11	10		1									
2		9				3							7					6									5	1									4		11	10			8								
2		9				3							7					6									5									8		4		11	10		1									
2		9				3	6			11	1		7					4	10									5									8																			
2						3	6							7					4										5	1	10					8				11					9								
2					11	3	6				1		7					4										5									8										10						9		
2						3	6							7					4										5	1							8	10			11												9		
2						3	6				1		7	10				4										5										8			11												9		
2	11					3	6								10													5	1					7		8	4															9		
	7					3	6								10				4										5						11		8											2	1				9		
9	7					3	6																								5								8	10	4								2	1		11				
2	7					3	6				1			10														5						11		8	4																9		
2					7	3	6								11				5																		8	10	4										1				9		
2			9		11	3	6											7	5																		8	10	4										1						
17	4	3	1		3	16	15			1	4	2	7	5		1	1	12	1				1			14	7	1		2	7	13	8	12		10	7		2	6	2	4	1	1		7		
1	1	2																										1						1	10	3			1	1			5					3		

Ashley Jack	Barton Harry	Beddows John	Briscoe Jim	Brown Wilf	Burton Stan	Catlin Ted	Cockroft Joe	Curnow Jack	Donaldson Harry	Driver Allenby	Drury Bill	Everitt Richard	Fox Oscar	Froggatt Redfern	Gabsby Ken	Goodson Harry	Hall Arthur	Herbert Frank	Hinsley George	Hunt Doug	Ibbotson Wilf	Laking George	Lowes Arnold	McCarter Jimmy	Massarella Len	Millership Walt	Morton Albert	Napier Charlie	Poulston Len	Pickering Bill	Reynolds Walter	Robinson Jackie	Rogers Alf	Russell Dave	Scholfield Ernest	Swift Hugh	Thompson Jackie	Thompson Ron	Wakley Ivor	Ward Tommy	Westlake Frank	Wilkinson Norman	Wiseman Ken	Woodhead Dennis	Wright Frank	Wright Horace		
2						3	6							11				5															7	8	10	4								1			9			
9						3	6							11				5															7		8	4							2	1				10		
9						3	6							11				5															7		8	4							2	1				10		
9						3	6							11	1			5															7		8	4							2					10		
9						3	6							11	1			5															7		8	4							2					10		
						3	6							11				5								9	1					7		8	4							2					10		
						3	6							11						9						5	1						8	7	4							2					10		
						3	6	1						11														5							7	9	8	4							2					10		
2						3	6	1		9				11				4									5							7		8															10		
						3	6	1						11				4									5							7		8			9					2					10		
						3	6	1										5					11			9							7		8	4							2					10		
9						3	6	1						8				5							7											4	11							2					10		
2						3	6	1										4			9				7	5								8		11					10								
						3	4		1	9				11				5						10							6	7	8				2													
						3	6		1	9				11				4							7	5							8			2		10										
5				3					1					11		4					9				7					6			8			2		10										
2									1				10	11		4					9				7	5				6			8			3													
						3	4		1				10	11				5			9										6	7		8			2													
							4		1					10				5			9			11	7					6			8			3					2						
						3	4		1									5				2			7				6			9	8		11		10												
10				1		17	18	6	7	3			2	17	2	2		16		1	5	1	2	1	7	9	2		1	5	12	5	18	10	3	7	1	2		1	11	3			1	11		
1							2			3			1	4												4							2		7	1														5		

1944-45

Football League North (1st Competition)

Manager: Eric Taylor

Did you know that?

Final League Position: 23rd
Final League Position: 33rd

On 26 May 1945, a game against Sheffield United counted as both a Football League (North) game and the second leg of the County Cup Final, with Wednesday winning 4–2 for the League game, and the Cup 7–3 on aggregate. The crowd ran onto the pitch with five minutes still to go, thinking the whistle had gone, holding the game up for six minutes.

Match No.	Date	Venue	Opponents		Round	Result	HT Score	Position	Scorers	Attendance
1	Aug 26	H	Sheffield United	D		1-1	1-0		Ward	17,888
2	Sep 2	A	Sheffield United	W		1-0	0-0		Ibbotson	15,684
3	9	A	Notts County	L		0-2	0-1			6,000
4	16	H	Notts County	W		6-1	3-0		Catlin, Massarella (2), Froggatt, Thompson (2)	9,430
5	23	H	Chesterfield	L		0-1	0-0	15th		10,459
6	30	A	Chesterfield	L		2-5	1-1		Thompson, Robinson	9,889
7	Oct 7	A	Mansfield Town	L		0-2	0-0			4,300
8	14	H	Mansfield Town	L		1-6	0-3		Massarella	7,908
9	21	H	Rotherham United	W		1-0	0-0		Robinson	16,321
10	28	A	Rotherham United	D		3-3	1-1		Tomlinson, Fox, Massarella	12,994
11	Nov 4	A	Lincoln City	W		3-0	2-0		Robinson (3)	4,572
12	11	H	Lincoln City	W		2-1	0-0		Massarella, Cockroft	9,332
13	18	A	Grimsby Town	W		2-1	2-1		Fox, Massarella	5,113
14	25	H	Grimsby Town *	L		2-3	2-1		Rogers (2)	3,026
15	Dec 2	H	Nottingham Forest	W		2-1	2-0		Hawkswell, Tomlinson	8,092
16	9	A	Nottingham Forest	L		0-1	0-1			5,902
17	16	A	Barnsley	W		3-2	2-2		Ward, Massarella, Tomlinson	5,811
18	23	H	Barnsley	W		5-0	2-0	23rd	Tomlinson (2), Rogers, Hawkswell, Robinson	10,000

* Played at Doncaster

Apps
Goals

FOOTBALL LEAGUE NORTH (2nd Competition)

Match No.	Date	Venue	Opponents		Round	Result	HT Score	Position	Scorers	Attendance
19	Dec 25	H	Sheffield United	L	*	1-2	0-2		Hawkswell	18,580
20	30	A	Sheffield United	L	*	0-1	0-0			19,011
21	Jan 6	A	Grimsby Town	L	*	1-4	1-2		Tomlinson	3,000
22	13	H	Grimsby Town	D	*	2-2	1-0		Hawkswell, Scholfield	5,539
23	20	H	Rotherham United	L	*	1-4	1-1		J. Thompson	6,501
24	27	A	Rotherham United	D	*	1-1	1-1		Herbert	8,000
25	3	A	Doncaster Rovers	W	*	3-1	1-1		J. Thompson (2), Robinson	9,340
26	10	H	Doncaster Rovers	L	*	1-6	1-3		Herbert	13,804
27	17	A	Lincoln City	L	*	3-5	1-2		Rogers (2), Tomlinson	2,725
28	24	H	Lincoln City	L	*	1-3	1-1	55th	Lowes	5,859
29	Mar 3	A	Leeds United	L		3-4	1-3		Herbert, Lindsay (2)	7,000
30	10	H	Doncaster Rovers	W	#	1-0	0-0		Froggatt	8,827
31	17	H	Leeds United	D		1-1	1-1		Rogers	7,941
32	24	A	Blackburn Rovers	D		2-2	1-2		Lindsay (2)	3,000
33	31	H	Blackburn Rovers	W		2-0	0-0		Lindsay, R. Thompson	9,178
34	Apr 2	A	Leicester City	L		1-2	1-2		Bates	7,500
35	7	A	Halifax Town	L		2-3	1-1		Lindsay (2)	3,000
36	14	H	Halifax Town	W		7-0	3-0		Lindsay (3), Tomlinson (2), Turton, Rogers	4,819
37	21	H	Bradford Park Avenue	W		3-1	1-1		Robinson (2), Tomlinson	10,237
38	28	A	Bradford Park Avenue	L		3-5	2-3		Hawkswell, Tomlinson, Froggatt	3,578
39	May 5	A	Barnsley	D	# S/F	3-3	3-0		Rogers, Robinson, Froggatt	3,624
40	9	A	Sheffield United	L	##	0-2	0-0			15,045
41	12	H	Barnsley	W	# S/F Re	4-1	2-0		Lindsay (2), Rogers, Froggatt	9,155
42	19	A	Sheffield United	W	# F 1L	3-1	3-0		Robinson, Rogers, Tomlinson	16,359
43	26	H	Sheffield United	W	# F 2L	4-2	2-1		Robinson, Tomlinson (2), Lindsay	15,464

* Also League Cup qualifying competition # Sheffield County Cup ## VE Match

Apps
Goals

Guest players: A. Calverley (Huddersfield T), J. Cockroft (West Ham), S. Fisher (Barnsley), J. Hawkswell (Chesterfield), H. Medhurst (Crystal Palace), J. Smith (Sheffield United), F. White (Sheffield United), F. Wright (Crystal Palace)

Ashley Jack	Bannister Keith	Bates George	Beach Doug	Calverley Alf	Catlin Ted	Cockroft Joe	Donaldson Harry	Driver Allenby	Fisher Stan	Fox Oscar	Froggatt Redfern	Gabsby Ken	Gale Tom	Goodson Harry	Hanford Harry	Hawkswell Jim	Herbert Frank	Ibbotson Wilf	Kippax Dennis	Lindsay Jack	Lowes Arnold	Massarella Len	Medhurst Harry	Millership Walt	Parkin Fred	Pickering Bill	Robinson Jackie	Rogers Alf	Scholfield Ernest	Smith Jack	Stewart Reg	Swift Hugh	Thompson Jackie	Thompson Ron	Tomlinson Charlie	Turton Cyril	Wakley Ivor	Ward Tommy	Westlake Frank	White Fred	Wright Frank
					3	6					10	1		4								7		5			8					2			11			9			
					3	6					7	1		4				9						5			8					2	10		11						
					3	6	7	8				1		4										5							9	2	10		11						
					3	6					8	1		4				9				7		5								2	10		11						
					3	6		9			8	1					4					7		5								2	10		11						
					3	6		9			7	1		4										5			8					2	10		11						
					2	6	1	8		10	7							9						5		3									11			4			
					3	4	1	8		10								9				7				6									11	5			2		
						6				7														5		3	8					2	10		11			4		1	9
						6				10							4					7		5		3		8				2			11					1	9
						6				10							4					7				3	8					2			11	5				1	9
						6				10												7		5		3		8				2			11		1	4			9
						6				10												7		5		3		8				2			11		1	4			9
						6				10	7					9										3		8				2			11	5	1	4			
						6				10						9								5		3	8	7				2			11		1	4			
						6				10	7													5		3	9	8				2			11		1	4			
						6				10						9						7		5		3		8				2			11		1	4			
					2	6										9						7				3	10	8							11	5	1	4			
					9	18	3	5		11	8	6		5		4	3	4				10		14		12	8	8			1	15	6		18	4	7	10	1	3	5
					1	1				2	1					2		1				7					6	3					3		5			2			

Ashley Jack	Bannister Keith	Bates George	Beach Doug	Calverley Alf	Catlin Ted	Cockroft Joe	Donaldson Harry	Driver Allenby	Fisher Stan	Fox Oscar	Froggatt Redfern	Gabsby Ken	Gale Tom	Goodson Harry	Hanford Harry	Hawkswell Jim	Herbert Frank	Ibbotson Wilf	Kippax Dennis	Lindsay Jack	Lowes Arnold	Massarella Len	Medhurst Harry	Millership Walt	Parkin Fred	Pickering Bill	Robinson Jackie	Rogers Alf	Scholfield Ernest	Smith Jack	Stewart Reg	Swift Hugh	Thompson Jackie	Thompson Ron	Tomlinson Charlie	Turton Cyril	Wakley Ivor	Ward Tommy	Westlake Frank	White Fred	Wright Frank
						6				10						9			7							3	8					2			11	5	1	4			
						6				10						9	4					7		5		3						2			11		1	8			
						6				10						9						7		5		3						2	8		11		1	4			
						6				8	7					9								5		3			11			2			10	4				1	
						6				10	7													5		3	8					2	9		11	4				1	
				11		6			9								8					7		5		3						2			10	4				1	
						6				7							9							5		3	8					2	10		11			4		1	
						6											9					7		5		3	8					2	10		11			4		1	
	3		2			4				7							9									6		8					10		11		1	5			
			2			6				7							5				9					3		8					10		11	4	1				
	4					6				7		1					8			9						3		10				2			11	5					
						6				7	10			4			8			9					1	3						2			11	5					
		7				6					10			4						9					1	3		8				2			11	5					
		7				6					10			4						9					1	3		8				2			11	5					
2		7				6					10			4	5					9					1	3								8	11						
		7				6					10			4						9					1	3						2		8	11	5					
		7				6				10			5							9					1	3		8				2			11	4					
		7				6					10		5							9					1	3		8				2			11	4					
						6					10		5							9					1	3	8	7				2			11	4					
		7				6					10		5			9									1	3		8				2			11	4					
						6					10		5							9					1	3	8	7				2			11	4					
		7				6					10	1								9						3		8				2			11	5		4			
2		7				6					10		5							9								8		1		3			11	4					
2						6					10		5							9			1				8	7				3			11	4					
2						6					10		5							9			1				8	7				3			11	4					
4	2	9	2	1		25			1	11	15	2	8	5	1	5	8		1	14	1	4	2	7	10	22	8	14	1	1		22	6	2	25	19	5	7		5	
		1									4					3	3			13	1						6	7	1				3	1	9	1					

1945-46

Football League North

Manager: Eric Taylor

Did you know that?

Final League Position: 5th

During the season, Wednesday wore blue-and-white-hooped shirts.

Match No.	Date	Venue	Opponents		Round	Result	HT Score	Position	Scorers	Attendance
1	Aug 25	H	Sunderland	W		6-3	4-2		Robinson (pen + 2), Rogers (3)	19,219
2	Sep1	A	Sunderland	L		0-1	0-0			22,300
3	8	A	Sheffield United	W		3-1	0-1		Robinson, Lindsay, Tomlinson	30,542
4	12	A	Manchester City	W		5-1	3-0		R. Thompson, Tomlinson, Fox, Eastwood (og), Lindsay	7,000
5	15	H	Sheffield United	W		2-1	0-1	4th	Robinson (2)	32,512
6	22	H	Middlesbrough	W		2-1	1-0	2nd	Froggatt, Lindsay	20,334
7	29	A	Middlesbrough	L		0-2	0-0	3rd		12,506
8	Oct 6	A	Stoke City	L		0-3	0-2			24,000
9	13	H	Stoke City	W		1-0	1-0	7th	Lindsay	33,389
10	20	H	Grimsby Town	W		4-1	1-1	6th	J. Thompson (2), Lindsay, Rogers (pen)	18,444
11	27	A	Grimsby Town	W		2-1	2-1	2nd	Lindsay, Tomlinson	10,083
12	Nov 3	A	Blackpool	L		1-5	1-3		Lindsay	14,087
13	10	H	Blackpool	W		3-2	2-1	2nd	Lindsay, Robinson (2)	25,619
14	17	H	Liverpool	L		2-3	2-0		Rogers, Froggatt	23,514
15	24	A	Liverpool	W		2-0	0-0		Lindsay, Tomlinson	33,000
16	Dec 1	A	Bury	W		2-1	1-0		R.Thompson, Froggatt	9,834
17	8	H	Bury	W		2-0	0-0	2nd	Cockroft (pen), Lindsay	16,963
18	15	H	Blackburn Rovers	D		1-1	0-0	2nd	Cockroft	17,768
19	22	A	Blackburn Rovers	L		1-2	0-1	3rd	Hunt	7,500
20	25	A	Bradford Park Avenue	L		2-3	2-0		Robinson, Lindsay	18,900
21	26	H	Bradford Park Avenue	W		3-0	0-0	5th	Robinson (1 + pen), Froggatt	32,078
22	29	H	Manchester City	D		1-1	1-0		Tomlinson	24,684
23	Jan 1	A	Newcastle United	L		0-2	0-0	6th		47,228
24	12	A	Burnley	D		2-2	1-1		Froggatt, Ward	10,807
25	19	H	Burnley	D		1-1	1-0		Hunt	15,109
26	Feb 2	A	Huddersfield Town	L		2-3	1-2		Froggatt (2)	8,912
27	4	H	Huddersfield Town	W		3-0	1-0		Lindsay, Froggatt, Tomlinson	10,090
28	16	H	Chesterfield	W		1-0	1-0		Tomlinson	31,304
29	20	A	Chesterfield	D		1-1	1-0		Driver	12,700
30	23	H	Barnsley	L		0-3	0-2			24,657
31	Mar 2	A	Barnsley	L		0-4	0-3			17,000
32	9	A	Everton	D		2-2	0-1	4th	J. Thompson, Ward	48,440
33	16	H	Everton	D		0-0	0-0			27,301
34	30	A	Bolton Wanderers	L		1-2	1-2		Ward	20,531
35	Apr 1	H	Bolton Wanderers	D		0-0	0-0			13,500
36	6	A	Preston North End	W		1-0	1-0		Robinson	15,000
37	13	H	Preston North End	W		2-0	2-0		Robinson (2)	16,804
38	20	A	Manchester United	L		0-4	0-3			34,000
39	22	A	Leeds United	W		1-0	0-0		Driver	14,000
40	23	H	Leeds United	W		2-0	1-0		Wands, Robinson (pen)	14,000
41	27	H	Manchester United	W		1-0	0-0		Robinson	12,000
42	May 4	H	Newcastle United	L		2-3	0-2		Kippax, Robinson (pen)	20,000
										Apps
									One own-goal	Goals

FA Cup

Match No.	Date	Venue	Opponents		Round	Result	HT Score	Position	Scorers	Attendance
43	Jan 5	A	Mansfield Town	D	3R 1L	0-0	0-0			9,000
44	10	H	Mansfield Town	W	3R 2L	5-0	1-0		J. Thompson, Ward, Froggatt, Aveyard, Tomlinson	22,208
45	26	H	York City	W	4R 1L	5-1	3-1		J. Thompson, Driver (2), Aveyard, Froggatt	33,363
46	30	A	York City	W	4R 2L	6-1	1-0		Tomlinson (3), Driver, J. Thompson, Froggatt	10,447
47	Feb 9	A	Stoke City	L	5R 1L	0-2	0-1			40,452
48	11	H	Stoke City	D	5R 2L	0-0	0-0			62,728
										Apps
										Goals

Aveyard Walter	Cockroft Joe	Driver Allenby	Fox Oscar	Froggatt Redfern	Gale Tom	Goodfellow Derwick	Goodson Harry	Hunt Doug	Kippax Dennis	Lindsay Jack	Lowes Arnold	Mackenzie Laurie	McCarter Jimmy	Morton Albert	Napier Charlie	Packard Edgar	Pickering Bill	Robinson Jackie	Rogers Alf	Smith Roy	Stewart Reg	Swift Hugh	Thompson Jackie	Thompson Ron	Tomlinson Charlie	Turton Cyril	Wakley Ivor	Wands Alex	Ward Tommy	Westlake Frank
	6			10	5					9				1			3	8	7			2			11	4				
	6			10	5					9	8			1			3		7			2			11	4				
	6			10	5					9				1			3	8	7			2			11	4				
	6		7	10	5					9				1			3					2		8	11	4				
	6			7	5					9				1	10		3	8				2			11	4				
	6			10	5					9				1			3	8				2			11	4			7	
	6	7		10	5					9				1			3		8			2			11	4				
	6			10	5					9				1			3		7			2		8	11	4				
	6			10	5					9				1			3	8	7			2			11	4				
	6				5					9				1			3		7			2	10	8	11	4				
	6				5					9				1			3		7			2	10	8	11	4				
	6				5					9				1			3	8	7			2		10	11	4				
	6			10						9				1		5	3	8	7			2			11	4				
	6			10	5					9				1			3		7			2		8	11	4				
	6			10	5					9				1			3		7			2		8	11	4				
	6		7	10	5					9				1			3					2		8	11	4				
	6		7	10	5					9				1			3					2		8	11	4				
	6		7		5	1				9	10						3	8				2			11	4				
				10	5	1		9		7							3	8	6			2			11	4				
				10	5	1				9							3	8	7			2			11	4		6		
				10	5	1				9							3	8				2			11	4		6	7	
				10	5	1				9							3					2		8	11	4		6	7	
	4			10		1				9							3	8				2			11	5		6	7	
	6			10			4			9							3					2		8	11	5	1		7	
9	4				5	1		10									3					2	8		11			6	7	
	4	7		10	5	1		9														2		8	11			6		3
	4	7		10	5					9												3			11		1	6	8	2
	6	8		10	5	1		9					11									2			7	4				3
	6	8		10	5					9			11							1		2			7	4				3
	6	8		10	5	1		9					11									2			7	4				3
	4			10	5	1			7	9							3					2			11			6	8	
	4			10	5	1			7								3					2	8		11			6	9	
	4			10	5	1			7								3					2	8		11			6	9	
	6			10		1			7							5	3	8				2			11	4			9	
				10		1			7			6				5	3	8				2			11	4			9	
	4	8				1			7							5		10				3			11			6	9	2
	4	8				1			7							5		10				3			11			6	9	2
	4	8				1			7	9						5		10				3			11			6		2
		8	7			1				9		4				5		10				3			11			6		2
	4		7	8		1				9						5		10				3			11			6		2
	4			8		1			7	9						5		10				3			11			6		2
	4			8		1			7	9						5		10				3			11			6		2
1	36	10	6	33	30	22	1	5	10	32	2	2	3	17	1	10	30	21	14	1		42	5	12	42	29	2	17	14	12
	2	2	1	8				2	1	12								17	5				3	2	7			1	3	

Aveyard Walter	Cockroft Joe	Driver Allenby	Fox Oscar	Froggatt Redfern	Gale Tom	Goodfellow Derwick	Goodson Harry	Hunt Doug	Kippax Dennis	Lindsay Jack	Lowes Arnold	Mackenzie Laurie	McCarter Jimmy	Morton Albert	Napier Charlie	Packard Edgar	Pickering Bill	Robinson Jackie	Rogers Alf	Smith Roy	Stewart Reg	Swift Hugh	Thompson Jackie	Thompson Ron	Tomlinson Charlie	Turton Cyril	Wakley Ivor	Wands Alex	Ward Tommy	Westlake Frank
9	4			10		1											3	8			5	2			11			6	7	
9	4			10		1											3				5	2	8		11			6	7	
9	4	7		10	5	1											3					2	8		11			6		
9	4	7		10	5	1											3					2	8		11			6		
9	4	7		10	5	1											3					2	8		11			6		
9	4	7		10	5	1											3	8				2			11			6		
6	6	4		6	4	6											6	2			2	6	4		6			6	2	
2		3		3																			3		4				1	

1946-47

Division Two

Manager: Eric Taylor

Did you know that?

Final League Position: 20th

On 7 June 1947 Chesterfield's George Milburn netted three penalties as his side beat Wednesday 4–2 at Saltergate. This is the latest date that Wednesday have finished a League season.

Match No.	Date	Venue	Opponents		Round	Result	HT Score	Position	Scorers	Attendance
1	Aug 31	A	Luton Town	L		1-4	1-2		Robinson	20,950
2	Sep 2	H	Barnsley	L		2-4	1-3		Ward, Lindsay	30,028
3	7	H	Plymouth Argyle	W		2-1	2-0	18th	Robinson, Aveyard	27,326
4	9	A	Barnsley	L		1-4	1-3	19th	Robinson	27,250
5	14	A	Leicester City	W		5-3	1-2	12th	Tomlinson, Ward (2), Robinson (2)	26,181
6	16	H	Fulham	D		1-1	0-1	12th	Robinson	21,000
7	21	H	Chesterfield	L		0-1	0-1	16th		28,476
8	28	A	Millwall	D		2-2	1-1	18th	Aveyard (2)	27,700
9	Oct 5	H	Bradford Park Avenue	L		1-2	0-2	19th	Froggatt	20,590
10	12	A	Manchester City	L		1-2	0-0	21st	Briscoe	36,413
11	19	H	Burnley	L		1-2	0-2	21st	Briscoe	22,083
12	26	A	Tottenham Hotspur	L		0-2	0-2	21st		33,216
13	Nov 2	H	Swansea Town	W		3-0	0-0	20th	Briscoe, Lowes (2)	22,793
14	9	A	Newcastle United	L		0-4	0-1	21st		46,916
15	16	H	West Bromwich Alb	D		2-2	0-1	21st	Lowes (pen), Dailey	23,964
16	23	A	Birmingham City	L		1-3	1-2	21st	Ward	32,425
17	30	H	Coventry City	W		4-2	1-1	21st	Dailey (2), Hunt, Ward	24,590
18	Dec 7	A	Nottingham Forest	D		2-2	2-1	20th	Ward, Dailey	18,307
19	14	H	Southampton	W		3-0	1-0	18th	Ward (2), Dailey	15,404
20	21	A	Newport County	L		3-4	1-1	20th	Ward (2), Slynn	10,680
21	25	A	Bury	L		2-4	2-1	21st	Dailey, Slynn	11,913
22	26	H	Bury	L		2-5	0-5	21st	Dailey, Hunt	41,183
23	28	H	Luton Town	D		1-1	0-0	21st	Ward	29,495
24	Jan 1	H	West Ham United	D		1-1	1-0	21st	Wands	31,192
25	4	A	Plymouth Argyle	L		1-4	1-2	21st	Slynn	21,698
26	18	H	Leicester City	L		1-3	1-0	21st	Dailey	34,858
27	Feb 1	H	Millwall	W		3-0	0-0	20th	Ward, Hunt, Dailey	25,082
28	22	A	Burnley	L		0-2	0-1	21st		25,083
29	Mar 1	H	Tottenham Hotspur	W		5-1	2-1	19th	Dailey (3), Tomlinson, Hunt	23,144
30	12	A	Bradford Park Avenue	D		1-1	1-0	19th	Dailey	5,718
31	22	A	West Bromwich Alb	L		1-2	0-0	20th	Hunt	35,448
32	29	H	Birmingham City	W		1-0	1-0	20th	Harris (og)	27,500
33	Apr 5	A	Coventry City	L		1-5	1-3	20th	Tooze (og)	19,478
34	7	A	Fulham	W		2-1	2-0	20th	Hunt, Ward	26,651
35	12	H	Nottingham Forest	W		2-0	1-0	19th	Ward, Slynn	30,092
36	19	A	Southampton	L		1-3	1-1	19th	Ward	13,514
37	26	H	Newport County	W		2-1	0-0	19th	Tomlinson, Cockroft (pen)	21,564
38	May 3	A	West Ham United	L		1-2	0-1	20th	Ward	20,977
39	10	A	Swansea Town	L		0-2	0-0	20th		22,356
40	24	H	Newcastle United	D		1-1	1-0	20th	Ward	28,405
41	26	H	Manchester City	W		1-0	1-0	20th	Ward	33,390
42	Jun 7	A	Chesterfield	L		2-4	1-1	20th	Slynn, Hunt	11,161
										Apps
									Two own-goals	Goals

FA Cup

Match No.	Date	Venue	Opponents		Round	Result	HT Score	Position	Scorers	Attendance
43	Jan 11	H	Blackpool	W	3R	4-1	2-0		Fox, Froggatt (2), Wands	31,240
44	25	H	Everton	W	4R	2-1	2-1		Froggatt, Tomlinson	62,250
45	Feb 20	H	Preston North End	L	5R	0-2	0-0			50,247
										Apps
										Goals

Aveyard Walter	Bannister Keith	Briscoe Jim	Cockroft Joe	Dailey Jimmy	Fox Oscar	Froggatt Redfern	Gale Tom	Godfellow Derwick	Hunt George	Kenny Mick	Kippax Dennis	Lindsay Jack	Logan Johnny	Lowes Arnold	Mackenzie Laurie	McCarter Jimmy	Marriott Jackie	Packard Edgar	Robinson Jackie	Rogers Alf	Slynn Frank	Smith Roy	Stewart Reg	Swift Hugh	Thompson Ron	Tomlinson Charlie	Turton Cyril	Wands Alex	Ward Tommy	Westlake Frank	Witcomb Doug	Woodhead Dennis
			6			10		1							4				8	7				3		11	5		9	2		
			4			10		1				9		6				5	8					3		11			7	2		
9			4			10		1						6				5	8					3		11			7	2		
9			4			10		1						6				5	8					3		11			7	2		
			4			7				3				10					8			1		2		11	5	6	9			
			4			7								10					8			1		2		11	5	6	9	3		
			4			7				3				10					8			1		2		11	5	6	9			
9			4			10				3	7			8		11						1		2			5	6				
9			4			10				3				8		11				7		1		2			5	6				
		9			7	10				3				8		11		4				1	5	2				6				
		9	10			7				3				8		11		4				1	5	2				6				
		9	6		7	10				3				8		11		4				1	5	2								
		9	6		7	10				3				8		11		4				1	5	2								
			6		7	10			8	3				9				4				1	5	2		11						
			6	9		7			8	3				10				4				1	5	2		11						
				9	7				8	3				6	4			5			11	1		2					10			
				9		7			8	3				6	4			5				1		2		11			10			
				9					8	3				6	4			5		7	11	1		2					10			
				9		7			8					6	4			5			11	1		3					10	2		
			4	9		7			8					6				5			11	1		3					10	2		
	6		4	9		7			8									5			11	1		3					10	2		
	6			9		7			8	3				4				5			11	1							10	2		
						7		1	9				4	10				5			11			3				6	8	2		
						7		1	8				4	9				5			11			3				6	10	2		
		9	6			10		1	8				4					5			11			3					7	2		
			4	9		10	5		8												11	1		3				6	7	2		
				9		10	5		8				6								7	1		3		11			4	2		
			4	9		10	5		8								7				11	1		2				6		3		
			6	9		10	5		8												7	1		3		11				2	4	
			6	9		10	5		8												7	1		3		11				2	4	
			6	9		10			8									5			7	1		3		11				2	4	
			6	9		10			8								7	5			11	1		3						2	4	
			6	9		10	5		8								7				11	1		3						2	4	
			6			10			8								7				11	1		3			5		9	2	4	
			6			10			8								7	5			11	1		3					9	2	4	
			6			10			8								7	5			11	1		3					9	2	4	
			6						8								7	5			11	1		3		10			9	2	4	
			6						8								7	5			11	1		3		10			9	2	4	
			6	9					10								7	5			11	1		3					8	2	4	
			6						8									5			7	1		3		10			9	2	4	11
			6						8									5			7	1		3		10			9	2	4	11
			6						8									5			7	1		3		10			9	2	4	11
4	2	5	33	17	5	34	6	7	29	14	1	1	4	22	5	6	9	29	7	3	26	35	6	41		19	7	11	28	29	14	3
3		3	1	13		1			7			1		3					6		5						3		1	18			

Aveyard Walter	Bannister Keith	Briscoe Jim	Cockroft Joe	Dailey Jimmy	Fox Oscar	Froggatt Redfern	Gale Tom	Godfellow Derwick	Hunt George	Kenny Mick	Kippax Dennis	Lindsay Jack	Logan Johnny	Lowes Arnold	Mackenzie Laurie	McCarter Jimmy	Marriott Jackie	Packard Edgar	Robinson Jackie	Rogers Alf	Slynn Frank	Smith Roy	Stewart Reg	Swift Hugh	Thompson Ron	Tomlinson Charlie	Turton Cyril	Wands Alex	Ward Tommy	Westlake Frank	Witcomb Doug	Woodhead Dennis
			4	9	7	10	5		8												11	1		3				6		2		
			6	9		10	5		8				4									1		3	7	11				2		
				9		10	5		8				6								7	1		3		11			4	2		
			2	3	1	3	3		3				2								2	3		3	1	2		1	1	3		
					1	3																				1		1				

League Table

	P	W	D	L	F	A	Pts
Manchester City	42	26	10	6	78	35	62
Burnley	42	22	14	6	65	29	58
Birmingham City	42	25	5	12	74	33	55
Chesterfield	42	18	14	10	58	44	50
Newcastle United	42	19	10	13	95	62	48
Tottenham Hotspur	42	17	14	11	65	53	48
West Bromwich Albion	42	20	8	14	88	75	48
Coventry City	42	16	13	13	66	59	45
Leicester City	42	18	7	17	69	64	43
Barnsley	42	17	8	17	84	86	42
Nottingham Forest	42	15	10	17	69	74	40
West Ham United	42	16	8	18	70	76	40
Luton Town	42	16	7	19	71	73	39
Southampton	42	15	9	18	69	76	39
Fulham	42	15	9	18	63	74	39
Bradford Park Avenue	42	14	11	17	65	77	39
Bury	42	12	12	18	80	78	36
Millwall	42	14	8	20	56	79	36
Plymouth Argyle	42	14	5	23	79	96	33
SHEFFIELD WEDNESDAY	42	12	8	22	67	88	32
Swansea Town	42	11	7	24	55	83	29
Newport County	42	10	3	29	61	133	23

1947-48

Division Two

Manager: Eric Taylor

Did you know that?

Final League Position: 4th

On top of the South Stand the incorrect formation date of 1866 was replaced by the correct figures of 1867.

On 17 May Wednesday played Sheffield United in a friendly in Douglas, Isle of Man, with the game finishing as a 2–2 draw.

On 23 December 1947, when Wednesday played away at Millwall, the match programme had the name of Wednesday's A team that had been telephoned to Millwall in error.

Match No.	Date	Venue	Opponents		Round	Result	HT Score	Position	Scorers	Attendance
1	Aug 23	H	Millwall	W		3-2	1-0		Ward, Froggatt, Woodhead	29,860
2	27	A	Southampton	L		1-3	1-0	14th	Hunt	16,615
3	30	A	Tottenham Hotspur	L		1-5	1-4	17th	Rogers	36,796
4	Sep 1	H	Southampton	L		1-2	1-1	18th	Dailey	23,289
5	6	H	Barnsley	W		5-2	2-2	15th	Dailey (5)	33,925
6	10	A	Bury	W		2-1	2-0	13th	Lowes, Woodhead	14,265
7	13	H	Cardiff City	W		2-1	1-1	9th	Woodhead, Witcomb	36,289
8	15	H	Bury	D		2-2	1-1	8th	Froggatt, Dailey	27,230
9	20	A	Bradford Park Avenue	L		0-2	0-1	13th		21,818
10	27	H	Nottingham Forest	W		2-1	1-1	8th	Lowes, Woodhead	33,052
11	Oct 4	A	Doncaster Rovers	W		1-0	0-0	7th	Dailey	28,199
12	11	A	Plymouth Argyle	W		2-0	0-0	6th	Dailey, Woodhead	21,699
13	18	H	Luton Town	W		1-0	0-0	5th	Dailey	40,297
14	25	A	Brentford	L		0-1	0-0	6th		29,024
15	Nov 1	H	Leicester City	D		1-1	1-1	6th	Froggatt	38,992
16	8	A	Leeds United	D		2-2	1-2	7th	Quigley (2)	32,500
17	15	H	Fulham	W		2-0	1-0	6th	Rogers, Quigley	32,102
18	22	A	Coventry City	L		1-3	1-1	6th	Quigley	21,187
19	29	H	Newcastle United	W		1-0	0-0	6th	Froggatt	41,355
20	Dec 6	A	Birmingham City	L		0-1	0-1	7th		31,217
21	13	H	West Bromwich Alb	L		1-2	0-1	8th	Witcomb	36,200
22	20	A	Millwall	D		0-0	0-0	8th		18,661
23	26	H	West Ham United	W		5-3	4-1	8th	Quigley (4), Lowes	37,343
24	27	A	West Ham United	W		4-1	3-0	7th	Froggatt, Quigley (2), Woodhead	28,480
25	Jan 3	H	Tottenham Hotspur	W		1-0	1-0	4th	Quigley	48,007
26	17	A	Barnsley	L		1-3	0-2	5th	Rogers	33,060
27	31	A	Cardiff City	L		1-2	0-1	7th	Froggatt	33,147
28	Feb 7	H	Bradford Park Avenue	W		3-1	1-1	5th	Quigley (2), Jordan	36,806
29	14	A	Nottingham Forest	D		0-0	0-0	6th		29,702
30	28	H	Plymouth Argyle	D		1-1	0-1	6th	Quigley	27,083
31	Mar 6	A	Luton Town	D		1-1	1-1	6th	Woodhead	16,888
32	20	A	Leicester City	W		3-2	0-1	6th	Quigley (2), Jordan	26,963
33	26	A	Chesterfield	W		2-0	2-0	5th	Froggatt, Quigley	25,600
34	27	H	Leeds United	W		3-1	1-1	5th	Jordan, Quigley (2)	38,557
35	29	H	Chesterfield	W		1-0	0-0	5th	Froggatt	40,650
36	Apr 3	A	Fulham	W		2-0	0-0	3rd	Froggatt, Woodhead	22,000
37	5	H	Doncaster Rovers	W		2-0	1-0	3rd	Froggatt, Quigley	51,467
38	10	H	Coventry City	D		1-1	1-1	3rd	Quigley	38,695
39	12	H	Brentford	D		1-1	0-0	3rd	Witcomb (pen)	36,170
40	17	A	Newcastle United	L		2-4	1-1	3rd	Witcomb (pen), Marriott	66,480
41	24	H	Birmingham City	D		0-0	0-0	4th		25,990
42	May 1	A	West Bromwich Alb	D		1-1	1-0	4th	Quigley	24,818
										Apps
										Goals

FA Cup

Match No.	Date	Venue	Opponents		Round	Result	HT Score	Position	Scorers	Attendance
43	Jan 10	A	Cardiff City *	W	3R	2-1	0-1		Quigley (pen), Lowes	47,000
44	Jan 24	A	Leicester City	L	4R	1-2	0-2		Lowes	36,517
										Apps
										Goals

* After extra-time. Score at full-time 1-1

Cockroft Joe	Dailey Jimmy	Fox Oscar	Froggatt Redfern	Hunt George	Ibbotson Wilf	Jordan Clarrie	Lowes Arnold	McIntosh Dave	Mackenzie Laurie	Marriott Jackie	Morton Albert	Packard Edgar	Quigley Eddie	Rogers Alf	Slynn Frank	Smith Roy	Swift Hugh	Tomlinson Charlie	Turton Cyril	Ward Tommy	Westlake Frank	Witcomb Doug	Woodhead Dennis
6			10	8							1				7		3		5	9	2	4	11
			10	8					6		1				7		3		5	9	2	4	11
6			10	9							1			8	7		3		5		2	4	11
6	9		10				8				1				7		3		5		2	4	11
6	9		10				8				1				7		3		5		2	4	11
6	9		10				8				1				7		3		5		2	4	11
6	9		10				8				1				7		3		5		2	4	11
6	9		10				8				1				7		3		5		2	4	11
6	9		10				8				1				7		3		5		2	4	11
6	9		10				8				1				7		3		5		2	4	11
6	9		10				8				1				7		3		5		2	4	11
6	9		10								1		8		7		3		5		2	4	11
6	9		10								1		8		7		3		5		2	4	11
6	9		10								1		8		7		3		5		2	4	11
6	9		10							7	1		8				3		5		2	4	11
6			10							7	1		8				3		5	9	2	4	11
6										7	1	5	8	10			3			9	2	4	11
6					10					7	1	5	8				3			9	2	4	11
6	9		10							7	1		8				3		5		2	4	11
6	9		10							7	1		8				3		5		2	4	11
6	9		10							7	1		8				3		5		2	4	11
6			10				8				1	5	9		7		3				2	4	11
6			10				8				1	5	9		7		3				2	4	11
6		7	10				8					5	9			1	3				2	4	11
6		7	10				8					5	9			1	3				2	4	11
6		7					8						9	10		1	3		5		2	4	11
6		7	10				8						9			1	3		5		2	4	11
6			10			9							8			1	3	11	5	7	2	4	
6			10			9							8			1	3	11	5	7	2	4	
6		7	10			9							8			1	3	11	5		2	4	
6		7	10			9							8			1	3		5		2	4	11
6		7	10			9							8			1	3		5		2	4	11
6		7	10			9							8			1	3		5		2	4	11
6			10			9				7			8			1	3	11	5		2	4	
6			10			9				7			8			1	3	11	5		2	4	
6			10			9		1		7			8				3		5		2	4	11
6			10			9		1		7			8				3	11	5		2	4	
6			10			9		1		7			8				3		5		2	4	11
6			10			9		1		7			8				3		5		2	4	11
6			10			9		1		7			8				3		5		2	4	11
6			10			9		1		7				8			3		5		2	4	11
6			10			9		1		7			8				3		5		2	4	11
41	15	8	39	3	1	15	14	7	1	16	23	6	30	4	16	12	42	6	36	7	42	42	36
	10		10	1		3	3			1			22	3						1		4	8

Cockroft Joe	Dailey Jimmy	Fox Oscar	Froggatt Redfern	Hunt George	Ibbotson Wilf	Jordan Clarrie	Lowes Arnold	McIntosh Dave	Mackenzie Laurie	Marriott Jackie	Morton Albert	Packard Edgar	Quigley Eddie	Rogers Alf	Slynn Frank	Smith Roy	Swift Hugh	Tomlinson Charlie	Turton Cyril	Ward Tommy	Westlake Frank	Witcomb Doug	Woodhead Dennis
6		7					8						10			1	3		5	9	2	4	11
6		7	10				8						9			1	3		5		2	4	11
2		2	1				2						2			2	2		2	1	2	2	2
							2						1										

League Table

	P	W	D	L	F	A	Pts
Birmingham City	42	22	15	5	55	24	59
Newcastle United	42	24	8	10	72	41	56
Southampton	42	21	10	11	71	53	52
SHEFFIELD WEDNESDAY	42	20	11	11	66	53	51
Cardiff City	42	18	11	13	61	58	47
West Ham United	42	16	14	12	55	53	46
West Bromwich Albion	42	18	9	15	63	58	45
Tottenham Hotspur	42	15	14	13	56	43	44
Leicester City	42	16	11	15	60	57	43
Coventry City	42	14	13	15	59	52	41
Fulham	42	15	10	17	47	46	40
Barnsley	42	15	10	17	62	64	40
Luton Town	42	14	12	16	56	59	40
Bradford Park Avenue	42	16	8	18	68	72	40
Brentford	42	13	14	15	44	61	40
Chesterfield	42	16	7	19	54	55	39
Plymouth Argyle	42	9	20	13	40	58	38
Leeds United	42	14	8	20	62	72	36
Nottingham Forest	42	12	11	19	54	60	35
Bury	42	9	16	17	58	68	34
Doncaster Rovers	42	9	11	22	40	66	29
Millwall	42	9	11	22	44	74	29

1948-49

Division Two

Manager: Eric Taylor

Did you know that?

Final League Position: 8th

Hillsborough was used as the venue for a boxing match, with the ring being erected on the pitch. Sheffield boxer Henry Hall took on Belfast-born Tommy Armour for the British Welterweight title on 16 August 1948.

On 3 December 1948 Wednesday paid Bury a British transfer record £20,050, which equalled the sum that Sunderland had paid to Newcastle United for Len Shackleton in February of the same year.

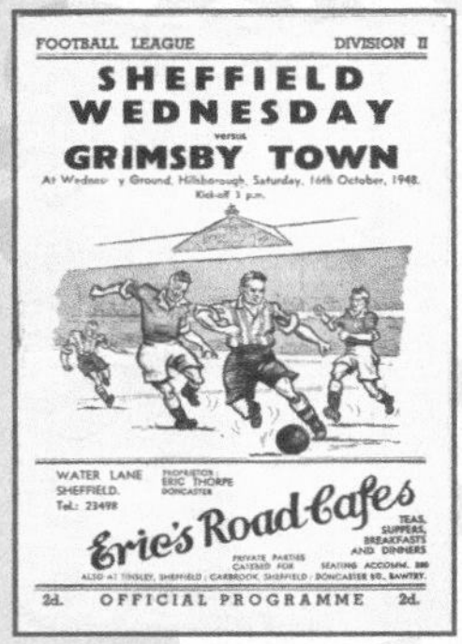

Match No.	Date	Venue	Opponents		Round	Result	HT Score	Position	Scorers	Attendance
1	Aug 21	A	Tottenham Hotspur	L		2-3	2-3		Cockroft, Jordan	51,265
2	23	H	West Ham United	W		3-0	0-0		Quigley (2), Witcomb (pen)	35,720
3	28	H	Brentford	D		0-0	0-0	7th		36,148
4	30	A	West Ham United	D		2-2	2-1	6th	Quigley, Jordan	28,000
5	Sep 4	A	Leicester City	D		2-2	2-1	8th	Quigley, Jordan	32,046
6	8	A	Bury	L		1-2	1-2	14th	Froggatt	20,397
7	11	H	Leeds United	W		3-1	1-1	11th	Witcomb (pen), Fox, Jordan	31,479
8	13	H	Bury	L		1-2	1-1		Quigley	32,602
9	18	A	Coventry City	W		4-3	4-1	8th	Woodhead, Jordan (2), Froggatt	23,790
10	25	H	Southampton	W		2-0	0-0	7th	Woodhead (2)	38,347
11	Oct 2	H	Lincoln City	D		2-2	0-0	8th	Froggatt, Quigley	42,327
12	9	A	Barnsley	L		0-4	0-1	9th		35,125
13	16	H	Grimsby Town	W		4-1	2-1	7th	Quigley (2), Froggatt, Woodhead	33,849
14	23	A	Nottingham Forest	W		2-1	1-0	6th	Woodhead (2)	28,851
15	30	H	Fulham	L		1-2	0-1	7th	Rogers	33,976
16	Nov 6	A	Plymouth Argyle	L		2-3	1-3	10th	Froggatt, Quigley	22,458
17	13	H	Blackburn Rovers	W		3-0	2-0	7th	Froggatt, Quigley, Dailey	29,998
18	20	A	Cardiff City	D		1-1	1-1	6th	Quigley	30,000
19	27	H	Queen's Park Rangers	W		2-0	0-0	5th	Jordan (2)	34,346
20	Dec 4	A	Luton Town	L		1-2	0-0	7th	Woodhead	18,558
21	11	H	Bradford Park Avenue	W		2-1	1-0	5th	Quigley, Woodhead	36,693
22	18	H	Tottenham Hotspur	W		3-1	2-1	4th	Woodhead, Jordan (2)	40,251
23	25	A	West Bromwich Alb	L		0-1	0-0			35,000
24	27	H	West Bromwich Alb	W		2-1	0-1	5th	Tomlinson, Quigley	59,924
25	Jan 1	A	Brentford	L		1-2	1-1	5th	Woodhead	16,894
26	22	A	Leeds United	D		1-1	0-1	6th	Quigley (pen)	42,000
27	Feb 5	H	Coventry City	W		2-1	0-0	6th	Quigley (2)	36,171
28	19	A	Southampton	L		0-1	0-0	6th		29,445
29	26	A	Lincoln City	L		1-3	1-1	8th	Woodhead	20,660
30	Mar 5	H	Barnsley	D		1-1	1-0	9th	Froggatt	27,725
31	12	A	Grimsby Town	L		0-2	0-2	9th		18,000
32	19	H	Nottingham Forest	W		2-1	1-1	9th	Froggatt, Woodhead	27,870
33	26	A	Fulham	D		1-1	1-1	9th	Kilshaw	35,000
34	Apr 2	H	Plymouth Argyle	W		2-1	1-0	8th	Woodhead, Jordan	27,090
35	9	A	Blackburn Rovers	L		1-2	0-2	8th	Jordan	17,700
36	11	H	Leicester City	L		0-1	0-0	8th		25,081
37	15	A	Chesterfield	D		1-1	0-1	8th	Froggatt	23,493
38	16	H	Cardiff City	D		1-1	0-1	8th	Quigley	32,374
39	19	H	Chesterfield	D		0-0	0-0	8th		30,293
40	23	A	Queen's Park Rangers	W		3-1	2-0	8th	Jordan, Woodhead, Froggatt	25,000
41	30	H	Luton Town	D		0-0	0-0	8th		18,829
42	May 7	A	Bradford Park Avenue	D		1-1	0-1	8th	Jordan	7,132
										Apps
										Goals

FA Cup

Match No.	Date	Venue	Opponents		Round	Result	HT Score	Position	Scorers	Attendance
43	Jan 8	H	Southampton	W	3R	2-1	1-1		Dailey, Quigley	44,292
44	29	A	Portsmouth	L	4R	1-2	1-1		Quigley	47,100
										Apps
										Goals

Bannister Keith	Cockroft Joe	Dailey Jimmy	Fletcher Doug	Fox Oscar	Froggatt Redfern	Gannon Eddie	Jordan Clarrie	Kenny Mick	Kilshaw Eddie	Locherty Joe	McIntosh Dave	Marriott Jackie	Packard Edgar	Parker Ray	Quigley Eddie	Rogers Alf	Swift Hugh	Tomlinson Charlie	Turton Cyril	Westlake Frank	Witcomb Doug	Woodhead Dennis
	6			7	10		9				1				8		3		5	2	4	11
	6			7	10		9				1				8		3		5	2	4	11
	6			7	10		9				1				8		3		5	2	4	11
	6			7	10		9				1				8		3		5	2	4	11
	6			7	10		9				1				8		3		5	2	4	11
	6			7	10		9				1				8		3		5	2	4	11
	6			7	10		9				1				8		3		5	2	4	11
	6			7	10		9				1				8		3		5	2	4	11
	6			7	10		9				1				8		3		5	2	4	11
	6			7	10		9				1				8		3		5	2	4	11
	6			7	10		9				1				8		3		5	2	4	11
	6			7	10		9				1				8		3		5	2	4	11
	6			7	10		9				1				8		3		5	2	4	11
6				7	10		9				1				8		3		5	2	4	11
6				7	10		9				1			5		8	3			2	4	11
6				7	10		9				1				8		3		5	2	4	11
6		9		7	10						1				8		3		5	2	4	11
6		9		7	10						1				8		3		5	2	4	11
6				7	10		9				1				8		3		5	2	4	11
6					10		9		7		1				8		3		5	2	4	11
6					10		9		7	4	1				8		3		5	2		11
6					10		9		7	4	1				8		3		5	2		11
6					10		9		7	4	1				8		3		5	2		11
6		9							7		1				8		3	10	5	2	4	11
6		9							7	4	1				8		3	10	5	2		11
		9			10				7	4	1				8		3		5	2	6	11
					10				7	4	1				9	8	3		5	2	6	11
							9		7	6	1				10	8	3		5	2	4	11
					10		9		7	6	1				8		3		5	2	4	11
					10		9		7		1				8	6	3	11	5	2	4	
					10	4	9		7		1				8	6	3	11	5	2		
					10	4	9		7		1				8		3		5	2	6	11
				8	10	4	9		7		1						3		5	2	6	11
				8	10	4	9		7		1						3		5	2	6	11
				8	10	4	9		7		1						3		5	2	6	11
			9		10	4			7		1				8		3		5	2	6	11
6					10	4	9				1	7	5		8		3			2		11
6			9		10	4		3			1	7	5		8		2					11
			9		8	4		3			1	7	5				2	10			6	11
					8		9	3		4	1	7	5				2	10			6	11
					8	4	9	2			1	7	5				3	10			6	11
					8	4	9	2			1	7	5				3	10			6	11
14	13	5	3	22	39	11	33	5	17	9	42	6	6	1	34	5	42	8	35	37	35	40
	1	1		1	10		14		1						17	1		1			2	14

Bannister Keith	Cockroft Joe	Dailey Jimmy	Fletcher Doug	Fox Oscar	Froggatt Redfern	Gannon Eddie	Jordan Clarrie	Kenny Mick	Kilshaw Eddie	Locherty Joe	McIntosh Dave	Marriott Jackie	Packard Edgar	Parker Ray	Quigley Eddie	Rogers Alf	Swift Hugh	Tomlinson Charlie	Turton Cyril	Westlake Frank	Witcomb Doug	Woodhead Dennis
6		9			10				7	4	1				8		3		5	2		11
					10		9		7	4	1				8		3		5	2	6	11
1		1			2		1		2	2	2				2		2		2	2	1	2
		1													2							

League Table

	P	W	D	L	F	A	Pts
Fulham	42	24	9	9	77	37	57
West Bromwich Albion	42	24	8	10	69	39	56
Southampton	42	23	9	10	69	36	55
Cardiff City	42	19	13	10	62	47	51
Tottenham Hotspur	42	17	16	9	72	44	50
Chesterfield	42	15	17	10	51	45	47
West Ham United	42	18	10	14	56	58	46
SHEFFIELD WEDNESDAY	42	15	13	14	63	56	43
Barnsley	42	14	12	16	62	61	40
Luton Town	42	14	12	16	55	57	40
Grimsby Town	42	15	10	17	72	76	40
Bury	42	17	6	19	67	76	40
Queen's Park Rangers	42	14	11	17	44	62	39
Blackburn Rovers	42	15	8	19	53	63	38
Leeds United	42	12	13	17	55	63	37
Coventry City	42	15	7	20	55	64	37
Bradford Park Avenue	42	13	11	18	65	78	37
Brentford	42	11	14	17	42	53	36
Leicester City	42	10	16	16	62	79	36
Plymouth Argyle	42	12	12	18	49	64	36
Nottingham Forest	42	14	7	21	50	54	35
Lincoln City	42	8	12	22	53	91	28

1949-50

Division Two

Manager: Eric Taylor

Did you know that?

Final League Position: 2nd

On 22 October 1949 Charlie Tomlinson netted after only 12 seconds for Wednesday's fastest-ever goal, as Wednesday beat Preston by that single goal.

On 14 December 1949 Eddie Quigley was transferred to Preston North End for a British transfer record of £26,000.

On 6 May 1950 Wednesday held Spurs, the Second Division champions, to a 0–0 draw and duly gained promotion by finishing ahead of Sheffield United by a goal average of 0.008!

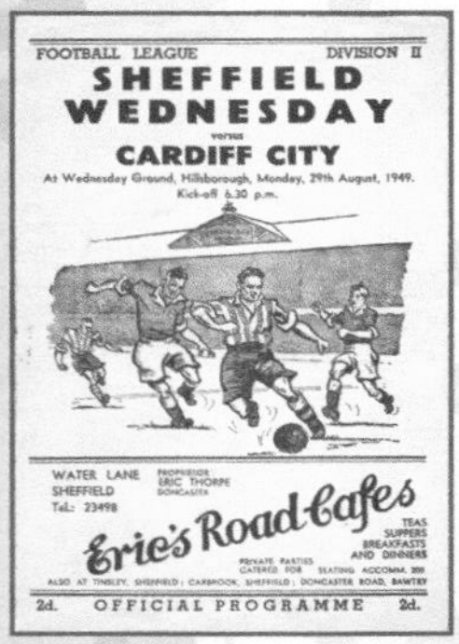

Match No.	Date	Venue	Opponents		Round	Result	HT Score	Position	Scorers	Attendance
1	Aug 20	H	Leicester City	W		3-1	3-1		Quigley (2), Froggatt	35,431
2	22	A	Cardiff City	L		0-1	0-0			37,913
3	27	A	Bradford Park Avenue	W		3-1	1-1	5th	Marriott, Rogers, Witcomb	18,745
4	29	H	Cardiff City	D		1-1	1-0	3rd	Froggatt	32,873
5	Sep 3	H	Chesterfield	W		4-2	1-1	4th	Quigley (4)	41,159
6	5	A	Tottenham Hotspur	L		0-1	0-1	5th		37,697
7	10	A	Plymouth Argyle	W		1-0	0-0	4th	Quigley	18,137
8	17	H	Sheffield United	W		2-1	2-1	3rd	Jordan, Quigley (pen)	55,555
9	24	H	Hull City	W		6-2	4-0	2nd	Jordan (4), Quigley (pen), Froggatt	52,869
10	Oct 1	A	Brentford	D		1-1	1-1	2nd	Quigley	25,270
11	8	A	Grimsby Town	L		1-4	1-1	3rd	Froggatt	25,062
12	15	H	Queen's Park Rangers	W		1-0	1-0	2nd	Jordan	31,748
13	22	A	Preston North End	W		1-0	1-0	2nd	Tomlinson	32,569
14	29	H	Swansea Town	W		3-0	1-0	2nd	Rogers, Jordan, Froggatt	34,564
15	Nov 5	A	Leeds United	D		1-1	1-1	2nd	Rogers	33,733
16	12	H	Southampton	D		2-2	0-2	2nd	Froggatt, Witcomb	32,146
17	26	H	Luton Town	D		1-1	1-1	3rd	Jordan	29,533
18	Dec 3	A	Barnsley	W		4-3	2-3	3rd	Froggatt (2), Rickett, Jordan	24,923
19	10	H	West Ham United	W		2-1	2-1	2nd	Packard, Rogers	26,405
20	17	A	Leicester City	D		2-2	1-1	2nd	Froggatt (2)	27,513
21	24	H	Bradford Park Avenue	D		1-1	0-1	2nd	Woodhead	37,851
22	26	H	Blackburn Rovers	W		2-0	1-0	2nd	Tomlinson, Froggatt	52,939
23	27	A	Blackburn Rovers	D		0-0	0-0	2nd		30,400
24	31	A	Chesterfield	W		2-1	1-0	2nd	Froggatt, Jordan	25,025
25	Jan 14	H	Plymouth Argyle	L		2-4	1-2	2nd	Gannon, Froggatt	39,318
26	21	A	Sheffield United	L		0-2	0-0	3rd		51,644
27	Feb 4	A	Hull City	D		1-1	0-0	3rd	Fox	50,103
28	11	A	Coventry City	L		0-3	0-2	3rd		18,003
29	18	H	Brentford	D		3-3	1-2	2nd	Fox, Jordan (2)	37,923
30	Mar 4	A	Queen's Park Rangers	D		0-0	0-0	3rd		23,273
31	11	H	Preston North End	L		0-1	0-1	5th		49,222
32	18	A	Swansea Town	W		2-1	2-0	3rd	McJarrow, Marriott	18,917
33	25	H	Leeds United	W		5-2	2-2	3rd	McJarrow (2), Henry (pen +1), Rickett	50,487
34	Apr 1	A	Luton Town	D		0-0	0-0	3rd		15,273
35	7	A	Bury	D		0-0	0-0	3rd		18,989
36	8	H	Barnsley	W		2-0	2-0	3rd	Henry, Marriott	48,119
37	10	H	Bury	W		1-0	1-0	2nd	Henry	30,449
38	15	A	Southampton	L		0-1	0-0	3rd		28,529
39	22	H	Coventry City	D		1-1	0-1	3rd	McJarrow	44,035
40	26	H	Grimsby Town	W		4-0	3-0	2nd	Rickett (3), McJarrow	40,862
41	29	A	West Ham United	D		2-2	0-2	3rd	Woodhead, Froggatt	10,361
42	May 6	H	Tottenham Hotspur	D		0-0	0-0	2nd		50,853
										Apps
										Goals

FA Cup

43	Jan 7	A	Arsenal	L	3R	0-1	0-0			54,193
										Apps

Abandoned match due to fog after 63 minutes

44	Nov 19	A	Coventry City			0-1	0-1			17,541

Bannister Keith	Dooley Derek	Fletcher Doug	Fox Oscar	Froggatt Redfern	Gannon Eddie	Henry Gerry	Jackson Norman	Jordan Clarrie	Kenny Mick	Locherty Joe	McIntosh Dave	McJarrow Hugh	Marriott Jackie	Morton Albert	Packard Edgar	Quigley Eddie	Rickett Walter	Rogers Alf	Swift Hugh	Tomlinson Charlie	Westlake Frank	Witcomb Doug	Woodhead Dennis
				10	4			9	2		1		7		5	8			3			6	11
					4			9	2		1		7		5	10		8	3	11		6	
			7	10	4			9	2		1		11		5			8	3			6	
		9	7	10	4				2		1		11		5			8	3			6	
			7	10	4				2		1		11		5	9		8	3			6	
			7	10	4				2		1		11		5	9		8	3			6	
			7	10	4			9	2		1		11		5	8			3			6	
			7	10	4			9	2		1		11		5	8			3			6	
				10	4			9	2		1		7		5	8			3	11		6	
				10	4			9	2		1		7		5	8			3	11		6	
				10				9	2	4	1		7		5	8			3	11		6	
				10	4			9	2		1		7		5			8	3	11		6	
				10	4			9	2					1	5		7	8	3	11		6	
				10	4			9	2		1				5		7	8	3	11		6	
				10	4			9	2		1				5		7	8	3	11		6	
				10	4			9	2		1				5		7	8	3	11		6	
				10				9	2		1				5	8	7	4	3	11		6	
				10	4			9	2		1		7		5		11	8	3			6	
				10	4			9	2		1		7		5		11	8	3			6	
				10	4			9	2		1		7		5		11	8	3			6	
				10	4			9	2		1				5		7	8	3			6	11
				8	4			9	2		1				5		7		3	10		6	11
				8	4			9	2		1		7		5		11		3	10		6	
				8	4			9	2		1		7		5		11		3	10		6	
				8	4			9			1		7		5		11		3	10	2	6	
2				10	4			9			1		7		5		11	8	3			6	
			10		4			9	2				7	1	5		11	8	3			6	
			10	8	4				2					1	5		7	9	3			6	11
3			10		4	8		9	2		1				5		7					6	11
3					4	8		9	2		1	10	7		5		11					6	
3	9			10	4	8			2		1		7		5		11					6	
3					4	8			2		1	9	7		5		11			10		6	
3					4	8			2		1	9	7		5		11			10		6	
3					4	8			2		1	9	7		5		11			10		6	
3					4	8	6		2		1	9	7		5		11			10			
					4	8			2		1	9	7		5		11		3	10		6	
					4	8			2		1	9	7		5		11		3	10		6	
					4	8			2		1	9	7		5		11		3	10		6	
					4	8			2		1	9	7		5		11		3	10		6	
				10	4	8			2		1	9			5		7		3			6	11
				10	4	8			2		1	9			5		7		3			6	11
				10	4	8			2		1	9			5		7		3			6	11
8	1	1	9	30	40	14	1	26	40	1	39	12	30	3	42	10	30	18	35	22	1	41	8
			2	14	1	4		12				5	3		1	10	5	4		2		2	2

				8	4			9	2		1		7		5		11		3	10		6	
				1	1			1	1		1		1		1		1		1	1		1	

				10			4	9	2		1				5		7	8	3	11		6	

League Table

	P	W	D	L	F	A	Pts
Tottenham Hotspur	42	27	7	8	81	35	61
SHEFFIELD WEDNESDAY	42	18	16	8	67	48	52
Sheffield United	42	19	14	9	68	49	52
Southampton	42	19	14	9	64	48	52
Leeds United	42	17	13	12	54	45	47
Preston North End	42	18	9	15	60	49	45
Hull City	42	17	11	14	64	72	45
Swansea Town	42	17	9	16	53	49	43
Brentford	42	15	13	14	44	49	43
Cardiff City	42	16	10	16	41	44	42
Grimsby Town	42	16	8	18	74	73	40
Coventry City	42	13	13	16	55	55	39
Barnsley	42	13	13	16	64	67	39
Chesterfield	42	15	9	18	43	47	39
Leicester City	42	12	15	15	55	65	39
Blackburn Rovers	42	14	10	18	55	60	38
Luton Town	42	10	18	14	41	51	38
Bury	42	14	9	19	60	65	37
West Ham United	42	12	12	18	53	61	36
Queen's Park Rangers	42	11	12	19	40	57	34
Plymouth Argyle	42	8	16	18	44	65	32
Bradford Park Avenue	42	10	11	21	51	77	31

1950-51

Division One

Manager: Eric Taylor

Did you know that?

Final League Position: 21st

On 15 March 1951 Wednesday broke the British transfer record by paying Notts County £35,000 for the transfer of Jackie Sewell.

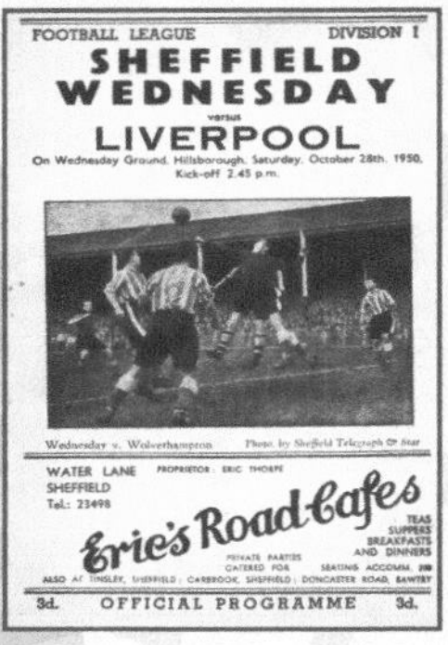

Match No.	Date	Venue	Opponents		Round	Result	HT Score	Position	Scorers	Attendance
1	Aug 19	A	Chelsea	L		0-4	0-3			48,468
2	21	H	Portsmouth	W		2-1	0-0	16th	McJarrow, Woodhead	46,740
3	26	H	Burnley	L		0-1	0-1	19th		44,079
4	30	A	Portsmouth	L		1-4	1-2		McJarrow	27,952
5	Sep 2	A	Arsenal	L		0-3	0-2	22nd		45,647
6	4	H	Stoke City	D		1-1	0-0	22nd	Tomlinson	37,500
7	9	H	Charlton Athletic	L		1-2	0-0	22nd	McJarrow	40,580
8	11	A	Stoke City	D		1-1	0-0	21st	Froggatt	23,277
9	16	H	Middlesbrough	L		0-1	0-1	22nd		46,954
10	23	A	Huddersfield Town	W		4-3	1-2	20th	McJarrow (2), Froggatt, Marriott	28,645
11	30	H	Newcastle United	D		0-0	0-0	20th		40,096
12	Oct 7	A	Manchester United	L		1-3	0-3	21st	McJarrow	40,651
13	14	H	Wolverhampton W	D		2-2	1-0	21st	Froggatt, Rickett	47,033
14	21	A	Derby County	L		1-4	1-1	21st	McJarrow	31,162
15	28	H	Liverpool	W		4-1	1-1	20th	Froggatt (3), Woodhead (pen)	43,643
16	Nov 4	A	Sunderland	L		1-5	0-2	21st	Witcomb	48,939
17	11	H	Aston Villa	W		3-2	2-0	20th	Rickett, Henry (2)	37,160
18	18	A	Fulham	L		2-4	1-2	21st	McJarrow (2)	26,357
19	25	H	Bolton Wanderers	L		3-4	2-2	21st	Froggatt, Howe (og), Henry	37,033
20	Dec 2	A	Blackpool	L		2-3	1-0	21st	Froggatt, McJarrow	19,732
21	9	H	Tottenham Hotspur	D		1-1	1-0	21st	McJarrow	44,346
22	23	A	Burnley	L		0-1	0-0	22nd		21,272
23	25	A	West Bromwich Alb	W		3-1	2-0	22nd	Jordan, McJarrow, Froggatt	27,610
24	26	H	West Bromwich Alb	W		3-0	2-0	22nd	McJarrow (2), Jordan	44,819
25	30	H	Arsenal	L		0-2	0-2	22nd		39,583
26	Jan 13	A	Charlton Athletic	L		1-2	0-1	22nd	Woodhead	21,785
27	20	A	Middlesbrough	L		1-2	1-0	22nd	Woodhead	34,031
28	Feb 3	H	Huddersfield Town	W		3-2	3-1	22nd	Froggatt (2), Woodhead (pen)	40,805
29	17	A	Newcastle United	L		0-2	0-1	22nd		47,075
30	24	H	Chelsea	D		2-2	0-1	22nd	Hughes (og), Quixall	40,943
31	26	H	Manchester United	L		0-4	0-2	22nd		25,693
32	Mar 3	A	Wolverhampton W	L		0-4	0-3	22nd		37,482
33	17	A	Liverpool	L		1-2	0-1	22nd	Sewell	31,413
34	24	H	Sunderland	W		3-0	1-0	22nd	Woodhead, Froggatt, Rickett	48,467
35	26	A	Everton	D		0-0	0-0	22nd		32,381
36	31	A	Aston Villa	L		1-2	0-1	22nd	Woodhead (pen)	29,321
37	Apr 7	H	Fulham	D		2-2	2-1	22nd	Froggatt, Sewell	31,328
38	14	A	Bolton Wanderers	W		1-0	0-0	21st	Woodhead	20,085
39	18	H	Derby County	W		4-3	3-3	21st	Woodhead (1 + pen), Oliver (og), Sewell	40,183
40	21	H	Blackpool	W		3-1	2-0	20th	Woodhead, Sewell, Witcomb	53,420
41	28	A	Tottenham Hotspur	L		0-1	0-1	22nd		46,645
42	May 5	H	Everton	W		6-0	3-0	21st	Woodhead (2), Sewell (2), Finney, Froggatt	41,166
										Apps
									Three own-goals	Goals

FA Cup

Match No.	Date	Venue	Opponents		Round	Result	HT Score	Position	Scorers	Attendance
43	Jan 6	A	Fulham	L	3R	0-1	0-0			29,200
										Apps

Bannister Keith	Curtis Norman	Davies George	Dooley Derek	Finney Alan	Froggatt Redfern	Gannon Eddie	Henry Gerry	Jackson Norman	Jordan John	Kenny Mick	Kirby Eric	McIntosh Dave	McJarrow Hugh	Marriott Jackie	Morton Albert	Packard Edgar	Quixall Albert	Rickett Walter	Sewell Jackie	Slynn Frank	Swift Hugh	Thomas Keith	Tomlinson Charlie	Turton Cecil	Witcomb Doug	Woodhead Dennis
					10	4	8			2		1	9			5		7			3				6	11
					8		4			2		1	9			5		7			3		10		6	11
					8		4			2		1	9			5		7			3		10		6	11
					8		4			2		1	9			5		7			3		10		6	11
					8		4			2		1	9			5		7			3		10		6	11
					8		4			2		1	9			5		7		6	3		10			11
					10	4	8			2		1	9			5		7		6	3					11
					8	4				2			9		1	5		7			3		10		6	11
					8	4				2			9		1	5		7			3		10		6	11
					10	4			8	2		1	9	7		5					3		11		6	
2					10	4			8			1	9	7		5					3		11		6	
2					10	4			8			1	9	7		5					3		11		6	
2					10	4			8			1	9			5		7			3		11		6	
2					10	4			8			1	9			5		7			3		11		6	
2					10	4	8					1	9			5		7			3				6	11
2					10	4	8					1	9			5		7			3				6	11
2					10	4	9		8			1						7			3			5	6	11
2					10	4	9					1	8					7			3			5	6	11
2	3				10	4	9					1	8					7			5				6	11
2	3				10	4	9					1	8					7						5	6	11
2	3				10	4	8						9		1	5		7							6	11
2	3				10	4	8						9		1	5		7							6	11
2	3				10	4			8				9	7	1	5									6	11
2	3				10	4			8				9	7	1	5									6	11
2	3				10	4			8				9	7	1	5									6	11
2	3		9			4			8				10	7	1	5									6	11
2	3					4	8						8	7	1	5							10		6	11
2	3				10		8				4		9	7	1	5									6	11
2	3				10	4	8						9		1	5		7							6	11
	3			7	10	4							9		1	5	8				2				6	11
	3			7	10	4							9		1	5	8				2				6	11
	3				8	4		2						7	1	5		9				10			6	11
	3				10	4		2					9	7	1	5			8						6	11
	3				10	4		2				1		7		5		11	8						6	9
	3				10	4		2				1		7		5		11	8						6	9
	3				10	4		2				1		7				11	8					5	6	9
	3				10	4		2				1		7		5		11	8						6	9
	3	4		7	10			2				1				5		11	8						6	9
	3			7	10		4	2				1				5		11	8						6	9
	3			7	10		4	2				1				5		11	8						6	9
	3			7	10		4	2				1				5		11	8						6	9
	3			7	10		4	2				1				5		11	8						6	9
19	24	1	1	7	40	31	22	11	10	10	1	27	31	15	15	37	2	30	10	2	21	1	13	4	40	37
				1	14		3		2				14	1			1	3	6				1		2	13

Bannister Keith	Curtis Norman	Davies George	Dooley Derek	Finney Alan	Froggatt Redfern	Gannon Eddie	Henry Gerry	Jackson Norman	Jordan John	Kenny Mick	Kirby Eric	McIntosh Dave	McJarrow Hugh	Marriott Jackie	Morton Albert	Packard Edgar	Quixall Albert	Rickett Walter	Sewell Jackie	Slynn Frank	Swift Hugh	Thomas Keith	Tomlinson Charlie	Turton Cecil	Witcomb Doug	Woodhead Dennis
2	3				10	4			8				9		1	5		7							6	11
1	1				1	1			1				1		1	1		1							1	1

League Table

	P	W	D	L	F	A	Pts
Tottenham Hotspur	42	25	10	7	82	44	60
Manchester United	42	24	8	10	74	40	56
Blackpool	42	20	10	12	79	53	50
Newcastle United	42	18	13	11	62	53	49
Arsenal	42	19	9	14	73	56	47
Middlesbrough	42	18	11	13	76	65	47
Portsmouth	42	16	15	11	71	68	47
Bolton Wanderers	42	19	7	16	64	61	45
Liverpool	42	16	11	15	53	59	43
Burnley	42	14	14	14	48	43	42
Derby County	42	16	8	18	81	75	40
Sunderland	42	12	16	14	63	73	40
Stoke City	42	13	14	15	50	59	40
Wolverhampton W.	42	15	8	19	74	61	38
Aston Villa	42	12	13	17	66	68	37
West Bromwich Albion	42	13	11	18	53	61	37
Charlton Athletic	42	14	9	19	63	80	37
Fulham	42	13	11	18	52	68	37
Huddersfield Town	42	15	6	21	64	92	36
Chelsea	42	12	8	22	53	65	32
SHEFFIELD WEDNESDAY	42	12	8	22	64	83	32
Everton	42	12	8	22	48	86	32

1951-52

Division Two

Manager: Eric Taylor

Did you know that?

Final League Position: 1st

On 1 December 1951, when Wednesday played Coventry City at home, a member of the Sheffield Police took the line until the proper linesman arrived. Wednesday went on to win 3–1.

On 13 May 1952 Wednesday played under floodlights for the first time in a friendly match in Bellinzona, Switzerland, which ended 2–2. The next day, in Berne, Wednesday had to play a near International Swiss team as they used this as a national trial for the forthcoming game with England. Wednesday lost 2–1 but had been expecting to play a local team.

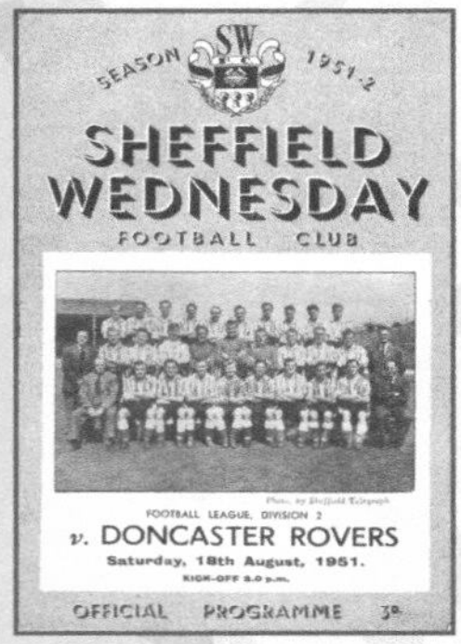

Match No.	Date	Venue	Opponents		Round	Result	HT Score	Position	Scorers	Attendance
1	Aug 18	H	Doncaster Rovers	W		3-1	1-0		Woodhead, Witcomb, Sewell	42,005
2	20	A	Leicester City	L		1-3	1-3		Sewell	23,395
3	25	A	Everton	D		3-3	0-2	12th	Woodhead, Sewell (2)	42,025
4	27	H	Leicester City	W		1-0	0-0	4th	Sewell	28,517
5	Sep 1	H	Southampton	W		3-1	2-0	3rd	Witcomb, Woodhead (1 + pen)	32,016
6	3	H	Birmingham City	D		1-1	1-0	2nd	Woodhead	32,490
7	8	A	Sheffield United	L		3-7	1-2	8th	Thomas, Woodhead (2)	52,045
8	12	A	Birmingham City	D		0-0	0-0	6th		13,894
9	15	A	Leeds United	L		2-3	1-1	10th	Woodhead, McJarrow	20,016
10	22	H	Rotherham United	L		3-5	0-1	12th	Sewell (2), McJarrow	54,684
11	29	A	Cardiff City	L		1-2	0-1	17th	Sewell	30,352
12	Oct 6	H	Barnsley	W		2-1	0-1	13th	Dooley (2)	34,207
13	13	A	Hull City	W		1-0	1-0	10th	Finney	34,011
14	20	H	Blackburn Rovers	W		2-0	0-0	9th	Sewell, Rickett (pen)	31,454
15	27	A	Queen's Park Rangers	D		2-2	1-2	7th	Finney, Dooley	18,541
16	Nov 3	H	Notts County	W		6-0	1-0	4th	Sewell, Dooley (5)	46,570
17	10	A	Luton Town	L		3-5	1-1	8th	Sewell, Dooley (2)	19,091
18	17	H	Bury	W		2-1	1-1	8th	Dooley (2)	35,882
19	24	A	Swansea Town	W		2-1	1-0	7th	Dooley (2)	9,934
20	Dec 1	H	Coventry City	W		3-1	2-0	6th	Dooley (2), Froggatt	35,739
21	8	A	West Ham United	W		6-0	4-0	3rd	Dooley (3), Froggatt (2), Quixall	17,798
22	15	A	Doncaster Rovers	D		1-1	1-1	4th	Dooley	27,763
23	22	H	Everton	W		4-0	0-0	1st	Dooley (4)	38,986
24	25	H	Nottingham Forest	D		1-1	0-0	2nd	Rickett (pen)	61,187
25	26	A	Nottingham Forest	L		1-2	0-2	2nd	Dooley	39,380
26	29	A	Southampton	W		4-1	3-1	1st	Finney (2), Dooley (2)	21,534
27	Jan 5	H	Sheffield United	L		1-3	1-1	2nd	Dooley	65,384
28	19	H	Leeds United	L		1-2	0-0	3rd	Dooley	42,357
29	26	A	Rotherham United	D		3-3	1-1	4th	Woodhead, Sewell, Dooley	25,149
30	Feb 9	H	Cardiff City	W		4-2	0-2	1st	Sewell (4)	42,881
31	16	A	Barnsley	L		4-5	2-2	3rd	Sewell, Froggatt (2), Dooley	29,795
32	Mar 1	H	Hull City	W		6-0	3-0	2nd	Sewell (2), Dooley (4)	41,811
33	12	A	Blackburn Rovers	D		0-0	0-0	2nd		20,100
34	15	H	Queen's Park Rangers	W		2-1	1-0	2nd	Sewell (2)	41,706
35	22	A	Notts County	D		2-2	1-1	3rd	Dooley (2)	33,230
36	Apr 2	H	Luton Town	W		4-0	2-0	1st	Sewell, Dooley (2), Rickett	25,848
37	5	A	Bury	W		2-1	2-1	1st	Quixall, Dooley	14,705
38	11	A	Brentford	W		3-2	2-0	1st	Dooley (3)	35,827
39	12	H	Swansea Town	D		1-1	0-0	2nd	Quixall	49,002
40	14	H	Brentford	W		2-0	1-0	1st	Sewell, Munro (og)	43,949
41	19	A	Coventry City	W		2-0	1-0	1st	Dooley (2)	36,337
42	26	H	West Ham United	D		2-2	0-2	1st	Froggatt, Dooley	44,011
										Apps
									One own-goal	Goals

FA Cup

Match No.	Date	Venue	Opponents		Round	Result	HT Score	Position	Scorers	Attendance
43	Jan 12	A	Bradford Park Avenue	L	3R	1-2	1-1		Dooley	28,449
										Apps
										Goals

Bannister Keith	Curtis Norman	Davies George	Dooley Derek	Edwards Len	Finney Alan	Froggatt Redfern	Gannon Eddie	Henry Gerry	Jackson Norman	Jordan Clarrie	Kenny Mick	McIntosh Dave	McJarrow Hugh	Marriott Jackie	O'Donnell Ralph	Packard Edgar	Quixall Albert	Rickett Walter	Sewell Jackie	Thomas Keith	Turton Cyril	Whitaker Colin	Witcomb Doug	Woodhead Dennis
	3				7			4	2			1				5		11	8	10			6	9
	3				7			4	2			1				5		11	8	10			6	9
					7		4		2		3	1						11	8	10	5		6	9
					7		4		2		3	1						11	8	10	5		6	9
					7		4		2		3	1						11	8	10	5		6	9
					7		4		2		3	1						11	8	10	5		6	9
					7		4		2		3	1						11	8	10	5		6	9
	3						4		2			1	9	7					8	10	5		6	11
	3						4	10	2			1	9	7					8		5		6	11
	3						4	10	2			1	9	7					8		5		6	11
	3	6			7		4				2	1						9	8	10	5			11
2		6	9		7		4				3	1					10	11	8		5			
2		6	9		7		4				3	1					8	11	10		5			
2		6	9		7		4				3	1					8	11	10		5			
2		6	9		7		4				3	1					10	11	8		5			
2		6	9		7		4				3	1				5	10	11	8					
2		6	9		7		4				3	1				5	10	11	8					
2		6	9		7		4				3	1			5		10	11	8					
2		6	9		7	8	4				3	1			5		10	11						
2		6	9		7	8	4				3	1			5		10	11						
2			9	6	7	8	4				3	1					10	11			5			
2			9	6	7	8	4				3	1			5		10	11						
2		6	9		7	8	4				3	1			5			11	10					
2		6	9		7	10	4				3	1			5			11	8					
2		6	9		7	10	4				3	1			5			11	8					
2		6	9		7	8	4				3	1		11	5		10							
2		6	9		7	8	4				3	1		11	5		10							
2	3	6	9		7	8	4					1			5		10	11						
2	3	6	9			7	4					1			5		10		8					11
2	3	6				7	4			9		1			5		10		8					11
2	3	6	9			7	4					1			5		10		8					11
2	3		9			7	4					1		10					8		5		6	11
2	3		9			7	4					1		10					8		5		6	11
2	3		9		7		4					1					10		8		5	11	6	
2	3		9			7	4					1					10	11	8		5		6	
2	3		9			7	4					1					10	11	8		5		6	
2	3		9			7	4					1					10	11	8		5		6	
2	3		9			7	4					1					10	11	8		5		6	
2	3		9			7	4					1					10	11	8		5		6	
2	3		9			7	4					1					10	11	8		5		6	
2	3		9			7	4					1					10	11	8		5		6	
2	3		9			7	4					1		11			10		8		5		6	
31	21	19	30	2	26	23	40	4	10	1	22	42	3	8	13	4	26	30	35	9	25	1	21	16
			46		4	6							2				3	3	23	1			2	9

Bannister Keith	Curtis Norman	Davies George	Dooley Derek	Edwards Len	Finney Alan	Froggatt Redfern	Gannon Eddie	Henry Gerry	Jackson Norman	Jordan Clarrie	Kenny Mick	McIntosh Dave	McJarrow Hugh	Marriott Jackie	O'Donnell Ralph	Packard Edgar	Quixall Albert	Rickett Walter	Sewell Jackie	Thomas Keith	Turton Cyril	Whitaker Colin	Witcomb Doug	Woodhead Dennis
2		6	9		7	8	4				3	1			5				10					11
1		1	1		1	1	1				1	1			1				1					1
			1																					

League Table

	P	W	D	L	F	A	Pts
SHEFFIELD WEDNESDAY	42	21	11	10	100	66	53
Cardiff City	42	20	11	11	72	54	51
Birmingham City	42	21	9	12	67	56	51
Nottingham Forest	42	18	13	11	77	62	49
Leicester City	42	19	9	14	78	64	47
Leeds United	42	18	11	13	59	57	47
Everton	42	17	10	15	64	58	44
Luton Town	42	16	12	14	77	78	44
Rotherham United	42	17	8	17	73	71	42
Brentford	42	15	12	15	54	55	42
Sheffield United	42	18	5	19	90	76	41
West Ham United	42	15	11	16	67	77	41
Southampton	42	15	11	16	61	73	41
Blackburn Rovers	42	17	6	19	54	63	40
Notts County	42	16	7	19	71	68	39
Doncaster Rovers	42	13	12	17	55	60	38
Bury	42	15	7	20	67	69	37
Hull City	42	13	11	18	60	70	37
Swansea Town	42	12	12	18	72	76	36
Barnsley	42	11	14	17	59	72	36
Coventry City	42	14	6	22	59	82	34
Queen's Park Rangers	42	11	12	19	52	81	34

1952-53

Division One

Manager: Eric Taylor

Did you know that?

Final League Position: 18th

On 14 February 1953, playing away at Preston North End, Derek Dooley collided with Preston's 'keeper, George Thompson, breaking his leg. A few days later he had to have his leg amputated to save his life, thus ending his footballing career (his debut for Wednesday in 1950 was also against Preston).

Match No.	Date	Venue	Opponents		Round	Result	HT Score	Position	Scorers	Attendance
1	Aug 23	H	Newcastle United	D		2-2	0-2		Sewell, Froggatt	55,126
2	27	A	Liverpool	L		0-1	0-0			46,614
3	30	A	Cardiff City	L		0-4	0-2	21st		43,478
4	Sep 3	H	Liverpool	L		0-2	0-1	22nd		41,183
5	6	H	Charlton Athletic	L		0-3	0-3	22nd		35,203
6	13	H	Tottenham Hotspur	W		2-0	0-0	22nd	Sewell, Finney	42,174
7	17	H	Middlesbrough	W		2-0	1-0	18th	Sewell, Dooley	41,456
8	20	A	Burnley	D		1-1	0-0	18th	Dooley	33,049
9	27	H	Preston North End	D		1-1	1-1	18th	Woodhead	47,729
10	Oct 4	A	Stoke City	W		3-1	2-0	16th	Dooley (2), Woodhead	29,278
11	11	A	Arsenal	D		2-2	1-0	14th	Froggatt, Woodhead	54,678
12	18	H	Derby County	W		2-0	2-0	12th	Curtis (2 pens)	51,597
13	25	A	Blackpool	W		1-0	0-0	11th	Woodhead	28,162
14	Nov 1	H	Chelsea	W		1-0	1-0	8th	Froggatt	48,186
15	8	A	Manchester United	D		1-1	1-0	9th	Dooley	48,571
16	15	H	Portsmouth	L		3-4	1-3	11th	Froggatt, Curtis (2 pens)	44,187
17	22	A	Bolton Wanderers	D		1-1	0-1	12th	Dooley	34,435
18	29	H	Aston Villa	D		2-2	2-1	11th	Dooley (2)	30,153
19	Dec 6	A	Sunderland	L		1-2	1-0	11th	Sewell	49,854
20	13	H	Wolverhampton W	L		2-3	2-1	15th	Shorthouse (og), Dooley	43,108
21	20	A	Newcastle United	W		5-1	2-0	12th	Dooley (2), Sewell (2), Marriott	37,927
22	26	H	West Bromwich Alb	L		4-5	3-2	13th	Woodhead (2), Froggatt, Dooley	59,389
23	27	A	West Bromwich Alb	W		1-0	0-0	11th	Dooley	49,510
24	Jan 1	A	Middlesbrough	D		2-2	1-1	12th	Sewell, Marriott	30,036
25	3	H	Cardiff City	W		2-0	2-0	10th	Dooley (2)	40,109
26	17	A	Charlton Athletic	L		0-3	0-2	11th		21,282
27	24	A	Tottenham Hotspur	L		1-2	1-2	11th	Dooley	43,241
28	31	A	Wolverhampton W	L		1-3	1-2	11th	Marriott	28,983
29	Feb 7	H	Burnley	L		2-4	1-2	11th	Sewell, Curtis (pen)	41,864
30	14	A	Preston North End	L		0-1	0-0	12th		28,629
31	21	H	Stoke City	W		1-0	0-0	12th	Sewell	38,187
32	Mar 2	H	Arsenal	L		1-4	0-2	11th	Jordan	32,814
33	7	A	Derby County	L		1-2	0-0	16th	Curtis (pen)	23,085
34	14	H	Blackpool	W		2-0	1-0	14th	Sewell, Marriott	40,904
35	21	A	Chelsea	L		0-1	0-1	15th		36,191
36	28	H	Manchester United	D		0-0	0-0	16th		31,101
37	Apr 3	A	Manchester City	L		1-3	1-2	17th	Sewell	45,435
38	4	A	Portsmouth	L		2-5	0-5	18th	Froggatt, Quixall	29,614
39	6	H	Manchester City	D		1-1	0-1	18th	Woodhead	43,520
40	11	H	Bolton Wanderers	D		1-1	0-0	19th	Sewell	40,158
41	18	A	Aston Villa	L		3-4	3-1	20th	F. Moss (og), Sewell, Marriott	26,654
42	25	H	Sunderland	W		4-0	2-0	18th	Sewell (3), Aitken (og)	45,168
										Apps
									Three own-goals	Goals
FA Cup										
43	Jan 10	H	Blackpool	L	3R	1-2	0-1		Sewell	60,199
										Apps
										Goals

Bannister Keith	Capewell Ron	Codd Ron	Curtis Norman	Davies George	Dooley Derek	Finney Alan	Froggatt Redfern	Gannon Eddie	Jackson Norman	Jordan Clarrie	Kenny Mick	McAnearney Tom	McIntosh Dave	Marriott Jackie	O'Donnell Ralph	Quixall Albert	Rickett Walter	Sewell Jackie	Shadbolt Bill	Slater Brain	Storrar Dave	Turton Cyril	Witcomb Doug	Woodhead Dennis
			3		9		7	4	2				1			10	11	8				5	6	
			3		9		7	4	2				1			10	11	8				5	6	
			3		9		7	4	2				1			10	11	8				5	6	
			3		9		7		2			4	1			10	11	8				5	6	
2	1		3				7	4		9						10	11	8				5	6	
	1		3	6	9	7		4			2					10		8				5		11
	1		3	6	9	7		4			2					10		8				5		11
	1		3	6	9	7		4			2					10		8				5		11
	1		3	6	9	7		4			2					10		8				5		11
	1		3	6	9	7	10				2					8						5	4	11
	1		3	6	9	7	10				2					8						5	4	11
	1		3	6	9	7	10				2					8						5	4	11
	1		3	6	9	7	10				2					8						5	4	11
	1		3	6	9	7	10				2					8						5	4	11
	1		3	6	9		10		2							7		8				5	4	11
	1		3	6	9	7	10		2									8				5	4	11
	1		3	6	9	7	10				2							8				5	4	11
	1		3	6	9	7	10				2							8				5	4	11
	1		3	6	9	7	10				2					11		8				5	4	
	1		3		9	7	10	4			2					8						5	6	11
	1		3		9		10	4			2			7				8				5	6	11
	1		3		9		10	4			2			7				8				5	6	11
	1		3		9			4			2			7				8		10	11	5	6	
	1		3		9			4			2			7		10		8			11	5	6	
	1		3		9			4			2			7		10		8			11	5	6	
	1		3		9		10	4			2			7				8			11	5	6	
	1		3		9	7	10				2	4		11				8				5	6	
	1		3	6	9		10				2			7				8				5	4	11
	1		3	6	9	7	10				2							8				5	4	11
			3	6	9	7					2	4	1			8		10	11			5		
			3	6		7			2	9		4	1			8		10	11			5		
			3	6		7	10		2	9		4	1					8	11			5		
			3	6			10			9	2		1	7	5	8			11				4	
			3	6			10				2		1	7	5			8	11				4	9
		9	3	6			10				2		1	7	5			8					4	11
		9	3	6			10				2		1	7				8				5	4	11
			3	6		7	10				2		1			8		9	11			5	4	
			3	6			10	4	2				1	7		8		9	11			5		
			3	6			10	4			2		1	7	5	8		9						11
			3	6			10	4			2		1	7	5			9		8				11
			3	6				4			2		1	7	5	8		9		10				11
			3	6			10				2		1	7	5	8		9					4	11
1	25	2	42	29	29	20	32	19	9	4	32	5	17	17	7	27	5	35	7	3	4	35	31	25
			6		16	1	6			1				5		1		16						7

	1		3		9		10	4			2			7		11		8				5	6	
	1		1		1		1	1			1			1		1		1				1	1	
																		1						

League Table

	P	W	D	L	F	A	Pts
Arsenal	42	21	12	9	97	64	54
Preston North End	42	21	12	9	85	60	54
Wolverhampton W.	42	19	13	10	86	63	51
West Bromwich Albion	42	21	8	13	66	60	50
Charlton Athletic	42	19	11	12	77	63	49
Burnley	42	18	12	12	67	52	48
Blackpool	42	19	9	14	71	70	47
Manchester United	42	18	10	14	69	72	46
Sunderland	42	15	13	14	68	82	43
Tottenham Hotspur	42	15	11	16	78	69	41
Aston Villa	42	14	13	15	63	61	41
Cardiff City	42	14	12	16	54	46	40
Middlesbrough	42	14	11	17	70	77	39
Bolton Wanderers	42	15	9	18	61	69	39
Portsmouth	42	14	10	18	74	83	38
Newcastle United	42	14	9	19	59	70	37
Liverpool	42	14	8	20	61	82	36
SHEFFIELD WEDNESDAY	42	12	11	19	62	72	35
Chelsea	42	12	11	19	56	66	35
Manchester City	42	14	7	21	72	87	35
Stoke City	42	12	10	20	53	66	34
Derby County	42	11	10	21	59	74	32

1953-54

Division One

Manager: Eric Taylor

Did you know that?

Final League Position: 19th

In November 1953 Wednesday played in a friendly against Derby at the Baseball Ground for their first game in Britain under floodlights, wearing silk shirts of blue with white arms, and lost 3–1.

Sheffield United submitted a £15,000 bid for Redfern Froggatt, which was rejected after he was put on the transfer list at his own request.

Match No.	Date	Venue	Opponents		Round	Result	HT Score	Position	Scorers	Attendance
1	Aug 19	H	Manchester City	W		2-0	1-0		Jordan, Sewell	40,139
2	22	H	Tottenham Hotspur	W		2-1	1-1	1st	Sewell (2)	39,118
3	26	A	Preston North End	L		0-6	0-1	9th		33,118
4	29	A	Burnley	L		1-4	1-4	15th	Froggatt	25,813
5	Sep 2	H	Preston North End	W		4-2	2-0	9th	Woodhead, Froggatt, Shaw, Marriott	37,528
6	5	H	Charlton Athletic	L		1-2	1-1	14th	Woodhead	41,723
7	9	A	Bolton Wanderers	L		1-2	1-0	15th	Froggatt	31,143
8	12	A	Sheffield United	L		0-2	0-2	15th		45,805
9	16	H	Bolton Wanderers	W		2-1	0-1	14th	Sewell, Woodhead	27,107
10	19	A	Middlesbrough	L		1-4	0-3	16th	Jordan	22,638
11	23	H	Newcastle United	W		3-0	3-0	11th	Jordan (2), Marriott	29,271
12	26	H	West Bromwich Alb	L		2-3	0-1	14th	Sewell, Woodhead	45,508
13	Oct 3	A	Liverpool	D		2-2	0-2	12th	Sewell, Woodhead	38,647
14	10	H	Chelsea	W		2-0	1-0	11th	Froggatt, Shaw	32,217
15	17	A	Blackpool	W		2-1	2-0	8th	Woodhead, Finney	35,910
16	24	H	Portsmouth	D		4-4	2-0	8th	Sewell (2), Jordan (2)	37,091
17	31	A	Arsenal	L		1-4	1-3	9th	Woodhead	52,543
18	Nov 7	H	Aston Villa	W		3-1	2-0	9th	Quixall, Shaw, Finney	31,124
19	14	A	Huddersfield Town	L		0-2	0-1	11th		30,671
20	21	H	Sunderland	D		2-2	0-1	12th	Woodhead, Sewell	38,120
21	28	A	Wolverhampton W	L		1-4	1-2	14th	Woodhead	35,154
22	Dec 5	H	Cardiff City	W		2-1	1-0	10th	Froggatt, Sewell	28,183
23	12	A	Manchester City	L		2-3	2-2	13th	Froggatt, Curtis (pen)	27,710
24	19	A	Tottenham Hotspur	L		1-3	1-1	14th	Froggatt	25,957
25	25	A	Manchester United	L		2-5	1-1		Gannon, Woodhead	27,123
26	26	H	Manchester United	L		0-1	0-0	17th		44,196
27	Jan 2	H	Burnley	W		2-0	2-0	15th	Mather (og), Woodhead	34,040
28	16	A	Charlton Athletic	L		2-4	0-3	17th	Sewell, Shaw	19,655
29	23	H	Sheffield United	W		3-2	2-1	17th	Sewell, Shaw (2)	43,231
30	Feb 6	H	Middlesbrough	W		4-2	0-2	13th	Sewell, Woodhead (2), Shaw	31,159
31	13	A	West Bromwich Alb	L		2-4	2-2	15th	Woodhead, Shaw	38,475
32	24	H	Liverpool	D		1-1	0-0	13th	Woodhead	18,000
33	27	A	Chelsea	W		1-0	0-0	13th	Greenwood (og)	54,498
34	Mar 6	H	Blackpool	L		1-2	0-1	14th	Woodhead	42,183
35	20	H	Arsenal	W		2-1	0-1	14th	Gannon, Sewell	42,072
36	31	A	Aston Villa	L		1-2	1-2	15th	Woodhead	9,609
37	Apr 3	H	Huddersfield Town	L		1-4	0-2	17th	Shaw	31,106
38	7	A	Portsmouth	L		1-2	0-1	17th	Shaw	15,179
39	10	A	Sunderland	W		4-2	3-0	16th	Finney, Shaw (2), Froggatt	36,982
40	16	A	Newcastle United	L		0-3	0-1	18th		43,945
41	17	H	Wolverhampton W	D		0-0	0-0	17th		41,278
42	24	A	Cardiff City	D		2-2	1-2	19th	Sewell, Woodhead	15,777
										Apps
									Two own-goals	Goals

FA Cup

Match No.	Date	Venue	Opponents		Round	Result	HT Score	Position	Scorers	Attendance
43	Jan 9	H	Sheffield United	D	3R	1-1	0-1		Shaw	61,250
44	13	A	Sheffield United	W	3R Re	3-1	0-1		Finney, Davies, Sewell	40,847
45	30	H	Chesterfield	D	4R	0-0	0-0			46,188
46	Feb 3	A	Chesterfield	W	4R Re	4-2	1-1		Shaw (2), Sewell, Woodhead	21,808
47	20	H	Everton	W	5R	3-1	1-0		Shaw, Sewell, Woodhead	65,000
48	Mar 13	H	Bolton Wanderers	D	6R	1-1	0-0		Woodhead	65,000
49	17	A	Bolton Wanderers	W	6R Re	2-0	0-0		Sewell, Shaw	52,568
50	27	N	Preston North End *	L	S/F	0-2	0-0			75,213
										Apps
										Goals

* At Maine Road, Manchester

Butler Barry	Capewell Ron	Conwell Tony	Curtis Norman	Davies George	Finney Alan	Froggatt Redfern	Gannon Eddie	Jordan Clarrie	Kenny Mick	McAnearney Jim	McAnearney Tom	McIntosh Dave	Marriott Jackie	O'Donnell Ralph	Quixall Albert	Ryalls Brian	Seemley Ivor	Sewell Jackie	Shaw Jack	Turton Cyril	Woodhead Dennis
		2	3	6		10		9			4	1	7	5				8			11
		2	3	6		10		9			4	1	7	5				8			11
		2	3	6		10		9			4	1	7	5				8			11
	1	2	3	6		10					4		7	5				8	9		11
	1	2	3	6		10					4		7	5	8				9		11
	1	2	3	6		10					4		7	5	8				9		11
	1	2	3	6		10	4						7	5	8				9		11
		2	3	6		10					4		7	5	8	1		9			11
			3	6		10	4	9	2				7	5		1		8			11
			3	6		10	4	9	2				7	5		1		8			11
		2	3			10	6	9			4		7	5		1		8			11
		2	3		7		6	9			4			5	8	1		10			11
		2	3		7		6	9			4			5	8	1		10			11
		2	3		7	10	6				4			5		1		8	9		11
		2	3		7		6	9			4			5	8	1		10			11
		2	3		7		6	9			4			5	8	1		10			11
		2	3		7	10	6				4			5		1		8	9		11
		2	3		7		6				4			5	8	1		10	9		11
		2	3		7		6				4			5	8	1		10	9		11
		2	3		7		6	9			4			5	8	1		10			11
		2	3	6	7		4	9						5	8	1		10			11
		2	3	6		9	4						7		8	1		10		5	11
		2	3			9	6				4		7	5	8	1		10			11
			3		7	9	6		2		4				8	1		10		5	11
			3		7	9	6		2		4				8	1		10		5	11
			3		7		4		2				11		8	1	6	10		5	9
5				6	7		4		2						8	1	3	10	9		11
5				6	7		4		2						8	1	3	10	9		11
5				6	7		4		2				11		8	1	3	10	9		
5				6	7		4		2						8	1	3	10	9		11
5				6	7				2		4				8	1	3	10	9		11
5			3	6			4		2	8		1	7					10	9		11
5			3	6	7		4		2			1			8			10	9		11
5			3	6			4		2	8		1	7					10	9		11
5			2	6			4					1	7		8		3	10	9		11
5			2	6		10	4					1	7		8		3		9		11
5				6	7	10	4		2	8		1					3		9		11
			3	6	7	10	4		2				11	5	8	1			9		
			3	6	7	10	4		2			1	11	5	8				9		
			3	6		10	4			7		1	11	5	8		2		9		
			3	6		10	4		2			1	7	5	8				9		11
			3			10	4		2			1	7	5	6			8	9		11
11	4	21	36	27	22	24	34	12	18	4	21	13	24	27	30	25	10	33	24	4	38
			1		3	8	2	6					2		1			15	12		18

Butler Barry	Capewell Ron	Conwell Tony	Curtis Norman	Davies George	Finney Alan	Froggatt Redfern	Gannon Eddie	Jordan Clarrie	Kenny Mick	McAnearney Jim	McAnearney Tom	McIntosh Dave	Marriott Jackie	O'Donnell Ralph	Quixall Albert	Ryalls Brian	Seemley Ivor	Sewell Jackie	Shaw Jack	Turton Cyril	Woodhead Dennis
5				6	7		4		2						8	1	3	10	9		11
5				6	7		4		2						8	1	3	10	9		11
5				6	7		4		2				11		8	1	3	10	9		
5				6	7		4		2						8	1	3	10	9		11
5			2	6	7		4					1			8		3	10	9		11
5				6	7		4		2			1			8		3	10	9		11
5			2	6	7		4					1			8		3	10	9		11
5			2	6	7		4					1			8		3	10	9		11
8			3	8	8		8		5			4	1		8	4	8	8	8		7
				1	1													4	5		3

League Table

	P	W	D	L	F	A	Pts
Wolverhampton W.	42	25	7	10	96	56	57
West Bromwich Albion	42	22	9	11	86	63	53
Huddersfield Town	42	20	11	11	78	61	51
Manchester United	42	18	12	12	73	58	48
Bolton Wanderers	42	18	12	12	75	60	48
Blackpool	42	19	10	13	80	69	48
Burnley	42	21	4	17	78	67	46
Chelsea	42	16	12	14	74	68	44
Charlton Athletic	42	19	6	17	75	77	44
Cardiff City	42	18	8	16	51	71	44
Preston North End	42	19	5	18	87	58	43
Arsenal	42	15	13	14	75	73	43
Aston Villa	42	16	9	17	70	68	41
Portsmouth	42	14	11	17	81	89	39
Newcastle United	42	14	10	18	72	77	38
Tottenham Hotspur	42	16	5	21	65	76	37
Manchester City	42	14	9	19	62	77	37
Sunderland	42	14	8	20	81	89	36
SHEFFIELD WEDNESDAY	42	15	6	21	70	91	36
Sheffield United	42	11	11	20	69	90	33
Middlesbrough	42	10	10	22	60	91	30
Liverpool	42	9	10	23	68	97	28

1954-55

Division One

Manager: Eric Taylor

Did you know that?

Final League Position: 22nd

On 9 March 1955, the first floodlit match was played at Hillsborough between a Sheffield XI and an International XI, for Derek Dooley's benefit match, which was won 5–1 by the International team.

Match No.	Date	Venue	Opponents		Round	Result	HT Score	Position	Scorers	Attendance
1	Aug 21	A	Wolverhampton W	L		2-4	1-2		Finney, Curtis (pen)	44,753
2	23	H	Manchester United	L		2-4	1-2	17th	Shaw, Curtis (pen)	38,118
3	28	H	Aston Villa	W		6-3	5-1	14th	Quixall, Sewell (2), Shaw (2), Finney	34,243
4	Sep 1	A	Manchester United	L		0-2	0-2	17th		29,563
5	4	A	Sunderland	L		0-2	0-0	20th		52,112
6	6	H	Huddersfield Town	W		4-1	3-0	18th	Finney, Sewell, Froggatt, Shaw	25,825
7	11	H	Tottenham Hotspur	D		2-2	0-0	15th	Shaw, Sewell	34,681
8	13	A	Huddersfield Town	L		0-3	0-1	17th		20,570
9	18	A	Sheffield United	L		0-1	0-0	20th		37,308
10	25	A	Portsmouth	L		1-2	0-1	21st	Quixall	28,579
11	Oct 2	H	Blackpool	W		2-1	1-0	19th	Sewell, Quixall	32,107
12	9	H	Arsenal	L		1-2	0-1	20th	Shaw	39,167
13	16	A	West Bromwich Alb	W		2-1	1-1	18th	Shaw, Davies	35,257
14	23	H	Burnley	D		1-1	1-0	19th	Shaw	30,005
15	30	A	Preston North End	L		0-6	0-5	19th		23,401
16	Nov 6	H	Manchester City	L		2-4	1-1	22nd	McAnearney, Froggatt	19,152
17	13	A	Cardiff City	L		3-5	2-2	22nd	Sewell (2), Gannon	15,998
18	20	H	Chelsea	D		1-1	1-0	22nd	Sewell	25,906
19	27	A	Leicester City	L		3-4	2-4	22nd	Hukin (2), Sewell	28,474
20	Dec 4	H	Newcastle United	L		0-3	0-1	22nd		20,221
21	11	A	Everton	L		1-3	1-1	22nd	Hukin	36,849
22	18	H	Wolverhampton W	D		2-2	2-1	22nd	Sewell, Marriott	33,102
23	25	A	Charlton Athletic	L		0-3	0-2	22nd		17,786
24	27	H	Charlton Athletic	D		2-2	1-1	22nd	Hammond (og), Curtis (pen)	43,114
25	Jan 1	A	Aston Villa	D		0-0	0-0	22nd		22,990
26	15	H	Sunderland	L		1-2	0-1	22nd	Sewell	16,975
27	22	A	Tottenham Hotspur	L		2-7	1-4	22nd	Sewell, Watson	26,310
28	Feb 5	H	Sheffield United	L		1-2	0-2	22nd	Marriott	36,176
29	12	H	Portsmouth	L		1-3	1-1	22nd	Woodhead	21,176
30	19	A	Blackpool	L		1-2	1-2	22nd	Butler	18,959
31	26	A	Arsenal	L		2-3	0-2	22nd	Marriott, Quixall	26,910
32	Mar 5	H	Everton	D		2-2	0-1	22nd	Sewell, Marriott	22,214
33	12	A	Burnley	L		0-2	0-0	22nd		20,082
34	19	H	Preston North End	W		2-0	0-0	22nd	Shaw, Marriott	21,048
35	30	A	Manchester City	D		2-2	1-0	22nd	Ewing (og), Ellis	14,825
36	Apr 2	H	Cardiff City	D		1-1	0-0	22nd	Curtis (pen)	20,295
37	8	A	Bolton Wanderers	D		2-2	1-0	22nd	Quixall, Marriott	22,828
38	9	A	Newcastle United	L		0-5	0-2	22nd		40,883
39	11	H	Bolton Wanderers	W		3-2	2-0	22nd	Froggatt (2), Curtis (pen)	17,267
40	16	H	Leicester City	W		1-0	1-0	22nd	Froggatt	20,539
41	23	A	Chelsea	L		0-3	0-1	22nd		51,421
42	30	H	West Bromwich Alb	W		5-0	1-0	22nd	Curtis (pen), Sewell, Marriott, Finney (2)	16,664
										Apps
									Two own-goals	Goals

FA Cup

Match No.	Date	Venue	Opponents		Round	Result	HT Score	Position	Scorers	Attendance
43	Jan 8	H	Hastings United	W	3R	2-1	0-1		Shaw, Greensmith	25,965
44	29	H	Notts County	D	4R	1-1	0-0		Watson	53,138
45	Feb 3	A	Notts County *	L	4R Re	0-1	0-0			35,488
										Apps
										Goals

* After extra-time.

Butler Barry	Conwell Tony	Curtis Norman	Davies George	Ellis Keith	Finney Alan	Froggatt Redfern	Gannon Eddie	Greensmith Ron	Howells Peter	Hukin Arthur	Jordan Clarrie	Kay Tony	Kenny Mick	McAnearney Jim	McAnearney Tom	McEvoy Don	McIntosh Dave	Marriott Jackie	Martin Jack	O'Donnell Ralph	Quixall Albert	Ryalls Brian	Seemley Ivor	Sewell Jackie	Shaw Jack	Turley Mike	Watson Don	Wilkinson Derek	Woodhead Dennis
		3	6		7		4						2				1			5	8			10	9				11
		3	6		7		4						2					11		5	8	1		10	9				
	2	3	6		7	11	4										1			5	8			10	9				
	2	3	6		7	11	4										1			5	8			10	9				
5	2	3	6		7	11	4										1				8			10	9				
5	2	3	6		7	11	4							8			1							10	9				
5	2	3	6		7	11	4							8			1							10	9				
5	2	3	6		7	10								8			1			4				9					11
5	2	3	6			11	4				9						1	7			8			10					
5	2	3	6			11	4										1	7			8			10	9				
5	2	3	6		7	11	4										1				8			10	9				
5	2	3	6		7	11	4										1				8			10	9				
5	2	3	6		7	11	4										1				8			10	9				
5	2	3	6		7	11	4										1				8			10	9				
5	2	3	6		7	11	4										1				8			10	9				
5	2	3			7	10			11					8			1			6	4				9				
	2	3				10	4							8			1	11		5				9	6			7	
	2	3			7	10	4											11		5	8	1		9	6				
	2	3			7		4			9								11		5	10	1		8	6				
	2	3					4			9							1	7		5	10			8	6				11
		2					4			9							1			5	10		3	8	6			7	11
		2	6				8			9						5	1	7					3	10	4				11
		2	6				8			9						5	1	7					3	10	4				11
	2	3					4			9						5	1	7			8			10	6				11
	2	3					4	11						10		5	1	7			8				9	6			
	2	3			11		4							8		5	1	7			10			9		6			
		2	6		7											5	1	11			10		3	8		4	9		
5	2	3	6			10	4										1	7			8						9		11
5	2						4						3				1	7			8			10	6		9		11
9		3	6		7											5	1	11	2		8				4		10		
		3	6		7										4	5	1	11	2		8			10	9				
		3	6													5	1	7	2	4	10			8	9				11
					7										4	5	1	11	2	6	10		3	8	9				
		3		9	7		4								6	5	1	11	2		8				10				
		3		9	7		6								4	5	1	11	2		8				10				
		3		9	7		6								4	5	1	11	2		8				10				
		3		9	7							6			4	5	1	11	2		8			10					
		3		9	7							6			4	5	1	11	2		8			10					
		3			7	9						6			4	5	1	11	2		8			10					
		3			7	9						6			4	5	1	11	2		8			10					
		3			7	9						6			4	5	1	11	2		8			10					
		3			7	10						6			4	5	1	11	2					8			9		
15	23	40	22	5	30	21	29	1	1	6	1	6	3	7	11	19	39	28	13	13	35	3	5	35	31	3	5	2	10
1		6	1	1	5	5	1			3				1				7			5			14	9		1		1

Butler Barry	Conwell Tony	Curtis Norman	Davies George	Ellis Keith	Finney Alan	Froggatt Redfern	Gannon Eddie	Greensmith Ron	Howells Peter	Hukin Arthur	Jordan Clarrie	Kay Tony	Kenny Mick	McAnearney Jim	McAnearney Tom	McEvoy Don	McIntosh Dave	Marriott Jackie	Martin Jack	O'Donnell Ralph	Quixall Albert	Ryalls Brian	Seemley Ivor	Sewell Jackie	Shaw Jack	Turley Mike	Watson Don	Wilkinson Derek	Woodhead Dennis
	2	3					4	11						10		5	1	7			8				9	6			
5	2	3	6		7		4										1	11			10			8			9		
5	2	3	6		7	10	4										1	11			8						9		
2	3	3	2		2	1	3	1						1		1	3	3			3			1	1	1	2		
								1																	1		1		

League Table

	P	W	D	L	F	A	Pts
Chelsea	42	20	12	10	81	57	52
Wolverhampton W.	42	19	10	13	89	70	48
Portsmouth	42	18	12	12	74	62	48
Sunderland	42	15	18	9	64	54	48
Manchester United	42	20	7	15	84	74	47
Aston Villa	42	20	7	15	72	73	47
Manchester City	42	18	10	14	76	69	46
Newcastle United	42	17	9	16	89	77	43
Arsenal	42	17	9	16	69	63	43
Burnley	42	17	9	16	51	48	43
Everton	42	16	10	16	62	68	42
Huddersfield Town	42	14	13	15	63	68	41
Sheffield United	42	17	7	18	70	86	41
Preston North End	42	16	8	18	83	64	40
Charlton Athletic	42	15	10	17	76	75	40
Tottenham Hotspur	42	16	8	18	72	73	40
West Bromwich Albion	42	16	8	18	76	96	40
Bolton Wanderers	42	13	13	16	62	69	39
Blackpool	42	14	10	18	60	64	38
Cardiff City	42	13	11	18	62	76	37
Leicester City	42	12	11	19	74	86	35
SHEFFIELD WEDNESDAY	42	8	10	24	63	100	26

1955-56

Division Two

Manager: Eric Taylor

Did you know that?

Final League Position: 1st

On 4 October 1955 Wednesday played Sheffield United in a secret, behind-closed-doors friendly to help the players acclimatise to playing under lights. Two reporters were allowed into the game but sworn to secrecy. However, a reporter leaked the score – Wednesday won 7–2, with Jackie Sewell and Ron Shiner both getting hat-tricks, while Albert Quixall got the other goal. Six days later, Wednesday played a friendly against Vasas of Budapest, losing 7–1 under lights.

On 21 March 1956 Wednesday played their first Football League game at home under floodlights, beating Barnsley 3–0.

Match No.	Date	Venue	Opponents		Round	Result	HT Score	Position	Scorers	Attendance
1	Aug 20	H	Plymouth Argyle	W		5-2	1-1		Sewell (3), Quixall (2)	31,716
2	24	A	Liverpool	W		3-0	1-0		Froggatt, Shiner, Sewell	41,791
3	27	A	Stoke City	L		0-2	0-2	5th		24,529
4	31	H	Liverpool	D		1-1	0-0	5th	Broadbent	30,853
5	Sep 3	H	Bristol Rovers	W		4-2	1-1	4th	Froggatt, Sewell,Shiner (2)	30,526
6	7	A	Lincoln City	D		2-2	1-1	6th	Sewell (2)	21,088
7	10	A	Doncaster Rovers	D		2-2	2-2	5th	Shiner, Broadbent	26,790
8	12	H	Leicester City	D		1-1	0-1	4th	Shiner	25,819
9	17	H	Swansea Town	D		2-2	0-1	5th	Sewell (2)	29,128
10	24	H	Nottingham Forest	L		1-2	0-0	10th	Sewell	29,304
11	Oct 1	A	Hull City	D		2-2	1-1	9th	Froggatt, Quixall	16,748
12	8	A	Notts County	D		1-1	1-1	10th	Froggatt	23,500
13	15	H	Leeds United	W		4-0	2-0	6th	Shiner (2), Sewell (2)	28,646
14	22	A	Port Vale	W		1-0	0-0	4th	Quixall	23,129
15	29	H	Bury	D		3-3	2-2	5th	Quixall, Froggatt, Sewell	25,138
16	Nov 5	A	Barnsley	W		3-0	0-0	3rd	Shiner (2), Broadbent	21,544
17	12	H	Middlesbrough	W		3-1	3-0	3rd	Shiner, Wilkinson, Gibson	25,180
18	19	A	Bristol City	L		2-3	1-2	3rd	Broadbent, Shiner (pen)	32,731
19	26	H	West Ham United	D		1-1	0-1	4th	Shiner (pen)	21,670
20	Dec 3	A	Fulham	W		2-1	1-1	2nd	Shiner, Broadbent	23,286
21	10	H	Rotherham United	L		0-2	0-2	2nd		23,108
22	17	A	Plymouth Argyle	D		1-1	1-0	3rd	Staniforth (pen)	17,276
23	24	H	Stoke City	W		4-0	1-0	1st	Shiner, Froggatt, Broadbent, Quixall	23,579
24	26	A	Blackburn Rovers	D		2-2	0-0	1st	Shiner (2)	24,139
25	27	H	Blackburn Rovers	W		5-1	2-0	1st	Froggatt (2), Broadbent, Shiner, Finney	31,574
26	31	A	Bristol Rovers	L		2-4	1-0	1st	Quixall, Shiner	30,887
27	Jan 14	H	Doncaster Rovers	W		5-2	0-2	1st	Froggatt, Quixall (2), Shiner (2)	18,281
28	21	A	Swansea Town	L		1-2	0-1	1st	Quixall	14,285
29	Feb 4	A	Nottingham Forest	W		1-0	1-0	1st	Broadbent	16,508
30	11	H	Hull City	W		4-1	2-0	1st	Froggatt, Shiner (2), Quixall	19,481
31	18	H	Bristol City	W		2-1	1-1	1st	Quixall (2)	22,539
32	25	A	Leeds United	L		1-2	0-1	1st	Broadbent	43,268
33	Mar 3	H	Port Vale	W		4-0	2-0	1st	Quixall, Shiner, O'Donnell, Finney	30,587
34	10	A	Rotherham United	W		3-2	0-2	1st	Quixall, Shiner, Froggatt	19,781
35	21	H	Barnsley	W		3-0	0-0	1st	Shiner (2), Froggatt	31,577
36	24	A	Middlesbrough	D		2-2	1-1	1st	Shiner, Quixall	19,026
37	31	H	Notts County	W		1-0	0-0	1st	Staniforth	32,263
38	Apr 2	A	Leicester City	W		2-1	1-1	1st	Froggatt (2)	37,624
39	7	A	West Ham United	D		3-3	2-1	1st	Broadbent (2), Howells	17,549
40	14	H	Fulham	L		2-3	0-2	1st	Shiner, Finney (pen)	27,439
41	21	A	Bury	W		5-2	3-0	1st	Broadbent, Shiner (2), Finney, Quixall	23,333
42	28	H	Lincoln City	W		5-3	2-3	1st	Shiner (3), Finney (1 + pen)	32,129
										Apps
										Goals
FA Cup										
43	Jan 7	H	Newcastle United	L	3R	1-3	0-0		Gibson	48,198
										Apps
										Goals

Bingley Walt	Broadbent Albert	Curtis Norman	Finney Alan	Froggatt Redfern	Gibson Don	Howells Peter	Kay Tony	Martin Jack	McAnearney Jim	McAnearney Tom	McEvoy Don	McIntosh Dave	O'Donnell Ralph	Quixall Albert	Sewell Jackie	Shiner Roy	Staniforth Ron	Swan Peter	Wilkinson Derek	Williams Les
	11	3	7		4					6		1	5	10	8	9	2			
	11	3		7	4					6		1	5	10	8	9	2			
	11	3		7	4					6		1	5	10	8	9	2			
	11	3		7	4					6			5	10	8	9	2			1
3	11			7	4					6			5	10	8	9	2			1
3	11			7	4					6			5	10	8	9	2			1
3	11			7	4					6			5	10	8	9	2			1
3	11			7	4			2	10	6		1	5		8	9				
	11	3		7	4					6		1	5	10	8	9	2			
3	11			7	4					6	5	1		10	8	9	2			
3	11			7	4					6	5	1		10	8	9	2			
3	11			7	4		6				5	1		10	8	9	2			
3	11			7	4		6				5	1		10	8	9	2			
3	11			7	4		6				5	1		10	8	9	2			
3	11			7	4		6					1	5	10	8	9	2			
3	11			10	4		6							8		9	2	5	7	1
3	11			10	4		6							8		9	2	5	7	1
3	11			10	4		6				2			8		9		5	7	1
3	11		7	10	4		6	2			5				8	9				1
3	11		7	10	4					6	5	1		8		9	2			
3	11		7	10						4		1	6	8		9	2	5		
3			7	10	4	11					5	1	6	8		9	2			
3	11		7	10	4						5	1	6	8		9	2			
3	11		7	10	4						5	1	6	8		9	2			
3	11	2	7	10	4						5		6	8		9				1
3	11	2	7	10	4						5	1	6	8		9				
	11	3	7	10	4						5	1	6	8		9	2			
	11	3	7	10	4						5	1	6	8		9	2			
	11	3	7	10						4	5	1	6	8		9	2			
	11	3	7	10						4	5	1	6	8		9	2			
	11	3	7	10						4	5	1	6	8		9	2			
	11	3	7	10						4	5	1	6	8		9	2			
	11	3	7	10						4	5	1	6	8		9	2			
	11	3	7	10						4	5	1	6	8		9	2			
	11	3	7	10						4	5	1	6	8		9	2			
	11	3	7	10						4	5	1	6	8		9	2			
	11	3	7	10						4	5	1	6	8		9	2			
	11	3	7	10						4	5	1	6	8		9	2			
	10	3	7	8		11				4	5	1	6			9	2			
	11	3	7	10						4	5	1	6	8		9	2			
	11	3	7	10						4	5	1	6	8		9	2			
	11	3	7	10						4	5	1	6	8		9	2			
21	41	23	25	41	27	2	8	2	1	27	29	33	32	39	16	42	37	4	3	9
	12		6	14	1	1							1	17	13	33	2		1	

Bingley Walt	Broadbent Albert	Curtis Norman	Finney Alan	Froggatt Redfern	Gibson Don	Howells Peter	Kay Tony	Martin Jack	McAnearney Jim	McAnearney Tom	McEvoy Don	McIntosh Dave	O'Donnell Ralph	Quixall Albert	Sewell Jackie	Shiner Roy	Staniforth Ron	Swan Peter	Wilkinson Derek	Williams Les
3	11		7	10	4						5	1	6	8		9	2			
1	1		1	1	1						1	1	1	1		1	1			
					1															

League Table

	P	W	D	L	F	A	Pts
SHEFFIELD WEDNESDAY	42	21	13	8	101	62	55
Leeds United	42	23	6	13	80	60	52
Liverpool	42	21	6	15	85	63	48
Blackburn Rovers	42	21	6	15	84	65	48
Leicester City	42	21	6	15	94	78	48
Bristol Rovers	42	21	6	15	84	70	48
Nottingham Forest	42	19	9	14	68	63	47
Lincoln City	42	18	10	14	79	65	46
Fulham	42	20	6	16	89	79	46
Swansea Town	42	20	6	16	83	81	46
Bristol City	42	19	7	16	80	64	45
Port Vale	42	16	13	13	60	58	45
Stoke City	42	20	4	18	71	62	44
Middlesbrough	42	16	8	18	76	78	40
Bury	42	16	8	18	86	90	40
West Ham United	42	14	11	17	74	69	39
Doncaster Rovers	42	12	11	19	69	96	35
Barnsley	42	11	12	19	47	84	34
Rotherham United	42	12	9	21	56	75	33
Notts County	42	11	9	22	55	82	31
Plymouth Argyle	42	10	8	24	54	87	28
Hull City	42	10	6	26	53	97	26

1956-57

Division One

Manager: Eric Taylor

Did you know that?

Final League Position: 14th

On 14 January 1957 no programme was produced for the FA Cup third-round second replay against Preston North End, played at Goodison Park, Liverpool.

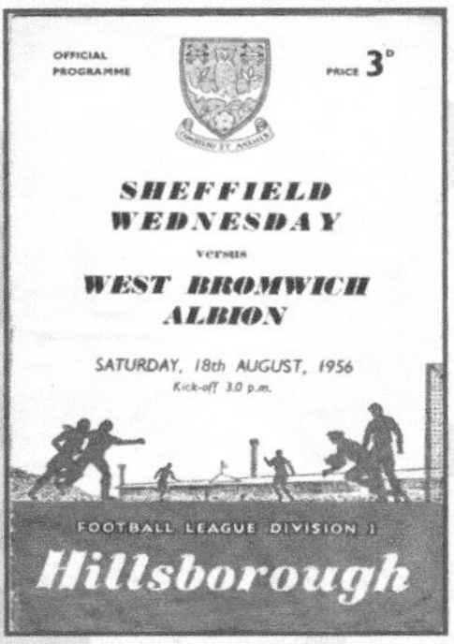

Match No.	Date	Venue	Opponents		Round	Result	HT Score	Position	Scorers	Attendance
1	Aug 18	H	West Bromwich Alb	W		4-2	1-1		Shiner (2), Finney, Quixall	22,586
2	22	H	Chelsea	W		4-0	2-0	1st	Shiner (2), Quixall (2)	36,543
3	25	A	Portsmouth	L		1-3	0-2	5th	Froggatt	23,983
4	Sep 1	H	Newcastle United	W		4-0	3-0	7th	Finney, Broadbent, Shiner, Quixall	36,270
5	5	A	Cardiff City	L		1-2	1-2	10th	Shiner	12,983
6	8	A	Charlton Athletic	D		4-4	3-1	9th	Finney, Shiner (2), Froggatt	21,335
7	12	H	Cardiff City	W		5-3	2-2	7th	Stitfall (og), Froggatt (2), Quixall (pen), Finney	38,721
8	15	A	Manchester United	L		1-4	0-3	9th	Quixall	48,306
9	19	A	Chelsea	D		0-0	0-0	8th		21,971
10	22	H	Arsenal	L		2-4	1-1	9th	Quixall (2)	40,629
11	29	A	Burnley	L		1-4	0-3	12th	Shiner	23,339
12	Oct 6	H	Sunderland	W		3-2	1-1	11th	Shiner, Broadbent, Froggatt	33,423
13	13	A	Luton Town	L		0-2	0-0	12th		19,202
14	20	H	Blackpool	L		1-2	1-1	14th	Broadbent	46,539
15	27	A	Manchester City	L		2-4	1-1	14th	Watson, McEvoy	29,259
16	Nov 3	H	Bolton Wanderers	L		1-2	0-2	14th	Watson	24,691
17	10	A	Leeds United	L		1-3	1-1	18th	Finney	31,857
18	17	H	Tottenham Hotspur	W		4-1	2-0	16th	Quixall, Finney (3)	32,214
19	24	A	Everton	L		0-1	0-0	19th		34,247
20	Dec 1	H	Aston Villa	W		2-1	1-1	17th	Quixall (2)	24,353
21	8	A	Wolverhampton W	L		1-2	1-2	19th	Wilkinson	27,453
22	15	A	West Bromwich Alb	W		4-1	2-0	16th	Froggatt (2), Quixall, Shiner	17,029
23	25	A	Birmingham City	L		0-4	0-2	17th		24,380
24	29	A	Newcastle United	W		2-1	1-0	17th	Finney, Froggatt	42,649
25	Jan 12	H	Charlton Athletic	W		3-1	3-0	15th	Froggatt, Gibson, Finney	24,589
26	19	H	Manchester United	W		2-1	1-0	14th	Shiner, Quixall	51,068
27	Feb 2	A	Arsenal	L		3-6	0-1	15th	Shiner, Quixall (pen), Broadbent	40,217
28	9	H	Burnley	D		0-0	0-0	15th		30,358
29	16	A	Sunderland	L		2-5	2-2	15th	Quixall, O'Donnell	44,135
30	23	H	Manchester City	D		2-2	2-1	16th	Quixall, Ellis	11,271
31	Mar 2	A	Blackpool	L		1-3	0-0	16th	Finney	18,444
32	9	H	Wolverhampton W	W		2-1	0-0	16th	J. McAnearney, Quixall	30,130
33	16	A	Bolton Wanderers	L		2-3	0-2	16th	J. McAnearney, Finney	18,424
34	26	H	Leeds United	L		2-3	2-1	17th	Quixall, Froggatt	33,205
35	30	A	Tottenham Hotspur	D		1-1	0-0	18th	Froggatt	34,370
36	Apr 6	H	Everton	D		2-2	0-1	18th	Quixall (pen), Curtis	23,258
37	9	H	Portsmouth	W		3-1	2-1	16th	Shiner (2), Wilkinson	19,890
38	13	A	Aston Villa	L		0-5	0-2	16th		28,134
39	19	A	Preston North End	L		0-1	0-1	17th		20,075
40	20	H	Luton Town	W		3-0	0-0	16th	Quixall (pen), Froggatt, Ellis	22,497
41	22	H	Preston North End	W		3-1	1-0	15th	Quixall (2 pens), Ellis	21,131
42	29	H	Birmingham City	W		3-0	2-0	14th	Ellis (3)	15,307
										Apps
									One own-goal	Goals

FA Cup

Match No.	Date	Venue	Opponents		Round	Result	HT Score	Position	Scorers	Attendance
43	Jan 5	A	Preston North End	D	3R	0-0	0-0			28,777
44	9	H	Preston North End *	D	3R Re	2-2	1-0		Quixall, Shiner	60,168
45	14	N	Preston North End #	L	3R 2Re	1-5	1-3		Quixall	32,108
										Apps
										Goals

* Score at full-time 1-1

2nd Replay at Goodison Park, Liverpool

Bingley Walt	Broadbent Albert	Cargill Dave	Curtis Norman	Ellis Keith	Finney Alan	Froggatt Redfern	Gibson Don	Greensmith Ron	Hill Brian	Hinchcliffe Alan	Martin Jack	McAnearney Jim	McAnearney Tom	McEvoy Don	McIntosh Dave	O'Donnell Ralph	Pllu Charlie	Quixall Albert	Shiner Roy	Staniforth Ron	Swan Peter	Watson Don	Whitham Terry	Wilkinson Derek	Williams Les	Young Garry
	11		3		7	10							4	5	1	6		8	9	2						
	11		3		7	10							4	5	1	6		8	9	2						
	11		3		7	10							4	5	1	6		8	9	2						
	11		3		7	10							4	5	1	6		8	9	2						
	11		3		7	10							4	5	1	6		8	9	2						
	11		3		7	10							4	5	1	6		8	9	2						
			3		7	10							4		1	6		8	9	2	5			11		
			3		7	10							4		1	6		8	9	2	5			11		
	10	11	3		7								4		1	6			9	2	5	8				
	10	11	3		7								4		1	6		8	9	2	5					
3		11			7	10					2		4			6		8	9	5					1	
3	11				7	10							4	5	1	6		8	9	2						
	11		3		7	10								5	1	6		8	9	2			4			
	11		3		7	10								5	1	6		8	9	2			4			
	11		3		7	10	4							5		6		8		2		9			1	
3	11		2		7		4			1				5		6		8	9			10				
3		11	2		7	10	6			1			4	5				8	9							
		11	3		7	10	6						4	5	1			8	9	2						
		11	3		7	10	6						4	5	1			8	9	2						
		11	3		7	10	6						4	5	1			8	9	2						
			3		11	10	6						4	5	1			8	9	2				7		
			3		11	10	6						4	5	1			8	9	2				7		
		11	3		7	10	6						4	5	1			8	9	2						
		11	3		7	10							4	5	1	6		8	9	2						
	11		3		7	10	6						4	5	1			8	9	2						
	11		3		7							10	4	5	1	6		8	9	2						
	11		3		7							10	4	5	1	6		8	9	2						
	11		3		7							10	4	5	1	6		8	9	2						
	11		3		7	10							4	5	1	6		8	9	2						
	11		3	9	7							10	4	5	1	6		8		2						
			3	9	7			11	6		2		4	5	1			8								10
			3		7			11				10	4	5	1	6		8	9	2						
			3		7			11			2	10	4	5	1	6		8	9							
	11		3		7	10					2		4	5	1	6		8	9							
	11		3		7	10					2		4	5	1	6		8	9							
	11		3		7	10					2		4	5		6	1	8	9							
	11		3			10					2		4	5		6	1	8	9					7		
	11		3			10					2		6	5			1	8	9		4			7		
	11		3	9		10							4	5		6	1	8		2				7		
	11		3	9		10							4	5		6	1	8		2				7		
	11		3	9		10					2		4	5		6	1	8						7		
	11		3	9							2	10	4	5		6	1	8						7		
4	28	9	40	6	36	31	10	3	1	2	10	7	38	37	31	32	7	41	35	31	5	3	2	10	2	1
	4		1	6	12	12	1					2		1		1		22	15			2		2		

Bingley Walt	Broadbent Albert	Cargill Dave	Curtis Norman	Ellis Keith	Finney Alan	Froggatt Redfern	Gibson Don	Greensmith Ron	Hill Brian	Hinchcliffe Alan	Martin Jack	McAnearney Jim	McAnearney Tom	McEvoy Don	McIntosh Dave	O'Donnell Ralph	Pllu Charlie	Quixall Albert	Shiner Roy	Staniforth Ron	Swan Peter	Watson Don	Whitham Terry	Wilkinson Derek	Williams Les	Young Garry
		11	3		7	10	6						4	5	1			8	9	2						
		11	3		7	10	6						4	5	1			8	9	2						
	11		3		7							10	4	5	1	6		8	9	2						
	1	2	3		3	2	2					1	3	3	3	1		3	3	3						
																		2	1							

League Table

	P	W	D	L	F	A	Pts
Manchester United	42	28	8	6	103	54	64
Tottenham Hotspur	42	22	12	8	104	56	56
Preston North End	42	23	10	9	84	56	56
Blackpool	42	22	9	11	93	65	53
Arsenal	42	21	8	13	85	69	50
Wolverhampton W.	42	20	8	14	94	70	48
Burnley	42	18	10	14	56	50	46
Leeds United	42	15	14	13	72	63	44
Bolton Wanderers	42	16	12	14	65	65	44
Aston Villa	42	14	15	13	65	55	43
West Bromwich Albion	42	14	14	14	59	61	42
Chelsea	42	13	13	16	73	73	39
Birmingham City	42	15	9	18	69	69	39
SHEFFIELD WEDNESDAY	42	16	6	20	82	88	38
Everton	42	14	10	18	61	79	38
Luton Town	42	14	9	19	58	76	37
Newcastle United	42	14	8	20	67	87	36
Manchester City	42	13	9	20	78	88	35
Portsmouth	42	10	13	19	62	92	33
Sunderland	42	12	8	22	67	88	32
Cardiff City	42	10	9	23	53	88	29
Charlton Athletic	42	9	4	29	62	120	22

1957-58

Division One

Manager: Eric Taylor

Did you know that?

Final League Position: 22nd

The first two games of the season, against Manchester City and Newcastle United, both away, had to be postponed due to the Wednesday players being ill with flu. A weakened Wednesday team did eventually start their season late, losing 2–1 at home to Nottingham Forest.

Christmas Day 1957 was the last time Wednesday had to play on this day in a 4–4 home draw with Preston North End.

Match No.	Date	Venue	Opponents		Round	Result	HT Score	Position	Scorers	Attendance
1	Aug 31	H	Nottingham Forest	L		1-2	1-1	21st	J. McAnearney	31,495
2	Sep 4	H	Newcastle United	W		1-0	0-0	17th	Broadbent	23,060
3	7	A	Portsmouth	L		2-3	0-1	21st	J. McAnearney, Ellis	29,141
4	11	H	Leicester City	W		2-1	1-0	13th	J. McAnearney, Ellis	18,270
5	14	H	West Bromwich Alb	L		1-2	1-2	16th	Ellis	23,395
6	18	A	Leicester City	L		1-4	0-3	20th	T. McAnearney	22,449
7	21	A	Tottenham Hotspur	L		2-4	1-2	22nd	Hopkins (og), Ellis	39,954
8	25	A	Newcastle United	D		0-0	0-0	21st		27,630
9	28	H	Birmingham City	W		5-3	1-1	19th	Smith (og), Quixall (2), Ellis (2)	20,311
10	Oct 5	A	Chelsea	L		0-1	0-0	21st		38,722
11	9	A	Manchester City	L		0-2	0-1	21st		24,036
12	12	H	Blackpool	L		0-3	0-1	21st		31,163
13	19	A	Luton Town	L		0-2	0-1	22nd		14,473
14	26	H	Sunderland	D		3-3	0-0	21st	Young, Quixall, Froggatt	22,618
15	Nov 2	A	Bolton Wanderers	L		4-5	3-2	22nd	Finney, Shiner (2), Quixall	18,072
16	9	H	Leeds United	W		3-2	3-1	21st	J. McAnearney, Froggatt (2)	22,641
17	16	A	Manchester United	L		1-2	1-2	21st	Finney	41,066
18	23	H	Arsenal	W		2-0	1-0	21st	Quixall (pen), Froggatt	23,904
19	30	A	Everton	D		1-1	1-1	21st	Finney	31,011
20	Dec 7	H	Aston Villa	L		2-5	0-3	21st	Ellis (2)	16,144
21	14	A	Wolverhampton W	L		3-4	1-1	22nd	Finney, Wilkinson, Shiner	28,082
22	21	H	Manchester City	L		4-5	2-3	21st	Froggatt, Wilkinson, Shiner, Quixall	22,042
23	25	H	Preston North End	D		4-4	2-1	21st	Froggatt, Finney (2), Wilkinson	26,825
24	26	A	Preston North End	L		0-3	0-1	22nd		28,055
25	28	A	Nottingham Forest	L		2-5	2-3	22nd	Wilkinson, Shiner	31,783
26	Jan 11	H	Portsmouth	W		4-2	1-0	22nd	Quixall (pen), Shiner, Wilkinson, Froggatt	21,308
27	18	A	West Bromwich Alb	L		1-3	0-3	22nd	Shiner	28,819
28	Feb 1	H	Tottenham Hotspur	W		2-0	1-0	22nd	Wilkinson, Shiner	23,696
29	15	H	Chelsea	L		2-3	1-2	22nd	Quixall (2 pens)	17,588
30	22	A	Blackpool	D		2-2	0-1	22nd	Johnson (2)	13,771
31	Mar 1	H	Luton Town	W		2-1	0-1	21st	Shiner (2)	17,747
32	8	A	Sunderland	D		3-3	2-1	21st	Aitken (og), Wilkinson, O'Donnell	22,549
33	12	A	Birmingham City	L		0-1	0-1	21st		15,937
34	15	H	Bolton Wanderers	W		1-0	1-0	20th	Quixall	25,825
35	22	A	Arsenal	L		0-1	0-1	22nd		28,074
36	29	H	Manchester United	W		1-0	1-0	22nd	Shiner	35,608
37	Apr 4	A	Burnley	L		0-2	0-1	22nd		18,165
38	5	A	Leeds United	D		2-2	1-1	22nd	Wilkinson, Shiner	26,212
39	7	H	Burnley	L		1-2	1-1	22nd	Shiner	23,714
40	12	H	Everton	W		2-1	0-0	21st	Quixall, Curtis	18,715
41	19	A	Aston Villa	L		0-2	0-0	22nd		25,955
42	26	H	Wolverhampton W	W		2-1	2-0	22nd	Wilkinson, Shiner	25,254
										Apps
									Three own-goals	Goals

FA Cup

Match No.	Date	Venue	Opponents		Round	Result	HT Score	Position	Scorers	Attendance
43	Jan 4	A	Hereford United	W	3R	3-0	1-0		Froggatt (2), Shiner	18,114
44	29	H	Hull City	W	4R	4-3	1-1		Wilkinson, Shiner, Durham (og), Froggatt	47,119
45	Feb 19	A	Manchester United	L	5R	0-3	0-1			59,848
										Apps
									One own-goal	Goals

Baker Peter	Bingley Walt	Broadbent Albert	Cargill Dave	Clark Harry	Curtis Norman	Ellis Keith	Fantham John	Finney Alan	Froggatt Redfern	Gibson Don	Greensmith Ron	Hill Brian	Johnson Peter	Kay Tony	Martin Jack	McAnearney Jim	McAnearney Tom	McEvoy Don	McIntosh Dave	O'Donnell Ralph	Pinner Mike	Pllu Charlie	Quixall Albert	Ryalls Brian	Shaw Jack	Shiner Roy	Springett Ron	Staniforth Ron	Swan Peter	Wilkinson Derek	Young Gerry
	3	11				9		7								10	4	5		6		1	8					2			
2	3	11				9		7								10	4	5		6		1	8								
2	3	11				9		7								10	4	5		6		1	8								
2	3	11				9		7								10	4	5		6		1	8								
2	3	11				9		7								10	4	5		6		1	8								
		11			3			7	10	6					2		4	5				1	8			9					
2	3	11				9		7		6						10	4	5				1	8								
2	3	11						7		6							4	5					8	1		9					10
2	3	11				9		7		6							4	5					8	1							10
2	3							7		6							4	5					8	1		9				11	10
	3							7		8	11						4	5		6				1		9		2			10
	3	11		10				7		8							4	5		6				1	9			2			
	3	11				9		7	10	4		6			2			5				1	8								
	3	11						7	9			6			2		4	5				1	8								10
					3			11	10			6			2		4	5				1	8			9				7	
					3			11	10			6			2	8	4			5		1				9				7	
					3			11	10			6			2	8	4			5		1				9				7	
					3			11	10			6			2		4		1	5			8			9				7	
					3	9		11	10			6					4		1	5			8					2		7	
					3	9		11	10			6					4		1	5			8					2		7	
					3			11	10			6			2		4			5	1		8			9				7	
					3			11	10			6			2		4			5	1		8			9				7	
					3			11	10	4			2					5		6	1		8			9				7	
					3			11	10	4			2				6			5	1		8			9				7	
			11		3			10		4			2				6			5	1		8			9				7	
					3			11	10					4	2			5		6			8	1		9				7	
					3			11	10					4	2			5		6			8	1		9				7	
							8	11	10				3	4	2			5		6				1		9				7	
								11	10				3	4	2			5		6			8	1		9				7	
3								11	10				9		2		4			6			8	1					5	7	
3								11	10						2		4			6			8	1		9			5	7	
3								11	10						2		4			6			8	1		9			5	7	
					3		11	7	10								4			6			8	1		9		2	5		
					3		11	7	10	6							4						8			9	1	2	5		
					3			11	10	6							4						8			9	1	2	5	7	
					3			11	10								4			6			8			9	1	2	5	7	
					3			11					10				4			6			8			9	1	2	5	7	
					3		10	11									4			6			8			9	1	2	5	7	
					3		10	11		4										6			8			9	1	2	5	7	
					3		10	11		4			2							6			8			9	1		5	7	
					3			11	10	4										6			8			9	1	2	5	7	
					3		10	11									4			6			8			9	1	2	5	7	
11	13	12	1	1	24	10	7	42	25	16	1	10	8	4	16	8	33	20	3	32	5	12	37	13	1	29	9	14	13	27	5
		1			1	8		6	7				2			4	1			1			11			14				9	1

Baker Peter	Bingley Walt	Broadbent Albert	Cargill Dave	Clark Harry	Curtis Norman	Ellis Keith	Fantham John	Finney Alan	Froggatt Redfern	Gibson Don	Greensmith Ron	Hill Brian	Johnson Peter	Kay Tony	Martin Jack	McAnearney Jim	McAnearney Tom	McEvoy Don	McIntosh Dave	O'Donnell Ralph	Pinner Mike	Pllu Charlie	Quixall Albert	Ryalls Brian	Shaw Jack	Shiner Roy	Springett Ron	Staniforth Ron	Swan Peter	Wilkinson Derek	Young Gerry
					3			11	10						2		4	5		6			8	1		9				7	
					3			11	10				2	4				5		6		1	8			9				7	
3			11						10				9	4	2					6			8	1					5	7	
1			1		2			2	3				2	2	2		1	2		3		1	3	2		2			1	3	
									3																	2				1	

League Table

	P	W	D	L	F	A	Pts
Wolverhampton W.	42	28	8	6	103	47	64
Preston North End	42	26	7	9	100	51	59
Tottenham Hotspur	42	21	9	12	93	77	51
West Bromwich Albion	42	18	14	10	92	70	50
Manchester City	42	22	5	15	104	100	49
Burnley	42	21	5	16	80	74	47
Blackpool	42	19	6	17	80	67	44
Luton Town	42	19	6	17	69	63	44
Manchester United	42	16	11	15	85	75	43
Nottingham Forest	42	16	10	16	69	63	42
Chelsea	42	15	12	15	83	79	42
Arsenal	42	16	7	19	73	85	39
Birmingham City	42	14	11	17	76	89	39
Aston Villa	42	16	7	19	73	86	39
Bolton Wanderers	42	14	10	18	65	87	38
Everton	42	13	11	18	65	75	37
Leeds United	42	14	9	19	51	63	37
Leicester City	42	14	5	23	91	112	33
Newcastle United	42	12	8	22	73	81	32
Portsmouth	42	12	8	22	73	88	32
Sunderland	42	10	12	20	54	97	32
SHEFFIELD WEDNESDAY	42	12	7	23	69	92	31

1958-59

Division Two

Manager: Harry Catterick

Did you know that?

Final League Position: 1st

On the 10 September 1958 Wednesday's twins Eric and Derek Wilkinson played together in an away game at Sunderland, which ended 3–3. This was Eric's only first-team appearance.

Manchester United, rebuilding after the Munich air disaster, broke the British transfer record in paying Wednesday £45,000 to make Albert Quixall their first signing by Matt Busby since Munich.

Wednesday netted a club-record 106 League goals in winning the Second Division Championship.

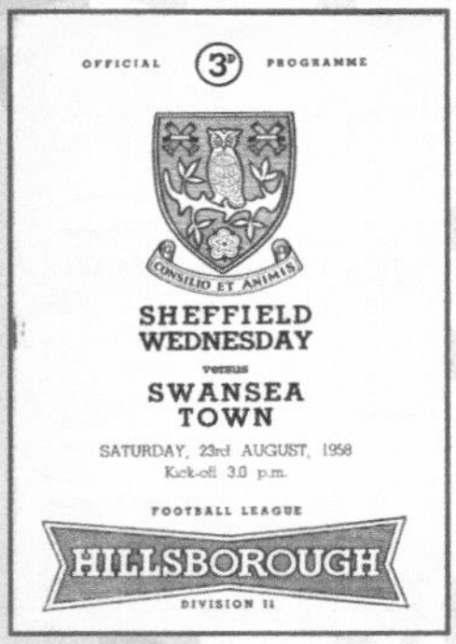

Match No.	Date	Venue	Opponents		Round	Result	HT Score	Position	Scorers	Attendance
1	Aug 23	H	Swansea Town	W		2-1	1-1		Finney, Froggatt	24,748
2	27	A	Stoke City	L		0-3	0-1	11th		24,126
3	30	A	Ipswich Town	W		2-0	1-0	6th	Young, Shiner	19,837
4	Sep 3	H	Stoke City	W		4-1	4-0	3rd	Shiner, Wilkinson, Froggatt (2)	23,622
5	6	H	Bristol Rovers	W		3-1	3-1	3rd	Quixall, Wilkinson (2)	28,968
6	10	A	Sunderland	D		3-3	2-1	3rd	Shiner, Froggatt (2)	33,684
7	13	A	Derby County	W		4-1	1-0	2nd	J. McAnearney, Wilkinson (2), Froggatt	24,227
8	17	H	Sunderland	W		6-0	2-0	2nd	Shiner, Quixall, Wilkinson, Froggatt (3)	33,398
9	20	H	Leyton Orient	W		2-0	1-0	2nd	Froggatt (2)	28,443
10	27	A	Scunthorpe United	W		4-1	3-1	2nd	Shiner (3), Wilkinson	17,488
11	Oct 4	H	Sheffield United	W		2-0	1-0	2nd	Froggatt, Shiner	46,404
12	11	A	Brighton & Hove Alb	W		3-1	1-1	1st	Shiner, Fantham, Froggatt	28,048
13	18	H	Grimsby Town	W		6-0	4-0	1st	Player (2 own-goals), Wilkinson, Froggatt (2), Fantham	29,866
14	25	A	Liverpool	L		2-3	2-0	1st	Shiner, Froggatt	39,912
15	Nov 1	H	Rotherham United	W		5-0	2-0	1st	Curtis (pen), Shiner, Fantham (2), Froggatt	32,183
16	8	A	Charlton Athletic	D		3-3	2-2	1st	Froggatt, Shiner (2)	23,369
17	15	H	Bristol City	L		2-3	2-1	2nd	Finney (2)	30,164
18	22	A	Cardiff City	D		2-2	2-0	2nd	Froggatt, Shiner	20,195
19	29	H	Huddersfield Town	W		4-1	2-1	2nd	Froggatt, Finney, Shiner (2)	25,394
20	Dec 6	A	Barnsley	W		1-0	0-0	1st	Shiner	23,073
21	13	H	Middlesbrough	W		2-0	1-0	1st	Finney, Curtis (pen)	28,115
22	20	A	Swansea Town	L		0-4	0-2	1st		13,721
23	26	H	Lincoln City	W		7-0	5-0	1st	Froggatt (2), Fantham (2), Shiner (2), Finney	36,403
24	27	A	Lincoln City	W		1-0	1-0	1st	Shiner	15,623
25	Jan 3	H	Ipswich Town	W		3-1	1-0	1st	Froggatt, Finney, Shiner	25,023
26	31	H	Derby County	D		1-1	0-1	1st	Moore (og)	31,199
27	Feb 7	A	Leyton Orient	W		2-0	2-0	1st	Curtis (pen), Finney	11,845
28	14	H	Scunthorpe United	W		2-0	1-0	1st	J. McAnearney, Wilkinson	22,877
29	21	A	Sheffield United	L		0-1	0-1	1st		43,919
30	27	H	Charlton Athletic	W		4-1	4-0	1st	Finney, Fantham, Ellis, Kay	29,470
31	Mar 7	A	Grimsby Town	W		2-0	2-0	1st	Kay, Curtis (pen)	13,109
32	21	A	Rotherham United	L		0-1	0-1	1st		18,050
33	27	A	Fulham	L		2-6	1-2	1st	Wilkinson, Shiner	39,377
34	28	H	Brighton & Hove Alb	W		2-0	1-0	2nd	Fantham, Curtis (pen)	20,949
35	30	H	Fulham	D		2-2	1-1	2nd	Shiner, Fantham	32,170
36	Apr 4	A	Bristol City	W		2-1	2-1	2nd	Fantham, Kay	21,211
37	11	H	Cardiff City	W		3-1	0-1	2nd	Shiner (2), Fantham	23,106
38	14	H	Liverpool	W		1-0	0-0	1st	Froggatt	28,264
39	18	A	Huddersfield Town	W		2-1	1-1	1st	Finney, T. McAnearney	19,960
40	22	A	Middlesbrough	D		2-2	1-1	1st	Fantham, Shiner	25,572
41	25	H	Barnsley	W		5-0	3-0	1st	Wilkinson, Froggatt (2), Shiner (2)	17,917
42	30	A	Bristol Rovers	L		1-2	0-1	1st	J. McAnearney	16,653
										Apps
									Three own-goals	Goals

FA Cup

Match No.	Date	Venue	Opponents		Round	Result	HT Score	Position	Scorers	Attendance
43	Jan 19	H	West Bromwich Alb	L	3R	0-2	0-1			50,455
										Apps

Ballagher John	Curtis Norman	Ellis Keith	Fantham John	Finney Alan	Froggatt Redfern	Gibson Don	Griffin Billy	Hill Brian	Johnson Peter	Kay Tony	Martin Jack	McAnearney Jim	McAnearney Tom	McLaren Roy	O'Donnell Ralph	Pinner Mike	Quixall Albert	Shiner Roy	Springett Ron	Staniforth Ron	Swan Peter	Whitham Terry	Wilkinson Derek	Wilkinson Eric	Young Gerry
	3		10	11	8	4				6	2							9	1		5		7		
	3		10		9	4				6	2	8						11	1		5		7		
10	3				8	6					2		4					9	1		5		7		11
10	3				8	6					2		4					9	1		5		7		11
	3				10	6					2		4				8	9	1		5		7		11
	3				10						2		4				8	9	1	6	5		7	11	
	3			11	9	6						10	4				8		1	2	5		7		
	3			11	10	6							4				8	9	1	2	5		7		
	3			11	10	6					2	8	4					9	1		5		7		
	3			11	10	6					2	8	4					9	1		5		7		
	3		10	11	8	6				4	2							9	1		5		7		
	3		10	11	8	6					2		4					9	1		5		7		
	3		10	11	8	6					2		4					9	1		5		7		
	3		10	11	8	6					2		4					9	1		5		7		
	3		10	11	8	6					2		4					9	1		5		7		
	3		10	11	8	6							4					9	1	2	5		7		
	3		10	11	8	6					2		4					9	1		5		7		
	3		10	11	8		7			6			4					9	1	2	5				
	3		10	11	8					6			4					9	1	2	5		7		
	3		10	11	8	4				6								9	1	2	5		7		
	3		10	11	8	4				6								9	1		5	2	7		
	3		10	11	8	4				6								9	1		5	2	7		
	3		10	11	8	4				6								9	1	2	5		7		
	3		10	11	8					6			4					9	1	2	5		7		
	3			11	8	4			2	6		10						9	1		5		7		
	3		10	11	8	4				6					5			9	1	2			7		
7	3		10	11	8					6			4		5			9	1	2					
	3		10	11						6		8	4		5			9	1	2			7		
	3		10	11						6		8	4					9	1	2	5		7		
	3	9	10	11						6		8	4						1	2	5		7		
	3	9	10	11						6		8	4						1	2	5		7		
	3	9	10	11	8					6			4						1	2	5		7		
	3		8	11	10					6			4			1		9		2	5		7		
	3		10	11	8				2	6			4			1		9			5		7		
	3		10	11	8					6			4	1				9		2	5		7		
	3		10	11	8					6			4	1				9		2	5		7		
	3		10	11	8					6			4	1				9		2	5		7		
	3		10	11	8				2	6			4	1				9			5		7		
	3		10	11	8				2	6			4	1				9			5		7		
	3		10	11	8				2	6		7	4	1				9			5				
	3		10	11	8				2	6			4	1				9			5		7		
	3		10	11		6			2			8	4	1				9			5		7		
3	42	3	33	37	37	23	1		7	27	14	11	33	8	3	2	4	38	32	20	39	2	39	1	3
	5	1	12	10	26					3		3	1				2	28					11		1

Ballagher John	Curtis Norman	Ellis Keith	Fantham John	Finney Alan	Froggatt Redfern	Gibson Don	Griffin Billy	Hill Brian	Johnson Peter	Kay Tony	Martin Jack	McAnearney Jim	McAnearney Tom	McLaren Roy	O'Donnell Ralph	Pinner Mike	Quixall Albert	Shiner Roy	Springett Ron	Staniforth Ron	Swan Peter	Whitham Terry	Wilkinson Derek	Wilkinson Eric	Young Gerry
	3			11	8	6		10		4					5			9	1	2			7		
	1			1	1	1		1		1					1			1	1	1			1		

League Table

	P	W	D	L	F	A	Pts
SHEFFIELD WEDNESDAY	42	28	6	8	106	48	62
Fulham	42	27	6	9	96	61	60
Sheffield United	42	23	7	12	82	48	53
Liverpool	42	24	5	13	87	62	53
Stoke City	42	21	7	14	72	58	49
Bristol Rovers	42	18	12	12	80	64	48
Derby County	42	20	8	14	74	71	48
Charlton Athletic	42	18	7	17	92	90	43
Cardiff City	42	18	7	17	65	65	43
Bristol City	42	17	7	18	74	70	41
Swansea Town	42	16	9	17	79	81	41
Brighton & Hove Albion	42	15	11	16	74	90	41
Middlesbrough	42	15	10	17	87	71	40
Huddersfield Town	42	16	8	18	62	55	40
Sunderland	42	16	8	18	64	75	40
Ipswich Town	42	17	6	19	62	77	40
Leyton Orient	42	14	8	20	71	78	36
Scunthorpe United	42	12	9	21	55	84	33
Lincoln City	42	11	7	24	63	93	29
Rotherham United	42	10	9	23	42	82	29
Grimsby Town	42	9	10	23	62	90	28
Barnsley	42	10	7	25	55	91	27

1959-60

Division One

Manager: Harry Catterick

Did you know that?

Final League Position: 5th

On 22 August, 1959, Wednesday featured for the first time on the BBC *Sports Special* in an away game played against Arsenal, winning 1–0, with Johnny Fantham scoring the goal.

On 28 November 1959 League leaders West Ham United came to Hillsborough, and within 10 minutes Wednesday were 3–0 up, going on to win 7–0.

Match No.	Date	Venue	Opponents		Round	Result	HT Score	Position	Scorers	Attendance
1	Aug 22	A	Arsenal	W		1-0	1-0		Fantham	47,430
2	26	A	Wolverhampton W	L		1-3	0-3		Fantham	37,397
3	29	H	Manchester City	W		1-0	0-0	10th	T. McAnearney	34,093
4	Sep 2	H	Wolverhampton W	D		2-2	2-1	8th	Shiner, Froggatt	45,145
5	5	A	Blackburn Rovers	L		1-3	1-0	14th	Froggatt	32,700
6	9	A	Nottingham Forest	L		1-2	0-1	17th	Shiner	26,042
7	12	H	Blackpool	W		5-0	2-0	10th	Fantham, Finney, Froggatt, Wilkinson, Shiner	30,238
8	16	H	Nottingham Forest	L		0-1	0-0	14th		34,249
9	19	A	Everton	L		1-2	1-0	17th	Hill	37,375
10	26	H	Luton Town	W		2-0	1-0	13th	Curtis (pen), Fantham	25,138
11	Oct 3	A	Bolton Wanderers	L		0-1	0-1	15th		23,990
12	10	A	Birmingham City	D		0-0	0-0	16th		21,769
13	17	H	Tottenham Hotspur	W		2-1	1-1	11th	Young, Wilkinson	37,743
14	24	A	Manchester United	L		1-3	1-1	14th	T. McAnearney	39,723
15	31	H	West Bromwich Alb	W		2-0	1-0	13th	Ellis, Froggatt	26,178
16	Nov 7	A	Leicester City	L		0-2	0-1	14th		21,232
17	14	H	Burnley	D		1-1	1-1	14th	Ellis	19,283
18	21	A	Leeds United	W		3-1	2-0	13th	Ellis (2), Fantham	21,260
19	28	H	West Ham United	W		7-0	4-0	9th	Fantham (2), Wilkinson, Finney (2), Craig, Ellis	38,307
20	Dec 5	A	Chelsea	W		4-0	2-0	8th	Craig, Fantham (2), Ellis	33,177
21	12	H	Preston North End	D		2-2	0-0	9th	Wilkinson, Craig	42,614
22	19	H	Arsenal	W		5-1	1-1	8th	Finney, Craig (2), Kay, Ellis	25,135
23	26	H	Fulham	D		1-1	0-1	8th	Ellis	50,240
24	28	A	Fulham	W		2-1	1-0	8th	Finney, Wilkinson	36,856
25	Jan 2	A	Manchester City	L		1-4	1-1	9th	Craig	44,167
26	16	H	Blackburn Rovers	W		3-0	1-0	6th	Craig, Fantham (2)	27,589
27	23	A	Blackpool	W		2-0	1-0	4th	Griffin (2)	16,343
28	Feb 6	H	Everton	D		2-2	1-0	4th	Kay, T. McAnearney (pen)	33,066
29	13	A	Luton Town	W		1-0	0-0	4th	Fantham	14,392
30	24	H	Bolton Wanderers	W		1-0	0-0	4th	Finney	36,392
31	27	H	Chelsea	D		1-1	1-1	3rd	Fantham	41,403
32	Mar 5	A	Tottenham Hotspur	L		1-4	1-2	4th	Finney	53,822
33	19	A	Preston North End	W		4-3	2-2	4th	Wilkinson, Ellis (2), Craig	16,497
34	30	H	Manchester United	W		4-2	1-0	4th	Griffin (2), Fantham, Wilkinson	26,821
35	Apr 2	A	Burnley	D		3-3	1-0	4th	Ellis, Finney, Craig	23,123
36	6	H	Leicester City	D		2-2	1-2	3rd	Griffin, Ellis	26,844
37	9	H	Leeds United	W		1-0	1-0	3rd	Finney	28,984
38	15	A	Newcastle United	D		3-3	2-2	4th	Wilkinson, Fantham, Ells	39,540
39	16	A	West Bromwich Alb	L		1-3	1-1	4th	Griffin	27,700
40	18	H	Newcastle United	W		2-0	1-0	4th	Fantham, Froggatt	33,332
41	23	H	Birmingham City	L		2-4	1-2	4th	Wilkinson, Froggatt	26,248
42	30	A	West Ham United	D		1-1	1-1	5th	Fantham	21,964
										Apps
										Goals

FA Cup

43	Jan 9	H	Middlesbrough	W	3R	2-1	1-0		T. McAnearney (pen), Ellis	49,580
44	30	H	Peterborough United	W	4R	2-0	0-0		Craig (2)	51,114
45	Feb 20	A	Manchester United	W	5R	1-0	0-0		T. McAnearney (pen)	66,350
46	Mar 12	A	Sheffield United	W	6R	2-0	2-0		Wilkinson (2)	61,180
47	26	N	Blackburn Rovers *	L	S/F	1-2	0-1		Fantham	74,135
										Apps
										Goals

* At Maine Road, Manchester

Craig Bobby	Curtis Norman	Ellis Keith	Fantham John	Finney Alan	Froggatt Redfern	Gibson Don	Griffin Billy	Hill Brian	Johnson Peter	Kay Tony	Kirby George	Martin Jack	McAnearney Tom	McLaren Roy	Megson Don	O'Donnell Ralph	Quinn John	Shiner Roy	Springett Ron	Swan Peter	Wilkinson Derek	Young Gerry
	3		10	11	8				2	6			4					9	1	5	7	
	3		10	11	8				2	6			4					9	1	5	7	
	3		10	11	8			6	2				4					9	1	5	7	
	3		10	11	8			6	2				4					9	1	5	7	
	3		10	11	8			6	2				4					9	1	5	7	
	3		10	11	8	4						2				6		9	1	5	7	
	3		10	11	8	4		6	2									9	1	5	7	
	3		10	11	8	4		6	2									9	1	5	7	
	3		10	11	9	6		8				2	4						1	5	7	
	3		10	11	8			6				2	4				7	9	1	5		
	3		10	11	8					6	9	2	4				7		1	5		
	3		10	11	8				2	6	9		4						1	5	7	
	3		10	11					2	6	9		4						1	5	7	8
	3	9	10	11					2	6			4						1	5	7	8
	3	9	10	11	8				2	6			4						1	5	7	
	3	9	10	11	8				2	6			4						1	5	7	
	2	9	10	11						6			4		3				1	5	7	8
8		9	10	11					2	6			4		3				1	5	7	
8		9	10	11					2	6			4		3				1	5	7	
8		9	10	11				6	2				4		3				1	5	7	
8		9	10	11					2	6			4		3				1	5	7	
8		9	10	11					2	6			4		3				1	5	7	
8		9	10	11					2	6			4		3				1	5	7	
8			10	11					2	6			4		3				1	5	7	9
8		9	10	11					2	6			4		3				1	5	7	
8		9	10	11					2	6			4		3				1	5	7	
8			10	11			9		2	6			4		3				1	5	7	
8	2		10	11			9			6			4		3				1	5	7	
8		9	10	7					2	6			4		3				1	5		11
8		9	10	7					2	6			4		3				1	5		11
8			10	11	9				2	6			4		3				1	5	7	
8		9	10	11						6		2	4		3				1	5	7	
8		9	10	11						6		2	4		3				1	5	7	
8		9	10				11		2	6			4		3				1	5	7	
8		9	10	11					2	6			4		3				1	5	7	
8		9	10				11		2	6			4	1	3					5	7	
8		9	10	11					2	6			4	1	3					5	7	
8		9	10	11					2	6			4		3				1	5	7	
		9	10	11			8		2	6			4		3				1	5	7	
8			10	7	9		11	6	2				4		3				1	5		
8			10	11	9			6	2				4		3				1	5	7	
8			10	11	9				2	6			4		3				1	5	7	
24	18	22	42	40	18	4	6	10	34	31	3	6	39	2	26	1	2	9	40	42	37	6
9	1	13	17	9	6		6	1		2			3					3			9	1

Craig Bobby	Curtis Norman	Ellis Keith	Fantham John	Finney Alan	Froggatt Redfern	Gibson Don	Griffin Billy	Hill Brian	Johnson Peter	Kay Tony	Kirby George	Martin Jack	McAnearney Tom	McLaren Roy	Megson Don	O'Donnell Ralph	Quinn John	Shiner Roy	Springett Ron	Swan Peter	Wilkinson Derek	Young Gerry
8		9	10	11					2	6			4		3				1	5	7	
10			8	11			9		2	6			4		3				1	5	7	
8		9	10	7					2	6			4		3				1	5		11
8		9	10	11						6		2	4		3				1	5	7	
8		9	10	11					2	6			4		3				1	5	7	
5		4	5	5			1		4	5		1	5		5				5	5	4	1
2		1	1										2								2	

League Table

	P	W	D	L	F	A	Pts
Burnley	42	24	7	11	85	61	55
Wolverhampton W.	42	24	6	12	106	67	54
Tottenham Hotspur	42	21	11	10	86	50	53
West Bromwich Albion	42	19	11	12	83	57	49
SHEFFIELD WEDNESDAY	42	19	11	12	80	59	49
Bolton Wanderers	42	20	8	14	59	51	48
Manchester United	42	19	7	16	102	80	45
Newcastle United	42	18	8	16	82	78	44
Preston North End	42	16	12	14	79	76	44
Fulham	42	17	10	15	73	80	44
Blackpool	42	15	10	17	59	71	40
Leicester City	42	13	13	16	66	75	39
Arsenal	42	15	9	18	68	80	39
West Ham United	42	16	6	20	75	91	38
Everton	42	13	11	18	73	78	37
Manchester City	42	17	3	22	78	84	37
Blackburn Rovers	42	16	5	21	60	70	37
Chelsea	42	14	9	19	76	91	37
Birmingham City	42	13	10	19	63	80	36
Nottingham Forest	42	13	9	20	50	74	35
Leeds United	42	12	10	20	65	92	34
Luton Town	42	9	12	21	50	73	30

1960-61

Division One

Manager: Harry Catterick

Did you know that?

Final League Position: 2nd

After losing on 3 December 1960 to Everton, Wednesday were then unbeaten for the next 19 games, before losing on April 17 1961 to Spurs.

On 21 January 1961 Fulham's Alan Mullery scored an own-goal 30 seconds after the start of the game, with Wednesday not having touched the ball. Wednesday went on to record a 6–1 away victory.

Match No.	Date	Venue	Opponents		Round	Result	HT Score	Position	Scorers	Attendance
1	Aug 20	H	West Bromwich Alb	W		1-0	1-0		Craig	34,177
2	24	A	Cardiff City	W		1-0	0-0		Finney	31,335
3	27	A	Birmingham City	D		1-1	0-0	2nd	Fantham	27,197
4	31	H	Cardiff City	W		2-0	2-0	2nd	Quinn (2)	28,493
5	Sep 3	H	West Ham United	W		1-0	0-0	2nd	Fantham	28,359
6	7	A	Manchester City	D		1-1	1-1	2nd	Fantham	35,188
7	10	H	Fulham	W		2-0	1-0	2nd	Finney, Craig	27,842
8	14	H	Manchester City	W		3-1	1-0	2nd	Ellis (2), Craig	30,221
9	17	A	Preston North End	D		2-2	2-1	2nd	Fantham, Ellis	17,497
10	24	H	Burnley	W		3-1	3-1	2nd	Ellis, Griffin, Fantham	37,779
11	Oct 1	A	Nottingham Forest	W		2-1	1-0	2nd	Fantham, Craig	30,073
12	15	H	Blackpool	W		4-0	2-0	2nd	Gratrix (og), Ellis (2), Fantham	34,124
13	22	A	Wolverhampton W	L		1-4	1-3	2nd	Ellis	30,270
14	29	H	Bolton Wanderers	W		2-0	1-0	2nd	Ellis, Griffin	27,595
15	Nov 5	A	Manchester United	D		0-0	0-0	2nd		36,855
16	12	H	Tottenham Hotspur	W		2-1	1-1	2nd	Griffin, Fantham	56,363
17	19	A	Leicester City	L		1-2	1-2	2nd	Griffin	25,567
18	26	H	Aston Villa	L		1-2	1-2	2nd	Griffin	27,939
19	Dec 3	A	Everton	L		2-4	2-1	4th	Ellis, Craig	60,702
20	10	H	Blackburn Rovers	W		5-4	5-1	4th	Fantham, Lodge (2), Craig (2)	22,455
21	17	A	West Bromwich Alb	D		2-2	2-2	5th	Fantham (2)	17,862
22	23	H	Arsenal	D		1-1	0-0	4th	Quinn	29,311
23	26	A	Arsenal	D		1-1	0-1	5th	Ellis	43,555
24	31	H	Birmingham City	W		2-0	1-0	4th	Wilkinson, Fantham	24,946
25	Jan 14	A	West Ham United	D		1-1	1-0	3rd	Ellis	20,620
26	21	A	Fulham	W		6-1	4-1	3rd	Mullery (og), McAnearney, Fantham, Ellis (2), Finney	17,920
27	Feb 4	H	Preston North End	W		5-1	2-0	3rd	Griffin (2), Fantham (2), Ellis	21,115
28	11	A	Burnley	W		4-3	3-2	3rd	Craig (2), Fantham, McAnearney (pen)	25,512
29	21	H	Nottingham Forest	W		1-0	1-0	3rd	Finney	35,199
30	25	H	Chelsea	W		1-0	0-0	2nd	Finney	25,000
31	Mar 11	H	Wolverhampton W	D		0-0	0-0	3rd		35,180
32	15	A	Blackpool	W		1-0	0-0	2nd	Fantham	17,738
33	18	A	Bolton Wanderers	W		1-0	0-0	2nd	Fantham	19,418
34	25	H	Manchester United	W		5-1	2-0	2nd	Cantwell (og), Young (3), Craig	35,901
35	31	A	Newcastle United	W		1-0	0-0	2nd	Craig	42,070
36	Apr 1	A	Blackburn Rovers	D		1-1	0-1	2nd	Young	21,300
37	3	H	Newcastle United	D		1-1	1-1	2nd	Craig (pen)	35,273
38	8	H	Leicester City	D		2-2	2-1	2nd	Wilkinson, Fantham	29,904
39	17	A	Tottenham Hotspur	L		1-2	1-2	2nd	Megson	61,200
40	22	H	Everton	L		1-2	1-1	3rd	Wilkinson	28,521
41	26	A	Chelsea	W		2-0	2-0	2nd	McAnearney (pen), Fantham	24,258
42	29	A	Aston Villa	L		1-4	1-2	2nd	Griffin	26,023
										Apps
							Three own-goals			Goals

FA Cup

Match No.	Date	Venue	Opponents		Round	Result	HT Score	Position	Scorers	Attendance
43	Jan 7	H	Leeds United	W	3R	2-0	1-0		Quinn, Ellis	36,225
44	28	H	Manchester United	D	4R	1-1	1-1		Wilkinson	58,000
45	Feb 1	A	Manchester United	W	4R Re	7-2	4-1		Fantham (2), Finney (2), Ellis (3)	65,243
46	18	A	Leyton Orient	W	5R	2-0	2-0		Fantham, Ellis	31,000
47	Mar 4	H	Burnley	D	6R	0-0	0-0			55,000
48	7	A	Burnley	L	6R Re	0-2	0-0			49,113
										Apps
										Goals

Craig Bobby	Ellis Keith	Fantham John	Finney Alan	Frye John	Griffin Billy	Hill Brian	Johnson Peter	Kay Tony	Lodge Bobby	Martin Jack	McAnearney Tom	McLaren Roy	Megson Don	Meredith John	O'Donnell Ralph	Quinn John	Springett Ron	Swan Peter	Wilkinson Derek	Young Gerry
8		10	11				2	6			4		3			9	1	5	7	
8		10	11				2	6			4		3			9	1	5	7	
8		10	11				2	6		3	4					9	1	5	7	
8	9		11				2	6		3	4					10	1	5	7	
8		10	11				2	6			4		3			9	1	5	7	
8	9	10	11				2	6			4		3				1	5	7	
8	9	10	11				2	6			4		3				1	5	7	
8	9	10	11				2	6			4		3				1	5	7	
8	9	10	11				2	6			4		3				1	5	7	
8	9	10	11		7		2	6			4		3				1	5		
8	9	10	11		7		2	6			4		3				1	5		
8	9	10	11		7		2	6			4		3				1	5		
8	9	10	11		7		2	6			4		3				1	5		
8	9	10	11		7		2	6			4		3				1	5		
8	9	10	11		7		2	6			4	1	3					5		
8	9	10	11		7		2	6			4	1	3					5		
8	9	10	11		7		2	6			4	1	3					5		
8	9	10	11		7		2	6			4	1	3					5		
8	9	10	11		7		2	6			4		3				1	5		
8	9	10	11				2	6	7				3				1	5		4
8	9	10	11			3	2	6	7		4						1	5		
8		10	11			3	2	6	7		4					9	1	5		
	9	10	11				2	6			4		3			8	1	5	7	
	9	10	11				2	6			4		3		5	8	1		7	
	9	10	11				2	6			4		3		5	8	1		7	
	9	10	11				2	6			4		3		5	8	1		7	
	9	10	11		8		2	6			4		3		5		1		7	
8	9	10	11				2	6			4		3		5	7	1			
8	9		11				2	6			4		3			10	1	5	7	
8	9		11				2	6			4		3			10	1	5	7	
8	9	10	7				2	6			4		3	11	5		1			
8		10	7				2	6			4		3				1	5	11	9
8		10	7				2	6			4		3				1	5	11	9
8		10	7				2	6			4		3				1	5	11	9
8		10	7				2	6			4		3				1	5	11	9
8		10	7				2	6			4		3				1	5	11	9
8		10	7			4	2	6					3				1	5	11	9
8	9	10	7				2	6			4		3				1	5	11	
8	9	10	7			4	2	6					3				1	5	11	
8	9	10	7				2	6			4		3				1	5	11	
8	9	10	7				2	6			4		3				1	5	11	
8	9	10	7		11		2	6			4		3				1	5		
37	31	39	42		12	4	42	42	3	2	39	4	38	1	6	13	38	36	26	7
12	14	20	5		8				2		3		1			3			3	4

Craig Bobby	Ellis Keith	Fantham John	Finney Alan	Frye John	Griffin Billy	Hill Brian	Johnson Peter	Kay Tony	Lodge Bobby	Martin Jack	McAnearney Tom	McLaren Roy	Megson Don	Meredith John	O'Donnell Ralph	Quinn John	Springett Ron	Swan Peter	Wilkinson Derek	Young Gerry
	9	10	11				2	6			4		3		5	8	1		7	
	9	10	11				2	6			4		3		5	8	1		7	
8	9	10	11				2	6			4		3		5		1		7	
8	9	10	11				2	6			4		3		5		1		7	
	9	10	11				2	6			4		3		5	8	1		7	
	9	10	11	8			2	6			4		3		5	7	1			
2	6	6	6	1			6	6			6		6		6	4	6		5	
	5	3	2													1			1	

League Table

	P	W	D	L	F	A	Pts
Tottenham Hotspur	42	31	4	7	115	55	66
SHEFFIELD WEDNESDAY	42	23	12	7	78	47	58
Wolverhampton W.	42	25	7	10	103	75	57
Burnley	42	22	7	13	102	77	51
Everton	42	22	6	14	87	69	50
Leicester City	42	18	9	15	87	70	45
Manchester United	42	18	9	15	88	76	45
Blackburn Rovers	42	15	13	14	77	76	43
Aston Villa	42	17	9	16	78	77	43
West Bromwich Albion	42	18	5	19	67	71	41
Arsenal	42	15	11	16	77	85	41
Chelsea	42	15	7	20	98	100	37
Manchester City	42	13	11	18	79	90	37
Nottingham Forest	42	14	9	19	62	78	37
Cardiff City	42	13	11	18	60	85	37
West Ham United	42	13	10	19	77	88	36
Fulham	42	14	8	20	72	95	36
Bolton Wanderers	42	12	11	19	58	73	35
Birmingham City	42	14	6	22	62	84	34
Blackpool	42	12	9	21	68	73	33
Newcastle United	42	11	10	21	86	109	32
Preston North End	42	10	10	22	43	71	30

1961-62

Division One

Manager: Vic Buckingham

Did you know that?

Final League Position: 6th

On 23 August 1961 Wednesday played Bolton, and their new £150,000 North Cantilever Stand was officially opened by Sir Stanley Rous, Secretary of the FA, as Wednesday won 4–2.

Match No.	Date	Venue	Opponents		Round	Result	HT Score	Position	Scorers	Attendance
1	Aug 19	A	West Bromwich Alb	W		2-0	1-0		Finney, Ellis	27,250
2	23	H	Bolton Wanderers	W		4-2	2-0		Craig, Wilkinson, Ellis (2)	36,470
3	26	H	Birmingham City	W		5-1	2-1	1st	Ellis, Finney, Fantham (3)	30,595
4	30	A	Bolton Wanderers	L		3-4	1-2	2nd	Ellis (2), Fantham	19,559
5	Sep 2	A	Everton	W		4-0	1-0	1st	Kay, McAnearney (pen), Craig, Ellis	42,578
6	9	H	Fulham	D		1-1	0-1	3rd	Fantham	35,773
7	16	A	Sheffield United	L		0-1	0-0	6th		38,497
8	20	H	Arsenal	D		1-1	1-1	5th	McAnearney (pen)	35,903
9	23	A	Leicester City	L		0-1	0-1	7th		21,338
10	30	H	Ipswich Town	L		1-4	1-3	9th	Fantham	27,565
11	Oct 7	H	Chelsea	W		5-3	2-2	8th	Fantham (2), Craig, Dobson, Griffin	28,093
12	16	A	Aston Villa	L		0-1	0-1			34,932
13	21	H	Blackburn Rovers	W		1-0	0-0	9th	Griffin	26,491
14	28	A	West Ham United	W		3-2	2-1	7th	Griffin (2), Megson,	26,453
15	Nov 4	H	Manchester United	W		3-1	2-1	5th	Fantham, Kay, Ellis	36,808
16	11	A	Cardiff City	L		1-2	0-1	6th	Fantham	17,987
17	14	A	Arsenal	L		0-1	0-0	6th		19,331
18	18	H	Tottenham Hotspur	D		0-0	0-0	6th		45,058
19	25	A	Blackpool	W		3-1	1-1	5th	Young, Finney, Craig	16,569
20	Dec 2	H	Nottingham Forest	W		3-0	2-0	4th	Wilkinson, Young (2)	30,083
21	9	A	Wolverhampton W	L		0-3	0-2	6th		20,964
22	16	H	West Bromwich Alb	W		2-1	2-0	6th	Dobson, Fantham	25,168
23	23	A	Birmingham City	D		1-1	1-1	6th	Finney	19,078
24	26	A	Burnley	L		0-4	0-0	7th		28,947
25	Jan 13	H	Everton	W		3-1	1-1	6th	Ellis, Dobson (2)	32,130
26	20	A	Fulham	W		2-0	1-0	6th	McAnearney, Fantham	19,966
27	Feb 3	H	Sheffield United	L		1-2	0-2	6th	Dobson	50,937
28	10	H	Leicester City	L		1-2	0-0	7th	Finney	28,179
29	24	A	Chelsea	L		0-1	0-1	8th		23,760
30	Mar 3	H	Aston Villa	W		3-0	2-0	7th	Wilkinson, Dobson (2)	23,896
31	9	A	Ipswich Town	L		1-2	1-1	7th	Dobson	23,713
32	17	H	West Ham United	D		0-0	0-0	8th		31,403
33	24	A	Manchester United	D		1-1	0-1	9th	Fantham	31,222
34	Apr 3	H	Cardiff City	W		2-0	1-0	8th	Megson, Fantham	18,434
35	7	A	Tottenham Hotspur	L		0-4	0-3	9th		40,360
36	14	H	Blackpool	W		3-2	3-0	8th	Quinn, Griffin (2)	20,090
37	20	A	Manchester City	L		1-3	0-0	10th	Fantham	32,131
38	21	A	Nottingham Forest	L		1-3	1-1	12th	Fantham	18,349
39	23	H	Manchester City	W		1-0	0-0	10th	Finney	22,048
40	26	A	Blackburn Rovers	W		2-0	1-0		Wilkinson, Dobson	12,171
41	28	H	Wolverhampton W	W		3-2	1-1	6th	Wilkinson, Holliday, Fantham	20,079
42	30	H	Burnley	W		4-0	1-0	6th	Dobson (2), Fantham, Wilkinson	20,501
										Apps
										Goals

FA Cup

Match No.	Date	Venue	Opponents		Round	Result	HT Score	Position	Scorers	Attendance
43	Jan 9	H	Swansea Town	W	3R	1-0	0-0		Finney	35,184
44	27	A	Nottingham Forest	W	4R	2-0	1-0		Craig, Ellis	46,000
45	Feb 17	A	Manchester United	D	5R	0-0	0-0			65,623
46	21	H	Manchester United	L	5R Re	0-2	0-1			65,009
										Apps
										Goals

Inter-Cities Fairs Cup

Match No.	Date	Venue	Opponents		Round	Result	HT Score	Position	Scorers	Attendance
47	Sep 12	A	Olympique Lyonnais	L	1R 1L	2-4	0-3		Young, Ellis	5,000
48	Oct 4	H	Olympique Lyonnais	W	1R 2L	5-2	3-1		Fantham (2), Griffin, McAnearney (pen), Dobson	30,303
49	Nov 29	H	A.S.Roma	W	2R 1L	4-0	3-0		Young (3), Fantham	42,589
50	Dec 13	A	A.S.Roma	L	2R 2L	0-1	0-0			45,000
51	Feb 28	H	Barcelona	W	Q/F 1L	3-2	2-2		Fantham (2), Finney	28,956
52	Mar 28	A	Barcelona	L	Q/F 2L	0-2	0-2			75,000
										Apps
										Goals

Craig Bobby	Dobson Colin	Ellis Keith	Fantham John	Finney Alan	Griffin Billy	Hardy Robin	Holliday Eddie	Johnson Peter	Kay Tony	McAnearney Tom	McLaren Roy	Megson Don	O'Donnell Ralph	Quinn John	Springett Ron	Swan Peter	Wilkinson Derek	Young Gerry
8		9	10	11				2	6	4		3			1	5	7	
8		9	10	11				2	6	4		3			1	5	7	
8		9	10	11				2	6	4		3			1	5	7	
8		9	10	11				2	6	4		3			1	5	7	
8		9	10	11				2	6	4		3			1	5	7	
8		9	10	11				2	6	4		3			1	5	7	
8		9	10	11				2	6	4		3			1	5	7	
	8	9	10	11				2	6	4		3			1	5	7	
	8	9	10	11				2	6	4		3			1	5	7	
8	11	9	10					2	6	4		3			1	5	7	
8	11		9	7	10			2	6	4		3			1	5		
8	11		9	7	10	4		2	6			3			1	5		
8	11		9	7	10	4		2	6			3			1	5		
	11	9	10	7	8			2	6	4		3			1	5		
	11	9	10	7	8			2	6	4		3			1	5		
	11	9	10	7	8			2	6	4		3			1	5		
	11	9	10	7	8			2	6	4		3			1	5		
8			10	7				2	6	4		3			1	5	11	9
8			10	7				2	6	4		3			1	5	11	9
8			10	7				2	6	4		3			1	5	11	9
8			10	7				2	6	4		3			1	5	11	9
8	11		10	7		4		2	6			3			1	5		9
8	11		10	7				2	6	4		3			1	5		9
8	11		10	7				2	6	4		3			1	5		9
8	11	9	10	7				2	6	4		3			1	5		
8	11	9	10	7				2	6	4		3			1	5		
8	11	9	10	7				2	6	4		3			1	5		
8	11	9	10	7				2	6	4		3			1	5		
8	11	9	10	7				2	6	4		3			1	5		
	8		10	11		4		2	6			3			1	5	7	9
	8		10	11		4		2	6			3			1	5	7	9
	8		10	7		4	11	2	6			3			1	5		9
	8		10	7		4	11	2	6			3			1	5		9
	8	9	10	7		4	11	2	6		1	3	5					
	8	9	10	7		4	11	2	6			3			1	5		
			10	7	8	4	11	2	6		1	3	5	9				
			10	7	8	4	11		6		1	3	2	9		5		
			10	7	8	4	11		6			3	2	9	1	5		
	8		10	7		4	11	2	6			3			1	5	9	
	8		10	7		4	11	2	6			3			1	5	9	
	8		10	7		4	11	2	6			3			1	5	9	
	8		10	7		4	11	2	6			3			1	5	9	
23	28	21	42	41	10	16	11	40	42	26	3	42	4	3	39	40	20	11
4	11	9	18	6	6		1		2	3		2		1			6	3

Craig Bobby	Dobson Colin	Ellis Keith	Fantham John	Finney Alan	Griffin Billy	Hardy Robin	Holliday Eddie	Johnson Peter	Kay Tony	McAnearney Tom	McLaren Roy	Megson Don	O'Donnell Ralph	Quinn John	Springett Ron	Swan Peter	Wilkinson Derek	Young Gerry
8	11	9	10	7				2	6	4		3			1	5		
8	11	9	10	7				2	6	4		3			1	5		
8		9	10	11				2	6	4		3			1	5	7	
8		9	10	11				2	6	4		3			1	5	7	
4	2	4	4	4				4	4	4		4			4	4	2	
1		1		1														

Craig Bobby	Dobson Colin	Ellis Keith	Fantham John	Finney Alan	Griffin Billy	Hardy Robin	Holliday Eddie	Johnson Peter	Kay Tony	McAnearney Tom	McLaren Roy	Megson Don	O'Donnell Ralph	Quinn John	Springett Ron	Swan Peter	Wilkinson Derek	Young Gerry
8		9		11				2	6	4		3			1	5	7	10
8	11		9	7	10			2	6	4		3			1	5		
8			10	7				2	6	4		3			1	5	11	9
8	11		10	7				2	6	4		3			1	5		9
	8		10	11		4		2	6			3			1	5	7	9
	8	9	10	7		4	11	2	6			3			1	5		
4	4	2	5	6	1	2	1	6	6	4		6			6	6	3	4
	1	1	5	1	1					1								4

League Table

	P	W	D	L	F	A	Pts
Ipswich Town	42	24	8	10	93	67	56
Burnley	42	21	11	10	101	67	53
Tottenham Hotspur	42	21	10	11	88	69	52
Everton	42	20	11	11	88	54	51
Sheffield United	42	19	9	14	61	69	47
SHEFFIELD WEDNESDAY	42	20	6	16	72	58	46
Aston Villa	42	18	8	16	65	56	44
West Ham United	42	17	10	15	76	82	44
West Bromwich Albion	42	15	13	14	83	67	43
Arsenal	42	16	11	15	71	72	43
Bolton Wanderers	42	16	10	16	62	66	42
Manchester City	42	17	7	18	78	81	41
Blackpool	42	15	11	16	70	75	41
Leicester City	42	17	6	19	72	71	40
Manchester United	42	15	9	18	72	75	39
Blackburn Rovers	42	14	11	17	50	58	39
Birmingham City	42	14	10	18	65	81	38
Wolverhampton W.	42	13	10	19	73	86	36
Nottingham Forest	42	13	10	19	63	79	36
Fulham	42	13	7	22	66	74	33
Cardiff City	42	9	14	19	50	81	32
Chelsea	42	9	10	23	63	94	28

1962-63

Division One

Manager: Vic Buckingham

Did you know that?

Final League Position: 6th

On 18 August 1962 Wednesday played Bolton in a 1–1 draw, wearing their new shirts of narrow-blue-and-white stripes, which became known as butcher aprons.

Wednesday, along with Birmingham, were banned by the FA and Football League from accepting an invitation to compete in the Inter-Cities Cup which, at the time, was by invitation only. The League and FA had nominated Burnley and Sheffield United to take their places. Only Everton took part that year.

On 22 October 1962 Wednesday played the world club champions, Santos of Brazil, at Hillsborough in a friendly, with Pele playing and scoring in a 4–2 win for the Brazilians.

Match No.	Date	Venue	Opponents		Round	Result	HT Score	Position	Scorers	Attendance
1	Aug 18	H	Bolton Wanderers	D		1-1	0-1	14th	Dobson	28,036
2	22	A	Leicester City	D		3-3	0-2	15th	Layne (2), Dobson	22,000
3	25	A	Everton	L		1-4	1-2	15th	Layne	51,544
4	29	H	Leicester City	L		0-3	0-0	18th		25,307
5	Sep 1	H	West Bromwich Alb	W		3-1	3-0	17th	Dobson (2), Fantham	23,042
6	8	A	Arsenal	W		2-1	1-1	14th	Layne (2)	31,115
7	12	H	Fulham	W		1-0	1-0	8th	Holliday	21,062
8	15	H	Birmingham City	W		5-0	1-0	7th	Dobson, Holliday (2), Layne (2)	22,255
9	19	A	Fulham	L		1-4	0-3	7th	Layne	22,635
10	22	A	Leyton Orient	W		4-2	1-1	9th	Layne, Dobson, Kay, Quinn	20,125
11	29	H	Manchester United	W		1-0	0-0	7th	Kay	40,520
12	Oct 6	A	Sheffield United	D		2-2	1-0	7th	Layne (2)	42,687
13	13	H	Nottingham Forest	D		2-2	2-1	8th	Kay, Layne	29,784
14	20	A	Manchester City	L		2-3	1-1	9th	Dobson (1 + pen)	20,700
15	27	H	Blackpool	D		0-0	0-0	8th		22,227
16	Nov 3	A	Wolverhampton W	D		2-2	2-2	8th	Wilkinson, Layne	24,300
17	10	H	Aston Villa	D		0-0	0-0	8th		20,507
18	17	A	Tottenham Hotspur	D		1-1	0-0	8th	Finney	42,390
19	24	H	West Ham United	L		1-3	1-3	8th	Fantham	23,764
20	Dec 1	A	Ipswich Town	L		0-2	0-2	10th		17,256
21	8	H	Liverpool	L		0-2	0-1	13th		15,939
22	22	H	Everton	D		2-2	1-0	13th	Quinn, Layne	28,279
23	29	A	Burnley	L		0-4	0-2	15th		20,848
24	Jan 12	A	West Bromwich Alb	W		3-0	1-0	11th	Layne, Quinn, Johnson	17,500
25	Mar 2	A	Nottingham Forest	W		3-0	2-0	9th	Dobson, Fantham (2)	25,421
26	9	H	Manchester City	W		4-1	1-0	9th	Dobson, Layne (3)	19,424
27	16	A	Blackpool	W		3-2	0-2	8th	Fantham, Layne, Wilkinson	10,200
28	23	H	Wolverhampton W	W		3-1	1-1	8th	Fantham, Layne, Dobson	26,495
29	30	A	Birmingham City	D		1-1	0-0	8th	Fantham	12,800
30	Apr 2	A	West Ham United	L		0-2	0-1	9th		20,048
31	8	H	Tottenham Hotspur	W		3-1	1-0	9th	Layne (2), Fantham	42,245
32	12	A	Blackburn Rovers	L		0-3	0-3	8th		14,400
33	13	A	Aston Villa	W		2-0	0-0	8th	Quinn, Layne	23,800
34	15	H	Blackburn Rovers	W		4-0	1-0	8th	Dobson, Layne (2), Young	25,707
35	20	H	Ipswich Town	L		0-3	0-2	8th		17,268
36	23	H	Burnley	L		0-1	0-1	9th		25,751
37	29	A	Liverpool	W		2-0	1-0	8th	Johnson, Layne	29,144
38	May 1	A	Manchester United	W		3-1	3-0		Finney, Quinn, Megson	31,873
39	4	H	Leyton Orient	W		3-1	1-1	6th	Dobson, Fantham, Finney	19,696
40	6	A	Bolton Wanderers	W		4-0	3-0	6th	Dobson, McAnearney, Johnson, Layne	12,833
41	15	H	Sheffield United	W		3-1	0-1	6th	Layne (2), McAnearney	41,585
42	18	H	Arsenal	L		2-3	1-2	6th	Fantham, Young	20,514
										Apps
										Goals

FA Cup

Match No.	Date	Venue	Opponents		Round	Result	HT Score	Position	Scorers	Attendance
43	Feb 21	A	Shrewsbury Town	D	3R	1-1	1-0		Layne	11,428
44	Mar 7	H	Shrewsbury Town	W	3R Re	2-1 *	1-1		Finney, Fantham	24,207
45	12	A	Arsenal	L	4R	0-2	0-0			40,367
										Apps
										Goals

* Score at full-time 1-1

Birks Graham	Dobson Colin	Ellis Keith	Eustace Peter	Fantham John	Finney Alan	Griffin Billy	Hardy Robin	Hill Brian	Holliday Eddie	Horrobin Tom	Johnson Peter	Kay Tony	Layne David	McAnearney Tom	McLaren Roy	Megson Don	Quinn John	Springett Ron	Swan Peter	Wilkinson Derek	Young Gerry
	8			10	7		6		11		2		9	4		3		1	5		
	8				7		6		11		2	10	9	4		3		1	5		
	10				7		6		11		2	8	9	4		3		1	5		
	10		4		7		6	3	11		2	8	9					1	5		
3	8		4	10	7			2	11			6	9					1	5		
3	8		4	10		7			11		2	6	9					1	5		
3	8		4	10		7			11		2	6	9					1	5		
	10		4						11		2	6	9			3	8	1	5	7	
	8		4						11		2	6	9			3	10	1	5	7	
	10		4						11		2	6	9			3	8	1	5	7	
	8		4						11	2		6	9			3		1	5	7	10
	10		4			8			11		2	6	9			3		1	5	7	
	11		4	10		8			7		2	6	9			3		1	5		
	11		4	10		8			7		2	6	9		1	3			5		
	8			10	7				11		2	6		4		3		1	5		9
	8			10			6		11	2			9	4		3		1	5	7	
	8					10	6		11	2			9	4		3		1	5	7	
				10	7				11		2	6	9	4		3		1	5	8	
3				10	7				11		2	6	9	4				1	5	8	
				10	7				11		2	6	9	4		3		1	5	8	
		9		10	7				11		2	6		4		3		1	5	8	
	11			10					7		2	6	9	4		3	8	1	5		
	11		6	10							2		9	4		3	8	1	5	7	
	11		6	10	7						2		9	4		3	8	1	5		
	11		6	10	7						2		9	4		3	8	1	5		
	11		6	10	7						2		9	4		3	8	1	5		
	11			10							2		9	4		3	8	1	5	7	6
	11			10							2		9	4		3	8	1	5	7	6
	11			10							2		9	4		3	8	1	5	7	6
	11			10	7						2			4		3	8	1	5	9	6
	11			10							2		9	4		3	8	1	5	7	6
	11			10							2		9	4		3	8	1	5	7	6
	11			10							2		9	4		3	8	1	5	7	6
	11			10							2		9	4		3	8	1	5	7	6
	11			10							2		9	4		3	8	1	5	7	6
	11			10	7						2		9	4		3	8	1	5		6
	11			10	7						2		9	4		3	8	1	5		6
	11			10	7						2		9	4		3	8	1	5		6
	11			10	7						2		9	4		3	8	1	5		6
	11				7						2		9	4		3	8	1	5	10	6
	11			10	7						2		9	4		3	8	1	5		6
	11			10	7						2		9	4		3		1	5	8	6
4	38	1	15	32	21	6	6	2	22	3	38	19	39	31	1	37	23	41	42	23	18
	14			10	3				3		3	3	29	2		1	5			2	2

Birks Graham	Dobson Colin	Ellis Keith	Eustace Peter	Fantham John	Finney Alan	Griffin Billy	Hardy Robin	Hill Brian	Holliday Eddie	Horrobin Tom	Johnson Peter	Kay Tony	Layne David	McAnearney Tom	McLaren Roy	Megson Don	Quinn John	Springett Ron	Swan Peter	Wilkinson Derek	Young Gerry
	8		6	10	7				11		2		9	4	1	3			5		
	11		6	10	7						2		9	4		3	8	1	5		
	11		6	10	7						2		9	4		3	8	1	5		
	3		3	3	3				1		3		3	3	1	3	2	2	3		
				1	1								1								

League Table

	P	W	D	L	F	A	Pts
Everton	42	25	11	6	84	42	61
Tottenham Hotspur	42	23	9	10	111	62	55
Burnley	42	22	10	10	78	57	54
Leicester City	42	20	12	10	79	53	52
Wolverhampton W.	42	20	10	12	93	65	50
SHEFFIELD WEDNESDAY	42	19	10	13	77	63	48
Arsenal	42	18	10	14	86	77	46
Liverpool	42	17	10	15	71	59	44
Nottingham Forest	42	17	10	15	67	69	44
Sheffield United	42	16	12	14	58	60	44
Blackburn Rovers	42	15	12	15	79	71	42
West Ham United	42	14	12	16	73	69	40
Blackpool	42	13	14	15	58	64	40
West Bromwich Albion	42	16	7	19	71	79	39
Aston Villa	42	15	8	19	62	68	38
Fulham	42	14	10	18	50	71	38
Ipswich Town	42	12	11	19	59	78	35
Bolton Wanderers	42	15	5	22	55	75	35
Manchester United	42	12	10	20	67	81	34
Birmingham City	42	10	13	19	63	90	33
Manchester City	42	10	11	21	58	102	31
Leyton Orient	42	6	9	27	37	81	21

1963-64

Division One

Manager: Vic Buckingham

Did you know that?

Final League Position: 6th

On 13 April 1964 Eric Taylor announced to the crowd at half-time of the game against Spurs that the two players involved in the bribery affair, which had been broken in a national Sunday newspaper, were to be suspended by the club while the League investigated the matter. Wednesday won the game 2–0.

Match No.	Date	Venue	Opponents		Round	Result	HT Score	Position	Scorers	Attendance
1	Aug 24	H	Manchester United	D		3-3	2-1		Quinn, McAnearney (pen), Holliday	32,177
2	28	A	Fulham	L		0-2	0-2			20,873
3	31	A	Burnley	L		1-3	0-2	21st	Wilkinson	20,374
4	Sep 4	H	Fulham	W		3-0	0-0	17th	Fantham (2), Layne	22,045
5	7	H	Ipswich Town	W		3-1	2-0	10th	Layne, Fantham, McAnearney (pen)	19,127
6	11	A	Leicester City	L		0-2	0-1	15th		27,296
7	14	A	Sheffield United	D		1-1	0-1	15th	Finney	35,276
8	21	A	Everton	L		2-3	1-1	17th	Fantham, McAnearney (pen)	48,894
9	28	H	Birmingham City	W		2-1	0-0	14th	Fantham, Holliday	18,903
10	Oct 2	H	Leicester City	L		1-2	0-1	17th	Quinn	21,420
11	5	A	West Bromwich Alb	W		3-1	1-1	13th	Holliday, Layne (2)	23,000
12	9	A	Liverpool	L		1-3	1-1	13th	Holliday	46,107
13	12	H	West Ham United	W		3-0	0-0	12th	Dobson, Pearson, Holliday	23,503
14	19	A	Chelsea	W		2-1	1-1	11th	Finney (2)	31,948
15	26	H	Aston Villa	W		1-0	1-0	11th	Pearson	20,616
16	Nov 2	A	Blackburn Rovers	D		1-1	0-1	12th	Wilkinson	17,780
17	9	H	Nottingham Forest	W		3-1	3-0	10th	Dobson (2), Wilkinson	23,231
18	16	A	Stoke City	D		4-4	1-3	10th	Layne (2), Pearson (2)	30,695
19	23	H	Wolverhampton W	W		5-0	1-0	8th	Finney (2), Layne, Dobson (2)	22,650
20	30	A	Tottenham Hotspur	D		1-1	0-0	9th	Johnson	39,498
21	Dec 7	H	Blackpool	W		1-0	0-0	6th	Holliday	20,397
22	14	A	Manchester United	L		1-3	0-2	9th	Layne	35,139
23	21	H	Burnley	W		3-1	1-0	7th	McAnearney (pen), Layne, Dobson	19,390
24	26	H	Bolton Wanderers	W		3-0	2-0	4th	Dobson (2), Pearson	31,301
25	28	A	Bolton Wanderers	L		0-3	0-0	6th		12,205
26	Jan 11	A	Ipswich Town	W		4-1	2-1	5th	Layne (3), Dobson	15,206
27	18	H	Sheffield United	W		3-0	2-0	4th	Layne, Wilkinson (2)	42,898
28	Feb 1	H	Everton	L		0-3	0-1	5th		30,722
29	8	A	Birmingham City	W		2-1	1-0	4th	Fantham, Layne	15,460
30	15	H	West Bromwich Alb	D		2-2	1-2	7th	Layne, Fantham	19,048
31	22	A	West Ham United	L		3-4	1-2	7th	Finney, Dobson, Fantham	24,578
32	29	H	Chelsea	W		3-2	2-1	6th	McAnearney, Layne, Finney	20,212
33	Mar 4	H	Liverpool	D		2-2	1-0		Holliday, Pearson	23,703
34	7	A	Aston Villa	D		2-2	1-1	6th	Layne (1 + pen)	13,972
35	21	A	Nottingham Forest	L		2-3	1-0	6th	Layne (pen + 1)	17,692
36	24	A	Arsenal	D		1-1	0-0	6th	Layne	24,364
37	28	H	Blackburn Rovers	W		5-2	4-1	6th	Hardy, Fantham, Holliday, Layne (1 + pen)	20,791
38	30	H	Arsenal	L		0-4	0-3	7th		26,433
39	Apr 4	A	Wolverhampton W	D		1-1	1-0	6th	Fantham	14,900
40	8	H	Stoke City	W		2-0	0-0	6th	Dobson, Fantham	17,487
41	13	H	Tottenham Hotspur	W		2-0	2-0	5th	Wilkinson (2)	31,377
42	18	A	Blackpool	D		2-2	1-1	6th	Fantham, Wilkinson	12,905
										Apps
										Goals

FA Cup

Match No.	Date	Venue	Opponents		Round	Result	HT Score	Position	Scorers	Attendance
43	Jan 4	A	Newport County	L	3R	2-3	1-0		Holliday, Finney	12,342
										Apps
										Goals

Inter-Cities-Fairs Cup

Match No.	Date	Venue	Opponents		Round	Result	HT Score	Position	Scorers	Attendance
44	Sep 25	A	D.O.S.Utrecht	W	1R 1L	4-1	2-0		Holliday, Layne, Quinn, Mijnals (og)	15,000
45	Oct 15	H	D.O.S.Utrecht	W	2R 2L	4-1	2-1		Layne (2 + pen), Dobson	20,643
46	Nov 6	A	Cologne	L	2R 1L	2-3	0-3		Pearson (2)	15,000
47	Nov 27	H	Cologne	L	2R 2L	1-2	1-0		Layne	36,929
										Apps
									One own-goal	Goals

Dobson Colin	Ellis Keith	Fantham John	Finney Alan	Hardy Robin	Hickton John	Hill Brian	Holliday Eddie	Johnson Peter	Layne David	McAnearney Tom	McLaren Roy	Megson Don	Mobley Vic	Noble Frank	Pearson Mark	Quinn John	Springett Ron	Swan Peter	Wilkinson Derek	Young Gerry
	9	10	7				11	2		4		3				8	1	5		6
		10	11					2	9	4		3				8	1	5	7	6
11		10							9	4		3		2		8	1	5	7	6
11		10				2			9	4		3				8	1	5	7	6
11		10				2			9	4		3				8	1	5	7	6
11			7			2			9	4		3				8	1	5	10	6
11			7			2			9	4		3				8	1	5	10	6
11		10	7			2			9	4		3				8	1	5		6
		10				2	11		9	4	1	3				8		5	7	6
		10	7			2	11		9	4		3				8	1	5		6
			7			2	11		9	4		3			10	8	1	5		6
			7			2	11		9	4		3			10	8	1	5		6
10			7			2	11		9	4		3			8		1	5		6
8	9		7			2	11			4		3			10		1	5		6
11	9		7			2				4		3			10	8	1	5		6
8			7			2	11			4		3			10		1	5	9	6
8			7			2	11			4		3			10		1	5	9	6
11			7					2	9	4		3			10		1	5	8	6
8			7				11	2	9	4		3			10		1	5		6
8			7	4			11	2	9			3			10		1	5		6
8			7			2	11		9	4		3			10		1	5		6
8			7			2	11		9	4	1	3			10			5		6
8			7			2	11		9	4	1	3			10			5		6
8						2	11		9	4	1	3			10			5	7	6
8			7			2	11		9	4	1	3			10			5		6
11			7	4		2			9		1	3			10			5	8	6
11			7	4		2			9		1	3			10			5	8	6
11			7			2			9	4		3			10		1	5	8	6
11		10	7			2			9	4		3					1	5	8	6
11		10				2			9	4		3			8		1	5	7	6
11		10	7			2			9	4		3			8		1	5		6
11		10	7			2			9	4		3			8		1	5		6
8			7			2	11		9	4	1	3			10			5		6
8			7	4	2		11		9		1	3			10			5		6
8			7	4	2		11		9		1	3			10			5		6
8		10	7	4		2	11		9		1	3						5		6
8		10	7	4		2	11		9		1	3						5		6
10		8	7	4			11	2	9		1	3						5		6
11		10	7					2	9	4		3	5		8		1			6
11		10	7					2	9	4		3			8		1	5		6
11		10	7					2		4		3	5		8		1		9	6
11		10	7					2		4		3	5		8		1		9	6
36	3	19	36	8	2	29	22	10	35	34	13	42	3	1	28	13	29	39	18	42
11		12	7	1			8	1	23	5					6	2			8	
8			7			2	11		9	4	1	3			10			5		6
1			1			1	1		1	1	1	1			1			1		1
			1				1													
		10	7			2	11		9	4		3				8	1	5		6
10			7			2	11		9	4		3				8	1	5		6
8			7			2	11			4		3			10		1	5	9	6
8			7	4			11	2	9			3			10		1	5		6
3		1	4	1		3	4	1	3	3		4			2	2	4	4	1	4
1							1		5						2	1				

League Table

	P	W	D	L	F	A	Pts
Liverpool	42	26	5	11	92	45	57
Manchester United	42	23	7	12	90	62	53
Everton	42	21	10	11	84	64	52
Tottenham Hotspur	42	22	7	13	97	81	51
Chelsea	42	20	10	12	72	56	50
SHEFFIELD WEDNESDAY	42	19	11	12	84	67	49
Blackburn Rovers	42	18	10	14	89	65	46
Arsenal	42	17	11	14	90	82	45
Burnley	42	17	10	15	71	64	44
West Bromwich Albion	42	16	11	15	70	61	43
Leicester City	42	16	11	15	61	58	43
Sheffield United	42	16	11	15	61	64	43
Nottingham Forest	42	16	9	17	64	68	41
West Ham United	42	14	12	16	69	74	40
Fulham	42	13	13	16	58	65	39
Wolverhampton W.	42	12	15	15	70	80	39
Stoke City	42	14	10	18	77	78	38
Blackpool	42	13	9	20	52	73	35
Aston Villa	42	11	12	19	62	71	34
Birmingham City	42	11	7	24	54	92	29
Bolton Wanderers	42	10	8	24	48	80	28
Ipswich Town	42	9	7	26	56	121	25

1964-65

Division One

Manager: Alan Brown

Did you know that?

Final League Position: 8th

Peter Wicks was Wednesday's youngest player when he kept goal against Liverpool on 16 January 1965 in a 4–2 away defeat.

Match No.	Date	Venue	Opponents		Round	Result	HT Score	Position	Scorers	Attendance
1	Aug 22	H	Blackburn Rovers	W		1-0	0-0	8th	Finney	21,620
2	25	A	Arsenal	D		1-1	1-0		Quinn	35,590
3	29	A	Blackpool	L		0-1	0-1	10th		18,461
4	Sep 2	H	Arsenal	W		2-1	1-1		Dobson, Pearson	22,555
5	5	H	Sheffield United	L		0-2	0-1	14th		32,684
6	9	A	Chelsea	D		1-1	1-0	15th	Pearson	31,973
7	12	H	Liverpool	W		1-0	1-0	8th	Quinn	22,701
8	16	H	Chelsea	L		2-3	1-1	15th	Dobson, Fantham	18,176
9	19	A	Aston Villa	L		0-2	0-1	16th		18,859
10	23	H	Burnley	W		5-1	5-0	9th	Fantham (3), Mobley, Dobson	17,366
11	26	H	Wolverhampton W	W		2-0	1-0	8th	McAnearney (pen), Dobson	19,881
12	Oct 10	A	Everton	D		1-1	1-0	10th	Fantham	41,911
13	17	H	Birmingham City	W		5-2	3-1	9th	Wilkinson (2), Quinn, Fantham (2)	16,161
14	24	A	West Ham United	W		2-1	1-0	9th	Fantham, Quinn	22,800
15	31	H	West Bromwich Alb	D		1-1	0-0	9th	Fantham	19,004
16	Nov 7	A	Manchester United	L		0-1	0-1	9th		50,178
17	14	H	Fulham	D		1-1	0-0	8th	Hickton	18,027
18	21	A	Nottingham Forest	D		2-2	0-2	10th	Dobson (pen + 1)	29,920
19	28	H	Stoke City	D		1-1	1-0	10th	Fantham	17,266
20	Dec 5	A	Tottenham Hotspur	L		2-3	0-1	9th	Hickton (2)	23,072
21	19	H	Blackpool	W		4-1	1-0	8th	Dobson (1 + pen), Hickton, Fantham	16,172
22	26	A	Leicester City	D		2-2	1-1	9th	Dobson (pen), Fantham	23,278
23	28	H	Leicester City	D		0-0	0-0	8th		18,046
24	Jan 2	A	Sheffield United	W		3-2	1-1	9th	Hickton, Fantham (2)	37,190
25	16	A	Liverpool	L		2-4	1-1	11th	Pearson, Hickton	42,422
26	29	A	Blackburn Rovers	W		1-0	1-0		Fantham	12,202
27	Feb 6	A	Wolverhampton W	L		1-3	1-1	10th	Hickton	18,665
28	13	H	Sunderland	W		2-0	0-0	8th	Finney, Eustace	17,909
29	20	H	Everton	L		0-1	0-1	10th		17,135
30	27	A	Birmingham City	D		0-0	0-0	10th		12,138
31	Mar 6	H	West Ham United	W		2-0	0-0	9th	Mobley, Hickton	14,931
32	13	A	Burnley	L		1-4	0-2	8th	Fantham	12,362
33	15	H	Aston Villa	W		3-1	1-0	7th	Hickton (2), Quinn	12,223
34	20	H	Manchester United	W		1-0	0-0	6th	Fantham	33,549
35	27	A	Fulham	L		0-2	0-2	6th		12,146
36	Apr 3	H	Nottingham Forest	D		0-0	0-0	8th		18,096
37	10	A	Stoke City	L		1-4	0-2	7th	Quinn	16,047
38	17	H	Tottenham Hotspur	W		1-0	1-0	7th	Eustace	23,099
39	19	H	Leeds United	W		3-0	2-0	7th	Fantham (2), Hunter (og)	39,054
40	20	A	Leeds United	L		0-2	0-2	7th		45,065
41	24	A	West Bromwich Alb	L		0-1	0-1	7th		16,000
42	28	A	Sunderland	L		0-3	0-1	8th		22,467
										Apps
									One own-goal	Goals

FA Cup

Match No.	Date	Venue	Opponents		Round	Result	HT Score	Position	Scorers	Attendance
43	Jan 9	A	Everton	D	3R	2-2	0-1		Fantham, Quinn	44,732
44	13	H	Everton	L	3R Re	0-3	0-3			50,080
										Apps
										Goals

Burgin Andy	Dobson Colin	Eustace Peter	Fantham John	Finney Alan	Hickton John	Hill Brian	Johnson Peter	McAnearney Tom	McLaren Roy	Megson Don	Mobley Vic	Pearson Mark	Quinn John	Smith Wilf	Springett Ron	Wicks Peter	Wilkinson Derek	Wilkinson Howard	Young Gerry
	11		10	7		2		4		3	5	8	9		1				6
	11		10	7		2		4		3	5	8	9		1				6
	11		10	7		2		4		3	5	8	9		1				6
	11		10	7		2		4		3	5	8	9		1				6
	11		10	7		2		4		3	5	8	9		1				6
	11		10			2		4		3	5	8	9		1			7	6
	11		10			2		4		3	5	8	9		1			7	6
	11		10			2		4		3	5	8	9		1			7	6
	11		10			2		4		3	5	8	9		1			7	6
	11		10			2		4		3	5	8	9		1		7		6
	11		10	7		2		4		3	5		8		1		9		6
	11	4	10	7		2				3	5		8		1		9		6
	11	4	10	7		2				3	5		8		1		9		6
	11	4	10	7		2				3	5		8		1		9		6
	11	4	10	7		2				3	5		8		1		9		6
	11	4	10	7		2				3	5		8		1		9		6
	11	4	10	7	9	2				3	5		8		1				6
	11	4	10	7	9	2		6		3	5		8		1				
	11	4	10	7	9	2		6		3	5		8		1				
	11	4	10	7	9	2				3	5		8		1				6
	11	4	10	7	9	2				3	5		8	6	1				
	11	4	10	7	9	2				3	5		8	6	1				
	11	4	10	7	9		2			3	5		8	6	1				
	11	4	10	7	9		2			3	5		8	6	1				
2	11	4		7	9					3	5	10	8	6		1			
	11	4	10	7	9	2				3	5		8	6	1				
	11	4	10	7	9	2				3	5		8	6	1				
	11	8	10	7	9	2		4		3	5			6	1				
	11	8	10	7	9	2		4		3	5			6	1				
	11	4	10	7	9	2				3	5		8	6	1				
	11	4	10	7	9	2				3	5		8	6	1				
	11	4	10	7	9	2				3	5		8	6	1				
	11	4	10		9	2				3	5		8	6	1			7	
	11	4	10		9	2				3	5		8	6	1			7	
	11	4	10		9	2				3	5		8	6	1			7	
	11	4	10		9	2				3	5		8	6	1			7	
	11	4	10		9	2				3	5		8	6	1			7	
	11	4	10		9	2				3	5		8		1			7	6
	11	4	10		9	2				3	5		8		1			7	6
	11	4	10		9	2				3	5		8		1			7	6
	11	4	10		9	2				3	5		8		1			7	6
	11	4	10		9	2				3	5		8	6	1			7	
1	42	31	41	27	26	39	2	15		42	42	11	40	18	41	1	7	14	22
	9	2	19	2	10			1			2	3	6				2		

Burgin Andy	Dobson Colin	Eustace Peter	Fantham John	Finney Alan	Hickton John	Hill Brian	Johnson Peter	McAnearney Tom	McLaren Roy	Megson Don	Mobley Vic	Pearson Mark	Quinn John	Smith Wilf	Springett Ron	Wicks Peter	Wilkinson Derek	Wilkinson Howard	Young Gerry
2	11	4	10	7	9					3	5		8	6	1				
2	11	4	10	7	9				1	3	5		8	6					
2	2	2	2	2	2				1	2	2		2	2	1				
			1										1						

League Table

	P	W	D	L	F	A	Pts
Manchester United	42	26	9	7	89	39	61
Leeds United	42	26	9	7	83	52	61
Chelsea	42	24	8	10	89	54	56
Everton	42	17	15	10	69	60	49
Nottingham Forest	42	17	13	12	71	67	47
Tottenham Hotspur	42	19	7	16	87	71	45
Liverpool	42	17	10	15	67	73	44
SHEFFIELD WEDNESDAY	42	16	11	15	57	55	43
West Ham United	42	19	4	19	82	71	42
Blackburn Rovers	42	16	10	16	83	79	42
Stoke City	42	16	10	16	67	66	42
Burnley	42	16	10	16	70	70	42
Arsenal	42	17	7	18	69	75	41
West Bromwich Albion	42	13	13	16	70	65	39
Sunderland	42	14	9	19	64	74	37
Aston Villa	42	16	5	21	57	82	37
Blackpool	42	12	11	19	67	78	35
Leicester City	42	11	13	18	69	85	35
Sheffield United	42	12	11	19	50	64	35
Fulham	42	11	12	19	60	78	34
Wolverhampton W.	42	13	4	25	59	89	30
Birmingham City	42	8	11	23	64	96	27

1965-66

Division One

Manager: Alan Brown

Did you know that?

Final League Position: 17th

On 21 August 1965 Wilf Smith was picked as the first substitute for Wednesday after the new law allowing substitutes was introduced for League games only. On 23 October 1965 David Ford was the first one to be used when he replaced the injured Don Megson after only eight minutes.

Match No.	Date	Venue	Opponents		Round	Result	HT Score	Position	Scorers	Attendance
1	Aug 21	A	Manchester United	L		0-1	0-1			37,524
2	25	H	Everton	W		3-1	0-1		Hickton (2), Quinn	26,986
3	28	H	Newcastle United	W		1-0	1-0	5th	Dobson	23,391
4	31	A	Everton	L		1-5	0-3	5th	Fantham	49,460
5	Sep 4	A	West Bromwich Alb	L		2-4	2-2	16th	Eustace, Hickton	17,000
6	11	H	Nottingham Forest	W		3-1	2-1	16th	Megson, Eustace, Hickton	18,368
7	15	A	Chelsea	D		1-1	0-0	14th	Fantham	26,183
8	18	A	Sheffield United	L		0-1	0-0	17th		35,655
9	25	A	Northampton Town	D		0-0	0-0	16th		16,298
10	Oct 9	H	Leeds United	D		0-0	0-0	16th		35,105
11	16	A	West Ham United	L		2-4	2-1	19th	Brown (og), Wilkinson	21,000
12	23	H	Sunderland	W		3-1	1-0	16th	Hickton, Dobson, Irwin (og)	21,381
13	30	A	Aston Villa	L		0-2	0-1	18th		23,247
14	Nov 6	H	Liverpool	L		0-2	0-0	19th		24,456
15	13	A	Tottenham Hotspur	W		3-2	3-1	16th	Dobson, Fantham, Mobley	29,848
16	20	H	Fulham	W		1-0	1-0	15th	Ford	16,030
17	27	A	Blackpool	L		1-2	0-0	15th	Thompson (og)	9,807
18	Dec 4	H	Blackburn Rovers	W		2-1	0-0	14th	Hickton, Finney	15,716
19	11	A	Leicester City	L		1-4	0-2	15th	Fantham	16,438
20	18	H	West Ham United	D		0-0	0-0	15th		12,996
21	27	H	Arsenal	W		4-0	3-0	14th	Hickton (3) Usher	33,101
22	28	A	Arsenal	L		2-5	0-3	14th	Fantham, Hickton	21,035
23	Jan 1	A	Leeds United	L		0-3	0-1	15th		34,841
24	8	H	Leicester City	L		1-2	1-2	16th	Wilkinson	15,165
25	26	A	Sunderland	W		2-0	0-0	16th	Fantham, McCalliog	25,033
26	29	H	Manchester United	D		0-0	0-0	15th		39,281
27	Feb 5	A	Newcastle United	L		0-2	0-1	16th		31,150
28	19	H	West Bromwich Alb	L		1-2	1-2	17th	Eustace	18,358
29	Mar 12	H	Sheffield United	D		2-2	1-1	18th	Fantham, Eustace	34,045
30	19	H	Northampton Town	W		3-1	1-0	16th	Ford (2), Fantham	17,020
31	30	H	Stoke City	W		4-1	1-1	17th	McCalliog, Ford, Dobson, Fantham	19,898
32	Apr 4	H	Blackpool	W		3-0	1-0	14th	Ford (2), Fantham	20,945
33	6	A	Liverpool	L		0-1	0-1			44,792
34	9	H	Tottenham Hotspur	D		1-1	1-0	13th	Ford	18,009
35	11	A	Burnley	L		1-2	1-0	15th	McCalliog	17,340
36	16	A	Fulham	L		2-4	2-1	19th	Ford, McCalliog	20,980
37	27	H	Aston Villa	W		2-0	0-0	16th	Fantham (2)	28,008
38	30	A	Blackburn Rovers	W		2-1	1-0	14th	Fantham, Ford	7,683
39	May 2	H	Chelsea	D		1-1	1-0		Davies	27,089
40	4	A	Stoke City	L		1-3	1-2	14th	Ford	11,602
41	7	A	Nottingham Forest	L		0-1	0-0	15th		16,413
42	9	H	Burnley	L		0-2	0-0	17th		21,049
										Apps
										Subs
									Three own-goals	Goals

FA Cup

43	Jan 22	A	Reading	W	3R	3-2	1-0	Fantham (2), McCalliog	23,000
44	Feb 12	A	Newcastle United	W	4R	2-1	2-1	Dobson, McGrath (og)	39,500
45	Mar 5	A	Huddersfield Town	W	5R	2-1	0-1	Ford, Usher	49,612
46	26	A	Blackburn Rovers	W	6R	2-1	1-1	Ford (2)	33,188
47	Apr 23	N	Chelsea *	W	S/F	2-0	0-0	Pugh, McCalliog	61,321
48	May 14	N	Everton #	L	Final	2-3	1-0	McCalliog, Ford	100,000
									Apps
								One own-goal	Goals

* At Villa Park, Birmingham
# At Wembley, London

Branfoot Ian	Davies Brian	Dobson Colin	Ellis Sam	Eustace Peter	Fantham John	Finney Alan	Ford David	Hickton John	Hill Brian	McCalliog Jim	Megson Don	Mobley Vic	Noble Frank	Pugh Graham	Quinn John	Smith Wilf	Springett Ron	Usher Brian	Wicks Peter	Wilkinson Howard	Woodall Brian	Young Gerry
		11		4	10			9	2		3	5			8	U	1	7				6
		11		4	10			9	2		3	5			8	U	1	7				6
		11		4	10			9	2		3	5			8		1	7		U		6
		11		4	10		U	9	2		3	5			8		1			7		6
		11		4	10		U	9	2		3	5			8		1	7				6
		11		4	10		U	9	2		3	5			8	6	1	7				
		11		4	10			9	2		3	5			8	6	1	7				U
		11		4	10			9	2		3	5			8	6	1	7				U
		11		4	10			9			3	5			8	2	1	7		U		6
		11		4	10			9	U		3	5			8	2	1	7				6
		11		4	10			9	U		3	5			8	2	1			7		6
		11		10			S*	9	2		3*	5			8	4	1			7		6
							11	9	2	10		5	3		8	4	1			7	U	6
		11		4				9	U	10	3	5			8	2	1			7		6
		11		4	8		10	U		9	3	5			7	2			1			6
		11			10		8	U	2	9	3	5			7	4			1			6
		11			8		10		2	9	3	5			U	4			1	7		6
					8	7		10	2	9	3*	5			S*	4	1	11				6
		11		4	8		10		U	9	3	5				2	1	7				6
		11		4	8			10	2	9		5			U	3	1	7				6
		11		4	8			10	2	9		5			U	3	1	7				6
		11		4*	8	7		10	2	9	3				S*	6	1					5
U		11			8	7		10	2	9	3				4	6	1					5
		11			8			10	2	9	3	5			U	4	1			7		6
		11		4	8			10		9	3	5			U	2	1	7				6
		11		4	8			10*		9	3	5			S*	2	1	7				6
		11			8			10	2	9	3*	5			S*	4	1	7				6
		11		4	8		10		U	9	3	5				2	1	7				6
		11		4	8		10	S*			3	5			9	2	1	7*				6
		11		4	8		10		U		3	5			9	2			1	7		6
		11		4	8		10	U		9	3	5			7	2	1					6
		11	5	4	8		10		U	9	3				7	2	1					6
		11	5	4	8		10		U	9	3				7	2	1					6
			5	4	8		10		U	9	3			7	11	2	1					6
			5	4	8		10		S*	9	3			7*	11	2	1					6
				4	8		10		U	9	3	5		7	11	2	1					6
			5	4	8		10			9	3		U	7	11	2	1					6
			5	4	8		10		U	9	3			7	11	2	1					6
U	8		5	4			10		2	9	3			7	11				1			6
	U	11	5	4	8		10		2	9	3			7					1			6
	10	11	5	4	8				U		3			7	9	2	1					6
6	8	U	5	4				10		9	3			7	11	2	1					
1	3	33	10	35	37	3	18	24	21	27	39	30	1	9	30	35	36	18	6	8		38
							1	1	1						4							
	1	4		4	13	1	10	10		4	1	1			1			1		2		

Branfoot Ian	Davies Brian	Dobson Colin	Ellis Sam	Eustace Peter	Fantham John	Finney Alan	Ford David	Hickton John	Hill Brian	McCalliog Jim	Megson Don	Mobley Vic	Noble Frank	Pugh Graham	Quinn John	Smith Wilf	Springett Ron	Usher Brian	Wicks Peter	Wilkinson Howard	Woodall Brian	Young Gerry
		11		4	8			10		9	3	5				2	1	7				6
		11		4	8		10			9	3	5				2	1	7				6
		11		4	8		10			9	3	5				2	1	7				6
				4	8		10			9	3	5			11	2	1	7				6
				4	8		10			9	3	5		7	11	2	1					6
			5	4	8		10			9	3			7	11	2	1					6
		3	1	6	6		5	1		6	6	5		2	3	6	6	4				6
		1			2		4			3				1				1				

League Table

	P	W	D	L	F	A	Pts
Liverpool	42	26	9	7	79	34	61
Leeds United	42	23	9	10	79	38	55
Burnley	42	24	7	11	79	47	55
Manchester United	42	18	15	9	84	59	51
Chelsea	42	22	7	13	65	53	51
West Bromwich Albion	42	19	12	11	91	69	50
Leicester City	42	21	7	14	80	65	49
Tottenham Hotspur	42	16	12	14	75	66	44
Sheffield United	42	16	11	15	56	59	43
Stoke City	42	15	12	15	65	64	42
Everton	42	15	11	16	56	62	41
West Ham United	42	15	9	18	70	83	39
Blackpool	42	14	9	19	55	65	37
Arsenal	42	12	13	17	62	75	37
Newcastle United	42	14	9	19	50	63	37
Aston Villa	42	15	6	21	69	80	36
SHEFFIELD WEDNESDAY	42	14	8	20	56	66	36
Nottingham Forest	42	14	8	20	56	72	36
Sunderland	42	14	8	20	51	72	36
Fulham	42	14	7	21	67	85	35
Northampton Town	42	10	13	19	55	92	33
Blackburn Rovers	42	8	4	30	57	88	20

1966-67

Division One

Manager: Alan Brown

Did you know that?

Final League Position: 11th

On 28 January 1967 John Quinn was the first Wednesday substitute to be used in an FA Cup game, as he replaced Gerry Young after seven minutes. Substitutes were now allowed in Cup games.

On 14 September 1966 Wednesday played their first game in the League Cup, a 1–0 home defeat against Rotherham United. Wednesday had not entered the competition in its first six seasons.

On 1 October 1966 Wednesday were awarded a penalty at Southampton, which was scored by Peter Eustace, in a 4–2 defeat. This was the first penalty awarded to Wednesday since 26 December 1964, 81 games before.

Gary Scothorn became the youngest player for Wednesday at 16 years and 257 days, when he kept goal for Wednesday in a 4–0 home FA Cup defeat of Mansfield Town on 18 February 1967.

On 6 May 1967 Jack Whitham came off the bench to net twice against his home-town team, Burnley, to become Wednesday's first goal scorer as a substitute.

Match No.	Date	Venue	Opponents		Round	Result	HT Score	Position	Scorers	Attendance
1	Aug 20	H	Blackpool	W		3-0	2-0		Ford, Quinn, Eustace	21,008
2	22	A	Aston Villa	W		1-0	0-0		Ford	14,575
3	27	A	Chelsea	D		0-0	0-0	3rd		33,489
4	31	H	Aston Villa	W		2-0	1-0	1st	Pugh, Fantham	25,992
5	Sep 3	H	Leicester City	D		1-1	0-1	1st	Pugh	31,252
6	6	A	Arsenal	D		1-1	0-0	1st	Ford	28,898
7	10	A	Liverpool	D		1-1	1-1	2nd	Fantham	48,717
8	17	H	West Ham United	L		0-2	0-1	5th		29,171
9	24	H	Sheffield United	D		2-2	1-2	7th	Munks (og), McCalliog	43,557
10	Oct 1	A	Southampton	L		2-4	1-4	9th	Ford, Eustace (pen)	21,595
11	8	H	Stoke City	L		1-3	0-2	11th	Fantham	28,047
12	15	A	Everton	L		1-2	0-2	13th	Eustace	38,355
13	22	H	Fulham	D		1-1	1-1	12th	McCalliog	20,044
14	29	A	West Bromwich Alb	W		2-1	1-0	11th	Eustace, Pugh	19,466
15	Nov 5	H	Everton	L		1-2	1-0	11th	Fantham	28,072
16	12	A	Manchester United	L		0-2	0-2	14th		46,942
17	19	H	Tottenham Hotspur	W		1-0	0-0	13th	Ford	32,990
18	26	A	Newcastle United	L		1-3	1-2	13th	Ritchie	26,860
19	Dec 3	H	Leeds United	D		0-0	0-0	13th		35,264
20	10	A	Nottingham Forest	D		1-1	1-0	12th	Ford	22,540
21	17	A	Blackpool	D		1-1	0-1	13th	Ritchie	10,862
22	27	H	Manchester City	W		1-0	0-0	14th	Young	34,005
23	31	H	Chelsea	W		6-1	2-0	12th	McCalliog, Ford (2), Ritchie (2), Fantham	31,032
24	Jan 2	A	Manchester City	D		0-0	0-0	12th		32,198
25	7	A	Leicester City	W		1-0	1-0	10th	Ritchie	22,241
26	14	H	Liverpool	L		0-1	0-1	12th		43,951
27	21	A	West Ham United	L		0-3	0-0	13th		29,220
28	Feb 4	A	Sheffield United	L		0-1	0-0	15th		43,490
29	11	H	Southampton	W		4-1	2-0	14th	Fantham (2 + pen), McCalliog	26,199
30	25	A	Stoke City	W		2-0	2-0	12th	Ford, Ritchie	27,164
31	Mar 18	A	Fulham	W		2-1	0-0	11th	Fantham (2)	21,771
32	24	A	Sunderland	L		0-2	0-1	11th		35,698
33	25	H	Nottingham Forest	L		0-2	0-2	13th		43,118
34	28	H	Sunderland	W		5-0	2-0	12th	Megson, Ritchie (2) Symm, Ford	26,094
35	Apr 1	A	Burnley	L		0-2	0-0	12th		14,430
36	10	H	Manchester United	D		2-2	0-2	13th	Fantham, Ritchie	51,018
37	15	A	Tottenham Hotspur	L		1-2	1-0	14th	Fantham	36,062
38	19	H	West Bromwich Alb	W		1-0	0-0	12th	Ford	23,056
39	22	H	Newcastle United	D		0-0	0-0	12th		25,007
40	May 6	H	Burnley	W		7-0	2-0	11th	Ford (3), McCalliog, Whitham (2), Quinn	21,103
41	13	H	Arsenal	D		1-1	1-0	11th	Ritchie	23,222
42	15	A	Leeds United	L		0-1	0-1	11th		23,052
										Apps
										Subs
									One own-goal	Goals

League Cup

Match No.	Date	Venue	Opponents		Round	Result	HT Score	Position	Scorers	Attendance
43	Sep 14	H	Rotherham United	L	2R	0-1	0-0			20,204
										Apps

FA Cup

Match No.	Date	Venue	Opponents		Round	Result	HT Score	Position	Scorers	Attendance
44	Jan 28	H	Queen's Park Rangers	W	3R	3-0	1-0		Ritchie (3)	40,038
45	Feb 18	H	Mansfield Town	W	4R	4-0	1-0		Ritchie (2), Fantham, McCalliog	49,049
46	Mar 11	A	Norwich City	W	5R	3-1	2-0		Quinn, Ford, Fantham	41,000
47	Apr 8	A	Chelsea	L	6R	0-1	0-0			52,481
										Apps
										Subs
										Goals

Branfoot Ian	Burgin Andy	Davies Brian	Ellis Sam	Eustace Peter	Fantham John	Ford David	Hill Brian	McCalliog Jim	Megson Don	Mobley Vic	Noble Frank	Pugh Graham	Quinn John	Ritchie John	Scothorn Gary	Smith Wilf	Springett Ron	Symm Colin	Usher Brian	Whitham Jack	Wicks Peter	Woodall Brian	Young Gerry
			5	4	8	10		9	3		U	7	11			2	1						6
			5	4	8	10		9	3		U	7	11			2	1						6
	U		5	4		10		9	3			8	11			2	1		7				6
			5	4	8	10	U	9	3			7	11			2	1						6
			5	4	8	10	U	9	3			7	11			2	1						6
U			5	4	8	10		9	3			7	11			2	1						6
			5	4	8	10	U	9	3			7	11			2	1						6
U			5	4	8	10		9	3			7	11			2	1						6
			5	4	8	10	U	9	3			7	11			2	1						6
			5	4	8	10	U	9	3			7	11			2	1						6
			5	4	8	10		9	3		U	7	11			2	1						6
			U	4		10		9	3	5		7	11			2	1	8					6
			5	4		10		9	3	U		7	11			2	1	8					6
			5	4	8	10		9	3		U	7	11			2	1						6
			5	4	8	10		9	3			7	11			2	1	U					6
U			5	4		10		8	3			7	11	9		2	1						6
11			5	4	7	10		8	3				U	9		2	1						6
11			5	4*	7	10		8	3				S*	9		2	1						6
11			5		7	10		8	3	4		U		9		2	1						6
11			5		7	10		8	3	4			U	9		2	1						6
U			5	11	7	10		8	3	4				9		2	1						6
11			5		7	10		8	3	4			U	9		2	1						6
			5		7	10		8	3	4		11	U	9		2	1						6
			5		7	10		8	3	4		11	U	9		2	1						6
			5		7	10	U	8	3	4		11		9		2	1						6
			5		7*	10		8	3	4		11		9		2	1	S*					6
2			5	11		10		8	3	4		7	9				1	U					6
			5	6	7	10		8	3	4		11		9		2		U			1		
			5		7	10		8	3	4		11	6	9		2	1	U					
			5		7	10		8	3	4		11	6	9		2			U		1		
			5	11	7	U		8	3	4			6	9		2	1	10					
11			5			10		8	3	4			6	9		2	1	7	U				
			5	11*		10		8	3	4			6	9		2	1	7	S*				
U			5			10		8	3	4			6	9		2	1	7	11				
6			5		7	10		8	3	4		11				2	1	9	U				
			5		7			8	3	4		11	6	9		2	1	U	10				
			5		7	10			3	4		11	6	9		2	1	U	8				
			5			10		8	3	4		11	6	9		2	1	U	7				
			5			10		8	3	4		11*	6	9		2	1		7				S*
			5			10		8	3	4			6	9		2	1		7*	S*			11
U			5			11			3	4			6	10		2	1	7		9			8
11			5			10			3	4			6			2	1	8	7	9		U	
9			41	23	29	40		39	42	25		29	30	24		41	40	9	8	2	2		29
													1					1	1	1			1
				4	12	14		5	1			3	2	10				1		2			1

Branfoot Ian	Burgin Andy	Davies Brian	Ellis Sam	Eustace Peter	Fantham John	Ford David	Hill Brian	McCalliog Jim	Megson Don	Mobley Vic	Noble Frank	Pugh Graham	Quinn John	Ritchie John	Scothorn Gary	Smith Wilf	Springett Ron	Symm Colin	Usher Brian	Whitham Jack	Wicks Peter	Woodall Brian	Young Gerry
U		10	5	4				9	3			8	11			2	1		7				6
		1	1	1				1	1			1	1			1	1		1				1

Branfoot Ian	Burgin Andy	Davies Brian	Ellis Sam	Eustace Peter	Fantham John	Ford David	Hill Brian	McCalliog Jim	Megson Don	Mobley Vic	Noble Frank	Pugh Graham	Quinn John	Ritchie John	Scothorn Gary	Smith Wilf	Springett Ron	Symm Colin	Usher Brian	Whitham Jack	Wicks Peter	Woodall Brian	Young Gerry
			5		7	10		8	3	4		11	S*	9		2	1						6*
			5		7	10		8	3	4		11	6	9	1	2		U					
			5	11	7	10		8	3	4			6	9		2	1	U					
			5		7	10*		8	3	4		11	6	9		2	1	S*					
			4	1	4	4		4	4	4		3	3	4	1	4	3						1
													1					1					
					2	1		1					1	5									

League Table

	P	W	D	L	F	A	Pts
Manchester United	42	24	12	6	84	45	60
Nottingham Forest	42	23	10	9	64	41	56
Tottenham Hotspur	42	24	8	10	71	48	56
Leeds United	42	22	11	9	62	42	55
Liverpool	42	19	13	10	64	47	51
Everton	42	19	10	13	65	46	48
Arsenal	42	16	14	12	58	47	46
Leicester City	42	18	8	16	78	71	44
Chelsea	42	15	14	13	67	62	44
Sheffield United	42	16	10	16	52	59	42
SHEFFIELD WEDNESDAY	42	14	13	15	56	47	41
Stoke City	42	17	7	18	63	58	41
West Bromwich Albion	42	16	7	19	77	73	39
Burnley	42	15	9	18	66	76	39
Manchester City	42	12	15	15	43	52	39
West Ham United	42	14	8	20	80	84	36
Sunderland	42	14	8	20	58	72	36
Fulham	42	11	12	19	71	83	34
Southampton	42	14	6	22	74	92	34
Newcastle United	42	12	9	21	39	81	33
Aston Villa	42	11	7	24	54	85	29
Blackpool	42	6	9	27	41	76	21

1967-68

Division One

Manager: Alan Brown/Jack Marshall

Did you know that?

Final League Position: 19th

For the game against Fulham on 6 September 1967, the nearest game to Wednesday's centenary birthday, fans were admitted at half-price and presented with a birthday card and a badge. Wednesday won 4–2 and moved to the top of the First Division.

Match No.	Date	Venue	Opponents		Round	Result	HT Score	Position	Scorers	Attendance
1	Aug 19	A	West Ham United	W		3-2	1-0		Fantham, Ritchie, McCalliog	29,603
2	23	H	Leicester City	W		2-1	1-0	1st	Ritchie (2)	30,190
3	26	H	Burnley	W		2-1	2-0	1st	Fantham, Ritchie	29,725
4	30	A	Leicester City	L		0-3	0-0	1st		20,443
5	Sep 2	A	Sheffield United	W		1-0	0-0	1st	Ritchie	36,258
6	6	H	Fulham	W		4-2	0-1	1st	Mobley, Ritchie (2), Ford	26,551
7	9	A	Tottenham Hotspur	L		1-2	0-1	3rd	Ford	43,314
8	16	H	Manchester United	D		1-1	1-0	3rd	Usher	47,274
9	23	A	Sunderland	W		2-0	0-0	3rd	McCalliog, Ritchie	29,003
10	30	H	Wolverhampton W	D		2-2	1-1	2nd	Mobley, Ritchie	35,177
11	Oct 7	H	Coventry City	W		4-0	3-0	1st	McCalliog, Mobley, Eustace, Fantham	33,931
12	14	A	Nottingham Forest	D		0-0	0-0	2nd		38,005
13	23	H	Stoke City	D		1-1	0-1	1st	Fantham	33,000
14	28	A	Liverpool	L		0-1	0-1	3rd		50,399
15	Nov 4	H	Southampton	W		2-0	1-0	3rd	Whitham, McCalliog	26,941
16	11	A	Chelsea	L		0-3	0-2	4th		29,569
17	18	H	West Bromwich Alb	D		2-2	1-0	5th	Ritchie, Williams (og)	28,256
18	25	A	Newcastle United	L		0-4	0-2	6th		28,100
19	Dec 2	H	Manchester City	D		1-1	0-0	7th	Fantham	38,137
20	16	H	West Ham United	W		4-1	3-1	5th	Ritchie (2), Fantham, Whitham	24,003
21	23	A	Burnley	L		1-2	1-2	5th	Ritchie (pen)	13,133
22	26	H	Leeds United	L		0-1	0-1	9th		51,055
23	30	A	Leeds United	L		2-3	0-2	11th	Ritchie, Whitham	36,409
24	Jan 6	H	Sheffield United	D		1-1	0-0	10th	Fantham	43,020
25	17	H	Tottenham Hotspur	L		1-2	1-1	10th	Fantham	32,150
26	20	A	Manchester United	L		2-4	0-1	11th	Whitham (2)	55,254
27	Feb 3	H	Sunderland	L		0-1	0-1	13th		25,004
28	24	A	Coventry City	L		0-3	0-3	14th		28,528
29	28	A	Fulham	L		0-2	0-0	15th		15,391
30	Mar 2	H	Newcastle United	D		1-1	0-0	15th	Whitham	24,762
31	16	A	Stoke City	W		1-0	0-0	13th	Ritchie	15,785
32	19	A	Wolverhampton W	W		3-2	2-1	11th	Whitham, Woodall (2)	32,869
33	23	H	Liverpool	L		1-2	0-1	12th	Ford	32,177
34	30	A	Southampton	L		0-2	0-1	13th		17,852
35	Apr 6	H	Chelsea	D		2-2	0-2	13th	Ritchie, Fantham	26,773
36	13	A	West Bromwich Alb	D		1-1	0-1	12th	Ritchie	20,246
37	15	A	Everton	L		0-1	0-1	13th		44,482
38	16	H	Everton	D		0-0	0-0	14th		24,766
39	20	H	Nottingham Forest	D		0-0	0-0	13th		28,496
40	25	A	Manchester City	L		0-1	0-1	16th		32,999
41	30	A	Arsenal	L		2-3	0-0	16th	Ritchie, Eustace (pen)	11,262
42	May 4	H	Arsenal	L		1-2	0-1	19th	McCalliog	25,066
										Apps
										Subs
									One own-goal	Goals

League Cup

Match No.	Date	Venue	Opponents		Round	Result	HT Score	Position	Scorers	Attendance
43	Sep 13	A	Stockport County	W	2R	5-3	1-1		McCalliog (2), Fantham (2), Ritchie	15,065
44	Oct 11	H	Barrow	W	3R	3-1	2-0		McCalliog, Fantham (2)	21,829
45	Nov 1	H	Stoke City	D	4R	0-0	0-0			26,001
46	15	A	Stoke City	L	4R Re	1-2	0-0		Young	21,185
										Apps
										Subs
										Goals

FA Cup

Match No.	Date	Venue	Opponents		Round	Result	HT Score	Position	Scorers	Attendance
47	Jan 27	H	Plymouth Argyle	W	3R	3-0	2-0		Whitham, Fantham, Ritchie (pen)	29,283
48	Feb 17	H	Swindon Town	W	4R	2-1	0-1		Smith, Ritchie	37,457
49	Mar 9	H	Chelsea	D	5R	2-2	2-1		Ritchie, Megson	49,186
50	12	A	Chelsea	L	5R Re	0-2	0-1			55,013
										Apps
										Subs
										Goals

Match Abandoned after 47 minutes due to a snow storm

Match No.	Date	Venue	Opponents		Round	Result	HT Score	Position	Scorers	Attendance
51	Dec 9	A	Arsenal				0-1			25,842

Branfoot Ian	Ellis Sam	Eustace Peter	Fantham John	Ford David	McCalliog Jim	Megson Don	Mobley Vic	Prendergast Mike	Pugh Graham	Quinn John	Ritchie John	Scothorn Gary	Smith Wilf	Springett Peter	Symm Colin	Usher Brian	Wall Adrian	Whitham Jack	Wicks Peter	Woodall Brian	Young Gerry
	5	S*	10		8	3	4			11*	9		2	1		7					6
U	5	6	10		8	3	4			11	9		2	1		7					
	5	6	10		8	3	4			11	9		2*	1	S*	7					
	5	6	10	11	8	3	4			2	9			1	U	7					
	5	S*	8*	11	10	3	4			2	9			1		7					6
	5	8	S*	11	10	3	4			2	9			1		7*					6
	5	8	S*	11	10	3*	4			2	9			1		7					6
	5	7	8*		10		4			2	9		3	1		11		S*			6
	5	11	8		10		4			2	9		3	1		7		U			6
	5	11	8*		10	3	4			S*	9		2	1		7					6
S*	5	11	8		10*	3	4			2	9			1		7					6
	5	11	8		10*	3	4			S*	9		2			7			1		6
	5	11	8		10	3	4			U	9		2	1		7					6
	5	11*	8		10	3	4			S*	9		2	1		7					6
	5	11	8		10	3	4			U	9		2	1				7			6
	5	11			9	3	4			8	U		2	1		7		10			6
	5	11	8		10	3	4			U	9		2	1		7					6
	5	11	8	S*	10	3	4				9		2	1		7*					6
	5	11	8		10	3	4				9		2	1	U			7			6
11	5		8		10	3	4				9		2	1		U		7			6
11	5		8		10	3	4				9		2	1	U			7			6
6	5				10	3	4				9		2	1	8	11		7			U
6	5				10	3	4				9		2	1	8	11		7			U
4			11		10	3	5				9		2	1	8	U		7			6
4			11		10	3	5				9		2	1	8	U		7			6
4			7		10	3	5				9		2	1	8	11		S*			6*
6	4		8		10*	3	5				9		2	1	S*	7		11			
6	4				10	3	5				9		2	1	8	11*		7		S*	
U		4		10	8	3	5				9		2	1		11		7			6
U		6			8	3	5				9	1	2			7		10		11	4
U		6	10		8	3	5				9		2	1		11		7			4
		4		U	8	3	5				9		2	1		7		10		11	6
		4		S*	8	3	5				9		2	1		7		10		11*	6
		6		11	8	3	5				9		2	1		7		10		U	4
		6	11	10	8	3	5	U			9		2	1			7				4
		6	11*	10	8	3	5				9		2	1			7			S*	4
		6	S*	10	8	3	5				9		2	1			7*			11	4
		6	7	10	8	3	5				9		2	1	U					11	4
		6	7	10	8	3	5				9		2	1	U					11	4
U		6		10	8	3	5				9		2	1		7				11	4
		6	7	10	8	3	5		11		9		2						1	U	4
		6	S*	10	8	3	5		11		9		2	1				7*			4
9	25	31	28	14	42	40	42		2	11	41	1	37	39	6	29	3	18	2	7	35
1		2	4	2						3					2			2		2	
		2	9	3	5		3				18					1		7		2	

Branfoot Ian	Ellis Sam	Eustace Peter	Fantham John	Ford David	McCalliog Jim	Megson Don	Mobley Vic	Prendergast Mike	Pugh Graham	Quinn John	Ritchie John	Scothorn Gary	Smith Wilf	Springett Peter	Symm Colin	Usher Brian	Wall Adrian	Whitham Jack	Wicks Peter	Woodall Brian	Young Gerry
	5	7	8		10		4			2	9		3	1	U			11			6
	5	11	8		10	3				2	9		U		6	7			1		4
	5	11*	8		10	3	4			S*	9		2	1		7					6
	5	11	8		10	3	4			U	9		2	1		7					6
	4	4	4		4	3	3			2	4		3	3	1	3		1	1		4
										1											
			4		3						1										1

Branfoot Ian	Ellis Sam	Eustace Peter	Fantham John	Ford David	McCalliog Jim	Megson Don	Mobley Vic	Prendergast Mike	Pugh Graham	Quinn John	Ritchie John	Scothorn Gary	Smith Wilf	Springett Peter	Symm Colin	Usher Brian	Wall Adrian	Whitham Jack	Wicks Peter	Woodall Brian	Young Gerry
6	4		7		10	3	5				9		2	1	8*	S*		11			
6	4		U		10	3	5				9		2	1	8	7		11			
U		6	10		8	3	5				9		2	1		11		7			4
U		6	10		8	3	5				9		2	1		11		7			4
2	2	2	3		4	4	4				4		4	4	2	3		4			2
																1					
			1			1					3		1					1			

Branfoot Ian	Ellis Sam	Eustace Peter	Fantham John	Ford David	McCalliog Jim	Megson Don	Mobley Vic	Prendergast Mike	Pugh Graham	Quinn John	Ritchie John	Scothorn Gary	Smith Wilf	Springett Peter	Symm Colin	Usher Brian	Wall Adrian	Whitham Jack	Wicks Peter	Woodall Brian	Young Gerry
	11	5	8		10	3	4				9		2	1		U		7			6

League Table

	P	W	D	L	F	A	Pts
Manchester City	42	26	6	10	86	43	58
Manchester United	42	24	8	10	89	55	56
Liverpool	42	22	11	9	71	40	55
Leeds United	42	22	9	11	71	41	53
Everton	42	23	6	13	67	40	52
Chelsea	42	18	12	12	62	68	48
Tottenham Hotspur	42	19	9	14	70	59	47
West Bromwich Albion	42	17	12	13	75	62	46
Arsenal	42	17	10	15	60	56	44
Newcastle United	42	13	15	14	54	67	41
Nottingham Forest	42	14	11	17	52	64	39
West Ham United	42	14	10	18	73	69	38
Leicester City	42	13	12	17	64	69	38
Burnley	42	14	10	18	64	71	38
Sunderland	42	13	11	18	51	61	37
Southampton	42	13	11	18	66	83	37
Wolverhampton W.	42	14	8	20	66	75	36
Stoke City	42	14	7	21	50	73	35
SHEFFIELD WEDNESDAY	42	11	12	19	51	63	34
Coventry City	42	9	15	18	51	71	33
Sheffield United	42	11	10	21	49	70	32
Fulham	42	10	7	25	56	98	27

1968-69

Division One

Manager: Jack Marshall

Did you know that?

Final League Position: 15th

On 31 August 1968, Wednesday beat Manchester United 5–4 at Hillsborough, with Jack Whitham netting a hat-trick; however, General Manager Eric Taylor tried to credit Whitham with a fourth goal when Nobby Stiles headed David Ford's free-kick into his own net, as Whitham was the nearest Wednesday player to Stiles.

Match No.	Date	Venue	Opponents		Round	Result	HT Score	Position	Scorers	Attendance
1	Aug 10	A	West Bromwich Alb	D		0-0	0-0			24,765
2	14	H	Newcastle United	D		1-1	1-1		Ford	27,258
3	17	H	Coventry City	W		3-0	1-0	4th	Fantham (2), Ritchie	26,235
4	20	A	Nottingham Forest	D		0-0	0-0	3rd		27,819
5	24	A	Tottenham Hotspur	W		2-1	1-0	5th	McCalliog, Whitham	30,542
6	28	A	Chelsea	L		0-1	0-0	5th		33,402
7	31	H	Manchester United	W		5-4	3-4	4th	Whitham (3), Ritchie, Stiles (og)	51,931
8	Sep 7	H	Ipswich Town	W		2-1	1-0	5th	Whitham, Eustace	27,128
9	14	A	Everton	L		0-3	0-1	6th		44,517
10	21	H	Burnley	W		1-0	1-0	6th	Whitham	23,183
11	28	A	West Ham United	D		1-1	1-1	7th	Whitham	31,182
12	Oct 5	H	Sunderland	D		1-1	0-0	7th	Whitham	27,932
13	9	H	Chelsea	D		1-1	0-0	7th	Whitham	30,991
14	12	A	Queen's Park Rangers	L		2-3	0-1	7th	Eustace, Whitham	19,044
15	19	H	Wolverhampton W	L		0-2	0-2	9th		23,928
16	26	A	Southampton	D		1-1	1-0	10th	McCalliog	20,047
17	Nov 9	A	Manchester City	W		1-0	0-0	10th	Eustace	23,861
18	16	H	Liverpool	L		1-2	0-1	10th	McCalliog	31,245
19	23	A	Leicester City	D		1-1	1-0	10th	Fantham	21,217
20	30	H	Stoke City	W		2-1	2-0	10th	Ritchie, Eustace	23,027
21	Dec 7	A	Leeds United	L		0-2	0-1	10th		32,718
22	14	H	Queen's Park Rangers	W		4-0	1-0	8th	Mobley, Fantham, Ford, McCalliog	22,004
23	21	A	Wolverhampton W	W		3-0	2-0	7th	Ritchie (2), Irvine	24,724
24	26	A	Sunderland	D		0-0	0-0	7th		26,233
25	28	H	Southampton	D		0-0	0-0	7th		27,398
26	Jan 11	A	Arsenal	L		0-2	0-1	7th		39,005
27	18	H	Manchester City	D		1-1	0-0	7th	Smith	33,074
28	Feb 1	A	Liverpool	L		0-1	0-0	9th		45,406
29	Mar 1	H	Arsenal	L		0-5	0-2	10th		21,987
30	5	H	West Bromwich Alb	W		1-0	0-0	10th	Mobley	18,960
31	8	A	Coventry City	L		0-3	0-2	10th		30,131
32	22	A	Manchester United	L		0-1	0-1	15th		45,527
33	Apr 1	H	Leeds United	D		0-0	0-0	13th		34,278
34	5	H	West Ham United	D		1-1	1-1	14th	Warboys	24,268
35	7	H	Nottingham Forest	L		0-1	0-0	14th		26,178
36	9	A	Newcastle United	L		2-3	0-1		Prendergast, McCalliog	31,800
37	12	A	Burnley	L		0-2	0-2	16th		9,595
38	14	H	Leicester City	L		1-3	0-1	16th	Woodall	18,155
39	19	H	Everton	D		2-2	1-0	16th	Ritchie, Woodall	23,173
40	22	A	Stoke City	D		1-1	1-0		Ford	8,826
41	25	A	Ipswich Town	L		0-2	0-0	15th		17,709
42	May 12	H	Tottenham Hotspur	D		0-0	0-0	15th		28,368
										Apps
										Subs
									One own-goal	Goals

League Cup

Match No.	Date	Venue	Opponents		Round	Result	HT Score	Position	Scorers	Attendance
43	Sep 4	A	Exeter City	L	2nd	1-3	0-1		Ford	15,962
										Apps
										Subs
										Goals

FA Cup

Match No.	Date	Venue	Opponents		Round	Result	HT Score	Position	Scorers	Attendance
44	Jan 4	H	Leeds United	D	3rd	1-1	1-1		Ritchie	52,111
45	8	A	Leeds United	W	3rd Re	3-1	1-1		Woodall (2), Ritchie	48,234
46	25	H	Birmingham City	D	4th	2-2	0-1		McCalliog, Young	52,062
47	28	A	Birmingham City	L	4th Re	1-2	0-1		Young	51,463
										Apps
										Subs
										Goals

Branfoot Ian	Burton Ken	Craig Tommy	Ellis Sam	Eustace Peter	Fantham John	Ford David	Irvine Archie	McCalliog Jim	Megson Don	Mobley Vic	Prendergast Mike	Pugh Graham	Ritchie John	Smith Wilf	Springett Peter	Symm Colin	Warboys Alan	Whitham Jack	Wicks Peter	Woodall Brian	Young Gerry
			4		7	11		8	3	5			9	2	1	10		U			6
				6	7	10		8	3	5		11	9	2	1			S*			4*
			4	6	7	10		8	3	5		11*	9	2	1			S*			
			4	6	7	10		8	3	5			9	2	1		U	11			
			4	6	11	10		8	3	5				2	1		9	7			U
			4	6	7	10		8	3	5				2	1		9	11			U
			4	6	11	10		8	3	5			9		1		U	7			2
			4	6		10		8	3	5		U			1		9	7		11	2
			4	6	11*	10		8	3	5					1		9	7		S*	2
			4	6	11	10		8	3	5					1		9	7		U	2
			4	6	11	10		8	3	5					1		9	7		U	2
			4	11*	S*	10		8	3	5				2	1		9	7			6
			4	8	11	10		9	3	5				2	1		U	7			6
			4	8		S*	7*	10	3	5				2	1		9	11			6
			4	11		10	S*	8	3	5				2	1		9	7*			6
U			4	8	10	11		9	3	5				2	1			7			6
			4	10	7	11		8	3	5				2	1		9			U	6
			4	10	7	11		8	3	5				2	1		9			U	6
S*			4	10	9		7*	8	3	5				2	1					11	6
	3		4	10	7		U	8		5			9	2	1					11	6
3			4	10	7	S*		8		5			9	2	1					11*	6
			4	10	7	11		8	3	5		U	9	2	1						6
			4	10		11	7	8	3	5		U	9	2	1						6
			4	10		11	7	8	3	5		U	9	2	1						6
			4	10	U	11	7	8	3	5			9	2	1						6
U			4	10			7	8	3	5			9	2	1					11	6
			4	10			7	8	3	5		U	9	2	1					11	6
2			4	10	U		7	8	3	5			9		1			11			6
			4		S*	11	7	8	3*	5		10	9	2	1						6
U	3				10	11	7	8		5		6	9	2	1						4
S*	3				10	11	7	8		5		6*	9	2	1						4
	3		S*	4	9		7	8		5		10		2	1					11*	6
	3		6	4	11		7	8	U	5			9	2	1		10				
			U	4	11		7	8	3	5			9	2	1		10				6
			U	4	11		7	8	3	5			9	2	1		10				6
U			4	10	11		7	8	3	5	9			2	1						6
2				10	11*		S*	8	3	5	7			4	1		9				6
3			4				7	8	U	5	10			2	1		9			11	6
	3			4			7*	8		5			10	2	1		9	S*		11	6
	3			4	U	7		8		5			9	2	1			10		11	6
	3			4		7	S*	8	2	5			10					9	1	11*	6
	3	6		7	9	11		8		5			S*	2	1		10*				4
4	9	1	31	37	27	27	18	42	32	42	3	6	23	35	41	1	18	16	1	11	37
2			1		2	2	3						1					3		1	
				4	4	3	1	5		2	1		6	1			1	10		2	

Branfoot Ian	Burton Ken	Craig Tommy	Ellis Sam	Eustace Peter	Fantham John	Ford David	Irvine Archie	McCalliog Jim	Megson Don	Mobley Vic	Prendergast Mike	Pugh Graham	Ritchie John	Smith Wilf	Springett Peter	Symm Colin	Warboys Alan	Whitham Jack	Wicks Peter	Woodall Brian	Young Gerry
			4	6	11	10		8	3	5			9*		1		S*	7			2
			1	1	1	1		1	1	1			1		1			1			1
																	1				
						1															

Branfoot Ian	Burton Ken	Craig Tommy	Ellis Sam	Eustace Peter	Fantham John	Ford David	Irvine Archie	McCalliog Jim	Megson Don	Mobley Vic	Prendergast Mike	Pugh Graham	Ritchie John	Smith Wilf	Springett Peter	Symm Colin	Warboys Alan	Whitham Jack	Wicks Peter	Woodall Brian	Young Gerry
			4	10		11	7	8	3	5		U	9	2	1						6
			4	10			7	8	3	5		U	9	2	1					11	6
S*			4	10			7	8	3	5			9	2*	1					11	6
2			4	10	S*		7*	8	3	5			9		1					11	6
1			4	4		1	4	4	4	4			4	3	4					3	4
1					1																
								1					2							2	2

League Table

	P	W	D	L	F	A	Pts
Leeds United	42	27	13	2	66	26	67
Liverpool	42	25	11	6	63	24	61
Everton	42	21	15	6	77	36	57
Arsenal	42	22	12	8	56	27	56
Chelsea	42	20	10	12	73	53	50
Tottenham Hotspur	42	14	17	11	61	51	45
Southampton	42	16	13	13	57	48	45
West Ham United	42	13	18	11	66	50	44
Newcastle United	42	15	14	13	61	55	44
West Bromwich Albion	42	16	11	15	64	67	43
Manchester United	42	15	12	15	57	53	42
Ipswich Town	42	15	11	16	59	60	41
Manchester City	42	15	10	17	64	55	40
Burnley	42	15	9	18	55	82	39
SHEFFIELD WEDNESDAY	42	10	16	16	41	54	36
Wolverhampton W.	42	10	15	17	41	58	35
Sunderland	42	11	12	19	43	67	34
Nottingham Forest	42	10	13	19	45	57	33
Stoke City	42	9	15	18	40	63	33
Coventry City	42	10	11	21	46	64	31
Leicester City	42	9	12	21	39	68	30
Queen's Park Rangers	42	4	10	28	39	95	18

1969-70

Division One

Manager: Danny Williams

Did you know that?

Final League Position: 22nd

On 17 January 1970, away at Derby, the referee stopped Derby's Ron Webster from playing as he had a plastic cover over a broken arm.

Match No.	Date	Venue	Opponents		Round	Result	HT Score	Position	Scorers	Attendance
1	Aug 9	A	Manchester City	L		1-4	0-3		Eustace (pen)	32,582
2	13	A	Newcastle United	L		1-3	0-2		Warboys	41,200
3	16	H	Wolverhampton W	L		2-3	1-3	22nd	Warboys, Ford	23,167
4	20	H	Newcastle United	W		1-0	1-0	19th	Eustace	19,213
5	23	A	Sunderland	W		2-1	1-0	14th	Craig, Eustace	15,559
6	26	A	Everton	L		1-2	0-1	16th	Smith	46,480
7	30	H	Liverpool	D		1-1	1-1	18th	Warboys	33,600
8	Sep 6	A	Arsenal	D		0-0	0-0	18th		28,605
9	13	H	Leeds United	L		1-2	1-2	19th	Burton	31,998
10	17	H	Manchester United	L		1-3	1-1	20th	Pugh	39,938
11	20	A	West Ham United	L		0-3	0-1	20th		23,491
12	27	H	Derby County	W		1-0	1-0	19th	Warboys	45,086
13	Oct 4	A	Ipswich Town	L		0-1	0-0	21st		17,034
14	8	A	Wolverhampton W	D		2-2	0-2	20th	Smith, Eustace	27,759
15	11	H	Southampton	D		1-1	0-1	19th	Eustace	20,488
16	18	A	Burnley	L		2-4	1-0	21st	Craig, Prendergast	13,212
17	25	H	Crystal Palace	D		0-0	0-0	20th		19,162
18	Nov 1	A	Tottenham Hotspur	L		0-1	0-0	21st		31,650
19	8	H	Chelsea	L		1-3	0-1	21st	Prendergast	18,044
20	15	H	Stoke City	L		0-2	0-1	21st		16,444
21	22	A	West Bromwich Alb	L		0-3	0-0	22nd		20,751
22	Dec 6	A	Nottingham Forest	L		1-2	0-2	22nd	Whitham	19,039
23	13	A	Leeds United	L		0-2	0-0	22nd		31,014
24	20	H	Arsenal	D		1-1	0-1	22nd	Whitham	17,165
25	26	H	Sunderland	W		2-0	1-0	22nd	Downes, Prophett	35,126
26	Jan 10	H	West Ham United	L		2-3	0-1	22nd	Craig, Prophett	28,135
27	17	A	Derby County	L		0-1	0-0	22nd		32,991
28	28	H	Coventry City	L		0-1	0-0	22nd		18,149
29	31	H	Ipswich Town	D		2-2	2-0	22nd	Smith, Sinclair	17,814
30	Feb 7	A	Southampton	L		0-4	0-4	22nd		19,470
31	21	A	Crystal Palace	W		2-0	1-0	21st	Sinclair, Whitham	25,723
32	28	H	Burnley	W		2-0	1-0	20th	Whitham (2)	23,188
33	Mar 10	H	West Bromwich Alb	W		2-0	2-0	19th	Whitham, Warboys	21,990
34	14	A	Coventry City	D		1-1	1-1	19th	Whitham	25,586
35	16	A	Liverpool	L		0-3	0-0	19th		31,931
36	21	H	Nottingham Forest	W		2-1	0-0	19th	Craig, Warboys	23,916
37	25	A	Chelsea	L		1-3	1-2	20th	Sinclair	29,590
38	28	A	Stoke City	L		1-2	0-0	19th	Craig	16,632
39	30	H	Tottenham Hotspur	L		0-1	0-1	21st		30,224
40	Apr 4	H	Everton	L		0-1	0-0	22nd		30,896
41	15	A	Manchester United	D		2-2	1-2	22nd	Coleman, Whitham	39,273
42	22	H	Manchester City	L		1-2	0-1	22nd	Coleman	45,258
										Apps
										Subs
										Goals

League Cup

Match No.	Date	Venue	Opponents		Round	Result	HT Score	Position	Scorers	Attendance
43	Sep 3	H	Bournemouth	D	2R	1-1	1-0		Pugh	14,363
44	9	A	Bournemouth	L	2R Re	0-1	0-1			15,894
										Apps
										Subs
										Goals

FA Cup

Match No.	Date	Venue	Opponents		Round	Result	HT Score	Position	Scorers	Attendance
45	Jan 3	H	West Bromwich Alb	W	3R	2-1	0-0		Whitham (2)	29,174
46	24	H	Scunthorpe United	L	4R	1-2	1-1		Whitham	38,047
										Apps
										Subs
										Goals

Branfoot Ian	Burton Ken	Coleman Tony	Craig Tommy	Downes Steve	Ellis Sam	Eustace Peter	Fantham John	Ford David	Grummitt Peter	Irvine Archie	Lawson Willie	Megson Don	Mobley Vic	Prendergast Mike	Prophett Colin	Pugh Graham	Sinclair Jackie	Smith Wilf	Springett Peter	Warboys Alan	Whitham Jack	Wicks Peter	Wilcockson Harold	Woodall Brian	Young Gerry
	3		6		4	8	7	11					5			U		2	1	9					10
	3		6		11	8		10		7*			5	S*				2	1	9					4
2	3		6			8	7	11		U			5	10					1	9					4
2	3		6		5	8	U	11		7								10	1	9					4
2	3		6		5	8		11		U						7		10	1	9					4
2*	3		6		5	8	S*	10								7		11	1	9					4
	3		6		5	8		11		7					S*	10		2	1	9*					4
	3				5	8	U	10						7	6	11		2	1	9					4
	3		6		5		11*			7				10	S*	8		2	1	9					4
	3		6		5		8	10		7				U		11		2	1	9					4
7			6		5		11*	10				3		9	S*	8		2				1			4
3			6		5	8		10						S*		7		2	1	9				11*	4
3		11	6		5	8		10							U	7		2	1	9					4
3		11	6		5	8		10						9	S*	7*		2	1						4
3		11*	6		5	8		10						9	S*	7		2	1						4
	3		6		5	8					11			9	10	7		2	1					U	4
	3	11	6		5	8					7*			10		S*		2	1	9					4
	3	11	6		5	8		10							U	7		2	1	9					4
	3	11	6		5	8*		7						10		S*		2	1	9					4
	3	11	6		U					7					5	8		2	1	9	10				4
2	3	11	6		U					7					5	8			1	9	10				4
	3	11	6			8		7							5	9		2	1	U	10				4
		11	6			8		7				3			5	9*		2	1	S*	10				4
	S*	11	6									3			5	8*	7	10	1		9		2		4
		11	6	8		S*						3			5		7	10	1		9*		2		4
		11	6	9								3			5	4	7	10	1	S*	8*		2		
		11	U	10	4							3			5	6	7	8	1	9			2		
	3	11	6	9					1						5	10*	7	4		S*	8		2		
	3	10	6	9					1		11				5		7*	8			S*		2		4
	3	10	6	9					1		11				5		7*	8		S*			2		4
		11	6	10*	4				1						5		7	3		9	S*		2		8
		11	6	U	4				1						5		7	3		9	10		2		8
			6	S*	4				1		11				5		7	3		9*	10		2		8
			6	S*	4				1		11				5		7	3		9	10*		2		8
		11	6		4				1						5	S*	7*	3		9	10		2		8
		11	6	U	4				1						5		7	3		9	10		2		8
		U	6		4				1		11				5		7	3		9	10		2		8
		11	6	10*	4				1						5		7	3		9	S*		2		8
		S*	6		4				1		11				5		7	3		9	10		2		8*
		11*	6		4				1					S*	5		7	3		9	10		2		8
		11*	6	S*	4				1						5		7	3		9	10		2		8
		11	6	S*	4				1						5		7	3*		9	10		2		8
10	20	25	40	8	31	18	5	18	15	7	8	6	3	9	25	21	19	40	26	30	18	1	19	1	39
	1	1		4		1	1							3	5	3				4	3				
	1	2	5	1		5		1						2	2	1	3	3		6	8				

Branfoot Ian	Burton Ken	Coleman Tony	Craig Tommy	Downes Steve	Ellis Sam	Eustace Peter	Fantham John	Ford David	Grummitt Peter	Irvine Archie	Lawson Willie	Megson Don	Mobley Vic	Prendergast Mike	Prophett Colin	Pugh Graham	Sinclair Jackie	Smith Wilf	Springett Peter	Warboys Alan	Whitham Jack	Wicks Peter	Wilcockson Harold	Woodall Brian	Young Gerry
2	3				5	8		10		7					U	11		6	1	9					4
	3		6		4		9*	11		7					S*	10		2	1	8					5
1	2		1		2	1	1	2		2						2		2	2	2					2
															1										
																1									

Branfoot Ian	Burton Ken	Coleman Tony	Craig Tommy	Downes Steve	Ellis Sam	Eustace Peter	Fantham John	Ford David	Grummitt Peter	Irvine Archie	Lawson Willie	Megson Don	Mobley Vic	Prendergast Mike	Prophett Colin	Pugh Graham	Sinclair Jackie	Smith Wilf	Springett Peter	Warboys Alan	Whitham Jack	Wicks Peter	Wilcockson Harold	Woodall Brian	Young Gerry
	U	7	6								11	3			5	2		10	1	9	8				4
	S*	11	6		4							3*			5	2	7	10	1	9	8				
		2	2		1						1	2			2	2	1	2	2	2	2				1
	1																								
																					3				

League Table

	P	W	D	L	F	A	Pts
Everton	42	29	8	5	72	34	66
Leeds United	42	21	15	6	84	49	57
Chelsea	42	21	13	8	70	50	55
Derby County	42	22	9	11	64	37	53
Liverpool	42	20	11	11	65	42	51
Coventry City	42	19	11	12	58	48	49
Newcastle United	42	17	13	12	57	35	47
Manchester United	42	14	17	11	66	61	45
Stoke City	42	15	15	12	56	52	45
Manchester City	42	16	11	15	55	48	43
Tottenham Hotspur	42	17	9	16	54	55	43
Arsenal	42	12	18	12	51	49	42
Wolverhampton W.	42	12	16	14	55	57	40
Burnley	42	12	15	15	56	61	39
Nottingham Forest	42	10	18	14	50	71	38
West Bromwich Albion	42	14	9	19	58	66	37
West Ham United	42	12	12	18	51	60	36
Ipswich Town	42	10	11	21	40	63	31
Southampton	42	6	17	19	46	67	29
Crystal Palace	42	6	15	21	34	68	27
Sunderland	42	6	14	22	30	68	26
SHEFFIELD WEDNESDAY	42	8	9	25	40	71	25

1970-71

Division Two

Manager: Danny Williams/Derek Dooley

Did you know that?

Final League Position: 15th

Hillsborough was chosen for a possible replay of the FA Cup Final and also the European Cup Final if the two games, staged at Wembley, finished in draws.

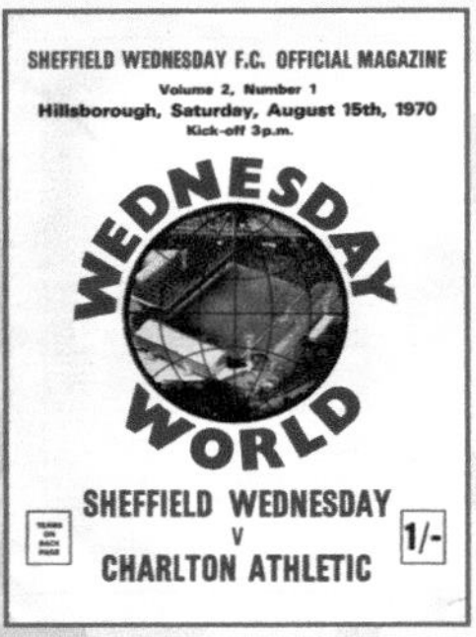

Match No.	Date	Venue	Opponents		Round	Result	HT Score	Position	Scorers	Attendance
1	Aug 15	H	Charlton Athletic	W		1-0	0-0		Downes	17,152
2	19	A	Bolton Wanderers	L		1-2	0-0		Prophett	13,130
3	22	A	Oxford United	D		1-1	1-0	10th	Prendergast	11,090
4	26	H	Cardiff City	L		1-2	1-2	10th	Prendergast	17,186
5	29	H	Blackburn Rovers	D		1-1	1-1	7th	Prendergast	15,188
6	Sep 2	H	Bolton Wanderers	D		1-1	0-0	9th	Downes	12,920
7	5	A	Portsmouth	L		0-2	0-2	15th		18,712
8	12	H	Queen's Park Rangers	W		1-0	0-0	9th	Wilcockson	14,920
9	19	A	Sunderland	L		1-3	1-0	13th	Downes	15,328
10	26	H	Carlisle United	W		3-0	3-0	11th	Warboys, Prendergast, Sissons	13,181
11	Oct 3	A	Sheffield United	L		2-3	0-2	16th	Craig, Sinclair	39,983
12	10	H	Luton Town	L		1-5	0-3	17th	Sinclair	15,189
13	17	A	Charlton Athletic	W		3-2	1-2	13th	Warboys (2), Reeves (og)	10,636
14	19	A	Orient	D		1-1	1-1	11th	Warboys	10,219
15	24	H	Leicester City	L		0-3	0-1	16th		23,160
16	31	A	Bristol City	W		2-1	0-0	14th	Prendergast, Sissons	13,093
17	Nov 7	H	Millwall	W		1-0	1-0	11th	Todd	12,668
18	14	A	Norwich City	D		0-0	0-0	11th		13,344
19	21	H	Middlesbrough	W		3-2	2-1	9th	Warboys, Prendergast, Craig (pen)	15,773
20	28	A	Swindon Town	L		0-3	0-2	11th		15,412
21	Dec 5	H	Watford	W		2-1	1-0	11th	Prophett, Prendergast	12,139
22	12	A	Birmingham City	L		0-1	0-0	12th		14,239
23	19	H	Oxford United	D		1-1	1-1	13th	Warboys	11,134
24	26	A	Hull City	D		4-4	1-1	12th	Prendergast, Sinclair (2), Ellis (pen)	24,399
25	Jan 9	A	Cardiff City	L		0-4	0-1	13th		21,490
26	16	H	Orient	W		2-1	1-1	13th	Prendergast, Prophett	11,149
27	30	H	Swindon Town	D		2-2	1-2	13th	Pugh, Sissons	12,964
28	Feb 6	A	Watford	L		0-3	0-1	14th		12,840
29	13	H	Birmingham City	D		3-3	3-1	13th	Prendergast, Craig (pen), Sinclair	13,138
30	20	A	Middlesbrough	L		0-1	0-1	13th		25,916
31	27	H	Bristol City	W		2-0	2-0	13th	Prendergast (2)	12,481
32	Mar 10	A	Leicester City	L		0-1	0-1	13th		25,843
33	13	H	Norwich City	W		2-1	1-0	12th	Prendergast (2)	13,136
34	20	A	Millwall	L		0-1	0-0	15th		7,284
35	30	H	Portsmouth	W		3-1	0-0	15th	Sinclair, Prendergast, Sunley	14,134
36	Apr 3	A	Blackburn Rovers	L		2-3	0-1	14th	Craig (pen), Burton	6,820
37	6	A	Queen's Park Rangers	L		0-1	0-1			11,371
38	10	H	Hull City	D		1-1	0-0	14th	Craig (pen)	22,150
39	12	H	Sheffield United	D		0-0	0-0	15th		47,592
40	17	A	Luton Town	D		2-2	1-1	15th	Sinclair, Sunley	12,308
41	24	H	Sunderland	L		1-2	1-0	15th	Prendergast	9,720
42	May 1	A	Carlisle United	L		0-3	0-2	15th		9,512
										Apps
										Subs
									One own-goal	Goals
League Cup										
43	Sep 9	H	Chelsea	D	2R	1-1	0-0		Sinclair	15,869
44	22	A	Chelsea	L	2R Re	1-2	1-2		Downes	26,646
										Apps
										Subs
										Goals
FA Cup										
45	Jan 2	A	Tottenham Hotspur	L	3R	1-4	1-2		Sunley	34,170
										Apps
										Subs
										Goals

Burton Ken	Craig Tommy	Downes Steve	Ellis Sam	Grummitt Peter	Lawson Willie	Mullen Jimmy	Potts Eric	Prendergast Mike	Prophett Colin	Prudham Eddie	Pugh Graham	Rodrigues Peter	Sinclair Jackie	Sissons John	Smith Wilf	Springett Peter	Sunley David	Thompson Allan	Todd Sammy	Warboys Alan	Wilcockson Harold	Young Gerry
	6	9		1	11			S*	5				7		3*				8	10	2	4
3	6	9		1	U			11	5				7						8	10	2	4
3	6	9	U	1				11	5				7						8	10	2	4
3*	6	9	S*	1				11	5				7						4	10	2	8
	6	9	U	1				8	5				7	11					4	10	2	3
	6	S*	3	1				10	5				7	11					4	9*	2	8
	6	9	5	1				10	2*		S*		7	11					4		3	8
	10	9	5	1					S*		8		7	11				4	6		2	3*
	10	9	5	1				8	2		6		7	11*				4	S*		3	
	10	9	5	1				8	2*				7	11				4	6	S*	3	
	6	9	5	1				8			U		7	11				2	4	10		3
3	6	9	5	1				8			U		7	11				4		10	2	
	8	9		1			S*				6	2	7	11				4*		10	3	5
	6	9		1			U				8	2	7	11				4		10	3	5
	6	9*		1				S*			8	2	7	11				4		10	3	5
	S*		5	1				8			6	2*	7	11				4	10	9	3	
	S*		5	1				8			6	2	7*	11				4	10	9	3	
S*	6		5	1				9			7	2		11*				4	8	10	3	
	S*		5	1				8	4		6*	2	7	11					10	9	3	
	S*		5	1				9	4		8*	2	7	11					6	10	3	
3	10		5	1		U		8	2		6		7					4	11	9		
3	10*		5						2		8		7	11		1	9	4	6			S*
U			2	1				9	5		8		7	11				4		10	6	3
			5	1		4		10	9		6		7	U			11	8			2	3
3			S*	1		4		10	5	7	6	2*		11			9	8				
3	9*		5	1		S*		10	4		6	2	7	11					8			
3	8			1		4		10	S*		6	2	7	11			9	5*				
3	8		U	1		4		9	5		6	2	7	11			10					
3	8			1				9	5		6	2	7	11			10	4	U			
3	8			1				9	5		6	2	7	11			10	4	U			
3	8		U	1				10	5		6		7	11			9	4	2			
3	8	9		1				10	5		4	2	7	11				6	U			
3	8	9		1				10	5		6	2	7	11				4	U			
3	8			1		U		10	5		6	2	7	11			9	4				
3	8			1		U		10	5		6	2	7	11			9	4				
3	8			1		6	S*	10	5		7	2		11*			9	4				
3	8			1		U	7	10	5		6	2		11			9	4				
3	8			1		S*		10	5		6	2	7	11			9	4*				
3	8			1		U		10	5		6	2	7	11			9	4				
3	8			1		U		10	5		6	2	7	11			9	4				
3	8			1			S*	10	5		6	2	7*	11			9	4				
3	8			1				10	5		6	2	7	11			9	4	U			
24	35	16	17	41	1	5	1	36	32	1	32	25	38	36	1	1	17	31	19	18	21	14
1	4	1	2			2	3	2	2		1								1	1		1
1	5	3	1					16	3		1		7	3			2		1	6	1	

Burton Ken	Craig Tommy	Downes Steve	Ellis Sam	Grummitt Peter	Lawson Willie	Mullen Jimmy	Potts Eric	Prendergast Mike	Prophett Colin	Prudham Eddie	Pugh Graham	Rodrigues Peter	Sinclair Jackie	Sissons John	Smith Wilf	Springett Peter	Sunley David	Thompson Allan	Todd Sammy	Warboys Alan	Wilcockson Harold	Young Gerry
	10	9	5	1				8*			S*		7	11				4	6		2	3
	10	9	5	1	11			8			U		7					4	2		3	6
	2	2	2	2	1			2					2	1				2	2		2	2
											1											
		1											1									

Burton Ken	Craig Tommy	Downes Steve	Ellis Sam	Grummitt Peter	Lawson Willie	Mullen Jimmy	Potts Eric	Prendergast Mike	Prophett Colin	Prudham Eddie	Pugh Graham	Rodrigues Peter	Sinclair Jackie	Sissons John	Smith Wilf	Springett Peter	Sunley David	Thompson Allan	Todd Sammy	Warboys Alan	Wilcockson Harold	Young Gerry
	S*		5			4		9	10		6		7*			1	11	8			3	2
			1			1		1	1		1		1			1	1	1			1	1
	1																					
																	1					

League Table

	P	W	D	L	F	A	Pts
Leicester City	42	23	13	6	57	30	59
Sheffield United	42	21	14	7	73	39	56
Cardiff City	42	20	13	9	64	41	53
Carlisle United	42	20	13	9	65	43	53
Hull City	42	19	13	10	54	41	51
Luton Town	42	18	13	11	62	43	49
Middlesbrough	42	17	14	11	60	43	48
Millwall	42	19	9	14	59	42	47
Birmingham City	42	17	12	13	58	48	46
Norwich City	42	15	14	13	54	52	44
Queen's Park Rangers	42	16	11	15	58	53	43
Swindon Town	42	15	12	15	61	51	42
Sunderland	42	15	12	15	52	54	42
Oxford United	42	14	14	14	41	48	42
SHEFFIELD WEDNESDAY	42	12	12	18	51	69	36
Portsmouth	42	10	14	18	46	61	34
Orient	42	9	16	17	29	51	34
Watford	42	10	13	19	38	60	33
Bristol City	42	10	11	21	46	64	31
Charlton Athletic	42	8	14	20	41	65	30
Blackburn Rovers	42	6	15	21	37	69	27
Bolton Wanderers	42	7	10	25	35	74	24

1971-72

Division Two

Manager: Derek Dooley

Did you know that?

Final League Position: 14th

On 23 February 1972 Pele and his Brazilian team Santos made their second visit to Hillsborough in a midweek afternoon kick-off, which drew a crowd of 36,996 as Santos won 2–0.

On 28 March 1972, Trevor Pearson, a 19-year-old amateur 'keeper on Wednesday's books, had to appear in goal for Wednesday in an away game at Fulham, as Wednesday's two senior 'keepers were both out injured and the League refused Wednesday permission to sign a loan 'keeper after the end of the transfer period. He then had to play in the next three League games.

Match No.	Date	Venue	Opponents		Round	Result	HT Score	Position	Scorers	Attendance
1	Aug 14	A	Queen's Park Rangers	L		0-3	0-3	22nd		13,270
2	21	H	Bristol City	L		1-5	0-3	22nd	Prendergast	12,738
3	28	A	Blackpool	L		0-1	0-1	22nd		16,557
4	31	A	Middlesbrough	L		1-2	1-1	22nd	Sissons	23,963
5	Sep 4	H	Portsmouth	D		1-1	1-1	22nd	Joicey	13,170
6	11	A	Cardiff City	L		2-3	0-1	21st	Craig, Joicey	17,195
7	18	H	Sunderland	W		3-0	0-0	22nd	Pugh, Joicey, Sinclair	13,710
8	25	A	Oxford United	L		0-1	0-0	22nd		8,173
9	27	A	Millwall	D		1-1	1-0	22nd	Craig	12,019
10	Oct 2	H	Fulham	W		4-0	1-0	21st	Prophett, Craig, Sissons, Joicey	14,955
11	9	A	Charlton Athletic	D		2-2	2-1	19th	Joicey (2)	9,107
12	16	H	Queen's Park Rangers	D		0-0	0-0	20th		16,716
13	20	H	Carlisle United	W		2-1	1-1	17th	Sissons, Prendergast	15,672
14	23	H	Swindon Town	W		1-0	0-0	15th	Sinclair	19,933
15	30	A	Watford	D		1-1	1-0	13th	Prendergast	11,314
16	Nov 6	H	Burnley	W		2-1	2-0	12th	Sissons, Joicey	23,743
17	13	A	Preston North End	L		0-1	0-0	14th		16,903
18	20	H	Norwich City	D		1-1	0-0	13th	Joicey	19,902
19	27	A	Orient	W		3-0	1-0	11th	Joicey (2), Prendergast	6,673
20	Dec 4	H	Hull City	W		2-1	0-1	11th	Joicey, Prendergast	20,173
21	11	A	Birmingham City	D		0-0	0-0	12th		29,272
22	18	A	Portsmouth	W		2-1	0-0	10th	Pugh, Craig (pen)	10,280
23	27	H	Luton Town	D		2-2	0-1	10th	Craig (pen), Holsgrove	31,391
24	Jan 1	A	Sunderland	L		0-2	0-1	10th		23,228
25	8	H	Blackpool	L		1-2	1-0	11th	Craig	17,113
26	22	H	Millwall	D		1-1	0-1	13th	Craig (pen)	16,829
27	29	A	Carlisle United	D		2-2	1-1	13th	Prendergast (2)	9,011
28	Feb 12	A	Swindon Town	L		0-1	0-1	15th		11,589
29	19	H	Watford	W		2-1	0-0	13th	Sinclair, Joicey	13,934
30	26	A	Burnley	L		3-5	2-2	14th	Sissons (2 + pen)	10,592
31	Mar 4	H	Preston North End	W		1-0	0-0	14th	Craig (pen)	12,162
32	18	A	Bristol City	L		0-1	0-1	17th		12,568
33	25	H	Cardiff City	D		2-2	1-2	15th	Sissons, Craig (pen)	12,910
34	28	A	Fulham	L		0-4	0-1	15th		7,947
35	Apr 1	A	Luton Town	L		1-3	1-0	16th	Joicey	9,121
36	3	H	Oxford United	D		0-0	0-0	18th		13,993
37	8	A	Norwich City	L		0-1	0-0	18th		27,244
38	10	H	Charlton Athletic	W		2-1	1-1	16th	Sinclair, Sunley	13,800
39	17	H	Orient	W		3-1	2-0	15th	Joicey (3)	15,188
40	22	A	Hull City	L		0-1	0-1	16th		13,177
41	26	H	Middlesbrough	W		1-0	1-0	16th	Craig pen)	14,151
42	29	H	Birmingham City	L		1-2	0-0	14th	Sunley	28,132
										Apps
										Subs
										Goals

League Cup

43	Aug 17	A	Rotherham United	W	1 R	2-0	0-0		Sissons, Sinclair	8,983
44	Sep 7	A	Carlisle United	L	2 R	0-5	0-4			10,338
										Apps
										Subs
										Goals

FA Cup

45	Jan 15	A	Sunderland	L	3R	0-3	0-1			25,310
										Apps

Burton Ken	Craig Tommy	Clements Dave	Downes Steve	Ellis Sam	Grummitt Peter	Holsgrove John	Johnson Kevin	Joicey Brian	Mullen Jimmy	Pearson Trevor	Prendergast Mike	Prophett Colin	Prudham Eddie	Pugh Graham	Rodrigues Peter	Sinclair Jackie	Sissons John	Springett Peter	Sunley David	Taylor Paul	Thompson Allan	Todd Sammy
3	8		9		1	5	S*				10	4		6	2	7				11*		
3	8		9		1	5*					10	4		6	2	7	11				S*	
	8		U		1	5					10	4	9		2	7	11			6	3	
	8	6			1	5		9			10	4	U		2	7	11				3	
	8	6			1	5		9			10	4	U		2	7	11				3	
	8	6			1	5		9			10	4		7	2	U	11				3	
	8	6			1	5		9			10	4		7	2*	S*	11				3	
	8	6			1	5		9			10	4		7*	2	S*	11				3	
	8	3			1	5		9			10*	4		6	2	7	11			S*		
	8	3			1	5		9			10	4	U	6	2	7	11					
	8	3			1	5		9			10	4	U	6	2	7	11					
	8	3			1	5		9			10	4	U	6	2	7	11					
	8	3			1	5		9			10	4	U	6	2	7	11					
	8	3			1	5		9			10	4		6	2	7	11				U	
	8	3			1	5		9			10	4*		6	2	7	11				S*	
	8	3			1	5		9			10	4		6	2	7	11				U	
	8	3			1	5		9			10	4		6	2	7	11*				S*	
	8	3			1	5		9			10	4		6		7	11		U		2	
	8	3			1	5		9			10	4		6		7	11		U		2	
	8	3			1	5		9			10	4		6*	2	7	11				S*	
	8	3			1	5		9			10	4		6	2	7	11				U	
	8	3			1	5		9			10	4		6	2	7	11				U	
	8	3			1	5		9			10*	4		6	2	7	11				S*	
	8	3			1	5		9				4		6	2*	7	11		10		S*	
	8	3			1	5		9				4		6	2	7	11		10		U	
	8	3			1	5		9				4	U	6	2	7	11		10			
		8			1	5		9	3		10	4		6*	2	7	11		S*			
	8	3			1			9			10	4		6	2	7	11		U		5	
	8	3			1	5		9			10*	4		6	2	7	11		S*			
S*	8	3			1	5		9				4		6	2	7*	11		10			
U	8	3			1	5		9				4		6	2	7	11		10			
U	8	3			1	5		9				4		6		7	11		10		2	
	8	6			1	5		9				4		U	2	7	11		10		3	
	8	6						9		1		4*		S*	2	7	11		10		3	5
U	8	3						9		1				4	2	7	11		10		5	6
		6						9		1		4		7	2	S*	11		10	8*	3	5
		6				5		9		1		4		7	2	U	11		10	8	3	
		6				5		9				4		8	2	7	11	1	10	U	3	
	U	6				5		9				4		8	2	7	11	1	10		3	
	U	6				5		9				4		8	2	7	11	1	10		3	
	8	3						9	5			4		6		7	11	1	10	U	2	
	8	3						9	5			4		6		7	11	1	10	U	2	
2	36	39	2		33	36		39	3	4	26	41	1	37	37	37	41	5	16	4	20	3
1							1							1		3			2	1	6	
	10					1		16			7	1		2		4	8		2			

Burton Ken	Craig Tommy	Clements Dave	Downes Steve	Ellis Sam	Grummitt Peter	Holsgrove John	Johnson Kevin	Joicey Brian	Mullen Jimmy	Pearson Trevor	Prendergast Mike	Prophett Colin	Prudham Eddie	Pugh Graham	Rodrigues Peter	Sinclair Jackie	Sissons John	Springett Peter	Sunley David	Taylor Paul	Thompson Allan	Todd Sammy
3	8		10		1	5					9	4		6	2	7	11				U	
	8	6		5	1			9			10	4			2	7	11			U	3	
1	2	1	1	1	2	1		1			2	2		1	2	2	2				1	
																1	1					

Burton Ken	Craig Tommy	Clements Dave	Downes Steve	Ellis Sam	Grummitt Peter	Holsgrove John	Johnson Kevin	Joicey Brian	Mullen Jimmy	Pearson Trevor	Prendergast Mike	Prophett Colin	Prudham Eddie	Pugh Graham	Rodrigues Peter	Sinclair Jackie	Sissons John	Springett Peter	Sunley David	Taylor Paul	Thompson Allan	Todd Sammy
	8	3			1	5		9				4		6	2	7	11		10		U	
	1	1			1	1		1				1		1	1	1	1		1			

League Table

	P	W	D	L	F	A	Pts
Norwich City	42	21	15	6	60	36	57
Birmingham City	42	19	18	5	60	31	56
Millwall	42	19	17	6	64	46	55
Queen's Park Rangers	42	20	14	8	57	28	54
Sunderland	42	17	16	9	67	57	50
Blackpool	42	20	7	15	70	50	47
Burnley	42	20	6	16	70	55	46
Bristol City	42	18	10	14	61	49	46
Middlesbrough	42	19	8	15	50	48	46
Carlisle United	42	17	9	16	61	57	43
Swindon Town	42	15	12	15	47	47	42
Hull City	42	14	10	18	49	53	38
Luton Town	42	10	18	14	43	48	38
SHEFFIELD WEDNESDAY	42	13	12	17	51	58	38
Oxford United	42	12	14	16	43	55	38
Portsmouth	42	12	13	17	59	68	37
Orient	42	14	9	19	50	61	37
Preston North End	42	12	12	18	52	58	36
Cardiff City	42	10	14	18	56	69	34
Fulham	42	12	10	20	45	68	34
Charlton Athletic	42	12	9	21	55	77	33
Watford	42	5	9	28	24	75	19

1972-73

Division Two

Manager: Derek Dooley

Did you know that?

Final League Position: 10th

On 31 March 1973 Peter Fox, at 15 years, eight months and 26 days, became the youngest player for Wednesday when he played against Orient in a 2–0 home win.

Match No.	Date	Venue	Opponents		Round	Result	HT Score	Position	Scorers	Attendance
1	Aug 12	H	Fulham	W		3-0	2-0		Prendergast, Holsgrove, Joicey	23,109
2	16	H	Swindon Town	W		2-1	0-0	1st	Joicey, Craig	20,841
3	19	A	Queen's Park Rangers	L		2-4	0-3	2nd	Sunley (2)	12,977
4	26	H	Hull City	W		4-2	2-2	1st	Sunley, Joicey (2), Craig (pen)	20,153
5	29	A	Swindon Town	L		0-1	0-0	2nd		11,376
6	Sep 2	A	Bristol City	W		2-1	1-0	3rd	Joicey (2)	12,373
7	9	H	Portsmouth	W		2-1	1-1	1st	Prendergast, Sunley	17,830
8	16	A	Sunderland	D		1-1	0-0	2nd	Joicey	16,960
9	20	A	Oxford United	L		0-1	0-1	3rd		11,333
10	23	H	Luton Town	W		4-0	2-0	2nd	Holsgrove, Rodrigues, Prendergast, Eustace	18,913
11	27	H	Huddersfield Town	W		3-2	1-1	1st	Prendergast, Henderson, Craig (pen)	22,185
12	30	A	Carlisle United	D		1-1	0-0	2nd	Sissons	7,306
13	Oct 7	A	Preston North End	D		1-1	0-0	2nd	Eustace (pen)	15,600
14	14	H	Burnley	L		0-1	0-0	2nd		30,197
15	21	A	Brighton & Hove Alb	D		3-3	1-0	2nd	Sissons, Ley (og), Sunley	18,699
16	28	H	Nottingham Forest	L		1-2	0-0	5th	Sissons	21,887
17	Nov 4	A	Huddersfield Town	L		0-1	0-1	6th		12,806
18	11	H	Oxford United	L		0-1	0-0	7th		13,163
19	18	H	Middlesbrough	W		2-1	1-1	6th	Mullen, Craig	16,174
20	25	A	Orient	L		2-3	1-2	8th	Eustace, Craig	5,254
21	Dec 2	H	Millwall	D		2-2	0-0	9th	Joicey, Wylde	13,906
22	9	A	Cardiff City	L		1-4	0-3	9th	Henderson	9,909
23	16	A	Blackpool	W		2-1	2-1	9th	Henderson, Craig	10,270
24	23	H	Aston Villa	D		2-2	1-2	8th	Craig, Joicey	20,961
25	26	A	Luton Town	D		0-0	0-0	8th		15,799
26	30	H	Queen's Park Rangers	W		3-1	1-1	7th	Craig, Sunley, Joicey	20,185
27	Jan 6	A	Hull City	D		1-1	1-0	8th	Sunley	11,537
28	27	A	Portsmouth	L		0-1	0-1	9th		9,705
29	Feb 10	H	Sunderland	W		1-0	0-0	9th	Henderson	16,949
30	17	A	Fulham	L		0-1	0-0	9th		11,686
31	28	H	Blackpool	W		2-0	0-0	9th	Joicey, Craig (pen)	13,930
32	Mar 3	H	Preston North End	W		2-1	0-0	6th	Sunley, Prophett	13,427
33	10	A	Burnley	W		1-0	0-0	5th	Sunley	16,927
34	14	H	Bristol City	W		3-2	0-0	3rd	Joicey (2), Sunley	13,819
35	17	H	Brighton & Hove Alb	D		1-1	1-0	4th	Joicey	16,122
36	24	A	Nottingham Forest	L		0-3	0-2	4th		10,488
37	31	H	Orient	W		2-0	0-0	4th	Sunley, Joicey	10,003
38	Apr 7	A	Millwall	L		1-2	1-1	5th	Craig (pen)	8,557
39	14	H	Cardiff City	W		1-0	1-0	5th	Dwyer (og)	10,952
40	21	A	Middlesbrough	L		0-3	0-1	6th		8,119
41	23	H	Carlisle United	D		0-0	0-0	8th		8,895
42	24	A	Aston Villa	L		1-2	1-0	10th	Prudham	20,710
										Apps
										Subs
									Two own-goals	Goals

League Cup

43	Sep 6	H	Bolton Wanderers	W	2R	2-0	2-0		Joicey, Eustace	15,903
44	Oct 4	A	Wolverhampton W	L	3R	1-3	0-2		Munro (og)	17,549
										Apps
										Subs
									One own-goal	Goals

FA Cup

45	Jan 13	H	Fulham	W	3R	2-0	1-0		Prendergast, Joicey	21,028
46	Feb 3	H	Crystal Palace	D	4R	1-1	1-0		Craig (pen)	35,156
47	6	A	Crystal Palace	D	4R Re	1-1 *	0-0		Sunley	44,071
48	19	N	Crystal Palace #	W	4R 2R	3-2 **	0-1		Joicey (3)	19,151
49	24	H	Chelsea	L	5R	1-2	1-1		Coyle	46,910
* Score at full-time 1-1			** Score at full-time 2-2			# Played at Villa Park, Birmingham				Apps
										Subs
										Goals

League Match Abandoned after 56 minutes

50	Jan 20	H	Bristol City			0-0	0-0			11,185

Clements Dave	Coyle Roy	Craig Jim	Craig Tommy	Eustace Peter	Fox Peter	Grummitt Peter	Henderson Willie	Holsgrove John	Joicey Brian	Mullen Jimmy	Potts Eric	Prendergast Mike	Prophett Colin	Prudham Eddie	Rodrigues Peter	Sinclair Jackie	Sissons John	Springett Peter	Sunley David	Swan Peter	Taylor Paul	Thompson Allan	Todd Sammy	Wylde Rodger
6			8			1	7	5	9	3		10			2		11		U	4				
6			8			1	7*	5	9	3		10			2		11		S*	4				
6			8			1	7	5	9	3			U		2		11		10	4				
3			6	8		1		5	9			10			2	U	11		7	4				
3			6	8		1	U	5	9			10			2		11		7	4				
3			6	8		1	S*	5	9			10			2		11		7	4*				
3			6	8		1	7*	5	9			10			2		11		S*	4				
3			6	8		1	S*	5	9*	4		10			2		11		7					
3			6	8		1	7	5		4		10			2		11		9	U				
3			6*	8		1	7	5		4		10			2		11		9	S*				
3			6	8		1	7	5	9	4		10			2		11		U					
3			6			1		5	9	4		10*			2		11		7	S*	8			
3				8		1		5	9	6	U					7	11		10	4		2		
3				8		1	7	5	9	6					2	U	11		10	4				
3			6	8		1	7	5*	9	S*					2		11		10	4				
3			6*	8		1	7	5	9						2	S*	11		10	4				
6				8		1	7	5	9	3	U				2		11		10	4				
6			8			1		5	9	3	U				2	7	11		10	4				
3			6	8		1	7	5	9	4							11		U			2		10
3			6	8		1	7	5	9	4					2	11						U		10
11			6	8		1	7	5	9	3					2				S*			4		10*
10			6	8		1	7	5	9	3					2		11*		S*			4		
3	11		6	8		1	7	5	9	U		10			2							4		
3	11*		6	8		1	7	5	9			10			2		S*					4		
3	11		6	8		1		5	9			10			2	U			7			4		
3	8		6					5	9			10			2	U	11	1	7			4		
3	8		6*					5	9			10	S*		2		11	1	7			4		
3	8	2	6	S*			7	5						10			11	1	9*			4		
3	8		6				7	5	9*		S*		4		2		11	1	10					
	8	2	6	U		1	7	5			10		4				11		9			3		
3	8		6			1		5	9		7		4		2		11		10			U		
3	8*		6			1	7	5	9		S*		4		2		11		10					
	8*		6	S*		1	7		9	3			5		2		11		10			4		
	8		6			1	7		9	3	S*		4		2		11*		10			5		
	8		6	S*			7		9	3	11		4		2			1*	10			5		
3	8*		6	11		1	7		9		S*		4		2				10			5		
3	8		6	U	1				9		7		4		2		11		10			5		
3	8		6	S*		1			9		7		4		2		11*		10			5		
11	8		6				7		9	3	U		4		2			1	10			5		
3	8		6	11			7		9*	4	S*				2			1	10			5		
3	8		6	11					9	5	7		4	U	2			1	10					
3			6	11					9	5	7		4	8*	2			1	10				S*	
38	19	2	39	24	1	32	27	32	38	23	7	16	13	2	38	3	31	9	32	13	1	19		3
				4			2			1	5		1			1	1		4	2			1	
			10	3			4	2	15	1		4	1	1	1		3		11					1

Clements Dave	Coyle Roy	Craig Jim	Craig Tommy	Eustace Peter	Fox Peter	Grummitt Peter	Henderson Willie	Holsgrove John	Joicey Brian	Mullen Jimmy	Potts Eric	Prendergast Mike	Prophett Colin	Prudham Eddie	Rodrigues Peter	Sinclair Jackie	Sissons John	Springett Peter	Sunley David	Swan Peter	Taylor Paul	Thompson Allan	Todd Sammy	Wylde Rodger
3			6	8		1	7	5	9			10			2		11		U	4				
6				8		1		5	9	3	S*					7	11		10	4		2*		
2			1	2		2	1	2	2	1		1			1	1	2		1	2		1		
											1													
				1					1															

Clements Dave	Coyle Roy	Craig Jim	Craig Tommy	Eustace Peter	Fox Peter	Grummitt Peter	Henderson Willie	Holsgrove John	Joicey Brian	Mullen Jimmy	Potts Eric	Prendergast Mike	Prophett Colin	Prudham Eddie	Rodrigues Peter	Sinclair Jackie	Sissons John	Springett Peter	Sunley David	Swan Peter	Taylor Paul	Thompson Allan	Todd Sammy	Wylde Rodger
3	8		6	U				5	9			10			2		11	1	7			4		
3	8		6	S*			7	5				10*			2		11	1	9			4		
3	8		6				7*	5	10		S*		4		2		11	1	9					
3	8		6			1	7*	5	9		S*		4		2		11		10					
3	8		6			1	7	5	9		U		4		2		11		10					
5	5		5			2	4	5	4			2	3		5		5	3	5			2		
				1							2													
	1		1						4			1							1					

Clements Dave	Coyle Roy	Craig Jim	Craig Tommy	Eustace Peter	Fox Peter	Grummitt Peter	Henderson Willie	Holsgrove John	Joicey Brian	Mullen Jimmy	Potts Eric	Prendergast Mike	Prophett Colin	Prudham Eddie	Rodrigues Peter	Sinclair Jackie	Sissons John	Springett Peter	Sunley David	Swan Peter	Taylor Paul	Thompson Allan	Todd Sammy	Wylde Rodger
3	8		6				7	5			U	10			2		11	1	9			4		

League Table

	P	W	D	L	F	A	Pts
Burnley	42	24	14	4	72	35	62
Queen's Park Rangers	42	24	13	5	81	37	61
Aston Villa	42	18	14	10	51	47	50
Middlesbrough	42	17	13	12	46	43	47
Bristol City	42	17	12	13	63	51	46
Sunderland	42	17	12	13	59	49	46
Blackpool	42	18	10	14	56	51	46
Oxford United	42	19	7	16	52	43	45
Fulham	42	16	12	14	58	49	44
SHEFFIELD WEDNESDAY	42	17	10	15	59	55	44
Millwall	42	16	10	16	55	47	42
Luton Town	42	15	11	16	44	53	41
Hull City	42	14	12	16	64	59	40
Nottingham Forest	42	14	12	16	47	52	40
Orient	42	12	12	18	49	53	36
Swindon Town	42	10	16	16	46	60	36
Portsmouth	42	12	11	19	42	59	35
Carlisle United	42	11	12	19	50	52	34
Preston North End	42	11	12	19	37	64	34
Cardiff City	42	11	11	20	43	58	33
Huddersfield Town	42	8	17	17	36	56	33
Brighton & Hove Albion	42	8	13	21	46	83	29

1973-74

Division Two

Manager: Derek Dooley/Steve Burtenshaw

Did you know that?

Final League Position: 19th

Wednesday played their first match on a Sunday in England, on 10 February 1974, beating Bristol City 3–1 before a crowd of 15,888.

Match No.	Date	Venue	Opponents		Round	Result	HT Score	Position	Scorers	Attendance
1	Aug 25	A	Swindon Town	L		1-3	1-2		Sunley	8,267
2	Sep 1	H	Blackpool	D		0-0	0-0	19th		15,834
3	8	A	Nottingham Forest	L		1-2	0-1	19th	Mullen	13,452
4	12	H	West Bromwich Alb	W		3-1	0-1		Sunley, Potts, Joicey	15,927
5	15	H	Carlisle United	W		1-0	0-0	12th	Thompson	15,080
6	17	A	Millwall	L		0-1	0-0	15th		9,167
7	22	A	Bristol City	L		0-2	0-1	21st		13,829
8	29	H	Crystal Palace	W		4-0	2-0	12th	Prendergast (3), Sunley	12,861
9	Oct 3	H	Millwall	W		3-2	2-2		Potts, Dorney (og), Prendergast	13,881
10	6	A	Sunderland	L		1-3	0-1	13th	Coyle	28,955
11	13	H	Portsmouth	L		1-2	1-0	15th	Joicey	12,690
12	20	A	Cardiff City	W		1-0	0-0	14th	Knighton	7,748
13	24	A	West Bromwich Alb	L		0-2	0-1			12,679
14	27	H	Notts County	D		0-0	0-0	16th		14,977
15	Nov 3	A	Aston Villa	L		0-1	0-1	18th		28,559
16	10	H	Orient	L		1-2	0-1	18th	Joicey	9,961
17	17	A	Luton Town	L		1-2	1-2	17th	Joicey	9,543
18	24	H	Oxford United	L		0-1	0-1	19th		7,998
19	Dec 8	H	Middlesbrough	D		2-2	1-1	20th	Prendergast, Joicey	11,992
20	15	H	Fulham	L		0-3	0-2	20th		7,925
21	22	A	Crystal Palace	D		0-0	0-0	20th		16,240
22	26	H	Hull City	D		1-1	0-1	20th	Prudham	15,600
23	29	H	Nottingham Forest	D		1-1	0-1	20th	Craig	16,332
24	Jan 1	A	Blackpool	D		0-0	0-0	20th		11,362
25	12	A	Carlisle United	D		2-2	2-1	20th	Coyle, Mullen	7,332
26	19	H	Swindon Town	W		2-1	1-1	20th	Sunley, Potts	11,944
27	Feb 2	A	Fulham	L		1-4	1-2	20th	Cameron	6,594
28	10	H	Bristol City	W		3-1	1-1	19th	Joicey, Henderson, Shaw	15,888
29	16	A	Bolton Wanderers	L		2-4	0-4	19th	Joicey, Ritson (og)	13,405
30	20	A	Portsmouth	D		1-1	0-1		Potts	8,669
31	23	H	Sunderland	L		0-1	0-1	20th		17,816
32	Mar 2	A	Hull City	L		1-2	0-1	20th	Potts	8,193
33	9	A	Notts County	W		5-1	3-0	19th	Prendergast (2), Joicey (2), Potts	9,378
34	16	H	Cardiff City	W		5-0	2-0	17th	Potts, Craig, Joicey (2), Thompson	13,841
35	23	A	Orient	W		1-0	1-0	17th	Craig	9,392
36	Apr 1	H	Aston Villa	L		2-4	1-2	18th	Prendergast, Thompson	22,094
37	6	A	Oxford United	L		0-1	0-1	18th		7,223
38	12	A	Preston North End	D		0-0	0-0	19th		11,286
39	13	H	Luton Town	D		2-2	1-0	18th	Joicey, Potts	16,492
40	15	H	Preston North End	W		1-0	1-0	18th	Craig	17,332
41	20	A	Middlesbrough	L		0-8	0-3	19th		25,287
42	27	H	Bolton Wanderers	W		1-0	0-0	19th	Knighton	23,264
										Apps
										Subs
									Two own-goals	Goals

League Cup

Match No.	Date	Venue	Opponents		Round	Result	HT Score	Position	Scorers	Attendance
43	Oct 10	A	Bournemouth	D	2R	0-0	0-0			11,017
44	15	H	Bournemouth *	D	2R RE	2-2	1-1		Craig (pen), Prendergast	5,883
45	29	H	Bournemouth **	W	2R RE	2-1	0-1		Prudham, Prendergast	8,894
46	Nov 6	A	Queens' Park Rangers	L	3R	2-8	2-3		Knighton, Prendergast	16,043
										Apps
										Subs
										Goals

* After extra-time. Score at full-time 2-2. ** After extra-time. Score at full-time 1-1

FA Cup

Match No.	Date	Venue	Opponents		Round	Result	HT Score	Position	Scorers	Attendance
47	Jan 5	H	Coventry City	D	3R	0-0	0-0			16,799
48	8	A	Coventry City	L	3R Re	1-3	0-1		Sunley	13,709
										Apps
										Subs
										Goals

Cameron Danny	Clements Dave	Coyle Roy	Craig Jim	Craig Tommy	Eustace Peter	Ferguson Bobby	Henderson Willie	Holsgrove John	Joicey Brian	Kent Mick	Knighton Ken	Mullen Jimmy	Potts Eric	Prendergast Mike	Prudham Eddie	Rodrigues Peter	Shaw Bernard	Sissons John	Springett Peter	Sunley David	Thompson Allan
	3	U		6	8			5	9			4	7				2	11	1	10	
				6	8		7	5	9			4	U			2	3	11	1	10	
		8		6	U			5			11	4	7		10	2	3		1	9	
			5	6	U				9		11		7	8		2	3		1	10	4
			5	6	U				9		11		7	8		2	3		1	10	4
			5	6	U				9		11		7	10		2	3		1	8	4
				6	U			5	9		11		7	10		2	3		1	8	4
			S*	6				5	9		11*		7	10		2	3		1	8	4
				6			S*	5	9		11*		7	10		2	3		1	8	4
		8		6	11		U					5	7	10		2	3		1	9	4
				6			7		9	8*	11	5		10		2	3		1	S*	4
		8			U					4	6	5	7	10		2	3	11	1	9	
2		8*			S*						6	5	7	10			3	11	1	9	4
2		8			U		7				6	5	11		9		3		1	10	4
2		8			S*				9		6*	5	11	10	7		3		1		4
					6				9		11	5	7	10	U	2	3		1	8	4
				6	U		7		9	5	8		11	10		2	3		1		4
				6			7		9	5	8		11	10	U	2	3		1		4
				6			7		9		8	5	11	10		2	3		1	U	4
				6			7		9*		8	5	11	10		2	3		1	S*	4
		8		6	5						3		7	10	U	2		11	1	9	4
		6		8	5						3		7	10	S*	2*		11	1	9	4
2		U		10	5						3		7	9	11		6		1	8	4
2		8		10	5				U		3		7		11		6		1	9	4
2		8		10	5		7		9		3	6	U						1	11	4
2		8		10	5		7*		9		3		S*				6		1	11	4
2		8*		10	5				9		3	S*	7				6		1	11	4
2		S*		10	5*	1	7		9		3		11				6			8	4
		7		10	5	1			9		3	U	11			2	6			8	4
		7		10	5	1			9*		3		11	S*		2	6			8	4
		5*		10		1	11				6		7	9	S*	2	3			8	4
				10	5	1	11				6*	S*	7	9		2	3			8	4
11				10	U			5	9		6		7	8		2	3		1		4
11				10			S*	5	9		6		7	8		2*	3		1		4
11				10				5	9		6	U	7	8		2	3		1		4
11*				10			S*	5	9		6		7	8		2	3		1		4
11		S*		10				5	9		6*	4	7	8		2	3		1		
11		6		10			S*	5	9			4	7	8*		2	3		1		
		6		10			11	5	9			4	7		S*	2	3		1	8*	
		6		10			11	5	9			4	7		S*	2	3		1	8*	
11		6*		10	S*			5	9			4	7		8	2	3		1		
2				10	S*		11	5	9		6	4	7				3		1	8*	
17	1	19	3	37	15	5	15	16	31	4	35	19	38	27	6	31	39	6	37	29	32
		2	1		4		4					2	1	1	4					2	
1		2		4			1		12		2	2	8	8	1		1			4	3

Cameron Danny	Clements Dave	Coyle Roy	Craig Jim	Craig Tommy	Eustace Peter	Ferguson Bobby	Henderson Willie	Holsgrove John	Joicey Brian	Kent Mick	Knighton Ken	Mullen Jimmy	Potts Eric	Prendergast Mike	Prudham Eddie	Rodrigues Peter	Shaw Bernard	Sissons John	Springett Peter	Sunley David	Thompson Allan
		8		6			11		9	S*		5	7	10		2*	3		1		4
				6*				5	9	4	11	3	7	10		2	8		1	S*	
2		8					7*		S*		6	5	11	10	9		3		1		4
2					6				9		11	5	7	10	U		3		1	8	4
2		2		2	1		2	1	3	1	3	4	4	4	1	2	4		4	1	3
									1	1										1	
				1							1			3	1						

Cameron Danny	Clements Dave	Coyle Roy	Craig Jim	Craig Tommy	Eustace Peter	Ferguson Bobby	Henderson Willie	Holsgrove John	Joicey Brian	Kent Mick	Knighton Ken	Mullen Jimmy	Potts Eric	Prendergast Mike	Prudham Eddie	Rodrigues Peter	Shaw Bernard	Sissons John	Springett Peter	Sunley David	Thompson Allan
2		8		11	5				S*		3		7	10*			6		1	9	4
2		8			5		11		10		3	6	7		S*				1	9*	4
2		2		1	2		1		1		2	1	2	1			1		2	2	2
									1						1						
																				1	

League Table

	P	W	D	L	F	A	Pts
Middlesbrough	42	27	11	4	77	30	65
Luton Town	42	19	12	11	64	51	50
Carlisle United	42	20	9	13	61	48	49
Orient	42	15	18	9	55	42	48
Blackpool	42	17	13	12	57	40	47
Sunderland	42	19	9	14	58	44	47
Nottingham Forest	42	15	15	12	57	43	45
West Bromwich Albion	42	14	16	12	48	45	44
Hull City	42	13	17	12	46	47	43
Notts County	42	15	13	14	55	60	43
Bolton Wanderers	42	15	12	15	44	40	42
Millwall	42	14	14	14	51	51	42
Fulham	42	16	10	16	39	43	42
Aston Villa	42	13	15	14	48	45	41
Portsmouth	42	14	12	16	45	62	40
Bristol City	42	14	10	18	47	54	38
Cardiff City	42	10	16	16	49	62	36
Oxford United	42	10	16	16	35	46	36
SHEFFIELD WEDNESDAY	42	12	11	19	51	63	35
Crystal Palace	42	11	12	19	43	56	34
Preston North End	42	9	14	19	40	62	31
Swindon Town	42	7	11	24	36	72	25

1974-75

Division Two

Manager: Steve Burtenshaw

Did you know that?

Final League Position: 22nd

When Brian Joicey scored in the 90th minute against Oxford United on 19 April 1975 to earn a 1–1 draw, it was the first goal scored by Wednesday at home since 14 December 1974 when Bobby Brown scored – a total of 14 hours and 25 minutes.

Match No.	Date	Venue	Opponents		Round	Result	HT Score	Position	Scorers	Attendance
1	Aug 17	A	Oldham Athletic	L		1-2	1-0		Craig (pen)	14,583
2	24	H	Bristol Rovers	D		1-1	0-1	17th	Eustace	14,343
3	31	A	Norwich City	D		1-1	1-0	17th	Craig	20,714
4	Sep 7	H	Cardiff City	L		1-2	1-2	22nd	Lamour (og)	9,850
5	14	A	Bolton Wanderers	W		1-0	1-0	20th	Brown	14,597
6	17	A	Bristol Rovers	D		1-1	1-1	15th	Rodrigues	12,330
7	21	H	Nottingham Forest	L		2-3	1-1	19th	Craig, Joicey	15,295
8	25	H	West Bromwich Alb	D		0-0	0-0			12,333
9	28	A	Orient	L		0-1	0-1	21st		7,378
10	Oct 2	H	Sunderland	L		0-2	0-1	21st		11,490
11	5	H	Bristol City	D		1-1	0-0	21st	Holsgrove	10,088
12	12	A	Oxford United	L		0-1	0-0	21st		6,562
13	15	A	Sunderland	L		0-3	0-3	21st		28,155
14	19	H	Hull City	W		2-1	2-1	21st	McMordie, Harvey	11,498
15	26	A	Aston Villa	L		1-3	1-3	21st	Craig	23,977
16	Nov 2	A	Blackpool	L		1-3	1-2	22nd	McMordie	6,243
17	9	H	York City	W		3-0	1-0	20th	Ferguson, McMordie, Potts	12,495
18	16	A	Notts County	D		3-3	1-0	21st	McMordie (2), Potts	14,170
19	23	H	Fulham	W		1-0	0-0	19th	McMordie	12,373
20	30	A	Portsmouth	L		0-1	0-0	20th		9,786
21	Dec 7	H	Manchester United	D		4-4	3-1	19th	Sunley (2), Harvey, Shaw	35,067
22	14	H	Oldham Athletic	D		1-1	1-0	19th	Brown	13,339
23	21	A	Millwall	L		1-2	0-0	21st	Brown	6,265
24	26	H	Bolton Wanderers	L		0-2	0-1	21st		17,153
25	28	A	Southampton	W		1-0	1-0	21st	Potts	15,243
26	Jan 11	A	Manchester United	L		0-2	0-1	21st		45,662
27	18	H	Portsmouth	L		0-2	0-0	22nd		11,032
28	31	A	York City	L		0-3	0-0	22nd		9,899
29	Feb 8	H	Blackpool	D		0-0	0-0	22nd		14,342
30	22	H	Notts County	L		0-1	0-0	22nd		14,734
31	25	A	Fulham	L		1-2	0-1	22nd	Holsgrove	8,550
32	Mar 8	A	West Bromwich Alb	L		0-4	0-0	22nd		10,385
33	15	H	Orient	L		0-1	0-0	22nd		8,492
34	22	A	Cardiff City	D		0-0	0-0	22nd		6,637
35	29	H	Millwall	L		0-1	0-0	22nd		8,171
36	31	H	Southampton	L		0-1	0-1	22nd		8,505
37	Apr 1	A	Nottingham Forest	L		0-1	0-0	22nd		14,077
38	8	H	Norwich City	L		0-1	0-0	22nd		7,483
39	12	A	Bristol City	L		0-1	0-0	22nd		11,976
40	19	H	Oxford United	D		1-1	0-1	22nd	Joicey	7,444
41	23	H	Aston Villa	L		0-4	0-2	22nd		23,605
42	26	A	Hull City	L		0-1	0-1	22nd		7,652
										Apps
										Sub
									One own-goal	Goals

League Cup

43	Aug 20	A	Scunthorpe United	L	1R	0-1	0-0			5,214
										Apps
										Sub

FA Cup

44	Jan 4	A	Chelsea	L	3R	2-3	1-0		Thompson (pen), Shaw	24,679
										Apps
										Sub
										Goals

Brown Bobby	Cameron Danny	Coyle Roy	Craig Tommy	Dowd Hugh	Eustace Peter	Ferguson Ronnie	Fox Peter	Harvey Colin	Henson Phil	Herbert Dave	Holsgrove John	Joicey Brian	Knighton Ken	McIver Fred	McMordie Eric	Mullen Jimmy	Potts Eric	Prendergast Mike	Prudham Eddie	Quinn Jimmy	Rodrigues Peter	Shaw Bernard	Springett Peter	Sunley David	Thompson Allan	Wylde Rodger
	U		6	2	10						5	9		8		3	7						1	11	4	
S*			6		10						5	9		8			7		11		2	3	1		4*	
			10	4	6						5	9		8		U	7		11		2	3	1			
			6	4	3*						5	9	10	8			7		11		2		1	S*		
11			10	4				8			5	9	6	3			7				2	U	1			
11			10	4				8			5	9	6	3			7				2*	S*	1			
11			10	4				8			5	9	6	3*			7				2		1	S*		
11			10	4				8			5	9*	6	3			7				2		1	S*		
11*			10	4				8			5	9	6	3		S*	7				2		1			
			10	4				8			5	U	6				7				2	3	1	11		9
			10	4				8			5	9	6				7		S*		2	3	1	11*		
			10	4				8*			5		6	3			7		9		2	S*	1	11		
			10	4				8			5	9	6	11			7				2*	S*	1		3	
11			10					8			5	9	3	U	6		7				2		1		4	
11			10					8*			5	9	3	S*	6		7				2		1		4	
11			10	5							S*	9*	3	8	6		7				2		1		4	
11*			10	5		9		8					3		6		7				2		1	S*	4	
			10	5		9		8						U	6		7				2	3	1	11	4	
U			10	5		9		8							6		7				2	3	1	11	4	
			10	5		9		8						U	6		7				2	3	1	11	4	
9*			10	5				8							6		7				2	3	1	11	4	S*
9			10	5				8*					3		6		7					2	1	11	4	S*
9				5			1	8					3	10		S*	7				2	6*		11	4	
9*				5		10	1	8					6	S*			7				2	3		11	4	
					U		1	8				9	6	10		5	7				2	3		11	4	
							1	8					6*	11		5	7	10			2	3		9	4	S*
11						S*	1	8					3	10		5	7				2	6		9	4*	
				5		9	1	8				11		10		U	7			3	2	6			4	
							1	8	10		5	9					7	11		3	2	6			4	U
							1	8*	10		5	9					7	11		3	2	6			4	S*
11					2		1		10		5		6	8		U	7			3					4	9
				S*	8		1		10	11	5		6				7			3	2				4	9*
S*				5	8		1		10	11			6*	2		4	7			3						9
				5	6		1	8*	10				3	2		4	7					S*		11		9
				5	6		1		10	S*			8	2		4	7			3*				11		9
S*						9	1	8	10				3			4	7	11			2*	6			5	
U	8					9	1		10				3			4	7	11			2	6			5	
U	2					9	1	8	10			11	3			4	7					6			5	
	2			5		9	1	8	10			11	3	U		4	7					6				
	2			5*			1	8	10			11				4	7			3		6		9		S*
	2						1		10*			11	8			4	7			3		6		9	5	S*
	2						1		10			11	8	U		4	7			3		6		9	5	
15	6		22	27	9	10	20	30	14	2	19	23	31	21	9	14	42	5	4	10	31	24	22	19	27	6
3				1		1				1	1			2		2			1			4		4		6
3			4		1	1		2			2	2			6		3				1	1		2		

Brown Bobby	Cameron Danny	Coyle Roy	Craig Tommy	Dowd Hugh	Eustace Peter	Ferguson Ronnie	Fox Peter	Harvey Colin	Henson Phil	Herbert Dave	Holsgrove John	Joicey Brian	Knighton Ken	McIver Fred	McMordie Eric	Mullen Jimmy	Potts Eric	Prendergast Mike	Prudham Eddie	Quinn Jimmy	Rodrigues Peter	Shaw Bernard	Springett Peter	Sunley David	Thompson Allan	Wylde Rodger
		S*	6	2	10*						5	9		8		3	7						1		4	11
			1	1	1						1	1		1		1	1						1		1	1
		1																								

Brown Bobby	Cameron Danny	Coyle Roy	Craig Tommy	Dowd Hugh	Eustace Peter	Ferguson Ronnie	Fox Peter	Harvey Colin	Henson Phil	Herbert Dave	Holsgrove John	Joicey Brian	Knighton Ken	McIver Fred	McMordie Eric	Mullen Jimmy	Potts Eric	Prendergast Mike	Prudham Eddie	Quinn Jimmy	Rodrigues Peter	Shaw Bernard	Springett Peter	Sunley David	Thompson Allan	Wylde Rodger
				5			1					9*	6	10		S*	7				2	3		11	4	8
				1			1					1	1	1			1				1	1		1	1	1
																1										
																						1			1	

League Table

	P	W	D	L	F	A	Pts
Manchester United	42	26	9	7	66	30	61
Aston Villa	42	25	8	9	79	32	58
Norwich City	42	20	13	9	58	37	53
Sunderland	42	19	13	10	65	35	51
Bristol City	42	21	8	13	47	33	50
West Bromwich Albion	42	18	9	15	54	42	45
Blackpool	42	14	17	11	38	33	45
Hull City	42	15	14	13	40	53	44
Fulham	42	13	16	13	44	39	42
Bolton Wanderers	42	15	12	15	45	41	42
Oxford United	42	15	12	15	41	51	42
Orient	42	11	20	11	28	39	42
Southampton	42	15	11	16	53	54	41
Notts County	42	12	16	14	49	59	40
York City	42	14	10	18	51	55	38
Nottingham Forest	42	12	14	16	43	55	38
Portsmouth	42	12	13	17	44	54	37
Oldham Athletic	42	10	15	17	40	48	35
Bristol Rovers	42	12	11	19	42	64	35
Millwall	42	10	12	20	44	56	32
Cardiff City	42	9	14	19	36	62	32
SHEFFIELD WEDNESDAY	42	5	11	26	29	64	21

1975-76

Division Three

Manager: Steve Burtenshaw/Len Ashurst

Did you know that?

Final League Position: 20th

The February 1976 home game against Chesterfield and the away game at Shrewsbury Town had to be postponed due to 'flu among the players being at epidemic proportions.

Hillsborough was chosen for the League Cup Final replay if the game at Wembley finished all-square.

On 28 January 1976 the Wednesday team, who had not won for 11 games, were taken onto Broomhead moor – part of the Yorkshire Moors – in freezing temperatures to spend the night in a survival exercise by trainer Tony Toms to toughen the players up. The next game at home to Chester was won 2–0.

Match No.	Date	Venue	Opponents		Round	Result	HT Score	Position	Scorers	Attendance
1	Aug 16	A	Southend United	L		1-2	1-0		Prendergast	6,775
2	23	H	Brighton & Hove Alb	D		3-3	2-1	17th	Prendergast, Joicey, Winstanley (og)	10,326
3	30	A	Hereford United	L		1-3	0-1	22nd	Henson	7,017
4	Sep 6	H	Wrexham	W		1-0	0-0	17th	Herbert	7,585
5	13	A	Swindon Town	L		1-2	1-0	20th	Herbert	6,993
6	20	H	Grimsby Town	W		4-0	2-0	16th	Prendergast, Herbert, Gray (og), Potts	11,345
7	24	A	Chesterfield	L		0-1	0-1	19th		12,959
8	27	A	Crystal Palace	D		1-1	1-0	16th	Potts	14,840
9	Oct 4	H	Peterborough United	D		2-2	1-1	18th	Prendergast, Lee (og)	11,412
10	11	H	Millwall	W		4-1	1-1	13th	Potts (2), Henson (2)	10,144
11	18	A	Cardiff City	L		0-2	0-0	20th		7,930
12	21	A	Chester	L		0-1	0-0	19th		6,248
13	25	H	Shrewsbury Town	D		1-1	1-0	20th	Joicey	12,045
14	Nov 5	H	Gillingham	W		1-0	0-0		Joicey	8,235
15	8	H	Port Vale	L		0-3	0-1	20th		10,880
16	15	A	Aldershot	D		1-1	0-0	21st	Henson	5,181
17	29	H	Rotherham United	D		0-0	0-0	21st		18,691
18	Dec 2	A	Walsall	D		2-2	1-0		Prendergast (2)	4,148
19	6	A	Colchester United	L		1-2	0-0	21st	Potts	3,534
20	20	H	Preston North End	D		2-2	0-0	21st	Potts, Herbert	8,553
21	26	A	Bury	D		0-0	0-0	20th		9,657
22	27	H	Mansfield Town	D		0-0	0-0	22nd		15,430
23	Jan 10	H	Hereford United	L		1-2	1-1	22nd	Shaw	8,155
24	17	A	Grimsby Town	D		1-1	0-0	22nd	Wylde	7,167
25	24	H	Swindon Town	L		0-2	0-1	22nd		8,342
26	31	H	Chester	W		2-0	2-0	19th	Nimmo, Prendergast	7,558
27	Feb 7	A	Gillingham	D		0-0	0-0	19th		8,090
28	16	A	Port Vale	L		0-1	0-0	21st		5,557
29	21	H	Aldershot	W		3-1	2-1	20th	Nimmo, Prendergast, Feely	8,286
30	Mar 2	A	Halifax Town	D		0-0	0-0	20th		5,876
31	6	H	Walsall	W		2-1	0-0	18th	Henson, Nimmo	9,713
32	10	A	Peterborough United	D		2-2	1-1		Nimmo, O'Donnell	8,209
33	13	A	Millwall	L		0-1	0-1	21st		6,769
34	17	H	Cardiff City	L		1-3	0-0	21st	Quinn	8,867
35	20	A	Rotherham United	L		0-1	0-1	22nd		13,500
36	24	H	Chesterfield	L		1-3	1-2	23rd	Prendergast	10,653
37	27	H	Colchester United	W		1-0	0-0	21st	Henson	6,905
38	30	A	Preston North End	L		2-4	0-1	22nd	Bell, Henson	6,899
39	Apr 7	H	Crystal Palace	W		1-0	0-0	20th	Prendergast	11,909
40	10	A	Wrexham	L		0-3	0-0	21st		4,190
41	13	A	Shrewsbury Town	D		0-0	0-0	22nd		2,968
42	17	H	Bury	W		1-0	0-0	21st	Nimmo	10,585
43	19	A	Mansfield Town	L		0-3	0-1	22nd		13,410
44	20	H	Halifax Town	W		1-0	1-0	19th	Henson	13,143
45	24	A	Brighton & Hove Alb	D		1-1	1-0	21st	Potts	11,859
46	29	H	Southend United	W		2-1	2-0	20th	Prendergast, Potts	25,802
										Apps
										Subs
									Three own-goals	Goals

League Cup

No.	Date	Venue	Opponents		Round	Result	HT Score	Position	Scorers	Attendance
47	Aug 19	A	Darlington	W	1R 1L	2-0	0-0		Prendergast, Potts	3,581
48	27	H	Darlington	L	1R 2L	0-2	0-0			7,452
49	Sep 3	H	Darlington * (#)	L	1st Re	0-0	0-0			6,276
										Apps
										Subs
										Goals

* After extra-time

(#) Lost on penalties 3-5

FA Cup

No.	Date	Venue	Opponents		Round	Result	HT Score	Position	Scorers	Attendance
50	Nov 22	H	Macclesfield Town	W	1R	3-1	1-1		Proudlove, Knighton, Prendergast	12,940
51	Dec 13	H	Wigan Athletic	W	2R	2-0	0-0		Sunley, Nimmo	12,436
52	Jan 3	A	Charlton Athletic	L	3R	1-2	0-1		Sunley	12,284
										Apps
										Subs
										Goals

Match abandoned after 26 minutes

No.	Date	Venue	Opponents		Round	Result	HT Score	Position	Scorers	Attendance
53	Nov 1	A	Walsall				0-0			5,836

Bell Derek	Brown Bobby	Cameron Danny	Cusack Dave	Dowd Hugh	Feely Peter	Fisher Paul	Fox Peter	Harvey Colin	Henson Phil	Herbert Dave	Hull Gary	Joicey Brian	Knighton Ken	McIver Fred	Mullen Jimmy	Nimmo Ian	O'Donnell Neil	Potts Eric	Prendergast Mike	Proudlove Andy	Quinn Jimmy	Ramsbottom Neil	Shaw Bernard	Sunley David	Thompson Allan	Walden Richard	Watling Barry	Wylde Rodger
	11*	2					1	6	8			9	S*		4			7	10		3				5			
		2		5				8*	11	S*		9		6	4			7	10		3	1						
		2		5				8	11	9			S*	6	4			7	10*		3	1						
	11*	2		5				8	6	9			S*		4			7	10		3	1						
	S*	2		5				8	11	9			6	3*	4			7	10			1						
		2		5				8	10	11					4			7	9*	S*	3	1	6					
		2		5				8	10*	11					4			7	9	S*	3	1	6					
		2		5				8	10	11*					4			7		S*	3	1	6	9				
				5				6	10	8		S*			4			7	9*	11	3	1	2					
			6	5				4	10			9	S*		3			7		11	2*	1	8					
			6	5				4	10			9*	S*		3			7		11	2	1	8					
			5	4				6	S*	10*					3			11	9	8	2	1	7					
			5	4				6	8			9						11	10	U	3	1	7		2			
			5					7	8*	S*		9					6	11		10	3	1	2		4			
			5					7	S*			9					6	11		8	3	1	2	10*	4			
			5	S*					8				7				6	11		10	3	1	2	9	4*			
			5									10	8*		7		6	11	9	S*	3	1	2		4			
			5									10	8		7		6	11	9	U	3	1	2		4			
			5									10*	8		7		6	11	9	S*	3	1	2		4			
			5				1			8					7		6	11		9*	3		2	10	4			S*
			5				1			S*					7		6	11		9*	3		2	8	4			10
			5				1			10				S*	7		6	11		9*	3		2	8	4			
			5				1					9			7*		6	11	S*		3		8		4	2		10
			5				1					9*			3	S*	6	11					7	10	4	2		8
			5												3	S*	6	11	9				7	10	4	2*	1	8
			5				1		8					7	3	9	6	11	10				2		4*			S*
			5				1		8					7	4	9	6	11	10		3		2					U
			5		10		1		8					7*	4		6	11	9		3		2					S*
			5		10	U	1				4			7		11	6		9				3			2		8
			5		10		1		U					7	4	11	6		9		3		2					8
			5		10		1		8					7*	4	S*	6	11	9		3		2					
			5		10		1		8		U				4	11	6	7	9		3		2					
			5		10		1		8*		S*				4	11	6	7	9		3		2					
			5		10		1		8						4	11*	6		S*		3		2		7			9
			5		10		1				S*	9			4		6	11			3		2		7			8*
11			5				1		S*						4	10	6		9		3		8		7	2*		
11			5				1		8		2			7*	4	S*		9	10		3							6
11			5		S*		1		8		2				4		6*	9	10		3							7
10*			5		S*		1		8		2				4		6	11	9		3							7
10			5		9		1		8		2				4	S*	6*	11			3							7
			5				1			U	2			8	4	10		11	9				3		6			7
			5		10*		1		8					6	3	S*		11	9				2		4			7
			5				1			S*				6	8	9		11	10		3*		2		4			7
			5		U		1		7						4	10	6	11	9				3			2		8
			5				1		8		U				4	10	6	11	9				3			2		7
			5				1		8		U				4	9	6	11	10				3			2		7
5	2	8	37	12	10		27	15	29	10	6	13	5	13	41	13	29	42	32	10	36	18	37	8	21	8	1	18
	1			1	2				3	4	2	1	5	1		6			2	5								3
1					1				8	4		3				5	1	8	11		1		1					1

Bell Derek	Brown Bobby	Cameron Danny	Cusack Dave	Dowd Hugh	Feely Peter	Fisher Paul	Fox Peter	Harvey Colin	Henson Phil	Herbert Dave	Hull Gary	Joicey Brian	Knighton Ken	McIver Fred	Mullen Jimmy	Nimmo Ian	O'Donnell Neil	Potts Eric	Prendergast Mike	Proudlove Andy	Quinn Jimmy	Ramsbottom Neil	Shaw Bernard	Sunley David	Thompson Allan	Walden Richard	Watling Barry	Wylde Rodger
		2		5				8	11			9	U	6	4			7	10		3	1						
		2		5					11	S*		9	8	6	4			7	10		3*	1						
		2		5				8*	11	9		S*		6	4			7	10		3	1						
		3		3				2	3	1		2	1	3	3			3	3		3	3						
										1		1																
																		1	1									

Bell Derek	Brown Bobby	Cameron Danny	Cusack Dave	Dowd Hugh	Feely Peter	Fisher Paul	Fox Peter	Harvey Colin	Henson Phil	Herbert Dave	Hull Gary	Joicey Brian	Knighton Ken	McIver Fred	Mullen Jimmy	Nimmo Ian	O'Donnell Neil	Potts Eric	Prendergast Mike	Proudlove Andy	Quinn Jimmy	Ramsbottom Neil	Shaw Bernard	Sunley David	Thompson Allan	Walden Richard	Watling Barry	Wylde Rodger
			5					8				S*	7				6	11	9	10*	3	1	2		4			
			5				1								7	S*	6	11	9*	8	3		2	10	4			
			5				1		10			S*			7		6*	11			3		2	8	4			9
			3				2	1	1				1		2		3	3	2	2	3	1	3	2	3			1
												2				1												
													1			1			1	1				2				

Bell Derek	Brown Bobby	Cameron Danny	Cusack Dave	Dowd Hugh	Feely Peter	Fisher Paul	Fox Peter	Harvey Colin	Henson Phil	Herbert Dave	Hull Gary	Joicey Brian	Knighton Ken	McIver Fred	Mullen Jimmy	Nimmo Ian	O'Donnell Neil	Potts Eric	Prendergast Mike	Proudlove Andy	Quinn Jimmy	Ramsbottom Neil	Shaw Bernard	Sunley David	Thompson Allan	Walden Richard	Watling Barry	Wylde Rodger
			5					7	8			9					6	11	10*	S*	3	1	2		4			

League Table

	P	W	D	L	F	A	Pts
Hereford United	46	26	11	9	86	55	63
Cardiff City	46	22	13	11	69	48	57
Millwall	46	20	16	10	54	43	56
Brighton & Hove Albion	46	22	9	15	78	53	53
Crystal Palace	46	18	17	11	61	46	53
Wrexham	46	20	12	14	66	55	52
Walsall	46	18	14	14	74	61	50
Preston North End	46	19	10	17	62	57	48
Shrewsbury Town	46	19	10	17	61	59	48
Peterborough United	46	15	18	13	63	63	48
Mansfield Town	46	16	15	15	58	52	47
Port Vale	46	15	16	15	55	54	46
Bury	46	14	16	16	51	46	44
Chesterfield	46	17	9	20	69	69	43
Gillingham	46	12	19	15	58	68	43
Rotherham United	46	15	12	19	54	65	42
Chester	46	15	12	19	43	62	42
Grimsby Town	46	15	10	21	62	74	40
Swindon Town	46	16	8	22	62	75	40
SHEFFIELD WEDNESDAY	46	12	16	18	48	59	40
Aldershot	46	13	13	20	59	75	39
Colchester United	46	12	14	20	41	65	38
Southend United	46	12	13	21	65	75	37
Halifax Town	46	11	13	22	41	61	35

1976-77

Division Three

Manager: Len Ashurst

Did you know that?

Final League Position: 8th

In April 1977 Wednesday launched an appeal fund to bring their floodlights up to European standards in the close season, and Director Ernest Barron ran from the Town Hall in the City to Hillsborough in a sponsored run. The run took him 24 minutes to complete.

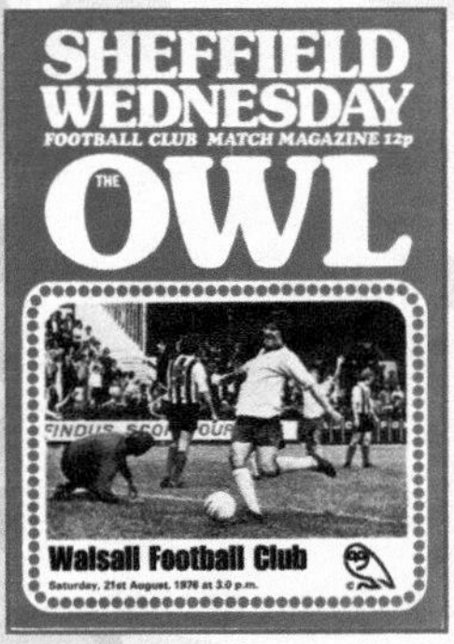

Match No.	Date	Venue	Opponents		Round	Result	HT Score	Position	Scorers	Attendance
1	Aug 21	H	Walsall	D		0-0	0-0			12,046
2	25	H	Northampton Town	W		2-1	1-1		Wylde (1 + pen)	11,511
3	28	A	Port Vale	L		0-2	0-0	11th		5,033
4	Sep 4	H	Portsmouth	D		1-1	0-0	13th	Prendergast	12,131
5	11	A	Swindon Town	L		2-5	1-1	17th	Tynan, Potts	8,698
6	18	H	Chesterfield	W		4-1	2-1	15th	Wylde (pen +1), Tynan, Hope	13,456
7	25	A	Wrexham	D		2-2	1-2	12th	Wylde, Bradshaw	8,672
8	Oct 2	A	Lincoln City	D		1-1	1-1	13th	Wylde	14,706
9	5	H	Chester	W		3-0	0-0	10th	Wylde, Hope, Tynan	13,209
10	9	H	Gillingham	W		2-0	1-0	5th	Wylde, Feely	15,133
11	16	A	Reading	W		1-0	0-0	4th	Johnson	9,449
12	23	H	Shrewsbury Town	L		0-1	0-1	6th		17,030
13	30	H	Mansfield Town	L		0-2	0-2	11th		15,559
14	Nov 2	H	Rotherham United	L		1-3	1-0	11th	Wylde	18,204
15	6	A	Bury	W		3-1	1-0	11th	Tynan (2), Hope	7,959
16	9	H	Crystal Palace	W		1-0	1-0	8th	Bradshaw	14,899
17	27	A	Peterborough United	W		2-1	0-1	7th	Tynan (2)	8,683
18	Dec 4	H	Tranmere Rovers	W		3-1	1-1	6th	Bradshaw, Henson (pen), Leman	12,315
19	18	A	Oxford United	D		1-1	0-0	6th	Tynan	4,674
20	27	H	York City	W		3-2	3-0	6th	Leman, Tynan, Rushbury	22,004
21	28	A	Grimsby Town	D		1-1	0-1	7th	Wylde	8,000
22	Jan 8	H	Brighton & Hove Alb	D		0-0	0-0	6th		17,000
23	11	A	Mansfield Town	L		0-1	0-0	7th		13,714
24	15	A	Northampton Town	W		2-0	1-0	5th	Bradshaw, Wylde	5,828
25	22	A	Walsall	L		1-5	1-1	7th	Wylde	7,297
26	25	H	Bury	W		1-0	1-0	6th	Leman	12,026
27	Feb 5	H	Port Vale	L		1-2	0-1	7th	Wylde	12,933
28	12	A	Portsmouth	W		3-0	0-0	6th	Tynan (2), Wylde	14,279
29	15	A	Chester	L		0-1	0-0	6th		5,613
30	19	H	Swindon Town	W		3-1	1-1	4th	Bradshaw, Hope (pen), Wylde	11,265
31	26	A	Chesterfield	L		0-2	0-1	6th		15,125
32	Mar 5	H	Wrexham	W		3-1	2-0	5th	Leman, Wylde, Hope (pen)	13,317
33	12	H	Lincoln City	D		1-1	1-1	7th	Rushbury	14,854
34	19	A	Gillingham	L		0-1	0-1	7th		6,022
35	26	H	Reading	W		2-1	0-1	7th	Hope (pen), Leman	9,854
36	29	A	Preston North End	L		1-4	1-2	7th	Hope (pen)	11,753
37	Apr 2	A	Shrewsbury Town	D		1-1	1-0	9th	Wylde	3,657
38	9	H	Grimsby Town	W		1-0	1-0	9th	Wylde	10,182
39	11	A	York City	W		2-0	2-0	8th	Tynan, Leman	5,568
40	12	A	Rotherham United	W		1-0	0-0	6th	Wylde	17,356
41	16	H	Preston North End	W		1-0	0-0	6th	Tynan	13,217
42	23	A	Crystal Palace	L		0-4	0-3	7th		20,018
43	30	H	Peterborough United	W		4-0	1-0	7th	Bradshaw (2), Wylde, Potts	8,727
44	May 3	A	Brighton & Hove Alb	L		2-3	1-0	8th	Rushbury, Nimmo	30,756
45	6	A	Tranmere Rovers	L		0-1	0-0	8th		3,826
46	14	H	Oxford United	W		2-0	0-0	8th	Wylde, Tynan	8,955
										Apps
										Subs
										Goals
League Cup										
47	Aug 14	A	Grimsby Town	W	1R 1L	3-0	2-0		Wylde (2), O'Donnell	6,222
48	18	H	Grimsby Town	D	1R 2L	0-0	0-0			10,207
49	31	A	Wolverhampton W	W	2R	2-1	1-0		Potts, Wylde	15,823
50	Sep 21	H	Watford	W	3R	3-1	2-0		Hope, Potts (2)	15,787
51	Oct 27	A	Millwall	L	4R	0-3	0-2			11,478
										Apps
										Subs
										Goals
FA Cup										
52	Nov 20	H	Stockport County	W	1R	2-0	0-0		Tynan, Wylde	13,886
53	Dec 15	A	Darlington	L	2R	0-1	0-0			7,474
										Apps
										Subs
										Goals

Bradshaw Paul	Bryant Steve	Collins John	Cusack Dave	Davis John	Dowd Hugh	Feely Peter	Fox Peter	Henson Phil	Hope Bobby	Jefferson Derek	Johnson Jeff	Leman Denis	McKeown Lindsay	Mullen Jimmy	Nimmo Ian	O'Donnell Neil	Owen Niel	Potts Eric	Prendergast Mike	Rushbury Dave	Simmonite Gordon	Turner Chris	Tynan Tommy	Walden Richard	Wylde Rodger
		3*	S*		5	10		6			8			4	9			11				1		2	7
	11		4		5	10*					8			3	9	6		S*				1		2	7
	11		5		4	10*					8			3	9	6		S*				1		2	7
		3			5	10*					8			4	S*	6		11	9			1		2	7
	S*	3*			5	10					8			4		6		11				1	9	2	7
		3			5			S*	10		8			4		6		11*				1	9	2	7
11		3			5			U	10		8			4		6						1	9	2	7
11			U		5			8	10	4				3		6						1	9	2	7
11					5	U			10	4	8			3		6						1	9	2	7
					5	11		S*	10*	4	8			3		6						1	9	2	7
11			4		5			10			8			3	S*	6						1	9*	2	7
11			U		5			10		4	8			3		6						1	9	2	7
11		3			5	9		6	10	4	8								7*			1		2	S*
11		3			5		1	U	10		8			4				6					9	2	7
11			4		5			S*	10		8							6*		3		1	9	2	7
11			4		5			U	10		8							6		3		1	9	2	7
11			4		5			7	10		8				S*			6*		3		1	9	2	
11			4		5			7	10		8	6						U		3		1	9	2	
11			4		5			U	10		8	6								3		1	9	2	7
11			4		5			U	10		8	6								3		1	9	2	7
11			4		5				10		8	6						U		3		1	9	2	7
11			4		5*			S*	10		8	6								3		1	9	2	7
11			4					U	10		8	6		5						3		1	9	2	7
11*			4						10		8	6		5					S*	3		1	9	2	7
11			4					8	10			6*		5					S*	3		1	9	2	7
11			4					8	10			6		5					S*	3		1	9*	2	7
6			4					S*	10		8			5					11*	3		1	9	2	7
11			4		5			U	10		8	6								3		1	9	2	7
11			4		5			U	10		8	6								3		1	9	2	7
11			4		5				10		8	6*						S*		3		1	9	2	7
11					5				10		8							6	S*	3	4	1	9	2*	7
11					5				10		8	6		4				U		3		1	9	2	7
11					5				10*		8	6		4				S*		3		1	9	2	7
11			4		5			10				6	8					S*		3		1	9*	2	7
11			4		5			8	10			6	S*							3		1	9*	2	7
11			4		5			8	10			6	9*					S*		3		1		2	7
11			4*		5			8	10			6	9	3								1	S*	2	7
11					5			3	10			6	8	4				9				1	U	2	7
11*					5			8	10			6	S*	4						3		1	9	2	7
11					5			8	10			6	U	4						3		1	9	2	7
11*					5			8	10			6	S*	4						3		1	9	2	7
					5			8	10			6*	11	4				S*		3		1	9	2	7
11					5			10			8	6		4*				S*		3		1	9	2	7
11			4					10			8	6			S*			5		3		1	9	2	7*
			5					3			9	7*	11		S*			6		4		1	10	2	8
11			5	8				6			10				U		4			3		1	9	2	7
37	2	7	26	1	38	7	1	22	34	5	34	26	6	27	3	11	1	12	3	30	1	45	38	46	43
	1		1					5					3		5			8	4				1		1
7						1		1	7		1	6			1			2	1	3			14		21

Bradshaw Paul	Bryant Steve	Collins John	Cusack Dave	Davis John	Dowd Hugh	Feely Peter	Fox Peter	Henson Phil	Hope Bobby	Jefferson Derek	Johnson Jeff	Leman Denis	McKeown Lindsay	Mullen Jimmy	Nimmo Ian	O'Donnell Neil	Owen Niel	Potts Eric	Prendergast Mike	Rushbury Dave	Simmonite Gordon	Turner Chris	Tynan Tommy	Walden Richard	Wylde Rodger
		3			5	10		U			8			4	9	6		11				1		2	7
		3	U		5	10		6			8			4	9			11				1		2	7
		3			5	10		U			8			4		6		11	9			1		2	7
		3			5	7		U	10		8			4		6		11				1	9	2	
					5	S*		10		4	8			3		6			11*			1	9	2	7
		4			5	4		2	1	1	5			5	2	4		4	2			5	2	5	4
						1																			
									1							1		3							3

Bradshaw Paul	Bryant Steve	Collins John	Cusack Dave	Davis John	Dowd Hugh	Feely Peter	Fox Peter	Henson Phil	Hope Bobby	Jefferson Derek	Johnson Jeff	Leman Denis	McKeown Lindsay	Mullen Jimmy	Nimmo Ian	O'Donnell Neil	Owen Niel	Potts Eric	Prendergast Mike	Rushbury Dave	Simmonite Gordon	Turner Chris	Tynan Tommy	Walden Richard	Wylde Rodger
11			4		5			U	10		8							6		3		1	9	2	7
11			4		5			7			8		10*		S*			6		3		1	9	2	
2			2		2			1	1		2		1					2		2		2	2	2	1
															1										
																							1		1

League Table

	P	W	D	L	F	A	Pts
Mansfield Town	46	28	8	10	78	42	64
Brighton & Hove Albion	46	25	11	10	83	40	61
Crystal Palace	46	23	13	10	68	40	59
Rotherham United	46	22	15	9	69	44	59
Wrexham	46	24	10	12	80	54	58
Preston North End	46	21	12	13	64	43	54
Bury	46	23	8	15	64	59	54
SHEFFIELD WEDNESDAY	46	22	9	15	65	55	53
Lincoln City	46	19	14	13	77	70	52
Shrewsbury Town	46	18	11	17	65	59	47
Swindon Town	46	15	15	16	68	75	45
Gillingham	46	16	12	18	55	64	44
Chester	46	18	8	20	48	58	44
Tranmere Rovers	46	13	17	16	51	53	43
Walsall	46	13	15	18	57	65	41
Peterborough United	46	13	15	18	55	65	41
Oxford United	46	12	15	19	55	65	39
Chesterfield	46	14	10	22	56	64	38
Port Vale	46	11	16	19	47	71	38
Portsmouth	46	11	14	21	53	70	36
Reading	46	13	9	24	49	73	35
Northampton Town	46	13	8	25	60	75	34
Grimsby Town	46	12	9	25	45	69	33
York City	46	10	12	24	50	89	32

1977-78

Division Three

Manager: Len Ashurst/Jack Charlton

Did you know that?

Final League Position: 14th

On 5 November, in the game against Carlisle United, the kick-off was brought forward due to the possibility of power cuts during the 'Winter of Discontent', which would prevent the use of the floodlights.

Match No.	Date	Venue	Opponents		Round	Result	HT Score	Position	Scorers	Attendance
1	Aug 20	H	Swindon Town	D		1-1	0-1		Tynan	12,095
2	27	H	Walsall	D		0-0	0-0	13th		10,634
3	Sep 3	A	Bury	L		0-3	0-2	20th		6,769
4	10	H	Shrewsbury Town	L		0-1	0-1	22nd		10,324
5	14	A	Chester	L		1-2	0-0	22nd	Tynan	4,520
6	17	A	Port Vale	D		0-0	0-0	23rd		5,135
7	24	H	Peterborough United	L		0-1	0-0	24th		9,620
8	27	H	Plymouth Argyle	D		1-1	1-0	24th	Wylde	8,515
9	Oct 1	A	Portsmouth	D		2-2	1-2	24th	Bradshaw, Tynan	12,020
10	4	A	Preston North End	L		1-2	1-2	24th	Baxter (og)	7,627
11	8	H	Chesterfield	W		1-0	1-0	24th	Tynan	12,920
12	12	A	Exeter City	L		1-2	1-1	24th	Wylde	4,564
13	15	A	Wrexham	D		1-1	1-1	24th	Tynan	9,145
14	22	H	Lincoln City	W		2-0	2-0	24th	Bradshaw, Rushbury	13,166
15	29	A	Bradford City	L		2-3	1-3	24th	Tynan, Mullen	12,825
16	Nov 5	H	Carlisle United	W		3-1	3-0	22nd	Hamilton (og), Prendergast, Tynan	12,285
17	12	A	Oxford United	L		0-1	0-0	23rd		6,481
18	19	H	Gillingham	D		0-0	0-0	24th		9,762
19	Dec 3	H	Colchester United	L		1-2	0-1	24th	Wylde	9,000
20	10	A	Cambridge United	L		0-3	0-2	24th		6,236
21	26	A	Tranmere Rovers	L		1-3	0-2	24th	Tynan	5,619
22	27	H	Rotherham United	W		1-0	0-0	24th	Prendergast	18,803
23	31	H	Hereford United	W		1-0	0-0	23rd	Wylde	11,029
24	Jan 2	A	Carlisle United	L		0-1	0-0	24th		11,309
25	14	A	Swindon Town	D		2-2	0-1	24th	Rushbury (pen), Mullen	7,609
26	17	H	Exeter City	W		2-1	1-0	20th	Rushbury (pen), Wylde	9,596
27	28	H	Bury	W		3-2	3-2	19th	Wylde (2), Tynan	9,054
28	Feb 11	H	Port Vale	W		3-1	2-1	18th	Leman, Mullen, Tynan	9,516
29	22	A	Peterborough United	L		1-2	0-1	17th	Cusack	4,252
30	25	H	Portsmouth	D		0-0	0-0	18th		10,241
31	28	A	Shrewsbury Town	D		0-0	0-0	18th		2,801
32	Mar 4	A	Chesterfield	D		2-2	0-1	18th	Tynan, Prendergast	12,395
33	7	H	Chester	D		1-1	1-1	16th	Grant	10,678
34	18	A	Lincoln City	L		1-3	1-2	20th	Hedley (pen)	8,811
35	21	H	Bradford City	W		2-0	0-0	19th	Tynan, Wylde	12,304
36	25	A	Rotherham United	W		2-1	2-1	18th	Johnson, Hornsby	12,630
37	27	H	Tranmere Rovers	W		1-0	0-0	17th	Tynan	12,976
38	Apr 1	A	Hereford United	W		1-0	0-0	16th	Porterfield	5,358
39	4	A	Plymouth Argyle	D		1-1	1-1	16th	Wylde	7,694
40	8	H	Oxford United	W		2-1	1-0	16th	Hornsby, Mullen	10,674
41	15	A	Gillingham	L		1-2	0-0	17th	Leman	7,238
42	18	H	Preston North End	W		1-0	0-0	15th	Tynan	12,426
43	22	H	Cambridge United	D		0-0	0-0	15th		11,512
44	25	A	Walsall	D		1-1	1-1		Tynan	5,232
45	29	A	Colchester United	D		1-1	0-1	16th	Rushbury	4,337
46	May 3	H	Wrexham	W		2-1	2-0	14th	Hornsby (pen), Tynan	15,700
										Apps
										Subs
									Two own-goals	Goals

League Cup

Match No.	Date	Venue	Opponents		Round	Result	HT Score	Position	Scorers	Attendance
47	Aug 13	H	Doncaster Rovers	W	1R 1L	5-2	3-2		Wylde (3), Porterfield, Walden	7,230
48	16	A	Doncaster Rovers	W	1R 2L	3-0	1-0		Porterfield, Wylde, Tynan	7,602
49	30	A	Blackpool	D	2R	2-2	0-1		Bradshaw, Tynan	10,101
50	Sep 5	H	Blackpool	W	2R Re	3-1	2-1		Bradshaw, Tynan, Johnson	13,260
51	Oct 25	H	Walsall	W	3R	2-1	0-0		Wylde, Tynan	18,350
52	Nov 29	H	Everton	L	4R	1-3	1-1		Tynan	36,079
										Apps
										Goals

FA Cup

Match No.	Date	Venue	Opponents		Round	Result	HT Score	Position	Scorers	Attendance
53	Nov 26	H	Bury	W	1R	1-0	1-0		Hope	11,571
54	Dec 17	A	Wigan Athletic	L	2R	0-1	0-0			13,871
										Apps
										Subs
										Goals

Bolder Bob	Bradshaw Paul	Cusack Dave	Darling Malcolm	Dowd Hugh	Grant David	Gregson Colin	Hedley Graeme	Hinch Jim	Hope Bobby	Hornsby Brian	Johnson Jeff	Leman Denis	McKeown Lindsay	Mullen Jimmy	Nimmo Ian	Owen Gordon	Porterfield Ian	Prendergast Mike	Rushbury Dave	Smith Mark	Turner Chris	Tynan Tommy	Walden Richard	Wylde Rodger
	11	4		5							8	6	U				10	7	3		1	9	2	
	11	4		5							8	6	S*				10		3		1	9	2	7*
	11	4	S*	5					7		8	6					10*		3		1	9	2	
	11	4	7	5					S*		8	6		3			10*				1	9	2	
	11	4		5					S*		8	6					10		3		1	9	2	7*
	11	5							10		8	6		4			U		3		1	9	2	7
	11	5							10		8	6		4	S*				3		1	9*	2	7
	11	5									8	6		4			10	9	3		1	U	2	7
	11	5				10					8	6		4				9*	3		1	S*	2	7
	11	5		S*					10*		8	6		4					3		1	9	2	7
	10	5		4							8	7		6		U			3		1	11	2	9
	10*	5		4		S*					8	7		6					3		1	11	2	9
		5		4							8	U		6			10	9	3		1	11	2	7
	11	5		4							8	U		6			10		3		1	9	2	7
	11	5		4*							8	S*		6			10		3		1	9	2	7
	11*	5							S*		8			4			6	10	3		1	9	2	7
	11	5		4							U			6			10	8	3		1	9	2	7
	11	5		4					U					6			10	8	3		1	9	2	7
	8	5		4					11					6			10*	S*	3		1	9	2	7
	11	5		4				S*			8			6			10		3		1	9	2	7*
		5*		4	3						8			7			11	S*	6		1	9	2	10
1	11				3							S*		5		6*	8	10	4			9	2	7
1	11	U			3							6		5			8	10	4			9	2	7
1	11	U			3							6		5			8	10	4			9	2	7
1	U	5			3						10	11		6			8		4			9	2	7
1	U	5			3						10	11		6			8		4			9	2	7
1	U	5			3						10	11		6			8		4			9	2	7
1	S*	5			3						10	11		6			8		4			9	2	7*
1	7	5			3						10	11		6			8	U	4			9	2	
1	7	S*			3*		6				10	11		5			8		4			9	2	
1	U	5					6				10	11		4			8	7	3			9	2	
1	S*	5		4			8				10	11*		6				7	3			9	2	
1	11*	5			3		8				10	S*		6				7	4			9	2	
1		S*			3		11			6	10			5			8		4*			9	2	7
1					3		11*			6	10	S*		5			8		4			9	2	7
1				5	3					11	10	U		6			8		4			9	2	7
1				5	3*					11	10	S*		6			8		4			9	2	7
1				5	3					11	10	U		6			8		4			9	2	7
1				5	3					11	10	U		6			8		4			9	2	7
1				5	3					11	10	U		6			8		4			9	2	7
1				5	3*					11	10	S*		6			8		4			9	2	7
1				5	3					11	10	S*		6			8		4			9	2	7*
1				5	3					11	10	S*		6			8		4			9	2	7*
1				5	3					11	10	U		6	7		8		4			9	2	
				5*	3					11		10	S*		7	9	8		4	6	1		2	
					3					11	10	S*		6			8*		4	5	1	9	2	7
23	25	29	1	26	24	1	6		5	13	39	23		41	2	2	38	13	45	2	23	43	46	36
	2	2	1	1		1		1	3			9	2		1			2				1		
	2	1			1		1			3	1	2		4			1	3	4			16		9

Bolder Bob	Bradshaw Paul	Cusack Dave	Darling Malcolm	Dowd Hugh	Grant David	Gregson Colin	Hedley Graeme	Hinch Jim	Hope Bobby	Hornsby Brian	Johnson Jeff	Leman Denis	McKeown Lindsay	Mullen Jimmy	Nimmo Ian	Owen Gordon	Porterfield Ian	Prendergast Mike	Rushbury Dave	Smith Mark	Turner Chris	Tynan Tommy	Walden Richard	Wylde Rodger
	11	4		5		U					8	6					10		3		1	9	2	7
	11	4		5							8	6	U				10		3		1	9	2	7
	11	4	U	5		7					8	6					10		3		1	9	2	
	11	4	7	5							8	6		3	U		10				1	9	2	
	11	5		4							8	U		6			10		3		1	9	2	7
	11	5		4					7		U			6			10	8	3		1	9	2	
	6	6	1	6		1			1		5	4		3			6	1	5		6	6	6	3
	2										1						2					5	1	5

Bolder Bob	Bradshaw Paul	Cusack Dave	Darling Malcolm	Dowd Hugh	Grant David	Gregson Colin	Hedley Graeme	Hinch Jim	Hope Bobby	Hornsby Brian	Johnson Jeff	Leman Denis	McKeown Lindsay	Mullen Jimmy	Nimmo Ian	Owen Gordon	Porterfield Ian	Prendergast Mike	Rushbury Dave	Smith Mark	Turner Chris	Tynan Tommy	Walden Richard	Wylde Rodger
	11	5		4					10			U		6			7	8	3		1	9	2	
	11*	5		4	3						8			6				S*	10		1	9	2	7
	2	2		2	1				1		1			2			1	1	2		2	2	2	1
																		1						
									1															

League Table

	P	W	D	L	F	A	Pts
Wrexham	46	23	15	8	78	45	61
Cambridge United	46	23	12	11	72	51	58
Preston North End	46	20	16	10	63	38	56
Peterborough United	46	20	16	10	47	33	56
Chester	46	16	22	8	59	56	54
Walsall	46	18	17	11	61	50	53
Gillingham	46	15	20	11	67	60	50
Colchester United	46	15	18	13	55	44	48
Chesterfield	46	17	14	15	58	49	48
Swindon Town	46	16	16	14	67	60	48
Shrewsbury Town	46	16	15	15	63	57	47
Tranmere Rovers	46	16	15	15	57	52	47
Carlisle United	46	14	19	13	59	59	47
SHEFFIELD WEDNESDAY	46	15	16	15	50	52	46
Bury	46	13	19	14	62	56	45
Lincoln City	46	15	15	16	53	61	45
Exeter City	46	15	14	17	49	59	44
Oxford United	46	13	14	19	64	67	40
Plymouth Argyle	46	11	17	18	61	68	39
Rotherham United	46	13	13	20	51	68	39
Port Vale	46	8	20	18	46	67	36
Bradford City	46	12	10	24	56	86	34
Hereford United	46	9	14	23	34	60	32
Portsmouth	46	7	17	22	41	75	31

1978-79

Division Three

Manager: Jack Charlton

Did you know that?

Final League Position: 14th

First Division Arsenal beat Third Division Wednesday after four replays in the third round of the FA Cup. They then went on to beat Manchester United 3–2 in the Final.

Match No.	Date	Venue	Opponents		Round	Result	HT Score	Position	Scorers	Attendance
1	Aug 19	A	Peterborough United	L		0-2	0-0			7,468
2	26	H	Colchester United	D		0-0	0-0	20th		10,685
3	Sep 2	A	Lincoln City	W		2-1	1-1	17th	Tynan, Hornsby	7,005
4	9	H	Southend United	W		3-2	2-0	11th	Hornsby (pen + 1), Grant	11,309
5	12	A	Gillingham	D		0-0	0-0	12th		5,835
6	16	A	Mansfield Town	D		1-1	0-1	13th	Hornsby (pen)	11,366
7	23	H	Plymouth Argyle	L		2-3	1-0	16th	Wylde, Nimmo	12,088
8	26	H	Bury	D		0-0	0-0	14th		9,000
9	30	A	Swindon Town	L		0-3	0-1	18th		5,857
10	Oct 7	A	Rotherham United	W		1-0	0-0	17th	Wylde	13,746
11	14	H	Carlisle United	D		0-0	0-0	16th		10,980
12	17	H	Oxford United	D		1-1	1-1	15th	Wylde	9,431
13	21	A	Shrewsbury Town	D		2-2	0-0	17th	Hornsby, Wylde	6,294
14	24	H	Exeter City	W		2-1	0-0	9th	Hornsby, Lowey	11,139
15	28	H	Walsall	L		0-2	0-1	14th		12,019
16	Nov 4	A	Blackpool	W		1-0	1-0	11th	Hornsby	9,403
17	11	H	Lincoln City	D		0-0	0-0	11th		12,590
18	18	A	Colchester United	L		0-1	0-0	13th		4,346
19	Dec 2	A	Swansea City	L		2-4	2-2	14th	Wylde, Hornsby	10,000
20	9	H	Chester	D		0-0	0-0	14th		8,872
21	26	A	Chesterfield	D		3-3	2-2	16th	Wylde, Porterfield, Johnson	13,322
22	Jan 27	A	Plymouth Argyle	L		0-2	0-1	18th		8,596
23	Feb 13	A	Southend United	L		1-2	0-1	20th	Wylde	4,559
24	19	A	Tranmere Rovers	D		1-1	1-1		Wylde	2,445
25	24	A	Carlisle United	D		0-0	0-0	20th		5,675
26	Mar 3	H	Shrewsbury Town	D		0-0	0-0	19th		11,284
27	6	H	Gillingham	W		2-1	1-1	18th	Owen, Wylde	8,205
28	10	A	Walsall	W		2-0	1-0	17th	Lowey, Hornsby	5,120
29	13	H	Brentford	W		1-0	1-0	15th	Wylde	10,229
30	24	A	Exeter City	D		2-2	0-1	16th	Wylde, Hornsby	4,521
31	27	H	Peterborough United	W		3-0	0-0	13th	Hornsby (pen), Wylde, Johnson	9,868
32	31	A	Watford	L		0-1	0-0	16th		15,394
33	Apr 3	H	Mansfield Town	L		1-2	0-2	16th	Nimmo	11,065
34	7	H	Swansea City	D		0-0	0-0	16th		12,101
35	13	A	Hull City	D		1-1	0-1		Curran	10,936
36	14	H	Chesterfield	W		4-0	2-0	16th	Rushbury, Wylde (2), Johnson	12,960
37	17	A	Brentford	L		1-2	0-2	17th	Nimmo	9,050
38	21	H	Tranmere Rovers	L		1-2	1-1	17th	Hornsby (pen)	9,815
39	25	A	Oxford United	D		1-1	0-0		Hornsby	3,243
40	28	A	Chester	D		2-2	0-1	16th	Owen, Lowey	4,200
41	May 1	A	Bury	D		0-0	0-0	16th		3,424
42	5	H	Watford	L		2-3	2-1	17th	Hornsby, Shirtliff	13,746
43	7	H	Rotherham United	W		2-1	1-1	16th	Mullen, Fleming	12,094
44	11	H	Swindon Town	W		2-1	1-0	16th	Hornsby, Nimmo	9,057
45	17	H	Blackpool	W		2-0	2-0	14th	Porterfield, Owen	7,310
46	19	H	Hull City	L		2-3	1-2	14th	Sterland, Hornsby	8,950
										Apps
										Subs
										Goals

League Cup

Match No.	Date	Venue	Opponents		Round	Result	HT Score	Position	Scorers	Attendance
47	Aug 12	A	Doncaster Rovers	W	1R 1L	1-0	1-0		Robinson (og)	7,232
48	15	H	Doncaster Rovers	L	1R 2L	0-1	0-0			8,055
49	22	A	Doncaster Rovers	W	1R Re	1-0	1-0		Hornsby	8,472
50	30	A	Aston Villa	L	2R	0-1	0-1			31,152
										Apps
										Subs
									One own-goal	Goals

FA Cup

Match No.	Date	Venue	Opponents		Round	Result	HT Score	Position	Scorers	Attendance
51	Nov 25	A	Scunthorpe United	D	1R	1-1	0-0		Nimmo	8,697
52	28	H	Scunthorpe United	W	1R Re	1-0	0-0		Nimmo	9,760
53	Dec 16	A	Tranmere Rovers	D	2R	1-1	0-1		Leman	4,250
54	19	H	Tranmere Rovers	W	2R Re	4-0	0-0		Wylde (2), Lowey, Hornsby (pen)	7,316
55	Jan 6	H	Arsenal	D	3R	1-1	0-1		Johnson	33,635
56	9	A	Arsenal #	D	3R Re	1-1	1-0		Wylde	37,987
57	15	N	Arsenal * #	D	3R Re	2-2	1-1		Hornsby (1 + pen)	25,011
58	17	N	Arsenal * #	D	3R Re	3-3	0-0		Rushbury, Lowey, Hornsby (pen)	17,008
59	22	N	Arsenal *	L	3R Re	0-2	0-2			30,275
										Apps
										Subs
										Goals

* At Filbert Street, Leicester

After extra-time (Match 56 Score at full-time 1-1) (Match 57 & 58 Score at full-time 2-2)

Blackhall Ray	Bolder Bob	Cox Brian	Curran Terry	Cusack Dave	Dowd Hugh	Fleming Ian	Grant David	Hornsby Brian	Johnson Jeff	Leman Denis	Lowey John	McKeown Lindsay	Mullen Jimmy	Nimmo Ian	Owen Gordon	Pickering Mike	Porterfield Ian	Rushbury Dave	Shirtliff Peter	Smith Mark	Sterland Mel	Strutt Brian	Taylor Kevin	Turner Chris	Tynan Tommy	Wylde Rodger
	1				5		3	11	10			U	6		7		8		2	4					9	
2	1				5		3		10	S*			7		11		8*	4		6					9	
3	1							11	10				6		7*		8	4	2	5					9	S*
2	1				5		3	11	10				6		U		8	4							9	7
2	1				5		3	11	10				6	S*			8	4							9*	7
2	1				5		3	11	10				6				8	4		S*					9*	7
2	1						3	11	10				6	S*			8	4		5					9*	7
2	1				5		3	11	10				6	S*			8	4							9*	7
2*	1				5		3	11	10				6		S*		8	4		9						7
2	1						3	11	10	9						5	8	6		4		U				7
2	1*						3	11	10	9					S*	5	8	6		4						7
2		1					3	11		9	10*				6	5	8	S*		4						7
2		1					3	11		9	S*				10*	5	8	4		6						7
2		1						11	6*	9	S*				10	5	8	3		4						7
2		1						11	6	9	10				S*	5	8*	3		4						7
2								11	6	9	10				U	5	8	3		4				1		7
2								11	6	9	10					5	8	3		4		U		1		7
2								11		9	S*		6		10*	5	8	3		4				1		7
2								11	6	9				10	U	5	8	3		4				1		7
2							6*	11	7					10	9	5	8	3		4				1		S*
2								11	6	9	10				U	5	8	3		4				1		7
2							S*	11	6		10		4			5	8*	3					9	1		7
						9*	4	11	6		10		5	S*			8	3	2					1		7
							4	11	6	9	10		5				8	3	2				U	1		7
							U	11	6	9	10		4			5	8	3	2					1		7
								11	6	9	10		4			5	8*	3	2				S*	1		7
								11	6		10		4		9	5	S*	3	2				8*	1		7
								11	6	9	10		4		U	5	8	3	2					1		7
								11	6	9*	10		4		S*	5	8	3	2					1		7
							3	11	6		10		4		S*	5	8		2	9*				1		7
							3	11	6		10*		4	S*	9	5	8		2					1		7
			S*				3	11	6		10		4			5	8		2	9				1		7*
			7			9*	3	11	6		10		4	S*		5	8		2					1		
			7					11	6		10		4	9	U	5	8	3	2					1		
			9					11	6		10		4		U	5	8	3	2					1		7
			9*					11	6				4	10	S*	5	8	3	2					1		7
			9					11	6		10		4	S*		5	8	3*	2					1		7
			10				3	11	6		S*		4	9*		5	8		2					1		7
	1		9				3	11	10*		S*		4			5	8		2	6						7
	1		9				3	11			10		4		S*	5	8	6	2*							7
	1		9				3	11			10		4		U	5	8	6	2							7
	1		9					11	6*		10		4		S*	5	8	3	2							7
	1		7			9		11	S*		10		4		6	5	8*	3	2							
	1					9	3	11	U				4	10	7	5	8	6	2							
	1					9	3	11*					4	10	7	5	8		2		S*		6			
	1					9	3	S*					4	11	10*	5	8		2		7		6			
21	19	4	11		7	6	26	44	37	16	24		35	8	14	35	45	36	26	20	1		4	23	8	36
			1				1	1	1	1	5			7	8		1	1		1	1		1			2
			1			1	1	16	3		3		1	4	3		2	1	1		1				1	14

Blackhall Ray	Bolder Bob	Cox Brian	Curran Terry	Cusack Dave	Dowd Hugh	Fleming Ian	Grant David	Hornsby Brian	Johnson Jeff	Leman Denis	Lowey John	McKeown Lindsay	Mullen Jimmy	Nimmo Ian	Owen Gordon	Pickering Mike	Porterfield Ian	Rushbury Dave	Shirtliff Peter	Smith Mark	Sterland Mel	Strutt Brian	Taylor Kevin	Turner Chris	Tynan Tommy	Wylde Rodger
	1			5*	4		3	11	10				6		S*		8		2						9	7
	1				5		3	11	10				6		S*		8	4	2*						9	7
2*	1				5		3	11	10				7		S*		8	4		6					9	
2	1				5		3	11	10				7		S*		8*	4		6					9	
2	4			1	4		4	4	4				4				4	3	2	2					4	2
															4											
								1																		

Blackhall Ray	Bolder Bob	Cox Brian	Curran Terry	Cusack Dave	Dowd Hugh	Fleming Ian	Grant David	Hornsby Brian	Johnson Jeff	Leman Denis	Lowey John	McKeown Lindsay	Mullen Jimmy	Nimmo Ian	Owen Gordon	Pickering Mike	Porterfield Ian	Rushbury Dave	Shirtliff Peter	Smith Mark	Sterland Mel	Strutt Brian	Taylor Kevin	Turner Chris	Tynan Tommy	Wylde Rodger
2								11	6	9				10	U	5	8	3		4				1		7
2								11	6	9				10	S*	5	8	3		4				1		7*
2							U	11	6	9	10					5	8	3		4				1		7
2								11	6	9	10				U	5	8	3		4				1		7
2							U	11	6	9	10		5				8	3		4				1		7
2							U	11	6	9	10		5				8	3		4				1		7
2							U	11	6	9	10					5	8	3		4				1		7
2							S*	11	6	9*	10					5	8	3		4				1		7
2							S*	11	6		10				9	5	8	3		4*				1		7
9								9	9	8	7		2	2	1	7	9	9		9				9		9
							2								1											
								4	1	1	2			2				1								3

League Table

	P	W	D	L	F	A	Pts
Shrewsbury Town	46	21	19	6	61	41	61
Watford	46	24	12	10	83	52	60
Swansea City	46	24	12	10	83	61	60
Gillingham	46	21	17	8	65	42	59
Swindon Town	46	25	7	14	74	52	57
Carlisle United	46	15	22	9	53	42	52
Colchester United	46	17	17	12	60	55	51
Hull City	46	19	11	16	66	61	49
Exeter City	46	17	15	14	61	56	49
Brentford	46	19	9	18	53	49	47
Oxford United	46	14	18	14	44	50	46
Blackpool	46	18	9	19	61	59	45
Southend United	46	15	15	16	51	49	45
SHEFFIELD WEDNESDAY	46	13	19	14	53	53	45
Plymouth Argyle	46	15	14	17	67	68	44
Chester	46	14	16	16	57	61	44
Rotherham United	46	17	10	19	49	55	44
Mansfield Town	46	12	19	15	51	52	43
Bury	46	11	20	15	59	65	42
Chesterfield	46	13	14	19	51	65	40
Peterborough United	46	11	14	21	44	63	36
Walsall	46	10	12	24	56	71	32
Tranmere Rovers	46	6	16	24	45	78	28
Lincoln City	46	7	11	28	41	88	25

1979-80

Division Three

Manager: Jack Charlton

Did you know that?

Final League Position: 3rd

On 13 October 1979, a wall around the pitch at the Rotherham's Millmoor ground collapsed a week after part of the same wall had collapsed when Rotherham played Sheffield United. Thirty people were hurt in a game that Wednesday won 2–1. The game was not held up.

Match No.	Date	Venue	Opponents		Round	Result	HT Score	Position	Scorers	Attendance
1	Aug 18	A	Barnsley	W		3-0	1-0		Curran, McCulloch, Mellor	22,360
2	21	H	Hull City	D		0-0	0-0			14,376
3	25	H	Blackburn Rovers	L		0-3	0-1	12th		14,228
4	Sep 1	A	Plymouth Argyle	W		3-1	1-0	8th	McCulloch, Porterfield, Curran	6,208
5	8	H	Brentford	L		0-2	0-1	14th		11,612
6	15	A	Colchester United	D		0-0	0-0	14th		3,473
7	18	A	Millwall	D		3-3	1-2	11th	Smith (pen), Hornsby, Owen	7,500
8	22	H	Swindon Town	W		4-2	2-1	8th	McCulloch, Smith (pen), Wylde (2)	11,636
9	29	A	Chesterfield	L		1-2	1-2	11th	Smith (pen)	14,950
10	Oct 2	H	Millwall	W		2-0	1-0	6th	Curran, Wylde	12,232
11	6	H	Mansfield Town	D		0-0	0-0	7th		13,072
12	9	A	Hull City	D		1-1	0-0	5th	Wylde	10,306
13	13	A	Rotherham United	W		2-1	2-1	5th	Mullen, Curran	18,500
14	20	H	Oxford United	D		2-2	1-1	5th	Wylde (2)	13,035
15	23	H	Grimsby Town	W		2-0	0-0	4th	Mullen, Curran	13,855
16	27	A	Wimbledon	W		4-3	2-1	4th	Lowey, Curran (2), Smith (pen)	6,009
17	Nov 3	H	Barnsley	L		0-2	0-0	6th		23,230
18	6	A	Grimsby Town	L		1-3	1-2	6th	Mellor	14,900
19	10	A	Blackpool	D		1-1	0-1	6th	Mellor	8,355
20	17	H	Southend United	W		2-0	0-0	6th	Mellor, King	10,563
21	Dec 1	A	Chester	D		2-2	1-1	5th	Wylde, Curran	6,241
22	8	H	Exeter City	L		0-1	0-1	8th		11,530
23	21	A	Reading	W		2-0	2-0	6th	Curran, Mellor	5,349
24	26	H	Sheffield United	W		4-0	1-0	6th	Mellor, Curran, King, Smith (pen)	49,309
25	Jan 12	H	Plymouth Argyle	L		0-1	0-1	8th		13,287
26	19	A	Brentford	D		2-2	1-0	8th	Hornsby, Mellor	8,390
27	Feb 2	H	Colchester United	W		3-0	2-0	5th	Smith (2 pens), Curran	11,958
28	5	H	Bury	W		5-1	3-0	4th	Curran (2), Taylor, Grant, Smith (pen)	12,425
29	9	A	Swindon Town	W		2-1	1-0	4th	Johnson, Taylor	16,415
30	16	H	Chesterfield	D		3-3	0-1	4th	Mellor (2), Wylde	23,433
31	23	H	Rotherham United	W		5-0	2-0	3rd	McCulloch (3), Curran, King	20,557
32	26	A	Carlisle United	W		2-0	2-0	3rd	Taylor, McCulloch	6,223
33	Mar 1	A	Oxford United	W		2-0	1-0	2nd	Hornsby, Curran	9,353
34	8	H	Wimbledon	W		3-1	2-0	1st	McCulloch, Curran (2)	20,803
35	15	A	Mansfield Town	D		1-1	0-0	2nd	McCulloch	16,109
36	18	A	Gillingham	D		1-1	1-0	1st	McCulloch	6,717
37	22	H	Blackpool	W		4-1	1-0	1st	McCulloch, Curran (2), Taylor	19,552
38	29	A	Southend United	D		1-1	1-1	2nd	Mellor	7,455
39	Apr 1	H	Reading	D		1-1	1-1	2nd	Curran	20,678
40	5	A	Sheffield United	D		1-1	0-1	2nd	Curran	45,156
41	7	H	Gillingham	W		1-0	0-0	2nd	Smith (pen)	22,717
42	12	A	Bury	L		0-1	0-0	2nd		11,622
43	19	H	Chester	W		3-0	1-0	2nd	McCulloch, Taylor, Curran	19,130
44	22	A	Blackburn Rovers	W		2-1	0-1	2nd	Taylor, Mellor	26,130
45	26	A	Exeter City	L		0-1	0-1	3rd		10,461
46	May 3	H	Carlisle United	D		0-0	0-0	3rd		32,734
										Apps
										Subs
										Goals

League Cup

Match No.	Date	Venue	Opponents		Round	Result	HT Score	Position	Scorers	Attendance
47	Aug 11	H	Hull City	D	1R 1L	1-1	1-0		Curran	9,152
48	14	A	Hull City	W	1R 2L	2-1	0-1		Fleming, Curran	7,059
49	28	H	Manchester City	D	2R	1-1	0-1		King	24,095
50	Sep 4	A	Manchester City	L	2R Re	1-2	0-0		Smith (pen)	24,074
										Apps
										Subs
										Goals

FA Cup

Match No.	Date	Venue	Opponents		Round	Result	HT Score	Position	Scorers	Attendance
51	Nov 24	H	Lincoln City	W	1R	3-0	1-0		Smith (pen), King, McCulloch	11,226
52	Dec 15	A	Carlisle United	L	2R	0-3	0-2			7,823
										Apps
										Subs
										Goals

Blackhall Ray	Bolder Bob	Cox Brian	Curran Terry	Fleming Ian	Grant David	Hornsby Brian	Johnson Jeff	King Jeff	Leman Denis	Lowey John	McCulloch Andy	Mellor Ian	Mullen Jimmy	Owen Gordon	Pickering Mike	Porterfield Ian	Shirtliff Peter	Smith Mark	Sterland Mel	Strutt Brian	Taylor Kevin	Williamson Charlie	Wylde Rodger
2	1		7	9	3	6	U				10	11			5	8		4					
2	1		7	9	3	6		8			10	11*			5	S*		4					
2	1		7	9	3	6		8			10	11			5*	S*		4					
2		1	7	9	3	6		11			10	U	5			8		4					
2		1	7	9*	3	6		11			10	S*	5			8		4					
2		1		9	3	6		11				U	5	10		8		4					7
2		1			3	6		11			9	U	5	10		8		4					7
2		1			3	6		11			9	U	5	10		8		4					7
2		1			3	6	S*	11			9*		5	10		8		4					7
		1	11		3		2	10	6	9		U	5			8	4						7
		1	11		3		2	10	6	9		U	5			8	4						7
2*		1	11		3			10	6	9		S*	5			8		4					7
		1	11		3	6*	2	10		9		S*	5			8		4					7
		1	11		3		2	10		9		S*	5			8		4			6*		7
		1	11		3		2	10	6	9			5			8		4		U			7
		1	11		3		2	10	6	9		U	5			8		4					7
		1	11	7*	3		2	10	6	9		S*	5			8		4					
		1	11		3	6*	2	10		9		7			5	8		4	S*				
	1		11		3	6		10		9		7			5	8		4	U	2			
	1				3	6		11			9	10		U	5	8	2	4					7
2	1		11		3	6	S*	10				9			5	8*		4					7
2	1		11		3	6	S*	10				9			5	8*		4					7
2	1		11			6	8	10	U		7	9			5			4				3	
2	1		11			6	8	7	U		9	10			5			4				3	
2	1		11			6	8	7*	S*		9	10			5			4				3	
2	1		11		3	6	8	7*			10	9			5			4	S*				
2	1		11		3	6	8				10	9			5			4			7		U
2	1		11		3	6	8				10	9			5			4			7		U
2	1		11		3*	6	8			S*	10	9			5			4			7		
2	1		11		3	6	8	S*				9			5			4			7*		10
	1		11		3	6	8	S*			10*	9			5			4		2	7		
2	1		11		3	6	8			U	10	9			5			4			7		
2	1		11		3	6	8			U	10	9			5			4			7		
2	1		11		3	6	8	U			10	9			5			4			7		
2	1		11		3	6	8	U			10	9			5			4			7		
2	1		11		3	6*	8	S*			10	9			5			4			7		
2	1		11		3		8	6	S*		10*	9			5			4			7		
2	1		11		3*		8	6		S*	10	9			5			4			7		
2	1		11		3	6	8	10		U		9			5			4			7		
2	1		11		3	6	8	U		10		9			5			4			7		
2	1		11		3	6	8	U			10	9			5			4			7		
2	1		11		3	6	8				10	9	S*		5			4			7*		
2*	1		11		3		8	6	S*		10	9			5			4			7		
2	1		11		3		8	6	U		10	9			5			4			7		
2	1		11		3		8	6	S*		10	9*			5			4			7		
2	1		11		3		8	6			10	9	U		5			4			7		
35	31	15	41	7	43	33	32	32	6	11	30	32	14	4	32	20	3	44		2	21	3	15
							3	3	4	2		5	1			2			2				
			22		1	3	1	3		1	12	11	2	1		1		9			6		8

Blackhall Ray	Bolder Bob	Cox Brian	Curran Terry	Fleming Ian	Grant David	Hornsby Brian	Johnson Jeff	King Jeff	Leman Denis	Lowey John	McCulloch Andy	Mellor Ian	Mullen Jimmy	Owen Gordon	Pickering Mike	Porterfield Ian	Shirtliff Peter	Smith Mark	Sterland Mel	Strutt Brian	Taylor Kevin	Williamson Charlie	Wylde Rodger
2	1		7*	9	3	6		8			10	11			5	S*		4					
2	1		7	9	3	6		8			10	11			5	U		4					
2		1	7	9	3	6		11			10	U	5			8		4					
2		1	7	9		6	U	11			10	3	5			8		4					
4	2	2	4	4	3	4		4			4	3	2		2	2		4					
																1							
			2	1				1										1					

Blackhall Ray	Bolder Bob	Cox Brian	Curran Terry	Fleming Ian	Grant David	Hornsby Brian	Johnson Jeff	King Jeff	Leman Denis	Lowey John	McCulloch Andy	Mellor Ian	Mullen Jimmy	Owen Gordon	Pickering Mike	Porterfield Ian	Shirtliff Peter	Smith Mark	Sterland Mel	Strutt Brian	Taylor Kevin	Williamson Charlie	Wylde Rodger
2	1				3	6		8			10	9		U	4	7		5					11
2	1		11		3		8	10				9	6*		4			5	S*				7
2	2		1		2	1	1	2			1	2	1		2	1		2					2
																			1				
								1			1							1					

League Table

	P	W	D	L	F	A	Pts
Grimsby Town	46	26	10	10	73	42	62
Blackburn Rovers	46	25	9	12	58	36	59
SHEFFIELD WEDNESDAY	46	21	16	9	81	47	58
Chesterfield	46	23	11	12	71	46	57
Colchester United	46	20	12	14	64	56	52
Carlisle United	46	18	12	16	66	56	48
Reading	46	16	16	14	66	65	48
Exeter City	46	19	10	17	60	68	48
Chester	46	17	13	16	49	57	47
Swindon Town	46	19	8	19	71	63	46
Barnsley	46	16	14	16	53	56	46
Sheffield United	46	18	10	18	60	66	46
Rotherham United	46	18	10	18	58	66	46
Millwall	46	16	13	17	65	59	45
Plymouth Argyle	46	16	12	18	59	55	44
Gillingham	46	14	14	18	49	51	42
Oxford United	46	14	13	19	57	62	41
Blackpool	46	15	11	20	62	74	41
Brentford	46	15	11	20	59	73	41
Hull City	46	12	16	18	51	69	40
Bury	46	16	7	23	45	59	39
Southend United	46	14	10	22	47	58	38
Mansfield Town	46	10	16	20	47	58	36
Wimbledon	46	10	14	22	52	81	34

1980-81

Division Two

Manager: Jack Charlton

Did you know that?

Final League Position: 10th

On 19 August in an away game at Bolton. The referee had to replace the ball twice as they deflated.

On April 28 When Paul Shirtliff came on as a substitute against Grimsby Town at Hillsborough to join his brother Peter. It was the first pair of brothers to play for Wednesday Since Jim and Tom McAnearney in April 1959.

Match No.	Date	Venue	Opponents		Round	Result	HT Score	Position	Scorers	Attendance
1	Aug 16	H	Newcastle United	W		2-0	0-0		McCulloch, Taylor	26,164
2	19	A	Bolton Wanderers	D		0-0	0-0			15,926
3	23	A	Notts County	L		0-2	0-1	13th		10,246
4	30	H	Preston North End	W		3-0	2-0	4th	McCulloch (2), King	16,724
5	Sep 6	A	Oldham Athletic	L		0-2	0-1	9th		11,700
6	13	H	Bristol City	W		2-1	1-1	6th	Pearson, King	15,054
7	20	H	Queens Park Pangers	W		1-0	1-0	5th	Pearson	15,195
8	27	A	Swansea City	W		3-2	1-1	8th	Hornsby, Pearson, McCulloch	9,764
9	Oct 4	A	Derby County	L		1-3	0-2	4th	McCulloch	18,554
10	7	H	Blackburn Rovers	W		2-1	2-1	4th	Hornsby, Curran	16,707
11	11	H	Cardiff City	W		2-0	1-0	4th	Hornsby, McCulloch	15,396
12	18	A	Bristol Rovers	D		3-3	2-1	5th	Blackhall, McCulloch, Grant	4,401
13	21	A	Grimsby Town	D		0-0	0-0	6th		10,298
14	25	H	Orient	D		2-2	1-0	6th	McCulloch, Mirocevic	18,018
15	Nov 1	A	Luton Town	L		0-3	0-0	6th		12,092
16	8	H	Wrexham	W		2-1	0-0	6th	Curran (pen + 1)	15,736
17	11	H	Bolton Wanderers	W		2-0	1-0		Jones (og), Curran (pen)	16,262
18	15	A	Newcastle United	L		0-1	0-1	4th		19,161
19	22	A	Chelsea	L		0-2	0-0	4th		24,947
20	29	H	Watford	W		1-0	1-0	4th	McCulloch	14,761
21	Dec 6	A	West Ham United	L		1-2	1-2	6th	Mirocevic	30,476
22	13	H	Bristol Rovers	W		4-1	1-0	6th	Smith, Curran, McCulloch (2)	14,008
23	26	H	Shrewsbury Town	D		1-1	0-0	9th	Pearson	22,863
24	Jan 10	H	Chelsea	D		0-0	0-0	11th		25,113
25	24	A	Cambridge United	W		2-0	2-0	6th	Leman, Sterland	9,231
26	31	H	Notts County	L		1-2	0-1	10th	Mirocevic	22,449
27	Feb 7	A	Bristol City	L		0-1	0-0	10th		11,639
28	14	H	Oldham Athletic	W		3-0	2-0	9th	Curran (2), McCulloch	16,679
29	21	H	Swansea City	W		2-0	1-0	7th	Sterland, McCulloch	17,887
30	28	A	Queens Park Pangers	W		2-1	0-0	3rd	Taylor (2)	15,104
31	Mar 4	A	Cardiff City	D		0-0	0-0	3rd		7,002
32	7	H	Derby County	D		0-0	0-0	3rd		28,301
33	14	A	Blackburn Rovers	L		1-3	0-2	6th	McCulloch	19,222
34	28	A	Orient	L		0-2	0-0	9th		6,561
35	Apr 4	H	Luton Town	W		3-1	1-0	6th	Mirocevic, Curran (2)	17,006
36	11	A	Wrexham	L		0-4	0-1	7th		8,001
37	14	A	Preston North End	L		1-2	0-0	7th	McCulloch	9,537
38	18	H	Cambridge United	W		4-1	0-1	8th	McCulloch (3), Taylor	14,315
39	21	A	Shrewsbury Town	L		0-2	0-1	9th		8,118
40	28	H	Grimsby Town	L		1-2	0-2	9th	Mirocevic	16,747
41	May 2	A	Watford	L		1-2	1-1	10th	Taylor	12,351
42	8	H	West Ham United	L		0-1	0-0	10th		21,087
										Apps
										Subs
									One own-goal	Goals

League Cup

Match No.	Date	Venue	Opponents		Round	Result	HT Score	Position	Scorers	Attendance
43	Aug 9	H	Sheffield United	W	1R 1L	2-0	2-0		Taylor, Johnson	23,989
44	12	A	Sheffield United	D	1R 1L	1-1	0-1		Curran	25,588
45	26	A	Wimbledon	L	2R 1L	1-2	1-2		Owen	3,549
46	Sep 2	H	Wimbledon	W	2R 2L	3-1	1-1		Owen, Grant, Curran	15,151
47	23	H	Watford	L	3R	1-2	0-0		Pearson	14,085
										Apps
										Subs
										Goals

FA Cup

Match No.	Date	Venue	Opponents		Round	Result	HT Score	Position	Scorers	Attendance
48	Jan 3	A	Newcastle United	L	3R	1-2	1-1		Pearson	22,499
										Apps
										Subs
										Goals

Blackhall Ray	Bolder Bob	Campbell Phil	Cox Brian	Curran Terry	Grant David	Hornsby Brian	Johnson Jeff	King Jeff	Leman Denis	Lowey John	Matthewson Trevor	McCulloch Andy	Mellor Ian	Mirocevic Ante	Oliver Gavin	Owen Gordon	Pearson John	Pickering Mike	Shirtliff Paul	Shirtliff Peter	Smith Mark	Sterland Mel	Taylor Kevin	Williamson Charlie
2	1			11			8	6				10	9			U		5			4		7	3
2	1			11			8	6				10	9			U		5			4		7	3
2	1			11			8	6				10	9*			S*		5			4		7	3
2	1			11	3		8	6				10	U			9		5			4		7	
2	1			11	3		8	6					10*		S*	9		5			4		7	
2	1	S*			3		8	6					11			9*	10	5			4		7	
2	1				3		8*	6					11		S*	9	10	5			4		7	
2			1		3	6			9			10	8				11	5			4	U	7	
2			1	11	3	7*		6	9			10					S*	5			4		8	
2			1	11	3	6	8	9				10	S*					5*			4		7	
2	1			11	3	6	8	9	U			10								5	4		7	
2	1			11	3	6	8	9*				10						5			4	S*	7	
2	1			11*	3	6	8					10	S*							5	4	9	7	
2	1				3	6	8					10*	S*	11						5	4	9	7	
2	1			11	3	6	8					10		S*				5			4	9	7*	
2	1			7	3	6	8	9				10	S*	11				5*			4			
2	1			7	3	6	8	9				10	U	11						5	4			
2	1			7	3	6	8	9				10	S*	11*						5	4			
2	1			11			8		9			10		7*			S*			5	4	6		3
2	1			11	3		8		9			10		7			U			5	4	6		
2	1			11	3		8		9			10		7*		S*				5	4	6		
2	1			11	3		8		9*			10		7			S*			5	4	6		
2	1			11	3		8		9			10		7*			S*			5	4	6		
2	1			11	3		8		9			10		U			7			5	4	6		
2	1			11					9			10		U			7			5	4	6	8	3
2	1			11			8		9*			10		S*			7			5	4	6		3
2	1			11	3		8*		9			10		7			S*			5	4	6		
2	1			11	3				9			10		7			S*			5	4	6	8*	
2	1				3*			11	9			10		7			S*			5	4	6	8	
2	1				3			11	9			10		7			U			5	4	6	8	
	1			S*	3			11*	9			10		7						5	4	6	8	2
2	1			11	3			9	U			10		7						5	4	6	8	
2	1			11			S*		9			10		7*						5	4	6	8	3
2	1			11	3	S*	9					10		7						5	4	6	8*	
2	1			11	3	S*	8					10	6	7						5	4		9*	
2	1			11	3		8					10	6	S*						5	4	7*	9	
2	1			11	3		6					10	7				8			5	4	U	9	
2	1			11	3	U	6					10	7	9				5			4		8	
2	1			11	3		6					10	7	9				5*		8	4		S*	
2	1			11	3	9*	8	6				10		7					S*	5		4		
2	1			11	3		6				7	10	S*	9						5	4		8*	
2	1			11	3		6	9*				10	7				S*			5	4		8	
41	39		3	35	35	12	33	20	16		1	39	13	22		4	7	15		28	41	21	29	8
		1		1		2	1						6	3	2	2	8		1			1	1	
1				9	1	3		2	1			18		5			4				1	2	5	

Blackhall Ray	Bolder Bob	Campbell Phil	Cox Brian	Curran Terry	Grant David	Hornsby Brian	Johnson Jeff	King Jeff	Leman Denis	Lowey John	Matthewson Trevor	McCulloch Andy	Mellor Ian	Mirocevic Ante	Oliver Gavin	Owen Gordon	Pearson John	Pickering Mike	Shirtliff Paul	Shirtliff Peter	Smith Mark	Sterland Mel	Taylor Kevin	Williamson Charlie
2	1			11	3		8	6				10				9		5		U	4		7	
2	1			11				6		U		10	9			8		5			4		7	3
2	1			11	3		8	6		9		10			U	7		5			4			
2		U	1	11	3		8	6				10				9		5			4		7	
2			1		3			6*				10	8		S*	9	11	5			4		7	
5	3		2	4	4		3	5		1		5	2			5	1	5			5		4	1
															1									
				2	1		1									2	1						1	

Blackhall Ray	Bolder Bob	Campbell Phil	Cox Brian	Curran Terry	Grant David	Hornsby Brian	Johnson Jeff	King Jeff	Leman Denis	Lowey John	Matthewson Trevor	McCulloch Andy	Mellor Ian	Mirocevic Ante	Oliver Gavin	Owen Gordon	Pearson John	Pickering Mike	Shirtliff Paul	Shirtliff Peter	Smith Mark	Sterland Mel	Taylor Kevin	Williamson Charlie
2	1			11	3*		8		9			10		S*			7			5	4	6		
1	1			1	1		1		1			1					1			1	1	1		
														1										
																	1							

League Table

	P	W	D	L	F	A	Pts
West Ham United	42	28	10	4	79	29	66
Notts County	42	18	17	7	49	38	53
Swansea City	42	18	14	10	64	44	50
Blackburn Rovers	42	16	18	8	42	29	50
Luton Town	42	18	12	12	61	46	48
Derby County	42	15	15	12	57	52	45
Grimsby Town	42	15	15	12	44	42	45
Queen's Park Rangers	42	15	13	14	56	46	43
Watford	42	16	11	15	50	45	43
SHEFFIELD WEDNESDAY	42	17	8	17	53	51	42
Newcastle United	42	14	14	14	30	45	42
Chelsea	42	14	12	16	46	41	40
Cambridge United	42	17	6	19	53	65	40
Shrewsbury Town	42	11	17	14	46	47	39
Oldham Athletic	42	12	15	15	39	48	39
Wrexham	42	12	14	16	43	45	38
Orient	42	13	12	17	52	56	38
Bolton Wanderers	42	14	10	18	61	66	38
Cardiff City	42	12	12	18	44	60	36
Preston North End	42	11	14	17	41	62	36
Bristol City	42	7	16	19	29	51	30
Bristol Rovers	42	5	13	24	34	65	23

1981-82

Division Two

Manager: Jack Charlton

Did you know that?

Final League Position: 4th

Wednesday finished in fourth place in Division Two one point behind promoted Norwich City. The first season when you get 3 points for a win. If it had been still two points for a win, Wednesday would had finished above Norwich to be promoted.

On March 29 1982 Wednesday played at Q.P.R. Loftus Road on their Astroturf artificial surface for the first time in a League game losing 2–0.

Match No.	Date	Venue	Opponents		Round	Result	HT Score	Position	Scorers	Attendance
1	Aug 29	A	Blackburn Rovers	W		1-0	1-0		Curran	14,980
2	Sep 5	H	Crystal Palace	W		1-0	0-0	5th	Bannister	18,476
3	8	H	Rotherham United	W		2-0	1-0	1st	Williamson, McCulloch	26,826
4	12	A	Luton Town	W		3-0	0-0	1st	McCulloch, Megson, Bannister	12,131
5	19	H	Derby County	D		1-1	0-1	1st	Megson	23,764
6	22	A	Barnsley	L		0-1	0-1	1st		28,870
7	26	A	Grimsby Town	W		1-0	0-0	1st	Curran	13,110
8	Oct 3	H	Wrexham	L		0-3	0-1	2nd		18,526
9	10	H	Cardiff City	W		2-1	0-1	3rd	Taylor, McCulloch	15,621
10	17	A	Charlton Athletic	L		0-3	0-2	4th		8,258
11	24	H	Oldham Athletic	W		2-1	0-0	3rd	Bannister, Shirtliff	17,839
12	31	A	Leicester City	D		0-0	0-0	3rd		19,125
13	Nov 7	A	Orient	L		0-3	0-1	4th		5,179
14	14	H	Queens Park Pangers	L		1-3	0-2	6th	Bannister	17,024
15	21	A	Cambridge United	W		2-1	0-1	6th	McCulloch (pen), Bannister	6,461
16	24	H	Barnsley	D		2-2	0-1	6th	McCulloch, Taylor	30,621
17	28	H	Watford	W		3-1	2-0	5th	Pearson, Bannister, Taylor	15,990
18	Dec 5	A	Chelsea	L		1-2	0-1	8th	Bannister	17,033
19	Jan 16	H	Blackburn Rovers	D		2-2	2-0	7th	McCulloch, Megson	13,120
20	19	A	Crystal Palace	W		2-1	1-1	6th	Bannister, Pickering	8,289
21	30	A	Derby County	L		1-3	1-0	8th	Bannister	11,215
22	Feb 3	A	Norwich City	W		3-2	1-1	6th	Bannister (2), Shirtliff	15,767
23	6	H	Luton Town	D		3-3	1-1	7th	Pearson (2), Bannister	18,012
24	13	A	Wrexham	W		1-0	0-0	4th	Bannister	4,907
25	16	H	Bolton Wanderers	L		0-1	0-0	5th		16,555
26	20	H	Grimsby Town	D		1-1	1-1	5th	Bannister (pen)	14,654
27	24	A	Newcastle United	L		0-1	0-1	6th		18,967
28	27	A	Cardiff City	W		2-0	2-0	6th	Bannister (pen), Taylor	5,674
29	Mar 2	H	Shrewsbury Town	D		0-0	0-0	4th		13,254
30	6	H	Charlton Athletic	D		1-1	1-1	5th	Taylor	12,853
31	13	A	Oldham Athletic	W		3-0	1-0	4th	Pearson, Megson, Bannister	9,027
32	20	H	Leicester City	W		2-0	0-0	3rd	Bannister, Pearson	18,962
33	27	H	Orient	W		2-0	0-0	3rd	Taylor, Megson	16,460
34	29	A	Queens Park Pangers	L		0-2	0-1	3rd		11,710
35	Apr 10	A	Shrewsbury Town	W		1-0	0-0	3rd	Bannister	8,103
36	12	H	Newcastle United	W		2-1	2-1	3rd	Shelton, Pearson	29,917
37	17	H	Cambridge United	W		2-1	1-0	3rd	Taylor, Pearson	18,314
38	24	A	Watford	L		0-4	0-4	3rd		23,987
39	May 1	H	Chelsea	D		0-0	0-0	3rd		19,259
40	4	A	Rotherham United	D		2-2	1-1	4th	Bannister (2)	20,513
41	8	A	Bolton Wanderers	L		1-3	1-1	5th	Curran	13,522
42	15	H	Norwich City	W		2-1	0-0	4th	McCulloch, Bannister	24,687

Apps
Subs
Goals

League Cup

43	Oct 7	A	Blackburn Rovers	D	2R 1L	1-1	0-0		Taylor	7,900
44	27	H	Blackburn Rovers	L	2R 2L	1-2	1-2		Bannister	13,099

Apps
Subs
Goals

FA Cup

45	Jan 2	A	Coventry City	L	3R	1-3	1-2		McCulloch	14,213

Apps
Subs
Goals

Bannister Gary	Blackhall Ray	Bolder Bob	Curran Terry	Grant David	Hornsby Brian	King Jeff	Leman Denis	Matthewson Trevor	McCulloch Andy	Megson Gary	Mellor Ian	Mirocevic Ante	Owen Gordon	Pearson John	Pickering Mike	Shelton Gary	Shirtliff Paul	Shirtliff Peter	Simmons Tony	Smith Mark	Sterland Mel	Taylor Kevin	Williamson Charlie
9	2	1	11						10	7		8						5		4	U	6	3
9	2	1	11						10	7	U	8						5		4		6	3
9	2	1	11						10	7	U	8						5		4		6	3
9		1	11				U		10	7		8						5		4	2	6	3
9		1	11						10	7	S*	8*						5		4	2	6	3
9		1	11						10	7	S*	8						5		4	2	6*	3
9	2	1	11	3	U				10	7		8						5		4		6	
9	2	1	11	3					10	7	S*	8						5		4		6*	
9	2	1	11						10	7		8*		S*				5		4		6	3
9	2	1	11						10	7		8*		S*				5		4		6	3
9	2	1	11						10	7				S*				5		4	8*	6	3
9		1	11				U		10	7		8						5		4	2	6	3
9		1	11					U		7		8		10				5		4	2	6	3
9		1	11					4	10	7		8*		S*	5						2	6	3
9		1	11			8		U	10	7					5					4	2	6	3
9		1	11			8			10*	7	S*				5					4	2	6	3
9	2	1	11				8			7	S*			10*				5		4		6	3
9		1	11		S*		8		10*	7								5		4	2	6	3
9		1		3					10	7		8	11	U	4			5		6	2		
9		1		3*					10	7	6	8	11	S*	5					4	2		
9		1							10	7	3	8	11		4			5		6	2	U	
9		1								7	11		S*	10	4		8*	5		6	2		3
9		1								7	11*		S*	10	4		8	5		6	2		3
9		1	U							7	11			10	5		8	4		6	2		3
9		1	S*							7*	11			10	5		8	4		6	2		3
9		1	11								7	U		10	5		8	2		4		6	3
9		1	11							10	7*			S*	5		8	2		4		6	3
9		1	11						10	7				U	5			4		8	2	6	3
9		1	11						10	7				S*	5			4		6*	2	8	3
9		1	11						10	7				S*	5			4		6*	2	8	3
9		1	11						10	7				S*	5			4		6	2*	8	3
9	2	1	11						10*	7		8		S*	5					4		6	3
9	2	1	11*							7		8		10	5	S*				4		6	3
9	2	1	11							7		8*		10	5	S*				4		6	3
9	3	1	11							7				10	5	8		U		4	2	6	
9	3	1	11							7		U		10	5	8				4	2	6	
9	3	1	11							7	U	8		10	5					4	2	6	
9	3	1	11									U		10	5	7		4		8	2	6	
9	3	1	11						10	7				S*	5	8				4	2*	6	
9	2	1	11						10	7				U		8		5		4		6	3
9		1	11						10	7	3		S*			8*		5		4		6	2
9		1	11*						10	7						8		5	S*	4	2	6	3
42	18	42	35	4		2	2	1	28	40	9	20	3	13	24	7	6	31		41	27	35	32
			1		1						5		3	11		2			1				
21			3						7	5				7	1	1		2				7	1

Bannister Gary	Blackhall Ray	Bolder Bob	Curran Terry	Grant David	Hornsby Brian	King Jeff	Leman Denis	Matthewson Trevor	McCulloch Andy	Megson Gary	Mellor Ian	Mirocevic Ante	Owen Gordon	Pearson John	Pickering Mike	Shelton Gary	Shirtliff Paul	Shirtliff Peter	Simmons Tony	Smith Mark	Sterland Mel	Taylor Kevin	Williamson Charlie
9	2	1	11*						10	7	S*	8						5		4		6	3
9	2	1	11						10	7				S*				5		4	8	6*	3
2	2	2	2						2	2		1						2		2	1	2	2
											1			1									
1																						1	

Bannister Gary	Blackhall Ray	Bolder Bob	Curran Terry	Grant David	Hornsby Brian	King Jeff	Leman Denis	Matthewson Trevor	McCulloch Andy	Megson Gary	Mellor Ian	Mirocevic Ante	Owen Gordon	Pearson John	Pickering Mike	Shelton Gary	Shirtliff Paul	Shirtliff Peter	Simmons Tony	Smith Mark	Sterland Mel	Taylor Kevin	Williamson Charlie
9		1	11						10	7	S*	8						5		4	2	6*	3
1		1	1						1	1		1						1		1	1	1	1
											1												
									1														

League Table

	P	W	D	L	F	A	Pts
Luton Town	42	25	13	4	86	46	88
Watford	42	23	11	8	76	42	80
Norwich City	42	22	5	15	64	50	71
SHEFFIELD WEDNESDAY	42	20	10	12	55	51	70
Queen's Park Rangers	42	21	6	15	65	43	69
Barnsley	42	19	10	13	59	41	67
Rotherham United	42	20	7	15	66	54	67
Leicester City	42	18	12	12	56	48	66
Newcastle United	42	18	8	16	52	50	62
Blackburn Rovers	42	16	11	15	47	43	59
Oldham Athletic	42	15	14	13	50	51	59
Chelsea	42	15	12	15	60	60	57
Charlton Athletic	42	13	12	17	50	65	51
Cambridge United	42	13	9	20	48	53	48
Crystal Palace	42	13	9	20	34	45	48
Derby County	42	12	12	18	53	68	48
Grimsby Town	42	11	13	18	53	65	46
Shrewsbury Town	42	11	13	18	37	57	46
Bolton Wanderers	42	13	7	22	39	61	46
Cardiff City	42	12	8	22	45	61	44
Wrexham	42	11	11	20	40	56	44
Orient	42	10	9	23	36	61	39

1982-83

Division Two

Manager: Jack Charlton

Did you know that?

Final League Position: 6th

On 7 September 1982 John Pearson scored after only 13 seconds against Bolton at home, as Wednesday went on to win 3–1.

On 16 April 1983, when Wednesday were to play Brighton in the FA Cup semi-final at Arsenal's Highbury ground, Wednesday left two players – Pat Heard and David Mills – behind in the hotel. Wednesday lost 2–1.

Match No.	Date	Venue	Opponents		Round	Result	HT Score	Position	Scorers	Attendance
1	Aug 28	H	Middlesbrough	W		3-1	0-0		Bannister (pen), Pearson (2)	18,611
2	Sep 4	A	Charlton Athletic	W		3-0	1-0	1st	Taylor, Bannister (pen), Pearson	8,327
3	7	H	Bolton Wanderers	W		3-1	1-0	1st	Pearson (2), Shelton	17,307
4	11	H	Leeds United	L		2-3	0-2	4th	Bannister, Megson	29,050
5	18	A	Queens Park Pangers	W		2-0	1-0	3rd	McCulloch, Bannister	13,733
6	25	H	Chelsea	W		3-2	1-0	3rd	Shelton, Bannister (pen), Smith	18,833
7	28	A	Carlisle United	L		2-4	0-0	3rd	Smith, Owen	6,127
8	Oct 2	A	Blackburn Rovers	W		3-2	1-1	3rd	Bannister (pen + 1), Megson	10,362
9	9	H	Wolverhampton W	D		0-0	0-0	3rd		21,519
10	16	A	Cambridge United	D		2-2	0-0	4th	Bannister (2)	5,677
11	23	H	Grimsby Town	W		2-0	1-0	2nd	Lyons, Shelton	17,904
12	30	A	Leicester City	W		2-0	1-0	1st	Mirocevic, Shelton	17,341
13	Nov 6	H	Derby County	W		2-0	0-0	1st	Bannister (pen + 1)	17,703
14	13	A	Shrewsbury Town	L		0-1	0-0	1st		8,033
15	20	H	Burnley	D		1-1	1-1	3rd	Taylor	16,117
16	27	A	Fulham	L		0-1	0-1	3rd		13,864
17	Dec 4	H	Oldham Athletic	D		1-1	0-0	4th	Bannister	15,096
18	11	A	Crystal Palace	L		0-2	0-2	4th		8,498
19	18	H	Newcastle United	D		1-1	0-1	4th	Haddock (og)	16,310
20	27	A	Barnsley	D		0-0	0-0	4th		23,275
21	28	H	Rotherham United	L		0-1	0-0	5th		25,024
22	Jan 1	A	Burnley	L		1-4	0-2	6th	McCulloch	9,644
23	3	H	Charlton Athletic	W		5-4	1-3	5th	McCulloch (2), Bannister, Gritt (og), Lyons	11,799
24	15	A	Middlesbrough	D		1-1	0-0	4th	Pearson	11,863
25	22	H	Carlisle United	D		1-1	1-1	4th	Taylor	12,874
26	Feb 15	H	Blackburn Rovers	D		0-0	0-0	7th		11,468
27	26	H	Cambridge United	W		3-1	2-0	6th	McCulloch (2) D. Mills	12,815
28	Mar 1	A	Wolverhampton W	L		0-1	0-1	6th		16,656
29	5	A	Grimsby Town	D		1-1	0-0	6th	Pearson	9,472
30	19	A	Derby County	D		0-0	0-0	9th		16,925
31	22	H	Leicester City	D		2-2	0-1	8th	McCulloch, Megson	14,036
32	26	H	Shrewsbury Town	D		0-0	0-0	9th		14,320
33	Apr 2	A	Rotherham United	W		3-0	0-0	7th	Bannister (2), D. Mills	11,250
34	4	H	Barnsley	L		0-1	0-0	9th		22,427
35	9	A	Bolton Wanderers	W		2-0	2-0	6th	Megson, Bannister	6,408
36	19	H	Queens Park Pangers	L		0-1	0-0	9th		11,713
37	23	A	Oldham Athletic	D		1-1	1-1	10th	Bannister	5,088
38	27	A	Leeds United	W		2-1	1-1	6th	Hart (og), Bannister	16,591
39	30	H	Fulham	W		2-1	0-0	6th	D.Mills, Lyons	12,531
40	May 2	A	Chelsea	D		1-1	0-1	6th	Bannister	10,462
41	7	A	Newcastle United	L		1-2	0-0	6th	Heard	29,812
42	14	H	Crystal Palace	W		2-1	1-0	6th	Heard, Bannister	11,154
										Apps
										Subs
									Three own-goals	Goals

League Cup

Match No.	Date	Venue	Opponents		Round	Result	HT Score	Position	Scorers	Attendance
43	Oct 4	A	Bristol City	W	2R 1L	2-1	2-0		Taylor (2)	4,486
44	26	H	Bristol City *	D	2R 2L	1-1	0-0		Taylor	7,920
45	Nov 9	A	Crystal Palace	W	3R	2-1	2-0		Megson, Bannister	8,146
46	30	H	Barnsley	W	4R	1-0	1-0		McCulloch	33,354
47	Jan 18	A	Arsenal	L	5R	0-1	0-0			30,937
										Apps
										Subs
										Goals

* After extra-time. Score at full-time 0-1

FA Cup

Match No.	Date	Venue	Opponents		Round	Result	HT Score	Position	Scorers	Attendance
48	Jan 8	A	Southend United	D	3R	0-0	0-0			6,973
49	11	H	Southend United *	D	3R Re	2-2	1-1		Smith, Megson	11,093
50	24	H	Southend United	W	3R Re	2-1	1-0		Taylor (1 + pen)	10,767
51	29	A	Torquay United	W	4R	3-2	1-1		Lyons, Sterland, Megson	7,823
52	Feb 19	A	Cambridge United	W	5R	2-1	1-0		Megson (2)	10,834
53	Mar 12	A	Burnley	D	6R	1-1	1-0		Bannister	23,134
54	15	H	Burnley	W	6R Re	5-0	3-0		Shelton (2), Megson (pen), McCulloch (2)	41,731
55	Apr 16	N	Brighton & Hove Alb	L	S/F #	1-2	0-1		Mirocevic	54,627
										Apps
										Subs
										Goals

* After extra-time. Score at full-time 1-1
# Played at Highbury, London

Bailey Ian	Bannister Gary	Bolder Bob	Heard Pat	Lyons Mike	Matthewson Trevor	McCulloch Andy	Megson Gary	Mills David	Mills Simon	Mirocevic Ante	Oliver Gavin	Owen Gordon	Pearson John	Pickering Mike	Shelton Gary	Shirtliff Paul	Shirtliff Peter	Simmons Tony	Smith Mark	Sterland Mel	Taylor Kevin	Williamson Charlie
3	10	1		5			8			11			9		6			S*	4	2*	7	
3	9	1		5		U	7			10			11		6		2		4		8	
3	9	1		5		U	7			10			11		6		2		4		8	
3	9	1		5		S*	7*			10			11		6				4	2	8	
3	9	1		5		10	8			11*				S*	6				4	2	7	
3	9	1		5			7					10	11	U	6				4	2	8	
3	9	1		5			8					10	11	S*	6				4	2	7*	
3	9	1		5			8					10	11	U	6				4	2	7	
3	9	1		5			8					10	11	U	6				4	2	7	
3	9	1		5		10	8					11*		S*	6				4	2	7	
3	9	1		5		10	8						11	U	6				4	2	7	
3	9	1		5		10	8			11*				S*	6				4	2	7	
3	9	1		5		10	8			11				U	6				4	2	7	
3	9	1		5			8			11					6	S*		10*	4	2	7	
3	9	1		5		10	8			11				U	6		2		4		7	
3	9	1		5		10	8			11			S*		6*		2		4		7	
3	9	1		5		10	8			6			11						4	2	7	U
3	9	1		5		10	8									6	U		4	2	7	11
3	9	1		5		10	8			11			S*		6				4	2	7*	
3	9	1		5		U	8			10			11		6				4	2	7	
3	9	1		5		S*	8			10*			11		6				4	2	7	
6	9	1		5	3	S*	7			10*			11		8				4	2		
3*	9	1		5		10	7		S*				11		6				4	2	8	
3	9	1	11	5			7					S*	10		6				4	2	8*	
3	9	1	11	5						7		S*	10		6				4	2	8*	
3		1	11	5		10	7	9					S*		6				4	2	8*	
3	9	1	11	5		10	7	8					U		6				4	2		
3	9	1	11	5		10*	7	8					S*		6				4	2		
3	9	1	11	5			7	8					10		6			S*	4	2*		
3		1	11			10*	7	8					S*		6		5		4	2	9	
3		1	11	5		10	7						9		6	U			4	2	8	
3	9	1	11	5		10	7						S*		6*		4			2	8	
3	9	1	11	5		10*	7	8					S*		6				4	2		
3	9	1	11	5		10*	7	8					S*		6				4			2
3*	9	1	11	5		10	7	8							6				4	2	S*	
	9	1	11			10	7	8*			5		S*		6		2		4			3
	9	1	11				7	8			5		10		6		2	U	4			3
	9	1	11	5		10	7	8					U		6				4	2		3
	9	1	11	5		10	7	8					S*		6*				4	2		3
	9	1	11	5		10	7	8					U		6				4	2		3
	9	1	11	5			7	8					10		6			U	4	2		3
	9	1	11	5		10	7	8							6				4	2	U	3
35	39	42	19	39	1	25	41	15		16	2	5	20		40	1	8	1	41	35	28	9
						3			1			2	10	4		1		2			1	
	20		2	3		7	4	3		1		1	7		4				2		3	

Bailey Ian	Bannister Gary	Bolder Bob	Heard Pat	Lyons Mike	Matthewson Trevor	McCulloch Andy	Megson Gary	Mills David	Mills Simon	Mirocevic Ante	Oliver Gavin	Owen Gordon	Pearson John	Pickering Mike	Shelton Gary	Shirtliff Paul	Shirtliff Peter	Simmons Tony	Smith Mark	Sterland Mel	Taylor Kevin	Williamson Charlie
3	9	1		5			7*					10		S*	6			11	4	2	8	
3	9	1		5		10	7					11		S*		6*			4	2	8	
3	9	1		5		10*	7			11				4	6		S*			2	8	
3	9	1		5		10	7			6			11						4	2	8	U
3	9	1		5			7			11*			10		6		S*		4	2	8	
5	5	5		5		3	5			3		2	2	1	3	1		1	4	5	5	
														2			2					
	1					1	1														3	

Bailey Ian	Bannister Gary	Bolder Bob	Heard Pat	Lyons Mike	Matthewson Trevor	McCulloch Andy	Megson Gary	Mills David	Mills Simon	Mirocevic Ante	Oliver Gavin	Owen Gordon	Pearson John	Pickering Mike	Shelton Gary	Shirtliff Paul	Shirtliff Peter	Simmons Tony	Smith Mark	Sterland Mel	Taylor Kevin	Williamson Charlie
	9	1		5	3	10	7		U				11		6				4	2	8	
	9	1		5	3	10*	7			S*			11		6		2		4		8	
3	9	1		5					7	11			10		6			U	4	2	8	
3	9	1	11	5		10	7						S*		6				4	2	8*	
3		1	11	5		10	7	8					9		6				4	2	U	
3	9*	1	11	5		10	7	8					S*		6				4	2		
3		1	11			10	7	8					U		6		5		4	2	9	
	9	1	3	5		10	7	8		11					6		U		4	2		
5	6	8	5	7	2	7	7	4	1	2			4		8		2		8	7	5	
										1			2									
	1			1		2	5			1					2				1	1	2	

League Table

	P	W	D	L	F	A	Pts
Queen's Park Rangers	42	26	7	9	77	36	85
Wolverhampton W.	42	20	15	7	68	44	75
Leicester City	42	20	10	12	72	44	70
Fulham	42	20	9	13	64	47	69
Newcastle United	42	18	13	11	75	53	67
SHEFFIELD WEDNESDAY	42	16	15	11	60	47	63
Oldham Athletic	42	14	19	9	64	47	61
Leeds United	42	13	21	8	51	46	60
Shrewsbury Town	42	15	14	13	48	48	59
Barnsley	42	14	15	13	57	55	57
Blackburn Rovers	42	15	12	15	58	58	57
Cambridge United	42	13	12	17	42	60	51
Derby County	42	10	19	13	49	58	49
Carlisle United	42	12	12	18	68	70	48
Crystal Palace	42	12	12	18	43	52	48
Middlesbrough	42	11	15	16	46	67	48
Charlton Athletic	42	13	9	20	63	86	48
Chelsea	42	11	14	17	51	61	47
Grimsby Town	42	12	11	19	45	70	47
Rotherham United	42	10	15	17	45	68	45
Burnley	42	12	8	22	56	66	44
Bolton Wanderers	42	11	11	20	42	61	44

1983-84

Division Two

Manager: Howard Wilkinson

Did you know that?

Final League Position: 2nd

Wednesday started the season by going undefeated in 15 League games and three League Cup ties until they lost to Crystal Palace 1–0, on 26 November 1983.

On 11 March 1984 the Sunday FA Cup game against Southampton was the first home Owls game to be shown live on television and ended 0–0.

Match No.	Date	Venue	Opponents		Round	Result	HT Score	Position	Scorers	Attendance
1	Aug 27	A	Swansea City	W		1-0	1-0	1st	Lyons	10,900
2	29	A	Derby County	D		1-1	0-1	1st	Bannister	10,241
3	Sep 3	H	Carlisle United	W		2-0	1-0	1st	O'Riordan (og), Bannister	14,544
4	6	H	Cambridge United	W		1-0	1-0	1st	Varadi	14,947
5	10	A	Charlton Athletic	D		1-1	1-1	1st	Dowman (og)	6,904
6	17	H	Chelsea	W		2-1	0-1	1st	Lyons, Megson	20,596
7	24	A	Oldham Athletic	W		3-1	1-1	1st	Varadi, Shelton, Sterland	9,269
8	Oct 1	H	Blackburn Rovers	W		4-2	1-1	1st	Sterland, Bannister, Lyons, Varadi	16,849
9	8	H	Leeds United	W		3-1	1-0	1st	Shelton, Pearson, Morris	26,814
10	15	A	Portsmouth	W		1-0	0-0	1st	Megson	16,335
11	22	A	Brighton & Hove Alb	W		3-1	2-0	1st	Pearson, Madden, Bannister	14,827
12	29	H	Huddersfield Town	D		0-0	0-0	1st		27,824
13	Nov 5	H	Barnsley	W		2-0	1-0	1st	Smith, Sterland (pen)	27,491
14	11	A	Fulham	D		1-1	1-0	1st	Cunningham	9,687
15	19	H	Newcastle United	W		4-2	1-1	1st	Varadi (2), Cunningham, Bannister	41,134
16	26	A	Crystal Palace	L		0-1	0-0	1st		11,263
17	Dec 3	H	Shrewsbury Town	D		1-1	1-0	1st	Varadi	17,703
18	10	A	Manchester City	W		2-1	1-1	1st	Varadi (2)	41,862
19	17	H	Cardiff City	W		5-2	3-0	1st	Varadi (2), Shelton, Bannister, Lyons,	14,580
20	26	A	Grimsby Town	L		0-1	0-0	1st		16,197
21	27	H	Middlesbrough	L		0-2	0-2	1st		24,818
22	31	A	Carlisle United	D		1-1	0-0	2nd	Megson	10,475
23	Jan 2	H	Oldham Athletic	W		3-0	0-0	1st	Varadi, Cunningham, Bannister	18,690
24	14	H	Swansea City	W		6-1	3-0	1st	Lyons, Pearson, Toshack (og) Megson,Heard. Varadi	13,787
25	21	A	Chelsea	L		2-3	0-2	2nd	Smith, Bannister	35,147
26	Feb 4	A	Blackburn Rovers	D		0-0	0-0	2nd		16,158
27	11	H	Charlton Athletic	W		4-1	1-0	2nd	Bannister, Shirtliff, Cunningham,Varadi	18,510
28	25	H	Brighton & Hove Alb	W		2-1	1-0	1st	Bannister, Varadi	21,614
29	Mar 3	A	Barnsley	W		1-0	1-0	2nd	Sterland (pen)	20,322
30	7	H	Fulham	D		1-1	0-0	2nd	Pearson	20,440
31	17	A	Cambridge United	W		2-1	1-0	2nd	Bannister, Varadi	5,562
32	31	A	Leeds United	D		1-1	0-0	2nd	Bannister	25,343
33	Apr 7	H	Portsmouth	W		2-0	1-0	1st	Shelton, Sterland	20,239
34	10	H	Derby County	W		3-1	1-0	1st	Varadi (2), Sterland (pen)	21,792
35	14	A	Newcastle United	W		1-0	0-0	1st	Shelton	36,725
36	21	H	Grimsby Town	W		1-0	0-0	1st	Sterland (pen)	25,828
37	25	A	Middlesbrough	L		0-2	0-1	1st		12,362
38	28	H	Crystal Palace	W		1-0	0-0	1st	Sterland (pen)	27,287
39	May 1	A	Huddersfield Town	W		1-0	0-0	1st	Worthington	18,488
40	5	A	Shrewsbury Town	L		1-2	0-0	1st	Bannister	7,885
41	7	H	Manchester City	D		0-0	0-0	2nd		36,763
42	12	A	Cardiff City	W		2-0	0-0	2nd	Bannister, Cunningham	14,171
										Apps
										Subs
									Three own-goals	Goals

League Cup

Match No.	Date	Venue	Opponents		Round	Result	HT Score	Position	Scorers	Attendance
43	Oct 4	H	Darlington	W	2R 1L	3-0	3-0		Bannister, Morris, Madden	9,060
44	25	A	Darlington	W	2R 2L	4-2	0-1		Madden, Shelton, Bannister (2)	3,615
45	Nov 8	A	Preston North End	W	3R	2-0	1-0		Varadi, Shelton	11,060
46	30	A	Stoke City	W	4R	1-0	0-0		Bannister	18,653
47	Jan 17	H	Liverpool	D	5R	2-2	1-1		Megson, Bannister	49,357
48	25	A	Liverpool	L	5R Re	0-3	0-1			40,485
										Apps
										Subs
										Goals

FA Cup

Match No.	Date	Venue	Opponents		Round	Result	HT Score	Position	Scorers	Attendance
49	Jan 7	H	Barnsley	W	3R	1-0	1-0		Pearson	29,638
50	30	H	Coventry City	W	4R	3-2	1-2		Shirtliff, Bannister, Sterland (pen)	26,154
51	Feb 18	A	Oxford United	W	5R	3-0	2-0		Varadi, Bannister (2)	14,167
52	Mar 11	H	Southampton	D	6R	0-0	0-0			43,030
53	20	A	Southampton	L	6R Re	1-5	1-2		Shirtliff	20,590
										Apps
										Subs
										Goals

Bannister Gary	Cunningham Tony	Heard Pat	Hodge Martin	Lyons Mike	Madden Lawrie	Megson Gary	Mills Simon	Morris Chris	Oliver Gavin	Pearson John	Shelton Gary	Shirtliff Peter	Smith Mark	Sterland Mel	Taylor Kevin	Varadi Imre	Williamson Charlie	Worthington Nigel
9			1	5	6	8		7		10*	11	4		2		S*	3	
9			1	5	6	8		7*		10	11	4		2		S*	3	
8			1	5	6	7		U		10	11	4		2		9	3	
8*			1	5	6	7		S*		10	11	4		2		9	3	
8*			1	5	6	7		S*		10	11	4	3	2		9		
8			1	5	6	7		U		10	11		4	2		9	3	
8*			1	5	6	7		S*		10	11		4	2		9	3	
8			1	5	6	7				10	11*		4	2	S*	9	3	
8			1	5	6	7		9		10	11		4	2	U		3	
8			1	5	6	7		9	S*	10*	11	3	4	2				
8			1	5	6	7		9		10*	11	3	4	2	S*			
8			1	5	6	7		10			11	3	4	2		9	U	
8			1	5	6	7		10*			11	3	4	2	S*	9		
8	10		1	5	6	7					11	3	4	2	U	9		
8	10		1	5	6	7		U			11	3	4	2		9		
8	10		1	5	6	7		S*			11	3	4	2*		9		
8		11	1	5	6	7		U		10		3	4	2		9		
8	10		1	5	6	7				U	11	3	4	2		9		
8	10		1	5	6	7		S*			11	3	4	2		9*		
8	10	S*	1	5	6*	7					11	3	4	2		9		
	10	S*	1	5	6	7		8			11	3	4*	2		9		
8	10		1	5	6	7				U	11	3	4	2		9		
8	10	S*	1	5	6	7					11	3	4*	2		9		
8	10*	11	1	5	6	7				9		3	4	2		S*		
8	S*		1	5	6	7				10	11	3	4	2		9*		
8	10*		1	5	6	7			3	S*	11		4	2		9		
8	10		1	5	6	7				U	11	3	4	2		9		
8	10		1	5		7				S*	11	3	4	2		9*		6
8	10		1	5		7*				9	11	3	4	2	S*			6
8	10		1	5		7*				S*	11	3	4	2		9		6
8	10*		1	5	4	7				S*	11	3		2		9		6
8	10		1	5		7			4	U	11				3	9	2	6
8*	10		1	5	4	7				S*	11	3		2		9		6
	10		1	5	4	7		U		8	11	3		2		9		6
	10*		1	5	6	7			S*	8	11	3	4	2		9		
	10		1	5	6	7			S*	8	11	3		2*		9		4
	10		1	5	4	7			U	8	11	3		2		9		6
S*	10*		1	5	4	7				8	11	3		2		9		6
10	S*		1	5	4	7				8	11	3		2*		9		6
8	10		1	5	4	7	S*		2		11	3*				9		6
8	10		1	5	6	7	2				11*	4				9	S*	3
8	10		1	5	6	7				S*	11	4		2		9*		3
36	26	2	42	42	38	42	1	8	3	21	40	36	27	39	1	35	9	14
1	2	3					1	5	3	6					4	3	1	
14	5	1		5	1	4		1		4	5	1	2	8		17		1

Bannister Gary	Cunningham Tony	Heard Pat	Hodge Martin	Lyons Mike	Madden Lawrie	Megson Gary	Mills Simon	Morris Chris	Oliver Gavin	Pearson John	Shelton Gary	Shirtliff Peter	Smith Mark	Sterland Mel	Taylor Kevin	Varadi Imre	Williamson Charlie	Worthington Nigel
8			1	5	6	7		9*		10	11	2	4		S*		3	
8			1	5	6	7		10	S*		11	3	4	2		9*		
8			1	5	6	7		10			11*	3	4	2	S*	9		
8		11	1	5	6	7		10*		S*		3	4	2		9		
8		U	1	5	6	7				10	11	3	4	2		9		
8			1	5	6	7			U	10	11	3	4	2		9		
6		1	6	6	6	6		4		3	5	6	6	5		5	1	
									1	1					2			
5					2	1		1			2					1		

Bannister Gary	Cunningham Tony	Heard Pat	Hodge Martin	Lyons Mike	Madden Lawrie	Megson Gary	Mills Simon	Morris Chris	Oliver Gavin	Pearson John	Shelton Gary	Shirtliff Peter	Smith Mark	Sterland Mel	Taylor Kevin	Varadi Imre	Williamson Charlie	Worthington Nigel
8	10	11	1	5	6	7		S*		9*		3	4	2				
8	S*		1	5	6	7				10	11	3*	4	2		9		
8	10*		1	5	6	7				S*	11	3	4	2		9		
8	10		1	5	6					S*	11	3	4	2	7	9*		
8	10*		1	5	6	7			4	S*	11	3		2		9		
5	4	1	5	5	5	4			1	2	4	5	4	5	1	4		
	1							1		3								
3										1		2		1		1		

League Table

	P	W	D	L	F	A	Pts
Chelsea	42	25	13	4	90	40	88
SHEFFIELD WEDNESDAY	42	26	10	6	72	34	88
Newcastle United	42	24	8	10	85	53	80
Manchester City	42	20	10	12	66	48	70
Grimsby Town	42	19	13	10	60	47	70
Blackburn Rovers	42	17	16	9	57	46	67
Carlisle United	42	16	16	10	48	41	64
Shrewsbury Town	42	17	10	15	49	53	61
Brighton & Hove Albion	42	17	9	16	69	60	60
Leeds United	42	16	12	14	55	56	60
Fulham	42	15	12	15	60	53	57
Huddersfield Town	42	14	15	13	56	49	57
Charlton Athletic	42	16	9	17	53	64	57
Barnsley	42	15	7	20	57	53	52
Cardiff City	42	15	6	21	53	66	51
Portsmouth	42	14	7	21	73	64	49
Middlesbrough	42	12	13	17	41	47	49
Crystal Palace	42	12	11	19	42	52	47
Oldham Athletic	42	13	8	21	47	73	47
Derby County	42	11	9	22	36	72	42
Swansea City	42	7	8	27	36	85	29
Cambridge United	42	4	12	26	28	77	24

1984-85

Division One

Manager: Howard Wilkinson

Did you know that?

Final League Position: 8th

On 8 December 1984 Wednesday drew at home 1–1 with Chelsea in their 2,000th First Division game.

In November 1984 Andy Blair scored three penalties as Wednesday beat Luton Town 4–2 in a League Cup game at Hillsborough.

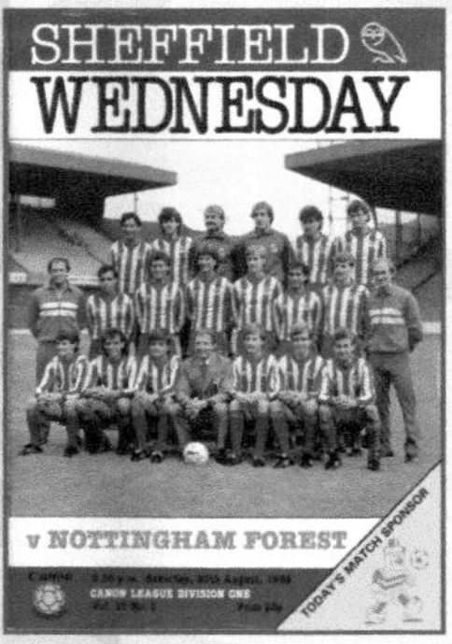

Match No.	Date	Venue	Opponents		Round	Result	HT Score	Position	Scorers	Attendance
1	Aug 25	H	Nottingham Forest	W		3-1	1-1		Sterland (pen), Varadi, Pearson	31,925
2	27	A	Newcastle United	L		1-2	1-1		Chapman	29,700
3	Sep 1	A	Stoke City	L		1-2	0-2	13th	Worthington	13,032
4	4	H	Southampton	W		2-1	1-0	8th	Varadi, Shelton	23,784
5	8	H	Tottenham Hotspur	W		2-1	2-1	4th	Varadi, Marwood	33,421
6	15	A	West Bromwich Alb	D		2-2	0-1	5th	Varadi, Shelton	16,439
7	22	H	Ipswich Town	D		2-2	0-1	5th	Marwood, Chapman	25,558
8	29	A	Liverpool	W		2-0	1-0	5th	Varadi, Shelton	40,196
9	Oct 6	H	Sunderland	D		2-2	2-0	4th	Chapman, Marwood	27,766
10	13	A	Luton Town	W		2-1	1-0	3rd	Chapman, Lyons	10,285
11	20	H	Leicester City	W		5-0	2-0	2nd	Varadi (3), Blair, Ryan	23,621
12	27	A	Coventry City	L		0-1	0-1	4th		14,348
13	Nov 3	H	Norwich City	L		1-2	0-1	6th	Sterland	21,847
14	10	A	Queen's Park Rangers	D		0-0	0-0	5th		13,390
15	17	A	Watford	L		0-1	0-1	7th		18,346
16	25	H	Arsenal	W		2-1	1-0	6th	Chapman, Smith	25,575
17	Dec 1	A	Everton	D		1-1	1-1	7th	Blair	35,440
18	8	H	Chelsea	D		1-1	0-0	8th	Varadi	29,373
19	15	A	West Ham United	D		0-0	0-0	7th		14,896
20	22	H	Stoke City	W		2-1	1-1	7th	Varadi, Chapman	19,799
21	26	H	Aston Villa	D		1-1	0-1	9th	Lyons	30,971
22	29	A	Southampton	W		3-0	1-0	6th	Chapman (2), Varadi	18,922
23	Jan 1	A	Manchester United	W		2-1	1-0	5th	Varadi (2)	47,638
24	12	H	West Bromwich Alb	W		2-0	1-0	4th	Chapman, Varadi	24,345
25	Feb 2	H	Liverpool	D		1-1	0-0	5th	Marwood	48,246
26	24	H	Watford	D		1-1	0-1	5th	Lyons	27,871
27	Mar 2	H	Coventry City	W		1-0	1-0	4th	Pearson	20,422
28	9	A	Leicester City	L		1-3	1-0	5th	Varadi	14,037
29	16	H	Luton Town	D		1-1	1-0	6th	Varadi	18,856
30	20	A	Nottingham Forest	D		0-0	0-0	6th		17,648
31	30	H	Newcastle United	W		4-2	2-1	5th	Marwood, Chapman (2), Shelton	26,525
32	Apr 3	A	Norwich City	D		1-1	1-1	5th	Haylock (og)	15,138
33	6	A	Aston Villa	L		0-3	0-1	6th		18,308
34	9	H	Manchester United	W		1-0	1-0	5th	Chapman	39,380
35	13	A	Ipswich Town	W		2-1	1-0	5th	Marwood (pen), Cooper (og)	16,268
36	16	A	Sunderland	D		0-0	0-0	6th		16,119
37	23	H	Queen's Park Rangers	W		3-1	1-0	6th	Stainrod, Marwood (pen), Blair	22,394
38	27	A	Arsenal	L		0-1	0-0	5th		23,803
39	May 4	H	Everton	L		0-1	0-1	6th		37,381
40	6	A	Chelsea	L		1-2	1-1	7th	Smith	17,085
41	11	H	West Ham United	W		2-1	2-0	7th	Chapman (2)	24,314
42	14	A	Tottenham Hotspur	L		0-2	0-1	8th		15,679
										Apps
										Subs
									Two own-goals	Goals

League Cup

Match No.	Date	Venue	Opponents		Round	Result	HT Score	Position	Scorers	Attendance
43	Sep 25	H	Huddersfield Town	W	2R 1L	3-0	1-0		Sterland (pen), Marwood, Chapman	16,139
44	Oct 9	A	Huddersfield Town	L	2R 2L	1-2	1-1		Sterland	7,163
45	30	H	Fulham	W	3R	3-2	1-1		Marwood, Lyons, Varadi	15,665
46	Nov 20	H	Luton Town	W	4R	4-2	2-0		Blair (3 pens), Marwood	18,313
47	Jan 28	A	Chelsea	D	5R	1-1	1-1		Madden	36,028
48	30	H	Chelsea *	D	5R Re	4-4	3-0		Lyons, Chapman, Marwood, Sterland (pen)	36,509
49	Feb 6	A	Chelsea	L	5R Re	1-2	1-1		Shelton	36,395
										Apps
										Subs
										Goals

* After extra-time. Score at full-time 4-4

FA Cup

Match No.	Date	Venue	Opponents		Round	Result	HT Score	Position	Scorers	Attendance
50	Jan 5	A	Fulham	W	3R	3-2	2-1		Sterland, Chapman (2)	11,433
51	26	H	Oldham Athletic	W	4R	5-1	2-0		Varadi (3), Chapman, Marwood	24,006
52	Mar 4	A	Ipswich Town	L	5R	2-3	1-0		Varadi, Lyons	17,459
										Apps
										Subs
										Goals

Blair Andy	Chapman Lee	Heard Pat	Hodge Martin	Jonsson Siggi	Lyons Mike	Madden Lawrie	Marwood Brian	Mills Simon	Morris Chris	Oliver Gavin	Pearson John	Ryan John	Shelton Gary	Shirtliff Peter	Smith Mark	Stainrod Simon	Sterland Mel	Varadi Imre	Worthington Nigel
8	10		1		5*		7				S*		11	3	4		2	9	6
8	10		1			5	7*				S*		11	3	4		2	9	6
8	10		1			5	7				S*		11	3*	4		2	9	6
8	10		1			5	7*		S*				11	3	4		2	9	6
8	10		1			5	7*		S*				11	3	4		2	9	6
8	10		1		5		7*	S*					11	3	4		2	9	6
8	10	11	1		5		7				S*			3	4*		2	9	6
8	10		1		5	S*	7					6*	11	3	4		2	9	
8	10		1		5		7				S*	6	11	3*	4		2	9	
8	10		1		5		7			3*		6	11		4		2	9	S*
8	10		1		5		7					S*	11*	3	4		2	9	6
8	10		1		5		7				U		11	3	4		2	9	6
8	10		1		5		7				S*		11	3	4		2	9	6*
8	10		1		5		U			2	7		11	3	4			9	6
8	10		1		5		7			2	U		11	3	4			9	6
8	10		1		5		7*			2		S*	11	3	4			9	6
8	10		1		5		7*			2		S*	11	3	4			9	6
8	10		1		5		7			2	U		11	3	4			9	6
8	10		1		5		7			2			11*	3	4		S*	9	6
8	10*		1		5	4	7			2			11	3			S*	9	6
8	10		1		5	4	7			2*			11	3			S*	9	6
8	10		1		5	4	7			U			11	3			2	9	6
8	10		1		5	4	7			U			11	3			2	9	6
8	10		1		5	4	7		U				11	3			2	9	6
8	10		1		5	4	7*			S*			11	3			2	9	6
8	10		1		5	3	7		U				11		4		2	9	6
8			1		5	3	7		U		10		11		4		2	9	6
	10		1	8	5	3	7						11	2	4	U		9	6
3	10		1	8	5*		7		S*				11	2	4			9	6
8	10		1			5	7		3				11	2	4	U		9	6
8	10		1		5		7		3				11	2	4	U		9	6
8	10		1		5		7*		3				11	2	4	S*		9	6
8	10		1	U	5		7		3				11	2	4	9			6
8	10		1	S*	5		7*		3				11	2	4	9			6
8	10		1		5		7	S*	3				11	2	4	9*			6
8	10		1		5		7	U	3				11	2	4	9			6
8	10		1		5		7		3				11	2	4	9*		S*	6
8	10		1		5		7		3				11	2	4	U		9	6
8	10		1		5	6	7*		3			2	11		4	S*		9	
8			1		5	6	7*		3		10	2	11		4	S*		9	
8	10		1	U	5	6	7						11		4		2	9	3
8	10		1		5	3	7						11		4	S*	2	9*	6
41	40	1	42	2	37	18	41		11	9	3	5	41	35	36	5	21	37	37
				1		1		2	3	1	6	3				4	3	1	1
3	14				3		7				2	1	4		2	1	2	16	1

Blair Andy	Chapman Lee	Heard Pat	Hodge Martin	Jonsson Siggi	Lyons Mike	Madden Lawrie	Marwood Brian	Mills Simon	Morris Chris	Oliver Gavin	Pearson John	Ryan John	Shelton Gary	Shirtliff Peter	Smith Mark	Stainrod Simon	Sterland Mel	Varadi Imre	Worthington Nigel
8	10	11	1		5		7		S*					3	4		2	9	6*
8	10*		1		5		7		S*	3	9	6	11		4		2		
8	10*		1		5		7				S*		11	3	4		2	9	6
8	10		1		5*		7		S*	2			11	3	4			9	6
8	10		1		5	4	7*			S*			11	3			2	9	6
8	10*		1		5	4	7			S*			11	3			2	9	6
8	10		1		5	4	7		S*				11	3			2	9*	6
7	7	1	7		7	3	7			2	1	1	6	6	4		6	6	6
									4	2	1								
3	2				2	1	4						1				3	1	

Blair Andy	Chapman Lee	Heard Pat	Hodge Martin	Jonsson Siggi	Lyons Mike	Madden Lawrie	Marwood Brian	Mills Simon	Morris Chris	Oliver Gavin	Pearson John	Ryan John	Shelton Gary	Shirtliff Peter	Smith Mark	Stainrod Simon	Sterland Mel	Varadi Imre	Worthington Nigel
8	10		1		5	4	7		U	3			11				2	9	6
8	10		1		5		7			S*			11*	3	4		2	9	6
8*			1		5	3	7				10		11	S*	4		2	9	6
3	2		3		3	2	3			1	1		3	1	2		3	3	3
										1				1					
	3				1		1										1	4	

League Table

	P	W	D	L	F	A	Pts
Everton	42	28	6	8	88	43	90
Liverpool	42	22	11	9	68	35	77
Tottenham Hotspur	42	23	8	11	78	51	77
Manchester United	42	22	10	10	77	47	76
Southampton	42	19	11	12	56	47	68
Chelsea	42	18	12	12	63	48	66
Arsenal	42	19	9	14	61	49	66
SHEFFIELD WEDNESDAY	42	17	14	11	58	45	65
Nottingham Forest	42	19	7	16	56	48	64
Aston Villa	42	15	11	16	60	60	56
Watford	42	14	13	15	81	71	55
West Bromwich Albion	42	16	7	19	58	62	55
Luton Town	42	15	9	18	57	61	54
Newcastle United	42	13	13	16	55	70	52
Leicester City	42	15	6	21	65	73	51
West Ham United	42	13	12	17	51	68	51
Ipswich Town	42	13	11	18	46	57	50
Coventry City	42	15	5	22	47	64	50
Queen's Park Rangers	42	13	11	18	53	72	50
Norwich City	42	13	10	19	46	64	49
Sunderland	42	10	10	22	40	62	40
Stoke City	42	3	8	31	24	91	17

1985-86

Division One

Manager: Howard Wilkinson

Did you know that?

Final League Position: 5th

On 3 May 1986 Wednesday's home game against Ipswich Town was the last League game to be played in front of an uncovered Kop. Wednesday won 1–0.

Match No.	Date	Venue	Opponents		Round	Result	HT Score	Position	Scorers	Attendance
1	Aug 17	H	Chelsea	D		1-1	1-1		Lyons	26,164
2	21	A	Nottingham Forest	W		1-0	1-0		Stainrod	18,367
3	24	A	Manchester City	W		3-1	1-0	2nd	Thompson, Marwood (2)	26,934
4	26	H	Watford	W		2-1	1-0	2nd	Sterland, Chapman	21,962
5	31	A	Oxford United	W		1-0	0-0	2nd	Jonsson	9,334
6	Sep 3	H	Everton	L		1-5	1-1	3rd	Marwood (pen)	30,065
7	7	H	West Ham United	D		2-2	1-1	3rd	Chapman, Thompson	19,287
8	14	A	Arsenal	L		0-1	0-1	7th		23,108
9	21	A	Tottenham Hotspur	L		1-5	1-1	9th	Chapman	23,601
10	28	H	Luton Town	W		3-2	2-1	7th	Marwood (1 + pen), Chapman	17,887
11	Oct 5	A	Birmingham City	W		2-0	1-0	6th	Sterland, Armstrong (og)	11,708
12	12	H	Coventry City	D		2-2	2-0	5th	Chapman, Shutt	19,132
13	19	A	Leicester City	W		3-2	1-0	5th	Marwood, Jonsson, Chapman	10,259
14	26	H	West Bromwich Alb	W		1-0	1-0	3rd	Chapman	19,873
15	Nov 2	A	Queen's Park Rangers	D		1-1	0-0	3rd	Snodin	12,123
16	9	H	Manchester United	W		1-0	0-0	3rd	Chapman	48,105
17	16	A	Aston Villa	D		1-1	1-1	5th	Hart	13,849
18	23	H	Southampton	W		2-1	1-0	5th	Chapman, Marwood	18,955
19	30	A	Ipswich Town	L		1-2	1-1	5th	Yallop (og)	12,918
20	Dec 7	H	Nottingham Forest	W		2-1	0-0	5th	Marwood, Chamberlain	22,495
21	14	A	Chelsea	L		1-2	0-1	5th	Marwood (pen)	19,658
22	21	H	Manchester City	W		3-2	3-1	5th	Thompson, Megson, Sterland	23,177
23	26	H	Newcastle United	D		2-2	1-0	6th	Marwood, Thompson	30,269
24	28	A	Everton	L		1-3	0-2	6th	Thompson	41,536
25	Jan 1	A	Liverpool	D		2-2	1-0	6th	Shutt, Thompson	38,964
26	18	H	Oxford United	W		2-1	1-0	6th	Shotton (og), Marwood	18,565
27	Feb 1	A	Watford	L		1-2	0-1	8th	Megson	13,144
28	22	H	Tottenham Hotspur	L		1-2	1-0	9th	Thompson	22,232
29	Mar 1	A	Luton Town	L		0-1	0-1	9th		10,206
30	8	H	Birmingham City	W		5-1	3-0	8th	Shutt (3), Chapman, Chamberlain	17,491
31	15	A	Coventry City	W		1-0	0-0	6th	Sterland	10,168
32	18	H	Leicester City	W		1-0	1-0	6th	Sterland	18,874
33	22	A	West Ham United	L		0-1	0-1	6th		16,604
34	29	H	Liverpool	D		0-0	0-0	7th		37,946
35	31	A	Newcastle United	L		1-4	0-3	7th	Shutt	25,614
36	Apr 8	H	Queen's Park Rangers	D		0-0	0-0	10th		13,157
37	13	A	Manchester United	W		2-0	0-0	9th	Shutt, Sterland (pen)	32,331
38	16	H	Arsenal	W		2-0	1-0	6th	Sterland (pen), Shutt	16,344
39	19	H	Aston Villa	W		2-0	1-0	6th	Megson, Sterland	19,782
40	22	A	West Bromwich Alb	D		1-1	1-0	6th	Marwood	6,201
41	26	A	Southampton	W		3-2	1-0	6th	Shutt, Shelton, Hart	15,375
42	May 3	H	Ipswich Town	W		1-0	0-0	5th	Marwood	22,369
										Apps
										Subs
									Three own-goals	Goals

League Cup

Match No.	Date	Venue	Opponents		Round	Result	HT Score	Position	Scorers	Attendance
43	Sep 25	A	Brentford	D	2R 1L	2-2	0-1		Chapman (2)	5,352
44	Oct 15	H	Brentford	W	2R 2L	2-0	1-0		Sterland (pen), Chapman	11,132
45	29	A	Swindon Town	L	3R	0-1	0-1			12,110
										Apps
										Subs
										Goals

FA Cup

Match No.	Date	Venue	Opponents		Round	Result	HT Score	Position	Scorers	Attendance
47	Jan 13	H	West Bromwich Alb	D	3R	2-2	1-1		Sterland, Smith	17,042
48	16	A	West Bromwich Alb	W	3R Re	3-2	2-1		Marwood (pen), Chapman, Chamberlain	11,152
49	25	H	Orient	W	4R	5-0	3-0		Thompson, Chapman, Sterland, Blair, Marwood	19,087
50	Feb 26	A	Derby County	D	5R	1-1	1-1		Christie (og)	22,781
51	Mar 5	H	Derby County	W	5R Re	2-0	1-0		Shutt (2)	29,077
52	12	H	West Ham United	W	6R	2-1	2-0		Worthington, Shutt	35,522
53	Apr 5	N	Everton * #	L	S/F	1-2	0-0		Shutt	47,711
										Apps
										Subs
									One own-goal	Goals

* At Villa Park, Birmingham

After extra-time. Score at full-time 1-1

Blair Andy	Chamberlain Mark	Chapman Lee	Gregory Tony	Hart Paul	Hodge Martin	Jonsson Siggi	Knight Ian	Lyons Mike	Madden Lawrie	Marwood Brian	Megson Gary	Morris Chris	Shelton Gary	Shirtliff Peter	Shutt Carl	Smith Mark	Snodin Glynn	Stainrod Simon	Sterland Mel	Thompson Garry	Worthington Nigel
8*		9		6	1			5		7			11	4				S*	2	10	3
		10*		6	1	8		5		7			11	4				9	2	S*	3
		S*	11	6	1	8		5		7				4				9*	2	10	3
		S*	11	6	1	8		5		7				4				9	2	10	3*
		9		6	1	10		5		7			11	4	S*				2	8*	3
		9		6*	1	10		5		7			11	4				S*	2	8	3
		9			1	10		5	6	7		2	11			4		S*		8*	3
	S*	9*			1	10		5	6	7		2	11			4				8	3
	U	9			1	10		5	6	7		2	11			4	3			8	
10	S*	9			1			5		7			11	6		4	3		2	8*	
10	S*	9*		5	1					7		3	11	6		4			2	8	
8	7	9		5	1							3	11	6	10	4			2		U
8		9		6	1	11		5		7					10	4	3		2		U
8		9		6	1				5	7		11	4		10		3		2		U
8		9		6	1				4	7		5	11				3		2	10	U
8	S*	9		6	1				4	7*		5	11				3		2	10	
8		9		6	1				4	7		5	11				3		2	10	U
8	U	9		6	1				4	7		5	11				3		2	10	
8*		9		6	1	S*			4	7		5	11				3		2	10	
8*	S*	9		6	1				4	7		5	11				3		2	10	
8	S*	9		6	1				4	7		5*	11				3		2		10
	S*	9*		6	1				4	7	8	5	11				3		2	10	
	S*	9		6	1				4	7	8	5	11				3*		2	10	
8	11		S*		1				4	7	10	5		2		6*				9	3
	7		11		1				4		6	5		2	8	3			S*	9	10*
10	S*			5*	1					7	6	11		4	8	3			2	9	
8		10		4	1				5	7	6	U				3	11		2	9	
8		10		4	1				5*	7	6	3	S*				11		2	9	
				4	1					7	8	3	10*	5	S*	6	11		2	9	
	S*	9			1					7	8	3	6*	5	10	4	11		2		
	U	9		4	1					7	8	3		5	10		11		2		6
	S*	9*		4	1					7	8	3		5			11		2	10	6
				4	1					7	8	3	U	5	9		11		2	10	6
	S*				1				4	7	8	3		5	10		11		2	9	6*
	S*			5	1				4	7	8	3	6*		10		11		2	9	
	S*	7		5	1				4		8		6*	3	10		11		2	9	
	S*	7*		5	1				4		8		6	3	10		11		2	9	
	S*	7*		5	1				4		8	3	6		10		11		2	9	
	S*			5	1		11		4	7	8	3	6		10*				2	9	
				5	1		11		4	7	8*	3	6		10		S*		2	9	
			8	5	1		11		4*	7		S*	6		10		3		2	9	
	S*			5	1		11			7	8		6	4	10		3		2	9*	
17	3	29	4	34	42	9	4	11	25	37	20	29	30	21	17	13	27	3	37	35	15
	18	2	1			1						1	1		2		1	3	1	1	
	2	10		2		2		1		13	3		1		9		1	1	8	7	

Blair Andy	Chamberlain Mark	Chapman Lee	Gregory Tony	Hart Paul	Hodge Martin	Jonsson Siggi	Knight Ian	Lyons Mike	Madden Lawrie	Marwood Brian	Megson Gary	Morris Chris	Shelton Gary	Shirtliff Peter	Shutt Carl	Smith Mark	Snodin Glynn	Stainrod Simon	Sterland Mel	Thompson Garry	Worthington Nigel
10	S*	9			1			5	6	7*			11			4	3		2	8	
8		9		5	1							3	11*	6	10	4	S*		2	7	
8		9		6	1			5	4	7			11		10*		3		2	S*	
3		3		2	3			2	2	2		1	3	1	2	2	2		3	2	
	1																1			1	
		3																	1		

Blair Andy	Chamberlain Mark	Chapman Lee	Gregory Tony	Hart Paul	Hodge Martin	Jonsson Siggi	Knight Ian	Lyons Mike	Madden Lawrie	Marwood Brian	Megson Gary	Morris Chris	Shelton Gary	Shirtliff Peter	Shutt Carl	Smith Mark	Snodin Glynn	Stainrod Simon	Sterland Mel	Thompson Garry	Worthington Nigel
10		S*	6	5	1				4	7		11			8*	3			2	9	
10	S*	8	6*	5	1					7		11		4		3			2	9	
8		10			1				5	7	6		S*	4*		3	11		2	9	
8*	S*	10			1					7	6	3		5		4	11		2	9	
	S*	9			1					7*	8	3	6	5	10	4	11		2		
	S*	9			1					7*	8	3		5	10	4	11		2		6
	S*	7*		5	1				4		8		6	3	10		11		2	9	
4		6	2	3	7				3	6	5	5	2	6	4	6	5		7	5	1
	5	1											1								
1	1	2								2					4	1			2	1	1

League Table

	P	W	D	L	F	A	Pts
Liverpool	42	26	10	6	89	37	88
Everton	42	26	8	8	87	41	86
West Ham United	42	26	6	10	74	40	84
Manchester United	42	22	10	10	70	36	76
SHEFFIELD WEDNESDAY	42	21	10	11	63	54	73
Chelsea	42	20	11	11	57	56	71
Arsenal	42	20	9	13	49	47	69
Nottingham Forest	42	19	11	12	69	53	68
Luton Town	42	18	12	12	61	44	66
Tottenham Hotspur	42	19	8	15	74	52	65
Newcastle United	42	17	12	13	67	72	63
Watford	42	16	11	15	69	62	59
Queen's Park Rangers	42	15	7	20	53	64	52
Southampton	42	12	10	20	51	62	46
Manchester City	42	11	12	19	43	57	45
Aston Villa	42	10	14	18	51	67	44
Coventry City	42	11	10	21	48	71	43
Oxford United	42	10	12	20	62	80	42
Leicester City	42	10	12	20	54	76	42
Ipswich Town	42	11	8	23	32	55	41
Birmingham City	42	8	5	29	30	73	29
West Bromwich Albion	42	4	12	26	35	89	24

1986-87

Division One

Manager: Howard Wilkinson

Did you know that?

Final League Position: 13th

On 25 October 1986, at Hillsborough, Coventry 'keeper Steve Ogrizovic punted a long clearance that was carried by the strong wind. It bounced and went in over the head of Wednesday's 'keeper, Martin Hodge, to score.

On 12 December 1986 the Queen came to Hillsborough to officially open the new covered Spion Kop.

Match No.	Date	Venue	Opponents		Round	Result	HT Score	Position	Scorers	Attendance
1	Aug 23	A	Charlton Athletic	D		1-1	0-0		Shelton	8,510
2	25	H	Everton	D		2-2	1-0		Shutt, Hirst	33,007
3	30	H	Chelsea	W		2-0	1-0	7th	Chamberlain, Gregory	25,853
4	Sep 2	A	Arsenal	L		0-2	0-1	12th		20,101
5	6	A	Newcastle United	W		3-2	2-0	9th	Shutt (2), Sterland	22,010
6	13	H	Leicester City	D		2-2	1-0	9th	Chapman (2)	21,603
7	20	A	Watford	W		1-0	0-0	7th	Terry (og)	14,329
8	27	H	West Ham United	D		2-2	1-0	8th	Madden, Megson	25,715
9	Oct 4	H	Oxford United	W		6-1	3-0	4th	Shutt (2), Chapman, Chamberlain, Shelton, Megson	20,205
10	11	A	Manchester United	L		1-3	1-1	6th	Chamberlain	45,890
11	18	A	Tottenham Hotspur	D		1-1	0-1	8th	Megson	26,876
12	25	H	Coventry City	D		2-2	1-1	9th	Chapman (2)	20,035
13	Nov 1	A	Nottingham Forest	L		2-3	0-2	11th	Chapman (2)	23,303
14	8	H	Southampton	W		3-1	0-0	9th	Marwood (pen), Chapman (2)	20,802
15	16	A	Liverpool	D		1-1	0-0	9th	Chapman	28,020
16	22	H	Luton Town	W		1-0	0-0	8th	Megson	21,171
17	29	A	Queen's Park Rangers	D		2-2	1-2	8th	Bradshaw, Chapman	10,241
18	Dec 6	H	Aston Villa	W		2-1	1-1	6th	Marwood (pen), Chapman	21,144
19	13	A	Wimbledon	L		0-3	0-2	8th		6,010
20	21	H	Newcastle United	W		2-0	2-0	5th	Chapman, Bradshaw	28,897
21	26	A	Manchester City	L		0-1	0-1	7th		30,193
22	27	H	Liverpool	L		0-1	0-0	9th		40,959
23	Jan 1	H	Norwich City	D		1-1	0-0	10th	Shelton	20,956
24	3	A	Leicester City	L		1-6	1-1	12th	Megson	10,851
25	17	A	Everton	L		0-2	0-2	12th		33,011
26	24	H	Charlton Athletic	D		1-1	0-1	12th	Shutt	17,365
27	Feb 7	A	Chelsea	L		0-2	0-0	12th		12,493
28	14	H	Arsenal	D		1-1	0-1	14th	Chamberlain	24,792
29	28	H	Watford	L		0-1	0-1	15th		20,530
30	Mar 7	A	Coventry City	L		0-1	0-0	15th		12,878
31	21	H	Manchester United	W		1-0	0-0	14th	Hirst	29,888
32	24	A	West Ham United	W		2-0	1-0	14th	Chapman, Shutt	13,514
33	28	A	Oxford United	L		1-2	1-1	14th	Chapman	7,981
34	Apr 7	H	Tottenham Hotspur	L		0-1	0-0	16th		19,488
35	14	H	Nottingham Forest	L		2-3	0-1	16th	Chapman, Hirst	18,597
36	18	A	Norwich City	L		0-1	0-1	17th		17,924
37	20	H	Manchester City	W		2-1	1-1	16th	Marwood (pen), Chapman	19,769
38	22	A	Southampton	D		1-1	1-0	16th	Chapman	13,014
39	25	A	Luton Town	D		0-0	0-0	16th		9,278
40	May 2	H	Queen's Park Rangers	W		7-1	4-1	14th	Hirst (2), Marwood (2), Megson, Sterland, Chamberlain	16,501
41	4	A	Aston Villa	W		2-1	2-0	12th	Chapman, Hirst	15,007
42	9	H	Wimbledon	L		0-2	0-0	13th		18,823
										Apps
										Subs
									One own-goal	Goals

Full Members Cup

43	Nov 25	H	Portsmouth	L	3R	0-1	0-0			7,846
										Apps
										Subs
										Goals

League Cup

44	Sep 23	H	Stockport County	W	2R 1L	3-0	1-0		Sterland, Shutt, Marwood (pen)	10,466
45	Oct 6	A	Stockport County *	W	2R 2L	7-0	1-0		Hart, Sterland (2), Walker (3), Jonsson	2,089
46	28	A	Everton	L	3R	0-4	0-2			24,638
										Apps
										Subs
										Goals

* Played at Maine Road, Manchester

FA Cup

47	Jan 26	H	Derby County	W	3R	1-0	1-0		Bradshaw	25,695
48	31	A	Chester City	D	4R	1-1	0-1		Chapman	8,146
49	Feb 4	H	Chester City	W	4R Re	3-1	2-1		Chapman, Abel (og), Bradshaw	20,726
50	21	H	West Ham United	D	5R	1-1	1-1		Shelton	31,134
51	25	A	West Ham United	W	5R Re	2-0	2-0		Chapman, Bradshaw	30,257
52	Mar 14	H	Coventry City	L	6R	1-3	0-1		Megson	48,005
										Apps
										Subs
									One own-goal	Goals

Bradshaw Carl	Brannigan Kenny	Chamberlain Mark	Chapman Lee	Gregory Tony	Hart Paul	Hazel Des	Hirst David	Hodge Martin	Jonsson Siggi	Knight Ian	Madden Lawrie	Marwood Brian	May Larry	Megson Gary	Morris Chris	Shelton Gary	Shutt Carl	Smith Mark	Snodin Glynn	Sterland Mel	Tomlinson David	Walker Colin	Worthington Nigel
			9	8	5		S*	1		4	6	7			2	11	10‡		3				
			9	8	4		S*	1			6	7			2	11	10		3				5*
		7	9	8	4			1		5	6			U	2	11	10		3				
		7	9	8	5			1		4	6*			S*	2	11	10		3				
		7	9	8*	5			1		4		S*		6		11	10		3	2			
		6	9		4		U	1		5		7		8		11	10		3	2			
		6	9	S*				1		5	4	7		8		11	10		3*	2			
		6	9	U				1		5	4	7		8		11	10			2			3
		6	9					1		5	4	7		8		11	10‡		S*	2			3
		6	9		5			1			4	7		8		11	10‡		S*	2			3
		6*	9		4			1		5		7		8	S*	11				2		10	3
		6	9	11	4			1		5		7		8					S*	2		10*	3
		S*	9		4		10	1		5*	6	7		8		11				2			3
		6*	9		4		10	1	S*		5	7		8		11				2			3
			9		4		10*	1	6	5		7		8		11			S*	2			3
			9		4		10*	1	6		5	7		8		11			S*	2			3
10			9		4			1	6		5			8	S*	11			7	2*			3
10			9		4			1	6		5	7*		8		11			S*	2			3
10			9		4			1			5			8	7	11	U		6	2			3
10*		S*	9		4			1	7		5			8		11			6	2			3
			9		4		S*	1	7		5			8	2	11‡	10		6				3
		11	9	8			10*	1	7	4	5				2		S*		6				3
		8	9					1	6	4	5				S*	11	10		7	2*			3
	7*		9	11				1			5			8	2		10	4	6		S*		3
10		S*	9					1	7		5			8	2	11‡		4	6				3
			9					1		6	5	7		8		11	10	4	U	2			3
10*		S*	9					1	4		6	7		8	2	11		5	3				
10		9					S*	1			5	7*		8		11		4	3	2			6
10		S*	9					1				7	5	8		11		4	3*	2			6
10*			9				S*	1			3	7	5	8		11		4		2			6
			9				S*	1	8		5	7*	3				10	4	11	2			6
			9				S*	1			5	7		8		11	10‡	4	3	2			6
			9				S*	1				7*	5	8		11	10	4	3	2			6
U			9				10	1			5	7	4	8		11			3	2			6
			9	2*			10	1			5	7	4	8		11	S*		3				6
			9				10	1			5	7	4	8	S*	11			3	2*			6
		S*	9				10*	1			5	7	4	8		11		3		2			6
		S*	9					1			5	7	4	8	2	11	10*	3					6
			9				10*	1			5	7	4	8	11			3	S*	2			6
		S*	9				10	1			5	7*	4	8		11		3		2			6
		S*	9				10	1	8*		5	7	4			11		3		2			6
		S*	9				10	1			5	7	4	8	2	11		3*					6
9	1	14	41	9	18		13	42	12	15	35	31	13	34	13	37	18	16	24	30		2	35
		10		1			8		1			1		1	4		2		7		1		
2		5	19	1			6				1	5		6		3	7			2			

		S*	9		4		10	1	6		5			8	U	11			7	2			3*
			1		1		1	1	1		1			1		1			1	1			1
		1																					

		6*	9				S#	1		5	4	7		8	S*	11	10#			2			3
9#				S*	4	6	10	1	11		5	7		8*					3	2		S#	
		6	9		4		10	1			5	7		8	U				11	2		U	3
1		2	2		2	1	2	3	1	1	3	3		3		1	1		2	3			2
				1			1								1							1	
					1				1			1					1			3		3	

10		S#	9					1		6	5	7#		8	S*	11		4		2*			3
10*		S*	9					1		6	5	7		8	2	11		4	U				3
10		S#	9					1	S*	6*	5	7#		8	2	11		4	3				
9							10#	1			5	7		8	S*	11	S#	4	3	2*			6
10#		S#	9					1			5	7		8	S*	11		4	3	2*			6
10#			9				S#	1			5	7		8	S*	11		4	3	2*			6
6			5				1	6		3	6	6		6	2	6		6	4	4			5
		4					1		1						4		1						
3			3											1		1							

League Table

	P	W	D	L	F	A	Pts
Everton	42	26	8	8	76	31	86
Liverpool	42	23	8	11	72	42	77
Tottenham Hotspur	42	21	8	13	68	43	71
Arsenal	42	20	10	12	58	35	70
Norwich City	42	17	17	8	53	51	68
Wimbledon	42	19	9	14	57	50	66
Luton Town	42	18	12	12	47	45	66
Nottingham Forest	42	18	11	13	64	51	65
Watford	42	18	9	15	67	54	63
Coventry City	42	17	12	13	50	45	63
Manchester United	42	14	14	14	52	45	56
Southampton	42	14	10	18	69	68	52
SHEFFIELD WEDNESDAY	42	13	13	16	58	59	52
Chelsea	42	13	13	16	53	64	52
West Ham United	42	14	10	18	52	67	52
Queen's Park Rangers	42	13	11	18	48	64	50
Newcastle United	42	12	11	19	47	65	47
Oxford United	42	11	13	18	44	69	46
Charlton Athletic	42	11	11	20	45	55	44
Leicester City	42	11	9	22	54	76	42
Manchester City	42	8	15	19	36	57	39
Aston Villa	42	8	12	22	45	79	36

1987-88

Division One

Manager: Howard Wilkinson

Did you know that?

Final League Position: 11th

On 23 April 1988 Wednesday became the last visiting team to play on Queen's Park Rangers's Loftus Road plastic pitch in a 1–1 draw. After this game, the plastic was to be replaced by grass for the following season.

Match No.	Date	Venue	Opponents		Round	Result	HT Score	Position	Scorers	Attendance
1	Aug 15	A	Chelsea	L		1-2	0-1		Chapman	21,929
2	18	H	Oxford United	D		1-1	1-1		Chapman	17,868
3	22	H	Newcastle United	L		0-1	0-1	17th		22,031
4	29	A	Everton	L		0-4	0-1	19th		29,649
5	31	H	Coventry City	L		0-3	0-2	19th		17,171
6	Sep 5	A	Southampton	D		1-1	1-0	20th	Chapman	12,526
7	12	H	Watford	L		2-3	1-2	20th	West, Chapman	16,144
8	19	A	Derby County	D		2-2	0-2	21st	Megson, Sterland	15,869
9	26	H	Charlton Athletic	W		2-0	2-0	20th	Chapman (2)	16,350
10	Oct 3	A	Tottenham Hotspur	L		0-2	0-0	20th		24,331
11	10	H	Manchester United	L		2-4	1-1	20th	Robson (og), Sterland	32,779
12	17	A	Nottingham Forest	L		0-3	0-1	20th		17,685
13	24	H	Norwich City	W		1-0	1-0	19th	Pearson	15,861
14	31	A	Portsmouth	W		2-1	1-1	18th	West (2)	13,582
15	Nov 7	A	West Ham United	W		1-0	1-0	16th	Bradshaw	16,277
16	14	H	Luton Town	L		0-2	0-1	18th		16,960
17	28	H	Queen's Park Rangers	W		3-1	2-0	17th	Proctor, Megson, Fenwick (og)	16,933
18	Dec 5	A	Arsenal	L		1-3	1-0	17th	West	23,760
19	12	H	Wimbledon	W		1-0	0-0	16th	Chapman	14,289
20	19	A	Liverpool	L		0-1	0-0	17th		35,383
21	26	A	Watford	W		3-1	3-1	16th	Pearson, West, Chapman	12,026
22	28	H	Derby County	W		2-1	2-0	12th	Chapman, West	26,191
23	Jan 1	H	Everton	W		1-0	1-0	10th	Proctor	26,433
24	2	A	Newcastle United	D		2-2	0-0	10th	Marwood, Chapman	25,503
25	16	H	Chelsea	W		3-0	1-0	9th	May, Marwood (pen), Bradshaw	19,859
26	Feb 6	H	Southampton	W		2-1	0-1	9th	Sterland, Chapman	14,769
27	13	A	Coventry City	L		0-3	0-1	9th		14,382
28	20	A	Charlton Athletic	L		1-3	0-3	9th	Chapman	4,517
29	27	H	Tottenham Hotspur	L		0-3	0-1	10th		18,046
30	Mar 5	H	Nottingham Forest	L		0-1	0-1	12th		19,509
31	12	A	Manchester United	L		1-4	0-2	12th	Chapman	33,318
32	19	H	Portsmouth	W		1-0	1-0	9th	Sterland (pen)	13,731
33	26	A	Norwich City	W		3-0	1-0	9th	Sterland (pen), Jonsson, Chapman	13,280
34	Apr 2	H	West Ham United	W		2-1	1-0	8th	Hirst, Chamberlain	18,435
35	5	A	Luton Town	D		2-2	0-0	8th	Chapman, Sterland	7,337
36	13	A	Oxford United	W		3-0	2-0	8th	Chapman (2), Sterland	5,727
37	23	A	Queen's Park Rangers	D		1-1	1-0	9th	West	12,531
38	30	H	Arsenal	D		3-3	3-1	8th	Sterland, Hirst, Chapman	16,681
39	May 3	A	Wimbledon	D		1-1	0-1	9th	Chapman	7,854
40	7	H	Liverpool	L		1-5	0-2	11th	Hirst	35,893
										Apps
										Subs
									Two own-goals	Goals

Full Members' Cup

Match No.	Date	Venue	Opponents		Round	Result	HT Score	Position	Scorers	Attendance
41	Nov 10	H	AFC Bournemouth	W	1R	2-0	0-0		Galvin, West	3,756
42	Dec 1	H	Stoke City	L	2R	0-1	0-0			5,228
										Apps
										Subs
										Goals

League Cup

Match No.	Date	Venue	Opponents		Round	Result	HT Score	Position	Scorers	Attendance
43	Sep 22	A	Shrewsbury Town	D	2R 1L	1-1	1-1		Fee	4,364
44	Oct 6	H	Shrewsbury Town	W	2R 2L	2-1	1-0		West (2)	8,572
45	27	A	Barnsley	W	3R	2-1	1-1		Chamberlain, Hirst	19,439
46	Nov 18	A	Aston Villa	W	4R	2-1	1-1		Chapman, West	25,302
47	Jan 20	H	Arsenal	L	5R	0-1	0-0			34,535
										Apps
										Subs
										Goals

FA Cup

Match No.	Date	Venue	Opponents		Round	Result	HT Score	Position	Scorers	Attendance
48	Jan 9	H	Everton	D	3R	1-1	0-0		West	33,304
49	13	A	Everton *	D	3Rr	1-1	1-0		Chapman	32,935
50	25	A	Everton *	D	3Rr	1-1	0-0		Chapman	37,414
51	27	H	Everton	L	3Rr	0-5	0-5			38,953
										Apps
										Subs
										Goals

* After extra-time. Score at full-time 1-1

Bradshaw Carl	Brannigan Kenny	Chamberlain Mark	Chapman Lee	Cranson Ian	Fee Greg	Galvin Tony	Hazel Des	Hirst David	Hodge Martin	Jacobs Wayne	Jonsson Siggi	Madden Lawrie	Marwood Brian	May Larry	McCall Steve	Megson Gary	Owen Gary	Pearson Nigel	Pressman Kevin	Proctor Mark	Shutt Carl	Sterland Mel	West Colin	Worthington Nigel
S*		11*	9					10	1			4	7	5	3	8	U					2		6
S*			9					10	1	11#		4	7*	5	3	8	S#					2		6
10			9				7	11	1	U		4		5	3	8	U					2		6
U			9		5		7	10	1		11	4			3	8	U					2		6
S*			9		U	11	7	10	1			4		5	3*	8						2		6
10#			9		5	11	7*	S#			S*	4				8			1	6		2		3
			9		5	11#	7*	S#			S*	4				8			1	6		2	10	3
10			9		5	11			1	S*	U	4				8				6	7*	2		3
S*			9		U	11			1	7		4		5		8				6		2	10*	3
S*			9			11*			1	U		4	7	5		8				6		2	10	3
		7*	9			11		S*	1	U		4		5		8				6		2	10	3
S*			9			S#		7	1	11#				5		8		4		6		2	10*	3
S#		7*	9		S*	11			1			4				8		5		6		2	10#	3
		7			S*	11		10	1	U		5				8		4		6		2*	9	3
10#		8*			S#	11			1	2		5				6	S*	4		7			9	3
		7	9		U	11*			1	2		4	S*			8		5		6			10	3
		7	9		U				1			4	U			8	11	5		6		2	10	3
		7	9		U			S*	1			4	11*				8	5		6		2	10	3
S*		11	9		S#				1			4	7*				8	5		6		2	10#	3
		7*	9						1			4	11	S#		10	8#	5		6		2	S*	3
		S*	9*		S#				1			4	7			8	11#	5		6		2	10	3
		S*	9		U				1			4	7*			8	11	5		6		2	10	3
S#		S*	9						1			4	7*	11		8#		5		6		2	10	3
11		S*	9						1			4	7	U		8		5		6		2	10*	3
9		S#			S*				1			4	7	11			8#	5		6		2*	10	3
S*			9					S#	1			4	7			8	11	5*		6		2	10#	3
U			9		4			U	1				7	5		8	11			6		2	10	3
		10	9		U	S*			1			4	7			8	11*	5		6		2		3
S*			9			S#		10*	1			4	7			8	11#	5		6		2		3
		S*	9					10	1		U	4	7*	11		8		5		6		2		3
		7	9		S*			10	1		11	4	U			8		5*		6		2		3
S#		7	9		5			10#			11*	4	S*			8			1	6		2		3
S*		7	9	5	U			10*			11	4				8			1	6		2		3
S*		7*	9	5	S#			10#			11	4				8			1	6		2		3
			9	5		S*		10#			11	4		7		8			1	6*		2	S#	3
			9	5		11		10			7	4		U		8			1	6		2	U	3
			9		U	S*		10*			11	4		5		8			1	6		2	7	3
			9		S#		S*	10			11	4		5		8	3#		1	6		2	7*	
U			9		3	U		10			11	4		5		8			1	6		2	7	
			9		U	S*		10			11	4		5		8			1	6		2	7*	3
6		15	37	4	7	12	5	19	29	5	11	38	16	17	5	37	12	19	11	35	1	38	23	38
14		6			9	6	1	5		1	2		2	1			2						2	
2		1	19					3			1		2	1		2		2		2		8	7	

Bradshaw Carl	Brannigan Kenny	Chamberlain Mark	Chapman Lee	Cranson Ian	Fee Greg	Galvin Tony	Hazel Des	Hirst David	Hodge Martin	Jacobs Wayne	Jonsson Siggi	Madden Lawrie	Marwood Brian	May Larry	McCall Steve	Megson Gary	Owen Gary	Pearson Nigel	Pressman Kevin	Proctor Mark	Shutt Carl	Sterland Mel	West Colin	Worthington Nigel
9#		7*	S#		2	11	S*		1	3		5				8		4		6			10	
		7	9						1	U		4	S*			8*	11	5		6		2	10	3
1		2	1		1	1			2	1		2				2	1	2		2		1	2	1
			1				1						1											
						1																	1	

Bradshaw Carl	Brannigan Kenny	Chamberlain Mark	Chapman Lee	Cranson Ian	Fee Greg	Galvin Tony	Hazel Des	Hirst David	Hodge Martin	Jacobs Wayne	Jonsson Siggi	Madden Lawrie	Marwood Brian	May Larry	McCall Steve	Megson Gary	Owen Gary	Pearson Nigel	Pressman Kevin	Proctor Mark	Shutt Carl	Sterland Mel	West Colin	Worthington Nigel
S*	U		9		5	11*			1	6	7	4				8						2	10	3
		7*	9		U	11		S*	1	6		4		5		8						2	10	3
		7	9		S*	11		S#	1	6		4		5*		8						2	10#	3
S*		7	9		4	11*			1	U		5				8	6					2	10	3
U		S*	9		5*				1			4	7	11		8	6					2	10	3
		3	5		3	4			5	3	1	5	1	3		5	2					5	5	5
2		1			1			2																
		1	1		1			1															3	

Bradshaw Carl	Brannigan Kenny	Chamberlain Mark	Chapman Lee	Cranson Ian	Fee Greg	Galvin Tony	Hazel Des	Hirst David	Hodge Martin	Jacobs Wayne	Jonsson Siggi	Madden Lawrie	Marwood Brian	May Larry	McCall Steve	Megson Gary	Owen Gary	Pearson Nigel	Pressman Kevin	Proctor Mark	Shutt Carl	Sterland Mel	West Colin	Worthington Nigel
U		U	9						1			4	7	11		8		5		6		2	10	3
S#		S*	9#						1			4	7*	11		8		5		6		2	10	3
		S*	9						1			4	7#	11*		8	S#	5		6		2	10	3
		11	9*		U				1				7	4		8	S*	5		6		2	10	3
		1	4						4			3	4	4		4		4		4		4	4	4
1		2															2							
			2																				1	

League Table

	P	W	D	L	F	A	Pts
Liverpool	40	26	12	2	87	24	90
Manchester United	40	23	12	5	71	38	81
Nottingham Forest	40	20	13	7	67	39	73
Everton	40	19	13	8	53	27	70
Queen's Park Rangers	40	19	10	11	48	38	67
Arsenal	40	18	12	10	58	39	66
Wimbledon	40	14	15	11	58	47	57
Newcastle United	40	14	14	12	55	53	56
Luton Town	40	14	11	15	57	58	53
Coventry City	40	13	14	13	46	53	53
SHEFFIELD WEDNESDAY	40	15	8	17	52	66	53
Southampton	40	12	14	14	49	53	50
Tottenham Hotspur	40	12	11	17	38	48	47
Norwich City	40	12	9	19	40	52	45
Derby County	40	10	13	17	35	45	43
West Ham United	40	9	15	16	40	52	42
Charlton Athletic	40	9	15	16	38	52	42
Chelsea	40	9	15	16	50	68	42
Portsmouth	40	7	14	19	36	66	35
Watford	40	7	11	22	27	51	32
Oxford United	40	6	13	21	44	80	31

1988-89

Division One

Manager: Howard Wilkinson/Peter Eustace/Ron Atkinson

Did you know that?

Final League Position: 15th

On 22 October 1988 Wednesday's away game at Southampton saw the home side field three Wallace brothers together, making post-war Football League history. Wednesday won 2–1.

On 15 April 1989 96 people died from crush related injuries in the Hillsborough disaster during a game between Liverpool and Nottingham Forest. On 9 May 1989 Wednesday played their first senior game at home since the disaster, with the Leppings Lane end of the ground closed and covered in blue plastic sheets.

Match No.	Date	Venue	Opponents		Round	Result	HT Score	Position	Scorers	Attendance
1	Aug 27	H	Luton Town	W		1-0	0-0		Sterland	16,433
2	Sep 3	A	Nottingham Forest	D		1-1	0-1	7th	Sterland	18,963
3	10	H	Coventry City	L		1-2	0-0	9th	Hirst	15,633
4	17	A	Queen's Park Rangers	L		0-2	0-1	12th		8,011
5	24	H	Arsenal	W		2-1	1-0	12th	Megson, Pearson	17,830
6	Oct 1	H	Aston Villa	W		1-0	1-0	7th	Hirst	18,301
7	22	A	Southampton	W		2-1	1-1	5th	Varadi, Reeves	12,725
8	29	A	Charlton Athletic	L		1-2	0-1	10th	Hodgson	5,933
9	Nov 5	H	Everton	D		1-1	0-0	13th	Sterland	21,761
10	12	A	Norwich City	D		1-1	0-1	13th	Sterland	14,353
11	20	H	Tottenham Hotspur	L		0-2	0-0	13th		15,386
12	23	A	Manchester United	D		1-1	0-0	10th	West	30,867
13	26	A	Middlesbrough	W		1-0	1-0	10th	Sterland	19,310
14	Dec 3	H	Derby County	D		1-1	1-0	11th	Sterland	20,609
15	10	A	West Ham United	D		0-0	0-0	11th		16,676
16	17	A	Millwall	L		0-1	0-0	12th		11,197
17	26	H	Newcastle United	L		1-2	1-2	13th	Hirst	25,573
18	31	H	Nottingham Forest	L		0-3	0-3	16th		20,407
19	Jan 2	A	Coventry City	L		0-5	0-2	17th		15,191
20	14	H	Liverpool	D		2-2	2-0	17th	Proctor, Varadi	31,524
21	21	A	Arsenal	D		1-1	0-0	18th	Varadi	33,490
22	Feb 4	A	Aston Villa	L		0-2	0-2	18th		19,334
23	11	H	Manchester United	L		0-2	0-1	18th		34,820
24	18	H	Southampton	D		1-1	0-0	18th	Proctor	16,677
25	25	A	Wimbledon	L		0-1	0-1	18th		4,384
26	Mar 4	H	Charlton Athletic	W		3-1	1-1	18th	Hirst, Jonsson, Galvin	16,081
27	11	A	Everton	L		0-1	0-1	18th		22,542
28	18	A	Luton Town	W		1-0	0-0	15th	Hirst	7,776
29	25	H	Queen's Park Rangers	L		0-2	0-0	17th		18,804
30	27	A	Newcastle United	W		3-1	2-0	14th	Barrick, Pearson, Hirst	31,040
31	Apr 1	H	Millwall	W		3-0	1-0	13th	Palmer, Whitton (2)	18,358
32	5	H	Wimbledon	D		1-1	0-0	14th	Hirst	15,777
33	8	A	Liverpool	L		1-5	0-2	14th	Barrick	39,672
34	12	A	Tottenham Hotspur	D		0-0	0-0	14th		17,270
35	22	A	Derby County	L		0-1	0-0	16th		17,529
36	May 9	H	West Ham United	L		0-2	0-0	18th		19,905
37	13	H	Middlesbrough	W		1-0	0-0	16th	Whitton	20,582
38	17	H	Norwich City	D		2-2	0-0	15th	Linighan (og), Reeves	16,238
										Apps
										Subs
									One own-goal	Goals
Full Members' Cup										
39	Feb 1	H	Queen's Park Rangers	L	3R	0-1	0-0			3,957
* After extra-time. Score at full-time 0-0										Apps
										Subs
										Goals
League Cup										
40	Sep 27	A	Blackpool	L	2R 1L	0-2	0-2			5,492
41	Oct 12	H	Blackpool * #	W	2R 2L	3-1	1-1		Varadi, Reeves, Hirst	12,237
* Lost on away goals										Apps
# After extra-time. Score at full-time 3-1										Subs
										Goals
FA Cup										
42	Jan 7	H	Torquay United	W	3R	5-1	2-1		Jonsson, Hodgson, Varadi (2), Proctor	11,384
43	28	A	Blackburn Rovers	L	4R	1-2	0-0		Hirst	16,235
										Apps
										Subs
										Goals

Barrick Dean	Bennett Dave	Bradshaw Carl	Cranson Ian	Fee Greg	Galvin Tony	Gregory Tony	Harper Alan	Hirst David	Hodgson David	Jonsson Siggi	Knight Ian	Madden Lawrie	McCall Steve	Megson Gary	Palmer Carlton	Pearson Nigel	Pressman Kevin	Proctor Mark	Reeves David	Rostron Wilf	Sterland Mel	Turner Chris	Varadi Imre	West Colin	Whitton Steve	Wood Darren	Worthington Nigel
		U			11*		6	S*		10		5		7		4	1	8			2			9			3
		U			11		6	S*		10		5		7		4	1	8*			2			9			3
		S#	S*		11#		6*	8		10		5		7		4	1				2			9			3
		S*	6	U	11*			8		10		5		7		4	1				2			9			3
		11#	6		S*			8*		10		5		7		4	1		9		2			S#			3
			6		S*			8#		10*		5		7		4	1		9		2		11	S#			3
			6	U					S*			5		7		4		11	8*		2	1	9	10			3
			6	U					S*			5		7		4		11	8*		2	1	9	10			3
			6						10	S#		5		7#		4		11	S*		2	1	9*	8			3
			4			U		S*	11*	6				7		5		8	10		2	1		9			3
			4			U		S*	11*	7		6				5		8	10		2	1		9			3
			4					10*	11#	7		6		S*		5		8			2	1	S#	9			3
			4					10*	S#	7		6		11		5		8			2#	1	S*	9			3
			4				S*	10#		8*		6		7		5		11	S#		2	1		9			3
			4				10	8	9	6	U			7		5	1	11			2*		S*				3
			4			S#	10	8	S*	11		6		7#		5	1	2					9*				3
			4			U		8		11		6		7		5	1	2			10		9*	S*			3
			4			7		8*		11		6		S#		5		2	S*			1	9	10			3#
					S*	S#	2		8	11	4	6		7		5#		3				1	9*	10			
			4		S*					11	U	6				5		7	8	3	2	1	10*	9			
			4				11		S#		6					5		7	8	3	2*	1	10	9#		S*	
			4				11	10		8	U	6				5		7		3	2	1	S*	9*			
			4		U		11	10		8		6				5		7	S*	3	2	1	9*				
			4		7		11	8*		9						5		6	S*	3	2	1	10			U	
			6		11			10		U		3			4	5		7	S*		2	1	9*			8	
			6		11		2	10		8		U				5		7				1	S*		9*	4	3
			U		11*		2	10		8		6			4	5		7	S*			1			9		3
					S*		2	10				6#	8		4	5		7		11*		1	S#		9		3
	7		6		S*		2	10		11			8*		4	5						1	U		9		3
11	7*		6	8	S*		2	10							4	5						1	U		9	3	
11	7		6*	8			2	10		S*					4	5						1	U		9		3
11	7			8	U		2	10		6					4	5						1			9	U	3
11	7			8	U		2	10		6					4					5		1	U		9		3
11	7			8			2	10		U					4	5						1	U		9	6	3
11	7			U	U		2	10				8			4	5						1	9			6	3
11	7#			8	S*		2	10				6			4	5			S#			1			9		3*
11	7*			8	S#		2	10#		S*		6			4	5						1			9	3	
	7		U	8	11*		2	10				6			4	5			S*			1			9	3	
8	10	1	25	8	9	1	23	28	6	25	2	27	2	16	13	37	9	24	8	7	22	29	14	17	12	7	28
		2	1		9	2	1	4	5	3				2					9				6	3		1	
2					1			7	1	1				1	1	2		2	2		6		3	1	3		

Barrick Dean	Bennett Dave	Bradshaw Carl	Cranson Ian	Fee Greg	Galvin Tony	Gregory Tony	Harper Alan	Hirst David	Hodgson David	Jonsson Siggi	Knight Ian	Madden Lawrie	McCall Steve	Megson Gary	Palmer Carlton	Pearson Nigel	Pressman Kevin	Proctor Mark	Reeves David	Rostron Wilf	Sterland Mel	Turner Chris	Varadi Imre	West Colin	Whitton Steve	Wood Darren	Worthington Nigel
			4		S#		11#	8*				6				5		7	S*	3	2	1	10	9			
			1				1	1				1				1		1		1	1	1	1	1			
					1														1								

Barrick Dean	Bennett Dave	Bradshaw Carl	Cranson Ian	Fee Greg	Galvin Tony	Gregory Tony	Harper Alan	Hirst David	Hodgson David	Jonsson Siggi	Knight Ian	Madden Lawrie	McCall Steve	Megson Gary	Palmer Carlton	Pearson Nigel	Pressman Kevin	Proctor Mark	Reeves David	Rostron Wilf	Sterland Mel	Turner Chris	Varadi Imre	West Colin	Whitton Steve	Wood Darren	Worthington Nigel
		11*	6	U	S*			8		10		5		7		4	1		9		2						3
			6		S*			8*				5		7		4		11	S#		2	1	9#	10			3
		1	2					2		1		2		2		2	1	1	1		2	1	1	1			2
					2														1								
								1											1				1				

Barrick Dean	Bennett Dave	Bradshaw Carl	Cranson Ian	Fee Greg	Galvin Tony	Gregory Tony	Harper Alan	Hirst David	Hodgson David	Jonsson Siggi	Knight Ian	Madden Lawrie	McCall Steve	Megson Gary	Palmer Carlton	Pearson Nigel	Pressman Kevin	Proctor Mark	Reeves David	Rostron Wilf	Sterland Mel	Turner Chris	Varadi Imre	West Colin	Whitton Steve	Wood Darren	Worthington Nigel
			3		U				8	11	4	6				5		7	S*		2	1	9	10*			
			4				11	S#			6*	S*				5		7	8	3	2	1	10#	9			
			2				1		1	1	2	1				2		2	1	1	2	2	2	2			
								1				1							1								
								1	1	1								1					2				

League Table

	P	W	D	L	F	A	Pts
Arsenal	38	22	10	6	73	36	76
Liverpool	38	22	10	6	65	28	76
Nottingham Forest	38	17	13	8	64	43	64
Norwich City	38	17	11	10	48	45	62
Derby County	38	17	7	14	40	38	58
Tottenham Hotspur	38	15	12	11	60	46	57
Coventry City	38	14	13	11	47	42	55
Everton	38	14	12	12	50	45	54
Queen's Park Rangers	38	14	11	13	43	37	53
Millwall	38	14	11	13	47	52	53
Manchester United	38	13	12	13	45	35	51
Wimbledon	38	14	9	15	50	46	51
Southampton	38	10	15	13	52	66	45
Charlton Athletic	38	10	12	16	44	58	42
SHEFFIELD WEDNESDAY	38	10	12	16	34	51	42
Luton Town	38	10	11	17	42	52	41
Aston Villa	38	9	13	16	45	56	40
Middlesbrough	38	9	12	17	44	61	39
West Ham United	38	10	8	20	37	62	38
Newcastle United	38	7	10	21	32	63	31

1989-90

Division One

Manager: Ron Atkinson

Did you know that?

Final League Position: 18th

On 30 August 1989 Wednesday played Everton, and before the game Everton's captain placed a bunch of flowers at the Leppings Lane end of the ground. On 29 November 1989, when Liverpool played at Hillsborough, Chris Turner of Wednesday and Alan Hansen of Liverpool both layed wreaths before a minute's silence.

On 17 February 1990 Arsenal's Steve Bould headed into his own goal at Hillsborough after only 15 seconds for the only goal of the game.

Match No.	Date	Venue	Opponents		Round	Result	HT Score	Position	Scorers	Attendance
1	Aug 19	H	Norwich City	L		0-2	0-1			19,142
2	22	A	Luton Town	L		0-2	0-1			9,503
3	26	A	Chelsea	L		0-4	0-3	20th		16,265
4	30	H	Everton	D		1-1	0-1	20th	Atkinson	19,657
5	Sep 9	A	Arsenal	L		0-5	0-1	20th		30,058
6	16	H	Aston Villa	W		1-0	1-0	13th	Atkinson	17,509
7	23	A	Millwall	L		0-2	0-0	20th		11,294
8	30	H	Coventry City	D		0-0	0-0	20th		15,054
9	Oct 14	A	Manchester United	D		0-0	0-0	20th		41,492
10	21	A	Tottenham Hotspur	L		0-3	0-2	20th		26,909
11	28	H	Wimbledon	L		0-1	0-0	20th		13,728
12	Nov 4	A	Nottingham Forest	W		1-0	0-0	20th	Wilson (og)	21,864
13	11	H	Charlton Athletic	W		3-0	1-0	20th	Atkinson, Hirst (2)	16,740
14	18	A	Derby County	L		0-2	0-1	20th		18,085
15	25	H	Crystal Palace	D		2-2	0-1	20th	Whitton, Hirst (pen)	17,227
16	29	H	Liverpool	W		2-0	0-0	17th	Hirst, Atkinson	32,732
17	Dec 2	A	Norwich City	L		1-2	1-2	17th	Hirst	15,341
18	9	H	Luton Town	D		1-1	1-0	18th	Dreyer (og)	16,339
19	16	H	Queen's Park Rangers	W		2-0	2-0	17th	Atkinson, Hirst	14,569
20	26	A	Liverpool	L		1-2	0-1	18th	Atkinson	37,488
21	30	A	Southampton	D		2-2	1-1	18th	Atkinson, Shirtliff	16,417
22	Jan 1	H	Manchester City	W		2-0	1-0	16th	Hirst, Pearson	28,756
23	14	H	Chelsea	D		1-1	0-1	15th	Atkinson	18,042
24	20	A	Everton	L		0-2	0-2	16th		25,545
25	Feb 3	H	Millwall	D		1-1	1-1	15th	Hirst	17,737
26	10	A	Aston Villa	L		0-1	0-0	17th		27,168
27	17	H	Arsenal	W		1-0	1-0	14th	Bould (og)	20,640
28	24	A	Crystal Palace	D		1-1	1-0	14th	Worthington	11,857
29	Mar 3	H	Derby County	W		1-0	1-0	14th	Sheridan	21,811
30	17	A	Coventry City	W		4-1	1-1	14th	Hirst, Worthington, Sheridan, Atkinson	13,339
31	21	H	Manchester United	W		1-0	1-0	14th	Hirst	33,260
32	24	A	Wimbledon	D		1-1	0-0	13th	Shirtliff	5,034
33	31	H	Tottenham Hotspur	L		2-4	1-1	14th	Hirst, Atkinson	26,582
34	Apr 7	H	Southampton	L		0-1	0-0	14th		18,329
35	14	A	Manchester City	L		1-2	0-1	17th	Hirst	33,022
36	21	A	Queen's Park Rangers	L		0-1	0-1	17th		10,448
37	28	A	Charlton Athletic	W		2-1	1-0	17th	Hirst (2)	7,029
38	May 5	H	Nottingham Forest	L		0-3	0-1	18th		29,762
										Apps
										Subs
									Three own-goals	Goals

Full Members' Cup

Match No.	Date	Venue	Opponents		Round	Result	HT Score	Position	Scorers	Attendance
39	Nov 21	H	Sheffield United *	W	2R	3-2	1-1		Atkinson, Palmer, Sheridan	30,464
40	Dec 20	A	Middlesbrough	L	3R	1-4	1-2		Bennett	8,716
										Apps
										Subs
										Goals

* After extra-time. Score at full-time 2-2

League Cup

Match No.	Date	Venue	Opponents		Round	Result	HT Score	Position	Scorers	Attendance
41	Sep 20	H	Aldershot	D	2R 1L	0-0	0-0			9,237
42	Oct 3	A	Aldershot	W	2R 2L	8-0	4-0		Whitton (4), Atkinson (3), Shakespeare	4,011
43	25	A	Derby County	L	3R	1-2	0-0		Hirst (pen)	18,042
										Apps
										Subs
										Goals

FA Cup

Match No.	Date	Venue	Opponents		Round	Result	HT Score	Position	Scorers	Attendance
44	Jan 6	A	Wolverhampton W	W	3R	2-1	0-0		Shirtliff, Atkinson	23,800
45	28	H	Everton	L	4R	1-2	1-2		Hirst	31,754
										Apps
										Subs
										Goals

Atkinson Dalian	Barrick Dean	Bennett Dave	Carr Franz	Fee Greg	Francis Trevor	Harper Alan	Hirst David	King Phil	Lycett David	Madden Lawrie	McCall Steve	Newsome Jon	Nilsson Roland	Palmer Carlton	Pearson Nigel	Pressman Kevin	Shakespeare Craig	Sheridan John	Shirtliff Peter	Taylor Mark	Turner Chris	Varadi Imre	Whitton Steve	Wood Darren	Worthington Nigel
10	8	7		U		2	S*			6				4	5		11				1		9*		3
9		S*		2		8*	10			6				4	5		11			7	1		U		3
9		U		U		2	10			6					5		11			7	1		4	8	3
9		S*		U		8	10			6					5		11			7	1		4	2*	3
9		S*				8*	10#			6		S#			5		11		2	7	1		4		3
9		U				U	10			6				4		1	11		5	7			8	2	3
9						S*	10			6		2		4		1	11		5	7#		S#	8*		3
9		U				S*	10			6		2*		4		1	11		5	7			8		3
10		7					S*			6		2		4	8	1	11		5	U			9*		3
10							7			6		2		4	8		11#		5	S#	1	S*	9*		3
10	11#					3	9			6		2		4	8		S#		5	7*	1		S*		
10		7		S*		2	9	3*		6				4		1	11	8	5				U		
10		7				2	9	3		6				4		1	11	8	5				U		U
10		7*				2	9	3	U	6					4	1	S*	8	5						11
10		7					9	3		6				4	2*	1	U	8	5				S*		11
10		7				U	9	3						4	6	1	11	8	5				U		2
10		7				U	9	3						4	6	1	11#	8	5				S*		2
10		7*				U	9	3					2	4	6	1		8	5				S*		11
10		7*					9	3		U			2	4	6	1		8	5				S*		11
10		U	7				9	3		U			2	4	6	1		8	5						11
10		U	7				9	3					2	4	6	1	U	8	5						11
10		S*	7				9	3					2	4	6	1*	U	8	5						11
10			7				9	3		S*			2*	4	6			8	5		1		U		11
10			7				9	2		U				4	6		11#	8	5		1		S*		3
10			7*		S*		9	3					2	4	6			8	5		1		U		11
10			7		S*		9	3		U			2	4	6			8	5		1				11*
10			S*		7*		9	3		S#			2	4	6			8	5#		1				11
10	U		S*		7*		9	3		5			2	4	6			8			1				11
10			S*		7#		9*	3		S#			2	4	6			8	5		1				11
10		S#	7				9#	3*		S*			2	4	6			8	5		1				11
10			7		U		9	3		U			2	4	6			8	5		1				11
10		S#			7#		9	3		S*			2	4	6			8	5		1				11*
10	11	S*			7*		9	3#		S#			2	4	6			8	5		1				
10		S*			7		9			3	U		2	4	6			8	5		1		11*		
10	U				7*		9			3	11		2	4	6			8	5		1		S*		
10					7		9	3			S*		2	4	6			8#	5		1		S#		11*
10					7#		9	3*		S#	S*		2	4	6			8	5		1				11
10					7*		9	3		U			2	4	6			8	5		1		S*		11
38	3	10	9	1	10	9	36	25		18	1	5	20	34	33	15	15	27	33	8	23		10	3	32
		8	3	1	2	2	2			7	2	1					2			1		2	9		
10							14								1			2	2				1		2

10		7*					9	3	U	6				4	2	1	S*	8	5						11
10		7*					9	3		U			2	4	6	1		8	5				S*		11
2		2					2	2		1			1	2	2	2		2	2						2
																	1						1		
1		1												1				1							

9						S*	10			6		2		4		1	11		5	7		U	8*		3
10		7				8	S*			6		2		4*		1	11		5			S#	9#		3
10						U	S*			6		2		4	8		11		5	7	1		9*		3
3		1				1	1			3		3		3	1	2	3		3	2	1		3		3
						1	2															1			
3							1										1						4		

10			7				9	3		U			2	4	6			8	5		1		U		11
10			7*				9	3		U			2	4	6			8	5		1		S*		11
2			2				2	2					2	2	2			2	2		2				2
																							1		
1							1												1						

League Table

	P	W	D	L	F	A	Pts
Liverpool	38	23	10	5	78	37	79
Aston Villa	38	21	7	10	57	38	70
Tottenham Hotspur	38	19	6	13	59	47	63
Arsenal	38	18	8	12	54	38	62
Chelsea	38	16	12	10	58	50	60
Everton	38	17	8	13	57	46	59
Southampton	38	15	10	13	71	63	55
Wimbledon	38	13	16	9	47	40	55
Nottingham Forest	38	15	9	14	55	47	54
Norwich City	38	13	14	11	44	42	53
Queen's Park Rangers	38	13	11	14	45	44	50
Coventry City	38	14	7	17	39	59	49
Manchester United	38	13	9	16	46	47	48
Manchester City	38	12	12	14	43	52	48
Crystal Palace	38	13	9	16	42	66	48
Derby County	38	13	7	18	43	40	46
Luton Town	38	10	13	15	43	57	43
SHEFFIELD WEDNESDAY	38	11	10	17	35	51	43
Charlton Athletic	38	7	9	22	31	57	30
Millwall	38	5	11	22	39	65	26

1990-91

Division Two

Manager: Ron Atkinson

Did you know that?

Final League Position: 3rd

On 8 December 1990 due to a snowstorm only about 200 Wednesday fans were able to get to Ashton Gate to see Bristol City and Wednesday draw 1–1. The rest of the fans were stranded on snow-covered motorways.

On 21 April 1991 Wednesday won the League Cup with John Harkes the first American to play in a major English Cup Final.

On 11 May 1991 Wednesday played the last game on Oldham's artificial pitch before it was replaced by grass for the following season.

Match No.	Date	Venue	Opponents		Round	Result	HT Score	Position	Scorers	Attendance
1	Aug 25	A	Ipswich Town	W		2-0	2-0	4th	Williams, Shirtliff	17,284
2	Sep 1	H	Hull City	W		5-1	2-1	2nd	Hirst (4), Williams	23,673
3	8	A	Charlton Athletic	W		1-0	0-0	2nd	Sheridan	7,407
4	15	H	Watford	W		2-0	1-0	2nd	Pearson, Worthington	22,061
5	18	H	Newcastle United	D		2-2	1-1	2nd	Hirst, McCall	30,628
6	22	A	Leicester City	W		4-2	2-1	2nd	Hirst (2), Wilson, Williams	16,156
7	29	H	West Ham United	D		1-1	1-0	2nd	Hirst	28,786
8	Oct 3	A	Brighton & Hove Alb	W		4-0	2-0	2nd	Wilson, Sheridan, Williams, Pearson	10,379
9	6	A	Bristol Rovers	W		1-0	1-0	2nd	Francis	6,413
10	13	H	Plymouth Argyle	W		3-0	2-0	1st	Wilson, Sheridan (2)	23,489
11	20	H	Port Vale	D		1-1	1-0	2nd	Williams	24,527
12	23	A	Barnsley	D		1-1	0-0	2nd	Palmer	23,079
13	27	A	Millwall	L		2-4	2-0	3rd	Hirst (2)	12,835
14	Nov 3	H	Oldham Athletic	D		2-2	0-2	3rd	Sheridan (2 pens)	34,845
15	10	A	Blackburn Rovers	L		0-1	0-1	3rd		13,437
16	17	H	Swindon Town	W		2-1	1-0	3rd	Williams, Pearson	22,715
17	24	A	West Bromwich Alb	W		2-1	0-1	3rd	Francis, Shirtliff	16,546
18	Dec 1	H	Notts County	D		2-2	2-0	4th	Sheridan (pen), Hirst	23,474
19	8	A	Bristol City	D		1-1	1-1	3rd	Wilson	11,254
20	15	H	Ipswich Town	D		2-2	1-2	3rd	Francis, Pearson	20,431
21	22	A	Oxford United	D		2-2	2-1	3rd	Hirst, Wilson	6,061
22	26	H	Wolverhampton W	D		2-2	2-0	4th	McCall, Palmer	29,686
23	29	H	Portsmouth	W		2-1	1-0	3rd	Hirst (2)	22,885
24	Jan 1	A	Middlesbrough	W		2-0	1-0	3rd	Hirst, Williams	22,869
25	12	A	Hull City	W		1-0	1-0	3rd	Williams	10,907
26	19	H	Charlton Athletic	D		0-0	0-0	3rd		22,318
27	Feb 2	A	Watford	D		2-2	0-2	3rd	Harkes, Williams	10,338
28	19	A	Swindon Town	L		1-2	0-0	3rd	Hirst	8,274
29	Mar 2	A	Notts County	W		2-0	1-0	3rd	Williams, Thomas (og),	15,546
30	9	H	West Bromwich Alb	W		1-0	0-0	3rd	Sheridan (pen)	26,934
31	13	H	Brighton & Hove Alb	D		1-1	1-0	3rd	Anderson	23,969
32	16	A	West Ham United	W		3-1	1-0	3rd	Hirst, Williams (2)	26,182
33	19	A	Plymouth Argyle	D		1-1	0-0	3rd	MacKenzie	7,806
34	23	H	Bristol Rovers	W		2-1	0-0	3rd	Clarke (og), Williams	25,074
35	30	A	Wolverhampton W	L		2-3	0-2	3rd	Pearson (2)	18,011
36	Apr 1	H	Oxford United	L		0-2	0-0	3rd		28,682
37	6	A	Portsmouth	L		0-2	0-1	3rd		10,390
38	10	H	Blackburn Rovers	W		3-1	0-1	3rd	Anderson, Sheridan (1 + pen)	23,139
39	13	H	Middlesbrough	W		2-0	0-0	3rd	Williams (2)	30,598
40	17	A	Newcastle United	L		0-1	0-1	3rd		18,330
41	24	H	Leicester City	D		0-0	0-0	3rd		31,308
42	27	H	Barnsley	W		3-1	1-1	3rd	Hirst, Harkes, MacKenzie	30,693
43	May 4	H	Millwall	W		2-1	1-0	3rd	Hirst (2)	30,278
44	6	A	Port Vale	D		1-1	0-0	3rd	Hirst	13,317
45	8	H	Bristol City	W		3-1	1-0	3rd	Hirst (2), Francis	31,706
46	11	A	Oldham Athletic	L		2-3	1-0	3rd	Hirst, Wilson	18,809
										Apps
										Subs
									Two own-goals	Goals

Full Members' Cup

Match No.	Date	Venue	Opponents		Round	Result	HT Score	Position	Scorers	Attendance
47	Dec 18	H	Barnsley	L	2R	3-3*	1-0		Hirst (3)	5,942
										Apps
										Subs
										Goals

* (Lost 2-4 on Penalties)

League Cup

Match No.	Date	Venue	Opponents		Round	Result	HT Score	Position	Scorers	Attendance
48	Sep 26	H	Brentford	W	2R 1L	2-1	0-1		Hirst, Pearson	11,027
49	Oct 9	A	Brentford	W	2R 2L	2-1	2-1		Francis, Pearson	8,227
50	31	H	Swindon Town	D	3R	0-0	0-0			13,900
51	Nov 6	A	Swindon Town	W	3R Re	1-0	1-0		Pearson	9,043
52	28	H	Derby County	D	4R	1-1	1-1		Hirst	25,649
53	Dec 12	A	Derby County	W	4R Re	2-1	1-0		Harkes, Williams	17,050
54	Jan 23	A	Coventry City	W	5R	1-0	1-0		Pearson	20,712
55	Feb 24	A	Chelsea	W	S/F 1L	2-0	0-0		Shirtliff, Hirst	34,074
56	27	H	Chelsea	W	S/F 2L	3-1	2-0		Pearson, Wilson, Williams	34,669
57	Apr 21	N	Manchester United *	W	Final	1-0	1-0		Sheridan	77,612
										Apps
										Subs
										Goals

* Played at Wembley

FA Cup

Match No.	Date	Venue	Opponents		Round	Result	HT Score	Position	Scorers	Attendance
58	Jan 5	A	Mansfield Town	W	3R	2-0	1-0		Shirtliff, Sheridan (pen)	9,076
59	26	A	Millwall	D	4R	4-4	2-2		Hirst, Francis, Pearson, Anderson	13,663
60	30	H	Millwall	W	4R Re	2-0	1-0		Anderson, Hirst	25,140
61	Feb 16	A	Cambridge United	L	5R	0-4	0-1			9,624
										Apps
										Subs
										Goals

Anderson Viv	Barrick Dean	Francis Trevor	Harkes John	Hirst David	King Phil	MacKenzie Steve	Madden Lawrie	McCall Steve	Newsome Jon	Nilsson Roland	Palmer Carlton	Pearson Nigel	Pressman Kevin	Sheridan John	Shirtliff Peter	Turner Chris	Watson Gordon	Wetherall David	Wood Darren	Whitton Steve	Williams Paul	Wilson Danny	Worthington Nigel
		U		9	3					2	4	5	1	8	6				U		10	7	11
		S*		9	3			S#		2	4	6*	1	8	5						10	7	11#
		U		9	3			U		2	4	6	1	8	5						10	7	11
		U		9	3			U		2	4	6	1	8	5						10	7	11
		S*		9	3			S#		2	4	6	1	8	5						10	7*	11#
		S*		9*	3			U		2	4	6	1	8	5						10	7	11
		S*		9	3			U		2	4	6	1	8	5						10	7*	11
		9			3		S#	S*		2	4	6	1	8*	5						10#	7	11
		9*			3		S*	U		2	4	6	1	8	5						10	7	11
		9*			3			S#		2	4	6	1	8	5					S*	10	7	11#
		9*		S*	3			U		2	4	6	1	8	5						10	7	11
		S*		9	3*		U			2	4	6	1	8	5						10	7	11
		S*		9	3		S#			2*	4	6#	1	8	5						10	7	11
		S*	2	9	3*			U			4	6	1	8	5						10	7	11
		S*	2	9	U			11*			4	6	1	8	5						10	7	3
		S*	2	9*	3			S#			4	6	1	8	5						10	7	11#
		S*	2	9	3			U			4	6	1	8	5						10*	7	11
		10	2	9	3			U			4	6	1	8*	5						S*	7	11
		10*	2	9	3			U			4	6	1	8	5						S*	7	11
		S*	2	9	3*			U			4	6	1	8	5						10	7	11
		11	2	9	3		U				4	6	1	8	5					U	10	7	
		U	2	9	3		U	11			4	6	1	8	5						10	7	
		10	2	9	3			11#			4	6		8	5	1					S*	7*	S#
		S*	2	9*	3		U	11			4	6		8	5	1					10	7	
2		U		9	3			11*			4	6		8	5	1					10	7	S*
2		S*		9	3			U			4	6		8	5	1					10	7*	11
2		S*	7	9	3			5			4	6		8		1		U			10		11*
2		10	7	9				11*			4	6		8	5	1					S*	U	3
2		10*	7			S#		11#			4	6		8	5	1	S*				9		3
2		10	7		3						4	6		8	5	1	U				9	U	11
2		10		S*	3	S#		11#			4	6		8	5	1					9	7*	
2		S*		9*	3	S#		11			4	6		8	5	1					10	7#	
2		7*		9	3	S#		11#			4	6		8	5	1	S*				10		
2		11*		9	3	7		S*			4	6		8	5	1	U				10		
2		S#		9	3	7		11#			4	6		8*	5	1					10	S*	
2		11		9	3	S*					4	6		8	5*	1	S#				10	7#	
5		S*	7	9	3	U		11*		2	4	6		8		1					10		
6		11	7	9	3	U				2	4			8	5	1	U				10		
5		U	7*	9	3	S*				2	4	6		8		1					10		11
6		S#		9	3	8				2	4			S*	5	1					10	7*	11#
S#		S*	4*	9	3					2		6#		8	5	1					10	7	11
6		11#	2	9	3	S*					4			8	5*	1	S#				10	7	
6		U	7	9	3	5*	S*			2	4			8		1					10		11
6		S*	11	9	3	5*	U			2	4			8		1					10	7	
6		10#	S*	9	3		5			2*	4			8		1					S#	7	11
6			U	9	3				5	2	4		1	8			10*				S*	7	11
21		18	22	39	43	5	1	13	1	22	45	39	23	45	39	23	1				40	35	31
1		20	1	2		7	4	6						1			4			1	6	1	2
2		4	2	24		2		2			2	6		10	2						15	6	1

Anderson Viv	Barrick Dean	Francis Trevor	Harkes John	Hirst David	King Phil	MacKenzie Steve	Madden Lawrie	McCall Steve	Newsome Jon	Nilsson Roland	Palmer Carlton	Pearson Nigel	Pressman Kevin	Sheridan John	Shirtliff Peter	Turner Chris	Watson Gordon	Wetherall David	Wood Darren	Whitton Steve	Williams Paul	Wilson Danny	Worthington Nigel
		10*	2	9	U			S*			4	6	1	8	5						11	7	3
		1	1	1							1	1	1	1	1						1	1	1
								1															
				3																			

Anderson Viv	Barrick Dean	Francis Trevor	Harkes John	Hirst David	King Phil	MacKenzie Steve	Madden Lawrie	McCall Steve	Newsome Jon	Nilsson Roland	Palmer Carlton	Pearson Nigel	Pressman Kevin	Sheridan John	Shirtliff Peter	Turner Chris	Watson Gordon	Wetherall David	Wood Darren	Whitton Steve	Williams Paul	Wilson Danny	Worthington Nigel
	U	8		9	3			S*		2	4	6	1		5						10	7*	11
		9			3		2	U			4	6	1	8	5					U	10	7	11
		S*	2	9	3		6	S#			4		1	8	5						10*	7	11#
		U	2	9			S*	3*			4	6	1	8	5						10	7	11
		10	2	9	3*			U			4	6	1	8	5						S*	7	11
		U	2	9	3		U				4	6	1	8	5						10	7	11
		U		9	2			11	U		4	6		8	5	1					10	7	3
		10*	2	9	3			U			4	6		8	5	1					S*	7	11
		10*	2	9	3			S#			4	6		8	5	1					S*	7#	11
		U	4*	9	3		S*			2		6		8	5	1					10	7	11
		5	7	9	9		2	2		2	9	9	6	9	10	4					7	10	10
		1					2	3													3		
		1	1	3								5		1	1						2	1	

Anderson Viv	Barrick Dean	Francis Trevor	Harkes John	Hirst David	King Phil	MacKenzie Steve	Madden Lawrie	McCall Steve	Newsome Jon	Nilsson Roland	Palmer Carlton	Pearson Nigel	Pressman Kevin	Sheridan John	Shirtliff Peter	Turner Chris	Watson Gordon	Wetherall David	Wood Darren	Whitton Steve	Williams Paul	Wilson Danny	Worthington Nigel
		U	2	9	3		U	11			4	6		8	5	1					10	7	
2		10*	7	9	3						4	6		8	5	1					S*	U	11
2		10*	7	9	3			U			4	6		8	5	1					S*		11
2		S*	S#	9	3*						4	6		8	5	1					10#	7	11
3		2	3	4	4			1			4	4		4	4	4					2	2	3
		1	1																		2		
2		1		2								1		1	1								

League Table

	P	W	D	L	F	A	Pts
Oldham Athletic	46	25	13	8	83	53	88
West Ham United	46	24	15	7	60	34	87
SHEFFIELD WEDNESDAY	46	22	16	8	80	51	82
Notts County	46	23	11	12	76	55	80
Millwall	46	20	13	13	70	51	73
Brighton & Hove Albion	46	21	7	18	63	69	70
Middlesbrough	46	20	9	17	66	47	69
Barnsley	46	19	12	15	63	48	69
Bristol City	46	20	7	19	68	71	67
Oxford United	46	14	19	13	69	66	61
Newcastle United	46	14	17	15	49	56	59
Wolverhampton W.	46	13	19	14	63	63	58
Bristol Rovers	46	15	13	18	56	59	58
Ipswich Town	46	13	18	15	60	68	57
Port Vale	46	15	12	19	56	64	57
Charlton Athletic	46	13	17	16	57	61	56
Portsmouth	46	14	11	21	58	70	53
Plymouth Argyle	46	12	17	17	54	68	53
Blackburn Rovers	46	14	10	22	51	66	52
Watford	46	12	15	19	45	59	51
Swindon Town	46	12	14	20	65	73	50
Leicester City	46	14	8	24	60	83	50
West Bromwich Albion	46	10	18	18	52	61	48
Hull City	46	10	15	21	57	85	45

1991-92

Division One

Manager: Trevor Francis

Did you know that?

Final League Position: 3rd

Trevor Francis brought Eric Cantona to Sheffield for a trial, and he played in a 6-a-side game versus Baltimore Blast, played at Sheffield Arena, but after refusing to extend his trial for a further week he walked out and joined Leeds.

On 14 August 1991 Chris Woods became the first million-pound player for Wednesday when they paid £1.2 million to Glasgow Rangers.

Match No.	Date	Venue	Opponents		Round	Result	HT Score	Position	Scorers	Attendance
1	Aug 17	H	Aston Villa	L		2-3	2-1	18th	Hirst, Wilson	36,749
2	24	A	Leeds United	D		1-1	0-0	20th	Hirst	30,260
3	28	H	Everton	W		2-1	0-0	15th	Wilson, Anderson	28,690
4	31	H	Queen's Park Rangers	W		4-1	3-0	9th	Palmer (3), Sheridan	25,022
5	Sep 3	A	Notts County	L		1-2	1-1	12th	Pearson	12,297
6	7	H	Nottingham Forest	W		2-1	1-0	8th	Williams, Francis	31,289
7	14	A	Manchester City	W		1-0	0-0	5th	Williams	29,453
8	18	A	Norwich City	L		0-1	0-1	8th		12,503
9	21	H	Southampton	W		2-0	1-0	4th	Williams, Worthington	27,291
10	28	A	Liverpool	D		1-1	0-1	4th	Harkes	37,071
11	Oct 2	A	Wimbledon	L		1-2	0-0	5th	Pearson	3,121
12	5	H	Crystal Palace	W		4-1	3-1	4th	Worthington, Hirst (2), Palmer	26,230
13	19	A	Luton Town	D		2-2	1-1	5th	Hirst, Sheridan	9,401
14	26	H	Manchester United	W		3-2	1-2	5th	Hirst, Jemson (2)	38,260
15	Nov 2	H	Tottenham Hotspur	D		0-0	0-0	4th		31,573
16	17	A	Sheffield United	L		0-2	0-1	7th		31,832
17	23	H	Arsenal	D		1-1	1-0	7th	Hirst	32,174
18	30	A	West Ham United	W		2-1	1-0	4th	Harkes, Jemson	24,116
19	Dec 7	H	Chelsea	W		3-0	0-0	3rd	Hirst (2), Williams	27,383
20	21	H	Wimbledon	W		2-0	0-0	3rd	Sheridan (pen + 1)	20,574
21	26	A	Everton	W		1-0	0-0	3rd	Hirst	30,788
22	28	A	Queen's Park Rangers	D		1-1	0-1	3rd	Hirst	12,990
23	Jan 1	H	Oldham Athletic	D		1-1	0-0	3rd	Sharp (og)	32,679
24	12	H	Leeds United	L		1-6	1-3	5th	Sheridan	32,228
25	18	A	Aston Villa	W		1-0	0-0	5th	Jemson	28,036
26	Feb 1	H	Luton Town	W		3-2	1-2	5th	Hirst, Williams, Harkes	22,291
27	8	A	Manchester United	D		1-1	1-1	4th	Hirst	47,074
28	15	A	Arsenal	L		1-7	1-1	5th	Worthington	26,805
29	22	H	West Ham United	W		2-1	0-1	4th	Palmer, Anderson	26,150
30	29	A	Chelsea	W		3-0	3-0	4th	Wilson, Worthington, Williams	17,538
31	Mar 7	H	Coventry City	D		1-1	0-0	3rd	Anderson	23,959
32	11	H	Sheffield United	L		1-3	0-2	3rd	King	40,327
33	14	A	Tottenham Hotspur	W		2-0	0-0	3rd	Hirst, Williams	23,027
34	21	H	Notts County	W		1-0	0-0	3rd	Hirst	23,910
35	28	A	Oldham Athletic	L		0-3	0-1	3rd		15,897
36	Apr 4	A	Nottingham Forest	W		2-0	2-0	3rd	Williams, Hirst	26,105
37	8	A	Coventry City	D		0-0	0-0	3rd		13,293
38	11	H	Manchester City	W		2-0	0-0	3rd	Hirst, Worthington	32,138
39	18	A	Southampton	W		1-0	0-0	3rd	Hirst	17,715
40	20	H	Norwich City	W		2-0	2-0	3rd	Nilsson, Sheridan	27,362
41	25	A	Crystal Palace	D		1-1	1-0	3rd	Williams	21,573
42	May 2	H	Liverpool	D		0-0	0-0	3rd		34,861
										Apps
										Subs
									One own-goal	Goals

Full Members' Cup

Match No.	Date	Venue	Opponents		Round	Result	HT Score	Position	Scorers	Attendance
43	Oct 23	H	Manchester City	W	2R	3-2	1-1		Hirst, Hyde, Jemson	7,951
44	Nov 26	A	Notts County	L	Q/F	0-1	0-0			4,118
										Apps
										Subs
										Goals

League Cup

Match No.	Date	Venue	Opponents		Round	Result	HT Score	Position	Scorers	Attendance
45	Sep 24	A	Leyton Orient	D	2R 1L	0-0	0-0			6,231
46	Oct 9	H	Leyton Orient	W	2R 2L	4-1	2-0		Anderson, P.Williams, Francis (2)	14,398
47	30	H	Southampton	D	3R	1-1	1-0		Hirst	17,627
48	Nov 20	A	Southampton	L	3R Re	0-1	0-0			10,801
										Apps
										Subs
										Goals

FA Cup

Match No.	Date	Venue	Opponents		Round	Result	HT Score	Position	Scorers	Attendance
49	Jan 4	A	Preston North End	W	3R	2-0	0-0		Sheridan, Bart-Williams	14,337
50	Feb 4	H	Middlesbrough	L	4R	1-2	1-1		Hirst	29,772
										Apps
										Subs
										Goals

Anderson Viv	Bart-Williams Chris	Francis Trevor	Harkes John	Hirst David	Hyde Graham	Jemson Nigel	Johnson David	King Phil	MacKenzie Steve	Nilsson Roland	Palmer Carlton	Pearson Nigel	Pressman Kevin	Sheridan John	Shirtliff Peter	Warhurst Paul	Watson Gordon	Williams Paul	Williams Mike	Wilson Danny	Wood Darren	Woods Chris	Worthington Nigel
		S*	S#	9				3		2	4	6		8#		5		10*		7		1	11
S*		S#		9#				3		2	4	6		8		5		10*		7		1	11
6		S*#		9				3	S#	2	4			8		5		10*		7		1	11
6		S*		9*				3	S#	2	4			8		5		10		7		1	11#
2		S*		9*				3	S#		4	6		8		5		10		7		1	11#
S#		S*						3		2	4	6		8		5	9*	10#		7		1	11
U		S*			8			3		2	4	6				5	9*	10		7		1	11
			S*		8*	S#		3		2	4	6				5	9#	10		7		1	11
S*		S#	8			9#		3		2	4	6*				5		10		7		1	11
U		S*	8			9*		3		2	4	6				5		10		7		1	11
S#		S*	8			9*		3#		2	4	6				5		10		7		1	11
8		S*		9*				3		2	4	6				5		10		7	U	1	11
5				9	S#	S*		3		2	4	6		8				10		7#		1	11*
6			S#	9#		S*		3		2	4			8		5		10		7		1	11*
6			S*	9		S#		3#		2	4			8		5		10		7*		1	11
6			S*	9		S#		3		2	4			8		5		10		7*		1	11#
S*	11		7	9		10#		3		2*	4	5		8		6		S#				1	
S*	7		2	9		10		3			4*	5		8		6		U				1	11
	7		S*	9		10#		3		2	4	5	1	8		6*		S#					11
S#	7		11	9*		10		3		2#	4	5		8		6		S*				1	
	7		11	9		10*		3		2	4	5		8#		6		S*		S#		1	
	7*		11	9	S#	S*		3		2	4	5				6		10#		8		1	
	7		2	9*	S#	10		3			4			8#	5			S*		6		1	11
6	9		S*			10		3		2	4	5*		8			7	S#				1	11#
6			S*		8	10	9	3		2*	4				5		U			7		1	11
U		S*	7	9	8			3		2	4	6				5		10				1	11*
			S#	9	8		10*	3		2	4	5				6		S*		7		1	11#
5			S*	9	8*		10	3		2	4#					6		S#		7		1	11
5	S*		11	9	8*		10#			2	4				6			S#		7		1	3
5	8#			9			S*	3		2	4				6	S#		10*		7		1	11
5	8#			9		S*		3		2	4				6	S#		10		7		1	11*
5			S*	9	8	S#		3		2	4	11#			6			10		7*		1	
	S#		11	9*	8#	S*				2	4	5			6	3		10		7		1	
	8#	S*	11	9	S#					2	4	5			6	3		10		7*		1	
	8#	S#	11	9				S*		2	4	5			6	3*		10		7		1	
		U	S*	9				3		2	4	5		8*	6			10		7		1	11
		S#	S*	9				3		2	4	5		8	6*			10#		7		1	11
		S*	S#	9				3		2	4	5		8#		6		10*		7		1	11
S*		S#		9*				3		2	4	5		8		6		10#		7		1	11
		S*	S#				9*	3		2	4	5		8#		6		10		7		1	11
		S*		9*				3		2	4	5		8	6	U		10		7		1	11
	S*	S#		9				3		2	4	5		8#		6		10*		7		1	11
15	12		14	33	9	11	5	38		39	42	31	1	24	12	31	4	31		35		41	34
8	3	20	15		4	9	1	1	3							2		9		1			
3		1	3	18		4		1		1	5	2		6				9		3			5

5			7*	9	8	S#		3		2	4							10		S*	6	1	11#
2	S*		7	9		10		3#			4	6				5	S#	11		8*		1	
2			2	2	1	1		2		1	2	1				1		2		1	1	2	1
	1					1											1			1			
				1	1	1																	

6		U	8			9		3		2						5	10		U	7	4	1	11
2		S*		9*	8#			3			4	6				5		10		7	S#	1	11
5			6	9		S*		3		2	4			8				10*		7	U	1	11
5			11*	9		S*		3		2	4	6		8				10		7		1	U
4			3	3	1	1		4		3	3	2		2		2	1	3		4	1	4	3
		1				2															1		
1		2		1														1					

5	7		6*		S#	10		3		2	4			8#			9			S*		1	11
S#		S*	7	9	8			3		2	4	5				6		10#				1	11*
1	1		2	1	1	1		2		2	2	1		1		1	1	1				2	2
1		1			1															1			
	1			1										1									

League Table

	P	W	D	L	F	A	Pts
Leeds United	42	22	16	4	74	37	82
Manchester United	42	21	15	6	63	33	78
SHEFFIELD WEDNESDAY	42	21	12	9	62	49	75
Arsenal	42	19	15	8	81	46	72
Manchester City	42	20	10	12	61	48	70
Liverpool	42	16	16	10	47	40	64
Aston Villa	42	17	9	16	48	44	60
Nottingham Forest	42	16	11	15	60	58	59
Sheffield United	42	16	9	17	65	63	57
Crystal Palace	42	14	15	13	53	61	57
Queen's Park Rangers	42	12	18	12	48	47	54
Everton	42	13	14	15	52	51	53
Wimbledon	42	13	14	15	53	53	53
Chelsea	42	13	14	15	50	60	53
Tottenham Hotspur	42	15	7	20	58	63	52
Southampton	42	14	10	18	39	55	52
Oldham Athletic	42	14	9	19	63	67	51
Norwich City	42	11	12	19	47	63	45
Coventry City	42	11	11	20	35	44	44
Luton Town	42	10	12	20	38	71	42
Notts County	42	10	10	22	40	62	40
West Ham United	42	9	11	22	37	59	38

1992-93

Premiership

Manager: Trevor Francis

Did you know that?

Final League Position: 7th

Wednesday and Arsenal met in the Final of the FA and League Cup in the same season, with Arsenal coming out on top in both. In the League Cup Final on 18 April 1993 John Harkes became the first American to score in a major English Cup Final.

Match No.	Date	Venue	Opponents		Round	Result	HT Score	Position	Scorers	Attendance
1	Aug 15	A	Everton	D		1-1	1-1	13th	Pearson	27,687
2	19	H	Nottingham Forest	W		2-0	1-0	5th	Hirst (2)	29,623
3	22	H	Chelsea	D		3-3	2-0	8th	Hirst (1 + pen), Wilson	26,338
4	25	A	Crystal Palace	D		1-1	0-1	8th	Williams	14,005
5	29	A	Arsenal	L		1-2	1-2	10th	Hirst	23,389
6	Sep 2	H	Coventry City	L		1-2	0-1	14th	Bart-Williams	22,874
7	5	H	Manchester City	L		0-3	0-1	17th		27,169
8	12	A	Nottingham Forest	W		2-1	1-0	14th	Warhurst, Hyde	19,420
9	19	A	Norwich City	L		0-1	0-1	16th		13,367
10	27	H	Tottenham Hotspur	W		2-0	2-0	11th	Bright, Anderson	24,895
11	Oct 3	A	Liverpool	L		0-1	0-0	13th		35,785
12	17	H	Oldham Athletic	W		2-1	2-1	12th	Palmer, Bright	24,485
13	24	A	Middlesbrough	D		1-1	1-1	13th	Bright	18,414
14	31	H	Blackburn Rovers	D		0-0	0-0	13th		31,044
15	Nov 8	A	Sheffield United	D		1-1	0-0	13th	Hirst	30,039
16	21	H	Ipswich Town	D		1-1	1-0	14th	Thompson (og)	24,270
17	28	A	Wimbledon	D		1-1	1-0	15th	Bart-Williams	5,740
18	Dec 5	H	Aston Villa	L		1-2	1-1	16th	Bright	29,964
19	12	A	Leeds United	L		1-3	1-1	17th	Nilsson	29,770
20	19	H	Queen's Park Rangers	W		1-0	1-0	15th	Bright	23,164
21	26	H	Manchester United	D		3-3	2-0	14th	Hirst, Bright, Sheridan	37,708
22	28	A	Southampton	W		2-1	1-0	14th	Sheridan (pen), Hirst	17,426
23	Jan 10	H	Norwich City	W		1-0	1-0	11th	Worthington	23,360
24	16	A	Tottenham Hotspur	W		2-0	0-0	10th	Bright, Hirst	25,702
25	30	A	Chelsea	W		2-0	1-0	9th	Warhurst, Harkes	16,261
26	Feb 6	H	Everton	W		3-1	2-0	9th	Warhurst, Harkes, Waddle	24,979
27	20	H	Crystal Palace	W		2-1	1-0	6th	Warhurst, Wilson	26,459
28	23	A	Manchester City	W		2-1	0-0	4th	Anderson, Warhurst	23,619
29	27	H	Liverpool	D		1-1	0-1	4th	Anderson	33,964
30	Mar 3	A	Coventry City	L		0-1	0-1	4th		13,206
31	10	A	Ipswich Town	W		1-0	0-0	4th	Hirst	16,538
32	20	A	Aston Villa	L		0-2	0-1	4th		38,024
33	24	H	Wimbledon	D		1-1	0-0	5th	Bright	20,918
34	Apr 7	A	Oldham Athletic	D		1-1	0-1	6th	Watson	12,312
35	10	A	Manchester United	L		1-2	0-0	8th	Sheridan (pen)	40,102
36	12	H	Southampton	W		5-2	2-0	6th	Bright, Bart-Williams (3), King	26,184
37	21	H	Sheffield United	D		1-1	0-1	6th	Warhurst	38,688
38	May 1	H	Middlesbrough	L		2-3	0-2	10th	Bart-Williams, Morris (og)	25,949
39	4	H	Leeds United	D		1-1	0-1	7th	Hirst	26,855
40	6	H	Arsenal	W		1-0	1-0	5th	Bright	23,645
41	8	A	Blackburn Rovers	L		0-1	0-0	6th		14,956
42	11	A	Queen's Park Rangers	L		1-3	0-2	7th	Bright	12,177
										Apps
										Subs
									Two own-goals	Goals

UEFA Cup

Match No.	Date	Venue	Opponents		Round	Result	HT Score	Position	Scorers	Attendance
43	Sep 16	H	Spora Luxembourg	W	1R 1L	8-1	4-1		Waddle, Anderson (2), Warhurst (2), Bart-Williams (2), Worthington	19,792
44	Oct 1	A	Spora Luxembourg	W	1R 2L	2-1	2-1		Watson, Warhurst	2,379
45	20	A	Kaiserslautern	L	2R 1L	1-3	1-1		Hirst	20,802
46	Nov 4	H	Kaiserslautern	D	2R 2L	2-2	1-0		Wilson, Sheridan	27,597
										Apps
										Subs
										Goals

League Cup

Match No.	Date	Venue	Opponents		Round	Result	HT Score	Position	Scorers	Attendance
47	Sep 23	H	Hartlepool United	W	2R 1L	3-0	0-0		Watson, Bright, Wilson	10,112
48	Oct 6	A	Hartlepool United	D	2R 2L	2-2	1-0		Bright, Warhurst	4,667
49	27	H	Leicester City	W	3R	7-1	2-0		Hirst, Worthington, Bright (2), Watson (2) Bart-Williams	17,326
50	Dec 2	H	Queen's Park Rangers	W	4R	4-0	2-0		Bright, Hirst, Palmer, Nilsson	17,161
51	Jan 19	A	Ipswich Town	D	5R	1-1	0-0		Sheridan	19,374
52	Feb 3	H	Ipswich Town	W	5R Re	1-0	0-0		Warhurst	26,328
53	10	A	Blackburn Rovers	W	S/F 1L	4-2	4-2		Harkes, Sheridan, Warhurst (2)	17,283
54	Mar 14	H	Blackburn Rovers	W	S/F 2L	2-1	0-1		Hirst, Bright	30,048
55	Apr 18	N	Arsenal *	L	F	1-2	1-1		Harkes	74,007
										Apps
										Subs
										Goals

* At Wembley

FA Cup

Match No.	Date	Venue	Opponents		Round	Result	HT Score	Position	Scorers	Attendance
56	Jan 13	A	Cambridge United	W	3R	2-1	0-0		Harkes, Bright	7,754
57	24	H	Sunderland	W	4R	1-0	0-0		Bright	33,422
58	Feb 13	H	Southend United	W	5R	2-0	1-0		Warhurst (2)	26,466
59	Mar 8	A	Derby County	D	6R	3-3	2-1		Sheridan (pen), Warhurst (2)	22,811
60	17	H	Derby County	W	6R Re	1-0	1-0		Warhurst	32,033
61	Apr 3	N	Sheffield United * #	W	S/F	2-1	1-1		Waddle, Bright	75,365
62	May 15	N	Arsenal * #	D	F	1-1	0-1		Hirst	79,347
63	20	N	Arsenal * #	L	F Re	1-2	0-1		Waddle	62,267
										Apps
										Subs
										Goals

* At Wembley
# After extra-time (Score at 90 minutes 1-1)

Anderson Viv	Bart-Williams Chris	Beresford Marlon	Bright Mark	Francis Trevor	Harkes John	Hirst David	Hyde Graham	Jemson Nigel	Jones Ryan	Key Lance	King Phil	Nilsson Roland	Palmer Carlton	Pearson Nigel	Pressman Kevin	Sheridan John	Shirtliff Peter	Stewart Simon	Waddle Chris	Warhurst Paul	Watson Gordon	Watts Julian	Williams Michael	Williams Paul	Wilson Danny	Woods Chris	Worthington Nigel
	S*					9#	8				3	2	4	5	U				7*	6	S#			10		1	11
	8			U	S*	9					3*	2	4	5	U					6				10	7	1	11
	8	U		S*	7#	9					3*	2	4	5						6				10	S#	1	11
	S*	U		U		9	8				3		4*	5			6			2				10	7	1	11
	8				S*	9#	4	S#				2		5	U		6			3				10	7*	1	11
	8			S*				7*				2	4	5	U		6		9	3#				10	S#	1	11
	8			S#	S*							2*	4	5	U				9	6	7			10	3#	1	11
3	10		9		2		7						4		U		5		8*	6#	S#				S*	1	11
6	10		9	11*	2			S*#					4	S#	U		5		8						7	1	3
6	10		9		2			U				7*	4		U		5		8		11				S*	1	3
6	10#		9		2		S*					7	4		U		5		8	11*	S#					1	3
6	10		11		7	9*							4		U		5		8#	2	S#				S*	1	3
6	10		9		2		7						4	5	U				8	11*	S*				U	1	3
6	U		10		2	9							4	5	U	11			8		U				7	1	3
	6		10		U	9						2	4	5	U	11*			8	S*					7	1	3
	S*		10		U	9						2	4	5	U	11			8	6*					7	1	3
4	5		10		S*	9						2			U	11	U		8	6					7*	1	3
5	S*		10		7*	9						2	4		U	11#			8	6	S#					1	3
	S*		10		7	9						2	4	5	U	11			8*	6	U					1	3
5	S*		10			9						2	4		U	11			8	6*	U				7	1	3
5	U		10		S*	9						2	4		U	11	6		8						7*	1	3
5	U		10		U	9						2	4		U	11	6		8						7	1	3
5*	S#		10		4	9#						2			U	11	6		8	S*					7	1	3
	U		10		4	9	7*					2		5	U	11	6		8	S*						1	3
	10#				5		S#					2*	4	S*	U	11	6		8	9					7	1	3
					5		S*	10*				2	4	S#	U	11	6		8	9					7#	1	3
U	10*				5			S*				2	4		U	11	6		8	9					7	1	3
S*	10#		S#		5							2	4		U	11	6		8	9					7*	1	3
S*	S#		10		5		7#					2	4		U	11	6*		8	9						1	3
6			10				7#	S#	5*		2		4		U	11			8	9		S*				1	3
6			10	S#		9*	7	8	11		2#				U			4			S*	5				1	3
6			10				S*	U				2	4		U	11		5*	8	9					7	1	3
6	9#		10					S#	5			2*	4		U	11			8			S*			7	1	3
6	S*				5*		7	10	9		S#	2			U			4	8#		11					1	3
6	S*		S#					10#			9	2	4		U	5			8		11				7*	1	3
6#	10		9		4*		7	S#	8		3				1			5				2	S*			U	11
	S#		10		5	9	S*		7*			2	4		U	11			8#	6						1	3
6	S*		10		7	9*	U					2	4		U	11	5			8						1	3
	10				S*	9	8		6		3#	2	4		U		5			S#					7*	1	11
5	10#		9		2		4	S#	8*	U	3				1	11		6	S*				7				
6	S#		10		7	9	S*					2	4		U	11*	5		8#							1	3
6	10		9				8	S*	4		3	2	S#		1	11		5#					7*			U	
24	21		28	1	23	22	14	5	9		11	32	33	13	3	25	20	6	32	25	4	2	2	7	21	39	40
2	13		2	4	6		6	8			1		1	3					1	4	7	2	1		5		
3	6		11		2	11	1				1	1	1	1		3			1	6	1			1	2		1

Anderson Viv	Bart-Williams Chris	Beresford Marlon	Bright Mark	Francis Trevor	Harkes John	Hirst David	Hyde Graham	Jemson Nigel	Jones Ryan	Key Lance	King Phil	Nilsson Roland	Palmer Carlton	Pearson Nigel	Pressman Kevin	Sheridan John	Shirtliff Peter	Stewart Simon	Waddle Chris	Warhurst Paul	Watson Gordon	Watts Julian	Williams Michael	Williams Paul	Wilson Danny	Woods Chris	Worthington Nigel
3	10			9	2		7*	S#					4		U		5		8	6#	U		U		S*	1	11
					2		6	10				3*	S#	5	1		U		S*	9#	11	4	8		7	U	U
6	S*				2	9	11*						4	5	U	U			8	10#	S#		U		7	1	3
6	S#				2*			U				S*	4	5#	U	11	U		8	10	9				7	1	3
3	1			1	4	1	3	1				1	3	3	1	1	1		3	4	2	1	1		3	3	3
	2							1				1	1						1		1				1		
2	2					1										1			1	3	1				1		1

Anderson Viv	Bart-Williams Chris	Beresford Marlon	Bright Mark	Francis Trevor	Harkes John	Hirst David	Hyde Graham	Jemson Nigel	Jones Ryan	Key Lance	King Phil	Nilsson Roland	Palmer Carlton	Pearson Nigel	Pressman Kevin	Sheridan John	Shirtliff Peter	Stewart Simon	Waddle Chris	Warhurst Paul	Watson Gordon	Watts Julian	Williams Michael	Williams Paul	Wilson Danny	Woods Chris	Worthington Nigel
6	10		9		2			U					4		1		5		8		11		U		7		3
2	S*		9				11						4	6	1		5		8*	10					7	U	3
6	S#		10		2	9*							4	5		11#			8		S*				7	1	3
5	S*		10#		7	9						2	4*			11			8	6	S#					1	3
U	S*		10		4	9*								5		11	6		8	2					7	1	3
	10*				5			U				2	4	S*		11	6		8	9					7	1	3
	10*				5			S#				2	4	S*#		11	6		8	9					7	1	3
6			10			S*	5				3*	2	4			11#		S#	8	9					7	1	
5			10		6	S*	S#				3#	2	4			11			8	9					7*	1	
6	3		7		7	3	2				2	5	8	3	2	7	5		9	7	1				8	7	7
	4					2	1	1						2				1			2						
	1		6		2	3						1	1			2				4	3				1		1

Anderson Viv	Bart-Williams Chris	Beresford Marlon	Bright Mark	Francis Trevor	Harkes John	Hirst David	Hyde Graham	Jemson Nigel	Jones Ryan	Key Lance	King Phil	Nilsson Roland	Palmer Carlton	Pearson Nigel	Pressman Kevin	Sheridan John	Shirtliff Peter	Stewart Simon	Waddle Chris	Warhurst Paul	Watson Gordon	Watts Julian	Williams Michael	Williams Paul	Wilson Danny	Woods Chris	Worthington Nigel
	U		10		4	9*						2		5		11	6		8	S*					7	1	3
	S#		10		4							2	S*	5*		11	6		8		9#				7	1	3
S#	10*				5			S*				2	4			11	6		8	9#					7	1	3
6			10		5#		S*	S#				2	4			11*			8	9					7	1	3
6			10			S*	U				5*	2	4			11			8	9					7	1	3
6			10		5	S*	S#					2	4			11#			8	9*					7	1	3
6*	S#		9		11	5	S*					2	4			10			7#	8						1	3
	S#		9		11	5	S*					2#	4			10			7	8					6*	1	3
4	1		7		7	3					1	8	6	2		8	3		8	6	1				7	8	8
1	3					2	4	2					1							1							
			3		1	1										1			2	5							

League Table

	P	W	D	L	F	A	Pts
Manchester United	42	24	12	6	67	31	84
Aston Villa	42	21	11	10	57	40	74
Norwich City	42	21	9	12	61	65	72
Blackburn Rovers	42	20	11	11	68	46	71
Queen's Park Rangers	42	17	12	13	63	55	63
Liverpool	42	16	11	15	62	55	59
SHEFFIELD WEDNESDAY	42	15	14	13	55	51	59
Tottenham Hotspur	42	16	11	15	60	66	59
Manchester City	42	15	12	15	56	51	57
Arsenal	42	15	11	16	40	38	56
Chelsea	42	14	14	14	51	54	56
Wimbledon	42	14	12	16	56	55	54
Everton	42	15	8	19	53	55	53
Sheffield United	42	14	10	18	54	53	52
Coventry City	42	13	13	16	52	57	52
Ipswich Town	42	12	16	14	50	55	52
Leeds United	42	12	15	15	57	62	51
Southampton	42	13	11	18	54	61	50
Oldham Athletic	42	13	10	19	63	74	49
Crystal Palace	42	11	16	15	48	61	49
Middlesbrough	42	11	11	20	54	75	44
Nottingham Forest	42	10	10	22	41	62	40

1993-94

Premiership

Manager: Trevor Francis

Did you know that?

Final League Position: 7th

On 4 December 1993 Wednesday beat Liverpool in a home game 3–1, with Neil Ruddock netting an own-goal after only 30 seconds, and then Mark Wright repeating the same feat after 59 minutes.

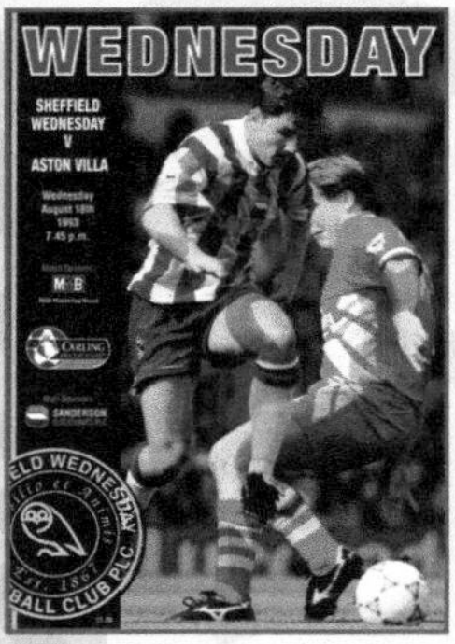

Match No.	Date	Venue	Opponents		Round	Result	HT Score	Position	Scorers	Attendance
1	Aug 14	A	Liverpool	L		0-2	0-1	18th		44,004
2	18	H	Aston Villa	D		0-0	0-0	17th		28,450
3	21	H	Arsenal	L		0-1	0-1	20th		26,023
4	25	A	West Ham United	L		0-2	0-0	21st		19,441
5	28	A	Chelsea	D		1-1	1-1	21st	Bright	16,652
6	Sep 1	H	Norwich City	D		3-3	0-0	21st	Bart-Williams, Bright, Sinton	25,175
7	13	A	Newcastle United	L		2-4	1-1	21st	Sinton (2)	33,890
8	18	H	Southampton	W		2-0	0-0	19th	Sheridan (pen), Hirst	22,503
9	25	A	Blackburn Rovers	D		1-1	0-0	21st	Hyde	13,917
10	Oct 2	H	Manchester United	L		2-3	0-0	19th	Bart-Williams, Bright	34,548
11	16	H	Wimbledon	D		2-2	1-0	19th	Waddle, Jones	21,752
12	23	A	Sheffield United	D		1-1	1-1	19th	Palmer	30,044
13	30	H	Leeds United	D		3-3	2-1	20th	Waddle, Jones, Bright	31,892
14	Nov 6	A	Ipswich Town	W		4-1	1-0	17th	Jemson (2), Bright, Palmer	15,070
15	20	H	Coventry City	D		0-0	0-0	17th		23,379
16	24	H	Oldham Athletic	W		3-0	2-0	16th	Watson (2), Jemson	18,509
17	27	A	Manchester City	W		3-1	0-0	14th	Jones (2), Jemson	23,416
18	Dec 4	H	Liverpool	W		3-1	1-1	12th	Ruddock (og), Wright (og), Bright	32,177
19	8	A	Aston Villa	D		2-2	1-1	12th	Bart-Williams, Teale (og)	20,304
20	12	A	Arsenal	L		0-1	0-0	15th		22,026
21	18	H	West Ham United	W		5-0	1-0	13th	Marsh (og), Bright, Waddle, Jemson, Palmer	26,350
22	27	A	Everton	W		2-0	2-0	10th	Bright, Palmer	16,777
23	29	H	Swindon Town	D		3-3	1-2	10th	Bright, Watson (2)	30,570
24	Jan 1	A	Queen's Park Rangers	W		2-1	0-0	9th	Bright, Watson	16,858
25	3	H	Tottenham Hotspur	W		1-0	1-0	6th	Bright	32,514
26	15	A	Wimbledon	L		1-2	0-2	8th	Pearce	5,536
27	22	H	Sheffield United	W		3-1	0-0	7th	Bright, Pearce, Watson	34,959
28	Feb 5	A	Tottenham Hotspur	W		3-1	1-0	6th	Coleman, Bright (2)	23,078
29	26	A	Norwich City	D		1-1	0-0	8th	Watson	18,311
30	Mar 5	H	Newcastle United	L		0-1	0-0	8th		33,224
31	12	A	Southampton	D		1-1	0-0	8th	Bart-Williams	16,391
32	16	A	Manchester United	L		0-5	0-4	8th		43,669
33	20	H	Blackburn Rovers	L		1-2	1-1	9th	Watson	24,699
34	30	H	Chelsea	W		3-1	2-0	9th	Bart-Williams, Palmer, Sheridan (pen)	20,433
35	Apr 2	H	Everton	W		5-1	2-0	7th	Jones, Bart-Williams, Worthington, Bright (2)	24,096
36	4	A	Swindon Town	W		1-0	0-0	6th	Watson	13,727
37	9	H	Queen's Park Rangers	W		3-1	3-0	6th	Bright (2) Sheridan (pen),	22,437
38	16	A	Coventry City	D		1-1	0-1	6th	Jones	13,013
39	23	H	Ipswich Town	W		5-0	2-0	6th	D.Linighan (og), Watson, Pearce, Bart-Williams, Bright	23,457
40	30	A	Oldham Athletic	D		0-0	0-0	7th		12,967
41	May 3	A	Leeds United	D		2-2	1-0	7th	Bart-Williams, Watson	33,806
42	7	H	Manchester City	D		1-1	1-0	7th	Watson	33,773
										App
										Sub
									Five own-goals	Goals

League Cup

Match No.	Date	Venue	Opponents		Round	Result	HT Score	Position	Scorers	Attendance
43	Sep 21	A	Bolton Wanderers	D	2R 1L	1-1	0-0		Bart-Williams	11,590
44	Oct 6	H	Bolton Wanderers	W	2R 2L	1-0	0-0		Bright	16,194
45	27	A	Middlesbrough	D	3R	1-1	0-0		Palmer	14,765
46	Nov 10	H	Middlesbrough *	W	3R Re	2-1	1-1		Watson, Palmer	19,482
47	Dec 1	A	Queen's Park Rangers	W	4R	2-1	1-1		Jemson, Jones	13,253
48	Jan 11	A	Wimbledon	W	5R	2-1	0-0		Watson, Bright	8,784
49	Feb 13	A	Manchester United	L	S/F 1L	0-1	0-1			43,294
50	Mar 2	H	Manchester United	L	S/F 2L	1-4	1-3		Hyde	34,878
										App
										Sub
										Goals

* After extra-time. Score at full-time 1-1

FA Cup

Match No.	Date	Venue	Opponents		Round	Result	HT Score	Position	Scorers	Attendance
51	Jan 8	H	Nottingham Forest	D	3R	1-1	1-0		Bright	32,488
52	19	A	Nottingham Forest	W	3R Re	2-0	0-0		Pearce, Bart-Williams	25,268
53	29	A	Chelsea	D	4R	1-1	0-1		Hyde	26,094
54	Feb 9	H	Chelsea *	L	4R Re	1-3	1-1		Bright	26,114
										App
										Sub
										Goals

* After extra-time. Score at full-time 1-1

14 Bart-Williams Chris	10 Bright Mark	29 Briscoe Lee	28 Coleman Simon	26 Francis Trevor	9 Hirst David	16 Hyde Graham	19 Jemson Nigel	21 Jones Ryan	23 Key Lance	18 King Phil	6 Linighan Brian	2 Nilsson Roland	4 Palmer Carlton	12 Pearce Andy	7 Poric Adem	5 Pearson Nigel	13 Pressman Kevin	11 Sheridan John	15 Sinton Andrew	8 Waddle Chris	17 Walker Des	7 Warhurst Paul	20 Watson Gordon	24 Watts Julian	25 Williams Michael	1 Woods Chris	3 Worthington Nigel
8*	S#				9	S*				3		2	7	5			U	6			4	10#				1	11
U	S*				9*	7				3		2	8	5			U	6			4	10				1	11
S*	S#				9	8				3#			7	5			U	6*	11		4	10				1	2
8	S*				9#	7						2	5			S#	U		11	6	4	10*				1	3
9	10					7					U	2				5	U	8	11	6	4		U			1	3
9	10					7						2		U		5	U	8	11	6	4		U			1	3
9*	10					7						2		U		5	U	8	11	6	4		S*			1	3
S#	10				9	S*						2	8			5*	U	7	11	6	4					1	3#
9*	10					7#		S#		3		2		5			U	8	11	6	4					1	S*
9	10					8		U		3		2	5	U			U	7	11	6	4					1	
6*	9					8	U	11					7	5	S*		1		3	10	4				2	U	
	9*					8	S*	11				2	7	5	6		1		3	10	4				U	U	
	9						10*	8				2	7	5			1	S*	11	6	4				U	U	3
	9					S*	10*	7				2	8	5	U		1		11	6	4					U	3
				S*		7	10*	8	U			2	9	5	U		1		11	6	4						3
S*						S#	10	8	U			2	7	5#			1		11*	6	4		9				3
S*	9					7	10	8	U			2	5		U		1		11*	6	4						3
7*	9		S#			11	10#	8	U			2	5		S*		1			6	4						3
8*	9		S*			6	10	7	U			2	5		U		1			11	4						3
6#	9		3			7	10*	8	U			2	5	S#	S*		1				4						11
11	9					8	10					2	7	5	U		1			6	4		U			U	3
7*	9					8	10#	S*				2	11	5			1			6	4		S#			U	3
S#	9					7		S*				2	8	5*			1		11#	6	4		10			U	3
6*	9					7	S#	8				2	5	S*			1		11#		4		10			U	3
6*	9					7	S#	8				2	5	S*			1		11#		4		10			U	3
S*	9		3			8	U	7	U		2*		6	5			1		11		4		10				
S*	9		3			7	U	8				2	6	5			1		11*		4		10			U	
6	9	S*	3		S#	7		11*				2	8	5			1				4		10#			U	
6*	10#		3		9	7			U			2	8	5	S*		1		11		4		S#				
6	9*		3			8#	S*		U	S#		2	7	5			1		11		4		10				
6	9		7				U		U	3		2	8	5	U		1		11		4		10				
10	9		3				U			8		2*		5	7		1		11		4		S*	6		U	
6	9		3			7	S*			S#		2	5				1	8#	11		4		10*			U	
10#	9					S#		11				2	7	5			1	8			4		S*		6*	U	3
10	9							11		S#		2	7	5			1	8#			4		S*		6*	U	3
10	9#		S#					11				2	7	5			1	8			4		S*		6*	U	3
6	9		S*				U	11				2	7	5			1	8			4*		10			U	3
10*	9		S#			6		11				2#	7	5			1	8			4		S*			U	3
6	9					S*	S#	11				2	7	5			1	8*			4		10#			U	3
6*	9					S*	S#	11				2	7	5			1	8#			4		10			U	3
6	9#		2			S*	S#	11					7	5			1	8*			4		10			U	3
6	9					S*	U	11				2	7	5			1	8			4*		10			U	3
30	36		10		6	27	10	24		7	1	38	37	29	2	4	32	19	25	19	42	4	15	1	4	10	30
7	4	1	5	1	1	9	8	3		3				3	4	1		1					8				1
8	19		1		1	1	5	6					5	3				3	3	3			12				1

14 Bart-Williams Chris	10 Bright Mark	29 Briscoe Lee	28 Coleman Simon	26 Francis Trevor	9 Hirst David	16 Hyde Graham	19 Jemson Nigel	21 Jones Ryan	23 Key Lance	18 King Phil	6 Linighan Brian	2 Nilsson Roland	4 Palmer Carlton	12 Pearce Andy	7 Poric Adem	5 Pearson Nigel	13 Pressman Kevin	11 Sheridan John	15 Sinton Andrew	8 Waddle Chris	17 Walker Des	7 Warhurst Paul	20 Watson Gordon	24 Watts Julian	25 Williams Michael	1 Woods Chris	3 Worthington Nigel
S*	9					8			U	3		2	6	5*				7	10	11	4		U			1	
9	10					8				3#		2	5	S#			U	7	11	6*	4		S*			1	
	9					6	S*	8*				2	7	5			1		11	10	4#				S#	U	3
						S*	9	8	U				7	5	S#		1		11	6	4		10*		2#		3
11*	9		U			7	10	8	U			2	5		S*		1			6	4						3
U	9		3			7		8			2		6	5	U		1		11		4		10			U	
S*	10		3		9	7						2	8	5			1		11	6*	4		U			U	
6	10		3		9	7			U			2	8	5	U		1		11*		4		S*				
3	7		3		2	7	2	4		2	1	6	8	6			6	2	7	6	8		2		1	2	3
2						1	1							1	2								2		1		
1	2					1	1	1					2										2				

14 Bart-Williams Chris	10 Bright Mark	29 Briscoe Lee	28 Coleman Simon	26 Francis Trevor	9 Hirst David	16 Hyde Graham	19 Jemson Nigel	21 Jones Ryan	23 Key Lance	18 King Phil	6 Linighan Brian	2 Nilsson Roland	4 Palmer Carlton	12 Pearce Andy	7 Poric Adem	5 Pearson Nigel	13 Pressman Kevin	11 Sheridan John	15 Sinton Andrew	8 Waddle Chris	17 Walker Des	7 Warhurst Paul	20 Watson Gordon	24 Watts Julian	25 Williams Michael	1 Woods Chris	3 Worthington Nigel
6	9					7	10	8				2*	5	S*			1		11		4		S#			U	3#
6	9					8	S*	11			2		7	5	U		1		3		4		10*			U	
7			3		S*	8	9	11*				2	6	5			1				4		10	U		U	
6	9		3			8						2	7	5	U		1		11	S*	4		10*			U	
4	3		2			4	2	3			1	3	4	3			4		3		4		3				1
					1		1							1						1			1				
1	2					1								1													

League Table

	P	W	D	L	F	A	Pts
Manchester United	42	27	11	4	80	38	92
Blackburn Rovers	42	25	9	8	63	36	84
Newcastle United	42	23	8	11	82	41	77
Arsenal	42	18	17	7	53	28	71
Leeds United	42	18	16	8	65	39	70
Wimbledon	42	18	11	13	56	53	65
SHEFFIELD WEDNESDAY	42	16	16	10	76	54	64
Liverpool	42	17	9	16	59	55	60
Queen's Park Rangers	42	16	12	14	62	61	60
Aston Villa	42	15	12	15	46	50	57
Coventry City	42	14	14	14	43	45	56
Norwich City	42	12	17	13	65	61	53
West Ham United	42	13	13	16	47	58	52
Chelsea	42	13	12	17	49	53	51
Tottenham Hotspur	42	11	12	19	54	59	45
Manchester City	42	9	18	15	38	49	45
Everton	42	12	8	22	42	63	44
Southampton	42	12	7	23	49	66	43
Ipswich Town	42	9	16	17	35	58	43
Sheffield United	42	8	18	16	42	60	42
Oldham Athletic	42	9	13	20	42	68	40
Swindon Town	42	5	15	22	47	100	30

1994-95

Premiership

Manager: Trevor Francis

Did you know that?

Final League Position: 13th

On 1 April 1995 Wednesday suffered their heaviest-ever home defeat in the League, 7–1 to Nottingham Forest.

Match No.	Date	Venue	Opponents		Round	Result	HT Score	Position	Scorers	Attendance
1	Aug 20	H	Tottenham Hotspur	L		3-4	0-2	16th	Petrescu, Calderwood (og), Hirst	34,051
2	24	A	Queen's Park Rangers	L		2-3	1-1	21st	Sheridan, Hyde	12,788
3	27	A	Wimbledon	W		1-0	0-0	14th	Watson	7,453
4	31	H	Norwich City	D		0-0	0-0	12th		25,072
5	Sep 10	A	Nottingham Forest	L		1-4	0-1	15th	Hyde	22,022
6	17	H	Manchester City	D		1-1	0-1	16th	Watson	26,776
7	26	H	Leeds United	D		1-1	1-1	17th	Bright	23,227
8	Oct 1	A	Liverpool	L		1-4	1-0	18th	Nolan	31,493
9	8	H	Manchester United	W		1-0	1-0	16th	Hirst	33,441
10	16	A	Ipswich Town	W		2-1	1-0	13th	Bright, Hirst	13,073
11	22	A	Newcastle United	L		1-2	0-2	14th	Taylor	34,408
12	29	H	Chelsea	D		1-1	0-1	15th	Bright	25,450
13	Nov 2	H	Blackburn Rovers	L		0-1	0-0	17th		24,207
14	6	A	Arsenal	D		0-0	0-0	16th		33,705
15	19	H	West Ham United	W		1-0	1-0	16th	Petrescu	25,300
16	27	A	Aston Villa	D		1-1	0-1	15th	Atherton	25,082
17	Dec 3	H	Crystal Palace	W		1-0	1-0	14th	Bart-Williams	21,930
18	10	A	Tottenham Hotspur	L		1-3	1-0	14th	Nolan	25,912
19	17	H	Queen's Park Rangers	L		0-2	0-0	18th		22,766
20	26	A	Everton	W		4-1	2-1	15th	Bright, Whittingham (2), Ingesson	37,080
21	28	H	Coventry City	W		5-1	3-1	13th	Bright (2), Waddle, Whittingham (2)	26,056
22	31	A	Leicester City	W		1-0	1-0	9th	Hyde	20,624
23	Jan 2	H	Southampton	D		1-1	1-0	10th	Hyde	28,424
24	14	A	Chelsea	D		1-1	0-1	10th	Nolan	17,285
25	21	H	Newcastle United	D		0-0	0-0	9th		31,215
26	23	A	West Ham United	W		2-0	1-0	7th	Waddle, Bright	14,554
27	Feb 4	H	Arsenal	W		3-1	2-1	8th	Petrescu, Ingesson, Bright	23,468
28	12	A	Blackburn Rovers	L		1-3	1-2	8th	Waddle	22,223
29	18	H	Aston Villa	L		1-2	0-2	8th	Bright	24,063
30	25	H	Liverpool	L		1-2	1-1	9th	Bart-Williams	31,964
31	Mar 4	A	Leeds United	W		1-0	1-0	8th	Waddle	33,750
32	8	A	Norwich City	D		0-0	0-0	8th		13,530
33	11	H	Wimbledon	L		0-1	0-0	8th		20,395
34	14	A	Crystal Palace	L		1-2	1-0	8th	Whittingham	10,422
35	18	A	Manchester City	L		2-3	2-1	9th	Whittingham, Hyde	23,355
36	Apr 1	H	Nottingham Forest	L		1-7	0-2	11th	Bright (pen)	30,060
37	8	H	Leicester City	W		1-0	1-0	10th	Whittingham	22,551
38	15	A	Coventry City	L		0-2	0-1	11th		15,710
39	17	H	Everton	D		0-0	0-0	13th		27,880
40	29	A	Southampton	D		0-0	0-0	14th		15,189
41	May 7	A	Manchester United	L		0-1	0-1	14th		43,868
42	14	H	Ipswich Town	W		4-1	1-0	13th	Whittingham (2), Williams, Bright	30,213
										App
										Sub
									One own-goal	Goal
League Cup										
43	Sep 21	H	Bradford City	W	2R 1L	2-1	0-0		Taylor, Hyde	15,705
44	Oct 4	A	Bradford City	D	2R 2L	1-1	1-0		Bart-Williams	13,092
45	26	H	Southampton	W	3R	1-0	0-0		Bart-Williams	16,715
46	Nov 30	A	Arsenal	L	4R	0-2	0-2			27,390
										App
										Sub
										Goal
FA Cup										
47	Jan 7	A	Gillingham	W	3R	2-1	2-1		Waddle, Bright	10,425
48	30	H	Wolverhampton W	D	4R	0-0	0-0			21,757
49	Feb 8	A	Wolverhampton W *	L	4R Re	1-1	0-1		Bright	28,136
										App
										Sub
										Goal

* After extra-time. Score at full-time 1-1. Lost 3-4 on penalties

2 Atherton Peter	14 Bart-Williams Chris	10 Bright Mark	29 Briscoe Lee	28 Coleman Simon	27 Donaldson O'Neill	22 Hardwick Matthew	9 Hirst David	16 Hyde Graham	18 Ingesson Klas	21 Jones Ryan	23 Key Lance	3 Nolan Ian	12 Pearce Andy	5 Petrescu Dan	7 Poric Adem	13 Pressman Kevin	11 Sheridan John	15 Sinton Andrew	4 Taylor Ian	8 Waddle Chris	17 Walker Des	20 Watson Gordon	24 Watts Julian	19 Whittingham Guy	25 Williams Michael	1 Woods Chris
5	8	9*		U			10				U	3		2		1	7	11	6		4	S*				
2	S#						9	7#		S*	U	3		5		1	8	11*	6		4	10				
2	10#						9	S*		11	U	3	5	6*		1	8		7		4	S#				
2	S*	10#					9				U	3	5	6		1	8	11	7*		4	S#				
2	S#			4			9	7	11		U	3	5	6*		1	8#	10				S*				
4	6	10#					9	7	S*		U	3	5	2		1	8	11*				S#				
5	11	9#					S#	7			U	3		2		1	8	6*	S*		4	10				
5	7	9					S*	6			U	3	U	2		1	8	11			4	10*				
2	6*	9#	11				10	7			U	3	5			1	8		S*		4	S#				
2	6#	10	11*				9	8			U	3	5			1	7	S*	S#		4					
2#	S*	10					9*	8			U	3	5	S#		1	7	11	6		4					
2	10#	9						7			U	3	5	S#		1	8*	11	6		4	S*				
2*	10#	9						7			U	3	5	S*		1	8	11	6		4	S#				
2	10	9						7			U	3	5	S#		1	8	11*	6		4#	S*				
2	10#	9						7			U	3	5	6*		1	8	11	S*		4	S#				
2	10							7			U	3	5	6	U	1	8	11	S*		4	9*				
4	10	9						7			U	3	5	2		1	8	11	6*	S*			U			
4	10	9	3					7			U	2	5			1	8	11	U	6			U			
2#	10	9*						7	S*	11	U	3	5	S#		1	8			6	4					
2	11	9						7	6		U	3	5		S*	1	8*			U	4			10		
2	11	9#						7	6*		U	3	5			1	8			S*	4	S#		10		
2	11	9						7			U	3	5	S*		1	8			6*	4	S#		10#		
2	11	9						7			U	3	5	S*		1	8			6*	4	S#		10#		
5	11	9*	3#						7		U	2		S#		1	8			6	4	S*		10		
5	7	S*							11		U	3		2			8			6	4	9*		10	U	1
2	8	9						7	11			3	5	S#		1				6#	4	S*		10*		U
2	8#	9						7	11			3	5	6		1	S*			10	4*			S#		U
2	7	9										3	5	6+		1	8#	11*		10	4			S#	S+	S*
5	S#	9	3*					7				2		6		1	8	11#		10	4			S*		U
5	8	9						7				3		2#		1	S*	11		6*	4	S#		10		U
6	11	9						7			U	3	5	2*				S*		10	4	U			8	1
6	7	9	2					11			U	3	5					U		10*	4	S*			8	1
6		9						8#				3	5	2*	S*	1		11		10	4			S#	7	U
2		9						7		8#	U	3	5			1		11*		S*	4	S#		10	6	
2	11	9			S#			7*				3#	5			1	8			6	4			10	S*	U
	6	9						7				3	5	2		1	8*	11		10	4		U	S*		U
2		S#					9*		11*			3	5			U	8	S*		6	4			10	7	1
6	S#						9	7	11#			3	5	2*		U	8			S*	4			10		1
2	8	S#					9#	11*	S*			3	5			1	7			6	4			10		U
2	11	9							S#	S*		3	5		7*	U				6#	4			10	8	1
2	11	9						7*				3	5		S#	U	8			S*	4			10#	6	1
2		S#					9#	S*				3	5			U	8*	11		6	4			10	7	1
41	32	33	6	1			13	33	9	3		42	34	20	1	34	34	22	9	20	38	5		16	8	8
	6	4			1		2	2	4	2				9	3		2	3	5	5		18		5	2	1
1	2	11					3	5	2			3		3			1		1	4		2		9	1	

2 Atherton Peter	14 Bart-Williams Chris	10 Bright Mark	29 Briscoe Lee	28 Coleman Simon	27 Donaldson O'Neill	22 Hardwick Matthew	9 Hirst David	16 Hyde Graham	18 Ingesson Klas	21 Jones Ryan	23 Key Lance	3 Nolan Ian	12 Pearce Andy	5 Petrescu Dan	7 Poric Adem	13 Pressman Kevin	11 Sheridan John	15 Sinton Andrew	4 Taylor Ian	8 Waddle Chris	17 Walker Des	20 Watson Gordon	24 Watts Julian	19 Whittingham Guy	25 Williams Michael	1 Woods Chris
4	6	10#					9	7	11*		U	3	5	2		1	8		S*			S#				
2	6	9#					S#	7			U	3	5			1	8	11*	S*		4	10				
2	10	9				U		7			U	3	5	U		1	8	11	6		4					
4	10							7		S*	U	3	5	2		1	8	11	6			9*	U			
4	4	3					1	4	1			4	4	2		4	4	3	2		2	2				
							1			1									2			1				
	2							1											1							

2 Atherton Peter	14 Bart-Williams Chris	10 Bright Mark	29 Briscoe Lee	28 Coleman Simon	27 Donaldson O'Neill	22 Hardwick Matthew	9 Hirst David	16 Hyde Graham	18 Ingesson Klas	21 Jones Ryan	23 Key Lance	3 Nolan Ian	12 Pearce Andy	5 Petrescu Dan	7 Poric Adem	13 Pressman Kevin	11 Sheridan John	15 Sinton Andrew	4 Taylor Ian	8 Waddle Chris	17 Walker Des	20 Watson Gordon	24 Watts Julian	19 Whittingham Guy	25 Williams Michael	1 Woods Chris
2	11	9						7			S*	3	5	S#		1	8			6#	4	U		10*		
2	11	9						7				3	5	S#		1	8#			6	4	S*		10*		U
2	8	9						7	6*			3	5			1	S*	11#		10	4			S#		U
3	3	3						3	1			3	3			3	2	1		3	3			2		
											1			2			1					1		1		
		2																		1						

League Table

	P	W	D	L	F	A	Pts
Blackburn Rovers	42	27	8	7	80	39	89
Manchester United	42	26	10	6	77	28	88
Nottingham Forest	42	22	11	9	72	43	77
Liverpool	42	21	11	10	65	37	74
Leeds United	42	20	13	9	59	38	73
Newcastle United	42	20	12	10	67	47	72
Tottenham Hotspur	42	16	14	12	66	58	62
Queen's Park Rangers	42	17	9	16	61	59	60
Wimbledon	42	15	11	16	48	65	56
Southampton	42	12	18	12	61	63	54
Chelsea	42	13	15	14	50	55	54
Arsenal	42	13	12	17	52	49	51
SHEFFIELD WEDNESDAY	42	13	12	17	49	57	51
West Ham United	42	13	11	18	44	48	50
Everton	42	11	17	14	44	51	50
Coventry City	42	12	14	16	44	62	50
Manchester City	42	12	13	17	53	64	49
Aston Villa	42	11	15	16	51	56	48
Crystal Palace	42	11	12	19	34	49	45
Norwich City	42	10	13	19	37	54	43
Leicester City	42	6	11	25	45	80	29
Ipswich Town	42	7	6	29	36	93	27

1995-96

Premiership

Manager: David Pleat

Did you know that?

Final League Position: 15th

On 10 February 1996 Mark Platts came on for Chris Waddle, with five minutes to go, in a 2–1 home win over Wimbledon in a Premier League fixture. He became the youngest outfield player for Wednesday at 16 years and 263 days.

Match No.	Date	Venue	Opponents		Round	Result	HT Score	Position	Scorers	Attendance
1	Aug 19	A	Liverpool	L		0-1	0-0	18th		40,535
2	23	H	Blackburn Rovers	W		2-1	1-0	8th	Waddle, Pembridge	25,544
3	27	H	Newcastle United	L		0-2	0-0	14th		24,815
4	30	A	Wimbledon	D		2-2	1-1	12th	Degryse, Hirst	6,352
5	Sep 9	A	Queen's Park Rangers	W		3-0	0-0	8th	Bright (2), Donaldson	12,459
6	16	H	Tottenham Hotspur	L		1-3	1-1	13th	Hirst	26,565
7	23	H	Manchester United	D		0-0	0-0	12th		34,101
8	30	A	Leeds United	L		0-2	0-1	13th		34,076
9	Oct 15	H	Middlesbrough	L		0-1	0-0	15th		21,177
10	21	A	Coventry City	W		1-0	1-0	12th	Whittingham	13,998
11	28	H	West Ham United	L		0-1	0-1	13th		23,917
12	Nov 4	A	Chelsea	D		0-0	0-0	13th		23,216
13	18	H	Manchester City	D		1-1	1-0	14th	Hirst (pen)	24,422
14	21	A	Arsenal	L		2-4	2-1	14th	Hirst, Waddle	34,556
15	25	A	Everton	D		2-2	2-1	15th	Bright (2)	35,898
16	Dec 4	H	Coventry City	W		4-3	2-2	14th	Whittingham, Hirst, Degryse, Bright	16,229
17	9	A	Manchester United	D		2-2	0-1	14th	Bright, Whittingham	41,849
18	16	H	Leeds United	W		6-2	3-1	14th	Degryse (2),Whittingham, Bright, Hirst (2)	24,573
19	23	H	Southampton	D		2-2	1-1	14th	Hirst (2 pens)	25,115
20	26	A	Nottingham Forest	L		0-1	0-1	14th		27,810
21	Jan 1	H	Bolton Wanderers	W		4-2	2-0	13th	Kovacevic (2), Hirst (pen + 1)	24,872
22	13	H	Liverpool	D		1-1	1-0	13th	Kovacevic	32,747
23	20	A	Blackburn Rovers	L		0-3	0-2	13th		24,732
24	Feb 3	A	Newcastle United	L		0-2	0-0	14th		36,567
25	10	H	Wimbledon	W		2-1	0-0	13th	Degryse, Watts	19,085
26	17	H	Queen's Park Rangers	L		1-3	1-1	14th	Hyde	22,442
27	24	A	Tottenham Hotspur	L		0-1	0-1	14th		32,047
28	Mar 2	H	Nottingham Forest	L		1-3	0-1	14th	Kovacevic	21,930
29	6	A	Aston Villa	L		2-3	1-0	14th	Blinker (2)	27,893
30	16	H	Aston Villa	W		2-0	0-0	14th	Whittingham, Hirst	22,964
31	20	A	Southampton	W		1-0	1-0	14th	Degryse	13,216
32	23	A	Bolton Wanderers	L		1-2	1-1	14th	Whittingam	18,368
33	Apr 5	A	Middlesbrough	L		1-3	0-0	14th	Pembridge	29,751
34	8	H	Arsenal	W		1-0	0-0	14th	Degryse	24,349
35	13	A	Manchester City	L		0-1	0-0	15th		30,898
36	17	H	Chelsea	D		0-0	0-0	15th		25,094
37	27	H	Everton	L		2-5	1-3	15th	Hirst, Degryse	32,724
38	May 5	A	West Ham United	D		1-1	0-0	15th	Newsome	23,790
										Apps
										Sub
										Goals

Uefa Intertoto Cup

39	Jun 24	A	FC Basel	L	QR	0-1	0-0			5,200
40	Jul 8	H	Gornik Zabrze *	W	QR	3-2	2-1		Krzetowski (og), Bright, Waddle	5,592
41	15	A	Karlsruher SC	D	QR	1-1	0-1		Bright	13,000
42	22	H	AGF Aarhus *	W	QR	3-1	1-1		Bright (2), Petrescu	6,990
										Apps
										Sub
									One own-goal	Goals

* Played at Millmoor Rotherham

League Cup

43	Sep 19	A	Crewe Alexandra	D	2R 1L	2-2	2-1		Degryse (2)	5,702
44	Oct 4	H	Crewe Alexandra	W	2R 2L	5-2	3-2		Degryse, Hirst, Bright (3)	12,039
45	25	A	Millwall	W	3R	2-0	1-0		Pembridge, Whittingham	12,822
46	Nov 29	A	Arsenal	L	4R	1-2	1-1		Degryse	35,361
										Apps
										Sub
										Goals

FA Cup

47	Jan 6	A	Charlton Athletic	L	3R	0-2	0-2			13,815
										Apps
										Sub
										Goals

2 Atherton Peter	Bailey Gavin	Barker Richard	15 Blinker Regi	Bowler Martin	Bowling Ian	Brien Tony	10 Bright Mark	29 Briscoe Lee	14 Degryse Marc	27 Donaldson O'Neill	Faulkner David	German David	9 Hirst David	Holmes Darren	30 Humphreys Ritchie	16 Hyde Graham	18 Ingesson Klas	21 Key Lance	18 Kovacevic Darko	6 Linighan Brian	20 Newsome Jon	5 Nicol Steve	3 Nolan Ian	12 Pearce Andy	Pearson John	4 Pembridge Mark	5 Petrescu Dan	31 Platts Mark	7 Poric Adem	13 Pressman Kevin	11 Sheridan John	15 Sinton Andrew	Smith Gavin	12 Stefanovic Dejan	22 Stewart Simon	8 Waddle Chris	17 Walker Des	24 Watts Julian	19 Whittingham Guy	Williams Andy	25 Williams Michael	1 Woods Chris
6							9						S*			8							3*			11	2			1	10	S#				7#	4	5				U
6							10		U				9			U							3			11	2			1	7	S*				8*	4	5				
6							10		7				9+			S*	S#						3			11	2#			1	8*	S+					4	5				
6							10	U	7				9*				S*						3			11	2			1	8						4	5			U	
6							10	U		9*					S*	7							3			11	2			1	8						4	5			U	
6							10		7				9										3			11	2			1	8#					S*	4	5*	S#		U	
6							S#	S*	10				9#			7							3	5		11*	2			1	U					8	4					
6							S+	S#	10+				9			7							3*	5		11	2#			1	S*					8	4					
5							9	3	10*							7#	U						2			11				1	S#	6				8	4		S*			
6							9	3*								S#	5						2			11				1		7				8#	4		10		S*	U
2							S#		S*				9				5			U			3			11				1		7				8	4		10#		6*	
6							10	2	11				9				5						3	U		7*				1						8	4		U		S*	
4								3	10				9			S*							2	5		8*				1		11				7		U	U		6	
4							S#	3	S*#				9			6				U			2			8*				1		7				11		5	10			
6							9	3*	S#							8						5	2							1		11				7	4		10		S*#	U
6							10	3	7				9			S*						5	2							1		U				8*	4	U	11			
6							10	3	7				9			U						5	2							1	S*	U				8*	4		11			
6							10	3	7				9			S*						5	2							1		U				8	4	U	11*			
6							10#	3	7*				9			S*			S#			5	2							1				U		8	4		11			
6							S#	3*	7				9#			U			10			5	2							1				S*		8	4		11			
5							S*		6				9			U			10*				2							1	U	7		3		8	4		11			
6							S*	3	7#				9			S#			10*			5	2											U		8	4		11			1
6							S#	S+	7				9			11			S*#			5	2											3+		10*	4		8			1
2							10		6				9*			U			S*			7	3					U		1						8	4	5	11			
5							S*		9*							6			10			7	2					S#		1				3+		11#	4	S+	8			
5							S*		9							6*			10			7	2					U		1				3		11	4	U	8			
5								3+	11*				9			6			10#			7	2					S+								S*	4	S#	8			1
6									11						S#	6+			9			7	2			S+								3#		S*	4	5	10			1*
5			11					3	S#						S+	8#			9+			S*	2*			10										6	4		7			1
			11					3	8				9#			S*			S#		5	2				10*					7						4	U	6			1
			11*					3	8				9#			S*			S#		5	2				10					7						4	U	6			1
2								3	10				9*		11#	S+			S*		5					8					7+					S#	4		6			1
2			11					S#	10				9+			S*			S+		5	3#				8				1	7*						4		6			
2			11*					3	10				9#						S#		5	U				8				1	7					S*	4		6			
6			11					3	10+	S+			9								5	2*				8#				1	S#					S*	4		7			
2			11*					3	10	U			9								5	U				8				1	7					S*	4		6			
5			11					3	10	S#			9#			S+						2				8+				1	7*					S*	4		6			
2			11*					3	10#				9		S#	7					5	U				8				1						S*	5		6			
36			9				15	22	30	1			29		1	14	3		8		8	18	29	3		24	8			30	13	7		5		23	36	9	27		2	8
							10	4	4	2			1		4	12	2		8			1				1		2			4	3		1		9		2	2		3	
			2				7		8	1			13			1			4		1					2										2		1	6			

	S#	9#		U	1	6		4			S*	2*		7	U	8									10								U		3					5	11	
5		S#					9#	3						U		8		U		U			2						7*			11				10	4	6	S*			1
2		U					10	U					9*			6		U					3						U			11				8	4	5	7		S*	1
6							10	S#					9*			7+							3#	5		11	2			U	8	S+					4		S*		U	1
3		1			1	1	3	2				1	2	1		4							3	1	1	1	1		1		1	2			1	2	3	2	1	1	1	3
	1	1						1			1																					1							2		1	
							4																				1									1						

2							9	U	6							S*							3	5		8	U			1		7				11	4		9*			
5							10	3	11*				9#			6							2			7				1						8	4		S*		S#	U
2							S*						9*				5						3	U		7				1		11				8	4		10		6	U
2							9*		6				S*			8							3						U	1		7				11	4	5	10			U
4							3	1	3				2			2	1						4	1		3				4		3				4	4	1	3		1	
							1						1			1																							1		1	
							3		4				1													1													1			

6							U		7				9			U			10				2							1		3		5		8	4		11			U
1									1				1						1				1							1		1		1		1	1		1			

League Table

See page 509

1996-97

Premiership

Manager: David Pleat

Did you know that?

Final League Position: 7th

On September 16 1996, in a match live on the televsion, David Hirst hit a shot in the 30th minute against Arsenal that hit the bar and was recorded at 114mph – the fastest recorded shot.

Match No.	Date	Venue	Opponents		Round	Result	HT Score	Position	Scorers	Attendance
1	Aug 17	H	Aston Villa	W		2-1	0-0	6th	Humphreys, Whittingham	26,861
2	20	A	Leeds United	W		2-0	1-0	1st	Humphreys, Booth	31,011
3	24	A	Newcastle United	W		2-1	1-1	1st	Atherton, Whittingham	36,452
4	Sep 2	H	Leicester City	W		2-1	1-1	1st	Humphreys, Booth	17,657
5	7	H	Chelsea	L		0-2	0-1	1st		30,983
6	16	A	Arsenal	L		1-4	1-0	5th	Booth	33,461
7	21	H	Derby County	D		0-0	0-0	5th		23,934
8	28	A	Everton	L		0-2	0-1	7th		34,160
9	Oct 12	A	Wimbledon	L		2-4	1-2	7th	Booth, Hyde	10,512
10	19	H	Blackburn Rovers	D		1-1	1-0	9th	Booth	22,191
11	26	A	Coventry City	D		0-0	0-0	8th		17,267
12	Nov 2	H	Southampton	D		1-1	1-0	9th	Newsome	20,106
13	18	H	Nottingham Forest	W		2-0	0-0	9th	Trustfull, Carbone	16,390
14	23	A	Sunderland	D		1-1	0-0	10th	Oakes	20,644
15	30	H	West Ham United	D		0-0	0-0	10th		22,321
16	Dec 7	A	Liverpool	W		1-0	1-0	9th	Whittingham	39,507
17	18	H	Manchester United	D		1-1	0-0	9th	Carbone	37,671
18	21	A	Tottenham Hotspur	D		1-1	1-1	10th	Nolan	30,996
19	26	H	Arsenal	D		0-0	0-0	10th		23,245
20	28	A	Chelsea	D		2-2	1-2	9th	Pembridge, Stefanovic	27,467
21	Jan 11	H	Everton	W		2-1	1-0	8th	Pembridge, Hirst	24,175
22	18	A	Middlesbrough	L		2-4	1-2	8th	Pembridge (2)	29,485
23	29	A	Aston Villa	W		1-0	0-0	8th	Booth	26,726
24	Feb 1	H	Coventry City	D		0-0	0-0	8th		21,793
25	19	A	Derby County	D		2-2	1-1	8th	Collins, Hirst	18,060
26	22	A	Southampton	W		3-2	0-2	8th	Hirst (2), Booth	15,062
27	Mar 1	H	Middlesbrough	W		3-1	2-0	8th	Booth, Hyde, Pembridge (pen)	28,206
28	5	A	Nottingham Forest	W		3-0	0-0	6th	Carbone (2), Blinker	21,485
29	12	H	Sunderland	W		2-1	1-1	5th	Hirst, Stefanovic	20,294
30	15	A	Manchester United	L		0-2	0-1	5th		55,267
31	22	H	Leeds United	D		2-2	1-2	7th	Hirst, Booth	30,373
32	Apr 9	H	Tottenham Hotspur	W		2-1	1-1	6th	Atherton, Booth	22,667
33	13	H	Newcastle United	D		1-1	0-1	5th	Pembridge	33,798
34	19	H	Wimbledon	W		3-1	1-0	6th	Donaldson, Trustfull (2)	26,957
35	22	A	Blackburn Rovers	L		1-4	0-3	6th	Carbone (pen)	20,845
36	May 3	A	West Ham United	L		1-5	0-3	7th	Carbone	24,960
37	7	A	Leicester City	L		0-1	0-0	7th		20,793
38	11	H	Liverpool	D		1-1	0-0	7th	Donaldson	38,943
										Apps
										Sub
										Goals

League Cup

39	Sep 18	H	Oxford United	D	2R 1L	1-1	1-0		Whittingham	7,499
40	24	A	Oxford United	L	2R 2L	0-1	0-0			6,863
										Apps
										Sub
										Goals

FA Cup

41	Jan 4	H	Grimsby Town	W	3R	7-1	3-0		Humphreys (2),Booth (2),Fickling (og),Hyde,Pembridge	20,590
42	25	A	Carlisle United	W	4R	2-0	1-0		Whittingham, Booth	16,104
43	Feb 16	A	Bradford City	W	5R	1-0	0-0		Mohan (og)	17,830
44	Mar 9	H	Wimbledon	L	6R	0-2	0-0			25,032
										Apps
										Sub
									Two own-goals	Goals

2 Atherton Peter	11 Blinker Regi	10 Booth Andy	8 Bright Mark	17 Briscoe Lee	8 Carbone Benny	13 Clarke Matt	20 Collins Wayne	22 Donaldson O'Neill	9 Hirst David	25 Humphreys Ritchie	12 Hyde Graham	24 Linighan Brian	5 Newsome Jon	14 Nicol Steve	3 Nolan Ian	19 Oakes Scott	4 Pembridge Mark	1 Pressman Kevin	16 Sheridan John	18 Stefanovic Dejan	26 Trustfull Orlando	6 Walker Des	7 Whittingham Guy	23 Williams Michael
2	11	10				U	7			9#	S*			U	3	S#	8*	1	U	5		4	6	
2	11	10				U	7#			9*	S*			S#	3	U	8	1	U	5		4	6	
2	11					U	7	U		9*	S#			U	3	10#	8	1		5	S*	4	6	
2	11	10	S#			U	7		9#	8*				U	3	U		1	S*	5		4	6	
2	11	10				U	7#		9	8*				U	3	S+		1	S*	5	S#	4	6+	
2	11#	10				U	7		9	U				S*	3	S#	8	1		5*	S+	4	6+	
2	11+	10#				U			9	S#	7			U	3	S+	8*	1		5	S*	4	6	
2	11	10				U			9*	S*	S+		U	8+	3			1		5	7	4	6#	S#
2+	11	10				U			9	U	7		4	S+	3	S#	8	1		5#	S*		6*	
2	11	10			6*	U			9+	S*	7		5	U	3		S#	1			8#	4	S+	
2	11*	10			6+	U				S#	7		5	U	3	S*	10	1			8#	4	S+	
2	S+	10			6*	U				S*	7		5		3	11#	9	1		U	8+	4	S#	
2	11	10+			6	U				S+	7#		5		3	S*	9	1		S#	8*	4	U	
2		10		U	6	U				S#	7		5		3	11#	9	1		U	8*	4	S*	
5		10		3*	6	U				S#	8			S*	2+	S+	9	1		U	11#	4	7	
6	S*	10			9*	U				U	8			3	2	U	11	1		5	U	4	7	
8	S+	10#			9+	U			S#		6*			3	2	U	7	1		5	S*	4	11	
2	S*	10#			9	U			S#	S+				7	3	U	11	1		5	7*	4	6+	
8	S*	S#			10	U			9#	U				3	2	7*	11	1		5	U	4	6	
8	S#	10			6#	U		S+		9+				3*	2	S*	7	1		5	U	4	11	
8	U	10*				U	U		S*	9	6			3	2		7	1		5	U	4	11	
8	S*	10				U	S#		S+	9#	7			2*	3		11	1		5	U	4	6+	
8	S*	10				U	U		9*	U	7			2	3		11	1		5	U	4	6	
8	S*	10				U	U		9#	U	7			2	3		11	1		5	S#	4	6*	
8	S*	10			9#	U	7	S#	S+	6+			5	2*	3		11	1		U		4		
8	S*	S+		U	10#	U	7+		9	6*			4	2	3	S#	11	1		5				
8	S*	10		U	6*	U			9+	S+	7#		5	2	3		11	1		S#		4		
7	11	10+		3	S*	U			9*	S+			5		2	6#	8	1		U	S#	4		
8		10		3	7*	U	U		9	S*					2	U	11	1		5	U	4	6	
7	11#	S*		S#	10	U	U		9	8+				3*	2			1		5	S+	4	6	
	S#	10		3	8#	U	S*	U	9	7*		U			2		11	1		5		4	6	
8	S#	10		3	7	U	U		9*	S*				5	2	U	11	1				4	6#	
8	S+	10*		U	9	U	S#			S*				2+	3	7	11	1		5		4#	6	
7	11*				10	U	U	9		U				2	3	U	8	1		5	S*	4	6	
5	S+			U	10	U	S*	9		S#				11*	3	2	7	1			8#	4	6+	
8	S*	10			11	U		U	9	U				2#	3	S#	7	1		5		4	6*	
8	S*	10			7	U		U	9*	3				U	2	U	11	1		5		4	6	
7	U	10			8	S+		S*	9*	3#				U	2	S#	11	1+		5		4	6	
37	15	32		5	24		8	2	20	14	15		10	19	38	7	33	38		27	9	36	29	
	18	3	1	1	1	1	4	3	5	15	4			4		12	1		2	2	10		4	1
2	1	10			6		1	2	6	3	2		1		1	1	6			2	3		3	

2 Atherton Peter	11 Blinker Regi	10 Booth Andy	8 Bright Mark	17 Briscoe Lee	8 Carbone Benny	13 Clarke Matt	20 Collins Wayne	22 Donaldson O'Neill	9 Hirst David	25 Humphreys Ritchie	12 Hyde Graham	24 Linighan Brian	5 Newsome Jon	14 Nicol Steve	3 Nolan Ian	19 Oakes Scott	4 Pembridge Mark	1 Pressman Kevin	16 Sheridan John	18 Stefanovic Dejan	26 Trustfull Orlando	6 Walker Des	7 Whittingham Guy	23 Williams Michael
4	11	10				U			9	S*			5#	S#	3		7	1			6*		8	2
2#	11	10				U				9	7			S*	3	S#		1		5	8	4*	6	
2	2	2							1	1	1		1		2		1	2		1	2	1	2	1
										1				2		1								
																							1	

2 Atherton Peter	11 Blinker Regi	10 Booth Andy	8 Bright Mark	17 Briscoe Lee	8 Carbone Benny	13 Clarke Matt	20 Collins Wayne	22 Donaldson O'Neill	9 Hirst David	25 Humphreys Ritchie	12 Hyde Graham	24 Linighan Brian	5 Newsome Jon	14 Nicol Steve	3 Nolan Ian	19 Oakes Scott	4 Pembridge Mark	1 Pressman Kevin	16 Sheridan John	18 Stefanovic Dejan	26 Trustfull Orlando	6 Walker Des	7 Whittingham Guy	23 Williams Michael
2	11*	10				U				9	6#			S#	3		7	1		5	S*	4	8	
2		10				U	7		U	9	8		5	U	3		11	1				4	6	
7	U	10			9*	U			S*	6	8		5	3	2		11	1				4		
8		10			9	U			S#	S*	7#		5*	2	3		11	1				4	6	
4	1	4			2		1			3	4		3	2	4		4	4		1		4	3	
									2	1				1							1			
		3								2	1						1						1	

League Table 1995-96

	P	W	D	L	F	A	Pts
Manchester United	38	25	7	6	73	35	82
Newcastle United	38	24	6	8	66	37	78
Liverpool	38	20	11	7	70	34	71
Aston Villa	38	18	9	11	52	35	63
Arsenal	38	17	12	9	49	32	63
Everton	38	17	10	11	64	44	61
Blackburn Rovers	38	18	7	13	61	47	61
Tottenham Hotspur	38	16	13	9	50	38	61
Nottingham Forest	38	15	13	10	50	54	58
West Ham United	38	14	9	15	43	52	51
Chelsea	38	12	14	12	46	44	50
Middlesbrough	38	11	10	17	35	50	43
Leeds United	38	12	7	19	40	57	43
Wimbledon	38	10	11	17	55	70	41
SHEFFIELD WEDNESDAY	38	10	10	18	48	61	40
Coventry City	38	8	14	16	42	60	38
Southampton	38	9	11	18	34	52	38
Manchester City	38	9	11	18	33	58	38
Queen's Park Rangers	38	9	6	23	38	57	33
Bolton Wanderers	38	8	5	25	39	71	29

League Table

	P	W	D	L	F	A	Pts
Manchester United	38	21	12	5	76	44	75
Newcastle United	38	19	11	8	73	40	68
Arsenal	38	19	11	8	62	32	68
Liverpool	38	19	11	8	62	37	68
Aston Villa	38	17	10	11	47	34	61
Chelsea	38	16	11	11	58	55	59
SHEFFIELD WEDNESDAY	38	14	15	9	50	51	57
Wimbledon	38	15	11	12	49	46	56
Leicester City	38	12	11	15	46	54	47
Tottenham Hotspur	38	13	7	18	44	51	46
Leeds United	38	11	13	14	28	38	46
Derby County	38	11	13	14	45	58	46
Blackburn Rovers	38	9	15	14	42	43	42
West Ham United	38	10	12	16	39	48	42
Everton	38	10	12	16	44	57	42
Southampton	38	10	11	17	50	56	41
Coventry City	38	9	14	15	38	54	41
Sunderland	38	10	10	18	35	53	40
Middlesbrough	38	10	12	16	51	60	39
Nottingham Forest	38	6	16	16	31	59	34

1997-98

Premiership

Manager: David Pleat/Ron Atkinson

Did you know that?

Final League Position: 16th

On 25 April 1998 Wednesday played at Goodison Park against Everton. This game was chosen to experiment with a yellow fluorescent ball, to give better visibility in all weather and lighting conditions. Wednesday went on to win 3–1.

On 8 April 1998, in a testimonial game against Glasgow Rangers, Wednesday's new signing Francesco Sanetti played under Krystof Kotylo's name, as his international clearance had not been received.

Match No.	Date	Venue	Opponents		Round	Result	HT Score	Position	Scorers	Attendance
1	Aug 9	A	Newcastle United	L		1-2	1-1	16th	Carbone	36,711
2	13	H	Leeds United	L		1-3	0-2	18th	Hyde	31,520
3	23	A	Wimbledon	D		1-1	0-1	16th	Di Canio	11,503
4	25	A	Blackburn Rovers	L		2-7	1-5	16th	Carbone (2)	19,618
5	30	H	Leicester City	W		1-0	0-0	15th	Carbone (pen)	24,851
6	Sep 13	A	Liverpool	L		1-2	0-0	19th	Collins	34,705
7	20	H	Coventry City	D		0-0	0-0	19th		21,087
8	24	H	Derby County	L		2-5	2-3	19th	Di Canio, Carbone (pen)	22,391
9	27	A	Aston Villa	D		2-2	2-1	18th	Collins, Whittingham	32,044
10	Oct 4	H	Everton	W		3-1	0-0	16th	Carbone (1+ pen), Di Canio	24,486
11	19	A	Tottenham Hotspur	L		2-3	0-3	17th	Collins, Di Canio	25,097
12	25	H	Crystal Palace	L		1-3	0-1	18th	Collins	22,072
13	Nov 1	A	Manchester United	L		1-6	0-4	20th	Whittingham	55,259
14	8	H	Bolton Wanderers	W		5-0	5-0	19th	Di Canio, Whittingham, Booth (3)	25,027
15	22	H	Arsenal	W		2-0	1-0	16th	Booth, Whittingham	34,373
16	29	A	Southampton	W		3-2	1-0	14th	Atherton, Collins, Di Canio	15,244
17	Dec 8	H	Barnsley	W		2-1	1-1	13th	Stefanovic, Di Canio	29,086
18	13	A	West Ham United	L		0-1	0-0	13th		24,344
19	20	H	Chelsea	L		1-4	0-1	14th	Pembridge	28,334
20	26	H	Blackburn Rovers	D		0-0	0-0	14th		33,502
21	28	A	Leicester City	D		1-1	0-1	15th	Booth	20,800
22	Jan 10	H	Newcastle United	W		2-1	1-1	12th	Di Canio, Newsome	29,446
23	17	A	Leeds United	W		2-1	0-0	11th	Newsome, Booth	33,166
24	31	H	Wimbledon	D		1-1	1-1	10th	Pembridge	22,655
25	Feb 7	A	Coventry City	L		0-1	0-0	14th		18,375
26	14	H	Liverpool	D		3-3	1-1	12th	Carbone, Di Canio, Hinchcliffe	35,405
27	21	H	Tottenham Hotspur	W		1-0	1-0	12th	Di Canio	29,871
28	28	A	Derby County	L		0-3	0-1	13th		30,203
29	Mar 7	H	Manchester United	W		2-0	1-0	12th	Atherton, Di Canio	39,427
30	14	A	Bolton Wanderers	L		2-3	1-1	13th	Booth, Atherton	24,847
31	28	A	Arsenal	L		0-1	0-1	13th		38,087
32	Apr 4	H	Southampton	W		1-0	0-0	13th	Carbone	29,677
33	11	A	Barnsley	L		1-2	0-0	14th	Stefanovic	18,692
34	13	H	West Ham United	D		1-1	0-1	14th	Magilton	28,036
35	19	A	Chelsea	L		0-1	0-1	14th		29,075
36	25	A	Everton	W		3-1	2-0	13th	Pembridge (2), Di Canio	35,497
37	May 2	H	Aston Villa	L		1-3	0-2	14th	Sanetti	34,177
38	10	A	Crystal Palace	L		0-1	0-0	16th		16,876
										Apps
										Sub
										Goals
League Cup										
39	Sep 17	A	Grimsby Town	L	2R 1L	0-2	0-1			6,429
40	Oct 1	H	Grimsby Town	W	2R 2L	3-2	1-0		Davison (og), Di Canio (2)	11,120
										Apps
										Sub
									One own-goal	Goals
FA Cup										
41	Jan 3	A	Watford	D	3R	1-1	0-0		Alexandersson	18,306
42	14	H	Watford *	W	3R Re	0-0	0-0			18,707
43	26	H	Blackburn Rovers	L	4R	0-3	0-2			15,940
										Apps
										Sub
										Goals

* After extra-time. Won 5-3 on penalties

23 Agogo Junior	26 Alexandersson Niclas	2 Atherton Peter	27 Barrett Earl	15 Blondeau Patrick	10 Booth Andy	17 Briscoe Lee	8 Carbone Benny	13 Clarke Matt	25 Clough Nigel	20 Collins Wayne	11 Di Canio Paulo	22 Donaldson O'Neill	26 Grobbelaar Bruce	20 Hinchcliffe Andy	9 Hirst David	16 Humphreys Ritchie	12 Hyde Graham	24 Magilton Jim	15 Mayrleb Christian	5 Newsome Jon	14 Nicol Steve	3 Nolan Ian	19 Oakes Scott	4 Pembridge Mark	21 Poric Adem	1 Pressman Kevin	28 Quinn Alan	25 Rudi Petter	30 Sanetti Francesco	21 Sedloski Goce	18 Stefanovic Dejan	22 Thome Emerson	6 Walker Des	7 Whittingham Guy
S+		7		2			9	U		S*	S#	10#				U	8*					3		11		1					5		4	6+
		7		2	10		9+	U		8*	11	S+				6#	S*					3	S#			1					5		4	U
		7		2	10		9	U		S*	11						6			5	U	3	U	8*		1							4	U
		7		2	10#		9	U		S*	11				S+		8			5	S#	3	U			1							4*	6+
		7				S#	10	U		S*	11				9	8+	6*			5	2	3#			U	1							4	S+
		7				S*		U	U	S#	10				9			8		5	3*	2		11#		1					U		4	6
		7*						S#	U	S*	10				9	U		8+		5	3	2	S+	11		1#							4	6
				2		U	9	1	10#	S+	11		U		S#			7		5*	S*	3		8									4	6+
						3	9	1	U	8	10		U					7			U	2	U	11*	S*						5		4	6
						S*	9	U		7	10				S#			8+			3*	2	U	11#	S+	1					5		4	6
						3+	9			S*	10	S+	U					7		5	U	2		11		1		8*			6#		4	S#
						3*	9			8#	10	S+	U					7		5	U	2		11	S#	1		S*					4	6+
				U			9#			7+	10*		U			S#		8		5	S*	2		3	S+	1		11					4	6
		8#		S+	10*			U		U	9+	S*					S#	7		5		2		3		1		11					4	6
		8		U	10		S*	U			9*					U	S#	7#		5		2		3		1		11					4	6
		8			10#		S#	U		S*	9					U	U	7*		5		2		3		1		11					4	6
				U	10		11*	U		7	9					U	S*	U				2		3		1		8			5		4	6
	U				10+		S#	U		6	9					S+	7*			5		2		S*		1		8			3		4	11#
	S+				10		S#	U		6*	9#					U	S*			5		2		7		1		8			3		4	11+
	6	7			10		9#	U		S*						U	U			5		2		11		1		8			3*		4	S#
	11	6			10		9	U		S*+						S+	S#			5		2		7*		1		8#			3		4	U
	6	7			S#		9	U			10#					S*	8*			5		2	U	3		1		11			U		4	
	6*	8			10			U			9+					S+	7#	S#		5		2		3		1		11			U		4	S*
	6*	7			10		9#	U						3		U		U	S#	5		2		8		1		11					4	S*
		7					10	U			9			3			8#	S#	S+	5	U	2		11+		1		6*					4	S*
		6					10	U			9			3			11*	S*	U	5		2	U	7#		1		8					4	S#
		6			U		10	U			9			3			11#	S#		5		2*	S*	7+		1		8			S+		4	
		8	2		S*		10	U			9+			3			7*	S#	S+	5			U	11#		1		6					4	
		6	2		10		8	U			9#			3					U	5	U		S#	7*		1					11		4	S*
		6	2		10		8	U			9			3				U		5*				7#		1		S#		S*	11		4	U
		6	2		10		8*	U			9			3			S*	U						7#		1				5	11	U	4	S#
		7	2		10		6	U			9			3			U	U						11*		1				5	8	U	4	S*
			2		10		S#	U			9			3			S*	U					U	11#		1				5*	8	7	4	6
			2		10		6	U			9			3		U		7					U	S*		1		11*			8	5	4	U
		7	2#		10		6	U			9			3				S#					U	S*		1		11*			8	5	4	U
		2			10	S*		U			9			3		U	8#	7*	U					11		1	S#					5	4	6
		7	2+			U	10	U			9			3			6	S+						11#		1			S#		8	5*	4	S*
		7	2			U	11*	U			9			3			6#	S#								1		S*	10		8	5	4	U
	5	27	10	5	21	3	28	2	1	8	34	1		15	3	2	14	13		25	4	27		31		36		19	1	3	19	6	38	17
1	1			1	2	4	5	1		11	1	4			3	5	8	8	3		3		4	3	4		1	3	1	1	1			11
		3			7		9			5	12			1			1	1		2				4					1		2			4

23 Agogo Junior	26 Alexandersson Niclas	2 Atherton Peter	27 Barrett Earl	15 Blondeau Patrick	10 Booth Andy	17 Briscoe Lee	8 Carbone Benny	13 Clarke Matt	25 Clough Nigel	20 Collins Wayne	11 Di Canio Paulo	22 Donaldson O'Neill	26 Grobbelaar Bruce	20 Hinchcliffe Andy	9 Hirst David	16 Humphreys Ritchie	12 Hyde Graham	24 Magilton Jim	15 Mayrleb Christian	5 Newsome Jon	14 Nicol Steve	3 Nolan Ian	19 Oakes Scott	4 Pembridge Mark	21 Poric Adem	1 Pressman Kevin	28 Quinn Alan	25 Rudi Petter	30 Sanetti Francesco	21 Sedloski Goce	18 Stefanovic Dejan	22 Thome Emerson	6 Walker Des	7 Whittingham Guy
		2				S*		U	10	7*	11							6		5	U	3		8		1							4	9
						3	9#	U		7*	11					S*		6				2		8	S#	1					5		4	10
		1				1	1		1	2	2							2		1		2		2		2					1		2	2
						1										1									1									
											2																							

23 Agogo Junior	26 Alexandersson Niclas	2 Atherton Peter	27 Barrett Earl	15 Blondeau Patrick	10 Booth Andy	17 Briscoe Lee	8 Carbone Benny	13 Clarke Matt	25 Clough Nigel	20 Collins Wayne	11 Di Canio Paulo	22 Donaldson O'Neill	26 Grobbelaar Bruce	20 Hinchcliffe Andy	9 Hirst David	16 Humphreys Ritchie	12 Hyde Graham	24 Magilton Jim	15 Mayrleb Christian	5 Newsome Jon	14 Nicol Steve	3 Nolan Ian	19 Oakes Scott	4 Pembridge Mark	21 Poric Adem	1 Pressman Kevin	28 Quinn Alan	25 Rudi Petter	30 Sanetti Francesco	21 Sedloski Goce	18 Stefanovic Dejan	22 Thome Emerson	6 Walker Des	7 Whittingham Guy
	11	6			10*		9	U			7					S*		U		5	U	2		3		1		8					4	U
	11#	6			10			U			9					S*	7	U		5		2	S#	3		1		8					4*	U
		6					10	U			9					S*		7*		5	U	2	S#	3		1		8			U		4	11#
	2	3			2		2				3						1	1		3		3		3		3		3					3	1
																3							2											
	1																																	

League Table

	P	W	D	L	F	A	Pts
Arsenal	38	23	9	6	68	33	78
Manchester United	38	23	8	7	73	26	77
Liverpool	38	18	11	9	68	42	65
Chelsea	38	20	3	15	71	43	63
Leeds United	38	17	8	13	57	46	59
Blackburn Rovers	38	16	10	12	57	52	58
Aston Villa	38	17	6	15	49	48	57
West Ham United	38	16	8	14	56	57	56
Derby County	38	16	7	15	52	49	55
Leicester City	38	13	14	11	51	41	53
Coventry City	38	12	16	10	46	44	52
Southampton	38	14	6	18	50	55	48
Newcastle United	38	11	11	16	35	44	44
Tottenham Hotspur	38	11	11	16	44	56	44
Wimbledon	38	10	14	14	34	46	44
SHEFFIELD WEDNESDAY	38	12	8	18	52	67	44
Everton	38	9	13	16	41	56	40
Bolton Wanderers	38	9	13	16	41	61	40
Barnsley	38	10	5	23	37	82	35
Crystal Palace	38	8	9	21	37	71	33

1998-99

Premiership

Manager: Danny Wilson

Did you know that?

Final League Position: 12th

On 26 September 1998 Paolo Di Canio pushed over the referee, Paul Alcock, after he had been sent-off in a game against Arsenal which Wednesday won 1–0.

On 3 March 1999, before the home game against Wimbledon, their manager Joe Kinnear was watching his team warm up and was taken ill. Wednesday's club doctor, Ravin Naik, saved his life as he suffered a heart attack. He recovered in a Sheffield hospital.

Match No.	Date	Venue	Opponents		Round	Result	HT Score	Position	Scorers	Attendance
1	Aug 15	H	West Ham United	L		0-1	0-0	19th		30,236
2	22	A	Tottenham Hotspur	W		3-0	2-0	7th	Atherton, Di Canio, Hinchcliffe	32,129
3	29	H	Aston Villa	L		0-1	0-1	12th		25,989
4	Sep 9	A	Derby County	L		0-1	0-1	17th		26,209
5	12	H	Blackburn Rovers	W		3-0	2-0	9th	Atherton, Hinchcliffe, Di Canio	20,846
6	19	A	Wimbledon	L		1-2	0-1	13th	Di Canio	13,163
7	26	H	Arsenal	W		1-0	0-0	10th	Briscoe	27,949
8	Oct 3	A	Middlesbrough	L		0-4	0-2	15th		34,163
9	18	A	Coventry City	L		0-1	0-0	16th		16,006
10	24	H	Everton	D		0-0	0-0	16th		26,592
11	31	H	Southampton	D		0-0	0-0	16th		30,078
12	Nov 8	A	Leeds United	L		1-2	1-1	16th	Booth	30,012
13	14	A	Newcastle United	D		1-1	0-1	15th	Charvet (OG)	36,698
14	21	H	Manchester United	W		3-1	1-1	15th	Alexandersson (2), Jonk	39,475
15	28	A	Chelsea	D		1-1	0-1	16th	Booth	34,451
16	Dec 7	H	Nottingham Forest	W		3-2	1-0	14th	Alexandersson, Carbone (2)	19,321
17	12	H	Charlton Athletic	W		3-0	1-0	13th	Booth, Carbone, Rudi	26,010
18	19	A	Liverpool	L		0-2	0-2	14th		40,003
19	26	H	Leicester City	L		0-1	0-1	15th		33,513
20	28	A	Aston Villa	L		1-2	1-1	15th	Carbone	39,217
21	Jan 9	H	Tottenham Hotspur	D		0-0	0-0	15th		28,204
22	16	A	West Ham United	W		4-0	2-0	13th	Hinchcliffe, Rudi, Humphreys, Carbone (pen)	25,642
23	30	H	Derby County	L		0-1	0-0	14th		24,440
24	Feb 6	A	Leicester City	W		2-0	0-0	14th	Jonk, Carbone	20,113
25	20	A	Blackburn Rovers	W		4-1	3-0	12th	Sonner, Rudi (2), Booth	24,643
26	27	H	Middlesbrough	W		3-1	1-0	10th	Booth (2), Sonner	24,534
27	Mar 3	H	Wimbledon	L		1-2	0-2	11th	Thome	24,116
28	9	A	Arsenal	L		0-3	0-0	11th		37,792
29	13	H	Leeds United	L		0-2	0-1	12th		28,142
30	20	A	Southampton	L		0-1	0-1	13th		15,201
31	Apr 3	H	Coventry City	L		1-2	0-1	14th	Rudi	28,136
32	5	A	Everton	W		2-1	0-1	13th	Carbone (2)	35,270
33	17	A	Manchester United	L		0-3	0-2	14th		55,270
34	21	H	Newcastle United	D		1-1	0-1	14th	Scott	21,545
35	25	H	Chelsea	D		0-0	0-0	14th		21,652
36	May 1	A	Nottingham Forest	L		0-2	0-2	14th		20,480
37	8	H	Liverpool	W		1-0	0-0	13th	Cresswell	27,383
38	16	A	Charlton Athletic	W		1-0	0-0	12th	Sonner	20,043
										Apps
										Sub
									One own-goal	Goals

League Cup

39	Sep 16	H	Cambridge United	L	2R 1L	0-1	0-1			8,921
40	22	A	Cambridge United	D	2R 2L	1-1	0-0		Campbell (og)	8,502
										Apps
										Sub
									One own-goal	Goals

FA Cup

41	Jan 3	H	Norwich City	W	3R	4-1	3-1		Humphreys (2), Rudi, Stefanovic	18,737
42	23	H	Stockport County	W	4R	2-0	1-0		Thome, Carbone	20,984
43	Feb 13	H	Chelsea	L	5R	0-1	0-0			29,410
										Apps
										Sub
										Goals

23 Agogo Junior	26 Alexandersson Niclas	2 Atherton Peter	27 Barrett Earl	10 Booth Andy	17 Briscoe Lee	8 Carbone Benny	13 Clarke Matt	15 Cobian Juan	21 Cresswell Richard	11 Di Canio Paulo	35 Haslam Steve	36 Higgins Alex	20 Hinchcliffe Andy	16 Humphreys Ritchie	12 Hyde Graham	4 Jonk Wim	24 Magilton Jim	31 McKeever Mark	34 Morrison Owen	5 Newsome Jon	19 Oakes Scott	1 Pressman Kevin	28 Quinn Alan	25 Rudi Petter	14 Sanetti Francesco	12 Scott Philip	32 Sonner Danny	33 Srnicek Pavel	18 Stefanovic Dejan	22 Thome Emerson	6 Walker Des	7 Whittingham Guy
		7	U	10		6	U	2		9			3		U	8					U	1		11						5	4	U
		7	S*	10	S+	6#	U	2*		9+			3		S#	8					U	1		11						5	4	
		7	S*	10	U	6	U	2*		9			3		U	8						1		11						5	4	U
		7	S#	10	S*	6	U	2#					3		U	8						1		11	U					5	4	9*
		7	S*	10		6	U	2*		9#			3		U	8						1		11	S#					5	4	U
		7	U	10	11#	9	U			S*			3			8	S#			2	U	1	6*							5	4	
	6#	7	U	10*	S#		U	2		9			3	S*		8+	S+					1		11						5	4	
	10	6	S#				U	2#					3	9		7	8+			U	S*	1		11*	S+					5	4	
	11	2		10	3	9*	U							8		7	U	U		U		1					6			5	4	S*
	6	2		10	11		U						3	9		8	U			U		1			U		7			5	4	U
	6	2		10	11*		U						3	9		8	U			U		1		S*	S#		7#			5	4	
	11	2		10	U		U						3	9#		7*	S*			S#		1		8	U		6			5	4	
	11	2		10		9#	U						3	S#		7	S*			U				6			8*	1	U	5	4	
	6	2		10		9	U						3	U		8	U							11	U		7	1	U	5	4	
	11	2		10#	U	9	U						3	S#		7	S*							6			8*	1	U	5	4	
	6	2		10	S*	9#	U						3	U		8	U							11*			7	1	S#	5	4	
	6*	2		10	S*	9	U						3	U		8	U							11#			7	1	S#	5	4	
	11*	2		10	S*	9	U						3	S#		8	U							6#			7	1	U	5	4	
	6#	2		10	S#								3	9*		8	U		S*			U		11			U	1	7	5	4	
	6#	2		10	S#	9							3	S*		8	U					U		11*			U	1	7	5	4	
	6	2			U	9							3	10		8				U		U		11	U		U	1	7	5	4	
U	6	2			S*	9							3*	10		8				U		U		11			7	1		5	4	U
	6+	2		10*	U	9		U					3	S*		8#				S#		S+		11				1	7	5	4	
	6	2		10*	U	9							3	S*		8				U		U		11			7	1	U	5	4	
U	6	2		10	S*	9	U	S#					3	U		8						1		11			7#			5	4*	
	6	2		10	U	9	U	U					3	U		8						1		11			7		U	5	4	
	6	2		10	U	9	U						3	S*		8				U				11			7*	1	U	5	4	
	6	2		10	U	9	U						3	U		8				U				11			7	1	U	5	4	
S#	6	2		10	S*								3	9#		8				U		U		11			7*	1	U	5	4	
	6	2		10	U	9							3*	S#		8#				U		U		11			7	1	S*	5	4	
U	6	2			3	9			7					10#		8+				S*		U		11		S+	S#	1		5	4*	
U	6*	2		10	U	9#			S#				3			8				4		U		11		S*	7	1		5		
	6*	2		10#	U	9			S#				3			8						U		11		S*	7	1	U	5	4	
	6	2		10		9		U	U				3			8*						U		11		S*	7	1	U	5	4	
	6	2		10*		9		U	S*		U					8		11		U		U					7	1	3	5	4	
	6+	2		10		9		S*	S+		U					8		S#				U		11#			7	1	3	5*	4	
	S*	6		10#		9			S#		2*	U				8		S+				U		11+			7	1	3	5	4	
	6	7		10		9#			S*		2*			U		8		U				U		11			S#	1	3	5	4	
	31	38		34	5	31		7	1	5	2		32	10		38	1	1		2		14	1	33			24	24	8	38	37	1
1	1		5		11			2	6	1				9	1		5	2	1	3	1	1		1	3	4	2		3			1
	3	2		6	1	8			1	3			3	1		2								5		1	3			1		

23 Agogo Junior	26 Alexandersson Niclas	2 Atherton Peter	27 Barrett Earl	10 Booth Andy	17 Briscoe Lee	8 Carbone Benny	13 Clarke Matt	15 Cobian Juan	21 Cresswell Richard	11 Di Canio Paulo	35 Haslam Steve	36 Higgins Alex	20 Hinchcliffe Andy	16 Humphreys Ritchie	12 Hyde Graham	4 Jonk Wim	24 Magilton Jim	31 McKeever Mark	34 Morrison Owen	5 Newsome Jon	19 Oakes Scott	1 Pressman Kevin	28 Quinn Alan	25 Rudi Petter	14 Sanetti Francesco	12 Scott Philip	32 Sonner Danny	33 Srnicek Pavel	18 Stefanovic Dejan	22 Thome Emerson	6 Walker Des	7 Whittingham Guy
		7	U	10#		6	U	2		9			3		U	8						1		11*	S#					5	4	S*
	S*	6	S#	10	8	11*	U			9			3			7+	U			2#		1			S+					5	4	
		2		2	1	2		1		2			2			2				1		2		1						2	2	
	1		1																						2							1

23 Agogo Junior	26 Alexandersson Niclas	2 Atherton Peter	27 Barrett Earl	10 Booth Andy	17 Briscoe Lee	8 Carbone Benny	13 Clarke Matt	15 Cobian Juan	21 Cresswell Richard	11 Di Canio Paulo	35 Haslam Steve	36 Higgins Alex	20 Hinchcliffe Andy	16 Humphreys Ritchie	12 Hyde Graham	4 Jonk Wim	24 Magilton Jim	31 McKeever Mark	34 Morrison Owen	5 Newsome Jon	19 Oakes Scott	1 Pressman Kevin	28 Quinn Alan	25 Rudi Petter	14 Sanetti Francesco	12 Scott Philip	32 Sonner Danny	33 Srnicek Pavel	18 Stefanovic Dejan	22 Thome Emerson	6 Walker Des	7 Whittingham Guy
	6	2			S#	10							3	9		8*	U		U			U		11			S*	1	7	5#	4	
	6	2		S*	U	10							3	9*		8				S#		U		11			7	1	U	5	4#	
S#	6	2		10	S*	9	U							U		8				U		1		11*			7#		3	5	4	
	3	3		1		3							2	2		3						1		3			2	2	2	3	3	
1				1	2															1							1					
						1								2										1					1	1		

League Table

	P	W	D	L	F	A	Pts
Manchester United	38	22	13	3	80	37	79
Arsenal	38	22	12	4	59	17	78
Chelsea	38	20	15	3	57	30	75
Leeds United	38	18	13	7	62	34	67
West Ham United	38	16	9	13	46	53	57
Aston Villa	38	15	10	13	51	46	55
Liverpool	38	15	9	14	68	49	54
Derby County	38	13	13	12	40	45	52
Middlesbrough	38	12	15	11	48	54	51
Leicester City	38	12	13	13	40	46	49
Tottenham Hotspur	38	11	14	13	47	50	47
SHEFFIELD WEDNESDAY	38	13	7	18	41	42	46
Newcastle United	38	11	13	14	48	54	46
Everton	38	11	10	17	42	47	43
Coventry City	38	11	9	18	39	51	42
Wimbledon	38	10	12	16	40	63	42
Southampton	38	11	8	19	37	64	41
Charlton Athletic	38	8	12	18	41	56	36
Blackburn Rovers	38	7	14	17	38	52	35
Nottingham Forest	38	7	9	22	35	69	30

1999-2000

Premiership

Manager: Danny Wilson

Did you know that?

Final League Position: 19th

On 11 December 1999 Alan Quinn was sent-off in a third-round FA Cup game at home to Bristol City a minute after coming on as a substitute for Gilles De Bilde in the 88th minute. Wednesday won 1–0.

Wednesday played Chelsea in the last Premier League game of the century, with Chelsea starting without a British player on the field. Chelsea won 3–0.

Match No.	Date	Venue	Opponents		Round	Result	HT Score	Position	Scorers	Attendance
1	Aug 7	H	Liverpool	L		1-2	0-0	15th	Carbone	34,853
2	11	A	Manchester United	L		0-4	0-2	20th		54,941
3	14	A	Bradford City	D		1-1	1-0	19th	Dreyer (og)	18,276
4	21	H	Tottenham Hotspur	L		1-2	1-2	20th	Carbone (pen)	24,027
5	25	H	Derby County	L		0-2	0-0	20th		20,943
6	28	A	Southampton	L		0-2	0-0	20th		14,815
7	Sep 11	H	Everton	L		0-2	0-2	20th		23,539
8	19	A	Newcastle United	L		0-8	0-4	20th		36,619
9	25	A	Sunderland	L		0-1	0-0	20th		41,132
10	Oct 2	H	Wimbledon	W		5-1	2-1	20th	Jonk, De Bilde (2), Rudi, Sibon	18,077
11	16	A	Leeds United	L		0-2	0-0	20th		39,437
12	23	H	Coventry City	D		0-0	0-0	20th		23,296
13	30	A	Leicester City	L		0-3	0-2	20th		19,046
14	Nov 6	H	Watford	D		2-2	0-1	20th	De Bilde (1 + pen)	21,658
15	21	A	West Ham United	L		3-4	1-1	20th	Rudi, Jonk, Booth	23,015
16	Dec 5	A	Liverpool	L		1-4	1-2	20th	Alexandersson	42,517
17	18	A	Aston Villa	L		1-2	1-0	20th	De Bilde (pen)	23,885
18	26	H	Middlesbrough	W		1-0	1-0	20th	Atherton	28,531
19	29	A	Chelsea	L		0-3	0-2	20th		32,938
20	Jan 3	H	Arsenal	D		1-1	0-1	20th	Sibon	26,155
21	15	H	Bradford City	W		2-0	0-0	20th	Alexandersson, O'Brien (og)	24,682
22	22	A	Tottenham Hotspur	W		1-0	1-0	19th	Alexandersson	35,897
23	Feb 2	H	Manchester United	L		0-1	0-0	19th		39,640
24	5	A	Derby County	D		3-3	1-0	19th	De Bilde, Sibon, Donnelly	30,100
25	12	H	Southampton	L		0-1	0-1	19th		23,470
26	26	H	Newcastle United	L		0-2	0-1	19th		29,212
27	Mar 4	A	Everton	D		1-1	0-1	19th	Quinn	32,020
28	11	H	West Ham United	W		3-1	0-1	19th	Cresswell, Hinchcliffe, Alexandersson	21,147
29	18	A	Watford	L		0-1	0-0	19th		15,840
30	25	A	Middlesbrough	L		0-1	0-1	19th		32,748
31	Apr 5	H	Aston Villa	L		0-1	0-0	19th		18,136
32	12	A	Wimbledon	W		2-0	1-0	19th	De Bilde, Sibon	8,248
33	15	H	Chelsea	W		1-0	0-0	18th	Jonk (pen)	21,743
34	22	H	Sunderland	L		0-2	0-0	18th		28,072
35	30	H	Leeds United	L		0-3	0-1	19th		23,416
36	May 6	A	Coventry City	L		1-4	0-1	19th	De Bilde	19,921
37	9	A	Arsenal	D		3-3	0-1	19th	Sibon, De Bilde, Quinn	37,271
38	14	H	Leicester City	W		4-0	2-0	19th	Quinn, Booth, Alexandersson, De Bilde	21,656
										Apps
										Sub
									Two own-goals	Goals

League Cup

Match No.	Date	Venue	Opponents		Round	Result	HT Score	Position	Scorers	Attendance
39	Sep 14	A	Stoke City	D	2R 1L	0-0	0-0			9,313
40	22	H	Stoke City	W	2R 2L	3-1	2-0		Alexandersson (2), De Bilde	10,993
41	Oct 13	H	Nottingham Forest	W	3R	4-1	1-0		Cresswell, Booth, Sonner, Rudi	15,524
42	Nov 30	A	Bolton Wanderers	L	4R	0-1	0-0			12,543
										Apps
										Sub
										Goals

FA Cup

Match No.	Date	Venue	Opponents		Round	Result	HT Score	Position	Scorers	Attendance
43	Dec 11	H	Bristol City	W	3R	1-0	1-0		Booth	11,644
44	Jan 8	H	Wolverhampton W	D	4R	1-1	1-0		Alexandersson	18,506
45	18	A	Wolverhampton W *	W	4R Re	0-0	0-0			25,201
46	29	A	Gillingham	L	5R	1-3	1-0		Sibon	10,130
										Apps
										Sub
										Goals

* After extra-time. Won 4-3 on penalties.

16 Alexandersson Niclas	2 Atherton Peter	10 Booth Andy	21 Briscoe Lee	8 Carbone Benny	36 Crane Tony	12 Cresswell Richard	23 De Bilde Gilles	18 Donnelly Simon	29 Hamshaw Matthew	22 Haslam Steve	3 Hinchcliffe Andy	26 Horne Barry	20 Humphreys Richie	4 Jonk Wim	24 McKeever Mark	19 Newsome Jon	38 Nicholson Kevin	17 Nolan Ian	11 O'Donnell Phil	1 Pressman Kevin	33 Quinn Alan	13 Richardson Barry	14 Rudi Petter	15 Scott Philip	9 Sibon Gerald	7 Sonner Danny	28 Srnicek Pavel	37 Staniforth Tom	5 Thome Emerson	6 Walker Des
7			S#	S+		S*	9+	8#		U	3					2				U			11		10*	6	1		5	4
6	8		S#	S*		S+	9+			U	3					2				U			11		10*	7#	1		5	4
6	8	S+	S*	10		U	9+	S#			3*			7#		2				1			11				U		5	4
6	2	S*		10			9	U		8				7#		U		3		1			11*	S#			U		5	4
6	8			10		S#	9#	U		2+				7		S*		3		1			11		S+		U		5	4*
6	4		3			9	10*	S*	U	8#						2		U		1			11	7	S#		U		5	
6#	7	10	3	S+			9+	S#								U		2	S*	1			11*			8	U		5	4
6		10*		S*			9	8+		S#						2		3	U	1			11#		S+	7	U		5	4
7		10	3			S*	9*	6+		U				S#				2		U			11#		S+	8	1		5	4
6	2	10#				U	9	S*						7		U		3		U			11		S#	8*	1		5	4
6	2	10	U			U	9				3			7				U		U			11		U	8	1		5	4
6	2	10#	S*			U	9				3*			7				U		U			11		S#	8	1		5	4
6	2		U		U	S*	9			U	3			7						U			11*		10	8	1		5	4
6*	2#	10	U			S*	9				3			7				S#		1			11		U	8	U		5	4
6	5	10	U			S*	9				3			7				2#		1			11*		U	8	U		S#	4
6	7	10	3#			S*	9*			U				8				2		1	S+		11+		S#		U		5	4
6	3	10				U	9			S*				8#			U	2		U	11*				S#	7	1		5	4
6	5	10			U	S#	9			S*	3			7	11#			2		U					U	8*	1			4
6	5	10+	11#			S+	9			S*	3			8	U			2		U					S#	7*	1			4
6	5		11*			S#	9				3			7	S*		U	2		U					10#	8	1	U		4
6*	5					U	9	S*		8	3			7				2		U	11				10	U	1	U		4
6	5					U	9#	S#		7	3			8				2		U	11*			S*	10	U	1			4
6	5					S#	9+	S+		8	3			7				2		U			S*	11*	10#		1	U		4
6*	5					U	9+	S+		7	3			8#				2		U	11			S*	10	S#	1			4
6	5	S#				U	9+	S+		7#	3							2		U	8		11*		10	S*	1			4
6	5		U			S*	9*			7	3							2		U	11		S#		10	8#	1	U		4
6	5		S*			U	9			7	3							2*		U	11		U		10	8	1	U		4
6	5		U			S*	9			7	3			8#				2		U	11				10*	S#	1	U		4
6	5		U			10	9			7	3			8				2		S*	11#		U		S#	U	1*			4
6	5		U			S#	9#			7*	3	U		8				2		1	11	U	10			S*				4
6	5	10#	11*			S#	9			U	3	U		8				2		1	7	U				S*				4
6	5	10	S#				9*			S+	3	7		8+				2		1	11#	U			S*	U				4
6	5	10	S*			U	9#			2	3	7*		8						1	11				S#	U	U			4
6+	5	10*				S*	9			2	3	7#		8				U		1	11				S#	S+	U			4
6+	5	10	S#				9#			U	3	7*		8				2		1	11				S*	S+	U			4
6#	5	10				U	9			S*	3	7+		8				2		1	11				S#	S+	U			4*
	5	10	S+				S*			11#	3	7+	U	8				2		1	9				S#	6*	U			4
6*	5	10				S+	9			S#	3	7+		8				2		1	11				U	S*	U			4#
37	35	20	7	3		2	37	3		16	29	7		29	1	5		28		18	18		18	2	12	18	20		16	37
		3	9	4		18	1	9		7				1	1	1		1	1	1	1		2	3	16	9			1	
5	1	2		2		1	10	1			1			3							3		2		5					

16 Alexandersson Niclas	2 Atherton Peter	10 Booth Andy	21 Briscoe Lee	8 Carbone Benny	36 Crane Tony	12 Cresswell Richard	23 De Bilde Gilles	18 Donnelly Simon	29 Hamshaw Matthew	22 Haslam Steve	3 Hinchcliffe Andy	26 Horne Barry	20 Humphreys Richie	4 Jonk Wim	24 McKeever Mark	19 Newsome Jon	38 Nicholson Kevin	17 Nolan Ian	11 O'Donnell Phil	1 Pressman Kevin	33 Quinn Alan	13 Richardson Barry	14 Rudi Petter	15 Scott Philip	9 Sibon Gerald	7 Sonner Danny	28 Srnicek Pavel	37 Staniforth Tom	5 Thome Emerson	6 Walker Des
6	7*	10	3	S#			9#	S*								U		2		1			11		U	8	U		5	4
6		10	3*			S#	9#	7	U	S*								2		U			11+		S+	8	1		5	4
6#	2	10	S*			9		S#			3+			7*				S+		U			11		U	8	1		5	4
7	5	10				U	9				3*			8	S+			2		1			11		6+	S#	U		S*	4#
4	3	4	2			1	3	1			2			2				3		2			4		1	3	2		3	4
			1	1		1		2		1					1			1							1	1			1	
2		1				1	1																1			1				

16 Alexandersson Niclas	2 Atherton Peter	10 Booth Andy	21 Briscoe Lee	8 Carbone Benny	36 Crane Tony	12 Cresswell Richard	23 De Bilde Gilles	18 Donnelly Simon	29 Hamshaw Matthew	22 Haslam Steve	3 Hinchcliffe Andy	26 Horne Barry	20 Humphreys Richie	4 Jonk Wim	24 McKeever Mark	19 Newsome Jon	38 Nicholson Kevin	17 Nolan Ian	11 O'Donnell Phil	1 Pressman Kevin	33 Quinn Alan	13 Richardson Barry	14 Rudi Petter	15 Scott Philip	9 Sibon Gerald	7 Sonner Danny	28 Srnicek Pavel	37 Staniforth Tom	5 Thome Emerson	6 Walker Des
6	8	10				U	9+				3*			7#	S*			2		U	S+				S#	11	1		5	4
6	5					S*	9*	S+		2	11			7+				3#		U				S#	10	8	1	U		4
	5					S*	9*	S#		8	3			7				2		U	11+			6#	10	S+	1	U		4
6	5					S+	9*	S*		7+	3			8				2		U	11#		S#	U	10		1			4
3	4	1					4			3	4			4				4			2			1	3	2	4		1	4
						3		3							1						1		1	1	1	1				
1		1																							1					

League Table

	P	W	D	L	F	A	Pts
Manchester United	38	28	7	3	97	45	91
Arsenal	38	22	7	9	73	43	73
Leeds United	38	21	6	11	58	43	69
Liverpool	38	19	10	9	51	30	67
Chelsea	38	18	11	9	53	34	65
Aston Villa	38	15	13	10	46	35	58
Sunderland	38	16	10	12	57	56	58
Leicester City	38	16	7	15	55	55	55
West Ham United	38	15	10	13	52	53	55
Tottenham Hotspur	38	15	8	15	57	49	53
Newcastle United	38	14	10	14	63	54	52
Middlesbrough	38	14	10	14	46	52	52
Everton	38	12	14	12	59	49	50
Coventry City	38	12	8	18	47	54	44
Southampton	38	12	8	18	45	62	44
Derby County	38	9	11	18	44	57	38
Bradford City	38	9	9	20	38	68	36
Wimbledon	38	7	12	19	46	74	33
SHEFFIELD WEDNESDAY	38	8	7	23	38	70	31
Watford	38	6	6	26	35	77	24

2000-01

Division One

Manager: Paul Jewell/Peter Shreeves

Did you know that?

Final League Position: 17th

On 13 August 13 2000 Wednesday's first game of the season was away at Wolves. In a match live on the television Kevin Pressman ran out of goal and outside the area, saved a shot and was sent-off after only 13 seconds, which is the fastest-ever sending-off in British football.

On 17 October 2000 Wednesday lost for their eighth League game in a row to set a new club record.

On 16 December 2000, Wednesday drew 1–1 with Sheffield United at Bramall Lane in a game that contained only one offside.

Match No.	Date	Venue	Opponents		Round	Result	HT Score	Position	Scorers	Attendance
1	Aug 13	A	Wolverhampton W	D		1-1	0-1	11th	Booth	19,086
2	19	H	Huddersfield Town	L		2-3	1-3	15th	Booth, Hinchcliffe (pen)	22,704
3	26	A	Grimsby Town	W		1-0	1-0	10th	Di Piedi	7,755
4	28	H	Blackburn Rovers	D		1-1	1-1	11th	Westwood	15,646
5	Sep 9	H	Wimbledon	L		0-5	0-0	20th		15,856
6	13	H	Nottingham Forest	L		0-1	0-1	22nd		15,700
7	16	A	Tranmere Rovers	L		0-2	0-1	23rd		9,352
8	23	H	Preston North End	L		1-3	1-0	23rd	Morrison	17,379
9	30	A	Gillingham	L		0-2	0-1	24th		9,099
10	Oct 8	H	West Bromwich Alb	L		1-2	1-1	24th	Morrison	15,338
11	14	A	Portsmouth	L		1-2	0-1	24th	Morrison	13,376
12	17	A	Burnley	L		0-1	0-0	24th		16,372
13	22	H	Birmingham City	W		1-0	0-0	23rd	Harkness	14,695
14	25	A	Queen's Park Rangers	W		2-1	0-1	22nd	Cooke, Quinn	10,353
15	28	H	Fulham	D		3-3	1-0	21st	Sibon, Morrison, Westwood	17,559
16	Nov 4	A	Crystal Palace	L		1-4	0-3	22nd	Sibon (pen)	15,333
17	7	A	Watford	W		3-1	1-0	20th	Haslam, Crane, Quinn	11,166
18	11	H	Norwich City	W		3-2	1-1	18th	Hinchcliffe (pen), Crane, De Piedi	16,956
19	18	A	Barnsley	L		0-1	0-1	19th		19,989
20	25	A	Crewe Alexandra	L		0-1	0-0	20th		7,103
21	Dec 2	H	Queen's Park Rangers	W		5-2	3-1	17th	Sibon (3), Morrison, Ekoku	21,782
22	9	H	Stockport County	L		2-4	2-2	19th	Morrison, Ekoku	16,337
23	16	A	Sheffield United	D		1-1	0-0	21st	Hendon	25,156
24	23	H	Wolverhampton W	L		0-1	0-1	21st		17,787
25	26	A	Bolton Wanderers	L		0-2	0-1	23rd		21,216
26	30	A	Huddersfield Town	D		0-0	0-0	22nd		18,931
27	Jan 1	H	Grimsby Town	W		1-0	0-0	21st	Sibon	17,004
28	13	A	Blackburn Rovers	L		0-2	0-2	22nd		19,308
29	20	H	Bolton Wanderers	L		0-3	0-2	22nd		17,638
30	Feb 3	H	Watford	L		2-3	2-2	24th	Sibon, Ekoku	16,134
31	10	A	Wimbledon	L		1-4	1-2	24th	Ekoku	6,741
32	13	H	Tranmere Rovers	W		1-0	0-0	21st	Ekoku	15,444
33	21	A	Nottingham Forest	W		1-0	0-0	21st	Sibon	23,266
34	24	A	Preston North End	L		0-2	0-0	22nd		14,379
35	Mar 3	H	Gillingham	W		2-1	1-0	19th	Ekoku, Di Piedi	18,702
36	7	H	Portsmouth	D		0-0	0-0	19th		20,503
37	10	A	West Bromwich Alb	W		2-1	1-1	18th	Soltvedt, Booth	18,662
38	17	H	Burnley	W		2-0	1-0	17th	Hendon, Sibon (pen)	20,184
39	24	A	Birmingham City	W		2-1	1-0	15th	De Bilde, Di Piedi	19,733
40	Apr 1	H	Sheffield United	L		1-2	0-0	17th	Sibon	38,433
41	7	A	Stockport County	L		1-2	0-1	17th	De Bilde	9,666
42	14	H	Crystal Palace	W		4-1	3-1	16th	Ekoku, De Bilde, Sibon, Ripley	19,877
43	16	A	Fulham	D		1-1	1-0	18th	Sibon	17,500
44	21	H	Barnsley	W		2-1	0-1	14th	Sibon, Donnelly	23,498
45	28	A	Norwich City	L		0-1	0-1	17th		21,241
46	May 6	H	Crewe Alexandra	D		0-0	0-0	17th		28,007
										Apps
										Sub
										Goals

League Cup

47	Sep 19	A	Oldham Athletic	W	2R 1L	3-1	1-1		Morrison, De Bilde, Westwood	3,213
48	27	H	Oldham Athletic	W	2R 2L	5-1	1-1		Hamshaw, Westwood, Di Piedi, Sibon, Quinn	4,773
49	Nov 1	H	Sheffield United *	W	3R	2-1	1-1		Ekoku (2)	32,383
50	29	A	West Ham United	W	4R	2-1	1-0		Morrison, Westwood	25,857
51	Dec 12	A	Birmingham City	L	5R	0-2	0-1			22,911
										Apps
										Sub
										Goals

* After extra-time. Score at full-time 1-1

FA Cup

52	Jan 6	H	Norwich City	W	3R	2-1	1-0		Hamshaw, Sibon	15,971
53	27	A	Southampton	L	4R	1-3	0-1		Booth	15,251
										Apps
										Sub
										Goals

13 Beresford Marlon	25 Billington David	27 Blatsis Con	9 Booth Andy	26 Bromby Leigh	23 Cooke Terry	36 Crane Tony	11 Cresswell Richard	10 De Bilde Gilles	17 Di Piedi Michele	18 Donnelly Simon	22 Ekoku Efan	30 Geary Derek	5 Grayson Simon	16 Hamshaw Matthew	5 Harkness Steve	2 Haslam Steve	12 Hendon Ian	34 Higgins Alex	3 Hinchcliffe Andy	12 Humphreys Richie	31 Hutton John	28 Johansson Jesper	4 Jonk Wim	14 Lescott Aaron	24 McKeever Mark	32 Morrison Owen	19 Muller Adam	38 Nicholson Kevin	11 O'Donnell Phil	23 Palmer Carlton	1 Pressman Kevin	7 Quinn Alan	9 Ripley Stuart	14 Rudi Petter	8 Sibon Gerald	20 Soltvedt Trond	22 Stockdale Robbie	29 Stringer Chris	6 Walker Des	21 Westwood Ashley
			10				6*	9+	S+				2	U		7			3#	U			8								1	11			S#			S*	4	5
			10				6+	9*	S*				2	U					3				7#						8		1	11		S#	S+			U	4	5
						U	8		9*				2	7					3	U	U						S*		6		1	11			10			U	4	5
	U		10			U	11						2	6					3*	U							U	S*	8			7			9			1	4	5
			10			U		S*	7			U	2	6					3	U									8*		1	11			9			U	4	5
			10			S+		S*	9*			U		6		7+				3									8#		1	11			S#		2	U	4	5
			10			6		9*				U		7#						3						11	S*	U			1	8			S#		2	U	4	5
			10*		6	S+		9	S*			U		S#						3						8#					1	11			7+		2	U	4	5
					6	U			9+			S#		U	3					11						S*	S+		7*			8			10		2#	1	4	5
					6+	U		9*	S*						3					U				7		11	S+		S#			8			10#		2	1	4	5
					S#	U			S*						5	2	3			9				8		10	U		7*		S+	6				11#		1+	4	
					9	S#			S*					6*	8	2	5	U		3				U		11	10#				1	7						U	4	
					6	S#					9			U	8	7	5			3*				U		10#					1	11			S*			U	4	2
					6	S*					9			U	3	8	2			U				U		11*					1	7			10			U	4	5
					6	U					9			S#	3	7	2			U				S*		11#					1	8			10*			U	4	5
					6	S*			S#		9	U		U	5	3	2							8*		11#					1	7			10			U	4	
			9		6	7			S*			U			8#	5	2		3					S#		U					1	11			10*			U	4	
			10*		6	7			S*		9	U		U		5	2		3	U				8		11					1							U	4	
					6	7			10#		9			U		5	2		3*	U				8		S#					1	11			S*			U	4	
			10		6	7			S+		9+				3*	8#	2							S*		U					1	11			S#			U	4	5
			10*			U			S*		9			U	3	7	2							S#		11					1	8			6#			U	4	5
			10*						S*		9			U	3	7	2							S#		11			U		1	8			6			U	4	5#
			10*	U	6	8#			U		9			S*	3	7	2							S#		11					1							U	4	5
				5*	6				S#		9#			S+	3	7	2							U		11+			S*		1	8			10			U	4	
					10*	S+					9			S#	3	7#	2							6+		11			U		1	8			S*			U	4	5
		5		U							9			6#	8	3	7							S*		10+			S+		1	11			S#			U	4	2*
		5			6+				9#			U		S*	7	2	3							S#		11*			S+		1	8			10			U	4	
1		5	S#	U				S*			9#			S+	8	3*	2							6		10						11						U	4	7+
1		5	10+	U				9#			S+			S#	3	8	2*							6		S*						7			11			U		4
1		5+		2		U		S#			9	S+		6#	3	8*								7		S*						11			10			U	4	
1		5*		3+				S#			9			U	8	7#	2							6		S+						11			10			U	4	S*
				S*				10#			9				3*	U	2							S#		U				11	1	6			7	8		U	4	5
				3				U			9	U				U	2							7		U				8	1	11			10	6		U	4	5
				3		7#		S#			9	U				U	2									S*				8	1	11*			10	6		U	4	5
				3				U	S*		9			6*		S#	2							8#		S+					1	11+			10	7		U	4	5
			10#	3				U	S#		9						2							U		S*				8	1	11*			6	7		U	4	5
			10#	3				U			9				S#		2							S*		U				8	1	11*			6	7		U	4	5
			10	3				U			9			U		U	2							S*						8	1	11*			6	7		U	4	5
				3		U		10#	S#		9			U	11		2*							S*						8	1				6	7		U	4	5
				2				10#	S+		9				S#	U								3+						8	1	11*	S*		6	7		U	4	5
				2		S+		S*			9	U			11#	S#			3+					8		10*				5	1				6	7		U	4	
				2				10+	S+		9	U			3	8*								S*		S#				5	1		11#		6	7		U	4	
				2				10*	S*	U	9	U			3	S#								8						5	1		11		6	7#		U	4	
				5				10*	U	S+	9	S#			3+		2							7#		S*					1		11		6	8		U	4	
				5				10#		S*	9	S+		S#	3+	U	2							8*							1		11		6	7		U		4
				5				S*		S#	9*	3		U			2							U		11#				8	1		6		11	7		U		4
4		6	17	17	16	7	4	13	6		31	1	5	9	28	24	31		9	7			2	17		20	1		7	12	38	37	5		32	15	6	4	43	32
			1	1	1	8		8	19	3	1	4		9	2	3								13		10	4	1	4		1		1	1	9			1		1
			3		1	2		3	4	1	7				1	1	2		2							6						2	1		13	1				2

13 Beresford Marlon	25 Billington David	27 Blatsis Con	9 Booth Andy	26 Bromby Leigh	23 Cooke Terry	36 Crane Tony	11 Cresswell Richard	10 De Bilde Gilles	17 Di Piedi Michele	18 Donnelly Simon	22 Ekoku Efan	30 Geary Derek	5 Grayson Simon	16 Hamshaw Matthew	5 Harkness Steve	2 Haslam Steve	12 Hendon Ian	34 Higgins Alex	3 Hinchcliffe Andy	12 Humphreys Richie	31 Hutton John	28 Johansson Jesper	4 Jonk Wim	14 Lescott Aaron	24 McKeever Mark	32 Morrison Owen	19 Muller Adam	38 Nicholson Kevin	11 O'Donnell Phil	23 Palmer Carlton	1 Pressman Kevin	7 Quinn Alan	9 Ripley Stuart	14 Rudi Petter	8 Sibon Gerald	20 Soltvedt Trond	22 Stockdale Robbie	29 Stringer Chris	6 Walker Des	21 Westwood Ashley
			10			7		9				2		6*						3		U				11	U	U			1	8			S*			U	4	5
						7*		9+	S+			2		6				U		3						11	S*	U			1#	8			10			S#	4	5
						S#			S+		9	S*		6		7+				3*				2		11	U				1	8			10			U	4	5#
			S*			6			U		9	3		U		7				U				2		11					1	8			10*			U	4	5
			10	U		S#			S+		9+	3#				7								2		11*			S*		1	8			6			U	4	5
			2			3		2			3	4		3		3				3				3		5					5	5			4				5	5
			1			2			3			1															1		1						1			1		
								1	1		2			1												2						1			1					3

13 Beresford Marlon	25 Billington David	27 Blatsis Con	9 Booth Andy	26 Bromby Leigh	23 Cooke Terry	36 Crane Tony	11 Cresswell Richard	10 De Bilde Gilles	17 Di Piedi Michele	18 Donnelly Simon	22 Ekoku Efan	30 Geary Derek	5 Grayson Simon	16 Hamshaw Matthew	5 Harkness Steve	2 Haslam Steve	12 Hendon Ian	34 Higgins Alex	3 Hinchcliffe Andy	12 Humphreys Richie	31 Hutton John	28 Johansson Jesper	4 Jonk Wim	14 Lescott Aaron	24 McKeever Mark	32 Morrison Owen	19 Muller Adam	38 Nicholson Kevin	11 O'Donnell Phil	23 Palmer Carlton	1 Pressman Kevin	7 Quinn Alan	9 Ripley Stuart	14 Rudi Petter	8 Sibon Gerald	20 Soltvedt Trond	22 Stockdale Robbie	29 Stringer Chris	6 Walker Des	21 Westwood Ashley
		5		S*+		S+			U		9			11*	7	2#	3							6		S#			U			8			10			1	4	
		5	10	7		S+					S*			U	11	2*	3							6+		S#					1	8#			9			U	4	
		2	1	1							1			1	2	2	2							2							1	2			2			1	2	
				1		2					1															2														
			1											1																					1					

League Table

See page 532

2001-02

Division One

Manager: Peter Shreeves/Terry Yorath

Did you know that?

Final League Position: 20th

On 21 August 2001, in an away League Cup game at Bury, Wednesday's fans chanted the name of Tom Staniforth for 15 minutes. He was a Wednesday reserve player who had died two days before the game while leaving a nightclub in York.

Match No.	Date	Venue	Opponents		Round	Result	HT Score	Position	Scorers	Attendance
1	Aug 12	H	Burnley	L		0-2	0-0	20th		21,766
2	18	A	Crewe Alexandra	W		2-0	1-0	11th	Sibon, McLaren	7,933
3	25	H	West Bromwich Albion	D		1-1	1-1	13th	Sibon	18,844
4	27	A	Norwich City	L		0-2	0-1	18th		16,820
5	Sep 8	A	Birmingham City	L		0-2	0-1	21st		19,421
6	15	A	Wimbledon	D		1-1	1-0	21st	T. Johnson	7,348
7	17	H	Bradford City	D		1-1	0-0	18th	Di Piedi	18,012
8	22	H	Manchester City	L		2-6	1-2	21st	Bonvin, Bromby	25,731
9	25	A	Rotherham United	D		1-1	0-0	21st	Westwood	8,679
10	29	A	Crystal Palace	L		1-4	1-3	21st	T. Johnson	17,066
11	Oct 7	H	Sheffield United	D		0-0	0-0	21st		29,281
12	13	A	Watford	L		1-3	1-2	23rd	T. Johnson	14,456
13	16	H	Preston North End	L		1-2	1-0	24th	Sibon	15,592
14	20	H	Walsall	W		2-1	0-1	21st	Sibon, Bonvin	16,275
15	24	H	Barnsley	W		3-1	1-1	20th	Sibon, Bonvin (2)	21,008
16	27	A	Coventry City	L		0-2	0-1	21st		17,381
17	31	A	Nottingham Forest	W		1-0	0-0	21st	Morrison	20,206
18	Nov 3	H	Portsmouth	L		2-3	1-2	21st	Donnelly, Sibon (pen)	18,212
19	10	H	Grimsby Town	D		0-0	0-0	21st		17,507
20	18	A	Wolverhampton W	D		0-0	0-0	22nd		19,947
21	24	H	Stockport County	W		5-0	1-0	19th	Maddix, Sibon (pen), Morrison, Soltvedt, Ekoku	17,365
22	Dec 2	A	Barnsley	L		0-3	0-2	20th		16,714
23	8	H	Millwall	D		1-1	0-0	20th	Ekoku	21,304
24	15	A	Gillingham	L		1-2	1-2	21st	Sibon (pen)	8,586
25	22	A	West Bromwich Albion	D		1-1	0-0	21st	Ekoku	20,340
26	26	H	Birmingham City	L		0-1	0-0	22nd		24,335
27	29	H	Norwich City	L		0-5	0-4	23rd		19,205
28	Jan 12	H	Crewe Alexandra	W		1-0	1-0	22nd	Sibon	16,737
29	19	A	Burnley	W		2-1	1-0	21st	McLaren, Kuqi	16,081
30	29	A	Sheffield United	D		0-0	0-0	21st		29,364
31	Feb 2	H	Crystal Palace	L		1-3	1-3	22nd	Ekoku	20,099
32	5	A	Preston North End	L		2-4	1-2	22nd	Quinn, Ekoku (pen)	14,038
33	9	A	Walsall	W		3-0	1-0	21st	Ekoku, Kuqi, Sibon	8,290
34	16	H	Watford	W		2-1	0-1	20th	Ekoku (pen), Kuqi	18,244
35	23	H	Rotherham United	L		1-2	0-0	20th	Kuqi	28,179
36	27	A	Manchester City	L		0-4	0-2	20th		33,682
37	Mar 2	A	Bradford City	W		2-0	1-0	19th	D. Johnson, Kuqi	16,904
38	6	H	Wimbledon	L		1-2	1-1	20th	D. Johnson	18,930
39	9	H	Gillingham	D		0-0	0-0	20th		20,361
40	16	A	Millwall	W		2-1	0-0	19th	Donnelly (2)	13,074
41	23	A	Portsmouth	D		0-0	0-0	20th		14,819
42	29	H	Coventry City	W		2-1	1-1	18th	Sibon (2)	21,470
43	Apr 1	A	Grimsby Town	D		0-0	0-0	18th		9,236
44	6	H	Nottingham Forest	L		0-2	0-1	18th		21,782
45	13	A	Stockport County	L		1-3	1-1	21st	Quinn	8,706
46	21	H	Wolverhampton W	D		2-2	1-1	20th	Donnelly, Kuqi	29,772
										Apps
										Sub
										Goals

League Cup

Match No.	Date	Venue	Opponents		Round	Result	HT Score	Position	Scorers	Attendance
47	Aug 21	A	Bury	W	1R	3-1	1-0		Ekoku, Maddix, McLaren	3,129
48	Sep 12	H	Sunderland *	W	2R	4-2	2-1		Ekoku, Morrison (pen), Di Piedi, Bonvin	12,074
49	Oct 10	H	Crystal Palace #	W	3R	2-2	0-1		Westwood, Crane	8,796
50	Nov 28	A	Aston Villa	W	4R	1-0	1-0		Ekoku	26,526
51	Dec 19	H	Watford	W	5R	4-0	1-0		Sibon, Hamshaw, O'Donnell, Soltvedt	20,319
52	Jan 8	H	Blackburn Rovers	L	S/F 1L	1-2	0-2		Ekoku	30,883
53	22	A	Blackburn Rovers	L	S/F 2L	2-4	0-2		Ekoku (pen), Soltvedt	26,844
										Apps
										Sub
										Goals

* After extra-time. Score at 90 minutes 2-2

After extra-time. Score at 90 minutes 1-1 (Won 3-1 on penalties)

FA Cup

Match No.	Date	Venue	Opponents		Round	Result	HT Score	Position	Scorers	Attendance
54	Jan 15	A	Crewe Alexandra	L	3R	1-2	1-1		Hamshaw	6,271
										Apps
										Sub
										Goals

34 Armstrong Craig	10 Bonvin Pablo	5 Bromby Leigh	14 Broomes Marlon	35 Burrows David	20 Crane Tony	17 Di Piedi Michele	18 Donnelly Simon	28 Djordjic Bojan	9 Ekoku Efan	29 Gallacher Kevin	22 Geary Derek	32 Gibson Neil	16 Hamshaw Matthew	15 Harkness Steve	12 Haslam Steve	31 Heald Paul	2 Hendon Ian	3 Hinchcliffe Andy	33 Johnson David	27 Johnson Tommy	28 Kuqi Shefki	14 Lescott Aaron	37 McCarthy Jon	4 McLaren Paul	25 Maddix Danny	11 Morrison Owen	24 O'Donnell Phil	26 Palmer Carlton	1 Pressman Kevin	7 Quinn Alan	30 Roberts Sean	8 Sibon Gerald	36 Siddall Richard	6 Soltvedt Trond Egil	13 Stringer Chris	21 Westwood Ashley	26 Windass Dean
		4				S#			9		3				10		2+					S+		7*	5	S*			U	6#		11		8	1	U	
		4					U		9		3				7		2					S*		6#	5	S#			1	11*		10		8	U	U	
	S#	4							9		3				11		2					U		7#	5	S*			1	6*		10		8	U	U	
	S#	4							9		3				7		2*					U		6	5	S+			1	11+		10#		8	U	S*	
	S*	4				S+			9		3				2					10*				6+	5	11		7#	1	S#				8	U	U	
	U	3				S*	U		9						2#					10*		S#		6	5			7	1	11				8	U	4	
	S#	3				S+			9+						2*					10#		U		6	5	S*		7	1	11				8	U	4	
	9+	3				10	S+						S#		U							S*		7*	5	11#		2	1	6				8	U	4	
	9*	3				S*					2				S#					10+		U		6#	5	S+		7	1	11				8	U	4	
	9*	3				S*					2				S+					10		S#		6+	5	U		7	1	11				8	U	4#	
	S#	2				9#	S*				3		6*		U					10				U	5			7	1	11				8	U	4	
		2			9	U					3+				8					10				6	5	S+		7*	1	S*		S#		11	U	4#	
					S+	S*					3		S#		7		2			10+					5	11		4	1	6#		9*		8	U	U	
	S#	11+			10#		U								6		3*								5	S*	S+	4	1	10		9		8	U	2	
	10				U	S#	S*				3				7		2							S+	5	11+			1	6*		9#		8	U	4	
	10*	U				S*	6				3				7		2							U	5	11#	S#		1			9		8	U	4	
	U	3			U		10							U			2					7		U	5	11			1	6		9		8	U	4	
	S*	3			S#		10				2			U								7*		U	5#	11			1	6		9		8	U	4	
	10*	2			S#	S+	6+				3													S*	5#	11	U		1	7		9		8	U	4	
		5			S+	U	10				2		S*		7									S#		11	3		1	6#		9+		8	U	4*	
	S#	4					10		S*		2		U		7									U	5	11#	3		1	6*		9		8	U		
	S*	4					6*		10		2			U	7									S#	5	11#	3		1			9		8	U	U	
	S#	4+						11	9		2*				7									S*	S+	U	3		1			6#		8	U	5	10
	S*		4		S#		U	11#	9		3*		U		7										2				1			6		8	U	5	10
	U		4		S*		U	11*	10		2				7									6	5		3		1	U		9		8	U		
	S#		3		S+		6*	11#	10+		2			U	7									S*	5				1			9		8	U	4	
	U		4		S#		U	S*	10		2#		6		8									7	5		3*		1			9		11	U		
	U	4	S*		U				9		2		6		7			3*			10				U				1	8		9			U	5	
	U	4	3*						9		S*		6#		2						10			7	U				1+	S#	S+	11		8		5	
	S*	4	3		U				9				10*		2	1								7	U		U			6	U	11		8		5	
	S+	4	3						9		S*		S#		2	1					10			7	U					6#	U	11+		8		5*	
	S#	4*			S+		U		9		3		6#		2	1			10					7	S*					11	U			8		5+	
	U				5		S*		9#		3	U	6*		2	1			7		10				4					11	U	S#		8			
3	U				11#		S*		9				S#		2	1			7		10			6	4*						U	S+		8		5+	
3	U		U				U		9				S*		2	U			11		10			7					1	8		6*		4		5	
3			4				U		S*				6*		2	U			9		10			7	U				1	11		U		8		5	
3+	S#		4				S*				2		6*		7	U			9#		10			8	S+				1	11		U		5			
3			4				S*		S#		2		6+		7	U			9#		10			8*	U				1	11		S+		5			
7	9#		5	3			S*				2		S#		8	U					10				U	S+			1	11		6+		5*			
7	U		5	3	S#		9#						6*		2	U					10			8	4	S*			1	11		U					
	U		5	3	S#		9*		S*				6#		2						10			8	4	U			1	7		11	U				
			5	3			9#		U	S#	U				2	U					10		6	8	4	S*			1	7		11*					
			5	3			9*		S+	U	S*		S#		2						10+		6	8	4				1	7		11#	U				
S*			5	3			9#		S#	S+	U				2						10		6+	8	4				1	7		11*	U				
			5	3			S#			S+	2				7#						10		6*	8+	4	S*			1	11		9	U			U	
		4	5	3			9			S*			6		2						10		U	8*		S#			1	7		11#	U			U	
7	7	26	18	8	4	2	14	4	21		29		13		39	5	9	1	7	8	17	2	4	29	33	11	6	10	40	35		31		38	1	25	2
1	16		1		11	10	9	1	6	4	3		8		2							5		6	3	13	2			3	1	4				1	
	4	1				1	4		7										2	3	6			2	1	2				2		12		1		1	

34 Armstrong Craig	10 Bonvin Pablo	5 Bromby Leigh	14 Broomes Marlon	35 Burrows David	20 Crane Tony	17 Di Piedi Michele	18 Donnelly Simon	28 Djordjic Bojan	9 Ekoku Efan	29 Gallacher Kevin	22 Geary Derek	32 Gibson Neil	16 Hamshaw Matthew	15 Harkness Steve	12 Haslam Steve	31 Heald Paul	2 Hendon Ian	3 Hinchcliffe Andy	33 Johnson David	27 Johnson Tommy	28 Kuqi Shefki	14 Lescott Aaron	37 McCarthy Jon	4 McLaren Paul	25 Maddix Danny	11 Morrison Owen	24 O'Donnell Phil	26 Palmer Carlton	1 Pressman Kevin	7 Quinn Alan	30 Roberts Sean	8 Sibon Gerald	36 Siddall Richard	6 Soltvedt Trond Egil	13 Stringer Chris	21 Westwood Ashley	26 Windass Dean
	S+	4							9		3				7		2*					S*		6+	5	S#			1	11#		10		8	U	U	
	S#	2				S+			9#				S*		3					10+		U		7	5	11*			1	6				8	U	4	
	9*	2			S*	10	U				3		U		7									U	5	11			1	6				8	U	4	
	U	4					10		S*		2				7									S#	5	11#	3		1	6*		9+		8	U	S+	
	S#				S*		11*		10#		3		6+		2									7	5		S+		1	U		9		8	U	4	
	10+	4#			S*				9		2		6		8			S#						7	U	S+	3*		1	11					U	5	
	S*	4					U		10		3#		6*		2	1								7	U		S#			11	U	9		8		5	
	2	6				1	2		5		6		3		7	1	1			1				5	5	3	2		6	6		4		6		5	
	4				3	1			1				1					1				1		1		2	2									1	
	1				1	1			5				1											1	1	1	1					1		2		1	

34 Armstrong Craig	10 Bonvin Pablo	5 Bromby Leigh	14 Broomes Marlon	35 Burrows David	20 Crane Tony	17 Di Piedi Michele	18 Donnelly Simon	28 Djordjic Bojan	9 Ekoku Efan	29 Gallacher Kevin	22 Geary Derek	32 Gibson Neil	16 Hamshaw Matthew	15 Harkness Steve	12 Haslam Steve	31 Heald Paul	2 Hendon Ian	3 Hinchcliffe Andy	33 Johnson David	27 Johnson Tommy	28 Kuqi Shefki	14 Lescott Aaron	37 McCarthy Jon	4 McLaren Paul	25 Maddix Danny	11 Morrison Owen	24 O'Donnell Phil	26 Palmer Carlton	1 Pressman Kevin	7 Quinn Alan	30 Roberts Sean	8 Sibon Gerald	36 Siddall Richard	6 Soltvedt Trond Egil	13 Stringer Chris	21 Westwood Ashley	26 Windass Dean
	S*	4	3		S#				10		2#		6		7									8	U		U		1	11*		9			U	5	
		1	1						1		1		1		1									1					1	1		1				1	
	1				1																																
													1																								

League Table

See page 532

2002-03

Division One

Manager: Terry Yorath/Chris Turner

Did you know that?

Final League Position: 22nd

On 21 September 2002 Wednesday played their 2,000th home game in the League – a 0–0 draw with Leicester City.

On 26 April relegated Wednesday played away at Burnley and won 7–2. This was the first time that they had scored seven goals away in the League game. During the match, both 'keepers were injured and were replaced. This is Wednesday's record away win in the League.

Match No.	Date	Venue	Opponents		Round	Result	HT Score	Position	Scorers	Attendance
1	Aug 10	H	Stoke City	D		0-0	0-0	11th		26,746
2	13	A	Reading	L		1-2	1-0	16th	Sibon	13,638
3	17	A	Nottingham Forest	L		0-4	0-1	22nd		21,129
4	24	H	Rotherham United	L		1-2	1-1	23rd	Armstrong	22,873
5	27	A	Wolverhampton W	D		2-2	1-0	21st	Kuqi (2)	27,096
6	Sept 1	H	Sheffield United	W		2-0	0-0	20th	Owusu, Kuqi	27,075
7	14	A	Preston North End	D		2-2	1-1	21st	Kuqi, McLaren	13,632
8	18	A	Coventry City	D		1-1	0-0	21st	Knight	14,178
9	21	H	Leicester City	D		0-0	0-0	22nd		22,219
10	25	H	Crystal Palace	D		0-0	0-0	20th		16,112
11	28	A	Walsall	L		0-1	0-1	21st		6,792
12	Oct 5	H	Burnley	L		1-3	0-1	22nd	Donnelly	17,004
13	12	A	Ipswich Town	L		1-2	0-2	22nd	Donnelly	23,410
14	19	H	Bradford City	W		2-1	1-1	21st	Sibon (1 + pen)	17,191
15	26	A	Watford	L		0-1	0-1	21st		15,058
16	30	H	Millwall	L		0-1	0-1	22nd		16,791
17	Nov 2	H	Derby County	L		1-3	0-1	23rd	Hamshaw	19,747
18	9	A	Norwich City	L		0-3	0-2	23rd		20,667
19	16	A	Gillingham	D		1-1	0-1	23rd	Knight	8,028
20	23	H	Portsmouth	L		1-3	1-1	23rd	Knight	16,601
21	30	A	Wimbledon	L		0-3	0-1	23rd		2,131
22	Dec 7	H	Brighton & Hove Albion	D		1-1	0-1	23rd	Kuqi	18,008
23	14	H	Gillingham	L		0-2	0-1	23rd		17,715
24	21	A	Grimsby Town	L		0-2	0-0	24th		8,224
25	26	H	Nottingham Forest	W		2-0	1-0	24th	Sibon, Johnston	26,362
26	28	A	Stoke City	L		2-3	1-1	24th	Sibon, Proudlock	16,042
27	Jan 1	A	Rotherham United	W		2-0	0-0	23rd	Kuqi, Proudlock	11,480
28	11	H	Reading	W		3-2	0-2	23rd	Quinn, Sibon, Johnston	17,715
29	17	A	Sheffield United	L		1-3	0-0	23rd	Quinn	28,179
30	Feb1	H	Wolverhampton W	L		0-4	0-2	23rd		21,381
31	8	H	Norwich City	D		2-2	0-2	23rd	Robinson, Quinn	19,114
32	15	A	Derby County	D		2-2	1-0	24th	Barton (og), Crane	26,311
33	22	A	Crystal Palace	D		0-0	0-0	23rd		16,707
34	Mar 1	H	Preston North End	L		0-1	0-0	24th		18,912
35	5	H	Coventry City	W		5-1	1-0	23rd	Reddy, Kuqi (2), McLaren, Bradbury	19,536
36	8	A	Leicester City	D		1-1	1-0	23rd	McLaren	27,463
37	15	H	Ipswich Town	L		0-1	0-1	24th		24,726
38	18	A	Bradford City	D		1-1	0-1	24th	Crane	14,452
39	22	A	Millwall	L		0-3	0-2	24th		7,338
40	29	H	Watford	D		2-2	0-1	24th	Bradbury (pen), Maddix	17,086
41	Apr 5	H	Wimbledon	W		4-2	1-0	24th	Reddy, Owusu (2), Bradbury	17,649
42	12	A	Portsmouth	W		2-1	0-1	23rd	Westwood, Reddy	19,524
43	19	H	Grimsby Town	D		0-0	0-0	23rd		26,082
44	21	A	Brighton & Hove Albion	D		1-1	1-0	23rd	Holt	6,928
45	26	A	Burnley	W		7-2	3-1	23rd	McLaren,Westwood,Wood,Evans,Haslam,Gnohere (og), Quinn	17,435
46	May 4	H	Walsall	W		2-1	0-0	22nd	Owusu, Quinn	20,864
										Apps
										Sub
									Two own-goals	Goals

League Cup

47	Sept 11	H	Rochdale	W	1R	1-0	1-0		Sibon	8,815
48	Oct 2	H	Leicester City *	L	2R	1-2	1-0		Sibon	10,472
										Apps
										Sub
										Goals

* After extra-time (Score at 90 minutes 1-1)

FA Cup

49	Jan 7	A	Gillingham	L	3R	1-4	1-3		Sibon	6,434
										Apps
										Sub
										Goals

14 Armstrong Craig	38 Barry-Murphy Brian	3 Beswetherick Jon	30 Bradbury Lee	5 Bromby Leigh	15 Burrows David	20 Crane Tony	26 Di Piedi Michele	18 Donnelly Simon	23 Evans Paul	40 Evans Richard	22 Geary Derek	19 Green Ryan	16 Hamshaw Matthew	12 Haslam Steve	2 Hendon Ian	28 Holt Grant	29 Johnston Allan	11 Knight Leon	9 Kuqi Shefki	4 McLaren Paul	25 Maddix Danny	27 Monk Garry	17 Morrison Owen	24 O'Donnell Phil	10 Owusu Lloyd	35 Powell Darryl	1 Pressman Kevin	28 Proudlock Adam	7 Quinn Alan	37 Reddy Michael	36 Robinson Carl	32 Shaw Jon	34 Shaw Matt	8 Sibon Gerald	39 Smith Dean	6 Soltvedt Trond Egil	13 Stringer Chris	21 Westwood Ashley	33 Wood Richard
7		11		4	3	U		6	U		2			U					9		U			U			1		8					10		5			
7		11		4	3	S#		8*	U		2		U	S*					9		U						1		6					10		5#			
7		11#		4	3			8*	U		2		U					S*	9	S#	U						1		6					10		5			
7		11*		4	3	U		U	U		2							8	9	S*							1		6					10		U		5	
11				4	3			U	U		2		U		U			6	9	7	U						1							10		8		5	
7				4	3			10*	U				S*		2#			6	9	7	U				S#		1		S+							8+		5	
11				4	3						U		U		2			6#	9	7	5				S#		1		S*					10		8*	U		
8				4	3						S+		S*		2+			10#	9	7	5				S#		1		11					6*		U	U		
7				4	3						2		S*					10#	9	8	5				S#		1		11					6*		U	U	U	
7#				4	3						S+		S*		2			10	9	8+	5				S#		1		11					6*		U	U		
8#				4	3+			S#			2		6*					S*	9	7	5				10		1		11							U	U	S+	
3				4				S*			2			U				6	9	8	5				10*		1		7					11		U	U	U	
U				4				10			3		S+	7	2*			6+		S#	5				S*		1		11					9		8#	U		
U				4				7			3		U	2				6*	10	S*	5				S#		1		11#					9		8	U		
U				4				6			3+		S+	2				S*	10	7*	5				S#		1		11#					9		8	U		
U				4				7			3		S+		2			6*	10	S#	5				S*		1		11+					9		8#	U		
11				4				6#			3		S#	5	2			U	10	7					S*		1		U					9*		8	U		
11				4				U			3		U	5	6			S*	9	7					10		1		U					8*		2	U		
8		S#		4		2		U			11		U	5	3#			S*	9*						10		1							7		6	U		
8		11*		4		2		S#			3		S*	5	U			9					U		10#		1		6					7			U		
				4	U	2		U			8	3	S*	5				11*	9#						10		1		7					S#		6	U		
7				U	3	4					2	6	S+	8+				9#	S#	11					10*		1							S*		5	U		
U					3*	4						2	6	S*			11	U	10	7		5					1	S#						9#		8	U		
U						4					3		6#	2			11	S#	10*	7		5					1	S*						9		8	U	U	
			S+			4					3		6#	2			11		U	7		5					1*	10	S#					9+		8	S*	U	
			10			4			U		3			2			11		U	7		5	S*					6	U					9*		8	1	U	
			10#	S#		4					3			U			11		9	7*		5	U				1	6	S*							8	U	2	
						4*	S+		U		3	6#		U			11	S#	10		S*	5					1		7					9+		8		2	
						U	9*		U		3	U		U			11	S*	10		4	5				7	1		6		8							2	
	3					U			U					S*			11		10		4	5			S#	7	1		6	9#	8					U		2*	
	3					U			U					U			11		10*		4	5			S*	7	1		6	9	8					U		2	
	3					S#			1					U			11		S*	U	4	5			10*	7			6	9#	8						U	2	
	11					S#			1			U		U			8		S*	6	4	5			10*				7	9#					2		U	3	
	3		9+			S+			1								11		10#	8*	U	5			S#	7	U		6	S*					4			2	
	3		9#						1					S+				S*	10	8	U	5			S#	7	U		11*	6					4			2+	
	3		9			S*			1					U					10*	8	U	5			U	7	U		11	6					4			2	
	3		9			S#			1					S*					10#	8	U	5			S+	7*	U		11	6					4			2+	
	3		9			10		S*	1			U		7*					U	8	5				U		U		11	6					4			2	
	3		9#			10+		8*				U		S*					S#	7	5				S+		1		11	6					4		U	2	
	3		9	U		10*		S+		11				8+		S#				7	5				S*#		1			6					4		U	2	
	3		9*	U						11				S+		S#			S*	7	5				10#		1		8+	6					4		U	2	
	3			6						U				8		S*			9*	7	5				10#		1		11	S#					4		U	2	U
	3			2				U		11*				S+		S#		S*	9+	7	5				10#		1		8	6					4		U		
	11			2						U				6		10+			S+	7	5				S*		1		8	9*					4		U	3#	S#
	11			2						S#				7		10+			9	6				U	S+		1*		8			U			4#		S*	3	5
	11			2						U				7		10#			9*	6				U	S*		1		8			S#			4		U	3	5
17	17	5	10	26	13	13	1	10	7	3	24	4	4	18	9	3	12	14	34	31	22	15			12	8	38	3	33	13	4			23	14	21	1	22	2
		1	1	1		6	1	5		1	2		11	8		4		10	6	5	1		1		20			2	4	2		1		2			2	1	1
1			3			2		2		1			1	1		1	2	3	8	4	1				4			2	5	3	1			6				2	1

14 Armstrong Craig	38 Barry-Murphy Brian	3 Beswetherick Jon	30 Bradbury Lee	5 Bromby Leigh	15 Burrows David	20 Crane Tony	26 Di Piedi Michele	18 Donnelly Simon	23 Evans Paul	40 Evans Richard	22 Geary Derek	19 Green Ryan	16 Hamshaw Matthew	12 Haslam Steve	2 Hendon Ian	28 Holt Grant	29 Johnston Allan	11 Knight Leon	9 Kuqi Shefki	4 McLaren Paul	25 Maddix Danny	27 Monk Garry	17 Morrison Owen	24 O'Donnell Phil	10 Owusu Lloyd	35 Powell Darryl	1 Pressman Kevin	28 Proudlock Adam	7 Quinn Alan	37 Reddy Michael	36 Robinson Carl	32 Shaw Jon	34 Shaw Matt	8 Sibon Gerald	39 Smith Dean	6 Soltvedt Trond Egil	13 Stringer Chris	21 Westwood Ashley	33 Wood Richard
7				4	3						S#		S+		2#			6	9*	8	5				S*+		1		11					10		U	U		
8				4	3#			S+			2		S*	U				6+	9		5				10		1		11					7*			U	S#	
2				2	2						1				1			2	2	1	2				1		2		2					2					
								1			1		2												1													1	
																																		2					

14 Armstrong Craig	38 Barry-Murphy Brian	3 Beswetherick Jon	30 Bradbury Lee	5 Bromby Leigh	15 Burrows David	20 Crane Tony	26 Di Piedi Michele	18 Donnelly Simon	23 Evans Paul	40 Evans Richard	22 Geary Derek	19 Green Ryan	16 Hamshaw Matthew	12 Haslam Steve	2 Hendon Ian	28 Holt Grant	29 Johnston Allan	11 Knight Leon	9 Kuqi Shefki	4 McLaren Paul	25 Maddix Danny	27 Monk Garry	17 Morrison Owen	24 O'Donnell Phil	10 Owusu Lloyd	35 Powell Darryl	1 Pressman Kevin	28 Proudlock Adam	7 Quinn Alan	37 Reddy Michael	36 Robinson Carl	32 Shaw Jon	34 Shaw Matt	8 Sibon Gerald	39 Smith Dean	6 Soltvedt Trond Egil	13 Stringer Chris	21 Westwood Ashley	33 Wood Richard
		3		7		4			U					2				S*	10		U		6*						11			S#	U	9#		8	1	5	
		1		1		1								1					1				1						1					1		1	1	1	
																		1														1							
																																		1					

League Table

See page 532

2003-04

Division Two

Manager: Chris Turner

Did you know that?

Final League Position: 16th

On 27 September 2003, in a game against Grimsby Town, Wednesday's 'keeper Kevin Pressman was injured. Goalkeeper-coach, Eric Nixon, who was on the bench, had to take his place to become the oldest player for Wednesday at 40 years and 358 days (because the age of Jerry Jackson is not known, he may have been the actual oldest player in 1923).

On 14 February 2004, Valentine's Day, a Wednesday fan proposed to his girlfriend on the pitch with Wednesday's Kop singing 'You don't know what you're doing'.

Match No.	Date	Venue	Opponents		Round	Result	HT Score	Position	Scorers	Attendance
1	Aug 9	A	Swindon Town	W		3-2	3-1	7th	Robinson (og), Owusu, Kuqi	10,573
2	16	H	Oldham Athletic	D		2-2	1-1	5th	Kuqi (2)	24,630
3	23	A	Peterborough United	W		1-0	1-0	2nd	Kuqi	10,194
4	25	H	Wrexham	L		2-3	1-1	10th	Quinn, P. Smith	24,478
5	Sep 1	A	Wycombe Wanderers	W		2-1	2-1	5th	Owusu, Quinn	6,444
6	6	H	Tranmere Rovers	W		2-0	0-0	2nd	P. Smith, Cooke	21,705
7	13	H	Stockport County	D		2-2	2-0	2nd	Kuqi, Quinn	22,535
8	16	A	AFC Bournemouth	L		0-1	0-0	7th		8,219
9	20	A	Brighton & Hove Albion	L		0-2	0-1	10th		6,602
10	27	H	Grimsby Town	D		0-0	0-0	9th		21,918
11	Oct 1	H	Notts County	W		2-1	1-0	6th	McLaren (2)	20,354
12	4	A	Brentford	W		3-0	2-0	4th	Holt (2), Owusu	8,631
13	10	A	Hartlepool United	D		1-1	0-0	4th	Owusu	7,448
14	18	H	Rushden & Diamonds	D		0-0	0-0	4th		22,599
15	22	H	Plymouth Argyle	L		1-3	0-1	8th	Reddy	20,090
16	25	A	Bristol City	D		1-1	1-0	10th	Proudlock	13,668
17	Nov 1	H	Blackpool	L		0-1	0-0	11th		21,450
18	15	A	Colchester United	L		1-3	0-1	14th	Bromby	5,018
19	22	H	Luton Town	D		0-0	0-0	17th		21,027
20	29	A	Queen's Park Rangers	L		0-3	0-1	17th		17,393
21	Dec 13	A	Barnsley	D		1-1	1-1	17th	Ndumbu-Nsungu	20,438
22	20	H	Chesterfield	D		0-0	0-0	18th		25,296
23	26	H	Port Vale	L		2-3	2-1	18th	Robins, Lee	24,991
24	28	A	Tranmere Rovers	D		2-2	2-0	18th	Lee, Ndumbu-Nsungu	9,645
25	Jan 3	A	Wrexham	W		2-1	1-0	15th	Ndumbu-Nsungu, Quinn	8,497
26	10	H	Swindon Town	D		1-1	0-0	15th	Robins	22,751
27	17	A	Oldham Athletic	L		0-1	0-1	16th		9,316
28	24	H	Peterborough United	W		2-0	0-0	15th	Robins, Proudlock	21,474
29	30	H	Wycombe Wanderers	D		1-1	0-1	15th	Proudlock	19,596
30	Feb 7	A	Port Vale	L		0-3	0-1	16th		7,958
31	14	H	Hartlepool United	W		1-0	0-0	13th	Ndumbu-Nsungu (pen)	20,732
32	21	A	Rushden & Diamonds	W		2-1	1-0	12th	Ndumbu-Nsungu (2 pens)	5,685
33	28	H	Bristol City	W		1-0	0-0	12th	Lee	24,154
34	Mar 2	A	Plymouth Argyle	L		0-2	0-1	12th		17,218
35	7	A	Chesterfield	L		1-3	0-1	12th	Ndumbu-Nsungu	7,695
36	13	H	Barnsley	W		2-1	1-0	12th	Ndumbu-Nsungu (2)	25,664
37	17	H	AFC Bournemouth	L		0-2	0-2	12th		18,799
38	20	A	Stockport County	L		0-1	0-1	12th		8,011
39	27	H	Brighton & Hove Albion	W		2-1	1-1	12th	Brunt, Mustoe	19,707
40	Apr 3	A	Grimsby Town	L		0-2	0-2	14th		6,641
41	10	H	Brentford	D		1-1	0-0	15th	D. Smith	20,004
42	12	A	Notts County	D		0-0	0-0	14th		9,601
43	17	A	Blackpool	L		1-4	1-2	15th	Brunt	7,388
44	24	H	Colchester United	L		0-1	0-0	16th		20,464
45	May 1	A	Luton Town	L		2-3	2-0	16th	Shaw, Cooke	7,157
46	8	H	Queen's Park Rangers	L		1-3	0-1	16th	Shaw	29,313
										Apps
										Sub
									One own-goal	Goals

League Cup

47	Aug 13	H	Hartlepool United *	L	1R	2-2	0-0	Lee, Wood	13,410
									Apps
									Sub
									Goals

* After extra-time. Score at 90 mins 1-1. Lost 4-5 on penalties.

Football League Trophy

48	Oct 15	H	Grimsby Town **	W	1R	1-1	0-1	Proudlock	7,323
49	Nov 12	H	Barnsley	W	2R	1-0	0-0	Reddy	13,575
50	Dec 9	A	Carlisle United	W	3R	3-0	1-0	Lee, Robins (2)	2,869
51	Jan 20	H	Scunthorpe United	W	S/F	4-0	2-0	Robins (2), Proudlock (2)	10,236
52	Feb 10	A	Blackpool	L	NF 1L	0-1	0-0		7,482
53	25	H	Blackpool	L	NF 2L	0-2	0-2		21,390
									Apps
									Sub
									Goals

** After extra-time. Score at 90 mins 1-1. Won on penalties 5-4. NF = Northern Final

FA Cup

54	Nov 9	H	Salisbury City	W	1R	4-0	1-0	Proudlock (2 + pen), Owusu	11,419
55	Dec 6	A	Scunthorpe United	D	2R	2-2	0-1	Ndumbu-Nsungu, Holt	7,418
56	Dec 17	H	Scunthorpe United *	L	2R Re	0-0	0-0		11,722
									Apps
									Sub
									Goals

* After extra-time. Lost on penalties 1-3.

30 Antoine-Curier Mickael	16 Armstrong Craig	3 Barry-Murphy Brian	20 Beswetherick Jon	6 Bromby Leigh	35 Brunt Chris	35 Burchill Mark	28 Carr Chris	15 Chambers Adam	23 Cooke Terry	17 Evans Richard	2 Geary Derek	12 Haslam Steve	9 Holt Grant	15 Kuqi Shefki	4 Lee Graeme	27 Lucas David	8 McLaren Paul	33 McMahon Lewis	22 Mustoe Robbie	24 Ndumbu-Nsungu Guylain	30 Needham Liam	26 Nixon Eric	25 Ogden Adam	9 Olsen Kim	10 Owusu Lloyd	32 Poulter Robert	1 Pressman Kevin	31 Proudlock Adam	7 Quinn Alan	28 Reddy Michael	34 Robins Mark	18 Shaw Jon	5 Smith Dean	11 Smith Paul	13 Stringer Chris	21 Tidman Ola	29 Wilson Laurie	30 Wilson Mark	19 Wood Richard
	8	3							6	11*	2	S+	S#	9	4										10#		U		7+				5	U		1			S*
		7							6	11#	2	S#	S*	9	4										10*		U		8			U	5	U		1			3
		3							6	11+	2	S#	S*	9#	4		7								10*		U		8				5	S+		1			U
		3							6	11#	2*	U	10	9	4		7								S*		U		8				5	S#		1			U
		3							6	11*	2	S+	9#		4		7		S#						10+		U		8				5	S*		1			U
	S#	3							6+	S+	2	U	S*		4		7		8#						10*		1	9					5	11		U			
	S#	3+							6		2			10	4		7			S+			U		S*		1	9*	8#				5	11					U
		U	3						6*			2		10	4		7			U			U		S*		1	9	8				5	11					U
		S+	3+	4					6			2		10#			7			S#		U			S*		1	9	8				5	11*					U
			3*	4					11			S*	U		4		6+		8	10		S#			S+		1#	9	7				5						U
		11#		2					8		3	U	10		4	1	6		7	U		U			S*			9*					5						S#
		11		2					8		3	7	10*		4	1	6		U	S#			U		9#					S*			5						U
		11		2					8		3	S+	10*		4	1	6		7+				U		9#			S*		S#			5						U
		11		2					8#		3	S#	10*		4	1	6		7								U	9		S*		U	5						U
		11*		2							3	U	10		4	1	7		8						S#		U	9#		6			5	S*					U
				2							3	U	U		4	1	6		7						10		U	9		11		U	5	U					8
				2							3	U	U		4	1	6		7	U					10		U	9		11			5	S*					8*
		11*		2							3	S*	S#		4		6		7	U					10		1	9#		8			5			U			U
S*		11*	U	2							3	6			4				7	U					10	U	1	9		8			5						U
		6	U	3								7	S*		4				8	U					10	U	1	9*		11			5				U		2
		3		5							2	7	9		4	1			8	11					U		U	S*		6*	10		U				U		
	8*	3		5							2	7	9#		4	1	S*			11					S+		U			6+	10		U	S#					
		3		5		S*					2	U	U		4	1	7		8	9							U			6*	10		U	11					
	S+	S#		2		9+					3	S*			4	1	6*		7	8							U				10		5#	11			U		
	S+	S*				9+					3	2	S#		4	1			7	8							U		6		10#		5	11*			U		
		4	U			9*					3	2	U			1			7	8							U	S*	6		10	U	5	11					
	S#	4				9*					3	2	U			1			7#	8							U	S*	6		10	U	5	11					
	7*	4		U					S*		3	2	S#			1											U	9	6		10#	U	5	11				8	
	U	4		U					S*		3	2				1				7*							U	9	6		10	U	5	11				8	
	7*	4		U							3	2				1#				S+				S*			S#	9	6		10	U	5	11				8+	
	8*	3		4							2	7								11				9		U		6	S*		10#	U	5	S#		1			U
		3		4				7			2	10						U		6	U			9		U			11			8	5			1	U		U
		8	U	4				7				3			2			U		9	U					U	1		6			10	5				U		11
		8	S*	4				7			3				2*			U		9	U					U			6			10	5			1	U		11
		8	11	4	U			7			3				2			U		9						U			6			10	5			1	U		U
		3		4	U			8			2				5			6	S*	11				10*			1	9#	7			S#				U			U
		3		4	S#			8			2				5			6	7*	11				10			1	9#				S*	U			U			U
		11		4				8	S#		3				5			6	7#	10				S*			1	9				U	2*			U			U
		3		4	11			S#	6#		2							7	8	10*				U		U	1	9				S*	5						U
		3		4	11			S#	6#		2							7	8*	10				U			1	9				S*	5			U			U
		3		4	11			U	6+		2						S*	7	8*	10#				S#		U	1	9				S+	5						
		U		4	11			8	U		2						7*	U						10		U	1	9	6			S*	5						3
		3		4	11			U			2						8	S*						9#			1	6*	7		S#	10	5			U			U
		3			11		U		S+		2						7#	8	S#								1	9*	6		10+	S*	5			U			4
		3			11		S+	S#	6#		2+						7	8						S*			1				10*	9	5	U		U			4
		3			11		S*	U	6		2						7	8	U					U			1				10	9	5*			U			4
	5	38	4	29	8	4		8	19	5	41	16	9	7	30	17	23	9	22	20				6	12		20	26	23	9	14	7	41	12		9		3	10
1	5	3	1		1	1	2	3	4	1		9	8				2	1	3	4		1		4	8		1	4	1	3	1	7		7					2
				1	2				2				2	5	3		2		1	9					4			3	4	1	3	2	1	2					

	7#	8							S#	11	2	U	S*	9	4										10*		U		6				5	U		1			3
	1	1								1	1			1	1										1				1				1			1			1
									1				1																										
															1																								1

	U	8	11	2							3	6	S#		4					7*			U				1	9		10#		S*	U						5
		11		2					S*+		3	S#	U		4*		6#		7	S+					10		1	9		8			5			U			
		3	S#	5							2	7	9*		4					11#					S+	U	1	S*		8	10+						6		U
	7	4							U		3+	2	S#			1		S+		8							U	9*	6		10#	S*	5	11					
	7	6		4*							3	2						U		8				S#		U		9			10#	U	5	11		1			S*
		3		2				8				7			U			U		10	U			9		S*			6			11	5			1*	U		4
	2	6	1	5				1			5	5	1		3	1	1		1	5				1	1		3	4	2	3	3	1	4	2		2	1		2
			1						1			1	2					1		1				1	1	1		1				2							1
															1													3		1	4								

			8	2					S+		3	S#	U		4		6		7#						10		1	9*		11+		S*	5		U				
		3	U	5							2	7	9		4				8	S*					10*	U	1	6#		11+							S#		S+
	U	3	S#	5							2	7	9#		4				8	11					10+	U	1	6*					S+				S*		
		2	1	3							3	2	2		3		1		3	1					3		3	3		2			1						
			1						1			1								1												1	1				2		1
													1							1					1			3											

League Table

See page 532

2004-05

League One

Manager: Chris Turner/Paul Sturrock

Did you know that?

Final League Position: 5th (Promoted Via Play-off)

On 23 February 2005 Wednesday beat Peterborough United 2–1 at home. This was the first time Wednesday had won, having to come from behind, since beating Walsall 2–1 on 4 May 2003.

May 2005 was Wednesday's first time in the promotion Play-offs, and they beat Brentford home and away in the semi-final before going on to beat Hartlepool United in the final, played at the Millennium Stadium, Cardiff. Wednesday took a record number of fans for a club game at this ground.

Match No.	Date	Venue	Opponents		Round	Result	HT Score	Position	Scorers	Attendance
1	Aug 7	H	Colchester United	L		0-3	0-0	24th		24,138
2	10	A	Blackpool	W		2-1	1-0	15th	Bullen, McMahon	6,713
3	14	A	Torquay United	W		4-2	1-1	8th	MacLean (pen), Lee, Peacock, Heckingbottom	5,005
4	21	H	Huddersfield Town	W		1-0	1-0	4th	MacLean	26,264
5	27	A	Tranmere Rovers	L		2-4	2-3	5th	MacLean, Ndumbu-Nsungu	9,506
6	30	H	Oldham Athletic	D		1-1	0-0	9th	Brunt	21,530
7	Sep 4	H	Luton Town	D		0-0	0-0	10th		20,806
8	11	A	Walsall	D		1-1	1-1	12th	Whelan	6,403
9	18	H	AFC Bournemouth	L		0-1	0-1	14th		19,203
10	25	A	Wrexham	W		3-0	1-0	7th	MacLean, Brunt, Proudlock	5,688
11	Oct 2	H	Milton Keynes Dons	D		1-1	0-0	11th	McGovern	20,245
12	17	H	Barnsley	W		1-0	1-0	11th	Proudlock	25,391
13	19	A	Peterborough United	D		1-1	0-1	10th	Bullen	5,875
14	23	A	Bradford City	L		1-3	0-0	12th	Bullen	13,717
15	27	A	Swindon Town	L		2-3	1-0	13th	Bullen, MacLean	6,972
16	30	H	Chesterfield	D		2-2	2-1	15th	Proudlock, MacLean (pen)	24,271
17	Nov 6	A	Stockport County	W		3-0	1-0	12th	Proudlock, McGovern, McMahon	7,222
18	20	H	Hartlepool United	W		2-0	0-0	10th	MacLean, Hamshaw	19,919
19	27	A	Bristol City	W		4-1	1-0	7th	Proudlock (2), Brunt, Collins	14,852
20	Dec 8	H	Hull City	L		2-4	1-3	8th	O'Brien, McGovern	28,701
21	11	H	Brentford	L		1-2	1-0	10th	MacLean (pen)	21,592
22	19	A	Doncaster Rovers	W		4-0	2-0	9th	MacLean (3), Jones	10,131
23	26	H	Walsall	W		3-2	1-1	8th	Jones, McShane (og), MacLean (pen)	26,996
24	28	A	Port Vale	W		2-0	2-0	4th	Jones, McGovern	8,671
25	Jan 1	A	Luton Town	D		1-1	1-0	6th	Jones	9,500
26	3	H	Wrexham	W		4-0	0-0	4th	MacLean (pen), Jones (2), Heckingbottom	24,253
27	8	H	Swindon Town	W		2-0	1-0	4th	O'Brien, Jones	20,804
28	15	A	AFC Bournemouth	D		1-1	0-1	4th	Heckingbottom	8,847
29	21	H	Port Vale	W		1-0	1-0	4th	MacLean	18,465
30	29	A	Milton Keynes Dons	D		2-2	1-0	4th	Quinn, Chorley (og)	7,325
31	Feb 5	A	Barnsley	D		0-0	0-0	4th		19,659
32	12	H	Bradford City	L		1-2	0-1	4th	MacLean	23,232
33	19	A	Chesterfield	W		3-1	1-0	4th	MacLean (2), Peacock	7,831
34	23	H	Peterborough United	W		2-1	1-1	4th	MacLean (pen), Heckingbottom	19,648
35	26	A	Brentford	D		3-3	2-1	4th	Peacock (2), Bullen	8,323
36	Mar 6	H	Doncaster Rovers	W		2-0	1-0	3rd	Bullen, Talbot	28,712
37	12	H	Blackpool	W		3-2	1-0	3rd	Rocastle, Talbot (2)	21,539
38	19	A	Colchester United	D		1-1	0-0	4th	McGovern	4,169
39	26	H	Torquay United	D		2-2	0-1	4th	Bullen, Barrett	21,526
40	29	A	Huddersfield Town	L		0-1	0-1	4th		17,292
41	Apr 2	H	Tranmere Rovers	L		1-2	1-1	4th	Brunt (pen)	22,925
42	9	A	Oldham Athletic	D		1-1	0-1	4th	Whelan	9,645
43	15	A	Hartlepool United	L		0-3	0-2	6th		6,429
44	23	H	Stockport County	D		0-0	0-0	5th		22,331
45	30	A	Hull City	W		2-1	1-0	4th	Talbot, Quinn	24,277
46	May 7	H	Bristol City	L		2-3	0-2	5th	McGovern, Wood	28,798
										Apps
										Sub
									Two own-goals	Goals

League Cup

Match No.	Date	Venue	Opponents		Round	Result	HT Score	Position	Scorers	Attendance
47	Aug 25	H	Walsall	W	1R	1-0	1-0		Peacock	8,959
48	Sep 22	A	Coventry City	L	2R	0-1	0-1			8,362
										Apps
										Sub
										Goals

Football League Trophy

Match No.	Date	Venue	Opponents		Round	Result	HT Score	Position	Scorers	Attendance
49	Sep 29	H	Chester City	L	1R	1-2	1-0		MacLean	7,640
										Apps
										Sub
										Goals

FA Cup

Match No.	Date	Venue	Opponents		Round	Result	HT Score	Position	Scorers	Attendance
50	Nov 13	A	Swindon Town	L	1R	1-4	0-1		Whelan	6,160
										Apps
										Sub
										Goals

League One Play-Off

Match No.	Date	Venue	Opponents		Round	Result	HT Score	Position	Scorers	Attendance
51	May 12	H	Brentford	W	S/F 1L	1-0	1-0		McGovern	28,625
52	16	A	Brentford	W	S/F 2L	2-1	1-0		Peacock, Brunt	10,823
53	29	N	Hartlepool United * **	W	Final	4-2	1-0		McGovern, MacLean (pen), Whelan, Talbot	59,808
										Apps
										Sub
										Goals

*Played at the Millennium Stadium, Cardiff
** After extra-time. Score at 90 mins 2-2.

5 Adams Steve	21 Adamson Chris	25 Aljofree Hasney	24 Aranalde Zigor	39 Armstrong Craig	27 Barrett Graham	5 Branston Guy	18 Bruce Alex	11 Brunt Chris	2 Bullen Lee	22 Carr Chris	12 Collins Patrick	17 Evans Richard	34 Foster Luke	15 Gallacher Paul	24 Green Adam	28 Greenwood Russ	8 Hamshaw Matt	3 Heckingbottom Paul	15 Jones Kenwyne	4 Lee Graeme	1 Lucas David	26 Marsden Chris	9 MacLean Steve	7 McGovern Jon-Paul	20 McMahon Lewis	24 Ndumbu-Nsungu Guylain	30 Needham Liam	18 O'Brien Joey	14 Olsen Kim	10 Peacock Lee	33 Poulter Robert	31 Proudlock Adam	22 Quinn James	23 Rocastle Craig	18 Shaw Jon	39 Spurr Tommy	19 Smith Paul	25 Talbot Drew	21 Tidman Ola	6 Whelan Glenn	16 Wood Richard
						S*		11	2		5						S+	3		4*	1	7	9	6	8+	U				S#		10#							U		
						5		S*#	3	U	2									4	1	7	9	6	8	U				10					S#		11*		U		
						5		S#	3		2							S*		4	1	7	9	6	8*	S+				10+					U		11#		U		
						5		11+	2		4						S*	3			1	8	9#	6		S+				10		S#							U	7*	U
						5		U	2		4							3			1	8	9	6*	U	11#				10	U	S*								7	S#
								S*	4	U	2							3			1		9	6	8	11*				10		S#			U				U	7#	5
								11#	4	U	2							3			1	8	9*	7		S*				10		6			U		S#		U		5
								S#	4	U	2										1	8	9	11		S*			U			6#			10*		3		U	7	5
						5		S#	4	U	2										1	8	9*	6		S*				10	U	U					11#			7	3
		4						11	2		5	U				S#					1	8	9*	6#	7	U					U	10			S*		3				
		4						11*	2		5					U	S*				1	8	9	6	7		U					10			U		3		U		
								11	4		2						U			S*	1	8	9	6	7							10					3*	U	U	U	5
								11#	4		2						U	3		S#	1*	8	9	6+	7										U			S+	S*	10	5
								U	4		2						S*	3		S#		11	9	6*	7+						U	10#						S+	1	8	5
								U	4		2					U	U	3				11	9	6	7						U	10						U	1	8	5
								11*	4		2					U	S#	3				7	9+	6#	S*						U	10						S+	1	8	5
						5		11*	2		4						S*	3		U	1		9	6	7	U						10							U	8	U
				U		5		11	2		4						S*	3		U	1		9	6	7	10*	U												U	8	
						5		11	2		4						S*	3		U	1		9	6	7*	S#						10#							U	8	U
				U		5		11	2		4						U	3			1		9	6		10*		7		S*	U									8	U
						5#		11	2		4					U	S*	3			1		9	6				7		10*	U							S#		8	U
								S#	2							U	11#	3	10*	4	1		9+	6		S+		7		S*	U									8	5
						U		S*	2							U	11*	3	10	4	1		9	6				7			U							U		8	5
						U		S*	2							U	11*	3	10#	4	1		9	6				7			U							S#		8	5
				U				S*	2							U	11*	3	10	4	1		9	6				7			U							U		8	5
				U				S*	2#							S#	11	3	10*	4	1		9+	6				7			U							S+		8	5
								S*	2		U						11*	3	10	4	1		9	6		U		7			U							U		8	5
				U				11	2		U							3	10	4	1		9	6				7*			U		S*					S#		8	5#
								11	2		U							3		4	1		9	6			U	7		S*	U		10*					U		8	5
	U							11	2					3	U					4	1	U	9	6				7		S*			10*					U		8	5
								S+	2		U			11+				3		4	1		9*	6				7		S*			10#	U				S#		8	5
								S*	2		U			11#				3		4	1		9	6*				7		S+			10+	S#				U		8	5
	U							11	2		U							3		4	1		9*	6	U					10#			S#	7				S*		8	5
	U							11	2		U							3		4	1		9	6				S*		10#			U	7*				S#		8	5
	U							11	2		U							3		4	1		9	6				7		10*			S*	U				U		8	5
	U							11	2		U							3		4	1		9*	6	U					10			U	7				S*		8	5
U	S*						S#	11	2								U	3		4#	1*			6						10			9+	7				S+		8	5
S*	1						2+	11	4		S+			U			U	3						6						10			9#	7*				S#		8	5
7	U		U		9#		2		4		U			1			11	3						6						10*			S#	8				S*			5
7			3		9#		2	S+	4		S*			1			U	U						6*						10				11+				S#		8	5
7	U		S*		9#			11	4		2			1		U	U	3						6						S#								10		8	5*
2	U				U			11	4		5			1			S*	3*						6						10			9#	7		U		S#		8	
7	U				9+			11*	2		4			1		U	8	3						6	S*					10#			S#					S+			5
7	U				9*		U	S+	4		2			1			11+	3						6						S#			10#	8				S*			5
7*	U		U				2	11#	4					1			S#	3						6						S*			9	S+				10*		8	5
7+					S#		2	11	4		S+			1			U	3						6						S*			9*	U				10#		8	5
8	1	2	1		5	10	5	27	46		25			8	3		9	37	7	19	34	15	36	46	13	4		14		18		11	10	9	1		7	3	3	36	33
1	1		1		1	1	1	15			3					2	11	1		3					2	7		1		11		3	5	2	2		1	18	1		1
					1			4	7		1						1	4	7	1			18	6	2	1		2		4		6	2	1				4		2	1

						5		11*	2		4							3			1	8	9	6#	S+	S*				10+	U	S#								7	U
								S*	5		4		U			2					1	8	9	6	11#		U				U	10*			S#		3			7	
						1		1	2		2					1		1			2	2	2	2	1					1		1					1			2	
								1																1	1						1			1						
																													1											

		4						11#	2	U	5					S*					1	8	9	6	7*		S#					10			U		3		U		
		1						1	1		1										1	1	1	1	1							1					1				
																1											1														
																							1																		

				U		5		11			2	U				U	S*			4	1		9	6	7													10*	U	8	3
						1		1			1									1	1		1	1	1													1		1	1
																	1																								
																																								1	

	U						2	S+	4		U						11	3			1			6	S#					10*			9+	7#				S*		8	5
S+	U						2	S*	4		U						11*	3			1			6						10			9#	7+				S#		8	5
U	U						2+	11	4		S+							3			1		S#	6						10*			9#	7				S*		8	5
							3	1	3								2	3			3			3						3			3	3						3	3
1								2			1												1		1													3			
								1															1	2						1								1		1	

League Table

See page 533

2005-06

Championship

Manager: Paul Sturrock

Did you know that?

Final League Position: 19th

31 January 2006 was the first game at Hillsborough where one of the referee's assistants was a woman, in a game against Luton Town.

Match No.	Date	Venue	Opponents		Round	Result	HT Score	Position	Scorers	Attendance
1	Aug 6	A	Stoke City	D		0-0	0-0	13th		18,744
2	9	H	Hull City	D		1-1	1-1	17th	Best	29,910
3	13	H	Southampton	L		0-1	0-1	18th		26,688
4	20	A	Ipswich Town	L		1-2	0-1	22nd	Peacock	24,238
5	26	A	Queen's Park Rangers	D		0-0	0-0	21st		12,131
6	Sep 10	A	Leicester City	L		0-2	0-2	23rd		22,618
7	13	H	Leeds United	W		1-0	1-0	20th	Eagles	29,986
8	17	H	Millwall	L		1-2	0-0	24th	Coughlan	22,446
9	23	A	Luton Town	D		2-2	1-1	22nd	Lee, Graham	8,267
10	27	A	Crystal Palace	L		0-2	0-1	24th		17,413
11	Oct 1	H	Coventry City	W		3-2	2-1	22nd	Coughlan, Brunt (1 + pen)	22,732
12	15	A	Plymouth Argyle	D		1-1	1-0	22nd	Buzsaky (og)	16,534
13	18	H	Watford	D		1-1	0-0	22nd	Brunt	21,187
14	24	H	Brighton and Hove Albion	D		1-1	0-0	21st	Peacock	21,787
15	29	A	Norwich City	W		1-0	0-0	18th	Brunt	25,383
16	Nov 1	A	Reading	L		0-2	0-1	21st		16,188
17	5	H	Derby County	W		2-1	0-1	16th	Brunt, Graham	26,334
18	9	H	Cardiff City	L		1-3	0-3	17th	Eagles	20,324
19	19	A	Watford	L		1-2	0-2	18th	Whelan	16,988
20	22	H	Plymouth Argyle	D		0-0	0-0	19th		20,244
21	26	H	Stoke City	L		0-2	0-1	20th		21,970
22	Dec 3	A	Sheffield United	L		0-1	0-1	21st		30,558
23	10	A	Hull City	L		0-1	0-0	21st		21,329
24	17	H	Ipswich Town	L		0-1	0-0	21st		21,716
25	26	A	Preston North End	D		0-0	0-0	22nd		18,867
26	28	H	Wolverhampton W	L		0-2	0-1	23rd		24,295
27	31	A	Burnley	W		2-1	1-0	22nd	Eagles, Coughlan	14,607
28	Jan 2	H	Crewe Alexandra	W		3-0	1-0	20th	Wood, Tudgay, McCready (og)	25,656
29	14	H	Leicester City	W		2-1	2-1	19th	Brunt, Coughlan	25,398
30	21	A	Leeds United	L		0-3	0-0	19th		27,843
31	31	H	Luton Town	L		0-2	0-0	20th		23,965
32	Feb 4	A	Millwall	W		1-0	0-0	20th	Simek	11,896
33	11	H	Crystal Palace	D		0-0	0-0	20th		24,784
34	15	A	Coventry City	L		1-2	0-1	21st	Brunt	20,021
35	18	H	Sheffield United	L		1-2	0-2	21st	MacLean (pen)	33,439
36	25	A	Southampton	L		0-3	0-1	21st		26,236
37	Mar 4	A	Cardiff City	L		0-1	0-1	21st		11,851
38	11	H	Queen's Park Rangers	D		1-1	1-1	21st	Burton	22,788
39	18	H	Preston North End	W		2-0	1-0	21st	Burton, O'Brien	23,429
40	25	A	Wolverhampton W	W		3-1	1-0	21st	Tudgay (2), Burton	25,161
41	Apr 1	H	Burnley	D		0-0	0-0	21st		24,485
42	8	A	Crewe Alexandra	L		0-2	0-2	21st		8,007
43	15	H	Norwich City	W		1-0	1-0	21st	Tudgay	30,755
44	17	A	Brighton and Hove Albion	W		2-0	1-0	21st	Hart (og), O'Brien	7,573
45	22	H	Reading	D		1-1	0-1	21st	MacLean (pen)	27,307
46	30	A	Derby County	W		2-0	1-0	19th	Tudgay, Best	30,391
										Apps
										Sub
									Three own-goals	Goals

League Cup

47	Aug 23	A	Stockport County *	W	1R	4-2	1-1		Peacock, Partridge, Proudlock (2)	3,001
48	Sep 20	H	West Ham United	L	2R	2-4	0-1		Coughlan, Graham	14,976
										Apps
										Sub
										Goals

* After extra-time. Score at 90 Mins 1-1.

FA Cup

49	Jan 7	H	Charlton Athletic	L	3R	2-4	1-3		Heckingbottom (2)	14,851
										Apps
										Sub
										Goals

15 Adams Steve	21 Adamson Chris	28 Agbonlahor Gabriel	10 Best Leon	29 Bischoff Mikkel	11 Brunt Chris	2 Bullen Lee	19 Burton Deon	22 Carson Scott	12 Collins Patrick	26 Corr Barry	5 Coughlan Graham	17 Diallo Drissa	19 Eagles Chris	4 Folly Yoann	35 Gilbert Peter	30 Graham David	3 Heckingbottom Paul	14 Hills John	27 Kirby Ben	4 Lee Graeme	1 Lucas David	9 MacLean Steve	33 McAllister Sean	7 McGovern Jon-Paul	29 Murphy Daryl	8 O'Brien Burton	18 Partridge Richie	10 Peacock Lee	31 Proudlock Adam	34 Reet Danny	23 Rocastle Craig	24 Ross Maurice	20 Simek Frankie	32 Spurr Tommy	38 Thorpe Matt	40 Tudgay Marcus	22 Weaver Nicky	6 Whelan Glenn	16 Wood Richard
U			9*		11								6#				U	3		4	1					U	S#	10	S*		8		2					7	5
U			9*		11						U		6#					3		4	1					U	S#	10	S*		8		2					7	5
U					11						U		6#			9*		3		4	1					S+	S#	10	S*		8+		2					7	5
10#					11						4	S#	6*			9+		3			1					8	U	S*	S+		U		2					7	5
					S*						4	5+	U			9		3		U	1					8	6	10#	S#		11		2					7*	S+
	U				S*	S#				S+	4		6			9#				U	1					8		10			11*	3+	2					7	5
					11#	S*				U	4		6			9*		3			1			U		8		10			S#	U	2					7	5
					11+	S*					4		6*			9#		3			1			U		8		10	S#		S+	U	2					7	5
					11	S*				U			6#			8		3		4	1			S#		8+		10*			S+	U	2					7	5
					11#	S*				S+	U		6			9+		3		4	1					8	S#	10			U		2*					7	5
					11	S#				U	5		6*			9#		3		4	1					S*	U	10			8		2					7	U
					11+	S#				U	5		6			9#		3		4	1					S*	U	10			8		2					7*	S+
					11	U				U	5#		6			9*		3		4	1					S*	S+	10			8+		2					7	S#
					11	S*				U	5		6			9#		3		4	1					S#	U	10			8		2*					7	U
		9#			11+	U							6*			S#	U	3		4	1					S+	S*	10			8		2					7	5
		9			11	U							S*			S+	U	3+		4	1					S#	6*	10#			8		2					7	5
		9#			11	S+							6			S#	U	3		4						S*	U	10+			8*		2				1	7	5
	U	S+			11	S*				10*			6#			9+	3			4						8	S#				U		2				1	7	5
	U	S#			11	2*						4	6			9#	3			S*						8	U	10			U						1	7	5
	U	10#			11					S*		4	6+			S#	3			9*						8	S+				U		2				1	7	5
		S+			11					U	5	4				9#	3*							S#	10	S*	6+				8		2				1	7	U
	U	U			11						4		S*		3	9				U					10	S#	6*				8#		2				1	7	5
7		S+			S*						4		S#		3	9+		U		U					10	11		6#					2				1	8*	5
7#					S*					S+	4		S#		3	9*		U		U					10	11		6+					2				1	8	5
7					10*					9#	4	U	6		3	S*		U								11	U	S#					2				1	8	5
7*					S*					9#	4	U	6		3	9+		U								11	S+	S#					2				1	8	5
7*					10	S#				9+	4	S+	6#		3			11								8	U			U			2				1	S*	5
					S*	S#	9#			S+	4	U			3			11+								8	6*				U		2			10	1	7	5
					6	S#	9			S*	4	U			3			11			U					8	U						2			10*	1	7#	5
					6	U	9		U	S#	4				3			11			U					8	S*						2			10#	1	7*	5
	U		S*		6	U	9			S#	4			7	3#			11*			1					8	U						2			10			5
			U		6	4	9			10#		S*		7	3						1*	U				11	U						2			S#		8	5
	1		S*		6	11	9*			10#	4+	2		7	3				U			S#				8	U									S+			5
	1		S#		S*	6				10#	4	5*		7+	3				U			9				11	S+						2			U		8	
	1		10*		6	5			U		4			7#	3				U			9	U			11	S#						2			S*		8	
	1				11	5	S#		3	S+	4								U			9#	S*			8+	6*						2	U		10		7	
	1		S*		11*	5	9		3		4			8					U							7	U				U		2	U		10		6	
	U		S#	5+	6#	2	9	1			4			7	3			U				S*				11							S+			10*		8	
	U		U	5	6	U	9	1			4			7	3			U				U				11							2			10		8	
			U	5	6#	S#	9	1			4			7	3*			S*				U		U		11							2			10		8	
	U		S#	5*	6#	S*	9+	1			4			7				3				U		S+		11							2			10		8	
	U		S+		S*	S#	9	1	5		4			7				3				U		6#		11+							2			10		8*	
8*			U		6#	5	9	1			4			7				3				U		S#		11							2	U		10		S*	
8			6*		S*	5	9	1			4							3				U	U	U		11							2	U		10		7	
			10#			5	S#	1	U			4		8				6*				9		7+		11	U						2	3		S+		S*	
	U		S*			5	9	1	U		4	2		7								U	11	6*		8	U							3		10			
8	5	4	5	4	35	12	15	9	3	7	33	8	21	14	17	19	4	26		14	18	4	1	3	4	34	6	19			14	1	42	2		14	14	40	27
		4	8		9	16	2			9		3	4			5		1		1		2	1	4		10	12	3	6		3		1			4		3	3
			2		7		3				4		3			2				1		2				2		2					1			5		1	1

	U				11+						4#	5				9*		3		U	1					8	6	10	S*		S+		2					7	S#
	U				11	3				10#	4					9		S+		U	1			6+		S*		S#			8	2						7*	5
					2	1				1	2	1				2		1			2			1		1	1	1			1	1	1					2	1
																		1								1		1	1		1								1
											1					1											1	1	2										

	U				11	S*				9	4	U					3				1					8	6*				U		2		U	10		7	5
					1					1	1						1				1					1	1						1			1		1	1
						1																																	
																	2																						

League Table

See page 533

2006-07

Championship

Manager: Paul Sturrock/Brian Laws

Did you know that?

Final League Position: 9th

On 23 December 2006 Wednesday's 'keeper, Mark Crossley, headed in Chris Brunt's corner in the 93rd minute to earn Wednesday a 3–3 draw with Southampton in a League game.

Match No.	Date	Venue	Opponents		Round	Result	HT Score	Position	Scorers	Attendance
1	Aug 5	A	Preston North End	D		0-0	0-0	12th		15,650
2	8	H	Luton Town	L		0-1	0-1	15th		22,613
3	12	H	Burnley	D		1-1	0-0	19th	MacLean (pen)	22,425
4	19	A	Plymouth Argyle	W		2-1	0-1	16th	McAllister, O'Brien	14,507
5	27	H	Leeds United	L		0-1	0-0	18th		23,792
6	Sep 9	A	Southend United	D		0-0	0-0	19th		9,639
7	12	H	Stoke City	D		1-1	1-1	19th	Brunt (pen)	19,966
8	15	A	Hull City	L		1-2	1-2	19th	Burton (pen)	17,685
9	23	H	Derby County	L		1-2	0-0	23rd	Brunt	23,659
10	30	A	Sunderland	L		0-1	0-0	24th		36,764
11	Oct 14	H	Barnsley	W		2-1	1-0	21st	Whelan, Brunt	28,687
12	18	A	Colchester United	L		0-4	0-1	21st		5,097
13	21	H	Queen's Park Rangers	W		3-2	2-0	20th	Tudgay (2), MacLean (pen)	23,813
14	28	A	Wolverhampton W	D		2-2	1-1	20th	Small, Brunt	20,637
15	31	H	Crystal Palace	W		3-2	1-1	19th	Tudgay, Coughlan, MacLean	19,034
16	Nov 4	H	Leicester City	W		2-1	1-0	16th	Tudgay (2)	22,451
17	11	A	Ipswich Town	W		2-0	1-0	13th	Tudgay, Bougherra	21,830
18	18	A	Coventry City	L		1-3	1-1	16th	Brunt	19,489
19	25	H	Cardiff City	D		0-0	0-0	17th		23,935
20	28	H	West Bromwich Albion	W		3-1	2-0	15th	Whelan, Bougherra, MacLean (pen)	21,695
21	Dec 2	A	Leicester City	W		4-1	1-0	13th	Brunt (pen + 1), Whelan, Tudgay	22,693
22	9	A	Norwich City	W		2-1	0-0	11th	Camp (og), Burton	24,816
23	16	H	Birmingham City	L		0-3	0-1	13th		26,083
24	23	H	Southampton	D		3-3	1-2	13th	Whelan (2), Crossley	23,739
25	26	A	Stoke City	W		2-1	1-0	12th	MacLean, Burton	23,003
26	30	A	Barnsley	W		3-0	1-0	10th	Andrews, Brunt, MacLean	21,253
27	Jan 1	H	Hull City	L		1-2	0-1	12th	Burton	28,600
28	13	A	Derby County	L		0-1	0-0	11th		28,936
29	20	H	Sunderland	L		2-4	0-2	11th	Brunt, Small	29,103
30	31	A	Southampton	L		1-2	0-1	12th	MacLean	20,230
31	Feb 3	H	Preston North End	L		1-3	1-2	13th	Burton	22,441
32	10	A	Burnley	D		1-1	0-0	13th	Burton	12,745
33	20	A	Luton Town	L		2-3	1-1	14th	Burton, Whelan	8,011
34	24	H	Southend United	W		3-2	2-1	14th	Tudgay, Prior (og), MacLean (pen)	24,116
35	Mar 3	A	Leeds United	W		3-2	2-0	13th	Tudgay, Brunt, Johnson	25,297
36	6	H	Plymouth Argyle	D		1-1	1-0	13th	MacLean	19,449
37	10	A	Queen's Park Rangers	D		1-1	0-0	13th	Brunt	15,188
38	13	H	Colchester United	W		2-0	2-0	12th	Simek, Mills (og)	18,752
39	17	H	Wolverhampton W	D		2-2	1-1	12th	Burton, MacLean	24,181
40	31	A	Crystal Palace	W		2-1	0-0	11th	Burton, Tudgay	21,523
41	Apr 7	A	Cardiff City	W		2-1	1-1	11th	Clarke, Burton	13,621
42	9	H	Ipswich Town	W		2-0	0-0	11th	Whelan. MacLean	23,232
43	13	A	West Bromwich Albion	W		1-0	0-0	10th	Burton	20,415
44	21	H	Coventry City	W		2-1	1-1	10th	Tudgay, MacLean	23,632
45	28	A	Birmingham City	L		0-2	0-0	10th		29,317
46	May 6	H	Norwich City	W		3-2	2-0	9th	Johnson, Burton, Etuhu (og)	28,287
										Apps
										Sub
									Four own-goals	Goals

League Cup

Match No.	Date	Venue	Opponents		Round	Result	HT Score	Position	Scorers	Attendance
47	Aug 23	H	Wrexham	L	1R	1-4	0-2		Whelan	8,047
										Apps
										Sub
										Goals

FA Cup

Match No.	Date	Venue	Opponents		Round	Result	HT Score	Position	Scorers	Attendance
48	Jan 7	H	Manchester City	D	3R	1-1	0-0		MacLean	28,487
49	16	A	Manchester City	L	3R Re	1-2	0-1		Bullen	25,621
										Apps
										Sub
										Goals

12 Adams Steve	22 Adamson Chris	17 Andrews Wayne	24 Beevers Mark	27 Boden Luke	21 Bougherra Madjid	34 Bowman Matt	11 Brunt Chris	2 Bullen Lee	10 Burton Deon	18 Clarke Leon	26 Corr Barry	5 Coughlan Graham	1 Crossley Mark	31 Folly Yoann	3 Gilbert Peter	30 Graham David	14 Hills John	23 Johnson Jermaine	1 Jones Brad	25 Lekaj Rocky	4 Lunt Kenny	9 MacLean Steve	33 McAllister Sean	23 McArdle Rory	28 McClements David	35 McMenamin Liam	8 O'Brien Burton	29 O'Donnell Richard	17 Sam Lloyd	20 Simek Frankie	15 Small Wade	32 Spurr Tommy	25 Talbot Andrew	7 Tudgay Marcus	19 Turner Iain	17 Watson Steve	6 Whelan Glenn	16 Wood Richard
	U				4		10#	6				5		7			3		1		U	9*	S#				11			2	S*	U					8	
	U				4		6					5		7#			3		1		10*	9	S#		U		11+			2	S*	S+					8	
	U			U	4		10					5					11		1		6*	9#	S#	U			8			2	S*	3					7	
	U			S+	4		10					5#					11		1		6+		S*	S#	U		8			2	9*	3					7	
	S*				4		10+	S#	9			5					11*		1		S+		U		U		8		6#	2		3					7	
7#	U				4		S#	S*	9			5							1		S+		U				11		6*	2		3		10+			8	
	U				4		11	S#	9			5							1		S*		S+		U		8		6+	2		3		10#			7*	
8*	U				4		S+	S#	9			5							1		S*		U				11		6+	2		3#		10			7	
	1				4		6	U	9*		S+	5									7#	S*	U				11			2		3	S#	10+			8	
S#					4		11	U	9*			5		7#					1		U	S+					8			2	S*	3	10+	6				
	U				4		11	U	S+					7			3		1			9+					S*			2	6	5	10#	S#			8*	
	U				4			6*	S#			5		7			3		1		S*	9#					8			2	11	U	S+	10+				
	U				4		11	U	9*					7			3		1		8	S*								2	6	5	S#	10#			U	
	U				4		11	U	9#					7			3		1		8	S#								2	6*	5	S+	10+			S*	
	U				4		11	S#	9*			5#		7			3		1		8	S*								2	6		U	10			U	
	U				4		11	5	9					7			3		1		8	S#					U			2	6*		S*	10#			U	
	U				4		11*	5	9+			U	1	7			3				8	S+					S*			2	6#			10			S#	
	U				4		11	5	9*			S#	1	7			3				8	S+					S*			2#	6	U		10+				
	U	6#			4+			5	9*			S+	1	7			3				8	S*					11			2		U		10			S#	
	U	6#			4		11	5	9+			U	1				3*				8	S+					S#			2		S*		10			7	
	U	6			4#		11	5	9*			S#	1	8								S*	U				S+			2		3+		10			7	
	U	6*			4		11	5	9			S+	1	S#							8#	S*					U			2+		3		10			7	
	U	6*			4		11	5	9+			U	1	7#							8	S*					S+			2		3	S#	10				
	U	S#			4		11	5	9#			U	1	6*							8	S*					U			2		3		10			7	
	U	6*			4		11#	5	S*			U	1	U							8	9					S#			2		3		10			7	
	U	6*			4		11#	5	S*			U	1	S+							8	9+					S#			2		3		10			7	
	U	S#			4		11	5	9			U	1	6							8#	S*					S+			2		3+		10*			7	
	U				4		11*	5	9			U	1	U		S#					8	10#								2	S*	3		6			7	
	U						11	5	S+	S*		4#	1	2		U					8	9+	S#				3*				6			10			7	
	U		4				11	5	S#	S*			1	7		U					U	9#								2	6*	3		10			8	
	U		4				11	5	9	S#			1	S*		U					7*	S+								2	6+	3		10#			8	
	U		U				11	5	9	S*			1	8	U						7	10#								2	6*	3		S#		4		
	U						11	5	9			U	1	S*		S+		6+			7*	10#								2		3		S#		4	8	
	U						11*	5	9#	S*		4		U		U		6				S#								2		3		10	1	7	8	
	U						11	5	9#					U	U			6*				S#								2	S*	3		10	1	7	8	4
	U						11	5	9#						U	S#		6*			U	10								2	S*	3			1	7	8	4
	U						11	5	9						U	S#				U	S*	10#								2		3		6	1	7*	8	4
	U						11	5	9					S*	3#	U				S+	7	10+								2		S#		6	1		8*	4
	U						11	5	9					U	3*					U	S#	10#								2		S*		6	1	7	8	4
	U						11#	2	9*					S*	3		U			U	7	10										S#		6	1	5	8	4
	U						11	2	9#	10+				S*	3					S+	7*	S#										U		6	1	5	8	4
	U						11	2	S*	10*				S#			U			U	7#	9										3		6	1	5	8	4
	U						11	5	9	S#				S*			S+	U			7	10#								2+		3		6	1		8*	4
	U						11	5	9+	10#					S+			S*			U	S#								2		3		6*	1	8	7	4
	1						11	5	9	S#				U	U			S*			8*	10						U		2#		3		6			7	4
	1						11	5	9	U				2	3			6*		U	8	S*	U				U							10			7	4
2	3	7	2		28		42	33	35	3		14	17	20	5		15	5	15		30	20					13		4	41	13	31	2	37	11	11	35	12
1	1	2		1			2	5	7	7	1	4		9	1	4	1	2		2	7	21	6	1			9				7	5	6	3			3	
		1			2		10		13	1		1	1					2				12	1				1			1	2			11			7	

12 Adams Steve	22 Adamson Chris	17 Andrews Wayne	24 Beevers Mark	27 Boden Luke	21 Bougherra Madjid	34 Bowman Matt	11 Brunt Chris	2 Bullen Lee	10 Burton Deon	18 Clarke Leon	26 Corr Barry	5 Coughlan Graham	1 Crossley Mark	31 Folly Yoann	3 Gilbert Peter	30 Graham David	14 Hills John	23 Johnson Jermaine	1 Jones Brad	25 Lekaj Rocky	4 Lunt Kenny	9 MacLean Steve	33 McAllister Sean	23 McArdle Rory	28 McClements David	35 McMenamin Liam	8 O'Brien Burton	29 O'Donnell Richard	17 Sam Lloyd	20 Simek Frankie	15 Small Wade	32 Spurr Tommy	25 Talbot Andrew	7 Tudgay Marcus	19 Turner Iain	17 Watson Steve	6 Whelan Glenn	16 Wood Richard
	1			9#	5	S#	10	4									11				6		7*	U	S*	U		U		2		3					8	
	1			1	1		1	1									1				1		1							1		1					1	
						1																			1													
																																					1	

12 Adams Steve	22 Adamson Chris	17 Andrews Wayne	24 Beevers Mark	27 Boden Luke	21 Bougherra Madjid	34 Bowman Matt	11 Brunt Chris	2 Bullen Lee	10 Burton Deon	18 Clarke Leon	26 Corr Barry	5 Coughlan Graham	1 Crossley Mark	31 Folly Yoann	3 Gilbert Peter	30 Graham David	14 Hills John	23 Johnson Jermaine	1 Jones Brad	25 Lekaj Rocky	4 Lunt Kenny	9 MacLean Steve	33 McAllister Sean	23 McArdle Rory	28 McClements David	35 McMenamin Liam	8 O'Brien Burton	29 O'Donnell Richard	17 Sam Lloyd	20 Simek Frankie	15 Small Wade	32 Spurr Tommy	25 Talbot Andrew	7 Tudgay Marcus	19 Turner Iain	17 Watson Steve	6 Whelan Glenn	16 Wood Richard
	U		U				11	4	10			5	1	U							8	9					U			2	S*	3		6*			7	
	U						11	4	10#			5	1	S*		U					8*	9								2+	S#	3		6			7	S+
							2	2	2			2	2								2	2								2		2		2			2	
														1																	2							1
								1														1																

League Table

See page 533

2007-08

Championship

Manager: Brian Laws

Did you know that?

Final League Position: 16th

On 19 August 2007, in Wednesday's game versus Wolves, the kick-off was delayed due to traffic problems as someone had threatened to jump off a motorway bridge. (The police got him down safely.)

Wednesday lost their first six games of the season to register their worst-ever start to a season.

When Wednesday drew with West Bromwich Albion, on 6 November 2007, it was their first draw in 24 games – a new club record.

Match No.	Date	Venue	Opponents		Round	Result	HT Score	Position	Scorers	Attendance
1	Aug 11	A	Ipswich Town	L		1-4	0-3	23rd	Clarke	23,099
2	19	H	Wolverhampton W	L		1-3	1-1	24th	Small	22,131
3	25	A	Charlton Athletic	L		2-3	2-0	24th	O'Brien, Spurr	22,033
4	Sep 1	H	Bristol City	L		0-1	0-1	24th		17,559
5	15	A	Preston North End	L		0-1	0-1	24th		13,062
6	18	H	Burnley	L		0-2	0-1	24th		18,359
7	22	H	Hull City	W		1-0	1-0	24th	Jeffers	21,518
8	29	A	Norwich City	W		1-0	0-0	23rd	Small	23,293
9	Oct 2	A	Watford	L		1-2	1-2	23rd	Kavanagh	15,473
10	6	H	Leicester City	L		0-2	0-2	23rd		20,010
11	20	A	Stoke City	W		4-2	2-2	22nd	J. Johnson, Tudgay (2), Burton	14,019
12	23	H	Scunthorpe United	L		1-2	1-2	23rd	Burton (pen)	21,557
13	27	H	Blackpool	W		2-1	0-1	21st	Tudgay, Hinds	19,238
14	Nov 3	A	Plymouth Argyle	W		2-1	0-0	17th	Sodje, O'Brien	12,145
15	6	A	West Bromwich Albion	D		1-1	0-0	18th	Watson	19,807
16	10	H	Southampton	W		5-0	1-0	16th	Whelan (pen + 1), Sodje (2), O'Brien	19,442
17	24	A	Queen's Park Rangers	D		0-0	0-0	16th		15,241
18	27	H	Barnsley	W		1-0	0-0	16th	Sodje	27,769
19	Dec 1	H	Colchester United	L		1-2	1-2	15th	Sodje	22,331
20	4	A	Southampton	D		0-0	0-0	16th		17,981
21	15	A	Crystal Palace	L		1-2	1-1	17th	Hinds	14,865
22	22	H	Watford	L		0-1	0-1	20th		19,641
23	26	A	Burnley	D		1-1	1-1	21st	Burton (pen)	15,326
24	30	A	Hull City	L		0-1	0-1	22nd		21,252
25	Jan 1	H	Preston North End	W		2-1	0-1	19th	Sodje, Jeffers (pen)	20,690
26	12	A	Cardiff City	L		0-1	0-1	20th		14,015
27	19	H	Sheffield United	W		2-0	1-0	20th	Sodje, Tudgay	30,486
28	29	A	Wolverhampton W	L		1-2	1-1	21st	Tudgay	22,746
29	Feb 2	H	Ipswich Town	L		1-2	1-1	21st	Tudgay	19,092
30	9	A	Bristol City	L		1-2	0-1	22nd	Bullen	15,520
31	12	H	Charlton Athletic	D		0-0	0-0	22nd		17,211
32	23	H	Cardiff City	W		1-0	1-0	21st	Tudgay	18,539
33	Mar 1	A	Barnsley	D		0-0	0-0	22nd		18,257
34	4	H	West Bromwich Albion	L		0-1	0-0	22nd		18,805
35	8	H	Queen's Park Rangers	W		2-1	1-1	22nd	Kavanagh, Burton (pen)	18,555
36	11	A	Colchester United	W		2-1	2-1	21st	Burton, Small	5,086
37	15	A	Coventry City	D		0-0	0-0	22nd		19,283
38	22	H	Crystal Palace	D		2-2	1-1	22nd	Sahar, Small	19,875
39	29	H	Stoke City	D		1-1	0-1	22nd	Songo'o	21,857
40	Apr 1	H	Coventry City	D		1-1	0-0	20th	Wood	21,110
41	5	A	Scunthorpe United	D		1-1	0-1	21st	Sahar	7,425
42	8	A	Sheffield United	D		2-2	1-0	20th	Bolder (2)	31,760
43	14	H	Plymouth Argyle	D		1-1	0-1	19th	Spurr	20,635
44	19	A	Blackpool	L		1-2	1-2	22nd	Wood	9,633
45	26	A	Leicester City	W		3-1	1-1	20th	Slusarski, Watson, Clarke	31,892
46	May 4	H	Norwich City	W		4-1	1-1	16th	Burton (pen + 1), Sahar, Clarke	36,208
										Apps
										Sub
										Goals

League Cup

Match No.	Date	Venue	Opponents		Round	Result	HT Score	Position	Scorers	Attendance
47	Aug 16	A	Rotherham United	W	1R	3-1	1-1		Whelan, Burton, Small	6,416
48	28	H	Hartlepool United *	W	2R	2-1	0-0		Burton, Folly	8,751
49	Sep 26	H	Everton	W	3R	0-3	0-0			16,463
										Apps
										Sub
										Goals

* After extra-time. Score at 90 min 1-1.

FA Cup

Match No.	Date	Venue	Opponents		Round	Result	HT Score	Position	Scorers	Attendance
50	Jan 6	A	Derby County	D	3R	2-2	2-2		Beevers, Tudgay	20,612
51	22	H	Derby County *	L	3R Re	1-1	1-0		Watson	18,020
										Apps
										Sub
										Goals

* After extra-time. Score at 90 minutes 1-1. Lost 2-4 on penalties

Match abandoned after 28 minutes due to a rain socked pitch

Match No.	Date	Venue	Opponents		Round	Result	HT Score	Position	Scorers	Attendance
52	Dec 8	H	Coventry City #				0-0			18,192

15 Beevers Mark	24 Boden Luke	29 Bolder Adam	11 Brunt Chris	2 Bullen Lee	27 Burch Robert	10 Burton Deon	18 Clarke Leon	11 Esajas Etienne	31 Folly Yoann	3 Gilbert Peter	1 Grant Lee	5 Hinds Richard	9 Jeffers Francis	23 Johnson Jermaine	29 Johnson Michael	6 Kavanagh Graham	12 Lekaj Rocky	4 Lunt Kenny	14 McAllister Sean	21 McClements David	25 McMenamin Liam	8 O'Brien Burton	22 O'Donnell Richard	34 Sahar Ben	31 Showunmi Enoch	20 Simek Frankie	36 Slusarski Bartosz	26 Small Wade	30 Sodje Akpo	35 Songo'o Franck	32 Spurr Tommy	7 Tudgay Marcus	33 Wallwork Ronnie	17 Watson Steve	6 Whelan Glenn	16 Wood Richard
			11	5*	U		S#			3	1	U	9#	6+				S*								2		S+				10		8	7	4
				5	U	9	S*			U	1	S+	10*	6				8+				S#				2		11			3				7#	4
				U	U	9	10*		S#	S+	1	5		6#				8				11				2					3+	S*			7	4
				S*	1	9		S#			U	5*		6+				U				11#				2			S+		3	10		8	7	4
					U	S*		11+	8		1	S+	9*	S#				U								2		6#	10		3			5	7	4
					U	S+		11			1	S*	9#	U				8								2		6	10+		3	S#		5*	7	4
					U	10		11			1	S*	9#		5	8										2		S+	U		3*	S#		7+	6	4
					U	10					1	S+	9*	S#	5	8										2		11	U		3+	S*		7#	6	4
U				S*	1	10		S#		3		4*		6	5	8		U				U				2#			9			11			7	
S*				4	U	10+		6		3	1	2	S#		5*	8		U				S+							9#			11			7	
				2#		S*		U			1	S#	9*	6+	5	8		U				11							S+		3	10			7	4
				S*	U	9#		S+			1	2		6	5	8		U				11+							S#		3	10			7	4*
U					U	S*		S+			1	4		6+	5	8						11				2			9*		3	10		S#	7#	
U					U	S*		S#	7		1	4		6#	5			U				11				2			9*		3	10		8		
5				U		S#		S+	U		1	4		6*								11#				2		S*	9+		3	10		7	8	
S+						S#		U	U		1	4		6#	5+							11				2		S*	9*		3	10		7	8	
U						S*		U	8		1	4		6#	5			U				11				2		S#	9*		3	10		7		
U						S#		U	8		1	4		6*	5			U				11				2		S*	9		3	10#		7		
5				U	U			S#			1	4		6				U				11#				2		S*	9		3	10*		7	8	
5	U			2	U			S#	7		1	4		6				U				11						10#	9*		3	S*			8	
U				S*				S#	U		1	4		6	5			U				11				2*		10#			3	9		7	8	
U				2		S*		S+	S#		1	4		6*	5			U				11+						10			3	9		7#	8	
5	S#			2		9#		S+	S*	U	1	4						U				11						6*			3	10		7+	8	
5				2	U	10#		S*	7*	U	1	4	S#					U				11							9		3	6			8	
5				2		10#		S*	7+	U	1	4	S#	6*				U				11							9		3	S+			8	
5				2		S+	9+	11*			1	4		S*								6						U			3	10	S#	7#	8	U
5				2		U	S*				1	4		11#								6						S#	9*		3	10	7	U	8	U
5	U			2		S#				U	1	4		6*								S*						11	9#		3	10	7		8	U
5				2		S+	S#			U	1	4		6+		8						11			9#			S*			3	10	7*			U
5	S#	7		2	U	9				3	1	4+				8			S*			11*						6				10#	U			S+
5		7		2		S#				U	1	U		6#		8*			U						9			11			3	10	S*			4
5		7		2*		S+				3	1	S*		6#		8						U		S#	9+			11				10	U			4
5		7			U	S+				3#	1	2				8						11		S*	9+			6*			S#	10	U			4
5		7			U	U					1	2		6		8			U			11*		S*	9						3	10	U			4
5	U				U	S#					1	2				8			S*			S+			9#			6+		11	3	10	7*			4
5	U				U	9					1	2				8			7			S#			S*			6#		11*	3	10	U			4
5		S+			U	9+				U	1	2				8			7			S*			S#			6		11*	3	10#				4
5		U			U	9					1	2				8			7			U		10	S*			6*		11	3			U		4
5		U				9					1	2*		S#		8			7					10+	S+		U	6#		11	3			S*		4
5		S*			U	9				U	1			2		8#			7*			6+		10			S+			11	3			S#		4
		7			U	9				3	1			6		8					U			10#			S#	S*		11*	5		U	2		4
5	U	7			U	9					1	S+		6		8*						S*		10#			S#			11+	3			2		4
5		7			U	9				2	1			6*							U	8		10#			S#	S*		11	3		U			4
5		7		S#	U	9		U		2	1			6#		S*						8*		S+			10+			11	3					4
5		7		2*	U	9	S+	U			1			S*										8+			10			11#	3		S#	6		4
5		7			U	9	S+	U			1			2		S*			S#					8+			10			11#	3			6*		4
26		11	1	17	2	23	2	5	7	9	44	30	7	30	13	21		3	5			26		8	6	17	3	18	16	12	40	29	4	20	25	26
2	2	2		5		17	6	13	3	1		8	3	5		2		1	3			7		4	4		4	11	3		1	6	3	3		1
		2		1		7	3					2	2	1		2						3		3			1	4	7	1	2	7		2	2	2

				U	U	9	S*			U	1	U		6				8								2		11			3	10*		4	7	5
	S+			S*	1	9			S#	U	U	4		6				8+				11+				2					3	10*			7	5
				U	U	S*				3	1	4	9#	6*		8+		S+								2		11	S#			10			7	5
					1	2				1	2	2	1	3		1		2				1				3		2			2	3		1	3	3
	1			1		1	1		1									1											1							
						2			1																			1							1	

5	U			2		S*		11		U	1	4	9*	6					U			7									3	10			8	U
5				2		S+	S#			U	1	4		11				S*										6+	9#		3	10		7*	8	U
2				2				1			2	2	1	2								1						1	1		2	2		1	2	
						2	1											1																		
1																																1		1		

U				U				U	U		1	4		6	5			U				11				2		10			3	9		7	8	

League Table

See page 533

League tables 2000-08

League Table 00-01

	P	W	D	L	F	A	Pts
Fulham	46	30	11	5	90	32	101
Blackburn Rovers	46	26	13	7	76	39	91
Bolton Wanderers	46	24	15	7	76	45	87
Preston North End	46	23	9	14	64	52	78
Birmingham City	46	23	9	14	59	48	78
West Bromwich Albion	46	21	11	14	60	52	74
Burnley	46	21	9	16	50	54	72
Wimbledon	46	17	18	11	71	50	69
Watford	46	20	9	17	76	67	69
Sheffield United	46	19	11	16	52	49	68
Nottingham Forest	46	20	8	18	55	53	68
Wolverhampton W.	46	14	13	19	45	48	55
Gillingham	46	13	16	17	61	66	55
Crewe Alexandra	46	15	10	21	47	62	55
Norwich City	46	14	12	20	46	58	54
Barnsley	46	15	9	22	49	62	54
SHEFFIELD WEDNESDAY	46	15	8	23	52	71	53
Grimsby Town	46	14	10	22	43	62	52
Stockport County	46	11	18	17	58	65	51
Portsmouth	46	10	19	17	47	59	49
Crystal Palace	46	12	13	21	57	70	49
Huddersfield Town	46	11	15	20	48	57	48
Queen's Park Rangers	46	7	19	20	45	75	40
Tranmere Rovers	46	9	11	26	46	77	38

League Table 01-02

	P	W	D	L	F	A	Pts
Manchester City	46	31	6	9	108	52	99
West Bromwich Albion	46	27	8	11	61	29	89
Wolverhampton W.	46	25	11	10	76	43	86
Millwall	46	22	11	13	69	48	77
Birmingham City	46	21	13	12	70	49	76
Norwich City	46	22	9	15	60	51	75
Burnley	46	21	12	13	70	62	75
Preston North End	46	20	12	14	71	59	72
Wimbledon	46	18	13	15	63	57	67
Crystal Palace	46	20	6	20	70	62	66
Coventry City	46	20	6	20	59	53	66
Gillingham	46	18	10	18	64	67	64
Sheffield United	46	15	15	16	53	54	60
Watford	46	16	11	19	62	56	59
Bradford City	46	15	10	21	69	76	55
Nottingham Forest	46	12	18	16	50	51	54
Portsmouth	46	13	14	19	60	72	53
Walsall	46	13	12	21	51	71	51
Grimsby Town	46	12	14	20	50	72	50
SHEFFIELD WEDNESDAY	46	12	14	20	49	71	50
Rotherham United	46	10	19	17	52	66	49
Crewe Alexandra	46	12	13	21	47	76	49
Barnsley	46	11	15	20	59	86	48
Stockport County	46	6	8	32	42	102	26

League Table 02-03

	P	W	D	L	F	A	Pts
Portsmouth	46	29	11	6	97	45	98
Leicester City	46	26	14	6	73	40	92
Sheffield United	46	23	11	12	72	52	80
Reading	46	25	4	17	61	46	79
Wolverhampton W.	46	20	16	10	81	44	76
Nottingham Forest	46	20	14	12	82	50	74
Ipswich Town	46	19	13	14	80	64	70
Norwich City	46	19	12	15	60	49	69
Millwall	46	19	9	18	59	69	66
Wimbledon	46	18	11	17	76	73	65
Gillingham	46	16	14	16	56	65	62
Preston North End	46	16	13	17	68	70	61
Watford	46	17	9	20	54	70	60
Crystal Palace	46	14	17	15	59	52	59
Rotherham United	46	15	14	17	62	62	59
Burnley	46	15	10	21	65	89	55
Walsall	46	15	9	22	57	69	54
Derby County	46	15	7	24	55	74	52
Bradford City	46	14	10	22	51	73	52
Coventry City	46	12	14	20	46	62	50
Stoke City	46	12	14	20	45	69	50
SHEFFIELD WEDNESDAY	46	10	16	20	56	73	46
Brighton & Hove Albion	46	11	12	23	49	67	45
Grimsby Town	46	9	12	25	48	85	39

League Table 03-04

	P	W	D	L	F	A	Pts
Plymouth Argyle	46	26	12	8	85	41	90
Queen's Park Rangers	46	22	17	7	80	45	83
Bristol City	46	23	13	10	58	37	82
Brighton & Hove Albion	46	22	11	13	64	43	77
Swindon Town	46	20	13	13	76	58	73
Hartlepool United	46	20	13	13	76	61	73
Port Vale	46	21	10	15	73	63	73
Tranmere Rovers	46	17	16	13	59	56	67
Bournemouth	46	17	15	14	56	51	66
Luton Town	46	17	15	14	69	66	66
Colchester United	46	17	13	16	52	56	64
Barnsley	46	15	17	14	54	58	62
Wrexham	46	17	9	20	50	60	60
Blackpool	46	16	11	19	58	65	59
Oldham Athletic	46	12	21	13	66	60	57
SHEFFIELD WEDNESDAY	46	13	14	19	48	64	53
Brentford	46	14	11	21	52	69	53
Peterborough United	46	12	16	18	58	58	52
Stockport County	46	11	19	16	62	70	52
Chesterfield	46	12	15	19	49	71	51
Grimsby Town	46	13	11	22	55	81	50
Rushden & Diamonds	46	13	9	24	60	74	48
Notts County	46	10	12	24	50	78	42
Wycombe Wanderers	46	6	19	21	50	75	37

League Table 04-05

	P	W	D	L	F	A	Pts
Luton Town	46	29	11	6	87	48	98
Hull City	46	26	8	12	80	53	86
Tranmere Rovers	46	22	13	11	73	55	79
Brentford	46	22	9	15	57	60	75
SHEFFIELD WEDNESDAY	46	19	15	12	77	59	72
Hartlepool United	46	21	8	17	76	66	71
Bristol City	46	18	16	12	74	57	70
Bournemouth	46	20	10	16	77	64	70
Huddersfield Town	46	20	10	16	74	65	70
Doncaster Rovers	46	16	18	12	65	60	66
Bradford City	46	17	14	15	64	62	65
Swindon Town	46	17	12	17	66	68	63
Barnsley	46	14	19	13	69	64	61
Walsall	46	16	12	18	65	69	60
Colchester United	46	14	17	15	60	50	59
Blackpool	46	15	12	19	54	59	57
Chesterfield	46	14	15	17	55	62	57
Port Vale	46	17	5	24	49	59	56
Oldham Athletic	46	14	10	22	60	73	52
Milton Keynes Dons	46	12	15	19	54	68	51
Torquay United	46	12	15	19	55	79	51
Wrexham	46	13	14	19	62	80	43
Peterborough United	46	9	12	25	49	73	39
Stockport County	46	6	8	32	49	98	26

League Table 05-06

	P	W	D	L	F	A	Pts
Reading	46	31	13	2	99	32	106
Sheffield United	46	26	12	8	76	46	90
Watford	46	22	15	9	77	53	81
Preston North End	46	20	20	6	59	30	80
Leeds United	46	21	15	10	57	38	78
Crystal Palace	46	21	12	13	67	48	75
Wolverhampton W.	46	16	19	11	50	42	67
Coventry City	46	16	15	15	62	65	63
Norwich City	46	18	8	20	56	65	62
Luton Town	46	17	10	19	66	67	61
Cardiff City	46	16	12	18	58	59	60
Southampton	46	13	19	14	49	50	58
Stoke City	46	17	7	22	54	63	58
Plymouth Argyle	46	13	17	16	39	46	56
Ipswich Town	46	14	14	18	53	66	56
Leicester City	46	13	15	18	51	59	54
Burnley	46	14	12	20	46	54	54
Hull City	46	12	16	18	49	55	52
SHEFFIELD WEDNESDAY	46	13	13	20	39	52	52
Derby County	46	10	20	16	53	67	50
Queen's Park Rangers	46	12	14	20	50	65	50
Crewe Alexandra	46	9	15	22	57	86	42
Millwall	46	8	16	22	35	62	40
Brighton & Hove Albion	46	7	17	22	39	71	38

League Table 06-07

	P	W	D	L	F	A	Pts
Sunderland	46	27	7	12	76	47	88
Birmingham City	46	26	8	12	67	42	86
Derby County	46	25	9	12	62	46	84
West Bromwich Albion	46	22	10	14	81	55	76
Wolverhampton W.	46	22	10	14	59	56	76
Southampton	46	21	12	13	77	53	75
Preston North End	46	22	8	16	64	53	74
Stoke City	46	19	16	11	62	41	73
SHEFFIELD WEDNESDAY	46	20	11	15	70	66	71
Colchester United	46	20	9	17	70	56	69
Plymouth Argyle	46	17	16	13	63	62	67
Crystal Palace	46	18	11	17	59	51	65
Cardiff City	46	17	13	16	57	53	64
Ipswich Town	46	18	8	20	64	59	62
Burnley	46	15	12	19	52	49	57
Norwich City	46	16	9	21	56	71	57
Coventry City	46	16	8	22	47	62	56
Queen's Park Rangers	46	14	11	21	54	68	53
Leicester City	46	13	14	19	49	64	53
Barnsley	46	15	5	26	53	85	50
Hull City	46	13	10	23	51	67	49
Southend United	46	10	12	24	47	80	42
Luton Town	46	10	10	26	53	81	40
Leeds United	46	13	7	26	46	72	36

League Table 07-08

	P	W	D	L	F	A	Pts
West Bromwich Albion	46	23	12	11	88	55	81
Stoke City	46	21	16	9	69	55	79
Hull City	46	21	12	13	65	47	75
Bristol City	46	20	14	12	54	53	74
Crystal Palace	46	18	17	11	58	42	71
Watford	46	18	16	12	62	56	70
Wolverhampton W.	46	18	16	12	53	48	70
Ipswich Town	46	18	15	13	65	56	69
Sheffield United	46	17	15	14	56	51	66
Plymouth Argyle	46	17	13	16	60	50	64
Charlton Athletic	46	17	13	16	63	58	64
Cardiff City	46	16	16	14	59	55	64
Burnley	46	16	14	16	60	67	62
Queen's Park Rangers	46	14	16	16	60	66	58
Preston North End	46	15	11	20	50	56	56
SHEFFIELD WEDNESDAY	46	14	13	19	54	55	55
Norwich City	46	15	10	21	49	59	55
Barnsley	46	14	13	19	52	65	55
Blackpool	46	12	18	16	59	64	54
Southampton	46	13	15	18	56	72	54
Coventry City	46	14	11	21	52	64	53
Leicester City	46	12	16	18	42	45	52
Scunthorpe United	46	11	13	22	46	69	46
Colchester United	46	7	17	22	62	86	38

2008-09

Championship

Manager: Brian Laws

Did you know that?

Final League Position: 12th

On 19 October 2008, in a match live on television against Sheffield United, Jermaine Johnson, who had already been substituted, was called back from the dressing room and booked for kicking a bottle as he left the field. This was his second booking of the game, so he received a red card. Wednesday won the match 1–0.

On 7 February 2009 Wednesday completed the double over United for the first time since the 1913–14 season, winning 2–1 at Bramall Lane. The game was beamed back to Hillsborough, where 9,000 fans watched on a giant screen.

Match No.	Date	Venue	Opponents		Round	Result	HT Score	Position	Scorers	Attendance
1	Aug 9	H	Burnley	W		4-1	3-1	1st	Tudgay (2), Sodje (2)	23,793
2	16	A	Wolverhampton W	L		1-4	1-1	13th	Esajas	22,491
3	23	H	Preston North End	D		1-1	1-0	11th	McAllister	17,963
4	30	A	Swansea City	D		1-1	0-1	14th	Watson	16,702
5	Sep 13	H	Watford	W		2-0	1-0	6th	Tudgay, Spurr	17,066
6	16	A	Reading	L		0-6	0-3	13th		18,159
7	20	H	Ipswich Town	D		0-0	0-0	14th		17,198
8	27	A	Charlton Athletic	W		2-1	2-1	9th	Small,Tudgay	20,278
9	30	H	Nottingham Forest	W		1-0	0-0	5th	Esajas	20,823
10	Oct 4	A	Plymouth Argyle	L		0-4	0-3	10th		10,795
11	19	H	Sheffield United	W		1-0	1-0	5th	Watson	30,441
12	21	A	Barnsley	L		1-2	0-1	10th	Clarke (pen)	17,784
13	25	A	Birmingham City	L		1-3	1-3	12th	Esajas	17,300
14	28	H	Plymouth Argyle	L		0-1	0-1	15th		16,515
15	Nov 1	A	Crystal Palace	D		1-1	1-0	15th	Clarke	14,650
16	8	H	Doncaster Rovers	W		1-0	1-0	12th	Clarke	20,872
17	15	A	Derby County	L		0-3	0-1	14th		30,111
18	22	H	Coventry City	L		0-1	0-0	16th		16,119
19	25	A	Blackpool	W		2-0	0-0	15th	Tudgay, Burton	7,054
20	29	H	Norwich City	W		3-2	0-1	12th	McMahon, Clarke, Tudgay	18,883
21	Dec 6	A	Southampton	D		1-1	0-1	12th	Tudgay	15,440
22	9	H	Queen's Park Rangers	W		1-0	0-0	10th	Clarke	14,792
23	13	H	Bristol City	D		0-0	0-0	10th		15,542
24	20	A	Cardiff City	L		0-2	0-0	11th		17,600
25	26	H	Blackpool	D		1-1	0-0	11th	Slusarski	25,044
26	28	A	Coventry City	L		0-2	0-1	13th		19,602
27	Jan 10	A	Ipswich Town	D		1-1	0-0	12th	Watson	22,213
28	17	H	Charlton Athletic	W		4-1	2-0	12th	Potter, Tudgay (1 + pen), Jeffers	28,766
29	27	A	Nottingham Forest	L		1-2	1-1	13th	Johnson	22,618
30	31	H	Birmingham City	D		1-1	0-0	13th	Buxton	18,409
31	Feb 7	A	Sheffield United	W		2-1	2-1	12th	Spurr, Tudgay	30,786
32	14	A	Doncaster Rovers	L		0-1	0-1	12th		14,823
33	17	H	Barnsley	L		0-1	0-1	13th		25,820
34	21	H	Crystal Palace	W		2-0	0-0	12th	McAllister, Clarke	22,687
35	28	A	Burnley	W		4-2	1-0	12th	Tudgay (2), Clarke (2)	12,449
36	Mar 3	H	Reading	L		1-2	1-0	12th	McAllister	19,268
37	7	H	Wolverhampton W	L		0-1	0-1	12th		23,703
38	10	A	Preston North End	D		1-1	1-0	12th	Jeffers	12,381
39	14	A	Watford	D		2-2	1-1	13th	Tudgay, Jeffers (pen)	16,294
40	21	H	Swansea City	D		0-0	0-0	13th		22,564
41	Apr 4	A	Norwich City	W		1-0	0-0	12th	Johnson	25,385
42	11	H	Derby County	L		0-1	0-1	12th		24,392
43	13	A	Queen's Park Rangers	L		2-3	1-0	12th	Mahon (og), Tudgay (pen)	13,742
44	18	H	Southampton	W		2-0	1-0	12th	Varney (2)	24,145
45	25	A	Bristol City	D		1-1	0-1	12th	Potter	17,486
46	May 3	H	Cardiff City	W		1-0	0-0	12th	Johnson	30,658
										Apps
										Sub
									One own-goal	Goals

League Cup

47	Aug 12	H	Rotherham United *	L	1R	2-2	1-1		Esajas (2)	16,298

* After extra-time (Score at full-time 1-1) — Apps

Lost 5-3 on Penalties — Sub

Goals

FA Cup

48	Jan 3	H	Fulham	L	3R	1-2	1-1		Spurr	18,377

Apps

Sub

Goals

15 Beevers Mark	24 Boden Luke	10 Burton Deon	21 Buxton Lewis	18 Clarke Leon	11 Esajas Etienne	3 Gilbert Peter	1 Grant Lee	19 Gray Michael	5 Hinds Richard	27 Jameson Arron	9 Jeffers Francis	23 Johnson Jermaine	12 Lekaj Rocky	28 Liversidge Sam	4 Lunt Kenny	8 McAllister Sean	19 McMahon Tony	25 McMenamin Liam	32 Modest Nathan	17 O'Connor James	22 O'Donnell Richard	10 Potter Darren	20 Simek Frankie	29 Slusarski Bartosz	26 Small Wade	14 Smith Jimmy	30 Sodje Akpo	2 Spurr Tommy	7 Tudgay Marcus	14 Varney Luke	6 Watson Steve	33 Wragg Max	16 Wood Richard
5		10		S*	U		1		2			6#				7				8+	U					S#	9*	3	11		S+		4
5	S+	10		S*	11*	U	1		2			9+				7				8	U					S#		3			6#		4
5		10#		S#	11	U	1					6*				7	2			8	U					S*		3	9		U		4
5		10#		S#	11+	U	1					S*				7	2			8	U					6*		3	9		S+		4
		S*		S+	11#	3	1					10+				7*	2			8	U				S#	U		5	9		6		4
		10+		U	11*	3	1				S+	9				7#	2			8	U				S*	S#		5	6				4
		S*		U	11*	3	1				S+	9#				7+	2			8					S#	U		5	9		6		4
		S*		U	S#	3	1				U	10*				7	2			8					6#	S+		5	9		11+		4
S*		10		U	11	3	1				S#					7	2			8	U				6#	U		5	9				4*
5		10+		U	11#		1				S#	S*				7	2			8	U				6*	S+		3	9		4		
5		10+	U		S#		1				S+	11*				6	2			8#						U	S*	3	9		7		4
5	U	S*	4	S+	U	11	1				10#					8	2								6+	7		3	9*		S#		
		S#	2	9#	11	3	1				U	10*				8					U		U		S*	7		5			6		4
	U	S#	2	9	11+	3	1				10#	6				8							S*		U		S+	5			7		4*
5		U	2	9#	11*	U	1				U	S*				7				8							S#	3	10		6		4
5		U	2*	9+	11#		1					S#				6	S*			8					U		S+	3	10		7		4
5		S#	U	9+			1				S+	S*				11*	2			8	U						10#	3	6		7		4
5		S*	3	10*			1				9#	11	U			7	2			8	U		U			S#			6				4
5		10	3	9	S#		1				U	11#				7*	2			8			U			U			6		S*		4
5			3	9	11		1				10#					S*	2			8	U		U	S#		U			6		7*		4
5			3	9	11#		1				10*					7				8	U		2	S*	S#	U		U	6				4
5				9	11*		1				10+					7				8	U		2#	S+	S*	U		3	6		S#		4
5			2	9			1				10#		U			7			U	8	U			11*		S#		3	6		S*		4
5	6		2				1						S#	U		7			11*	8	U			10#		S*		3	9				4
5	S#		2				1				10#		U			S*			S+	7+				11	6*	U		3	9		8		4
5	S+		2				1				S*		S#			6*			U	7+				10	11#	U		3	9		8		4
5	6		2				1	11*		U	9	10		U	U	8			S*									3			7	U	4
5	S#		2				1	11	U		9#	6*				S+			U	7		8+			S*			3	10				4
5	S+		2	S*			1	11	U		9	6*							U	7+		8			S#			3	10#				4
5	U		2	9			1	11	U			6*				U				7		8			S*			3	10		U		4
5	U		2	9			1	11	U			6*				U				7		8			U			3	10		S*		4
5	U		2	9			1	11	U			6				U				7	U	8			U			3	10				4
	S+		2	9+			1	11*	5		S*	6#				U				7	U	8			S#			3	10				4
5	U			S*			1	11*	4		9#	6+				7				S+	U	8	2		S#			3	10				
5			2	9			1	11+	4		S+	6*				7#				S#		8	U		S*			3	10				U
5			2	9			1	11*	U		S+	6+				7				S#		8#	U		S*			3	10				4
U	S+		2	9*			1	11#	5		S*	6				7				8+			U				S#	3	10				4
5			2				1	11	U		9*	6#				7				S#	U	8	U				S*	3	10				4
5	S*		2				1	11*	S+		9	6				7		U		8+	U		S#					3#	10				4
U	S#		2				1		5		9#	6				7*				11	U	8	U					3	10	S*			4
S#			2		U		1		5		9*	11#				7				U		8	U				S*	3	10	6			4
U	U		3	S*	S+		1		5		9#	11+				7				6*		8	2				S#		10				4
S*			2	9+	11#		1		5		U	S#				U				7		8					S+	3	6	10			4*
U	U		2		11#		1		5		9*	S*				7				S#		8	U					3	6	10			4
U	U		2	10	11*		1		5		9#	S*				7				S#	U	8						3	6				4
S*	S#		2				1		5*		9#	11				6+			S+	8	U	7	U					3	10				4
30	2	9	32	20	18	8	46	13	13		20	29				37	14		1	35		17	4	4	6	3	2	41	42	3	15		42
4	10	8		9	4				1		11	8	2			3	1		3	6			2	3	13	9	9			1	7		
		1	1	8	3						3	3				3	1					2		1	1		2	2	14	2	3		

15 Beevers Mark	24 Boden Luke	10 Burton Deon	21 Buxton Lewis	18 Clarke Leon	11 Esajas Etienne	3 Gilbert Peter	1 Grant Lee	19 Gray Michael	5 Hinds Richard	27 Jameson Arron	9 Jeffers Francis	23 Johnson Jermaine	12 Lekaj Rocky	28 Liversidge Sam	4 Lunt Kenny	8 McAllister Sean	19 McMahon Tony	25 McMenamin Liam	32 Modest Nathan	17 O'Connor James	22 O'Donnell Richard	10 Potter Darren	20 Simek Frankie	29 Slusarski Bartosz	26 Small Wade	14 Smith Jimmy	30 Sodje Akpo	2 Spurr Tommy	7 Tudgay Marcus	14 Varney Luke	6 Watson Steve	33 Wragg Max	16 Wood Richard
5	S#	10*		9	11	2	1						S+		U	S*		U		7	U					6+		3			8#		4
1		1		1	1	1	1													1						1		1			1		1
	1												1			1																	
					2																												

15 Beevers Mark	24 Boden Luke	10 Burton Deon	21 Buxton Lewis	18 Clarke Leon	11 Esajas Etienne	3 Gilbert Peter	1 Grant Lee	19 Gray Michael	5 Hinds Richard	27 Jameson Arron	9 Jeffers Francis	23 Johnson Jermaine	12 Lekaj Rocky	28 Liversidge Sam	4 Lunt Kenny	8 McAllister Sean	19 McMahon Tony	25 McMenamin Liam	32 Modest Nathan	17 O'Connor James	22 O'Donnell Richard	10 Potter Darren	20 Simek Frankie	29 Slusarski Bartosz	26 Small Wade	14 Smith Jimmy	30 Sodje Akpo	2 Spurr Tommy	7 Tudgay Marcus	14 Varney Luke	6 Watson Steve	33 Wragg Max	16 Wood Richard
5	6		2				1			U	9	10#	S#	U		7			S*	8					11*			3				U	4
1	1		1				1				1	1				1				1					1			1					1
													1						1														
																												1					

League Table

	P	W	D	L	F	A	Pts
Wolverhampton W.	46	27	9	10	80	52	90
Birmingham City	46	23	14	9	54	37	83
Sheffield United	46	22	14	10	64	39	80
Reading	46	21	14	11	72	40	77
Burnley	46	21	13	12	72	60	76
Preston North End	46	21	11	14	66	54	74
Cardiff City	46	19	17	10	65	53	74
Swansea City	46	16	20	10	63	50	68
Ipswich Town	46	17	15	14	62	53	66
Bristol City	46	15	16	15	54	54	61
Queen's Park Rangers	46	15	16	15	42	44	61
SHEFFIELD WEDNESDAY	46	16	13	17	51	58	61
Watford	46	16	10	20	68	72	58
Doncaster Rovers	46	17	7	22	42	53	58
Crystal Palace	46	15	12	19	52	55	57
Blackpool	46	13	17	16	47	58	56
Coventry City	46	13	15	18	47	58	54
Derby County	46	14	12	20	55	67	54
Nottingham Forest	46	13	14	19	50	65	53
Barnsley	46	13	13	20	45	58	52
Plymouth Argyle	46	13	12	21	44	57	51
Norwich City	46	12	10	24	57	70	46
Southampton	46	10	15	21	46	69	45
Charlton Athletic	46	8	15	23	52	74	39

2009-10

Championship

Manager: Brian Laws/Alan Irvine

Did you know that?

Final League Position: 22nd

On 26 September 2009, at the start of the game against Cardiff City, Wednesday and their fans held a minute's applause for one of their former players who had died in the week, but the referee had not been told, and the game kicked off with the fans still applausing.

Match No.	Date	Venue	Opponents		Round	Result	HT Score	Position	Scorers	Attendance
1	Aug 8	H	Barnsley	D		2-2	2-0	7th	Johnson, Gray	30,644
2	15	A	Peterborough United	D		1-1	1-0	12th	O'Connor	10,747
3	19	A	Newcastle United	L		0-1	0-1	16th		43,904
4	22	H	Scunthorpe United	W		4-0	3-0	11th	Wood, Johnson, Tudgay, Potter	20,215
5	29	A	Plymouth Argyle	W		3-1	1-0	8th	Wood, Tudgay (pen + 1)	10,228
6	Sep 12	H	Nottingham Forest	D		1-1	1-1	9th	Tudgay	25,270
7	15	H	Middlesbrough	L		1-3	1-1	11th	Varney	21,722
8	18	A	Sheffield United	L		2-3	0-3	12th	Tudgay, Esajas	29,210
9	26	H	Cardiff City	W		3-1	1-1	12th	Esajas, Varney, Clarke	18,959
10	29	A	Crystal Palace	D		0-0	0-0	13th		12,476
11	Oct 3	A	Derby County	L		0-3	0-1	13th		30,116
12	17	H	Coventry City	W		2-0	2-0	13th	Purse, Clarke (pen)	20,026
13	20	H	Preston North End	L		1-2	1-1	15th	Gray	20,882
14	23	A	Watford	L		1-4	1-2	15th	Tudgay	14,591
15	31	A	Bristol City	D		1-1	0-0	14th	Varney	15,005
16	Nov 7	H	Queen's Park Rangers	L		1-2	1-1	14th	Johnson	19,491
17	21	A	Ipswich Town	D		0-0	0-0	17th		19,636
18	28	H	West Bromwich Albion	L		0-4	0-3	19th		20,824
19	Dec 5	H	Reading	L		0-2	0-0	20th		22,090
20	8	A	Doncaster Rovers	L		0-1	0-0	21st		12,825
21	12	A	Leicester City	L		0-3	0-2	22nd		22,236
22	19	H	Swansea City	L		0-2	0-2	22nd		18,329
23	26	H	Newcastle United	D		2-2	1-2	22nd	Varney, O'Connor	30,030
24	Jan 16	A	Barnsley	W		2-1	2-1	22nd	Spurr, Johnson	17,844
25	19	A	Blackpool	W		2-1	0-0	21st	Soares, Clarke	8,007
26	23	H	Peterborough United	W		2-1	1-0	20th	Tudgay (2)	24,882
27	27	A	Scunthorpe United	L		0-2	0-1	21st		7,038
28	30	H	Plymouth Argyle	W		2-1	2-1	19th	Varney (2)	22,590
29	Feb 6	A	Nottingham Forest	L		1-2	0-1	20th	Varney	27,900
30	9	H	Blackpool	W		2-0	1-0	18th	O'Connor, Potter	19,058
31	16	H	Doncaster Rovers	L		0-2	0-1	19th		22,252
32	20	H	Ipswich Town	L		0-1	0-1	21st		21,641
33	27	A	Reading	L		0-5	0-2	22nd		17,573
34	Mar 6	H	Leicester City	W		2-0	1-0	22nd	Clarke (2)	21,647
35	9	A	West Bromwich Albion	L		0-1	0-0	22nd		20,458
36	13	A	Swansea City	D		0-0	0-0	20th		14,167
37	16	A	Preston North End	D		2-2	0-1	21st	Miller, Tudgay	12,311
38	20	H	Derby County	D		0-0	0-0	21st		21,827
39	24	H	Watford	W		2-1	0-0	20th	Nolan, Varney	18,449
40	27	A	Coventry City	D		1-1	0-0	19th	Varney	17,608
41	Apr 3	A	Queen's Park Rangers	D		1-1	0-1	20th	Soares	13,405
42	5	H	Bristol City	L		0-1	0-0	22nd		19,688
43	10	A	Middlesbrough	L		0-1	0-1	22nd		19,932
44	18	H	Sheffield United	D		1-1	1-0	22nd	Potter	35,485
45	25	A	Cardiff City	L		2-3	1-1	22nd	Johnson, Tudgay	23,304
46	May 2	H	Crystal Palace	D		2-2	1-1	22nd	Clarke, Purse	37,121
										Apps
										Sub
										Goals
League Cup										
47	Aug 11	H	Rochdale	W	1R	3-0	2-0		Esajas, Johnson (2)	6,696
48	25	A	Port Vale	L	2R	0-2	0-0			6,667
										Apps
										Sub
										Goals
FA Cup										
49	Jan 2	H	Crystal Palace	L	3R	1-2	1-1		Hill (og)	8,690
										Apps
										Sub
									One own-goal	Goals

15 Beevers Mark	24 Boden Luke	3 Buxton Lewis	18 Clarke Leon	11 Esajas Etienne	29 Feeney Warren	1 Grant Lee	33 Gray Michael	5 Hinds Richard	25 Jameson Arron	9 Jeffers Francis	23 Johnson Jermaine	12 Lekaj Rocky	8 McAllister Sean	6 Miller Tommy	28 Modest Nathan	32 Nolan Eddie	17 O'Connor James	22 O'Donnell Richard	29 Palmer Liam	14 Potter Darren	4 Purse Darren	20 Simek Frankie	30 Soares Tom	10 Sodje Akpo	2 Spurr Tommy	7 Tudgay Marcus	19 Varney Luke	21 Wood Nick	16 Wood Richard	26 Wragg Max
S#		2		S*		1	11	U		9*	6#		U	U			7	U		8	4	U			3	10			5	
U	U	2		S#		1	11	S+			10#		6*	S*			8	U		7+	4	U			3	9			5	
U		2		S*		1	11#	U		S+	10		6*	S#			8+	U		7	4	U			3	9			5	
		2		S*		1	11	U		S#	6*		U	S+			8+	U		7	4			U	3	10	9#		5	
U		2		U		1	11#	U			7*		S#	S*			7	U		8	4			S+	3	10	9+		5	
S+		2	U	U		1	11	U			6		S*	8*				U		7	4			S#	3	10#	9		5+	
5*		2	S+	U		1	11+	S*			6		S#	8#				U		7	4	U		U	3	10	9			
		2	S#	S*		1	11				6*		U	S+			8+	U		7	4	U		U	3	10	9#		5	
U		2	S*	6#		1	11				S#			U			8	U		7	4	U		S+	3	10*	9+		5	
U		2	10#	6+		1	11				S+			U			8	U		7	4	U		S*	3	S#	9*		5	
U		2	9*	6#		1	11				S#		U	S+			8+	U		7	4	U		S*	3	10			5	
5		2	10*			1	11#	U		U	6+		S#	S+			8	U		7	4	U		S*	3		9			
5		2	10*			1	11+	U		S+	11		U	S#			8#	U		7	4	U		S*	3		9			
5		2		S#		1	11#	U		U	6+		U	S*			8*	U		7	4			S+	3	10	9			
	U	4	S*			1		5		U	11			8*	U		7	U		6		2			3	10	9	U		U
U		4	S+	U		1		5			11+		S*	6*			8	U		7		2#		U	3	10	9		S#	
U		4	S*	U		1	11	5		U	6*		U				8	U		7	U	2			3	10	9			
S*		4	9	U	U	1	11	5			6*		U				8	U		7		2	S*		3*	10+	S+			
4		2	S#	6#	S+	1	11*	5			S*		U				8	U		7	U		U		3	10	9+			
5		2	9*	S#	U	1	U				11#		6				8+	U		7	4	U	S+		3	10	S*			
5		2	9+	U	U	1	S#	U			11#		6				8	U		7*	4		S*		3	10	S+			
5		2#	9	U		1		U		S*	11+		6*				8	U		7	4	S#	U		3	10	S+			
5		U	S#	S*		1	U	U		U	6*						8	U		7	4	2	11		3	10	9#			
5	U	2		U		1	11		U		6*	U	U				8			7	4	U	9	S*	3	10				
5		2	S*	U		1	11	S+	U		10*		U				8			7	4	U	6	U	3+	9				
5		2	9*	U		1	11	U	U				U				8			7	4	U	6	U	3	10	S*			
5		2	10	S#		1	11#	U	U				U				8+			7	4	U	6*	S+	3	10	S*			
5		2*		U		1	11	U	U	U			U				8			7	4	S*	6#	S#	3	10	9			
5	U		S*	S#		1	11#	U	U			U	U				8			7	4	2	6*		3	10	9			
5	U		S*	U		1	11	U	U			U	U				8			7	4	2	6		3	10	9*			
5	U		S*	S#		1	11#	U	U			U	U				8			7	4	2	6*		3	10	9			
5	U		S*	6#		1	11*	5	U				S#			U	8		U	7		2	U		3	10	9			
5	U		S#	U		1	11*	4					S+	S*		2	8+	U		7		U	6#		3	10	9			
5			9+			1	U			U	11#		U	6		2	8	U		7	4	S*	S+		3*	10	S#			
5			9			1	U	U		S#	11*		U	6		2	8#	U		7	4	U	S*		3		10			
5			9	U		1	U	U			11			6		2	8	U		7	4	U	U		3	S*	10*			
5			S#			1	U	U		U	11*			6		2	8	U		7	4	U	S*		3	9	10#			
5			9#	S+		1	U	S*		S#				6		2	8+	U	U	7	4*	U	11		3	10				
5			S*	U		1	S+	U		S#				6*		2	8	U		7	4	U	11#		3	10	9+			
5	U		9#	U		1	S*	U		S#						2	8	U		7	4	U	11*		3	10	6			
5		2	S#			1	U	U		U	S*					6	8	U		7#	4	U	11		3	10	9*			
5	U		9	U		1	U	U		S*						2	8	U		7*	4	U	11		3	6	10			
5	U			S*		1	U	U		S#	6					2	8*	U		7	4	U	11		3	10#	9			
5			9*	U		1	U	U		U	6					2	8	U		7	4	U	S*		3	11	10			
5		U	S*	S+		1	U	U		S#	6*					2	8	U		7	4		11#		3	10	9+			
5		U	9*	S#		1	U	U		S+	6					2+	8#	U		7	4		S*		3	10	11			
32		28	18	5		46	27	7		1	29		5	10		14	44			46	39	9	17		46	41	32		10	
3			18	15	1		3	4		12	5		7	10								3	8	11		2	7		1	
			6	2			2				5			1		1	3			3	2		2		1	10	9		2	

4	U			11		1	S+	S*		S#	10+		7	6			U	U		8	5	2			3*	9#			U	
4		U		6*		1		5		9	S*		11#	7+			S+	U		8	U	2		S#	3	10			U	
2				2		2		1		1	1		2	2						2	1	2			2	2				
							1	1		1	1						1							1						
				1							2																			

4#	U	S#	10	S+		1			U	9	S*		U				8		U	6	5	2	7*		3	11+				
1			1			1				1							1			1	1	1	1		1	1				
		1		1							1																			

League Table

	P	W	D	L	F	A	Pts
Newcastle United	46	30	12	4	90	35	102
West Bromwich Albion	46	26	13	7	89	48	91
Nottingham Forest	46	22	13	11	65	40	79
Cardiff City	46	22	10	14	73	54	76
Leicester City	46	21	13	12	61	45	76
Blackpool	46	19	13	14	74	58	70
Swansea City	46	17	18	11	40	37	69
Sheffield United	46	17	14	15	62	55	65
Reading	46	17	12	17	68	63	63
Bristol City	46	15	18	13	56	65	63
Middlesbrough	46	16	14	16	58	50	62
Doncaster Rovers	46	15	15	16	59	58	60
Queen's Park Rangers	46	14	15	17	58	65	57
Derby County	46	15	11	20	53	63	56
Ipswich Town	46	12	20	14	50	61	56
Watford	46	14	12	20	61	68	54
Preston North End	46	13	15	18	58	73	54
Barnsley	46	14	12	20	53	69	54
Coventry City	46	13	15	18	47	64	54
Scunthorpe United	46	14	10	22	62	84	52
Crystal Palace	46	14	17	15	50	53	49
SHEFFIELD WEDNESDAY	46	11	14	21	49	69	47
Plymouth Argyle	46	11	8	27	43	68	41
Peterborough United	46	8	10	28	46	80	34

2010-11

League One

Manager: Alan Irvine/Gary Megson

Did you know that?

Final League Position: 15th

On 30 November 2010, in an away Cup game at Carlisle, the lines on the snow-covered pitch were painted blue.

Match No.	Date	Venue	Opponents		Round	Result	HT Score	Position	Scorers	Attendance
1	Aug 7	H	Dagenham and Redbridge	W		2-0	2-0	4th	Doe (OG), C.Morrison	23,081
2	14	A	Colchester United	D		1-1	0-0	5th	Mellor	6,011
3	21	H	Brighton and Hove Albion	W		1-0	1-0	4th	Coke	18,674
4	28	A	Hartlepool United	W		5-0	3-0	1st	Murray (OG), Coke, Mellor, Tudgay (Pen), C.Morrison	4,084
5	Sept 5	A	Brentford	L		0-1	0-1	1st		5,396
6	11	H	Carlisle United	L		0-1	0-1	6th		20,282
7	18	A	Plymouth Argyle	L		2-3	1-1	11th	O'Connor, Miller	7,916
8	25	H	Southampton	L		0-1	0-0	14th		18,198
9	28	H	Oldham Athletic	D		0-0	0-0	16th		16,609
10	Oct 2	A	Notts County	W		2-0	0-0	10th	Tudgay, Potter	11,355
11	9	H	Leyton Orient	W		1-0	0-0	5th	Buxton	17,445
12	16	A	Yeovil Town	W		2-0	0-0	4th	Johnson, Miller (Pen)	5,927
13	23	H	AFC Bournemouth	D		1-1	0-1	4th	Mellor	17,868
14	30	A	Charlton Athletic	L		0-1	0-1	7th		17,365
15	Nov 2	H	Huddersfield Town	L		0-2	0-2	10th		20,540
16	13	H	Rochdale	W		2-0	0-0	9th	Coke, C.Morrison	16,520
17	20	A	Milton Keynes Dons	W		4-1	2-1	5th	Mellor (3), Chadwick (OG)	10,552
18	23	H	Walsall	W		3-0	1-0	4th	Potter, Beevers, C.Morrison	15,228
19	Dec 4	A	Swindon Town	L		1-2	1-1	4th	Morrison	9,123
20	11	H	Bristol Rovers	W		6-2	4-1	2nd	Sedgwick,Miller,Teale,Johnson,O'Connor,Heffernan	19,242
21	18	A	Exeter City	L		1-5	1-1	2nd	Miller	5,524
22	Jan 3	A	Huddersfield Town	L		0-1	0-1	6th		17,024
23	15	H	Charlton Athletic	D		2-2	0-2	9th	Heffernan, R.Johnson	19,051
24	22	A	Leyton Orient	L		0-4	0-0	12th		6,449
25	25	H	Yeovil Town	D		2-2	1-1	10th	Madine, R.Johnson	16,618
26	Feb 1	A	Peterborough United	L		3-5	3-2	12th	J.Johnson, Madine, Sedgwick	6,480
27	5	H	Milton Keynes Dons	D		2-2	0-2	12th	Mellor, C.Morrison	17,631
28	12	A	Rochdale	L		1-2	0-2	14th	Madine	6,154
29	15	A	Tranmere Rovers	L		0-3	0-0	16th		5,941
30	22	A	AFC Bournemouth	D		0-0	0-0	16th		7,268
31	26	A	Carlisle United	W		1-0	1-0	16th	Miller	6,834
32	Mar 5	H	Plymouth Argyle	L		2-4	0-2	16th	Coke, R.Johnson	18,474
33	8	A	Oldham Athletic	W		3-2	2-2	15th	Beevers, Sedgwick (2)	4,133
34	12	H	Notts County	L		0-1	0-1	16th		17,835
35	15	H	Peterborough United	L		1-4	0-3	16th	Heffernan	16,014
36	19	A	Southampton	L		0-2	0-0	16th		20,234
37	26	A	Dagenham and Redbridge	D		1-1	1-0	16th	Teale	3,549
38	29	H	Brentford	L		1-3	1-2	17th	R.Jones	14,797
39	April 2	H	Colchester United	W		2-1	1-0	16th	Mellor (2)	15,663
40	5	H	Tranmere Rovers	W		4-0	3-0	15th	Miller (1+Pen), Madine, Mellor	15,235
41	9	A	Brighton and Hove Albion	L		0-2	0-1	16th		8,107
42	16	H	Hartlepool United	W		2-0	1-0	15th	Miller (Pen), Madine	16,358
43	23	A	Walsall	D		1-1	1-1	15th	Mellor	6,387
44	25	H	Swindon Town	W		3-1	2-1	14th	Potter, Mellor (2)	17,348
45	30	A	Bristol Rovers	D		1-1	1-1	13th	Miller (Pen)	8,340
46	May 7	H	Exeter City	L		1-2	1-0	15th	J.Johnson	21,085
										Apps
										Sub
									3 Own goals	Goals

League Cup

Match No.	Date	Venue	Opponents		Round	Result	HT Score	Position	Scorers	Attendance
47	Aug 10	H	Bury	W	1R	1-0	0-0		Coke	7,390
48	24	A	Scunthorpe United	L	2R	2-4	0-1		Tudgay (Pen), Mellor	4,680
										Apps
										Sub
										Goals

Football League Trophy

Match No.	Date	Venue	Opponents		Round	Result	HT Score	Position	Scorers	Attendance
49	Sept 1	H	Notts County	W	1R	2-1	2-1		O'Connor (2)	10,551
50	Oct 6	H	Chesterfield	W*	2R	2-2	1-1		Mellor, Tudgay.	15,003
51	Nov 10	H	Hartlepool United	W	3R	4-1	2-1		Mellor (2 + Pen), Teale	10,909
52	30	A	Carlisle United	L	NAS/F	1-3	0-1		Purse	3,149
										Apps
										Sub
										Goals

* Won 8-7 on penalties

FA Cup

Match No.	Date	Venue	Opponents		Round	Result	HT Score	Position	Scorers	Attendance
53	Nov 7	A	Southport	W	1R	5-2	1-0		Teale, Mellor, C.Morrison (2), Spurr	4,490
54	Nov 27	H	Northampton Town	W	2R	3-2	2-0		Beevers, Miller (2 x Pens)	8,932
55	Jan 8	A	Bristol City	W	3R	3-0	0-0		Teale, Mellor, Morrison.	11,378
56	29	H	Hereford United	W	4R	4-1	1-1		Potter, C.Morrison (2 x Pens), J.Johnson	16,578
57	Feb 19	A	Birmingham City	L	5R	0-3	0-2			14,607
										Apps
										Sub
										Goals

12 Batth Danny	15 Beevers Mark	19 Boden Luke	3 Buxton Lewis	10 Coke Giles	34 Cuff Sean	9 Heffernan Paul	5 Hinds Richard	25 Jameson Arron	23 Johnson Jermaine	22 Johnson Reda	11 Jones Daniel	27 Jones Rob	32 Madine Gary	33 Mellor Neil	8 Miller Tommy	28 Modest Nathan	30 Morrison Clinton	6 Morrison Michael	16 Nicholls Lee	18 O'Brien Joey	17 O'Connor James	13 O'Donnell Richard	4 Osbourne Isaiah	36 Otsemobor Jon	29 Palmer Liam	14 Potter Darren	4 Purse Darren	7 Reynolds Mark	24 Sedgwick Chris	2 Spurr Tommy	21 Teale Gary	7 Tudgay Marcus	1 Weaver Nicky
	5		2	8		U		U			S+			S*			9*				7#			U	U	S#	4		6	3	11+	10	1
	5		2	8		U					S+			S*			9				7#	U		U	U	S#	4		6	3+	11*	10	1
	5		2	8+		S*	U	U			U			9*							S#			U	S+	7	4		6#	3	11	10	1
	5		2	8+		U		U			U			9#	S+		S#				S*			U		7	4		6	3	11*	10	1
	5		2	8		S+		U			U			9#	U		S#				S*			U		7	4		6*	3	11+	10	1
	5		2	8		S*		U			U				S+		9*				S#			U	U	7#	4		6	3	11+	10	1
	5		2	8		U		U			S+			9	S#		S*				7			U		11*	4		6#	3+	U	10	1
	5		2	8		U		U			3			9	S+		S#				7			S*		6#	4*		U	U	11+	10	1
	5		U	8		S+		U			S*			U	11		9				7+			3		U	4		6#	2*	S#	10	1
	5		U	8		9#		U			U			S*	11		10*				7			3		S#	4		U	2	U	11	1
			5			U	U	U	U		U			S*	6		9*				7			3		8	4		U	2	11	10	1
			5			U	U	U	S*		2			S#	6		9+				7			3		8	4		S+	U	11*	10#	1
	5		3	8		S+	U	U			2			S*	6		9*				7#					8	4		U	U	S#	10+	1
	5		3	8		U	U	U	S*		2			9	6		S#				U					8			U	4	11*	10#	1
	5		3	8		U	U	U	11		2			9			S#				S*					8*	4		6+	U	S+	10#	1
	5		3	8		U	U	U			U			9	6		10#				7					U	4		S*	3	11*	S#	1
	5		3			S#	U	1	U		U			9+	7#		10					U			S+	8	4		6*	3	11	S*	
	5					U	U	U	S*		3			9	7#		10				U				S#	8	4		6*	2	11	U	1
	5		3*	S#		S+	U	U	10+		S*				7		9				U				U	8	4		6#	2	11		1
	5	U				S*	U	U	10*		3				7+	U	9				S#				S+	8#	4		6	2	11		1
	5	U				U	U	U	10		3			S*	7		9				U				U	8	4		6*	2	11		1
	5					S+	U	U	6		S#			9	7		10				8+			2#	U	U	4		S*	3	11*		1
	U					S*		U	S#	5	3			9*	7		10	2			8				U	U	4		6	U	11#		1
	S*		2*			U		U	S+	5	3		9#	S#	7+		10	4			8					U			6	U	11		1
	U			7		S*		U	6	5	U		9	10			S#	4+			U					8		3#	S+	2	11*		1
	U		2	7		U		U	11*	5	S+		9	10#			U	4			S#					8		3	6+		S*		1
	U		2	7		S#		1	6	5	3		9*	S*			10	4			8	U						U	U	U	11#		
	5		2	8+		U	U	U			11		S*	9*			10	4			6		S#			7#		3	S+		U		1
	U			8		S*	U	U		5	S#		9	U			10	4			6		7					3#	U	2	11*		1
	4					U	3	U		5	U		9	U	8		U				S*		6		10*	U			11	2	7		1
	4					U	3	U		5	S+		9#	U	8		S#	U					6		10*	S*			11	2	7+		1
	4			S*		U	3		S+	5			9		8		S#				U	U	6+		10*	U			11#	2	7		1
	4					U			U	5	U		9*	U	8		S*	3			10	U	6#			S#			11	2	7		1
	4			U		U			S*	5	S#			9*	8		10	3			S+	U	6+			U			11#	2	7		1
	4*			10		S#	3+		11#		S*		9	U	8		U	5			U	U	6			S+		2			7		1
4			U	10	U	10			S*			5	9	U	8#			3			S+	1	6*			S#		2		U	7+		
4			S*			U			U			5	9	U	8#		U	3	U	7	S#	1				10		2*	11		6		
4			3			10#			S+			5*	9		U		S#	U	U	7		1	6	S*		11+			U	2	8		
4			3	S#					11*	5	U		9	10	7		U		U	U	8	1		2		U			S*		6#		
4			3	U					11	5	U		9+	10	7*		S+		U	S*	8	1		2		U			S#		6#		
4			3	S*		U			11#	5		U	S#	10			9		U	8*	7	1		2		S+			6+		U		
4			3	S#		U			11#		U	5	9	10+	7*		S+		U		8	1		2	U	S*					6		
4			3	11*					S*	S#	U	5#	9	10	7		U				8	1		2		U			U		6		U
			3			U			11#	4	6+	5	9*	10	S*		U				8	U		2	S+	7			S#		U		1
4			3						S*	U	U	5	9	10	7		U				8#	U		2	6+	S+			S#		11*		1
4			3						11	U	S*	5*	9	10	7		U				8	S+		2	U	S#			U		6#		1+
10	27		29	22		3	4	2	15	15	13	8	20	24	29		22	12		3	25	8	9	13	4	22	22	7	24	26	37	15	36
	1		1	5		14			11	1	12		2	9	5		13			1	11	1	1	2	5	11			9		4	2	
	2		1	4		3			4	3		1	5	13	9		6				2					3			4		2	2	

	5	U	U	S#		9*	U	U			11#			10			S*				S+			2	7+	8	4			3	6		1
	5		U	U		9*	4	U			3			S*	S#		10				8			2		7			6#	U	11+	S+	1
	2					2	1				2			1			1				1			2	1	2	1		1	1	2		2
				1										1	1		1				1											1	
				1										1																		1	

	5		U			U		U			3			S#	S*		9#				8			2		7	4		6*		11	10	1
	5+		2	8		S*		U			3			9*			10#							S+	U	7	4		6		11	S#	1
	S*		5	8		U		U						9+	6		10				7			2*			4#		S#	3	11	S+	1
	5			S*		S#	U	U	11+		2			9*	8		10				S+					7	4		6#	3			1
	3		2	2					1		3			3	2		4				2			2		3	4		3	2	3	1	4
	1			1		2								1	1						1			1					1			2	
														4							2						1				1	1	

	5		U	8		S+		U			U			9*	6#		10+				7			2		U	4		S#	3	11	S*	1
	5			S#		U	U	U	S*		3			9	7		10				U				U	8	4		6*	2	11#		1
	U					U		U	U	2	3			9	7		10	5			8				U	U	4		6	U	11		1
	U			7#		10		U	6	5	2			U			10	4			S*					8*		U	S#	3	11		1
	S#					U	S*	U		5	11			9			10	4#			6+		8		S+	U		2*	U	3	11		1
	2			2		1			1	3	4			4	3		5	3			3		1	1		2	3	1	2	4	5		5
	1			1		1	1		1												1				1				2			1	
	1								1					2	2		5									1				1	2		

League Table

	P	W	D	L	F	A	Pts
Brighton & Hove Albion	46	28	11	7	85	40	95
Southampton	46	28	8	10	86	38	92
Huddersfield Town	46	25	12	9	77	48	87
Peterborough United	46	23	10	13	106	75	79
Milton Keynes Dons	46	23	8	15	67	60	77
Bournemouth	46	19	14	13	75	54	71
Leyton Orient	46	19	13	14	71	62	70
Exeter City	46	20	10	16	66	73	70
Rochdale	46	18	14	14	63	55	68
Colchester United	46	16	14	16	57	63	62
Brentford	46	17	10	19	55	62	61
Carlisle United	46	16	11	19	60	62	59
Charlton Athletic	46	15	14	17	62	66	59
Yeovil Town	46	16	11	19	56	66	59
SHEFFIELD WEDNESDAY	46	16	10	20	67	67	58
Hartlepool United	46	15	12	19	47	65	57
Tranmere Rovers	46	15	11	20	53	60	56
Oldham Athletic	46	13	17	16	53	60	56
Notts County	46	14	8	24	46	60	50
Walsall	46	12	12	22	56	75	48
Dagenham & Redbridge	46	12	11	23	52	70	47
Bristol Rovers	46	11	12	23	48	82	45
Plymouth Argyle	46	15	7	24	51	74	42
Swindon Town	46	9	14	23	50	72	41

Wednesday's League record against other Clubs

Opponents		HOME					AWAY				
	P	W	D	L	F	A	W	D	L	F	A
Accrington	2	1	0	0	5	2	0	0	1	2	4
Aldershot	2	1	0	0	3	1	0	1	0	1	1
Arsenal	108	24	15	15	91	73	8	15	31	59	115
Aston Villa	128	38	8	18	132	88	10	9	45	67	159
Barnsley	58	18	4	7	56	30	8	8	13	33	44
Birmingham City	78	22	7	10	96	54	5	14	20	28	61
Blackburn Rovers	122	34	16	11	122	59	14	16	31	70	111
Blackpool	68	21	5	8	76	35	15	7	12	50	46
Bolton Wanderers	98	31	10	8	100	44	12	11	26	63	79
Bournemouth	6	0	1	2	1	4	0	2	1	1	2
Bradford City	34	8	5	4	35	22	2	6	9	18	33
Bradford Park Avenue	18	6	1	2	18	7	1	4	4	9	15
Brentford	22	2	5	4	13	17	2	4	5	17	18
Brighton & Hove Albion	20	4	6	0	14	9	4	3	3	19	14
Bristol City	44	14	3	5	40	26	7	7	8	28	29
Bristol Rovers	12	5	1	0	20	8	1	3	2	9	11
Burnley	86	23	8	12	78	46	11	6	26	53	97
Burton Swifts	2	1	0	0	6	0	1	0	0	5	0
Bury	72	23	6	7	75	42	9	10	17	44	68
Cambridge United	10	4	1	0	10	3	3	1	1	8	7
Cardiff City	58	18	6	5	58	31	5	6	18	29	52
Carlisle United	20	5	4	1	12	4	2	5	3	11	14
Charlton Athletic	42	12	6	3	45	24	6	5	10	30	40
Chelsea	100	25	19	6	102	60	12	17	21	50	66
Chester City	10	3	2	0	9	1	0	2	3	5	8
Chesterfield	28	7	5	2	26	13	3	3	8	18	25
Colchester United	18	4	1	4	10	9	1	4	4	7	14
Coventry City	74	19	12	6	68	37	7	10	20	30	65
Crewe Alexandra	6	2	1	0	4	0	1	0	2	2	3
Crystal Palace	48	15	6	3	44	20	4	9	11	18	36
Dagenham & Redbridge	2	1	0	0	2	0	0	1	0	1	1

Opponents		HOME					AWAY				
	P	W	D	L	F	A	W	D	L	F	A
Darlington	2	1	0	0	4	0	0	0	1	1	5
Darwen	2	1	0	0	5	0	0	0	1	1	2
Derby County	106	25	16	12	83	62	10	13	30	63	118
Doncaster Rovers	12	5	0	1	13	5	2	2	2	8	5
Everton	128	26	19	19	118	93	10	18	36	75	134
Exeter City	8	2	0	2	5	5	0	1	3	4	10
Fulham	60	17	9	4	59	32	7	5	18	35	61
Gainsborough Trinity	2	1	0	0	5	1	1	0	0	2	0
Gillingham	16	5	2	1	8	4	0	4	4	4	9
Grimsby Town	46	17	5	1	48	10	7	5	11	24	38
Halifax Town	2	1	0	0	1	0	0	1	0	0	0
Hartlepool United	6	3	0	0	5	0	1	1	1	6	4
Hereford United	4	1	0	1	2	2	1	0	1	2	3
Huddersfield Town	40	9	5	6	36	33	3	3	14	15	41
Hull City	42	13	5	3	50	20	4	10	7	21	25
Ipswich Town	36	7	5	6	29	23	8	2	8	25	22
Leeds United	80	19	8	13	69	53	8	11	21	44	74
Leicester City	102	25	14	12	79	54	13	14	24	72	100
Leyton Orient	32	10	4	2	27	10	4	5	7	16	21
Lincoln City	14	4	3	0	18	6	3	2	2	10	11
Liverpool	116	23	17	18	98	81	13	9	36	67	116
Loughborough Town	2	1	0	0	5	0	0	1	0	0	0
Luton Town	56	14	10	4	53	28	6	10	12	36	46
Manchester City	96	30	13	5	96	50	12	11	25	63	100
Manchester United	112	31	12	13	101	71	6	13	37	50	116
Mansfield Town	8	0	2	2	1	4	0	2	2	2	6
Middlesbrough	90	30	5	10	88	49	9	9	27	49	107
Millwall	32	9	4	3	30	16	2	4	10	13	26
MK Dons	4	0	2	0	3	3	1	1	0	6	3
Nelson	2	1	0	0	5	0	0	1	0	1	1
New Brighton Tower	2	1	0	0	4	0	0	1	0	2	2
Newcastle United	120	26	21	13	90	63	12	9	39	66	128
Newport County	2	1	0	0	2	1	0	0	1	3	4
Northampton Town	4	2	0	0	5	2	1	1	0	2	0
Norwich City	44	12	6	4	40	28	6	7	9	19	24
Nottingham Forest	118	30	10	19	90	77	18	13	28	71	86
Notts County	60	16	8	6	49	22	9	8	13	35	42
Oldham Athletic	42	11	8	2	40	17	3	6	12	19	33
Oxford United	26	4	6	3	18	13	3	4	6	12	12
Peterborough United	16	5	1	2	16	9	2	3	3	11	14
Plymouth Argyle	36	5	6	7	27	28	7	5	6	27	29

Opponents		HOME					AWAY				
	P	W	D	L	F	A	W	D	L	F	A
Portsmouth	62	15	8	8	58	43	9	5	17	40	51
Port Vale	28	8	1	5	23	14	3	3	8	12	18
Preston North End	90	26	8	11	74	47	8	12	25	43	86
Queen Park Rangers	56	18	3	7	53	29	6	11	11	32	41
Reading	12	2	2	2	8	9	2	0	4	4	15
Rochdale	2	1	0	0	2	0	0	0	1	1	2
Rotherham United	30	8	1	6	25	16	8	4	3	22	15
Rushden & Diamonds	2	0	1	0	0	0	1	0	0	2	1
Scunthorpe United	6	2	0	1	7	2	1	1	1	5	4
Sheffield United	112	24	15	17	84	67	11	20	25	60	88
Shrewsbury Town	16	0	6	2	3	5	1	4	3	5	8
Southampton	72	18	12	6	58	28	11	9	16	43	59
Southend United	8	4	0	0	10	5	0	2	2	3	5
South Shields	12	3	1	2	9	5	2	4	0	7	5
Stockport County	20	6	3	1	30	13	4	0	6	10	10
Stoke City	78	21	8	10	70	40	12	9	18	45	64
Sunderland	112	26	15	15	108	66	14	11	31	64	111
Swansea City	26	6	6	1	24	10	5	4	4	16	20
Swindon Town	28	9	4	1	28	17	3	1	10	16	30
Torquay United	2	0	1	0	2	2	1	0	0	4	2
Tottenham Hotspur	96	28	9	11	79	49	10	8	30	64	111
Tranmere Rovers	16	6	0	2	15	5	1	2	5	10	17
Walsall	18	6	2	1	14	7	2	5	2	12	12
Watford	36	9	4	5	30	23	3	3	12	18	33
West Bromwich Albion	106	31	7	15	109	78	19	18	16	76	82
West Ham United	86	22	11	10	82	46	14	12	17	69	73
Wimbledon	34	7	4	6	27	24	3	6	8	20	31
Wolverhampton W.	94	22	14	11	87	55	6	12	29	55	104
Wrexham	14	5	0	2	14	9	3	2	2	9	11
Wycombe Wanderers	2	0	1	0	1	1	1	0	0	2	1
Yeovil Town	2	0	1	0	2	2	1	0	0	2	0
York City	4	2	0	0	6	2	1	0	1	2	3

Play-off games not included.

Sheffield Wednesday – First Team 1889–2011

Alliance League/Football League/Premiership Seasonal results

			Home					Away							
Season	Division	P	W	D	L	F	A	W	D	L	F	A	Pts	Pos.	GA/GD
1889–90	C Alliance League	22	11	0	0	48	19	4	2	5	22	20	32	1st	1.79
1890–91	Alliance League	22	4	3	4	30	26	0	2	9	9	40	13	12th	0.59
1891–92	Alliance League	22	10	0	1	45	16	2	4	5	20	19	28	4th	1.86
	TOTAL	**66**	**25**	**3**	**5**	**123**	**61**	**6**	**8**	**19**	**51**	**79**			
1892–93	First Division	30	8	2	5	34	28	4	1	10	21	37	27	12th	0.85
1893–94	First Division	30	7	3	5	32	21	2	5	8	16	36	26	12th	0.84
1894–95	First Division	30	10	2	3	36	19	2	2	11	14	36	28	8th	0.91
1895–96	First Division	30	10	2	3	31	18	2	3	10	13	35	29	8th	0.83
1896–97	First Division	30	9	4	2	29	11	1	7	7	13	26	31	6th	1.14
1897–98	First Division	30	12	0	3	39	15	3	3	9	12	27	33	5th	1.21
1898–99	R First Division	34	8	2	7	26	24	0	6	11	6	37	24	18th	0.52
1899–1900	C Second Division	34	17	0	0	61	7	8	4	5	23	15	54	1st	3.82
1900–01	First Division	34	13	2	2	38	16	0	8	9	14	26	36	8th	1.24
1901–02	First Division	34	9	5	3	30	14	4	3	10	18	38	34	9th	0.92
1902–03	C First Division	34	12	3	2	31	7	7	1	9	23	29	42	1st	1.50
1903–04	C First Division	34	14	3	0	34	10	6	4	7	14	18	47	1st	1.71
1904–05	First Division	34	10	3	4	39	22	4	2	11	22	35	33	9th	1.07
1905–06	First Division	38	12	5	2	40	20	6	3	10	23	32	44	3rd	1.21
1906–07	First Division	38	8	5	6	33	26	4	6	9	16	34	35	13th	0.82
1907–08	First Division	38	14	0	5	50	25	5	4	10	23	39	42	5th	1.14
1908–09	First Division	38	15	0	4	48	24	2	6	11	19	37	40	5th	1.10
1909–10	First Division	38	11	4	4	38	28	4	5	10	22	35	39	11th	0.95
1910–11	First Division	38	10	5	4	24	15	7	3	9	23	33	42	6th	0.98
1911–12	First Division	38	11	3	5	44	17	5	6	8	25	32	41	5th	1.41
1912–13	First Division	38	12	4	3	44	23	9	3	7	31	32	49	3rd	1.36
1913–14	First Division	38	8	4	7	34	34	5	4	10	19	36	34	18th	0.76
1914–15	First Division	38	10	7	2	43	23	5	6	8	18	31	43	7th	1.13
1919–20	R First Division	42	6	4	11	14	23	1	5	15	14	41	23	22nd	0.44
1920–21	Second Division	42	9	7	5	31	14	6	4	11	17	34	41	10th	1.00
1921–22	Second Division	42	12	4	5	31	24	3	10	8	16	26	44	10th	0.94
1922–23	Second Division	42	14	3	4	36	16	3	9	9	18	31	46	8th	1.15

			Home					Away							
Season	Division	P	W	D	L	F	A	W	D	L	F	A	Pts	Pos.	GA–GD
1923–24	Second Division	42	15	5	1	42	9	1	7	13	12	42	44	8th	1.06
1924–25	Second Division	42	12	3	6	36	23	3	5	13	14	33	38	14th	0.89
1925–26	C Second Division	42	19	0	2	61	17	8	6	7	27	31	60	1st	1.83
1926–27	First Division	42	15	3	3	49	29	0	6	15	26	63	39	16th	0.82
1927–28	First Division	42	9	6	6	45	29	4	7	10	36	49	39	14th	1.04
1928–29	C First Division	42	18	3	0	55	16	3	7	11	31	46	52	1st	1.39
1929–30	C First Division	42	15	4	2	56	20	11	4	6	49	37	60	1st	1.84
1930–31	First Division	42	14	3	4	65	32	8	5	8	37	43	52	3rd	1.36
1931–32	First Division	42	14	4	3	60	28	8	2	11	36	54	50	3rd	1.17
1932–33	First Division	42	15	5	1	46	20	6	4	11	34	48	51	3rd	1.18
1933–34	First Division	42	9	5	7	33	24	7	4	10	29	43	41	11th	0.93
1934–35	First Division	42	14	7	0	42	17	4	6	11	28	47	49	3rd	1.09
1935–36	First Division	42	9	8	4	35	23	4	4	13	28	54	38	20th	0.82
1936–37	R First Division	42	8	5	8	32	29	1	7	13	21	40	30	22nd	0.77
1937–38	Second Division	42	10	5	6	27	21	4	5	12	22	35	38	17th	0.88
1938–39	Second Division	42	14	4	3	47	18	7	7	7	41	41	53	3rd	1.49
1946–47	Second Division	42	10	5	6	39	28	2	3	16	28	60	32	20th	0.76
1947–48	Second Division	42	13	6	2	39	21	7	5	9	27	32	51	4th	1.25
1948–49	Second Division	42	12	6	3	36	17	3	7	11	27	39	43	8th	1.13
1949–50	P Second Division	42	12	7	2	46	23	6	9	6	21	25	52	2nd	1.40
1950–51	R First Division	42	9	6	6	43	32	3	2	16	21	51	32	21st	0.77
1951–52	C Second Division	42	14	4	3	54	23	7	7	7	46	43	53	1st	1.52
1952–53	First Division	42	8	6	7	35	32	4	5	12	27	40	35	18th	0.86
1953–54	First Division	42	12	4	5	43	30	3	2	16	27	61	36	19th	0.77
1954–55	R First Division	42	7	7	7	42	38	1	3	17	21	62	26	22nd	0.63
1955–56	C Second Division	42	13	5	3	60	28	8	8	5	41	34	55	1st	1.63
1956–57	First Division	42	14	3	4	55	29	2	3	16	27	59	38	14th	0.93
1957–58	R First Division	42	12	2	7	45	40	0	5	16	24	52	31	22nd	0.75
1958–59	C Second Division	42	18	2	1	68	13	10	4	7	38	35	62	1st	2.21
1959–60	First Division	42	12	7	2	48	20	7	4	10	32	39	49	5th	1.36
1960–61	First Division	42	15	4	2	45	17	8	8	5	33	30	58	2nd	1.66
1961–62	First Division	42	14	4	3	47	23	6	2	13	25	35	46	6th	1.24
1962–63	First Division	42	10	5	6	38	26	9	5	7	39	37	48	6th	1.22
1963–64	First Division	42	15	3	3	50	24	4	8	9	34	43	49	6th	1.25
1964–65	First Division	42	13	5	3	37	15	3	6	12	20	40	43	8th	1.04
1965–66	First Division	42	11	6	4	35	18	3	2	16	21	48	36	17th	0.85
1966–67	First Division	42	9	7	5	39	19	5	6	10	17	28	41	11th	1.19
1967–68	First Division	42	6	10	5	32	24	5	2	14	19	39	34	19th	0.81
1968–69	First Division	42	7	9	5	27	26	3	7	11	14	28	36	15th	0.76
1969–70	R First Division	42	6	5	10	23	27	2	4	15	17	44	25	22nd	0.56
1970–71	Second Division	42	10	7	4	32	27	2	5	14	19	42	36	15th	0.74

			Home					Away							
Season	Division	P	W	D	L	F	A	W	D	L	F	A	Pts	Pos.	GA–GD
1971–72	Second Division	42	11	7	3	33	22	2	5	14	18	36	38	14th	0.88
1972–73	Second Division	42	14	4	3	40	20	3	6	12	19	35	44	10th	1.07
1973–74	Second Division	42	9	6	6	33	24	3	5	13	18	39	35	19th	0.81
1974–75	R Second Division	42	3	7	11	17	29	2	4	15	12	35	21	22nd	0.45
1975–76	Third Division	46	12	6	5	34	25	0	10	13	14	34	40	20th	0.81
1976–77	Third Division	46	15	4	4	39	18	7	5	11	26	37	53	8th	10
1977–78	Third Division	46	13	7	3	28	14	2	9	12	22	38	46	14th	-2
1978–79	Third Division	46	9	8	6	30	22	4	11	8	23	31	45	14th	0
1979–80	P Third Division	46	12	6	5	44	20	9	10	4	37	27	58	3rd	34
1980–81	Second Division	42	14	4	3	38	14	3	4	14	15	37	42	10th	2
1981–82	Second Division	42	10	8	3	31	23	10	2	9	24	28	70	4th	4
1982–83	Second Division	42	9	8	4	33	23	7	7	7	27	24	63	6th	13
1983–84	P Second Division	42	16	4	1	47	16	10	6	5	25	18	88	2nd	38
1984–85	First Division	42	12	7	2	39	21	5	7	9	19	24	65	8th	13
1985–86	First Division	42	13	6	2	36	23	8	4	9	27	31	73	5th	9
1986–87	First Division	42	9	7	5	39	24	4	6	11	19	35	52	13th	-1
1987–88	First Division	40	10	2	8	27	30	5	6	9	25	36	53	11th	-14
1988–89	First Division	38	6	6	7	21	25	4	6	9	13	26	42	15th	-17
1989–90	R First Division	38	8	6	5	21	17	3	4	12	14	34	43	18th	-16
1990–91	P Second Division	46	12	10	1	43	23	10	6	7	37	28	82	3rd	29
1991–92	First Division	42	13	5	3	39	24	8	7	6	23	25	75	3rd	13
1992–93	Premiership	42	9	8	4	34	26	6	6	9	21	25	59	7th	4
1993–94	Premiership	42	10	7	4	48	24	6	9	6	28	30	64	7th	22
1994–95	Premiership	42	7	7	7	26	26	6	5	10	23	31	51	13th	-8
1995–96	Premiership	38	7	5	7	30	31	3	5	11	18	30	40	15th	-13
1996–97	Premiership	38	8	10	1	25	16	6	5	8	25	35	57	7th	-1
1997–98	Premiership	38	9	5	5	30	26	3	3	13	22	41	44	16th	-15
1998–99	Premiership	38	7	5	7	20	15	6	2	11	21	27	46	12th	-1
1999–2000	R Premiership	38	6	3	10	21	23	2	4	13	17	47	31	19th	-32
2000–01	Division One	46	9	4	10	34	38	6	4	13	18	33	53	17th	-19
2001–02	Division One	46	6	7	10	28	37	6	7	10	21	34	50	20th	-22
2002–03	Division One	46	7	7	9	29	32	3	9	11	27	41	46	22nd	-17
2003–04	Division Two	46	7	9	7	25	26	6	5	12	23	38	53	16th	-16
2004–05	P League One	46	10	6	7	34	28	9	9	5	43	31	72	5th	18
2005–06	Championship	46	7	8	8	22	24	6	5	12	17	28	52	19th	-13
2006–07	Championship	46	10	6	7	38	36	10	5	8	32	30	71	9th	4
2007–08	Championship	46	9	5	9	29	25	5	8	10	25	30	55	16th	-1
2008–09	Championship	46	11	6	6	26	14	5	7	11	25	44	61	12th	-7
2009–10	R Championship	46	8	6	9	30	31	3	8	12	19	38	47	22nd	-20
2010–11	League One	46	10	5	8	38	29	6	5	12	29	38	58	15th	0
	TOTALS	4406	1170	538	495	4038	2463	512	572	1119	2540	3929			

Non-competitive & minor cup ties 1867-2011

Date	Comp	Opposition	Venue	Res	Att	Scorers
12 Oct 1867	PR	Inter-club practice match	HF			
19 Oct 1867	FR	Mechanics	A	3-0*		*won by 3 goals & 4 rouges to 1 rouge
28 Oct 1867	FR	Milton	A			
23 Nov 1867	FR	Heeley	A	0-1*		
28 Dec 1867	FR	Milton	A			* lost by 1 goal and 3 rouges
31 Dec 1867	FR	Dronfield	A	1-0		* won by 1 goal to 4 rouges
11 Jan 1868	FR	Heeley	A	0-4		
25 Jan 1868	FR	Broomhall	HF			
1 Feb 1868	CRC SF	Exchange	N	4-0		
1 Feb 1868	FR	Mechanics	HF	0-1		
8 Feb 1868	FR	Wellington	A			
15 Feb 1868	CRC FI	Garrick	BL	1-0	600	AET
14 Mar 1868	PR	Inter-club practice match	HF			
3. Oct 1868	PR	Inter-club practice match	HF			
24 Oct 1868	FR	Broomhall	HF			
7 Nov 1868	FR	Heeley	HF			
14 Nov 1868	FR	Heeley	HF			
25 Nov 1868	FR	MacKenzie				
28 Nov 1868	FR	Broomhall	A			
5 Dec 1868	FR	Mechanics				
15 Dec 1868	FR	Pitsmoor				
26 Dec 1868	FR	Dronfield	A			
2 Jan 1869	PR	Inter-club practice match	HF			
23 Jan 1869	FR	Broomhall	HF			
30 Jan 1869	FR	Heeley	A			
9 Feb 1869	FR	Wellington	A			
13 Feb 1869	FR	Broomhall	HF			
20 Feb 1869	PR	Inter-club practice match	HF			
27 Feb 1869	FR	Dronfield	HF			
12 Mar 1869	FR	Norfolk Park				
12 Apr 1869	FR	Heeley				
23 Oct 1869	FR	Pitsmoor	A			
6 Nov 1869	FR	Heeley	A	1-3		Ward
13 Nov 1869	FR	Broomhall	HF	2-0*		n/k

Date	Comp	Opposition	Venue	Res	Att	Scorers
20 Nov 1869	FR	Broomhall	HF	0-4		
23 Nov 1869	FR	Fir Vale	A	3-0		n/k
27 Nov 1869	FR	United Mechanics	HF	2-1		n/k
4 Dec 1869	FR	Broomhall	A	1-2		Littlehales
11 Dec 1869	FR	Pitsmoor	A	1-0		Littlehales
27 Dec 1869	FR	Dronfield	A	Won		
28 Dec 1869	FR	United Mechanics	A	2-3		n/k
15 Jan 1870	FR	United Mechanics	HF	1-0		n/k
22 Jan 1870	FR	Broomhall	A	1-2		Littlehales
29 Jan 1870	FR	Pitsmoor	HF	1-1		Butler
5 Feb 1870	FR	United Mechanics	A	0-3		
12 Feb 1870	FR	Heeley	HF	1-1		Sampson
19 Feb 1870	FR	Broomhall	HF	1-1		Ward
19 Feb 1870	FR	Pitsmoor	HF	0-0		
26 Feb 1870	FR	Fir Vale	HF	1-0		Mills
5 Mar 1870	FR	Dronfield	HF	1-1		Ward
8 Oct 1870	FR	Mackenzie	MR*	1-0		Sampson
* Played at Myrtle Road but contemporary reports suggest the match was a MacKenzie home fixture						
22 Oct 1870	FR	Broomhall	A	1-0		Deans
5 Nov 1870	FR	Heeley	A	1-0		Croft
19 Nov 1870	FR	Derby St Andrews	A	7-0		Sampson 2, Reaney 3, W. Clegg, Slowe
26 Nov 1870	FR	Fir Vale	A	1-0		Donovan
7 Jan 1871	FR	Derby St Andrews	A	4-0		Littlehales, W. Clegg 2, Cawthorn
9 Jan 1871	FR	Mackenzie	MR	1-1		Parker
21 Jan 1871	FR	Heeley	MR	0-0		
4 Feb 1871	FR	Broomhall	MR	0-1		
25 Feb 1871	FR	Fir Vale	MR	3-0		Anthony, Sampson, Orton
7 Oct 1871	FR	Attercliffe Christ Church	A	3-0		Cawthron 2, Croft
11 Nov 1871	FR	Rotherham	A	4-1		Rycroft, Anthony, Tingle, Parker
18 Nov 1871	FR	Derby St Andrews	MR	8-0		Reaney 3, Deans, Cawthron, Carr 2, Wright
28 Nov 1871	FR	Attercliffe Christ Church	A	0-2		
9 Dec 1871	FR	Fir Vale	A	0-1		
16 Dec 1871	FR	Broomhall	MR	1-2		
13 Jan 1872	FR	Derby St Andrews	A	4-0		Marsh, T. Butler, Hollingworth, Littlehales
20 Jan 1872	FR	Mackenzie	MR	1-0		F. Butler
10 Feb 1872	FR	Heeley	A	0-1		
17 Feb 1872	FR	Attercliffe Christ Church	MR	3-0		Cawthorn, Littlehales, Staniland
24 Feb 1872	FR	Fir Vale	MR	0-1		
5 Oct 1872	FR	Attercliffe Christ Church	A	4-2		Pinter, Orton, Cawthron, n/k
12 Oct 1872	FR	Heeley	A	2-0		F. Butler, n/k
26 Oct 1872	FR	Broomhall	A	1-1		Sampson
23 Nov 1872	FR	Derbyshire	BL	0-1	500	
30 Nov 1872	FR	Fir Vale	A	1-0		

Date	Comp	Opposition	Venue	Res	Att	Scorers
14 Dec 1872	FR	Brincliffe	A	1-0		W. Stacey
11 Jan 1873	FR	Heeley	MR	1-0		Anthony
25 Jan 1873	FR	Broomhall	MR	3-0		F. Butler, Carr, Hill
3 Feb 1873	FR	Derbyshire	A	2-1	400	Orton, W. Clegg
15 Feb 1873	FR	Fir Vale	MR	5-0		W. Stacey, Wood 2, F. Butler 2
22 Feb 1873	FR	Attercliffe Christ Church	MR	0-4		
1 Mar 1873	FR	Brincliffe	MR	4-0		Bailey 2, Orton 2
4 Oct 1873	FR	Attercliffe	A	4-0		J. Clegg, F. Butler, Cawthorn, W. Stacey
11 Oct 1873	FR	Heeley	A			
25 Oct 1873	FR	Broomhall	MR	2-2	200-300	Orton, Ellis
8 Nov 1873	FR	Exchange Brewery	MR	5-0		Hatherley 3, West, Rycroft
22 Nov 1873	FR	Fir Vale	MR	0-0		
29 Nov 1873	FR	Heeley	MR	3-1		Cawthorn 2, Wilson
13 Dec 1873	FR	Rotherham	A	0-1		
27 Dec 1873	FR	Derbyshire	BL	6-0	1,500	J. Clegg, F. Butler 2, Orton, Gregory, G. Anthony
10 Jan 1874	FR	Rotherham	MR	2-0		Cawthorn, T. Butler
17 Jan 1874	FR	Attercliffe	MR	1-0		F. Butler
31 Jan 1874	FR	Broomhall	A	1-2		Middleton
7 Feb 1874	FR	Fir Vale	A	2-1		T. Butler 2
28 Feb 1874	FR	Derbyshire	A	0-0	2,000	
21 Mar 1874	FR	Exchange Brewery	A			
3 Oct 1874	FR	Attercliffe	A	1-0		Cawthorn
10 Oct 1874	PR	Inter-club practice match	MR			
17 Oct 1874	FR	Fir Vale	A	0-4		
24 Oct 1874	FR	Thurlstone Crystal Palace	A	4-0	500	Cawthorn, Fay, Orton 2
31 Oct 1874	FR	Heeley	A	2-1		W. Clegg, Deans
5 Dec 1874	FR	105th Regiment	MR	1-0		Wardley
9 Dec 1874	FR	Hallam				
26 Dec 1874	FR	Broomhall	A			
16 Jan 1875	FR	Attercliffe	MR	1-1		Wilson
23 Jan 1875	FR	Derby Derwent	BL	3-1	700	F. Butler 2, T. Butler
25 Jan 1875	FR	105th Regiment	MR	3-0		Brownhill 2, Heath
6 Feb 1875	FR	Broomhall	MR	1-0		J Hanson
13 Feb 1875	FR	Exchange Brewery	A			
27 Feb 1875	FR	Heeley	MR	1-0*		
13 Mar 1875	FR	Derby Derwent	A	1-0		W. Clegg
20 Mar 1875	FR	Fir Vale #	MR	1-0		R. Gregory # Only five Fir Vale players so practice match played
30 Oct 1875	FR	Thurlestone Crystal Palace	A	3-0		Mosforth 2, Jones
27 Nov 1875	FR	Derby Derwent	BL	4-0	150	T. Butler 2, Mosforth, F. Butler
11 Dec 1875	FR	Spital United	MR	2-2		F. Butler, Houseley
18 Dec 1875	FR	Broomhall	MR	0-0		
8 Jan 1876	FR	Nottingham Forest	A	5-0		T. Butler, Gregory 2, Mosforth 2
15 Jan 1876	FR	Derby Derwent	A	3-0		F. Butler 2, Jones

Date	Comp	Opposition	Venue	Res	Att	Scorers
22 Jan 1876	FR	Attercliffe	MR	2-0		F. Butler, Hanson
31 Jan 1876	FR	Heeley	MR	0-1		
5 Feb 1876	FR	Thurlestone Crystal Palace	MR	3-0		Hoyland/F. Butler, Ellis, Stacey
21 Feb 1876	FR	Nottingham Castle	A	1-1		Beardshaw
26 Feb 1876	FR	Spital United	A	2-1		Hanson 2
18 Mar 1876	FR	Nottingham Forest	BL	9-1*	1,000	J. Clegg 3, Houseley, F. Butler 3, Gregory
1 Apr 1876	FR	Clydesdale (Scotland)	A	0-2	17,500	
7 Oct 1876	FR	Attercliffe	A	0-4	300	
21 Oct 1876	SCC1	Parkwood Springs	A	3-1	1,000	F. Butler 2, Tomlinson
28 Oct 1876	FR	Spital Chesterfield	MR	5-0		J. Clegg, W. Clegg, F. Butler, Gregory 2
18 Nov 1876	FR	Crystal Palace Thurlstone	MR	?		
25 Nov 1876	FR	Hallam	MR	1-1		T. Butler
2 Dec 1876	SCC2	Kimberworth	A	1-0		W. Clegg
26 Dec 1876	FR	Derby Town	MR	5-1		F. Butler 2, T. Butler, Houseley, n/k
1 Jan 1877	SCC3	Attercliffe	A	1-0		Lang
13 Jan 1877	FR	Nottingham Forest	A	1-2		Beardshaw
20 Jan 1877	FR	Heeley	MR	0-0	500	
27 Jan 1877	FR	Nottingham Forest	MR	0-1		
3 Feb 1877	SCC SF	Exchange	BL	3-1	6,000	Bishop 2, J. Clegg
8 Feb 1877	FR	Derby Town	A	1-0		
10 Feb 1877	FR	Attercliffe	MR	1-2	1,000	Hessey
13 Feb 1877	FR	Nottingham Forest	A	1-0		Butler
17 Feb 1877	FR	Derby Town	A	2-1		F. Butler, Tomlinson
10 Mar 1877	SCC F	Heeley	BL	4-3	8,000	F. Butler, T. Butler, W. Clegg, Skinner
17 Mar 1877	FR	Spital Chesterfield	A	1-1	600	J. Clegg
6 Oct 1877	FR	Attercliffe	A	0-1		
13 Oct 1877	FR	Exchange	A	1-1		F. Butler
20 Oct 1877	FR	Heeley	MR	0-0		
27 Oct 1877	FR	Endcliffe	A	3-1		Anthony, F. Butler, n/k
3 Nov 1877	FR	Derby	A	0-6		
10 Nov 1877	SCC1	Exchange Brewery	SH	5-0		F. Butler 2, J. Clegg, W. Clegg, Carr
24 Nov 1877	FR	Spital Chesterfield	A	1-0		Patterson
26 Dec 1877	FR	Derby	SH	1-0		T. Butler
19 Jan 1878	FR	Heeley	SH	1-5		Billings
26 Jan 1878	SCC3	Hallam	BL	2-0	2,000	Bishop, T. Butler
26 Jan 1878	FR	Nottingham Forest	A	1-4	1,500	Anthony
2 Feb 1878	FR	Exchange Brewery	SH	0-1		
18 Feb 1878	FR	Glasgow Rangers (Scotland)	BL	1-2		Patterson
23 Feb 1878	SCC SF	Derby	BL	2-0	3,000	Bishop, J. Clegg *AET
25 Feb 1878	FR	Heeley	A	0-1		
2 Mar 1878	SCC F	Attercliffe	BL	2-0	7,000	F. Butler, Bishop
5 Mar 1878	FR	Nottingham Forest	A	1-0		Muscroft
30 Mar 1878	FR	Spital Chesterfield	A	3-1		W. Clegg, J. Clegg, Gregory

Date	Comp	Opposition	Venue	Res	Att	Scorers
5 Oct 1878	FR	Attercliffe	A	0-1	800	
12 Oct 1878	FR	Heeley	A	0-1		
19 Oct 1878	FR	Endcliffe	A	1-4		
26 Oct 1878	FR	Staveley	SH	1-1		Sheel
2 Nov 1878	SCC1	Oxford	A	2-1	300	Sheel, F. Butler
9 Nov 1878	FR	Spital Chesterfield	SH	0-0		
23 Nov 1878	FR	Albion	A	2-2		Orton, n/k
30 Nov 1878	SCC2	Hallam	A	0-3		
7 Dec 1878	FR	Nottingham Forest	SH	1-0	1,500	Bingley
11 Jan 1879	FR	Albion	SH	2-0		Richards, F. Butler
18 Jan 1879	FR	Thurlestone Crystal Palace	SH	3-0		W. Stacey, Orton, Wells
25 Jan 1879	FR	Mr Beardshaw's Team	BL	2-3		Woodcock 2
1 Feb 1879	FR	Endcliffe	SH	2-4		
8 Feb 1879	FR	Staveley	A	0-2	300	
22 Feb 1879	FR	Heeley	SH	0-4	500	
1 Mar 1879	FR	Spital Chesterfield	A	1-2		Gregory
8 Mar 1879	FR	Derby	A	0-1		
10 Mar 1879	FR	Exchange Brewery	SH	0-1		
15 Mar 1879	WCC - F	Heeley	BL	3-2	3,000	Woodcock 3
22 Mar 1879	FR	Attercliffe	SH	0-1		
4 Oct 1879	FR	Attercliffe	A	2-1		Ambler, Lang
11 Oct 1879	FR	Heeley	A	0-3		
13 Oct 1879	FR	Exchange Brewery	A	3-1		Sheel, Lang, F. Butler
18 Oct 1879	SCC1	Exchange Brewery	A	0-1		
1 Nov 1879	FR	Spital Chesterfield	SH	1-0		McKenzie
3 Nov 1879	FR	Holmes	A	2-1		F. Butler, Ramsden
8 Nov 1879	WCC1	Hallam	SH	2-1	2,000	J. Clegg, n/k
15 Nov 1879	FR	Broomhall	SH	0-6		
13 Dec 1879	FR	Derby	A	0-2		
27 Dec 1879	FR	Endcliffe	SH	2-2*		
30 Dec 1879	FR	Walsall Town	A	1-2		Mosforth
31 Dec 1879	FR	Wednesbury Strollers	A	1-1		Bishop
1 Jan 1880	WCC SF	Spital	SH	3-0		Lang, Ambler, n/k
3 Jan 1880	FR	Vale of Leven (Scotland)	SH	0-3	1,500	
10 Jan 1880	FR	Endcliffe	A	0-1		
17 Jan 1880	WCC - F	Heeley	SH	1-2		Hawley
19 Jan 1880	FR	Eckington Rovers	A	1-3		Hinchcliffe
7 Feb 1880	FR	Nottingham Forest	A	0-2	800	
10 Feb 1880	FR	Derby	SH	2-2	200	
21 Feb 1880	FR	Nottingham Forest	SH	1-0		Gregory
28 Feb 1880	FR	Staveley	A	0-7		
6 Mar 1880	FR	Spital Chesterfield	A	3-1		Worrall, Gregory, Andrews
13 Mar 1880	FR	Staveley	SH	1-3		

Date	Comp	Opposition	Venue	Res	Att	Scorers
25 Sep 1880	FR	Attercliffe	A	0-0		
2 Oct 1880	FR	Heeley	BL	4-2		Lang, Charles, Mosforth, Gregory
9 Oct 1880	FR	Staveley	BL	3-3		Gregory, Sheel, Lang
11 Oct 1880	FR	Exchange	A	2-1		Gregory 2
16 Oct 1880	SCC1	White Cross	A	4-1		Lang, Hawley, Bingley, Newbould
21 Oct 1880	FR	Queens Park (Scotland)	BL	0-5	500	
30 Oct 1880	FR	Exchange	A	0-0		
6 Nov 1880	FR	Derby	A	4-0		Cawley, 3 n/k
13 Nov 1880	SCC2	Phoenix Bessemer	BL	8-1	300	Gregory 4, Mosforth 2, Lang, 1 n/k
20 Nov 1880	WCC SF	Heeley	BL	2-2	1,200	H. Newbould, Mosforth
27 Nov 1880	FR	Heeley	BL	5-2	1,500	Pilling 2, E. Buttery, Mosforth, Lang
4 Dec 1880	FR	Walsall Town	A	1-1		C. Rhodes
11 Dec 1880	SCC3	Providence	BL	7-0	700	Mosforth 2, Gregory 2, Lang, Bingley, Hudson
13 Dec 1880	FR	Exchange	BL	4-1	150	Stratford 2, Gregory, n/k
27 Dec 1880	FR	Blackburn Olympic	A	3-1*		Lang, Sheel
8 Jan 1881	FR	Walsall Town	BL	1-2		H. Newbould
15 Jan 1881	SCC S/F	Lockwood Brothers	BL	7-1	1,500	Bingley 4, Mosforth, Gregory, Lang
24 Jan 1881	WCC SFr	Heeley #	BL	7-2		Mosforth 2, Cawley 2, Rhodes, Lang, H. Newbould
# Final not played						
19 Feb 1881	FR	Wednesbury Elwell's	A	6-1*		Bingley, 4 n/k
1 Mar 1881	FR	Attercliffe	BL	8-1		F. Newbould 3, Pilling 2, 3 n/k
12 Mar 1881	FR	Staveley	A	0-9	1,000	
19 Mar 1881	SCC F	Ecclesfield	BL	8-1	3,000	Gregory 5, Mosforth 2, Bingley
26 Mar 1881	Charity	Exchange	SH	0-2	1,000	
9 Apr 1881	FR	Blackburn Rovers	A	3-7	4,000	Lang, Anthony, Malpas
1 Oct 1881	FR	Attercliffe	A	1-4	500	Gregory
8 Oct 1881	SCC1	Eckington Colliery	BL	4-1		Mosforth, Gregory, Sheel, Bingley
17 Oct 1881	FR	Hallam	A	1-2		
29 Oct 1881	FR	Heeley	BL	5-1*	1,000	Bingley 2, Sheel, Gregory
12 Nov 1881	FR	Darwen	A	2-7	2,000	Rhodes, Wilson
19 Nov 1881	SCC2	Heeley	BL	3-3	2,000	Anthony 2, Guest
26 Nov 1881	FR	Spital Chesterfield	A	0-0		
3 Dec 1881	SCC2	Heeley	BL	1-1	1,000	Sheel
10 Dec 1881	SCC2r	Heeley	BL	1-2	2,000	Anthony
2 Jan 1882	WCC SF	Lockwood Brothers	BL	7-2*	2,000	Rhodes 2, Gregory 2, Anthony, Mosforth
7 Jan 1882	FR	Accrington	A	1-4	1,500	Sheel
16 Jan 1882	FR	Exchange	MR	0-1	300	
28 Jan 1882	FR	Spital Chesterfield	MR	0-4		
13 Feb 1882	FR	Heeley	BL	3-3		
4 Mar 1882	WCC F	Heeley	BL	5-0	4,000	Cawley 3, Gregory, Hibbert
23 Sep 1882	FR	Attercliffe	A	3-1		F. Newbould, Sheel, 1 n/k
30 Sep 1882	FR	Darwen	A	1-6	4,000	West
7 Oct 1882	FR	Spital Chesterfield	BL	2-2		Sheel, Mosforth

Date	Comp	Opposition	Venue	Res	Att	Scorers
14 Oct 1882	FR	Aston Villa	A	1-6		Allen
21 Oct 1882	SCC1	Leeds Oulton	A	8-0		
11 Nov 1882	SCC2	Walkley	A	7-0	400	H. Newbould 2, Anthony, Gregory, F. Newbould, 2 n/k
18 Nov 1882	FR	Blackburn Rovers	A	1-2	3,000	Gregory
25 Nov 1882	FR	Thurlestone	HB	5-0		H. Newbould 2, Cawthorne, C. Stratford, Bingley
26 Dec 1882	FR	Brigg Representative	A	5-0		
27 Dec 1882	FR	Thurlestone	A	3-3		E. Bingley, 2 n/k
30 Dec 1882	SCC3	Pyebank	BL	3-2	500	Stratford, Gregory, F. Newbould
20 Jan 1883	FR	Walsall Town	A	0-2	1,200	
5 Feb 1883	WCC1	Walkley	BL	3-0		Cawley 2, Wilson
17 Feb 1883	FR	Darwen	HB	2-2	600	Gregory, H. Newbould
3 Mar 1883	WCC SF	Attercliffe	A	4-2	1,700	Wilson, Gregory, Malpas, Cawley
17 Mar 1883	SCC -SF	Attercliffe	BL	3-3	3,000	Gregory 2, H. Newbould *AET 90 mins – 2-2
24 Mar 1883	SCC -SFr	Attercliffe	BL	2-0	3,000	Gregory, n/k
27 Mar 1883	SCC F	Lockwood Brothers	BL	2-2	2,000	Gregory, Mosforth
31 Mar 1883	WCC F	Pyebank	BL	4-0*	2,500	Hudson, H. Newbould, 1 n/k
7 Apr 1883	SCC Fr	Lockwood Brothers	BL	2-1	5,000	F. Newbould, Mosforth
14 Apr 1883	FR	Surrey	A	0-2		
16 Apr 1883	FR	Blackburn Rovers	H*	0-1	300	*played at Newhall Grounds
15 Sep 1883	FR	Attercliffe	A	6-1		
22 Sep 1883	FR	Rotherham	HB	4-2		Newbould 2, Gregory, n/k
6 Oct 1883	FR	Spital Chesterfield	A	3-0		Mosforth 2, Winterbottom
13 Oct 1883	SCC1	Redcar	BL	7-1	3,000	Bentley 3, Cawley 3, Winterbottom
27 Oct 1883	FR	Blackburn Rovers	BL	2-0	4,000	Winterbottom, Cawley
29 Oct 1883	FR	Deepcar	A	3-0		
5 Nov 1883	TST	Heeley (Martin)	BL	0-2	1,200	
10 Nov 1883	FR	Derby Midland	A	1-1*	1,500	
3 Dec 1883	SCC2	Lockwood Brothers	BL	1-2	1,000	Mosforth
8 Dec 1883	FR	Astley Bridge (Bolton)	HB	0-4	100	
15 Dec 1883	FR	Darwen	BL	1-0	700	Newbould
24 Dec 1883	FR	Walsall Town	BL	1-3	3,000	
29 Dec 1883	FR	Darwen	A	2-5	1,500	Ibbotson, n/k
1 Jan 1884	WCC1	Park Grange	BL	1-3	1,000	H. Newbould
2 Jan 1884	FR	Bolton Wanderers	A	1-4	5,000	H. Newbould
7 Jan 1884	FR	Heeley	BL	6-3	1,000	Sugg 4, Naylor 2
12 Jan 1884	FR	Wednesbury Town	BL	0-4		
26 Jan 1884	FR	Notts County	BL	0-0		
2 Feb 1884	FR	Derby Midland	H*	8-1		Bentley 4, Stokes 2, H. Newbould 2
*played at Eccleshall Road						
26 Feb 1884	TST	Lockwood Brothers (T. Buttery)	A	5-2	800	Sugg, Cawley, Winterbottom, Sayer, n/k
8 Mar 1884	FR	Nottingham Forest	A	2-0	800	Winterbottom 2
15 Mar 1884	FR	Lockwood Brothers	HB	1-1		Winterbottom
22 Mar 1884	FR	Wednesbury Town	A	2-0		Mosforth, Jeeves

Date	Comp	Opposition	Venue	Res	Att	Scorers
5 Apr 1884	FR	Walsall Town	A	0-2		
21 Apr 1884	FR	Blackburn Rovers	A	1-3	500	Cawley
20 Sep 1884	FR	Aston Villa	A	3-2		Bentley 2, Winterbottom
20 Sep 1884	FR	Spital Chesterfield	HB	5-2		
27 Sep 1884	FR	Bolton Wanderers	A	1-2	3,000	Winterbottom or Mastin
4 Oct 1884	FR	Mexborough	BL	5-1*		W. Hiller 2, C. Hiller, Winterbottom
11 Oct 1884	SCC1	Hallam	BL	5-1*		Stratford, Mosforth, Stokes, Brayshaw
18 Oct 1884	FR	Notts County	A	0-0	2,000	
27 Oct 1884	FR	Heeley	BL	1-1	1,000	
1 Nov 1884	FR	Notts County	BL	0-1	2,000	
10 Nov 1884	SCC2	Attercliffe	BL	2-1	2,000	Mastin, Naylor
15 Nov 1884	FR	Nottingham Forest	A	5-0	600	Stokes 2, Bentley, Winterbottom, Turner
22 Nov 1884	FR	Blackburn Rovers	A	1-3	600	Bentley
29 Nov 1884	FR	Blackburn Olympic	A	0-12	500	
6 Dec 1884	SCC3	Lockwood Brothers	BL	0-1	4,000	
20 Dec 1884	FR	Blackburn Rovers	BL	1-1	1,500	Bentley
26 Dec 1884	FR	Blackburn Olympic	BL	6-0	3,000	W. Hiller 2, Mosforth, Cawley, Winterbottom, 1 n/k
1 Jan 1885	WCC1	Mexborough	BL	3-1	3,000	Bentley, Winterbottom, Mosforth
10 Jan 1885	FR	Astley Bridge (Bolton)	A	3-1	1,000	West, Bennett, Eadon
17 Jan 1885	FR	Mexborough	A	2-2		Parton, Winterbottom
24 Jan 1885	FR	Bolton Wanderers	BL	2-6	700	C. Hiller, W. Hiller
26 Jan 1885	FR	Heeley	BL	0-3	800	
7 Feb 1885	FR	Rotherham	HB	4-0		
17 Feb 1885	FR	Preston North End	BL	0-4	700	
21 Feb 1885	FR	Preston North End	A	1-8	2,000	Nicholson
28 Feb 1885	WCC SF	Lockwood Brothers	A	1-1		
14 Mar 1885	WCC SFr	Lockwood Brothers	BL	1-0	3,000	Winterbottom
28 Mar 1885	WCC F	Heeley	BL	1-1	5,000	Nicholson
30 Mar 1885	FR	Aston Villa	BL	1-2	600	Nicholson
4 Apr 1885	FR	Nottingham Forest	BL	0-7	2,000	
6 Apr 1885	WCC Fr	Heeley	BL	0-4	6,000	
11 Apr 1885	TST	Lockwood Brothers (Malpas)	A	3-2		Davy 2, Nicholson
19 Sep 1885	FR	Long Eaton Rangers	SH	2-1	1,000	Cawley 2
26 Sep 1885	FR	Lockwood Brothers	BL	0-0	2,000	
28 Sep 1885	FR	Park Grange	SH	1-2		Nicholson
1 Oct 1885	FR	Notts County	A	1-6	4,000	Nicholson
3 Oct 1885	FR	Spital Olympic	A	1-3		n/k
3 Oct 1885	FR	Walsall Town	A	1-5		Haslam
10 Oct 1885	FR	Notts Olympic	A	4-2*		Hammond, Cawley, Shaw
17 Oct 1885	FR	Attercliffe	A	2-1		
19 Oct 1885	FR	Owlerton	A	1-1		
2 Nov 1885	FR	Rotherham	A	1-2		Watson
7 Nov 1885	SCC2	Holmes	BL	7-1		Davy 4, Nicholson, F. Newbould, Shaw

Date	Comp	Opposition	Venue	Res	Att	Scorers
21 Nov 1885	FR	Attercliffe	A	0-0		
23 Nov 1885	FR	Derby County	BL	2-8		Cawley, n/k
7 Dec 1885	FR	Burslem Port Vale	A	0-3	3,000	
12 Dec 1885	SCC3	Hallam	HB	2-0		Davy 2
19 Dec 1885	FR	Nottingham Forest	BL	1-1	800	Watson
24 Dec 1885	FR	Heeley	BL	0-0	1,000	
26 Dec 1885	TST	Lockwood Brothers (Brears)	A	2-2		Dungworth, Needham
1 Jan 1886	WCC1	Walkley	BL	4-1		F. Newbould 2, Cawley, Naylor
2 Jan 1886	FR	London Hotspur	BL	2-1		Winterbottom 2
18 Jan 1886	FR	Mexborough	A	1-3	400	Cawley
23 Jan 1886	FR	Derby County	A	0-6		
30 Jan 1886	FR	Walsall Town	SH	1-4		Dungworth
6 Feb 1886	SCC SF	Heeley	BL	1-1	3,000	Cawley
13 Feb 1886	FR	Halliwell	A	0-9	300	
20 Feb 1886	FR	Preston North End	A	1-3	3,000	Aizlewood
9 Mar 1886	FR	Preston North End	BL	0-3	3,000	
15 Mar 1886	WCC SF	Lockwood Brothers	BL	6-0		Brayshaw, Shaw, Davy, Cawley, H. Newbould, Haslam
20 Mar 1886	SCC SFr	Heeley	N*	1-3*		*played at Eccleshall Road
27 Mar 1886	FR	Notts County	SH	1-1	1,000	Davy
5 Apr 1886	MRC SF	Attercliffe	SH	4-1		Cawley 2, Shaw, Brayshaw
12 Apr 1886	MRC F	Heeley	SH	1-2	1,800	Davy
17 Apr 1886	WCC F	Heeley	Brightside	2-0	2,000	Mosforth, Davy
26 Apr 1886	FR	Everton	A	1-3		
11 Sep 1886	FR	Attercliffe	A	0-2	400	
18 Sep 1886	FR	Grimsby Town	A	1-1*		
20 Sep 1886	FR	Lockwood Brothers	A	1-0		
25 Sep 1886	FR	Derby Midland	SH	0-0	800	
2 Oct 1886	FR	Aston Villa	A	0-7	2,000	
7 Oct 1886	FR	Nottingham Forest	A	1-4	1,000	E. Buttery
9 Oct 1886	SCC1	Eckington Works	BL	3-0		Wilson, Cawley, Parkin
11 Oct 1886	FR	Staveley	A	1-3		Hird
16 Oct 1886	FR	Derby County	A	0-3	1,000	
1 Nov 1886	FR	Rotherham Town	A	1-5		Mosforth
15 Nov 1886	FR	Staveley	SH	2-6		Cawley, n/k
20 Nov 1886	FR	Mexborough	SH	2-1	300	Parkin, Mosforth/Naylor
22 Nov 1886	FR	Clinton	A	2-4		Waller, n/k
27 Nov 1886	SCC2	Park Grange	BL	4-1	1,500	Naylor 2, Mosforth, Needham
29 Nov 1886	FR	Owlerton	A	0-1		
4 Dec 1886	FR	Heeley	BL	2-1	2,000	Davy, Needham/Cawley
6 Dec 1886	FR	Derby County	SH	2-2	700	Mosforth, Ingram
11 Dec 1886	FR	Long Eaton Rangers	A	0-4		
24 Dec 1886	FR	Heeley	BL	1-1		Sellars
27 Dec 1886	WCC1	Attercliffe	BL	3-1	2,000	Beckett, Mosforth/Watson, Cawley

Date	Comp	Opposition	Venue	Res	Att	Scorers
30 Dec 1886	FR	London Hotspur	SH	4-0		Nicholson, 3 n/k
8 Jan 1887	FR	Halliwell	A	0-16	1,000	
22 Jan 1887	WCC SF	Lockwood Brothers	BL	3-0	3,000	Cawley/Mosforth, Naylor, Dungworth
12 Feb 1887	FR	Mexborough	A	1-3		Bennett
19 Feb 1887	WCC F	Staveley	BL	0-3	3,500	
21 Feb 1887	FR	Clinton	SH	1-2		Needham
22 Feb 1887	FR	Preston North End	BL	0-5	4,000	
26 Feb 1887	FR	Derby Midland	A	1-3		Naylor
7 Mar 1887	SCC SF	Lockwood Brothers	BL	4-1	2,000	Naylor 2, Needham, Mosforth
19 Mar 1887	TST	Lincoln City (Strawson)	A	0-1		
26 Mar 1887	SCC F	Sheffield Collegiate	BL	2-1		Mosforth, Brayshaw
9 Apr 1887	HE	Heeley	SH	1-0		Cawley
12 Apr 1887	HE	Heeley	SH	1-0	1,000	Cawley
3 Sep 1887	FR	West Bromwich Albion	A	1-4		Needham
12 Sep 1887	FR	Blackburn Rovers	H	4-4	2,000	Wilson 2, Mosforth, Cawley
17 Sep 1887	FR	Aston Villa	A	1-6	5,000	Cawley
19 Sep 1887	FR	Lockwood Brothers	H	2-0		Winterbottom 2
24 Sep 1887	FR	Notts Rangers	A	2-1		Winterbottom, Cawley
1 Oct 1887	FR	Sheffield	H	1-0		Brayshaw
6 Oct 1887	FR	Nottingham Forest	A	1-2		Cawley
8 Oct 1887	SCC1	Owlerton	A	3-3		C. Hiller, Mosforth, n/k
22 Oct 1887	SCC1r	Owlerton	H	2-0	4,000	Cawley, Waller
24 Oct 1887	FR	Mexborough	H	9-0*		Cawley 4, Ingram 2, C. Hiller, Mosforth
29 Oct 1887	SCC2	Holmes	H	6-0		Waller 3, C. Hiller, Cawley, n/k
7 Nov 1887	FR	Rotherham Town	A	1-3		Ingram
19 Nov 1887	SCC3	Eckington Works	H	10-0	3,000	Cawley 3, Ingram 2, Waller, C. Hiller 2, Winterbottom 2
26 Nov 1887	FR	Burnley	A	0-5		
28 Nov 1887	FR	Lincoln City	H	5-1*		Cawley 2, C. Hiller, Ingram
5 Dec 1887	FR	Park Grange	H	5-1		Ingram 3, W. Hiller 2
24 Dec 1887	FR	Derby County	H	8-0	2,000	Ingram 3, Cawley 3, Dungworth, Waller
26 Dec 1887	WCC1	Heeley	BL	7-0	3,000	Waller 2, Betts 2, Winterbottom, Ingram, Wilson
28 Dec 1887	FR	Heeley	A	1-1		Ingram
31 Dec 1887	FR	Sheffield Collegiate	H	8-1		Waller 3, Betts 2, Cawley, Ingram, Dungworth
9 Jan 1888	FR	Lockwood Brothers	H	3-0	1,000	Cawley 2, Ingram
14 Jan 1888	FR	Clinton	H	9-0	900	Ingram 3, C. Hiller 2, Winterbottom, Drabble, Waller, n/k
16 Jan 1888	FR	Mexborough	A	3-0		Cooper, C. Hiller, Mumford
4 Feb 1888	SCC SF	Staveley	BL	1-0	6,000	Mosforth
6 Feb 1888	FR	Park Grange	A	4-0	1,000	Mosforth, Cawley, Brayshaw, n/k
11 Feb 1888	FR	Ecclesfield	H	2-1	1,000	Dungworth, Thompson
14 Feb 1888	FR	Derby Midland	H	6-1		C. Hiller 2, Cawley, Winterbottom, Ingram, n/k
18 Feb 1888	WCC SF	Staveley	BL	3-2	4,000	Ingram, Mosforth, C.Hiller
25 Feb 1888	WCC F	Rotherham Town	BL	2-0	2,000	Cawley, Ingram
3 Mar 1888	SCC F	Ecclesfield	BL	3-2	4,000	Winterbottom, Ingram, C. Hiller

Date	Comp	Opposition	Venue	Res	Att	Scorers
5 Mar 1888	FR	Notts County	H	3-4	1,500	Ingram 2, Waller
10 Mar 1888	FR	Rotherham Town	H	3-2	2,000	Cawley, Dungworth, Winterbottom
19 Mar 1888	FR	Ecclesfield	H	0-0		
24 Mar 1888	FR	Lincoln City	A	2-1	2,000	Waller, n/k
31 Mar 1888	FR	Welsh Amateurs	H	8-4	1,500	Waller 4, Mosforth 2, Chapman, Brayshaw
2 Apr 1888	FR	Halliwell	H	2-2	3,000	Cawley, Hardman
3 Apr 1888	FR	Staveley	H	7-1	1,500	Ingram 2, Cawley 2, Mumford, 2 n/k
7 Apr 1888	FR	Heeley	H	4-0	1,000	Cawley 2, Ingram, Drabble
14 Apr 1888	FR	Derby County	A	2-2		Hawnt, Winterbottom
28 Apr 1888	FR	Doncaster Rovers	H	3-1	1,000	Mosforth, Thompson, Cawley
1 Sep 1888	FR	West Bromwich Albion	H	1-3	3,000	Wilkinson
8 Sep 1888	FR	Nottingham Forest	H	2-2		Cawley 2
12 Sep 1888	FR	Doncaster Rovers	A	3-1	500	Woolhouse, Ingram, n/k
15 Sep 1888	FR	Witton	H	5-2	3,000	Ingram 2, Woolhouse 2, Mumford
17 Sep 1888	PR	First Team v Reserves	H	5-0		
22 Sep 1888	FR	Birmingham St George's	A	4-9	1,000	Winterbottom, Mumford, Cawley or Winterbottom, Woolhouse
29 Sep 1888	FR	Derby Junction	H	3-1	3,000	Cawley, Woolhouse, Mumford
1 Oct 1888	FR	Park Grange	A	13-0		Cawley 2, Woolhouse 2, Betts, Ingram, Winterbottom, 6 n/k
6 Oct 1888	FR	Sunderland	A	1-2	3,000	
13 Oct 1888	FR	Leeds Association	H	6-0*	2,000	Ingram, Winterbottom, Waller, Woolhouse, Mumford
20 Oct 1888	FR	Nottingham Forest	A	3-1	1,000	Winterbottom 2, Woolhouse
22 Oct 1888	FR	Halliwell	H	0-1	1,000	
27 Oct 1888	FR	Notts Rangers	H	8-0	3,000	Ingram 3, Cawley 2, Mumford 2, Brayshaw
3 Nov 1888	FR	Ecclesfield	H	11-0	400	Ingram 3, Woolhouse 3, Cawley 2, Mumford, Waller, n/k
5 Nov 1888	FR	Sheffield	H	10-1	400	Cawley 5, Mumford 3, Brayshaw, n/k,
10 Nov 1888	FR	Lincoln City	A	6-1		Ingram, Cawley, Mumford, 3 n/k
17 Nov 1888	FR	Derby Junction	A	0-1		
19 Nov 1888	FR	Heeley	H	2-0	1,000	Woolhouse 2
24 Nov 1888	FR	Birmingham St George's	H	5-2	4,000	Woolhouse 3, Ingram 2
1 Dec 1888	FR	Wolverhampton Wanderers	A	0-1		
8 Dec 1888	FR	Derby St Lukes	H	4-0		Ingram 2, Woolhouse 2
10 Dec 1888	FR	Preston North End	H	2-1	5,000	Ingram 2
15 Dec 1888	FR	Derby County	A	1-3	2,000	Ingram
22 Dec 1888	FR	Gainsborough Trinity	A	1-1	1,200	Mumford
24 Dec 1888	FR	Lincoln City	H	5-0	2,000	Cawley 2, Winterbottom, Ingram, Mumford
27 Dec 1888	FR	Staveley	H	1-3		Brayshaw
29 Dec 1888	FR	Newcastle West End	A	1-0		Cawley
31 Dec 1888	FR	Clyde (Scotland)	H	1-2	3,500	Mumford
1 Jan 1889	FR	Halliwell	A	3-2		
2 Jan 1889	FR	Heart of Midlothian (Scotland)	H	3-0	2,000	Ingram 2, White
5 Jan 1889	FR	Gainsborough Trinity	H	1-0	1,000	Winterbottom
12 Jan 1889	FR	Newton Heath	H	2-1	1,500	Mumford, Woolhouse
19 Jan 1889	GNC2	Doncaster Rovers	H	10-0	2,500	Ingram 4, Cawley 4, Betts, Winterbottom

Date	Comp	Opposition	Venue	Res	Att	Scorers
26 Jan 1889	GNC3	Gainsborough Trinity	H	4-0	4,000	Woolhouse 2, Mumford, Ingram
4 Feb 1889	FR	Sheffield	BL	3-0	1,000	Mumford 2, Winterbottom
23 Feb 1889	FR	Sunderland	H	1-2	3,000	Waller
25 Feb 1889	GNC SF	Grimsby Humber Rovers	H	4-0	1,500	Mumford 3, White
5 Mar 1889	FR	Aston Villa	H	2-1	3,000	Cawley, Woolhouse
18 Mar 1889	FR	Heeley	A	3-0	1,500	Cawley, Woolhouse, Mumford
23 Mar 1889	FR	Witton	A	1-0		Ingram
30 Mar 1889	FR	Burnley	H	3-1	1,500	Woolhouse, Winterbottom, Ingram
1 Apr 1889	TST	Blackburn Rovers (Hudson)	H	1-1	2,000	Dungworth
6 Apr 1889	FR	Heeley	H	9-1	1,500	Ingram 3, Woolhouse 2, White 2, Winterbottom, Cawley
13 Apr 1889	GNC F	Burton Swifts	N	4-1*	2,000	Waller, Mumford, Winterbottom
* played at Northolme, Gainsborough						
19 Apr 1889	FR	Preston North End	A	0-2	7,000	
20 Apr 1889	FR	Newton Heath	A	2-1	6,000	Ingram, Mumford
22 Apr 1889	FR	Crewe	H	5-2	3,000	Cawley 2, Woolhouse 2, White
23 Apr 1889	FR	Staveley	H	3-0	2,000	Mumford, Cawley, Betts
27 Apr 1889	FR	Burnley	A	0-5	3,000	
28 Aug 1889	PR	First Team v Reserves	H			
2 Sep 1889	PR	Forwards v Backs	H		800	
4 Sep 1889	PR	First Team v Reserves	H	0-1		
9 Sep 1889	FR	Wolverhampton Wanderers	H	2-0	2,000	Mumford 2
21 Sep 1889	FR	Witton	H	5-0	3,000	Winterbottom 2, Mumford, Woolhouse, Betts
23 Sep 1889	FR	Stoke	A	0-5	1,500	
3 Oct 1889	FR	Notts County	A	1-6	3,000	Cawley
5 Oct 1889	FR	Blackburn Rovers	H	2-1	3,000	Mumford, Winterbottom
2 Nov 1889	FR	Burton Swifts	H	6-0	3,000	Cawley 2, Mumford, Ingram, Betts, n/k
9 Nov 1889	FR	Witton	A	3-0	1,000	Ingram, Cawley, Mumford
23 Nov 1889	FR	St Augustine's Darlington	H	6-0**	3,000	Mumford 2, Winterbottom, Bennett
14 Dec 1889	FR	Sunderland Albion	H	4-1*	4,000	3 n/k
20 Jan 1890	FR	Clifton	H	13-1	1,000	Ingram 4, Winterbottom 3, Mumford 2, Cawley, Bennett, Betts, Waller
3 Feb 1890	TST	Stoke FC (Cawley)	H	3-2	5,793	Ingram 2, Bennett
18 Feb 1890	FR	Preston North End	H	5-3	6,000	Mumford 2, Bennett 2, Cawley
7 Apr 1890	FR	Middlesbrough Ironopolis	H	3-2	3,000	Woolhouse, W. Hiller, Ingram
14 Apr 1890	FR	Derby County	H	1-1	2,000	Woolhouse
3 May 1890	FR	Derby County	A	3-5	1,500	Bennett 2, Woolhouse
10 May 1890	FR	Blackburn Rovers	A	2-5	2,000	W. Hiller, Ingram
18 Aug 1890	PR	First Team v Reserves	H	4-3	3,000	
20 Aug 1890	PR	First Team v Reserves	H	2-2		
25 Aug 1890	PR	First Team v Reserves	H	4-4	4,000	
28 Aug 1890	PR	Married players v Single players	H	5-2		
1 Sep 1890	FR	Newcastle East End	A	1-1	2,000	Ingram
2 Sep 1890	FR	Middlesbrough Ironopolis	A	1-1	2,000	Betts
6 Sep 1890	FR	Lincoln City	H	3-3	4,000	Cawley, Ingram, Thompson

Date	Comp	Opposition	Venue	Res	Att	Scorers
8 Sep 1890	FR	Burnley	A	1-8	4,000	Hodder
13 Sep 1890	FR	Lincoln City	A	1-2	3,000	Ingram
18 Sep 1890	PR	First Team v Reserves	H	5-3	200	
22 Sep 1890	FR	Everton	A	1-5	3,000	Mumford
25 Sep 1890	FR	Accrington	H	0-1	1,500	
4 Oct 1890	FR	Notts County	A	1-3	6,000	Ingram
13 Oct 1890	FR	Burnley	H	4-1	4,000	Hodder 2, Woolhouse, Ingram
20 Oct 1890	FR	Wolverhampton Wanderers	A	3-3*	3,000	Woolhouse, Brown
3 Nov 1890	FR	Burton Swifts	H	5-3	2,000	Woolhouse 2, J.Brandon, Winterbottom, Ingram
10 Nov 1890	FR	Wolverhampton Wanderers	H	3-0	3,000	Bennett, Hodder, Mumford
29 Nov 1890	FR	Bolton Wanderers	A	0-3	1,000	
6 Dec 1890	FR	Bolton Wanderers	H	3-6	4,000	Hodder, Winterbottom, n/k
15 Dec 1890	FR	Sheffield United	H	2-1	10,000	Woolhouse, Winterbottom
27 Dec 1890	FR	Middlesbrough Ironopolis	H	5-1	4,000	Hodder 2, R. Brandon, Bennett, Mumford
1 Jan 1891	FR	Glasgow Battlefield (Scotland)	H	3-2	5,000	Woolhouse 2, R. Brandon
3 Jan 1891	FR	Partick Thistle (Scotland)	H	3-2	3,000	Betts, Mumford, n/k
12 Jan 1891	FR	Sheffield United	A	2-3	15,000	Ingram, R. Brandon
2 Feb 1891	FR	Everton	H	2-3	5,000	H. Brandon, Winterbottom
10 Feb 1891	FR	Preston North End	H	0-2	9,000	
23 Feb 1891	TST	Stoke FC (Winterbottom)	H	4-1	5,000	Woolhouse 2, Winterbottom, Ingram
16 Mar 1891	FR	West Bromwich Albion	H	1-2	3,000	Winterbottom
30 Mar 1891	FR	Notts County	H	3-2	10,000	Woolhouse, H. Brandon, Winterbottom
31 Mar 1891	FR	Glasgow Celtic	H	1-3	7,000	Gemmell
11 Apr 1891	FR	Derby County	A	1-5	2,000	Richardson
13 Apr 1891	FR	Glasgow Rangers	H	3-3	2,000	Gibson, Woolhouse, H. Brandon
18 Apr 1891	FR	Derby County	H	4-2	2,000	Gibson 2, Woolhouse, Gibson or Gemmell
23 Apr 1891	WCC SF	Sheffield United	H	2-1	3,000	Woolhouse, Gibson
25 Apr 1891	FR	Accrington	H	6-2	3,000	Gemmell 3, Woolhouse, Richardson, Gibson
27 Apr 1891	FR	Rotherham Town	H	2-0	2,500	Ferguson, Woolhouse
13 Aug 1891	PR	Blues v Whites	H	2-1	2,000	
18 Aug 1891	PR	Blues v Whites	H		4,000	
20 Aug 1891	PR	Blues v Whites	H			
24 Aug 1891	PR	Blues v Whites	H			
27 Aug 1891	PR	Blues v Whites	H			
2 Sep 1891	FR	Sunderland Albion	A	1-2	2,000	Spiksley
3 Sep 1891	FR	Stockton	A	1-3	1,000	Spiksley
5 Sep 1891	FR	Canadian Touring side	H	4-1	6,000	Woolhouse 3, Gemmell
12 Sep 1891	FR	Lincoln City	H	7-4	5,000	Thompson 4, Spiksley, Mumford, Gemmell
14 Sep 1891	FR	Stockton	H	1-5	3,000	Woolhouse
21 Sep 1891	FR	Burslem Port Vale	A	3-4		
3 Oct 1891	FR	Middlesbrough	H	5-3*	8,000	Mumford, Gemmell, Thompson, Spiksley
5 Oct 1891	FR	Middlesbrough Ironopolis	H	3-2*	4,000	Gemmell, H. Brandon
19 Oct 1891	FR	Royal Arsenal	A	8-1	3,000	Gemmell 2, Thompson 2, Richardson, Spiksley, Mumford, Betts

Date	Comp	Opposition	Venue	Res	Att	Scorers
20 Oct 1891	FR	Millwall Athletic	A	5-3	1,500	Gemmell 2, Mumford, Thompson, Richardson
26 Oct 1891	FR	Sheffield United	A	0-5	22,900	
3 Nov 1891	FR	Rotherham Town	A	2-1	5,000	Richardson, Shaw
9 Nov 1891	FR	Sunderland Albion	H	2-1	3,000	McConachie, Hall
16 Nov 1891	FR	Sheffield United	H	4-1	11,000	Woolhouse 2, Spiksley 2
30 Nov 1891	FR	Royal Arsenal	H	5-1	2,000	Brown 2, Gemmell, Richardson, Thompson
1 Jan 1892	FR	Glasgow Battlefield (Scotland)	H	4-2	5,000	Thompson, Woolhouse, Betts, Brown
2 Jan 1892	FR	St Mirren (Scotland)	H	2-2	6,000	Brown 2
16 Jan 1892	FR	Bolton Wanderers	H	2-1	16,000	Brown, Thompson
6 Feb 1892	FR	Middlesbrough	A	0-0	4,139	
22 Feb 1892	FR	Blackburn Rovers	H	0-6	4,000	
1 Mar 1892	FR	Preston North End	H	6-1	4,000	Gemmell 2, Brown, Thompson, Spiksley, H. Brandon
7 Mar 1892	FR	Sunderland	H	0-3	3,000	
14 Mar 1892	FR	Notts County	H	2-5	3,000	Gemmell, Spiksley
21 Mar 1892	FR	Accrington	H	6-0	1,500	McConachie 3, Richardson, Ingram, H. Brandon
2 Apr 1892	FR	Notts County	A	5-2	2,000	Spiksley 2, Richardson, Gemmell, Thompson
4 Apr 1892	FR	Partick Thistle (Scotland)	H	9-1	2,000	Spiksley 4, Ingram 3, Gemmell, Mumford
6 Apr 1892	FR	Middlesbrough Ironopolis	A	0-1	1,500	
9 Apr 1892	FR	Derby County	A	2-6	3,000	Gemmell, Winterbottom
15 Apr 1892	FR	Ardwick	A	0-0	7,000	
16 Apr 1892	FR	Third Lanark (Scotland)	H	2-1	3,000	H. Brandon, Richardson
19 Apr 1892	FR	St Mirren (Scotland)	H	6-3	2,000	Spiksley 2, J. Brandon 2, Ingram, Richardson
23 Apr 1892	FR	Accrington	A	0-1	1,000	
28 Apr 1892	FR	Bolton Wanderers	H	1-1	500	Spiksley
30 Apr 1892	FR	Derby County	H	0-0	2,000	

KEY:

*	Own-goal scored for SWFC	BL	Bramall Lane	CRC	Cromwell Cup
FR	Friendly	GNC	Gainsborough News Charity Cup	HE	Heeley Sports Cup
HF	Highfields	HB	Hunter's Bar	MR	Myrtle Road
MRC	Mayor's Relief Charity Cup	N	Neutral venue	PR	Practice Match
SCC	Sheffield Challenge Cup	SH	Sheaf House	WCC	Wharncliffe Charity Cup
TST	Testimonial/Benefit (recepient in brackets)	All home games from 1887 played at Olive Grove			

Minor and Non Competitive games – 1892–2011

17 Aug 1892	PR	Narrow Stripes v Broad Stripes	H	3-2	7,000	
19 Sep 1892	FR	Rotherham Town	H	4-0	2,000	Spiksley 2, Dunlop, Brady
8 Oct 1892	FR	Stoke FC	H	1-1	4,000	Rowan
17 Oct 1892	FR	Sheffield United	H	1-1	18,000	Rowan or Brady
8 Nov 1892	FR	Rotherham Town	A	1-2	5,000	Rowan
12 Nov 1892	FR	Grimsby Town	A	1-0	4,000	Brady
14 Nov 1892	FR	Notts County	H	2-3	3,000	Spiksley, Dunlop
21 Nov 1892	FR	Sheffield United	A	3-1	12,000	Davis, Woolhouse, n/k
5 Dec 1892	FR	Darwen	H	2-2	500	Davis, Woolhouse

Date	Comp	Opposition	Venue	Res	Att	Scorers
15 Dec 1892	FR	Mount St Mary's College	A	5-2		Davis, Brown, Brady, Thompson, n/k
26 Dec 1892	FR	Newcastle East End	H	1-0	2,000	Rowan
28 Dec 1892	FR	Grimsby Town	H	3-1	2,000	Rowan 2, O'Neil
31 Dec 1892	FR	Glasgow Battlefield (Scotland)	H	6-2	5,000	Spiksley 2, McIntosh 2, Rowan, Brady
25 Feb 1893	FR	Glasgow Northern (Scotland)	H	4-0	2,000	Brady 2, Spiksley, Davis
6 Mar 1893	FR	Middlesbrough Ironopolis	H	4-1	1,500	Rowan 3, Spiksley
8 Apr 1893	FR	Nottingham Forest	H	2-1	1,500	Rowan, T. Brandon
12 Apr 1893	Charity	Everton	A	3-3	7,000	Brady 2, Woolhouse
15 Apr 1893	FR	Middlesbrough Ironopolis	A	0-4	2,000	
22 Apr 1893	FR	Blackburn Rovers	H	5-4	1,000	Davis 2, Woolhouse, Hall, Rowan
24 Apr 1893	WCC F	Sheffield United	H	0-0	4,000	# Trophy shared
29 Apr 1893	FR	Middlesbrough Ironopolis	H	6-0		Brown 3, H. Brandon, Woolhouse, Davis
18 Aug 1893	PR	Stripes v Whites	H	2-3	3,000	
24 Aug 1893	PR	Stripes v Whites	H	?		
11 Sep 1893	FR	Rotherham Town	H	4-1	1,000	Woolhouse, Rowan, Smith, Webster
9 Oct 1893	FR	Notts County	H	1-2	1,500	Davis
25 Oct 1893	Club Benefit	Gainsborough Trinity	A	2-2	2,000	Spiksley, Rowan
7 Nov 1893	FR	Rotherham Town	A	2-3	1,500	Woolhouse, H. Brandon
4 Dec 1893	TST	Attercliffe & District (Briggs)	H	4-1	700	Barlow 2, McIntosh, Webster
14 Dec 1893	TST	Nottingham Forest (Higgins)	A	1-3	3,000	H. Woolhouse
20 Jan 1894	UCL	Nottingham Forest	H	2-2	6,000	Miller, Jamieson
3 Mar 1894	UCL	Derby County	A	1-1	4,000	H. Brandon
17 Mar 1894	UCL	Notts County	A	1-2	4,000	Brady
24 Mar 1894	FR	Glasgow Battlefield (Scotland)	H	7-1	2,000	Priestley 4, Brown/Mumford, Smith, Lowe
27 Mar 1894	UCL	Sheffield United	A	0-2	9,000	
31 Mar 1894	FR	Queens Park (Scotland)	A	2-1	8,000	Davis 2
7 Apr 1894	UCL	Derby County	H	5-2	1,000	Davis 2, H. Brandon, Brady, F. Woolhouse
9 Apr 1894	UCL	Notts County	H	4-0	800	Davis 2, Spiksley, Brady
14 Apr 1894	UCL	Sheffield United	H	1-1	3,000	Brady
21 Apr 1894	UCL	Nottingham Forest	A	1-5	3,000	Webster
23 Apr 1894	TST	Liverpool (Betts)	H	4-0*	3,000	Davis, Brady, R. Brown
26 Apr 1894	WCC F	Sheffield United	H	0-1	1,000	
28 Apr 1894	FR	Barnsley St Peters	A	2-7	2,000	Davis, H. Woolhouse
21 Aug 1894	PR	Stripes v Whites	H	?		
24 Aug 1894	PR	Stripes v Whites	H	?		
12 Sep 1894	FR	Lincoln City	A	3-5	900	Clifford, 2 n/k
24 Sep 1894	FR	Leicester Fosse	A	3-5	1,000	H. Woolhouse, Brady, Ferrier
1 Oct 1894	FR	Lincoln City	H	5-0	300	Brady 2, F. Woolhouse, H. Woolhouse, Webster
11 Oct 1894	FR	Barnsley St Peters	A	2-3	2,000	Crawshaw, Webster
20 Oct 1894	FR	Blackpool	A	2-2	2,500	Spiksley, Davis
23 Oct 1894	FR	Gainsborough Trinity	A	4-2		Mumford 2, Gribben, n/k
12 Nov 1894	FR	Heart of Midlothian	H	2-3		H. Brandon, Spiksley
26 Nov 1894	FR	Rotherham Town	H	2-1	500	H. Brandon, Crawshaw

Date	Comp	Opposition	Venue	Res	Att	Scorers
24 Dec 1894	FR	Rotherham Town	A	1-2		Ferrier
26 Jan 1895	FR	Long Eaton Rangers	H	5-2	1,500	Fox, F. Woolhouse, Lowe, Gribben, H. Woolhouse
9 Feb 1895	UCL	Notts County	A	2-0	1,000	Ferrier, Brady
4 Mar 1895	UCL	Notts County	H	5-2	200	Spiksley 2, Brash 2, Brady
8 Apr 1895	UCL	Sheffield United	A	0-0	3,000	
20 Apr 1895	UCL	Sheffield United	H	1-1	3,000	T. Crawshaw
25 Apr 1895	TST	Ardsley & District (Mahon)	A	1-0		Fox
21 Aug 1895	PR	Stripes v Whites	H	?		
9 Sep 1895	FR	Liverpool	H	4-2		Davis 2, Bell, Callaghan
21 Sep 1895	FR	Millwall Athletic	A	2-2*	4,000	Spiksley
23 Sep 1895	FR	Woolwich Arsenal	A	1-2	2,000	Davis
14 Oct 1895	FR	Wath Upon-Dearne	A	2-0	2,000	Richards, n/k
18 Nov 1895	FR	St Bernard's (Scotland)	H	1-0	1,000	Brady
5 Dec 1895	TST	Notts County (Calderhead)	A	3-1	500	Brash, Ferrier, Callaghan
13 Jan 1896	BSC1	Small Heath	H	2-1	2,000	Bell, Davis
23 Jan 1896	FR	Millwall Athletic	A	3-1	2,000	Davis, Bell, Brash
25 Jan 1896	FR	Swindon Town	N*	4-0	250	Davis, T. Crawshaw, Brady, Ferrier *played at the Crystal Palace, London
10 Feb 1896	BSC2	Aston Villa	H	3-4	8,000	Brash, Davis, Brandon
2 Mar 1896	TST	Sheffield United (Mumford)	H	0-5	2,000	
8 Apr 1896	FR	Liverpool	A	0-1		
27 Apr 1896	FR	Newcastle United	A	4-1	5,000	Callaghan 2, Richards, Ferrier
28 Apr 1896	FR	Third Lanark	A	0-1	2,000	
29 Apr 1896	FR	Heart of Midlothian	A	0-3	4,000	
30 Apr 1896	FR	St Mirren	A	1-0		Brash
24 Aug 1896	PR	Stripes v Whites	H	0-2		
27 Aug 1896	PR	Stripes v Whites	H	?		
30 Dec 1896	TST	The Corinthians (Spiksley)	H	4-4*	6,000	Brady 2, Brash
13 Feb 1897	SDL	Sheffield United	A	0-0	8,000	
20 Mar 1897	FR	The Corinthians	A	2-1	4,000	T. Crawshaw, Davis
22 Mar 1897	FR	Southampton St Mary's	A	1-4	4,000	Gillies
24 Mar 1897	FR	Eastbourne	A	4-0	2,500	Ferrier 3, Davis
25 Mar 1897	FR	Brighton Athletic	A	2-0		Ferrier 2
27 Mar 1897	FR	Crystal Palace	A	4-0		Ferrier, Spiksley, Brady, Brash
19 Apr 1897	SDL	Sheffield United	H	2-1	2,000	Bell, Davis
24 Apr 1897	FR	Leicester Fosse	A	0-1	2,000	
23 Aug 1897	PR	Stripes v Whites	H	1-1	5,000	
30 Oct 1897	FR	Corinthians	A	0-2	7,000	
28 Dec 1897	TST	Notts County (H. Brandon)	H	1-1	3,000	Dryburgh
26 Feb 1898	FR	Sheffield United	A	4-1	2,500	Brady 2, Kaye 2
23 Mar 1898	FR	Casuals	A	2-4	2,000	Beech, Davis
2 Apr 1898	FR	Millwall Athletic	A	1-2	5,000	Davis
12 Apr 1898	FR	Distillery	N. Ireland	3-0	6,000	Kaye 3
30 Apr 1898	FR	Cumberland County	A	6-2	4,000	Brady 2, Earp 2, Davis, Spiksley

Date	Comp	Opposition	Venue	Res	Att	Scorers
23 Aug 1898	PR	Stripes v Whites	H	2-1	4,000	
26 Aug 1898	PR	Stripes v Whites	H	?		
29 Aug 1898	PR	Stripes v Whites	H	?		
30 Jan 1899	TST	Notts County (Davis)	H	1-3	<1,000	Ernest
13 Mar 1899	TST	Aston Villa (Davis)	H	2-0	3,000	Richards 2
3 Apr 1899	FR	Queens Park	H	0-0	6,000	
8 Apr 1899	FR	Queens Park	Scotland	0-1	6,000	
21 Aug 1899	PR	Stripes v Whites	H*		2,000	
24 Aug 1899	PR	Stripes v Whites	H*	?		* played at Niagara Grounds, Wadsley Bridge
28 Aug 1899	PR	Stripes v Whites	H*			
28 Oct 1899	FR	The Corinthians	A	1-1	5,000	Millar
26 Dec 1899	FR	Sheffield United	A	1-0	18,000	Wright
20 Aug 1900	PR	Stripes v Whites	H	1-4	3,000	
22 Aug 1900	PR	Stripes v Whites	H	4-1		
27 Aug 1900	PR	Stripes v Whites	H			
3 Sep 1900	FR	Barnsley	A	1-1	1,500	Millar
28 Dec 1900	TST	The Casuals (Langley)	H	4-2*	3,000	Chapman 2, Simpson
23 Feb 1901	FR	The Corinthians	A	2-1	1,500	Spiksley, Chapman
14 Mar 1901	TST	Notts County (Bull)	A	2-1	1,000	Pryce 2
21 Aug 1901	PR	Stripes v Whites	H	1-2	3,000	
28 Aug 1901	PR	Stripes v Whites	H	2-0	2,000	
28 Sep 1901	FR	Barrow	A	5-2	5,000	Spiksley 2, Chapman, Wright, Wilson
30 Dec 1901	TST	The Corinthians (T. Crawshaw)	H	3-4	8,000	Wilson, Malloch, Spiksley
8 Feb 1902	FR	The Corinthians	A	4-1	1,000	Ruddlesdin 2, Dryburgh 2
24 Apr 1902	TST	Doncaster Rovers (Longdon)	A	1-0	1,500	Wilson
3 May 1902	Charity	(Ibrox) Sheffield United	H	3-0	4,747	Beech, Wilson, Spiksley
22 Aug 1902	PR	Stripes v Whites	H	0-2	4,000	
25 Oct 1902	FR	The Corinthians	A	1-1	2,000	Malloch
29 Dec 1902	TST	The Corinthians (Ferrier)	H	5-3	7,000	G. Simpson 2, Bartlett, Davis, V. Simpson
21 Feb 1903	FR	Portsmouth	A	2-1	8,000	Wilson, Spiksley
7 Mar 1903	FR	Heavy Woollen League (Dewsbury)	A	2-2	3,000	T. Crawshaw, Chapman
25 Apr 1903	PB	Notts County	N*	2-0	16,000	Malloch, Ruddlesdin *played at Plymouth
27 Apr 1903	FR	Bristol City	A	2-2	300	Spiksley, Chapman
28 Apr 1903	FR	Aberaman	Wales	6-0		Spiksley 2, Chapman, Ferrier, T. Crawshaw, n/k
22 Aug 1903	PR	Stripes v Whites	H	3-3	7,000	
5 Oct 1903	FR	Sheffield United	A	3-1	10,158	G. Simpson, Wilson, Stewart
29 Dec 1903	TST	The Corinthians (Layton)	H	1-1	4,815	Hoyland
24 Aug 1904	PR	Stripes v Whites	H	3-0	4,000	
29 Aug 1904	PR	Stripes v Whites	H	0-2	2,000	
3 Oct 1904	Charity	Sheffield United	H	0-2	7,991	
19 Apr 1905	FR	Buxton	A	3-4	n/k	Stewart, Brittleton, Davis
24 Apr 1905	SLC	The Corinthians	N*	2-1	15,000	Wilson 2 * played at Crystal Palace
24 Aug 1905	PR	Stripes v Whites	H	0-1	2,000	

Date	Comp	Opposition	Venue	Res	Att	Scorers
2 Oct 1905	Charity	Sheffield United	A	3-3	8,493	Brittleton 2, Wilson
23 Aug 1906	PR	Stripes v Whites	H	0-4		
25 Aug 1906	PR	Stripes v Whites	H	1-1	7,000	
1 Oct 1906	Charity	Sheffield United	H	3-0	6,500	Wilson, Tummon, Davis (pen)
30 Apr 1907	FR	Buxton	A	5-1		Wilson 3, Bradshaw, T. Crawshaw
24 Aug 1907	PR	Stripes v Whites	H	1-2	5,000	
18 Sep 1907	FR	Gainsborough Trinity	A	3-2	2,000	Bradshaw 2, Foxall
7 Oct 1907	Charity	Sheffield United	A	1-1	11,000	Chapman
1 Feb 1908	FR	Bradford Park Avenue	A	0-2	8,000	
22 Aug 1908	PR	Stripes v Whites	H	2-2	4,000	
5 Oct 1908	Charity	Sheffield United	H	0-0	7,306	
28 Aug 1909	PR	Stripes v Whites	H	0-1	4,000	
4 Oct 1909	Charity	Sheffield United	A	3-1	10,264	Rollinson 3
27 Aug 1910	PR	Stripes v Whites	H	3-0	4,500	
3 Oct 1910	Charity	Sheffield United	H	2-0	5,000	Dowling, Wilson
27 Apr 1911	HHC	Hull City	A	1-3	6,000	McLean
21 May 1911	FR	Orgryte	Sweden	5-0		Spoors (pen), McLean, Kirkman, Wilson, Robertson
23 May 1911	FR	Swedish Select	Sweden	2-1		McLean 2
25 May 1911	FR	Denmark	Denmark	3-2	8,000	McLean, Glennon, n/k
26 May 1911	FR	Copenhagen XI	Denmark	3-2		McLean, Kirkman, Glennon
28 May 1911	FR	Denmark	Denmark	3-2		Wilson 2, n/k
26 Aug 1911	PR	Stripes v Whites	H	2-3	7,000	
2 Oct 1911	Charity	Sheffield United	A	0-2	8,326	
24 Aug 1912	PR	Stripes v Whites	H	1-0	8,000	
7 Oct 1912	Charity	Sheffield United	H	3-0	7,566	Wright 2, Lloyd
23 Aug 1913	PR	Stripes v Whites	H	5-4	12,000	
30 Apr 1914	Charity	Sheffield United	H	0-2	5,000	
22 Aug 1914	PR	Stripes v Whites	H	5-3	15,652	
5 Oct 1914	Charity	Sheffield United	H	2-0	6,000	Glennon, McLean
23 Aug 1915	PR	Stripes v Whites	H	3-2	4,000	
6 May 1916	Charity	Sheffield United	A	0-3	6,000	
7 Apr 1917	FR	Birmingham FC	A	0-0	5,000	
5 May 1917	Charity	Sheffield United	A	2-1	5,000	Glennon, Burkinshaw
13 Apr 1918	Charity	Sheffield United	H	2-0	6,000	Salt, Capper
20 Apr 1918	Charity	Sheffield United	A	1-1	6,000	Brittleton
4 May 1918	FR	Liverpool	A	1-1		Burkinshaw
11 May 1918	FR	Liverpool	H	3-1	6,000	Glennon 2, Lamb
5 Apr 1919	FR	Sheffield United	A	1-0	12,000	Spoors (pen)
12 Apr 1919	FR	Sheffield United	H	0-1	8,000	
3 May 1919	Charity	Rotherham County	H	3-1	5,000	Gill 2, Glennon
24 May 1919	FR	Everton	H	1-4	8,000	Glennon
31 May 1919	FR	Everton	A	2-1	5,000	Glennon 2
23 Aug 1919	PR	Stripes v Whites	H	2-1	7,000	

Date	Comp	Opposition	Venue	Res	Att	Scorers
31 Jan 1920	FR	Derby County	H	2-1	5,000	MacKay, W. Taylor
13 Dec 1920	FR	Merthyr Town	Wales	1-0	1,000	Binney
14 May 1921	SHCC SF	Rotherham County	H	1-0	10,000	S. Taylor
21 May 1921	SHCC F	Sheffield United	H	1-2	21,203	S. Taylor
20 Aug 1921	PR	Stripes v Whites	H	1-1	8,000	
24 Apr 1922	SHCC SF	Rotherham County	H	1-0	6,000	Lofthouse
13 May 1922	SHCC F	Barnsley	A	1-2	15,000	Binks
19 Aug 1922	PR	Stripes v Whites	H	2-2	9,283	
25 Sep 1922	FR	Swansea Town	Wales	0-1	10,000	
26 Sep 1922	FR	Ton Pentre	Wales	1-1	2,000	Lowdell
10 Mar 1923	FR	The Corinthians	H	3-2	12,000	Binks 2, S. Taylor
26 Mar 1923	FR	Bishop Auckland	A	0-2	4,000	
3 Apr 1923	FR	Boscombe	A	1-0		Harron
9 Apr 1923	SHCC SF	Rotherham County	A	0-1		
19 Apr 1923	TST	Sheffield United (Waller)	A	2-0	25,000	Petrie, Harron
18 Aug 1923	PR	Stripes v Whites	H	3-4	6,000	
19 Sep 1923	FR	York City	A	1-1	1,500	S. Taylor
31 Dec 1923	SHCC SF	Barnsley	H	5-1	15,419	Walker 3, S. Taylor, Binks
28 Apr 1924	FR	Bishop Auckland	A	3-2		Kean 3
10 May 1924	SHCC F	Sheffield United	H	0-2	15,000	
23 Aug 1924	PR	Stripes v Whites	H	3-2	10,352	
18 Sep 1924	TST	Sheffield United (Nicholson)	A	2-2	17,572	Marsden, Binks
16 Oct 1924	FR	Royal Air Force	H	3-0	5,500	Trotter 2, Weaver
20 Apr 1925	SHCC SF	Barnsley	A	1-2	5,300	Trotter
27 Apr 1925	TST	Rotherham County (Bailey)	A	1-4	2,500	S. Powell
22 Aug 1925	PR	Stripes v Whites	H	4-4	10,594	
9 Nov 1925	SHCC SF	Barnsley	H	3-2	6,000	Prince, Whitworth, Marsden
6 Mar 1926	FR	Kilmarnock	H	6-1	12,000	S. Powell 2, Barress 2, Lowdell, Trotter
3 May 1926	SHCC F	Sheffield United	A	1-3	39,698	Lowdell
21 Aug 1926	PR	Stripes v Whites	H	2-5		
6 Dec 1926	SHCC SF	Rotherham County	A	4-0		Trotter 3, Kirkwood
14 May 1927	SHCC F	Barnsley	H	4-1	15,856	Trotter 2, Strange, Kean
22 Aug 1927	PR	Stripes v Whites	H	4-4	5,000	
14 Nov 1927	FR	Huddersfield Town	H	1-6	4,000	Gilmour
28 Nov 1927	SHCC SF	Sheffield United	H	3-1	10,339	Strange 2, Hill
25 Apr 1928	SHCC F	Rotherham County	H	5-2	15,419	Allen 3, Hill, Wilkinson
18 Aug 1928	PR	Stripes v Whites	H	1-1	9,000	
26 Nov 1928	SHCC SF	Barnsley	H	3-0	4,500	Allen 3
6 May 1929	SHCC F	Sheffield United	H	2-0	11,800	Whitehouse, Hooper
9 May 1929	FR	Young Fellows Club	Switzerland	3-0	6,000	Trotter 2, Gregg
11 May 1929	FR	Nordstern	Switzerland	2-1	10,000	Allen, Trotter
19 May 1929	FR	Cantonal	Switzerland	3-0	6,000	Marsden, Wilson, Hooper
20 May 1929	FR	Grasshoppers	Switzerland	4-0	25,000	Trotter 3, Hooper

Date	Comp	Opposition	Venue	Res	Att	Scorers
22 May 1929	FR	Berne	Switzerland	4-1	4,000	Hooper 2, Allen, n/k
26 May 1929	FR	Lausanne	Switzerland	4-0	1,500	Allen 2, Hooper, Whitehouse
24 Aug 1929	PR	Stripes v Whites	H	10-3	7,000	
9 Sep 1929	TST	Chesterfield (Wass)	A	2-3	1,575	Burgess, Rimmer
21 Oct 1929	SHCC SF	Rotherham United	H	5-2*	3,000	Burgess 4
5 May 1930	SHCC F	Sheffield United	A	1-3	20,000	Leach
23 Aug 1930	PR	Stripes v Whites	H	5-2	3,973	
29 Sep 1930	TST	Stockport County (Bocking/Boardman)	A	1-1	3,000	Allen
3 Nov 1930	SHCC SF	Sheffield United	H	1-2	5,000	Ball
10 Nov 1930	FR	Rotherham United	A	6-0	4,500	Rimmer 3, Gregg 2, Wright
30 Apr 1931	TST	Doncaster Rovers (Buckley)	A	6-2	3,886	Rimmer 2, Allen 2, Stephenson, Jones
22 Aug 1931	PR	Stripes v Whites	H	3-3	5,724	
12 Oct 1931	SHCC SF	Sheffield United	H	4-1	6,000	Burgess, Rimmer, Jones, Ball
25 Apr 1932	SHCC F	Barnsley	N	3-0	4,000	Millership 2, Burgess
15 May 1932	FR	H.B.S (The Hague)	Holland	8-1	8,000	Ball 2, Leach (pen), Millership 2, Hooper, Burgess 2
16 May 1932	FR	Nicholson (Austria)	Holland	2-2	10,000	Burgess, Rimmer
20 Aug 1932	PR	Stripes v Whites	H	6-4	4,000	
19 Sep 1932	HIC	Huddersfield Town	A	1-3	5,025	Law
10 Oct 1932	SHCC F	Sheffield United	A	2-4	8,182	Burgess, Starling
28 Jan 1933	FR	The Corinthians	H	3-1	2,831	Leach, Jones, Millership
18 Apr 1933	TST	Sheffield United (Gibson)	A	1-2	8,182	Leach
24 Apr 1933	SCHC	Scunthorpe United	A	2-1	7,000	Burgess, Hooper
1 May 1933	FR	Linfield	N.Ireland	2-0	15,000	Rimmer, Burgess
3 May 1933	FR	Shelbourne	Eire	4-1*	15,000	Rimmer, Ball, Starling
15 Aug 1933	PR	Stripes v Whites	H	5-2		
19 Aug 1933	PR	Stripes v Whites	H	7-3	3,239	
30 Oct 1933	SHCC SF	Barnsley	A	6-1	3,300	Ball 4, Cooper, Hooper
19 Mar 1934	FR	St Johnstone	H	3-0	1,688	Rimmer, Leach, Law
23 Apr 1934	SCHC	Scunthorpe United	A	3-1	5,000	Starling 2, Burgess
2 May 1934	SCHS	Scarborough	A	2-1	2,700	Dewar, Burgess
12 May 1934	SHCC F	Doncaster Rovers	H	3-0	3,100	Dewar, Cooper, Hooper
27 May 1934	FR	Gaestrickland	Sweden	5-2	8,000	Dewar 4, Rimmer
30 May 1934	FR	AIK	Sweden	5-1		Dewar 2, Starling, Hooper, Oxley
1 Jun 1934	FR	Gothenburg Select	Sweden	3-3		Hooper, Dewar, Starling
3 Jun 1934	FR	Malmo Combined XI	Sweden	9-1		Burgess 4, Cooper 2, Dewar, Starling, Rimmer
6 Jun 1934	FR	Danish Select XI	Denmark	7-0	8,000	Dewar 5, Burgess, Oxley
8 Jun 1934	FR	Danish Select XI	Denmark	6-0	20,000	Dewar 2, Rimmer, Hooper, Oxley, Walker
18 Aug 1934	PR	Stripes v Whites	H	3-0	4,675	
17 Sep 1934	SHCC Pr	Doncaster Rovers	A	3-1	2,520	Dewar 2, Hooper
1 Oct 1934	TST	Halifax Town (Davies)	A	5-3	3,000	Dewar 3, Hooper, Cooper
29 Oct 1934	SHCC SF	Rotherham United	A	0-1	4,332	
10 Dec 1934	FR	FC Austria	H	3-0	12,445	Rimmer 2, Millership
12 Feb 1935	PR	Stripes v Whites	H	1-4	8,000	

Date	Comp	Opposition	Venue	Res	Att	Scorers
3 Apr 1935	TST	Sheffield United (Craig)	H	0-0	1,500	
2 May 1935	SCHC	Scunthorpe United	A	2-1	8,000	Starling, Hooper
6 May 1935	Charity	Grimsby Town	A	1-3	18,000	Starling
17 May 1935	FR	Copenhagen Combined	Denmark	2-1	15,000	Palethorpe 2
19 May 1935	FR	Copenhagen Combined	Denmark	8-2	10,000	Thompson 2, Hooper 2, Bargh 2, Starling 2
21 May 1935	FR	Copenhagen Combined	Denmark	6-2	30,000	Thompson 3, Hooper 2, Rimmer
23 May 1935	FR	AGF Aarhus	Denmark	5-0	7,000	Hooper 2, Rimmer 2, Palethorpe
25 May 1935	FR	Aalborg Select XI	Denmark	3-0*	6,000	Palethorpe, Rimmer
30 May 1935	FR	Racing Club de Paris	France	4-0	8,000	Palethorpe 2, Surtees, Starling
24 Aug 1935	PR	Stripes v Whites	H	2-2	4,431	
4 Sep 1935	FR	Glasgow Rangers	H	1-1	23,986	Dewar
18 Sep 1935	FR	Glasgow Rangers	Scotland	0-2	30,000	
30 Sep 1935	SHCC Pr	Barnsley	A	0-1	5,339	
7 Oct 1935	TST	Southend United (Jones)	A	2-2	3,000	Dewar 2
18 Nov 1935	FR	Sparta & Slavia Select XI	H	4-1	3,241	Dewar 2, Hooper, Rimmer
1 Dec 1935	FR	Ligue Du Nord	France*	2-3	19,000	Dewar 2 * played at Lille
5 May 1936	SCHC	Scunthorpe United	A	3-0	3,500	Rimmer 2, Starling
22 May 1936	FR	Copenhagen Select	Denmark	4-2	10,000	Robinson 3, Rimmer
25 May 1936	FR	Danish Select	Denmark	6-0	15,000	Ashley 3, Robinson 2, Hooper
27 May 1936	FR	Danish Select	Denmark	3-1	10,000	Grosvenor 2, Robinson
22 Aug 1936	PR	Stripes v Whites	H	2-1	4,812	
22 Sep 1936	FR	Swansea Town	Wales	2-3	7,000	Grosvenor, Millership
28 Sep 1936	SHCC Pr	Doncaster Rovers	H	3-0	1,433	Surtess 2, Robinson
30 Nov 1936	SHCC SF	Barnsley	A	1-3	1,871	Burrows (pen)
4 May 1937	SCHC	Scunthorpe United	A	0-3		
21 Aug 1937	PR	Stripes v Whites	H	6-3	3,782	
11 Oct 1937	SHCC Pr	Barnsley	H	0-2	1,086	
13 Aug 1938	PR	Stripes v Whites	H	4-2	4,841	
20 Aug 1938	FR	Sheffield United	H	4-1	14,917	Hunt 3, Lewis
24 Oct 1938	SHCC SF	Rotherham United	A	1-1	1,722	Driver
7 Nov 1938	SHCC SF r	Rotherham United	H	4-1		Hunt 4
8 May 1939	SHCC F	Sheffield United	A	0-0	13,907	* Trophy shared
10 May 1939	SCHC	Scunthorpe United	A	3-1	9,000	Robinson, Hunt 2
14 Aug 1939	PR	Stripes v Whites	H	2-1	1,857	
19 Aug 1939	FR	Sheffield United	H	2-4	11,378	Napier, Toseland
23 Sep 1939	FR	Barnsley	A	2-1	3,800	Lowes, Dillon
30 Sep 1939	FR	Rotherham United	A	2-4	2,900	Driver, Hunt
7 Oct 1939	FR	Nottingham Forest	A	2-1	4,352	Robinson, Massarella
14 Oct 1939	FR	Huddersfield Town	H	5-4	3,669	Millership 2, Ward, Hunt, Massarella
16 Dec 1939	FR	Stoke City	H	1-2	2,708	Ward
25 Dec 1939	FR	Sheffield United	A	1-2	15,000	Hunt
30 Dec 1939	FR	Halifax Town	A	0-0	1,500	
1 Jan 1940	FR	Barnsley	A	0-5	1,680	

Date	Comp	Opposition	Venue	Res	Att	Scorers
17 Feb 1940	FR	Manchester City	A	1-3*	3,000	
9 Mar 1940	FR	Bolton Wanderers	H	3-3	2,686	Massarella 2, Millership
25 Mar 1940	FR	Leicester City	A	2-5	2,500	Driver, Millership
25 May 1940	FR	Northampton Town	A	7-2	3,000	Thompson 4, Ward 2, Scholfield
4 Sep 1940	FR	Army XI	H	4-2		Thompson 3, Rogers
14 Sep 1940	FR	Notts County	H	3-1	2,052	Ward 3
8 Sep 1941	FR	Army XI	H	5-2		Ward 2, Drury 2, Cockroft (pen)
21 Aug 1943	FR	Sheffield United	A	2-3	6,889	Everitt, Rogers
19 Aug 1944	Charity	Huddersfield Town	H	3-2	3,767	Froggatt 2, Tomlinson
15 Apr 1946	SHCC Pr	Sheffield United	H	1-0	18,060	Robinson
29 Apr 1946	SHCC SF	Rotherham United	A	2-1	7,964	Lindsay 2
8 May 1946	SHCC F1L	Barnsley	A	1-1	10,242	Tomlinson
11 May 1946	SHCC F2L	Barnsley	H	1-0	18,279	Kippax
18 May 1946	FR	Copenhagen Select	Denmark	2-4	12,700	Robinson, Ward
20 May 1946	FR	Copenhagen Select	Denmark	2-2		Robinson 2
22 May 1946	FR	Copenhagen Select	Denmark	1-1	27,000	Froggatt
24 May 1946	FR	Malmo	Sweden	9-2		Froggatt 3, Driver 2, Robinson 2, Ward, Rogers
24 Aug 1946	PR	Stripes v Whites	H	1-2	4,079	
9 Dec 1946	FR	Copenhagen Combination (Denmark)	H	2-3	7,000	Ward 2
29 Apr 1948	TST	Scunthorpe United (Allcock/Lloyd)	A	3-2	8,080	Woodhead, Jordan, Witcomb (pen)
3 May 1948	SHCC SF	Rotherham United	A	4-1	12,200	Froggatt, Woodhead, Quigley, Jordan
8 May 1948	SHCC F	Barnsley	H	1-3	22,619	Froggatt
17 May 1948	FR	Sheffield United	Isle of Man*	2-2	8,000	Quigley 2 *played at Douglas
14 Aug 1948	PR	Stripes v Whites	H	2-0	9,051	
15 Jan 1949	FR	Chelsea	H	2-0	23,114	Dailey, Woodhead
12 Feb 1949	SHCC SF	Sheffield United	H	2-4	49,980	Quigley 2 (1 pen)
13 Aug 1949	PR	Stripes v Whites	H	2-1	8,708	
8 May 1950	SHCC SF	Barnsley	H	3-1	11,000	Henry (pen), Rogers, Tomlinson
13 May 1950	SHCC F	Sheffield United	H	2-1	31,861	Tomlinson, McJarrow
16 May 1950	FR	Norrkoping	Sweden	2-2	7,750	Henry 2 (1 pen)
18 May 1950	FR	Copenhagen Select	Denmark	1-0		Woodhead
20 May 1950	FR	Copenhagen Select	Denmark	4-0		Henry 3, Rogers
23 May 1950	FR	Denmark XI	Denmark	0-1		
12 Aug 1950	PR	Stripes v Whites	H	2-1	6,166	
27 Jan 1951	FR	Leicester City	A	0-1	7,859	
10 Feb 1951	SHCC SF	Sheffield United	H	2-0	40,660	Marriott, McJarrow
12 May 1951	SHCC F	Doncaster Rovers	H	2-1	24,081	Woodhead 2 (1 pen)
16 May 1951	FOB	Frem (Denmark)	H	0-0	13,900	
13 Aug 1951	PR	Stripes v Whites	H	5-3	3,523	
29 Apr 1952	WIC	Manchester City	Kendal	1-1	13,816	Quixall
5 May 1952	SHCC SF	Sheffield United	H	1-3	20,327	Marriott
13 May 1952	FR	Bellinzona XI	Switzerland	2-2	10,000	Sewell, Dooley
14 May 1952	FR	Swiss Trial Side	Switzerland	1-2	10,000	Froggatt

Date	Comp	Opposition	Venue	Res	Att	Scorers
18 May 1952	FR	Inter Milan (Italy)	Switzerland	1-2		Quixall * played at Geneva
21 May 1952	FR	St Gallen	Switzerland	5-1		Quixall 2, Dooley, Froggatt, Marriott
22 May 1952	FR	German Select XI	Switzerland	0-3		* played at Berne
16 Aug 1952	PR	Stripes v Whites	H	2-0	7,987	
28 Apr 1953	WIC	Huddersfield Town	Kendal	1-2	4,000	Froggatt
4 May 1953	SHCC Pr	Doncaster Rovers	H	2-1	8,100	Codd, Jordan
9 May 1953	SHCC SF	Rotherham United	A	0-7	9,732	
15 Aug 1953	PR	Stripes v Whites	H	2-0	4,000	
4 Nov 1953	FR	South Africa	H	9-3	5,298	Shaw 4, Sewell 2, Woodhead 2, Marriott
9 Nov 1953	FR	Derby County	A	1-3*	7,716	
27 Apr 1954	SHCC SF	Rotherham United	H	3-5	9,514	J.McAnearney 2, Gannon
9 May 1954	FR	Desportes (Brazil)	Belgium	0-6	10,000	* played at Antwerp
13 May 1954	FR	Bangu (Brazil)	France	5-3	25,000	Shaw 3, Froggatt, Woodhead * played at Paris
19 May 1954	FR	Sedan	France	0-4	25,000	* played at Paris
25 Oct 1954	SHCC SF	Doncaster Rovers	A	3-1	14,000	J.McAnearney, Shaw, Froggatt
14 May 1955	SHCC F	Rotherham United	H	2-4	11,979	Watson, McEvoy * AET 90 mins 2-2
10 Oct 1955	FR	Vasas Budapest (Hungary)	H	1-7	45,983	Quixall
2 Nov 1955	SHCC Pr	Sheffield United	H	2-5	16,158	Froggatt, Shiner
26 Jan 1956	FR	San Lorenzo (Argentina)	H	9-0	8,644	Finney 3, Shiner 3, Froggatt, Howells, Broadbent
28 Jan 1956	FR	Luton Town	H	2-2	11,000	Finney 2 (1 pen)
30 Apr 1956	FR	Leeds United	A	3-3	15,319	Shiner 2, Broadbent
5 May 1956	Charity	Vasco Da Gama (Brazil)	Holland	0-2	25,000	* played at Amsterdam
9 May 1956	FR	Wuppertal	Germany	3-3	10,000	Broadbent 2, Shiner
22 Oct 1956	FR	CCA (Romania)	H	3-3	35,811	Froggatt 2, Broadbent
29 Oct 1956	SHCC Pr	Rotherham United	H	0-1	8,912	
6 Dec 1956	FR	Zagreb (Croatia)	H	1-1	19,401	Shiner
1 Apr 1957	FR	Norwich City	A	2-0	9,650	Ellis, Shiner
27 Apr 1957	FR	Grimsby Town	A	1-1	6,000	Ellis
30 Apr 1957	FR	Stocksbridge Works	A	1-1		Broadbent
4 Nov 1957	FR	Gwardia (Poland)	H	4-4	14,735	Shiner 2, Froggatt, D. Wilkinson
28 Nov 1957	FR	Juventus (Italy)	H	3-4	44,560	Shiner, Quixall, Froggatt
4 Dec 1957	SHCC SF	Barnsley	H	7-0	4,900	Quixall 2, Ellis 2, D. Wilkinson 2, Froggatt
28 Apr 1958	TST	Kings Lynn (Bannister)	A	4-3		Quixall 2, Shiner, Hill
30 Apr 1958	SHCC F	Sheffield United	H	0-3	21,289	
1 May 1958	TST	Hyde United (Rodgers)	A	6-3*		Wilkinson 2, Gibson 2, Johnson
2 May 1958	FR	Bedford United	A	3-0*	5,500	Shiner, Fantham
5 Nov 1958	FR	Napoli (Italy)	H	6-0	29,589	Curtis 2 (2 pens), Finney, Fantham, J. McAnearney, Shiner
28 Apr 1959	SHCC SF	Doncaster Rovers	H	5-2		Griffin 2 (1 pen), Curtis (pen), Shiner, Finney
4 May 1959	SHCC F	Sheffield United	H	1-4	18,221	Shiner
12 Oct 1959	SHCC Pr	Sheffield United	A	1-3	10,953	Fantham
23 Nov 1959	FR	Torpedo Moscow (Russia)	H	2-1	35,098	Finney, Ellis
24 May 1960	FR	CSKA Moscow	Russia	0-1	50,000	
28 May 1960	FR	Dynamo Tblisi	Georgia	0-1	26,000	

Date	Comp	Opposition	Venue	Res	Att	Scorers
1 Jun 1960	FR	Lokomotiv Moscow	Russia	2-3		Finney 2
7 Nov 1960	FR	Dinamo Tblisi (Georgia)	H	5-0	38,778	Fantham 4, Ellis
29 Nov 1960	SHCC Pr	Doncaster Rovers	H	3-0	4,811	Griffin 2, Ballagher
10 May 1961	FR	Western Region	Nigeria	11-2		Young 5, 6 n/k
13 May 1961	FR	NFA Eagles	Nigeria	1-0		Ellis
17 May 1961	FR	Eastern Region	Nigeria	2-1		Dobson, T. McAnearney (pen)
21 May 1961	FR	Northern Nigeria	Nigeria	2-2		Frye, Ellis
13 Aug 1961	FR	Ajax	Holland	2-1		Craig, Fantham
2 May 1962	SHCC Pr	Sheffield United	A	2-3	12,089	Fantham, D.Wilkinson
12 Aug 1962	FR	Ajax Amsterdam	Holland	1-3		Dobson
17 Oct 1962	TST	Ajax Amsterdam (Froggatt)	H	2-2	21,810	Layne, Johnson
22 Oct 1962	FR	Santos	H	2-4	49,058	Griffin, Layne
30 Oct 1962	TST	Bristol Rovers (Williams)	A	6-2	7,061	Fantham 4, Ellis, Dobson
26 Jan 1963	FR	Grimsby Town	A	2-2	5,377	Dobson, Holliday
17 Aug 1963	FR	Southampton	A	3-3	7,606	Layne 2, Fantham
25 Jan 1964	FR	Norwich City	A	1-2	8,921	Layne
29 Apr 1964	TST	Buxton (Rennie)	A	9-0		Ford 2, Quinn 2, Dobson 2, Fantham 2, Young
8 Aug 1964	FR	Kaiserslautern	Germany	1-2	12,000	Fantham
13 Aug 1964	FR	Werder Bremen	Germany	0-1		
30 Sep 1964	FR	AGF Aarhus	Denmark	1-4	5,000	D. Wilkinson
6 Oct 1964	FR	German Select	Germany	0-0	30,000	* played at Dusseldorf
8 Mar 1965	FR	Werder Bremen	H	2-3	18,942	Hickton 2
1 May 1965	FR	Polish Select XI	Poland	1-2	70,000	Fantham * played at Katowice
5 May 1965	FR	Warsaw Combination	Poland	0-1	15,000	
8 May 1965	FR	Valencia	Spain	0-3		* played at Madrid
10 May 1965	FR	Shamrock Rovers	Eire	4-3		Hickton 2, Fantham, Dobson
5 Aug 1965	FR	Levski Sofia	Bulgaria	1-2	25,000	Hickton
7 Aug 1965	FR	Stara Zagore	Bulgaria	1-4		Hickton
8 Aug 1965	FR	Cherno More	Bulgaria	1-2		Quinn
6 Oct 1965	FR	Dutch International XI	Holland	3-3	25,000	Quinn, Hickton, Dobson(pen) * played at Rotterdam
19 May 1966	TST	Doncaster Rovers (Finney)	A	5-6	7,027	Eustace, Branfoot, Fantham, McCalliog, Ford
27 May 1966	FR	Hong Kong Select	Hong Kong	2-1	12,848	Quinn, Ellis (Ford, Ellis in foreign match report)
1 Jun 1966	FR	Fulham	Hong Kong	5-2	17,853	Ford 2, Pugh, Quinn, Eustace
5 Jun 1966	FR	Asian All Stars	Malaysia	5-1	20,000	Pugh 2, McCalliog 2, Eustace * played at Kuala-Lumpur
9 Jun 1966	FR	Asian Select XI	Malaysia	1-2	20,000	Ford * played at Ipoh
11 Jun 1966	FR	Fulham	Malaysia	3-5	12,000	Ford, Eustace (pen), McCalliog * played at Kuala-Lumpur
14 Jun 1966	FR	Fulham	Singapore	2-4	10,000	Usher, Ford
23 Jul 1966	FR	Spartak Varna	Bulgaria	2-2		Ford, Pugh
25 Jul 1966	FR	Cherno More	Bulgaria	4-4*		Quinn, Fantham 2
27 Jul 1966	FR	Drobuga	Bulgaria	1-1		Symm
8 Aug 1966	FR	Bulgarian Select XI	H	2-1	19,441	Pugh, McCalliog
26 Sep 1966	TST	All Star XI (Wilkinson)	H	8-7	10,096	Springett 4, Ford 2, Quinn, McCalliog
17 Oct 1966	TST	Northern All Stars (Keen)	A	3-6	1,311	Pugh 2, Ford * played at Gateshead

Date	Comp	Opposition	Venue	Res	Att	Scorers
16 Jan 1967	OL	Hartlepool United	A	3-3	6,241	Mobley, McCalliog, Branfoot
3 Mar 1967	FR	Charlton Athletic	A	1-1	6,011	Ritchie
26 Apr 1967	TST	Sheffield United (Shaw)	A	2-3	15,135	McCalliog, Ford
22 May 1967	Charity	Wellington Town	A	4-1	3,033	Whitham 2, Ford, Ritchie
4 Jun 1967	FR	Toluca	Mexico*	4-1	40,000	Ritchie 2, Ford 2
11 Jun 1967	FR	Mexican Select	Mexico*	0-5	45,000	
18 Jun 1967	FR	Deportivo Español (Spain)	Mexico*	0-2		
20 Jun 1967	FR	Bologna (Italy)	Mexico*	0-1		
22 Jun 1967	FR	FC América	Mexico*	1-1		Megson * all games played at the Aztec Stadium, Mexico City
25 Sep 1967	TST	Sheffield United (Springett)	H	3-2	23,070	Whitham, Ritchie, Eustace
18 Oct 1967	OL	Chesterfield	A	2-0	12,358	Symm, Usher
21 Nov 1967	TST	Barnsley (Brookes/Winstanley)	A	2-2	8,478	Ford, Eustace (pen)
16 May 1968	FR	GAZ Club	Austria	0-2		
18 May 1968	FR	Salzburg	Austria	2-0		Ford, Ritchie
29 Jul 1968	FR	Ards	N. Ireland	2-1		Fantham 2
1 Aug 1968	FR	Glentoran	N. Ireland	3-0	6,000	Fantham 2, Whitham
10 Sep 1968	TST	Sheffield United (Hodgkinson)	A	2-2	15,604	Woodall, Warboys
16 Oct 1968	FR	Flanders Select XI	France	1-3	2,000	Eustace (pen)
5 Feb 1969	TST	Hereford United (Evans/Purcell)	A	4-2	5,000	Whitham, Fantham, Pugh, Mobley
24 Mar 1969	FR	Bradford City	A	1-2	4,437	Ritchie
24 Jul 1969	FR	Rhyl	A	2-0	2,500	Ford, Woodall
30 Jul 1969	FR	Aberdeen	H	2-1	10,075	Fantham, Ford
2 Aug 1969	FR	Italy U21's	H	2-0	8,064	Fantham, Eustace
4 Aug 1969	FR	Airdrie	H	1-2	5,804	Prendergast
30 Sep 1969	TST	International XI (Megson)	H	7-7	10,961	Warboys 4, Young, Whitham, Ford
25 Apr 1970	TST	Sheffield United (Young)	H	3-3	12,120	Whitham 2, Warboys
2 May 1970	AIC	Napoli	H	4-3	10,166	Warboys 2, Downes 2
9 May 1970	AIC	Juventus	H	0-0	9,495	
16 May 1970	AIC	Napoli	Italy	1-5	30,000	Sinclair
20 May 1970	FR	Savoia	Italy	2-0		Craig 2
23 May 1970	AIC	Juventus	Italy	0-2	3,000	
1 Aug 1970	FR	Notts County	A	2-1	2,900	Lawson, Prendergast
4 Aug 1970	FR	Huddersfield Town	A	0-5	9,425	
7 Aug 1970	FR	Tranmere Rovers	A	0-0	2,661	
15 Mar 1971	FR	British Olympic XI	H	3-1	3,000	Prendergast, Pugh, Prudham
31 Jul 1971	FR	Ards	N. Ireland	2-0	1,000	Thompson, Sunley
2 Aug 1971	FR	Glentoran	N. Ireland	1-1	500	Downes
5 Aug 1971	FR	Drumcondra	Eire	4-1		Prendergast 2, Sinclair, Craig (pen)
9 Aug 1971	FR	Sheffield United	A	2-2	18,000	Downes, Prendergast
16 Nov 1971	FR	Werder Bremen	H	2-0	5,193	Joicey, Sinclair
2 Feb 1972	OL	Rhyl	A	3-1		Craig (pen), Holsgrove, Joicey
5 Feb 1972	FR	Chesterfield	A	1-2	8,673	Joicey
23 Feb 1972	FR	Santos	H	0-2	36,996	

Date	Comp	Opposition	Venue	Res	Att	Scorers
29 Jul 1972	FR	East Fife	Scotland	3-1	4,565	Joicey 2, Prendergast
2 Aug 1972	FR	St Johnstone	Scotland	3-1*	3,800	Holsgrove, Prendergast
5 Aug 1972	FR	Dunfermline	Scotland	4-2*	3,000	Holsgrove, Clements, Prendergast
1 Nov 1972	SHCC SF	Rotherham United	H	3-0	6,185	Sunley, Joicey, Eustace (pen)
20 Mar 1973	FR	Sheffield United	A	1-1	23,540	Joicey
20 Jul 1973	VIF	Vasterhaninge	Sweden	1-3	1,208	Joicey
23 Jul 1973	VIF	IFK Eskilstuna	Sweden	4-2	1,843	Sunley 2, Craig (pen), Mullen
27 Jul 1973	VIF 3PO	Sandvikens IF	Sweden	2-0	500	Sunley 2
30 Jul 1973	FR	Norrkoping	Sweden	2-1		Mullen, Craig
13 Aug 1973	FR	Southend United	A	0-0	2,845	
15 Aug 1973	FR	Gillingham	A	1-0	2,875	Prendergast
26 Jan 1974	SHCC F	Sheffield United	H	0-0	18,869	Won 4-3 on penalties
6 May 1974	SHCC SF	Rotherham United	A	0-0	4,506	Lost 4-3 on penalties
9 May 1974	TST	Sheffield United (Woodward)	A	3-3	10,543	Prudham 2, Potts
29 Jul 1974	FR	Clyde	Scotland	4-0	1,000	Craig 3 (1 pen), Sunley
31 Jul 1974	FR	Kilmarnock	Scotland	1-0	4,000	Prudham
3 Aug 1974	FR	Dundee United	Scotland	1-1		Sunley
10 Aug 1974	FR	Port Vale	A	1-2	1,596	Joicey
21 Oct 1974	TST	England All Star XI (Taylor)	H	0-5	10,939	
25 Jan 1975	FR	Burnley	H	1-3	2,587	Ferguson
4 Feb 1975	SHCC SF	Doncaster Rovers	H	1-1	2,100	Wylde
18 Feb 1975	SHCC SF r	Doncaster Rovers	A	2-0	4,207	Potts, Henson
14 Apr 1975	FR	Morton	H	2-0	1,676	Sunley 2
28 Apr 1975	TST	Worksop Town (Reid)	A	2-0	2,002	Henson, Herbert
8 May 1975	TST	Goole Town (Hague)	A	2-2	831	Mullen, Wylde
29 Jul 1975	FR	Kilmarnock	Scotland	0-1	4,000	
1 Aug 1975	FR	Motherwell	Scotland	0-2		
6 Aug 1975	FR	York City	A	2-1	2,097	Prendergast, Joicey
11 Aug 1975	FR	Coventry City	H	0-3	3,986	
14 Oct 1975	SHCC F	Sheffield United	A	2-1	14,663	Shaw, Joicey (1974–75 Final)
9 Feb 1976	SHCC Pr	Sheffield United	A	0-2	9,498	
8 May 1976	FR	Boston United	A	1-2		Nimmo
10 May 1976	TST	Sheffield United (Latham)	A	0-0	6,495	
31 Jul 1976	Shipp	Peterborough United	H	3-2	3,275	Feely, Prendergast, Potts
4 Aug 1976	Shipp	Lincoln City	H	1-0	3,923	Potts (pen)
7 Aug 1976	Shipp	Cambridge United	A	5-2	1,309	Wylde 2, Feely 2, Nimmo
12 Oct 1976	SHCC SF	Sheffield United	A	0-2	6,985	
13 Nov 1976	FR	Burnley	H	2-1	2,822	Wylde, Tynan
21 Feb 1977	TST	Norwich City (O'Donnell)	H	2-0	5,739	Wylde, McKeown
25 Apr 1977	TST	Leicester City (Prendergast)	H	2-3	3,179	Mullen, Nimmo
9 May 1977	TST	Select XI (Prendergast)	A	2-2		Tynan, Wylde * played at Denaby United FC
10 May 1977	FR	Hartlepool	A	6-0		Wylde, Tynan, Cusack (pen), Davis, Walden, Potts
30 Jul 1977	Shipp	Peterborough United	A	2-0	2,954	Rushbury, Tynan

Date	Comp	Opposition	Venue	Res	Att	Scorers
2 Aug 1977	Shipp	Cambridge United	A	2-3	1,973	Nimmo 2
6 Aug 1977	Shipp	Huddersfield Town	H	0-2	3,840	
7 Jan 1978	SHCC SF	Doncaster Rovers	H	1-1	1,937	Nimmo
13 Mar 1978	SHCC SF r	Doncaster Rovers	A	0-2	1,530	
4 Aug 1978	FR	Coventry City	H	1-1	3,235	Tynan
3 Oct 1978	TST	Gainsborough Trinity (Rose)	A	1-1	1,000	Hornsby (pen)
14 Nov 1978	SHCC SF	Doncaster Rovers	A	1-2	1,380	Lowey
6 Feb 1979	FR	Vale Recreation	A	5-0	362	Hornsby 2, Lowey 2, Taylor
3 Aug 1979	FR	York City	A	0-1	1,125	
11 Sep 1979	TST	Leeds United (Bradshaw)	H	4-2	4,079	Wylde 3, Leman
13 Nov 1979	SHCC SF	Barnsley	H	0-0	1,832	* won 5-4 on penalties
4 Jan 1980	FR	Coventry City	A	2-3	563	Mellor, Leman
7 May 1980	TST	Manchester City (Mullen)	H	3-1	4,531	Mullen (pen), King, Oliver
8 May 1980	SHCC F	Sheffield United	H	1-2	5,340	McCulloch
31 Jul 1980	FR	Queen of the South	Scotland	1-2	750	Lowey
2 Aug 1980	FR	Kilmarnock	Scotland	2-1	1,200	Johnson, Campbell
4 Aug 1980	FR	Olimpija Ljubljana (Slovenia)	H	1-1	4,177	Smith (pen)
14 Oct 1980	TST	Rotherham United (Wilson)	A	3-6	1,605	Curran 3
18 Mar 1981	FR	Vancouver Whitecaps (Canada)	H	2-1	2,385	Mellor, Taylor
4 May 1981	SHCC SF	Barnsley	H	2-1	1,276	Curran 2
15 Aug 1981	FR	Nigeria	H	3-1	4,116	Curran, Mellor, Bannister
18 Aug 1981	FR	Crewe Alexandra	A	1-1	1,098	Bannister
20 Aug 1981	FR	Wigan Athletic	A	1-4	2,173	Bannister
22 Aug 1981	FR	Middlesbrough	H	0-3	4,139	
14 Oct 1981	TST	Leeds United (Cherry)	A	3-3	9,331	Smith, McCulloch, Bannister (pen)
2 Nov 1981	SHCC F	Rotherham United	A	1-2	1,263	Mellor
23 Jan 1982	FR	Middlesbrough	H	1-2	2,854	Megson
9 Mar 1982	SHCC Pr	Rotherham United	H	2-2	619	Simmons, Owen * AET – 90 mins 2-2 (won 5-3 on pens)
2 Apr 1982	FR	Stoke City	H	0-0	1,984	
10 May 1982	TST	Mansfield Town (Foster)	A	6-3	1,000	Simmons 2, McCulloch 2, Shelton 2
17 May 1982	SHCC SF	Doncaster Rovers	H	9-1		Simmons 6, Pearson 2, Williamson
21 May 1982	SHCC F	Sheffield United	A	2-3		Pearson, Oliver
14 Aug 1982	FR	Notts County	H	5-0	2,673	Bannister 2, Pearson 2, Shelton
23 Aug 1982	FR	West Bromwich Albion	H	2-2	4,500	Bannister (pen), Taylor
9 May 1983	TST	Doncaster Rovers (Warboys)	A	4-4	1,007	Taylor 2, Pearson, Megson
8 Aug 1983	FR	Mexborough Town	A	2-0	1,000	Heard, Bannister
12 Aug 1983	FR	Chesterfield	A	0-0	3,105	
16 Aug 1983	FR	Lincoln City	A	2-2	1,208	Bannister, Pearson
19 Aug 1983	FR	Hull City	A	0-1	3,230	
22 Aug 1983	FR	West Bromwich Albion	H	1-0	3,409	Simmons
14 Nov 1983	TST	Sheffield United (Coldwell)	A	1-1	9,512	Cunningham
22 Jul 1984	Charity (NSPCC)	Royal Oak (Keswick)	A	25-1		Chapman 4, Morris 4, Heard 3, Hodge 3, Varadi 2, Pearson 2, Hesford, Wilkinson, Eustace, Marwood, Smith, Williamson, Sterland

Date	Comp	Opposition	Venue	Res	Att	Scorers
11 Aug 1984	FR	Grimsby Town	A	0-2	1,237	
14 Aug 1984	FR	York City	A	2-2	2,454	Lyons, S. Mills
18 Aug 1984	TST	Notts County (O'Brien)	A	1-1	1,507	Shelton
3 Oct 1984	FR	Halmstad BK	Sweden	1-1	5,252	Chapman
17 May 1985	TST	Chesterfield (O'Neill)	A	1-1	5,086	Varadi
30 May 1985	FR	Watford	Thailand	0-0	2,000	* played at Bangkok, won 3-2 on pens.
3 Aug 1985	FR	Scunthorpe United	A	6-2	1,172	Stainrod 2, Blair, Sterland (pen), Gregory, Shutt
6 Aug 1985	FR	Goole Town	A	4-0	280	Stainrod 2, Marwood, Chapman
9 Aug 1985	FR	Barnsley	A	3-0	2,894	Chapman 2, Marwood
12 Aug 1985	FR	Derby County	A	1-0	2,420	Sterland
6 May 1986	TST	Sheffield United (Kenworthy)	A	4-3	9,566	Megson 2, Chapman, Shutt
7 May 1986	TST	Matlock Town (Smith)	A	6-4	409	Chapman 3, Shelton, Hart, Hodge
8 May 1986	TST	Frickley Athletic (Meehan)	A	2-5	969	Snodin, Eustace
30 Jul 1986	FC	HJK Helsinki	Finland	2-3		Chapman, Gregory
31 Jul 1986	FR	Finnish Select XI (Hanko)	Finland	5-3	509	Walker, Morris, Marwood, Knight, Shutt
1 Aug 1986	FR	Kuuysi	Finland	2-1		Walker, Hart
9 Aug 1986	FR	Notts County	A	3-0	1,176	Shutt 2, Snodin
16 Aug 1986	FR	Hull City	A	2-2	2,138	Worthington, Chamberlain
8 Sep 1986	FR	Kuwait	Kuwait	5-2		Walker 2, Marwood, Chapman, Snodin
15 Sep 1986	TST	Sheffield United (Smith)	H	3-1	10,800	Varadi 2, Hirst
13 Oct 1986	TST	Grimsby Town (Moore)	A	9-3	1,600	Walker 4, Chapman 2, Shelton, Chamberlain, Megson
31 Mar 1987	FC	HJK Helsinki	H	4-0	3,979	Chapman 2, Hirst 2
13 May 1987	FR	Canada XI (Windsor)	Canada	1-2	2,500	Marwood (pen)
15 May 1987	FR	Team Canada (London)	Canada	5-1	1,300	Chapman 3, Marwood 2
18 May 1987	FR	Canadian Olympic Team (Aylmer)	Canada	1-2	4,200	Hirst
22 May 1987	FR	Calgary Kickers	Canada	0-0	1,500	
18 Jul 1987	FR	Arminia Bielefeld	Germany	0-0	1,800	
19 Jul 1987	FR	Witten	Germany	3-1		Hirst 3
25 Jul 1987	FR	Bad Honnefer	Germany	2-1		Megson, Chapman
26 Jul 1987	FR	Schalke 04	Germany	0-1	7,000	
2 Aug 1987	FC	HJK Helsinki	Finland	2-2	2,392	Chapman, Hirst * won 4-2 on pens
5 Aug 1987	Charity	Sheffield United	A	3-0	8,724	Megson, Sterland, Chamberlain
9 Aug 1987	FR	Scarborough	A	3-1	1,458	Fee, Hirst, Marwood
7 Sep 1987	TST	Chesterfield (Ferguson)	A	1-1	1,724	Walker
15 Feb 1988	FR	Kuwait	Kuwait	2-4		Bradshaw, Hirst
9 May 1988	TST	Frickley Athletic (Gill)	A	2-4		Jonsson, Chapman
17 Aug 1988	FR	Exeter City	A	0-0	1,403	
19 Aug 1988	FR	Torquay United	A	2-1*	1,575	Galvin
12 Sep 1988	TST	Colin Morris Select XI (Morris)	BL	3-1	2,999	Hodgson, Reeves, West * played at Bramall Lane
6 Oct 1988	OL	Harworth Colliery	A	6-2	480	Hirst 2, Megson, Sterland, Galvin, McCall
19 Apr 1989	TST	Kettering Town (Keast)	A	1-1	1,321	Hirst
24 Apr 1989	FR	Guernsey	A	6-0	800	Bennett 4, Palmer, Varadi
27 Jul 1989	FR	Witney Town	A	5-0	462	Shakespeare, Atkinson, Hirst, Whitton, Bennett

Date	Comp	Opposition	Venue	Res	Att	Scorers
29 Jul 1989	FR	Abingdon Town	A	4-0	473	Barrick 2, Hirst, Palmer
31 Jul 1989	FR	Cheltenham Town	A	5-1*	1,420	Shakespeare 2, Hirst, Whitton
7 Aug 1989	FR	Glentoran	N. Ireland	2-1	4,000	Bennett, Atkinson
12 Aug 1989	FR	Sheffield United	A	0-0	17,951	
10 Mar 1990	FR	Brondby (Denmark)	H	3-0	3,715	Hirst 2, Bennett
26 Mar 1990	FR	Ryde Sports	A	2-0	2,380	Shirtliff, Bennett
2 Apr 1990	FR	Malmo	Sweden	2-0	3,505	Hirst, Sheridan
4 Aug 1990	FR	Dawlish	A	8-0*	515	Francis 2, Johnson 2, Hirst, Nilsson, Mooney
6 Aug 1990	FR	Torquay United	A	3-0	2,227	Sheridan, Francis, Williams
9 Aug 1990	FR	Genoa	Italy	0-3		
14 Aug 1990	FR	Cremonese	Italy	0-2	9,000	
17 Aug 1990	TST	Sheffield United (Madden)	H	3-0	15,040	Williams 2, Shirtliff
19 Aug 1990	FR	Crewe Alexandra	A	8-1	1,530	Hirst 3 (2 pen), Pearson, Sheridan, Francis, Worthington, Bennett
12 Nov 1990	TST	Leeds United (Sterland)	A	7-2	6,246	Francis 3, Hirst 2 (1 pen), Mooney, Harkes
29 Jul 1991	FR	Maryland Bays	U.S.A	2-0	3,812	MacKenzie, Williams
2 Aug 1991	FR	USA	U.S.A	0-2	44,261	* played at Philadelphia
7 Aug 1991	FR	Glentoran	N. Ireland	6-0	4,000	Hirst 3, Pearson, Sheridan, MacKenzie
9 Aug 1991	FR	Portsmouth	A	1-1	5,800	Francis
14 Oct 1991	FR	Histon	A	5-1	653	Chambers 3, Jemson, Williams
24 Jul 1992	FR	Ards	N. Ireland	1-1	2,275	Hyde
26 Jul 1992	FR	League of Ireland Select XI	Eire	6-1	1,063	Jemson 2, Wilson, Hirst, Francis, Hyde
30 Jul 1992	FR	West Bromwich Albion	A	2-2	6,171	Williams, Harkes
1 Aug 1992	FR	Rotherham United	A	0-1	5,818	
5 Aug 1992	FR	AEK Athens	Greece	0-4	4,944	
11 Oct 1992	FR	Hellenic	South Africa	2-1	6,000	Warhurst 2
13 Oct 1992	FR	Mamelodi Sundowns	South Africa	2-2	30,000	Jemson, Anderson
19 Jul 1993	FR	Bodmin Town	A	9-2	3,000	Warhurst 3, Bright 2, Sherdian, Pearce, Waddle, Williams
21 Jul 1993	TST	Plymouth Argyle (Burrows)	A	5-0*	7,182	Nilsson, Warhurst, Palmer, Bright
23 Jul 1993	FR	Exeter City	A	6-0	3,490	Warhurst 2, Bright 2, Hyde, Bart-Williams
26 Jul 1993	FR	Glentoran	N. Ireland	7-1	4,842	Warhurst 3, Watson 2, Jemson, Williams
28 Jul 1993	FR	Bangor	N. Ireland	2-0	2,275	Jones, Warhurst
31 Jul 1993	FR	Glasgow Celtic	Scotland	1-1	24,876	Warhurst
7 Aug 1993	TST	Derby County (Worthington)	H	1-1	7,048	Warhurst
9 Aug 1993	TST	Sheffield United (Dooley)	A	1-0	8,829	Hirst
3 Nov 1993	FR	Enfield	A	6-1	1,100	Bright 3, Sinton 2, Francis
22 Mar 1994	FR	Real Madrid	Spain	1-3	17,000	Sheridan * played at Cordoba
18 Jul 1994	FR	Yomiuri Verdy (Tokyo)	Japan	1-2	45,041	Bright
20 Jul 1994	FR	Shimizu S-Pulse (Tokyo)	Japan	4-3	44,037	Hirst, Bright, Jones, Taylor
28 Jul 1994	FR	Dundalk	Eire	3-0	3,650	Sheridan (pen), Watson, Hirst
29 Jul 1994	FR	Glenavon	Eire	2-0	2,098	Hirst, Bright
5 Aug 1994	FR	Sunderland	A	2-1	7,467	Hirst, Watson
7 Aug 1994	FR	Hibernian	Scotland	2-3	6,934	Taylor, Bright
9 Aug 1994	FR	Sheffield United	H	2-3	13,724	Bart-Williams, Taylor

Date	Comp	Opposition	Venue	Res	Att	Scorers
12 Aug 1994	FR	Mansfield Town	A	3-0	3,911	Taylor, Jemson, Bright
9 Nov 1994	FR	Newry Town	N. Ireland	4-0	3,000	Watson, Jones, Bart-Williams, Nolan
24 Apr 1995	TST	Charlton Athletic (Bolder)	A	3-3	3,438	Atherton, Francis, Whittingham
1 Aug 1995	FR	Birmingham City	A	3-1	5,302	Bright 2, Petrescu
5 Aug 1995	SCCC	Sheffield United	A	3-1	13,254	Hirst, Atherton, Bright
8 Aug 1995	TST	Rotherham United (Johnson)	A	2-1	4,079	Bright 2
11 Aug 1995	FR	Kettering Town	A	5-2	2,276	Hirst 2, Sheridan, Waddle, Pembridge
26 Jul 1996	TST	Brighton & Hove Albion (Foster)	A	7-1	3,831	Hirst 3 (1 pen), Pembridge 2, Donaldson, Booth
28 Jul 1996	FR	Peterborough United	A	0-2	5,475	
30 Jul 1996	TST	Rotherham United (Goodwin)	A	1-0	3,912	Nolan
2 Aug 1996	FR	FC Gouda	Holland	12-0*		Booth 3, Whittingham 3, Pembridge 2, Hyde 2, Blinker
3 Aug 1996	FR	NEC Nijmegen	Holland	0-1		
4 Aug 1996	FR	HV & CV Quick	Holland	5-0		Hirst 3, Whittingham, Pembridge
7 Aug 1996	FR	Twente Enschede	Holland	1-1	5,000	Whittingham
9 Aug 1996	FR	FC Zwolle	Holland	4-1	3,000	Humphreys 2, Oakes, Blinker,
10 Aug 1996	FR	FC Utrecht	Holland	2-1	10,000	Booth, Humphreys
27 Aug 1996	SCCC	Sheffield United	A	1-4	7,271	Hyde
12 Nov 1996	FR	Merthyr Tydfil	Wales	3-0	2,327	Blinker, Humphreys, Trustfull
10 Feb 1997	FR	Shelbourne	Eire	2-3	5,100	Booth 2
21 Jul 1997	FR	Exeter City	A	3-1	4,042	Blinker 2, Hirst
23 Jul 1997	FR	Torquay United	A	1-0	1,515	Pembridge
25 Jul 1997	FR	Plymouth Argyle	A	0-2	4,354	
29 Jul 1997	FR	Leiden Select XI	Holland	4-1	1,300	Carbone 2, Donaldson 2
1 Aug 1997	FR	T.O.P. Oss	Holland	3-1	1,500	Humphreys, Whittingham, Donaldson
2 Aug 1997	FR	Sparta Rotterdam	Holland	1-2	6,000	Pembridge
4 Aug 1997	FR	Huddersfield Town	A	0-1	8,927	
28 Apr 1998	TST	Glasgow Rangers (Durrant)	Scotland	2-2	26,046	Carbone, Di Canio
5 May 1998	TST	Luton Town (Johnson)	A	2-0	2,504	Whittingham 2
15 Jul 1998	FR	Reading	A	0-3	7,157	
17 Jul 1998	FR	Peterborough United	A	2-1	2,060	Booth, Magilton
23 Jul 1998	FR	Manchester City	A	0-0	2,882	
25 Jul 1998	FR	Blackpool	A	0-1	3,401	
29 Jul 1998	FR	Lincoln City	A	3-0	2,986	Booth, Di Canio, Atherton
1 Aug 1998	FR	Birmingham City	A	0-4	8,643	
3 Aug 1998	FR	Walsall	A	1-2	2,416	Booth
3 Aug 1998	SHR	Shrewsbury Town	A	0-1	1,316	
18 May 1999	TST	Chesterfield (Hewitt)	A	1-1*	3,400	
20 Jul 1999	FR	Queen's Park Rangers	A	2-1*	3,685	Donnelly
23 Jul 1999	FR	Peterborough United	A	1-0	3,104	De Bilde
27 Jul 1999	TST	West Bromwich Albion (Raven)	A	2-1	2,989	De Bilde, Alexandersson
29 Jul 1999	FR	Stockport County	A	1-0	2,326	Donnelly
31 Jul 1999	FR	Rotherham United	A	1-0	5,979	Carbone
15 Jul 2000	FR	Chesterfield	A	1-2	3,813	Holmes

Date	Comp	Opposition	Venue	Res	Att	Scorers
17 Jul 2000	FR	Crawley Town	A	3-1	1,453	Sibon, Cresswell, Humphreys (pen)
19 Jul 2000	FR	Stevenage Borough	A	3-0	1,723	Sibon 2, Muller
22 Jul 2000	FR	Wrexham	A	4-1	1,493	Sibon 2 (1 pen), Booth, Hamshaw
29 Jul 2000	FR	Scunthorpe United	A	2-3	2,691	Quinn, Jonk
2 Aug 2000	FR	PSV Eindhoven (Holland)	H	2-2	9,097	De Bilde, Booth
5 Aug 2000	FR	Brighton & Hove Albion	A	0-2	4,004	
18 Jul 2001	FR	Dunfermline Athletic	Scotland	1-3	2,867	Sibon
20 Jul 2001	TST	Kilmarnock (MacPherson)	Scotland	0-0	2,145	
25 Jul 2001	FR	Hull City	A	0-0	5,775	
28 Jul 2001	FR	Derby County	H	0-0	4,635	
31 Jul 2001	FR	York City	A	2-1	2,011	McLaren, Quinn
4 Aug 2001	FR	Deportivo Alaves (Spain)	H	1-0	5,842	McLaren
16 Jul 2002	FR	FC Copenhagen	Denmark	1-1	2,002	O'Donnell
18 Jul 2002	FR	Trelleborgs XI	Sweden	4-1	1,120	Crane 2, Sibon, Armstrong
20 Jul 2002	FR	Ystads	Sweden	3-0	800	Sibon 2, Crane
24 Jul 2002	FR	Partick Thistle	Scotland	2-0	2,431	Sibon, Knight
27 Jul 2002	FR	Kilmarnock	Scotland	1-2	3,711	McLaren
30 Jul 2002	FR	Middlesbrough	H	1-2	5,940	Beswetherick
3 Aug 2002	FR	Oldham Athletic	A	2-1	2,049	Donnelly, Sibon
8 Jul 2003	FR	VV Dovo	Holland	5-0	1,500	Lee 3, Owusu, Watson
10 Jul 2003	FR	DOS Kampen	Holland	4-0	800	Evans 2, Holt, Shaw
15 Jul 2003	FR	Doncaster Rovers	A	2-0	6,255	Watson 2 (1 pen)
19 Jul 2003	FR	Macclesfield Town	A	3-1	2,136	Kuqi 3 (1 pen)
22 Jul 2003	FR	ADO Den Haag (Holland)	H	1-2	5,411	Quinn (pen)
26 Jul 2003	FR	Hartlepool United	A	3-1	1,398	Owusu, McLaren, Armstrong
1 Aug 2003	FR	Newcastle United	H	4-3	14,955	Owusu, D.Smith, Armstrong, Kuqi
12 May 2004	TST	Rotherham United (Hurst)	A	1-2	3,064	Quinn
13 Jul 2004	COPA SF	Preston North End	Ibiza	3-2	1,200	Marsden, MacLean, Proudlock
15 Jul 2004	COPA F	Watford	Ibiza	1-1	1,500	Proudlock * lost 5-4 on penalties
24 Jul 2004	FR	York City	A	2-1	2,648	Brunt, Peacock
28 Jul 2004	FR	Birmingham City	H	0-1	8,428	
31 Jul 2004	FR	Bolton Wanderers	H	2-2	6,729	MacLean 2 (1 pen)
3 Aug 2004	FR	Everton	H	3-6	9,613	Ndumbu-Nsungu 2, Proudlock
12 Jul 2005	FR	Sheffield	A	7-1	1,308	Peacock 2, Brunt 2, MacLean 2 (1 pen), Reet
14 Jul 2005	FR	Stocksbridge Park Steels	A	1-0	2,050	Brunt
18 Jul 2005	FR	Grimsby Town	A	2-1	2,016	MacLean, Proudlock
20 Jul 2005	FR	Partick Thistle	Scotland	0-0	1,463	
23 Jul 2005	CDC SF	Wolverhampton Wanderers	Scotland	0-0	6,695	* played at Dundee Utd FC – won 5-4 on penalties
24 Jul 2005	CDC F	Dundee United	Scotland	1-2	5,081	Peacock * played at Dundee FC
27 Jul 2005	FR	Mansfield Town	A	0-0	2,356	
31 Jul 2005	FR	Manchester City	H	1-1	12,796	Whelan
1 Aug 2005	FR	York City	A	1-2	1,117	Partridge
15 Jul 2006	FR	Wilmington Hammerheads	USA	1-1	3,156	Lunt

Date	Comp	Opposition	Venue	Res	Att	Scorers
19 Jul 2006	FR	USL Allstars	U.S.A	0-0	5,193	* played at Cary, North Carolina
22 Jul 2006	FR	Rochester Raging Rhinos	U.S.A	2-0	6,289	MacLean 2
26 Jul 2006	FR	Mansfield Town	A	0-4	3,665	
29 Jul 2006	FR	Middlesbrough	H	1-2	5,684	Brunt (pen)
14 Jul 2007	FR	Halifax Town	A	3-0	2,227	Brunt, Clarke, Tudgay
17 Jul 2007	FR	Go Ahead Eagles	Holland	2-1	1,900	Tudgay, Small
18 Jul 2007	FR	Heerenveen	Holland	2-2	2,000	Brunt(pen), Small
21 Jul 2007	FR	FC Groningen	Holland	1-1	2,800	Tudgay
24 Jul 2007	FR	Chesterfield	A	2-0	4,430	Brunt(pen), Small
28 Jul 2007	FR	Port Vale	A	0-3	1,890	
31 Jul 2007	FR	Oldham Athletic	A	0-2	2,596	
4 Aug 2007	FR	Birmingham City	H	0-2	5,689	
15 Jul 2008	FR	HFC Haarlem (at Heiloo)	Holland	2-0	800	Burton, Tudgay
17 Jul 2008	FR	Stormovogels Telstar (at Heiloo)	Holland	3-0	850	Tudgay, Burton, Johnson
22 Jul 2008	FR	MK Dons	A	4-1	3,510	Burton 2, Esajas, Johnson
26 Jul 2008	FR	Bury	A	2-0	1,929	Clarke 2
29 Jul 2008	FR	Chesterfield	A	0-1	3,621	
2 Aug 2008	FR	Wigan Athletic	H	2-3	7,067	Johnson, Burton (pen)
13 Jul 2009	MTT	Floriana*	Malta	1-0		McAllister
13 Jul 2009	MTT	Dingli Swallows*	Malta	1-0		Esajas
16 Jul 2009	MTT	Birkirkara*	Malta	0-0		* lost 5-4 on pens.
16 Jul 2009	MTT	Sliema Wanderers*	Malta	0-1		* all 45 minutes duration
21 Jul 2009	FR	Hartlepool United	A	2-0	1,625	Tudgay, France
25 Jul 2009	FR	Hull City	H	0-0	5,213	
28 Jul 2009	FR	Northampton Town	A	2-0	1,912	Johnson, Jeffers
1 Aug 2009	FR	Blackburn Rovers	H	2-2	5,579	Sodje, Tudgay
10 Jul 2010	FR	USF Anif	Austria	0-0	150	
13 Jul 2010	FR	Stocksbridge Park Steels	A	6-1	1,000	Mellor 4, Johnson 2
13 Jul 2010	FR	Hallam	A	9-0	600	Tudgay 3, Heffernan 2, Miller 2, Buxton, Boden
17 Jul 2010	FR	Grimsby Town	A	1-2	3,335	Boden
20 Jul 2010	FR	Darlington	A	1-1	1,261	Heffernan
24 Jul 2010	FR	Scunthorpe United	A	0-1	2,594	
27 Jul 2010	FR	Barnsley	A	0-2	8,534	
31 Jul 2010	FR	Doncaster Rovers	A	0-1	5,942	

KEY:

*	Own-goal scored for SWFC	AIC	Anglo Italian Cup	BSC	Birmingham Senior Cup
CS	Charity Shield	COPA	Copa de Ibiza	CDC	Dundee City of Discovery Cup
FIN	Finlux Cup	FOB	Festival of Britain	FR	Friendly
HHC	Hull Hospital Cup	HIC	Huddersfield Infirmary Cup	MTT	Maltese Triangular Tournaments
OL	Opening of Lights	PB	Plymouth Bowl	PR	Practice Match
SCCC	Steel City Challenge Cup	SCHC	Scunthorpe Hospital Cup	SCHS	Scarborough Hospital Shield
SDL	Sheffield & Derbyshire League	SHCC	Sheffield & Hallamshire County Cup	Shipp	Shipp Cup
SHR	Shropshire Senior Cup	SLC	Sheriff of London Charity Shield	TST	Testimonial/Benefit (recipient in brackets)
UCL	United Counties League	VIF	Vasterhaninge July Cup (Sweden)	WCC	Wharncliffe Charity Cup
WIC	Westmorland Invitation Cup				

Player of the Year

YEAR	WINNER
1969	John RITCHIE
1970	Peter EUSTACE
1971	Peter GRUMMITT
1972	John SISSONS
1973	Tommy CRAIG
1974	Mick PRENDERGAST
1975	Eric POTTS
1976	Eric POTTS
1977	Richard WALDEN
1978	Tommy TYNAN
1979	Ian PORTERFIELD
1980	Jeff JOHNSON
1981	Mark SMITH
1982	Gary BANNISTER
1983	Mel STERLAND
1984	Gary SHELTON
1985	Imre VARADI
1986	Martin HODGE
1987	Lee CHAPMAN
1988	Gary MEGSON
1989	Lawrie MADDEN
1990	David HIRST

YEAR	WINNER
1991	Nigel PEARSON
1992	Phil KING
1993	Chris WADDLE
1994	Des WALKER
1995	Peter ATHERTON
1996	Peter ATHERTON
1997	Des WALKER
1998	Paolo DI CANIO
1999	Emerson THOME
2000	Niclas ALEXANDERSSON
2001	Gerald SIBON
2002	Derek GEARY
2003	Alan QUINN
2004	Guylain NDUMBU-NSUNGU
2005	Steve MacLEAN
2006	Graham COUGHLAN
2007	Glenn WHELAN
2008	Mark BEEVERS
2009	Marcus TUDGAY
2010	Lee GRANT
2011	Neil MELLOR

Club Sponsors

1983–84	CROSBY KITCHENS
1984–85	MHS GROUP
1986–88	FINLUX LIMITED
1988–90	VT PLASTICS
1992	MR. TOM
1992–2000	SANDERSON ELECTRONICS LIMITED
2000–02	CHUPA CHUPS
2003–05	NAPOLEON'S
2005–09	PLUSNET
2009–11	SHEFFIELD CHILDREN'S HOSPITAL

Season Ticket Prices - Post War

South Stand - Centre

Season	Cost	Inflation Adjusted
1946–47	£5.00	£158.55
1947–48	£5.00	£153.80
1948–49	£5.00	£143.75
1949–50	£5.00	£133.60
1950–51	£5.00	£129.95
1951–52	£5.00	£126.05
1952–53	£7.00	£161.77
1953–54	£7.00	£148.12
1954–55	£7.00	£143.64
1955–56	£7.00	£141.12
1956–57	£7.00	£135.03
1957–58	£7.00	£128.73
1958–59	£7.00	£124.11
1959–60	£7.00	£120.47
1960–61	£8, 8s	£143.72
1961–62	£8, 8s	£142.30
1962–63	£8, 8s	£137.59
1963–64	£8, 8s	£131.88
1964–65	£8, 8s	£129.28
1965–66	£8, 8s	£125.16
1966–67	£8, 8s	£119.45
1967–68	£10.00	£136.90
1968–69	£10.00	£133.60
1969–70	£10.00	£127.60
1970–71	£11.00	£133.21
1971–72	£11.00	£125.18
1972–73	£14.50	£145.60
1973–74	£16.00	£155.36
1974–75	£20.00	£177.80
1975–76	£22.00	£168.52
1976–77	£27.00	£166.59
1977–78	£34.50	£182.85
1978–79	£38.00	£174.40

Season	Cost	Inflation Adjusted
1979–80	£41.40	£175.12
1980–81	£57.10	£212.98
1981–82	£56.70	£179.17
1982–83	£84.00	£236.88
1983–84	£84.00	£218.40
1984–85	£80.00	£199.20
1985–86	£95.00	£225.15
1986–87	£101.00	£225.23
1987–88	£101.00	£218.16
1988–89	£108.00	£223.56
1989–90	£116.00	£228.52
1990–91	£133.00	£243.39
1991–92	£205.70	£342.35
1992–93	£231.50	£364.98
1993–94	£240.00	£364.80
1994–95	£253.00	£379.50
1995–96	£253.00	£369.38
1996–97	£267.00	£376.47
1997–98	£281.00	£387.78
1998–99	£336.00	£450.24
1999–2000	£360.00	£468.00
2000–01	£332.50	£425.60
2001–02	£332.50	£412.30
2002–03	£342.00	£417.24
2003–04	£350.00	£420.00
2004–05	£368.00	£430.56
2005–06	£385.00	£438.90
2006–07	£425.00	£471.75
2007–08	£457.00	£493.56
2008–09	£515.00	£535.60
2009–10	£468.00	
2010–11	£492.00	
2011–12	£482.00	

Average Attendances

* All figures from 1889-1924 based on estimated crowds published in the local press

SEASON	AGGREGATE	AVERAGE
1889–90	41,500	3,773
1890–91	53,000	4,818
1891–92	81,000	7,364
1892–93	149,000	9,933
1893–94	120,500	8,033
1894–95	127,000	8,466
1895–96	123,787	8,252
1896–97	98,400	6,560
1897–98	142,000	9,467
1898–99	162,000	9,000
1899–1900	121,000	7,118
1900–01	210,000	12,353
1901–02	184,000	10,824
1902–03	253,000	14,882
1903–04	228,000	13,412
1904–05	235,000	13,824
1905–06	249,500	13,132
1906–07	218,000	11,474
1907–08	278,643	14,665
1908–09	248,000	13,053
1909–10	221,000	11,632
1910–11	225,000	11,842
1911–12	268,425	14,128
1912–13	386,000	20,316
1913–14	405,000	21,316
1914–15	288,000	15,158
1919–20	386,500	18,405
1920–21	406,000	19,333
1921–22	315,000	15,000
1922–23	378,000	18,000
1923–24	339,000	16,143
1924–25	397,206	18,915
1925–26	517,072	24,622
1926–27	484,273	23,061
1927–28	463,578	22,075
1928–29	567,376	27,018

SEASON	AGGREGATE	AVERAGE
1929–30	543,341	25,873
1930–31	418,140	19,911
1931–32	351,035	16,716
1932–33	353,927	16,854
1933–34	338,700	16,129
1934–35	394,621	18,791
1935–36	386,833	18,421
1936–37	426,737	20,321
1937–38	495,006	23,572
1938–39	571,045	27,193
1946–47	562,159	26,769
1947–48	753,359	35,874
1948–49	711,093	33,862
1949–50	854,341	40,683
1950–51	871,571	41,503
1951–52	870,686	41,461
1952–53	893,316	42,539
1953–54	754,394	35,924
1954–55	567,995	27,047
1955–56	570,537	27,168
1956–57	618,673	29,461
1957–58	491,323	23,396
1958–59	598,683	28,509
1959–60	689,042	32,812
1960–61	655,697	31,224
1961–62	625,704	29,795
1962–63	539,407	25,686
1963–64	507,431	24,163
1964–65	435,655	20,745
1965–66	486,397	23,162
1966–67	643,202	30,629
1967–68	666,454	31,736
1968–69	570,701	27,176
1969–70	559,001	26,619
1970–71	337,074	16,051
1971–72	360,315	17,158

SEASON	AGGREGATE	AVERAGE	SEASON	AGGREGATE	AVERAGE
1972–73	363,601	17,314	1992–93	572,535	27,264
1973–74	309,729	14,749	1993–94	570,920	27,187
1974–75	279,132	13,292	1994–95	558,509	26,596
1975–76	254,564	11,068	1995–96	472,665	24,877
1976–77	309,827	13,471	1996–97	488,745	25,723
1977–78	262,830	11,427	1997–98	545,423	28,706
1978–79	244,797	10,643	1998–99	508,161	26,745
1979–80	415,952	18,085	1999–2000	472,253	24,855
1980–81	386,472	18,403	2000–01	443,163	19,268
1981–82	400,734	19,083	2001–02	480,011	20,870
1982–83	348,611	16,601	2002–03	467,509	20,326
1983–84	472,250	22,488	2003–04	513,731	22,336
1984–85	583,374	27,780	2004–05	531,289	23,100
1985–86	484,134	23,054	2005–06	571,625	24,853
1986–87	486,100	23,148	2006–07	543,685	23,638
1987–88	395,933	19,796	2007–08	492,618	21,418
1988–89	380,699	20,037	2008–09	495,463	21,542
1989–90	397,616	20,927	2009–10	533,122	23,179
1990–91	611,899	26,604	2010–11	409,796	17,817
1991–92	621,140	29,578		**HISTORIC AVERAGE**	**20,537**

Attendance Graph 1889–2011

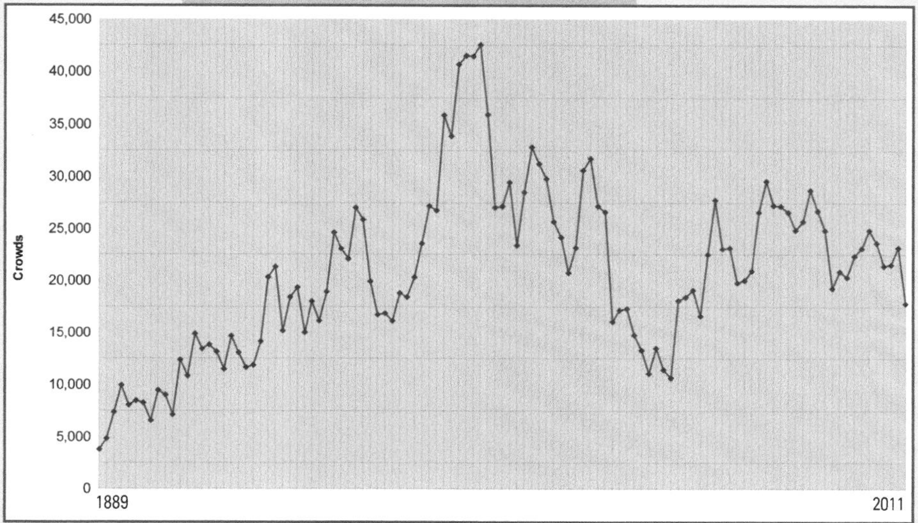

Finances

Year	Turnover £	Wages £	Wages to Turnover	Profit–Loss £
30 April 1900	5,356	3,076	57%	-579
30 April 1901	5,803	3,698	64%	-127
30 April 1902	5,940	3,789	64%	63
30 April 1903	8,007	3,840	48%	1,310
30 April 1904	9,758	4,364	45%	2,024
30 April 1905	9,293	4,334	47%	1,433
30 April 1906	8,676	4,889	56%	-439
30 April 1907	11,268	5,263	47%	1,018
30 April 1908	8,108	5,690	70%	-510
30 April 1909	8,970	5,376	60%	238
30 April 1910	6,140	5,968	97%	-2,067
30 April 1911	6,649	5,242	79%	-1,096
30 April 1912	9,334	4,691	50%	2,192
30 April 1913	13,437	4,652	35%	5,382
30 April 1914	14,203	5,414	38%	3,368
30 April 1915	9,593	5,004	52%	-1,564
30 April 1916	2,779	368	13%	-1,105
30 April 1917	2,225	266	12%	-1,312
30 April 1918	2,646	241	9%	-869
30 April 1919	4,133	373	9%	-209
30 April 1920	20,921	8,789	42%	-1,677
7 May 1921	28,305	11,147	39%	4,651
7 May 1922	16,316	12,956	79%	-5,572
7 May 1923	23,306	12,562	54%	-3,763
7 May 1924	21,576	11,833	55%	1,082
7 May 1925	24,453	13,125	54%	-3,265
7 May 1926	28,605	14,014	49%	3,402
7 May 1927	28,989	13,787	48%	1,373
7 May 1928	30,310	14,112	47%	-1,839
7 May 1929	41,054	14,981	36%	10,281
7 May 1930	38,092	16,669	44%	-1,614
7 May 1931	24,768	14,834	60%	94
7 May 1932	27,659	14,286	52%	450
7 May 1933	20,224	14,743	73%	-3,198
7 May 1934	26,754	13,813	52%	2,741
7 May 1935	32,000	15,554	49%	2,973
7 May 1936	28,158	14,481	51%	-16,824
7 May 1937	34,495	14,248	41%	8,286
7 May 1938	21,902	15,017	69%	-5,592
7 May 1939	33,280	15,274	46%	4,406
7 May 1940	5,232	5,679	109%	-4,129
7 May 1941	2,096	1,355	65%	-1,776
7 May 1942	3,281	1,166	36%	-769
7 May 1943	11,054	1,932	17%	3,099
7 May 1944	7,682	2,610	34%	-139
7 May 1945	8,183	3,141	38%	-1,103
7 May 1946	31,868	9,919	31%	2,079
7 May 1947	40,069	16,814	42%	2,269
7 May 1948	63,916	24,847	39%	2,596
7 May 1949	67,577	24,805	37%	1,077
7 May 1950	80,727	26,679	33%	10,591
7 May 1951	80,028	30,599	38%	-14,304
7 May 1952	89,077	36,183	41%	8,025

Year	Turnover £	Wages £	Wages to Turnover	Profit–Loss £
31 May 1953	95,462	34,854	37%	7,321
31 May 1954	91,082	36,602	40%	5,635
31 May 1955	78,781	33,938	43%	-12,384
31 May 1956	75,012	39,770	53%	1,015
31 May 1957	81,117	37,830	47%	2,006
31 May 1958	82,476	44,508	54%	-2,427
31 May 1959	117,259	53,665	46%	12,112
31 May 1960	124,505	57,320	46%	17,223
31 May 1961	131,056	61,925	47%	4,405
31 May 1962	#163,308	72,221	44%	4,810
31 May 1963	183,335	74,648	41%	13,571
31 May 1964	125,053	80,265	64%	-29,970
31 May 1965	142,990	77,961	55%	1,481
31 May 1966	166,006	89,060	54%	-45,320
31 May 1967	#238,641	99,458	42%	-30,963
31 May 1968	233,444	110,179	47%	27,003
31 May 1969	229,803	117,056	51%	-116,388
31 May 1970	372,234	115,765	31%	138,556
31 May 1971	200,435	116,891	58%	-24,261
31 May 1972	195,000	133,953	69%	-165,252
31 May 1973	290,349	177,511	61%	-47,544
31 May 1974	211,865	182,856	86%	-102,724
31 May 1975	#227,084	181,376	80%	-81,507
31 May 1976	256,093	188,889	74%	-55,807
31 May 1977	#361,325	196,976	55%	-43,966
31 May 1978	390,149	200,350	51%	129,265
31 May 1979	474,588	260,702	55%	97,078
31 May 1980	878,444	364,750	42%	450,180
31 May 1981	946,703	388,079	41%	219,553
31 May 1982	911,913	528,589	58%	-14,900
31 May 1983	1,280,440	595,096	46%	-27,878
31 May 1984	1,899,940	839,119	44%	119,931
31 May 1985	2,869,913	904,335	32%	498,579
31 May 1986	1,951,367	1,182,004	61%	385,452
31 May 1987	2,322,748	1,147,709	49%	242,673
31 May 1988	2,193,833	1,410,227	64%	-442,846
31 May 1989	2,336,510	1,731,232	74%	-53,862
31 May 1990	2,791,000	2,240,000	80%	-1,735,000
31 May 1991	5,880,000	3,461,000	59%	168,000
31 May 1992	7,516,000	3,627,000	48%	2,420,000
31 May 1993	12,806,000	4,702,000	37%	1,370,000
31 May 1994	11,914,000	5,427,000	46%	-199,000
31 May 1995	10,995,000	5,660,000	51%	982,000
31 May 1996	10,078,000	6,412,000	64%	-2,254,000
31 May 1997	14,335,000	7,571,000	53%	-3,254,000
31 May 1998	16,303,000	11,284,000	69%	-10,140,000
31 May 1999	19,124,000	13,539,000	71%	-9,432,000
31 May 2000	18,026,000	14,375,000	80%	-2,823,000
31 May 2001	13,228,000	13,416,000	101%	-9,072,000
31 May 2002	18,552,000	11,411,000	62%	-387,000
31 May 2003	8,512,000	9,801,000	115%	-8,361,000
31 May 2004	9,026,000	5,987,000	66%	-4,105,000
31 May 2005	9,661,000	5,508,000	57%	-3,007,000
31 May 2006	11,613,000	5,667,000	49%	-457,000
31 May 2007	11,321,000	6,297,000	56%	1,491,000
31 May 2008	12,317,000	7,169,000	58%	2,217,000
31 May 2009	11,170,000	8,180,000	73%	-3,708,000

Turnover re-stated in following year's accounts

Reserve Team Seasonal Records 1891-2011

Season	Competition	P	W	D	L	F	A	Pts	Pos.	Top Scorer
1891–92	Hallamshire League	14	10	2	2	53	26	22	3rd	n/k
1892–93	Sheffield & District League	26	18	2	6	92	34	38	1st	n/k
1893–94	Sheffield & District League	8	6	0	2	28	13	12	1st*	n/k
	*Lost in Championship Play-off									
1893–94	S & H Challenge Cup League	26	17	6	3	78	31	40	3rd	n/k
1894–95	Wharncliffe Charity Cup League	10	4	1	5	17	31	9	5th	H. Woolhouse 4
1894–95	S & H Challenge Cup League	28	23	1	4	106	26	47	1st	n/k
1895–96	S & H Challenge Cup League	28	19	2	7	129	47	40	3rd	Gooing
1895–96	Wharncliffe Charity Cup League	10	4	2	4	15	16	10	3rd	Gooing 5
1896–97	Sheffield Association League	18	11	3	4	55	18	25	2nd	n/k
1896–97	Sheffield & N. Derbyshire League	8	4	2	2	19	15	10	3rd	n/k
1896–97	Wharncliffe Charity Cup League	16	12	0	4	51	20	24	2nd	n/k
1897–98	United Counties League	16	14	1	1	53	19	29	1st	Dryburgh
1897–98	Yorkshire League	18	11	1	6	56	25	23	5th	n/k
1898–99	Midland League	26	10	5	11	42	52	25	10th	Beech 12
1898–99	Yorkshire League*	17	11	1	5	53	27	23	5th	n/k
	* Final game not played									
1899–1900	Sheffield Association League	16	14	1	1	55	9	29	1st	n/k
1899–1900	Wharncliffe Charity Cup League	16	12	4	0	68	10	28	1st	Beech
1900–01	Sheffield Association League	28	23	3	2	110	25	49	1st	n/k
1901–02	Midland Counties League	28	13	11	4	82	32	37	3rd	n/k
1901–02	Wharncliffe Charity Cup League	12	8	1	3	33	12	12	2nd	Hutton 7
1902–03	Midland Counties League	32	24	3	5	98	26	51	1st	n/k
1902–03	Wharncliffe Charity Cup League	14	12	1	1	51	10	25	1st	Marrison/Beech 9
1903–04	Midland Counties League	34	25	5	4	104	28	55	2nd	Stewart 32
1903–04	Wharncliffe Charity Cup League	12	6	3	3	32	15	15	3rd	Marrison 11
1904–05	Midland Counties League	32	18	6	8	80	43	42	4th	Stewart 22
1904–05	Wharncliffe Charity Cup League	14	10	1	3	42	11	21	1st	Tummon 14
1905–06	Midland Counties League	34	25	5	4	111	27	55	1st	Brittleton 19
1905–06	Wharncliffe Charity Cup League	14	12	0	2	39	5	24	1st	n/k
1906–07	Midland Counties League	38	25	5	8	84	44	55	3rd	Napier 18
1906–07	Wharncliffe Charity Cup League	14	4	3	7	24	23	11	7th	Rollinson 6
1907–08	Midland Counties League	38	27	2	9	106	37	56	1st	Rollinson 27
1908–09	Midland Counties League	38	17	8	13	80	45	42	6th	Tummon 14

Season	Competition	P	W	D	L	F	A	Pts	Pos.	Top Scorer
1908–09	Wharncliffe Charity Cup League	8	4	3	1	16	8	11	1st	Hamilton 3
1909–10	Midland Counties League	42	20	11	11	110	66	51	4th	Hamilton
1910–11	Midland Counties League	38	24	8	6	86	41	56	2nd	Stringfellow 13
1911–12	Midland Counties League	36	15	8	13	68	64	38	8th	Hemstock 11
1912–13	Midland Counties League	38	16	7	15	78	69	39	7th	n/k
1913–14	Midland Counties League	34	17	6	11	68	50	40	4th	McGregor 11
1914–15	Midland Counties League	38	20	7	11	92	56	47	5th	J. Burkinshaw 24
1919–20	Midland Counties League	34	16	6	12	50	44	38	6th	Edmondson 7
1920–21	Midland Counties League	38	16	7	15	66	50	39	9th	Ruddock 11
1921–22	Midland Counties League	42	23	10	9	98	49	56	3rd	Lunn 24
1922–23	Midland Counties League	42	28	7	7	88	37	63	1st	Trotter 20
1923–24	Central League	42	19	10	13	76	54	48	8th	Eyre 14
1924–25	Central League	42	24	9	9	81	38	57	4th	S. Taylor 15
1925–26	Central League	42	17	10	15	87	84	44	8th	S. Powell 15
1926–27	Central League	42	21	5	16	95	76	47	7th	S. Powell 33
1927–28	Central League	42	21	5	16	97	86	47	5th	S. Powell 26
1928–29	Central League	42	24	9	9	104	56	57	1st	Trotter 21
1929–30	Central League	42	25	6	11	114	71	56	4th	Johnson 29
1930–31	Central League	42	22	8	12	115	77	52	3rd	Jones 27
1931–32	Central League	42	21	8	13	99	79	50	7th	Millership 21
1932–33	Central League	42	19	8	15	81	80	46	9th	Law 27
1933–34	Central League	42	13	8	21	73	88	34	15th	Cooper 12
1934–35	Central League	42	15	7	20	87	97	37	16th	Law 17
1935–36	Central League	42	10	8	24	79	109	28	21st	Ashley 15
1936–37	Central League	42	13	12	17	90	87	38	16th	Shelley 12
1937–38	Central League	42	18	8	16	59	55	44	5th	Driver 9
1938–39	Central League	42	20	7	15	79	72	47	5th	Aveyard 13
1939–40	Central League	3	3	0	0	9	3	6	N/A	Ward 3
1941–42	Sheffield Association League	22	13	5	4	78	37	31	2nd/3rd	n/k
1942–43	Sheffield Association League	20	12	1	4	61	28	25	Top 4	* 3 results unknown
1943–44	Sheffield Association League	26	18	1	6	64	27	37	Top 4#	* 1 result unknown
	# won Championship Play-off									
1944–45	Sheffield Association League	34	11	5	16	70	66	27	Top 4	* 2 results unknown
1945–46	Central League	40	27	9	4	112	41	63	1st	Ward 16
1946–47	Central League	42	19	5	18	71	77	43	12th	Ward 12
1947–48	Central League	42	13	10	19	76	67	36	14th	Rogers 10
1948–49	Central League	42	17	12	13	62	56	46	10th	Fletcher 15
1949–50	Central League	42	18	8	16	54	54	44	10th	Dooley 12
1950–51	Central League	42	16	12	14	59	68	44	10th	Dooley 21
1951–52	Central League	42	23	7	12	83	62	53	4th	Dooley 13
1952–53	Central League	42	17	7	18	63	68	41	14th	Slater 17
1953–54	Central League	42	18	6	18	68	69	42	12th	Slater 13
1954–55	Central League	42	14	8	20	68	83	36	18th	J. McAnearney 11

Season	Competition	P	W	D	L	F	A	Pts	Pos.	Top Scorer
1955–56	Central League	42	19	11	12	78	59	49	5th	Greensmith 10
1956–57	Central League	42	25	10	7	91	51	60	2nd	J.McAnearney 21
1957–58	Central League	42	18	9	15	79	61	45	8th	J. McAnearney 11
1958–59	Central League	42	21	12	9	90	65	54	3rd	J. McAnearney 13
1959–60	Central League	42	21	9	12	74	57	51	7th	Griffin 14
1960–61	Central League	42	25	7	10	78	52	57	1st	Griffin 16
1961–62	Central League	42	14	8	20	78	77	36	16th	Quinn 14
1962–63	Central League	42	16	12	14	77	72	44	11th	Hickton 12
1963–64	Central League	42	23	6	13	92	60	52	6th	Ford 17
1964–65	Central League	42	15	9	18	73	74	39	13th	n/k
1965–66	Central League	42	13	12	17	66	78	38	16th	Davies/Whitham 12
1966–67	Central League	42	11	10	21	50	80	32	18th	Whitham 15
1967–68	Central League	42	11	7	24	47	92	29	19th	Whitham/Woodall 6
1968–69	Central League	42	16	8	18	49	52	40	12th	Prendergast 8
1969–70	Central League	42	10	13	19	53	82	33	19th	Prendergast 13
1970–71	Central League	42	12	16	14	45	60	40	13th	Sunley 12
1971–72	Central League	42	9	16	17	44	53	34	18th	Downes
1972–73	Central League	42	20	9	13	77	51	49	6th	Wylde 26
1973–74	Central League	42	16	13	13	54	45	45	10th	Prudham
1974–75	Central League	42	18	6	18	60	69	42	12th	Herbert 11
1975–76	Central League	42	9	15	18	42	60	33	17th	Herbert 11
1976–77	Central League	42	11	16	15	41	55	38	15th	Fisher
1977–78	Central League	42	12	7	23	37	60	31	21st	Owen 6
1978–79	Central League	42	19	6	17	74	68	44	8th	Strutt 13
1979–80	Central League	42	18	7	17	68	61	43	12th	Lowey
1980–81	Central League	42	15	10	17	52	60	40	11th	Pearson 12
1981–82	Central League	42	18	5	19	75	76	41	12th	Simmons 24
1982–83	Central League	30	16	6	8	59	39	38	5th	Simmons 15
1983–84	Central League	30	11	5	14	52	61	38	10th	Taylor 12
1984–85	Central League	34	18	4	12	69	55	58	6th	Pearson 14
1985–86	Central League	34	16	4	14	55	47	52	6th	Shutt 7
1986–87	Central League	34	13	10	11	57	51	49	10th	Reeves 10
1987–88	Central League	34	13	8	13	54	52	47	9th	Bradshaw 8
1988–89	Central League	34	8	8	18	40	70	32	R17th	Reeves
1989–90	Central League - Second Division	34	19	6	9	69	36	63	P3rd	Lycett 13
1990–91	Central League - First Division	34	23	6	5	69	36	75	1st	Watson 13
1991–92	Central League - First Division	34	10	9	15	44	49	39	13th	Watson 12
1992–93	Central League - First Division	34	13	10	11	51	48	49	8th	Watson 16
1993–94	Central League - First Division	34	7	12	15	46	63	33	R16th	Chambers 10
1994–95	Central League - Second Division	34	20	6	8	74	40	66	P3rd	Barker 20
1995–96	Central League - First Division	34	11	8	15	66	63	41	13th	Donaldson 16
1996–97	Central League - Premier Division	24	12	4	8	42	32	40	3rd	Donaldson 10
1997–98	Central League - Premier Division	24	4	7	13	27	40	19	R13th	Donaldson 5

Season	Competition	P	W	D	L	F	A	Pts	Pos.	Top Scorer
1998–99	Central League - First Division	24	9	8	7	26	23	35	6th	Douglas 7
1999–2000	FA Premier Reserve League	24	5	4	15	35	52	19	12th	Cresswell 5
2000–01	FA Premier Reserve League (North)	22	1	3	18	25	68	6	12th	Muller 5
2001–02	FA Premier Reserve League (North)	24	2	4	18	26	61	10	13th	Bonvin 5
2002–03	FA Premier Reserve League (North)	28	3	5	20	21	55	14	14th	Donnelly/Owusu 3
2003–04	Central League - Premier Division	22	8	3	11	32	33	27	7th	Shaw 11
	League Cup: Winners									
2004–05	Central League - Premier Division	22	11	4	7	36	28	37	3rd	Shaw 6
	League Cup: Runners Up									
2005–06	Central League - Division One (Central)	18	10	5	3	26	13	35	1st*	Corr 6
	League Cup: Q/F * lost in divisional Play-offs									
2006–07	Central League - Division One (Central)	22	12	4	6	36	25	40	4th	Graham 7
	League Cup: R1									
2007–08	Central League - East	22	11	4	7	37	23	37	3rd	Esajas 5
	League Cup: Did not enter									
2008–09	Central League - Central Division	16	6	3	7	24	27	21	4th	R. Lekaj 10
	League Cup: R1									
2009–10	Central League - Central Division	16	4	3	9	16	25	15	9th	Jeffers 4
2010–11	Central League - Central Division	14	0	2	12	7	42	2	8th	Seven with 1 goal

The reserve team was scrapped in April 2011 after almost 120 years of competitive football

Second/Third/A Team /Youth Friendlies & Minor Cups

R Reserves
3RD Third Team/'A' Team
Yth Youth/Junior team

9 Nov 1867	FR	R	Milton Res.	A	?	
25 Nov 1867	FR	R	Garrick Club Res.	A	0-0	* Lost 1 rouge to nil
26 Nov 1867	FR	R	Wellington Res.	A	?	
7 Dec 1867	FR	R	Milton Res.	HF	0-0	* Lost 4 rouges to nil
9 Dec 1867	FR	R	Garrick Club Res.	HF	0-1	
30 Dec 1867	FR	R	Broomhall Res.	HF	?	
7 Mar 1868	FR	R	Wellington Res.	HF	?	
7 Nov 1868	FR	R	Mechanics Res.	A	?	
21 Nov 1868	FR	R	Wellington Res.	HF	?	
5 Dec 1868	FR	R	Mechanics Res.	HF	?	
12 Dec 1868	FR	R	Broomhall Res.	A	?	
16 Jan 1869	FR	R	Wellington Res.	A	?	
13 Feb 1869	FR	R	Broomhall Res.	HF	?	
15 Oct 1870	FR	R	Heeley Res.	A	1-1	Butterell
24 Oct 1870	FR	3rd	Oxford 3rds	A	1-1	T. Butler
29 Oct 1870	FR	R	Mackenzie Res.	MR	0-0	
12 Nov 1870	FR	R	Fir Vale Res.	MR	1-0	
21 Nov 1870	FR	3rd	Broomhall 3rds	A	3-0	Fearnehough 2, Staniland
3 Dec 1870	FR	3rd	MacKenzie 3rds	A	0-1	
10 Dec 1870	FR	2nd	Broomhall 3rds	A	8-0	Ward 3, Orton 2, Croft, Staniland, Mill
17 Dec 1870	FR	R	Heeley Res.	MR	1-1	Jones
26 Dec 1870	FR	R	Fir Vale Res.	A	0-4	
14 Jan 1871	FR	3rd	Oxford 3rds	MR	5-0*	Booker 2, Roberts, Donovan
14 Jan 1871	FR	R	Broomhall Res.	A	4-1	Hill, Cawthorn, Hague, Jones
28 Jan 1871	FR	R	Mackenzie Res.		0-0	
11 Feb 1871	FR	3rd	Broomhall 3rds	MR	1-0	Mills
18 Feb 1871	FR	R	Mackenzie Res.	MR	2-1	Tingle, Staniland
14 Oct 1871	FR	R	Heeley Res.	A	0-1	
4 Nov 1871	FR	R	Fir Vale Res.	A	1-4	
13 Nov 1871	FR	3rd	Broomhall 3rds	MR	4-1	Brownhill 2, Lee, Parker

25 Nov 1871	FR	R	Mackenzie Res.	MR	1-0	Anthony (J)
13 Jan 1872	FR	R	Heeley Res.	MR	4-0	Glossop 2, White, Hill
27 Jan 1872	FR	R	Fir Vale Res.	MR	2-0	Brownhill, Hill
3 Feb 1872	FR	3rd	Broomhall 3rds	A	0-1	
12 Feb 1872	FR	3rd	MacKenzie 3rds	MR	2-1	Staniland 2
9 Mar 1872	FR	3rd	MacKenzie 3rds	MR	0-5	
19 Oct 1872	FR	??	Heeley	A	2-0	
1 Jan 1873	FR	??	Brincliffe	??	Won	
22 Feb 1873	FR	??	Rotherham	MR	9-0	???
18 Oct 1873	FR	R	Fir Vale Res.	A	5-0	Brownhill 2, Eliis, Hall, Procter
15 Nov 1873	FR	3rd	Norfolk Park 3rds	A	2-5	Hatherley, Graham
25 Nov 1873	FR	R	Fir Vale Res.	MR	?	
1 Dec 1873	FR	R	Broomhall Res.	Ecclesfield	Draw	
6 Dec 1873	FR	R	Rotherham Res.	A	1-1	Hill
10 Jan 1874	FR	R	Heeley Res.	MR	1-0	T. Butler
17 Jan 1874	FR	R	Broomhall Res.	MR	2-1	T. Butler, Wood
24 Jan 1874	FR	R	Norfolk Park Res.	A	1-3	
7 Feb 1874	FR	3rd	Broomhall 3rds	Ecclesfield	1-1	
21 Feb 1874	FR	3rd	Norfolk Park 3rds	MR	4-1	
7 Mar 1874	FR	R	Norfolk Park Res.	MR	3-1	
24 Oct 1874	FR	3rd	Broomhall 3rds	MR	1-5	
14 Nov 1874	FR	R	Exchange Brewery	MR	2-1*	Wilson
21 Nov 1874	FR	R	Norfolk Park Res.	A	8-0	Orton 5
28 Nov 1874	FR	3rd	Norfolk Park 3rds	MR	1-0	
12 Dec 1874	FR	R	Heeley Res.	A	0-0	
28 Dec 1874	FR	R	Broomhall Res.	A	?	
2 Jan 1875	FR	R	Norfolk Park Res.	MR	3-0	Wardley, Orton, Selby
9 Jan 1875	FR	R	Heeley Res.	MR	0-1	
30 Jan 1875	FR	3rd	Broomhall 3rds	MR	2-1	Hill 2
30 Jan 1875	FR	R	Crystal Palace Res. (Thurlstone)	A	?	
20 Feb 1875	FR	3rd	Norfolk Park 3rds	A	?	
6 Mar 1875	FR	R	Broomhall Res.	MR	1-0	Fay
16 Oct 1875	FR	R	Exchange Brewery Res.	MR	1-2	Pinder
23 Oct 1875	FR	R	Hallam Res.	A	1-3	Pinder
4 Dec 1875	FR	R	Heeley Res.	A	0-3	
1 Jan 1876	FR	R	Crystal Palace Res. (Thurlstone)	MR	3-0	Collins, Brooke, Siddall
3 Jan 1876	FR	3rd	Millhouses 3rds	A	?	
29 Jan 1876	FR	R	Hallam Res.	MR	1-1	H. Musforth
12 Feb 1876	FR	R	Broomhall Res.	A	0-3	
4 Mar 1876	FR	R	Heeley Res.	MR	1-4	Gill
14 Oct 1876	FR	R	Heeley Res.	MR	1-1	Selby
23 Oct 1876	FR	3rd	Exchange Brewery 3rds	A	1-2	C. Fletcher
4 Nov 1876	FR	R	Hallam Res.	A	3-0	Lindsay, Barker, Ellis

16 Dec 1876	FR	R	Exchange Brewery Res.	A	1-2		Staniforth
28 Dec 1876	FR	R	Crystal Palace Res. (Thurlstone)	A	?		
30 Dec 1876	FR	3rd	Millhouses 3rds	A	?		
29 Jan 1877	FR	3rd	Exchange Brewery 3rds	MR	?		
13 Feb 1877	FR	3rd	Millhouses 3rds	MR	1-3		
5 Jan 1878	FR	R	Heeley Res.	SH	1-1		T. Butler
7 Jan 1878	FR	3rd	Exchange Brewery 3rds	SH	0-2		
12 Jan 1878	FR	R	Spital Hill Res.	SH	4-0		Deans, T. Butler, Parker, Burrell
16 Mar 1878	FR	R	Exchange Brewery Res.	A	0-3		
7 Dec 1878	FR	3rd	Heeley 3rds	A	0-5		
22 Feb 1879	FR	3rd	Millhouses 3rds	A	0-8		
25 Oct 1879	FR	R	Heeley Res.	A	1-2		
29 Nov 1879	FR	R	Exchange Brewery Res.	A	0-0		
8 Dec 1879	FR	3rd	Heeley 3rds	SH	0-1		
22 Nov 1880	FR	R	Fir Vale Res.	A	1-6		
1 Jan 1881	FR	R	Oxford Res.	A	0-4		
21 Oct 1882	MC1	R	Walkley Res.	A	10-1		
18 Nov 1882	MC2	R	Lockwood Brothers Res.	H	0-10		
20 Jan 1883	FR	R	Broomhall Res.	H	7-2		Wilson 4, Hiller 2, Stokes
6 Oct 1883	FR	R	Surrey Res.	A	6-0		Walker, Robinson, Cawthorne, n/k
13 Oct 1883	MC1	R	Attercliffe Res.	A	2-2		Hiller, n/k
27 Oct 1883	MC1 r	R	Attercliffe Res.	HB	2-2		
3 Nov 1883	FR	R	St Matthias	HB	5-2		
10 Nov 1883	FR	R	Heeley Res.	A	0-2		
17 Nov 1883	FR	R	Rotherham Res.	A	?		
1 Dec 1883	FR	R	Cavendish	HB	0-2		
15 Dec 1883	MC1 2r	R	Attercliffe Res.	HB	2-2		
29 Dec 1883	FR	R	St Williams Walkley	HB	4-1		
1 Jan 1884	MC1 3r	R	Attercliffe Res.	A	0-2		
26 Jan 1884	FR	R	Heeley Res.	HB	?		
2 Feb 1884	FR	R	Lockwood Brothers Res.	A	?		
9 Feb 1884	FR	R	Park Grange Res.	A	?		
March 1884	FR	R	Caledonians	HB	5-0		
15 Mar 1884	FR	R	Walkley Res.	A	2-2		
22 Mar 1884	FR	R	Wesley College	HB	?		
27 Sep 1884	FR	R	Owlerton Res.	HB	5-1		
11 Oct 1884	MC1	R	Holmes Res.	HB	9-0		
1 Nov 1884	FR	R	Hallam Res.	HB	0-1		
10 Nov 1884	FR	R	Melville Res.	A	0-1		
15 Nov 1884	MC2	R	Rotherham Res.	HB	6-1		Hiller, Parton
22 Nov 1884	FR	R	Spital Chesterfield	A	2-3		
29 Nov 1884	MC3	R	Attercliffe Res.	A	1-1	600	Wilkinson
6 Dec 1884	MC3r	R	Attercliffe Res.	HB	1-2		

31 Jan 1885	FR	R	Heeley Res.	A	1-0	
21 Feb 1885	FR	R	Melville Res.	HB	1-6	
19 Sep 1885	FR	R	Pitsmoor Standard	HB	3-3	
10 Oct 1885	MC1	R	Milton Works	HB	2-2	
24 Oct 1885	MC1 - r	R	Milton Works	A	1-1	
7 Nov 1885	MC1 - 2r	R	Milton Works	HB	2-0	Needham, n/k
28 Nov 1885	MC2	R	Doncaster Rovers	HB	1-2	
26 Dec 1885	FR	R	Rotherham Res.	A	0-10	
16 Jan 1886	FR	R	Hallam Res.	HB	1-1	Smith
20 Jan 1886	FR	R	Lockwood Brothers Res.	A	3-1	
9 Oct 1886	MC1	R	Owlerton St Johns	A	0-1	
30 Oct 1886	FR	R	Bethel Reds	HB	1-4	
13 Nov 1886	FR	R	St Mary's	HB	0-1	
6 Dec 1886	FR	R	Sheffield Scottish	HB	2-0	
11 Dec 1886	FR	R	Bethel Reds	A	2-1	
7 Feb 1887	FR	R	Clarence	HB	8-0	
14 Feb 1887	FR	R	Lockwood Brothers Res.	HB	1-3	
10 Sep 1887	FR	R	Lockwood Brothers Res.	A	3-0	Swift, Hurd, Young
17 Sep 1887	FR	R	Hanover	H	9-1	
1 Oct 1887	FR	R	St Andrews	HB	1-2	
8 Oct 1887	MC1	R	Melville	A	1-1	
15 Oct 1887	MC1 - r	R	Melville	H	1-2	Dronfield
29 Oct 1887	FR	R	Hallam	A	2-1	Candlish, Young
5 Nov 1887	FR	R	Wadsley Asylum	A	6-1	
19 Nov 1887	FR	R	Hallam	A	1-5	
26 Nov 1887	FR	R	St Anne's	H	3-0	
10 Dec 1887	FR	R	Weston Street Reform	A	1-0	
31 Dec 1887	FR	R	Heeley Res.	A	0-2	
14 Jan 1888	FR	R	Spital Chesterfield	A	1-2	Elliott
21 Jan 1888	FR	R	St Mary's	A	1-4	
4 Feb 1888	FR	R	Hastings	H	7-2	
6 Feb 1888	FR	R	Lockwood Brothers Res.	A	0-5	
31 Mar 1888	FR	R	Heeley Res.	A	0-7	
9 Apr 1888	FR	R	Hastings	A	1-3	
16 Apr 1888	FR	R	Meadowhall	H	4-2	
22 Sep 1888	FR	R	Owlerton Res.	H	4-1	Marr 2, Hawnt, n/k
6 Oct 1888	FR	R	Fitzwalters	H	6-2	
15 Oct 1888	FR	R	Owlerton Res.	A	0-3	
20 Oct 1888	FR	R	Chesterfield	H	1-4	
10 Nov 1888	FR	R	Derby County Res.	H	1-5	White
24 Nov 1888	FR	R	Melville	A	2-1	
8 Dec 1888	FR	R	West End	A	7-0	50 mins game
22 Dec 1888	FR	R	Eckington	H	11-1	

27 Dec 1888	FR	R	Newark	A	1-1		Macredie
1 Jan 1889	FR	R	Chesterfield	A	3-4		
1 Jan 1889	FR	R	St Mary's	A	5-0		
7 Jan 1889	FR	R	Heeley Olympic	A	2-1		
12 Jan 1889	FR	R	St George's Athletic	A	2-1		
14 Jan 1889	FR	R	Millhouses	H	10-1		
26 Jan 1889	FR	R	Sheepbridge Works	A	3-5		White, Macredie, Hudson
18 Feb 1889	FR	R	Newark	H	5-3		White 2, W. Hiller 2, Wise
4 Mar 1889	FR	R	Stocksbridge Foresters	A	5-1		White
27 Apr 1889	FR	R	Sheffield FC Res.	H	2-0		
7 Sep 1889	FR	R	Exchange	A	3-0		
14 Sep 1889	FR	R	Worksop Town	H	4-0		S. Nicholson 2, n/k
28 Sep 1889	FR	R	Owlerton Res.	H	4-0		Thompson, Bramwell, n/k
12 Oct 1889	FR	R	Huddersfield Association XI	A	6-2		Thompson 2, Gill, White, Warburton, n/k
19 Oct 1889	FR	R	Bakewell	H	3-1		
26 Oct 1889	FR	R	Sheepbridge Works	H	2-0		
2 Nov 1889	FR	R	Long Eaton Athletic	A	1-2		White
9 Nov 1889	FR	R	Notts County Res.	H	1-1	500	White
16 Nov 1889	FR	R	Exchange Brewery	H	2-1		
2 Dec 1889	FR	R	15th East Yorks. Regiment	H	5-0		White 2, Cutts, Thompson, n/k
7 Dec 1889	FR	R	Mexborough	H	2-0		
9 Dec 1889	FR	R	Ecclesfield	H	3-1		
14 Dec 1889	FR	R	Gainsborough Trinity Res.	A	1-0		
26 Dec 1889	FR	R	Ecclesfield	A	0-3		
28 Dec 1889	FR	R	Scarborough	A	1-0		White
Dec 1889	FR	R	Whitby	A	1-5		
20 Jan 1890	FR	R	Worksop Town	A	3-0		
27 Jan 1890	FR	R	Owlerton Res.	A	0-2		
1 Feb 1890	FR	R	Retford Town	A	5-0		
8 Feb 1890	GNCC1	R	Gainsborough Trinity Res.	H	3-2		Ward 2, Holroyd
22 Feb 1890	FR	R	Notts County Res.	A	0-5		
17 Mar 1890	FR	R	Chesterfield	H	5-0	400	Cutts 2, Ward, W. Hiller, White
22 Mar 1890	FR	R	Sheepbridge Works	A	1-1		Ward
5 Apr 1890	TST	R	Bakewell (Robinson)	A	3-2		
12 Apr 1890	FR	R	Mexborough	A	2-6		Cutts, White
19 Apr 1890	GNCC SF	R	Notts Olympic	H	1-3	800	Holroyd
26 Apr 1890	FR	R	Carbrook Church	H	8-1		Webster 4, Holroyd 2, n/k
3 Sep 1890	PR		Probables v Improbables	H	2-1		
8 Sep 1890	FR	R	Ecclesfield	H	3-3	300	W. Hiller 2, Hill
13 Sep 1890	FR	R	Carbrook Church	H	7-3		Woolhouse 3, Gill, Webster, Cutts, n/k
27 Sep 1890	SCC1*	R	Clinton	H	3-2		Shaw, Bissett, Webster * AET – 90 mins 2-2
* Game ordered to be replayed after Shaw of Wednesday found to have been incorrectly registered							
4 Oct 1890	FR	R	Bradford Association	H	6-1	800	Bennett 2, Webster, Scott, P. Hiller, Shaw

25 Oct 1890	SCC1	R	Clinton	H	14-1	2,000	W. Hiller 5, Scott 4, Drabble 2, Hurd, Ingram, Cutts
1 Nov 1890	FR	R	Buxton	A	1-1		Shaw
8 Nov 1890	SCC2	R	Mexborough	A	4-2	500	Kennedy 2, P. Hiller, W. Hiller
22 Nov 1890	FR	R	Gainsborough WMC	A	3-2		Fairburn, Shaw, Webster
6 Dec 1890	FR	R	Fairfield (Manchester)	A	0-1		
13 Dec 1890	FR	R	Bradford Association	A	5-0	300	Bennett, n/k
20 Dec 1890	FR	R	Rotherham Town Res.	H	5-4		Shaw, n/k
26 Dec 1890	FR	R	Scarborough	A	2-0	2,000	Ingram, Shaw
31 Dec 1890	SCC3*	R	Ecclesfield	H	1-2	1,500	* Game ordered to be replayed
1 Jan 1891	FR	R	Chesterfield Town	A	2-3		
19 Jan 1891	SCC3	R	Ecclesfield	H	1-3	750	Winterbottom
24 Jan 1891	FR	R	Attercliffe	A	2-5		Mifflin, Dungworth
31 Jan 1891	FR	R	Sheepbridge Works	A	2-2	600	G. Shaw, W. Bennett
7 Feb 1891	FR	R	Rotherham Town Res.	A	5-5		White, Scott, Webster, n/k
7 Mar 1891	FR	R	Grimsby Town Res.	H	4-0		Webster 2, W. Bennett, n/k
14 Mar 1891	FR	R	Wath	A	2-4		Webster, n/k
23 Mar 1891	FR	R	Sheepbridge Works	H	12-0		W. Bennett 4, Hurd 4, Shaw 3, Webster
28 Mar 1891	TST	R	Belper Town (Stone)	A	1-4	1,000	H. Bennett
11 Apr 1891	FR	R	Scarborough	H	2-2	300	Ingram 2
5 Sep 1891	FR	R	Saltley (Birmingham)	A	5-2		
19 Sep 1891	FR	R	Buxton	A	1-3		Shaw
10 Oct 1891	FR	R	Attercliffe	H	5-3		Ingram 2, T. Dungworth 2, Webster
7 Nov 1891	SCC1	R	Eckington Works	H	5-0		T. Dungworth, Shaw, Winterbottom, H. Woolhouse, Swallow
14 Nov 1891	FR	R	Burton Swifts Res.	H	7-0		Shaw 3, Winterbottom 2, Webster 2
5 Dec 1891	FR	R	Nottingham Forest Res.	H	2-2		Shaw, T. Dungworth
19 Dec 1891	SCC2*	R	Attercliffe	H	2-0		Shaw 2 * game ordered to be replayed
25 Dec 1891	FR	R	Grimsby Town Res.	H	6-0		Cawley 5, Richardson
1 Jan 1892	FR	R	Barnsley St Peters	A	3-2		
2 Jan 1892	FR	R	Belper Town	A	4-4	500	Ingram, Webster, T. Dungworth, n/k
4 Jan 1892	SCC2r	R	Attercliffe	A	3-1	1,000	Ingram 3
23 Jan 1892	FR	R	Rotherham	A	2-2	1,000	Shaw 2
30 Jan 1892	SCC3	R	Rotherham	A	4-1	1,000	Webster 3, Winterbottom
20 Feb 1892	SCC SF	R	Barnsley St Peters	Carbrook	6-1	1,000	Ingram 3, Shaw, J. Brandon, Webster
12 Mar 1892	SCC F	R	Sheffield United Res.	BL	1-2	5,000	Winterbottom
28 Mar 1892	FR	R	Attercliffe	A	3-7*		Webster, Winterbottom
7 Apr 1892	WCC SF	R	Staveley	BL	4-1		Webster, H. Woolhouse, Winterbottom, J. Brandon
11 Apr 1892	FR	R	Minor League XI	H	3-7		
18 Apr 1892	FR	R	Burton Swifts Res.	A	2-3		
19 Apr 1892	FR	R	Minor League XI	H	3-1		Priest, Parkin, Murdoch
26 Apr 1892	FR	R	Minor League XI	H	3-2		Gray, n/k
19 Sep 1892	FR	R	Wombwell Town	A	3-2	500	Ingram 2, Bestall
3 Dec 1892	FR	R	Chesterfield	A	0-2		
12 Dec 1892	SCC3	R	Mexborough	H	4-2		Dunlop, H. Woolhouse, T. Dungworth, Cheffins

2 Jan 1893	FR	R	Attercliffe	A	1-1		Millar
14 Jan 1893	FR	R	Sheepbridge Works	A	2-4	1,000	Barlow, n/k
28 Jan 1893	SCC SF	R	Rotherham Town	BL	2-1	5,000	Reid, T. Dungworth
4 Feb 1893	FR	R	Buxton	A	0-2		
18 Feb 1893	FR	R	Matlock	A	2-3		Fairburn, Dunlop
20 Mar 1893	SCC F	R	Sheffield United Res.	BL	1-3	4,500	McIntosh
4 Apr 1893	FR	3rd	Minor League XI	H	4-1		Burridge, Wass, n/k
15 Apr 1893	FR	R	Gainsborough Trinity Res.	H	5-0	1,000	Ingram, Reid, Fairburn, Pike, H. Brandon
17 Apr 1893	FR	R	Rest of League	H	4-2		Dunlop, Hall, Barlow, H. Woolhouse
20 Apr 1893	FR	3rd	Minor League XI	H	2-1		Short, Fairburn
22 Apr 1893	FR	R	Mexborough	A	3-1		Gooing, Darroch (pen), Barlow
18 Sep 1893	FR	R	Kilnhurst	H	3-0	1,000	F. Woolhouse, Barlow, McIntosh
28 Oct 1893	FR	R	Blackburn Rovers Res.	A	1-3	1,000	Rowan
11 Dec 1893	FR	R	Pyebank Rovers	H	1-4		Ward
3 Feb 1894	FR	R	Doncaster Rovers	H	1-0		F. Woolhouse
20 Mar 1894	FR	R	Mount St Mary's College	A	3-1		F. Thompson, n/k
31 Mar 1894	FR	R	Ilkeston Town	A	0-3	2,000	
16 Apr 1894	FR	R	Pyebank Rovers	H	5-0		
21 Apr 1894	FR	R	Attercliffe	H	3-2		
19 Sep 1895	FR	R	Rest of League	H	2-2		Priestley, n/k
2 Dec 1895	FR	R	Eyam	H	4-0		Callaghan 3, Taylor
7 Apr 1896	FR	R	Eckington Works	H	4-0		Wastnage, Collinson, n/k
25 Apr 1896	FR	R	Channing Rovers	H	2-2	1,000	Bullivant, Jones
25 Jan 1897	SCC1	R	Sheffield United Res.	A	1-3	800	Gooing
25 Dec 1897	FR	R	Ilkeston Town	A	1-3		
8 Jan 1898	SCC1	R	Kilnhurst	H	2-0		Topham (pen), Richards
5 Feb 1898	SCC SF	R	Wath	Owlerton	4-1		Cole, Topham, Moffatt, Richards
2 Apr 1898	FR	R	Owlerton Swifts	A	1-2		
12 Apr 1898	FR	R	Rest of League	Leicester	1-2		Regan
14 Nov 1898	SCC F (held over)	R	Sheffield United Res.	A	1-3	2,000	Layton (pen)
9 Jan 1899	SCC1	R	Royston United	H	7-1		Topham 2, Beech 2, Maidment 2, Hutton
18 Feb 1899	SCC SF	R	Attercliffe	Owlerton	1-2		Hutton
1 Apr 1899	TST	R	Montrose Works	A	2-6		Brady, n/k
4 Apr 1899	TST	R	Attercliffe	A	1-0		P. Crawshaw
21 Oct 1899	FR	R	Montrose Works	A	1-1		Topham
6 Nov 1899	FR	R	Parkgate United	A	3-1		Beech 2, Nettleton
2 Dec 1899	SCC1	R	Attercliffe	A	2-2		Chapman, Hutton
30 Dec 1899	SCC1 - r	R	Attercliffe	H	8-0		Lee 2, Topham 2, Beech, Chapman, n/k
13 Jan 1900	SCC2	R	Mexborough	H	9-0		Hutton 3, Simmons 2, Beech, Thackeray, Chapman
3 Feb 1900	SCC SF	R	Rotherham	Carbrook	1-0		Beech
31 Mar 1900	SCC F	R	Worksop Town	Carbrook	2-0		Chapman, Saxby
16 Apr 1900	FR	R	Barnsley	A	1-3		Davis
1 Dec 1900	SCC2	R	Montrose Works	A	6-1		Lee 2, Simmons, Beech, Chapman, Topham

29 Dec 1900	WCC2	R	Sheffield United Res.	A	1-0	3,000	Chapman
5 Jan 1901	FR	R	Doncaster Rovers	A	1-1		McWhinnie
12 Jan 1901	SCC3	R	Denaby United	A	2-0		Beech, McWhinnie
16 Feb 1901	WCC SF	R	Monk Bretton	Wath	0-7		
19 Feb 1901	FR	R	Doncaster Rovers	H	1-2		Layton
4 Mar 1901	SCC SF	R	Sheffield United Res.	BL	2-3	5,000	Beech, McWhinnie
11 Jan 1902	SCC3	R	Wath Athletic	A	2-1		Topham, Dryburgh
15 Mar 1902	SCC SF	R	Sheffield United Res.	BL	1-0	8,000	Beech
29 Mar 1902	SCC F	R	Royston	Monk Bretton	1-0	3,000	Simmons
21 Apr 1902	FR	R	Channing Rovers	H	0-3		
8 Dec 1902	SCC2	R	Sheffield United Res.	A	1-1	2,000	Stewart
7 Jan 1903	SCC2r	R	Sheffield United Res.	H	4-1		Stewart 2, Marrison 2
10 Jan 1903	SCC SF	R	Thornhill United	Carbrook	7-0		Stewart 3, Marrison 3, Gosling
14 Feb 1903	SCC F	R	Roundel	BL	1-1	6,000	Ryalls
13 Apr 1903	SCC Fr	R	Roundel	BL	5-0*	7,000	Marrison 2, Beech, Stewart
14 Apr 1903	FR	R	Rest of League	H	1-0	3,500	Simms
16 Nov 1903	SCC2	R	Thorpe Hesley	H	4-2		Marrison 2, Stewart, Beech
16 Jan 1904	SCC3	R	Sheffield United Res.	H	4-2	4,000	Beech 2, Bartlett, Marrison
13 Feb 1904	SCC SF	R	Barnsley Res.	Mexborough	2-2*		Thackeray (pen)
28 Feb 1904	SCC SFr	R	Barnsley Res.	Wath	0-3		
5 Apr 1904	FR	R	Rest of League	H	4-1		Tummon 3, Marrison
17 Dec 1904	SCC2	R	Barnsley Res.	A	1-1		J. Stewart (pen)
9 Jan 1905	SCC2r	R	Barnsley Res.	H	3-0		Marrison, Bradshaw, Malloch
14 Jan 1905	SCC3	R	Rotherham Town	A	3-0	2,500	Marrison 2, n/k
11 Feb 1905	SCC SF	R	Wycliffe	Rotherham	2-0	1,000	Eyre, Bradshaw
11 Mar 1905	SCC F	R	Sheffield United Res.	Owlerton	1-3	6,000	Bradshaw
16 Dec 1905	SCC1	R	Doncaster Rovers	A	4-0		Brittleton 4
20 Jan 1906	SCC2	R	Hoyland Town	H	18-0		Bradshaw 7, Rollinson 5, Tummon 2, Reynolds, Holbem, Marrison, n/k
10 Feb 1906	SCC SF	R	Barnsley Res.	Intake	7-0		Hemmingfield 3, Rollinson 2, Bradshaw, Tummon
17 Mar 1906	SCC F	R	Denaby United	Rotherham	2-4	7,000	Bradshaw 2
30 Apr 1906	FR	R	Grimsby Town Res.	H	3-1	500	Rollinson 2, Tummon
15 Dec 1906	SCC1	R	Rotherham County	A	1-0		Lloyd
21 Jan 1907	SCC2	R	Tinsley Park	A	3-0		Reynolds, F. Wilson, Lloyd
18 Feb 1907	SCC SF	R	Rotherham Town	BL	2-1	5,000	Tellum, Rollinson
18 Mar 1907	SCC F	R	Sheffield United Res.	Owlerton	2-2	4,000	Bradshaw (pen), Malloch
18 Apr 1907	SCC Fr	R	Sheffield United Res.	BL	2-0	4,000	Tellum, Lloyd
2 Dec 1907	WCC1	R	South Kirkby Colliery	A	2-0		Napier, Holbem
14 Dec 1907	SCC2	R	Tinsley Park	A	6-0	600	Napier 2, Rollinson 2, Armstrong, Tummon
18 Jan 1908	SCC3	R	Doncaster Rovers	H	6-0		Rollinson 3, Armstrong, Tummon (pen), Miller
10 Feb 1908	SCC SF	R	Sheffield United Res.	BL	2-3	10,286	Rollinson 2
23 Mar 1908	WCC SF	R	Sheffield United Res.	H	1-0	3,000	Rollinson
4 Apr 1908	TST	R	Grasshoppers (Millhouses) (Lyall/Malloch)	A	8-0		
30 Nov 1908	WCC F	R	Rotherham County	BL	3-2	4,000	Spoors 2, Armstrong (1907-08 Final held over)

12 Dec 1908	SCC1	R	Wath Athletic	A	2-0		Stringfellow, Spoors (pen)
25 Jan 1909	SCC2	R	Rotherham County	H	0-4	2,000	
6 Feb 1909	FR	R	Buxton	A	1-1		
13 Apr 1909	TST	R	Ilkeston United (Roulstone)	A	2-1	2,000	O'Connell, Stringfellow
21 Oct 1909	WCC1	R	Hickleton Main	A	3-0	500	Stringfellow, n/k
11 Dec 1909	SCC1	R	South Kirkby Colliery	A	5-3		Lloyd 2, Stringfellow, Hamilton (pen), Weir
22 Jan 1910	SCC2	R	Wath Athletic	A	2-0		O'Connell 2 (1 pen)
12 Feb 1910	SCC SF	R	Barnsley Res.	Wath	1-3		Miller
14 Feb 1910	WCC2	R	Sheffield United Res.	A	0-1		
19 Nov 1910	WCC1	R	Hickleton Main	A	5-2		Glennon 3, Murray, Bradley
10 Dec 1910	SCC1	R	Rotherham County	A	2-6		Stringfellow, Wright
dnk	WCC2	R	Darfield United	A	2-0		
28 Jan 1911	FR	R	Licenced Victuallers Lge	H	3-1*		Warren (pen), Stringfellow
4 Feb 1911	WCC SF	R	Shiregreen	H	2-1		Burkinshaw 2
10 Apr 1911	WCC F	R	Sheffield United Res.	A	3-3	3,000	Wright 2, O'Connell (pen)
27 Apr 1911	WCC Fr	R	Sheffield United Res.	H	3-0	2,000	Glennon 3
16 Sep 1911	FR	R	Aston Villa Res.	A	2-5		Moore, Wright
2 Dec 1911	WCC1	R	Dinnington Main	H	4-0		O'Connell 2 (1 pen), Wright, Paterson
9 Dec 1911	SCC1	R	Rotherham Town	A	3-1	3,000	Beech, Lloyd, Wright
27 Jan 1912	SCC2	R	Rotherham County	A	0-2		
5 Feb 1912	WCC2	R	Sheffield United Res.	H	0-1		
dnk	WCC1	R	Darfield United	A	Won		
7 Dec 1912	SCC1	R	Wath Athletic	A	2-2		Armitage, Beech
12 Dec 1912	SCC1r	R	Wath Athletic	H*	3-2		Cawley, n/k * AET – 90 mins 2-2 * played at Wath
25 Jan 1913	SCC2	R	Rotherham County	A	2-4		Cawley 2
10 Feb 1913	WCC2	R	Rotherham County	A	2-2		Beech 2
3 Mar 1913	WCC2r	R	Rotherham County	H	4-3		Hemstock, Gill, Beech, Wright
17 Mar 1913	WCC SF	R	Doncaster Rovers	H	1-0		Beech
21 Apr 1913	WCC F	R	Gainsborough Trinity	Worksop	0-0	1,000	
23 Apr 1913	WCC Fr	R	Gainsborough Trinity	Worksop	1-3		Lloyd
27 Oct 1913	WCC1	R	Rotherham Town	A	5-3		Pickering 3, Armitage, Burkinshaw
6 Dec 1913	SCC1	R	Cammell's Sports	H	5-1		McGregor 2, Cawley, Monaghan, Barrett (pen)
26 Jan 1914	SCC2	R	Denaby United	H	6-1		Pickering 2, Glennon 2, Gill, Brelsford (pen)
14 Feb 1914	SCC SF	R	Worksop Town	BL	2-1		McGregor, Armitage
16 Feb 1914	WCC2	R	Rotherham County	A	1-2		Wright
2 Mar 1914	SCC F	R	Rotherham County	BL	0-1	8,000	
21 Mar 1914	FR	R	Sheffield Gas Co.	H	1-3		Wood
14 Apr 1914	FR	R	Blackburn FC	A	0-1		
12 Oct 1914	WCC1	R	Denaby United	H	8-0		Nicholson 2, T. Brelsford, Lamb, C. Brelsford, Platts, Tasker, Gill
26 Nov 1914	FR	R	Whitworth's (Sheffield)	A	5-0		
12 Dec 1914	SCC1	R	Mexborough Town	A	4-0*		Gill, Clarke, Capper
23 Jan 1915	SCC2	R	Sheffield United Res.	A	0-1	6,000	
1 Feb 1915	WCC2	R	Gainsborough Trinity	H	5-4		J. Burkinshaw 2, Gill, Capper, Tasker

12 Apr 1915	WCC SF	R	Rotherham County	H	3-0		Gill 2, J. Burkinshaw
1 May 1915	WCC F	R	Sheffield United Res.	A	4-1	6,000	Gill 4
1 Jan 1916	FR	R	Sheffield United Res.	H	0-3		
27 Dec 1918	Charity	R	Sheffield United Res.	N*	2-2	3,000	Roe, Glennon * played at Tankersley
12 Dec 1919	WCC1	R	Maltby MW	H	2-3		Cartlidge, Cooper
15 Dec 1919	SCC1	R	Sheffield United Res.	H	0-3		
31 Jan 1920	FR	3rd	High Green Swifts	A	3-2		
14 Feb 1920	FR	3rd	Staveley Old Boys	A	5-0		Anthony Cooper, Armitage, Harvey, n/k
26 Feb 1920	FR	3rd	Mr EH Baker XI	H	2-1		Foster, Armitage
28 Feb 1920	FR	R	Mexborough Athletic	A	1-5		Woolhouse
11 Dec 1920	SCC1	R	Worksop Town	A	2-1	3,500	W. Taylor, Harvey
3 Jan 1921	WCC1	R	Denaby United	H	7-0		Hall 3, W. Taylor 2, Prior, Kean
15 Jan 1921	SCC2	R	Rotherham Co Res.	H	0-0		
20 Jan 1921	SCC2 - r	R	Rotherham Co Res.	A	3-3		Reed, Shelton, Binney
22 Jan 1921	FR	R	Wombwell Town	A	0-1	1,500	
31 Jan 1921	SCC2 - 2r	R	Rotherham Co Res.	BL	4-1	3,000	Ruddock 3, Prior
12 Feb 1921	SCC SF	R	Rotherham Town	Wath	0-0		
19 Feb 1921	FR	R	Elsecar Main	A	3-0		
24 Feb 1921	WCC2	R	Wath Athletic	A	1-1		Eggo
29 Feb 1921	SCC SF - r	R	Rotherham Town	BL	3-1	10,000	Shelton, Ruddock, Taylor
7 Mar 1921	WCC2 - r	R	Wath Athletic	H	4-0	8,000	Binney 2, Shelton, W. Taylor
12 Mar 1921	FR	R	Sheffield University	H	1-4		Bingham
14 Mar 1921	SCC F	R	Barnsley Res.	BL	2-0	8,000	W. Taylor 2
11 Apr 1921	WCC S/F	R	Frickley Colliery	Clifton Lane	1-2	1,500	Binney
2 May 1921	FR	R	Sheffield Sunday School Lge.	H	2-0		Kean, Davis
5 May 1921	FR	3rd	Sheffield University	H	3-0		Davis, Levick, Foulstone
6 May 1921	FR	3rd	Osborn's Sports	H	8-3		Ruddock 4, Dent 2, Shelton, Styles
10 Dec 1921	SCC1	R	Denaby United	H	4-1		Binney 2, Froggatt, Shelton
7 Jan 1922	FR	R	Chesterfield	H	3-1		Hall, Levick, Shelton
12 Jan 1922	WCC1	R	Worksop Town	H	3-1	4,000	Binney, Lunn, S. Taylor
23 Jan 1922	SCC2	R	Rotherham Co Res.	A	2-0		Bellas, Binney
20 Feb 1922	SCC SF	R	Wombwell Town	BL	1-1	10,000	Shelton
28 Feb 1922	WCC2	R	Rotherham Town	H	3-0		Binney, Lunn, Brelsford (pen)
9 Mar 1922	SCC SFr	R	Wombwell Town	Millmoor	5-0	4,000	Hall 2, Lunn 2, Price
20 Mar 1922	SCC F	R	Barnsley Res.	BL	2-0		Lowdell 2
30 Mar 1922	WCC SF	R	Wath Athletic	H	6-0		Petrie 2 (1 pen), Thompson 2, Froggatt, Lowdell
2 Sep 1922	FR	R	York City	A	3-3	4,000	Trotter, Pennington, Binney
16 Oct 1922	WCC F	R	Sheffield United Res.	H	3-1	12,978	Binks 2, Binney (1921/22 Final held over)
11 Dec 1922	WCC1	R	Tinsley WMC	H	4-0		Trotter 2, Wolfe 2
1 Jan 1923	SCC1	R	Barnsley Res.	A	1-2		Binney
27 Jan 1923	FR	R	Attercliffe Alliance League XI	H	4-0		Binney 2, Trotter, Wolfe
1 Mar 1923	WCC2	R	Sheffield United Res.	A	1-1		Binney
22 Mar 1923	WCC2 - r	R	Sheffield United Res.	H	0-1		

23 Apr 1923	FR	R	The Rest	H	2-1		Trotter, Henshall
23 Apr 1923	TST	R	Ecclesfield District XI (Woolhouse)	A	1-1		Armitage
25 Dec 1923	WCC1	R	Rotherham Town	H	1-0		Eyre
25 Feb 1924	WCC2	R	Rotherham Amateurs	H	8-0		Eyre 4, Helliwell 2, Trotter 2
17 Mar 1924	WCC SF	R	Worksop Town	H	4-2		S. Taylor 3, Trotter
8 Apr 1924	FR	R	Kiveton Park	A	1-2	1,000	Laycock
26 Apr 1924	FR	R	Clay Cross Town	A	3-5		Harvey 3
28 Apr 1924	WCC F	R	Sheffield United Res.	H	1-2	5,000	Helliwell
12 Jan 1925	WCC1	R	Dinnington Main	H	3-0		Littlewood 2, Ayres
19 Feb 1925	WCC2	R	Anston	A	3-0		Lee 2, Littlewood
19 Mar 1925	WCC SF	R	Worksop Town	H	3-0		Taylor 2, Weaver
14 Apr 1925	WCC F	R	Rotherham Town	H	3-1	8,000	Helliwell 2, Ayres
16 Sep 1925	FR	R	Sutton Town	A	4-2		Shepherd, Weston, L. Carr, Cook
26 Sep 1925	FR	R	Long Eaton Town	A	1-3		Flanaghan
19 Oct 1925	SICC1	R	Sheffield United Res.	A	1-0		Hill
29 Oct 1925	WCC1	R	Worksop Town	A	4-3		Ayres, Marson, Whitworth, Sheperd
21 Nov 1925	FR	R	Wombwell Town	A	3-2		Weaver 2, Harvey
5 Dec 1925	SCC1	3rd	Brodsworth Main	A	1-3		Hallam
1 Feb 1926	SICC SF	R	Denaby United	H	4-2		S. Powell 4 (1 pen)
15 Feb 1926	WCC SF	R	Sheffield United Res.	H	3-4	6,000	Ayres 2, S. Powell
15 Mar 1926	SICC F	R	Doncaster Rovers Res.	BL	4-2		Ayres 2, W. Powell, Fletcher
26 Apr 1926	TST	R	Mexborough Athletic (Moralee)	A	1-4	2,000	Knock
4 Oct 1926	WCC1	R	Rotherham United Res.	A	5-0		S. Powell 2, Brown 2, Marson
15 Nov 1926	SICC1	R	Rotherham United Res.	A	2-0		Leach, Burridge
8 Jan 1927	WCC SF	R	Doncaster Rovers Res.	A	2-3		Smith, Marson
5 Feb 1927	FR	R	Norton Woodseats	A	10-2*		Antiss 4, Smith 2, McIlvenny, Ferrari, Bradford
28 Feb 1927	SICC SF	R	Mexborough Athletic	BL	3-2		Bradford 2, S. Powell
25 Apr 1927	SICC F	R	Sheffield United Res.	A	0-2		
31 Aug 1927	FR	R	Lopham Street UM	A	5-1		Green 2, Johnson 2, Winnell
22 Sep 1927	FR	R	Chesterfield	H	5-4		Broatch 2, Watson, Smith, Winnell
20 Oct 1927	FR	R	Dronfield Woodhouse	H	2-0		Dr Gordon, Green
31 Oct 1927	FR	R	Wombwell Town	A	2-4		Marson 2
19 Dec 1927	SICC1	R	Barnsley Res.	H	7-2		S. Powell 4, Strange, Prince, Johnson
25 Feb 1928	FR	R	Chesterfield	A	0-1		
27 Feb 1928	SICC SF	R	Sheffield United Res.	A	3-1		S. Powell 2, Trotter (pen)
28 Mar 1928	TST	R	Wath Athletic (Dennis)	A	1-1		Thorpe
30 Apr 1928	SICC F	R	Worksop Town	BL	4-0		Harper 2, Prince, Wilkinson
27 Aug 1928	FR	R	Sheffield Works Association	H	4-1		Hill 3, Simmons
18 Sep 1928	FR	R	Ecclesfield District XI	A	3-1		Balmforth 2, H. Sharpe
15 Oct 1928	WCC1	R	Rotherham United Res.	H	5-0*		Harper 2, Wilkinson, Goddard
24 Oct 1928	FR	R	Mansfield Town	A	5-1		Harper 5
19 Nov 1928	SICC1	R	Mexborough Athletic	H	11-2		Harper 5, Wilson 4, Wilkinson, Hill
24 Nov 1928	FR	R	Worksop Town	A	4-1		Hartson 2, Wilkinson, Dean

12 Jan 1929	FR	R	Doncaster Rovers	H	4-2		Hartson 2, Wilson, Hill
21 Jan 1929	SICC SF	R	Frickley Colliery	H	2-1		Harper 2 * abandoned fog - 67 mins
31 Jan 1929	SICC SF	R	Frickley Colliery	H	3-1		Hill, Harper, Wilson
25 Feb 1929	WCC SF	R	Sheffield United Res.	H	1-3	4,000	Trotman
10 Apr 1929	FR	R	Lopham Street UM	A	2-0		Hartson, Dean
15 Apr 1929	SICC F	R	Sheffield United Res.	BL	4-1		Trotter 2, Wilson 2
20 Apr 1929	FR	3rd	Worksop Town	A	4-0		Hartson 2, Dean 2
22 Apr 1929	FR	3rd	Sheffield City Police XI	A	3-3		Hartson 2, n/k
25 Apr 1929	TST	R	Frickley Colliery (Lax)	A	2-1		Hill, Hargreaves
11 Nov 1929	WCC1	R	Doncaster Rovers Res.	H	0-2		
25 Nov 1929	SICC1	R	Wombwell Town	H	5-1		Trotter 3, Wilkinson, Trotman
27 Jan 1930	SICC SF	R	Barnsley Res.	A	3-5		Johnson, Jones, Trotter
17 Nov 1930	SICC SF	R	Rotherham United Res.	H	14-3		Allen 7, Millership 3, Wright 2, Jones 2 (1 pen.)
10 Jan 1931	FR	R	Lincoln City	H	8-6		Johnson 3, Millership 3, Allison, Jones (pen.)
23 Mar 1931	WCC F	R	Sheffield United Res.	A	4-0	6,000	Johnson 2, Brown, Millership
13 Apr 1931	SICC F	R	Sheffield United Res.	H	3-1		Millership, Allen, Jones
5 Oct 1931	SICC SF	R	Barnsley Res.	A	3-1		Jones, Wright, Millership
7 Dec 1931	WCC F	R	Sheffield United Res.	H	0-2		
29 Feb 1932	SICC F	R	Wombwell Town	BL	3-1		Millership 3
1 May 1933	WCC F	R	Sheffield United Res.	A	2-1	1,930	Glasper, Short
6 Nov 1933	SICC1	R	Thurnscoe Victoria	A	4-2		Williams 2, Jones, Thompson
12 Mar 1934	SICC SF	R	Dinnington Athletic	A	1-0		McPhail
17 Mar 1934	TST	3rd	Mexborough Athletic	A	2-5		Dunderdale 2
12 Apr 1934	TST	R	Boston United	A	2-4		Wynn, McPhail
26 Apr 1934	SICC F	R	Barnsley Res.	A	0-8		
20 Apr 1936	FR	3rd	Lopham Street UM	A	1-3		Hutchinson
5 Nov 1936	FR	3rd	Nottingham University	H	8-1		Drury 3, Grange 3, Freeman, n/k
21 Apr 1937	WCC1	3rd	Norton Woodseats	H	4-1*		Webster 2, Hall
22 Apr 1937	SICC SF	R	Barnsley Res.	H	0-1		
27 Apr 1937	WCC2 SF	3rd	Dinnington Athletic	H	0-2		
20 Sep 1937	FR	3rd	Gringley Atheltic (Gainsboro')	A	4-0	1,200	Moss 2, Drury, Colley
21 Feb 1938	SICC Pr	R	Rotherham United Res.	A	2-4		Curry, Roy
12 Apr 1938	TST	R	Birley Carr	A	5-1	1,000	Driver 2, Curry 2, Hooper
20 Apr 1938	WCC SF	3rd	Sheffield Club	H	8-2		Curry 4, Driver, Lowes, Moss, Duers
6 May 1938	WCC F	3rd	Sheffield United A	H	2-1		Duers, Lowes
13 Mar 1939	WCC SF	3rd	Sheffield United A	H	2-0		Ward 2
23 Mar 1939	SICC Pr	R	Sheffield United Res.	A	0-2		
1 May 1939	WCC F	3rd	Norton Woodseats	A	5-3		Lumsden 3, Condron, Mulligan
6 May 1939	FR	3rd	Stocksbridge Works	A	3-1		Aveyard, D. Sewell, Hooper
6 Dec 1941	FR	R	The Army XI	H	5-1		Smith 3 (1 pen), Allard 2
17 Jan 1942	SCC1	R	Upton Colliery	A	1-2		Howsam
25 Apr 1942	WCC1	R	Beighton MW	H	3-2		n/k
2 May 1942	WCC SF	R	Wales St Johns	H	2-1		Crookes, Gill

23 May 1942	WCC F	R	RASC	H	1-4		Helsem
25 May 1942	SICC1	R	RASC	H	2-3		Rogers, Everitt
5 Dec 1942	WCC1	R	Thurcroft Main	H	5-1		Barber 2, Woodhead 2, Froggatt
30 Jan 1943	SCC3	R	Denaby United	H	9-4		Burgin 5, Rogers 2, Fox 2 (1 pen)
6 Feb 1943	FR	R	Attercliffe Radicals	A	4-1		
13 Mar 1943	SCC SF	R	Thurcroft Main	H	3-2		Everitt 2, Nibloe (pen)
20 Mar 1943	WCC SF	R	Sheffield United Res.	H	1-1		Fox
27 Mar 1943	FR	R	Barnsley Res.	A	1-5		Barber
3 Apr 1943	WCC SFr	R	Sheffield United Res.	A	4-5		Curry 2, Herbert, Fox (AET)
26 Apr 1943	SCC F	R	RASC	BL	3-3		Curry 2, Everitt
1 May 1943	SCC Fr	R	RASC	BL	0-1		
21 Aug 1943	FR	R	Sheffield United Res.	A	1-1		Scholfield
11 Sep 1943	SICC1	R	Sheffield United Res.	A	2-2		Ibbotson, Everitt
16 Oct 1943	SICC1r	R	Sheffield United Res.	H	1-2		Hall
20 Nov 1943	SCC2	R	Upton Colliery	A	1-0		Briscoe
27 Dec 1943	SCC SF	R	Norton Woodseats	H	1-2		Briscoe
29 Apr 1944	WCC SF	R	RASC	BL	0-4		
11 Nov 1944	SCC2	R	Thurcroft Main	A	2-0		Froggatt, Ibbotson
13 Jan 1945	SCC3	R	Barnsley Res.	BL	1-1		Briscoe
3 Mar 1945	SCC3r	R	Barnsley Res.	A	1-2		Hawkswell
7 Apr 1945	SICC SF	R	Norton Woodseats	H	2-1		Hawkswell, Kippax
21 Apr 1945	SICC F	R	Firbeck Main	Worksop	1-1		?
28 Apr 1945	SICC Fr	R	Firbeck Main	H	2-3		Davies, Ibbotson
10 Nov 1945	SCC2	3rd	Denaby United	H	0-0		
22 Nov 1945	SCC2r	3rd	Denaby United	A	5-2		Ward 4, Toone
12 Jan 1946	SCC3	3rd	Norton Woodseats	H	3-0		Kippax, Toone, Cornish
9 Mar 1946	SCC SF	3rd	Wombwell Town	A	0-6		
9 Oct 1948	SCC1	Yth	Sheffield FC	A	4-1		Wyatt 3, Foster
6 Nov 1948	SCC2	Yth	Norton Woodseats	A	0-6		
19 Sep 1949	TST	Yth	Sheffield YMCA (Lambert)	H	1-3	1,200	Levitt
5 Nov 1949	SCC1	Yth	Hamptons Sports	A	1-4		
24 Apr 1950	TST	R	Gainsborough Trinity (Carte)	A	2-0		Jordan, Woodhead
10 May 1950	Hospital Cup	R	Scunthorpe United	A	2-1	10,000	Dooley, Tomlinson
24 Sep 1951	TST	R	Oswestry Town (Cornes)	A	0-1		
30 Apr 1952	TST	R	Wisbech Town (Cockroft)	A	6-3*	6,000	J. McAnearney 2, Slater 2, Jordan
4 Oct 1952	SCC1	Yth	Steel, Peech & Tozer	A	4-2		Kaye 2, Hall, Waller
1 Nov 1952	SCC2	Yth	Grimethorpe MW	H	1-2		Whiteman
20 Apr 1953	TST	R	Ilkeston Town (4 players)	A	2-2	4,000	Codd 2
3 Oct 1953	SCC 1Q	Yth	Wickersley Institute	A	2-1		
31 Oct 1953	SCC 2Q	Yth	Hallam	A	1-1		Hukin * abandoned after 100 mins in extra-time
7 Nov 1953	SCC 2Qr	Yth	Hallam	H	4-0		Hukin 2, Slater 2
5 Dec 1953	SCC1	Yth	Houghton Main	A	4-0		Greensmith, Dixon, Lockwood, Kay
2 Jan 1954	SCC2	Yth	Hamptons Sports	A	3-1		Ellis, Greensmith, D. Wilkinson

13 Mar 1954	SCC SF	Yth	Norton Woodseats	A	2-1		Greensmith, Rooth
10 Apr 1954	FR	3rd	Northern Nomads	H	3-2		
19 Apr 1954	AFIC	Yth	Appleby Frodingham	A	2-1		
26 Apr 1954	SCC F	Yth	Worksop Town	A	2-1		Rooth, J. McAnearney (* AET - 90 mins 0-0)
6 Nov 1954	FR	Yth	Middlesbrough Yth	H	9-0		
4 Dec 1954	SCC1	3rd	Hamptons Sports	A	2-1		Jordan, Crompton
8 Jan 1955	SCC2	3rd	Frickley Colliery	A	1-1		Stewart
14 Apr 1955	SCC2r	3rd	Frickley Colliery	A	4-2		
25 Apr 1955	SCC SF	3rd	Worksop Town	A	1-2		D. Wilkinson (* AET – 90 mins 0-0)
2 May 1955	AFIC	3rd	Appleby Frodingham	A	2-0		Nevin, Howard
3 Dec 1955	SCC1	Yth	Beighton MW	A	1-3		Hill
14 Jan 1956	FR	3rd	Northern Nomads	A	3-0		
24 Mar 1956	FR	Yth	Balfours Sports	A	7-0		
6 Oct 1956	SCC1Q	Yth	Thorncliffe Rec	A	4-3		Nevin 2, Creswick, Mee
3 Nov 1956	SCC2Q	Yth	Sheffield FC	A	1-2		Creswick
9 Mar 1957	WCC1	Yth	David Brown's	A	5-2		n/k
April 1957	FR	Yth	Penistone Chruch	A	3-4		Crossan, n/k
13 Apr 1957	WCC2	Yth	Shardows Sports	A	3-0		n/k
8 May 1957	WCC SF	Yth	Grenoside Sports	A	11-2		Fantham 3, Jenkinson 3, Crossan 2, Creswick 2, Carr
11 May 1957	WCC F	Yth	Sheffield FC	High Green	3-2	1,000	Crossan, Creswick (pen), Jenkinson (AET - 90mins 2-2)
9 Nov 1957	SCC Q	Yth	Brown Bayleys	H	11-0		
7 Dec 1957	SCC1	3rd	Parkgate Welfare	H	4-2		Elliott 2, Fantham, Lawrence
1 Mar 1958	WCC1	Yth	Fulwood	H	4-1		n/k
4 Mar 1958	SCC2	3rd	Frickley Colliery	H	0-1		
21 Apr 1958	WCC2	Yth	Pimro Sports	H	2-1		n/k
5 May 1958	WCC SF	Yth	Parkgate Welfare	Rawmarsh	Won		
9 May 1958	WCC F	Yth	Grenoside Sports	High Green	6-0		Griffin 2, Nevin, Elliott, Calladine, Marklew
15 Nov 1958	WCC2	Yth	Wickersley Social	H	1-1		n/k
19 Nov 1958	SCCQ	3rd	Sheffield FC	BL	3-1		Griffin, Nainby, Ballagher
dnk	WCC2r	Yth	Wickersley Social	A	Won		
6 Dec 1958	SCC1	3rd	Dodworth	H	2-0		Nainby, Moulson
3 Jan 1959	SCC2	3rd	Stocksbridge Works	A	2-1		Colton, Nainby
24 Jan 1959	WCC3	Yth	Steel, Peech & Tozer	A	4-0		Wilkinson, Colton, Moulson, n/k
11 Apr 1959	WCC4	Yth	Hillsborough Select	H	4-0		n/k
dnk	WCC SF	Yth	?	?	Won		
24 Apr 1959	SCC SF	3rd	Bentley Colliery	A	0-3		
6 May 1959	WCC F	Yth	Thurcroft Main	High Green	4-3		K. Ford 3, Colton
28 Nov 1959	SCC1	3rd	Osborns Sports	A	6-1		Ballagher 2, McMillan 2, Dobson 2
16 Jan 1960	SCC2	3rd	Hamptons Sports	H	5-1		Jeffries, Dobson, Ballagher, McMillan, Gabbitas
13 Feb 1960	SCC3	3rd	Frickley Colliery	A	4-3		Ballagher 3, Dobson
5 Mar 1960	WCC2	Yth	Stocksbridge Works	A	2-0		Sellars, J. McAnearney
2 Apr 1960	WCC3	Yth	Sheffield YMCA	H	2-1		n/k
19 Apr 1960	SCC SF	3rd	Grimethorpe MW	A	0-2		

9 May 1960	WCC SF	Yth	Steel, Peech & Tozer	Swallownest	Won		
13 May 1960	WCC F	Yth	Thorncliffe Recreation	High Green	2-4		Lockwood 2 *AET – 90 mins 2-2
12 Oct 1960	FR	3rd	Sheffield University	A	5-1		Ballagher 2, Stone, Lockwood, Lodge
14 Jan 1961	SCC 2Q	3rd	Stocksbridge Works	A	2-2		Dickinson, Himsworth
21 Jan 1961	SCC 2Qr	3rd	Stocksbridge Works	H	1-2		Dickinson
4 Mar 1961	WCC1	Yth	Osborns Sports	A	2-3		n/k
23 Sep 1961	FR	R	The Rest (Central League)	H	1-3		Frye
17 Aug 1963	FR	R	Southampton Res.	A	3-5		Eustace, Ford, Little
4 Jan 1964	WCC1	Yth	Maltby Main	A	1-2		n/k
21 Apr 1964	FR	R	Hallam	A	6-4		Davies 2, Woodall, H. Wilkinson, Ford, Hickton (pen)
28 Apr 1965	FR	R	Brigg Town	A	2-1		
16 Aug 1965	FR	R	Bishop Auckland	A	1-2	835	Pugh
8 Nov 1965	FR	R	Gateshead	A	4-4		Symm 3, Wall
15 Aug 1966	FR	R	Retford Town	A	2-3		Whitham, Davies
26 Jul 1969	FR	R	Scarborough	A	1-2	1,235	Woodall
8 Aug 1970	FR	R	Gainsborough Trinity	A	2-4		
10 Aug 1971	FR	R	Scarborough	A	1-1	780	Potts
2 Aug 1972	FR	R	Worksop Town	A	3-2	1,060	Wylde, Potts, Downes
13 Aug 1973	FR	R	Alfreton Town	A	7-1		Wylde 3, Prudham 2, Hall, Clements
16 Aug 1973	FR	R	Bridlington Town	A	11-0		
5 Aug 1974	FR	R	Mexborough Town Athletic	A	2-0		
5 Aug 1975	FR	R	Mexborough Town Athletic	A	5-2		Herbert 4, Nimmo
9 Aug 1975	FR	R	Wolverton Town	A	1-1		Dowd
12 Aug 1975	FR	R	Farsley Celtic	A	1-3		Nimmo
17 Sep 1975	FR	R	Hallam	A	1-0		Sunley (pen)
3 Dec 1975	FR	R	Buxton	A	?		
7 Aug 1976	FR	R	Buxton	A	1-2		
9 Aug 1976	FR	R	Worksop Town	A	0-0	1,177	
8 Mar 1977	FR	R	Worksop Town	A	0-4	657	
12 Aug 1978	FR	R	Sutton Town	A	3-0	119	
30 Jul 1979	FR	R	Sutton Town	A	2-3	362	Lowey, n/k
7 Aug 1980	FR	R	Emley	A	2-0		Bentley, Lowey
11 Aug 1981	FR	R	Matlock Town	A	3-0		Owen 2, Sterland
11 Aug 1982	FR	R	Worksop Town	A	1-0	473	Bailey
24 Aug 1982	FR	R	Eastwood Town	A	3-0		Mossman 2, Kenney
10 Aug 1983	FR	R	Matlock Town	A	1-0		Pearson
1983/84	FR	R	Gainsborough Trinity	A	2-1		
9 Aug 1984	FR	R	Mexborough Town Athletic	A	3-0	700	Mossman, Oliver, Gregory
13 Aug 1984	FR	R	Frickley Athletic	A	1-3		Mossman
14 Aug 1984	FR	R	Worksop Town	A	2-5		Hazel 2
31 Jul 1985	FR	R	Sheffield FC	A	2-3		
5 Aug 1985	FR	R	Ilkeston Town	A	2-2		Cooke, Oliver
7 Aug 1985	FR	R	Fiery Fred (Darnall)	A	5-1		

2 Aug 1986	FR	R	Shepshed Charterhouse	A	?		
6 Aug 1986	FR	R	BSC Parkgate	A	2-0		
13 Aug 1986	FR	Yth	North Ferriby United	A	?		
8 Sep 1986	OL	R	Lincoln United	A	2-2	1,200	Reeves 2
28 Jul 1987	FR	R	Mexborough Town Athletic	A	3-0	400	Reeves, Barrick, Rinkcavage
4 Aug 1987	FR	R	Armthorpe Welfare	A	?		
7 Aug 1987	FR	R	Heswall	A	0-3	1,100	
26 Jul 1988	FR	R	Matlock Town	A	1-1	448	Reeves
15 Aug 1988	FR	R	Belper Town	A	1-2	176	Gregory
13 Oct 1988	OL	R	Armthorpe Welfare	A	0-2		
3 Aug 1989	FR	R	Buxton	A	0-0		
8 Aug 1989	FR	R	Harworth Colliery Institute	A	3-0		
10 Aug 1989	FR	R	Emley	A	0-1		
15 Aug 1989	FR	R	Maltby MW	A	1-1		
14 Mar 1990	FR	Yth	GAIS Gothenburg	H	6-1		Jones 3 (1 pen), Downing, Dickinson, Chambers
5 Apr 1990	FR	R	Wisbech Town	A	1-0*	1,150	
2 Aug 1990	FR	R	Buxton	A	?		
Aug 1990	FR	R	Ossett Town	A	?		
Aug 1990	FR	R	Frickley Athletic	A	3-4		Goodacre 2, Jones
10 Aug 1990	FR	R	Horwich RMI	A	3-0		Chambers, Lycett, Barrick
19 Aug 1990	FR	R	Crewe Alexandra Res.	A	1-3		Newsome
17 Oct 1990	OL	R	Stocksbridge Park Steels	A	4-1		Lycett, Barrick, Chambers, Jones
26 Apr 1991	FR	R	Bromsgrove Rovers	A	?		
July 1991	FR	R	Rotherham United Res.	A	1-0		
July 1991	FR	R	Scunthorpe United Res.	H	4-1		
26 Jul 1991	FR	R	Hallam	H	2-0		Shirtliff, n/k
30 Jul 1991	FR	R	Ossett Town	A	3-1		Shirtliff, n/k
1 Aug 1991	FR	R	Frickley Athletic	A	3-2		Chambers 2, Johnson
5 Aug 1991	FR	R	Maltby MW	A	6-0	1,000	Johnson 2, Jones 2, Taylor, Chambers
7 Aug 1991	FR	R	Buxton	A	3-2		Watson, Chambers, Wood
9 Aug 1991	FR	R	Sheffield Aurora	A	3-1		Jones, Chambers, Simmonite
12 Aug 1991	FR	R	Wisbech Town	A	4-2*		Chambers, Johnson, Taylor
15 Aug 1991	FR	R	Worksop Town	H	2-4		Taylor, Garwood
20 Jul 1992	FR	Yth	Hallam	H	0-1		
22 Jul 1992	FR	R	Pontefract Colleries	A	4-0	450	Rowntree 2, Wright, Curzon
24 Jul 1992	FR	R	Mexborough Town Athletic	H	2-1		Simpson, Jones
28 Jul 1992	FR	Yth	Quorn	H	1-1		Barker
31 Jul 1992	FR	R	Buxton	A	3-1	270	Johnson 2 (1 pen), B. Linighan
3 Aug 1992	FR	R	Brigg Town	A	2-2		Jemson, Chambers
5 Aug 1992	FR	R	Matlock Town	A	0-1	446	
			STUDIO 10 TOURNAMENT				
7 Aug 1992	FR	R	Tottenham Hotspur Res.	S/F (Penzance)	1-2Jemson		
9 Aug 1992	FR	R	Penzance	A	1-1		Jones

11 Aug 1992	FR	R	Maltby MW	A	2-4		Watson, Carter
13 Aug 1992	FR	R	Stocksbridge Park Steels	A	2-2	750	Francis, Watson
15 Nov 1992	FR	R	Goole Town	A	5-1*		Chambers 2, Johnson, Jemson
20 Jul 1993	FR	R	Hallam	H	3-2		B. Linighan, Holmes, Jones (pen)
23 Jul 1993	FR	R	Buxton	A	1-3		Watson
26 Jul 1993	FR	R	Pickering Town	A	3-3	400	B. Linighan 2, Guest
			TRANSPENNINE TROPHY				
27 Jul 1993	FR	R	Tottenham Hotspur Res.	S/F (York)	1-2	175	Faulkner
29 Jul 1993	FR	R	Liverpool Res.	York	3-4		Barker 2, B. Linighan
4 Aug 1993	FR	R	Newcastle Town (Staffs.)	A	2-0	935	Harkes, Bart-Williams
6 Aug 1993	FR	R	Maltby MW	A	3-0	500	Jemson, Poric, Watson
10 Aug 1993	FR	R	Gainsborough Trinity	A	1-3	400	Jemson (pen)
12 Aug 1993	FR	R	Stocksbridge Park Steels	A	4-1	800	Watson 3, Jemson
16 Aug 1993	FR	R	Worksop Town	A	5-0	945	Watson 2, Jemson, Chambers, Rowntree
31 Aug 1993	FR	U-21	Sheffield United Res.	H	5-0		Chambers, Boyce, Brown, Poric, Jones (pen)
2 Sep 1993	FR	R	Rowntree FC	A	1-0		Rowntree
7 Mar 1994	FR	Yth	Guernsey Youth	A	2-0		Jackson, Sykes
29 Mar 1994	FR	Yth	Tucson	H	12-0		Burkill 3, Bailey 3, Jackson 2, Sykes, Carter, Pass, Scargill
2 Apr 1994	FR	Yth	Guernsey Youth	H	7-0		Bailey 3, Jackson 2, Pass, Daley
22 Jul 1994	TST	R	Goole Select XI (Young)	A	7-2		Poric 3, King (pen), Guest, Barker, Holmes
25 Jul 1994	FR	R	Buxton	A	2-1		Guest, Jemson
27 Jul 1994	FR	R	Worksop Town	A	3-1	947	Brown 2, Jemson (pen)
			TRANSPENNINE TROPHY				
30 Jul 1994	FR	R	Leeds United Res.	S/F (York)	2-3		Poric, Jemson
31 Jul 1994	FR	R	Manchester United Res.	York	1-1		Burrows
2 Aug 1994	FR	R	Wigan Athletic	A	2-2	959	Ciantar, Burrows
4 Aug 1994	FR	R	Leicester United	A	3-0		Jemson, Barker, Carter
8 Aug 1994	FR	R	Newcastle Town (Staffs.)	A	3-1	666	Burrows, Jemson, Holmes
11 Aug 1994	FR	R	Stocksbridge Park Steels	A	3-0	1,000	Burrows, Holmes, Watt
22 Aug 1994	FR	R	Sheffield FC	A	2-0		Stewart, Watt
4 Oct 1994	FR	R	Oman Youth	Oman	0-2		
6 Oct 1994	FR	R	Oman Youth	Oman	1-0		Bailey
3 Nov 1994	OL	R	Cheddar	A	6-1	850	Barker 3, Jones, Guest, Ingesson
8 Dec 1994	FR	U-21	Nott'm Forest U-21	Grantham	1-1		Ingesson
3 Feb 1995	FR	U-21	Gainsborough Trinity	A	0-2		
14 Jul 1995	FR	Yth	Walsall Yth	H	3-0		Petrescu, Batty, Stevens
21 Jul 1995	FR	R	Doncaster Rovers Res.	H	0-0		
22 Jul 1995	FR	Yth	West Bromwich Alb. Yth	H	6-1		Kirkpatrick 2, Platts, Wood, Batty, James
25 Jul 1995	FR	R	Worksop Town	A	6-3	808	Sinton 2, Whittingham 2, Donaldson, Ingesson (pen)
28 Jul 1995	FR	Yth	Lincoln City Yth	H	2-1		Humphreys (pen), Stevens
31 Jul 1995	FR	R	Hallam	H	1-1		Bailey
2 Aug 1995	FR	R	Buxton	A	0-0		

			RYDALE TROPHY				
5 Aug 1995	FR	R	Nottingham Forest Res.	S/F (Goole)	0-0		(NF won 4-1 on penalties)
6 Aug 1995	FR	R	Leeds United Res.	York	0-0		
11 Aug 1995	FR	R	Burnley Res.	H	1-3		Barker
17 Aug 1995	FR	R	Stocksbridge Park Steels	A	6-2		Barker 2, Guest 2, Degryse, Jackson
8 Apr 1996	FR	U-16	Guernsey U-18	H	0-0		
			RYDALE TROPHY				
27 Jul 1996	FR	R	Dundee United Res.	S/F (York)	1-1		Barker (* won 4-2 on penalties)
28 Jul 1996	FR	R	Tottenham Hotspur Res.	Fnl (York)	0-1		
3 Aug 1996	FR	R	Hucknall Town	A	4-2	200	Donaldson 2, Barker, Jones
3 Aug 1996	FR	Yth	Singapore National U-19	H	1-0		Bettany
6 Aug 1996	FR	R	Maltby MW	A	4-2		Weaver, Donaldson, Kotylo, Barker
8 Aug 1996	FR	R	Worksop Town	A	1-0	902	Weaver
12 Aug 1996	FR	R	Mansfield Town	A	2-1	1,606	Platts, Donaldson
13 Aug 1996	FR	R	Denaby United	A	0-3		
15 Aug 1996	FR	R	Stocksbridge Park Steels	A	2-1	1,500	Trustfull, Bright
25 Oct 1996	FR	U-21	Halifax Town U-21	A	1-2	200	Daly
11 Jul 1997	FR	U-21	Manchester City U-21	H	0-3		
11 Jul 1997	FR	Yth	Manchester City Yth	H	0-0		
15 Jul 1997	FR	Yth	Bradford City Yth	H	6-1		Hibbins 2 (1 pen), Coubrough 2, N. Haslam 2
16 Jul 1997	FR	Yth	Blackburn Rovers Yth	H	0-2		
18 Jul 1997	FR	Yth	Wolves Yth	H	3-3		N. Haslam, Hiner, Coubrough
22 Jul 1997	FR	R	Nuneaton Boro'	A	1-0	1,011	Agogo
29 Jul 1997	FR	R	Ilkeston Town	A	2-2		Hirst 2
30 Jul 1997	FR	Yth	Sheffield United Yth	H	2-5		
1 Aug 1997	FR	R	Belper Town	A	6-0		Billington 2, Kotylo, Harrison, Batty, Agogo
4 Aug 1997	FR	Yth	Manchester City Yth	A	2-3		
5 Aug 1997	FR	R	Doncaster Rovers	A	2-0		Oakes, McKeever
8 Aug 1997	FR	R	Worksop Town	A	1-2	502	G. Smith
9 Aug 1997	FR	U-21	Sheffield FC	A	0-1		
12 Aug 1997	FR	R	Frecheville CA	A	2-2	200	Pringle (pen), Weaver
16 Aug 1997	FR	R	Altrincham	A	1-1	250	Agogo
4 Sep 1997	FR	R	Stocksbridge Park Steels	A	7-0	1,000	Donaldson 3, Poric 2, Platts 2
5 Oct 1997	FR	Yth	Dublin & District Select XI	Home Farm	1-0*		
12 Feb 1998	FR	R	Stalybridge Celtic	A	2-0		Wojtala, Kotylo
1 Apr 1998	FR	Yth	Japan Select XI	H	4-3		N. Haslam, Holmes, Coubrough, Hindley
14 Jul 1998	FR	R	Hallam	A	5-1*	300	Billington 2, McKeever, N. Haslam
16 Jul 1998	FR	Yth	Notts County Yth	H	2-1		Nelson, Fraser
17 Jul 1998	FR	R	Frickley Athletic	A	0-1		
21 Jul 1998	FR	R	Buxton	A	1-1		Holmes
23 Jul 1998	FR	R	Nuneaton Boro'	A	1-1		Douglas
28 Jul 1998	FR	R	Ilkeston Town	A	3-3	457	Nicholson 2, Hibbins
4 Aug 1998	FR	U-21	Worksop Town	A	0-3		

6 Aug 1998	FR	U-21	Alfreton Town	A	2-2	298	Brennan, Douglas
13 Aug 1998	FR	R	Stocksbridge Park Steels	A	3-0		Staniforth, Powell, Davis
15 Aug 1998	FR	U-16	Osgoode Rideau (Ottowa)	H	6-0		Pounder, Nelson, Cropper, Morrison, Vodden, Hamshaw
20 Jul 1999	FR	R	Billingham Synthonia	A	1-1		Douglas
24 Jul 1999	FR	R	Hartlepool United	A	1-4	1,381	Nicholson
29 Jul 1999	FR	R	Stocksbridge Park Steels	A	4-1	1,500	Carbone 3, Humphreys
31 Jul 1999	FR	R	Worksop Town	A	0-0	498	
3 Aug 1999	FR	R	Hallam	A	9-0	400	Holmes 2, Staniforth 2, Higgins 2, Brennan, Hibbins, Hamshaw
6 Aug 1999	FR	R	Staveley	A	5-3		Coubrough, Hindley, Nicholson, Hamshaw, Morrison (pen)
13 Aug 1999	FR	R	Cameroon U-23	H	?		
15 Jan 2000	FR	Yth	Huddersfield Town Yth	H	0-3		
29 Feb 2000	FR	R	Worksop Town	A	2-2		Humphreys (pen), Coubrough
18 Apr 2000	FR	R	Brunsmeer Athletic	A	0-1	500	
25 Jul 2000	FR	R	Garforth Town	A	6-2	570	Cropper 2, Liparoti, Morrison, Hamshaw, Callery
27 Jul 2000	FR	R	Sheffield FC	A	1-3		Morrison
31 Jul 2000	FR	Yth	Boca Juniors U-20	H	1-7		Morrison (pen)
1 Aug 2000	FR	R	Alfreton Town	A	3-0	389	Muller, Cropper,Morrison
2 Aug 2000	FR	R	Wensleydale League XI	A	4-1		Cropper 2, R. Dixon, J. Shaw
5 Aug 2000	FR	Yth	Doncaster Rovers Yth	H	3-6		Morrison 2, Tevendale (pen)
7 Aug 2000	FR	R	Worksop Town	A	1-1	987	Hamshaw
10 Aug 2000	FR	R	Stocksbridge Park Steels	A	3-1*		Morrison, Klomp
16 Jul 2001	FR	R	Harrogate Town	A	1-1	635	Connelly
23 Jul 2001	FR	R	Stocksbridge Park Steels	A	4-1	700	Di Piedi 2, Muller, Morrison (pen)
2 Aug 2001	FR	R	Emley	A	4-0		Hamshaw, Di Piedi, O'Donnell, Muller
6 Aug 2001	FR	R	Worksop Town	A	0-0	406	
22 Jul 2002	FR	Yth	Anglesley Select	A	3-2		J. Shaw 2, Stevenson
25 Jul 2002	FR	Yth	Porthmadog	A	2-1		McMahon, J.Shaw
5 Aug 2002	FR	R	Stocksbridge Park Steels	A	3-1	1,412	Knight, Di Piedi, Morrison
15 Aug 2002	FR	R	Worksop Town	A	2-3	224	Di Piedi 2
28 Aug 2002	FR	R	Sheffield FC	A	2-0	475	Di Piedi, Donnelly
7 Jul 2003	FR	Yth	South Normanton Athletic	A	0-2		
12 Jul 2003	FR	Yth	Dinnington Town	A	1-1	150	Needham
18 Jul 2003	FR	Yth	Staveley	A	2-0	150	McMahon, Cox
23 Jul 2003	FR	R	Stocksbridge Park Steels	A	0-2	840	
29 Jul 2003	FR	R	Hallam	A	5-0		J. Shaw 2, Wilson, R. Wood, Bromby
2 Aug 2003	FR	Yth	Bridlington Town	A	0-3	262	
5 Aug 2003	FR	R	Spennymoor United	A	3-2	300	J. Shaw. Foster, McLaren
7 Aug 2003	FR	Yth	Sheffield FC	A	4-5		Orlik, Jerome, Wilson, Greenwood
12 Aug 2003	FR	Yth	Stocksbridge Park Steels	A	1-2	400	White
20 Jul 2004	FR	R	Barrow	A	9-0	770	J. Shaw 3, Hamshaw 2, Collins, Ndumbu-Nsungu, Smith, McMahon
20 Jul 2004	FR	Yth	Gainsborough Trinity Res.	A	2-1		Mason, Fores-Chambers
23 Jul 2004	FR	Yth	Kimberley Town	A	6-0	50	Reet 4, Talbot, Needham
26 Jul 2004	FR	Yth	Hull City Yth	H	2-1		Brackenbridge

27 Jul 2004	FR	R	Alfreton Town	A	1-1	525	Talbot
28 Jul 2004	FR	Yth	Worksop Town Yth	A	6-1		Appleyard, Fores-Chambers, McArdle, Mason, Jones, Needham
30 Jul 2004	FR	Yth	Doncaster Rovers Yth	A	4-0		Brackenbridge 2 (1 pen), Jones, Damms
2 Aug 2004	FR	Yth	Bradford Park Avenue	A	1-2	256	Needham
6 Aug 2004	FR	Yth	Grimsby Town Yth	H	2-0		Reet, Mason
9 Aug 2004	FR	R	Stocksbridge Park Steels	A	3-0	543	Evans, Reet, Fores-Chambers
13 Aug 2004	FR	Yth	Leicester City Yth	H	5-3		Mason 2, Reet, Cockerill, Spurr
17 Aug 2004	FR	Yth	Hallam	A	0-5		
13 Sep 2004	FR	R	Sheffield FC	A	5-1		Talbot 3, Fores-Chambers 2
22 Jul 2005	FR	Yth	Gainsborough Trinity	A	4-1		Boden 2, Broadbent, Brackenbridge
27 Jul 2005	FR	Yth	Chesterfield College	H	2-1		Damms, Brackenbridge
Jul 2005	FR	Yth	Chesterfield Yth	?	3-3		Damms, Jordan, n/k
3 Aug 2005	FR	Yth	Rotherham United Yth	A	2-1		Boden, Brackenbridge
8 Aug 2005	FR	Yth	Hull City Yth	H	2-2		Reet, Brackenbridge
21 Jul 2006	FR	Yth	Chesterfield College	H	6-0		Jordan, Kee, McClements, Aston, Wood, Bowman
26 Jul 2006	FR	Yth	Rotherham United Yth	A	0-4		
28 Jul 2006	FR	Yth	Hull City Yth	H	0-3		
31 Jul 2006	FR	R	Burton Albion	A	1-2	874	Jordan
1 Aug 2006	FR	Yth	Sheffield FC U-19	A	2-1		Kay, Bowman
4 Aug 2006	FR	Yth	Scunthorpe United Yth	H	5-2		McClements 3, Bowman, Tawton
10 Aug 2006	FR	Yth	Stocksbridge Park Steels	A	1-2		Stothard
26 Oct 2006	OL	R	Dinnington Town	A	2-1	400	McMenamin, Brueton
10 Jul 2007	FR	Yth	Dearne Valley College U-18	A	8-3		
17 Jul 2007	FR	Yth	Cliftonville	N. Ireland	2-1		T. Wood, Fraser
19 Jul 2007	FR	Yth	Linfield	N. Ireland	2-2		McClements, Fraser
25 Jul 2007	FR	R	Sheffield FC	A	3-2	735	McClements, McAllister, T. Wood
31 Jul 2007	FR	Yth	Dinnington Town	A	0-0		
3 Aug 2007	FR	Yth	Sheffield FC U-18	A	2-1		Tunnard, Harrison
10 Aug 2007	FR	Yth	Stocksbridge Park Steels	A	1-3		R. Lekaj
4 Jul 2008	FR	Yth	Handsworth YC	H	4-4		
8 Jul 2008	FR	Yth	Dinnington Town	A	1-3		Modest
11 Jul 2008	FR	Yth	Hull City Yth	A	2-1		Palmer, Modest
22 Jul 2008	FR	Yth	Rotherham United Yth	H	2-1		Palmer, L. Lekaj
23 Jul 2008	FR	R	Stocksbridge Park Steels	A	1-1		N. Wood
29 Jul 2008	FR	Yth	Doncaster Rovers Yth	A	0-1		
30 Jul 2008	FR	R	Sheffield FC	A	2-2	865	Mohammed, Lunt
1 Aug 2008	FR	Yth	Grimsby Town Yth	H	1-1		L. Lekaj
6 Aug 2008	FR	Yth	Maltby Main	A	3-2		n/k
12 Aug 2008	FR	Yth	Buxton	A	2-2		Tunnard (pen), Modest
14 Aug 2008	FR	Yth	Tideswell United	A	3-1		Palmer 2, Oliver
14 Jul 2009	FR	Yth	Dinnington Town	A	4-3		Barnett 2, Cottingham, Trialist
18 Jul 2009	FR	Yth	Hull City Yth	A	2-1		Barnett, Kendall
22 Jul 2009	FR	R	Stocksbridge Park Steels	A	2-1		Modest, Sodje

24 Jul 2009	FR	Yth	Grimsby Town Yth	A	2-0		Oliver 2
29 Jul 2009	FR	R	Frickley Athletic	A	0-2		
31 Jul 2009	FR	Yth	Doncaster Rovers Yth	H	2-1		Modest, Harrison
4 Aug 2009	FR	Yth	Carlisle United Yth	H	2-1		Tunnard, Kirkland
6 Jul 2010	FR	Yth	Dinnington Town	A	0-2		
9 Jul 2010	FR	Yth	Doncaster Rovers Yth	A	1-2		Husbands
12 Jul 2010	FR	Yth	Chesterfield	A	1-4		Lacey
16 Jul 2010	FR	Yth	Grimsby Town Yth	A	1-1		Cottingham
19 Jul 2010	FR	Yth	York City Yth	A	3-1		Kendal 2, Oliver
21 Jul 2010	FR	Yth	Scunthorpe United Yth	A	0-2		
23 Jul 2010	FR	Yth	Bradford City Yth	H	0-0		
27 Jul 2010	FR	Yth	Bradford College	H	8-1		Cardwell 2, Kendall 2, Pinhorn, Haywood, Mir, Husbands
3 Aug 2010	FR	Yth	Barnoldswick Town	A	1-1		Nyoni
6 Aug 2010	FR	Yth	Hull City Yth	A	3-3		Husbands, Kendall, Oliver
10 Aug 2010	FR	Yth	Sheffield Parramore	A	2-1		Oliver, Husbands
12 Aug 2010	FR	Yth	Huddersfield Town	A	1-2		Lacey
14 Aug 2010	FR	Yth	Tideswell United	A	6-1	74	Lacey 2, Husbands 2, Cardwell, Kendall
29 Sep 2010	FR	Yth	Ilkeston Town Yth	A	3-2		n/k

KEY

*	Own-goal scored for SWFC
AFIC	Appleby Frodingham Inivitation Cup
FR	Friendly
GNCC	Gainsborough News Charity Cup
MC	Minor Cup
OL	Opening of Floodlights
SCC	Sheffield Challenge Cup
SICC	Sheffield Invitation Challenge Cup
TST	Testimonial/Benefit (recipient in brackets)
WCC	Wharncliffe Charity Cup

Miscellaneous Games

Testimonials & benefits

	Recipient	Team	Score	Team		Att:
9 Apr 1883	Bob Gregory	Wednesday Over 25's	4-0	Wednesday Under 25's	BL	1,080
27 Feb 1888	Billy Mosforth	Wednesday and District XI	1-8	Preston North End	BL	4,000
25 Apr 1892	Jack Dungworth	Englishmen	3-0	Scotchmen	H	7,500
10 Apr 1893	Jim Smith	Sheffield's English Players	4-3	Sheffield's Scottish Players	H	5,000
28 Sep 1931	Billy Marsden	Sheffield XI	1-0	FA XI	H	9,613
9 Mar 1955	Derek Dooley	Sheffield XI	1-5	International XI	H	55,000
31 Oct 1961	Duggie McMillan	Sheffield XI	5-8	Select XI	H	25,202
13 Oct 1970	John Fantham	Sheffield XI	4-8	John Fantham XI	H	6,234
1 Oct 2000	David Hirst	Owls 93'	9-7	Premier Allstars XI	H	11,000

Games not played over 90 minutes

Wednesday Competition

		Team	Round	Result	Scorers
27 Mar 1880	Sheaf House	Pyebank	QF	Won	
27 Mar 1880	Sheaf House	Spital	SF	2-1	Stacey, Buttery
27 Mar 1880	Sheaf House	Heeley	F	0-1	

Football League Centenary Trophy

	Venue	Team	Round	Result	Attn.	Scorers
16 Apr 1988	Wembley	Crystal Palace	1R	0-0		* won 2-1 on pens
16 Apr 1988	Wembley	Wigan Athletic	2R	1-1		Worthington (* won 3-2 on pens)
17 Apr 1988	Wembley	Manchester United	SF	2-1	17,000	Sterland (pen), West
17 Apr 1988	Wembley	Nottingham Forest	F	0-0	17,000	* lost 3-2 on pens

Soccer Sixes Tournament

	Team	Round	Result	Scorers
10 Dec 1986	Tottenham Hotspur	1R	1-2	Gregory
10 Dec 1986	Arsenal	1R	2-5	Shutt 2
8 Dec 1987	Southampton	1R	1-1	
8 Dec 1987	Nottingham Forest	1R	0-1	
5 Dec 1988	Luton Town	1R	1-2	Varadi
5 Dec 1988	Millwall	1R	3-1	Sterland, Jonsson, Hirst

Trans Atlantic Challenge

	Venue	Team	Result	Attn.	Scorers
29 Jan 1992	S. Arena	Baltimore Blast (USA)	3-8	8,206	Wilson, Palmer, Warhurst

Abandoned Games

	Match		Team	Result	Att	Scorers	Reason abandoned
28 Oct 1871	Friendly	MR	Mackenzie	0-0	n/k		Burst ball
22 Oct 1881	WCC1	BL	Staveley	1-1	500	Bayley	Staveley walk-off
28 Dec 1885	Friendly	BL	Heeley	0-0	n/k		Waterlogged pitch – 20 mins
4 Jan 1886	Friendly	n/k	Park Grange	1-1	n/k	Newbould	Serious injury – 2nd Half
6 Jan 1940	Friendly	A	West Bromwich A	3-0	1,426	Burrows, Thompson, Robinson	Fog

Seasonal Third/A Team Records 1921-64

Season	Competition	P	W	D	L	F	A	Pts	Pos.	Lge Cup	Top Scorer
1921–22	Sheffield Association League	36	18	9	9	78	47	45	5th	N/A	n/k
1922–23	Yorkshire Mid-Week League	18	7	1	10	24	36	15	n/k	N/A	Binney 4
1923–24	Yorkshire Mid-Week League	16	5	2	9	19	27	12	7th	N/A	n/k
1924–25	Yorkshire Mid-Week League	16	6	3	7	28	23	15	5th	N/A	n/k
1925–26	Yorkshire Mid-Week League	16	6	2	8	38	39	14	6th	N/A	n/k
1926–27	Yorkshire Mid-Week League	6	1	2	3	15	17	4	4th	N/A	W. Powell 3
1929–30	Yorkshire Mid-Week League	12	7	2	3	35	24	16	2nd	N/A	Hartson 8
1930–31	Yorkshire Mid-Week League	14	11	1	2	56	23	23	1st	N/A	Johnson 19
1931–32	Yorkshire Mid-Week League	12	3	4	5	21	25	10	4th	N/A	Johnson 6
1932–33	Yorkshire Mid-Week League	12	6	2	4	35	28	14	n/k	N/A	n/k
1934–35	Yorkshire League	34	23	4	7	125	60	50	3rd	R1	n/k
1935–36	Yorkshire League	38	26	3	9	124	62	55	2nd	R1	Smith 51 (min.)
1936–37	Yorkshire League	36	17	6	13	94	73	40	7th	R2	Webster/Wright 13
1937–38	Yorkshire League	38	17	4	17	100	91	38	9th	R2	n/k
1938–39	Yorkshire League	38	31	3	4	138	44	65	1st	R1	Curry 27
1945–46	Sheffield Association League	18*	7	2	7	39	35	16	n/k	N/A	n/k
1945–46	Sheffield Invitation Cup League	8	4	1	3	18	17	9	n/k	n/a	n/k
1946–47	Yorkshire League	38	14	7	17	69	88	35	13th	R2	n/k
1947–48	Yorkshire League	38	15	5	18	81	83	35	13th	n/k	n/k
1948–49	Yorkshire League	38	13	8	17	70	78	34	14th	R2	Wyatt
1949–50	Yorkshire League	34	12	7	15	52	55	31	11th	R1	n/k
1950–51	Yorkshire League	34	24	4	6	100	47	52	1st	Winners	Dooley 21
1951–52	Yorkshire League	34	17	4	13	84	64	38	7th	R2	Slater 17
1952–53	Yorkshire League	34	11	10	13	59	69	32	12th	R1	Price 19
1953–54	Yorkshire League	34	11	10	13	67	65	32	9th	R3	n/k
1954–55	Yorkshire League	34	15	5	14	56	64	35	9th	R1	n/k
1955–56	Yorkshire League	34	16	8	10	86	57	40	3rd	S/F	n/k
1956–57	Yorkshire League	34	18	8	8	86	42	44	2nd	Winners	n/k
1957–58	Yorkshire League	34	17	9	8	97	49	43	3rd	S/F	n/k
1958–59	Yorkshire League	34	18	7	9	62	35	43	4th	R1	n/k
1959–60	Yorkshire League	34	18	6	10	77	53	42	4th	Runners-up	n/k
1960–61	Yorkshire League	34	27	4	3	90	32	58	1st	R2	L Dickinson 19
1962–63	Hatchard League	26**	9	5	12	65	55	23	9th	n/a	n/k
1963–64	Hatchard League	30	14	4	12	78	70	32	7th	n/a	n/k

* 2 results unknown ** Due to bad weather, only the first 24 games of the season played

SEASONAL YOUTH TEAM RECORDS 1948-2011

Season	Competition	P	W	D	L	F	A	Pts	Pos.	Lge Cup	Top Scorer (inc. LC)
1948–49	Hatchard League	22*	4	2	16	42	74	10	n/k	n/a	n/k
1949–50	Hatchard League	28*	10	5	13	60	57	25	10/11th	n/a	n/k
1950–51	Hatchard League	30	22	4	4	141	57	48	2nd	n/a	n/k
1951–52	Hatchard League	26	10	1	15	73	60	21	9th	n/a	Lill/Price 9
1952–53	Hatchard League	26	16	5	5	58	36	37	4th	n/a	n/k
1953–54	Hatchard League	28*	18	4	6	86	39	40	n/k	n/a	n/k
1954–55	Hatchard League	30	21	6	3	99	41	48	2nd	n/a	n/k
1955–56	Hatchard League	30	18	4	8	97	61	40	2nd	n/a	n/k
1956–57	Hatchard League	30	17	3	10	99	75	37	5th	n/a	n/k
1957–58	Hatchard League	28*	22	1	5	100	32	45	n/k	n/a	n/k
* Final record n/k - 30 game season											
	TOTAL	**278**	**158**	**35**	**85**	**855**	**532**	**351**			
1958–59	Northern Intermediate League	28	12	6	10	62	48	30	7th	Group stages	n/k
1959–60	Northern Intermediate League	30	18	5	7	75	37	41	4th	R1	n/k
1960–61	Northern Intermediate League	30	19	6	5	84	27	44	2nd	Runners-up	n/k
1961–62	Northern Intermediate League	32	23	3	6	78	32	49	2nd	R1	Lockwood 17
1962–63	Northern Intermediate League	24*	12	2	10	57	45	26	7th	R1	Ford 11
* Due to bad weather, only the first 24 games of the season played											
1963–64	Northern Intermediate League	32	13	8	11	74	67	34	8th	S/F	Davies 27
1964–65	Northern Intermediate League	32	14	8	10	48	48	36	8th	Runners-up	Whitham 7
1965–66	Northern Intermediate League	32	4	5	23	23	80	13	16th	R2	Heard/Oliver/Wall 4
1966–67	Northern Intermediate League	28	5	9	14	41	57	19	13th	R2	Wall 9
1967–68	Northern Intermediate League	32	8	9	15	39	60	25	10th	R1	Fellows 6
1968–69	Northern Intermediate League	34	14	10	10	58	50	38	8th	Runners-up	Sunley 17
1969–70	Northern Intermediate League	34	15	5	14	53	72	35	8th	Runners-up	Hall 11
1970–71	Northern Intermediate League	28	10	6	12	51	50	26	9th	Runners-up	Musson 9
1971–72	Northern Intermediate League	30	20	4	6	67	27	44	3rd	Runners-up	Musson 15
1972–73	Northern Intermediate League	30	20	4	6	81	34	44	3rd	R1	Herbert 22
1973–74	Northern Intermediate League	32	13	6	13	61	53	32	8th	R2	Ferguson 19
1974–75	Northern Intermediate League	32	12	10	10	56	49	34	7th	S/F	Ferguson 19
1975–76	Northern Intermediate League	30	10	4	16	44	52	24	10th	R2	Strutt 14
1976–77	Northern Intermediate League	28	10	5	13	30	39	25	9th	R2	n/k
1977–78	Northern Intermediate League	30	16	7	7	52	35	39	2nd	R2	T. Smith

Season	Competition	P	W	D	L	F	A	Pts	Pos.	Lge Cup	Top Scorer (inc. LC)
1978–79	Northern Intermediate League	30	13	4	13	46	56	30	8th	R1	n/k
1979–80	Northern Intermediate League	30	12	3	15	59	61	27	10th	R1	n/k
1980–81	Northern Intermediate League	34	10	10	14	46	62	30	11th	Runners-up	n/k
1981–82	Northern Intermediate League	30	12	3	15	44	57	27	10th	Winners	n/k
1982–83	Northern Intermediate League	30	10	6	14	62	65	36	12th	R1	n/k
1983–84	Northern Intermediate League	28	7	7	14	56	66	28	11th	R1	n/k
1984–85	Northern Intermediate League	28	12	5	11	62	52	29	9th	R1	n/k
1985–86	Northern Intermediate League	34	19	8	7	78	45	46	3rd	Runners-up	n/k
1986–87	Northern Intermediate League	34	14	7	13	72	53	49	10th	S/F	Reeves 32
1987–88	Northern Intermediate League	34	16	8	10	51	32	56	7th	R1	n/k
1988–89	Northern Intermediate League	34	13	5	16	57	51	44	10th	Winners	n/k
1989–90	Northern Intermediate League	34	18	4	12	81	64	58	7th	Prel.	Goodacre 20
1990–91	Northern Intermediate League	34	11	10	13	47	51	43	13th	Prel.	Chambers 14
1991–92	Northern Intermediate League	34	15	10	9	47	31	55	7th	R1	Rowntree 13
1992–93	Northern Intermediate League	32	11	10	11	36	36	43	9th	Winners	Barker 7
1993–94	Northern Intermediate League	30	13	9	8	57	41	48	6th	R2	Jackson 10
1994–95	Northern Intermediate League	32	15	7	10	50	36	52	7th	R1	Bailey 23
1995–96	Northern Intermediate League	30	15	4	11	63	33	49	7th	R2	Thorpe 12
1996–97	Northern Intermediate League	34	13	11	10	63	47	50	8th	R1	Batty 16
1997–98	Northern Intermediate League	34	20	6	8	58	42	66	4th	R2	Powell 22
	TOTAL	**1248**	**537**	**259**	**452**	**2269**	**1943**	**1524**			
1997–98	FA Premier Youth League - Northern	22	12	5	5	40	28	41	1st*	n/a	Hibbins 13
	* Lost in Play-off semi-final										
	TOTAL	**22**	**12**	**5**	**5**	**40**	**28**	**41**			
1998–99	FA Academy League U-17	22	11	2	9	45	41	35	4th	n/a	Hindley 12
1998–99	FA Academy League U-19	22	10	5	7	37	36	35	2nd**	n/a	Brennan 12
	** Lost in Play-off Final										
1999–2000	FA Academy League U-17	22	9	6	7	41	33	33	4th	n/a	Cropper 9
1999–2000	FA Academy League U-19	22	10	1	11	39	49	31	3rd	n/a	Morrison 9
2000–01	FA Academy League U-17	24	3	3	18	29	75	12	8th	n/a	J. Shaw 9
2000–01	FA Academy League U-19	28	13	3	12	47	49	41	4th	n/a	Cropper 11
2001–02	FA Academy League U-17	24	3	5	16	29	61	14	9th	n/a	McMahon 11
2001–02	FA Academy League U-19	28	5	6	17	32	61	21	10th	n/a	Knowles 7
2002–03	FA Academy League U-17	22	5	3	14	28	53	18	7th	n/a	Mason 10
2002–03	FA Academy League U-19	28	7	3	18	46	67	24	10th	n/a	J. Shaw 14
2003–04	FA Academy League U-19	26	4	6	16	31	50	18	10th	n/a	McMahon/Talbot/White 4
2004–05	FA Academy League U-18	28	15	6	7	51	33	51	2nd	n/a	Reet 13
2005–06	FA Academy League U-18	28	7	4	17	29	55	25	9th	n/a	Reet 9
2006–07	FA Academy League U-18	28	9	7	12	30	40	34	6th	n/a	McClements 10
2007–08	FA Academy League U-18	28	5	7	16	24	53	22	9th	n/a	T. Wood 5

Season	Competition	P	W	D	L	F	A	Pts	Pos.	Lge Cup	Top Scorer (inc. LC)
2008–09	FA Academy League U-18	28	6	6	16	27	47	24	8th	n/a	Palmer 5
2009–10	FA Academy League U-18	28	3	8	17	24	57	17	10th	n/a	Oliver 9
2010–11	FA Academy League U-18	28	6	6	16	31	64	24	10th	n/a	Husbands 7
	TOTAL	**464**	**131**	**87**	**246**	**620**	**924**	**479**			

SHEFFIELD WEDNESDAY IN THE FA YOUTH CUP

Date	Venue	Team	Round	Res	Att	Scorers
8 Sep 1952	H	Hull City	1R	3-5		J.McAnearney, Turner, Fountain *AET
24 Oct 1953	A	Notts County	1R	7-2		
14 Nov 1953	A	Nottingham Forest	2R	0-2		
16 Oct 1954	A	Derby County	1R	9-1		Hukin 3, Nevin 3, Kay 2, Elliott
6 Nov 1954	A	Nottingham Forest	2R	2-1		Kay, Nevin
4 Dec 1954	A	Middlesbrough	3R	4-1		Bates 2, Kelsey, n/k
5 Feb 1955	A	Manchester United	4R	0-7		
26 Sep 1955	A	Rotherham United	1R	5-1		Elliott 2, Hukin, Fantham, Poole
19 Nov 1955	H	Notts County	2R	7-2*		Elliott 3, Fantham 2, Hukin
6 Dec 1955	A	Doncaster Rovers	3R	1-3		Hukin
25 Sep 1956	H	Lincoln City	1R	6-1		Fantham 3, Creswick, Crossan, Jenkinson
17 Oct 1956	H	Holbeach United	2R	13-0		Crossan 6, Jenkinson 3, Carr, Colton, Creswick, Fantham
20 Nov 1956	H	Barnsley	3R	5-2*		Jenkinson, Creswick, Crossan, Fantham
5 Feb 1957	A	Stoke City	4R	3-2	3,376	Fantham 3
12 Mar 1957	H	Sheffield United	QF	1-0	18,030	Carr (pen)
2 Apr 1957	H	West Ham United	SF- L1	0-0	14,250	
11 Apr 1957	A	West Ham United	SF - L2	0-2		
16 Oct 1957	H	Notts County	1R	5-2		Griffin 2, Marklew, Hardy, Goodison
18 Nov 1957	H	Chesterfield	2R	6-0		Lawrence 4, Dobson, Hardy
12 Dec 1957	A	Scunthorpe United	3R	3-1		Dobson 2, Ford
12 Mar 1958	H	Bolton Wanderers	4R	1-4		Griffin
15 Oct 1958	A	Sheffield United	1R	1-3		Griffin
24 Sep 1959	A	Scunthorpe United	1R	1-2		Dickinson
10 Oct 1960	H	Lincoln City	1R	4-1		Sellers, Jack McAnearney, Bardsley, Lockwood
25 Oct 1960	H	Grimsby Town	2R	2-1		Lee, Lockwood
20 Dec 1960	H	Coventry City	3R	3-1		Lockwood, Sellers, Hickton
30 Jan 1961	A	Sheffield United	4R	5-0		Jack McAnearney 2, Storf, Eustace, Radford (pen)
6 Mar 1961	H	Everton	QF	0-0		
14 Mar 1961	A	Everton	QF - R	0-5	7,254	
25 Sep 1961	A	Lincoln City	1R	1-0		Storf

Date	Venue	Team	Round	Res	Att	Scorers
14 Oct 1961	H	Stamford Youth Club	2R	16-0		Hickton 9, Slater 5, Eustace, Burkenshaw
13 Nov 1961	H	Rotherham United	3R	6-0		Hickton 5, Ford
24 Jan 1962	A	Sheffield United	4R	1-3		Ford
15 Dec 1962	A	The Corinthians	2R	4-0		n/k
25 Mar 1963	H	Stoke City	3R	5-1		Ford 3, Barraclough, Little
3 Apr 1963	A	Middlesbrough	4R	4-1		Denton, Davies, Mee, Ford
30 Apr 1963	H	Manchester United	QF	2-0		Hickton, Ford
14 May 1963	A	Liverpool	SF	0-4	9,798	
9 Dec 1963	H	Bradford City	2R	2-1		Woodall 2
22 Jan 1964	H	Leeds United	3R	0-1		
7 Dec 1964	H	Sheffield United	2R	3-1	2,025	Davies, Smith, Whitham
22 Jan 1965	H	Barnsley	3R	1-2		Heard
11 Dec 1965	H	Doncaster Rovers	2R	3-0		Pugh 2, Wall
10 Jan 1966	H	Sheffield United	3R	1-2		Wall
3 Dec 1966	H	Doncaster Rovers	2R	1-1		Lunn
7 Dec 1966	A	Doncaster Rovers	2R -R	1-0		Lunn
3 Jan 1967	A	Scunthorpe United	3R	0-1		
6 Dec 1967	H	Barnsley	2R	4-0		Prendergast 2, Burton, Fellows
1 Jan 1968	A	Hull City	3R	3-2		Fellows 2, Wall
31 Jan 1968	H	Sheffield United	4R	0-1		
2 Dec 1968	A	Hull City	2R	1-4		Johnson
3 Dec 1969	H	Leeds United	2R	1-2		Ken Johnson
28 Oct 1970	H	Leeds Ashley Road	1R	4-0		Hall 2, Musson 2
24 Nov 1970	H	Barnsley	2R	1-1		Wylde
1 Dec 1970	A	Barnsley	2R -R	0-2		
2 Nov 1971	A	Bradford Park Avenue	1R	2-0		Musson 2
30 Nov 1971	H	Doncaster Rovers	2R	1-0		Byron
22 Dec 1971	A	Everton	3R	2-3	6,249	Hall, Herbert
31 Oct 1972	A	Lincoln City	1R	7-0		Herbert 3, Ferguson 2, Burden, Nicholson
28 Nov 1972	H	Huddersfield Town	2R	1-2		Ferguson
3 Nov 1973	A	Grimsby Town	1R	3-1		Nicholson, Spacie, Herbert
1 Dec 1973	A	Hartlepool United	2R	0-0		
12 Dec 1973	H	Hartlepool United	2R -R	2-1		Ferguson, Spacie
1 Jan 1974	H	Everton	3R	1-0		Nicholson (pen)
22 Jan 1974	A	Arsenal	4R	1-3	500	Ferguson
30 Oct 1974	H	Barnsley	1R	5-2		Spacie 2, Ferguson 2, Nimmo
18 Nov 1974	H	Chesterfield	2R	1-0		Nimmo
18 Dec 1974	H	Rotherham United	3R	0-1		
19 Nov 1975	H	Nottingham Forest	2R	1-1		Nimmo
26 Nov 1975	A	Nottingham Forest	2R -R	0-2		
7 Dec 1976	A	Rotherham United	2R	2-1		Grant 2
3 Feb 1977	H	Derby County	3R	2-4		Strutt, Owen (G.)

Date	Venue	Team	Round	Res	Att	Scorers
1 Dec 1977	H	Hull City	2R	1-1		Grant
6 Dec 1977	A	Hull City	2R -R	0-2		
31 Oct 1978	H	Sheffield United	1R	2-1		Peter Shirtliff, Paul Shirtliff
20 Nov 1978	H	Bolton Wanderers	2R	2-2		Matthews, Williamson
12 Dec 1978	A	Bolton Wanderers	2R -R	1-2		Taylor
29 Oct 1979	A	Wigan Athletic	1R	4-2	1,100	Bentley 4
4 Dec 1979	H	Oldham Athletic	2R	1-0		Mills
8 Jan 1980	A	Bolton Wanderers	3R	2-0		Pearson 2
7 Feb 1980	A	Wimbledon	4R	3-0		Sterland, Pearson, Campbell
4 Mar 1980	H	Manchester City	QF	1-1	3,409	Pearson
11 Mar 1980	A	Manchester City	QF - R	2-3		Sterland, Mills * AET - 90 mins 2-2
2 Dec 1980	H	Manchester United	2R	1-2		Simmons
1 Dec 1981	H	West Bromwich Albion	2R	4-1		Beaumont, Simmons, Kenney, Mossman
21 Jan 1982	A	Bury	3R	0-2		*Mills & Mossman sent off
25 Nov 1982	H	Chester	2R	3-0		Simmons 2, Dwyer
19 Jan 1983	A	Blackpool	3R	4-3		Dwyer 2, Mills, Simmons
9 Feb 1983	A	Wrexham	4R	2-2		Dwyer, Riley
17 Feb 1983	H	Wrexham	4R - R	3-1		Simmons 2, Dwyer
3 Mar 1983	H	Chelsea	QF	4-2	942	Simmons 2, Showler, Mills
17 Mar 1983	H	Everton	SF L1	0-2		
7 Apr 1983	A	Everton	SF L2	0-7	2,315	
8 Dec 1983	H	Walsall	2R	2-3		Coombes, Showler
13 Dec 1984	H	Blackpool	2R	4-0		Brookes 2, Gregory (pen), C.Bradshaw
31 Jan 1985	A	Middlesbrough	3R	3-0		Hazel 2, Oliver
14 Feb 1985	H	Tottenham Hotspur	4R	0-1		
2 Dec 1985	A	Huddersfield Town	2R	3-2		Gregory, Taylor, Morris
14 Jan 1986	A	Mansfield Town	3R	1-1		Lee
20 Jan 1986	H	Mansfield Town	3R - R	0-1		
8 Dec 1986	H	Oldham Athletic	2R	0-3		
30 Nov 1987	A	Blackpool	2R	4-1		n/k
11 Jan 1988	A	Doncaster Rovers	3R	1-2		Newsome
5 Dec 1988	A	Middlesbrough	2R	2-2		n/k
19 Dec 1988	H	Middlesbrough	2R -R	2-0		Johnson 2
9 Jan 1989	H	Manchester United	3R	0-0		
18 Jan 1989	A	Manchester United	3R - R	0-2		
4 Dec 1989	H	Sheffield United	2R	5-1	700	Foster 2, Chambers, Holmshaw, Dickinson
4 Jan 1990	H	Wigan Athletic	3R	2-0		Dickinson, Chambers
8 Feb 1990	A	Manchester United	4R	1-3		Holmshaw
3 Dec 1990	H	Bury	2R	4-1		Chambers 2, Robinson, Smith
19 Dec 1990	A	Aston Villa	3R	3-2		Jones, Chambers, Robinson
4 Feb 1991	H	West Bromwich Albion	4R	2-1		Chambers, Jones
6 Mar 1991	H	Hull City	5R	1-1		Smith

Date	Venue	Team	Round	Res	Att	Scorers
19 Mar 1991	A	Hull City	5R - R	1-1		Rowntree * AET – 90 mins 1-1
28 Mar 1991	H	Hull City	5R - 2R	5-1		Jones 3, Curzon, B.Linghan
8 Apr 1991	H	Manchester United	S/F - L1	1-1		Curzon
18 Apr 1991	A	Manchester United	S/F - L2	1-0*		
1 May 1991	H	Millwall	FINAL - L1	0-3	1,666	
7 May 1991	A	Millwall	FINAL - L2	0-0	4,261	
2 Dec 1991	A	Shrewsbury Town	2R	0-3		
10 Dec 1992	H	Leeds United	2R	1-2		Faulkner
3 Nov 1993	A	Blackburn Rovers	1R	0-1		
19 Oct 1994	A	Grimsby Town	1R	3-1		Smith, Sykes, Bailey
23 Nov 1994	A	Sunderland	2R	1-1		Sykes
30 Nov 1994	H	Sunderland	2R - R	0-1		
11 Nov 1995	A	Blackburn Rovers	1R	0-2		
12 Nov 1996	A	Leeds United	1R	2-2		Platts, Batty
15 Nov 1996	H	Leeds United	1R - R	0-4		
22 Sep 1997	A	Preston North End	Qual.	0-1		
18 Dec 1998	A	Manchester City	3R	3-2		Morrison, Staniforth, Nicholson
2 Feb 1999	H	Leicester City	4R	1-0	404	Morrison
16 Feb 1999	H	Everton	5R	1-1	1,000	Morrison
1 Mar 1999	A	Everton	5R - R	1-3*	1,500	
1 Dec 1999	A	Wimbledon	3R	0-0		* played at Sutton United FC
7 Dec 1999	H	Wimbledon	3R - R	0-1		
4 Dec 2000	A	Burnley	3R	6-0	222	Cropper 3, Shaw, Barrett, Jubb
16 Jan 2001	A	Bolton Wanderers	4R	1-1		Tevendale (pen)
30 Jan 2001	H	Bolton Wanderers	4R - R	2-2		Cropper 2 * AET – 90 mins 1-1, lost 4-2 on penalties
10 Dec 2001	A	Tranmere Rovers	3R	1-4		Stevenson (pen) * McMahon sent off
2 Dec 2002	A	Reading	3R	2-1		Wood, McMahon * AET – 90 mins 1-1
21 Jan 2003	A	Manchester United	4R	0-2		* played at Altrincham FC
20 Oct 2003	H	Rochdale	1R	3-0		McAllister, Docker, Bermingham
4 Nov 2003	H	Tranmere Rovers	2R	2-4		Greenwood, Marsden
10 Nov 2004	A	Doncaster Rovers	1R	1-0		Cockerill
23 Nov 2004	H	Cambridge United	2R	0-1		
7 Dec 2005	H	Southend United	3R	2-0		McClements 2
18 Jan 2006	H	Newcastle United	4R	1-2	684	Broadbent
12 Dec 2006	H	Bolton Wanderers	3R	0-2		
11 Dec 2007	A	Carlisle United	3R	1-1	188	Harrison * AET – 90 mins 1-1 lost 4-2 on penalties
11 Dec 2008	H	Millwall	3R	1-3	329	Connelly
8 Dec 2009	H	Sunderland	3R	2-7		Oliver, Barnett
3 Nov 2010	A	Rotherham United	R1	3–2		Husbands, Magill, Lacey * AET – 90 mins 2–2
16 Nov 2010	A	Oldham Athletic	R2	2–3		Husbands, Lacey

Youth Tournaments

VOELKINGEN, THE SAAR, WEST GERMANY

Date	Opposition	Score	Scorers	Position
4 May 1957	Kaiserslautern	2-0		
4 May 1957	FC Basel	3-0		
5 May 1957	Voelkingen FC	1-1		
5 May 1957	MVV Maastricht (Final)	2-1	Fantham, Brian Finney	Winners

GOTTINGHAM, WEST GERMANY

Date	Opposition	Score	Scorers	Position
May 1961	2 x German sides +	3-0		
May 1961	1 Danish side	2-0		
May 1961		8-0		
May 1961	Hamburg (Final)	0-0	* won on the toss of a coin	Winners

MARL, NR ESSEN, WEST GERMANY

Date	Opposition	Score	Scorers	Position
8 Jun 1964	Belgrade	1-2	Barroclough	
June 1964	Malmo FF	?		
June 1964	Juniorenrauswal Marl	?	?	

AMSTERDAM, NETHERLANDS

Date	Opposition	Score	Scorers	Position
12-16 May 1967	Spandaver SV (Berlin)	0-0		
12-16 May 1967	SC Enschede	1-1	Middleton	
12-16 May 1967	Borussia Monchengladbach	5-1	Middleton 2, Stenson, McCall, Prendergast	3rd

DÜSSELDORF, WEST GERMANY

Date	Opposition	Score	Scorers	Position
May 1969	Offenbach Kickers	1-1	Warboys	
May 1969	Ujpest Dosza	2-2	Warboys, Fearnley	
May 1969	Fortuna Düsseldorf	0-0		
May 1969	Truro Düsseldorf	4-1	Prendergast 2, Fearnley, Burton	3rd

PARMA, ITALY

Date	Opposition	Score	Scorers	Position
12–16 Jun 1972	group?			
12–16 Jun 1972	Partizan Belgrade (Final)	1-0	Musson	Winners

VENIZE, ITALY (U-21)

Date	Opposition	Score	Scorers	Position
June 1973	Lost in quarter-finals		?	

ZILVEREN BOTTEN TOURNAMENT, VOLENDAM, NETHERLANDS

Date	Opposition	Score	Scorers	Position
4 Aug 1973	FC Brugge	0-0		
4 Aug 1973	ADO Den Haag	1-0	Nicholson	
4 Aug 1973	NAC	3-0	Hancock, Cameron, Ferguson	
5 Aug 1973	Ajax Amsterdam	0-0		
5 Aug 1973	Volendam (Final)	2-0	Nicholson, Spacie att: 3,500	Winners

ENSCHEDE, NETHERLANDS

Date	Opposition	Score	Scorers	Position
May 1980	VV Venlo	3-0	Oliver, Pearson, Mills	
May 1980	Sportklub Enschede	5-0	Pearson 2, Smith, Campbell, Taylor	
May 1980	Bayer Laverkusen	3-0	Smith, Williamson, own-goal	
May 1980	FC Twente '65 (Final)	3-0	Campbell, Pearson, Matthewson	Winners

ENSCHEDE, NETHERLANDS

May 1982	Won 3 group games	3-0, 3-0, 2-0	Beaumont 3, S. Mills, Oliver, Simmons, Pearson	
May 1982	Newcastle United (Final)	0-1		2nd

BOCHUM, WEST GERMANY

April 1985	Watenscheid	0-2		
April 1985	Langendreer	5-0	C. Bradshaw 3, Brookes, Gregory	
April 1985	Bochum	3-0	Kerr, Brookes, Smith	?

MONTHEY, SWITZERLAND

12 May 1989	Monthey	2-0	Newsome, Lycett	
13 May 1989	Liege	2-1	Johnson, Lycett	
13 May 1989	Nice	1-1	Lycett	
14 May 1989	Bologna (Final)	2-1	Hyde, own-goal	Winners

MONTHEY, SWITZERLAND

31 May 1990	Osijek			
1 Jun 1990	Barcelona			
2 Jun 1990	Sion			
3 Jun 1990	??		?	

ENSCHEDE, NETHERLANDS (U-20)

30 May 1992	Den Haag	0-0		
30 May 1992	PSV Eindhoven	0-0		
31 May 1992	IFK Gothenburg	3-1	Jones 2, Wright	
31 May 1992	KV Mechelen	0-1		4th

ROMAINVILLE, NR. PARIS, FRANCE

29 May 1993	Sarmata (Poland)	1-0	Curzon	
29 May 1993	Romainville	2-0	Curzon 2	
31 May 1993	Sedan (France)	2-0	Stewart, Curzon	
31 May 1993	Prague Select* (Final)	1-1	Frank	2nd

*AET - Prague won 4-2 on penalties

JARNY, FRANCE (U-19)

21 May 1994	Brondby	2-2	Carter, Jacks	
21 May 1994	Jarny	3-0	Bailey, Burkill, Carter	
22 May 1994	Aberdeen	1-1	Briscoe	
22 May 1994	Chelsea	0-2		
23 May 1994	Ghent	2-0	Jackson, Burkill	5th

ENSCHEDE, NETHERLANDS (U-20)

28 May 1994	FC Twente	0-1		
28 May 1994	Heerenveen	1-0	Stewart	
29 May 1994	Banik Ostrava	1-1	Barker	
29 May 1994	Werder Bremen	3-1	Barker, Guest (pen), Hardwick	3rd

MONTHEY, SWITZERLAND

1 Jun 1995	Sion	0-0		
2 Jun 1995	Fenerbahce	3-2	Jackson 2, own-goal	
3 Jun 1995	Read Madrid	0-3		
4 Jun 1995	Ascoli	3-0	Jackson 2, Bailey	3rd

ST JOSEPHS, FRANCE

7 Apr 1996	St Josephs	2-0	Todd, Hutchinson	
7 Apr 1996	Brugge FC	0-0	* Lost on penalties	
8 Apr 1996	Croavia FC	1-0	Weaver	
8 Apr 1996	St Eteinne	0-0	* Lost 1-0 on penalties	4th

ENSCHEDE, NETHERLANDS (U-20)

1 Jun 1996	Feyenoord	0-0		
1 Jun 1996	FC Metz	0-1		
2 Jun 1996	Deportivo Catolica	1-2	D. Smith	
2 Jun 1996	FC Twente	0-1		6th

PFORZHEIM, NR STUTTGART, GERMANY

16 May 1997	NK Osijek (Croatia)	1-1	Haslam	
17 May 1997	FC Pforzheim	4-0	Batty 3, Hibbins	
17 May 1997	Fortuna Düsseldorf	1-0	Bettney	
18 May 1997	MSV Duisburg	0-1		
18 May 1997	VFR Pforzheim	4-0	Powell, Harrison, Agogo, Woodward	
19 May 1997	Hansa Rostock	3-1	Powell, Hibbins, Hiner	
19 May 1997	VFL Bochum	0-1		4th

GILLETTE 9TH SOCCER 7S, SINGAPORE

16 May 1998	Balestier Central	1-0		
16 May 1998	Home United	4-1		
16 May 1998	Sembawang Rangers	4-1		
17 May 1998	Tanjong Pager (S/F)	4-1		
17 May 1998	Coventry City (Final)	1-0	Holmes	Winners

ENSCHEDE, NETHERLANDS

23 May 1998	Antwerp	2-0	Platts, Holmes	
23 May 1998	FC Twente	1-0	Higgins	
24 May 1998	Armenia Bielfeld	2-0	Douglas, Earnshaw	
24 May 1998	Universidad Catolica (Final)	0-2		2nd

STEMVADE, NR MINDE, GERMANY

21 May 1999	Eintracht Frankfurt	0-1		
22 May 1999	PD Guadalajara	0-1		
22 May 1999	Werder Bremen	0-1		
23 May 1999	Muhlenkreis	5-0	Higgins 3, Douglas, Holmes	7th

ENSCHEDE, NETHERLANDS

2 Jun 2000	Enschede	5-0	Cropper 2, Crane 2, Morrison	
3 Jun 2000	USA U-19	1-3	Cropper	
3 Jun 2000	Heracles	0-1		
4 Jun 2000	FC Twente (S/F)	1-0	Strutt	
4 Jun 2000	Cruz Azul (Mexico) (Final)	1-0	Tevendale	Winners

BARI, ITALY (U-16)

31 May 2006	Rosanaise	1-0	Kirkland	
2 Jun 2006	Reggio 2000	3-0		
3 Jun 2006	Catone	2-1		
4 Jun 2006	Sporting (Final)	2-2	* Lost 4-3 on penalties	2nd

AGATHE, NETHERLANDS

8 Aug 2009	Sparta Rotterdam	2-1	Oliver, Modest	
8 Aug 2009	Arminia Bielefeld	0-1		
9 Aug 2009	Botafogo (S/F)	0-0	* Won 4-3 on penalties (Eckhardt, Wood, Cottingham, Poulton)	
9 Aug 2009	Standard Liege (Final)	1-2	N. Wood	2nd

ROTTERDAM, NETHERLANDS

31 Jul 2010	Excelsior	0-2		
31 Jul 2010	FC Dordrecht	0-0		
1 Aug 2010	Excelsior	1-2	Modest	N/A

Sheffield Wednesday Internationals

Full Caps

England

Billy BETTS (1)	v Wales 23 February 1889
Ernie BLENKINSOP (26)	v France 17 May 1928, v Belgium 19 May 1928, v Ireland 22 October 1928, v Wales 17 November 1928, v Scotland 13 April 1929, v France 9 May 1929, v Belgium 11 May 1929, v Spain 15 May 1929, v Ireland 19 October 1929, v Wales 20 November 1929, v Scotland 5 April 1930, v Germany 10 May 1930, v Austria 14 May 1930, v Ireland 20 October 1930, v Wales 22 November 1930, v Scotland 28 March 1931, v France 14 May 1931, v Belgium 16 May 1931, v Ireland 17 October 1931, v Wales 18 November 1931, v Spain 9 December 1931, v Scotland 9 April 1932, v Ireland 17 October 1932, v Wales 16 November 1932, v Austria 7 December 1932, v Scotland 1 April 1933
Frank BRADSHAW (1)	v Austria 8 June 1908
Teddy BRAYSHAW (1)	v Ireland 5 February 1887
Tommy BRITTLETON (5)	v Ireland 10 February 1912, v Wales 11 March 1912, v Scotland 23 March 1912, v Scotland 5 April 1913, v Wales 16 March 1914
Jack BROWN (6)	v Wales 12 February 1927, v Scotland 2 April 1927, v Belgium 11 May 1927, v Luxembourg 21 May 1927, v France 26 May 1927, v Ireland 19 October 1929
Harry BURGESS (4)	v Ireland 20 October 1930, v Scotland 28 March 1931, v France 14 May 1931, v Belgium 16 May 1931
Horace BURROWS (3)	v Hungary 10 May 1934, v Czechoslovakia 16 May 1934, v Holland 18 May 1935
Ted CATLIN (5)	v Wales 17 October 1936, v Ireland 19 November 1936, v Hungary 2 December 1936, v Norway 14 May 1937, v Sweden 17 May 1937
Charles CLEGG (1)	v Scotland 30 November 1872
William CLEGG (1)	v Scotland 8 March 1873
Tommy CRAWSHAW (10)	v Ireland 9 March 1895, v Ireland 7 March 1896, v Wales 16 March 1896, v Scotland 4 April 1896, v Ireland 20 February 1897, v Wales 29 March 1897, v Scotland 3 April 1897, v Ireland 9 March 1901, v Wales 29 February 1904, v Ireland 12 March 1904

Harry DAVIS (3)	v Ireland 14 February 1903, v Wales 2 March 1903, v Scotland 4 April 1903
Teddy DAVISON (1)	v Wales 13 March 1922
John FANTHAM (1)	v Luxembourg 28 September 1961
Billy FELTON (1)	v France 21 May 1925
Redfern FROGGATT (4)	v Wales 12 November 1952, v Belgium 26 November 1952, v Scotland 18 April 1953, v USA 8 June 1953
Andy HINCHCLIFFE (2)	v Switzerland 25 March 1998, v Saudi Arabia 23 May 1998
David HIRST (3)	v Australia 1 June 1991, v New Zealand 8 June 1991, v France 19 February 1992
Jack HUDSON (1)	v Ireland 24 February 1883
Fred KEAN (7)	v Belgium 19 March 1923, v Scotland 14 April 1923, v Wales 3 March 1924, v Northern Ireland 22 October 1924, v Northern Ireland 24 October 1925, v Belgium 24 May 1926, v Luxembourg 21 May 1927
Tony LEACH (2)	v Ireland 20 October 1930, v Wales 22 November 1930
Billy MARSDEN (3)	v Wales 20 November 1929, v Scotland 5 April 1930, v Germany 10 May 1930
Billy MOSFORTH (9)*	v Scotland 3 March 1877, v Scotland 2 March 1878, v Wales 18 January 1879, v Scotland 5 April 1879, v Scotland 13 March 1880, v Wales 15 March 1880, v Wales 26 February 1881, v Scotland 11 March 1882, v Wales 13 March 1882

* *Records differ as to which club Mosforth was attached to when capped for England – the above list shows all caps won in his career.*

Carlton PALMER (18)	v CIS 29 April 1992, v Hungary 12 May 1992, v Brazil 17 May 1992, v Finland 3 June 1992, v Denmark 11 June 1992, v France 14 June 1992, v Sweden 17 June 1992, v Spain 9 September 1992, v Norway 14 October 1992, v Turkey 18 November 1992, v San Marino 17 February 1993, v Turkey 31 March 1993, v Holland 28 April 1993, v Poland 29 May 1993, v Norway 2 June 1993, v USA 9 June 1993, v Brazil 13 June 1993, v Holland 13 October 1993
Albert QUIXALL (5)	v Wales 10 October 1953, v Rest of the World 21 October 1953, v Northern Ireland 11 November 1953, v Spain 18 May 1955, v Portugal 22 May 1955
Ellis RIMMER (4)	v Scotland 5 April 1930, v Germany 10 May 1930, v Austria 14 May 1930, v Spain 9 December 1931
Jackie ROBINSON (4)	v Finland 20 May 1937, v Germany 14 May 1938, v Switzerland 21 May 1938, v Wales 22 October 1938
Herrod RUDDLESDIN (3)	v Wales 29 February 1904, v Ireland 12 March 1904, v Scotland 1 April 1905
Jackie SEWELL (6)	v Northern Ireland 14 November 1951, v Austria 25 May 1952, v Switzerland 28 May 1952, v Northern Ireland 4 October 1952, v Hungary 25 November 1953, v Hungary 23 May 1954

Andy SINTON (2)	v Holland 13 October 1993, v San Marino 17 November 1993
Fred SPIKSLEY (7)	v Wales 13 March 1893, v Scotland 1 April 1893, v Ireland 3 March 1894, v Scotland 7 April 1894, v Ireland 7 March 1896, v Wales 28 March 1898, v Scotland 2 April 1898
Ron SPRINGETT (33)	v Northern Ireland 18 November 1959, v Scotland 19 April 1960, v Yugoslavia 11 May 1960, v Spain 15 May 1960, v Hungary 22 May 1960, v Northern Ireland 8 October 1960, v Luxembourg 19 October 1960, v Spain 26 October 1960, v Scotland 15 April 1961, v Mexico 10 May 1961, v Portugal 21 May 1961, v Italy 24 May 1961, v Austria 27 May 1961, v Luxembourg 28 September 1961, v Wales 14 October 1961, v Portugal 25 October 1961, v Northern Ireland 22 November 1961, v Austria 4 April 1962, v Scotland 14 April 1962, v Switzerland 9 May 1962, v Peru 20 May 1962, v Hungary 31 May 1962, v Argentina 2 June 1962, v Bulgaria 7 June 1962, v Brazil 10 June 1962, v France 3 October 1962, v Northern Ireland 20 October 1962, v Wales 21 November 1962, v France 27 February 1963, v Switzerland 5 June 1963, v Wales 2 October 1965, v Austria 20 October 1965, v Norway 29 June 1966
Ron STARLING (1)	v Scotland 1 April 1933
George STEPHENSON (1)	v France 14 May 1931
Mel STERLAND (1)	v Saudia Arabia 16 November 1988
Jimmy STEWART (2)	v Wales 18 March 1907, v Scotland 6 April 1907
Alf STRANGE (20)	v Scotland 5 April 1930, v Germany 10 May 1930, v Austria 14 May 1930, v Ireland 20 October 1930, v Wales 22 November 1930, v Scotland 28 March 1931, v France 14 May 1931, v Belgium 16 May 1931, v Ireland 17 October 1931, v Wales 18 November 1931, v Spain 9 December 1931, v Scotland 9 April 1932, v Ireland 17 October 1932, v Austria 7 December 1932, v Scotland 1 April 1933, v Italy 13 May 1933, v Switzerland 20 May 1933, v Ireland 14 October 1933, v Wales 15 November 1933, v France 6 December 1933
Peter SWAN (19)	v Yugoslavia 11 May 1960, v Spain 15 May 1960, v Hungary 22 May 1960, v Northern Ireland 8 October 1960, v Luxembourg 19 October 1960, v Spain 26 October 1960, v Wales 23 November 1960, v Scotland 15 April 1961, v Mexico 10 May 1961, v Portugal 21 May 1961, v Italy 24 May 1961, v Austria 27 May 1961, v Luxembourg 28 September 1961, v Wales 14 October 1961, v Portugal 25 October 1961, v Northern Ireland 22 November 1961, v Austria 4 April 1962, v Scotland 14 April 1962, v Switzerland 9 May 1962
Des WALKER (1)	v San Marino 17 November 1993
George WILSON (12)	v Wales 14 March 1921, v Scotland 9 April 1921, v Belgium 21 May 1921, v Ireland 22 October 1921, v Scotland 8 April 1922, v Ireland 21 October 1922, v Wales 5 March 1923, v Belgium 19

	March 1923, v Scotland 14 March 1923, v Ireland 20 October 1923, v Wales 3 March 1924, v France 17 May 1924
Chris WOODS (19)	v Turkey 16 October 1991, v Poland 13 November 1991, v Germany 11 September 1991, v France 19 February 1992, v CIS 29 April 1992, v Brazil 17 May 1992, v Finland 3 June 1992, v Denmark 11 June 1992, v France 14 June 1992, v Sweden 17 June 1992, v Spain 9 September 1992, v Norway 14 October 1992, v Turkey 18 November 1992, v San Marino 17 February 1993, v Turkey 31 March 1993, v Holland 28 April 1993, v Poland 29 May 1993, v Norway 2 June 1993, v USA 9 June 1993
Gerry YOUNG (1)	v Wales 18 November 1964

SCOTLAND

Jimmy BLAIR (2)	v Ireland 13 March 1920, v England 10 April 1920
James CAMPBELL (1)	v Wales 3 March 1913
Jack LYALL (1)	v England 1 April 1905
Jim McCALLIOG (4)	v England 15 April 1967, v Northern Ireland 21 October 1967, v Russia 10 May 1967, v Denmark 16 October 1968
Davie McLEAN (1)	v England 23 March 1912
George ROBERTSON (3)	v Wales 2 March 1912, v Ireland 15 March 1913, v England 5 April 1913
Andrew WILSON (6)	v England 6 April 1907, v England 4 April 1908, v England 23 March 1912, v England 5 April 1913, v Wales 3 March 1913, v Ireland 14 March 1914

WALES

Harry HANFORD (4)	v Northern Ireland 11 March 1936, v Scotland 30 October 1937, v England 17 November 1937, v France 20 May 1939
Ryan JONES (1)	v Estonia 23 May 1994
Tommy JONES (2)	v Northern Ireland 5 December 1931, v France 25 May 1933
Mark PEMBRIDGE (17)	v Moldova 6 September 1995, v Germany 11 October 1995, v Albania 15 November 1995, v Switzerland 24 April 1996, v San Marino 2 June 1996, v San Marino 31 August 1996, v Holland 5 October 1996, v Holland 9 November 1996, v Turkey 14 December 1996, v Eire 11 February 1997, v Belgium 29 March 1997, v Scotland 27 May 1997, v Belgium 11 October 1997, v Brazil 12 November 1997, v Jamaica 25 March 1998, v Malta 3 June 1998, v Tunisia 6 June 1998
Peter RODRIGUES (17)	v Romania 11 November 1970, v Czechoslovakia 21 April 1971, v Scotland 15 May 1971, v England 19 May 1971, v Northern Ireland 22 May 1971, v Finland 13 October 1971, v Czechoslovakia 27 October 1971, v Romania 24 November 1971, v England 20 May 1972, v Northern Ireland 27 May 1972, v England 15 November 1972, v England 24 January

1973, v Poland 28 March 1973, v Scotland 12 May 1973, v England 15 May 1973, v Northern Ireland 19 May 1973, v Poland 26 September 1973

Rees WILLIAMS (4) v Scotland 17 March 1923, v Scotland 31 October 1925, v England 12 February 1927, v Ireland 9 April 1927

Doug WITCOMB (1) v Northern Ireland 16 April 1947

NORTHERN IRELAND

Chris BRUNT (10) v Switzerland 18 August 2004, v Germany 4 June 2005, v Malta 17 August 2005, v Wales 8 October 2005, v Austria 12 October 2005, v Portugal 15 November 2005, v Estonia 1 March 2006, v Wales 6 February 2007, v Liechtenstein 24 March 2007, v Sweden 28 March 2007

Dave CLEMENTS (13) v USSR 22 September 1971, v USSR 13 October 1971, v Spain 16 February 1972, v Scotland 20 May 1972, v England 23 May 1972, v Wales 27 May 1972, v Bulgaria 18 October 1972, v Cyprus 12 February 1973, v Portugal 28 March 1973, v Cyprus 8 May 1973, v England 12 May 1973, v Scotland 16 May 1973, v Wales 19 May 1973

Roy COYLE (5) v Portugal 28 March 1973, v Cyprus 8 May 1973, v Wales 19 May 1973, v Bulgaria 26 September 1973, v Portugal 14 November 1973

Hugh DOWD (2) v Norway 4 September 1974, v Sweden 30 October 1974

Bill GOWDY (1) v Scotland 12 September 1932

Jim MAGILTON (2) v Portugal 11 October 1997, v Spain 3 June 1998

Ian NOLAN (11) v Armenia 5 October 1996, v Germany 9 November 1996, v Albania 14 December 1996, v Portugal 29 March 1997, v Ukraine 2 April 1997, v Germany 20 August 1997, v Portugal 11 October 1997, v Germany 8 September 1999, v Finland 9 October 1999, v Malta 28 March 2000, v Hungary 26 April 2000

James QUINN (1) v Poland 30 March 2005

Danny SONNER (5) v Germany 27 March 1999, v Canada 27 April 1999, v Luxembourg 23 February 2000, v Malta 29 March 2000, v Hungary 25 April 2000

Sammy TODD (3) v Spain 11 November 1970, v Cyprus 3 February 1971, v Cyprus 21 April 1971

Danny WILSON (6) v Yugoslavia 12 September 1990, v Denmark 17 October 1990, v Austria 14 November 1990, v Faroe Islands 1 May 1991, v Austria 16 October 1991, v Scotland 19 February 1992

Nigel WORTHINGTON (50) v Wales 22 May 1984, v Finland 27 May 1984, v Israel 16 October 1984, v Spain 27 March 1985, v Turkey 11 September 1985, v Romania 16 October 1985, v England 13 November 1985, v Denmark 26 March 1986, v Algeria 3 June 1986, v Spain 7 June 1986, v England 15 October 1986, v Turkey 12 November 1986, v Israel 18 February 1987, v

	England 1 April 1987, v Yugoslavia 29 April 1987, v Yugoslavia 14 October 1987, v Turkey 11 November 1987, v Greece 17 February 1988, v Poland 23 March 1988, v France 27 April 1988, v Malta 21 May 1988, v Eire 14 September 1988, v Hungary 19 October 1988, v Spain 21 December 1988, v Malta 26 April 1989, v Hungary 6 September 1989, v Eire 11 October 1989, v Uruguay 18 May 1990, v Yugoslavia 12 September 1990, v Denmark 17 October 1990, v Austria 14 November 1990, v Faroe Islands 1 May 1991, v Austria 16 October 1991, v Denmark 13 November 1991, v Scotland 19 February 1992, v Lithuania 28 April 1992, v Germany 2 June 1992, v Albania 9 September 1992, v Spain 14 October 1992, v Denmark 18 November 1992, v Eire 31 March 1993, v Spain 28 April 1993, v Lithuania 25 May 1993, v Latvia 2 June 1993, v Latvia 8 September 1993, v Denmark 13 October 1993, v Eire 17 November 1993, v Liechtenstein 20 April 1994, v Colombia 4 June 1994, v Mexico 11 June 1994

Ireland (Pre-1924)

English McCONNELL (5)	v Scotland 15 March 1909, v Wales 20 March 1909, v England 12 February 1910, v Scotland 19 March 1910, v Wales 11 April 1910
James MURRAY (1)	v Wales 11 April 1910
Patrick O'CONNELL (2)	v England 10 February 1912, v Scotland 16 March 1912

Eire

Bill FALLON (4)	v Switzerland 18 September 1938, v Poland 13 November 1938, v Hungary 18 May 1939, v Germany 23 May 1939
Tony GALVIN (9)	v Luxembourg 9 September 1987, v Bulgaria 14 October 1987, v Romania 23 March 1988, v Poland 22 May 1988, v Norway 1 June 1988, v England 12 June 1988, v USSR 15 June 1988, v Holland 18 June 1988, v Spain 16 November 1988
Eddie GANNON (11)	v Belgium 24 April 1949, v Portugal 22 May 1949, v Sweden 2 June 1949, v Spain 12 June 1949, v Finland 8 September 1949, v Norway 26 November 1950, v West Germany 4 May 1952, v Austria 7 May 1952, v Luxembourg 28 October 1953, v France 25 November 1953, v Norway 7 November 1954
Alan QUINN (4)	v Norway 30 April 2003, v Australia 19 August 2003, v Jamaica 2 June 2004, v Holland 5 June 2004
John SHERIDAN (29)	v Wales 28 March 1990, v Turkey 27 May 1990, v Malta 2 June 1990, v Italy 30 June 1990, v Morocco 12 September 1990, v Turkey 17 October 1990, v Chile 22 May 1991, v USA 1 June 1991, v Hungary 11 September 1991, v Latvia 9 June 1993, v Spain 13 October 1993, v Holland 20 April 1994, v Bolivia 24 May 1994, v Germany 29 May 1994, v Czech Republic 5 June 1994, v Italy 18 June 1994, v Mexico 24 June 1994, v Norway

	28 June 1994, v Holland 4 July 1994, v Latvia 7 September 1994, v Liechtenstein 12 October 1994, v Northern Ireland 16 November 1994, v England 15 February 1995, v Northern Ireland 29 March 1995, v Portugal 26 April 1995, v Liechtenstein 3 June 1995, v Austria 11 June 1995, v Austria 6 September 1995, v Holland 13 December 1995

Algeria

Madjid BOUGHERRA (4)	v Gabon 15 August 2006, v Guinea 3 September 2006, v Gambia 7 October 2006, v Burkina Faso 15 November 2006

Benin

Reda JOHNSON (2)	v Libya 9 February 2011, v Ivory Coast 27 March 2011

Belgium

Gilles DE BILDE (8)	v England 10 October 1999, v Italy 13 November 1999, v Portugal 23 February 2000, v Holland 29 March 2000, v Norway 26 April 2000, v Denmark 3 June 2000, v Turkey 19 June 2000, v Bulgaria 16 August 2000
Marc DEGRYSE (3)	v Denmark 6 September 1995, v Cyprus 15 November 1995, v France 27 March 1996

Czech Republic

Pavel SRNICEK (15)	v Belgium 9 February 1999, v Lithuania 27 March 1999, v Scotland 31 March 1999, v Poland 28 April 1999, v Estonia 5 June 1999, v Scotland 9 June 1999, v Lithuania 4 September 1999, v Bosnia 8 September 1999, v Faroe Islands 9 October 1999, v Holland 13 November 1999, v Israel 26 April 2000, v Germany 3 June 2000, v Holland 11 June 2000, v France 16 June 2000, v Denmark 21 June 2000

Finland

Shefki KUQI (13)	v South Korea 20 March 2002, v Macedonia 17 April 2002, v Latvia 22 May 2002, v Eire 21 August 2002, v Wales 7 September 2002, v Azerbaijan 12 October 2002, v Yugoslavia 16 October 2002, v Northern Ireland 12 February 2003, v Italy 29 March 2003, v Norway 22 May 2003, v Serbia & Montenegro 7 June 2003, v Denmark 20 August 2003, v Wales 10 September 2003

Holland

Wim JONK (1)	v Denmark 18 August 1999

Iceland

Siggi JONSSON (14)	v Luxembourg 24 April 1985, v Scotland 28 May 1985, v Spain 25 September 1985, v Eire 25 May 1986, v France 10

September 1986, v USSR 24 September 1986, v East Germany 29 October 1986, v France 29 April 1987, v East Germany 3 June 1987, v Norway 9 September 1987, v USSR 31 August 1988, v Hungary 21 September 1988, v USSR 31 May 1989, v Austria 14 June 1989

Jamaica

Deon BURTON (9) v England 3 June 2006, v Trinidad & Tobago 27 March 2008, v St Vincent & Grenadines 3 June 2008, v Trinidad & Tobago 8 June 2008, v Grenada 11 June 2008, v Bahamas 15 June 2008, v Bahamas 18 June 2008, v Canada 20 August 2008, v Mexico 7 September 2008

Jermaine JOHNSON (11) v El Salvador 18 November 2007, v Trinidad & Tobago 8 June 2008, v Mexico 12 October 2008, v Canada 19 November 2008, v Nigeria 11 February 2009, v El Salvador 31 May 2009, v Panama 8 June 2009, v Canada 26 June 2009, v El Salvador 7 July 2009, v Costa Rica 10 July 2009, v South Africa 7 November 2009

Macedonia

Goce SEDLOSKI (6) v Bulgaria 25 March 1998, v Malta 6 September 1998, v Egypt 29 September 1998, v Croatia 14 October 1998, v Malta 18 November 1998, v Albania 10 February 1999

Norway

Petter RUDI (13) v Colombia 8 October 1997, v France 25 February 1998, v Mexico 20 May 1998, v Romania 19 August 1998, v Latvia 6 September 1998, v Egypt 18 November 1998, v Italy 10 February 1999, v Greece 27 March 1999, v Georgia 28 April 1999, v Jamaica 20 May 1999, v Georgia 30 May 1999, v Albania 5 June 1999, v Greece 4 September 1999

Romania

Dan PETRESCU (10) v Azerbaijan 7 September 1994, v France 8 October 1994, v England 12 October 1994, v Slovakia 12 November 1994, v Israel 14 December 1994, v Poland 29 March 1995, v Azerbaijan 26 April 1995, v Israel 7 June 1995, v Poland 6 September 1995, v France 11 October 1995

Sweden

Niclas ALEXANDERSSON (14) v Tunisia 10 February 1999, v Luxembourg 27 March 1999, v Poland 31 March 1999, v Eire 28 April 1999, v Austria 18 August 1999, v Bulgaria 4 September 1999, v Luxembourg 8 September 1999, v Poland 9 October 1999, v Italy 23 February 2000, v Denmark 26 April 2000, v Spain 3 June

	2000, v Belgium 10 June 2000, v Turkey 15 June 2000, v Italy 19 June 2000
Klas INGESSON (2)	v Iceland 7 September 1994, v Hungary 26 April 1995
Roland NILSSON (31)	v Belgium 21 February 1990, v Algeria 11 April 1990, v Wales 25 April 1990, v Finland 27 May 1990, v Brazil 10 June 1990, v Scotland 16 June 1990, v Costa Rica 20 June 1990, v Denmark 5 September 1990, v West Germany 10 October 1990, v Colombia 5 June 1991, v Denmark 15 June 1991, v Norway 8 August 1991, v Yugoslavia 4 September 1991, v Poland 7 May 1992, v Hungary 27 May 1992, v France 10 June 1992, v Denmark 14 June 1992, v England 17 June 1992, v Germany 21 June 1992, v Norway 26 August 1992, v Israel 11 November 1992, v France 28 April 1993, v Austria 19 May 1993, v Israel 2 June 1993, v Switzerland 11 August 1993, v France 22 August 1993, v Bulgaria 8 September 1993, v Finland 13 October 1993, v Austria 10 November 1993, v Wales 20 April 1994, v Nigeria 5 May 1994

USA

John HARKES (12)	v Eire 29 April 1992, v Eire 30 May 1992, v Portugal 3 June 1992, v Italy 6 June 1992, v Saudi Arabia 15 October 1992, v Brazil 6 June 1993, v England 9 June 1993, v Germany 13 June 1993, v Jamaica 10 July 1993, v Honduras 17 July 1993, v Costa Rica 21 July 1993, v Mexico 25 July 1993
Frank SIMEK (5)	v Guatemala 28 March 2007, v China 2 June 2007, v Trinidad & Tobago 9 June 2007, v El Salvador 12 June 2007, v Mexico 24 June 2007

Yugoslavia

Darko KOVACEVIC (4)	v Romania 27 March 1996, v Mexico 23 May 1996, v Japan 26 May 1996, v Malta 2 June 1996
Dejan STEFANOVIC (4)	v Romania 27 March 1996, v Japan 26 May 1996, v Russia 7 February 1997, v Argentina 24 February 1998

Other Caps

England B

Dalian ATKINSON (1)	v Eire 27 March 1990
Chris BART-WILLIAMS (1)	v Northern Ireland 10 May 1994
Alan FINNEY (1)	v Scotland 29 February 1956
Redfern FROGGATT (1)	v Switzerland 18 January 1950
David HIRST (3)	v Switzerland 20 May 1991, v Spain 18 December 1991, v Czechoslovakia 24 March 1992
Phil KING (1)	v Switzerland 20 May 1991

Carlton PALMER (5)	v Eire 27 March 1990, v Switzerland 20 May 1991, v Spain 18 December 1991, v France 18 February 1992, v Czechoslovakia 24 March 1992
Kevin PRESSMAN (3)	v Northern Ireland 10 May 1994, v Eire 13 December 1994, v Chile 10 February 1998
Albert QUIXALL (3)	v Scotland 11 March 1953, v Yugoslavia 16 May 1954, v Switzerland 22 May 1954
Walter RICKETT (1)	v Switzerland 18 January 1950
Mel STERLAND (1)	v Malta 14 October 1987
Hugh SWIFT (1)	v Switzerland 18 January 1950

England Under-23

Colin DOBSON (2)	v Yugoslavia 29 May 1963, v Romania 2 June 1963
Sam ELLIS (3)	v Wales 2 October 1968, v Wales 1 October 1969, v Russia 22 October 1969
John FANTHAM (1)	v Italy 2 November 1960
Alan FINNEY (3)	v Italy 20 January 1954, v Scotland 8 February 1956, v Scotland 26 February 1957
David FORD (2)	v Wales 12 October 1966, v Scotland 1 March 1967
Tony KAY (7)	v Italy 7 May 1959, v West Germany 10 May 1959, v Scotland 2 March 1960, v Holland 16 March 1960, v East Germany 15 May 1960, v Poland 18 May 1960, v Israel 22 May 1960
Vic MOBLEY (13)	v Wales 4 November 1964, v Romania 25 November 1964, v Scotland 24 February 1965, v Czechoslovakia 7 April 1965, v West Germany 25 May 1965, v Czechoslovakia 29 May 1965, v Austria 2 June 1965, v France 3 November 1965, v Yugoslavia 24 November 1965, v Austria 10 May 1967, v Greece 31 May 1967, v Bulgaria 3 June 1967, v Turkey 7 June 1967
Graham PUGH (1)	v Wales 1 October 1969
Albert QUIXALL (1)	v Scotland 8 February 1956
Wilf SMITH (6)	v Portugal 16 April 1969, v Holland 22 May 1969, v Portugal 28 May 1969, v Wales 1 October 1969, v Scotland 4 March 1970, v Bulgaria 8 April 1970
Peter SPRINGETT (6)	v Italy 20 December 1967, v Scotland 7 February 1968, v Hungary 1 May 1968, v Italy 25 May 1968, v West Germany 3 June 1968, v Belgium B 25 May 1969
Peter SWAN (3)	v France 11 November 1959, v Scotland 2 March 1960, v Holland 16 March 1960
Jack WHITHAM (1)	v Wales 2 October 1968

England Under-21

Gary BANNISTER (1)	v Poland 7 April 1982
Chris BART-WILLIAMS (14)	v Spain 8 September 1992, v Norway 13 October 1992, v Turkey 11 November 1992, v Denmark 8 March 1994, v

	Russia 29 May 1994, v France 31 May 1994, v Belgium 5 June 1994, v Portugal 7 June 1994, v Portugal 6 September 1994, v Austria 11 October 1994, v Eire 15 November 1994, v Eire 27 March 1995, v Latvia 25 April 1995, v Latvia 7 June 1995
Lee BRISCOE (5)	v Croatia 23 April 1996, v Belgium 24 May 1996, v Angola 28 May 1996, v Brazil 1 June 1996, v Switzerland 1 April 1997
David HIRST (7)	v USSR 7 June 1988, v France 12 June 1988, v Denmark 13 September 1988, v Bulgaria 5 June 1989, v Senegal 7 June 1989, v Eire 9 June 1989, v USA 11 June 1989
Richie HUMPHREYS (3)	v Poland 8 October 1996, v Georgia 8 November 1996, v Switzerland 1 April 1997
Ian KNIGHT (2)	v Sweden 9 September 1986, v Yugoslavia 11 November 1986
Carlton PALMER (4)	v Bulgaria 5 June 1989, v Senegal 7 June 1989, v Eire 9 June 1989, v USA 11 June 1989
Kevin PRESSMAN (1)	v Denmark 13 September 1988
Gary SHELTON (1)	v Finland 16 October 1984 **overage player*
Mark SMITH (5)	v Eire 25 February 1981, v Romania 28 April 1981, v Switzerland 31 May 1981, v Hungary 5 June 1981, v Poland 7 April 1982
Mel STERLAND (7)	v Denmark 20 September 1983, v Hungary 11 October 1983, v France 28 February 1984, v France 28 March 1984, v Italy 18 April 1984, v Spain 17 May 1984, v Spain 24 May 1984
Paul WARHURST (1)	v Germany 10 September 1991
Gordon WATSON (2)	v Senegal 27 May 1991, v USSR 31 May 1991

England Under-20

Matt HAMSHAW (6)	v Finland 13 February 2002, v Portugal 10 April 2002, v China 6 May 2002, v Poland 10 May 2002, v Brazil 14 May 2002, v Japan 17 May 2002
Steve HASLAM (3)	v USA 5 April 1999, v Cameroon 8 April 1999, v Japan 11 April 1999
Richie HUMPHREYS (2)	v Ivory Coast 18 June 1997, v Argentina 26 June 1997

England Under-19

Mark BEEVERS (1)	v Russia 25 March 2008

England Under-18

Tony CRANE (1)	v Luxembourg 27 April 2000
Matt HAMSHAW (8)	v France 8 March 2000, v Luxembourg 27 April 2000, v Israel 1 September 2000, v Andorra 7 October 2000, Faroe Islands 9 October 2000, v Italy 11 October 2000, v Belgium 16 November 2000, v Poland 22 March 2001
Steve HASLAM (5)	v Russia 27 October 1997, v Russia 14 November 1997, v Israel 12 February 1998, v Cyprus 30 May 1998, v France 1 June 1998
Mark PLATTS (2)	v Finland 11 October 1996, v Northern Ireland 13 October 1996

England Youth

Carl BRADSHAW (4)	v Brazil 29 March 1986, v Hungary 30 March 1986, v France 31 March 1986, v Thailand 7 May 1986
Kenny BURTON (3)	v Bulgaria 7 April 1968, v Holland 9 April 1968, v Russia 1 April 1968
Tony GREGORY (11)	v Russia 3 April 1985, v Italy 5 April 1985, v Holland 7 April 1985, v Iceland 11 September 1985, v Scotland 25 March 1986, v China 5 May 1986, v China Army 9 May 1986, v France 11 May 1986, v Brazil 13 May 1986, v Brazil 2 June 1987, v Uruguayan Interior Selection 7 June 1987
Simon MILLS (3)	v Israel Under-21 21 February 1983, v Israel Olympic XI 23 February 1983, v Belgium 13 April 1983
John PEARSON (3)	v Spain 25 May 1981, v Scotland 27 May 1981, v Scotland 23 March 1982
Kevin PRESSMAN (10)	v Algeria 22 April 1984, v USSR 8 August 1984, v Sweden 10 September 1984, v Yugoslavia 12 September 1984, v Brazil 29 March 1986, v Hungary 30 March 1986, v France 31 March 1986, v China Army 9 May 1986, v Uruguayan Interior Selection 7 June 1987, v Uruguay 10 June 1987
Tony SIMMONS (9)	v Norway 13 July 1982, v Denmark 15 July 1982, v Poland 17 July 1982, v USSR 4 September 1982, v Switzerland 6 September 1982, v Yugoslavia 9 September 1982, v Israel Under-21s 21 February 1983, v Israel Olympic XI 23 February 1983, v Belgium 13 April 1983
Wilf SMITH (6)	v Scotland 27 February 1965, v Belgium 15 March 1965, v Spain 17 March 1965, v Hungary 21 March 1965, v Italy 23 March 1965, v East Germany 25 March 1965
Peter SWAN (1)	v Holland 5 November 1955
Chris TURNER (5)	v Wales 9 March 1977, v Wales 23 March 1977, v Belgium 19 May 1977, v Iceland 21 May 1977, v Greece 23 May 1977
Peter WICKS (1)	v Italy 25 May 1966
Howard WILKINSON (5)	v Scotland 24 February 1962, v Yugoslavia 20 March 1962, v Holland 22 March 1962, v Bulgaria 24 March 1962, v Ireland 12 May 1962

English FA Tours

Teddy DAVISON (3)	v Australia 4 July 1925, 11 July 1925 and 25 July 1925
John FANTHAM (6)	v Malaya 13 May 1961, v Singapore 17 May 1961, v Hong Kong 21 May 1961, v Chinese XI 23 May 1961, v New Zealand 5 June 1961 and 10 June 1961
Redfern FROGGATT (1)	v Buenos Aires (Argentina) 14 May 1953
Don MEGSON (7)	v Tahiti 21 May 1969, v New Zealand 2 June 1969, 7 June 1969 and 11 June 1969, v Singapore 14 June 1969, v Hong Kong 16 June 1969, v Thailand 20 June 1969
Jimmy SEED (2)	v South Africa 15 June 1929 and 13 July 1929

Jackie SEWELL (6) v American Soccer League (New York) 9 May 1951, v Australia 26 May 1951, 30 June 1951, 7 July 1951, 14 July 1951 and 21 July 1951

England FA Services Tours

Doug HUNT (1) v Switzerland 21 July 1945

England Amateur

William HARVEY (1) v Ireland 15 November 1919

Haydn HILL (5) v Wales 19 January 1935, v Ireland 16 February 1935, v Scotland 23 March 1935, v Ireland 15 February 1936, v Scotland 14 March 1936

Mike PINNER (9) v Scotland 29 March 1958, v France 28 April 1958, v Ireland 27 September 1958, v Finland 11 October 1958, v South Africa 25 October 1958, v Wales 8 November 1958, v Scotland 14 March 1959, v Holland 20 May 1959, v Germany 27 May 1959

Scotland Under-23

Tommy CRAIG (1) v England 13 March 1974

Jim McCALLIOG (2) v Wales 30 November 1966, v England 1 March 1967

Scotland Under-21

Liam PALMER (2) v Northern Ireland 17 November 2010, v Belgium 24 March 2011

Scotland Under-19

Liam PALMER (4) v Luxembourg 14 April 2010, v Montenegro 19 May 2010, v Belgium 21 May 2010, v Croatia 24 May 2010

Scottish FA Tours

Jim McCALLIOG (7) v Israel 16 May 1967, v Hong Kong 25 May 1967, v Australia 28 May 1967, 31 May 1967, 3 June 1967, v New Zealand Under-23s 5 June 1967, v Canada 13 June 1967

Wales B

Ryan JONES (1) v Scotland 2 February 1994

Wales Under-21

Ryan JONES (4) v Romania 16 November 1993, v Bulgaria 13 December 1994 and 28 March 1995, v Germany 25 April 1995

Northern Ireland B

Danny SONNER (1) v Wales 9 February 1999

Northern Ireland Under-23

Chris BRUNT (1) v Serbia & Montenegro 27 April 2004

Northern Ireland Under-21

Chris BRUNT (2) v Scotland 8 February 2005, v Romania 16 August 2006

Rory McARDLE (4) v Wales 28 February 2006, v Liechenstein 10 May 2006, v Romania 16 August 2006, v Germany 1 September 2006

Liam McMENAMIN (4) v Poland 19 August 2008, v Ukraine 19 August 2008, v Germany 5 September 2008, v Scotland 18 November 2008

Owen MORRISON (4) v Bulgaria 27 March 2001, v Malta 5 October 2001, v Scotland 6 September 2002, v Finland 11 February 2003

Northern Ireland Under-20

Rory McARDLE (3) v Paraguay 28 July 2006, v Turkey 2 August 2006, v Denmark 4 August 2006

David McCLEMENTS (2) v Luxembourg 13 May 2008, v FC Metz 14 May 2008

Northern Ireland Under-19

Rory McARDLE (6) v Eire 16 October 2005, v Italy 18 October 2005, v Moldova 20 October 2005, v Serbia & Montenegro 18 May 2006, v England 20 May 2006, v Belgium 22 May 2006

David McCLEMENTS (3) v Switzerland 21 August 2007, v Austria 30 October 2007, v Cyprus 4 November 2007

Liam McMENAMIN (4) v Switzerland 21 August 2007, v Austria 30 October 2007, v Slovakia 1 November 2007, v Cyprus 4 November 2007

Northern Ireland Under-17

David McCLEMENTS (5) v Cyprus 14 September 2004, v Cyprus 16 September 2004, v Malta 27 September 2005, v Lithuania 29 September 2005, v Serbia 1 October 2005

Liam McMENAMIN (1) v Finland 26 March 2006

Eire B

Glenn WHELAN (1) v Scotland 20 November 2007

Eire Under-23

John SHERIDAN (1) v Northern Ireland 15 May 1990

Eire Under-21

David BILLINGTON (1) v Greece 24 April 2000

Mark McKEEVER (4) v Czech Republic 24 March 1998, v Sweden 27 April 1999, v Scotland 31 May 1999, v Northern Ireland 2 June 1999

Alan QUINN (7) v Czech Republic 22 February 2000, v Columbia 25 May 2000, v Ghana 27 May 2000, v Portugal 29 May 2000, v

	Holland 2 September 2000, v Portugal 6 October 2000, v Cyprus 23 March 2001
Glenn WHELAN (13)	v Bulgaria 17 August 2004, v Cyprus 3 September 2004, v Switzerland 7 September 2004, v France 8 October 2004, v Portugal 8 February 2005, v Israel 25 March 2005, v Israel 3 June 2005, v Northern Ireland 16 August 2005, v Cyprus 7 October 2005, v Switzerland 11 October 2005, v Sweden 28 February 2006, v Greece 16 August 2006, v Belgium 1 September 2006

DR CONGO UNDER-20

Guylain NDUMBU-NSUNGU (1)	v Cameroon 26 October 2003

NORWAY UNDER-19

Rexhap LEKAJ (1)	v France 27 March 2007

FOOTBALL LEAGUE

George BEESON (2)	v Irish League 4 October 1933, v Irish League 25 September 1935
Ernie BLENKINSOP (8)	v Scottish League 7 November 1928, v Irish League 22 September 1928, v Scottish League 2 November 1929, v Scottish League 6 November 1930, v Scottish League 7 November 1931, v Scottish League 9 November 1932, v Irish League 1 October 1932, v Scottish League 10 February 1934
Frank BRADSHAW (2)	v Scottish League 10 October 1908, v Irish League 27 February 1909
Tommy BRITTLETON (2)	v Scotland 26 February 1910, v Ireland 23 October 1913
Jack BROWN (2)	v Scottish League 19 March 1927, v Irish League 24 September 1930
Ted CATLIN (1)	v Scottish League 31 October 1936
Tommy CRAWSHAW (8)	v Scottish League 13 April 1895, v Scottish League 24 April 1897, v Scottish League 1 April 1899, v Irish League 5 November 1899, v Irish League 6 November 1902, v Irish League 10 October 1904, v Irish League 15 October 1905, v Irish League 12 October 1907
Harry DAVIS (1)	v Scottish League 14 March 1903
Jack EARP (1)	v Irish League 6 November 1898
John FANTHAM (3)	v Scottish League 22 March 1961, v Irish League 1 November 1961, v Italian League 8 November 1961
Redfern FROGGATT (1)	v Scottish League 25 March 1953
Tony KAY (3)	v League of Ireland 4 November 1959, v Irish League 1 November 1961, v Italian League 8 November 1961
Fred KEAN (4)	v Irish League 29 September 1923, 11 October 1924 and 9 October 1926, v Scottish League 10 March 1929

Ambrose LANGLEY (1)	v Scottish League 9 April 1898
Willie LAYTON (1)	v Irish League 10 November 1901
Tony LEACH (1)	v Scottish League 6 November 1930
Billy MARSDEN (1)	v Scottish League 2 November 1929
Don MEGSON (1)	v Italian League 1 November 1960
Vic MOBLEY (1)	v League of Ireland 8 November 1967
Albert QUIXALL (3)	v Irish League 23 September 1953 and 25 April 1956, v League of Ireland 19 September 1956
John RITCHIE (1)	v League of Ireland 8 November 1967
Jackie ROBINSON (1)	v Irish League 21 September 1939
Jackie SEWELL (4)	v Scottish League 31 October 1951, v Irish League 24 September 1952, v League of Ireland 10 February 1954, v Scottish League 28 April 1954
Wilf SMITH (3)	v League of Ireland 8 November 1967, v Scottish League 26 March 1969, v Scottish League 18 March 1970
Fred SPIKSLEY (2)	v Scottish League 21 April 1894, v Scottish League 14 March 1903
Ron SPRINGETT (9)	v Irish League 23 September 1959, v League of Ireland 4 November 1959, v Italian League 1 November 1960, v Scottish League 22 March 1961, v League of Ireland 11 October 1961, v Italian League 8 November 1961, v Italian League 29 November 1962, v Scottish League 21 March 1962, v Scottish League 16 March 1966
Mel STERLAND (1)	v Irish League 8 September 1987
Alf STRANGE (3)	v Scottish League 6 November 1930, v Irish League 24 September 1930, v Scottish League 6 November 1932
Peter SWAN (6)	v League of Ireland 4 November 1959, v Italian League 1 November 1960, v Scottish League 22 March 1961, v League of Ireland 11 October 1961, v Italian League 8 November 1961, v Scottish League 21 March 1962
Derek WILKINSON (2)	v Scottish League 8 October 1958, v League of Ireland 17 March 1959
George WILSON (4)	v Scottish League 12 March 1921, 18 March 1922 and 17 February 1923 v Irish League 29 September 1923

FOOTBALL ALLIANCE LEAGUE

Harry BRANDON (1)	v Football League 20 April 1891

Players Database

(*Intertoto, Full Members Cup, Play-offs and Associate Members Cup)

Player		1st Game	v	Last Game	v
ADAMS	Steve	19/03/2005	Colchester United	30/09/2006	Sunderland
ADAMSON	Chris	12/03/2005	Blackpool	06/05/2007	Norwich City
AGBONLAHOR	Gabby	29/10/2005	Norwich City	10/12/2005	Hull City
AGOGO	Junior	09/08/1997	Newcastle United	13/03/1999	Leeds United
ALEXANDERSSON	Niclas	20/12/1997	Chelsea	14/05/2000	Leicester City
ALJOFREE	Hasney	25/09/2004	Wrexham	02/10/2004	MK Dons
ALLAN	William	23/01/1892	Bolton Wanderers	11/01/1896	Blackburn Rovers
ALLEN	Jack	09/04/1927	Aston Villa	24/01/1931	Barnsley
ANDERSON	Viv	12/01/1991	Hull City	15/05/1993	Arsenal
ANDREWS	Wayne	25/11/2006	Cardiff City	01/01/2007	Hull City
ANSTISS	Harry	28/08/1926	Sheffield United	12/02/1927	Huddersfield Town
ANTHONY	Nudger	05/11/1881	Sheffield Providence	02/12/1882	Lockwood Brothers
ANTOINE-CURIER	Mickael	22/11/2003	Luton Town	22/11/2003	Luton Town
ARANALDE	Zigor	29/03/2005	Huddersfield Town	02/04/2005	Tranmere Rovers
ARMITAGE	Harry	02/05/1921	Bristol City	18/03/1922	Port Vale
ARMITAGE	Len	20/09/1919	Notts County	18/10/1919	Blackburn Rovers
ARMSTRONG	Craig	16/02/2002	Watford	14/02/2004	Hartlepool United
ARMSTRONG	Harold	26/10/1907	Liverpool	26/09/1908	Newcastle United
ARMSTRONG	James	03/09/1921	Barnsley	05/11/1921	Fulham
ASHLEY	Jack	18/04/1936	Stoke City	29/04/1939	Tottenham Hotspur
ATHERTON	Peter	20/08/1994	Tottenham Hotspur	14/05/2000	Leicester City
ATKINSON	Dalian	19/08/1989	Norwich City	05/05/1990	Nottingham Forest
AVEYARD	Walter	05/01/1946	Mansfield Town	05/10/1946	Bradford Park Avenue
AYRES	George	03/05/1924	Manchester United	17/10/1925	Derby County
BAILEY	Gavin	24/06/1995	FC Basel	24/06/1995	FC Basel
BAILEY	Ian	28/08/1982	Middlesbrough	09/04/1983	Bolton Wanderers
BAIRD	Walter	17/11/1934	Preston North End	17/11/1934	Preston North End
BAKER	Peter	04/09/1957	Newcastle United	08/03/1958	Sunderland
BALL	Jack	08/09/1930	Chelsea	23/12/1933	Stoke FC
BALLAGHER	John	30/08/1958	Ipswich Town	07/02/1959	Leyton Orient
BANNISTER	Gary	29/08/1981	Blackburn Rovers	12/05/1984	Cardiff City
BANNISTER	Keith	25/12/1946	Bury	06/09/1952	Charlton Athletic
BARGH	George	09/09/1935	Bolton Wanderers	19/02/1936	Derby County
BARKER	Richard	24/06/1995	FC Basel	08/07/1995	Gornik Zabrze
BARRASS	Matt	21/03/1925	Middlesbrough	17/04/1926	Clapton Orient
BARRETT	Earl	28/02/1998	Derby County	03/10/1998	Middlesbrough
BARRETT	Graham	26/03/2005	Torquay United	07/05/2005	Bristol City
BARRICK	Dean	27/03/1989	Newcastle United	31/03/1990	Tottenham Hotspur
BARRON	George	06/04/1903	Bury	06/04/1903	Bury
BARRY-MURPHY	Brian	01/02/2003	Wolverhampton Wanderers	08/05/2004	Queen's Park Rangers
BARTLETT	William	22/02/1904	Notts County	19/03/1910	Sheffield United
BART-WILLIAMS	Chris	23/11/1991	Arsenal	07/05/1995	Manchester United
BATTH	Danny	19/03/2011	Southampton	07/05/2011	Exeter City
BECKETT	Albert	05/11/1887	Long Eaton Rangers	05/11/1887	Long Eaton Rangers
BEDFORD	Lewis	29/08/1925	Fulham	17/10/1925	Derby County
BEECH	Jack	05/04/1897	Nottingham Forest	04/04/1904	Everton
BEESON	George	02/11/1929	Leicester City	24/03/1934	Huddersfield Town
BEEVERS	Mark	31/01/2007	Southampton		
BELL	Derek	24/03/1976	Chesterfield	10/04/1976	Wrexham
BELL	Lawrie	02/09/1895	Everton	17/04/1897	Bury
BELLAS	Jack	09/10/1920	Leeds United	05/05/1923	Port Vale
BENNETT	Dave	25/03/1989	Queen's Park Rangers	07/04/1990	Southampton
BENNETT	Mickey	20/01/1890	London Swifts	29/03/1890	Blackburn Rovers
BENTLEY	Harry	14/04/1914	Oldham Athletic	17/04/1920	Aston Villa

Lge	Sub	goals	FA Cup	Sub	goals	L Cup	Sub	goals	Euro	Sub	Goals	Other*	Sub	Goals	Total	Sub	Goals
18	2												1		18	3	0
9	2					1									10	2	0
4	4														4	4	0
	2			1											0	3	0
73	2	8	8		2	4	1	2							85	3	12
2												1			3	0	0
102			16												118	0	0
104		76	10		9										114	0	85
60	11	8	8	2	2	10		1	3		2	2			83	13	13
7	2	1													7	2	1
12		5													12	0	5
			5		3										5	0	3
	1														0	1	0
1	1														1	1	0
3															3	0	0
3															3	0	0
29	6	1				3						2			34	6	1
6															6	0	0
7															7	0	0
106		3	11												117	0	3
214		9	18			16			3						251	0	9
38		10	2		1	3		3				2		1	45	0	15
4		3	6		2										10	0	5
26		11													26	0	11
										1					0	1	0
35			5			5									45	0	0
1															1	0	0
11			1												12	0	0
132		90	3		4										135	0	94
3															3	0	0
117	1	55	12		4	13		7							142	1	66
75			3												78	0	0
5															5	0	0
									1	1					1	1	0
48		14	1												49	0	14
10	5						1								10	6	0
5	1	1													5	1	1
11		2													11	0	2
1															1	0	0
55	3		2			1						6			64	3	0
175		2	24		1										199	0	3
95	29	16	9	3	2	10	6	4	1	2	2		1		115	41	24
10															10	0	0
			1												1	0	0
11		2													11	0	2
20		5	2												22	0	5
74			1												75	0	0
117	10	2	6	1	2	5						3	1		131	12	4
5		1													5	0	1
46		10	7		3										53	0	13
45			6												51	0	0
20	8					1						2		1	23	8	1
			5		4										5	0	4
51		3	2												53	0	3

(*Intertoto, Full Members Cup, Play-offs and Associate Members Cup)

Player		1st Game	v	Last Game	v
BENTLEY	Willis	06/01/1883	Nottingham Forest	03/01/1885	Nottingham Forest
BERESFORD	Marlon	13/01/2001	Blackburn Rovers	10/02/2001	Wimbledon
BEST	Leon	06/08/2005	Stoke City	30/04/2006	Derby County
BESWETHERICK	Jon	10/08/2002	Stoke City	07/03/2004	Scunthorpe United
BETTS	Billy	06/01/1883	Nottingham Forest	13/04/1895	Preston North End
BINGLEY	Jack	08/01/1881	Turton	05/11/1881	Sheffield Providence
BINGLEY	Walter	03/09/1955	Bristol Rovers	26/10/1957	Sunderland
BINKS	Sid	26/08/1922	Rotherham United	27/09/1924	Manchester United
BINNEY	Chas	15/11/1919	Derby County	26/12/1922	Bradford City
BIRCH	Arnold	30/08/1919	Middlesbrough	06/01/1923	Blackpool
BIRKS	Graham	01/09/1962	West Bromwich Albion	24/11/1962	West Ham United
BISCHOFF	Mikkel	11/03/2006	Queen's Park Rangers	01/04/2006	Burnley
BLACKHALL	Ray	22/08/1978	Doncaster Rovers	04/05/1982	Rotherham United
BLAIR	Andy	25/08/1984	Nottingham Forest	26/02/1986	Derby County
BLAIR	Jimmy	26/09/1914	Bradford Park Avenue	13/11/1920	West Ham United
BLATSIS	Con	30/12/2000	Huddersfield Town	10/02/2001	Wimbledon
BLENKINSOP	Ernie	27/01/1923	Bury	10/03/1934	Wolverhampton Wanderers
BLINKER	Regi	06/03/1996	Aston Villa	07/05/1997	Leicester City
BLONDEAU	Patrick	09/08/1997	Newcastle United	08/11/1997	Bolton Wanderers
BODEN	Luke	19/08/2006	Plymouth Argyle	03/05/2009	Cardiff City
BOLDER	Adam	09/02/2008	Bristol City	04/05/2008	Norwich City
BOLDER	Bob	27/12/1977	Rotherham United	14/05/1983	Crystal Palace
BOLLAND	Tommy	18/01/1908	Notts County	20/03/1909	Bradford City
BOLSOVER	Henry	12/03/1900	Burton Swifts	17/03/1900	Arsenal
BONVIN	Pablo	21/08/2001	Bury	09/03/2002	Gillingham
BOOTH	Andy	17/08/1996	Aston Villa	17/03/2001	Burnley
BOSWORTH	Samuel	04/03/1899	Everton	22/04/1899	Preston North End
BOUGHERRA	Madjid	05/08/2006	Preston North End	13/01/2007	Derby County
BOWLING	Ian	24/06/1995	FC Basel	24/06/1995	FC Basel
BOWMAN	Matt	23/08/2006	Wrexham	23/08/2006	Wrexham
BOWNS	George	12/02/1883	Notts County	31/10/1885	Long Eaton Rangers
BRADBURY	Lee	26/12/2002	Nottingham Forest	05/04/2003	Wimbledon
BRADLEY	Martin	15/10/1910	Bury	28/01/1911	Notts County
BRADSHAW	Carl	29/11/1986	Queen's Park Rangers	27/09/1988	Blackpool
BRADSHAW	Frank	23/04/1906	Everton	19/02/1910	Notts County
BRADSHAW	Paul	25/09/1976	Wrexham	07/03/1978	Chester City
BRADY	Alec	03/09/1892	Notts County	28/01/1899	Stoke FC
BRANDON	Harry	17/01/1891	Halliwell	16/04/1898	Wolverhampton Wanderers
BRANDON	Robert	17/01/1891	Halliwell	14/02/1891	West Bromwich Albion
BRANDON	Tom	23/01/1892	Bolton Wanderers	03/04/1893	Notts County
BRANFOOT	Ian	09/05/1966	Burnley	22/11/1969	West Bromwich Albion
BRANNIGAN	Kenny	03/01/1987	Leicester City	03/01/1987	Leicester City
BRANSTON	Guy	07/08/2004	Colchester United	11/12/2004	Brentford
BRASH	Archie	01/09/1894	Everton	28/04/1900	Middlesbrough
BRATLEY	George	11/02/1933	West Bromwich Albion	25/03/1933	Portsmouth
BRAYSHAW	Teddy	08/11/1884	Long Eaton Rangers	14/02/1891	West Bromwich Albion
BREEDON	Jack	27/12/1930	Newcastle United	05/05/1934	Stoke FC
BRELSFORD	Chas	09/11/1912	Oldham Athletic	07/02/1914	Liverpool
BRELSFORD	Tom	10/03/1920	Liverpool	15/03/1924	Oldham Athletic
BRETNALL	Oscar	19/01/1920	Darlington	19/01/1920	Darlington
BRIEN	Tony	24/06/1995	FC Basel	24/06/1995	FC Basel
BRIGHT	Mark	12/09/1992	Nottingham Forest	02/09/1996	Leicester City
BRISCOE	James	12/10/1946	Manchester City	04/01/1947	Plymouth Argyle
BRISCOE	Lee	05/02/1994	Tottenham Hotspur	09/05/2000	Arsenal
BRITTLETON	Tommy	14/01/1905	Bury	01/05/1920	Oldham Athletic
BROADBENT	Albert	20/08/1955	Plymouth Argyle	26/10/1957	Sunderland
BROLLY	Tom	14/10/1933	Derby County	10/03/1934	Wolverhampton Wanderers
BROMBY	Leigh	23/12/2000	Wolverhampton Wanderers	17/04/2004	Blackpool
BROOMES	Marlon	15/12/2001	Gillingham	21/04/2002	Wolverhampton Wanderers
BROWN	Bobby	24/08/1974	Bristol Rovers	13/09/1975	Swindon Town

Lge	Sub	goals	FA Cup	Sub	goals	L Cup	Sub	goals	Euro	Sub	Goals	Other*	Sub	Goals	Total	Sub	Goals
			5		1										5	0	1
4															4	0	0
5	8	2													5	8	2
9	2		2	1								1	1		12	4	0
50		3	33		1										83	0	4
			2												2	0	0
38			1												39	0	0
77		29	6		4										83	0	33
40		6	3												43	0	6
27			2												29	0	0
4															4	0	0
4															4	0	0
115		1	12			13									140	0	1
58		3	7		1	10		3							75	0	7
57			4												61	0	0
6			2												8	0	0
393		5	31												424	0	5
24	18	3	1			2									27	18	3
5	1														5	1	0
2	13	0	1	0	0	1	2								4	15	0
11	2	2													11	2	2
196			12			16									224	0	0
13		1													13	0	1
2															2	0	0
7	16	4		1		2	4	1							9	21	5
124	9	28	9	1	5	10	1	1							143	11	34
7															7	0	0
28		2				1									29	0	2
									1						1	0	0
							1								0	1	0
			2												2	0	0
10	1	3													10	1	3
2															2	0	0
16	16	4	6	1	3	2	2					1			25	19	7
87		38	8		2										95	0	40
62	2	9	4			6		2							72	2	11
159		34	19		5										178	0	39
147		15	25		1										172	0	16
			2		1										2	0	1
30		2	8												38	0	2
33	3		3	1		1									37	4	0
1															1	0	0
10	1		1			1									12	1	0
119		17	12		6										131	0	23
3															3	0	0
			21												21	0	0
45			2												47	0	0
6			1												7	0	0
117		6	5												122	0	6
			1												1	0	0
									1						1	0	0
112	21	48	13		7	20	1	11	3		4				148	22	70
5		3													5	0	3
48	30	1		2		5	2		2	1					55	35	1
342		30	30		3										372	0	33
81		17	2												83	0	17
2															2	0	0
98	2	2	6	1		8						5			117	3	2
18	1		1												19	1	0
17	4	3													17	4	3

(*Intertoto, Full Members Cup, Play-offs and Associate Members Cup)

Player		1st Game	v	Last Game	v
BROWN	Jack	21/04/1923	Coventry City	20/03/1937	Liverpool
BROWN	James	02/01/1893	West Bromwich Albion	26/12/1893	Burnley
BROWN	Sparrow	23/01/1892	Bolton Wanderers	26/03/1894	Preston North End
BRUCE	Alex	12/03/2005	Blackpool	29/05/2005	Hartlepool United
BRUCE	Robert	12/10/1935	Derby County	09/11/1935	Leeds United
BRUNT	Chris	17/03/2004	Bournemouth	11/08/2007	Ipswich Town
BRYANT	Steve	25/08/1976	Northampton Town	11/09/1976	Swindon Town
BULLEN	Lee	07/08/2004	Colchester United	26/04/2008	Leicester City
BURCH	Rob	28/08/2007	Hartlepool United	02/10/2007	Watford
BURCHILL	Mark	26/12/2003	Port Vale	17/01/2004	Oldham Athletic
BURGESS	Harry	14/09/1929	Aston Villa	20/02/1935	Liverpool
BURGIN	Andy	09/01/1965	Everton	16/01/1965	Liverpool
BURKINSHAW	Jack	01/09/1913	Bolton Wanderers	14/01/1920	Darlington
BURKINSHAW	Laurie	23/09/1911	Notts County	25/04/1914	Tottenham Hotspur
BURRIDGE	Bert	28/08/1926	Sheffield United	28/12/1929	Portsmouth
BURROWS	David	09/03/2002	Gillingham	14/12/2002	Gillingham
BURROWS	Horace	27/12/1932	Manchester City	29/04/1939	Tottenham Hotspur
BURTON	Deon	02/01/2006	Crewe Alexandra	25/11/2008	Blackpool
BURTON	Harry	10/10/1903	Wolverhampton Wanderers	27/03/1909	Manchester City
BURTON	Ken	30/11/1968	Stoke City	26/02/1972	Burnley
BUTLER	Barry	02/01/1954	Burnley	19/02/1955	Blackpool
BUTTERY	Edward	18/12/1880	Blackburn Rovers	15/03/1882	Blackburn Rovers
BUTTERY	Thomas	18/12/1880	Blackburn Rovers	05/02/1881	Darwen
BUXTON	Lewis	21/10/2008	Barnsley		
CALLAGHAN	John	04/01/1896	Burnley	12/09/1896	West Bromwich Albion
CAMERON	Danny	24/10/1973	West Bromwich Albion	27/09/1975	Crystal Palace
CAMPBELL	James	18/02/1911	Bury	10/03/1920	Liverpool
CAMPBELL	Phil	13/09/1980	Bristol City	13/09/1980	Bristol City
CAPEWELL	Ron	06/09/1952	Charlton Athletic	09/09/1953	Bolton Wanderers
CAPPER	Alf	26/09/1914	Bradford Park Avenue	26/02/1921	Hull City
CARBONE	Benito	19/10/1996	Blackburn Rovers	19/09/1999	Newcastle United
CARGILL	David	19/09/1956	Manchester United	19/02/1958	Manchester United
CARR	Chris	01/05/2004	Luton Town	08/05/2004	Queen's Park Rangers
CARR	Franz	26/12/1989	Liverpool	21/03/1990	Manchester United
CARSON	Scott	11/03/2006	Queen's Park Rangers	30/04/2006	Derby County
CATLIN	Ted	28/03/1931	Leicester City	29/04/1939	Tottenham Hotspur
CAWLEY	Tom	05/11/1881	Sheffield Providence	23/01/1892	Bolton Wanderers
CHALMERS	Bruce	24/12/1892	Manchester United	23/12/1893	Everton
CHAMBERLAIN	Mark	14/09/1985	Arsenal	02/04/1988	West Ham United
CHAMBERS	Adam	21/02/2004	Rushden & Diamonds	01/05/2004	Luton Town
CHAPMAN	Harry	16/02/1901	Blackburn Rovers	28/01/1911	Notts County
CHAPMAN	Lee	25/08/1984	Nottingham Forest	07/05/1988	Liverpool
CHAPMAN	William	15/03/1924	Oldham Athletic	25/10/1924	South Shields
CHEDGZOY	Syd	28/08/1937	Chesterfield	16/09/1937	Tottenham Hotspur
CLARKE	Harry	12/10/1957	Blackpool	12/10/1957	Blackpool
CLARKE	Leon	20/01/2007	Sunderland	02/05/2010	Crystal Palace
CLARKE	Matt	11/05/1997	Liverpool	27/09/1997	Aston Villa
CLEMENTS	Dave	31/08/1971	Middlesbrough	25/08/1973	Swindon Town
CLOUGH	Nigel	17/09/1997	Grimsby Town	24/09/1997	Derby Country
COBIAN	Juan	15/08/1998	West Ham United	01/05/1999	Nottingham Forest
COCKROFT	Joe	05/01/1946	Mansfield Town	16/10/1948	Grimsby Town
CODD	Ronnie	21/03/1953	Chelsea	28/03/1953	Manchester United
COKE	Giles	07/08/2010	Dagenham & Redbridge		
COLE	William	17/09/1898	Bolton Wanderers	19/01/1901	Notts County
COLEMAN	Simon	04/12/1993	Liverpool	10/09/1994	Nottingham Forest
COLEMAN	Tony	04/10/1969	Ipswich Town	22/04/1970	Manchester City
COLLIER	William	30/08/1924	Crystal Palace	14/03/1925	Port Vale
COLLINS	John	14/08/1976	Grimsby Town	02/11/1976	Rotherham United
COLLINS	Patrick	07/08/2004	Colchester United	08/04/2006	Crewe Alexandra
COLLINS	Wayne	17/08/1996	Aston Villa	28/12/1997	Leicester City

Lge	Sub	goals	FA Cup	Sub	goals	L Cup	Sub	goals	Euro	Sub	Goals	Other*	Sub	Goals	Total	Sub	Goals
465			42												507	0	0
10															10	0	0
46		7	9		1										55	0	8
5	1											3			8	1	0
5															5	0	0
113	27	23	4			4	1					2	2	1	123	30	24
2	1														2	1	0
108	26	8	4	1	1	4	1					4			120	28	9
2						1									3	0	0
4	1														4	1	0
215		70	18		7										233	0	77
1			2												3	0	0
56		8	5		2										61	0	10
23		6	2		1										25	0	7
26															26	0	0
21						2									23	0	0
233		8	27												260	0	8
82	34	24	2	2		3	1	2							87	37	26
171			27												198	0	0
55	3	2		1		3									58	4	2
26		1	10												36	0	1
			11												11	0	0
			2												2	0	0
89	1	2	1	1								2			92	2	2
4		2													4	0	2
31		1	2			5									38	0	1
143		3	13												156	0	3
	1														0	1	0
29			1												30	0	0
59		4	3												62	0	4
86	10	25	7		1	3	1								96	11	26
10			3												13	0	0
	2														0	2	0
9	3		2												11	3	0
9															9	0	0
206			21												227	0	0
			37		22										37	0	22
23		1	5												28	0	1
32	34	8	1	11	1	5	2	1				2	1		40	48	10
8	3											1			9	3	0
270		93	29		7										299	0	100
147	2	62	17	1	10	17		6				2	1		183	4	78
4															4	0	0
4															4	0	0
1															1	0	0
43	40	18	1	1		1	1								45	42	18
2	2														2	2	0
78			6			3									87	0	0
1						1									2	0	0
7	2					1									8	2	0
87		2	10												97	0	2
2															2	0	0
22	5	4	2	1			1	1				2	1		26	8	5
8		1	2												10	0	1
11	5	1	2			3									16	5	1
25	1	2	2												27	1	2
14															14	0	0
7						4									11	0	0
28	3	1	1			2						1	1		32	4	1
16	15	6	1			2									19	15	6

(*Intertoto, Full Members Cup, Play-offs and Associate Members Cup)

Player		1st Game	v	Last Game	v
CONWELL	Tony	19/08/1953	Manchester City	12/02/1955	Portsmouth
COOKE	Terry	23/09/2000	Preston North End	08/05/2004	Queen's Park Rangers
COOPER	Alf	20/09/1919	Notts County	04/10/1919	Sheffield United
COOPER	Anthony	20/09/1919	Notts County	20/09/1919	Notts County
COOPER	Joe	07/05/1921	Bristol City	07/05/1921	Bristol City
COOPER	Sedley	28/10/1933	Wolverhampton Wanderers	09/11/1935	Leeds United
COOPER	William	15/10/1887	Belper	15/10/1887	Belper
CORR	Barry	10/09/2005	Leicester City	23/09/2006	Derby County
COUGHLAN	Graham	20/08/2005	Ipswich Town	24/02/2007	Burnley
COX	Brian	17/10/1978	Oxford United	07/10/1980	Blackburn Rovers
COYLE	Roy	16/12/1972	Blackpool	20/08/1974	Scunthorpe United
CRAIG	Jim	27/01/1973	Portsmouth	29/09/1973	Crystal Palace
CRAIG	Bobby	21/11/1959	Leeds United	24/02/1962	Chelsea
CRAIG	Tommy	12/05/1969	Tottenham Hotspur	14/12/1974	Oldham Athletic
CRANE	Tony	13/09/2000	Nottingham Forest	29/03/2003	Watford
CRANSON	Ian	26/03/1988	Norwich City	01/04/1989	Millwall
CRAPPER	Chris	23/04/1906	Everton	23/04/1906	Everton
CRAWSHAW	Percy	31/12/1899	Chesterfield	31/12/1904	Middlesbrough
CRAWSHAW	Tommy	01/09/1894	Everton	07/03/1908	Sheffield United
CRESSWELL	Richard	03/04/1999	Coventry City	28/08/2000	Blackburn Rovers
CRINSON	William	05/01/1907	Manchester City	08/04/1908	Middlesbrough
CROSSLEY	Mark	11/11/2006	Ipswich Town	20/02/2007	Luton Town
CRUICKSHANK	Alex	13/09/1926	Birmingham FC	18/09/1926	Blackburn Rovers
CUNNINGHAM	Tony	11/11/1983	Fulham	12/05/1984	Cardiff City
CURRAN	Terry	31/03/1979	Watford	15/05/1982	Norwich City
CURRY	Bob	18/09/1937	Aston Villa	18/09/1937	Aston Villa
CURTIS	Norman	25/11/1950	Bolton Wanderers	06/02/1960	Everton
CUSACK	Dave	11/10/1975	Millwall	12/08/1978	Doncaster Rovers
DAILEY	Jimmy	16/11/1946	West Bromwich Albion	22/01/1949	Leeds United
DARLING	Malcolm	03/09/1977	Bury	10/09/1977	Shrewsbury Town
DARROCH	Jack	15/10/1892	Blackburn Rovers	09/12/1893	Aston Villa
DAVIES	Brian	02/05/1966	Chelsea	14/09/1966	Rotherham United
DAVIES	George	14/04/1951	Bolton Wanderers	05/03/1955	Everton
DAVIS	Harry	03/09/1892	Notts County	27/03/1899	Stoke FC
DAVIS	Harry	02/02/1900	Manchester United	27/02/1907	Sunderland
DAVIS	John	14/05/1977	Oxford United	14/05/1977	Oxford United
DAVISON	Teddy	10/10/1908	Bristol City	20/12/1924	Hull City
DAVISON	Tommy	07/02/1931	Bolton Wanderers	13/02/1932	Chelsea
DE BILDE	Gilles	07/08/1999	Liverpool	06/05/2001	Crewe Alexandra
DEGRYSE	Marc	27/08/1995	Newcastle United	05/05/1996	West Ham United
DENT	Fred	20/11/1920	Fulham	18/12/1920	Leicester City
DEWAR	Neil	30/12/1933	Manchester City	01/05/1937	Huddersfield Town
DIALLO	Drissa	20/08/2005	Ipswich Town	30/04/2006	Derby County
DI CANIO	Paulo	09/08/1997	Newcastle United	26/09/1998	Arsenal
DI PIEDI	Michaelli	13/08/2000	Wolverhampton Wanderers	17/01/2003	Sheffield United
DICKINSON	Wally	18/11/1922	Hull City	20/01/1923	Bury
DILLON	Francis	29/10/1938	Sheffield United	04/03/1939	Sheffield United
DJORDJIC	Bojan	08/12/2001	Millwall	29/12/2001	Norwich City
DOBSON	Colin	20/09/1961	Arsenal	07/05/1966	Nottingham Forest
DODDS	Chris	22/11/1930	Leicester City	22/11/1930	Leicester City
DONALDSON	O'Neill	18/03/1995	Manchester City	08/11/1997	Bolton Wanderers
DONNELLY	Simon	07/08/1999	Liverpool	29/03/2003	Watford
DOOLEY	Derek	11/03/1950	Preston North End	14/02/1953	Preston North End
DOWD	Hugh	17/08/1974	Oldham Athletic	30/09/1978	Swindon Town
DOWLING	Michael	17/09/1910	Preston North End	08/04/1911	Nottingham Forest
DOWNES	Steve	26/12/1969	Sunderland	21/08/1971	Bristol City
DRISCOLL	John	23/10/1937	Manchester United	11/01/1938	Burnley
DRIVER	Allenby	01/01/1938	Chesterfield	11/02/1946	Stoke City
DRURY	George	07/11/1936	Grimsby Town	05/03/1938	Manchester United
DRYBURGH	William	01/09/1897	Aston Villa	22/03/1902	Blackburn Rovers

Lge	Sub	goals	FA Cup	Sub	goals	L Cup	Sub	goals	Euro	Sub	Goals	Other*	Sub	Goals	Total	Sub	Goals
44			3												47	0	0
35	5	3		1			1						1		35	8	3
3															3	0	0
1															1	0	0
1															1	0	0
19		4													19	0	4
			1												1	0	0
7	10		1			1									9	10	0
47	4	5	3			2		1							52	4	6
22						4									26	0	0
38	2	2	7		1	2	1								47	3	3
5	1														5	1	0
84		25	11		3				4						99	0	28
210	4	38	9	1	1	9		1							228	5	40
24	25	4	1	3		3	5	1							28	33	5
29	1		2			2						1			34	1	0
1															1	0	0
9															9	0	0
418		24	47		2										465	0	26
7	24	2		3		1	1	1							8	28	3
4															4	0	0
17		1	2												19	0	1
2															2	0	0
26	2	5	4	1											30	3	5
122	3	35	3			10		4							135	3	39
1															1	0	0
310		21	14												324	0	21
92	3	1	7			7									106	3	1
37		24	4		1										41	0	25
1	1					1									2	1	0
17			3												20	0	0
3		1				1									4	0	1
98		1	11		1										109	0	2
160		36	24		6										184	0	42
213		59	22		8										235	0	67
1															1	0	0
397			27												424	0	0
17			1												18	0	0
50	9	13	4			5		2							59	9	15
30	4	8	1			3		4							34	4	12
4		1													4	0	1
84		43	11		7										95	0	50
8	3					1									9	3	0
39	2	15	3			4		2							46	2	17
9	30	5				1	4	2							10	34	7
7			1												8	0	0
7			2												9	0	0
4	1														4	1	0
177		49	11		1				7		2				195	0	52
1															1	0	0
4	10	3													4	10	3
27	26	8		3		3	3								30	32	8
61		62	2		1										63	0	63
110	3		5			19									134	3	0
7															7	0	0
26	5	4				3		1							29	5	5
5		2	1												6	0	2
6		3	6		3										12	0	6
44		9	3		2										47	0	11
47		11	3												50	0	11

(*Intertoto, Full Members Cup, Play-offs and Associate Members Cup)

Player		1st Game	v	Last Game	v
DUNGWORTH	Jack	31/10/1885	Long Eaton Rangers	29/03/1890	Blackburn Rovers
DUNLOP	Walter	03/09/1892	Notts County	03/09/1892	Notts County
DUNN	John	28/08/1920	Barnsley	07/10/1920	Nottingham Forest
EAGLES	Chris	06/08/2005	Stoke City	31/12/2005	Burnley
EARP	Jack	07/10/1893	Stoke FC	31/03/1900	Leicester Fosse
EATON	Walter	03/04/1905	Derby County	03/04/1905	Derby County
EDMONSON	Joe	25/10/1919	Manchester City	19/04/1920	Bradford Park Avenue
EDWARDS	Len	08/12/1951	West Ham United	15/12/1951	Doncaster Rovers
EGGO	Robert	17/02/1920	Burnley	18/12/1920	Leicester City
EKOKU	Efan	22/10/2000	Birmingham City	06/04/2002	Nottingham Forest
ELLIS	Keith	19/03/1955	Preston North End	26/10/1963	Aston Villa
ELLIS	Sam	04/04/1966	Blackpool	07/09/1971	Carlisle United
ESAJAS	Etienne	01/09/2007	Bristol City	02/05/2010	Crystal Palace
EUSTACE	Peter	29/08/1962	Leicester City	29/03/1975	Millwall
EVANS	Paul	15/02/2003	Derby County	18/03/2003	Bradford City
EVANS	Richard	29/03/2003	Watford	06/09/2003	Tranmere Rovers
EYRE	Ron	22/03/1924	Oldham Athletic	22/03/1924	Oldham Athletic
EYRE	Issac	12/03/1904	Stoke FC	12/03/1904	Stoke FC
FALLON	Bill	19/03/1938	Barnsley	29/04/1939	Tottenham Hotspur
FANTHAM	John	01/02/1958	Tottenham Hotspur	20/09/1969	West Ham United
FAULKNER	David	24/06/1995	FC Basel	24/06/1995	FC Basel
FEE	Greg	29/08/1987	Everton	04/11/1989	Nottingham Forest
FEELY	Peter	16/02/1976	Port Vale	30/10/1976	Mansfield Town
FEENEY	Warren	05/12/2009	Reading	05/12/2009	Reading
FELTON	Billy	01/01/1923	Southampton	23/02/1929	Birmingham FC
FERGUSON	Bobby	10/02/1974	Bristol City	02/03/1974	Hull City
FERGUSON	Ron	09/11/1974	York City	12/04/1975	Bristol City
FERRIER	Bob	01/09/1894	Everton	26/04/1905	Newcastle United
FINNEY	Alan	24/02/1951	Chelsea	01/01/1966	Leeds United
FISH	Tom	30/03/1901	Everton	25/01/1902	Sunderland
FLEMING	Ian	13/02/1979	Southend United	03/11/1979	Barnsley
FLETCHER	Brough	03/04/1926	Hull City	05/04/1926	Stoke FC
FLETCHER	Doug	11/04/1949	Leicester City	29/08/1949	Cardiff City
FLETCHER	Henry	08/01/1881	Turton	08/01/1881	Turton
FOLLY	Yoann	31/01/2006	Luton Town	01/01/2008	Preston North End
FORD	David	23/10/1965	Sunderland	13/12/1969	Leeds United
FOX	Oscar	12/10/1946	Manchester City	18/02/1950	Brentford
FOX	Peter	31/03/1973	Leyton Orient	02/11/1976	Rotherham United
FOX	William	25/03/1895	Birmingham FC	22/04/1895	West Bromwich Albion
FOXALL	Frank	04/04/1907	Sheffield United	19/03/1910	Sheffield United
FRANCIS	Trevor	03/02/1990	Millwall	20/11/1993	Coventry City
FROGGATT	Frank	22/10/1921	Bradford Park Avenue	07/09/1927	Manchester United
FROGGATT	Redfern	05/01/1946	Mansfield Town	30/04/1960	West Ham United
FRYE	John	07/03/1961	Burnley	07/03/1961	Burnley
GALE	Tommy	26/01/1946	York City	05/04/1947	Coventry City
GALLACHER	Kevin	29/03/2002	Coventry City	21/04/2002	Wolverhampton Wanderers
GALLACHER	Paul	26/03/2005	Torquay United	07/05/2005	Bristol City
GALVIN	Tony	31/08/1987	Coventry City	17/05/1989	Norwich City
GANNON	Eddie	12/03/1949	Grimsby Town	02/04/1955	Cardiff City
GEARY	Derek	19/09/2000	Oldham Athletic	08/05/2004	Queen's Park Rangers
GEMMELL	Duncan	23/01/1892	Bolton Wanderers	13/02/1892	West Bromwich Albion
GERMAN	David	24/06/1995	FC Basel	24/06/1995	FC Basel
GIBSON	Don	20/08/1955	Plymouth Argyle	19/09/1959	Everton
GILBERT	Peter	03/12/2005	Sheffield United	28/10/2008	Plymouth Argyle
GILL	James	25/12/1913	Chelsea	17/04/1920	Aston Villa
GILLIES	Alex	06/03/1897	Burnley	13/03/1897	Wolverhampton Wanderers
GLEN	Bob	09/09/1893	Blackburn Rovers	09/09/1893	Blackburn Rovers
GLENNON	Teddy	24/12/1910	Oldham Athletic	17/04/1915	Bradford City
GOODFELLOW	Derwick	17/09/1936	Huddersfield Town	04/01/1947	Plymouth Argyle
GOOING	William	08/02/1896	Birmingham FC	07/03/1896	Sunderland

Lge	Sub	goals	FA Cup	Sub	goals	L Cup	Sub	goals	Euro	Sub	Goals	Other*	Sub	Goals	Total	Sub	Goals
			17		2										17	0	2
1															1	0	0
8															8	0	0
21	4	3													21	4	3
155		7	19		1										174	0	8
1															1	0	0
14		3													14	0	3
2															2	0	0
23															23	0	0
52	7	14	2	1		8	1	7							62	9	21
102		52	14		7				2		1				118	0	60
155	3	1	13			11									179	3	1
28	32	5	1	1		3		3							32	33	8
238	11	25	20	1		11		1							269	12	26
7															7	0	0
8	2	1				1									9	2	1
1															1	0	0
1															1	0	0
44		12	7		1										51	0	13
381	7	146	33	1	11	6		4	6		5				426	8	166
										1					0	1	0
16	10					3	1	1				1			20	11	1
17	2	2				4	1								21	3	2
	1														0	1	0
158			6												164	0	0
5															5	0	0
10	1	1													10	1	1
308		18	21		2										329	0	20
455		81	39		6				10		1				504	0	88
7			1												8	0	0
13		1				4		1							17	0	2
2															2	0	0
4															4	0	0
			1												1	0	0
41	12			1			1	1							41	14	1
117	5	31	10		5	3		1							130	5	37
44		3	3		1										47	0	4
49			3												52	0	0
4															4	0	0
44		9													44	0	9
29	47	5	2	2	1	5	2	3	1			1			38	51	9
91		1	5												96	0	1
434		139	24		9										458	0	148
			1												1	0	0
9			4												13	0	0
	4														0	4	0
8															8	0	0
21	15	1				4	2					1	1	1	26	18	2
204		4	15												219	0	4
95	9		4			12	2					5			116	11	0
			3												3	0	0
									1						1	0	0
80		2	4		1										84	0	3
39	2					2									41	2	0
38		9	5		1										43	0	10
2															2	0	0
1															1	0	0
121		41	12		1										133	0	42
69			8												77	0	0
3		1													3	0	1

(*Intertoto, Full Members Cup, Play-offs and Associate Members Cup)

Player		1st Game	v	Last Game	v
GOSLING	William	23/03/1901	Liverpool	21/12/1901	Birmingham FC
GOWDY	William	09/01/1932	Tottenham Hotspur	09/04/1932	Portsmouth
GRAHAM	David	13/08/2005	Southampton	10/03/2007	Queen's Park Rangers
GRANT	Dave	17/12/1977	Wigan Athletic	19/01/1982	Crystal Palace
GRANT	Lee	11/08/2007	Ipswich Town	02/05/2010	Crystal Palace
GRAY	George	03/12/1921	Clapton Orient	18/11/1922	Hull City
GRAY	Michael	10/01/2009	Ipswich Town	27/03/2010	Coventry City
GRAYSON	Simon	13/08/2000	Wolverhampton Wanderers	09/09/2000	Wimbledon
GREEN	Adam	29/01/2005	MK Dons	12/02/2005	Bradford City
GREEN	Albert	21/11/1936	Leeds United	16/09/1937	Tottenham Hotspur
GREEN	Ryan	30/11/2002	Wimbledon	11/01/2003	Reading
GREENSMITH	Ronald	01/01/1955	Aston Villa	09/10/1957	Manchester City
GREENWOOD	Ross	22/09/2004	Coventry City	03/01/2005	Wrexham
GREGG	Robert	08/09/1928	Sunderland	15/09/1930	Chelsea
GREGORY	Tony	24/08/1985	Manchester City	02/01/1989	Coventry City
GREGORY	Bob	18/12/1880	Blackburn Rovers	01/12/1883	Staveley
GREGSON	Colin	30/08/1977	Blackpool	12/10/1977	Exeter City
GRIFFIN	Billy	22/11/1958	Cardiff City	10/11/1962	Aston Villa
GROSVENOR	Tommy	19/02/1936	Derby County	01/05/1937	Huddersfield Town
GRUMMITT	Peter	28/01/1970	Coventry City	07/04/1973	Millwall
HALL	Sandy	23/01/1892	Bolton Wanderers	03/04/1893	Notts County
HALL	Harry	11/12/1920	Cardiff City	18/03/1922	Port Vale
HAMILTON	Henry	22/01/1910	Bristol City	14/03/1910	Tottenham Hotspur
HAMSHAW	Matt	26/08/2000	Grimsby Town	16/05/2005	Brentford
HANFORD	Harry	29/02/1936	Leeds United	29/04/1939	Tottenham Hotspur
HARDY	Robin	16/10/1961	Aston Villa	30/03/1964	Arsenal
HARGREAVES	Len	16/03/1929	Leicester City	23/03/1929	Manchester United
HARKES	John	31/10/1990	Swindon Town	20/05/1993	Arsenal
HARKNESS	Steve	30/09/2000	Gillingham	28/04/2001	Norwich City
HARPER	Alan	27/08/1988	Luton Town	18/11/1989	Derby County
HARPER	Ted	26/11/1927	Derby County	02/03/1929	Bury
HARRISON	W.	06/01/1883	Nottingham Forest	13/01/1883	Nottingham Forest
HARRON	Joe	15/03/1923	Stockport County	25/10/1924	South Shields
HART	Paul	17/08/1985	Chelsea	26/12/1986	Manchester City
HARVEY	Colin	14/09/1974	Bolton Wanderers	22/11/1975	Macclesfield Town
HARVEY	Edward	01/09/1919	Manchester United	01/01/1921	Leicester City
HARVEY	William	25/10/1919	Manchester City	17/04/1920	Aston Villa
HASLAM	Steve	08/05/1999	Liverpool	28/02/2004	Bristol City
HATFIELD	Ernie	13/04/1929	West Ham United	13/04/1929	West Ham United
HAZEL	Des	06/10/1986	Stockport County	30/04/1988	Arsenal
HEALD	Paul	22/01/2002	Blackburn Rovers	16/02/2002	Watford
HEARD	Pat	15/01/1983	Middlesbrough	25/09/1984	Huddersfield Town
HECKINGBOTTOM	Paul	07/08/2004	Colchester United	07/01/2006	Charlton Athletic
HEDLEY	Graeme	25/02/1978	Portsmouth	21/03/1978	Bradford City
HEESON	J.	08/11/1884	Long Eaton Rangers	08/11/1884	Long Eaton Rangers
HEFFERNAN	Paul	10/08/2010	Bury		
HEMMINGFIELD	Bill	10/09/1898	Nottingham Forest	25/04/1907	Birmingham FC
HENDERSON	Willie	12/08/1972	Fulham	27/04/1974	Bolton Wanderers
HENDON	Ian	14/10/2000	Portsmouth	16/11/2002	Gillingham
HENRY	Gerry	18/02/1950	Brentford	22/09/1951	Rotherham United
HENSHALL	Horace	09/12/1922	Leicester City	17/03/1923	South Shields
HENSON	Phil	08/02/1975	Blackpool	14/05/1977	Oxford United
HERBERT	David	08/03/1975	West Bromwich Albion	19/04/1976	Mansfield Town
HIBBERT	Henry	04/04/1908	Blackburn Rovers	18/04/1908	Birmingham FC
HICKTON	John	07/03/1964	Aston Villa	09/05/1966	Burnley
HILL	Brian	02/03/1957	Blackpool	04/05/1966	Stoke City
HILL	Harold	18/10/1924	Coventry City	01/09/1928	Blackburn Rovers
HILL	Haydn	06/04/1935	Tottenham Hotspur	26/12/1935	Everton
HILLER	Carl	01/12/1883	Staveley	01/12/1883	Staveley
HILLER	Walpole	03/01/1885	Nottingham Forest	03/01/1885	Nottingham Forest

Lge	Sub	goals	FA Cup	Sub	goals	L Cup	Sub	goals	Euro	Sub	Goals	Other*	Sub	Goals	Total	Sub	Goals
5															5	0	0
1			1												2	0	0
19	9	2				2		1							21	9	3
132	1	4	4	2		11		1							147	3	5
136			4			5									145	0	0
32			1												33	0	0
40	3	2					1								40	4	2
5															5	0	0
3															3	0	0
6		1													6	0	1
4															4	0	0
5			1		1										6	0	1
	2					1							1		1	3	0
37		7	2												39	0	7
14	4	1	2				1								16	5	1
			17		14										17	0	14
1	1					1									2	1	0
35		20	1						1		1				37	0	21
22		1	1												23	0	1
121			3			6									130	0	0
17		2	3												20	0	2
31		1													31	0	1
7															7	0	0
35	39	2	2	1	2	6	3	2				2			45	43	6
85		1	9												94	0	1
30		1							3						33	0	1
2		1													2	0	1
59	22	7	12	1	1	17		3	4			3			95	23	11
28	2	1	2												30	2	1
32	3		1			1	1					1			35	4	0
18		13	4		3										22	0	16
			2		3										2	0	3
61		5	3		1										64	0	6
52		2	3			4		1				1			60	0	3
45		2	1			2									48	0	2
12															12	0	0
19		1	1												20	0	1
115	29	2	9	1		10	1					5	1		139	32	2
1															1	0	0
5	1					1							1		6	2	0
5						1									6	0	0
22	3	3	6			2									30	3	3
41	1	4	1		2	1						3			46	1	6
6		1													6	0	1
			1												1	0	0
3	14	3	1	1		2							2		6	17	3
43		12	4		1										47	0	13
42	6	5	5			3									50	6	5
49		2	2			2									53	0	2
40		7													40	0	7
14		1	3												17	0	1
65	8	9	2			5									72	8	9
12	5	4				1	1								13	6	4
2															2	0	0
52	1	20	3												55	1	20
116	1	1	2						3						121	1	1
91		37	8		3										99	0	40
4															4	0	0
			5		1										5	0	1
			1												1	0	0

(*Intertoto, Full Members Cup, Play-offs and Associate Members Cup)

Player		1st Game	v	Last Game	v
HILLS	John	06/08/2005	Stoke City	13/04/2007	West Bromwich Albion
HINCH	Jim	10/12/1977	Cambridge United	10/12/1977	Cambridge United
HINCHCLIFFE	Alan	03/11/1956	Bolton Wanderers	10/11/1956	Leeds United
HINCHCLIFFE	Alfred	17/01/1920	Everton	17/01/1920	Everton
HINCHCLIFFE	Andy	31/01/1998	Wimbledon	12/01/2002	Crewe Alexandra
HINDS	Richard	19/08/2007	Wolverhampton Wanderers	15/03/2011	Peterborough United
HIRST	David	23/08/1986	Charlton Athletic	04/10/1997	Everton
HODDER	William	31/01/1891	Derby County	14/02/1891	West Bromwich Albion
HODGE	Martin	27/08/1983	Swansea City	12/03/1988	Manchester United
HODGKISS	Thomas	10/03/1928	Burnley	17/03/1928	Bury
HODGSON	David	22/10/1988	Southampton	21/01/1989	Arsenal
HOLBEM	Walter	26/01/1907	Preston North End	11/02/1911	Liverpool
HOLLIDAY	Eddie	17/03/1962	West Ham United	30/03/1964	Arsenal
HOLMES	Darren	24/06/1995	FC Basel	24/06/1995	FC Basel
HOLMES	George	17/09/1921	Notts County	13/03/1922	Coventry City
HOLSGROVE	John	14/08/1971	Queen's Park Rangers	08/03/1975	West Bromwich Albion
HOLT	Grant	29/03/2003	Watford	24/01/2004	Peterborough United
HOOPER	Mark	22/01/1927	Leicester City	07/05/1938	Tottenham Hotspur
HOPE	Bobby	18/09/1976	Chesterfield	03/12/1977	Colchester United
HORNE	Barry	12/04/2000	Wimbledon	14/05/2000	Leicester City
HORNSBY	Brian	18/03/1978	Lincoln City	05/12/1981	Chelsea
HORROBIN	Thomas	29/09/1962	Manchester United	10/11/1962	Aston Villa
HOUNSFIELD	Reg	03/10/1902	Notts County	04/10/1902	Liverpool
HOWELLS	Peter	06/11/1954	Manchester City	07/04/1956	West Ham United
HOYLAND	George	26/03/1904	Manchester City	17/12/1904	Newcastle United
HUDSON	Jack	18/12/1880	Blackburn Rovers	31/10/1885	Long Eaton Rangers
HUKIN	Arthur	27/11/1954	Leicester City	27/12/1954	Charlton Athletic
HULL	Gary	21/02/1976	Aldershot	13/04/1976	Shrewsbury Town
HULL	Jack	12/02/1936	Portsmouth	12/02/1936	Portsmouth
HUMPHREYS	Ritchie	09/09/1995	Queen's Park Rangers	01/11/2000	Sheffield United
HUNT	Doug	05/03/1938	Manchester United	29/04/1939	Tottenham Hotspur
HUNT	George	09/11/1946	Newcastle United	30/08/1947	Tottenham Hotspur
HUNTER	Andy	27/03/1909	Manchester City	30/04/1910	Sunderland
HUNTER	Jack	18/12/1880	Blackburn Rovers	05/02/1881	Darwen
HUTTON	Robert	27/03/1899	Stoke FC	11/01/1902	Notts County
HYDE	Graham	14/09/1991	Manchester City	22/08/1998	Tottenham Hotspur
IBBOTSON	Wilf	22/11/1947	Coventry City	22/11/1947	Coventry City
INGESSON	Klas	10/09/1994	Nottingham Forest	04/11/1995	Chelsea
INGLIS	Bill	08/09/1924	Derby County	14/03/1925	Port Vale
INGRAM	Billy	19/12/1887	Crusaders	31/01/1891	Derby County
IRVINE	Archie	12/10/1968	Queen's Park Rangers	22/11/1969	West Bromwich Albion
JACKSON	Jerry	27/08/1923	Port Vale	27/08/1923	Port Vale
JACKSON	Norman	07/04/1950	Bury	04/04/1953	Portsmouth
JACOBS	Wayne	18/08/1987	Oxford United	14/11/1987	Luton Town
JAMESON	Arron	20/11/2010	MK Dons		
JAMESON	Joe	04/04/1907	Sheffield United	27/02/1909	Preston North End
JAMIESON	James	02/09/1893	Sunderland	18/02/1899	Sunderland
JARVIS	Richard	02/04/1904	Notts County	01/04/1905	Notts County
JEEVES	Jack	01/12/1883	Staveley	01/12/1883	Staveley
JEFFERS	Francis	11/08/2007	Ipswich Town	02/05/2010	Crystal Palace
JEFFERSON	Derek	02/10/1976	Lincoln City	30/10/1976	Mansfield Town
JEMSON	Nigel	18/09/1991	Norwich City	03/05/1994	Leeds United
JOHNSON	David	18/01/1992	Aston Villa	20/04/1992	Norwich City
JOHNSON	David	05/02/2002	Preston North End	06/03/2002	Wimbledon
JOHNSON	George	04/04/1931	Blackpool	04/04/1931	Blackpool
JOHNSON	Jeff	14/08/1976	Grimsby Town	08/05/1981	West Ham United
JOHNSON	Jermaine	20/02/2007	Luton Town		
JOHNSON	Kevin	14/08/1971	Queen's Park Rangers	14/08/1971	Queen's Park Rangers
JOHNSON	Michael	22/09/2007	Hull City	22/12/2007	Watford
JOHNSON	Peter	25/12/1957	Preston North End	02/01/1965	Sheffield United

Lge	Sub	goals	FA Cup	Sub	goals	L Cup	Sub	goals	Euro	Sub	Goals	Other*	Sub	Goals	Total	Sub	Goals
41	2					2	1								43	3	0
	1														0	1	0
2															2	0	0
1															1	0	0
86		7	6			4	1								96	1	7
54	13	2	2	1		4	1								60	15	2
261	33	106	12	7	6	26	9	11	3		1	7		4	309	49	128
			2		1										2	0	1
197			25			24						3			249	0	0
2															2	0	0
6	5	1	1		1										7	5	2
86			3												89	0	0
55		12	2		1				5		1				62	0	14
									1						1	0	0
20			1												21	0	0
103	1	5	6			5									114	1	5
12	12	3	2		1		1					1	2		15	15	4
384		124	39		11										423	0	135
39	3	7	2		1	2		1							43	3	9
7															7	0	0
102	4	25	10		4	8		1							120	4	30
3															3	0	0
2															2	0	0
3		1													3	0	1
3		1													3	0	1
			16												16	0	0
6		3													6	0	3
6	2														6	2	0
1															1	0	0
34	33	4	5	4	4	4	2								43	39	8
42		30	6		1										48	0	31
32		8	3												35	0	8
15		3													15	0	3
			3												3	0	0
5		1													5	0	1
126	46	11	13	5	2	17	3	2	7			1		1	164	54	16
1															1	0	0
12	6	2	1			2									15	6	2
29			2												31	0	0
			16		8										16	0	8
25	3	1	4			2									31	3	1
1															1	0	0
31															31	0	0
5	1					3						1			9	1	0
2															2	0	0
7															7	0	0
125		3	10												135	0	3
6															6	0	0
			1												1	0	0
28	26	5	3			2	1								33	27	5
5						1									6	0	0
26	25	9	3	3		3	4	1	1	1		1	1	1	34	34	11
5	1														5	1	0
7		2													7	0	2
1		1													1	0	1
175	5	6	14		1	17		2							206	5	9
108	31	15	4	2	1	4	1	2				1			117	34	18
	1														0	1	0
13															13	0	0
181		6	19						7						207	0	6

(*Intertoto, Full Members Cup, Play-offs and Associate Members Cup)

Player		1st Game	v	Last Game	v
JOHNSON	Reda	08/01/2011	Bristol City		
JOHNSON	Tommy	08/09/2001	Birmingham City	16/10/2001	Preston North End
JOHNSTON	Allan	14/12/2002	Gillingham	01/03/2003	Preston North End
JOICEY	Brian	31/08/1971	Middlesbrough	20/03/1976	Rotherham United
JONES	Brad	05/08/2006	Preston North End	04/11/2006	Leicester City
JONES	Daniel	07/08/2010	Dagenham & Redbridge		
JONES	Kenwyne	19/12/2004	Doncaster Rovers	15/01/2005	Bournemouth
JONES	Rob	19/03/2011	Southampton	07/05/2011	Exeter City
JONES	Ryan	03/03/1993	Coventry City	29/04/1995	Southampton
JONES	Tommy	05/04/1930	Liverpool	14/04/1934	Leicester City
JONK	Wim	15/08/1998	West Ham United	19/08/2000	Huddersfield Town
JONSSON	Siggi	09/03/1985	Leicester City	13/05/1989	Middlesbrough
JORDAN	Clarrie	07/02/1948	Bradford Park Avenue	18/09/1954	Sheffield United
JORDAN	John	23/09/1950	Huddersfield Town	13/01/1951	Charlton Athletic
KAVANAGH	Graham	22/09/2007	Hull City	04/05/2008	Norwich City
KAY	Tony	08/04/1955	Bolton Wanderers	22/12/1962	Everton
KAYE	Albert	11/09/1897	Bury	25/02/1899	Wolverhampton Wanderers
KEAN	Fred	28/08/1920	Barnsley	08/09/1928	Sunderland
KELL	George	03/02/1921	Everton	26/02/1921	Hull City
KENNY	Vin	14/09/1946	Leicester City	12/02/1955	Portsmouth
KENT	Mick	10/10/1973	Bournemouth	24/11/1973	Oxford United
KEY	Lance	07/01/1995	Gillingham	07/01/1995	Gillingham
KILSHAW	Eddie	04/12/1948	Luton Town	11/04/1949	Leicester City
KING	Jeff	11/08/1979	Hull City	24/11/1981	Barnsley
KING	Phil	04/11/1989	Nottingham Forest	02/04/1994	Everton
KINGHORN	Henry	27/02/1909	Preston North End	31/12/1910	Tottenham Hotspur
KINMAN		15/10/1887	Belper	15/10/1887	Belper
KIPPAX	Dennis	28/09/1946	Millwall	28/09/1946	Millwall
KIRBY	Eric	03/02/1951	Huddersfield Town	03/02/1951	Huddersfield Town
KIRBY	George	03/10/1959	Bolton Wanderers	17/10/1959	Tottenham Hotspur
KIRKMAN	Sam	18/09/1909	Bury	01/05/1920	Oldham Athletic
KIKWOOD	Dan	20/11/1926	Aston Villa	11/02/1928	Middlesbrough
KITE	Percy	01/05/1920	Oldham Athletic	01/05/1920	Oldham Athletic
KNIGHT	Ian	19/04/1986	Aston Villa	28/01/1989	Blackburn Rovers
KNIGHT	Leon	17/08/2002	Nottingham Forest	19/04/2003	Grimsby Town
KNIGHTON	Ken	08/09/1973	Nottingham Forest	06/12/1975	Colchester United
KOVACEVIC	Darko	23/12/1995	Southampton	08/04/1996	Arsenal
KUQI	Shefki	12/01/2002	Crewe Alexandra	20/09/2003	Brighton & Hove Albion
LAMB	John	22/09/1913	Oldham Athletic	18/10/1919	Blackburn Rovers
LAMB	Walter	29/08/1921	Derby County	03/09/1921	Barnsley
LANG	James	18/12/1880	Blackburn Rovers	15/03/1882	Blackburn Rovers
LANGLEY	Ambrose	02/09/1893	Sunderland	19/12/1903	Newcastle United
LAW	Alex	09/12/1933	Liverpool	06/04/1935	Tottenham Hotspur
LAWSON	Willie	18/10/1969	Burnley	22/09/1970	Chelsea
LAYNE	David	18/08/1962	Bolton Wanderers	08/04/1964	Stoke City
LAYTON	Willie	08/01/1898	Everton	25/09/1909	Tottenham Hotspur
LEACH	Tony	02/02/1927	South Shields	03/03/1934	Sheffield United
LEDGER	H.	08/01/1881	Turton	13/01/1883	Nottingham Forest
LEE	George	16/09/1899	Bolton Wanderers	18/02/1900	Sheffield United
LEE	Graeme	09/08/2003	Swindon Town	22/11/2005	Plymouth Argyle
LEKAJ	Rexhep	13/03/2007	Colchester United	28/12/2008	Coventry City
LEMAN	Denis	04/12/1976	Tranmere Rovers	05/12/1981	Chelsea
LESCOTT	Aaron	08/10/2000	West Bromwich Albion	03/11/2001	Portsmouth
LESTER	Fred	23/10/1937	Manchester United	28/01/1939	Swansea Town
LEVICK	Oliver	22/01/1921	Port Vale	03/05/1924	Manchester United
LEWIS	Idris	27/08/1938	Bury	11/03/1939	Newcastle United
LINDSAY	Jack	02/09/1946	Barnsley	02/09/1946	Barnsley
LINIGHAN	Brian	11/01/1994	Wimbledon	19/01/1994	Nottingham Forest
LLOYD	Billy	29/12/1906	Bury	05/10/1912	Aston Villa
LOCHERTY	Joe	11/12/1948	Bradford Park Avenue	08/10/1949	Grimsby Town

Lge	Sub	goals	FA Cup	Sub	goals	L Cup	Sub	goals	Euro	Sub	Goals	Other*	Sub	Goals	Total	Sub	Goals
15	1	3	3												18	1	3
8		3				1									9	0	3
12		2													12	0	2
144	1	48	7	3	4	9	2	1							160	6	53
15															15	0	0
13	12		4			2						3			22	12	0
7		7													7	0	7
8		1													8	0	1
36	5	6	3			4	1	1							43	6	7
29		6													29	0	6
69	1	5	7			4									80	1	5
59	8	4	1	1	1	3		1				1			64	9	6
92		36	2												94	0	36
10		2	1												11	0	2
21	2	2				1									22	2	2
179		10	18						6						203	0	10
41		12	3		1										44	0	13
230		8	17												247	0	8
5			1												6	0	0
144			8												152	0	0
4						1	1								5	1	0
				1											0	1	0
17		1	2												19	0	1
54	3	5	2		1	9		1							65	3	7
124	5	2	9			17						4			154	5	2
25															25	0	0
			1		1										1	0	1
1															1	0	0
1															1	0	0
3															3	0	0
187		37	14		3										201	0	40
18		1	1												19	0	1
1															1	0	0
21			5			1									27	0	0
14	10	3		1		2									16	11	3
71	5	2	4		1	4		1							79	5	4
8	8	4	1												9	8	4
58	6	19	1			3									62	6	19
5															5	0	0
2															2	0	0
			5												5	0	0
295		14	23												318	0	14
9		4													9	0	4
9			1			1									11	0	0
74		52	4		1				3		5				81	0	58
331		2	30												361	0	2
238		12	22		2										260	0	14
			13												13	0	0
5		1	1												6	0	1
63	4	5	4			1		1				3		1	71	4	7
	4			1			1								0	6	0
89	14	9	9		1	4									102	14	10
19	18		2			3	1								24	19	0
17			4												21	0	0
21															21	0	0
18		7	5		1										23	0	8
1		1													1	0	1
1			1			1									3	0	0
79		6	5		1										84	0	7
10			2												12	0	0

(*Intertoto, Full Members Cup, Play-offs and Associate Members Cup)

Player		1st Game	v	Last Game	v
LODGE	Bobby	10/12/1960	Blackburn Rovers	23/12/1960	Arsenal
LOFTHOUSE	Jimmy	28/08/1920	Barnsley	02/12/1922	Leicester City
LOGAN	John	28/12/1946	Luton Town	20/02/1947	Preston North End
LOWDELL	Arthur	28/01/1922	Wolverhampton Wanderers	02/04/1927	Bolton Wanderers
LOWE	H.	08/12/1894	Stoke FC	15/12/1894	Nottingham Forest
LOWES	Arnold	10/09/1938	Tranmere Rovers	31/01/1948	Cardiff City
LOWEY	John	17/10/1978	Oxford United	26/08/1980	Wimbledon
LUCAS	David	01/10/2003	Notts County	04/02/2006	Millwall
LUKE	Charlie	19/02/1936	Derby County	04/12/1937	Newcastle United
LUNN	Fred	07/01/1922	Bradford Park Avenue	06/05/1922	Leicester City
LUNT	Kenny	08/08/2006	Luton Town	22/01/2008	Derby County
LYALL	Jack	21/09/1901	Bolton Wanderers	29/03/1909	Sunderland
LYONS	Mick	28/08/1982	Middlesbrough	29/10/1985	Swindon Town
MacKENZIE	Matt	31/08/1946	Luton Town	27/08/1947	Southampton
MacKENZIE	Steve	02/03/1991	Notts County	03/09/1991	Notts County
MACKEY	Thomas	28/04/1930	Birmingham FC	05/12/1931	Arsenal
MacLEAN	Steve	07/08/2004	Colchester United	06/05/2007	Norwich City
MADDEN	Lawrie	27/08/1983	Swansea City	08/05/1991	Bristol City
MADDIX	Danny	12/08/2001	Burnley	21/04/2003	Brighton & Hove Albion
MADINE	Gary	22/01/2011	Leyton Orient		
MAGILTON	Jim	13/09/1997	Liverpool	28/11/1998	Chelsea
MALLINSON	W.	05/02/1898	Everton	03/03/1900	New Brighton Tower
MALLOCH	Gavin	25/12/1931	Liverpool	24/03/1936	Grimsby Town
MALLOCH	Jock	01/09/1900	Manchester City	10/04/1907	Manchester United
MALPASS	Arthur	18/12/1880	Blackburn Rovers	08/11/1884	Long Eaton Rangers
MARRIOTT	Jackie	22/02/1947	Burnley	30/04/1955	West Bromwich Albion
MARRISON	Thomas	28/03/1903	Stoke FC	07/01/1905	Wolverhampton Wanderers
MARSDEN	Billy	30/08/1924	Crystal Palace	03/05/1930	Manchester City
MARSDEN	Chris	07/08/2004	Colchester United	30/10/2004	Chesterfield
MARSON	Fred	23/10/1926	Arsenal	08/10/1927	Birmingham FC
MARTIN	Jack	19/02/1955	Blackpool	31/08/1960	Cardiff City
MARWOOD	Brian	25/08/1984	Nottingham Forest	19/03/1988	Portsmouth
MASSARELLA	Len	15/01/1938	Swansea Town	21/01/1939	Chester
MASSEY	Jimmy	03/11/1894	Aston Villa	09/02/1901	Bury
MATTHEWS	Ernest	16/09/1937	Tottenham Hotspur	05/03/1938	Manchester United
MATTHEWSON	Thomas	24/12/1921	Coventry City	24/12/1921	Coventry City
MATTHEWSON	Trevor	02/05/1981	Watford	11/01/1983	Southend United
MAXWELL	James	29/03/1907	Arsenal	20/04/1908	Arsenal
MAY	Larry	28/02/1987	Watford	07/05/1988	Liverpool
MAYRLEB	Chistian	31/01/1998	Wimbledon	28/02/1998	Derby Country
McALLISTER	Sean	25/02/2006	Southampton	27/02/2010	Reading
McANEARNEY	Jim	24/02/1954	Liverpool	30/04/1959	Bristol Rovers
McANEARNEY	Tom	03/09/1952	Liverpool	20/02/1965	Everton
McARDLE	Rory	19/08/2006	Plymouth Argyle	19/08/2006	Plymouth Argyle
McCAFFERTY	Michael	01/04/1899	Burnley	01/04/1899	Burnley
McCALL	Steve	15/08/1987	Chelsea	06/04/1991	Portsmouth
McCALLIOG	Jim	30/10/1965	Aston Villa	12/05/1969	Tottenham Hotspur
McCAMBRIDGE	Joseph	10/10/1936	Arsenal	31/10/1936	Charlton Athletic
McCARTER	Jimmy	28/09/1946	Millwall	02/11/1946	Swansea Town
McCARTHY	Jon	29/03/2002	Coventry City	13/04/2002	Stockport County
McCLEMENTS	David	23/08/2006	Wrexham	23/08/2006	Wrexham
McCONACHIE	Robert	01/04/1893	Stoke FC	01/04/1893	Stoke FC
McCONNELL	English	01/09/1908	Leicester Fosse	09/04/1910	Chelsea
McCULLOCH	Andy	11/08/1979	Hull City	14/05/1983	Crystal Palace
McEVOY	Don	18/12/1954	Wolverhampton Wanderers	15/02/1958	Chelsea
McGOVERN	Jon-Paul	07/08/2004	Colchester United	30/04/2006	Derby County
McGREGOR	James	20/12/1913	Tottenham Hotspur	03/01/1914	Burnley
McILVENNY	Paddy	19/12/1925	Blackpool	19/12/1925	Blackpool
McINTOSH	Dave	03/04/1948	Fulham	07/12/1957	Aston Villa
McINTOSH	Tom	07/01/1893	Aston Villa	09/09/1893	Aston Villa

Lge	Sub	goals	FA Cup	Sub	goals	L Cup	Sub	goals	Euro	Sub	Goals	Other*	Sub	Goals	Total	Sub	Goals
3		2													3	0	2
95		13	3												98	0	13
4			2												6	0	0
108		6	8												116	0	6
2															2	0	0
42		8	2		2										44	0	10
35	7	4	7		2	1									43	7	6
69			2			4						5			80	0	0
42		8	1												43	0	8
11		4	1												12	0	4
33	8		2	1		3	1								38	10	0
263			32												295	0	0
129		12	15		2	20		2							164	0	16
6															6	0	0
5	10	2													5	10	2
4															4	0	0
60	23	32	3		1	2						1	1	2	66	24	35
200	12	2	20	1		26	2	3				5			251	15	5
55	4	2				7		1							62	4	3
20	2	5													20	2	5
14	13	1	1			2									17	13	1
5			1												6	0	0
84			5												89	0	0
144		11	9												153	0	11
			15												15	0	0
153		19	6												159	0	19
5		1													5	0	1
205		9	16												221	0	9
15						2						1			18	0	0
10															10	0	0
63			3												66	0	0
125	3	27	19		3	13		5					1		157	4	35
31		10	2												33	0	10
159			14												173	0	0
16		7													16	0	7
1															1	0	0
3			2												5	0	0
27		6													27	0	6
30	1	1	4			3									37	1	1
	3														0	3	0
48	20	4	1			3	1								52	21	4
38		10	2												40	0	10
352		19	23		2				7		1				382	0	22
	1														0	1	0
1															1	0	0
21	8	2	1			2	3						1		24	12	2
150		19	18		5	6		3							174	0	27
2															2	0	0
6															6	0	0
4															4	0	0
							1								0	1	0
1															1	0	0
44			6												50	0	0
122	3	44	10		4	14		1							146	3	49
105		1	7												112	0	1
49	4	6	1			3						4		2	57	4	8
6		2													6	0	2
1															1	0	0
293			15												308	0	0
9		1													9	0	1

(*Intertoto, Full Members Cup, Play-offs and Associate Members Cup)

Player		1st Game	v	Last Game	v
McINTYRE	Johnny	20/03/1920	Chelsea	10/12/1921	Clapton Orient
McIVER	Fred	17/08/1974	Oldham Athletic	19/04/1976	Mansfield Town
McJARROW	Hugh	04/03/1950	Queen's Park Rangers	22/09/1951	Rotherham United
McKAY	Colin	20/12/1919	Arsenal	26/04/1920	Oldham Athletic
McKEEVER	Mark	25/04/1999	Chelsea	03/01/2000	Arsenal
McKEOWN	Lindsay	15/12/1976	Darlington	29/04/1978	Colchester United
McLAREN	Roy	30/03/1959	Fulham	13/01/1965	Everton
McLAREN	Paul	12/08/2001	Burnley	08/05/2004	Queen's Park Rangers
McLEAN	David	18/02/1911	Bury	06/09/1919	Middlesbrough
McMAHON	Lewis	20/01/2004	Scunthorpe United	12/05/2005	Brentford
McMAHON	Tony	23/08/2008	Preston North End	29/11/2008	Norwich City
McMORDIE	Eric	19/10/1974	Hull City	14/12/1974	Oldham Athletic
McSKIMMING	Bob	14/03/1910	Tottenham Hotspur	14/02/1920	Preston North End
McWHINNIE	William	01/09/1900	Manchester City	16/02/1901	Blackburn Rovers
MEGSON	Don	14/11/1959	Burnley	24/01/1970	Scunthorpe United
MEGSON	Gary	29/08/1981	Blackburn Rovers	02/01/1989	Coventry City
MELIA	James	05/09/1896	Everton	01/01/1898	Nottingham Forest
MELLOR	Ian	11/08/1979	Hull City	08/05/1982	Bolton Wanderers
MELLOR	Neil	07/08/2010	Dagenham & Redbridge	07/05/2011	Exeter City
MELLOR	Billy	23/03/1894	Burnley	23/03/1894	Burnley
MELLORS	Richard	12/02/1927	Huddersfield Town	08/09/1930	Chelsea
MEREDITH	John	11/03/1961	Wolverhampton Wanderers	11/03/1961	Wolverhampton Wanderers
MILLAR	Harry	02/09/1899	Chesterfield	23/03/1901	Liverpool
MILLER	James	04/01/1913	Middlesbrough	14/02/1914	Aston Villa
MILLER	John	02/09/1893	Sunderland	15/01/1894	Darwen
MILLER	Tommy	11/08/2009	Rochdale	07/05/2011	Exeter City
MILLER	Walter	28/03/1908	Manchester United	08/04/1908	Middlesbrough
MILLERSHIP	Harry	05/04/1930	Liverpool	15/04/1939	Nottingham Forest
MILLS	David	15/02/1983	Blackburn Rovers	14/05/1983	Crystal Palace
MILLS	Simon	03/01/1983	Charlton Athletic	13/04/1985	Ipswich Town
MIROCEVIC	Ante	25/10/1980	Orient	16/04/1983	Brighton & Hove Albion
MOBLEY	Vic	04/04/1964	Wolverhampton Wanderers	16/08/1969	Wolverhampton Wanderers
MODEST	Nathan	20/12/2008	Cardiff City		
MONAGHAN	James	13/12/1913	West Bromwich Albion	20/12/1913	Tottenham Hotspur
MONK	Garry	14/12/2002	Gillingham	15/03/2003	Ipswich Town
MORALEE	Matt	11/01/1902	Notts County	10/10/1903	Wolverhampton Wanderers
MORLEY	Hayden	20/01/1890	London Swifts	29/03/1890	Blackburn Rovers
MORLEY	Lance	01/12/1883	Staveley	01/12/1883	Staveley
MORRIS	Chris	27/08/1983	Swansea City	09/05/1987	Wimbledon
MORRISON	Clinton	07/08/2010	Dagenham & Redbridge		
MORRISON	Michael	08/01/2011	Bristol City		
MORRISON	Owen	26/12/1998	Leicester City	07/01/2003	Gillingham
MORTON	Albert	23/08/1947	Millwall	17/03/1951	Liverpool
MOSFORTH	Billy	18/12/1880	Blackburn Rovers	30/01/1888	Preston North End
MOSS	Frank	14/11/1936	Liverpool	18/09/1937	Aston Villa
MOSS	William	31/10/1885	Long Eaton Rangers	31/10/1885	Long Eaton Rangers
MULLEN	Jimmy	26/12/1970	Hull City	12/04/1980	Bury
MULLER	Adam	26/08/2000	Grimsby Town	17/10/2000	Burnley
MUMFORD	Albert	02/02/1889	Notts Rangers	26/03/1894	Preston North End
MURPHY	Daryl	26/11/2005	Stoke City	17/12/2005	Ipswich Town
MURRAY	James	25/03/1910	Bradford City	26/11/1910	Blackburn Rovers
MUSTOE	Robbie	01/09/2003	Wycombe Wanderers	24/04/2004	Colchester United
NAPIER	Charlie	19/03/1938	Barnsley	29/04/1939	Tottenham Hotspur
NAPIER	Dan	26/12/1907	Sunderland	27/02/1909	Preston North End
NDUMBU-NSUNGU	Guylain	13/09/2003	Stockport County	19/12/2004	Doncaster Rovers
NEEDHAM	Liam	29/09/2004	Chester City	29/09/2004	Chester City
NEVIN	George	21/01/1933	Blackburn Rovers	22/04/1933	Middlesbrough
NEWBOULD	Herbert	18/12/1880	Blackburn Rovers	01/12/1883	Staveley
NEWSOME	Jon	09/09/1989	Arsenal	19/09/1999	Newcastle United
NIBLOE	Joe	25/08/1934	Stoke City	07/05/1938	Tottenham Hotspur

Lge	Sub	goals	FA Cup	Sub	goals	L Cup	Sub	goals	Euro	Sub	Goals	Other*	Sub	Goals	Total	Sub	Goals
67		36	3												70	0	36
34	3		1			4									39	3	0
46		21	1												47	0	21
12		3	2												14	0	3
2	3			1			1								2	5	0
6	5		1												7	5	0
31			3												34	0	0
83	13	8	2			6	1	1				1			92	14	9
135		88	12		12										147	0	100
22	3	2	1			1	1					1	2		25	6	2
14	1	1													14	1	1
9		6													9	0	6
181			13												194	0	0
9															9	0	0
386		6	41		1	5			10						442	0	7
230	3	25	27		6	23		2				3			283	3	33
7															7	0	0
54	16	11	2	1		5	1								61	18	11
24	9	13	4		2	1	1	1				3	1	4	32	11	20
1															1	0	0
14															14	0	0
1															1	0	0
32		16	2												34	0	16
30			1												31	0	0
13		8													13	0	8
39	15	10	3		2	2	1					2	1		46	17	12
3															3	0	0
210		25	26		9										236	0	34
15		3	4												19	0	3
1	4		1												2	4	0
58	3	6	3	2	1	4									65	5	7
187		8	19			4									210	0	8
1	3			1											1	4	0
2															2	0	0
15															15	0	0
4		1													4	0	1
			7												7	0	0
			1												1	0	0
61	13	1	7	5		5	5	1							73	23	2
22	13	6	5		5	1	1					4			32	14	11
12			3												15	0	0
31	25	8	1	2		8	2	3							40	29	11
41			1												42	0	0
			25		6										25	0	6
22			1												23	0	0
			1												1	0	0
222	8	10	9	1		23									254	9	10
1	4						1								1	5	0
23		1	19		6										42	0	7
4															4	0	0
13		4													13	0	4
22	3	1	3									1			26	3	1
48		9	8		1										56	0	10
11		2													11	0	2
24	11	10	1	1	1		1					5	1		30	14	11
													1		0	1	0
2															2	0	0
			8		4										8	0	4
56	5	4	6	1		6									68	6	4
116			12												128	0	0

(*Intertoto, Full Members Cup, Play-offs and Associate Members Cup)

Player		1st Game	v	Last Game	v
NICHOLLS	Harry	22/09/1934	Arsenal	10/11/1934	Aston Villa
NICHOLSON	George	31/10/1885	Long Eaton Rangers	31/10/1885	Long Eaton Rangers
NICHOLSON	Horace	03/01/1914	Burnley	14/04/1914	Oldham Athletic
NICHOLSON	Kevin	28/08/2000	Blackburn Rovers	28/08/2000	Blackburn Rovers
NICOL	Steve	25/11/1995	Everton	01/11/1997	Manchester United
NILSSON	Roland	09/12/1989	Luton Town	07/05/1994	Manchester City
NIMMO	Ian	13/12/1975	Wigan Athletic	19/05/1979	Hull City
NIXON	Eric	27/09/2003	Grimsby Town	27/09/2003	Grimsby Town
NOBLE	Frank	31/08/1963	Burnley	30/10/1965	Aston Villa
NOLAN	Eddie	27/02/2009	Reading	02/05/2010	Crystal Palace
NOLAN	Ian	20/08/1994	Tottenham Hotspur	14/05/2000	Leicester City
OAKES	Scott	17/08/1996	Aston Villa	03/10/1998	Middlesbrough
O'BRIEN	Burton	13/08/2005	Southampton	19/04/2008	Blackpool
O'BRIEN	Joey	08/12/2004	Hull City	09/042011	Brighton & Hove Albion
O'CONNELL	Paddy	24/04/1909	Bury	25/01/1912	Middlesbrough
O'CONNOR	James	09/08/2008	Burnley		
O'DONNELL	Neil	05/11/1975	Gillingham	27/10/1976	Millwall
O'DONNELL	Phil	11/09/1999	Everton	29/12/2001	Norwich City
O'DONNELL	Ralph	17/11/1951	Bury	21/04/1962	Nottingham Forest
O'DONNELL	Richard	19/03/2011	Southampton		
OLIVER	Gavin	06/09/1980	Oldham Athletic	02/02/1985	Liverpool
OLSEN	Kim	07/02/2004	Port Vale	01/05/2004	Luton Town
O'NEILL	Harry	25/10/1919	Manchester City	26/11/1921	Blackpool
OSBOURNE	Isaiah	12/02/2011	Rochdale	29/03/2011	Brentford
OTSEMOBOR	Jon	10/08/2010	Bury		
OWEN	Gary	18/08/1987	Oxford United	30/04/1988	Arsenal
OWEN	Gordon	27/12/1977	Rotherham United	22/01/1983	Carlisle United
OWEN	Niel	14/05/1977	Oxford United	14/05/1977	Oxford United
OWUSU	Lloyd	01/09/2002	Sheffield United	20/12/2003	Chesterfield
OXLEY	Bernard	05/05/1934	Stoke City	04/03/1935	Wolverhampton Wanderers
PACKARD	Edgar	02/09/1946	Barnsley	10/11/1951	Luton Town
PALETHORPE	Jack	15/12/1934	Everton	28/09/1935	Preston North End
PALMER	Carlton	25/02/1989	Wimbledon	20/10/2001	Walsall
PALMER	Liam	10/08/2010	Bury		
PARKER	Ray	30/10/1948	Fulham	30/10/1948	Fulham
PARKES	David	11/03/1914	Derby County	07/02/1920	Preston North End
PARTRIDGE	Richie	06/08/2005	Stoke City	25/02/2006	Southampton
PATERSON	Marr	11/02/1911	Liverpool	23/03/1912	Bolton Wanderers
PEACOCK	John	08/09/1930	Chelsea	08/09/1930	Chelsea
PEACOCK	Lee	07/08/2004	Colchester United	28/12/2005	Wolverhampton Wanderers
PEARCE	Andy	14/08/1993	Liverpool	18/11/1995	Manchester City
PEARSON	John	13/09/1980	Bristol City	24/06/1995	FC Basel
PEARSON	Mark	05/10/1963	West Bromwich Albion	16/01/1965	Liverpool
PEARSON	Nigel	17/10/1987	Nottingham Forest	18/09/1993	Southampton
PEARSON	Stanley	01/09/1919	Manchester United	06/09/1919	Middlesbrough
PEARSON	Trevor	28/03/1972	Fulham	08/04/1972	Norwich City
PEMBRIDGE	Mark	22/07/1995	AGF Aarhus	02/05/1998	Aston Villa
PETRESCU	Dan	20/08/1994	Tottenham Hotspur	30/09/1995	Leeds United
PETRIE	Charles	11/02/1922	Nottingham Forest	02/10/1924	Clapton Orient
PETRIE	Bob	01/09/1894	Everton	02/03/1897	Sheffield United
PICKERING	John	01/11/1913	Derby County	22/11/1913	Blackburn Rovers
PICKERING	Mick	07/10/1978	Rotherham United	09/11/1982	Crystal Palace
PICKERING	William	29/10/1938	Sheffield United	11/02/1946	Stoke City
PINNER	Mike	14/12/1957	Wolverhampton Wanderers	28/03/1959	Brighton & Hove Albion
PLATTS	Mark	10/02/1996	Wimbledon	24/02/1996	Tottenham Hotspur
PLLU	Charlie	06/04/1957	Everton	29/01/1958	Hull City
PORIC	Adem	16/10/1993	Wimbledon	01/11/1997	Manchester United
PORTERFIELD	Ian	13/08/1977	Doncaster Rovers	08/12/1979	Exeter City
POTTER	Darren	17/01/2009	Charlton Athletic		
POTTS	Eric	17/10/1970	Charlton Athletic	06/05/1977	Tranmere Rovers

Lge	Sub	goals	FA Cup	Sub	goals	L Cup	Sub	goals	Euro	Sub	Goals	Other*	Sub	Goals	Total	Sub	Goals
3															3	0	0
			1												1	0	0
3															3	0	0
	1														0	1	0
41	8		2	1			2								43	11	0
151		2	15			16		1	1	1		2			185	1	3
26	19	10	2	2	3	2									30	21	13
	1														0	1	0
2															2	0	0
14		1													14	0	1
164	1	4	15			15	1		3						197	2	4
7	17	1		2			1								7	20	1
73	26	6	2			2	1								77	27	6
17	2	2													17	2	2
18			3												21	0	0
104	17	5	5	1		2	2					2	1	2	113	21	7
40		1	3			4		1							47	0	2
13	7					2	3	1							15	10	1
170		3	13												183	0	3
8	1														8	1	0
14	6		2	1		2	4								18	11	0
6	4											1	1		7	5	0
49			2												51	0	0
9	1		1												10	1	0
13	2		1			2						2	1		18	3	0
12	2			2		2						1			15	4	0
32	15	5	1	1		7	4	2							40	20	7
1															1	0	0
24	28	8	3		1	2	1					1	1		30	30	9
14		4													14	0	4
124		1	2												126	0	1
28		13	6		4										34	0	17
226	1	14	18	1		31		3	3	1		5		1	283	3	18
4	5			1		1									5	6	0
1															1	0	0
47		1	3												50	0	1
6	12		1			1		1							8	12	1
21		2													21	0	2
1															1	0	0
37	14	6				2	1	2				3		1	42	15	9
66	3	3	6	1	1	11	1		1						84	5	4
64	41	24	8	5	2	7	3	1	1						80	49	27
39		9	1						2		2				42	0	11
176	4	14	15		1	17	2	5	3			7			218	6	20
2															2	0	0
4															4	0	0
88	5	12	7		1	6		1	1						102	5	14
28	9	3		2		2			1		1				31	11	4
58		22	2		1										60	0	23
52		3	10												62	0	3
4															4	0	0
106	4	1	9			8	2								123	6	1
3			6												9	0	0
7															7	0	0
	2														0	2	0
19			1												20	0	0
3	11						2		1						4	13	0
103	3	4	11			12	1	2							126	4	6
85	11	8	3		1	4						3			95	11	9
142	17	21	8	2		12	1	4							162	20	25

(*Intertoto, Full Members Cup, Play-offs and Associate Members Cup)

Player		1st Game	v	Last Game	v
POTTS	Harry	20/11/1897	Bury	18/02/1899	Sunderland
POULTER	Robert	25/02/2004	Blackpool	25/02/2004	Blackpool
POWELL	Darryl	17/01/2003	Sheffield United	15/03/2003	Ipswich Town
POWELL	Sam	21/03/1925	Middlesbrough	07/03/1928	Birmingham FC
POWELL	William	25/10/1924	South Shields	11/04/1925	Fulham
PRENDERGAST	Mick	09/04/1969	Newcastle United	07/03/1978	Chester
PRESSMAN	Kevin	05/09/1987	Southampton	08/05/2004	Queen's Park Rangers
PRICE	Arthur	25/10/1919	Manchester City	17/04/1922	Hull City
PRIESTLEY	R.	30/03/1895	Liverpool	01/04/1895	West Bromwich Albion
PRINCE	Arthur	01/09/1924	Derby County	31/03/1928	Leicester City
PRIOR	George	30/10/1920	Birmingham FC	15/03/1924	Oldham Athletic
PROCTER	Mark	05/09/1987	Southampton	18/03/1989	Luton Town
PROPHETT	Colin	30/08/1969	Liverpool	24/04/1973	Aston Villa
PROUD	Pattison	19/01/1907	Middlesbrough	19/01/1907	Middlesbrough
PROUDLOCK	Adam	14/12/2002	Gillingham	17/09/2005	Millwall
PROUDLOVE	Andy	20/09/1975	Grimsby Town	27/12/1975	Mansfield Town
PRUDHAM	Eddie	09/01/1971	Cardiff City	12/10/1974	Oxford United
PRYCE	Jack	04/03/1899	Everton	16/02/1901	Blackburn Rovers
PUGH	Graham	09/04/1966	Tottenham Hotspur	29/04/1972	Birmingham City
PURSE	Darren	08/08/2009	Barnsley	15/01/2011	Charlton Athletic
QUIGLEY	Eddie	11/10/1947	Plymouth Argyle	26/11/1949	Luton Town
QUINN	Alan	25/04/1998	Everton	24/04/2004	Colchester United
QUINN	James	31/01/1975	York City	19/04/1976	Mansfield Town
QUINN	James	15/01/2005	Bournemouth	29/05/2005	Hartlepool United
QUINN	John	26/09/1959	Luton Town	11/11/1967	Chelsea
QUIXALL	Albert	24/02/1951	Chelsea	17/09/1958	Sunderland
RAMSBOTTOM	Neil	19/08/1975	Darlington	06/12/1975	Colchester United
RAMSBOTTOM	Tom	10/12/1921	Clapton Orient	04/03/1922	South Shields
RATCLIFFE	Archie	27/08/1921	Barnsley	31/12/1921	Stoke FC
REDDY	Michael	01/02/2003	Wolverhampton Wanderers	26/12/2003	Port Vale
REED	Percy	13/09/1919	Notts County	03/02/1921	Everton
REEVES	David	24/09/1988	Arsenal	17/05/1989	Norwich City
REEVES	Fred	30/04/1921	Bury	30/04/1921	Bury
REGAN	William	01/09/1896	Liverpool	11/09/1897	Bury
REILLY	John	28/08/1920	Barnsley	06/11/1920	West Ham United
REYNOLDS	Jack	07/04/1906	Sunderland	30/03/1907	Stoke FC
REYNOLDS	Mark	25/01/2011	Yeovil Town		
RHODES	E.	08/01/1881	Turton	07/02/1882	Upton Park
RHODES	Richard	19/10/1935	Birmingham FC	19/03/1938	Barnsley
RICHARDS	Anthony	11/12/1895	Stoke FC	22/02/1896	Bury
RICHARDS	Fred	04/03/1899	Everton	25/03/1899	Aston Villa
RICHARDSON	Edward	29/11/1924	Wolverhampton Wanderers	14/02/1925	Stoke FC
RICHARDSON	R.	23/01/1892	Bolton Wanderers	13/02/1892	West Bromwich Albion
RICKETT	Walter	22/10/1949	Preston North End	06/09/1952	Charlton Athletic
RIMMER	Ellis	25/02/1928	Newcastle United	12/03/1938	Stockport County
RIPLEY	Stuart	01/04/2001	Sheffield United	06/05/2001	Crewe Alexandra
RITCHIE	John	12/11/1966	Manchester United	12/05/1969	Tottenham Hotspur
ROBERTS	Sean	19/01/2002	Burnley	19/01/2002	Burnley
ROBERTSON	George	25/03/1910	Bradford City	13/12/1919	Sunderland
ROBINS	Mark	09/12/2003	Carlisle United	08/05/2004	Queen's Park Rangers
ROBINSON	Carl	17/01/2003	Sheffield United	15/02/2003	Derby County
ROBINSON	Jackie	22/04/1935	West Bromwich Albion	21/09/1946	Chesterfield
ROBSON	Tom	28/03/1931	Leicester City	19/12/1931	Manchester City
ROCASTLE	Craig	12/02/2005	Bradford City	03/12/2005	Sheffield United
RODGRIGUES	Peter	17/10/1970	Charlton Athletic	01/04/1975	Nottingham Forest
ROGERS	Alf	31/08/1946	Luton Town	11/02/1950	Coventry City
ROLLINSON	Frank	25/12/1906	Derby County	27/12/1910	Newcastle United
ROSS	Maurice	10/09/2005	Leicester City	20/09/2005	West Ham United
ROSTRON	Wilf	14/01/1989	Liverpool	08/04/1989	Liverpool
ROWAN	Alexander	10/09/1892	Accrington	04/09/1893	Wolverhampton Wanderers

Lge	Sub	goals	FA Cup	Sub	goals	L Cup	Sub	goals	Euro	Sub	Goals	Other*	Sub	Goals	Total	Sub	Goals
2		1													2	0	1
													1		0	1	0
8															8	0	0
25		8	1												26	0	8
20			2												22	0	0
170	14	53	7	1	2	15		4							192	15	59
400	4		21			46			1			6			474	4	0
78		2	4		1										82	0	3
2		1													2	0	1
53		7	1												54	0	7
37															37	0	0
59		4	6		1	1						3			69	0	5
111	8	7	7			2	1								120	9	7
1															1	0	0
40	15	11	3		3	1	2	2				5	1	3	49	18	19
10	5		2		1										12	5	1
14	5	2		1		1		1							15	6	3
55		6	4												59	0	6
136	5	7	9		1	4	1	1							149	6	9
61	0	2	2			4						4		1	71	0	3
74		49	4		3										78	0	52
147	10	16	6	1		14		1				2			169	11	17
46		1	3			3									52	0	1
10	5	2										3			13	5	2
165	8	20	14	1	3	3	1		2		1				184	10	24
241		63	19		2										260	0	65
18			1			3									22	0	0
12															12	0	0
12		4													12	0	4
22	5	4	2									3		1	27	5	5
14			4												18	0	0
8	9	2	1	1		1	1	1					1		10	12	3
1															1	0	0
9															9	0	0
2															2	0	0
2															2	0	0
7			1												8	0	0
			6		8										6	0	8
57			2												59	0	0
7		1	1												8	0	1
3		1													3	0	1
9			2												11	0	0
			3		3										3	0	3
95		11	2												97	0	11
381		122	36		18										417	0	140
5	1	1													5	1	1
88	1	34	12		10	5		1							105	1	45
	1														0	1	0
163		30	10		1										173	0	31
14	1	3										3		4	17	1	7
4		1													4	0	1
108		34	11		5										119	0	39
3															3	0	0
23	5	1				1	1					3			27	6	1
162		2	7			5									174	0	2
30		8													30	0	8
41		16	3												44	0	16
1						1									2	0	0
7			1									1			9	0	0
29		13	5		1										34	0	14

(*Intertoto, Full Members Cup, Play-offs and Associate Members Cup)

Player		1st Game	v	Last Game	v
ROY	John	06/02/1937	Preston North End	15/01/1938	Swansea Town
RUDDLESDIN	Herrod	10/09/1898	Nottingham Forest	19/10/1907	Aston Villa
RUDI	Petter	19/10/1997	Tottenham Hotspur	19/08/2000	Huddersfield Town
RUSHBURY	Dave	06/11/1976	Bury	11/05/1979	Swindon Town
RUSSELL	David	27/08/1938	Bury	29/04/1939	Tottenham Hotspur
RYALLS	Brian	12/09/1953	Sheffield United	12/03/1958	Birmingham City
RYALLS	Joe	14/03/1903	Blackburn Rovers	09/04/1904	Sheffield United
RYAN	John	29/09/1984	Liverpool	06/05/1985	Chelsea
SAHAR	Ben	23/02/2008	Cardiff City	04/05/2008	Norwich City
SAM	Lloyd	27/08/2006	Leeds United	15/09/2006	Hull City
SANETTI	Francesco	02/05/1998	Aston Villa	31/10/1998	Southampton
SAYER	Jim	08/11/1884	Long Eaton Rangers	03/01/1885	Nottingham Forest
SCOTHORN	Gary	18/02/1967	Mansfield Town	02/03/1968	Chelsea
SCOTT	Phil	03/04/1999	Coventry City	05/02/2000	Derby Country
SEDGWICK	Chris	07/08/2010	Dagenham & Redbridge		
SEDLOSKI	Goce	14/03/1998	Bolton Wanderers	11/04/1998	Barnsley
SEED	Jimmy	27/08/1927	Everton	04/04/1931	Blackpool
SEEMLEY	Ivor	26/12/1953	Manchester United	12/03/1955	Burnley
SEWELL	Jackie	17/03/1951	Liverpool	26/11/1955	West Ham United
SHADBOLT	Bill	14/02/1953	Preston North End	04/04/1953	Portsmouth
SHAKESPEARE	Craig	19/08/1989	Norwich City	20/01/1990	Everton
SHARP	Wilf	08/12/1934	Leicester City	13/04/1936	Middlesbrough
SHAW	Bernard	31/10/1885	Long Eaton Rangers	31/10/1885	Long Eaton Rangers
SHAW	Bernard	25/08/1973	Swindon Town	29/04/1976	Southend United
SHAW	Jack	29/08/1953	Burnley	12/10/1957	Blackpool
SHAW	Jon	07/01/2003	Gillingham	25/09/2004	Wrexham
SHELLEY	Albert	02/01/1937	Wolverhampton Wanderers	21/04/1937	West Bromwich Albion
SHELTON	Gary	27/03/1982	Orient	09/05/1987	Wimbledon
SHELTON	George	14/02/1920	Preston North End	26/12/1921	Leeds United
SHEPHERD	James	23/09/1893	Sunderland	25/09/1893	Sunderland
SHERIDAN	John	04/11/1989	Nottingham Forest	07/09/1996	Chelsea
SHINER	Roy	20/08/1955	Plymouth Argyle	26/09/1959	Luton Town
SHIRTLIFF	Paul	28/04/1981	Grimsby Town	11/12/1982	Crystal Palace
SHIRTLIFF	Peter	12/08/1978	Doncaster Rovers	08/05/1993	Blackburn Rovers
SHORT	James	30/04/1932	Manchester City	07/05/1932	Grimsby Town
SHOWUMNI	Enoch	02/02/2008	Ipswich Town	29/03/2008	Stoke City
SHUTT	Carl	31/08/1985	Oxford United	19/09/1987	Derby County
SIBON	Gerald	07/08/1999	Liverpool	11/01/2003	Reading
SIMEK	Frankie	06/08/2005	Stoke City	06/03/2010	Leicester City
SIMMONITE	Gordon	26/02/1977	Chesterfield	26/02/1977	Chesterfield
SIMMONS	Tony	15/05/1982	Norwich City	05/03/1983	Grimsby Town
SIMMONS	William	19/01/1900	Loughborough	19/01/1900	Loughborough
SIMPSON	George	14/03/1903	Blackburn Rovers	29/03/1909	Sunderland
SIMPSON	Vivian	28/03/1902	Manchester City	09/03/1907	Liverpool
SINCLAIR	Jackie	20/12/1969	Arsenal	25/11/1972	Orient
SINTON	Andy	21/08/1993	Arsenal	06/01/1996	Charlton Athletic
SISSONS	John	29/08/1970	Blackburn Rovers	26/12/1973	Hull City
SLATER	Brian	27/12/1952	West Bromwich Albion	18/04/1953	Aston Villa
SLAVIN	Hugh	26/11/1904	Manchester City	25/09/1909	Tottenham Hotspur
SLUSARSKI	Bartosz	01/04/2008	Coventry City	28/12/2008	Coventry City
SLYNN	Frank	23/11/1946	Birmingham City	09/09/1950	Charlton Athletic
SMAILES	Andy	14/10/1922	Fulham	29/09/1923	Fulham
SMALL	Wade	05/08/2006	Preston North End	03/03/2009	Reading
SMELT	John	05/02/1921	Blackpool	29/08/1921	Derby County
SMITH	Dean	22/02/2003	Crystal Palace	08/05/2004	Queen's Park Rangers
SMITH	Jim	08/11/1884	Long Eaton Rangers	13/02/1892	West Bromwich Albion
SMITH	Jimmy	09/08/2008	Burnley	20/12/2008	Cardiff City
SMITH	Jock	02/09/1893	Sunderland	26/12/1893	Burnley
SMITH	Tom	28/01/1935	Blackburn Rovers	28/01/1935	Blackburn Rovers
SMITH	Mark	29/04/1978	Colchester United	09/05/1987	Wimbledon

Lge	Sub	goals	FA Cup	Sub	goals	L Cup	Sub	goals	Euro	Sub	Goals	Other*	Sub	Goals	Total	Sub	Goals
15		1	1												16	0	1
259		7	26												285	0	7
70	7	7	6	1	1	5		1							81	8	9
111	1	8	13		1	8									132	1	9
42			8												50	0	0
41			6												47	0	0
2															2	0	0
5	3	1				1									6	3	1
8	4	3													8	4	3
4															4	0	0
1	4	1					2								1	6	1
			2		1										2	0	1
1			1												2	0	0
2	7	1	1	1											3	8	1
24	9	4	2	2		1						3	1		30	12	4
3	1														3	1	0
134		33	12		5										146	0	38
15			8												23	0	0
164		87	11		5										175	0	92
7															7	0	0
15	2					3		1					1		18	3	1
48		2	10												58	0	2
			1												1	0	0
100	4	3	5		1	4									109	4	4
56		21	9		6										65	0	27
8	10	2		2			1					1	2		9	15	2
3		2													3	0	2
195	3	18	23	1	3	18		3				1			237	4	24
17			1												18	0	0
2															2	0	0
187	10	25	17	1	3	24		3	2		1	3		1	233	11	33
153		93	7		3										160	0	96
7	2					1									8	2	0
292		8	25	1	4	35	2	1	1			3			356	3	13
2															2	0	0
6	4														6	4	0
36	4	16	4	1	4	3		1							43	5	21
98	31	36	7	1	3	11	2	4							116	34	43
113	6	2	4			7									124	6	2
1															1	0	0
1	3					1									2	3	0
1															1	0	0
142		30	22		9										164	0	39
30		8	8		3										38	0	11
97	4	14	3			5		2							105	4	16
54	6	3	5			13			2	1					74	7	3
114	1	14	6			5		1							125	1	15
3															3	0	0
48			7												55	0	0
7	7	2													7	7	2
44		5	2												46	0	5
37		13	3		2										40	0	15
37	31	7	2	2		2		1							41	33	8
16		2													16	0	2
55		1	1	1		1						4			61	1	1
			22												22	0	0
3	9					1									4	9	0
18		1													18	0	1
1															1	0	0
281	1	16	39		3	29		1							349	1	20

(*Intertoto, Full Members Cup, Play-offs and Associate Members Cup)

Player		1st Game	v	Last Game	v
SMITH	Norman	17/12/1927	Sunderland	21/04/1928	Portsmouth
SMITH	Paul	23/08/2003	Peterborough United	17/10/2004	Barnsley
SMITH	Roy	26/03/1937	Bolton Wanderers	29/03/1948	Chesterfield
SMITH	Wilf	19/12/1964	Blackpool	15/08/1970	Charlton Athletic
SMITH	William	01/02/1930	Sheffield United	01/04/1933	Chelsea
SNODIN	Glynn	21/09/1985	Tottenham Hotspur	25/04/1987	Luton Town
SOARES	Tom	28/11/2009	West Bromwich Albion	02/05/2010	Crystal Palace
SODJE	Apko	01/09/2007	Bristol City	30/01/2010	Plymouth Argyle
SOLTVEDT	Trond-Egil	13/02/2001	Tranmere Rovers	11/01/2003	Reading
SONGO'O	Franck	08/03/2008	Queen's Park Rangers	04/05/2008	Norwich City
SONNER	Danny	18/10/1998	Coventry City	14/05/2000	Leicester City
SPIKSLEY	Fred	23/01/1892	Bolton Wanderers	18/04/1903	West Bromwich Albion
SPOORS	Jimmy	07/11/1908	Middlesbrough	05/04/1920	Bolton Wanderers
SPRINGETT	Peter	19/08/1967	West Ham United	14/12/1974	Oldham Athletic
SPRINGETT	Ron	15/03/1958	Bolton Wanderers	15/05/1967	Leeds United
SPURR	Tommy	22/04/2006	Reading		
SRNICEK	Pavel	14/11/1998	Newcastle United	18/03/2000	Watford
STACEY	William	18/12/1880	Blackburn Rovers	02/12/1882	Lockwood Brothers
STAINROD	Simon	03/04/1985	Norwich City	07/09/1985	West Ham United
STANIFORTH	Ron	20/08/1955	Plymouth Argyle	11/04/1959	Bristol City
STAPLETON	William	30/08/1919	Middlesbrough	01/05/1920	Oldham Athletic
STARLING	Ron	27/08/1932	Blackpool	02/01/1937	Wolverhampton Wanderers
STEFANOVIC	Dejan	26/12/1995	Nottingham Forest	16/05/1999	Charlton Athletic
STEPHENSON	George	07/02/1931	Bolton Wanderers	11/02/1933	West Bromwich Albion
STERLAND	Mel	17/05/1979	Blackpool	25/02/1989	Wimbledon
STEVENS	J.	09/01/1882	Staveley	15/03/1882	Blackburn Rovers
STEVENSON	Thomas	04/09/1897	Sunderland	22/01/1898	Nottingham Forest
STEWART	Jimmy	14/02/1903	Grimsby Town	25/04/1908	Everton
STEWART	Reg	05/01/1946	Mansfield Town	16/11/1946	West Bromwich Albion
STEWART	Simon	10/03/1993	Ipswich Town	24/06/1995	FC Basel
STOCKDALE	Robbie	13/09/2000	Nottingham Forest	14/10/2000	Portsmouth
STORRAR	David	27/12/1952	West Bromwich Albion	17/01/1953	Charlton Athletic
STRANGE	Alf	19/02/1927	Sunderland	22/04/1935	West Bromwich Albion
STRATFORD	Chas	05/02/1881	Darwen	03/01/1885	Nottingham Forest
STREETS	George	01/09/1913	Bolton Wanderers	03/01/1914	Burnley
STRINGER	Chris	13/08/2000	Wolverhampton Wanderers	26/04/2003	Burnley
STRINGFELLOW	Frank	27/02/1909	Preston North End	17/04/1911	Manchester United
STRUTT	Brian	10/11/1979	Blackpool	23/02/1980	Rotherham United
STUBBS	Frank	13/10/1900	Blackburn Rovers	20/12/1902	West Bromwich Albion
SUNLEY	David	12/12/1970	Birmingham City	24/01/1976	Brighton & Hove Albion
SURTESS	Jack	25/12/1934	Birmingham FC	17/10/1936	Chelsea
SUTHERLAND	George	17/11/1894	Wolverhampton Wanderers	22/04/1895	West Bromwich Albion
SWAN	Peter	05/11/1955	Barnsley	11/11/1972	Oxford United
SWIFT	Hugh	05/01/1946	Mansfield Town	26/02/1951	Man Utd
SYKES	Joe	10/03/1920	Liverpool	08/03/1924	Stockport County
SYMM	Colin	15/10/1966	Everton	10/08/1968	West Bromwich Albion
TALBOT	Andrew	19/10/2004	Peterborough United	16/12/2006	Birmingham City
TAYLOR	Charles	07/02/1920	Preston North End	01/05/1920	Oldham Athletic
TAYLOR	Ian	20/08/1994	Tottenham Hotspur	03/12/1994	Crystal Palace
TAYLOR	Jock	31/12/1907	Arsenal	09/04/1910	Chelsea
TAYLOR	Kevin	27/01/1979	Plymouth Argyle	31/03/1984	Leeds United
TAYLOR	Mark	22/08/1989	Luton Town	28/10/1989	Wimbledon
TAYLOR	Paul	14/08/1971	Queen's Park Rangers	30/09/1972	Carlisle United
TAYLOR	Sam	15/01/1921	Port Vale	07/02/1925	Leicester City
TAYLOR	William	29/04/1920	Aston Villa	14/01/1922	Stoke FC
TEALE	Gary	07/08/2010	Dagenham & Redbridge		
THACKERAY	Fred	09/03/1901	Aston Villa	04/04/1903	Everton
THOMAS	Walter	03/03/1951	Wolverhampton Wanderers	29/09/1951	Cardiff City
THOME	Emerson	11/04/1998	Barnsley	18/12/1999	Aston Villa
THOMPSON	Ernie	10/09/1921	Notts County	15/04/1922	Bury

Lge	Sub	goals	FA Cup	Sub	goals	L Cup	Sub	goals	Euro	Sub	Goals	Other*	Sub	Goals	Total	Sub	Goals
19			4												23	0	0
19	8	2				1						3			23	8	2
84			13												97	0	0
207		4	21		1	6									234	0	5
29		1													29	0	1
51	8	1	9			4	1					1			65	9	1
17	8	2	1												18	8	2
18	23	9	1				2								19	25	9
74		2	1			6		2							81	0	4
12		1													12	0	1
42	11	3	4	2		3	1	1							49	14	4
292		100	29		15										321	0	115
255		5	17												272	0	5
180			16			11									207	0	0
345			28			1			10						384	0	0
186	6	5	10		2	7						2			205	6	7
44			6			2									52	0	0
			5												5	0	0
8	7	2													8	7	2
102		2	5												107	0	2
20															20	0	0
176		30	17												193	0	30
59	7	4	4		1	2									65	7	5
39		18	6		2										45	0	20
271	8	37	34	1	5	30		7				3			338	9	49
			5												5	0	0
2															2	0	0
123		52	18		8										141	0	60
6			2												8	0	0
6							1		1						7	1	0
6															6	0	0
4															4	0	0
253		22	20												273	0	22
			11												11	0	0
2															2	0	0
6	3		2				1								8	4	0
20		5	1												21	0	5
2															2	0	0
18															18	0	0
121	12	21	12		5	2	1								135	13	26
40		5	10		3										50	0	8
3															3	0	0
273	2		14			2			10						299	2	0
181			14												195	0	0
29		1	2												31	0	1
16	3	1	2	1		1									19	4	1
5	24	4	1										3	1	6	27	5
7															7	0	0
9	5	1				2	2	1							11	7	2
20															20	0	0
118	7	21	7		2	11	2	5							136	9	28
8	1					2									10	1	0
5	1														5	1	0
120		36	8		3										128	0	39
16		4	1												17	0	4
37	4	2	5		2	2						3		1	47	4	5
9			1												10	0	0
10		1													10	0	1
60	1	1	4		1	5	1								69	2	2
23			1												24	0	0

(*Intertoto, Full Members Cup, Play-offs and Associate Members Cup)

Player		1st Game	v	Last Game	v
THOMPSON	Fred	15/10/1887	Belper	14/02/1891	West Bromwich Albion
THOMPSON	Garry	17/08/1985	Chelsea	03/05/1986	Ipswich
THOMPSON	Gavin	23/01/1892	Bolton Wanderers	13/02/1892	West Bromwich Albion
THOMPSON	Jackie	25/11/1933	Sunderland	09/02/1946	Stoke City
THOMPSON	Ron	25/01/1947	Everton	25/01/1947	Everton
THOMPSON	William	09/09/1970	Chelsea	19/04/1976	Mansfield Town
TIDMAN	Ola	09/08/2003	Swindon Town	30/10/2004	Chesterfield
TODD	Sammy	15/08/1970	Charlton Athletic	24/04/1973	Aston Villa
TOMLINSON	Charlie	05/01/1946	Mansfield Town	20/01/1951	Middlesbrough
TOMLINSON	David	03/01/1987	Leicester City	03/01/1987	Leicester City
TOONE	George	04/10/1924	Leicester City	10/04/1925	Oldham Athletic
TOPHAM	Jack	22/10/1898	Sunderland	31/03/1900	Leicester Fosse
TOSELAND	Ernie	18/03/1939	West Bromwich Albion	29/04/1939	Tottenham Hotspur
TROTTER	Jimmy	13/02/1922	Wolverhampton Wanderers	02/02/1929	Sheffield United
TRUSTFULL	Orlando	24/08/1996	Newcastle United	22/04/1997	Blackburn Rovers
TUDGAY	Marcus	02/01/2006	Crewe Alexandra	20/11/2010	MK Dons
TUMMON	Oliver	23/04/1906	Everton	05/03/1910	Liverpool
TURLEY	Mike	01/01/1955	Aston Villa	22/01/1955	Tottenham
TURNER	Chris	14/08/1976	Grimsby Town	08/05/1991	Bristol City
TURNER	Iain	24/02/2007	Southend United	21/04/2007	Coventry City
TURTON	Cyril	31/08/1946	Luton Town	26/12/1953	Manchester United
TYNAN	Tommy	11/09/1976	Swindon Town	26/09/1978	Bury
ULYETT	George	12/02/1883	Notts County	12/02/1883	Notts County
USHER	Brian	21/08/1965	Manchester United	25/04/1968	Manchester City
VARADI	Imre	27/08/1983	Swansea City	21/10/1989	Tottenham Hotspur
VARNEY	Luke	21/03/2009	Swansea City	02/05/2010	Crystal Palace
WADDLE	Chris	15/08/1992	Everton	05/05/1996	West Ham United
WALDEN	Richard	10/01/1976	Hereford United	03/05/1978	Wrexham
WALKER	Colin	06/10/1986	Stockport County	25/10/1986	Coventry City
WALKER	Cyril	23/10/1937	Manchester United	27/11/1937	Nottingham Forest
WALKER	Des	14/08/1993	Liverpool	21/04/2001	Barnsley
WALKER	Fred	16/09/1937	Tottenham Hotspur	07/05/1938	Tottenham Hotspur
WALKER	Tommy	03/04/1926	Hull City	22/04/1935	West Bromwich Albion
WALKER	William	20/10/1923	Nelson	03/05/1924	Manchester United
WALL	Adrian	06/04/1968	Chelsea	15/04/1968	Everton
WALLER	George	15/10/1887	Belper	29/03/1890	Blackburn Rovers
WALLWORK	Ronnie	12/01/2008	Cardiff City	26/04/2008	Leicester City
WANDS	Alex	05/01/1946	Mansfield Town	22/02/1947	Burnley
WARBOYS	Alan	24/08/1968	Tottenham Hotspur	19/12/1970	Oxford United
WARD	Tommy	05/01/1946	Mansfield Town	14/02/1948	Nottingham Forest
WARE	Harry	28/08/1937	Chesterfield	06/11/1937	Barnsley
WARHURST	Paul	17/08/1991	Aston Villa	25/08/1993	West Ham United
WARREN	Peter	13/11/1909	Arsenal	16/09/1911	Middlesbrough
WATLING	Barry	24/01/1976	Swindon Town	24/01/1976	Swindon Town
WATSON	Don	22/01/1955	Tottenham Hotspur	03/11/1956	Bolton Wanderers
WATSON	Gordon	02/03/1991	Notts County	14/03/1995	Crystal Palace
WATSON	J.	31/10/1885	Long Eaton Rangers	31/10/1885	Long Eaton Rangers
WATSON	Steve	10/02/2007	Burnley	07/02/2009	Sheffield United
WATTS	Julian	01/10/1992	Spora Luxembourg	02/03/1996	Nottingham Forest
WEAVER	Alex	01/01/1925	Oldham Athletic	07/03/1925	Bradford City
WEAVER	Nicky	05/11/2005	Derby County		
WEBSTER	Arnie	05/04/1937	Stoke City	05/04/1937	Stoke City
WEBSTER	Fred	15/10/1887	Belper	15/10/1887	Belper
WEBSTER	Johnny	16/09/1893	Newton Heath	22/04/1895	West Bromwich Albion
WEIR	Findlay	19/01/1910	Notts County	18/03/1912	Bury
WELSH	Fletcher	17/01/1920	Everton	04/09/1920	Barnsley
WEST	Colin	12/09/1987	Watford	04/02/1989	Aston Villa
WEST	Fred	28/12/1881	Staveley	15/03/1882	Blackburn Rovers
WESTLAKE	Frank	26/03/1938	Luton Town	14/01/1950	Plymouth Argyle
WESTWOOD	Ashley	13/08/2000	Wolverhampton Wanderers	04/05/2003	Walsall

Lge	Sub	goals	FA Cup	Sub	goals	L Cup	Sub	goals	Euro	Sub	Goals	Other*	Sub	Goals	Total	Sub	Goals
			12		1										12	0	1
35	1	7	5		1	2	1								42	2	8
			3		1										3	0	1
36		9	4		3										40	0	12
			1												1	0	0
150	6	3	9		1	8									167	6	4
12	1				1							2			14	1	1
22	2	1				2									24	2	1
68		7	9		5										77	0	12
	1														0	1	0
19			2												21	0	0
12		2	4												16	0	2
12		2													12	0	2
153		109	6		5										159	0	114
9	10	3		1		2									11	11	3
178	17	49	6	1	1	5	1	1				1	2	1	190	21	52
40		9	6		3										46	0	12
3			1												4	0	0
166			21			17						1			205	0	0
11															11	0	0
146			5												151	0	0
89	2	31	4		1	12		5							105	2	37
			1												1	0	0
55	1	2	7	1	1	4									66	2	3
86	12	36	9		7	12	1	3				1			108	13	46
35	8	11	0	0	0	0	0	0	0	0	0	0	0	0	35	8	11
94	15	10	12	1	3	19			5	1	2				130	17	15
100			4			11		1							115	0	1
2							1	3							2	1	3
4															4	0	0
307			24			28			3						362	0	0
10		1													10	0	1
258		3	29												287	0	3
18		5	1												19	0	5
3															3	0	0
			16		2										16	0	2
4	3														4	3	0
11		1	7		1										18	0	2
66	5	13	2			2	1								70	6	13
35		19	4		1										39	0	20
12		1													12	0	1
60	6	6	7	1	5	9		4	4		3	1			81	7	18
7															7	0	0
1															1	0	0
8		3	2		1										10	0	4
29	37	15	5	2		6	5	5	2	1	1		1		42	46	21
			1												1	0	0
46	10	5	1	0	1	2	0	0							49	10	6
12	4	1				1			3						16	4	1
6		1													6	0	1
50			5			2						4			61	0	0
1															1	0	0
			1												1	0	0
23		5	4												27	0	5
71		1	1												72	0	1
12		4													12	0	4
40	5	8	6		1	6		3				3		1	55	5	13
			7												7	0	0
110			7												117	0	0
79	3	5	2			10	2	4							91	5	9

(*Intertoto, Full Members Cup, Play-offs and Associate Members Cup)

Player		1st Game	v	Last Game	v
WHALLEY	Johnny	03/04/1920	Newcastle United	19/04/1920	Bradford Park Avenue
WHELAN	Glenn	21/08/2004	Huddersfield Town	29/01/2008	Wolverhampton Wanderers
WHITAKER	Colin	15/03/1952	Queen's Park Rangers	15/03/1952	Queen's Park Rangers
WHITEHOUSE	Jack	02/03/1929	Bury	07/12/1929	Middlesbrough
WHITHAM	Jack	06/05/1967	Burnley	22/04/1970	Manchester City
WHITHAM	Terry	13/10/1956	Luton Town	20/12/1958	Swansea Town
WHITTINGHAM	Guy	26/12/1994	Everton	18/10/1998	Coventry City
WHITTON	Steve	04/03/1989	Charlton Athletic	13/10/1990	Plymouth
WICKS	Peter	16/01/1965	Liverpool	20/09/1969	West Ham United
WILCOCKSON	Harold	20/12/1969	Arsenal	02/01/1971	Tottenham Hotspur
WILKINSON	Derek	13/11/1954	Cardiff City	07/11/1964	Manchester United
WILKINSON	Eric	10/09/1958	Sunderland	10/09/1958	Sunderland
WILKINSON	Harry	28/12/1881	Staveley	12/02/1883	Notts County
WILKINSON	Howard	09/09/1964	Chelsea	19/03/1966	Northampton Town
WILKINSON	Jack	03/04/1926	Hull City	08/03/1930	Leicester City
WILLIAMS	Andy	24/06/1995	FC Basel	24/06/1995	FC Basel
WILLIAMS	Len	26/01/1924	Leeds United	24/10/1925	Nottingham Forest
WILLIAMS	Les	31/08/1955	Liverpool	27/10/1956	Man City
WILLIAMS	Mike	01/10/1992	Spora Luxembourg	28/09/1996	Everton
WILLIAMS	Paul	25/08/1990	Ipswich Town	05/09/1992	Manchester City
WILLIAMS	Rees	26/08/1922	Rotherham United	29/08/1927	Manchester United
WILLIAMSON	Charlie	21/12/1979	Reading	07/05/1984	Manchester City
WILSON	Andrew	01/09/1900	Manchester City	10/03/1920	Liverpool
WILSON	Charles	25/02/1928	Newcastle United	13/01/1932	Tottenham Hotspur
WILSON	Danny	25/08/1990	Ipswich Town	20/05/1993	Arsenal
WILSON	George	13/03/1920	Liverpool	21/03/1925	Middlesbrough
WILSON	Joe	25/08/1923	Bradford City	11/02/1924	Leicester City
WILSON	Laurie	06/12/2003	Scunthorpe United	17/12/2003	Scunthorpe United
WILSON	Mark	24/01/2004	Peterborough United	07/02/2004	Port Vale
WILSON	S.	08/11/1884	Long Eaton Rangers	03/01/1885	Nottingham Forest
WINDASS	Dean	08/12/2001	Millwall	15/12/2001	Gillingham
WINTERBOTTOM	Harry	18/12/1880	Blackburn Rovers	14/02/1891	West Bromwich Albion
WISE	F.	15/10/1887	Belper	15/10/1887	Belper
WITCOMB	Doug	01/03/1947	Tottenham Hotspur	25/04/1953	Sunderland
WOOD	Darren	21/01/1989	Arsenal	23/10/1991	Manchester City
WOOD	Richard	21/04/2003	Brighton & Hove Albion	07/11/2009	Queen's Park Rangers
WOODALL	Brian	24/02/1968	Coventry City	27/09/1969	Derby County
WOODHEAD	Dennis	24/05/1947	Newcastle United	05/03/1955	Everton
WOODS	Chris	17/08/1991	Aston Villa	23/03/1996	Bolton Wanderers
WOOLHOUSE	Toddles	02/02/1889	Notts Rangers	16/03/1895	West Bromwich Albion
WORRALL	Teddy	21/01/1911	Preston North End	20/03/1915	Manchester City
WORTHINGTON	Nigel	25/02/1984	Brighton & Hove Albion	07/05/1994	Man City
WORTLEY	George	03/01/1885	Nottingham Forest	03/01/1885	Nottingham Forest
WRIGHT	Vic	03/10/1931	Aston Villa	10/10/1931	Leicester City
WRIGHT	Jimmy	20/03/1935	Derby County	12/02/1936	Portsmouth
WRIGHT	Jocky	26/11/1898	Aston Villa	17/03/1902	Derby County
WRIGHT	Percy	22/04/1911	Everton	31/01/1914	Wolverhampton Wanderers
WYLDE	Rodger	18/11/1972	Middlesbrough	16/02/1980	Chesterfield
YOUNG	Gerry	02/03/1957	Blackpool	02/01/1971	Tottenham Hotspur

Lge	Sub	goals	FA Cup	Sub	goals	L Cup	Sub	goals	Euro	Sub	Goals	Other*	Sub	Goals	Total	Sub	Goals
5															5	0	0
136	6	12	6		1	8		2				3		1	153	6	16
1															1	0	0
10		1													10	0	1
54	9	27	6		4	2									62	9	31
4															4	0	0
90	23	22	7	1	1	7	2	2	1	2					105	28	25
22	10	4		1		3		4					1		25	12	8
13						1									14	0	0
40		1	1			2									43	0	1
212		53	15		4				4						231	0	57
1															1	0	0
			12												12	0	0
22		2													22	0	2
72		16	7		1										79	0	17
									1						1	0	0
9															9	0	0
11															11	0	0
16	7	1				3	2		2	1					21	10	1
78	15	25	3	2		10	3	3				3			94	20	28
163		7	10												173	0	7
61	1	1	1			4									66	1	1
502		198	44		17										546	0	215
57		5	3												60	0	5
91	7	11	9	1		22		2	3	1	1	2	1		127	10	14
184		4	12												196	0	4
3															3	0	0
				2								1			1	2	0
3															3	0	0
			2												2	0	0
2															2	0	0
			22		10										22	0	10
			1												1	0	0
224		12	6												230	0	12
10	1					1	1					1			12	2	0
162	9	7	3	2		6	1	1				5	1		176	13	8
19	3	4	3		2										22	3	6
213		72	13		3										226	0	75
106	1		10			13			6			2			137	1	0
16		10	19		11										35	0	21
103			11												114	0	0
334	4	12	29		1	41		1	3		1	6			413	4	15
			1												1	0	0
2															2	0	0
3			1												4	0	0
103		41	7		1										110	0	42
20		6	2												22	0	6
157	12	54	15		4	10		8							182	12	66
307	2	13	17		2	10		1	8		4				342	2	20

Roll of Honour

Dr. Andrew Brodie
Jess Brodie
Keith King
Edwin John O'Sullivan
Danilo "Dan" Ronzani (Bologna)
James Hargreaves
Kevin James Carpenter
Ralph, Ian & Robin May
Paul Beal
Steven Miller
David Miller
Steve Rogers
Zak Berisford
Steve Deakin
Alan W. Woolley
Aiden Priestley
Ian White
Steve Goodison
John Eastie Eastwood
Tony Mazengarb
Keith Strickland
Paul Strickland
Stephen Paul York
Dennis Cox
Lee Cutts
Brett Carter
Jack Barratt
Mick Simpson
Neville Wright
Nevill Ashley Wright
Michael Wright
Matthew David Wright
Jo-Anne Sheree Wright
Sophie Elliott Oliver Ashton
Richard Havard
John Goodwin
Phil Aylen
Thomas Fogg
Jamie Kieron Oliver
David Melson
John B. Gath
Alex P. Gath
Derek Sowerby
Peter Bates
Vinay Mistry
Mr. Philip J. Lockwood
Alan Mark Tolley
Graham Clixby
Steven Goulden
Ian N. Oxley
Glyn Wragg
Jason R. Smith
Alan Bunker
Steve:Beastie
Hollie Morris
David J. Cranny
David Faukner Bendiksen

Adam Denovan
Rob 'Coops' Cooper
Nigel Lawes
Richard Major
Ed Thomas
Michael W. Scruton
David, Owen & Libby Haslehurst
Wilf Binns
Stuart Robert Ellershaw
David J. Lee
Ernie Jenkins
Martin Langhorn
Kris Wigfield
Ian Wigfield
Ewan Wigfield
Joe Rowbotham
Tracy Cundey
Alan Saxton
Rich Stokes
Alan North
Christian Brailsford
Michael Towers
Martin Hoyles
Richard Graney
Colin J. A. Hatcher
Martin Perryman
Robert (Bob) Green
David Herbert
Nigel R. Linfitt
Chris Ludford
James Newcombe
Benjamin Nield
Dave Williams
Dave & Chloe Major
Craig Barton
Tom Crabtree
Thomas Littlewood
Naomi Littlewood
Chris (Smudge) Smith
James Janiszewski
Daniel Saul
David Tunley
James Cockings
Tony Garfitt
Gary Claydon
Rory J. Galloway
Andy Marshall
Peter Broomhead
Nicholas Brown
Mr. Vorn Penaluna
Andrew 'Snozzer' Brownrigg
Thomas Ledger
Ben Clarke
Mark R. Jones
Graham David Benson
Terry James Maycock
Ken Vale

Malcolm Gray
Shaun Hockenhull
John Seeviour
Lee Hicklin
Simon Rowe
Craig Metcalfe
Colin Philip Walker
Dr. Helen J. Knight
Geoff Denbigh
Dave & Karen Parry
Ian Colley
Paul Glossop
Charlie Holmes
Daniel Hammond
Mark Plumley
Adam Sean Ogden
Nick Torlop
Phillip Bonsall
Nick Hobbs
Timothy Wilson Bott
Matthew Anderton
Derrick Devenport
Dave Hanson
Allan David Barr
Peter Adolfsen Løhmann
Bob Neville
David Bellamy
Jake & Andrew Bellamy
John Mason
Tony Mason
Tyrone & Shelley Briddon
Paul Kay
Stephen Waller
Charles Page
Graham Cryan
Andy Brockley
Graham Scott
Joe Ludlam
Justin & Shelley Biggin
Littlewood Family
Peter Frederick Goulty
Christopher D. McHugh
Andrew Bingham
Richard Gregg
Andy Sharpe
David Brooklyn
Derek Mounfield
Adam Tyson
John O'Brien
Ian Brownhill
Paul Richard Whitaker
David Andrew Ogden
Nathan Robert Langley
Peter Maycock
Tom Wraight
Callum Steven James Mellor
Grahame Morris

P. C. Carter
Andrew Appleby
David Parfitt
Liam Tankard
Kavan Tankard
Simon Needham
Danny Jones
Steve Rebbeck
Max Turley
John Flower
Glenn Poulton
Richard George
Steve Parkin
Glyn Speed
Jake Speed
Philip M. Allsop
Phil Lyle
Mark Quince 1969
Luca & Aidan Jeffery 2011
Jane Tweedy
Mark Tweedy
Daniel Spencer
Richard Crooks
Gareth Coe
Stephen Oxby
Islwyn Roberts
Helen Jones
Steve Whitehead
Adam White
Trevor Nichols
Derek Housley
Oliver David Rains
Steven D. Maxted
Antony Mills
Frank Rotchell
Adam Andrews
Peter Startup
Oliver George Thomas Eyre
Paul Stevens
Colin Geoffrey Turner
Lee Alan Bancroft
Jonathan James Joshua Watson
Andrew & Sue Sheppard
Eimear Harney
Matthew Brown
Ian Davies
Terry Douglas Cocker
David L. Cooke
Paul David Johnston
Lucy Jeffcock
Matt Hardwick
Steven Scarlett
Ernie Lockett
Wednesday Maya Morton
Neil & Russell Staniland
Richard A. Oldfield
Tony Curran
Nathan Knight
Russell Warner
Christopher Humphries
Séan Lathey
Geoffrey Easton

Richard Hughes
Andrew Webster
Dean Pearson
David R. Goddard
Neil Christopher Kitson
Richard Mark Josh Hull
Matthew Johnson
Joseph Davison
Christopher Radley
Darren Goucher
Steve Knight
Darren Lee Wilson
Carl Bennett
Paul Thomas Ward
Alan Page
Derek Broomhead
David O'Brien
Paul Rogers
Mick Green
Anton Le Saux
Thomas David Evans
Bailey Revill
Adrian Goodison
Michael Goodison
Andy Harvey
Michael F. Bennett
Eric Hall
David Enzor
Peter A. Tindle
Andrew Rossington
Aaron David Hukin
Alan, Rachel & Bradley Marples
C. A. & J. Varley
David G. Stark
Gordon John Harrold
Tony Peacock
Rebecca Langhorn
David H. Hawksworth
Nichola Starr
Gary Starr
Harry Coy
Carlo Flori
Paul Palgrave
Trevor C. Gill
Patrick John Hunt
Steve Guy
Richard Wright
Paul Gibbon
Jon Paul Luke Oxley
William South
Alan W. Staves
Mark W. Bottomley
Edward T. Bulmer
Phil Chetwynd
Henry & George Wragg
Ian Fraser
Dean A. S. Hedley
Chris Driver
Harris & Riley Goodinson
Tom & Josh Chapman
Tom Crawshaw
Ian Robert Christlo

Steve Beech
Kyle Beech
Andy Saunders
Tom Greaves
Steve Moffatt
Andrew Moffatt
Ian C. Wordsworth
Glynn Slattery
Denis Lumb
Clive Nicholson
John Ward
Ward 65
David John Ward
Paul Willis
Derrick A. Edwards
Susan Edwards
John Bowater
Paul McLellan
Janet Ethel Edwards
Reece C. Edwards
Lewis A. Edwards
Ryan Broadbent-Fluffy
Jamie Lee Ward
John Butcher
Michael John Morley
Martin Edwards
Jonathan & William Hurst
Karl Taylor
David Biggin
Michael Renshaw
Stephen Pepper
Alex Pepper
Neil Mclean
Lee Mclean
Ian Donaldson
John Donaldson
Stuart Stanniland
Robert Auckland
Jonathon Page
Andy Stevens
Roger M. Outram
Richard J.P. D'Silva
David Taylor
Dean Paul Maltby
Philip Downing
Michelle Boorer
Mark & Andrew Ford
Stephen Lovegrove
Peter Andrews
Andrew Thorpe
Niall Green
Roy Loon Bellamy
Paul Queeney
Roger Dale Yarnold
Dave Dobson
Richard Morton
Ian Bloom
Martyn Clarke
Ann Womersley
David John Reid
Graham Lane MBE
G. S. Briggs

The Hadfield Family
Glyndon Foster
John Clifford Fletcher
Jean Lindley
Mark Alan Lindley
Brendon Reid Flanagan
Terry Kennedy
Kevin Knight
Richard Woodward
Keith Roberts
Tony Lindsay
Paul Roberts
Peter Sturman
Tom Buckle
Phil Buckle
Maggie Brown
Malcolm Loveday
Neil Yates
Michael Lunn
The Andrews Family
Paul & Jack Douglas
Brent Humberstone
Robert Alexander Boyd
John Chadwick
Joshua Alexander Morgan
Jason Boddy
Daniel Beckett
Thomas S. Marshall
Dave Stillings
Claire Reaney
Ethan Turner
Mark Stenton
Joe Stickel
Jim, David, Robert Naylor
Brian Gee
Kenneth Cliffe
Harry Tibbitts
Dennis Cox
Adrian M. Pigott
Liam Urry
Nicholas Biggs
Adam M. Briggs
Richard S. Briggs
Mark Poulton
Sean Lovell
Richard Bell
Mick Pashley
Corey Lewis Parkin
Darren Parkin
Stephen Broadhead
Lucas Dylan Grady
Ray Parkin
Paul L. Redfern
Ian Bull
Lee Cartwright
Lorraine Cartwright
Ric Robinson
Stephen Michael Jackson
Harry Mills
Andrew Steele
Dr. James Spooner
Peter Brownhill

Lindsay Gauton
Sam Guy
Kevin J. Thompson
Bill Ross
Ross Siddons
Todd Siddons
Andrew Adlington
Alan Cusworth
Russell Gregory Taylor
Mark Worley
Jonathan Kirk
Andrew N. Goble
Roy Jackson
Glenn Creighton
John Figiel
Stephen Burns
Craig Webster
Ryan Maxwell
Peter Coussens
Rick Baines
Martyn Smith
Brad Fairhead
Stewart Askham
John Oxley
Lee Gurney
James Lavin
Alan Gregory
Mark Bryan
Andre Hill
J.F.S. Russell - Saw '35 Final
Neil Gingell
Darren Wilkinson Owl4Life
Thomas Corcoran
Mr. Nicholas Johnson
Michael Di Mattina
John Barton
David Mark Briggs
Daniel Warburton
Rob Johnston
Beryl & Garry Bennett
Michael A. Cole
Conor Joseph Webb
Barbara Ann Watson
Andy Clarke
Peter Beardsley
Thomas Bramall
John R. Mclean-Searle
Harry Edwin Searle
Richard Brook
Judith Brook
Brian Tanner
Jim Butterley
Stephen Malcolm James
Andrew D. Middleton
Adrian Abbey
Harry Martin 1946 Owl
Shaun McLoughlin
Richard Abberley
Malcolm G. Atkin
Graeme Whillance
David Harrington
Paul Chilcott

Kieran Webster
Sheila Buckley
John Topham
Alexander Paul Scott Ball
Timothy James Cox
Michael Chapman
The Jarvis Family
Mark J. N. Hempshall
Ron Cawthron
Richard Yeardley
Fletch 1971
John Michael Thompson
Richard Taff
Karl Ashley Linnell
Jason Lee Wright
Stephen Lovatt Foster
Taylor Jacob Andrews
Philip Bulloss
Pam Revington
Dexter George Barker
Derek Skidmore
Thomas David Hartley
Craig Weldon
David John Elsom
Graham Earnshaw
Philip Colin Purnell
Steve Lambarth
Denis George Handley
Nils Deleuran
Lars Grandt
Leslie Peter Robinson
Les Robinson
Ben Robinson
Wayne Elliott
Lane Wright
Neil Denver
Helen Crofts
Geoff Crofts
George Titman
Andrew Bell
Geoff Wilkenson
Robert Steven Dakin
Graham Oxby
Mick Lewis
John Nilen
Jack A. Burditt
Gary A. Burditt
Peter Doane
Ronald Pearson
Tom Rogers
Paul Harry George Bradshaw
David Metham
David Brian Thompson
Stephen Mark Elliott
Adam Jessop
Derek James Fox
Aidan Hardy
David Wales
Stephen Linley
Stephen Derek Wade
Steven Fleetwood
Wayne Billyard

Kieran Shaw
Stephen Hunt
Leon Jude Watson Clark
Richard Bruton
John Daubney
Gareth, Julie, Owen Davies
Sarah Parikh
Andrew Ramshaw
Paul Simmons
Richard Simmons
Stuart Quinton
Howard Whyman
Alan Stevenson
Michael Batty
Tom Wall
Dave Hawley
Andy Hawley
Lee Walker
Lee Vernon
Ian Richardson
Graham Lawrence
Judith Bigford
Andrew Everitt
Keith Brockelbank
Mark Bramhall
Neil B. Woolhouse
Paul Hopton
Stuart E. Smith (Grandpa)
John Sheader
Malcolm Ian Baker
Kyle Richardson
Adrian Leslie Hill
Ralph Desmond Hill
John Clayton
Thomas Eades
Mitchel Walker
Elliott Bermudez-Galton
Matt Gerrietty - Pompeyowl
Mike Deane
Michael Andrews
Richard Andrews
David Fox
Thomas Steel
Richard Cussens
Kenneth Batty
Ann & Roger Pace
Ailsa Jeanette Brookes
Alan Stinson
Stephen Edward Wilkinson
Lee Cooper
Glyn Evans
Christopher Birks
John Fidler
John Gray
Peter Marlow
Craig Hopper
Michael Bell
Ray Wallis
John Bonser
Pauline Hawley
Lewis & Steven Reynolds
Paul Ryder

John Anthony Civico
Martin Bogue
Stephan Davies
Paul Deane
Tony Dallman
Tom Foster
Stephen Ripley
David Hay
Michael C. Carnall
Graham Moore
Albert Lacey
Philip Lacey
Stephen Lacey
Chris Lacey
Stuart Butlin
Martin James Swift
Alistair Upton
John Roddison
Harrison Barker
Benjamin Harding
Mr. Gary Lee Biram
Chris Powell
Richard Powell
Jane Osborn
Neil Stuart Holt
Gary Thompson
Neil Taylor
Paul Goman
Iain R. Swallow
Philip Sherriff
Michael Larner
Ian Schofield
Phillip Rogers 17.09.52
Kevin Allsopp
Mr. T. W. D. Smith
Dr. N.W.P. Smith
Paul Flint
Mark Priest
Ben Scott (Australia)
Christopher Roberts 0782
Stephen Waldron
Myles Waldron
Adam Waldron
Steven Savage
Mike Timmons
James & Zach Holmes
Robert Christopher Ellis
Gary Hamilton
Ian Craft
Michael Stephen Turner
Joe & Robert Mortimer
David Mortimer
Niall O'Donovan
Liam O'Donovan
John Bradshaw 1948-2010
Edward J. H. Carnall
Charlie Daniel Kitchen
Alan Crazyhorse Pashley
Paul K. Hayden
James Speed
Brett B. Marsh
Kevin & Barrie Beck

Alexander James Fraser
Andrew Wild
Terry & Susan Dawson
Neil Jarvis
Paul Hinchliffe
Gordon Bradbury
Mark "Tank" Tomlinson
Christian Isaksen
Sebastian James Akers
Steven Smith
Mick Derrick
Stuart Rowland Thorpe
Janet & John Dickinson
Clare & Martin Jones
Marc Oxley
T. Peter Wild
Karl Frudd
Daniel Gambles
Jay Sanderson
Vivien Hambleton
Emily Barker
Joanna Barker
Thomas Buck
Paul John Hunsley
Dafydd Wyn Jones
Andrew Lawson
Jack Priestley
Graham Tindle
Paul "Bully" Bulmer
Lawrence Arthur West
Darryl Lomas
Thomas Lomas
Rebecca Lomas
Spencer Fearn
Jonathan Vidler
Pete Emsley
Ray Stewart-Kelcher
Matthew Kelcher
David Soden
David Winfield
James Austin Taylor
Bernard Peter Tomlinson
Rich & Arthur Topley
James Reid
Steven Ovenden
Peter New
Max & Martin Walters
Steve Ball
Steve Hoyland
Mick Hill
Ian Murdoch
Dylan Hughes
Hugh, Geoff & Sarah Hall
Stephen Dumigan
Ryan A. Houghton
David & Ray Rivers
Jacob Fisher
David Brooks
Richard Brooks
Tony & David Ptak
Chris Wathey
Koren Kyran Keegan Hanson

Gerald Bailey
Mark Garner
John Emson
Calvin & Myles Graves
Anthony Brian Pheasey
William Pike
Stuart J. Burgess
John Ripley
Neil Hinch
Tim Bloor
John Hilton
James Middleton
Alan John Mincher
Barry Peck
Josh Bibby
David Peck
Paul Phillips
Michael E. Revill
Adrian Waple
Jan "The Viking" Emerson
Andy (Wiz) Wilson
Chris Fletcher
Paul C. Maguire
Adam Rhys Moore
James Stephen Moore
David Land
Adam Cotton
Alexander Fuller
Russ Hague
Alfie Jay Bagnall
Graham Wallace
Marc Waring
David Young
Frank John Barton Coombes
Michael John Auckland
Stephen Armitage
Paul Armitage
Paul Evanson
Michael Grayson
Paul Adams
Thomas James Wilmot
Clive F. Wilson
Tony Cooper
Cluckie Lowedges Owls
David Middleton
Joshua Cooper
Thomas McGloin
Raphael Edwards
Dan Woodmansey
Tony Roper
Emily Louise Rowles
Lee & Emily Mason
Roger Pepper
David Vaughan
Dale Harrison
Robert Searle
Dave Collinson
Anthony Briggs
Steve Savage
Andrew Bishop
Steven Lenagh
Peter Coleman
Andy Gleadall
Paul Bruce
Christopher James Emsell
Richard Picton
Craig Mirfin
Patricia Mirfin
Alan Mark Hague
Paul Mark Bishop
Kev Cook
Martin Vincent Wild
Russell Seggar
Scott Taylor
Chris Williams
Brell Ewart
Steve Caron
James Caron
Matthew Caron
Daniel Caron
Shaun Jones
Michael S. G. Ward
Geoffrey W. Bly
Gregg Taylor
Dennis Stenton
Robert Pinder
Paul W. Dove
Kate Loftus
Peter H. Bailey
Garry Westley
The Asquiths
Colin Peskett
David Peskett
Ken Frith
Geoff Allen
Graham Smith
Mervyn Spink
Andrew Philip Damms
Lawrie Bacon
Dr. Brendan Hudson
Jack Wilkinson
David William Green
Nick Findlay
Gary Foster
Robert John Davies
Adam Manning
Kris Voakes
Andrew Fulford
Stuart Thomas Goff
Michael Howard
Tony Bennett
Paul Buckley
Vidar Hauge Halvorsen
Edward Sammy Thomas Davis